# Handbook of Development Policy Studies

# PUBLIC ADMINISTRATION AND PUBLIC POLICY

## A Comprehensive Publication Program

*Executive Editor*

**JACK RABIN**
Professor of Public Administration and Public Policy
School of Public Affairs
The Capital College
The Pennsylvania State University—Harrisburg
Middletown, Pennsylvania

*Additional Volumes in Preparation*

## ANNALS OF PUBLIC ADMINISTRATION

# Handbook of Development Policy Studies

edited by
## Gedeon M. Mudacumura
*Pennsylvania State University*
*Harrisburg, Pennsylvania, U.S.A.*

## M. Shamsul Haque
*National University of Singapore*
*Singapore*

MARCEL DEKKER, INC.        NEW YORK • BASEL

**Library of Congress Cataloging-in-Publication Data**
A catalog record for this book is available from the Library of Congress.

**ISBN: 0-8247-0602-1**

This book is printed on acid-free paper.

**Headquarters**
Marcel Dekker, Inc., 270 Madison Avenue, New York, NY 10016, U.S.A.
tel: 212-696-9000; fax: 212-685-4540

**Distribution and Customer Service**
Marcel Dekker, Inc., Cimarron Road, Monticello, New York 12701, U.S.A.
tel: 800-228-1160; fax: 845-796-1772

**Eastern Hemisphere Distribution**
Marcel Dekker AG, Hutgasse 4, Postfach 812, CH-4001 Basel, Switzerland
tel: 41-61-260-6300; fax: 41-61-260-6333

**World Wide Web**
http://www.dekker.com

The publisher offers discounts on this book when ordered in bulk quantities. For more information, write to Special Sales/Professional Marketing at the headquarters address above.

# Preface

During the postwar period, there was an unprecedented proliferation of development theories, models, policies, institutions, and experts worldwide. Many critics considered this massive development enterprise ethnocentric, reductionist, empiricist, hegemonic, and often impractical. In the 1970s, the development field began to overcome some of its alleged limitations in terms of constructing critical and emancipatory theories, emphasizing multidimensional views, exploring indigenous alternatives, and drawing attention to adverse human conditions such as poverty, inequality, dependence, and powerlessness.

But all this has fundamentally changed in the current age when everything is articulated as "new"—new right ideology, new political economy, new economic policy, new public management, and so on. Underlying these expressions, the central practical message is very simple, which is to reject the state as the dominant actor, and replace it with the private sector as the leading agent in national and international economic management. This position has been advocated by international market forces, reinforced by world events such as the collapse of socialist states, and realized through intensive globalization of capital, technology, information, and knowledge. In this global context, the state-centric approaches to development have come under challenge, intellectual progress in development thinking has almost reversed, reductionist economism has been revived, market-based economic growth has become national agenda, and concerns for the above-mentioned critical human conditions have largely been forgotten.

Due to contemporary trends toward diminishing diversity in development thinking, reduction of multidimensional development into economic calculus, exclusion of serious noneconomic issues from policy debates, and worsening developmental conditions worldwide, there is an urgent need to undertake serious development studies to counter such an antidevelopmental global context. Development scholars need to re-examine the recent changes in theoretical orientations, practical policies, sectoral priorities, institutional choices, and pertinent issues and challenges. This volume explores these unprecedented changes, evaluates their implications, and explores future alternatives. It brings together diverse contributions dealing with multiple facets of development, and represents a rich source of broad-based learning that highlights both theoretical underpinnings and practical policies and issues in development.

Concretely, development scholars and practitioners will find this handbook useful for updating themselves about current thoughts and practices in various parts of the world. Development students can also benefit from the mix of contributions made to this volume by credible scholars and experts. Moreover, the handbook is user-friendly in terms of its coherent structure of different parts and chapters, which encompass theoretical discourse, basic domains, policy issues, major institutions, inherent dilemmas, current challenges, and future directions related to development. Authors with diverse academic backgrounds and regional affiliations or identities address these major themes, and thus make this volume a valuable frame of reference for development scholars, experts, students, and practitioners worldwide.

We would like to thank all the chapter authors for their valuable and timely contributions to this volume. Special thanks must go to Professor Stuart S. Nagel whose insights laid the groundwork for this handbook. Finally, we would like to take this opportunity to express our deep gratitude to Paige Force, the production editor, for her patience and cooperation.

*Gedeon M. Mudacumura*
*M. Shamsul Haque*

# Contents

**Part III: Development Policy Issues in Major Sectors**

**Part IV: Development Institutions: Local and Global**

# Contents

## Part V: Development Dilemmas: How To Resolve?

## Part VI: Development Trends and Challenges

# Contributors

**Henry Adobor**  Associate Professor, Department of Management, Quinnipiac University, Hamden, Connecticut, U.S.A.

**Angeline L. Ames**  Department of Sociology, National University of Singapore, Singapore

**Todd T. Ames**  Department of Sociology, National University of Singapore, Singapore

**Zaheer Baber**  Department of Sociology, University of Saskatchewan, Saskatoon, Saskatchewan, Canada

**Noorjahan Bava***  Professor, Department of Political Science, University of Delhi, Delhi, India

**P. Dal Brodhead**  President, New Economy Development Group, Ottawa, Ontario, Canada

**Yongshun Cai**  Department of Political Science, National University of Singapore, Singapore

**Selina Ching Chan**  Department of Sociology, National University of Singapore, Singapore

**Thomas S. Chapman**  Graduate Student, Department of Agriculture, Environment, and Development Economics, The Ohio State University, Columbus, Ohio, U.S.A.

**Patricia A. Cholewka**  Teachers College, Columbia University, New York, New York, U.S.A.

**Cynthia Donovan**  Assistant Professor, Department of Agricultural Economics, Michigan State University, East Lansing, Michigan, U.S.A.

---

* Retired.

**Lloyd J. Dumas**  Professor, School of Social Sciences, University of Texas, Dallas, Texas, U.S.A.

**O. P. Dwivedi**  Professor, Department of Political Science, University of Guelph, Guelph, Ontario, Canada

**Svante Ersson**  Department of Political Science, Umea University, Umea, Sweden

**Barbara Fillip***  Consultant, Arlington, Virginia, U.S.A.

**R. Warren Flint**  Five E's Unlimited, Washington, D.C., U.S.A.

**Margaret Grieco**  Professor, Department of Transport and Society, Napier University, Edinburgh, United Kingdom

**Roberto P. Guimarães**  Economic Affairs Officer, Sustainable Development and Human Settlement Division, U.N. Economic Commission for Latin America and the Caribbean (ECLAC), Santiago, Chile

**M. Shamsul Haque**  Associate Professor, Department of Political Science, National University of Singapore, Singapore

**Elaine Ho**  Department of Geography, National University of Singapore, Singapore

**Monica Koubratova Hristova**  Researcher, Institute of Agrarian Economics, Sofia, Bulgaria

**Edward T. Jackson**  Associate Professor, School of Public Policy and Administration, Carleton University, Ottawa, Ontario, Canada

**R. B. Jain**  Professor, Department of Political Science, University of Delhi, Delhi, India

**Ho-Won Jeong**  Institute for Conflict Analysis and Resolution, George Mason University, Fairfax, Virginia, U.S.A.

**Rym A. Kaki**  School of Policy, Planning, and Development, University of Southern California, Los Angeles, California, U.S.A.

**Habibul Haque Khondker**  Department of Sociology, National University of Singapore, Singapore

**Alfred Lakwo**  Center for International Development Issues, Catholic University of Nijmegen, Nijmegen, The Netherlands

**Jan-Erik Lane**  Department of Political Science, University of Geneva, Geneva, Switzerland

**Seungjoo Lee**  Assistant Professor, Department of International Relations, Yonsei University, Wonju-si, Kangwon-do, South Korea

**Nadia Lisovskaya**  Department of Government, University of Manchester, Manchester, United Kingdom

---

*Current affiliation*: President, Knowledge for Development, LLC, Arlington, Virginia, U.S.A.

**Scott Loveridge**   Professor, Department of Agricultural Economics, Michigan State University, East Lansing, Michigan, U.S.A.

**Desta Mebratu\***   UNIDO Consultant, Addis Ababa, Ethiopia

**Eleftherios Michael**   Institute for Conflict Analysis and Resolution, George Mason University, Fairfax, Virginia, U.S.A.

**Sangho Moon**   Assistant Professor, Institute of Government, Tennessee State University, Nashville, Tennessee, U.S.A.

**Edson Mpyisi**   Department of Agricultural Economics, Michigan State University, East Lansing, Michigan, U.S.A.

**Gedeon M. Mudacumura**   Research and Development Analyst, Pennsylvania Treasury Department, and Adjunct Faculty, School of Public Affairs, Pennsylvania State University, Harrisburg, Pennsylvania, U.S.A.

**Jorge Nef**   Director, Center for Latin American, Caribbean, and Latino Studies, University of South Florida, Tampa, Florida, U.S.A.

**Heather Nel**   Professor, Raymond Mhlaba Institute of Public Administration and Leadership, University of Port Elizabeth, Port Elizabeth, South Africa

**Hindy Lauer Schachter**   School of Management, New Jersey Institute of Technology, Newark, New Jersey, U.S.A.

**Karin Schelzig**   Poverty Specialist, Agriculture and Economics Group, Development Alternatives, Inc., Bethesda, Maryland, U.S.A.

**Alex Sekwat**   Associate Professor, Institute of Government, Tennessee State University, Nashville, Tennessee, U.S.A.

**Keshav C. Sharma**   Professor, Faculty of Social Sciences, University of Botswana, Gaborone, Botswana

**Kristen Sheeran**   Assistant Professor, Economics Department, St. Mary's College of Maryland, St. Mary's City, Maryland, U.S.A.

**Theresa Wong**   Department of Geography, National University of Singapore, Singapore

**Brenda S. A. Yeoh**   Department of Geography, National University of Singapore, Singapore

**Habib Zafarullah**   Associate Professor, School of Social Science, University of New England, New South Wales, Australia

---

\**Current affiliation*: Program Officer, Regional Office for Africa, United Nations Environment Program, Nairobi, Kenya.

# 1

## Introduction
### *Development Discourse and Its Challenges and Directions*

**M. SHAMSUL HAQUE**

*National University of Singapore, Singapore*

### DEVELOPMENT DISCOURSE: LIMITS AND SIGNIFICANCE

In human history, there has always been a dominant mode development discourse shaped and reinforced by economic needs and demands, social class and political power structures, cultural norms and beliefs, and ideological and intellectual orientations. With the basic shifts in these various factors at the national and global levels, there emerged some significant changes in the nature of development thinking in different epochs. During the precolonial phase, diverse modes of human progress (often known as civilizations) occurred in different parts of the world based on distinct historical traditions (Chinese, Indian, Persian, Egyptian, European, and so on) with unique sets of human needs, social systems, political structures, and cultural beliefs (Haque, 1999a). These different traditions or civilizations became marginalized, impoverished, and eventually supplanted during the centuries of worldwide colonial conquests. The colonization process eroded human diversity, restructured various economies and political systems, transformed cultures and lifestyles, and imposed a Eurocentric development discourse on subjugated societies and peoples, which continued in different forms during the postcolonial phase.

Although the postwar period saw worldwide decolonization and the emergence of newly independent states in Asia, Africa, and Latin America, the colonial legacy remained influential in development thinking—in terms of imitative development outlook, borrowed development models, and aid-dependent development policies—which came to be viewed as a form of neocolonialism (Haque, 1999a; Streeten, 1983). While the former colonial powers remained most dominant in global finance, world

1

military structure, and international trade (Opitz, 1987), some Western scholars expressed concern about the academic domination or "imperialism" of advanced capitalist nations in development theory and research (Streeten, 1975; Wiarda, 1981). This condition of domination and dependence was further reinforced during the Cold War when the constitutional governments in many new states were replaced by the unconstitutional military regimes serving either of the two ideological camps. In fact, the whole development enterprise became an instrument of foreign policy and ideological containment for the superpowers in dealing with developing countries. In the process, there was a massive expansion of the development field in terms of the proliferation of development-related models, plans, policies, agencies, experts, conferences, books, and journals, although all these efforts hardly succeeded in realizing such development goals as poverty reduction, employment creation, income redistribution, and economic self-reliance.

In the 1970s, however, due to the growing worldwide concerns for the failure of the economic growth and modernization models to address poverty, inequality, and external debt and dependence, some of these issues were taken into account in the development debates introduced by the proponents of the basic needs approach, dependency theory, new world economic order, and so on. There also emerged such fragmented but unconventional ideas as authentic development, alternative development, indigenous development, and the development in the African, Chinese, or Indian ways (Steidlmeier, 1987; Goulet, 1980). Some hope was also created by the end of the Cold War that some of the existing development problems would be addressed. Unfortunately, the period since the demise of the Cold War and the collapse of major socialist states saw the intensive globalization of transnational capital and media, increasing dominance of capitalist states and international financial agencies, forced restructuring of the developing economies and polities in favor of global market forces, marginalization of such critical development concerns as poverty and inequality, and erosion of indigenous cultures and identities (Helleiner, 1990; Petras, 1990; Sanyal, 1993). In this context, there has been a reversal of progress in development discourse made in the earlier decades; in the atmosphere dominated by neoliberal market ideology, the emancipatory mode of development discourse has almost vanished. Despite the limitations of such development discourse, however, it has become more significant today, especially due to the worsening conditions of most of the world's population, which live in the poor, developing nations. In this regard, it is necessary to recapitulate some of the major limits of development study and explain the reasons why it remains so significant.

## Major Limits of Development Studies: Existing Critique

In the past, the development field came under attack for varieties of its alleged limitations or shortcomings. First, it is often mentioned by critics that the colonial legacy of an evolutionist and Eurocentric view of social progress based on the assumption of Western superiority has been always dominant in development thinking (Raghaviah, 1987; Said, 1983). Some scholars suggest that the Eurocentric notion of development—which emphasizes material progress, the dominance of science and industry, and Western history, society, and culture—was inherent in development theory and practice and imposed on the entire world during the postcolonial period through foreign aid and technical assistance (Merriam, 1988; Pieterse, 1991; Haque, 1999a).

The implications of such a prejudiced understanding of development, according to critics, have been the conceptual degradation of non-Western societies as "underdeveloped," the expansion of "diploma disease" (i.e., an obsession for foreign education), the retardation of indigenous knowledge construction, and the mystification of the common masses by the "myth" of development (Addo, 1985; Haque, 1999a).

Second, it is argued that the development industry has largely served the dominant classes and nations in most cases. According to Nandy (1989:35), the development initiatives have become an instrument of state domination, and "hundreds of thousands of citizens can be legitimately killed or maimed or jailed in the name of development." Although this interpretation may sound a bit extreme, there is no doubt that in many countries the political and bureaucratic elites used development programs to make economic gains and legitimize their repressive rule. At the international level, developmentalism is characterized by some critics as an ideology of neoimperialism and a superstructure of the world capitalist system that preserves unequal global economic structure and maintains the dominance of international institutions (Pieterse, 1991; Murphy, 1990). In particular, the field enhances the power and dominance of international development experts and advisors over Third World people by prescribing or imposing development policies and programs for which they themselves are hardly accountable (Goulet, 1980; Harrod, 1982). It has thus been pointed out that the development industry is a "big business" for such experts, advisors, and technocrats in terms of financially gaining from advising Third World regimes on development initiatives (Korten, 1990; Haque, 1999a).

Finally, the development field is said to suffer both from considerable ineffectiveness in resolving practical problems and from an impasse or inertia in making theoretical change or improvement. It is observed that the imitative development models worsened income inequality, external debt and dependence, cultural erosion, and environmental degradation and ecological crisis (Haque, 1999a). At the theoretical level, some scholars have expressed concern that development studies began to face an intellectual impasse, which led to a decline in confidence in the field, and thus perhaps required the revival of orthodox theories. (See Manzo, 1991; Preston, 1987; Munck, 1999.) This limitation of development studies has been repeatedly pointed out by various critical development scholars, who despite academically engaging themselves in the field, remained dissatisfied with its intellectual inertia.

## Contemporary Significance of Development Discourse

In the current age, there has been a significant decline in the mainstream theoretical discourse and practical policy debate in the development field that is not necessarily due to its above-mentioned limitations, which could in fact lead to more controversy, critique, and discussion. Perhaps the main reason for the diminishing academic attraction to development economics and the development field as a whole has to do with the field's predominantly state-centric approach, which is now considered obsolete in the contemporary national and international contexts dominated by market-driven policies and interests. In this new context, however, it has become imperative to revive and intensify critical development discourse for various reasons which are discussed below.

First, despite the above critiques of the development field, there are instances and studies that provide some favorable assessment of earlier development initiatives. It is pointed out that the state-led development models were undertaken in developing countries with the objectives of overcoming foreign ownership and domination, enhancing economic self-reliance, generating employment, redistributing income, developing infrastructure, and so on (Martin, 1993; Haque, 1999b). Based on development initiatives, some of these countries in Asia, Africa, and Latin America have managed to reduce poverty, expand employment, enhance literacy, improve public health, accelerate industrial growth, and so on (Bello et al., 1994; ILO, 1995). Some of the widely cited success stories of state-led development efforts include the "economic miracles" of Asia, such as Singapore, Japan, Taiwan, and South Korea (Clarke, 1994; Martin, 1993). On the other hand, the concerns for development failures led to a series of theoretical and strategic constructs in the development field, including dependency theory, the neo-Marxist approach, and the New World Economic Order, which drew attention to the problems of poverty, inequality, dependence, and hegemony (Randall and Theobald, 1985; Haque, 1999a). In other words, all development thoughts and constructs were not based on pro-systemic status quo, and some of the critical debates still remain extremely relevant today.

Second, the expansion of development discourse is also significant because of the emergence of an antidevelopmental, market-biased neoliberal ideology that now dominates state policies, interstate relations, foreign assistance, and academic debates. The adoption of structural adjustment programs based on neoliberal assumptions has worsened economic and social conditions in many developing countries and post-socialist nations, although it has considerably benefited business firms, transnational agencies, and ruling elites and their cronies in these countries (Martin, 1993; Carchedi, 1994). Under the worldwide dominance of market-driven neoliberal thinking, the earlier ideological and intellectual diversity in development discourse has diminished, and critical development issues, such as income disparity, external dependence, and cultural erosion, have become marginalized in policy debates (Berthoud, 1992; Esteva, 1992). The loss of ideological diversity and the exclusion of critical concerns have been reinforced by the process of intensive globalization of the media and information networks propagating market values and bourgeois lifestyles through advertising, news, films, and the entertainment industry, while overlooking adverse human conditions in poor countries (Angus and Jhally, 1989; Kellner, 1990). In this global context, expanding development discourse has become more crucial to confront the hegemony of neoliberal ideology, explore multiple perspectives and options, and allow alternative voices in the development debate.

Finally, the increasing significance of development discourse also lies in the fact that the above-mentioned critical human conditions identified in earlier decades—including severe poverty, income inequality, external dependence, cultural erosion, and ecological crisis—have not been resolved. In fact, the status of some urgent development concerns has worsened during the recent decades. For example, between 1990 and 1998, the number of people living in abject poverty in developing countries rose from 916 million to 986 million; between 1991 and 1997, the share of the world's income for the poorest 20% of its population fell from 1.4% to 1.1%; between 1992 and 1998, the income gap between the richest and poorest countries increased from a ratio of 72:1 to 84:1; and between 1990 and 1998, the amount of external debt increased to an alarming level in most countries, especially in China, India, Indonesia, South Korea, Thailand, Brazil, and Mexico (World Bank, 2000; 2001; Bjonnes, 2002; UNDP, 1997). Similarly, in most regions, there have been worsening forms of environmental degradation, such as air and water pollution, land degradation, deforestation, and biodiversity loss (UNESCAP, 2000).

All these worsening development conditions have been repeatedly emphasized at such major world forums as the U.N. Conference on Environment and Development in 1992 and the World Summit on Sustainable Development in 2002, which represent a reminder that today there is a greater need for development discourse in the current antidevelopmental global context. The question remains, however, as to the nature, objective, structure, and agent of such a development discourse. In order to decipher the situation in this regard, it is necessary to explore more specific scenarios of the contemporary challenges and directions of development.

## CURRENT DEVELOPMENT CHALLENGES AND DIRECTIONS

### Ideological Underpinnings

During the postwar period, while most Western capitalist nations pursued the liberal welfare model to address diverse societal problems and Eastern European countries introduced massive socialist planning largely based on ideological grounds, the postcolonial developing countries adopted mixed models of development representing varying combinations of nationalist protectionism, socialist planning, and the capitalist market. In most developing countries in Asia, Africa, and Latin America, irrespective of regime variations, these diverse modes of development initiatives representing different ideological fragments have often been generalized as developmentalism. In some African and South Asian cases, the postindependence period was characterized by the relative absence of a dominant class and the overwhelming autonomy and power of the bureaucratic–military oligarchy under which developmentalism was pursued in the form of accelerating socioeconomic progress and ensuring territorial unity and nation building (Westergaard, 1985; Haque, 1999c). In Latin America, on the other hand, developmentalism became the dominant theme even for various repressive regimes.

In the early 1980s, however, state-managed developmentalism was challenged because of its growing academic critique, public dissatisfaction, and more importantly, the global corporate demands to end state monopoly and expand the scope of market competition (Haque, 1999a). The ideological discredit to developmentalism was also reinforced by the worsening fiscal problems in developing countries, the collapse of the major socialist states, and the triumph of the capitalist market system. The final determining push came from the so-called Washington consensus, which pressured most governments in the developing world to replace the planned development model with a more market-based neoliberal approach (CPD, 1999; Williamson, 1999). Reinforced by the world's changing ideological circumstances, intensive globalization of transnational capital, and the growing power of market forces, the market-friendly neoliberal beliefs in individual choice, utilitarian self-interest, free trade and foreign investment, and antiwelfarism were gradually embraced by many countries in the developing world, often under the pressure of international financial agencies (Walton and Seddon, 1994; Haque, 1999c). With regard to this trend in Latin

America, for example, Alvarez et al. (1998:22) mention that neoliberalism has become "powerful and ubiquitous" in the region's design of democracy.

The neoliberal underpinnings of the current development paradigm, however, are likely to face serious challenge and public opposition in developing countries, in which market institutions are underdeveloped, cultural norms and ethics are hardly utilitarian, poverty and inequality is already severe, and most people still depend on public welfare services. In the early 1990s, this public dissatisfaction with or opposition to the neoliberal development framework became evident in the increasing number of annual labor strikes in such countries as Brazil, Chile, Colombia, India, Philippines, Mexico, Nigeria, South Africa, and South Korea (ILO, 1997–1998). In addition, overall public confidence in many neoliberal regimes in Asia, Africa, and Latin America is quite low (Haque, 2000). In the developing world, the main challenge to the current neoliberal mode of development is thus how to win popular support despite its unpopular socioeconomic implications.

## Theoretical Perspectives

Although development theories began with the concern for economic growth based on free market competition—as reflected in classical and neoclassical theories—they shifted to a more interventionist theoretical framework due to various challenges, such as the Great Depression in the capitalist world and the relative absence of private capital and market system in the developing world. These interventionist approaches include the Keynesian and post-Keynesian growth models, which emerged in response to the crisis in advanced market economies, but were adjusted in the context of developing economies into the so-called unbalanced growth theory, vicious circle theory, stages-of-growth theory, and so on. (See Haque, 1999a.)

Beyond this narrow concern for economic growth, however, there emerged various modernization theories to explain development in the noneconomic spheres of developing societies. In order to address the major flaws of these mainstream theories (e.g., their imitative frameworks based on the images of advanced capitalist nations, their incapacity to address unequal and dependent relationships between metropolitan and peripheral countries, and their inadequacy to deal with such issues as the mode of production and state-class relations) there emerged more radical theories of development, especially the dependency and neo-Marxist perspectives (Randall and Theobald, 1985). On the other hand, developing countries themselves articulated and demanded the New International Economic Order and the New World Information and Communication Order. Although these alternative theories or models were hardly put into practice, they created considerable debates in the development field, and became major parts of development studies. Despite the emergence of these radical and reformist theoretical constructs, which evolved as alternatives to mainstream growth and modernization theories, the development field as a whole came under attack for its theoretical inadequacies to address existing development problems (Haque, 1999a).

Despite its limits and problems, the dynamic field of development began to cover multiple dimensions of society and generated lively debates on basic human concerns, such as poverty, inequality, and dependence. With the advent of neoliberal market ideology worldwide, however, the development field has reversed back to its "primitive" age of neoclassical economic theory (combined with the public choice perspective), and whatever theoretical progress was made to address those critical human concerns seems to have eroded. It is observed by some scholars that national development planning has been replaced by market-led neoclassical economics in developing countries, and this revival of the neoclassical model of market competition represents a "counterrevolution" in development studies (Smith, 1991; Veltmeyer, 1993). There is a consensus among critics that this new form of the neoclassical framework—which assumes the superiority of market forces, accuses the public sector of inefficiency, and suggests that the role of government be limited to the protection of private property and the money supply—was mostly imposed on developing nations by the World Bank and the International Monetary Fund (IMF) through structural adjustment programs (Bello et al., 1994; Stein, 1994).

This recent revival and worldwide expansion of the neoclassical model and its variants, such as public choice theory, may face serious limitations in the developing world, in which its assumptions of individualistic self-interest are discouraged, political instability is a common syndrome, and the role of the state still remains crucial for delivering goods and services in the absence of a well-developed market system (Stein, 1994). In addition, the neoclassical model is less appropriate for developing countries (except the globally integrated small city states, such as Hong Kong, Singapore, and Taiwan), because it fails to address certain essential components of developmental reality, such as cultural norms, religious ethics, and class and ethnic affiliations, which affect the market behavior itself (Sinaceur, 1983; Haque, 1999a). In other words, although the World Bank has attempted to impose the criteria of individualistic market competition to replace the collective public sector norms in order to "cure all evils" (Helleiner, 1990; Clements, 1994), the effectiveness of such an approach remains questionable in the context of developing societies.

## Policies and Strategies

Based on the ideology of developmentalism, many Asian, African, and Latin American countries adopted various interventionist, state-led policies, including the establishment of public enterprises, expansion of state agencies, nationalization of private firms, regulation of market forces, control over export and import, and prohibition of foreign investment. These policies were introduced to achieve major developmental goals set by national development plans. This interventionist policy approach was even endorsed by such international agencies as the World Bank and the IMF prior to the late 1970s (Haque, 1999b). But since the early 1980s, in the global atmosphere dominated by the neoliberal market ideology and neoclassical approach discussed above, there has been a fundamental promarket shift in the policy orientation of developing nations, especially under the structural adjustment program. These countries embraced a new set of market-led policies, such as the downsizing of the public sector, privatization of state enterprises, corporatization of government agencies, deregulation of market controls, liberalization of trade and foreign investment, and withdrawal of welfare subsidies (Martinez and Garcia, 1999; Hildyard, 1997).

Prescribed or imposed by the World Bank and the IMF, in the 1980s and 1990s, privatization, deregulation, and liberalization were aggressively pursued by many countries in Asia (e.g., India, Indonesia, Malaysia, Pakistan, Philippines, South Korea, and Thailand), Africa (e.g., Ghana, Nigeria, South Africa, Tanzania, and Zambia), and Latin America (e.g., Argentina, Brazil, Chile, Colombia, and

Mexico) (CIPE, 1992; Haque, 1999c). For instance, the privatization policy affected almost all sectors (e.g., banking, insurance, airlines, electricity, petroleum, automobiles, tobacco, fertilizer, and telecommunications) in these developing regions, and the privatization transactions generated instant revenues (Shirley, 1998; Haque, 1999b). To varying degrees, under external pressure, most developing countries have also reduced trade barriers and introduced various incentives (e.g., tax exemption, profit repatriation, foreign ownership, and duty-free import) to attract foreign investors. These changes in policies have been pursued in order to enhance market competition, increase economic efficiency, and accelerate economic growth.

These basic changes in policy orientation, however, have done more harm than good to national economies and human well-being in many countries. For example, the privatization of profit-making enterprises to private firms (often to foreign investors) has permanently diminished the potential for government revenues from these enterprises. In addition, in the absence of market transparency and competitive local buyers in developing countries and transitional economies, valuable public assets have often been sold at nominal prices to the vested interests associated with the policy-making elites without much concern for public accountability (Martin, 1993; Ramanadham, 1995). In addition, the liberalization of foreign investment and the provision of attractive incentives have often discriminated and marginalized local investors, and even led to an initial process of deindustrialization in some developing countries (Sarkar, 1991). The expansion of foreign ownership under the current policy regime has also eroded economic self-reliance, and according to some critics, led to the economic recolonization of poor countries (Odle, 1993; Haque, 1999b). Finally, the policy of streamlining public agencies and reducing welfare subsidies has adverse impacts on low-income citizens. In Asia, Africa, and Latin America, the recent tendencies of diminishing government spending on education, health, housing, agriculture, and so on (UNDP, 2001; World Bank, 2000; 2001; Tevera, 1995), represent a major challenge to the realization of basic needs for poorer households.

## Concerns and Issues

During the earlier decades of development studies, the narrow objective of economic growth emphasized in the 1950s was expanded to accommodate the sociopolitical dimensions in various modernization theories, and such development concerns as basic needs, inequality, and dependence were emphasized in other theoretical constructs ranging from the basic need approach to dependency theory (Bloomstrom and Hettne, 1984). In the practical policy domain, the primary concerns for most state-run development policies and programs were to enhance nation building, generate employment, reduce inequality, end foreign ownership, enhance self-reliance, promote entrepreneurship, develop human resources, and so on (Onis, 1991; Haque, 1999b). The major development concerns and issues encompassed economic and noneconomic dimensions, addressed all sectors and income groups, and had some kind of macronational vision, although all these could be more rhetorical than real in many developing countries.

The situation has considerably changed today, however; the primary developmental concerns related to the market-driven policies discussed above are to overcome economic backwardness, monopoly, inefficiency, and waste and to enhance growth, competition, efficiency, economy, and value for money (Asmerom, 1994; Jiyad, 1995; Munck, 2000). In Asia, Africa, and Latin America, many countries have recently adopted such promarket policy reforms in order to improve economic performance in terms of greater efficiency, growth, and competitiveness (see Kelegama, 1995; World Bank, 1997). Today the earlier developmental concerns or problems—such as poverty, unemployment, inequality, dependence, and foreign ownership—have thus become secondary or obsolete. In the history of development thinking, there was hardly any period in which all development concerns were relegated or reduced to such a reductionist set of economic criteria and calculations found under the current neoliberal policy atmosphere.

The economic reductionism in development ideology, theory, and policy, however, is challenged by the alarming and worsening development conditions—including poverty, inequality, external debt, ecological crisis, and cultural hegemony—in different parts of the world. In the 1990s, poverty worsened in sub-Saharan Africa and hardly improved in South Asia and Latin America (World Bank, 2000; 2001). During the neoliberal policy period, the conditions of internal inequality and external debt have deteriorated in many developing countries in all these regions (World Bank, 2000; 2001). Similarly, various forms of environmental disorders have worsened under the market-oriented structural adjustment policies (Bello et al.; 1994), which unilaterally focus on economic growth based on hazardous industrial production and consumption without much concern for the environment. On the other hand, ethnic and religious conflicts have caused an alarming amount of death and suffering in such cases as Bosnia, Chechnya, Palestine, Sri Lanka, and Rwanda (Haque, 1999a). Another current major developmental concern is the process of unprecedented globalization that has widened international inequality, worsened Third World dependence, eroded national sovereignty, and destroyed indigenous cultures and identities. All these are serious developmental concerns overlooked by the current policy agenda of economic growth and efficiency.

## Main Actors and Target Groups

In the developing world, the state was always the main actor in planning development, formulating development policies, and carrying out development programs and projects. Even in cases in which the private sector was allowed to play a certain developmental role, the state remained central in overall economic management. It is this state-centric mode of development that largely led to the articulation of the concept of "developmental state" (Polidano, 1998). Such a state was crucial in the realization of rapid economic development in East and Southeast Asia. In addition, in the poverty-ridden developing countries, in the absence of a capable private sector, the state had to play the substitute role to deliver such basic services as health care, education, and housing.

During the 1980s and 1990s, however, the state and its bureaucracy came under attack for alleged inefficiency, mismanagement, elitism, patronage, and corruption (Clarke, 1994; Smith, 1991). Although there was a certain amount of truth in such accusations, the opposition to the state-centered approach largely came from the advocates of neoliberal ideology and promarket policies. This centrality of the state in Third World development was thus questioned and gradually replaced with the leading role played by the private sector (Chaudhry, 1994). This process of replacing the state by the private sector has been accentuated by the above-mentioned policies of downsizing, privatization, deregulation, and liberalization. More importantly, the role of the state has been redefined; it should not be the main actor in socioeconomic development, its main function is to support or facilitate the private sector by creating a conducive market-friendly atmosphere. Under the auspices of international agencies, especially the World Bank, today most countries in Asia, Africa, Latin America, and the Middle East have more or less decided to redefine the role of the state and restructure its bureaucracy to facilitate or enable the business sector to produce, manage, and deliver goods and services (Kaul, 1996; World Bank, 1996).

In line with this changing role of the state to enable the private sector to play the primary role in economic management and development, the main recipients or targets of such a role are also private firms or investors rather than common citizens. The main recipients of state support and incentives in various countries in Asia, Africa, and Latin America have often been the foreign investors; however. In many of these countries, the state has recently created a conducive financial, legal, and administrative atmosphere and infrastructure support for private firms and expanded the scope of public–private partnerships or joint ventures in all major sectors (World Bank, 1996; 1997; Haque, 1999b). In contrast, the common citizens have been worse off from this changing role of the state, as their basic services, such as health and education, have all been challenged due to the adoption of an antiwelfare option, the withdrawal of subsidies, and the introduction of user charges (Tevera, 1995; Walton and Seddon, 1994; Haque, 1999c). This trend represents a significant shift from the earlier state-led development approach counting all citizens (especially the poor) as development targets, to the current market-driven approach assuming local and foreign investors as the primary targets.

The above changes in the actors and targets of development may produce adverse outcomes for both states and citizens. For instance, the diminishing role of the state and the increasing role of the private sector in developing countries may erode the capacity and legitimacy of the state to exercise necessary controls over anarchic market forces and foreign investors in order to make them accountable to customers and citizens. On the other hand, the diversion of attention from the common citizens to the business elites (local and foreign) has serious repercussions for low-income households. It has been observed that under the market-friendly neoliberal approach, the erosion of citizens' entitlement to basic services has caused a serious decline in the living standards of poor people in many developing countries (Development Group, 1999). For instance, about 1.6 billion people worldwide have seen their average incomes dropped, and about 1 billion people have experienced a diminishing level of consumption during the recent decades (UNDP, 1998). This situation has made the age-old question—"development for whom"—more relevant to the current global context.

## IN THIS VOLUME

In the above discussion, a series of development issues, trends, and challenges has been examined. Although all these concerns cannot be systematically explored in edited books compiling contributions from authors with diverse backgrounds and interests, this volume makes an effort to present a coherent structure of chapters by categorizing and arranging them into these major development concerns. It covers the following major development themes sequentially: development discourse, development domains, development policy issues, development institutions, development dilemmas, and development trends and challenges.

## Part 1 Development Discourse: Change versus Continuity

In the past, theoretical discourse on development came under attack for its ethnocentric, reductionist, empiricist, and hegemonic nature. Although the nature of such discourse has considerably changed, its limitations have hardly been overcome. In this section, some generic and specific dimensions of such development discourse have been addressed. In her chapter, Rym Kaki explains the nature of development discourse in terms of Isaiah Berlin's contention that all "liberating" ideas end up as "suffocating" constructs, which are replaced with another set of constructs with the potential of being equally stifling. In this regard, she examines the major stages of development discourse that evolved in various disciplines during the postwar period. Her main emphasis, however, is on the use of "narratives" in development discourse. She specifically refers to Emory Roe's, *Except Africa: Remaking Development, Rethinking Power*, which was published in 1999, and cites examples of development narratives (stories, counterstories, untold stories) used in technical assistance, structural adjustment programs, and so on. She emphasizes that the less controversial, apolitical, and quantitative development studies should be transcended and more attention should be paid to the controversial, complex, and uncertain issues in development discourse.

On the other hand, Henry Adobor focuses on the theoretical underpinnings of sustainable development. Despite the conceptual ambiguity of sustainable development, according to the author, it is usually linked with the natural environment and resources and requires global social change in order to realize its objectives. He pays specific attention to the limitations of the linear framework, however, which stresses a rigid cause and effect relationship and produces only a short-term solution, in understanding such a complex and dynamic phenomenon as sustainable development. He instead proposes a nonlinear approach as more appropriate for explaining this issue involving the uncertain, unpredictable, and complex ecological system. In this regard, he examines the relevance of chaos theory to the basic imperatives of sustainable development. He also evaluates the policy implications of using a nonlinear framework for sustainable development in terms of its institutional choices and designs.

Although this topic of sustainable development is also discussed by Warren Flint, his focus is quite different. Flint observes that the existing debate tends to stress a dichotomy between economic development and the environment. In this regard, he presents sustainability not only as an effective measure to assess the stage at which human economic activities become a danger to the environment, but also as a means to identify the multidimensional links between human development and the ecological system. The author also recognizes that this essential issue of sustainability is not only a matter of science and economics, it is also related to values and ethics inherent in different cultures. In ensuring sustainability, people must believe in their shared future and mutual interdependence within the limits of natural systems. The chapter attempts to explore how communities are required to continuously evaluate and adjust their program activities in order to achieve sustainable development.

In his chapter, M. Shamsul Haque examines the conceptual and practical dominance of economic growth, especially the measure of gross national product (GNP), in development discourse. He attempts to reveal the "myths" of GNP in terms of its major limitations. He explains how the GNP figure represents the "commoditization" of material goods and human labor, counts certain goods and services that do not enhance human well-being, overlooks some major costs inherent in

economic growth, and includes goods and services resulting from pathological
outcomes of economic activities. The chapter then examines the major causes and
adverse implications of using the GNP measure, such as the continuation of economic inequality, legitimation of political repression, realization of vested interests,
domination of economic experts, and marginalization of indigenous cultures and
identities. The author recommends further critical studies to demystify the myths of
economic growth and to explore more authentic and comprehensive measures of
human development.

On the other hand, Zaheer Baber attempts to use the postmodern framework of
deconstructing the power–knowledge connections to examine modernization theory.
He explains that although modernization theory may have been eclipsed in academic
discussion, it remains the dominant worldview for policy makers and international
institutions and agencies. He attempts to explore a specific tenet of modernization
theory (and its structural and ideological contexts), developed between the 1950s and
1970s by some social scientists affiliated with the MIT Center for International Studies
and the Ford Foundation and their counterparts in India. The author suggests that
this intellectual endeavor was based on the assumption that the knowledge generated
from such a project could be used by the United States to prescribe social and
economic changes or reforms for South Asian countries based on its own interests.
For some observers, however, this group of social scientists perhaps considered this
MIT project an opportunity for career development.

## Part 2   Development Domains and Their Significance

Although development studies began with a narrow focus on economic growth
found in classical and neoclassical economic theories, gradually it expanded to
address the social, political, cultural, and environmental dimensions of development,
especially due to its extension to various social science disciplines. Today there is no
controversy over the fact that human development involves the multiple dimensions,
clusters, and layers of society. It has become imperative, however, to remind ourselves of this multidimensional and complex nature of development because of the
global triumph of one-dimensional neoliberal ideology that overemphasizes economic factors at the expense of noneconomic concerns.

In this regard, Noorjahan Bava reiterates this multivariate and multidimensional nature and scope of development. She presents a long list of developmental
domains, including the "political, legal, administrative, social, economic, cultural,
environmental, psychological, physical, mental, intellectual, moral, material, spiritual, individual, group, rural, urban, local, subnational, regional, national, international and global, and quantitative and qualitative dimensions." In order to deal
with this multidimensional concept of development, she suggests a comprehensive
and holistic perspective and interdisciplinary or multidisciplinary methodology. She
adds further that beyond this complex nature and scope of development, it can be
defined as freedom or liberation from all forms of adverse human conditions, such as
poverty, hunger, illiteracy inequality, insecurity, and exploitation.

On the other hand, O. P. Dwivedi and Jorge Nef focus on the administrative
dimension of development, with special reference to the recent transition from
"development administration" to "new public management" (NPM). They explain
how in the postcolonial context development administration emerged as a rational

and productive bureaucracy, often based on external inducements and foreign training. More recently, however, this development administration has been replaced by NPM, which originated in the 1980s, mainly in such Western countries as the United Kingdom and the United States. Based on a businesslike approach, this NPM, according to these authors, covers certain major components, such as budget cuts, downsizing, an emphasis on results, decentralization, contracting out, and performance-based pay. The authors conclude that although developing countries may have no choice but to adopt this NPM, it remains relatively ineffective because of the coexistence of colonial, neocolonial, and local factors in these countries.

In their chapter, Angeline L. Ames and Todd T. Ames examine the gender question with special reference to the emergence of waged female labor and its implication for women's socioeconomic development in Thailand. Compared to previous research, recent studies show that the integration of women into waged labor has not always benefited women, as they receive lower wages and inadequate social protection. In the case of Thailand, although the country's increasing Gross Domestic Product (GDP) growth rates and state policies have expanded the scope for women's waged labor and allowed them to pursue professional careers based on education, for most women wages remain very low, as their employment is primarily in the agriculture sector.

Selina Ching Chan also deals with the gender dimension, but with a different focus and in a different context. She explores how the patriarchal Chinese tradition about women's position in society (especially their inheritance rights) was invented and perpetuated (fossilized) under British colonial rule in Hong Kong. The fossilization of this patriarchal female inheritance tradition by the colonial government involved various stakeholders (women's groups, male villagers, and the general public), often faced women's active grievances, and required negotiation between the villagers and the colonial government. Such an inheritance tradition enforced by various legal orders constrained women's rights, interests, and development. The author realizes that this tradition-bound gender inequality is difficult to overcome, because beyond legal institutions, it requires a change in the male-dominated belief system.

A relatively new but crucial domain of development involves information and communication technologies (ICTs), which are explored by Barbara Fillip. She points out that although ICTs are essential today for development, the actual favorable outcome is not that simple and automatic. She refers to the examples of donor-funded pilot projects of ICT applications in developing countries, and observes that there is a tendency to oversimplify ICTs by confining them mainly to computers and the Internet. She stresses that the application of ICTs should be extended to such areas as health, education, E-commerce, and E-government. There is also a need to integrate ICTs with community needs, and to address the risk of creating unbalanced resource allocation for ICTs in poor countries.

## Part 3   Development Policy Issues in Major Sectors

Beyond academic discourse, the adoption of appropriate practical policies in various sectors—including agriculture, industry, population, education, health, housing, transport, and defense—is crucial for development. It involves the determination of sectoral priorities, selection of desirable alternatives within each sector, and allocation of scarce financial and human resources to achieve these priorities and alternatives. The selection of policy options should be based on contextual realities and human needs and demands. In many developing countries, however, inappropriate development policies are often undertaken due to international pressures, local vested interests, and/or lack of knowledge and information.

In this section, Cynthia Donovan examines agricultural policies vis-à-vis population pressure, with reference to Africa in general and the case of Rwanda in particular. She mentions that unlike other regions, the agriculture sector in Africa has stagnated, suffered lower yields of crops, and failed to keep up with the rate of population growth. One of the main causes of such agricultural failure has been the lack of policy initiatives and farmers' incentives to use modern innovations, technologies, and inputs. In the case of Rwanda, the past regimes adopted policies and techniques without much concern for farmers' incentives and without long-term investment in agricultural research. Although some adjustments have recently been made by farmers, in order to make significant improvements in agriculture, the author suggests the reduction of formal and informal barriers to trade among neighboring countries in the region, an agreed-upon regional system of reporting food prices, and investments in local agricultural research.

Monika Koubatrova Hristova also deals with the agriculture sector, but focuses on its structural adjustment policy in the case of Bulgaria. The transformation period since 1989 saw the adoption of structural adjustment in agriculture in Bulgaria within its broader national policy framework to shift from a planned economy to a market-oriented economy. She tries to explain the nature and impacts of such a transition in agriculture toward land reform, privatization, and private land ownership adopted for greater efficiency and performance. She mentions that in the current circumstances, land fragmentation will continue to be a concern, and thus the restructuring of ownership needs to be supplemented by a set of comprehensive policy measures to create a favorable condition for agricultural production.

Patricia Cholewka, on the other hand, looks into policy issues in the heath sector in postsocialist countries in Central and Eastern Europe that have recently experienced substantive changes in financing and delivering health care services. As these countries have shifted from a secondary (state responsibility) to a primary (individual responsibility) health care system, often with financial assistance from foreign donors, they face considerable challenges, such as the problem of reconciling planned controls with market incentives and the absence of coordination and accountability systems. The author recommends the adoption of the management technique of total quality management (used in the United States and Western Europe) for the health care system, which would emphasize the participation of health care practitioners both in planning and evaluating efficient and effective clinical services and in ensuring their accountability in this regard.

The health sector is also the focus of Alex Sekwat and Sangho Moon. More specifically, they examine the impacts of HIV/AIDS on economic development and its policy implications for countries in sub-Saharan Africa. In many countries in the region, this epidemic has adversely affected economic development by killing valuable human resources (farmers, teachers, civil servants, professionals, workers), diverting scarce financial resources and savings to health care expenditures, and so on. The authors recommend that the solutions to this catastrophic situation must go beyond technical measures (e.g., safe blood transfusions, treatment of sexually transmitted diseases), and include such preventive measures as information dissemination, proper education, community-level dialogue, voluntary testing, nondiscrimination against patients, and mobilization of all stakeholders and multiple sectors to combat the epidemic.

In his chapter, Desta Mebratu explores the nature of industrial policies and their limitations in African countries that have not done well in economic performance. He explains that these countries have pursued three types of development strategies since the 1960s, including the United Nations development initiatives, the regional development initiatives, and the Bretton Woods Institutions initiatives. Despite all these initiatives, the region experienced negative growth, although there has been some optimism in recent years. In general, the contribution of the manufacturing sector has been minimal in Africa. The author suggests that the African governments and their international partners should pay more attention to the role of the manufacturing industry in enhancing and sustaining development in the region. He feels optimistic that the region has great potential to achieve such development.

Habibul Haque Khondker focuses on science and technology policies practiced in Singapore. He emphasizes how science and technology can contribute to the realization of such developmental goals as poverty eradication, infrastructure building, disease control, and environmental management. In the case of Singapore, the author explains, the political leaders had a long-term view regarding science and technology, especially in terms of its role in accelerating economic growth based on export-led industrialization. Based on the changing global and local contexts, the government has increasingly shifted to information technology and biotechnology with considerable success. He points out that in Singapore, the state has played a crucial role in developing science and technology in coordination with education, infrastructure, and foreign human resources.

## Part 4  Development Institutions: Local and Global

Similar to development policies in the different sectors mentioned above, the choices of appropriate institutions at the global, national, and local levels remain crucial to achieve development. The history of development studies shows the evolution of institutional priorities; while the postwar period saw the expansive role of state institutions, the current age of globalization is dominated by international agencies, private sector institutions, and nongovernment organizations (NGO). The contemporary trend is toward decentralization, private initiatives, and global–local connections. Beyond the logic of effectiveness, however, there are often public opinions as well as vested interests behind these institutional choices, and these choices imply the configuration of local, national, and global power structures with implications for the major stakeholders involved in the enterprise of development.

In this regard, the chapter by Thomas Chapman identifies some major institutions or actors in development. His purpose is to familiarize the readers with these institutions and their profiles and data sources, which could be useful for exploring policy options and information related to such issues as population pressure, health care, food security, civil rights, and environmental problems. He provides the lists of certain major types of organizations, including U.S. government departments with international focus, foreign government agencies, international organizations, and NGOs. The author considers this chapter an information gateway to the institutional entities involved in development policies and issues.

At the local level, the institutional focus of Gedeon M. Mudacumura is on NGOs, especially their developmental role. He explains how NGOs have come to play an increasing developmental role in the developing world since the 1980s with active support from diverse international agencies. Although the number of NGOs has multiplied on the grounds that they are more capable of reaching rural people compared to state agencies and they have increasing sources of funding, close scrutiny would show the depressing statistics of poverty in developing countries. Despite certain institutional strengths of NGOs in terms of building local capacity, sustaining rural progress, and allowing the poor to resolve their own problems, the author questions their success in achieving these goals. He concludes by suggesting that development experts should investigate further to assess the role of NGOs in this regard.

Edward T. Jackson and P. Dal Brodhead also examine the role of NGOs with special reference to such microfinance institutions as *Palli Daridro Bimochon Foundation* (PDBF) or Rural Poverty Alleviation Foundation in Bangladesh. They explain that although there are several large microfinance NGOs in this country, they could cover only 10–20% of the rural poor, and thus it was necessary to create the PDBF to expand such financial support. After ten years of experimentation, the PDBF was established by the government as an autonomous microfinance institution to alleviate rural poverty. The authors emphasize that after such a long experimental process, the PDBF is not yet a perfect model and more remains to be accomplished.

In his chapter, Yong-shun Cai deals with the development roles and limits of local government institutions in China. There are rationales that decentralized local institutions are conducive to economic development, that because they have access to information about local conditions they can make better decisions regarding local problems, and that they generate competition and efficiency. Along this line of thinking, China adopted fiscal decentralization and allowed the participation of local leaders, but there are some serious problems with the local government system in China because of the emergence of local protectionism in each local unit; it imposes restrictions on external business enterprises from other local government units in order to maximize its own business interests. Such a situation diminishes competition among local government units, discourages them from improving their enterprises, and may have produced "collective bad" for China. Since the central government has not been very effective in resolving this problem of local protectionism, the author thinks that there is a need for "a strong and determined central state" to address the problem.

Noorjahan Bava also examines local government institutions, although her focus is on India. She explains how the local government system of *Panchayati Raj* (PR) evolved in India at different stages, from its emergence as one of the oldest traditions of local governance to its contemporary status. The failure of community development programs led to the establishment of the Mehta committee, which recommended a three-tiered PR system at the village and district levels to ensure citizens' participation, decentralized administration, and local self-governance in rural areas. The PR model faced some serious barriers, however, especially the efforts of central and state government leaders to reduce the autonomy exercised by the local government leaders. At the state level, however, because of the political ideology, stability, and commitment of political leaders, the PR institutions have been relatively successful in West Bengal.

In his chapter, Keshav C. Sharma explores decentralization for good governance in Botswana. After examining the features of good governance—democracy, decentralization, participation, and accountability—he emphasizes that some progress has been made in this regard in the case of Botswana. There are certain obstacles to decentralized development and public participation in this country, however, such as the weak vertical and horizontal coordination among institutions and the limited administrative capacity caused by inadequate financial and human resources. In order to achieve a decentralized and participatory mode of development, he recommends committed political leadership, further improvements in organizations and procedures, empowerment of grassroots organizations, and the involvement of traditional authorities.

## Part 5  Development Dilemma: How to Resolve It

The development field is full of dilemmas among sectors, policies, and institutions. National policy makers, international agencies, and nonstate actors have to make choices in development (e.g., between local and global orientations, rural and urban progress, export-led and import-led strategies, industrial and agricultural growth, labor-intensive and capital-intensive production, civilian and military use of resources, national resources and foreign loans, and economic growth and sustainability). What choices or options are made usually shape the fate of development in various regions and countries.

In his chapter, Roberto P. Guimaraes explores the dilemma and challenges inherent in the realization of sustainable development. He emphasizes that the current environmental crisis and resource scarcity require a sustainable mode of development, which in turn has implications for the choice of appropriate political institutions and development policies. There is also the challenge of paying attention to the *quality* rather than *quantity* of economic growth. At the global level, the author expresses concern for the continuing priority given to the economic interests of "hegemonic countries" while undermining the importance of poverty reduction, social equality, and the ecosystems. He regrets that, three decades after the sustainability debate in Stockholm, the challenge still continues.

Another development dilemma pointed out by Ho-Won Jeong and Eleftherios Michael is between the defense and security policy on the one hand and the concern for developmental issues on the other. They stress that although the end of the Cold War has created the potential for demilitarization, there are still new weapons being tested, produced, and deployed while millions of people suffer from poverty, hunger, and malnutrition. They suggest that to enhance development, the traditional security perspective based on military power and violence should be replaced by a more holistic approach that emphasizes peaceful settlement, cooperation, human rights, self-determination, nonviolence, and ecological balance. In the ultimate analysis, both security and development should be directed in such a way that they create conditions for realizing human capacity and expectations.

Lloyd J. Dumas deals with a similar topic that explains the dilemma of democracy, demilitarization, and development in Africa. For him, beyond elections, demilitarization is critical for democracy and development, because formal democratic institutions and informal civil society have little scope to function under the authoritarian structure of the military. Even when the military encourages cooperation and joint effort, it has the culture of obedience, structure of command, and so on. In Africa, demilitarization is essential, because there are too many weapons that kill people,

drain scarce resources, constrain political democracy, and harm economic development. There is also a need for developing human resources by investing in education
and skill development.

In their chapter, Yeoh Saw Ai Brenda, Theresa Wong, and Elaine Ho explore the
dilemma between labor migration and economic development in Southeast Asia. They
point out that there has emerged considerable literature explaining the consequences
of transnational migration for socioeconomic development in both the host and sending countries. The authors pay special attention to the impact of such labor migration
on the social development of women—in terms of their empowerment, gender equality, family matters, and so on—in the traditionally patriarchal countries in Southeast
Asia. In order to overcome the negative effects of female transmigration in the region,
it is emphasized that there should be political commitment to reforms, regional dialogue and bilateral agreements, support of civil society groups, networking among
female migrant workers, and so on.

Seungjoo Lee focuses on the growing dilemma between state autonomy and
globalization, and examines the changing role of the developmental state under globalization in South Korea. Based on his interpretation of the "developmental state," he
observes that because of the current reality of globalization, the related policy of
liberalization, and the recent financial crisis in the state-led Asian economies, there is a
common tendency to conclude that the existence of developmental states in Asia is in
doubt. Although he agrees with this conclusion to a certain extent, he finds the South
Korean case exceptional, because the developmental state in this country has continued to play a significant role in making the liberalization decisions in such sectors
as the Information Technology (IT) industry. From this particular case, he concludes
that the developmental state can adopt strategies to cope with new challenges posed by
the globalization process, which may largely depend on the state's historical, political,
and cultural contexts in various countries.

The chapter authored by Nadia Lisovskaya examines the gap between the
common perception and the actual nature of post-Soviet reforms. She underscores
the point that long after the collapse of the Soviet Union, because of the unique nature
of the post-Soviet transitional economies, their political economy is not properly
understood. In particular, she emphasizes that the lack of commodity exchange and
money economy has continued even after the end of state planning and adoption of
market mechanisms. This feature makes these transitional economies a specific group,
distinguishing them from other groups of countries in the world.

## Part 6   Development Trends and Challenges

In the development field, depending on global, national, and local circumstances,
there are continuous changes in the ideology, theory, and policy of development that
represent specific trends and challenges of development in different epochs. As
discussed earlier in this chapter, in recent decades there have emerged certain major
trends and challenges in the development field that need to be clearly understood in
order to pursue development policies and achieve their intended outcomes.

Globalization is one of the most widely known developmental trends and challenges, and is addressed by M. Shamsul Haque. He explains that the current globalization forces pose a serious challenge to a self-reliant mode of development in the
developing world. In this regard, he examines the extent of globalization and its
adverse impacts on self-reliance in three major development domains—the economic-

financial, politicoideological, and informational-cultural spheres. He also illustrates why the process of globalization continues to deepen despite its adverse developmental implications. In particular, he explains that the main beneficiaries and advocates of globalization (including transnational corporations, international agencies, and neo-liberal states) are the major forces behind its continuity and expansion. He recommends the dissemination of critical studies, generation of awareness, and solidarity among disadvantaged countries and peoples to encounter this globalization challenge.

H. J. Nel also focuses on globalization, but with special reference to its impact on the role of local government in South Africa. It is pointed out that under the new legislation in this country, local government has gained the power to act as an effective agency to develop local communities, provide basic services, and meet local needs. This role of local government has come under challenge, however, from the globalization process that requires a reduction in the role of both central and local governments and an increase in the private sector's role. In this context, the central government has to cut back public spending and deliver services through such alternative means as public–private partnership, which has financially affected the role of local government in South Africa. In this regard, the author suggests that various civil society organizations should endorse local government and act as alternatives to the private sector in delivering services.

Margaret Grieco deals with the developmental challenge of how to enhance the expression of concerns voiced by the poor through the Internet. She refers to the World Bank's initiative known as the Voices of the Poor, which aims to collect information and opinion exchanges and use them in project selection and design. The author suspects, however, that in this mechanism the aim is to "capture" voices without allowing "direct voicing," and that the "voicing" has been reduced to interviews and archived responses while the direct voices of the poor are missing. On the other hand, the author underscores the importance of the poor's "connectivity" based on their access to Information and Communication Technologies (ICTs), without which their community-driven initiatives remain localized. The use of ICTs by the community-driven initiatives may help overcome the problem of being too localized, and allow people to voice their needs and preferences through such means as Web pages, E-mail, and online forums.

With regard to the challenge of realizing sustainable development through good governance, R. B. Jain presents the case of India. He reiterates the important role played by governance or bureaucracy in accomplishing major developmental objectives in such developing countries as India. He realizes, however, that planning alone cannot ensure good governance; it requires the involvement of all levels of government in making tough decisions and monitoring and evaluating their impacts. The author is optimistic, however, that many countries now recognize the need to ensure good governance by combating corruption and adopting innovations in order to eventually realize sustainable development.

With regard to public governance, Hindy L. Schachter explores the recent challenge of diffusing the model of NPM—which largely emerged in Western countries—in such East Asian countries as China, Hong Kong, Malaysia, South Korea, and Taiwan. The author emphasizes that the transfer of such a businesslike, customer-oriented model has been quite rapid because of the availability and use of electronic communication. Regarding the transfer of NPM, however, there are observations that this customer model is culturally incompatible with the Asian context. The author finds that it is not the East–West cultural gap that shaped the observations made on NPM in East Asia; it is rather the inherent nature of the model itself that generated such observations. It is evident in the fact that the arguments and critical views on NPM made by the Asian and Western critics are very similar irrespective of their cultural differences. The problem in transferring NPM was thus not that much of a cultural gap; it was rather the inability of East Asian policy makers to foresee the model's inherent problems before it was transferred.

Another developmental challenge, the challenge of decentralization, is analyzed by Alfred Lakwo in the context of Uganda. It is pointed out by the author that development problems always generated new prescriptions, and decentralization policy represents one such prescription. Based on the experience of one district in Uganda, it is observed that decentralization still remains basically a top-down approach, that local power is largely concentrated in the hands of local elites, that the participation of nonstate actors is marginal, and that decentralization has often led to the recentralization of power at the local level. The author recommends a more people-centered governance based on citizenship building (without ethnic biases), changes in managerial orientation, and the devolution of power to the common people. The Ugandan experience is expected to be a source of lessons for other developing countries currently experimenting with decentralization.

## Part 7  Conclusions and Future Directions

Based on an understanding of the current trends and challenges mentioned above, it is the task of development scholars and experts to decipher the future directions of development in terms of its concepts, theories, policies, institutions, and so on. In this regard, Gedeon M. Mudacumura explains the problems and directions of development policy design. He suggests that policy analysts have not been forthcoming in designing solutions to various policy issues. In line with Laswell's emphasis on the policy context, it is stressed that policy analysts should seriously take into account all major contextual factors. In particular, the future policy experts addressing development issues must consider the multidimensional, uncertain, and complex nature of development. In this regard, the author recommends a participatory policy design that requires a team of multidisciplinary development scholars, practitioners, and other stakeholders to design necessary development policies.

Habib Zafarullah, on the other hand, examines the direction of decentralized local governance in Asia. He observes that a decentralized mode of governance has recently emerged in Asia because of either local pressures or the external influence of foreign donors. There are considerable variations among Asian countries such as India, the Philippines, Pakistan, Bangladesh, Indonesia, and Thailand with regard to the nature and extent of decentralization, especially because of their diversity in macropolitical structures. In general, there is hardly any genuine devolution of power, and privatization in local administration is not a preferred option in most Asian countries. There is also the risk that the opportunity for local-level participation might be manipulated by local elites. The author is optimistic about this new context of decentralization in Asia, although the success may depend on genuine political commitment, administrative support, public–private partnership, civil society's interaction with the state, and so on.

Kristen Sheeran focuses on the direction of global environmental policy with special reference to the Kyoto Protocol. For the author, this protocol is a crucial framework because of the global concern for climate change, although by giving concessions to developing countries, it compromises efficiency. It is argued that the participation of developing countries in climate control is essential for efficiency. In order to ensure both equity and efficiency in climate control, there are alternative approaches, such as paying developing countries for maintaining their forests and thus benefiting the global community. Without such payment, there will be very little incentive for tropical countries to stop cutting forests for fuel and timber. With regard to emissions, the author suggests that a climate control treaty such as the Kyoto Protocol could require all nations (including developing countries) to reduce emissions.

The main concern of Jan-Erik Lane and Svante Ersson is policy implementation in poor countries with regard to its economic and political preconditions. The authors seem to be indifferent toward the choice of approaches (top-down and bottom-up) to policy implementation, but they emphasize political stability and economic development as the primary two preconditions for policy success in poor countries. They observe that there is a positive correlation between affluence (economic development) and lack of corruption (political stability); affluence leads to political stability, which in turn helps to reduce poverty, because political instability or uncertainty adversely affects policies. The authors conclude by emphasizing that political corruption is a major cause of the failure of antipoverty policies in various developing countries.

Another crucial development concern for the future is the measurement of poverty, which is explored by Karin Schelzig. It is crucial because variations in the methods of poverty measurement may determine the number of people categorized as poor, and thus affect policy choices, program decisions, and project assessments. Although most studies recognize the multidimensional and complex nature of poverty, its assessment is often reduced to the level of income. The author recommends that the measurement of poverty should go beyond the economic interpretation, adopt a multidimensional approach, and include such factors as social capital, access to property, vulnerability, political rights, and popular perception.

Finally, the concluding chapter, by Gedeon M. Mudacumura, outlines the development agenda for the twentyfirst century. Based on the observations made in *World Development Report 2000/01* on the growing gap between the rich and the poor worldwide, it is reiterated that global economic growth has failed to trickle down to benefit all people. The author emphasizes the urgent need for improving the living conditions of the poor by expanding their access to basic services. Moreover, in order to pursue a holistic mode of development, the author offers his "general theory of sustainability," which incorporates six dimensions (economic, social, cultural, political, ecological, spiritual) of development. He suggests that the adoption of such a holistic approach may require policy makers to go beyond economic thinking and embrace other noneconomic domains of development.

## REFERENCES

Addo, H. (1985). Beyond Eurocentricity: Transformation and transformational responsibility. In: Addo, H., ed. Development as Social Transformation. Boulder, CO: Westview Press, pp. 12–47.

Alvarez, S. E., Dagnino, E., Escober, A. (1998). Introduction: The cultural and the political in

Latin American social movements. In: Alvarez, S. E., Dagnino, E., Escober, A., eds. Cultures of Politics and Politics of Cultures. Boulder, CO: Westview Press, pp. 1–29.

Angus, I. H., Jhally, S. (1989). Introduction. In: Angus, I., Jhally, S., eds. Cultural Politics in Contemporary America. New York: Routledge, pp. 1–14.

Asmerom, H. K. (1994). The impact of structural adjustment policy on administrative reform strategies. In: Jain, R. B., Bongartz, H., eds. Structural Adjustment, Public Policy and Bureaucracy in Developing Societies. New Delhi: Har-Anand, pp. 368–395.

Bello, W., Cunningham, S., Rau, B. (1994). Dark Victory: The United States, Structural Adjustment and Global Poverty. London: Pluto.

Berthoud, G. (1992). Market. In: Sachs, W., ed. The Development Dictionary: A Guide to Knowledge as Power. London: Zed Books, pp. 70–87.

Bjonnes, R. (2002). Strategies to eradicate poverty: Integral approach to development. In: UNESCO, ed. The Encyclopedia of Lifesupport Systems Paris: UNESCO, www.sustainablevillages.org/Resources/pages/eradicating_poverty. html.

Bloomstrom, M., Hettne, B. (1984). Development Theory in Transition. London: Zed Books.

Carchedi, G. (1994). Privatization: East meets West. In: Clarke, T., ed. International Privatization: Strategies and Practices. Berlin: Walter de Gruyter, pp. 289–323.

Chaudhry, K. A. (1994). Economic liberalization and the lineages of the Rentier State. Compar. Pol. 27(1):1–25.

CIPE (Center for International Private Enterprise) (1992). The economic reform survey: Regional findings. In: Economic Reform Today (3). Washington, DC: Center for International Private Enterprise.

Clarke, T. (1994). Reconstructing the public sector: Performance measurement, quality assurance, and social accountability. In: Clarke, T., ed. International Privatization: Strategies and Practices. Berlin: Walter de Gruyter, pp. 399–431.

Clements, L. (1994). Privatization American style: The "Grand Illusion". In: Clarke, T., ed. International Privatization: Strategies and Practices. Berlin: Walter de Gruyter, pp. 87–104.

CPD (Centre for Policy Dialogue). (1999). Policy Reform: The Need for a New Consensus. report no. 8. Dhaka: Centre for Policy Dialogue.

Development Group for Alternative Policies (1999). The All-Too-Visible-Hand: A Five-Country Look at the Long and Destructive Reach of the IMF. Washington, DC: Development Group of Alternative Policies.

Esteva, G. (1992). Development. In: Sachs, W., ed. The Development Dictionary: A Guide to Knowledge as Power. London: Zed Books, pp. 6–25.

Goulet, D. (1980). Development experts: The one-eyed giants. World Dev 8, (7/8):481–489.

Haque, M. S. (1999). Restructuring Development Theories and Policies: A Critical Study. Albany, NY: State University of New York Press.

Haque, M. S. (1999). Globalization of market ideology and its impact on third world development. In: Kouzmin, A., Hayne, A., eds. Essays in Economic Globalization, Transnational Policies and Vulnerability. Amsterdam: IOS Press, pp. 75–100.

Haque, M. S. (1999). The fate of sustainable development under the neoliberal regimes in developing countries. Internat. Polit. Sci. Rev. 20(2):199–222.

Haque, M. S. (2000). The diminishing publicness of public service under the current mode of governance. Pub. Admin. Rev. 61(1):65–82.

Harrod, J. (1982). Development studies: From change to stabilization. In: de Gaay Fortman, B., ed. Rethinking Development. The Hague: Institute of Social Studies, pp. 1–19.

Helleiner, G. K. (1990). The New Global Economy and the Developing Countries: Essays in International Economics and Development. Aldershot, England: Edward Elgar.

Hildyard, N. (1997). The World Bank and the State: A Recipe for Change? London: Bretton Wood Project.

ILO (International Labour Organization). (1995). Impact of Structural Adjustment in the Public Services. Geneva: International Labour Office.

ILO (International Labour Organization). (1997–1998). World Labour Report 1997–98: Industrial Relations, Democracy, and Social Stability. Geneva: International Labour Office.

Jiyad, A. M. (1995). The social balance sheet of privatization in the Arab countries. Third Nordic Conference on Middle Eastern Studies, 19–22, June. Finland: Joensuu.

Kaul, M. (1996). Civil service reforms: Learning from commonwealth experiences. Pub. Admin. Dev. 16(2):131–150.

Kelegama, S. (1995). The impact of privatization on distributional equity: The case of Sri Lanka. In: Ramanadham, V. V., ed. Privatization and Equity. London: Routledge, pp. 143–180.

Kellner, D. (1990). Television and the Crisis of Democracy. Boulder, CO: Westview Press.

Korten, D. C. (1990). Getting to the 21st Century. West Hartford, CI: Kumarian Press.

Manzo, K. (1991). Modernist discourse and the crisis of development theory. Stud. Compar. Internat. Dev. 26(2):3–36.

Martin, B. (1993). In the Public Interest: Privatization and Public Sector Reform. London: Zed Books.

Martinez, E., Garcia, A. Aug. 1999. What is "Neo-liberalism?" Alternatives.

Merriam, A. H. (1988). What does "third world" mean? In: Norwine, J. Gonzalez, A., eds. The Third World: States of Mind and Being. Boston: Unwin Hyman, pp. 15–22.

Munck, R. (1999). Deconstructing development discourses: Of impasses, alternatives and politics. In: Munck, R., O'Hearn, D., eds. Critical Development Theory: Contributions to a New Paradigm. Dhaka: University Press, pp. 196–210.

Munck, R. Deconstructing development discourses: Of impasses, alternatives and politics. paper presented at Development: The Need for Reflection, Centre for Developing Area Studies, McGill University, Montreal, Quebec, Sept. 21–23, 2000.

Murphy, C. N. (1990). Freezing the North–South bloc(k) after the East–West thaw. Socialist. Rev. 20(3):25–45.

Nandy, A. (1989). The idea of development: The experience of modern psychology as a cautionary tale and as an allegory. In: Augustine, J. S., ed. Strategies for Third World Development. New Delhi: Sage, pp. 34–46.

Odle, M. (1993). Towards a Stages Theory Approach to Privatization. Pub. Admin. Dev. 13(1): 17–35.

Onis, Z. (1991). The logic of the developmental state. Compar. Pol. 24(1):109–126.

Opitz, P. J. (1987). The United Nations and the emancipation of the third world. Law State 35:7–21.

Petras, J. F. (1990). The world market: Battleground for the 1990s. J. Contemp. Asia 20(2): 145–176.

Pieterse, J. N. (1991). Dilemmas of development discourse: The crisis of developmentalism and the comparative method. Dev. Change 22(1):5–29.

Polidano, C. Don't Discard State Autonomy: Revisiting the East Asian Experience of Development. Public Policy and Management Working Paper no. 9, Institute for Development Policy and Management, University of Manchester, Manchester, UK: Sept. 1998.

Preston, P. W. (1987). Rethinking Development: Essays on Development and Southeast Asia. London: Routledge & Kegan Paul.

Raghaviah, Y. (1987). Post-positivist bureaucratic theory and the third world predicament. Indian J. Pub. Admin. 33(1):1–13.

Ramanadham, V. V. (1995). The impact of privatization on distributional equity. In: Ramanadham, V. V., ed. Privatization and Equity. London: Routledge, pp. 1–34.

Randall, V., Theobald, R. (1985). Political Change and Underdevelopment. Durham, NC: Duke University Press.

Said, E. W. (1983). The World, the Text, and the Critic. Cambridge, MA: Harvard University Press.

Sanyal, K. K. (1993). Paradox of competitiveness and globalisation of underdevelopment. Econ. Pol. Wkly. 28 (June):1326–1330.

Sarkar, P. (1991). IMF/World Bank stabilisation programme: A critical assessment. Econ. Pol. Wkly. 5 (Oct.):2307–2310.

Shirley, M. M. (1998). Trends in privatization. Econ. Ref. Today 1:8–10.

Sinaceur, M. A. (1983). Foreword: Development—to what end? In: Perroux, F., ed. A New Concept of Development. London: Croom Helm, pp. 1–19.

Smith, B. (1991). The changing role of government in comparative perspective. In: Smith, B. C., ed. The Changing Role of Government: Management of Social and Economic Activities. London: Management Development Programme, Commonwealth Secretariat, pp. 27–43.

Steidlmeier, P. (1987). The Paradox of Poverty: A Reappraisal of Economic Development Policy. Cambridge, MA: Ballinger.

Stein, H. (1994). Theories of institutions and economic reform in Africa. World Dev. 22(12): 1833–1849.

Streeten, P. (1975). The Limits of Development Research. Oxford: Pergamon.

Streeten, P. (1983). Development Dichotomies. Brighton, England: IDS.

Tevera, D. (1995). The medicine that might kill the patient: Structural adjustment and urban poverty in Zimbabwe. In: Simon, D., et al., ed. Structurally Adjusted Africa: Poverty, Debt and Basic Needs. London: Pluto Press.

UNDP. (1997). Human Development Report 1997. New York: Oxford University Press.

UNDP. (1998). Human Development Report 1998. New York: Oxford University Press.

UNDP. (2001). Human Development Report 2001. New York: Oxford University Press.

UNESCAP (U.N. Economic and Social Commission for Asia and the Pacific). 2000; Review of the State of the Environment in Asia and the Pacific. Bangkok, Thailand: UNESCAP, http://www.unescap.org/mced2000/so1.htm.

Veltmeyer, H. (1993). Liberalisation and structural adjustment in Latin America: In search of an alternative. Econ. Pol. Wkly. 25 (Sept.):2080–2086.

Walton, J., Seddon, D. (1994). Free Markets & Food Riots: The Politics of Global Adjustment. Cambridge, MA: Blackwell.

Westergaard, K. (1985). State and Rural Society in Bangladesh: A Study of Relationship. London: Curzon.

Wiarda, H. J. (1981). The ethnocentrism of the social science implications for research and policy. Rev. of Pol. 43(2):163–197.

Williamson, J. 1999; What should the bank think about the Washington consensus? background paper for the World Bank's World Development Report 2000. Washington, DC: Institute of International Economics, http://www.iie.com/papers/williamson0799.htm.

World Bank. (1996). World Bank Annual Report 1996. Washington, DC: International Bank for Reconstruction and Development.

World Bank. (1997). World Development Report 1997: The State in a Changing World. New York: Oxford University Press.

World Bank. (2000). World Development Report 1999/2000. New York: Oxford University Press.

World Bank. (2001). World Development Report 2000/2001. New York: Oxford University Press.

# 2

# The Narrative Foundations of International Development

**RYM A. KAKI**

*University of Southern California, Los Angeles, California, U.S.A.*

## INTRODUCTION

The history of thought and action concerning international development, particularly since World War II, bears great similarity to what Isaiah Berlin (1962), largely inspired by Hegel, observed about the history of social and political theory. In fact, international development discourse has been no more, to use Berlin's words, than "a changing pattern of great liberating ideas which inevitably turn into suffocating straightjackets, and so stimulate their own destruction by new emancipating, and at the same time, enslaving conceptions" (Bernstein, 1976: 57). Each time a particular development policy—whether at the local, national, regional, or international level— is proclaimed to solve a particular development controversy, an underlying statement is being made about *its* "liberating" and "emancipatory" effects, and each time the proclaimed "great liberating ideas" fail to bring about the desired results in a particular development controversy, they inevitably become "suffocating straightjackets," breeding their own destruction and calling for "new emancipatory ideas" to emerge.

Along these lines, but using semantics more directly applicable to international development work, Emery Roe (1999) depicts a similar pattern of thinking and action in international development. He observed a pattern of thought and action built around the generation of "development narratives" and "counternarratives" to stabilize our assumptions for decision making in the face of unfolding development controversies.

*Development narratives* are the rule of thumb, arguments, "war stories" and other scenarios about development that enable decision makers to take decisions. [And] there can be no development without *counter-narratives*. The task of policy makers, development

**25**

specialists, and policy scholars is to come up with counter-narratives that are just as effective, if not more so, in stabilizing decision-making under uncertainty but which are far less noxious and pernicious than the development narratives currently guiding a great deal of that decision making (1999: 1–2).

Roe draws attention to being able to dig beneath the surface of the facts and figures that drive much of our contemporary international development practices and to focus on the "storytelling"; that is, the narrative structure underlying the thought and many of the decision-making processes that take place in the deliberation of international development strategies and plans. The nature of traditional inquiry in international development studies has long neglected the narrative foundations of international development discourse hinted at by both Berlin and Roe, however. This chapter clearly takes inspiration from the above conceptualization, as it calls attention to the narrative structure; that is, the stories animating thinking and action in international development. Before examining the nature of the storytelling underlying international development policies, various definitional and theoretical assumptions driving the meaning and usage of the terms *development*, *development narrative*, and *development narrative analysis* will be explored.

## THE MEANINGS OF DEVELOPMENT

The term development is widely used without having acquired an agreed-upon definition. Uphof and Ilchman refer to it as "probably one of the most depreciated terms in social science literature, having been used vastly more than it has been understood" (1972: ix). In the early postwar era there was a general tendency to discuss and use international development in segmented terms, such as "economic development" and "political development," and to concentrate both thinking and practice on the countries of the so-called Third World as the newly emergent scene (i.e., the geographic laboratory in which the experimentation of development ideas and practices is said to take place).

### Economic Interpretation of Development

For a long time development economists understood development as the pursuit of "economic growth"; that is, "the diversion of a nation's scarce resources and productive powers to the augmentation of its stock of productive wealth and to the progressive enlargement of its gross and net national product of goods and services" (Braibanti and Spengler, 1961: 9). Development economists, mostly living in the industrialized nations of the West, proposed "industrialization" for the so-called underdeveloped countries of the Third World as the "big push" strategy to accelerate national economic development. Industrialization meant shifting production from the primary sector—that is, traditional rural agriculture—to the more modern manufacturing sector, which is usually located in the urban industrial centers in which productivity is believed to increase. The gross national product (GNP) per capita was dubbed not only *the* measurement index of development, but also *the* end to development.

Although little disagreement was expressed over the relevance of economic growth as an analytical concept in the development debate, development economists' views diverged a great deal on the means and strategies to achieve it. No attempt can be made in this chapter to do justice to the abundant studies of international development economics that shaped thinking and practice in international development. Suffice it to say that from the second half of the twentieth century economic thinking on development included many scenarios and narratives on how development, primarily seen as a matter of economic growth, could materialize in Third World nations. From W. W. Rostow's *The Stages of Economic Growth,* which posited a linear path along which all countries are said to travel, to the *big push* theories, which considered manufacturing as inherently superior to primary production as a vehicle of development, to the subsequent *dual-sector modeling,* which called for the transfer of production from the traditional subsistence agrarian rural centers to the modern, commercialized, industrial urban centers in which productivity is believed to increase and growth to take place (Meier, 1984), all such strategies shared the common denominator of GNP-based national growth as an end.

Development economists of the mid-1970s and early 1980s increasingly began to express dissatisfaction with the idea of narrowly confining the term development to economic growth, thus calling for a reconsideration of the meaning of development and a fundamental redirection of development policy. Settling for an aggregate or per capita index of development was found to overlook the noneconomic dimensions of development, such as the achievement of better nourishment, health, education, physical living conditions, conditions of employment, and participation, especially for the low-end poverty groups in the so-called poor countries of the Third World (Meier, 1984: 5–9; Somjee, 1990). Moreover, economic development theorizing had to move from the simplistic, narrowly focused, linear, and deterministic conceptualizations that merely identify development with a set of determinants and conditions or a catalog of characteristics to broader political economy explanations that recognize national development beyond economic growth, encompassing social, political, legal, and administrative development. As early as the mid-1970s, political economy scholars also started to call for more interdisciplinary research to determine how economic and noneconomic forces acted and to guard against the uncontested worship of the concept of GNP as the ultimate measurement of a nation's development accomplishments.

> The questions to ask about a country's development are: what has been happening to poverty? What has been happening to employment? What has been happening to inequality? If all three of these central problems have been growing worse, it would be strange to call the result "development," even if per capita income had soared. This applies of course to the future too. A "plan" which conveys no targets for reducing poverty, unemployment and inequality can hardly be considered a "development plan" (Duddley Seers, in Meier, 1984:9).

This growing dissatisfaction with the GNP-based development approach also resonated amid the rank and file of Third World national development practitioners. A Pakistani government official once summarized the development practitioners' growing dissatisfaction as follows: "The problem of development must be defined as a selective attack on the worst forms of poverty... We were taught to take care of our GNP because it would take care of poverty. Let us reverse this and take care of poverty because it will take care of the GNP" (Meier, 1984:8).

Rethinking GNP-based development also made its way to international donors. Before 1970, development policy and research at the Bretton Woods institutions, namely the World Bank and the International Monetary Fund (IMF), was dominated by strong neoliberal themes. Neoliberalism, thought to be the principal route to economic growth, prescribed GNP maximization by domestically adopting capital accumulation via savings and investment and externally promoting export expansion and diversification. It was not until Robert McNamara's leadership that the World Bank's ideology was challenged and calls were made to stress poverty issues and income distribution programs (Ayres, 1983). McNamara's 1974 address in Nairobi, entitled *Redistribution with Growth*, signaled a major turning point in the World Bank's development research and policy:

> It is now clear that more than a decade of rapid growth in underdeveloped countries has been of little or no benefit to perhaps a third of their population. Although the average per capita income of the Third World has increased by 50 percent since 1960, this growth has been very unequally distributed among countries, regions within countries, and socioeconomic groups. Paradoxically, while growth policies have succeeded beyond the expectations of the first development decade, the very idea of aggregate growth as a social objective has increasingly been called into question (Chenery et al., 1974: xiii).

The realization that the GNP was an insufficient indicator to monitor a particular nation's development has led the World Bank to call for a reordering of national priorities and policies: "Instead of policies to foster growth in general, policies should be redesigned to direct investment to poverty groups in the form of education, access to credit, health care, public facilities and so on" (Meier, 1984: 136). The GNP-based approach to development was not the only issue that came under heavy criticism by political economy scholars, particularly during the last two decades of the twentieth century. The notion of "one style-fits-all" development also came under attack. Development in the so-called Third World countries had to mean more than the mere replication of the conditions and experience generally prevalent in Western industrialized countries. Commenting on what could be learned about various national development experiences since World War II, Meier observed that

> Clearly, there is more than one feasible route to equitable growth and development. Some countries have succeeded by pursuing market-oriented, outward-looking strategies, relying on entrepreneurial skills (such as Hong Kong and Korea) or physical resources (such as oil exporting countries) as the key to growth. By contrast, the People's Republic of China has followed a socialist, inward-looking strategy based on considerable natural resources, ideology, and highly effective social organization (1984: 49).

Political economy scholars of the mid-1970s and 1980s, along with disillusioned national and international development practitioners, have contributed a great deal to unfreezing economic thinking on international development from the misconceptions, rigidities, orthodoxies, and—to borrow Berlin's term—the suffocating straightjackets that prevailed throughout the first three decades of post-World War II development. Political economists, ranging from Marxist to neoliberal, not only "unfroze" the post-World War II economic development narratives by calling attention to the limitations of the GNP-based approach to development, but most important, provided us with a number of insightful arguments that could lay the theoretical grounds for a new counternarrative of development capable of garnering wider approval. Although not emanating from a single coherent theory of development, some of their most insightful arguments can be summarized as follows:

Development involves something more than economic growth. Development is taken to mean growth plus *change*; there are essential qualitative dimensions in the development process that may be absent in the simple process of expanding or widening an economy. While improving a nation's performance of its factors and techniques of production, emphasis should also be directed toward the nation's performance in such areas as unemployment, harsh income inequalities, discrimination, widespread rates of illiteracy, disease, malnutrition, crime, and violence.

Development is not an end but a *process*. Thinking in terms of process implies the operation of certain forces in an interconnected and causal fashion. To interpret development in terms of a process involving causal relationships should prove more meaningful than identifying development with a set of determinants or conditions. Development is a form of a progressive action—a working out of certain principal forces that reveal the inner structure of a society's development.

Development is *multipurposive*; there is a multitude of goals and subgoals underlying the development process. Although GNP growth has been traditionally pursued as the primary goal, other equally important goals are also being pursued (political stability, social justice, human resource development, poverty alleviation).

Development is about *sustainability*. There is a vital distinction between initiating development and the more difficult task of sustaining development over the long run.

Development surpasses the nation–state level as *the unit of development*. A nation's development path is the result of the interplay of endogenous as well as exogenous structures. On the endogenous level, state agencies alone are not capable of bringing about economic growth and political change. On the exogenous level, historically and currently established relations of interdependence bind national systems with supranational systems. Interdependence—whether via historical and/or colonial relations or via present industrial–financial relations, industrial–technological relations, trade relations, debt relations, foreign investment relations, or multinational corporate relations—significantly shapes the course and style of a nation's development experience.

Although insightful and refreshing, the above arguments are still far from bringing closure to the debate on what development is or is not. In fact, twenty-first century economic thinking on development is not likely to differ from the type of reasoning that evolved in the preceding century, at least *in pattern*, in that it will most likely continue to undergo the cycle of generating new narratives and counternarratives on what human development means and what it entails. The concept of development itself is most likely to be subjected to continuous deconstruction and reconstruction, and whatever definition is ascribed to its content and extent, it will most likely not be able to reach either a satisfactory or definitive closure. Moreover, whoever undertakes the deconstruction and reconstruction of development narratives will most likely do so through their disciplinary training and experiential knowledge, despite efforts to transcend disciplinary divisions and idiosyncratic experiences. The following section will turn to what political theorists have to offer on the subject.

## Political Explanation of Development

Among the political scientists of the first three decades following World War II, the term development was also assigned various meanings and was a cause of much dispute. Throughout much of the 1960s and 1970s, definitions "proliferated at an alarming rate" (Huntington and Dominguez, 1975). Political development referred to a myriad of societal situations and processes. For some, it pertained to the capacity of political systems of the newly decolonized countries to cope with the challenges of state building, nation building, participation, and welfare distribution (Almond and Powell, 1966; Binder et al., 1974). They further argued that development occurs if the political system has the capabilities for successfully adapting to the above-mentioned challenges; otherwise the result will be "negative development" (Almond and Powell, 1966: 34). For others, political development meant the capacity to close the gap between the rapid and disruptive demands for social and economic change (i.e., modernization) and the demands for political stability (i.e., institutionalization) (Jaguaribe, 1973). For dependency political theorists, causes of underdevelopment were attributed to the overwhelming impact of the external environment on developing countries, thus denouncing the uncontested propagation of Western political theory and its bias toward an Anglo-Saxon standard for modernity and development. Concepts such as colonialism, neocolonialism, economic stagnation, marginalization, and denationalization animated the dependency school discourse (Smith, 1985). Summarizing the overall thematic orientation of dependency theorists, Ferrel Heady noted

> The dominant note is that what is commonly called underdevelopment is the consequence of state of dependence by one society on another, and a secondary theme is that this dependency condition is repeated within the affected society by an internal colonialism which one segment of the society imposes on another segment. The net effect is a situation which allows little prospect for improvement without a drastic alteration of both the external environment and the internal system (1996: 131).

The dependency narrative used by the Cold War dependency theorists to account for the causes of underdevelopment throughout the developing world gained widespread acceptance. Dependency narratives have generally depicted a Third World trapped in an "interimperial" system, represented by a bipolar configuration; and, the United States and the ex-USSR. While Western Europe, Japan, and China were viewed as enjoying relatively high degrees of autonomy and self-determination, the rest of the world was viewed as being in a condition of dependency in which the future outlooks for autonomy and self-determination were bleak (Heady, 1996). Political elites in the developing world often mimicked much of the dependency scholars' posture and used their dependency arguments to mask what might be some of the endogenous causes to the persistent low levels of underdevelopment, such as the perceived state failure to foster a favorable environment for political stability, economic growth, and social justice. With the end of the Cold War era and in light of the new world system configuration, the dependency narrative had to play down the "conspiracy" undertones and revise the "victimization" of the so-called Third World.

The revisionist trend in international development scholarship was propelled by all branches in the social sciences, in particular development economics and political science, and resonated far beyond academic circles (Streeten et al. 1981). Even before the collapse of the bipolar world and its implications on the Third World, a growing number of development theorists of the early 1980s and throughout much of the 1990s began to express dissatisfaction with the usage of the term development. Efforts to rethink development were reflected in the writings of Alberto Guerreiro Ramos (1981), David Apter (1987), Joel Migdal (1988), Samuel Huntington (1991), Branislav Gosovic (2000), and many others to be included in this review, each taking a different angle. Ramos (1981) and later Gosovic (2000) both rejected conventional approaches to development, calling for the demystification of the term. Ramos advocated a model of development that promotes national self-reliance and inventiveness and rejects modernization by imitation of the so-called advanced industrial societies. Gosovic deplored Third World countries' endemic and continuous receptivity of the Western conceptualization of development and progress. Gosovic does not consider that Third World countries imitate the North by conviction; he views them as "trapped" in a world system configuration run by the "global ruling class," propagating an insufficiently understood "global intellectual hegemony." For Gosovic, a small number of influential global actors—including the International Monetary Fund (IMF), the World Bank, the World Trade Organization (WTO), and giant business entities from the North—are playing a critical role in the international system, which is based on neoliberal premises that have not been adequately understood, scrutinized, challenged, or questioned (2000: 448–452). As a result, Gosovic expects the emergence of a counternarrative in international development in order to challenge the current global intellectual hegemony that has dominated international development discourse and practice for so long (2000:455). He clearly interprets international development discourse in terms of a progression of narratives and counternarratives: "Any "[intellectual] hegemony is a passing phenomenon" and "hegemonies in general do not last." Such are Gosovic's valuable insights, which will be retained for discussion purposes throughout this chapter.

In addition to liberating the conventional development discourse dependency themes, state-centered narratives were declared empirically irrelevant. National government bureaucracies were no longer considered the only institutional agencies to bring about political stability and economic growth; a host of other formal and informal institutional arrangements came into play to either foster or hinder development (Apter, 1987; North, 1989). Migdal (1988) found that throughout Asia, Africa, and Latin America strong states had been more a rarity than a rule of thumb: "so many prevailing approaches—modernization theories, Marxist theories, dependency and world system theories, and empiricist descriptions—were both too uncritical about the power at the top and too state-centered" (1988: xvi–xvii). Migdal's frustration with the modernization theory's preoccupation with the effect of the center on the periphery, as well as the Marxist/dependency theory's exclusive focus on Third World societies and politics, interlocked with metropolitan countries, is not unique.

By the end of the twentieth century the focus of development theorizing went not only beyond modernity themes, dependency relations, and nation–states as the agents of development; it had also transcended the developed versus developing nations' dichotomy and the bipolar world configuration. The term Third World itself came under heavy attack (Heady, 1996:153). Geographically configured discussions of development had to be abandoned, as the post-Cold War geography of international development has changed. In fact, the post-Cold War world system changed configurations; thinking in "the old traditional ways" (i.e., in terms of First World, Second World, and Third World) while pondering the currently unfolding development controversies of the twenty-first century is not longer feasible. The post-Cold War era resulted in a more crisis-prone world, a sort of a *marché mondial*, increasingly characterized by the leakage of power from nation–states to supra- and subnational levels, the outbreak of cultural diversity, the globalization of production and trade systems, the internationalization of communication technologies, and the breakdown of traditional borders and national identities. All these profound changes are bringing more complex, uncertain, and unstable controversies, which require mindsets cognizant of the inherent complexity and uncertainty underlying political and social systems throughout the world. On the nature of the current world order, the French philosopher Jacques Rancière comments

> The notion of "marché mondial" that is everywhere but nowhere results in a confusion as there is no incarnation of the adversary on a specific issue. There is no statist scene to confront. Anti-imperialist movements of the 1960s addressed their own states as ones engaged in colonial and neo-colonial wars. Today, this scene is fractured. The responsibility of order is divided in an indecisive manner between nation-states, international institutions, and a faceless world-order: a center that is both everywhere and nowhere (2000:125–126).

In the face of a crisis-prone world in which complexity, uncertainty, and instability are the unchallenged governing principles, theorizing efforts about development ought to take a self-reflective pause. It is necessary to absorb the fast-changing configuration of world political systems and search for alternative analytical methods that can capture the high levels of complexity, uncertainty, and divisiveness that govern much of our international development work.

## Development Beyond Disciplinary Boundaries

From the above discussion, one might observe that no matter how hard scholars and practitioners attempted to present the concept of development and generate a body of universal laws to standardize the concept, they were bound to fall into disciplinary divisions and reductionist models, and inevitably make some judgment calls as to what is and is not important. Even those who attempted to engage in interdisciplinary research and apply the so-called broader political economy and institutionalist explanations to the process of development found it difficult to account for all the possible causal relationships underlying development.

Whether it is in the northern, southern, eastern, or western parts of the globe, whether the pondering issues are of economic growth, political stability, administrative reform, social justice, or environmental sustainability, actual development has not been realized. Development is about bringing out possibilities, about "unrealized potential" and the "pursuit of betterment," to use Gerald Caiden's terminology

(1991: 93). The trouble with theorizing efforts on the nature and scope of development is the overall reluctance to admit to the incoherent nature of the development context, the imperfectability of our conjectures and institutions, and the perpetual feeling of "unfinished business" whenever we want to assess progress. Speaking of progress in administrative reform, Caiden (1991:93) mentions that "mankind is still experimenting with what works and what does not work. Only the exceptionally privileged can be content with the status quo and even they have fears about the state of world affairs. It seems that for every two steps forward, mankind slips back a step and more."

By defining development as the unrealized potential, the pursuit of betterment, and slow progress, this chapter does not purport to lock the discussion on development in theoretical "relativism" or "escapism" or to elevate it to the realm of the unknown. Similarly, humankind will not tire of developing stories about what has been developed and what needs to be further developed by saying that development is about unfinished business and unrealized potential. Theory construction about development, whether explanatory, interpretive, or critical, is still relevant, possible, and even desirable. What is becoming irrelevant is the narrow pursuit of theoretical precision, neatness, simplicity, and elegance, a sort of a theoretical correctness thrust upon a world that is instead governed by incoherence, complexity, uncertainty, and instability, where "no one is really held constant and no one is really under control." Commenting on the nature of the policy world in development, Roe (2001) remarks that "in the policy world, the only thing complete are disasters...The policy world is a world of interruptions, and interruptions make for unfinished business." He recommends looking for new "techniques that frame uncertainty and complexity in ways we can do something about them, without at the same time supposing that the uncertainty and complexity can be dismissed, avoided, or otherwise dispelled" (Roe, 1998: 7–8).

In other terms, the sooner we acknowledge the limits of our "great liberating ideas" encapsulated in explanatory, interpretive and critical theories and models of development, the less confined, more creative and inventive will be our ideas and tools for "the pursuit of betterment" and the realization of the "unrealized potential" that is development. Theorizing about the "unrealized potential" and the "room for betterment" requires more than neatly delineated blueprints (1998). It requires a sense of intellectual humility and a return to some basic premises about the governing principles of our human-made society. As Roe noted, "not all development controversies come to us neatly defined," and "the probability of planned actions going wrong is high in an environment characterized by instability and uncertainty," adds Goren Hyden (1983:65). Having defined what development is, the following section explains the critical attributes of the development context that make development issues complex, uncertain, and controversial.

## Nature of the Development Context

By defining development as "unrealized potential", there emerges an area of thinking and action blurred by uncertainty, complexity, and controversy, which downplays the importance of producing results. Yet, we need to gain a deeper understanding on the nature of the context in which results are expected to occur. Results cannot be assessed nor appreciated without a delineation of the nature of the context. Although development research is replete with facts and figures on what works and what does not work, development practitioners continue to encounter situations in which they lack knowledge about what really matters while planning actions and evaluating results.

Development dilemmas, which involve multiple and often inconsistent objectives, many constraints, multiple and conflicting evaluative criteria, and constant trade-offs, abound by the thousands in the daily context of development. In pursuing economic development, for instance, while focusing on a country's stock of productive wealth and gross and net national products, it is necessary to consider its income distribution and levels of unemployment and impoverishment. For instance, when aiming to reduce poverty by giving the poor access to microcredit to start off a small-scale revenue-generating activity, access to microcredit alone would not guarantee a reduction in economic precariousness and feelings of vulnerability unless fair and affordable access is also provided to education, vocational training, health services, basic infrastructure, markets, and property rights. In pursuing political stability, the task of maintaining order and social control is often seen as being at odds with the task of protecting civil liberties and democratic participation in civic affairs. In the management of a rural development program, the interests and needs of local farmers are often difficult to synchronize with those of national bureaucrats or international donors. Such development dilemmas involve more than one causal relationship, constraint, solution, agency, and action. In addition, what matters most in pursuing trade-offs is often not known at all. Part of the answer might be that the context "contains more variables than we can comprehend at once, or that some of the variables are subject to influences we cannot control or predict" (Thompson, 1967:6); therefore, agreement is not always reached over the means and ends of development. When people are unable to reach agreement over the means and ends, uncertainty arises: "Uncertainty is not about risk or ignorance" (Viscusi, 1992:154); "It is rather about the analyst's lack of knowledge about what matters" (Roe, 1998: 15). When conventional analytical methods cease to make sense in the face of uncertain situations, "we seek inspiration, luck, leadership, intuition, or the high octane of political will, to propel us the rest of the journey" (Roe, 1998:15).

In addition to uncertainty, pondering about development means grappling with the issue of complexity. Complexity depends on the number of components involved in a particular development issue, the degree of differentiation among these components, and the degree of interconnectedness among them (Demshak, 1991; Roe, 1998). For instance, when local people are asked to get involved in the design of a particular rural development program in order to increase participation and feedback, the program's operations are expected to become more complex as more voices enter the decision-making process. Each voice articulates a different interpretation of the facts and values and a different scenario on how to tackle the issues at hand. Narratives are said to multiply as actors multiply in the decision-making process.

The other critical assumption about the nature of the development context is the controversial nature of the deliberation of certain complex and uncertain development goals and policies. Development actors do not know much about what precisely matters in the pursuit of development goals and policies, especially when they face situations with many unknowns and ambiguity and uncertainty. When disagreement arises, development actors concentrate around extreme and opposing views and positions, each using a different story line and arguments and proposing different courses of action. Polarization intensifies when the knowledge base guiding policy making becomes more inspirational than empirical.

Recognizing the importance of factoring in complexity, uncertainty, and polarization when practicing and reflecting on development is not the end of the argument. The mere recognition of such attributes without explanation of their practical implications for development thinking and policy making is not very helpful. One should not subscribe to "negative academics," to use Chambers's (1983) term (i.e., academics that rely on descriptive critique alone and fail to offer effective alternative arguments). The following section discusses the foundational premises, merits, and relevance of development narrative analysis, which is increasingly being proposed by a growing number of researchers from a variety of disciplines disenchanted with conventional analytical methods when trying to make sense of issues governed by so many unknowns and so little agreement.

## DEVELOPMENT NARRATIVE ANALYSIS: THEORETICAL AND METHODOLOGICAL PREMISES

### Connotation of the Narrative Analysis of Development

The emphasis on narrative, both as a concept and a method of analysis, grew out of the emerging trend of scholars who drew from different disciplines and who wanted to seek an alternative to the dominant hyperfactualism and positivist understanding of the thought process that guides much human thought and action. "It is not surprising," argued Martin Cortazzi (1993: 2), "to see scholars come to regard 'narratology' as an independent discipline studying the theory of narrative texts." More often researchers interested in narratives have regarded narrative as a field in which a number of disciplines converge, each with each its own focus.

Efforts at narrative research were more prevalent in such disciplines as literary theory, anthropology, psychology, sociolinguistics, social work, education, and philosophy than in economics, political science, or public policy. Definitions originating from the first above-mentioned group of disciplines abound. Narratives are defined as a "primary act of mind" (Hardy, 1987), as "the primary scheme by means of which human existence is rendered meaningful" (Polkinghorne, 1988), as "a means by which human beings represent and restructure the world" (Mitchell, 1981), and as "the organizing principle" by which "people organize their experience in, knowledge about, and transactions with the social world" (Bruner, 1990). When people articulate narratives, they are engaged in a "perceptual activity that organizes data into a special pattern which represents and explains experience" (Branigan, 1992, Cortazzi, 1993:1). Postmodernist philosophers, such a Jean Francois Lyotard, have also discussed the concept of narrative at great length. Drawing on Lyotard's understanding of a narrative, Jay White notes

> Knowledge in the traditional societies took on a narrative form: stories, fables, legends, or tales, handed down from generation to generation. [These] narratives served several important functions. They told people what to believe, how to act, and what to hope for in life. Norms and rules communicated through narratives established social, political and economic practices for those who chose to believe the narrative. Narratives gave legitimacy to the institutions that promulgated them (the church, the state, and practitioners of sorcery). Narratives also contained criteria for making statements about

truth, justice and beauty. . .Modernity, which replaced traditional narratives, is a product of the Enlightenment. The Enlightenment brought hope that a rational, objective science would allow for the control of natural and social forces. There was also hope that a rational, scientific attitude in the humanities and law would ensure moral progress, universal justice, autonomous art, and universal happiness (1999:155–156).

For Lyotard all is narrative. To use language, to communicate, or to promote common understanding, whether through scientific study, investigative journalism, or political argument, is to build a narrative structure and tell a story. John Fiske (1993) argues that "even statistical knowledge is narrative and therefore political." Stories situate people and provide them with a context, argues Joseph Kling (1997:161). As Sanford F. Schram and Philip Neisser further put it, "[story-telling] is an important way in which people, coalitions, and groups let others know who they are, what their interests are, and how those interests can be served, whether it is in terms of fulfilling 'the American dream,' the 'social contract,' or 'the global political economy'" (1997:7). "Those in privileged positions," Fiske argues, "need to learn to 'listen' to the knowing voices of the weak, the marginalized, the homeless, the poor, etc." (quoted in Schram and Neisser, 1997:7). Policy narratives are built around "structures of attention" and "structures of inattention," argues Mieke Bal (see Schram and Neisser, 1997:8). Narratives can structure silence, inattention, neglect, and exclusion. Schram and Neisser highlight such structures of inattention and neglect by invoking the example of welfare policy narratives: "the typical stories of welfare recipients as fraudulent render invisible the strength, hard work, sacrifice, caring, and survival skills of those who have almost no resources. To highlight this silence implicit in the narrative voice of welfare stories is to suggest a different narrative" (Schram and Neisser, 1997:8).

The turn to such interpretive research methods as narrative analysis has also started to echo among researchers from disciplines that have long neglected narrative analysis, including policy analysis, political science, and public administration. "A turn back to interpretation is going on," argues Jay White (1999:35), quoting Daniel Bell, "[with] people disappointed with what they can do with numbers, they are showing more interest in looking at the meaning of things." There is an increasingly shared feeling that conventional methods are unable to address the narrative foundations of such disciplines as public policy, public administration, and development economics and that alternative analytical methods need to be designed to enable us to classify and assess the significance of the factual data acquired by experiment and observation. The following section will discuss the writings of some of the prominent scholars—in particular Emory Roe—who have called attention to the utility of narrative analysis in such fields as public policy, public management, and development administration.

## Public Policy Insights in Narrative Analysis

Martin Rein was one of the first policy analysts to revive interest in the narrative foundations of public policy and public administration. In 1976, he advanced the notion that public policy analysis is about the "giving of advice," which he boldly equated with storytelling. When policy analysts tell stories, he argued, they do so by "deriv[ing] from past experience a narrative which interprets the events as they unfold and draws a moral for future actions, suggesting, for example, how the future might unfold if certain steps are taken" (1976: 265–266). He further explained that stories provide "an interpretation of a complex pattern of events with normative implications for action, and not with a universal law" (1976: 266). Even if giving advice entails normative choice, he believed it possible to argue objectively about the relevance of a policy story by examining the facts of the story in light of the situation it is supposed to describe. Stories can still weave together both facts and values. Thomas Kaplan (1986) and Martin Krieger (1986) both affirmed the relevance and centrality of stories and the telling of stories in policy making and the profession of policy analysis. Kaplan in particular argues that narratives and appeals to narratives must play an important role in the profession (1986). The study and interpretation of politics and policy making from institutional, individual, and rational choice perspectives need to take into account the narrative nature of what is being referred to, be it the institution, the self, or the objectively rational choice. Schram and Neisser further corroborate this argument, stating that

> Proponents of institutional, behavioral, rational choice, and other approaches ascendant among political scientists and policy analysts, often dismiss the narrative dimension of not only politics and public policy-making but also of their own texts. In fact what are institutions, individuals, and rational interest, if they are not understandings in narrative form about established practices, persons, and principles for making optimal decisions (1997: 9)?

Although Emery Roe was not the first thinker to draw attention to the relevance of the concept of narrative and counternarrative his writings offer the most relevant type of narrative analysis for public policy analysis. Roe not only discusses the utility of narrative analysis as it pertains to the discipline of public policy making in general, he also advocates the application of the method to issues pertaining to the field of international development, which makes his propositions quite novel for a field that has become overreliant on conventional research methods. "When development policies become so uncertain, complex and polarized and their empirical, political, legal and bureaucratic merits are unknown, not agreed upon, or both," argues Roe; "the only things left to examine are the different *stories* policy makers use to articulate and make sense of that uncertainty, complexity and polarization" (Roe, 1994:3). Development narratives, he further argues, "are the rules of thumb, arguments, and other scenarios that enable decision makers to take decisions" (Roe, 1999: 1). In his book *Except Africa: Remaking Development, Rethinking Power,* Roe defines development narratives as the "stories (scenarios and arguments) that underwrite and stabilize the assumptions for decision making in situations of high complexity and uncertainty" (Roe, 1999:9).

Decision makers generate narratives about development when they experience ambiguity over that development. The more uncertain the development context appears to be at the micro level, the greater the perceived need for explanatory narratives to stabilize uncertainty. When imprecision becomes the norm for development actors, Roe comments, "the tangled scenarios and arguments they tell can sometimes become the only means to expose issues of high uncertainty or little agreement in ways that make them more amenable to conventional policy tools" (Roe, 1999:13). Giving advice to policy analysts, Richard Neustadt and Ernest May (1986:106) suggest that "the best way to find out the real problems in a complicated issue of many unknowns is not by asking directly 'what is the problem?' but rather 'what's the story behind the issue.'"

The evolution of the international development discourse and practice is not just about narrative construction. Some narratives are said to be constructive and have policy relevance. Others are said to be pernicious, destructive, and self-destructive, therefore paving the way for a counternarrative to emerge (i.e., counterarguments that claim to better stabilize decision making). As they revolve around a sequence of events or positions, narratives have a beginning, a middle stage, and an end (Krieger, 1981). Some development narratives are able to dominate discourse and practice longer than others.

Roe distinguishes constructive development narratives that enhance our understanding of development and are conducive to possible and plausible plans of action from pernicious narratives that intoxicate our understanding of development, thus destabilizing decision making and policy making. One example of what Roe means by a disenchanting, intoxicating development narrative is what he likes to call the *except Africa* narrative. *Except Africa* stands for the scenario usually deployed by foreign as well as national development experts whenever reference is made to development work—namely, rural development—on the African continent. The following headlines summarize what Roe calls the *except Africa* narrative, a pernicious narrative that has come to dominate African development discourse and practice: "everything works…*except* in Africa," "Africa is the *exception* when it comes to development," "the world is likely to experience a decline in poverty *except Africa* where things will only get worse," "famine now coursing through Africa poses an immediate crisis of vast proportions," and so on (Roe, 1999: 2–5).

What is at issue with the above narratives, according to Roe, is not so much the crisis message they convey about the prospects of African development as the lack of little constructive guidance for the local African people. Such messages of crisis, argues Roe, have actually contributed to stabilizing policy making for international donors and development agencies with respect to African rural development. In fact, the continued use of such narratives secured employment and consultancy contracts for both national and international development experts. The perniciousness of such narratives resides in the little policy relevance for the African people themselves, whose perception for the most part has been marginalized if not ignored in the narrative weaving process. Moreover, such apocalyptic messages about Africa are based more on arguments of impossibility and exceptionalism than on local field research to gather local facts and values.

Roe calls for the "denarrativizing" of such pernicious discourse. Denarrativizing is achieved by addressing the factual shortcomings of what is believed to be a pernicious, destructive narrative based on factual fallacies and exclusions. In other words, denarrativizing means "getting both the facts and figures right" in order to get the story straight. A point–by-point rebuttal of the narrative found to be substantially wanting is not the end of the story, however, argues Roe; a counternarrative (i.e., an alternative development narrative that tells a better story and provides a better plan of action) is needed (1999: 13–27).

## Utility and Value of Narrative Analysis

Roe's use of development narrative analysis as applied to the African rural development context offers new insights and directions on what we ought to be looking for when a new development narrative emerges or an old one persists for too long in the field of international development. *Except Africa* is but one narrative in the panoply of popular development narratives that have animated post-World War II development discourse and practice. Examples include the so-called *Third World technical assistance* programs of the 1960s and 1970s (to stabilize the postcolonial nation-building experiments), the IMF-prescribed *structural adjustment programs* of the 1980s (to bring Third World economies in line with global standards of economic performance), the World Bank's marketing campaign in the 1990s of the so-called *Southeast Asian Tigers*' developmental state model (to revamp the developmental role of Third World states) (Johnson 1987; Amsden, 1994; Page, 1994), and the current global microfinance program for the poor (to disburse small doses of capital to the "entrepreneurial" poor to graduate them out of poverty). All are loaded with stories, counterstories, and untold stories about how to develop the so-called Third World countries.

A close text analysis of these development narratives will reveal that each narrative carries perhaps more than a story on how local, national, and global development is viewed and how to bring about desired results. Such development narratives are woven to aid development policy makers and practitioners in understanding, interpreting, and stabilizing the high levels of complexity and uncertainty that typically govern international development issues and controversies. Development narratives exist in different ways; some are created, others are pre-existing, some have to be discovered, and others are just not told. They also differ in their purposive value; some are constructive and bear practical policy relevance, and others are pernicious, as they obfuscate reality, cloud factual knowledge with ill-founded arguments, and bear no direct policy relevance. Development narratives have different life spans; while some narratives come and go, others persist and become hard to dislodge. Different individuals, groups, and alliances coalesce around development narratives. Development narratives can be woven by institutionalized groups, such as international development organizations, by state officials, such as leaders and government officials, or simply by individual local farmers. The analytical techniques used in development narrative analysis take a radically different direction from conventional policy analysis or social science research in general. One way to objectively assess the value of narrative analysis and its analytical merits is to address its common critiques.

## How Different Is Narrative Analysis from Fiction?

Narrative analysis stipulates first and foremost that for a development narrative to qualify to be called as such it needs to address a development issue that is governed by high levels of uncertainty, complexity, and divisiveness and expressed by stories that can be compared and evaluated. The primary goal of the narrative analyst, Schram and Neisser (1997:5) explicate, "is to interrogate all policy making activity for its narrativity and assess the consequences given the persuasiveness of particular tales." In assessing the narrativity of certain development stories, however, (i.e., the extent to which they make true claims about the reality under analysis), there is always the risk of some fiction infiltrating such stories or even being the basis for some stories. While it is important to distinguish implicit narrative structure from consciously told tales or gossip, Schram and Neisser argue that "stories, wherever told, whether unconsciously articulated through the invocation of prevailing discourse or consciously fashioned by participating in the rumor mill, are critical constitutive forces in politics and public policy making" (1997: 5). Addressing the fine line between fiction and narrative in policy making, Roe comments

> In the situations of high uncertainty and complexity for which narrative policy analysis is appropriate, it simply is not possible to decide if the policy narratives being analyzed are fiction, or if the science is right, or what form power and politics are really taking...We are, to put it simply, asked with increasing frequency to take positions on issues about which the only thing we have to analyze are the polarized arguments in favor or against, and for which truth claims cannot be the sole guide in deciding (1994: 8).

## How Analytically Objective Is Narrative Analysis?

Another common criticism directed to narrative analysis is its reduced prospects for analytic objectivity. The answer to that is that the closest an analyst can get to objectivity in narrative analysis, in which conditions of extreme uncertainty and complexity are taken as the point of departure, is identifying just whose uncertainty, complexity, and polarization is being analyzed. Narrative analysis is not about the narrative analyst's personal uncertainty in the development controversy, but about the uncertainties of the disputants in the controversy. Narrative analysis is not, however, a mere mechanical exercise of locating the different narratives of decision making on a particular development issue and constructing new counter narratives to recast the problem in such a way that it accounts for the diversity of perspectives and actors. Much of the narrative deconstruction and reconstruction work depends on the narrative analyst's methodology, and regardless of the methodology used, the analyst is not immune from misreporting or reconfiguring problems. The same argument can be made about policy analysts who use such conventional methods as statistics, however. Roe puts both narrative analysts and econometricians on an equal standing when he asserts that "Different [narrative] analysts could come up with different meta-narratives, depending on the type of non-story or counter-story used, is similar to the difficulty analysts have when developing scenarios based on different statistical packages and methods of economic analysis, each of which offers advantages the others do not" (Roe, 1994: 16).

What proponents of narrative analysis fail to emphasize is that the grounds for assessing the objectivity of narratives is not so much the degree of their purely factual basis as the political implications of their narrativity. Schram and Neisser argue that such standards of objectivity could "be unsettling for those looking for political or policy analysis to serve as some safe, stabilized site for the articulation of objective and rational analysis of politics or public policy" (1997: 9). Narrative analysis is objective to the extent it "highlights narrative exclusions and opens the door to a politics of inclusion and alters the political situation" (Shapiro, 1995). The grounds for assessing narratives are thus politics itself (Schram and Neisser, 1997).

## How Practically Relevant Is Narrative Analysis?

Narrative analysis takes into account the need of analysts, policy makers, and the concerned public to act upon what is perceived to be a development issue crying out for immediate action and to produce results on the ground. Narrative analysis is not just to reflect, retheorize, or denigrate, but also to do something about the scenarios and arguments driving issues of high controversy. By highlighting the excluded narrative, along with tolerating as many different and conflicting voices and acknowledging as many narratives as possible, narrative analysis brings pluralism to the decision-making process in development. More than one story can be told to make sense of any particular area of concern. Although narrative analysis does not guarantee to decrease the levels of technical uncertainties, simplify complexities, and reduce the divisiveness in development discourse, by bringing to the surface the variety of assumptions used to stabilize development decisions, narrative analysis does offer insights on how we ought to read the development context in question, where it begins, where it ends, who populates it and who does not, and which of the concerns are included and which are excluded. By doing so, it recasts the formulation of the controversy is such a way that makes it more understandable and more tractable to decision making.

For those for whom the terms stories, narratives, metanarratives, and narrative analysis bear little relevance to such practical fields as public policy and development administration, narrative analysis has the advantage of bringing a plurality of both told and untold stories that have dictated and continue to dictate the enactment of thousands of public policies. Having said that, the analysis of development narratives does not denigrate the importance of factual knowledge (i.e., the facts and figures necessary to argue the empirical merits of a particular policy), or tolerate the continued exclusion of the untold and neglected stories that could bring alternative understandings that are not accounted for in the dominant knowledge base and the mainstream empirical standards of decisions.

## CONCLUSION

While the analytical or conceptual framework discussed in this chapter acknowledges the contributions of economic and political reasoning as well as of more eclectic social science approaches in advancing our understanding of the nature of development work, it clearly departs from the conventional approach to development on two grounds. Theoretically, it rejects the notion of confining the discussion of development discourse and practice to only those issues that are the least controversial and political, yet more amenable to statistical analysis and more tractable to concrete plans of action. Development issues, especially the most controversial, complex, and uncertain, are the types of issues we should be busy investigating if we expect to define development as unrealized potential with room for improvement. On methodological grounds, while this chapter does not discredit the contribution of conventional statistical knowledge it strongly calls attention to the merits of narrative analysis in bringing to the surface the bulk of both told and untold storytelling that underlies much of our international development policy making.

## REFERENCES

Almond, G. A., Powell, G. B. (1966). *Comparative Politics: A Developmental Approach.* Boston: Little, Brown.

Amsden, A. H. (1994). Why isn't the whole world experimenting the East Asian model to develop? Review of the East Asian miracle. *World Dev* 22(4):627–633.

Apter, D. E. (1987). *Rethinking Development: Modernization, Dependency, and Postmodern Politics.* Beverly Hills, CA: Sage.

Ayres, R. (1983). *Banking on the Poor: The World Bank and World Poverty*. Cambridge, MA: MIT Press.

Bernstein, R. J. (1976). *The Restructuring of Social and Political Theory*. Philadelphia: University of Pennsylvania Press.

Binder, L., et al. Crises and sequences in political development. In: *Series Studies in Political Development*. Princeton, NJ: Princeton Paperback, pp. 64–65.

Braibanti, R., Spengler, J. J., eds. (1961). *Tradition, Values and Socio-economic Development*. Durham, NC: Duke University Press.

Branigan, E. (1992). *Narrative Comprehension and Film*. London: Routledge.

Bruner, J. (1990). *Acts of Meaning*. Cambridge, MA: Harvard University Press.

Caiden, G. E. (1991). *Administrative Reform Comes of Age*. Berlin: Walter de Gruyter.

Chambers, R. (1983). *Rural Development: Putting the Last First*. London: Longman.

Chenery, H., et al. (1974). *Redistribution with Growth*. A Joint study by the World Bank's Development Research and Institute of Development Studies at the University of Sussex. London: Oxford University Press.

Cortazzi, M. (1993). *Narrative Analysis*. London: Falmer.

Demshak, C. (1991). *Military Machines, Complex Machines*. Ithaca, NY: Cornell University Press.

Fiske, J. (1993). *Power Plays, Power Works*. London: Verso.

Gosovic, B. (Dec. 2000). Global intellectual hegemony and the international development agenda. *Internat Soc Sci J* 166:447–456.

Hardy, B. (1987). *The Collected Essays of Barbara Hardy*. Vol. 1. Sussex: Harvester.

Heady, F. (1996). *Public Administration: A Comparative Perspective*. New York: Marcel Dekker.

Huntington, S. (1991). *The Third Wave: Democratization in the Late Twentieth Century*. Norman, OK: University of Oklahoma Press.

Huntington, S., Dominguez, J. (1975). Political development. Greenstein, F. I., Plosby, N. W., eds. *Handbook of Political Science*. Vol. 3. Reading, MA: Addison-Wesley, pp 1–114.

Hyden, G. (1983). *No Shortcuts to Progress: African Development Management in Perspective*. Berkeley: University of California Press.

Jaguaribe, H. (1973). *A Comprehensive Theory of Political Development: A General Theory and a Latin American Case Study*. New York: Harper and Row. Chap. 9.

Johnson, C. (1987). Political institutions and economic performance: The government–business relationship in Japan, South Korea, and Taiwan. In: Deyo, F., ed. *The Political Economy of the New Asian Industrialism*. Ithaca, NY: Cornell University Press, pp. 136–164.

Kaplan, T. (1986). The narrative structure of policy analysis. *J Policy Anal Mgt* 5:4.

Kling, J. (1997). Tales of the city: The secret life of devolution. In: Schram, S. F., Neisser, P., eds. *Tales of the State*. Lanham, MD: Rowman and Littlefield, pp. 150–162.

Krieger, M. (1986). Big decisions and a culture of decision-making. *J Policy Anal Mgt* 5:4.

Krieger, M. (1981). *Advice and Planning*. Philadelphia: Temple University Press.

Meier, G. M. (1984). *Leading Issues in Economic Development*. New York: Oxford University Press.

Migdal, J. (1988). *Strong Societies and Weak States: State–Society Relations and State Capabilities in the Third World*. Princeton, NJ: Princeton University Press.

Mitchell, W. J. T. (1981). *On Narrative*. Chicago: Chicago University Press.

Neustadt, R., May, E. (1986). *Thinking in Time: The Uses of History for Decision-makers*. New York: Free Press.

North, D. C. (1989). *Institutions, Institutional Change and Economic Performance*. New York: Cambridge University Press.

Page, J. M. (1994). The East Asian miracle. *World Dev* 22(4):615–625.

Polkinghorne, D. E. (1988). *Narrative Knowing and the Human Sciences*. Albany, NY: State University of New York Press.

Ramos, A. G. (1981). *The New Science of Organizations: A Reconceptualization of the Wealth of Nations*. Toronto, Canada: University of Toronto Press.

Rancière, J. (2000). Dissenting words: A conversation with Jacques Rancière. *Diacrit Rev Contemp Crit* 30(summer):113–126.

Rein, M. (1976). *Social Science and Public Policy*. New York: Penguin.

Roe E. (2001). Policy optics for rethinking poverty, defense and the environment entirely. paper presented at the Center for Sustainable Resource Development, Berkeley, CA.

Roe, E. (1999). *Except Africa: Remaking Development, Rethinking Power*. New Brunswick, NJ: Transaction.

Roe, E. (1998). *Taking Complexity Seriously*. Boston: Kluwer Academic.

Roe, E. (1994). *Narrative Policy Analysis: Theory and Practice*. London: Duke University Press.

Schram, S. F., Neisser, P. (1997). *Tales of the State: Narrative in Contemporary Politics and Public Policy*. Lanham, MD: Rowman and Littlefield.

Shapiro M. (Feb. 1995). The ethics of encounter: Unreading/unmapping the imperium. paper presented at the Annual Meeting of the International Studies Association. Chicago.

Somjee, A. H. (1990). *Development Theory: Critiques and Explorations*. New York: St. Martin's.

Smith, T. (1985). The dependency approach. In: Wiarda, H. J., ed. *New Directions in Comparative Politics*. Boulder, CO: Westview Press, pp. 113–126.

Streeten, P., et al. *First Things First*. Oxford: Oxford University Press.

Thompson, J. (1967). *Organizations in Action*. New York: McGraw-Hill.

Uphof, N. T., Ilchman, W. F., eds. (1972). *The Political Economy of Development: Theoretical and Empirical Contributions*. Berkeley, CA: University of California Press.

Viscusi, W. K. (1992). *Fatal Tradeoffs*. New York: Oxford University Press.

White, J. D. (1999). *Taking Language Seriously: The Normative Foundations of Public Administration Research*. Washington, DC: Georgetown University Press.

White, J. D., Adams, G. (1995). Reason and post-modernity: The historical and social context of public administration research and theory. *Admin Theory Praxis* 17:1–19.

# 3

## Managing Social Change in Complex Environments
### A Chaos Approach to Environmental Impacts

**HENRY ADOBOR**

*Quinnipiac University, Hamden, Connecticut, U.S.A.*

### INTRODUCTION AND BACKGROUND

This chapter draws on some key ideas from the nonlinear sciences to explain social change in complex environments. I argue that policy inferences that posit direct relationships between cause and effect (linear frameworks) may be unsuitable for managing phenomena that are complex and nonlinear because linear frameworks represent an equilibrium-centered view of development and change. This chapter presents a nonlinear framework for analyzing social change, including the sort of institutional choices that may be more conducive to sustainability.

One of the most important social change objectives of our time is the promotion of the prudent utilization of the world's natural resources to achieve and maintain a certain level of intergenerations equity for future generations. The need to unravel the complex web of ecological, economic, political, and social forces that arise in achieving that objective has never been greater. For example, it is necessary to understand the dynamics of the ecology as well as social and political systems, including institutional choices that are required to effect the necessary social transformation and change.

The related issues that emerge for these concerns have come to be closely identified with the emerging paradigm of sustainable development. In some sense, sustainable development as a paradigm remains a vague concept because it is often conceptualized in different way, but as Gladwin et al. (1995) note, this sort of diversity of opinion on what sustainable development means is to be expected during the emergent phase of any potentially big idea of general usefulness. Despite existing definitional variety and a certain amount of ideological controversy (Levin, 1993), most people agree on two things: (1) the concept links the natural environment, development, and the prudent use of resources (see, e.g., Greene et al., 1990; Brundtland, 1987), and (2) global social change in one form or another is required if the objectives of sustainable development are to be realized (Rogers, 1993; Schmidheiny, 1992; Guastello, 1995; Holling, 1995).

Sustainable development has generated a bourgeoning amount of research (See, e.g., Rogers, 1993; Schmidheiny, 1992; Brown, 1993; Vivian, 1992; De La Court, 1990; Commoner, 1990; Pearce et al., 1990; Holling et al., 1995). This research has broadened our understanding of how human, social, and natural systems interact to generate the problems of sustainability. In addition, the human side of sustainable development is better understood. Despite this progress, some gaps remain. As Parson and Clark (1995) note, theories of social dynamics that may produce real understanding of long-term, largescale interactions of the environment and development are largely missing, and much remains to be done in terms of both theory development and policy application. For example, there is a need for a greater understanding of the structure and dynamics of the institutional choices and management systems that can advance our realization of sustainable development (Daneke, 1999).

This chapter responds to that need by exploring the usefulness of the emerging sciences of chaos and complexity (Briggs and Peat, 1989; Guastello, 1995; Glieck, 1988) for both our understanding of the complex issues of sustainability and the ecology of the institutional choices most conducive to that effort. This focus is important because moving sustainable development beyond the status of a grand agenda requires the development of suitable policy mechanisms and institutions for coping with the complex and dynamic challenges that are associated with sustainable development. The objective of this chapter is to present a theoretical framework for stimulating both empirical research and action to help the realization of the normative objectives of sustainable development. Theory development may be an integral part of normative policy development. As Holling (1995: 19) notes, the development of appropriate theory is sometimes a necessary prerequisite for social change effort. He writes evocatively: "investing in the development and testing of usable and useful theory is not an academic luxury, but a practical necessity, particularly at times of profound change."

The main argument in this chapter is that an inappropriate understanding of the complexities of change in social systems can lead to shortsighted responses to issues of social change in pursuit of sustainable development. Policy inferences that posit some direct relationship between cause and effect (linear frameworks) are unsuitable for managing phenomena that may be complex and nonlinear because they represent an equilibrium-centered view of development and change.

I assert that traditional mechanistic and adaptive paradigms of social change ignore the essential dynamism of the sustainable development paradigm and instead focus on adaptive responses and a search for stability. The use of a linear framework to approximate nonlinear problems and dynamic phenomena may be fundamentally flawed. The presumption is that linear and equilibrium-centered approaches tend to generate short-term solutions that are at best brittle and tentative. A nonlinear framework reveals that reliance on prediction, order, and stability as a way of understanding the impact of change and transformation may be counterproductive.

I suggest that a nonlinear framework may allow us to see the dynamic possibilities for change because it presents us with the concepts and tools that may be congenial for managing the complex and dynamic issues that are associated with sustainability. For example, Constanza et al. (1993) suggest that sustainable development involves an appreciation of the uncertainty, unpredictability, nonlinear interaction, and complex dynamics in ecological and social systems. It has also been observed that sustainability requires that we design institutions so that living systems can carry out self-organization or self-renewal (Norton, 1991).

Natural and social systems are constantly producing surprises. As a science of surprises, nonlinear theories may offer us the conceptual vocabulary for a greater understanding of systems in which surprises are ubiquitous. In some sense, a nonlinear framework informs us that complexity, change, uncertainty, and surprise may need to be savored and explored for their inherent potential for generating creative solutions.

This chapter will begin with a conceptual overview of sustainable development. The section will specifically (1) discuss the components of sustainable development and (2) demonstrate the need to conceptualize sustainable development as a dynamic and complex concept. Second, I will explore the core concepts of chaos and complexity theory shows that the revealed ontology of chaos theory may be more consistent with the imperatives of sustainable development, including social change. In some respects, the way we conceptualize, develop theory, and act on sustainable development (or any phenomenom for that matter) may be affected by our ways of seeing and knowing. These relate to *ontology*, our picture of how we see the world, and *epistemology*, our belief about how knowledge about the world is acquired.

In the third section, I explore the policy implications of a nonlinear framework for sustainable development. Guidelines on institutional choice and design are explored including the types of intervention, their timing, the prediction of outcomes and a greater understanding of institutional ecologies for sustainability. I will deal specifically with six issues that have been identified as important in sustainability literature: (1) intervention and responsive action, (2) complexity and holistic development, (3) interconnectivity and the imperatives of multiparty collaboration, (4) the imperatives of learning and creativity, (5) the imperatives of local action, and (6) temporal dynamics and sustainability. In the fourth and final section I will look at some of the research implications of the chapter.

## SUSTAINABLE DEVELOPMENT: A CONCEPTUAL OVERVIEW

A simple but widely accepted definition of sustainable development can be found in *Our Common Future*, the report by the World Commission on the Environment and Development (Brundtland, 1987). The commission defines sustainable development simply as "development, which meets the needs of the present without compromising the ability of future generations to meet their own needs."

The simplicity of this definition somewhat belies its inherent complexity and ideological contentiousness. (See, e.g., Rogers, 1993.) As a paradigm, sustainable development has generated several ontological and epistemological debates, including different development models of change. The complexity of both the concept and goals of sustainable development is recognized (Guastello, 1995; Constanza et al., 1991; Holling, 1995). Holling (1995) observes that sustainable development is a paradox because it reflects constancy or stability as well as instability and change. Constanza et al. (1991: 8) also characterize sustainable development in terms of this complexity and dynamism. They define the concept as "a relationship between dynamic economic systems and larger dynamic, but normally slower-changing ecological systems, in which (a) human life can continue indefinitely, (b) human individuals can flourish, and (c) human cultures can develop; but in which effects of human activities remain within bounds, so as not to destroy the diversity, complexity, and function of the ecological life support system."

Gladwin et al. (1995) content-analyzed several popular definitions of sustainable development and derived five principal components of shared ideas about sustainable development. These are: inclusiveness, connectivity, equity, prudence, and security. The authors define the terms as follows. *Inclusiveness* is defined in terms of human development over time and space. The authors observe that sustainable development embraces both environmental and human systems. Any action toward sustainability must therefore include a consideration of the underlying dynamics of economic, social, political, and technological change. Any attempt to decompose and deal with these elements as independent of each other will clearly be inadequate. This is consistent with at least one other categorization of sustainable development. As Holling (1995: 32) notes, "sustainable development is neither an ecological problem, a social problem, nor an economic problem. It is an integrated combination of all three."

*Connectivity* implies the recognition that the ecological, human, social, political, and technological dimensions of sustainability are all interdependent. The issue of connectivity is widely accepted. In fact, the preamble to Agenda 21 of the United Nations Conference in Rio de Janeiro in 1992 reflected this view of sustainability; a wide range of interrelated issues—deforestation, pollution, economic development, and women's rights, among others—became Agenda 21. *Equity* refers to behavior that recognizes our obligation to safeguard the natural environment so that it can support future generations. This raises the question of intergenerational equity that is at the core of sustainable behavior. *Prudence* means keeping the scale of human activity within sustainable limits. *Security* demands that emphasis be placed on human freedom and human rights. This and other conceptualizations of sustainable development clearly demonstrate the complex and dynamic nature of the concept.

## NONLINEAR DYNAMICS AS A MODEL FOR CHANGE AND TRANSFORMATION

The conceptual overview presented above shows that sustainable development is a complex and dynamic concept. The key revelations from the emerging sciences of chaos and complexity theory showing that our universe may be one of disorder, instability, and uncertainty may be more consistent with sustainability than what our traditional models of change teach us.

The emerging theories of nonlinear dynamical systems, what Glieck (1988) calls the "new sciences" (specifically chaos and complexity theory) may provide important tools for understanding and theorizing on the complex issues that arise in sustainable development. At least one area within sustainable development research, ecology, and earth system dynamics has seen some application of nonlinear dynamical theories to understand sustainability issues. (See e.g., Holling, 1992; 1995.) Dore (1994) has also modeled sustainable development with a nonlinear equation and concluded that the dynamic equilibrium of sustainable development is at a point at which environmental damage is zero and the growth rate of consumption is zero. Daneke (1999) suggests that a nonlinear framework may lead to a greater understanding of the inherent complexity of institutional ecologies that impact sustainable development and the design of more effective environmental policies.

As a metatheory of nonlinear systems, chaos theory, is a set of ideas about dynamic transformation in nonlinear systems. It reveals that most social phenomena are intrinsically dynamic, and complex and are often unpredictable. Systems exhibit nonlinear behavior when small changes in the system's variables can lead to disproportionate outcomes. A dynamic system is one whose state changes overtime. Complexity refers to a situation in which there are a number of interactions among elements that make up the system. There is some recognition that the revealed ontology of chaos theory may provide the concepts and tools that are most conducing in unraveling the complex issues of nature and the environment, including the nature of social transformation that sustainability requires (Wells, 1996; Peet, 1992; Kay, 1991; Holling, 1995). For example, Holling (1995) notes that nonlinear dynamics and other emerging theories may provide the focus for posing research questions that are the first steps toward usable understanding of the complex issues of sustainability.

Despite these efforts, the role of nonlinear dynamical systems in the natural and social transformation inherent in sustainability may need additional clarification. For example, current applications have stopped short of systematically deriving policy implications of nonlinear thinking for sustainability. The result is that our understanding of the policy implications of a nonlinear framework in the areas of institutional choice and ecological management remains sketchy at best. The tendency to use technical language has also meant that the material has not been easily accessible to nonexperts.

The social sciences have witnessed some application of the nonlinear sciences to shed light on phenomena. Researchers in fields as diverse as organization studies (Stacey, 1992) and sociology (Turner, 1997) have applied ideas from chaos and complexity to explain phenomena, largely at the level of metaphor. Like most applications of the framework, the metaphorical use of chaos theory may aid our understanding of sustainability. Although there are limits to the value of metaphors (Morgan, 1986), a careful application of metaphors can yield new understanding because metaphors allow us to create meaning. Black (1962: 236) notes: "metaphors are designed to bring two separate domains into cognitive and emotional relation by using language directly appropriate to the one as a lens for seeing the other." Kiel and Elliot (1996: 2–3) observe that the "obvious metaphorical value of applying a theory of chaos to the social realm has served as an impetus for the emergence of the application of this theory to social phenomena."

Chaos and complexity theory emerged in response to the realization that many systems, including those with purely deterministic properties, possess nonlinear dynamics. In the physical sciences in which it originated, chaos was engaged primarily to better understand complex, nonlinear, dynamical systems, such as the behavior of gases and liquids (Gleick, 1988; Waldrop, 1992). It is important to note that chaos does not mean indeterminacy. On the contrary, the power of chaos theory may be its ability to offer intelligible ways of understanding deterministic systems. A system is deterministic if it has precise points at which it undergoes transformation.

The distinguishing feature of nonlinear systems is that they undergo transformation and exhibit temporary behavior over time. Each transformation that arises after a bifurcation gives rise to a different behavioral regime. A behavioral regime is a temporary state that a system occupies as it evolves. These states range from order or stability to various levels of chaos or instability. Systems that are stable often do not change in any appreciable way, while instability implies that change will happen, but the results are unpredictable. An abrupt or sudden change in system behavior is called a bifurcation. A bifurcation describes radical or major systemic change in overall system behavior. The concept of bifurcation shows that the dynamics of the whole system can be radically altered by a small change in a causal element of the system (Feigenbaum, 1978; Briggs and Peat, 1989). For example, a small piece of rock in the path of a large flowing stream causes the water to branch out and flow in different directions. After each bifurcation, the multiple pathways a system develops will end up in end states called outcome basins. An outcome basin is a range of alternative outcomes available to a nonlinear system after each bifurcation.

Nonlinear dynamic systems do not just move from a state of order to disorder. They can also demonstrate the reverse, in which case they move from a state of disorder to order by a process known as self-organization (Prigogine and Stengers, 1984). Although dynamic systems can exhibit unpredictable and discontinuous behavior, such systems invariably get pulled toward either point or an attractor. During the process of moving from one behavioral regime to the other, chaotic systems often go through different phases. The seemingly random movement through phases gets organized around some key structure, an attractor (Maldelbrot, 1977). An attractor is simply any spot, point, or location within an orbit that seems to pull the system to it (Briggs and Peat, 1989). Attractors can be thought of as underlying guiding principles that ensure that there is always some order in chaos. This is why one can always discern a pattern in chaotic systems. Such patterns can represent behaviors that are either steady, in which case they are called "fixed" attractors or "cyclical" attractors when they exhibit behavior that is continuously repeating itself, or "strange" attractors, in which the behavior is discontinuous. A pendulum is an example of a point attractor. An automatic light switch that comes on at dusk and turns off at dawn is an example of a "limit" attractor. It is called a limit attractor because there are precise limits above and below which the behavior does not exceed.

One interesting and potentially useful insight for sustainability is that there is always some underlying pattern in a system, even if it is in state of disorder or chaos (Briggs and Peat, 1989). In order words, chaotic systems have a tendency to reveal orderliness. A system is orderly if its movements can be explained in the kind of cause-and-effect scheme represented by a linear differential equation (Briggs and Peat, 1989). Another very useful idea in chaos theory is that all nonlinear systems take a universal path as they undergo transformation over time (Peitgen et al., 1992). This behavior can be mapped on a sort of path diagram known as a *Feigenbaum diagram*. Chaos has some key characteristics. Together, these characteristics express the revealed ontology of chaos theory. These are: (1) nonlinearity, (2) sensitivity to initial conditions, and (3) emergence.

The first is nonlinearity. The defining element of chaos theory is nonlinearity. Since nonlinear systems produce changes that are often disproportionate and surprising, it is difficult if not impossible to make long-term prediction of such systems with any degree of accuracy. It is, however, possible to make short-term prediction in nonlinear regimes of chaos, because such systems do exhibit different regimes of temporal behavior in which there may be periods of order or stability.

Second is sensitivity dependence on initial conditions (SDIC). Although not wholly new, this phenomenon was brought to center stage within the chaos paradigm by Edward Lorenz. It has come to be known by the metaphor of the "butterfly" effect to express the inherent unpredictability of chaos. The concept of SDIC has three implications for our understanding of phenomena. The first is that small initial changes can have unexpected impacts and prediction of future events is possible only in the short run. The second is the idea that similar conditions can produce radically different outcomes over time. Finally, sensitivity to initial conditions implies that when one makes a small error in specifying initial conditions, this small error can be magnified exponentially over time. Conversely, small initial successes can yield exponential payoffs in the future. Examples of this phenomenon have been documented in organizational research. For example, research has found that organizational growth strongly depends on founding conditions (Stinchcombe, 1965). Eisenhardt and Schoonhoven (1990) also observed that small initial advantages created new advantages in the future for newly founded firms.

The final characteristic is emergence: chaotic systems possess "emergent" properties. Emergence is the process by which new macro structures arise out of the interaction of lower-level elements through the process of "self-organization." Stacey (1996) defines self-organization as a process by which the elements of a system interact with each other according to their own local rules of behavior without any overall blueprint telling them what to do. Complex natural systems are known to engage in self-organization (Prigogine and Stengers, 1984).

What has come to be known as the science of complexity is in reality a study of complex systems. Although there is some debate over what exactly constitutes a complex system (Stein, 1989), looking at some characteristics of complex systems may give us clues. A complex system is a dynamic system that evolves over time. The relationships between elements that make up a complex system are interrelated in several ways, and the key elements of a complex system will affect each other in nonlinear ways, including mutually. There is mutual causation between two variables when the size of influence in one direction has an effect upon the size of influence in the other direction and that same variable is in turn affected by it (Maruyama, 1963).

Loops can be formed in a model of causal processes. Each element affects other elements in the loop either directly or indirectly. It is also influenced through other elements. A mutual causal process is one formed by a closed loop in which the action of one element, initiated by itself or some element outside the loop, affects all the other elements in the loop, which in turn causes further changes in the original element. As Weick (1979) observes, a mutual loop thus represents the almost simultaneous influence of two variables on each other. It is important to note that there is no hierarchical causal priority in any of the elements. It is futile to think that one variable is more important than any other variable. It is also difficult to separate cause and effect in causal models.

Mutual causal models have both positive and negative feedback loops. A positive feedback loop is present when a change in one direction calls up reinforcing changes that move the variable even further in one direction. Positive feedback loops can lead to instability. For example, population growth may put pressure on land use. Overuse of marginal lands leads to environmental degradation, leading to greater poverty. As more hands are needed to work the marginal lands, people will tend to have more children, leading to an increase in population growth. This type of relationship is deviation-amplifying (Maruyama, 1963). In the case of deviation-amplifying models, deviations get amplified until some critical limit is reached. Such loops are not self-correcting, and unless some intervention is carried out, the system risks imminent collapse. In social systems in particular, human intervention appears to be the only option. It is also important to mention that in deviation-amplifying models, similar conditions may produce dissimilar outcomes (Maruyama, 1963). This is consistent with sensitive dependence on the initial conditions concept in chaos theory.

There is negative feedback when a change that pushes a variable in one direction calls up counterbalancing forces that restore the variable close to its original position. For example, if on increase in population were to lead to a reduction in the number of children born, population growth would be curtailed. Negative feedback ensures a system's stability since it produces self-correcting, deviation-counteracting models. Deviations are self-correcting only to a point, however. Once a system reaches a point of bifurcation, the ability of negative feedback to maintain system stability breaks down.

## MANAGING FOR SUSTAINABILITY: POLICY AND MANAGEMENT IMPLICATIONS OF A NONLINEAR FRAMEWORK

The metaphors and conceptual vocabulary of chaos and complexity theory may be more in tune with the realities and nature of change that sustainability requires. While it is generally recognized that some form of change in mindsets, attitude, and behavior is important for sustainability, there may be little by way of past experience that prepares us for the sort of social change that sustainability requires. The usual search for stability and planning-based systems in development are clearly inconsistent with the dynamism inherent in ecological and environmental management. As Michael (1995: 463) puts it, "our semantic baggage from past experience is not matched to a reality of systematic interactions, circular feedback processes, nonlinearity, or multiple causation and outcomes. Implicitly, our conventional language relates us to a world of linear relationships, simple cause and effect, and separate circumstances, whether they are events, simple causes, and effects. But that is not the world we live in." A look at one major theory of change can illuminate our understanding of the sort of social change effort that may be conducive to the attainment of the objectives of sustainability. Jantsch (1980) identified three views of change: (1) deterministic change, (2) equilibrium-based change, and (3) dissipative or transformational change.

Jantsch's first view of change is largely consistent with a linear view of change. A linear view of change posits some direct relationship between cause and effect. It also presumes that we can predict the future and anticipate what the consequences will be of any intervention we apply to a system. This model of change starts from a premise that order, stability, and prediction are possible or indeed, the reality. Under this view, the responsibility of those at the forefront of change is to search for order and ways of reducing uncertainty. The limits of this view are clear. When the realities of sustainability are disorder, uncertainty, and surprise rather than stability and order, a linear model is clearly unsuitable. There is some evidence that some of the present work linking interactions of the environment and development have applied this sort of linear, equilibrium-centered approach to development. Clark (1989) observes that the "bias of most research and policy programs has been toward institutions, processes, and practices that might maintain or restore some presumptive 'equilibrium' with nature."

Jantsch's second view of change is an adaptive model of change, which has its theoretical roots in systems theory (Boulding, 1964). While systemic thinking is consistent with the realities of sustainability, adaptation is in some sense a search for stability and order, because systems theory is focused on balance and equilibrium. Like linear thinking, adaptation views unpredictability and disorder as dysfunctional. Institutional choices based on an adaptive model will tend to "tinker" with the system instead of pursuing radical transformation and change. The temptation to engage in incremental planning is greatest when one adopts the adaptive view of change because the primary objective will be a focus on reducing error and variety. Worse yet, the search for conventional solutions means that there is hardly any incentive or opportunity for radically changing mental models. The fact is that stable systems tend to resist change. Individuals and organizations used to stability will resist change because once locked into specific mindsets, change is seen as a disturbance of the status quo. The pathologies of stability for radical transformation have been revealingly demonstrated in several case studies of forest management in New Brunswick, the Everglades, the Baltic, and Chesapeake Bay (Gunderson et al., 1995).

The third and final view of change is the dissipative view of change. This is more consistent with a nonlinear framework because it connotes radical transformation and renewal. Radical change occurs when old existing structures of a system break up and emerge as new forms through the process of self-organization. Under this view, change, uncertainty, and instability are accepted as a necessary part of transformation. Since sustainable development requires change and transformation, this view of change is most useful. In summary, we note that a nonlinear view of change and sustainability will be more consistent with the realities of sustainability. A number of policy and management implications can be derived from the preceding discussion.

## Intervention and Change in Social Systems

Chaos theory reveals that all systems undergo dynamic transformation that includes periods of relative stability, some instability, and total chaos or instability and disorder (Briggs and Peat, 1989). Managing a system during periods of stability may be easier, partly because one can still make predictions about the results of intervention. Determining cause and effect is still possible during relative periods of stability. One important lesson here is that we can try to prevent a system from moving to full-blown chaos. The clue is to look for bifurcation, because bifurcation points signal that a system is changing from one behavioral regime to the other. This may necessitate the taking of some form of "pre-emptive" action.

The need for timely intervention in social systems becomes even more urgent when one realizes that unlike physical systems, social systems face imminent collapse unless some human intervention is applied. In the case of sustainable development, it is imperative that action be taken to prevent the key parameters that drive either the whole system or subsystems from continuously exceeding their critical limits. For intervention to be effective, however, requires that it be timely, focus on the appropriate targets, and apply systemic thinking.

First, although theory suggests that complex systems have the ability to self-adapt, it is more probable that social systems that continuously hover on the brink of catastrophe will collapse without some human intervention, because positive feedback loops indicative of chaos and crisis dampen the ability of negative feedback to bring the system into some equilibrium. Indeed, the value of negative feedback loops as a corrective mechanism diminishes drastically as the system reaches a bifurcation point. One policy implication is that intervention needs to be instituted to prevent the system from reaching full-blown chaos. The existing evidence seems to suggest that intervention sometimes occurs when this point is passed. For example, on some occasions the World Bank and the IMF seem to have instituted or called for drastic policy changes in poorer regions of the world after the systems have reached total chaos (Klitgaard, 1990).

Second, an effort should be made to study the key driving forces or key parameters of the system. These should become the targets for change effort. This may be possible because we know that all systems, including social systems, obey certain rules. Peak and Frame (1994) note that any system that obeys rules, even chaotic systems, can be controlled once we know what the rules are. Byrne (1998) suggests that the rules that are important in social systems include both the specification of the controlling parameters or dynamical keys and knowledge of the nonlinear effects of changes in the dynamical keys. Key parameters are the forces that govern a system's path as it undergoes qualitative transformation. Dynamical keys may be one or a combination of several variables. We can identify these key variables by identifying those variables in which small changes produce nonlinear changes in the system's evolution. For example, population and land use may be control parameters in a system. Knowing what the effects are of changes in these variables will also be useful in deciding what to control.

Finally, it is important to apply systemic thinking in intervention. This calls for a holistic approach to development. The concept of holism in chaos theory teaches us that our understanding of sustainable development will be incomplete without a systemic framework. According to Daneke (1999), holism is simply the position that systems cannot be understood merely by looking at the parts individually. It means, for example, that we cannot reduce the sustainable problem into parts to be studied and managed separately. Piecemeal solutions and "tinkering" with the system will be a story half told. The idea that simple systems can generate complex and surprising behavior implies that simple solutions will only produce brittle results and surprises. It is therefore imperative that systemwide solutions that take into consideration all the relevant factors be developed for intervention to work. This may be especially crucial in the brittle environments of the poorer regions of the world.

## Chaos, Nonlinearity, and Action

The concept of sensitive dependence on initial conditions or the "butterfly" effect (Lorenz, 1986) reveals that small causes can yield unpredictable and totally unexpected effects. The potential for surprise in social systems therefore, is great. Describing ecosystems, Holling (1986: 294), notes that surprises occur when causes turn out to be sharply different than were conceived, when behaviors are profoundly unexpected, and when action produces a result opposite to that intended–in short, when perceived realities depart qualitatively from expectation. For example, even a well-intentioned program such as the much publicized structural adjustment program to correct imbalances in both micro and macro disequilibrium in the economies of developing countries has often resulted in severe hardships for the very poor and caused political instability (Kiltgaard, 1990; Abbey, 1990). Ecotourism is also supposed to help native communities, yet we know that there are unintended consequences and deleterious effects of the ensuing economic activity on the environment. Bringing the notion of surprises to the forefront of theorizing and policy formation on sustainable development can be particularly helpful. The inherent dynamism of systems, expressed by a system's sensitivity dependence on initial conditions, has some important management implications.

First, the concept suggests among other things that two systems or regions that exhibit close similarity in system conditions may ultimately develop or evolve in completely different ways. This has one important implication for development models. The tendency to extrapolate findings and replicate models from one region to another needs to be re-evaluated in the light of the new knowledge of system behavior.

Second, the idea that multiple outcomes can exist for systems that may have similar initial conditions has profound implications for sustainable development. It suggests, for example, that applying similar intervention strategies in systems that appear very similar may actually produce radically different results. For example, the Grameen model has become a model for micro financing in regions of the South. Originally developed in Bangladesh, the model has since been replicated in such diverse countries as Nigeria (Ekpenyong, 1992), Malawi, Sri Lanka, and Malaysia (Hulme, 1990). The fact that this model of micro financing worked in one place does not mean it can be universally applied. Worse yet, we may be unable to predict with any degree of certainty what the outcomes of introducing this idea would be in other settings. In practical terms, what this suggests is that planners and those at the forefront of developing intervention strategies ought to be sensitive to these possibilities and develop an acute understanding of each case. Again one must always be prepared for surprises. The insight is that intervention strategies and solutions must always reflect the specific needs and prevailing circumstances of a place and that there are no guarantees that a model that succeeds in one particular place can be successfully duplicated with the same result elsewhere, even if the system conditions appear similar.

Third, sensitivity to initial conditions alerts us to the fact that in certain cases small changes can lead to very profound outcomes, while in others even large initial kicks would hardly result in any changes at all. Finally, the concept of sensitivity to initial conditions implies that even small mistakes can have very serious consequences because error tends to grow exponentially over time (Glieck, 1988). By the same token, initial success in certain cases will feed on itself. These ideas pose serious challenges to policy planning on sustainability. Analysis and action must incorporate these guidelines if realistic solutions are to be generated on the complex and dynamic issues that define sustainability.

## Chaos, Learning, and Social Transformation

Social change requires that we develop a capacity for learning (Gray, 1985; Parson and Clark, 1995). This learning, however, may not come readily to individuals, social actors, and institutions. This is because there are often cognitive, sociocultural, and emotional constraints to learning (Michael, 1995). Institutions and individuals may fail to learn from experience, but this is crucial if the goals of sustainable development are to be attained. This may be because existing mindsets have not necessarily prepared us for the sort of collective learning that sustainability entails.

Argyris and Schön (1978) proposed that learning takes two forms: single-loop and double-loop or complex learning. Single-loop learning occurs when existing mindsets are reinforced through new information and experience. Single-loop learning focuses on error detection and incremental adaptation because experience becomes a point of reference. Novelty may therefore be dismissed as an aberration or something that needs to be explained away. The tendency to dismiss novelty, however, may lead single-loop learners to miss important opportunities to reframe their thinking and develop creative solutions, all qualities required for social learning on sustainability.

Double-loop learning occurs when behaviors are adapted in response to external stimuli and when existing schemas are changed. Double-loop learning promotes innovation and creativity. Michael (1995) observes that social learning on ecological management can be facilitated by acknowledging uncertainty and using crises as occasions for learning. Although important, there is little reason to believe that our existing mindset has prepared us to accept uncertainty, embrace error, and see crises as "desirable," but this is exactly what chaos theory reveals. Since our normal ways of seeing and knowing have led us to search for stability and see uncertainty as worrisome, the temptation to engage in single-loop learning must be resisted. Instead of seeing anomalies as aberrations, chaos theory teaches us that an anomaly or error may be an opportunity for creative learning. Accepting the ubiquity of uncertainty prepares one to be better prepared to deal with and learn from crises.

## Attractors and Local Context: Thinking Globally and Acting Locally

Sustainable development involves cross-scale issues in the sense that local actions have global implications. At the same time, it is important that action matches the scale. This brings the local context to the forefront of action. The concept of attractors in chaos theory may be useful for our understanding of the imperatives of local participation in managing social transformation.

At least two key insights from the concept can help the management of social change effort toward sustainability. First, those at the forefront of change can look for hidden attractors in a system. In every situation, the search for those dynamical keys that a system tends to be "pulled" to may lead to the identification of an attractor. Once that attractor is identified, policy management can be designed around that attractor. Second and related, there can be a deliberate effort to build specific attractors into a chaotic system (Wheatley, 1992).

For example, the grounding of development models in native systems and structures may be one way of building attractors into a chaotic system in the poorer regions of the world. Three examples are used to illustrate how attractors can be built into the system. These are: the retaining of traditional, low-input methods in land utilization, the concept of self-reliance, and the possibility of building development models on long-cherished value systems. A Buddhist economics example is used to illustrate this point.

First, the application of simple technologies may be a way of building attractors into a system; thus even when new ways of land use are adopted, the core philosophy of low-energy, low-input practices must be retained. Traditional land utilization systems determined to be appropriate can be blended with new ways, especially in the brittle environments of the poor South. The idea is that existing systems remain the core around which modern systems are built and not the other way around.

Second, a self-reliant approach to development may be one attractor that can be built into the system. The goals of a self-reliant strategy have been identified to include: (1) the promotion of human needs, (2) the facilitation of participation in the political economy, (3) the more efficient utilization of local factors of production, and (4) the attainment of ecologically sustainable development (Solomon, 1990). Although the tendency is for people to dismiss the idea of self-reliance as a simplistic option, a clear understanding of self-reliance reveals that it may be a powerful attractor under certain conditions. Of course, self-reliance should not mean isolation or autarky; it is perhaps the nature of the dependency equation between the North and South that must change. Perlmutter and Trist (1986: 19) note that self-reliance does not imply a denial of a two-way relationship of interdependence. They write evocatively that self-reliance "cannot exist unless each party has both independence value and need for the other. Such mutually advantageous symbiotic relations are desirable. Dominance and dependence are replaced by a balance of interdependence and independence."

Finally, the incorporation of existing systems of beliefs into development models can be one way of building attractors into the system. Speculation suggests that native religions, including animism, in most of the South have a veneration for nature. For example, Buddhism specifically calls for a veneration of nature. Indeed, the links between Buddhism and economics have been made for some time now (Alexandrin, 1993). Among other things, Buddhism enjoins reverent and nonviolent attitude toward nature and calls for simple living. It carefully distinguishes between renewable and nonrenewable resources. Nonrenewable resources are to be used only when absolutely necessary.

The value and resilience of local participation has been demonstrated. For example, Thibaukt and Blaney (2001) analyzed the perseverance of those who participated in a sustainability program in Gabon, in Africa, and concluded that village collaborators were more "sustainable" than government agents. They found that of government agents who attended their respective training sessions, 7.7% continued ecological surveys (one segment of the program) and 0% continued participatory rural appraisal (another segment of the program) two years after training; however, 76.2% and 60% of the members of local communities who received training were still active in ecological surveys and participatory rural appraisal, respectively, after two years.

## Institutional Choices and Multiparty Collaboration

Sustainability poses messy problems. Prior research has demonstrated that in order to be resolved, messy problems require input from a wide range of actors. Lessons from complexity theory, specifically the concept of self-organizing systems, can help explain some of the dynamics of the types of institutional arrangements that are most amenable to dealing with the messy problems that cut across several domains.

The complexity of sustainability requires input from a broad range of stakeholders with competing interests and different jurisdictions (Vredenburg and Westley, 1993). Everything from religious equity, ethical, political, social, economic, and gender equity has been listed as a part of global sustainability (Greene et al., 1990). Even if we work with the narrow and basic definition of sustainability (à la Brundtland), the need to involve a range of stakeholders and experts in the design of intervention strategies and policy choices is clear. This of course means that the issue of how to promote multiparty collaboration needs to be addressed.

Daneke (1999) observes that collaborative systems are more likely to emerge within highly participatory institutional arrangements, yet some evidence suggests that society generally lacks the ability to forge this form of collaboration (Vredenburg and Westley, 1993; Gray, 1985). Exploring the institutional ecology of this form of collaboration can be useful. Two key issues are important in that regard: the type of collaboration, including the structuring of the network, and leadership.

First is the type of collaboration. Westley and Vredenburg (1991) identified three types of collaboration on the basis of their origin: those that originate by the actions of a visionary leader, those that are mandated by the government, and those that seem to spring up spontaneously through the action of shared communities of interest, such as researchers and citizens' movements. Westley (1995) demonstrates that the three forms of collaboration vary in their ability to deal with the critical areas of issue definition, resource mobilization, action mobilization, and institutionalization, all critical tasks required for collaboration to succeed. Westley's research suggests that the third type of collaboration, the spontaneous one, seems better placed to succeed at these tasks.

Similar dynamics have been identified in political science in the theory of regimes. Young (1982: 277) defines regimes as social institutions governing the actions of those interested in specifiable activities. Young (1982) identifies three main forms of regimes: spontaneous, negotiated, and imposed. First are spontaneous regimes. Spontaneous orders are defined as the "product of the action of many men but not the result of human design." As Young (1982) notes, spontaneous orders do not often require explicit consent on the part of subjects or prospective subjects. This sort of regime closely resembles the spontaneous type of collaboration identified by Vredenburg and Westley (1993). Second are negotiated orders. These are regimes characterized by explicit consent on the part of individual participants. For example, the GAAT (General Agreement on Trade) may be an example of a regime in which member nations agree to be bound by rules and regulations of a negotiated order or regime. Environmental programs such as Agenda 21 of the Rio Conference (Rogers, 1993) may be one example of this type of regime.

Finally come imposed regimes. This occurs when norms of behavior are forced upon consortia of actors by a dominant actor. As in spontaneous orders, individual actors may not explicitly give their consent, but the dominant actor or actors succeeds in getting them to conform to the requirements of the regime through a combination of coercion, co-optation, and the manipulation of incentives. This is similar to the collaboration imposed by government. It is probably the least capable performance because stakeholders often have different visions and jurisdictions and getting actors to collaborate becomes very difficult. Worse yet, the task of leadership under such situations would often be turned over to bureaucrats and experts of all sorts. Short-term and fluid planning will often replace long-term systemic thinking. Experience teaches us that these types of efforts yield short-term successes that will prove increasingly brittle and fragile in the long run.

Case studies of ecosystems (see Gunderson et al., 1995) have demonstrated that government bureaucrats are often under pressure to produce results and tend to close issues without thorough deliberation. It is also known that bureaucrats are quintessential incrementalists (Lindblom, 1959) who may choose error-free management instead of seeking radical change and transformation, yet nonlinear frameworks suggest that social transformation on sustainability may only come through radical transformation.

Spontaneous emergence of collaboration is most consistent with a nonlinear framework. It is also consistent with the research of the sociologist Mark Granovetter (1985), who argued persuasively that weaker ties are preferable to stronger ties for cooperation and trust to emerge. Emery and Trist (1973) have also suggested that open and active participation by individuals and groups on social problems enhances adaptive capabilities. Spontaneous collaboration among communities of interest will tend to be evolutionary. To use the chaos metaphor, spontaneous collaborators benefit from self-organization (Prigogine and Stengers, 1984). Self-organization here refers to the stakeholder group's ability to generate self-renewal within the parties.

Management theorist Ralph Stacey (1996: 204) suggests that "spontaneous self-organization produces stable behavior in groups of people because of their need to belong. Spontaneous self-organization is a process of bottom-up cooperation and therefore a major source of the stability we observe in the behavior of organizations." Stacey's description of self-organization in organizations also stresses the key role of shadow networks in fostering collaboration. A shadow network comprises an informal group of individuals who "work" behind the scenes.

Although these people work informally, their need to gain the support of the larger group of members in the network makes them acutely sensitive to the views of others. This sort of shadow network finds some parallel in the concept of neural net organizations described by Michael (1991). Each individual engaged in this sort of behind-the-scene action can be liked to a "neuron" that is waiting to be excited. Individual actors are only excited when they form links with other people in the network, as well as form several communication patterns so that they can receive equal amounts of stimulation. These kinds of groups will tend to be adaptive groups that group and regroup over time. What is most useful is the capacity for self-regulation in these loose networks.

Stacey (1996) suggests that this sort of self-organization fosters creativity. These same ideas can be applied to groups engaged in social change. Indeed, the instrumental role of such "shadow networks" in ecosystem management has been documented in the series of cases in Gunderson et al. (1995). The most important policy implication here is that it may be preferable to encourage the action of loose networks of like-minded individuals and groups rather than design highly structured institutions to foster multiparty collaboration, because a loose structure is more likely to promote self-organization than a structured one. This is so because compared to structured forms, spontaneous, self-organizing systems have the most capacity for continuous change, self-renewal, and transformation, perhaps because self-organizing systems will also tend to see uncertainty, chaos, and instability as challenges for continuous adaptation and renewal.

The second important issue in multiparty collaboration has to do with leadership. In their description of ecosystem management in the Great Lakes basin, Francis and Regier (1995) demonstrated that the presence of a narrow range of professional expertise often became a barrier to social change. This may be because a certain measure of disciplinary parochialism makes experts reluctant to perceive new situations in ways that diminish their expertise. It is therefore important not to leave the process exclusively to elites and experts. It is common knowledge that while experts can have important and beneficial effects on the process, they may become obstacles to change for at least two reasons. First, they may be unwilling to change their frames of reference and by doing so miss the opportunity for recognizing new possibilities. Second, they may have their own ideological agendas that make them focus only on sections of problems that are in their domain of expertise.

For profound or transformational change to occur, however, requires that problems be reframed in new ways. Kahneman and Tversky (1981) suggest that choices in uncertain situations depend strongly on the way a situation is described or "framed," but all sorts of management rigidities may hamper a search for new solutions.

Although, except in a few cases and perhaps for short time periods, government mandated leadership may be unhelpful to the process, this is not to downplay the key role institutional leaders can and should play. In the developing countries of the South, their participation is necessary because perhaps more than any other group, they alone have some semblance of institutional adequacy. It will be preferable that their role be limited largely to a facilitative one, however. The example of Japan's Ministry of Trade (MITI) may be an example. Organized by the government, MITI has succeeded through a combination of incentives and threats to foster interfirm collaboration among Japanese firms (Hagen and Choe, 1998).

## Temporal Dynamics and Sustainability

It is important to consider the effect of time on the actions and consequences of human activity as well as its relationship to sustainable development. At least two characteristics of sustainability make this imperative. First, the stability of a system must be defined for a specific time and space because complex, large systems have several areas of equilibrium or stability regimes within which they move, depending on the magnitude of the outside forces or boundary conditions (Jansson and Velner, 1995). Second, the impact of environmental factors and actions are often not immediate and take time for the effects to be seen, and so a greater understanding of the temporal dynamics of environmental impacts may be useful. Chaos theory may offer some conceptual tools for incorporating the temporal lens in sustainability because it is focused on time-bound phenomena. The understanding of time lags and feedback loops will be particularly helpful to understanding the long-term impact of actions.

Time lag refers to the period between in which an effect Y is seen, given a cause X. Chaos theory suggests that our ability to predict when Y will occur given X is limited. When Y occurs may depend on the nature of each specific situation, and so a greater understanding of the local context is important. Chaos theory suggests that we look for the key driving forces in every system to determine when change in the system will take place. Identifying the key driving forces may give clues to when changes in related variables occur in the system. A bifurcation in any of these forces will often signal that change is about to happen or has already happened.

Chaos theory also alerts us to the importance of feedback in complex and dynamic systems. System theorists have traditionally conceptualized negative feedback as having a stabilizing effect because it allows for corrective action. We also know that positive feedback can lead to instability. In general, chaos allows us to look at time and change in new ways. The lesson of chaos is that analysts need to consider these and other temporal factors for a greater understanding of the consequences of both environmental and human action.

## CONCLUSION

This chapter presented a conceptual framework for a greater understanding of sustainability issues. An important criterion of any conceptual framework is whether it can stimulate empirical research and practice that aids in the resolution of problems. The hope is that the framework presented here achieves that objective, and a presentation of some possible areas for further study is in order. The need to study how we can identify the dynamical keys or driving forces in any system is urgent. A greater understanding of the role of shadow networks for collaboration will also be useful. Hass (1990) has studied the role of what he calls "epistemic communities" in saving the Mediterranean. Understanding the role of shadow networks in the promotion of sustainable development, especially in the poorer regions of the world, will be particularly useful.

Advances in the sciences of chaos and complexity present an opportunity for the next crucial phase of experimental testing of the claims of chaos. Chaos theory has developed its own mathematics as well as its own geometry (Briggs and Peat, 1989; Maldelbrot, 1977). Besides, existing research methods such as case studies, metaphorical essays, simulations, and time series modeling may all appropriate research techniques for studying dynamic systems (Dooley, 1997). Longitudinal and process-focused research is needed to capture the complex issues associated with sustainability.

In general, the epistemological and ontological implications of chaos theory in the social sciences require some additional clarification. For example, normal scientific views of paradigm development (Kuhn, 1962) in which successive approximations of theory lead to the development of grand theories, are clearly contrary to the revealed ontology of nonlinear sciences. Successive replication of prior studies is impossible where prediction and causality are difficult to ascertain. These and other issues await conceptual clarification.

There is some realization among researchers and policy planners that synoptic, planning-based approaches to sustainable development have their limits. For example, the U.S. National Research Council on Sustainable Development declares in its publication *Our Common Journey* that "because the pathway to sustainability cannot be charted in advance, it will have to be navigated through trial and error and conscious experimentation." This clearly suggests that institutional designs that foster creativity and experimentation are needed. A nonlinear framework may provide the guidelines for designing institutions and systems that can foster the sort of creativity and experimentation required to move the world toward a sustainable future.

## REFERENCES

Abbey, J. L. (1990). Ghana's experience with structural adjustment: Some lessons. In: Picket, J., Singer, H., eds. Toward Recovery in Sub-Saharan Africa. London: Rutledge.

Adams, W. M. (1990). Green Development: Environmental Management and Sustainability in the Third World. New York: Rutledge.

Alexandrin, G. (1993). Elements of Buddhist economics. Internat. J. Soc. Econ. 20:3–11.

Armitage, J., Schramm, G. (1989). Managing the supply and demand of fuel wood in Africa. In: Scram, G., Warlord, J. J., eds. Environmental Management and Economic Development. Baltimore: Johns Hopkins University Press, pp. 141–152.

Argyris, C., Schön, D. (1986). Organizational Learning: A Theory of Action Perspective. Reading, MA: Addison Wesley.

Black, M. (1962). Models and Metaphors: Studies in Language and Philosophy. Ithaca, NY: Cornel University Press.

Boulding, K. (1964). General systems as a point of view. In: Mesarovic, M. D., ed. Views on General Systems Theory. New York: Wiley.

Briggs, J., Peat, D. (1989). Turbulent Mirror: An Illustrated Guide to Chaos Theory and the Science of Wholeness. New York: Harper and Row.

Brown, L. D. (1993). Social change through collective reflection with Asian non-governmental development organizations. Human Relat. 46:249–273.

Brundtland, H. (1987). Our Common Future. Oxford: Oxford University Press; for the World Commission on Environment and Development.

Byrne, D. (1998). Complexity Theory and the Social Sciences. New York: Rutledge.

Clark, W. C. (1989). Managing planet Earth. Sci. Am. 261(3):47–54.

Commoner, B. (1990). Making Peace with the Planet. New York: Pantheon.

Constanza, R., Daly, H. E., Bartholomew, J. A. (1991). Goals, agenda and policy recommendations for ecological economics. In: Constanza, R., ed. Ecological Economics: The Science and Management of Sustainability. Washington, DC: Island Press.

Constanza, R., Waigner, L., Folke, C., Maler, K. G. (1993). Modeling complex ecological economic system. Bioscience 43(8):545–555.

Daneke, G. A. (1999). Systemic Choices. Ann Arbor, MI: University of Michigan Press.

De La Court, T. (1990). Beyond Brundtland: Green Development in the 1990's. New York: Horizon.

Dooley, K. (1997). A complex adaptive systems model of organizational change. Nonlin. Dynam. Psycho. Life Sci. 1(1):69–97.

Dore, M. H. (1994). Modeling intertemporary sustainable development: A nonlinear approach. Proceedings of the Sustainable Development Forum II, Naperville, IL, Oct. 22, pp. 15–16.

Eisenhardt, K. M., Schoonhoven, C. B. (1990). Organizational growth: Linking founding team, strategy, environment, and growth among U.S. semiconductor ventures. Admin. Sci. Quarterly 35(3):504–552.

Ekpenyong, D. (1992). Relevance of Bangladesh Grameen Bank experience for Nigerian small business financing: A case study of the Peoples Bank of Nigeria. J. Finan. Mgt. Anal. 5:1–9.

Feigenbaum, M. (1978). Quantitative universality for a class of nonlinear transformations. J. Stat. Physics 19:25–52.

Francis, G. R., Regier, H. A. (1995). Restoration of the Great Lakes Basin ecosystem. In:

Gunderson, L., Holling, C. S., Light, S., eds. Barriers and Bridges to the Renewal of Ecosystems and Institutions. New York: Columbia University Press, pp. 239–291.

Gladwin, T. N., Kennelly, J. J., Krause, T. (1995). Shifting paradigms for sustainable development: Implications for management theory and research. Acad. Mgt. Rev. 20(4):874–907.

Gleick, J. (1988). Chaos: Making a New Science. New York: Penguin.

Granovetter, M. S. (1985). Economic action and social structure: A theory of embeddedness. Amer. J. Sociol. 91:481–510.

Gray, B. (1985). Conditions facilitating interorganizational collaboration. Human Relat. 38(10):911–936.

Greene, G., Wright, D., Bregha, F., Ruitenbeek, J. 1990. A Sustainable Development Framework for CIDA. draft document for the Canadian Development Agency. Hull, Canada.

Guastello, S. J. (1995). Chaos, Catastrophe, and Human Affairs: Applications of Nonlinear Dynamics to Work, Organizations, and Social Evolution. Mahwah, NJ: Lawrence Erlbaum.

Gunderson, L., Holling, C. S., Light, S. S., eds. (1995). Barriers and bridges to the renewal of ecosystems and institutions. New York: Columbia University Press.

Hagen, J. M., Choe, S. (1998). Trust in Japanese interfirm relations: Institutional sanctions matter. Acad. Mgt. Rev. 23:589–600.

Hass, P. M. (1990). Saving the Mediterranean: The Politics of International Cooperation. New York: Columbia University Press.

Holling, C. S. (1986). The resilience of terrestrial ecosystems: Local surprise and global change. In: Clark, W. C., Munn, R. E., eds. Sustainable Development of the Biosphere. Cambridge: Cambridge University Press, pp. 292–317.

Holling, C. S. (1992). Cross-scale morphology, geometry and dynamics of ecosystems. Ecol. Monogr. 62(4):447–502.

Holling, C. S. (1995). What barriers? What bridges? In: Gunderson, L. H., Holling, C. S., Light, S., eds. Barriers and Bridges to the Renewal of Ecosystems and Institutions. New York: Columbia University Press, 3–34.

Hulme, D. (1990). Can the Grameen Bank be replicated? Recent experiments in Malaysia, Malawi and Sri Lanka. Devel. Policy Rev. 8:287–300.

Jansson, B, Velner, H. 1995. The Baltic: The sea of surprises. In: Gunderson, L., Holling, C.S., Light, S., eds. Barriers and Bridges to the Renewal of Ecosystems and Institutions. New York: Columbia University Press, pp. 429–372.

Jantsch, E. (1980). The Self-Organizing Universe: Scientific and Human Implications of the Emerging Paradigm of Evolution. Elmsford, NY: Pergamon.

Kahneman, D., Tversky, A. (1981). The framing of decisions and the psychology of choice. Science 211:453–458.

Kay, J. J. (1991). A non-equilibrium thermodynamic framework for discussing ecosystem integrity. Environ. Mgt. 15:483–495.

Kiel, L. D., Elliot, E. (1996). Chaos Theory in the Social Sciences. Ann Arbor, NI: University of Michigan Press.

Kiltgaard, R. (1990). Tropical Gangsters. New York: Basic Books.

Kuhn, T. (1962). The Structure of Scientific Revolutions. Chicago: University of Chicago Press.

Levin, S. A. (1993). Science and sustainability. Ecol. Appl. 3(4):1–2.

Lindblom, C. (1959). The "science" of muddling through. Pub. Admin. Rev. 19(2):79–88.

Maldelbrot, B. (1977). The Fractal Geometry of Nature. New York: Freeman.

Maruyama, M. (1963). The second cybernetics: Deviation-amplifying mutual causal processes. Amer. Sci. pp. 164–179.

Michael, M. D. (1991). Chaos constructions: A neural net model of organizations. In: Michaels, M. D., ed. Proceedings of the First Annual Chaos Network Conference. Savoy, IL: People Technologies, pp. 79–83.

Michael, D. N. (1995). Barriers and bridges to learning in turbulent human ecology. In: Gunderson, L., Holling, C. S., Light, S., eds. Barriers and Bridges to the Renewal of Ecosystems and Institutions. New York: Columbia University Press, pp. 461–485.

Morgan, G. (1986). Images of Organizations. Newborn Park, CA: Sage.

Nicolis, G., Prigogine, I. (1989). Exploring Complexity. New York: Freeman.

Norton, B. G. (1991). Toward Unity among Environmentalists. New York: Oxford University Press.

Parson, E. A., Clark, W. C. (1995). Sustainable development as social learning: Theoretical perspectives and practical challenges for the design of a research program. In: Gunderson, L., Holling, C. S., Light, S., eds. Barriers and Bridges to the Renewal of Ecosystems and Institutions. New York: Columbia University Press, pp. 428–460.

Peak, D., Frame, M. (1994). Chaos under Control. New York: Freeman.

Peet, J. (1992). Energy and the Ecological Economics of Sustainability. Washington, DC: Island Press.

Peitgen, H. O., Jurgens, H., Saupe, D. (1992). Chaos and Fractals: New Frontiers of Science. New York: Springer-Verlag.

Pearce D., Barbier, E., Markandyam, A., 1990. Sustainable Development, Economics and Environment in the Third World. Aldershot, England: Edward Elgar.

Perlmutter, H., Trist, E. L. (1986). Paradigms for societal transition. Human Relat. 39:1–27.

Prigogine, I., Stengers, I. (1984). Order Out of Chaos: Man's New Dialogue with Nature. New York: Bantam.

Rogers, A. (1993). The Earth Summit: A Planetary Reckoning. Los Angeles: Global View.

Schmidheiny, S. (1992). Changing Course: A Global Business Perspective on Development and Environment. Business Council for Sustainable Development. Cambridge, MA: MIT Press.

Solomon, L. D. (1990). Humanomics: A model for the third world development. George Wash. J. Internat. Law Econ. 25:447–475.

Stacey, R. D. (1992). Managing the Unknowable: Strategic Boundaries Between Order and Chaos in Organizations. San Francisco: Jossey-Bass.

Stacey, R. D. (1996). Complexity and Creativity in Organizations. San Francisco: Berrett-Koehler.

Stein, D. L. (1989). Lectures in the Sciences of Complexity. Redwood City, CA: Addison-Wesley for the Sante Fe Institute.

Stinchcombe, A. L. (1965). Organizations and social structure. In: March, J. G., ed. Handbook of Organizations. Chicago: Rand McNally, pp. 153–193.

Thibault, M., Blaney, S. (2001). Sustainable human resources in protected area in southwestern Gabon. Conversat. Biol. 15(3):591–595.

Turner, F. (1997). Foreword: Chaos and social science. In: Eve, R. A., Horsfall, S., Lee, M. E., eds. Chaos, Complexity, and Sociology. Thousand Oaks, CA: Sage, pp. xi–xxvii.

Vivian, J. M. (1992). Foundations for sustainable development. In: Ghai, D., Vivian, J., eds. Grassroots Environmental Action. New York: Rutledge.

Vredenburg, H., Westley, F. (1993). The creation and implementation of sustainable of sustainable development strategies in Canadian ecosystems: A participative action research. paper presented at the Administrative Science Association of Canada Conference (ASAC), Lake Louise, Alberta.

Waldrop, M. M. (1992). The Emerging Science at the Edge of Order and Chaos. New York: Simon and Schuster.

Weick, K. E. (1979). The Psychology of Organizing. Reading, MA: Addison-Wesley.

Wells, D. (1996). Environmental Policy. Upper Saddle River, NJ: Prentice Hall.

Westley, F., Vredenburg, H. (1991). Strategic bridging: The alliances of business and environmentalists. J. Appli. Behav. Sci. 27(1):65–90.

Westley, F. (1995). Governing design: The management of social systems and ecosystems management. In: Gunderson, L., Holling, C. S., Light, S., eds. Barriers and Bridges to the Renewal of Ecosystems and Institutions. New York: Columbia University Press, pp. 391–427.

Wheatley, M. (1992). Leadership and the New Science: Learning about Organizations from an Orderly Universe. San Francisco: Berret-Koehler.

Young, O. R. (1982). Regime dynamics: The rise and fall of international regimes. Internat. Org. 36(2):277–297.

# 4

## Sustainable Development
### What Does Sustainability Mean to Individuals in the Conduct of Their Lives and Businesses?

**R. WARREN FLINT**

*Five E's Unlimited, Washington, D.C., U.S.A.*

### INTRODUCTION

Society consistently faces issues related to economy, the environment, and fairness among people. Each of these human concerns is in some way impacted by the forces that drive the natural world. But traditionally international development models intended to tackle societal problems have most often taken a piecemeal, singular approach, addressing issues of economics, environment, or social health, sometimes in isolation from one another. Typically, socioeconomic systems have been caught up in the adversarial "economy versus environment" debate, operating in a linear direction—taking resources from the Earth, making them into products, and throwing them away to produce large amounts of waste (take–make–waste).

The purpose of this chapter is to make sense of the available information about how communities function and how they can choose alternative paths toward development improvements. This chapter will examine how the natural and human worlds are connected and what this means with regard to re-evaluation of traditional international development models. The following pages will demonstrate how sustainable development principles can promote a multidimensional way to achieve recovery and improve the quality of life for everyone.

The discussion further focuses on how achieving sustainable development requires communities to pursue an evolving and ever-changing program of activities, including a continuous process of evaluating current and emerging trends, an on-going means of encouraging citizen participation and negotiating conflicts, and an updating of plans. Since plans are intended to reflect substantive policy outcomes, the principles of sustainability will be defined to guide future international development actions. With these guiding principles a framework will exist for incorporating the concept into decision making at all levels of the public and private sector that finds itself focused on international development issues.

Recent discoveries emphasize that current and future generations must strive to achieve a decent standard of living for all people and live within the limits of natural systems. Despite this apparent simplicity, there is no general agreement on how sustainable development should be translated into practice. In fact, sustainability is not strictly a problem of science, engineering, or economics, but is also founded on values, ethics, and the equal contributions of different cultures. With this recognition, several examples are discussed that illustrate how sustainability can become part of mainstream development patterns in the near term.

## WHAT ARE THE BASIC FACTORS OF OUR WORLD?

Human settlements are placing significant burdens on both local ecosystems and the global environment. Many communities face enormous difficulties as their economic and environmental resources are damaged or depleted and their social and cultural systems disrupted (Bartlett, 1999; Flint and Houser, 2001). Because the environmental and socioeconomic dimensions of communities are interconnected, traditional, fragmented inquiry into specific problems generally offers no way to integrate knowledge into effective solutions. The challenge to seeking effective solutions requires cutting across traditional disciplines and demands new multi- and transdisciplinary means of generating knowledge. It also requires more effective mechanisms for conveying information to policy makers and the public.

To make sense of the available information about how communities function and how they can choose alternative paths toward improvements, basic factors affecting how our human and natural worlds operate should be examined. First, we consider how humans generally perceive their world in terms of economics, environment (or more specifically ecology), and social equality or equity.

Economy is the management and use of resources to meet household and community needs. The lack of economic security is today's reality. It compels us to find ways to make jobs, public health, and the environment truly compatible. Economic activity should serve the common good, be self-renewing, build local assets and self-reliance, and be efficient and prudent in using resources. Think of economy in the way you would when managing a household, which involves budgeting and planning your resources to secure decent housing, enough food and clothing, a safe environment (for health and protection from crime), the necessary utilities, and some entertainment or recreation. Just as households must meet certain economic needs, a vibrant community must meet the needs of a healthy local economy.

Ecology is the pattern of relationships between living things and their environment. Consider how we view a house as compared to a home. A *house* is an assemblage of materials put together to provide shelter. A *home*, on the other hand, includes the physical structure of the house plus all the inhabitants of that house and their various relationships. Just as humans are part of their home, we are also part of nature. Nature has limits, and human communities are responsible for protecting and building natural assets within these limits. Ecological considerations include the amount of air, land, water, and biological resources it takes to support us. Nearly every decision a community makes affects these resources in some way (Flint and Houser, 2001).

Equity involves the social characteristics of humans, including the ethics that influence their relationships to other people and nature. Usually some people do very well, while others face hardship in their lives. Where there is equity, decisions are based on fairness, and everyone has opportunity and is treated with dignity. The chance of full participation in all activities and decision making, along with equal responsibility and access to benefits for all members of society, is an integral part of a healthy, functional community.

To fully understand how the human world and natural world are interconnected, it is essential to also consider the principles that drive the natural world, then determine how humans can act more in harmony with functions of nature. It is acknowledged that the following basic principles dictate *how the natural world works* (Robert ct al., 1997).

1. Matter and energy can be neither created nor destroyed. For example, when we drive our car, the gasoline we use looks as though it disappears. In fact, no matter or energy has disappeared—it has simply lost its concentrated form and the energy released in the process has been used to power the car. The molecules that made up the gasoline in the tank have now been widely dispersed through the exhaust pipe as waste. Simply put: *Nothing disappears*. This is *the first law of thermodynamics, the conservation of matter*.

2. Energy and matter tend to disperse and/or spread spontaneously. All substances created by or introduced into human society eventually will disperse in nature. Simply put: *Everything spreads*. This is *the second law of thermodynamics, or the law of entropy*. Entropy is a measure of the disorder or randomness of a system. In every *closed system* entropy produced from the breakdown of matter (disorder) always increases. Earth is a *closed system* with respect to matter, therefore the disorder or entropy that occurs in the use of matter on Earth increases, which explains the accumulation of things in our natural world (i.e., pollution). Consider the fact that DDT, PCBs, and other persistent organic pollutants are showing up in such places as the Arctic, where they were never used (Auman et al., 1997).

3. Quality of a substance or material can be characterized by its concentration and structure. The higher its concentration or the more complex its structure, the higher its quality. Food and gasoline are valuable because they contain order. If the food or gasoline only consisted of a loose arrangement of molecules, then we nor our cars would benefit. We cannot consume energy or matter, only its concentration, purity, and structure. If you drop a glass and it breaks on the floor, some of the value from its structure is lost, but all of the original atoms (broken pieces of the glass) are still present. Simply put: *There is value in order and enhanced structure.*

4. How do all life forms in our natural world derive benefit from changes in the structure of matter and resulting improvements in its quality, as described in (3)? As an *open system* with respect to energy, Earth receives light energy from the sun. It is this flow of sunlight, being converted by photosynthesis in green plants, which is responsible for almost all increases in net

material quality on this planet (Rojstaczer et al., 2001). Simply put: *Plants create structure and order by absorbing and using energy from sunlight*, which provides energy for other forms of life, such as animals.

These four principles have direct ramifications on the outcomes of programs and projects enacted in the human sectors of economy and ecology (Flint and Houser, 2001). As we will see below, the consideration of direct connections (causes and effects) between these natural world principles and society's actions on economy and ecology can be instructive in guiding decision making that will prove more sustainable in its outcomes.

## WHY DO WE NEED TO THINK ABOUT SUSTAINABILITY?

Thirty years ago, there was a tremendous sense of optimism—science and technology would solve all the world's problems. If we can get a man on the moon, then we can do anything! Things are very different now. Global warming, deforestation, loss of soil fertility, pollution, chemical contamination, loss of biodiversity, overpopulation, the hole in the ozone layer all are having their effect upon life on Earth (Robbins, 1987; Hartmann, 1997; Lazaroff, 2000).

The nature of the problem can be summarized by the simple graph in Figure 1. The demand for resources is continuing to increase. This is being driven not only by an increasing world population, but also by the aspirations of that population for an ever-increasing standard of living (Bartlett, 1999). At the same time, the capacity of the planet to meet this demand is in decline through overharvesting, inappropriate

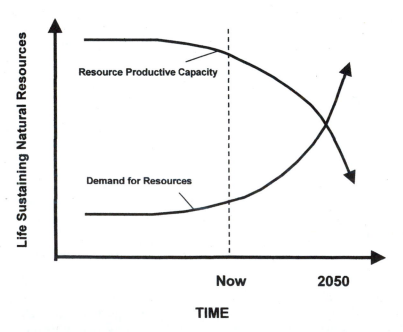

**Figure 1**  Comparison of increasing human demand for natural resources to the resulting decline in these natural resources and their productivity (EcoSteps, 2002).

agricultural practices, and pollution, to name just a few. These impacts on Earth are occurring because humans are not in line with the natural world principles described above (EcoSteps, 2002).

For example, the average North American needs twice the area required by the average Western European to produce the consumed natural resources and absorb the carbon dioxide, and some five times required by the average Asian, African, or Latin American (Brown, 1999; Giuliano, 2000). If every human alive today thus consumed natural resources and emitted carbon dioxide at the same rate as people in North America or in fact as in many other developed nations, at least another two Earths would be needed, according to the World Wide Fund for Nature's *Living Planet Report* (2000).

Herman Daly put it well (Daly, 1992): "The growth ideology (economics) is extremely attractive politically because it offers a solution to poverty without requiring the moral discipline of sharing (equity) and population control. Every system has a predefined carrying capacity (ecology) and it is becoming more apparent everyday that Earth is quickly reaching its carrying capacity with regards to human consumption and waste generation."

The natural step's (TNS) metaphorical use of a "funnel" developed by Dr. Karl-Henrik Robert (Robert et al., 1997; Gips, 1998) further illustrates how society's perceived needs are clashing with our natural environment (Figure 2). Society is "hitting the limits" (like hitting the wall of a funnel) in its never-ending use of natural resources and production of waste. The situation of people on the Earth can be viewed as a funnel with ever-diminishing room to maneuver. Life-support systems for our continued existence on the planet are in decline. At the same time, the global population and global demand for these resources are increasing, leading us to "hit the wall" of the funnel. For example, compare the similarities of the lines in Figure 1 with the two walls of the funnel in Figure 2. Where the lines in Figure 1 cross indicates when we have hit the funnel wall in Figure 2.

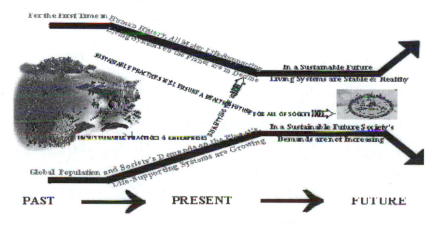

**Figure 2** Conceptual illustration of the "funnel" used by Dr. Karl-Henrik Robert to describe the natural step philosophy. Source from the original ideas of the Resort Municipality of Whistler (BC, Canada) public presentation (Whistler Center for Sustainability, 2001).

The science behind natural world function (described above) offers us direction in finding solutions to the sustainability problems we currently face. The concept of the TNS funnel instructs us that in a sustainable future society's demands on natural systems are not increasing and these systems are thus stable and healthy because they are in line with principles of nature and there is fairness in the use of resources. *The conventional economic imperative to maximize production is accountable to an ecological imperative to protect the ecosphere and a social equity imperative to minimize human suffering. This is the foundation of sustainable development.*

In summary, society consistently faces issues related to economy, the environment, and fairness among people. Each of these human concerns is in some way impacted by the principles that dictate how the natural world works (described on page 69 and identified here by number). Let's consider, for example, the use of timber from a forest. Trees that provide timber for human uses are originally grown from the energy of the sun (principle 4), and these trees also provide habitat for animals and ecological services for humans. Loggers cut trees down to harvest the timber. Pieces of timber are then manufactured into a selection of furniture, significantly increasing the timber's quality or value (principle 3). This manufacturing process is what economics is all about, adding value to natural things (resources), and in this case the economy is supported by the natural resource of the tree the timber came from.

The piece of manufactured furniture no longer resembles the original pieces of timber. The structure has changed (principle 3), and has improved in quality. The remaining wood waste from the pieces of timber after making the furniture has not disappeared either (principle 1). The waste wood has simply changed form, into wood shavings and sawdust (first law of thermodynamics), and the waste wood might be sold as materials for making prefabricated firewood (principle 3) to use for home heating, which is an additional use of the original energy from the sun (principle 4). The burned wood, however, does not disappear, but simply changes its structure again (principle 1). It provides energy in the form of heat and turns into $CO_2$ from the burning process, which goes up the chimney, dispersing (principle 2) into the atmosphere (second law of thermodynamics), and this dispersed $CO_2$, which is synonymous with the increase   in disorder (entropy) of matter, is driving society's concern for our environment because this $CO_2$ from the burned wood is adding to Earth's greenhouse gases (pollution), affecting climate change.

In addition, as the human demand for furniture (consumption) places pressure on the natural world's production of wood, fewer remaining forests produce less wood, which results in less production of furniture (e.g., the TNS funnel), as well as less habitat to support natural biodiversity. With this decrease in natural resources not every person will have the ability to buy furniture because of its increased cost from greater consumer demand. This leads to disproportionate impacts or inequality in society, as well as to a loss of natural habitat (forests), which affects all other living things and our atmosphere, because of the filtering effects of forests on air quality. Isn't it just amazing what a piece of timber represents?

## HOW DO WE BECOME SUSTAINABLE?

The word *sustainability* implies the ability to support life, to comfort, to nourish, and to keep alive (Webster's *New Collegiate Dictionary*). For all of human history, the

Earth has sustained human beings by providing food, water, air, and shelter. Likewise, the beauty of the Earth sustains our hearts and inspires our lives.

Sustainable also means continuing without lessening. *Development* means improving or bringing to a more advanced state, such as in our economy (Webster's *New Collegiate Dictionary*). *Sustainable development* can thus mean working to improve humans' productive power without damaging or undermining society or the environment.

Likewise, a *community* is a group of people who live and interact in a certain area supported by a common economy (Webster's *New Collegiate Dictionary*). A *sustainable community* is one that seeks to maintain and improve the economic, environmental, and social characteristics of an area so its members can continue to lead healthy, productive, and enjoyable lives.

Definitions of sustainability have varied and often remained vague, but it is possible to think about and discuss sustainable development in the context of things we all know about, such as our homes, our children, our jobs, nature, the air we breathe, and the food we eat. These topics are what sustainability is really about, and although variations in definition may occur, many share a number of basic principles, including: (1) a concern for the well-being of future generations, (2) an awareness of the multidimensional impacts of any decision (broadly categorized as economic, environmental, and social), and (3) the need for balance among the different dimensions across sectors, themes, and scales of place and time.

Traditional approaches to societal problems often take a piecemeal, singular approach, addressing issues of economics, environment, or social health, sometimes in isolation from one another (Flint and Danner, 2001), as demonstrated by the three separate circles in Figure 3. In addition, individual interests typically override a collective will to preserve the uniqueness of place. For example, as cities sprawl past nature's carrying capacity, those at ground level promote their individual interests, and thus political expediency is forced to ignore the deeper cost. This leads to communities being unsustainable!

In contrast, sustainability promotes a multidimensional way to achieve recovery and improve the quality of life for everyone, but how? Sustainable development simultaneously considers environment, life, and human well-being (Figure 4). It suggests reliable, responsible economic activity that considers tradition, a sense of history, a cyclical view of time, the significance of place, the benefit of personal

**Figure 3** Demonstration of how traditional problem solving is usually conducted by considering separately issues of economy, society, and the environment.

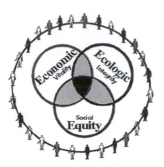

**Figure 4**  Conceptual presentation of the sustainability model in which the three overlapping circles indicate the integration of economic, ecologic, and social issues (black area of circles). The ring of people around the circles implies full public involvement.

relationships, and the importance of natural ecosystems (Flint and Houser, 2001), and when continued over the long term will: (1) not diminish the quality of the present environment, (2) not critically reduce the availability of renewable resources, (3) take into consideration the value of nonrenewable resources to future generations, and (4) not compromise the ability of other species or future generations to meet their needs.

Moreover, sustainable development not only implies wisdom and stewardship in environmental management to meet future needs, but also includes the equitable fulfillment of basic human needs now, such as food, shelter, clothing, and the economic means to achieve these. This view translates into an acceptable quality of life for everyone.

To better envision ideas of sustainability, consider the three overlapping circles diagram (Flint and Danner, 2001) illustrating the interconnectedness of a community's economic, social, and ecological dimensions (Figure 4). Members of a sustainable community would realize that long-term economic viability depends upon having a sound ecosystem, a healthy social environment, and a political system that facilitates full public involvement in governance (suggested by the ring of people around the three circles). Each of the circles characterizes the following basic elements of sustainability: (1) *economic viability* (compatible with nature)—development that protects and/or enhances natural resource quantities through improvements in management practices and policies, technology, efficiency, and changes in lifestyle, (2) *ecologic integrity* (natural ecosystem capacity)—understanding natural system processes of landscapes and watersheds to guide the design of sound economic development strategies that preserve these natural systems; and, (3) *social equity* (balancing the playing field)— guaranteeing equal access to jobs (income), education, natural resources, and services for all people (total societal welfare).

All three elements are equally important in establishing the foundation of sustainable communities, therefore any project, program, or regulatory issue seeking to promote sustainability must simultaneously address each of these three circles at their overlap, the area represented by the black intersection region of the three circles (Figure 4).

In understanding the three overlapping circles, it is also critical to recognize there is a "directionality" to each circle's dependence on the others. It is true that all life depends on natural resources (Wackernagel and Rees, 1996), but economy and society are no less important to humanity than ecology; rather, there is a "directionality" of dependence (Figure 5).

In examining these three ellipses inside one another, you can ask if there is any species of animal besides humans that possesses an economy. Probably not as we perceive economy, and through the ages our economy has changed significantly (e.g., from hunters and gathers, to a subsistence economy, to the industrial revolution), without changing the basic relationships defined by the idea of society. The existence of economies is based solely on the existence of societies, and the society ellipse will exist no matter what the economy ellipse represents. (Economy is inside the society ellipse.)

Furthermore, we can all agree that society cannot exist without an acceptable environment, therefore the society ellipse is inside the environment ellipse. In sum, this is the directionality for issues of ecology, society, and economy—or in terms of a three-stage rocket ship—propelling or building and enhancing natural capital (ecology) first, which powers human capital (society) second, and finally propels financial capital (economy) through the engines of society.

A sustainable community thus would not be one that has merely attained a "balance" between its economics and its environment as if they were two distinct entities (Flint and Danner, 2001); rather, it would be one that has a directionality by which economic and cultural activities are integrated into natural processes in a cyclic fashion so as not to degrade the environment upon which economic prosperity and social stability rest (the directionality of the ellipses in Figure 5).

**There is no economy outside of society**

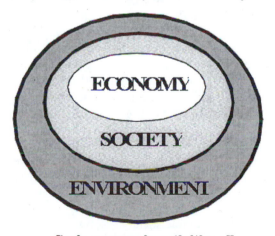

**Socio-economic activities all happen within the environment**

**Figure 5** Illustration of the directionality of sustainability, indicating how socioeconomic issues are directly related to the health of the environment.

## WHAT ARE THE PRINCIPLES OF SUSTAINABILITY?

Because plans reflect substantive policy outcomes that are based upon our technical understanding of issues, to incorporate ideas of sustainable development into planning, scientific principles of sustainability need to be defined. A framework will then exist for incorporating the concept into decision making at all levels of the public and private sectors.

To begin defining principles of sustainability, we can consider TNS, which recommends that humans maintain the integrity of the ecological systems that support life (Gips, 1998). The natural step provides a model for sustainable development that integrates the dictates of the natural world (four principles described earlier) with the major societal issues of economy, ecology, and equity into four system conditions. Using these four system conditions can provide a "compass" to guide organizations, communities, and individuals toward sustainable practices (Robert, 1991). The four conditions are the following:

1. *How can we reduce our dependence on mining and fossil fuels?* In a sustainable society nature's functions and diversity are not systematically subject to increasing concentrations of substances extracted from the Earth's crust. There are thresholds beyond which living organisms and ecosystems are adversely affected by these increases. Human activities such as the burning of fossil fuels and the mining of metals and minerals need not occur at a rate that causes them to systematically increase in the ecosphere.

2. *How can we reduce our dependence on persistent, unnatural substances?* In a sustainable society nature's functions and diversity are not systematically subject to increasing concentrations of substances produced by society. Synthetic organic compounds such as DDT, PCBs, and freon can remain in the environment for many years, concentrating in the Earth's atmosphere or accumulating in the tissue of organisms, causing profound deleterious effects on predators in the upper levels of the food chain (Flint and Vena, 1991; Flint, 1992). Society needs to find ways to reduce economic dependence on persistent human-made substances.

3. *How can we reduce our dependence on nature-consuming activities?* In a sustainable society nature's functions and diversity are not systematically impoverished by physical displacement, overharvesting, or other forms of ecosystem manipulation. Biodiversity, which includes the great variety of animals and plants found in nature, provides the foundation for the ecosystem services necessary to sustain all life on this planet (Robert et al., 1997). Humans should avoid taking more from the biosphere than can be replenished by natural systems or systematically encroaching upon nature by destroying the habitat of other species. Society's health and prosperity depends on the enduring capacity of nature to renew itself and rebuild waste into resources.

4. *How can we do more with less?* In a sustainable society resources are used fairly and efficiently in order to meet basic human needs globally. Humans need to be efficient and fair with regard to resource use and waste generation in order to be sustainable. Achieving greater fairness is essential for social stability and the cooperation needed for making large-scale changes within the framework laid out by the first three conditions (Gips, 1998). Economists believe in "growing the pie" so that poor people will get a "bigger slice."

> Even if Earth's capacity allows for growing the pie, providing a bigger slice from a larger pie to the poor is not decreasing the gap between rich and poor (fairness); it is actually increasing this gap.

The fourth TNS system condition brings attention to a long-held view. Because economic growth has become associated with progress, an economy that does not grow is considered a "bad" or unhealthy economy. But economist Herman Daly says (Daly, 1996a) that "sustainable development is development without growth—as growth means getting bigger while development means getting better." In theory this should not be too difficult to envision. Each of us does much the same thing in the course of our individual lives. We grow early in life and when we reach adult maturity we develop mentally, socially, and culturally instead of continuing to grow structurally. Physical growth during maturity usually means obesity or cancer. In summary, *sustainable development is progressive social betterment without growing beyond the ecological carrying capacity: achieving human well-being without exceeding the Earth's twin capacities for natural resource regeneration* (e.g., trees and water) *and waste absorption* (e.g., carbon dioxide and toxic chemicals).

## COMMUNITIES AND SUSTAINABILITY

The primary barriers to communities achieving sustainability include: (1) economic deprivation, (2) concentration of money and an imbalance of power (in a few hands), (3) an economy driven by profits at any cost, greed, and consumption, (4) communities competing with one another for jobs, (5) different languages with no translation and inaccurate perceptions of others, (6) lack of accountability in government, corporations, and individual behavior, (7) placing of blame "out there" rather than accepting responsibility, (8) barriers between work, home, and play—physical separation, sprawl, and isolation, (9) imbalance of power, (10) lack of trust in the "other," and (11) conflicting goals, strategies, and analyses.

Sustainable development in communities is not about walking a tightrope, seeking some mythical balance between economics and environment (Flint and Houser, 2001). This leads to habitats half protected, economies weakened, and personal principles bargained away. Instead communities must search for ways to create coaction and assume coresponsibility while doing no harm to the life-giving environmental elements that sustain the future of human. Economic activity can promote a healthy environment, and healthy ecosystems can enrich their inhabitants (Daly, 1996b).

How can a region achieve community synergy, simultaneously responding to economic pressures while also protecting the environment? A sustainable community emulates nature. Such a community is defined not by legal boundaries but in patterns of relationships, connection to place, and amount of citizen involvement. Moreover, a sustainable community is conscious of its obligations to future generations and develops leadership that can deal with change while paying attention to the imperatives of collective well-being that transcend the narrow economic interests of individuals. In addition effective processes exist for finding common ground. In a nutshell, a sustainable community is one that transmits shared values and honors them in good faith.

Sustainability requires communities to pursue an evolving and ever-changing program of activities, including a continuous process of evaluating current and emerging trends, an ongoing means of encouraging citizen participation and negoti-ating conflicts, and an updating of plans. These activities should be oriented toward searching for ways to continuously move communities in the direction of becoming more sustainable. The process of developing community sustainability will expose citizens to the effects of their actions on others and on their local environment while motivating and mobilizing them to pursue a responsible and shared vision for a col-lective future. Some of the key indicators of a sustainable community include ideas of sufficiency and sharing as core values, communities with strong leadership, solutions to economic problems that should also improve or enhance the environment, linking or connecting economic, environmental, and health concerns, the political will for change, acknowledgment that human health is integrally linked to environmental health, ability to seek common ground solutions, show of a spirit of cooperation and patterns of relationships, communities that emulate nature, inclusiveness (true col-laboration) and taking responsibility, cooperative efforts toward economic security, value of future generations, communities wanting to revisit "traditional" values, framework of cooperation not competition, and commitment to comprehensive planning and regionalism.

Sustainable communities thus might be identified by the following character-istics (Flint et al., 2001):

## Economic Security

*How well does the idea, project, or program take the total economic well-being of the community into account?* A sustainable community possesses a healthy and diverse economy (variety of businesses, industries, and institutions that are environmentally sound) that adapts to change, provides long-term material security to residents, and respects ecological limits by maximizing income generation while also maintaining or increasing the assortment of natural assets that yield benefits (Jacobs, 2000). Sustainable communities strive to price goods and services to reflect the full social and environmental costs of their provision and link area businesses, products and services, and resources and customers to increase the recycling of money and other resources that will remain in the community.

## Ecological Integrity

*How well does the idea, project, or program take ecological opportunities and limitations into account?* Sustainable communities are inhabited by people with a sense of stewardship who maintain and enhance the environment and natural ecosystems, for their own essential functions, their beauty, their livability as a landscape, and their ability to provide sustainable supplies of natural resources and waste assimilation capacity for all human use without undermining their function and longevity in the future. Communities use land prudently, preserving quality wild and productive lands and designing compact urban development that features pedestrian- and transit-oriented mixed-use development with extensive access to green space.

## Social Equity

*Does the idea, project, or program promote greater equity within the community and with people outside the community as well as between present and future generations?*

Social equity implies that diverse social and cultural systems are preserved and that tensions are able to be resolved by distributing costs and benefits equitably (Bryant and Mohai, 1992). A more sustainable community recognizes and supports individuals' evolving sense of well-being. Sustainable communities consider intragenerational equity (e.g., elimination of poverty, viable levels of welfare, protection of public health, provision of education) and intergenerational equity (e.g., leaving the world in a better condition than we found it, protecting future generations' rights to the opportunities of present generations).

## Citizen Engagement and Responsibility

*How well does an idea, project, or program contribute to a sense of community among neighbors and to key features that make a community strong—its residents, businesses, government, and institutions?* Engagement is a participatory approach to managing a region that blends concepts of good governance, consensus building, the assuming of civic responsibilities, and strategic planning. A more sustainable community enables people to feel empowered and to take responsibility based on a shared vision, equal opportunity, ability to access expertise and knowledge for their own needs, and a capacity to positively affect the outcome of decisions that influence them.

## Cultural Vitality

*How well does the idea, project, or program respect and use local people and their knowledge as well as local energy and materials?* A sustainable community is one that preserves cultural attributes developed over its history while also being open to alternative traditions that reflect changing conditions. There is much to be learned from society keeping a constant eye on the history of past civilizations, the cultural attributes that have developed in different societies through time, and the way their ancestors went about living, playing, working, and growing. The institutions and means communities implement to retain their cultural heritage benefit from the varied skills and perspectives of local peoples, and are a significant part of indicating a community's sustainability.

## Institutional Effectiveness

*How well does an idea, project, or program encourage the participation of all affected people in decision making and support the civic values of trust and cooperation?* Businesses, neighborhood and community groups, the media, and citizens, as well as governments and nongovernmental organizations (NGOs), influence governance through effective participation. Proponents of strong communities seek to make citizens' voices heard in governance and to achieve greater transparency in government decision making and programs. In sustainable communities institutions function effectively to satisfy the physical needs of their citizens while preserving the environment by providing citizens with the information and opportunities necessary to participate meaningfully.

## Making Connections and Trade-offs

*How well does the idea, project, or program consider the connections among issues, make balanced trade-offs where necessary, and seek to understand impacts?* Synergies and interconnections should be considered in a way that emphasizes the inadvisability of addressing bits of the picture in isolation and not accounting for links among social, economic, and environmental issues. Sustainable communities elicit support from businesses, local government, and citizen organizations and work with other communities in a larger context in a spirit of connectivity. In lieu of reaching full consensus, the community makes reasoned and balanced trade-offs informed by the community's core values.

## Resilience

*How well does the idea, project, or program provide systemic ways of responding to changes that can safeguard the community from failure?* Resilience can be characterized as the amount of disturbance in economies, relationships, and ecosystems that can be sustained by a community before a change may occur in its structure (Axelrod and Cohen, 1999). Resilience in communities is dictated by the state of *diversity* and *redundancy* represented in different community characteristics in the context of a "complex system." In this way, communities that are sustainable identify criteria having certain thresholds that should not be exceeded. A sustainable community also considers impacts on the community 175 years from now (the seven-generation test).

## Adaptive Management

*How well does the idea, project, or program identify adaptive behaviors that can be enacted by learning from doing?* Adaptive management is built upon the premise that people learn from their actions as well as their mistakes. An adaptive, learning-based approach to the practice of sustainability implies looking for ways to maintain flexibility by identifying feedback loops, making sure they give timely and relevant information and then paying attention to them, and being prepared to abandon unsuccessful strategies (Ruitenbeck and Cartier, 2001).

## HOW DO WE TURN THEORY INTO ACTION?

What we have discovered so far basically states that current and future generations must strive to achieve a decent standard of living for all people and live within the limits of natural systems. Despite this apparent simplicity, there is no general agreement on how sustainable development should be translated into practice. Better ideas and policy can be produced through a process of triangulation (EcoSteps, 2002) in which a problem is analyzed from a number of different perspectives, a multidimensional process that includes economic, social, political, psychological, ecological, and technical considerations. These dimensions are interdependent and cannot be fully understood in isolation. A task of the coming years is to work out the details and to narrow the gap between theory and practice.

The new worldview that can guide sustainability theory into practice includes the following components: a tripartite model integrating economic, social, and environmental goals and requirements; an ecological footprint measurement, to better evaluate how we are approaching or overshooting the very tangible threshold of Earth's carrying capacity; life cycle thinking and management; "total cost" analysis and decision making—making visible the impacts and costs often treated as externalities in our current systems; and a value creation continuum whereby rather than a "trade-off mentality," greater return and value result from a more proactive and comprehensive integration of economy, environment, and social needs.

Consider the following example, using a tripartite approach as an illustration of the new worldview described in the previous paragraph. According to the Chef's Collaborative Network, more restaurants are banking on sustainable cuisine (Kreitz, 2002): (1) procurement of more environmentally friendly ingredients helps many restaurants attract customers, adding to their economic bottom line, (2) "greening" restaurant buildings and purchasing products that are organically produced, or in the case of fish, caught by hook and line, supports low-impact environmental activities, and (3) the social benefits are tremendous, from healthier eating to support of local communities by the act of purchasing locally, providing more local job opportunities.

A significant modification to the use of environmental management systems (EMS) incorporates the next several components of this new worldview for sustainability. An environmental management system is "that part of the organization's overall management system which includes corporation structure, planning activities, responsibilities, practices, procedures, processes, and resources for developing, implementing, achieving, reviewing, and maintaining an organization's environmental policy" (Burns, 2001). The benefits of an EMS include minimizing environmental risk liabilities, maximizing the efficient use of resources, reducing waste, demonstrating a good corporate image, building awareness of environmental concern among employees, gaining a better understanding of the environmental impacts of business activities, and increasing profit while improving environmental performance through more efficient operations.

In response to the complexity of environmental management and a growing demand for a systematic and comprehensive EMS procedure, the International Standards Organization (ISO) developed criteria in the early 1990s for environmental management systems (Burns, 2001). The ISO 9000/14000 series, of which ISO 14001 is the most recent (late 1996), is a set of completely voluntary standards and guideline reference documents that include environmental management systems, eco-labeling, environmental auditing, life cycle assessment, environmental performance evaluation, and environmental aspects in product standards.

ISO 14001 is thus designed to provide customers with a reasonable assurance that the performance claims of a company are accurate. ISO 14001 increases environmental compliance, reduces costs and liabilities, reduces impact on the environment, offers a competitive advantage, and demonstrates that customers prefer certified suppliers.

Environmental management systems are gaining popularity around the world. They provide the structure for the integration of environmental issues into management and day-to-day operations, but they don't provide the vision that guides organizations and corporations on the path to sustainability nor do they provide an understanding of what constitutes a sustainable direction. The TNS framework and consideration of the three overlapping circles model (Figure 4), however, offer the compass to better direct the activities of the traditional EMS. Through a combination of ideas and tools, a new methodology is proposed, an environmentally sustainable management system (ESMS), designed after the ideas of the EMS. The ESMS then becomes a process for managing the impacts of an organization's activities on the environment by integrating elements of sustainability through the use of a variety of new tools. Once the vision and direction are set, an ESMS becomes a valuable methodology for guiding decisions, operationalizing the vision, and documenting the progress. It provides a structured approach to planning and implementing environmental protection measures that will enhance sustainability.

One of the guiding elements of the ESMS is the ecological footprint analysis (EcoSteps, 2002). The ecological footprint is the area of land and water required to support a defined economy or population at a specified standard of living. Also known as "appropriated carrying capacity" (Rees and Wackernagel, 1994), this concept incorporates the distributional aspects of sustainable production and consumption. Ecological footprinting is an integrated, comprehensive measuring tool to get a tangible overview of our performance with regard to sustainability, and is unique in its capacity to communicate very directly how lifestyle and technical competence relate to such a perspective.

Life cycle analysis (LCA) is also an important "proactive" environmental management technique that can further enhance an ESMS strategy. An LCA is an investigation that aims to quantify the level of energy and raw materials used, as well as the solid, liquid, and gaseous wastes produced at every stage of a product's life or process, identifying environmental impacts before they happen. End-of-pipe or re-active techniques generally have been unable to offer the potential environmental benefits that can be achieved with preventable techniques, such as LCA. Life cycle analysis provides a useful framework and philosophy for addressing the environmental impacts of a particular product. An LCA can also lead to the concept of "full cost accounting" (the fourth element of the new worldview described previously on page 80). The idea of full or total cost accounting is a way of accurately reflecting both the benefits and costs of natural resource use, as well as product manufacturing benefits and costs.

An ESMS is not prescriptive; that is, it does not specify how environmental targets should be met. It requires organizations to take a proactive role in examining their practices, making both the impacts and costs visible (economic, social and health-related, and environmental), and then determining themselves how their impacts should best be managed (Burns, 2001). This approach encourages creative and re-levant solutions from the organization itself, offering innovative opportunities for the proactive and comprehensive integration of economy, environment, and social needs (fifth element of the new worldview) improving both a company's profitability and its environmental performance.

This brings us back to the restaurant example cited above. *Practicing sustainability makes good business sense!* Another good business example of this new world view includes the Fairmont Hotels and Resorts Green Partnership Program, considered by many the most comprehensive environmental program in the North American hotel industry. Through this program contributions to the waste stream are being reduced and energy and water are conserved, along with habitat protection and donations to research, lessening the plight of endangered species. Also, visitors are being educated about the fragile beauty of the unique ecosystems in which Fairmont hotels operate. This hotel chain is making a difference economically, environmentally, and socially through subtle and not so subtle decision-making and operational changes (Nattrass and Altomare, 2002).

## ANATOMY OF SUSTAINABLE DECISION MAKING

Traditionally socioeconomic systems have been caught up in the adversarial "economy versus environment" debate, operating in a linear direction—taking resources from the Earth, making them into products, and throwing them away to produce large amounts of waste (take–make–waste). As we have learned from the principles of TNS, this can result in communities being unsustainable.

Individuals, companies, product producers, and community builders are now beginning to redefine the economic equation in our society. Similar to the way in which nothing is wasted by nature, "waste equals loss of energy" is the formula that is beginning to close the loops in our thinking (biomimickry), and in doing so is redefining the way we live (McDonough and Braungart, 1998). We are, however, early on in the learning curve of mimicking the patterns of nature in our human settlements. For example, ours is the first generation to gain awareness that every community within the larger global community has an ecological footprint. Understanding the nature and limits of that footprint is to live in a sustainable manner.

Within the context of biomimickry, the idea of industrial ecology is now being seriously considered by many businesses as a holistic and integrative approach to the traditional take–make–waste practices (McDonough and Braungart, 1998). This idea uses the metaphor of metabolism to analyze production and consumption by industry, government, organizations, and consumers, and the interactions between them. It involves tracking energy and material flows through industrial systems (e.g., a plant, region, or national or global economy), so that instead of the cradle-to-grave views, companies are now considering cradle-to-cradle perspectives, whereby waste from one process is food for another (McDonough and Braungart, 2002).

With these new approaches, sustainability becomes a yardstick for evaluating when collective human actions are endangering our relationship with nature—or simply put, a measure of the impact of our social and economic present on the environmental future. Applying this yardstick to our activities challenges us to examine the important multidimensional links between human development and ecological systems. A multidimensional approach to sustainability is characterized by processes that develop local assets to revitalize economies and conserve natural resources and that concurrently limit waste and pollution, improve the status of disadvantaged peoples, make valuable connections among people, and promote cooperation and efficiency.

It is imperative to find ways of integrating these multiple dimensions in order to produce a sustainable framework for decision making. For example, if an organization chooses to use the ISO 14001 guidelines in conjunction with a standard environmental management system, that organization will focus upon how to best comply with existing environmental regulations. What happens, however when regulations change—for example, becoming more limiting and restrictive with regard to environmental impacts than the company planned on in its original EMS development to meet current ISO 14001 guidelines? In other words, industry keeps reacting to constantly changing environmental regulations rather than getting ahead of the game and moving toward sustainability.

A good example is the case of ozone-depleting chemicals (Burns, 2001). When chlorofluorocarbons (CFCs) were initially restricted by law, companies re-engineered their products and factories to accommodate hydrochloroflurocarbons (HCFCs) instead, but these are problematic as well. Although they are less ozone-depleting than CFCs, they are persistent compounds, are greenhouse gases, and are toxic. Hydrochloroflurocarbons will eventually be phased out, necessitating companies to change course again. There is no doubt that benign substitutes can sometime be difficult to find; nevertheless there are many opportunities for companies to avoid these costly course corrections by thinking systematically about long-term sustainability.

Using such tools as TNS and the lessons from the three overlapping circles sustainability model (Figure 4) provides additional guidance and directions so that the company's EMS now becomes an ESMS and can move beyond goals compliance and incremental improvement to support goals such as market leadership and improved competitiveness (Burns, 2001). Sustainable-based decision making in an ESMS context considers the complexity of systems within the framework of adaptive management. An adaptive, learning-based approach to decision making implies developing, testing, and refining a common framework for learning from experience wherever promising approaches to problem solving are undertaken.

Adaptive management also suggests the constant attention to and evaluation (monitoring) of activities to ensure one's continuous awareness and understanding of changes in circumstances in order to feedback information to decision-making endeavors. Principles of adaptive management that can steer sustainable decision making include the following: decision-making processes should effectively integrate both long-term and short-term economic, environmental, social, and equity considerations; conservation of biological diversity and ecological integrity should be a fundamental consideration in decision making; it is necessary to anticipate and prevent decisions that avoid problematic situations in the future while remaining consistent with intergenerational equity; live off the interest to guarantee that the level of a resource will not fall below the threshold required to perpetuate this resource through all time; we must take into consideration the concept of an ecosystem approach; prevent environmental degradation if there are threats of serious or irreversible damage; unavoidable or inevitable projects should guarantee environmental and social benefits at a minimum; valuation, pricing, and incentive mechanisms in decision making should be improved to make the environment a forethought and not an afterthought; and equitable distribution of resources should be encouraged to create a sense of fairness, identifying and satisfying real needs before wants and leaving options open for future generations.

Pursuing the guidance of the overlapping circles model (Figure 4) and the TNS system conditions through an adaptive management approach to decision making causes us to transform the rhetoric of sustainable development into actions. For example, applying the philosophy suggested by the overlap of the three circles as a template we can test one's operations and guarantee each act, project, or program implemented will concurrently address issues of environment, economics, and social well-being. In this way one can ask of any project, program, or act (Flint and Houser, 2001) the following questions. Does this activity provide an economic benefit? What is it? Does this activity provide an environmental benefit? What is it? Does this activity offer equal benefits to all sectors of society? What are some? Was this activity agreed to through the participation of all people (stakeholders) impacted by the activity? If the answer to any one of these questions is *no*, then the project, program, or act should be rethought to better address the core principles of sustainability.

An extension of the three overlapping circle model can be found in the application of the triple bottom line (TBL) concept, which demonstrates a way of pursuing activities in the context of sustainability. The TBL is a term used to refer to the three pillars of social, environmental, and economic accountability (Elkington, 1997). The notion of reporting against these three components (or bottom lines) of performance is directly tied to the concepts and goals of sustainable development. If properly implemented, TBL reporting will provide information to enable others to assess how sustainable an organization's or community's operations are. For an organization (or a community) to be sustainable (a long-run perspective) it must be financially secure (as evidenced through such measures as profitability), it must minimize (or ideally eliminate) its negative environmental impacts, and it must act in conformity with societal expectations. These three factors are obviously highly interrelated.

Integrated TBL accounting and reporting implies that the three measures of value added are incorporated into a single, all-encompassing measurement (Elkington, 2001), so, for example, economic value-added measures would be adjusted for the environmental and social dimensions. Such approaches imply moving toward a single set of accounts. The near-term challenge is to identify a limited set of key performance indicators for each bottom line, with a constant eye on the degree to which—and how—progress can be measured and integrated into this overall set of accounts.

In summary, it is most important to recognize the fact that sustainability is not strictly a problem of science, engineering, or economics, but is also founded on values, ethics, and the equal contributions of different cultures. Additionally, all members of the community have a shared future; they are dependent on each other in ways that are both complex and profound. Ideals of preservation and protection on the one hand, and of economic vitality and opportunity on the other, are thus not in conflict, but in a sustainable future they are linked together. We recognize our ability to see the needs of the future is limited. Any attempt to define sustainability should therefore remain as open and flexible as possible, through the guidance of adaptive management. The workings of TNS instruct us on how to think about taking sustainable action by describing the A–B–C–D strategy, which stands for *a*wareness that society is presently trying to push beyond natural limits, *b*aseline establishment to test whether or not we are meeting the basic system conditions, *c*reate a clear, compelling vision of where we want to go, and get *d*own to action in taking steps to achieve our defined goals for sustainability (Whistler Center for Sustainability, 2001).

# REFERENCES

Auman, H. J., Ludwig, J. P., Summer, C. L., Verbrugge, D. A., Froese, K. L., Golborn, T., Giesy, J. P. (1997). PCBs, DDE, DDT, and TCDD-EQ in two species of albatross on Sand Island, Midway Atoll, North Pacific Ocean. Environ. Tox. Chem. 16(3):498–504.

Axelrod, R. M., Cohen, M. D. (1999). Harnessing Complexity: Organizational Implications of a Scientific Frontier. New York: Free Press.

Bartlett, A. A. (1999). Reflections on sustainability, population growth, and the Environment: Revisited. Focus 9(1):49–68.

Brown, L. (1999). State of the World: A Worldwatch Institute Report on Progress Toward a Sustainable Society. New York: Norton.

Bryant, B., Mohai, P. (1992). Environmental injustice: Weighing race and class as factors in the distribution of environmental hazards. Univ. Colo. Law Rev. 63:921–932.

Burns, S. (2001). A compass for environmental management systems, pp. 169–185. In: Nattrass, B.Altomare, M., eds. The Natural Step for Business. Gabriola Island, BC; Canada: New Society, pp. 222.

Daly, H. E. (1992). Allocation, distribution, and scale: Toward an economics that is efficient, just, and sustainable. Ecol. Econ. 6:185–194.

Daly, H. E. (1996a). Beyond Growth. Boston: Beacon.

Daly, H. E. (1996b). Beyond Growth. Boston: Beacon, pp. 90.

EcoSteps, 2002: Developing SD Capability: The Sustainability Tree. online at URL http://www.ecosteps.com.au/home.htm.

Elkington, J. (1997). Cannibals with Forks: The Triple Bottom Line of 21st Century Business (Conscientious Commerce). Gabriola, BC, Canada: New Society, pp. 416.

Elkington, J. (2001). The Chrysalis Economy: How Citizens, CEOs and Their Corporations Can Fuse Values and Value Creation. New York: Wiley, pp. 288.

Flint, R. W. (1992). Risks from environmental chemical exposure as exemplified in the Great Lakes Basin ecosystem of North America. Pharmacopsychoecologia 5:15–28.

Flint, R. W., Vena, J., 1991. Human Health Risks from Chemical Exposure: The Great Lakes Ecosystem. Boca Raton, FL: Lewis Publishers and CRC Press, pp. 268.

Flint, R. W., Rich, R. C., Lamphier, K. (2001). Sustainable communities: Their definition and science needs. Proceedings of the 25th Annual World-System Conference, Virginia Tech, Blacksburg, VA, http://filebox.vt.edu/users/wdunaway/flint2.htm.

Flint, R. W., Danner, M. J. E. (2001). The nexus of sustainability and social equity. Internat. J. Econ. Dev. 3(2); URL: http://spaef.com/IJEC_PUB/v3n2.html.

Flint, R. W., Houser, W. L. (2001). Living a Sustainable Lifestyle for Our Children's Children. Campbell, CA: IUniverse, pp. 288.

Gips, T. (1998). The natural step four conditions for sustainability or system conditions. Minneapolis: Alliance for Sustainability and Sustainability Associates.

Giuliano, J. A. (2000). Its Worse Than You Think. Healing Our World: weekly comment. Environment News Service (ENS), online at URL: http://ens.lycos.com/ens/feb2000/2000L-02-14g.html.

Hartmann, T. (1997). Last Hours of Ancient Sunlight. Northfield, VT: Mythical Books, pp. 77–79.

Jacobs, J. (2000). The Nature of Economies. New York: Modern Library, pp. 190.

Kreitz, K. (2002, March 6). Restaurateurs relish sustainability. Environmental News Network (ENN), online at URL: http://enn.com/news/enn-stories/2002/03/03062002/s_46464.asp.

Lazaroff, C. (2000). Growing Population Faces Diminishing Resources. Environment News Service (ENS), online at URL: http://ens.lycos.com/ens/jan2000/2000L-01-18-06.html.

McDonough, W., Braungart, M. (1998, Oct.). The Next Industrial Revolution. Atl Monthly pp. 82.

McDonough, W., Braungart, M. (2002). Cradle to Cradle: Remaking the Way We Make Things. New York: North Point, pp. 208.

Nattrass, B., Altomare, M. (2002). Dancing with the Tiger. Gabriola Island, BC; Canada: New Society, pp. 172–173.

Rees, W. E., Wackernagel, M. (1994). Ecological footprints and appropriated carrying capacity: Measuring the natural capital requirement of the human economy. In: Jansson, A. M., Hammer, M., Folke, C., Costanza, R., eds. Investing in Natural Capital: The Ecological Economics Approach to Sustainability. Washington, DC: Island Press.

Robert, K. H., 1991. Educating a Nation: The Natural Step. In Context #28 In Context Institute spring 1991: 10; online at URL: http://www.context.org/ICLIB/IC28/Robert.htm.

Robert, K. H., Daly, H., Hawken, P., Holmberg, J. (1997). A compass for sustainable development. Internat J Sust Dev World Ecol 4, 79–92.

Robbins, J. (1987). Diet for a New America. Tiburon, CA: Kramer, pp. 357.

Rojstaczer, S., Sterling, S. M., Moore, N. J. (2001). Human appropriation of photosynthesis products. Science. 294:2549–2552.

Ruitenbeck, J., Cartier, C. (2001). The Invisible Wand: Adaptive Co-management as an Emergent Strategy in Complex bio-economic Systems. occasional paper no. 34. Jakarta: Center for International Forestry Research (CIFOR).

Wackernagel, M., Rees, W. (1996). Our Ecological Footprint. Gabriola Island, BC; Canada: New Society, pp. 115.

Whistler Center for Sustainability. (2001). Whistler, It's Our Nature Household Toolkit. Whistler, BC, Canada.

# 5

# The Myths of Economic Growth (GNP)
## Implications for Human Development

**M. SHAMSUL HAQUE**

*National University of Singapore, Singapore*

## INTRODUCTION

In the development field, most mainstream development theories, irrespective of their differences in philosophical and ideological underpinnings, tend to focus largely on the economic sphere while overlooking the noneconomic domains (politics, culture, religion) or considering them to be secondary. This inclination toward economic reductionism could be observed in major conservative theoretical traditions, such as noninterventionist classical and neoclassical economic theories and interventionist Keynesian and post-Keynesian perspectives, which focus mostly on economic realities in advanced capitalist nations. Similar emphasis on the narrow economic dimension could be found in the reformist theories and approaches that emerged between the 1950s and 1970s, including unbalanced growth theory, vicious-circle theory, stages of growth theory, agriculture-first approach, and basic-needs approach, which attempt to address economic backwardness in developing countries (Haque, 1999). During this period, although certain modernization theories stressed political, cultural, and psychological factors (Appelbaum, 1973; Kim, 1984), in the ultimate analysis such factors were treated as causal variables related eventually to the realization of economic growth in these countries. What central concern inspires all these theories thus was often the issue of economic growth—the sources, causes, processes, obstacles, possibilities, and ends of such growth. Although the radical theoretical tradition of development theories covering various dependency and neo-Marxist analyses tried to explain issues such as dependency and underdevelopment, dependent development, class and the state, and articulation of the modes of production (Randall and Theobald, 1985; Simon and Ruccio, 1986), their primary emphasis remained on the economic sphere.

Even if one gives more credit to some of the above theories for their scope to address certain noneconomic factors, the fact remains that in real-life, development practices and experiences—including most development policies, programs, projects, and agencies—have been shaped by mainstream economic growth theories and guided by a narrow concern for growth indicated predominantly by such measure as gross national product (GNP). Under the challenges posed by the Great Depression and the Second World War, the practical historical circumstances reinforced this particular economic measure (Cobb et al., 1995). In the developing world, since the worldwide decolonization and emergence of newly independent nations, the measure of GNP has remained the most dominant concern in adopting national development plans, rationalizing development programs, evaluating the success of development projects, and providing development assistance by international agencies. As Robinson (1979) observes, GNP per capita has been treated as the primary measure of development objectives, economic success, and citizens' national welfare. According to Streeten (1979:21–22), due to the "result of the propaganda of politicians and economists, aided by the transistor radio, television, and jet planes, economic growth came to be regarded as a human right."

In addition, it is largely the measure of GNP per capita that has been used to determine a country's economic status and rank in the overall global hierarchy of levels of national development (Hoogvelt, 1982:15). Although historically, the biased ranking or profiling of various societies into categories—such as civilized vs. barbarian, traditional vs. modern, and backward vs. advanced—were guided by cultural and religious prejudices, in the current age it is the GNP measure that has dominated this ranking of nations into such categories as "least developed," "developing," and "developed." No matter how parochial, superficial, and misleading the GNP measure may be, it has been effectively used by development experts and agencies in stereotyping postcolonial societies, certifying their ranks in global economic order, imposing on them the inappropriate development policies and strategies, and encouraging them to follow the economic leadership of international institutions dominated by capitalist states. This reductionist framework often precludes the use of various noneconomic measures to determine the levels of development. In this regard, Merriam (1988:16) states the following about the importance of noneconomic factors:

> In some ways the "poor" cultures of the Third World are rich psychologically and spiritually, enjoying a contentment and sense of tradition sorely lacking in hectic, ulcer-ridden, depersonalised industrial societies. To many Buddhists, for example, inner peace is more valuable than a high Gross National Product. The highest divorce and suicide rates occur in the First and Second Worlds. If personal happiness were our criterion, the Third World might rank first.

The fact remains, however, that the measure of GNP not only continues to dominate development studies and policies; it has gained new significance in recent decades because of the global rise or revival of market-biased neoliberal ideology and new economic policy, which tend to prescribe the realization of economic growth and efficiency while ignoring the noneconomic spheres that are equally critical for authentic human development (Haque, 2002). It has been observed that today the measure of GNP is globally accepted as the indicator of human progress, level of civilization, sign of well-being, yardstick of economic success, and basis of policy debate (Bjonnes, 2002; Cobb et al., 1995; Cobb et al., 1999). The unilateral focus on economic growth by national governments, regional economic associations, and international institutions, however, has adverse developmental implications in terms of the biased and reductionist profiling of nations based on the GNP, rationalization of the dominance of advanced industrial states (with higher GNP) in world order, imposition of policies by these dominant states on countries with lower GNP, rapid depletion of resources and degradation of environment in the process of accelerating GNP, and so on. This chapter attempts to explore major paradoxes and limitations of the measure of GNP as the most widely used indicator of development and to evaluate the implications of this use of GNP for formulating development theories and policies. In pursuing these objectives, the next section presents a brief discussion on the connotation and existing critique of GNP.

## EXISTING CRITIQUE OF GNP: SOME EXAMPLES

In general, the GNP of a country represents the total money value of all goods and services produced by its residents in one year. More specifically, GNP includes the money value of the total annual domestic product of a country, plus incomes (e.g., investment earnings and remittances) earned abroad by its residents, minus payments made to nonresidents and foreign institutions (e.g., interest on foreign loans and repatriated profits made by foreign investors) (World Bank, 1985; David, 1986). On the other hand, the gross domestic product (GDP) is the total money value of annual goods and services produced by both residents and nonresidents (including profits made by foreign investors) in a country, minus incomes earned abroad by its residents. For developing countries, the GNP measure seems to be more realistic, because in these countries profits or incomes made by foreign investors are much more common and significant than profits made by their own residents in foreign countries (Cobb et al., 1995). In any case, the GNP measure has come to represent the "principal measure of economic progress" and the "criterion of success" (Brown, 1990; Robinson, 1979). As mentioned above, the measure is used to categorize nations along the continuum between the most the developed and least developed nations, with other categories (such as high-income, middle-income, lower-middle-income, and upper-middle-income countries) between the two (Gonzalez, 1988). Although the use of GNP to assess the level of development has been expanded and globalized, there are some criticisms of this development measure.

More specifically, first, it has been pointed out that the valuation of goods and services in terms of GNP requires the existence of perfect market competition, and since such a condition hardly exists, there is a certain skepticism about the use of this measure as an indicator of economic welfare (Bannock, 1975). The problem becomes more serious in many developing nations, in which market institutions are underdeveloped and the valuation of goods and services through the free market is often ineffective. Second, there are certain inherent limits of GNP pointed out by various authors. For David (1986), the cross-national comparison of GNP in terms of a common currency, such as the U.S. dollar, is problematic because the official exchange rates do not always reflect income and price differences among countries, and because of the existence of underground economy and unpriced economic activities in many countries. According to Estes (1988:24–25), another limitation of the GNP measure is that it is incapable of measuring the noneconomic (social) dimension of human welfare, which constitutes an essential part of overall development. In addition, this measure assumes all outputs as beneficial, without making any distinction between "productive and destructive activities" (Cobb et al., 1995).

Third, in opposition to the parochial economistic view of development held by mainstream economists, it is emphasized by some scholars that there is no direct compatibility between GNP growth rate and actual human development. As Daly (1989:75) points out, "Limits to growth do not imply limits to development." Similarly, for Trainer (1989:2), "Identifying development with sheer economic growth certainly does wonders for GNP, but it does very little for the poor majority." Fourth, going one step further and in line with dependency theorists, Alschuler (1988:6) mentions that sometimes economic growth may lead to national disintegration, internal colonialism, state repression, and thus maldevelopment. Shiva (1989) also points out how the GNP measure may eventually imply maldevelopment. There are indeed certain developing nations with high GNP growth rates (especially the newly industrialized countries) that have achieved these rates at the expense of internal state control and external dependence.

Finally, in order to overcome some of the major limits or shortcomings of GNP, there have emerged some alternative measures for assessing development. For example, there is the so-called physical quality-of-life index (PQLI) developed by Morris D. Morris and his associates, which covers such issues as life expectancy, infant mortality, and adult literacy (Barnett, 1988). On the other hand, the U.N. Expert Groups covered a broader range of items in defining the "level of living," including health, education, nutrition, housing, employment, transportation, security, freedom, and recreation (Estes, 1988). A very similar list of items was considered by the Organization for Economic Cooperation and Development (OECD) in its concept of "social well-being," which, according to Estes (1988), reflects the living status in developed nations rather than developing countries. Based on such a critique of existing measures of socioeconomic development, Estes (1988) himself presents a separate index called the "index of social progress" (ISP) in order to assess human welfare. It consists of forty-four social indicators that are classified into eleven subindexes, including health, education, defense, demography, geography, economics, political stability, and so on. Some other authors present indicators such as happy life expectancy, the genuine progress indicator, and the international human suffering index (Yeh et al., 2001). On the other hand, Gonzalez (1988) offers the so-called socioeconomic development index (SEDI), which consists of four factors, including income, diet, health, and education. He compares the above four measures or indexes (GNP, PQLI, ISP, SEDI), and explains how socioeconomic ranks of different countries vary when these diverse measures are used.

Although some of these measures to assess development are more comprehensive than GNP, they are still biased and reductionist in nature in terms of taking the indicators of affluent Western nations as the benchmarks of development, excluding structural factors of interclass variations in living conditions, and presenting all developmental issues in statistical figures. The former U.N. secretary general Javier Perez de Cuellar pointed out that the outcomes of economic development hardly benefited the poorest strata in society, and development concerns such as human dignity and well-being should not be treated as "a collection of numbers in a list of statistical tables" (De Cuellar, 1983:190). More important, the past and present assessments of development have largely been based on the GNP measure: most national development plans, regional development initiatives, and global development reports have been dominated by the GNP figures. Even in the academic sphere, although some scholars may pay attention to certain noneconomic factors, eventually they also begin to "rank the less developed countries in groups based on GNP or per capita GNP" (Thanawala, 1990:15). There is thus a need for more comprehensive critical studies of GNP as a measure of development. The next section thus attempts to present a more comprehensive critique of GNP.

## DECONSTRUCTING THE MYTHS AND REALITIES OF GNP

### GNP as Process of Commoditizing Life

It has been pointed out that most measures of "economic growth," especially GNP, tend to put emphasis mainly on the market value of production, and thus on "the rate at which resources are converted to commodities," without taking into account all the goods and services that are not exchanged in the market (Mander and Barker, 2001). In other words, GNP largely involves the process of commoditizing material goods and human labor by selling them in the marketplace at certain prices or wages.

First, with regard to material goods, an increase in GNP may occur simply because of the commoditization of these goods (i.e., the process of measuring the monetary value of those goods based on their market values). In other words, when goods are produced and consumed by the same individuals without going through the process of market valuation and exchange, they are unlikely to be taken into account in the GNP calculation. The rate of the GNP increase thus often reflects the pace of converting resources into commodities. In subsistence economies, although people's basic needs are usually satisfied through "self-provisioning mechanisms" (goods produced and consumed without involving market-based exchange), such mechanisms remain outside the GNP measure (Shiva, 1989). One main reason, of course, is the fact that the valuation and information of these self-provisioning products (outside the market) simply do not exist, and thus do not appear in the GNP tables in many developing countries (Robinson, 1979). While in developed capitalist economies almost every product has a market value, in many developing countries, significant portions of material goods are usually produced in the household economy, and thus remain in the "nonmarket sphere" beyond the scope of GNP (Barnett, 1988; Cobb et al., 1995).

As Shiva (1989) mentions, when people eat self-produced foods, live in self-built housing, and wear handmade garments, they are considered poor since these products have not been assigned with monetary values, but when they eat processed food, live in rented houses, and wear machine-made garments available in the market, they are considered rich. Historically, before the intervention of the world capitalist system in traditional developing societies, most indigenous people used to produce goods and services for their immediate consumption rather than for accumulation and sale, and in the absence of a money economy, they depended on barter as a means of exchange. Such a self-reliant lifestyle could hardly be measured in terms of GNP. In the case of India, according to Chopra (1983:217), "the unorganized barter economy" of rural India was largely excluded from the national income account. With the deeper incorporation of many developing societies into the world market, and the proliferation of the money economy into every sphere of life (Bjonnes, 2002), the GNP figures may show considerable progress, but often without much improvement in the actual quality of life. In some cases, a considerable portion of increased GNP may have nothing to do with real increases in goods and services, except the process of their marketization and valuation in monetary terms.

Second, in terms of human labor, the GNP figure increases with the commoditization of services involving paid labor, but the GNP measure fails to include unpaid labor involved in such household activities as caring for children and elderly parents at home, growing and preparing foods for family consumption, and providing volunteer services to the community (Cobb et al., 1999; Mander and Barker, 2001). With regard to the prevalence of such unpaid labor in most developing countries, Redclift (1987:15) observes that "informal activities are particularly important when we consider the environment in the South: collecting firewood, cooking food, feeding, clothing and housing people. None of these activities are adequately represented in GNP statistics." In traditional developing societies, the main reason for not including unpaid household labor (involved in parenting, caring, cooking, cleaning, repairing, etc.) in the GNP calculation is the fact that in these activities "no money changes hands" (Cobb et al., 1995).

In contrast, in advanced capitalist nations, because of the social realities of broken families, high divorce rates, single parenthood, the end of intergenerational bonds, and the dominance of individualistic choice and careerism, the above-mentioned household activities are performed by paid or waged labor counted in GNP. As a result, parenting is replaced by paid child care, home cooking is replaced by dining in restaurants, neighborhood watch is replaced by salaried security guards, and so on (Cobb et al., 1995). Thus as the families and communities declined in these societies, the GNP figures went up and economic experts became unnecessarily impressed (Cobb et al., 1995). With regard to the female workforce in these countries, Mishan (1986:114–115) observes that "the services that women now provide for industry and commerce continue to add to the value of GNP, the concomitant reduction of services they would otherwise provide in their homes . . .is ignored in the GNP computation."

While in developing countries the unpaid labor of housewives used in washing, cooking, cleaning, and caring is not counted in GNP, in developed nations most women add to GNP by earning wages as paid employees and by purchasing home appliances (e.g., washing machines, coffeemakers), using expensive child-care services, or hiring domestic helpers to replace their traditional household duties. In addition, in order to maintain their career image, these women spend a huge amount of money on expensive cosmetics, jewelry, clothes, diet pills, fitness program, and so on. All of these also increase the GNP figure. On the other hand, the grandparents (senior citizens) in developed nations cost billions of dollars in state-funded old-age security and care (as a part of GNP). In most developing countries, they stay with the family, take care of the grandchildren, and contribute to family stability through valuable advice based on their wisdom and experience. Even most children in developing countries often participate in household activities without being counted in GNP. Their education is relatively inexpensive, and their sources of recreation are local games and sports and handmade toys (also outside the GNP loop), whereas children in developed nations inflate the GNP figure by billions of dollars with their expensive education, child care, high-tech toys, cartoon shows, computer games, and so on.

It is clear from the above discussion that the commoditization of material goods, human labor, and lifestyle—in terms of determining their market values based on their supply and demand—is crucial to include them in the calculation of GNP. In the capitalist nations, because of the existence of advanced markets and an intensive process of commoditization, most products and work hours are counted in their GNP figures. But in developing societies characterized by self-serving rural economies and underdeveloped market systems (especially countries with minimal exposure to the world capitalist system), many people grow their foods themselves, build their own houses, perform their own household activities, and have care services for their family members, although these outputs and services outside the market do not appear in the GNP figures. One may thus conclude that in measuring GNP, it is quite misleading to compare the standards of living between the developed and the developing countries.

## GNP Without Human Well-Being

In modern market economies, a considerable portion of economic growth (in terms of GNP) is based on activities and goods and services that hardly contribute to human well-being in any form. As pointed out by Cobb et al. (1999), the GNP or GDP is simply the total amount of money spent on goods and services irrespective of whether they increase or diminish actual well-being. First, the money spent on and the revenue generated from the whole advertising industry has become colossal—although it publicizes various consumption items to attract customers, by itself it does not produce any goods for human consumption. In modern societies, the sale of most products involves extensive advertising, and customers are often attracted to such products not because of their actual needs, but because of their continuous manipulation through such advertising in various media. In fact, there is hardly any advertising for products related to primary human needs, such as basic food items, medicines, and education.

There is massive advertising for relatively unnecessary goods, however, ranging from cosmetics to private cars, alcoholic beverages to diet pills, airlines to hotels, and children's toys to adult entertainment. It is estimated that the average American observes 150,000 advertisements on television in his or her lifetime (UNDP, 1998). In the process of shaping the desires of consumers for various products, the global spending on advertising amounts to at least $435 billion, and its recent growth has been the fastest in such developing countries as South Korea, the Philippines, and Colombia (UNDP, 1998). Although this huge amount spent on advertising constitutes a part of GNP, it does not offer any tangible consumption goods; it basically produces sensational images and symbols for various products and services to attract customers and manipulate their consumption patterns. Even hazardous or harmful products can be made attractive through repetitive advertising. The capitalist market economy has to continue to advertise, however, in order to manufacture customers' needs and expectations, so that they never feel self-sufficient. As Weaver (1973:104) mentions, "The industrial economy is based on people wanting more and more material goods...advertising plays some part in this process."

Second, due to the above-mentioned proliferation of the advertising industry, many goods are produced and purchased by customers and thus counted in GNP, but they often do not enhance human well-being. Today there are dozens of overpublicized but ineffective products on the market that claim but fail to address human disorders associated with a modern lifestyle, including alcoholism, sexual dysfunction, job stress, and loneliness. It is the excessive publicity of products through advertising that leads to "addictive consumption," and without such publicity many customers would not spend money on these products (Cobb et al., 1995). Although such addictive consumption may not improve well-being, it increases GNP. In addition, since intensive advertising distorts human wants and manipulates them to possess more and more, many goods are purchased but only partially consumed or not consumed at all. In this regard, Mishan (1986:183) mentions some of such unused or underused products covered in GNP, including unread books and magazines, hardly used electronic goods, discarded sports equipments, and unused postcards and sales catalogues. In other words, although many products are sold through intensive publicity (often based on fabrication or misinformation), which boosts the nation's economic growth figure, they fail to enhance human well-being to the extent that they are usually underutilized, not to mention their adverse outcomes in terms of worsening the problem of garbage disposal.

Third, another item that adds to GNP but cannot be consumed or does not improve human well-being is the production of military hardware and lethal weapons (Mander and Barker, 2001), which represents one of the biggest sources of government expenditure in the world. In the United States, by the mid-1980s the national economy became heavily dependent on arms production, and it increasingly accounted for a major part of the nation's economic growth (Redclift, 1987; Mishan, 1986). In 2001, the world military expenditure was $839 billion, and a mere five rich, industrialized countries accounted for more than 50% of this expenditure (SIPRI, 2002). Although the global military expenditure declined during the period from 1987 to 1998, perhaps because of the end of the Cold War, it increased by 7% during the period from 1998 to 2001 (SIPRI, 2002). By 2003, while the estimated military budget rose to $379 billion in the United States, it also increased in China, India, and Russia (CDI, 2002; Walker, 2002). Although the colossal business of arms production boosts GNP figures, especially in advanced industrial countries, these products—including conventional arms, ballistic missiles, nuclear arms, and biological and chemical weapons—cannot contribute to human well-being in terms of living standards.

On the other hand, the opportunity costs of expansive military budgets in developing countries are significant, because the huge defense budget reduces the funds available for the education, health, transport, and housing sectors that are so critical for the well-being of poor populations. Of course one may argue that the strong defense sector contributes to human well-being in terms of greater national security, which is largely a self-serving argument, because interstate conflict and the arms race are not ordained by any supernatural power—they are human creations and often involve the vested interests underlying the whole political economy of the defense industry. If various nations would decide to have collective peace and security without military expansion and arms proliferation, a more genuine and long-lasting security could be achieved, the resources available for basic human needs would increase, and the human and environmental costs (e.g., the deaths caused by wars and the environmental disorders caused by nuclear arms) could also be avoided. Under such an ideal global situation, although the GNP figure might plummet, the extent of actual human well-being would certainly improve.

Finally, in advanced market economies, for most products there are many intermediaries involved between the production and consumption processes, many of which may be counted in GNP but do not enhance human well-being. For instance, before reaching the consumers, many food items have to pass through various stages, such as storage, packaging and repackaging, using preservatives, and transporting to various destinations. It has been mentioned that in the United States., the food supply system involves the intensive use of energy at its various stages, such as processing, transportation, and preparation (Brookfield, 1979). In the final analysis, however, an apple pie remains an apple pie regardless of how many times it is packaged, how much distance it travels, how long it is kept in cold storage, and how much it is treated by preservatives. Each of these stages between production and consumption involves other final products (such as packaging, transport, storage facilities, preservatives, and distribution outlets), which cannot be consumed but are taken into account in the GNP calculation. On the other hand, in the localized rural economies in developing countries, since people usually produce their own consumption goods or purchase them fresh from small local markets, the long chain of intermediaries between production and consumption that boost the GNP figure without enhancing actual well-being hardly exist in this context.

## GNP—Concealing the Hidden Costs

There are many hidden costs that are not taken into account in the calculation of GNP. While GNP includes the benefits of industrial and technological production in market economies, such as abundant food, comfortable shelter, increased mobility, and improved communication, it hardly takes into account the costs involved in such production processes, including the depletion of natural resources, air and water pollution, soil erosion, the risk of radiation, the destruction of entire species, economic disruption, urban congestion, low-quality processed foods, family breakdown, destruction of communities, and increases in crime (Bannock, 1975; Cobb et al., 1995). These serious shortcomings of the GNP measure require further clarifications.

First, the GNP figure is flawed because while it takes into account the depreciation of industrial plant, its fails to consider the depletion of such "natural capital" as fossil fuels and forest resources (Brown, 1990:7–8). As various nations, especially the advanced industrial nations, extract more oil and gas from the ground, the growth rate of GNP increases, but this measure overlooks the fact that the more these nonrenewable natural resources are exploited, the less will be available for future use (Cobb et al., 1999). As Mishan (1986:117) mentions, the rate of using such resources as fossil fuels, mineral reserves, and water reserves increased to such an extent that it might pose a threat to the use of such resources by future generations. Although the depletion of these natural resources may add to GNP in the current year, it makes such resources less available in the future years; therefore it is a violation of "basic accounting principles" if such depletion is not considered "a cost on the national accounts" in terms of the unavailability of such resources in the future (Cobb et al., 1995, 1999). Beyond resource depletion, the massive use of fossil fuels by growth-inducing industries and cars is responsible for the emission of greenhouse gases (especially carbon dioxide), which may eventually lead to global warming, a rise in the sea level, disastrous floods, and so on. Unfortunately, these catastrophic costs of growth-related products and activities are always overlooked in the GNP assessment.

This interpretation is also applicable in the case of renewable natural sources, such as forests and fisheries, because continuous overexploitation of these resources exhausts them so much that the rate of depletion often exceeds the regeneration capacity, and thus they eventually become nonrenewable resources (Shiva, 1989). With regard to the eventual destruction of forests due to their rapid depletion, Brown (1990:7–8) mentions that in the calculation of GNP "the trees cut down are counted as income but no subtraction is made to account for depletion of the forest, a natural asset." During the recent two decades, the loss of tropical forest was 7 million hectares in Latin America and the Caribbean, 4 million hectares in Asia, and another 4 million hectares in sub-Saharan Africa (UNDP, 1998). A similar observation has been made about the depletion of the fisheries—that it may improve the national account of economic growth only until the whole sector collapses (Cobb et al., 1995). The global fish stocks have already been depleted or are in danger of being depleted by 25% (UNDP, 1998). Once again, the point here is that the measure of economic growth only shows the rate of exploiting natural resources while ignoring its cost in terms of the unavailability of such depleted resources in the future. This form of economic growth based on the mindless depletion and waste of natural resources that endangers future generations has been interpreted by the UNDP (1996:4) as "futureless growth." In this regard, Brown (1990:9) mentions that if the environmental outcomes of economic growth, including resource depletion, are considered, "real economic progress would be much less than conventional economic measures indicate."

Second, another cost not counted in GNP is the process of land degradation (e.g., soil erosion, salinization, groundwater depletion, and desertification) caused by intensive cultivation, irrigation, fertilizer use, and so on. While such modern cultivation, often pursued for cash crops by commercial agriculture, brings immediate economic gains and boosts GNP, it leads to land degradation to such an extent that the rate of land productivity eventually declines, which is not taken into account in assessing economic growth. It has been observed that modern cultivation based on irrigation, fertilizer, and pesticides accounts for the salinization and desertification of land; thus one-sixth of the world's land area (about 2 billion hectares) has already been degraded, and almost 70% of dry land is at risk worldwide (UNDP, 1998; Redclift, 1987; Bjonnes, 2002). In both developed and developing countries, the expansion of agricultural modernization and the adoption of high-yielding varieties have usually caused the depletion of groundwater and the loss of soil quality (Brookfield, 1979; Redclift, 1987). Regarding the exclusion from economic assessment of this worsening problem of land degradation, it is mentioned that "with the existing economic accounting system, those who overplow and overpump appear to be doing well in the short run, even while facing a disastrous collapse over the long run" (Brown, 1990:9). Also, in most countries, in the process of economic development, the construction and expansion of highways, airports, pipelines, seaports, buildings, rail lines, industrial plants, and so on causes huge areas of cultivable land to be destroyed or degraded, and these are hardly taken into account in the GNP (Mander and Barker, 2001; Cobb et al., 1999).

Third, the measure of GNP fails to include its indirect cost to human health and lifestyle, especially in terms of serious health hazards resulting from the GNP-inducing commercial foods and industrial products and the loss of leisure and family time caused by the GNP-friendly waged labor. It has been reported by experts that in this industrial age, people are absorbing and inhaling toxic chemicals, synthetic materials, and harmful gases through the commercial food chain and intensive industrial atmosphere, which has a damaging effect on their livers, kidneys, lungs, and other organs (Caldwell, 1977). In the process of boosting economic growth, the replacement of home-cooked foods (overlooked in GNP) with manufactured foods (counted in GNP) has caused new diseases or the "diseases of civilization" in high-income nations, including diabetes, cancer, and blood pressure, which are relatively absent in traditional low-income countries (Caldwell, 1977). Ironically, the money spent on research, medicines, and hospital services for these modern diseases also increases the GNP figures of affluent nations, whereas the absence of these diseases and medical services implies less GNP for traditional societies.

On the other hand, in the process of generating incomes, most citizens in advanced market economies have no choice but to be engaged in waged labor in various organizations to earn their livelihood, which implies that they have to compromise their leisure time spent with family and friends. Even from a utilitarian perspective, since the eventual objective of any meaningful economic growth and income is supposed to be individual satisfaction, this loss of leisure time is an opportunity cost of waged labor. Such measures of economic growth as GNP or GDP, however, ignore the value of such leisure and recreation (Cobb et al., 1999). As a result, in some traditional societies, although people may lead happy and relaxed lives based on the satisfaction of basic material needs, leisure and recreation with family, and the pursuit of spiritual beliefs, their GNP figures are poor, since they do not add to the market-based indicator of economic growth (see Bjonnes, 2002).

## GNP Pathologies Leading to More GNP

The above-mentioned useless components and unaccounted hidden costs of GNP—such as advertising and overconsumption, industrialization and environmental hazards, waged labor and alienation—create a series of adverse or pathological outcomes (e.g., obesity, pollution, crimes) that require additional products and services (e.g., weight-loss programs, environmental regulation, crime control) that also add further to the GNP figure. In other words, the pathological consequences of GNP themselves lead to more GNP. In this regard Paul Streeten mentions that if "it were to be found that what we had been measuring was not goods, but anti-bads, produced in order to combat the bads produced by the process of growth, we might all agree that economic growth was not all that wonderful" (Streeten, 1988:7). This dimension of the GNP myth requires more specific explanations.

First, as mentioned earlier, due to continuous media manipulation of consumers' behavior through the huge advertising industry, there is a tendency toward overconsumption of manufactured or processed foods (usually with high sugar and fat content) contributing to the national account of GNP. This pathological consumption has led to the problem of obesity and thus to the proliferation of numerous diet pills, weight-loss programs, exercise machines, low-fat products, and fitness clubs, which contribute to a further boost in the GNP figure of affluent nations. In the United States, for example, more than 50% of adults are overweight or obese, the number of obese children increased by 50% in the last two decades, and more than two-thirds of the population is trying to lose weight; thus the annual spending on various weight-loss products and programs has reached about $33 billion (Redefining Progress, 1999; Cobb et al., 1995). In addition, about 300,000 people die every year from both an unhealthy diet and inactivity, the medical spending on various obesity-related diseases (e.g., breast and colon cancer, heart disease, and stroke) amounts to over $51 billion per year in the United States (Redefining Progress, 1999), and all these constitute part of this country's GNP. In contrast, in many developing countries in which the modern food industry—especially fast-food chains—has not yet entered in any significant way, the problem of obesity hardly exists, and thus the pathological GNP cannot add to their economic development indicators.

Second, in the process of generating GNP, the massive expansion of industries usually involves the burning of fossil fuels, use of hazardous chemicals, and pollution of air and water. As Weaver (1973:109) suggests, "Once growth is introduced as the primary goal, environmental pollution is inevitable. Each firm must pollute in order to compete with other firms." This situation creates the need for various environmental programs and agencies to regulate and monitor these industries and their products and to carry out cleanup operations. The management of human waste and garbage has become a great challenge in cities worldwide. It is estimated that in the past fifty years the rate of global carbon dioxide emissions from fossil fuels increased fourfold, and in the past twenty years the amount of per capita waste in industrial nations increased threefold (UNDP, 1998). As Mishan (1986:118–119) points out, the environmental pollution caused by private industries usually becomes the responsibility of the government, which must spend public money to clean up such pollution, and this expenditure appears in the national accounts as a component of GNP. Today in almost all nations there are environmental ministries, agencies, and departments spending a considerable part of the national budget to regulate environmental hazards, monitor environment-related industrial activities, clean up garbage, create conducive infrastructure, and maintain environmental health. There are also examples of environmental disasters, such as the Exxon Valdez oil spill, which required the government to spend money on the cleanup of toxic waste, also adding to the GNP figure (Cobb et al., 1999). Similarly, the medical bills paid for health problems caused by a hazardous environment become a part of GNP. In this regard, it is pointed out that it is a violation of accounting principles to incorporate such public and private expenditures on managing environmental degradation and its health effects into the calculation of GNP (Cobb et al., 1995).

Third, in most capitalist nations the pursuit of economic growth and accumulation based on market competition, utilitarian self-interest, and waged labor has reinforced individualistic motivation, family disintegration, community destruction, erosion of family and community support, feelings of loneliness and alienation, and so on. On the other hand, these sociopsychological patterns arising from capitalist economic growth have led to such pathological behavior as mental disorders, a sense of insecurity, alcoholism, and criminal acts (Weaver, 1973). Since the family and community support systems have virtually disappeared in modern industrial societies, numerous public and private sector organizations have emerged, and a considerable amount of money is spent to address these pathologies, which becomes a part of GNP (Cobb et al., 1999; Weaver, 1973). For instance, the erosion of the family in industrial nations is evident in the alarmingly high divorce rate, which has generated various services, including marriage counseling, sex-advice clinics, divorce settlement, single-parenthood consultation, and child care. Although these services are relatively unknown in low-income societies (Mishan, 1986), they now constitute a part of GNP in affluent nations.

Related to the fragmentation of family and community and the impersonal atmosphere at the workplace are the feelings of alienation, loneliness, and stress that often lead to artificial coping mechanisms, such as alcoholism, drug abuse, antidepressants, psychotherapy, and various types of recreation (often perverted), including gambling, nightclub, videos, adult movies, massage centers, computer games, hotline facilities, and commercial sports. All these services arising from the pathological outcomes of industrial societies add tremendously to the calculation of GNP. In European countries, for instance, the average cost of alcoholism represents 2–6% of GNP (Alcoweb, 1996). Social breakdown in these societies is also related to various types of crimes. In the United States, the expansive crime-prevention system and security industry (e.g., locks and electronic devices) generates $65 billion a year, and is included in the GNP (Cobb et al., 1995). In addition, due to the erosion of family and neighborhood support systems, most individuals feel vulnerable or insecure, and in order to overcome such a perceived or real sense of insecurity, there have emerged various insurance policies for virtually all aspects of life—health insurance, car insurance, property insurance, travel insurance, unemployment insurance, life insurance, and so on—which are also a plus for GNP (Cobb et al., 1999). In traditional developing countries, the guarantee of individual security is not based on such organized policies offered by the profit-making insurance companies; it is often ensured by family and community protection that does not appear in GNP. In short, in advanced industrial nations, the pathological outcomes of economic growth or GNP require the adoption of redress mechanisms and remedial services that boost the GNP figures of these countries further.

## CRITICAL IMPLICATIONS OF THE GNP MYTH

It has been discussed above that the development policies and programs pursued by countries all over the world have been dominated by the GNP indicator despite the availability of some alternative measures. The idea of economic growth in general and GNP in particular has serious limitations. As discussed in great detail in this chapter, the GNP figure may continue to increase by simply putting market prices without adding actual goods and services and without enhancing human well-being. In addition, GNP fails to include the unaccounted costs of economic growth, but incorporates expenditures made on activities related to the pathological outcomes of economic growth itself. Beyond these shortcomings or drawbacks of GNP, this section briefly explains some of the major critical implications of using GNP as the primary development agenda for various countries.

### Economic Impacts

First, in general, economic growth (especially the GNP indicator) has not only been used by such international agencies as the World Bank, International Monetary Fund (IMF), and World Trade Organization (WTO) to impose economic policies and conditions on developing countries; it has also been used by governments in these countries to justify policy reforms, invite foreign investments, and ask for foreign loans (Bjonnes, 2002; Streeten, 1979). As early as 1969, the report of the Commission on International Development submitted to the World Bank emphasized an increase in foreign aid to enhance the rates of economic growth in developing countries (Minhas, 1979). Earlier scholars such as Rostow interpreted development as "economic growth," and suggested that the objective of growth could have provided the rationale for international aid, technical assistance, and foreign investment (Streeten, 1979). In the name of GNP, the extent of external debt and dependence of these countries has thus increased considerably. Between 1970 and 1990, the combined total external debt of all developing nations increased from only $100 million to $1.3 trillion (O'Cleir-eacain, 1990). In the name of economic growth, developing countries borrowed heavily from external sources that worsened their conditions of dependence and diminished their economic self-reliance.

Second, whatever increase in GNP has been achieved through economic growth policies, the situation of poverty has not improved in many developing nations. The United Nations Development Programme (UNDP, 1996:2) calls it "ruthless growth," which may "benefit the rich, leaving millions of people struggling in ever-deepening poverty. During 1970–85 global GNP increased by 40%, yet the number of poor increased by 17%." In many instances, while the overall level of GNP has increased, growth-led policies have often diminished the living standards of common people (Bjonnes, 2002). In Africa, the average household consumes 20% less today than it did twenty-five years ago (UNDP, 1998). Globally, about 20% of the world's population has not benefited from the explosion in the growth of consumption, and in the developing world, 33% of the people are without safe drinking water, 20% are without adequate food, and 25% are without adequate housing (UNDP, 1998; Brandon, 2000; Karliner, 1997). Ironically, although the world's food supply is adequate, each year 30 million people still die of hunger, 800 million experience malnutrition, and millions more cannot afford to purchase enough food (Bjonnes, 2002).

Even in countries in which the GNP level has improved, because of rapid industrialization, agricultural modernization, urban development, and foreign investment, it is usually the affluent elite (industrialists, bureaucrats, and politicians) who have gained from such ventures, while impoverishing the majority of the population, including the rural and urban poor. In Africa, for example, large industrial projects and irrigation systems have benefited the rich minority, but they have destroyed the local production systems and the indigenous farming and fisheries on which the poorer sections have always depended (Postel, 1990:47). Similarly, in many developing countries, the environmental degradation and resource depletion caused by growth-led activities have devastated the livelihood of the poor (Mander and Barker, 2001). The measure of GNP has no scope for considering the worsening situation of poverty as long as the overall national economic figures keep increasing, even though such GNP figures are often deceptive in many ways discussed in this article. In addition, the GNP indicators often perpetuate a form of psychological poverty among people in traditional societies by ranking their nonmarket but self-reliant lifestyle at a much lower level in comparison with the market-driven lives of people in advanced market economies.

Third, an overemphasis on the realization of national economic growth understood in terms of GNP often conceals, justifies, and even worsens inequality between income groups and between nations. It has been pointed out that since the GNP or GDP measure overlooks the issue of income distribution, any economic gains made by a few high-income households may be understood as benefits to all; it does not make a distinction between the gainers and losers of higher economic growth (Cobb et al., 1995). At the international level, therefore, although the total global income reached $23 trillion by 1993, about 20% of the world's population living in industrial nations accounted for $18 trillion, while 80% of this population living in developing countries claimed only $5 trillion (UNDP, 1996). According to UNDP (1997), in fact, the share of global income for the poorest 20% of the world's population declined from 2.3% in 1960 to 1.4% in 1991 to 1.1% in 1997. Despite the continuous increase in the global GNP, the economic gap between the richest and poorest countries increased from a ratio of 3:1 in 1920, to 35:1 in 1950, to 72:1 in 1992, to 84:1 in 1998 (Bjonnes, 2002). Similarly, in terms of consumption, while the 20% of the world's population in the richest countries accounted for 86% of the world's private consumption expenditures in 1998, the poorest 20% accounted for as little as 1.3% of such expenditures (UNDP, 1998). At both the global and national levels, the rapid economic growth facilitated by globalization has benefited the rich; it has hardly trickled down to the poor (Mander and Barker, 2001).

## Political Implications

Beyond economics, the dominance of GNP as the primary national goal and development agenda has considerable political implications, because it tends to ignore, even legitimize, political repression, authoritarian rule, external interference, and international hegemony as long as the economic growth figures continue to increase. Such a scenario of economic growth is interpreted by the UNDP (1996:2–4) as "voice-less growth," under which economic growth does not expand democracy or empower people; it instead perpetuates authoritarian political controls. There are both the global and national dimensions to this scenario.

Internationally, it is widely recognized that the realization of economic growth and accumulation at the early stage of capitalism was inseparable from the worldwide colonial intervention involving political repression, forced labor, and the drainage of resources from South and Southeast Asia, Africa, and Latin America (Chopra, 1983; Furtado, 1983). It is pointed out that the early growth and prosperity of England and other Western countries cannot be understood without some reference to the exploitation of material and human resources in South Asian and African countries (Blacking, 1987). This repressive colonial means used for economic growth still continues in indirect form. After decolonization, the Western powers created and used such international institutions as the World Bank and the IMF to exercise economic dominance over developing nations (Robinson, 1979). Today the global economic powers, especially the United States, exercise politicoeconomic domination over the people and governments in the developing world through such international agencies and multinational corporations (Chossudovsky, 1994). In other words, the past economic achievements and the current higher GNP figures in developed nations have often been realized through the repressive means and external pressures used in former colonies that are now "dependent" independent nation-states.

Internally, the achievement of economic growth and accumulation has involved domestic repression in both developed and developing countries. It has been observed that instead of expanding citizens' democratic rights, economic growth has usually been accompanied by internal repression and control (Seers, 1979). For instance, in South Africa, the previous high rate of economic growth or GNP under the apartheid regime usually involved severe political and economic repression (Lipton, 1985). It has been mentioned by Worsely (1984) that the regimes in East Asian countries, which have been known for high growth rates of GNP, (especially in Taiwan and South Korea), practiced continuous political repression against popular organizations. A similar point is made by Chakravarty (1987:83)—that the high growth rates in East

Asia were pursued through economic nationalism based on an authoritarian framework. In fact, in almost all cases the realization of a higher growth rate requires that "all work is done in anonymous, undemocratic, faceless, impersonal, smoothly functioning institutions" (Weaver, 1973:105).

Recently, in most Latin American countries the realization of rapid economic growth through the market-driven neoliberal approach has been carried out by a centralized mode of governance. In order to enhance the GNP figures, pro-market policies, such as privatization, deregulation, and liberalization, were introduced by states through executive power without popular mandate. In cases such as Argentina, Brazil, and Peru, the neoliberal policy approach has usually been based on presidential decrees without any public support, legislative debate, and discussion with opposition parties (Pereira et al., 1993:208). Similarly, based on the rationale of enhancing economic growth and efficiency, most countries in Southeast Asia, sub-Saharan Africa, and the Middle East have embraced these neoliberal policies largely prescribed by the World Bank and the IMF under the so-called structural-adjustment programs (Schmidt, 1998; Corkery, 1997; Jiyad, 1995). It has been pointed out by Hildyard (1997) that in Africa these growth-led and market-centered policies, in fact, required repressive governments and authoritarian rules that did not allow any public opposition or resistance to such policies.

## Cultural Consequences

The realization of higher economic growth or GNP requires the reorganization of society and culture. For developing societies, it largely implies the replacement of indigenous cultural beliefs (which usually discourage competition, greed, and accumulation) by the commoditized cultural products that generate incomes and boost economic growth by reinforcing selfish possession, hedonistic consumerism, and individualistic competition. According to UNDP (1996:4), in the process of achieving this "rootless growth," individuals' cultural identities are being eroded, many of the world's 10,000 distinct cultures have been endangered, and certain minority cultures have been marginalized by the dominant culture of economic growth. Even in capitalist nations, the costs of growth-driven industrial goods and cultural commodities have been the loss of individuality and uniqueness and the destruction of local subsistence cultures (Mishan, 1986; Bjonnes, 2002). In recent years, because of the worldwide craze for enhancing economic growth through the deregulation of media networks, liberalization of information and communication technologies, and globalization of cultural products, the indigenous cultures of most developing countries have come under serious threats.

In the pursuit of economic growth, the recent expansion of free trade and foreign investment brought more foreign goods, consumerism, and bourgeois outlook in developing countries, especially through massive publicity or advertising (UNDP, 1998). On the other hand, the global media, including cable television, the film industry, and computer networks, have entered the remotest parts of developing countries with devastating impacts on their local cultures. Although these have enhanced enormous potential for economic growth by accelerating the speed and volume of information exchange and economic transaction, they have serious repercussions for indigenous cultural traditions. Similarly, many countries in the developing world have introduced an expansive tourism industry in order to increase GNP, especially by attracting affluent visitors from Western nations, which has had serious cultural impacts (Thanh-Dam, 1983). Although tourism has expanded worldwide and become a multibillion dollar industry, it seriously threatens indigenous cultures.

One good example of the cultural cost of economic growth is Southeast Asia. After decades of export-led policy, foreign investment, and tourism in most countries in the region—which are globally known for spectacular GNP growth rates—today a major part of their urban population speaks English, practices Western lifestyles, endorses Western mass culture, and eagerly follows Anglo-Saxon ideals and world-views (Schmidt, 1998). Guided by "growth fetishism," the policy makers in these countries have apparently paid inadequate attention to the long-run consequences of rapid economic growth (Chakravarty, 1987:92–93). The adverse cultural consequences of high growth rates in these newly industrialized countries—such as the replacement of local languages, destruction of indigenous lifestyles, loss of self-reliance, expansion of forced labor, proliferation of sex tourism, and erosion of identity and self-respect—should be a valuable lesson for other developing countries that take the cultural dimension of human development seriously.

## CONCLUDING OBSERVATIONS

In this chapter, it has been argued that the contemporary development debates and policies are dominated by economic measures or indicators such as GNP. There are major limits or drawbacks of GNP, however, in assessing the status of development in various countries. It has also been explained that there are considerable economic, political, and cultural implications of using GNP as an indicator of development or enhancing GNP as the primary national goal. Despite such conceptual shortcomings and practical demerits, most governments and international institutions continue to use GNP as the dominant indicator of progress. The critical reasons for preferring this economic measure by national and international policy makers is not just their ignorance of its limitations and implications, but also their vested interests, which are served by the use of such reductionist, unreliable, and harmful measures to assess human progress or development.

At the international level, the use of GNP to rank various countries creates images of superior and inferior nation-states, encourages developing countries to ask for foreign assistance, justifies the expansion of foreign investment, and thus perpetuates the external dependence of poor countries on rich nations based on an exploitative relationship. In the process, many developing countries in Asia, Africa, and Latin America have become the victims of huge external debt, which diminishes their economic autonomy to the extent that their major national policies are now dictated by the donor countries and agencies. Similarly, based on the perceived need for a higher GNP rate (reinforced by international development agencies and experts), most developing countries are now encouraged to provide maximum incentives to attract foreign investment. As a result, all major transnational corporations have penetrated into developing countries, made huge economic gains, and established corporate ownership and control in these countries (Alschuler, 1988; Karliner, 1997). In addition, (1) the policy experts (mostly economists) associated with international agencies often prefer to use the GNP figures because of their previous training in reductionist economics; (2) they do not have the capacity to deal with crucial noneconomic issues (family, community, environment, leisure) that may not be quantifiable in monetary terms; (3) their jobs in these organizations that function as the "foreign aid industry" are based on the GNP myth; and (4) their interest in exercising expert power is reinforced by the calculus of economic figures (Bjonnes, 2002; Helleiner, 1990).

At the national level, the use of GNP in articulating national policies often serves the interests of the ruling parties or regimes in various ways. For instance, many regimes in the developing world use the GNP figures to sell economic policies (e.g., privatization of basic services and liberalization of trade and investment) that are otherwise harmful to citizens in terms of their adverse implications for employment, basic services, and economic self-reliance. By continuously advocating the positive figures of GNP, even the dictatorial regimes—such as those in South Korea, Taiwan, and the Philippines in the 1980s—may try to justify their repressive modes of governance. In addition, by focusing on the "overall" national economic condition or the "average" economic situation of individuals, the GNP figures overlook serious inequalities among classes or income groups, and thus may help legitimize the growing affluence of local elites and the worsening poverty of low-income citizens. It is thus not surprising that in the case of the United States, while the political leaders may boast about improvement in the GNP or GDP figures, the average citizens feel unsure or left out (Cobb et al., 1999).

In the above context, there is a serious need for re-examining, rejecting, and replacing GNP as the dominant goal or indicator of human development, especially in developing countries, which have been the worst victims of the GNP myths in recent years. It is possible to decipher "what" major initiatives need to be taken in this regard, although it is difficult to identify "who" can adopt and implement such initiatives. First, perhaps in line with the main arguments in this chapter, it is necessary to undertake serious critical studies on the limits and dangers of such reductionist and futile measure as GNP and to disseminate these critical studies widely since this measure has been perpetuated for many years among academics, experts, policy makers, and institutions. These further studies on this measure of economic growth are essential to demonstrate its misleading nature, to show how it may have presented the wrong impressions of national affluence and poverty, and to emphasize the significance of a more "humanistic assessment" of social progress (Chakravarty, 1987; Mishan, 1986; Soedjatmoko, 1983).

Second, a more comprehensive measure of development has to be articulated to replace the GNP framework. In this regard, it is wise to consider some of the alternative measures that are already available, including the so-called genuine progress indicator (GPI), which addresses some unconventional but important factors, such as nonmonetary benefits (e.g., household work, parenting, volunteer work), expenses without well-being (e.g., defense expenditure), depletion of natural resources, and harm caused by environmental pollution and economic inequality (Cobb et al., 1999). The point here is that any comprehensive measure for assessing development must overcome the drawbacks of economic growth, consider the multiple dimensions (economy, politics, culture, ecology), accommodate diverse societies and traditions, and involve various actors or stakeholders (Bjonnes, 2002; Pearce et al., 1990). It may require a multidisciplinary approach and cross-cultural outlook to articulate such a comprehensive measure of development.

Finally, with regard to practical priorities, specially in developing countries, it is imperative to move away from the GNP mania and undertake policies in favor of basic human needs, such as food, housing, sanitation, medicine, and education (Chakravarty, 1987; Cole, 1987). These countries also need to overcome GNP-driven external debt and dependence and build economic self-reliance or self-determination so that they can adopt appropriate policies and programs based on local context, individuals' needs, social justice, and cultural beliefs (Bjonnes, 2002). These policies may include substantive land reforms, agricultural subsidies, small-scale industries, need-based education, grassroots development, citizens' empowerment, bottom-up planning, environmental protection, and cultural enrichment (Bjonnes, 2002). It does not really matter whether national policies and activities enhance economic growth and improve the GNP figures; the ultimate consideration should be whether such policies and activities lead to greater happiness, well-being, and freedom for current and future generations. It is time to overcome the fetish of economic growth and get out of the GNP trap, which according to Mishan (1986:114), represents a form of "statistical hallucination."

## REFERENCES

Alcoweb. (1996). Cost of alcoholism. http://www.alcoweb.com/english/gen_info/alcohol_health_society/eco_aspects/cost/cost.html.

Alschuler, L. R. (1988). Multinationals and Maldevelopment. New York: St. Martin's.

Appelbaum, R. P. (1973). Theories of Social Change. Chicago: Markham.

Bannock, G. (1975). Technology and the quality of life. In: Alexander, K. J. W., ed. The Political Economy of Change. Oxford: Basil Blackwell, pp. 45–56.

Barnett, T. (1988). Sociology and Development. London: Hutchinson.

Bjonnes, R. (2002). Strategies to eradicate poverty: Integral approach to development. In: UNESCO, ed. The Encyclopedia of Lifesupport Systems. Paris: UNESCO, http://www.sustainablevillages.org/Resources/pages/eradicating_poverty.html.

Blacking, J. (1987). Development studies and the reinvention of tradition. World Dev 15(4):527–532.

Brandon, J. J. (Jan. 3, 2000). Raising the world's standard of living. Chris Sci Mon 9.

Brookfield, H. (1979). Urban bias, rural bias, and the regional dimension: To the house of Tweedledee. In: Tothko Chapel Colloquium, ed. Toward a New Strategy for Development. New York: Pergamon, pp. 97–121.

Brown, L. R. (1990). The illusion of progress. In: the Worldwatch Institute, ed. State of the World. 1990. New York: Norton, pp. 3–16.

Caldwell, M. (1977). The Wealth of Some Nations. London: Zed Press.

CDI (Center for Defense Information). (2002). World Military Expenditures. Washington, DC: Center for Defense Information, http://www.cdi.org/issues/wme/.

Chakravarty, S. (1987). Development strategies in the Asian countries. In: Emmerij, L., ed. Development Policies and the Crisis of the 1980s. Paris: Development Centre of the Organisation for Economic Co-operation and Development, pp. 78–95.

Chopra, P. (1983). Development and society: an overview of the Indian experience. In: Mattis, A., ed. A Society for International Development: Prospectus, 1984. Durham, NC: Duke University Press, pp. 215–226.

Chossudovsky, M. (Aug. 12, 1994). Global impoverishment and the IMF–World Bank economic medicine. Frontline.

Cobb, C., Goodman, G. S., Wackernagel, M. (1999). Why Bigger Isn't Better: The Genuine Progress Indicator—1999 Update. Oakland, CA: Redefining Progress.

Cobb, C., Halstead, T., Rowe, J. (Oct. 1995). If the GDP is up, why is America down? Atlantic http://www.theatlantic.com/politics/ecbig/gdp.htm.

Cole, J. (1987). Development and Underdevelopment: A Profile of the Third World. London: Methuen.

Corkery, J. (March 1997). International Experience with Institutional Development and Administrative Reform: Some Pointers for Success. ECDPM working paper no. 15. Maastricht, Belgium: ECDPM.

Daly, H. E. (1989). Steady-state and growth concepts for the next century. In: Archibug, F. Nijkamp, P., eds. Economy and Ecology: Towards Sustainable Development. Dordrecht, Netherlands: Kluwer Academic, pp. 73–87.

David, W. L. (1986). Conflicting Paradigms in the Economics of Developing Nations. New York: Praeger.

De Cuellar, J. P. (1983). The imperative of international economic cooperation. In: Mattis, A., ed. A Society for International Development: Prospectus, 1984. Durham, NC: Duke University Press, pp. 190–193.

Estes, R. J. (1988). Toward a "quality-of-life" index: Empirical approaches to assessing human welfare internationally. In: Norwine, J., Gonzalez, A., eds. The Third World: States of Mind and Being. Boston: Unwin Hyman, pp. 23–36.

Furtado, C. (1983). Accumulation and Development. Oxford: Martin Robertson.

Gonzalez, A. (1988). Indexes of socioeconomic development. In: Norwine, J., Gonzalez, A., eds. The Third World: States of Mind and Being. Boston: Unwin Hyman, pp. 37–49.

Haque, M. S. (1999). Restructuring Development Theories and Policies: A Critical Study. New York: State University of New York Press.

Haque, M. S. (2002). Globalization, new political economy, and governance: a third world viewpoint. Admin Theory Praxis 24(1):103–124.

Helleiner, G. K. (1990). The New Global Economy and the Developing Countries: Essays in International Economics and Development. Surrey, England: Edward Elgar.

Hildyard, N. (1997). The World Bank and the State: A Recipe for Change? London: Bretton Wood Project.

Hoogvelt, A. M. M. (1982). The Third World in Global Development. London: Macmillan Education.

Jiyad, A. M. (1995). The social balance sheet of privatization in the Arab countries. paper presented at the Third Nordic Conference on Middle Eastern Studies: Ethnic Encounter and Culture Change. Joensuu, Finland, 19–22, June.

Karliner, J. (1997). The Corporate Planet: Ecology and Politics in the Age of Globalization. San Francisco: Sierra Club.

Kim, D. H. (1984). Development Theories and Strategies: Critical Perspectives. Seoul, Korea: Sung Kyun Kwan University Press.

Lipton, M. (1985). Capitalism and Apartheid: South Africa, 1910–1984. Totowa, NJ: Rowman & Allanheld.

Mander, J., Barker, D. (Dec. 19, 2001). The root of the problem. TomPain.Commonsense, http://www.tompaine.com/feature.cfm?ID = 4779.

Merriam, A. H. (1988). What does "third world" mean? In: Norwine, J., Gonzalez, A., eds. The Third World: States of Mind and Being. Boston: Unwin Hyman, pp. 15–22.

Minhas, B. S. (1979). The current development debate. In: Rothko Chapel Colloquium, ed., Toward a New Strategy for Development. New York: Pergamon, pp. 75–96.

Mishan, E. J. (1986). Economic Myths and the Mythology of Economics. Brighton, Sussex, UK: Wheatsheaf.

O'Cleireacain, S. (1990). Third World Debt and International Public Policy. New York: Praeger.

Pearce, D., Barbier, E., Markandya, A. (1990). Sustainable Development. Surrey, England: Edward Elgar.

Pereira, L. C. B., Maravall, J. M., Przeworski, A. (1993). Conclusions. In: Pereira, L. C. B., Maravall, J. M., Przeworski, A., eds. Economic Reforms in New Democracies: A Social Democratic Approach. New York: Cambridge University Press, pp. 199–220.

Postel, S. (1990). Saving water for agriculture. In: the Worldwatch Institute, ed. State of the World, 1990. New York: Norton, pp. 39–58.

Randall, V., Theobald, R. (1985). Political Change and Underdevelopment. Durham, NC: Duke University Press.

Redclift, M. (1987). Sustainable Development: Exploring the Contradictions. London: Methuen.

Redefining Progress. (1999). Food for Thought: The GDP Is Padded with Fat—Ours. Oakland, CA: Redefining Progress.

Robinson, J. (1979). Aspects of Development and Underdevelopment. Cambridge: Cambridge University Press.

Schmidt, J. D. (Feb. 1998). Southeast Asia Between Global Neoliberal Discipline and Local Quests for Welfare. Working paper no. 84. Australia: Asia Research Centre, Murdoch University.

Seers, D. (1979). The congruence of Marxism and other neoclassical doctrines. In: Rothko Chapel Colloquium, ed. Toward a New Strategy for Development. New York: Pergamon, pp. 1–17.

Shiva, V. (1989). Development, ecology, and women. In: Plant, J., ed. Healing the Wounds. Philadelphia: New Society.

Simon, L. H., Ruccio, D. F. (1986). A methodological analysis of dependency theory: Explanation in Andre Gunder Frank. World Dev 14(2):195–209.

SIPRI (Stockholm International Peace Research Institute). (2002). SIPRI Yearbook 2002: Armaments, Disarmament and International Security. Oxford, UK: Oxford University Press.

Soedjatmoko. (1983). The human and cultural dimensions of development: accomplishments and failures. In: Mattis, A., ed. A Society for International Development: Prospectus, 1984. Durham, NC: Duke University Press, pp. 18–25.

Streeten, P. (1979). Development ideas in historical perspective. In: Rothko Chapel Colloquium, ed. Toward a New Strategy for Development. New York: Pergamon, pp. 21–52.

Streeten, P. (1988). Intergenerational responsibilities or our duties to the future. In: Dell, S., ed. Policies of Development. London: Macmillan, pp. 3–21.

Thanawala, K. (1990). Economic development and all that. Internat J Soc Econ 17(12):14–21.

Thanh-Dam, T. (1983). The dynamics of sex tourism: The case of Southeast Asia. Dev Change 14(4):533–553.

Trainer, T. (1989). Developed to Death: Rethinking Third World Development. London: Green Print.

UNDP (United Nations Development Programme). (1996). Human Development Report 1996. New York: Oxford University Press.

UNDP (United Nations Development Programme). (1997). Human Development Report 1997. New York: Oxford University Press.

UNDP (United Nations Development Programme). (1998). Human Development Report 1998. New York: Oxford University Press.

Walker, M. (2002). World military spending on rise after Sept. 11. Reuters, June 13, http://www.globalpolicy.org/wtc/analysis/2002/0613military.htm.

Weaver, J. H. (1973). The social and environmental consequences of economic growth. In: Weaver, J. H., ed. Modern Political Economy. Boston: Allyn and Bacon, pp. 102–120.

World Bank. (1985). World Development Report 1985. Washington, DC: World Bank.

Worsely, P. M. (1984). The Three Worlds: Culture and World Development. Chicago: University of Chicago Press.

Yeh, J. R., Lo, S. L., Lee, L. L., Liu, J. T., Wang, J. C. S., Huang, S. L. (2001). Sustainable development indicators for Taiwan. Workshop on Sustainable Development Indicators. Taiwan, 17–19, Nov.

# 6

## Social Scientific Knowledge and American Interests
### An Episode in the Development of Development Theory*

**ZAHEER BABER**

*University of Saskatchewan, Saskatoon, Saskatchewan, Canada*

## INTRODUCTION

The recent proliferation of studies that have analyzed the intricate institutional and ideological connections between power and knowledge have contributed to a growing awareness of the diversity of mechanisms and modalities through which hegemonic relations are reproduced and contested. Deploying a variety of theoretical and methodological perspectives, Foucault (1973,1977,1980,1981), Escobar (1994), Said (1978,1993), Berman (1983), Asad (1973), Viswanathan (1989), Fisher (1980,1983, 1992), Gendzier (1985), Buxton (1985), Silva and Slaughter (1984), Huaco (1986), Rafael (1994), Lele (1993), and Gareau (1990), among others, have examined the reciprocal linkages between the exercise of power and the reproduction of specific systems of knowledge. Most of these studies have focused on the role of social scientific knowledge in the discursive construction of objects that become the sites of disciplinary and normalizing techniques and practices. In a more specific domain, a number of studies in the sociology of scientific knowledge have analyzed the complex and mediated linkages between natural scientific knowledge and power (Aronowitz,

*An earlier version of this chapter was presented at the World Congress of Sociology, organized by the International Sociological Association in Montreal, Canada, in 1998. I thank the Canada Research Chairs program funded by the SSHRC for generous financial support and time off from teaching to revise this chapter.

1988, Brown, 1993). Many of these studies have taken their analytical cues from Michel Foucault's inquiries into the nature of the relationship between knowledge and power. Based on extensive empirical studies, Foucault locates the emergence of specific fields of knowledge, such as criminology, clinical medicine, psychiatry, and the social sciences, in the context of an emerging "disciplinary society" with its associated mechanisms of power and social control over increasing numbers of people in specific institutional settings, such as schools, asylums, hospitals, prisons, and factories.

Michel Foucault's approach extends the scope of Max Weber's understanding of the increasing growth of instrumental rationality as a crucial and perhaps even dominant component of modernity. While Foucault himself was quite cautious in his analysis and did not seek to construct a cut and dried power/knowledge formula that could be applied to all settings, however, some of his more enthusiastic interlocutors have purged the element of ambiguity and ambivalence that were significant elements of the distinction between formal and substantial rationality invoked by Weber, Mannheim, and Foucault himself. Some of the excesses of the starry-eyed disciples of Foucault have ironically and possibly unwittingly contributed to a totalizing conception of power that envelops individuals from all sides, constituting subjects that are little more than "docile bodies" who lack any capacity for resistance. One need not accept the strong shade of pessimism in Foucault's own formulations, as evident in the famous debate with Noam Chomsky, in order to appreciate the methodological and indeed substantive value of his perspective in making sense of the complexities of the emergence of specific disciplinary knowledge and their intersection with the exercise of power, domination, and regulation.

Drawing upon the general analytical insights offered by the some of the writers discussed above, this chapter seeks to engage in a reflexive examination of some of the conditions of possibility for the emergence of one strand of "modernization theory" and its complicity with structures of power and domination. Given the existence of many excellent theoretical and empirical critiques of modernization theory, any further discussion might appear to be superfluous. As Irene Gendzier (1985) and Timothy Luke (1991: 272) have argued, however, while modernization theory may have been all but buried under the broadsides emanating from dependency and world-system theorists, it nevertheless constitutes the dominant worldview of policy makers and economists in many parts of the world; thus while modernization theory seems to have virtually disappeared in academic sociological discussions of development, the reverse is quite true when it comes to the assumptions underlying the strategies of major international development institutions, agencies, and organizations. Indeed, critiques of most of the theoretical suppositions of modernization theories have barely affected the policy-making and policy-implementing institutions and organizations. Most of these institutions continue to exhibit an inordinate amount of Comtean faith and confidence in the ability of positivistic social science to provide scientistic recipes for controlling and managing the trajectories of social change and economic growth on demand in various "developing societies."

In view of the fact that modernization theory continues to permeate the thinking and policy strategies of development experts, a critical and reflexive (Baber, 1992) look at the political and structural conditions that contributed to and sustained its emergence may help in understanding its appeal to theorists and practitioners of development policy. This chapter examines an extended period of engagement among social scientists formally affiliated with MIT, their counterparts in India, and Indian society. The aim of this chapter is to flesh out and unravel the structural and ideological conditions for the emergence of a specific element of modernization theory. The association of the MIT social scientists with the development process in India constituted a major element in what Arturo Escobar (1985) has called the "development of the discourse of development." In general, this chapter provides qualified support for the general arguments of Fisher (1980,1983,1992), Gendzier (1985), Escobar (1985), Luke (1991), and Leys (1982). Although the focus of this chapter is on a specific period and geographic zone of engagement between specific intellectuals and a specific society, the arguments advanced here have broader implications for a general understanding of the genesis and the role of "area study programs," as well as specific social scientific discourses (Lele, 1993).

The particular episode examined here involves the relationships among the social scientists associated with the MIT Center for International Studies (henceforth MITCIS), the Ford Foundation, the U.S. government and policy makers, and their counterparts in India between the early 1950s and 1970s. During the two decades of involvement, certain key American social scientists managed to convince the U.S. government that they were in a position to produce what Habermas (1971:309) and C. Wright Mills (1970) have called "instrumental" and "nomological" knowledge, respectively. The social scientists associated with the MITCIS had enormous faith in their ability to produce policy-relevant knowledge about South Asia. The assumption was that this kind of knowledge could presumably be used by the U.S. administration to direct the process of economic development and social change in accordance with its own strategic, ideological, and economic interests. Overall, then, this chapter examines the relationship among social scientists, the emergence of a particular theory of social change, and its connections with the larger social, economic, and political context.

## THE DISCOVERY OF UNDERDEVELOPMENT AND DEVELOPMENT

The genesis and development of "development studies," initially as a subdiscipline of economics, and later as a full-fledged field, occurred in the aftermath of the Second World War. The concept of "underdevelopment" as a problem did not emerge until around the 1940s, and up until this period there was an almost total absence of systematic theories that attempted to understand and explain the process and trajectory of change from underdeveloped to developed societies. Of course, a number of Western economists had been interested in the economy and social structure of the colonies, and this is hardly surprising, given the long history of colonialism. In the case of India, this interest, particularly by English economists, is evident in the title of Keynes's first book: Indian Currency and Finance. The work of Ambirajan (1978), Barber (1975), and Eric Stokes (1959) documents in further detail, the interest of English economists in the Indian economy and society. At that time, however, development studies as a formal and systematic subdiscipline had not yet emerged. By 1945 there were a number of universities in England in which courses on "colonial economics" were being offered, but there were no such facilities in the United States. As George Rosen (1985:19–20) points out, although several American universities were offering courses on South Asian culture and history, the economy of the region did not figure in the curriculum.

The depression, followed by the Second World War, served to focus the attention of American economists on issues related to development and underdevelopment. Both these events pointed toward the role of greater governmental intervention to effect substantial changes in the economy. In addition to these factors, the fact that the Soviet Union was quite unaffected by depression and had emerged as a major industrial power during the same period did not go unnoticed. In fact it was evident to the American economists that centralized planning had played a key role in the growth of the industrial base in the Soviet Union. Such an awareness prodded American economists and other social scientists to seriously consider planning as a possibility for effecting economic growth in nations identified as having a low industrial base and therefore been underdeveloped. Finally, the conception and eventual execution of the Marshall Plan in Europe after the war had imbued economists with a strong dose of confidence in the feasibility of redeveloping battered economies with the help of investment-related policies combined with the tools of economic planning. The overall effect of the depression, the war, and a fair measure of success in the execution of the Marshall Plan was to provide American economists with an unwarranted confidence in their ability to understand, explain, and control the trajectory of social change at the macro level (Rosen, 1985:26–27). To invoke Habermas's typology of three different forms of knowledge, economists came to acquire a high degree of faith in their ability to produce "instrumental knowledge" that could presumably help in predicting and controlling the process of social change along predetermined trajectories (Habermas, 1971:309).

## THE CONSTRUCTION OF SOUTH ASIA AS AN OBJECT OF DISCIPLINARY PRACTICES

In addition to the depression, the war, and the early success of the Marshall Plan, another key development made South Asia the center of attraction for some social scientists, the U.S. government, and the Ford Foundation. This was the Chinese Revolution of 1949. The Chinese Revolution, together with the gradual onset of the cold war, provided a convergence of focus on South Asia, and especially India. In many quarters of the U.S. administration and the Ford Foundation, the general sentiment was that the Chinese Revolution of 1949 signified a major "loss" for American interests. Most of them were convinced that unless some action was taken, there was a high probability of India following the Chinese example (Rosen, 1985:3–6). A number of steps for stalling such a development were explored and discussed.

In early 1951, Paul Hoffman, the first president of the highly expanded and newly reconstituted Ford Foundation paid a visit to India to explore the possibility of providing aid for "developmental" purposes. Hoffman, who had most recently been the administrator of the Marshall Plan, also wrote to his friend Chester Bowles (who was to become the U.S. ambassador to India) recounting the missed opportunity for providing such aid to China and its implication for India. Invoking the telling metaphors of disease and immunization against it, he wrote: "if in 1945 we had embarked on such a program [Rural Reconstruction Program in Formosa] and carried it on at a cost of not over two hundred million dollars a year, the end result would have been a China completely immunized against the appeal of the Communists. India, in my opinion, is today what China was in 1945" (cited in Rosen, 1985:11).

For his part, Chester Bowles, echoing the "domino theory" of the spread of communism, recounted that he was eventually persuaded to take the position of U.S. ambassador to India because: "If we lose India, as we have lost China, we shall certainly lose Southeast Asia with the repercussions running all the way through Africa. It is difficult under such circumstances to see how Japan could be held in line, and it would not be too long before we would find ourselves driven back into a 'citadel'" (cited in Rosen, 1985:11). After spending some time in India as the U.S. ambassador, Chester Bowles wrote to his friend Paul Hoffman of the Ford Foundation of his apprehension that

> the critical danger as I see it lies in the possibility that economic conditions may improve in China while the Indian situation remains stagnant....if such a contrast developed during the next four or five years...the growth of Communism in India might be great...another potentially strong Communist nation might be born...it is absolutely essential that the objectives of (the first Five Year Plan) should be attained....this will provide the essential strengthening of the Indian economy, and at the same time harden the Indian attitude towards the Communist threat (cited in Rosen, 1985: 15).

At about the same time, South Asia was emerging as an area of interest for economists and other social scientists in the United States and for roughly the same reasons that had attracted the attention of the U.S. administration and the Ford Foundation. Confident from their recent success with the Marshall Plan, these economists and social scientists were eager to actively plan and direct the process of "development" in South Asia in order to, as Hoffman put it, invoking the metaphor of disease and preventive medicine, "immunize" it from the appeals of communism.

A number of social scientists who were keen to offer their expertise for formulating policies and strategies to immunize South Asia from the specter of communism came together under the newly constituted Center for International Studies at MIT. Set up in 1951 with the economist Walt Whitman Rostow as its key figure, the center was conceived as part of a larger MIT effort to direct its research effort "toward problems affecting the national welfare [of the United States] in the current period of crisis" (Rosen, 1985:27). Although the MITCIS had already begun classified research on communist societies for the U.S. government, it also began actively exploring the possibilities of securing finances from private foundations for its proposed research on the theme of economic development and political stability in the developing areas. In the initial exchange between the MITCIS and the Ford Foundation—which was identified as a likely source of funds—the social scientists made it clear that "the ultimate aim of [all the nontechnical research]...will be the production of an alternative to Marxism" (Rosen, 1985:28).

In 1952, the economist Max Millikan quit his job as the director of economic research for the CIA and took up the newly created position of the director of the MITCIS. In one of the first formal proposals for funding to the Ford Foundation, Millikan defined the center's research program as "the application of basic social science research to problems of U.S. policy in the current world struggle" (Rosen, 1985:29). The same proposal identified the connection between economic development and political stability as the key area of research MITCIS would focus on. After a brief technical discussion of some issues relating to economic development, the specific ideological assumptions underpinning the goals of the MITCIS were clearly spelled out by Millikan. As he puts it

> the stable evolution of national societies towards effective democracy is probably essential to the establishment and maintenance of a world environment which will permit American society to evolve over the long run within the framework of its traditional principles and institutions...Economic development of the free nations...is obviously a prime determinant of their political stability. It is a determinant, moreover, on which U.S. policy and action has a major impact. It is, therefore, important for us to know as much as possible about the factors which limit and those which encourage such development (Rosen, 1985:30).

In the same proposal for funds, Millikan made it clear that the center's research would be policy-oriented. He pointed out that in the first instance the center would focus on "basic intellectual problems which really require the resources of a university for their solution." He was quick to specify the general orientation of the new institution, however, by asserting that "we should undertake no research that does not...grow out of the necessity to know something in order to be able to do something [about it]" (Rosen, 1985:30).

In this proposal, Millikan also indicated the MIT center's plans to supplement the studies conducted by economists with other forms of knowledge gained by the various disciplines of the social sciences. He hoped that the services of anthropologists and sociologists could be relied upon to conduct field studies of the village or the "microcosm." In later correspondence with the Ford Foundation, Millikan wrote that research at the center would aim to identify the "strategic factors" that determined a country's achievement. Elaborating further on this point, he noted, "By a strategic factor—(cultural, institutional, ideological, or administrative)—we mean both one that has an important effect in causing political and economic changes and one that can be influenced by the conscious policies of the governments of the countries, of the American government, of private organizations, or of international agencies" (Rosen, 1985:32). Once again, the importance of India for American policy was emphasized, and more so in view of the former's close relations with the Soviet Union. Finally, Millikan underscored the importance of presenting the results of the research conducted by MITCIS in such a way so as to create public support in the United States for "desirable American policies" (Rosen, 1985:32).

It should be evident that Max Millikan, a prominent academic economist and the then head of the MITCIS, was quite clear about his ideological position in the prevailing international context. He was also rather confident about the role and efficacy of social scientific knowledge in assisting the U.S. government and policy makers as well as private foundations in pursuing their interests. Finally, he was quite aware of the high degree of congruence of views between the intellectuals associated with the MITCIS, the government, policy makers, and the Ford Foundation. The ideological context in which a strand of development and modernization theory emerged can be gauged by the comments made by Walt W. Rostow quite a few decades after the center at MIT was set up. In a 1982 lecture, Rostow recalled the role of the Korean War in convincing Millikan and himself "that the struggle to deter and contain the thrust for expanded communist power would be long; and that new concepts would be required to underpin U.S. foreign policy in the generation ahead, quite aside from the task of dealing directly with the communist world. We believed that a portion of academic talent should be devoted to generating these concepts" (emphasis added; cited in Rostow, 1985:12).

By the 1960s, some of Rostow's now famous (or infamous) concepts—"takeoff," "self-sustained growth"—had become part of the standard repertoire of developmental economists and modernization theorists (Rostow, 1960).

## SOCIAL SCIENTIFIC KNOWLEDGE AND AMERICAN INTERESTS

The interest in South Asia was not limited to the Ford Foundation and social scientists at MIT. As mentioned earlier, the U.S. administration was also a key player in the attempt to develop immunity of a particular kind in India. In 1958, John F. Kennedy, then a senator from Massachussets, together with John Sherman Cooper, a Republican and former U.S. ambassador to India, introduced a resolution to the Senate. The Kennedy–Cooper resolution, as it came to be known, reads

> Resolved by the Senate (the House of Representatives concurring), that the Congress recognizes the importance of the economic development of the Republic of India to its people, to democratic values and institutions, and to peace and stability in the world. Consequently, it is the sense of the Congress that it is in the interest of the United States to join with other nations in providing support of the type, magnitude, and duration, adequate to assist India to complete successfully its current program for economic development (Congressional Record, 1958:4678).

The resolution was moved together with speeches from both Cooper and Kennedy. Kennedy's speech pleaded strongly for foreign aid for India's five-year plans, despite the fact that the Indian government had consistently been extremely critical of American foreign policy. Kennedy argued that the first five year plan in India (1951–1956) had demonstrated a capacity for progress, and went on to emphasize that its performance relative to that of China would have great political and ideological significance in the developing regions, and since the second five year plan (1956–1961) appeared to be headed for failure because of the shortage of foreign exchange, Kennedy urged the Congress for increased external assistance to India. Like Paul Hoffman of the Ford Foundation, Kennedy cited the success of the Marshall Plan in bringing about the reconstruction of Western Europe. He also attempted to address the fears of those senators who were critical of aid to a country that had close ties with the Soviet Union, that had an official policy of "neutrality," and that continued to be very critical of U.S. foreign policy. Kennedy urged fellow members of the congress not to be

> confused by talk of Indian neutrality...our nation also during the period of its formative growth adopted a policy of non-involvement in the great international controversies of the 19th century...Nothing serves the ultimate interests of all of the West better than the opportunity for the emergent uncommitted nations of the world to absorb their primary energies now in programs of real economic improvement...This is the only basis on which Asian and African nations can find the political balance and social stability which provide the true defense against communist penetration (Congressional Record, 1958:4679).

In the same speech, Kennedy also deflected criticism against providing foreign aid to a country that had embarked on five-year plans on the Soviet model and was spending more on public as opposed to private sector enterprises. His argument was that

> There is every reason to believe that future private investment in India will expand with the rise of Government assistance...Mr. G.D. Birla and Mr. J.R.D. Tata, perhaps the foremost exponents of private enterprise along western lines in India, have made it perfectly clear that the success of India's 5-year plan is essential if there is to be a sizeable increase in private investment...There are certain types of investments in underdeveloped countries—education, health, transport, fuel, and power—which private capital cannot underwrite. Yet they are essential to the creation of a setting in which efficient profitable private operations can grow (*Congressional Record*, 1958: 4678).

Finally, Kennedy specifically cited Walt Rostow's testimony (and used his signature concept of economic takeoff) to the Senate Foreign Relations Committee to argue that "India has passed the point of economic take-off and is launched upon an effort which will by the end of the century make her one of the big powers of the world...India today represents as great a hope, as commanding a challenge as Western Europe did in 1947" (Congressional Record, 1958:4678). The Kennedy–Cooper resolution was supported by a coalition of Democrats and liberal Republicans in the Senate, but it was rejected in the House of Representatives. In early 1959, Kennedy and Cooper tabled a revised concurrent resolution to the Senate, and on this occasion too, Kennedy's speech reiterated his earlier concerns. He emphasized that

> to nations in a hurry to emerge from the rut of development, Communist China offers a potential model. 1949 was their "round"...But 1959 could and should be our "round," our year...if we act now, on the right scale, in the right way, we may reverse the ever-widening gap — we may diminish the threat of a Communist takeover, and increase the chances of a peaceful evolution in India and other uncommitted, less developed areas (Kennedy, cited in Rostow, 1985: 158).

The proposed concurrent Kennedy–Cooper resolution reads as follows:

> Whereas the continued vitality and success of the Republic of India is a matter of common free world interest, politically because of her four hundred million people and vast land area; strategically because of her commanding geographic location; economically because of her organized national development effort; and morally because of their heartening commitment to the goals, values and institutions of democracy . . .
>
> Resolved by the Senate (The House of Representatives concurring), that it is the sense of Congress that the United States Government should invite other friendly and democratic nations to join in a mission to consult with India on the detailed possibilities for joint action to assure the fulfilment of India's second five-year plan and the effective design of its third plan. And that the secretary of state report to the Congress on the possibility of such a mission after consultation with interested governments and with the Republic of India (cited in Rostow, 1985: 158–1959).

As Rostow (1985:161) points out, much of the Kennedy–Cooper resolution was prepared in direct consultation with the economists at the MITCIS. After the concurrent resolution was tabled, the State Department raised some objections. One of these was the fact that Pakistan had been excluded from the resolution (Rostow, 1985: 161). Kennedy and Cooper agreed to make some changes in the resolution, and a revised version was presented to the Senate Foreign Relations Committee on July 14, 1959. The U.S. administration expressed cautious support, characterizing the revised resolution as a "purely exploratory measure and a useful one" (Rostow, 1985:162). In September 1959, the final drafting of the resolution was prepared with the help of Max Millikan, Paul Rosenstein Rosen (a British economist associated with the MITCIS), I. G. Patel (Indian economist, and until recently the director of the London School of Economics), Morarji Desai (the then minister of finance in the Indian government), B. K. Nehru (the then Indian ambassador to the United States), and Walt Rostow. Finally on September 10 1959, the amended resolution, substituting India with South Asia, was accepted without dissent in the Senate.

## ENGINEERING SOCIAL CHANGE IN SOUTH ASIA

So far I have discussed the views of the key officials of the Ford Foundation as well as some members of the U.S. administration about the changing international context and how they saw their role in encouraging a particular pattern of economic and political development in the developing areas. In this section, the focus will be on elaborating the view of the MITCIS as an institution. A couple of key documents put out by the center will be examined, and this will be followed by an evaluation of the degree of convergence of interests and views of these intellectuals, the U.S. government, and the Ford Foundation.

The first of these documents is a report originally prepared for a foreign policy conference at Princeton University in 1954. The letter of invitation sent out to the select participants at the proposed Princeton conference set the agenda in the following words:

> What the United States needs, in the development of its foreign policy, in its successful counter to Soviet expansion, in its determination to roll back communism by a peaceful means, is a bold, imaginative plan...a group of the best people we can find should sit down for a weekend to consider the broad shape such a synthesis should take...if a World Economic Plan contains those ingredients which will unmistakably add to the welfare and prosperity of this country and of the free world, the fact that the grass is indeed greener on freedom's side of the fence will cease to be merely an American statement, and become a reality (Jackson, cited in Rostow, 1985:245–249)

Among the select nineteen individuals invited to the Princeton conference were Edward Mason of Harvard, Max Millikan, director of the MITCIS, George Baldwin and Walt Rostow of MITCIS, Allen W. Dulles, director of the C.I.A., Lloyd Berkner, president, Associated Universities Inc., Abbot Washburn of the U.S. Information Agency, Thomas McKittric of Chase National Bank, and Robert Garner, vice-president, International Bank (Rostow, 1985:250–251).

At the Princeton conference Rostow and Millikan were asked to put together a paper outlining the linkages between the promotion of economic growth abroad and U.S. foreign policy. This report was further expanded with the help of other social scientists, such as Everett Hagen, Francis Bator, George Baldwin, Harold Issacs, and Ithiel Pool, and was eventually published in 1957 as A Proposal: Key to an Effective Foreign Policy. This report quickly became an important foreign policy document and was drawn upon by the U.S. administration for a number of years. Based on the accumulated knowledge of different developing areas studied by social scientists attached to the MITCIS, the thesis of the report was that a much expanded long-term program of American participation in the economic development of the underdeveloped areas can and should be one of the most important means for furthering the purposes of American foreign policy (Millikan and Rostow, 1957:1). It was envisaged that this program could be an effective instrument for achieving two crucial goals.

> (1) increasing the awareness elsewhere in the world that the goals, aspirations, and values of the American people are in large part the same as those of peoples in other countries; and (2) developing viable energetic, and confident societies through the Free World. We believe, therefore, that such a program could be a principal and effective instrument in our efforts to produce political, social, and psychological results in the national interest (Millikan and Rostow, 1957:2).

The authors of the proposal also cautioned that the program espoused by them would require U.S. government expenditure somewhat larger than the current spending for economic aid. This extra expense was justified, however, by the argument that "the amount of additional money needed would be small compared with what we shall have to spend in emergency efforts either to salvage situations which have been permitted to degenerate, such as South Korea and Indo-China, or to put out additional brush-fires if they got started. The total costs of such a program would be insignificant compared with the costs of waging limited wars "(Millikan and Rostow, 1957:2).

Overall, then, Millikan and Rostow's proposal promised to be cost-effective in promoting the development of underdeveloped areas according to the perceived interests of the United States. While it is impossible to go into all the details of the book, it is significant to note that Chapter Six, titled "The Stages of Growth," constituted the rough draft of Rostow's The Stages of Economic Growth: A Non-Communist Manifesto (1960). Overall, Millikan and Rostow's proposal identified the problems of U.S. foreign policy, the areas of study on which social scientists should focus, the institutions required to implement the blueprint for action, and finally an assessment of the levels of expenditure required to put the program in action.

The other key document that enables us to get some understanding of the worldview of the key intellectuals associated with the MITCIS is Max Millikan and Donald Blackmer's book, The Emerging Nations: Their Growth and United States Policy. Published in 1961 under the auspices of the MITCIS on a request from the Senate Committee on Foreign Relations, the book offers interesting insights about the assumptions and expectations of social scientists regarding the patterns of development in the "developing" societies. It also enables one to get some idea about the degree of rather Comtean confidence these social scientists had about their ability to control the direction and scale of social change in the developing areas of the world. The authors argue that the United States and other developed nations "must declare their hope of influencing the course of evolution of other nations with the consent and active participation of those nations themselves" (Millikan and Blackmer, 1961:132). Among other means and mechanisms, the authors suggest the need for "new apparatus and personnel and an unprecedented and skillfully co-ordinated use of the instruments of economic, military, and information policy" (Millikan and Blackmer, 1961:133).

In this book the authors also attempt to chart the process of evolution of underdeveloped societies form their "traditional" stages towards "modernity." They note that this transition from traditional to modern may go awry at times, or the resulting strains and lack of fulfillment of rising expectations may cause them to succumb to the "appeal of communism" (Millikan and Blackmer, 1961:102–104). The overall teleological evolutionary goal of "modernization" is never questioned, however, and the role of social scientists in both producing knowledge and directing the development of societies is outlined in the following manner:

> modernization is a dynamic process occurring through the interaction of the economic, political, social, and psychological forces in a society. Clearly, policy designed to have the maximum constructive influence on the course of modernization should coordinate every instrument of international policy...This is the time to help establish a wide variety of data-collecting and statistical-reporting procedures—surveys and projections of man-power, education, health, agricultural conditions, and resource availabilities...They can be designed to serve a double purpose: to provide essential information to the new governments and to put us in touch with a larger number of elements of the indigenous society. They will be crucial to more ambitious development efforts later (Millikan and Blackmer, 1961:136).

In this passage, the relationship between power and knowledge (or to use Michel Foucault's term, power-knowledge) should be evident. The above passage also clearly indicates that the authors conceived of social science and capable of producing what C. Wright Mills (1970) and Habermas (1971) have labeled "nomological" and "rational instrumental," respectively.

It is clear that the development of the discourse of development can be located in a particular social, economic, and political context. More specifically, the social scientists associated with MITCIS focused on the developing areas for a number of reasons. These ranged from a direct and self-conscious effort to produce knowledge that could be of use for the policy makers within the U.S. government to the creation of what Bourdieu and Passeron (1977) have termed "cultural capital" or what Ben Agger (1991: xi) has called "career capital." Although not all the rank-and-file social scientists associated with the MITCIS might have been self-consciously engaged in the process of reproducing the hegemony of the United States vis-à-vis the developing areas, their research invariably led to the production of knowledge that policy makers within the U.S. government believed could be used to direct the process of social change in these areas.

The key intellectuals involved in setting up the center had a specific conception of their role as intellectuals, and the nature of social scientific knowledge, and possessed a tremendous amount of confidence in the utility of this knowledge in influencing the course of social change in South Asia, thus such social scientists as Max Millikan, Rostow, Everett Hagen, and Lucien Pye actively sought to engage the U.S. government and the Ford Foundation with the MITCIS in order to coordinate the production of knowledge that they believed was necessary for U.S. interests and the perpetuation of global capitalism.

## CONCLUSION: POWER AND ITS LIMITS

While "modernization theory" has been criticized many times over, usually on logical, methodological, or empirical grounds, the focus of this particular chapter has been different from such critiques. One particular case has been examined to lend further support to the arguments of such other scholars as Irene Gendzier, Timothy Luke, and Arturo Escobar that a specific discourse of modernization and development emerged in the context of the cold war and the perceived needs of the U.S. government to combat the spread of communism. It was in this context that a group of eminent social scientists were able to convince some key actors within the U.S. government and the Ford Foundation about their ability to produce knowledge and theories that could be put into practice in directing the development of certain countries so that it would not be incompatible with what was perceived to be the interests of developed nations.

Although it is not claimed that the factors discussed above can provide an exhaustive explanation regarding the emergence and development of modernization theory, there seems to be little doubt that this particular case constituted one episodic element of a much larger process. Although elements of modernization theory continue to inform the practice of most agencies engaged in "development" projects, however, most of their actions seem to be based on an undemonstrated and unwarranted assumption of their ability to completely control and direct the process of social change in the developing areas. Consequently, while Foucault's writings are helpful in making sense of the emergence of the discourse of modernization and development studies, discourses may not always be as powerful, and developing and underdeveloped societies may not quite be the docile bodies that some of his more enthusiastic and uncritical followers seem to believe. Such an uncritical acceptance of developing societies as passive docile bodies comes out clearly in Timothy Luke's conclusion that

> For a "non-modern, non-developed, non-metropolitan, non-core society," the processes of "modernization" or "development" unfold as normalization and through sur-veillance and quiet coercion...These modern truths invalidate or subjugate the indi-genous knowledge of local culture, time and technology.... Acting under the directive discourse of development and within the disciplinary grids of the world economy, the national leaders of LDCs can only retrace the discursive leads of power/knowledge in imitative enactments of normalization, which prevent their peoples from becoming the individual subjects they might have been or from retaining the traditional subjectivity they have by inducing them to become normalized global subjects they actually are not (Luke, 1991:292).

Although Luke addresses the issue from quite a different political spectrum, his argu-ment displays the same unwarranted belief in the powers of discourse of moderniza-tion as exhibited by Walt Rostow and others associated with the MITCIS. Luke's conclusions further reproduce a theoretically and politically naive image of the "na-tional leaders of LDCs [less developed countries]" who cannot help but "retrace the discursive leads of power/knowledge in imitative enactments of normalization." As Wole Soyinka (1991) has argued in the context of Africa, the reality of the ravages of colonialism and imperialism notwithstanding, such reasoning, coupled with populist rhetoric, has been constantly appropriated by some "nationalist" leaders and intel-lectuals of LDCs to legitimize many oppressive policies and practices at home.

In the context of India, many intellectuals find it more comforting to point out the colonialist roots of almost all social problems without reflecting on the complex-ities of the role of contemporary agents and evolving social structures (Baber, 1998, 2001). As Aijaz Ahmad (1992:196–1967) has accurately and acutely observed, "colonialism is now being blamed not only for its own cruelties, but conveniently enough for ours too."

Although Luke's arguments are presented as a critique of the discourse of development, he seems to invest too much faith in the powers of positivistic social science to control the social world, and he seems to have too little faith in the resilience of such cultural constructs as "traditional subjectivities" and "traditional knowledges," which in any case hardly ever existed in their pristine, static forms.

Finally, he has ignored the unintended consequences of the application of the "discipline of modernity" to the developing societies. One should therefore be cautious against reading too much instrumentalism in the production of knowledge for the purposes of exercising power over and controlling the process of social change in developing societies. While there is no doubt that such intellectuals as Rostow and Millikan were consciously manipulating and hoping to direct the process of social change of South Asia in a particular direction, other social scientists saw MIT's India Project as nothing more than a good opportunity to accumulate "career capital." In the final analysis, Rostow and Millikan's endeavor seems to have been rooted in an unwarranted confidence and belief in Auguste Comte's positivist slogan: "Savoir pour prevoir, et prevoir pour pouvoir."

## REFERENCES

Agger, B. (1991). Why theorize? Curr. Persp. Soc. Theory 11:ix–xii.

Ahmad, A. (1992). In Theory: Classes, Nations, Literatures. London: Verso.

Ambirajan, S. (1978). Classical Political Economy and British Policy in India. Cambridge: Cambridge University Press.

Aronowitz, S. (1998). Science as Power: Discourse and Ideology in Modern Society. Minneapolis: University of Minnesota Press.

Asad, T. (1973). Anthropology and the Colonial Encounter. London: Ithaca.

Baber, Z. (1992). Sociology of scientific knowledge: Lost in the reflexive funhouse? Theory Soc. 21(2):105–119.

Baber, Z. (1998). Communalism and the nostalgic imagination in India. J. Contemp. Asia 28(1):27–44.

Baber, Z. (2001). Orientalism, occidentalism, nativism. The European Legacy 7(6):747–758.

Barber, W. (1975). British Economic Thought and India, 1600–1858: A Study in the History of Development Economics. Oxford: Clarendon.

Berman, E. H. (1983). The Influence of the Carnegie, Ford and Rockefeller Foundations on American Foreign Policy: The Ideology of Philanthropy. Albany: State University of New York Press.

Bourdieu, P., Passeron, J. (1977). Reproduction in Education, Society and Culture. London: Sage.

Brown, R. H. (1993). Modern science: Institutionalization of knowledge and rationalization of power. Soc. Q. 34:153–168.

Buxton, W. (1985). Talcott Parsons and the Capitalist Nation State: Political Sociology as a Strategic Vocation. Toronto: University of Toronto Press.

Congressional Record. (1958). 85th Congress, Second Session. Vol. 104. Washington, DC.

Escobar, A. (1985). Discourse and power in development: Michel Foucault and the relevance of his work to the third world. Alternatives X:377–400.

Escobar, A. (1994). Encountering Development: The Making and Unmaking of the Third World. Princeton; NJ: Princeton University Press.

Fisher, D. (1980). American philanthropy and the social sciences in Britain 1919–1939: The reproduction of a conservative ideology. Soc. Rev. 28:277–315.

Fisher, D. (1983). The role of philanthropic foundations in the reproduction and production of hegemony. Sociology. 17:206–233.

Fisher, D. (1992). Fundamental Development of the Social Sciences. Ann Arbor: University of Michigan Press.

Foucault, M. (1977). Discipline and Punish. London: Allen Lane.

Foucault, M. (1973). The Birth of the Clinic. London: Tavistock.

Foucault, M. (1981). The History of Sexuality. Harmondworth, UK: Penguin.

Foucault, M. (1980). Power/Knowledge. Brighton: Harvester.

Gareau, F. (1990). The political economy of social science: Where the trail leads. Internat. J. Compar. Soc. 31(1–2):49–66.

Gendzier, I. (1985). Managing Political Change: Social Scientists and the Third World. Boulder, CO: Westview Press.

Habermas, J. (1971). Knowledge and Human Interests. Boston: Beacon.

Huaco, G. A. (1986). Ideology and general theory: The case of sociological functionalism. Compar. Stud. Soc. Hist. 28:34–54.

Lele, J. (1993). Orientalism and the social sciences. In: Breckenridge, C. A., van der Veer, P., eds. Orientalism and the Postcolonial Predicament. Princeton, NJ: Princeton University Press, pp. 45–75.

Leys, C. (1982). Samuel Huntington and the end of classical modernization theory. In: Alavi, H., Shanin, T., eds., Introduction to the Sociology of "Developing Societies." New York: Monthly Review Press, pp. 332–349.

Luke, T. W. (1990). Social Theory and Modernity. Newbury Park, CA: Sage.

Luke, T. W. (1991). The discourse of development: A genealogy of "developing nations" and the discipline of modernity. Curr. Persp. Soc. Theory 11:271–293.

Millikan, M., Blackmer, D. (1961). The Emerging Nations: Their Growth and United States Policy. Boston: Little, Brown.

Millikan, M., Rostow, W. W. (1957). A Proposal: Key to an Effective Foreign Policy. New York: Harper and Brothers.

Mills, C. W. (1970). The Sociological Imagination. Harmondsworth, UK: Penguin.

Rafael, V. L. (1994). The cultures of area studies in the United States. Soc. Text 41:91–112.

Rosen, G. (1985). Western Economists and Eastern Societies: Agents of Social Change in South Asia, 1950–1970. Baltimore: Johns Hopkins University Press.

Rostow, W. W. (1960). The Stages of Economic Growth: A Non-Communist Manifesto. Cambridge: Cambridge University Press.

Rostow, W. W. (1985). Eisenhower, Kennedy and Foreign Aid. Austin: University of Texas Press.

Said, E. (1978). Orientalism. New York: Pantheon.

Said, E. (1993). Culture and Imperialism. London: Chatto and Windus.

Silva, E., Slaughter, S. (1984). Serving Power: The Making of the Academic Social Science Expert. Westport, CT: Greenwood Press.

Soyinka, W. (1991). Africa's culture producers. Society 28(2):32–40.

Stokes, E. (1959). The English Utilitarians and India. Oxford: Clarendon Press.

Viswanathan, G. (1989). Masks of Conquest: Literary Study and British Rule in India. New York: Columbia University Press.

# 7

# Development as a Multidimensional Concern

**NOORJAHAN BAVA**

*University of Delhi, Delhi, India*

## INTRODUCTION

Theoretical and empirical research studies and academic attempts at theorizing the concept of development in the past, present, and future have had to encounter the highly complex, dynamic, multivariate, multidimensional, and protean nature of development, resulting in scholars facing dilemmas related to its conceptualization. It would do well, therefore, to keep in mind the complex nature of development. Although it is true that the term development per se was not always used either in academic discourses, debates, and discussions or as the specific objective, goal, and value of governments' policies and administration, that does not mean that the human mind was unaware or unconscious of its need or importance. As a matter of fact, until sociologists (the first among social scientists) consciously and deliberately used the term development in their writings, scholars referred to the same notion by different names, such as progress, evolution, civilization, welfare, prosperity, and well-being. Even sociologists grappling with the problem of societal development gave up the usage of the "more dangerous" concept of development in favor of the "less dangerous" concept of social change. Since the eighteenth century four different concepts have been used to denote change in human society: progress, evolution, development, and modernization (Bava, 1993)*.

　　The idea of progress belongs to the post-Renaissance period of European history, more specifically to the eighteenth-century Enlightenment, when it was believed

---

*Professor Bava is retired.

that mankind could progress through the use of reason and science. In the nineteenth century, the notion of evolution surfaced when Spencer propounded the theory of social evolution. It held the view that human societies such as Darwin's naturally evolving species had a history of structural differentiation and functional specialization, and that those societies that did not follow the path of evolution would be left behind, become "inferior," and would soon be conquered and dominated by those that were at the vanguard of the evolution. History is replete with instances of how Spencer's theory of social evolution led to legitimization of colonization and the "white man's burden" of carrying on the evolution of backward and "retarded" colonial societies into its completion.

Development has been a key concept of social reality since 1945. With the emergence of the Third World nations following their liberation from the shackles of colonialism and imperialism, the concept of development was launched with full vigor and determination. Development has become the center of politics, administration, international relations, and trade the world over. In the last fifty years, immediately before the dawn of the twenty-first century and third millennium, the usage of the term development has conjured up images of prosperity, social harmony, social security, universal participation, mass literacy, and improvement in the living conditions of the poor, weak, and downtrodden. Development continues to reign supreme as the most desirable value of humanity, the focal point of human endeavors, and a chief objective of the governments of both developing nations and national and international bodies, such as the United Nations. Since the mid-1950's the term modernization has been in vogue as the mainstream theory of development, which is discussed in the section on approaches to development

The currency of the concept of development shows that it is not a "static" term, but has been changing with the march of human civilization. National development in the nineteenth century meant the building of a modern nation-state characterized by industrialization, and structural-functional differentiation. It also included new organizational forms, such as corporations in business, factories in industrial production and bureaucracies in public administration, capitalism based on private enterprises, and political democracy under the system of constitutional and representative government.

Many significant changes took place in the world in the period between the two world wars (1914–1939). These were: the technological revolution, comprising the technical and managerial parts; institutional shifts from individualism to collectivism following the establishment of the USSR in 1917, offering an alternative model of development based on Marxism–Leninism; and the emergence of the Third World. As a result, the nature of development objectives became much broader and more complex. Democracy came to be redefined to include not only political and economic democracy, but also freedom from want, hunger, disease, and ignorance. The "police" state gave way to the "welfare" state; a laissez-faire economy was replaced by a state-planned and -regulated one in which the "administrative" state performed multiple roles. In the changing environment, the earlier notion of development, meaning economic growth (i.e., an increase in the Gross National Product per capita) was rejected. Since the 1970s development objectives came to include: (1) equitable distribution of wealth and income, (2) full utilization of manpower, (3) better utilization of natural resources, and (4) protection of the human environment. The cumulative effects of the great changes have been the addition of social, political, and environmental dimensions of development to the originally restricted economic notion of development. New aspects, such as development as peace, sustainable development, and human rights realization, were born.

## NATURE OF THE CONCEPT OF DEVELOPMENT

### Development: A Difficult Term to Conceptualize

While a clear theoretical definition of the concept of development is imperative for meaningful analysis and resolution of any of its challenging problems, it is important to remember that there is no universally acceptable definition of the concept. On the contrary, scholars are unanimous in their perception that development is not an easy term to define. All exercises to bring the concept within the four walls of a definition have opened a Pandora's box. There is considerable confusion about the meaning of the term and the appropriateness of the models for ordering this elusive phenomenon. This explains why in discussions on development there is often an immediate redefinition in terms of another concept, such as progress, civilization, evolution, westernization, industrialization, modernization, economic growth as measured by increase in GNP per capita, self-sustained growth, structural differentiation and functional specificity, institutionalization, social mobilization, participation, social change, democracy, justice, liberty, and equality, or a shift to consideration of the requisite conditions, goals, or impact of development (Bava, 1993).

Sometimes attempts are made to overcome the problem by ignoring it and concentrating instead on specific case studies in which the meaning of the term is assumed to be self-evident. As Gunnel (1970) warns, no mere accumulation of case studies will in itself lead to an "adequate understanding" of development or produce a "viable concept," and if the concept of development is to be adequately delineated, it needs to be supplied with "substantive content" and yet apply in "cross-national and cross-cultural contexts" and encompass diverse goals and areas of endeavor, in both the public and private realms.

To speak meaningfully of development, some preconditions are essential. First, the issue of development must be placed in a wider perspective and context of social change within which any notion of development must inevitably be conceived, for if development is anything it is an aspect of social change (Gunnel, 1970). If development, development polity, development administration, or developing/developed economy are to become substantive concepts, however, they need to be defined narrowly to include certain instances of social change and exclude others. This is why, for example, equating development with "structural differentiation" is ultimately "unsatisfactory" in the view of Gunnel (1970). Differentiation and integration may be attributes and indicators or characteristics of development, but they do not meaningfully distinguish it from other forms of social change. Nathan Shamuyarira (1976) draws attention to the "dysfunctional" consequences of factionalism, instability, and chaos produced by increasing "differentiation" and "institutionalization" in such pluralist societies as Nigeria and Zaire.

Second, a meaningful discussion of development and its challenges calls for a broad global perspective (Webster, 1984; Waldo, 1977) and an understanding of the role of the highly unjust, unequal, and exploitative international system (Frank, 1969). The colonial and imperial policies of some developed industrialized countries of the

West were responsible for the poverty of the former colonial societies, which became new nations after the attainment of political freedom. Poverty is not a natural objective condition of any society; on the contrary, poverty is man-made. The continuing poverty in developing nations is augmented by the industrialized Western nations controlling the World Bank, International Monetary Fund (IMF), and the World Trade Organization (WTO), and the policies of privatization, liberalization, and globalization.

## Development: A Value-Loaded Concept

Another difficulty with the concept is that development is value-loaded, and value-based, involving value judgment in terms of both quality and quantity. In terms of quality, development implies improvement of some over others—improvement of the present product or source over the past or of some country over another. In terms of quantity, it is more in an arithmetic or a linear sense (Bava, 1993). It also involves the concept of "catching up" between the top group that has all the wants and so faces an endless void ahead of it, and the other groups—the lowest one which wants to catch up with the higher group like the developing countries trying to catch up with the developed ones. This paradigm applies to all countries regarding their economic and social systems (Adiseshiah, 1966).

   Lin (1976) rightly points out that there have been no value–free approaches or value–free definitions in the realm of development since there never existed either in practice or in theory a development approach that objectively accorded with the interests of all social sectors. Being value–centered development has given rise to many approaches, theories, and paradigms (Bava, 1981; 2000), which are discussed in the next section.

## Development: A Protean Concept

Development is a protean concept, appearing differently to different people. It looks increasingly "perplexing" for Fred W. Riggs (1966), and "elusive" to George Gant (1979), and it has "invidious implications" for Ferrell Heady (1966). Literally, develop means "to take out of an envelope." From the standpoint of the modernization theorists the envelope consists of traditional society and its cultural moorings, values, and traditions. These are looked upon as obstacles to change and development and as the fount of backwardness (Beck, 1988). The transformation of traditional society into a modern (industrial) one is regarded as development by some.

   For Edward Weidner (1977) development is fundamentally an equalitarian goal. It is equalitarian among the peoples of the world, and it is equalitarian "within a given people" (within different segments and regions of a nation). He also defines development as a state of mind—growth in a particular direction—but it is not an end state; it is never complete.

   One of the most prolific model builders of comparative public administration, Fred W. Riggs (1976), defines development as a "process of increasing autonomy (discretion) of social systems, made possible by rising level of diffraction." While "discretion" is the ability to choose among alternatives, diffraction refers "to the degree of differentiation and integration present in a social system." Of the twin elements of development, differentiation indicates the presence in a social system of a specialized structure for the performance of every function in a particular society. And integration is the presence of a mechanism to tie together, to link up, to mesh, or to coordinate the various kinds of specialized roles. Higher levels of differentiation and integration represent the diffracted (developed) society, whereas if a society is highly differentiated but poorly integrated, it is prismatic (undergoing development).

Riggs also observes that the level of differentiation in any society depends upon technological and nontechnological factors. The higher the development of technology, the higher the level of differentiation. Integration in any society depends on two important factors; namely, penetration and participation. While penetration is the ability of a government to make and carry out decisions throughout the country, participation denotes the willingness of the citizens to submit to laws and help carry out the laws and policies of the government. In turn, participation, depends upon two conditions: the willingness of the people to participate and the ability of the people to participate in the management of public affairs.

In Riggs's (1964) classification of societies into fused, prismatic, and diffracted models, the functionally diffused society is the traditional society (fused), which ranks high in terms of the "pattern variables" of particularism, ascriptive values, and functional diffusion. At the other end of the spectrum stands the modern, developed (diffracted) society, which ranks high in universalism, achievement orientation, and functional specificity. At the midpoint between the fused and diffracted society, stands the prismatic or developing society, with the pattern variables of selectivism, attainment, and polyfunctionalism. The prismatic society is characterized by three features; namely, heterogeneity, formalism, and overlap.

For George Gant (1979) development means "a condition of life, a goal to be achieved and the capacity to grow, change and develop." A Third World sociologist, M. S. Gore (1988), is of the view that development by definition is not a predetermined end state. It is on the one hand a process of improvement of levels of living. It is at the same time a process of hierarchization. There is no static duality of developed and undeveloped; there is a continuous grading of more developed less developed, and least developed. He says that at the core of the concept of development is the idea of achieving a state of relative affluence, not just attainment of a predetermined standard of adequacy in meeting life's needs. Needs being elastic, they increase with affluence. Development therefore implies a notion of achieving higher and higher levels of consumption. In this sense it has the potential of being insatiable, and therefore exploitative. At the same time it must be recognized that this insatiability is often the driving force behind the hard work, innovation, and technological progress achieved by the developed nations. It is also at the root of wars.

## Development: A Multivariate, Multilevel, Umbrella Concept

The concept of development has both normative and empirical referents. While some tend to see the former, others highlight the latter, but the fact is that both foci are interdependent and mutually reinforce each other. Development is a truly "umbrella" concept involving many aspects: political, legal, administrative, social, economic, cultural, environmental, psychological, physical, mental, intellectual, moral, material, spiritual, individual, group, rural, urban, local, subnational, regional, national, international, and global, and with both quantitative and qualitative dimensions. Development is indeed a multidimensional, interdisciplinary concept, progression toward which calls for the adoption of a holistic, integrated, comprehensive, and multidisciplinary methodology and approach since it is (development) is the mother of the social sciences.

Public policy and administration has emerged as the integrated social science (Bava, 1993). The public administration perspective is the interdisciplinary, integrated social science perspective (Bava, 1993; 2000). Public policy making on development and administration of development policies, plans, programs, and projects are the core areas of development administration. The formulation, implementation, and evaluation of development policies are multidisciplinary exercises calling for pooling of inputs of knowledge of all the sciences—social, natural, physical, and chemical-taught at the college level, as well as resources within a nation and between nations.

## Development as Human Ascent and Human Rights Realization

To Mahbub-ul Haq (1995) human welfare is the overall objective—the essence of development. Increased income should be regarded as a means to improve human welfare, not as an end to itself. Increased incomes and national economic growth are crucial preconditions for improvements in standards of living, but not the only preconditions (Martinussen, 1997).

The ultimate goal of development is human ascent (Bava, 1993). Development is another name for humanism, human development that encompasses development of all humans—women, men, children, people who belong to different societies, nations, races, ethnic groups, linguistic and religious groups, rich, poor, native and tribal people, and minorities. Development is liberation not only from political subjugation, but it is also freedom from hunger, disease, malnutrition, illiteracy, ignorance, superstition, and so on. It means restructuring the contemporary inegalitarian social order into a new society in which there will be full realization of all human rights—political, economic, social, and cultural—for all human beings, irrespective of age, gender, race, caste, class, complexion, nationality, and religion. The ushering in of a genuine democracy—social, political, cultural, and economic, wherein there will be intrinsic value and dignity of life, justice, freedom, and equality and opportunity (for personality development) for every human being—constitutes development from the human rights perspective.

From the human rights perspective (Bava, 1997) it is essential to ensure the development of women, who constitute half the population of any society and the world; the all-around growth and development of children by protecting and enforcing the childhood and personality development rights of every child; and the protection of the rights of the economically and socially weak, the poor, the downtrodden, the handicapped, widows, victims of crime, the aged, and the diseased, in order to bring them on par with the mainstream through affirmative action by the government.

Human resource development is an integral part of the human rights approach to development. Some thinkers (Gore, 1988) do not regard human beings as a "resource." The tendency to look upon development as a material good to be possessed or a state of material well–being to be achieved by a society is likely to lead us to look upon human beings as instruments, as a resource to be used to achieve social development. In a humanistic perspective, the human being is real, and society is an abstraction. The growth of the human being and the satisfaction of his needs is the goal. Society provides the context within which the content of such development is perceived and can be realized. On the contrary, such writers as Peter Drucker view human beings as the precious "human capital" of a society. Development of the human resource is considered essential for the economic, social, political, and cultural development of every society.

## THEORIES, APPROACHES, AND PARADIGMS OF DEVELOPMENT AND ITS DIMENSIONS

Being a time–honored and value-loaded concept in the social sciences and a perennial issue of humankind, development has spawned many varied approaches, theories, and paradigms (Kuhn, 1962). Szymon Chodak (1973) has identified the following approaches and theories: (1) theories of social change, (2) theories of development as a growing systemness, (3) theories of motivation and security, (4) theories of economic and political development, and (5) theories of modernization. I would like to expand the list by adding the following new approaches: (1) the Third World's perspectives on development, (2) the concept of sustainable development, and (3) the human rights and human resource perspective on development.

### Theories of Social Change

Theories of social change include four broad groups of theories, including evolutionary, linear, revolutionary, and cyclical theories.

#### Evolutionary Theories

According to evolutionary (also known as organismic, histiosophic) approaches, development or social change and progress is the result of natural evolutionary process. The concept of development (Harris, 1967) subsumes the essential evolutionary ideas of organism conceived as living systems; time; movement over time toward complexity of organization; hierarchization; and an end state of organization (equilibrium) that is maintained with stability and self–regulation.

Chodak (1973) admits that Harris's is a "good example " of an evolutionary interpretation of the idea of development, but he quickly adds that there are other definitions promoting evolutionary, organismic approaches. According to these definitions development is one or a combination of the following: a spontaneous process of gradual evolution toward higher stages of organization; a process of exteriorization of a potentiality and of the realization of an embryonic capacity in a unilinear process of maturation; a process of continuous structural–functional transformation, proceeding as a result of greater specialization and structural differentiation; and a self-generating, complex, ongoing process of change, containing factors inevitably and subsequently producing even more complex structures and interactions. A close look at these definitions would reveal their four diverse leanings. The first definition is based on a purely evolutionary understanding of the concept; the second on a genetic understanding; the third on a structural–functional understanding; and the fourth on the elements of inevitability and determinism.

*Critique.* It is difficult to agree with the evolutionary conception of development as a product of evolutionary, natural forces. First, it assigns an inactive, passive role to the human beings in society in the process of their own development and promotes a wrong feeling of fatalism among them. Second, it runs counter to the actual practice and empirical experience in developing countries in which development is a predetermined policy goal consciously and deliberately planned and implemented by the people and the government. Third, human intellectual development is the interplay of reason, science, pursuit of power, wealth, glory, fame, security, and achievement have been responsible for human progress.

The evolutionary conception of development, including Spencer's ideas, directly contributed to the rise of the structural–functional approach in the social sciences during the behavioral movement. Talcott Parsons in sociology, David Easton and Almond and Powell in political science, Fred W. Riggs in public administration, and others spun theories of development based on functionalism, which may be a characteristic of development, but it is not development per se.

## Linear Theories

Comte, Spencer, and Hobhouse are the most significant theorists of the linear type of social change (Bava, 1981). The linear approach emphasizes that change occurs in a linear or spiral fashion, the process of which involves several stages, levels, or states, each one unfolding to the next, and each an improvement over the last.

Comte (1898), the founder of sociology and positivist philosophy, ardently believed in the concept of human development and the possibility of directing it by means of science, especially by means of the positivist philosophy. He held the view that the development of humanity was the natural offshoot of the development of nature. He defined development as consisting of the intellectual and moral self-perfection of man and his increased humanization. He believed that with self–perfection mankind would propound perfect, more complex, and higher philosophies and approaches to life, polity, society, economy, and culture, and in the process rationality would increasingly prevail over emotionalism, altruism over egoism, and knowledge over ignorance. Comte identified three stages in the process of development of mankind: the theological, metaphysical, and positivist. Each of these stages is not a "different era in the history of humanity but a stage in the progressing capacity of the human mind and the growing complexity and interdependence of the world directed by man" (Chodak, 1973).

Taking into consideration the phenomenal advancement of science in the last half of the twentieth century that resulted in the harnessing of nuclear energy for constructive and destructive purposes, the revolutions in communications (information technology) and computers, the discovery of the human genome, and the advancements in human health, one tends to agree with Comte that the highest stage in the march of development is the positivist one wherein science will rule the roost.

Herbert Spencer viewed society as an organism comparable to a biological organism, and identified development with evolution, and characterized the processes, that led to new types of structures (biological and social), as "unilinear, spontaneous and continuous growth." His ideas not only led to the rise of structural–functionalism in the social sciences, but also the legitimization of colonialism and the white-man's burden, which played havoc in the non-Western world.

## Revolutionary Theory of Social Change

Marx viewed development as the dialectic, historical, and inevitable unilinear process of societal transformation involving various stages. He viewed development as an ongoing complex process of growth in a sequential transformation that leads spirally from lower to higher stages of matter, substance, and organization. In the process it resolves the contradictions, especially those of the class struggle, through revolutionary change, resulting in the perfection of the "mode of production" and the self-perfection of man himself. Marx asserted that as societies undergo change, the dominant mode of production emerges—slave, feudal, capitalist, or socialist. Each new and higher mode of production signifies a new and higher level or stage in the history of the development of mankind. In the Marxist perspective development also means an ongoing expansion of production; that is the continuous and sustained economic growth arising out of the increasing application of functional rationality and scientific knowledge. Marxism asserts that development is goal-oriented (i.e., the revolutionary overthrow of the capitalist economy, polity, and society by the Proletariat), that development or goal attainment is a historical inevitability, and above all that political development cannot take place independently of economic development, for the economy is the base and everything else—the polity, administration, society, culture, law, religion, and so on—the superstructure.

It is a well–known fact that Lenin and Mao Zedong—who came to power through revolutionary overthrow of the feudal regimes in Tzarist Russia and China, respectively—had to introduce a number of revisions and changes in the Marxist doctrine in order to make it an operational creed. These include many changes: (1) stages in the process of development, such as that of the capitalist society, may be bypassed or skipped entirely, (2) scientific socialism (communism) can be planned and achieved as a result of deliberate, planned development even with a feudal mode of production, (3) while Marxism is a macro theory applicable to the whole of humanity, the followers of the high priest admitted that it is possible that while some societies turn socialist, others remain feudal or capitalist, and (4) instead of being demolished or allowed to "wither away" the state can be used to bring about planned economic development. The state thus has to be maintained, even in postcapitalist societies. In China, a predominantly peasant society, the peasants, farmers, and farmworkers would lead the revolution under the vanguard of the revolutionary Communist Party led by Mao Zedong, Zhou Enlai, and others to establish the peoples' democracy of China by overthrowing the feudal, exploitative, and unjust regime. Mao's ideas of the Cultural Revolution and the commune system of rural government and economy represented the revisions that he effected on orthodox Marxism.

To the extent that Karl Marx believed that the process of social change involved a series of stages inevitably moving in a linear manner—from primitive to slave; feudal; capitalist, to socialist, and the corresponding socialist mode of production—it is possible to treat him as a linear social theorist, but it is wrong to consider him as an evolutionary social theorist because Marx strongly advocated revolution, the use of naked force and violence to overthrow the exploitative capitalists, landlords, and moneyed classes. Marx was thus a great revolutionary social theorist.

After the demise in 1989 of the erstwhile Soviet Union, the bastion of the Communist model of development, and the subsequent collapse of its satellite allies in Eastern Europe, there is no practical example of a communist country or communism as an ideology in the twenty-first century. Marxism will remain as a theory or philosophy in the social literature, however.

## Cyclical Theories

When human societies became more complex because of industrialization, mechanization, and structural differentiation, the concept of evolutionary social change was challenged, and cyclical theories were advocated by many, including Pareto, Sorokin, and Toynbee.

The notion that "civilization" is development is the contribution of history. Cyclical change theorists believe that every civilization passes through periods of genesis, growth, development, zenith, decay, and death in a cyclical manner. There is strong archaeological evidence today showing that the highly developed Indus Valley civilization existed some 5000 years ago and the ancient Chinese, Egyptian, Babylonian, and Assyrian civilizations also belonged to the same age, followed by the Greek and Roman civilizations. It is widely believed that they all met their ends; because of such natural factors as torrential rains and floods, earthquakes, climate changes and other unknown reasons. There is a strong possibility that the contemporary civilization that began in the eighteenth century may meet with the same end if a nuclear war breaks out or the great threats to the Earth from persistent and growing environmental disasters, such as the shrinkage of the ozone layer caused by increased greenhouse gases, climate change, and so on, are not averted imminently.

## Aspects of Social Development

The relevance of various social change theories lies in conceptualizing social development as something more than merely economic, political, social, and environmental development (Gore, 1973). It does not denote the limited sectoral target achievements as is often provided in national development plans for economic, physical, infrastructural, educational, and health and welfare targets of growth and expansion, but social development planning requires "the perception and delineation of the nature of inter-relationships between the different sectors. Social development is an integrative concept and this integration depends upon clear enunciation of the values and the type of society" toward which planners, policy makers, and the people of a particular society would decide to shape and usher in. Depending on the decisions taken by the government, social development can take place within the framework of a democracy or any other political system. In military dictatorships in some developing countries, the ruling dictator or the junta speaks of planning for social development.

The re-examination and rejection of the concept of economic development as an increase in economic growth as measured by per capita GNP in the 1970s by Third World scholars and the United Nations has led to its broadening and inclusion into the concept of social development. The concept of social development includes economic development, but differs from it in the sense that it emphasizes the development of the totality of society in its economic, social, political, administrative, and cultural aspects. Social development planning in the above sense does not mean planning only for social welfare services. On the contrary, social development encompasses other socially relevant policy domains, such as population policy, industrialization policy, urbanization policy, rural/urban development policies, environmental protection and prevention of ecological decay and degradation policy, regional development policy, income growth and income distribution policy, land reform and agricultural development policy, education policy, health policy, housing policy, development policies for women and children, the poor, downtrodden, and handicapped, and disabled persons, and eradication of poverty, unemployment, and inequality from societies.

From the perspective of social development, planning has to be done in an integrated and simultaneous manner for all the above areas and not in a fragmented or piecemeal fashion in which economic development comes first and is later followed by steps to ensure distributive justice through a modified income policy or an extended network of tax-supported social and welfare services.

At this juncture one can anticipate a poser or two: Is rational-comprehensive decision making at all necessary? Given the general trend of incremental decision making is it possible in democratic market-oriented societies? Our response to the questions is "yes." In my perception decision makers in democratic and market-oriented societies may do well to keep the comprehensive approach to social development in mind, for it would greatly help avert lopsided and imbalanced development, such as economic growth with unemployment or growth with poverty or environmental pollution. It would also prevent both the waste of valuable resources and social costs. Even in developing countries, most of which are not market economies, the government cannot leave the power of making vital decisions to the market forces in all matters of economic development on the grounds of wider common good, public interest, and national interest.

Development administration based on a holistic approach to social development calls for a number of steps. First, the government policy makers, planners, administrators, and experts must adopt and operationalize the concept of long- medium-, and short-term planning for development. Second, they have to assess the priority needs of their country and people, and the availability of resources at all levels of the internal and external environment. Third, the integrative orientation must be kept at the center stage in all the interfaces of the decision-making process—planning, formulation, implementation, monitoring, and evaluation of development policies, plans, programs, and projects. Last but not the least, in a democracy political leaders in government, parliament, and political parties, administrators, enlightened citizens, advocates of nongovernmental organizations, civil society groups, and the media must carry out midterm review and impact studies. Such evaluations may help the project administration to effect midcourse correction steps, including jettisoning of a project, enforcement of accountability, and prevention of cost and time overruns that result in an escalation of scarce resources and delay.

I agree with the view that social change is a product of both "endogenous and exogenous" factors, such as decisions based on the free will of persons in authority as opposed to the "inevitability" notion of the evolutionary perspective. Among the other factors are the influence of material factors and ideas, cultural contacts, conquest, revolution, growth of knowledge, technological inventions, industrialization, and social conflicts (Ogburn, 1922). I also concur with the view of Chodak (1973) that the historisophic and evolutionary interpretations of the idea of development are "Euro-centrically biased," although they make references to "other cultures and civilizations" in the early stages of evolution of humanity or culture. It is not difficult to see that the presumed universal laws and rules of historical inevitability as proclaimed, established, or anticipated within the evolutionary theories of societies are the "interpretations of European history." I reject the view that development is the inexorable march of Westernization to the nondeveloping world. It does not answer the question as to why the presumed laws of historical inevitability and the sequential stages in the change process did not manifest themselves to the same extent in the non-Western world or why the industrial revolution originated in Western Europe and not in other parts of the world. I also question the notion that "humanity and culture" are constituted as a single whole and not as separate organisms. There is historical evidence to show that cultures and civilizations developed separately and evolution of cultures of different societies differed more than they resembled one another.

According to Indian sociologists Srinivas, Seshiah, and Parthasarathy (1976), all those concerned with social change in India would have to address many dimensions of social development as concepts and methods, mobility, and stratification of society. Further, one must look at the reservation policy of the government for removal of both inequality and discrimination against women, scheduled caste and scheduled tribes, and backward classes in the field of education, government (public) employment, and political decision-making bodies (i.e., Parliament, state legislatures, panchayats, and municipal bodies). They also stress the need for affirmative action for the disabled, handicapped, war widows, and ex-serviceman; religion and change; rural social change; family, socialization, and change; communications and change; and civil society and development.

## Development as Growing Societal Systemness

Theories that view development as growing systemness discuss various social processes such as industrialization, urbanization, increasing communication, greater mobility, changing cultural patterns, and transformation of pattern variables on which the social structure is based or simply the changing character of social structures. Yet taken together they explain various aspects of one great process of transformation or movement in societal structure and in human relations, interactions, and interdependencies (modernization?). They identify factors such as industrialization, increased productivity, intensified urbanization, spread of education, increased social mobility, changing social division of labor, greater specialization, and changing cultural attitudes, and tell us how these transform the ongoing process of greater mutual interdependence of the individuals and the units, and of the agencies and subsystems of society. Finally, they explain how greater interrelatedness emerges between various societies of the world (i.e., growing societal interdependence and systemness) (Chodak, 1973). Those who subscribed to this view included Charles Cooley, Ferdinand Toennis, Durkheim, Max Weber, Talcott Parsons, and Edward Shils, to mention the most important ones.

According to the growing systemness perspective (Smelser, 1968) the ongoing process of growth of social systemness is "irreversible and directional." System development implies continuity, in which the pace of social development is not steady or rhythmic but in fact uneven and sometimes even invisible and at other times "frozen," and at still other times advancing in transformations, innovations, and transitions. Growing systemness does not, however, mean a movement toward an equifinality or predestination; it cannot be explained by technology; nor is it a process of unfolding a potential capacity of the various attributes of the progenitors of humanity of a given society. In each society, at each level of development decisions taken by planners, policy makers, and people bring about the next step in the growing systemness. Nothing is preordained. It is evident that developing societies are moving toward greater complexity and increasing systemness.

Under the influence of the above theory some system analysts (Hozelitz, 1960; Riggs, 1964) treated development as a continuum, as a transition from traditionalism to modernism, and from an agricultural society to an industrial society using the "pattern variables" of Talcott Parsons and Shills. Theories that view development as growing societal systemness do not discuss the development of humanity, the culture of mankind in all societies or areas, or the cumulative effects of continuity, or build bridges between past, present, and future of all societies at all times. They compare and contrast preindustrial and industrial periods, developed and developing, and traditional and modern societies (Chodak, 1973). As a rule, they apply dichotomies, that expose the contrasting features of such societies and the systems within them by means of descriptions, pattern variables, models, and the like. These are not theories strictly on societal growth and development.

The systems approach, however, is a powerful and useful theoretical framework for analyzing societies—past, present, and future—polities, administrations, economies, and cultures. It is an interdisciplinary and holistic approach to study and analyze any phenomenon in the real world in terms of such system parameters as groups of units or parts, the interdependence between parts, the interaction of parts between them, and the environment, boundary, structures, role, and functions.

## Motivational and Security Approaches

### Theories of Motivation and Security

Motivational theories explain the causes rather than the meaning of development. Max Weber (1958) thought that Europe became the cradle of industrialization because of the spirit of capitalism fostered and nurtured by the Protestant work ethic. Everett Hagen's (1962) theory of "status withdrawal" emphasizes that development or modernization can occur only where natural conditions can be found and both society as a whole and the individual in it have a burning need for change and innovation. David Mc Clelland (1961) sought an explanation for economic development in the "achievement syndrome." He says "the higher and wider the spread of the achievement motivation, the more likely that economic development will be intense."

Barry Buzan (1991) and others think that the quest for development begins with the quest for security, which in their opinion is the most common important enough social development. Today the state in developed and developing countries has to be concerned with development and participation, as well as security (Chai-Anan, 1991). It is concern for security—individual (personal), familial, neighborhood, state, national, and international—that has compelled contemporary states to embark upon scientific innovations, research in military weapons, arms, ammunitions, and the arms race between states on a scale that is a great threat to world peace. The threat of Pakistan to use nuclear weapons in its war against India over the Kashmir issue and the ongoing terrorism in Jammu and Kashmir is a case in point. International terrorism, which struck the United States on September 11, 2001, underscores the paramount importance of national security and the threat it poses to international peace and security. Development and peace are indivisible, and they mutually reinforce each other.

### Security and Peace Aspects of Development

Policy makers and planners of development at the national and international levels have to take into account various aspects of security. This includes national security, entailing such issues as disarmament, total elimination of nuclear weapons, peace initiatives, commitment to cooperate with the United Nations and its international agencies, and conflict resolution through negotiations, dialogues, and peaceful means. Next comes food security, which involves increasing food production, building buffer stocks, moving grains in a timely fashion to areas hit by droughts, floods, famines, and scarcities, and protecting and preserving food grains in warehouses by food administration. The health security of its people is an essential function of every government, including drinking water supply, sanitation, hygiene, health care, immunization and control of diseases, prevention of environmental pollution, and preventive and curative treatment for AIDS/HIV. Last but not the least, come social security for the physically and mentally disabled, the old, pensioners, ex-service personnel, war widows, orphans, and the destitute.

The achievement orientation emphasized by this approach is relevant to all societies for all times to come since it is an important facilitating factor of development. It motivates individuals, groups, societies, and nations to strive hard and achieve their values, goals, and purposes in personal and public life. It is the chief driving force behind great achievements, such as political independence from colonial rule, political and economic development, scientific inventions, new technologies, and spectacular leaps of mankind into space and medical sciences.

Likewise, the understanding that development and peace are indivisible and both goals are mutually reinforcing is very relevant for achieving a peaceful world. The idea that development is peace and security has to be at the center stage of public policies of all civilized governments. Such a perspective motivates the government to plan and execute programs not only for national security but also for other types of security.

## Economic and Political Development Approaches

### Theories of Economic Development

The theory of development has always remained at the center stage of economics and political science. Far from treating development as a spontaneous evolution, economists and political scientists view it as a goal–oriented activity.

While among classical economists—Adam Smith and others—the champions of laissez-faire equated economic development with capital formation, Marx identified it with the socialist system ushered in through the revolutionary overthrow of the capitalist state. Such neoclassical economists as Alfred Marshall and Pareto identified it with the stability and continuity of the capitalist system and the positive role of the state in the regulation of the market economy.

Joseph Schumpeter, who like Marx predicted the decline of capitalism and its succession by socialism, distinguished between "economic growth" and "economic development". Growth is a product of cumulative changes brought about by the material and nonmaterial forces of production. It is steady, continuous, and slow, whereas development, which is the effect of technological and social factors and to some extent economic growth, is discontinuous, disharmonious, uneven, cyclical, and unstable. Technological change is the determining factor and the entrepreneur is the propelling force of economic development.

In the 1950s and 1960s the economic development theories that were based on the experience of Western developed countries viewed development as economic growth measured by increasing GNP per capita. This limited definition and ethnocentric conceptualization of economic development became the dominant approach to the development policies pursued by both developing nations and the United Nations in the 1950s and 1960s. These theories followed the "stages" that all nations will pass through and believed the same unilinear growth process. Walt Rostow (Rostow, 1962), who regarded technological innovations as the crucial variables of economic development, distinguished only five stages of economic growth; namely, the "pre–Newtonian" or "traditional", "transitional", "takeoff", "maturity", and "mass consumption" stages. The common denominator for this categorization is the rate of saving and investment. Rostow defines the takeoff stage as one in which the rate of effective saving and investment will rise from 5% to 10% and more. At maturity it will become 10–20% of the national income, and at the mass consumption stage the economy will shift toward durable consumer goods and services and the capitalist state will have the policy options and choices to pursue international peace, develop a welfare state, or further increase consumption.

The classical economists interpreted development as only economic and equated it with economic growth that is, an increase in national income or GNP per capita. In other words, the output of the economy of a nation (i.e., GNP) is determined by the input (say, capital) as multiplied by its productivity or efficiency as measured by the output–input ratio. These economists further thought that economic development should be left to the market mechanism (market forces) to guide the economy to reach the optimum point and the role of the government in development should be minimal.

The early economic development theories argued for a high degree of state intervention in economic development processes, however, as the state was required as the engine of growth and economic transformation (Martrinussen, 1997). The structuralist economists, such as Rual Prebisch (1984), Furtado et al. (1972), and Myrdal (1968), focus on external factors as determinants of the development process. Economists such as Lewis (1955), Nurkse (1953), Rodan (1943), Rustow (1967), and Hirschman (1958) place themselves between the structuralists and neoclassicists. They hold the view that the economy can develop through sustained accumulation of capital since there can be a certain automatic spreading and trickling down of economic growth in the long run. At the same time, however, they recognize the need for structural reforms and conceive development as a discontinuous process with different stages.

As mentioned earlier, the narrow view of economic development as increase in per capita and national income has been rejected and the concept has been broadened to include social development. This happened in the 1970s. Since then social development is recognized as being closely related to economic development and refers to the improvement in the general well-being of the people, which in the ultimate analysis, is the objective of development. It is measured by the level of welfare, including not only the reduction of disease and poverty, but also the states of physical, mental, and social health and the standard of living (i.e., the level of satisfaction of the material needs of the population in terms of the per capita goods and services available at a given period of time).

A latest dimension of economic development is human resource development. The human being is the greatest and most important "Human capital." In order to develop human capital, investment in education, training in skills and capabilities, health, and housing, the fulfillment of the basic needs of life are essential. This should be part of the policy of the government towards infrastructure development, since no private sector company or enterprise would come forward to invest large and intensive capital for the long gestation periods involved in human development.

Meier (1989) defines "economic development as a process whereby real per capita income of a country increases over a long period of time while simultaneously poverty is reduced and the inequality in society is diminished".

Another dimension of economic development is the eradication of poverty, the creation of full employment opportunities for all able-bodied citizens, and the removal of inequalities, regional disparities, and disabilities of persons and such segments of the population as women, and poor, backward, and disabled people. Economic development also means sustainable development; that is, it should be planned in a manner that it is harmonious with the conservation of natural resources. This means that it doesn't cause environmental pollution, decay, and degradation, and that it makes provisions for future generations to meet their basic needs.

## Theories of Political Development

The idea of political development is as old as Plato and Aristotle, the founding fathers of political science who in their magnum opus—the Republic and Politics respectively—raised fundamental and perennial issues relevant to human society at all times and in all places. The substance of Plato's work is justice, which even today is relevant and stands at the center stage of the concept of development. Similarly, Politics shows ways of creating and maintaining an ideal (developed) state. Aristotle reminds his readers that man is a moral being and the state, which arises from the needs of man, continues to exist to promote the "good life" in society. He also warned that inequality in society would cause revolution. In the burgeoning literature on political development spawned between 1960 and 1976, American and Western political scientists used the term mainly to perform a "legitimizing" function. Huntington (1965) and Dominguez (1965) opine that the term political development has been used in four different senses: geographical, derivative, teleological, and functional. In the geographical sense it denotes the politics of the developing nations of Asia, Africa, and Latin America. The derivative usage links it with political modernization. Teleologically it denotes movement toward one or more goals for the political system. The goals may be simple or complex, one or many, including democracy, stability, legitimacy, participation, mobilization, institutionalization, equality, capability, differentiation, identity, penetration, integration, bureaucratization, security, peace, welfare, justice, and liberty. As Ferrel Heady (1979) says, there is no commonality among these goals but they indicate the value preferences of the political scientists who selected them.

Bava (1981) writes that theories of political development show three distinct approaches; namely, the structural–functional, the social process, and comparative history. In the view of Huntington, the structural-functional approach is weak in change, the social process is weak in politics, and the comparative history approach is weak in theory.

## Aspects of Political Development

Lucian Pye (1966), of the comparative history school, has equated political development with the political requisite of economic development, politics typical of industrial societies, political modernization, operation of the nation-state, administrative and legal development, mass mobilization and participation, building of democracy, stability and orderly change, mobilization, and power. Pye's development syndrome consists of "equality, capacity, and differentiation."

Within the systems approach, Gabriel Almond and Bingham Powell (1966), the ardent advocates of the structural-functional framework, view political development as an increase in the capabilities of the political system for successful adaptation to meet such challenges as state and nation building, the participation of organized groups in decision making, and welfare—demands, that may emanate either from the international environment or domestic society or from political elites within the political system itself. They conclude that political development is a cumulative process of structural and zonal differentiation, subsystem autonomy, and the secularization of political culture, the significance of which lies in the effectiveness of the political system and its increased capabilities.

Huntington (1965) has conceptualized political development as the "institutionalization of political organizations and procedure". A well-institutionalized polity, he says, would be marked by high levels of adaptability, complexity, autonomy, and coherence. The strength of political organizations varies with their scope; that is, the extent to which they encompass social activities and their level of institutionalization (i.e., the process by which they acquire their value and stability).

Karl Deutsch (1961) identified political development with social processes like industrialization, westernization, commercialization, mass education, and social mobilization, while such comparative historians as Eisenstadt, Barrington Moore, and Reinhard Bendix sought to compare the nature of evolution of two or more societies through both space and time.

Theories that view political development as political change distinguish among componential change, crisis change, and complex change. Huntington, identifying himself with componential change, believed that the relationship between political participation and political institutionalization should be taken as the central focus of political change. In Huntington's perception a political system consists of five components: culture, structure, groups, leadership, and policies. A clear understanding of the totality of political changes calls for the study of changes deep in each of the five components and the relation between changes in one component and changes in another.

While Almond and Rustow, the followers of crisis change, emphasize the choice to be made by the political leadership, Ronald Brunner and Garry Brewer associate political change with a complex amalgam of a number of significant demographic, economic, and political variables that could open before policy makers a vast field of choices for achieving the objectives they consider desirable. To Helio Jauguribe (1973), political development is an amalgam of both political modernization and institutionalization. In the view of Leonard Binder, developing polities are confronted with five types of crises of political development; namely, identity, legitimacy, participation, penetration, and distribution.

An important contribution of various theories of economic development is the widening of the concept to include not only an increase in GNP per capita, but also various dimensions of social development, including an increase in the well-being of people, sustainable and humane development, gender equality and justice for women, and political, economic, and social empowerment of women, marginalized sections of society, and minorities. Such a comprehensive connotation of environment-friendly, humane socioeconomic development will be a useful focus for planners and policy makers everywhere.

The ongoing economic liberalization policy of privatization, marketization, and globalization as a universal model of economic development for all countries, however, including the low-income countries, is biased in favor of the rich nations controlling the Wold Bank, IMF, and the WTO. As far as the level of economic development of developing nations is concerned, it is not on par with the developed countries, and as such these countries are not yet ripe for implementing economic reforms. Under such circumstances developed countries have to transfer more financial resource, give more trade-related concessions, and share the latest technology with the less developed ones.

It is worth remembering that today the most widely accepted definition of political development is the ushering in of a modern, secular, democratic polity in which there is constitutionally elected, responsible, responsive, good governance; rule of law; and fundamental rights and freedoms for all citizens, including the right to equality, justice, and progress through the increasing participation of people in the institutions and processes of governance and development.

## The Modernization (Mainstream) Approach

The paramount importance and need for development in the newly independent nations after the Second World War made the think tanks in the universities of United States and Western Europe evolve a development theory that because of its dominance was called the "mainstream version." Such critics of the mainstream theory as Lehman (1979) and Preston (1985) pointed out that the mainstream theory had a close resemblance with the socio economic studies published at the end of the nineteenth and beginning of the twentieth centuries, when traditional ideas and institutions of Western Europe underwent great changes in the wake of the industrial revolution, modernization, and urbanization. The theories of Spencer, Durkheim, and Weber were reformulated with an eye on the developing countries, especially in North American universities. It is here that the idea for the development scenario of the Third World calling for the replication and repeat performance of the Western model of development was born (Bava, 1993).

When sociologists came out with theories of modernization and viewed development as a wave against traditionalism and feudalism, political scientists—Apter, Myron Weiner, Black, Rustow, and Welch (1966–1967)—equated political modernization with the building of modern states, secular polity, democracy, liberty, equality, justice, participatory decision making, and so on. At the same time economists associated economic modernization with industrialization, urbanization, migration, mass literacy, transportation, communication, high growth rate in GNP, manipulation of technology, and social mobilization. The central features of the modernization theory are as follows:

1. Secularization of the value system by imparting a rational sociopolitical culture
2. Modernization of society through
   a. Devaluation of historical traditions
   b. Adoption of modern Western behavior patterns and communication of Western values and ideas
   c. Urbanization as the surest path of development
   d. Inculcation of cosmopolitan attitudes among people through mass media

3.  Economic growth by promotion of industrialization and marginalization of the tradition-ridden agricultural sector
4.  Nation building, with the state as the prime mover of development
5.  Priority for urban elites

Critics of the mainstream model challenged its relevance for Third World development by saying that far from aiming at the authentic development of the new nations it was designed to promote westernization in these countries. Some of them suggested an alternative: a program of full human development for all to forestall political protest movements in reaction to the model in developing countries. Increasing occurrences of coup d' etat and establishment of military dictatorships in some Asian, African, and Latin American countries were cited as proof of the failure of the first-generation leaders in their quest for modernization.

## Third World Perspectives

### Western Theories of Development: A Critique

Before enunciating their perceptions and perspectives on development, Third World scholars, thinkers, and statesmen subjected the Western theories of development to a close scrutiny in the context of the challenges that developing nations have had to encounter. Their critique can be summed up as follows. The Western theories of development are highly "ethnocentric," woven around the American paradigm of behavioralism, structural–functionalism, and system theory. The Third World rejects the action that the Western experience is the only consummated development experience and the only possible path to development everywhere today because it overlooks history prior to the eighteenth century and outside the Western world. The assumption that there was no political development prior to eighteenth century and the process began particularly after the French Revolution in 1789 and the industrial revolution in England is a travesty of historical facts (Arora, 1976). Shamuyarira (1976) and Inayatullah (1967) challenge the Western presumption that all history is inexorably moving toward the same destiny, goals, and value system, as the Western man has, and they take the West to task for conveniently ignoring the vast span of technological development before this period that traditional societies had developed and transmitted to Western societies. Samir Amin (1976) brings out the unequal development that took place and is taking place between the developed, industrialized, capitalist countries and the developing, economically poor nations. The American political scientist Huntington joins the issue when he raises the pertinent question: "if political development was merely to reflect the present state of western societies and it was assumed that all societies were to move in the same direction, what could one think of the Chinese, Greek, Roman, and Indian and other highly developed political systems in ancient time?"

More criticisms of Western theories of development were put forward by Indian and African scholars. While D. L. Sheth calls for a comparative theory of state and nation building, Shamuyarira focuses on the dysfunctional consequences of factionalism, instability, and chaos produced by increasing differentiation and institutionalization in such ethnic pluralistic countries as Nigeria and Zaire. Admitting that modernization is a powerful model of historical growth, equally shared by liberals and Marxists alike, its weakness lies in its "historicist teleological and apolitical nature," says Rajni Kothari (1976), who gives a call for a "linkage model" for the fulfillment of the values of freedom, justice, and democracy. Such Latin American scholars as Andre Gunter Frank, and Marcos have advanced development theories such as dependency. They point out that the center/metropolis was promoting capitalist development on its soil at the cost of economic underdevelopment of the periphery/satellite colonies, which led to the dependency of the latter. Jose A. Silva Michelena, another Third World scholar, questions the equilibrium, stability, and homeostasis assumptions of the model, rejects it for its incapacity to be the explanatory theory of social and political development, and calls for the study of historical processes with an integrated perspective. Challenging the division of societies into "developed" and "developing" and the linear view of development, Ralph Brainbanti (1977) advocates the "contextual nonlinear" approach. He calls for change in the context of profound comprehension of a cultural past, its existing social organization, its economic realities, and the psychic needs of the people.

## Third World Conceptions of Development

Nasir Islam and George M. Henault (1979) echo the development thinking of the Third World nations when they write that during the last three decades the notion of development has moved away from a narrow, largely economic conceptualization toward a wider, all-encompassing, socioeconomic one. New development thinking has shifted from industrialization to agriculture, from urbanization to rural development, from market-determined priorities to politically determined basic needs, from GNP per capita to individual welfare, and from top-down planning to participative planning.

Doh Joon Chien (1977) and Bava (1993) opine that the Third World has to examine the issue of mass poverty afresh and search for indigenous solutions to its problems. The time for parroting borrowed solutions from the West is over, for the Western model gives primacy to materials, systems, and institutions and treats growth in GNP, modernity, and system change as ends in themselves, whereas in fact they are only means to an end. The Western line of thinking needs to be rejected in favor of the alternative of people's development, with its emphasis on the provision of a minimum accepted standard of living for the vast majority of people, who are poor and underprivileged and live in developing countries.

Malcolm Adiseshiah (1970) succinctly sums up the development thinking of the Third World as follows:

> Development is a function of a series of variables and not just of the economic variables of industrialization, urbanization, international trade, and national income level; but also of the enlightenment variables of schooling, literacy and media exposure; the power variables of participation, party membership and voting; the personality variables of motivation, need achievement and sympathy; the cultural variables of local temporal aspects of socio-cultural behavior and the ecological variables of population, organization, environment and technology together with the principles of interdependence and differentiation.... Development must thus be conceived in a holistic, organic, dynamic, valuational manner. Its planning requires human centered approach.

In another place Adiseshiah (1977) reflected the perspective of developing nations in the following words: "Development is measured by the extent to which the skewed distribution of factor ownership is corrected by the number of people who are lifted above the poverty line by education, health facilities and housing provided to them, by the range of employment generation, by economic growth, price stability, political participation by the unorganized and disinherited majority and by cultural progress."

As Jagannadham (1978) observes, development is neither "unilinear" nor "uniform." Each country and culture has to discover its strategic growth factor. It has to assess its leads and lags and see that the former is able to take the latter along in the march to the goal.

Bava (1984) shares the perspective that development does not mean the maintenance of a social order in which there are glaring disparities among people arising from concentration of economic power, wealth, and resources in the hands of few people in society, leading to meaningful realization of freedom and equality only for those few who own such resources and the denial of these rights for the vast multitude who do not. As Dudley Seers observes, inequality cannot be really reduced as long as property ownership is heavily concentrated. An economic system with a large number of undernourished and unemployed people at the bottom end of a long social ladder can never provide a firm basis for political or civic order. A sociopolitical-economic system in which there is inequality, poverty, and unemployment and hence no scope for dignified human life for all people, can never be regarded as a developed society. In her perception not even a welfare state can be regarded as a developed one since in such a state the claim to dignified human life becomes a "concession" and not a matter of right. In her perception, development does not mean the use of violence and bloody revolution to create a just and equal society, however, for ends do not justify means and means are as important and must be as good as ends; man is a moral being, and observance of morality in public and private life is essential for an enduring system.

## Latin American Dependency Theories

The dependency theories propounded by Latin American scholars also form part of the Third World perspective on development. The most well known and oft-quoted dependency theorist is Andre Gunder Frank, whose contribution lies in two directions: a critique of the modernization theory and his metropolitan-satellite paradigm of development and underdevelopment. Frank showed that the modernization theory advocated by Hoselitz, Marian Levy, Everret Hagen, and Mc Clelland in particular was "theoretically inadequate, empirically untenable and practically incapable of stimulating development in the Third World."

In his book Capitalism and Underdevelopment, Frank came to the conclusion that it was the incorporation of national economies into the world capitalist system that led to development in some areas and underdevelopment in others. Following Baran and Sweezy (1968), he stressed that it was utilization of the surplus that caused development in the metropolitan area and underdevelopment in the satellite areas. The world capitalist system was characterized by metropolis-satellite structures wherein the former exploited the latter. This has resulted in the expropriation of the actual surplus of the underdeveloped (satellite) by the developed (metropolis) and prevented the satellite nations from realizing their potential surplus. He argued that the monopoly structures that existed at all levels—from international to the national and local—created a situation of exploitation that in turn caused a 'chainlike' flow of surplus from the remotest Latin American villages to Wall Street.

The satellite tended to be increasingly dominated by the metropolis as well as increasingly dependent upon it. The strength of this dependency might vary from time to time. A weakening might occur when the metropolis experiences such crises as depression or war, and some development might take place within satellite country during such crises. He concluded that the weaker the metropolis–satellite relations, the better the development prospect for the satellite. He also pointed out that the development of underdevelopment that had taken place in the periphery had continuously accentuated another fundamental contradiction of capitalism–that of continuity in change. That is why the development strategies formulated by the U.N. appointed Economic Commission for Latin America were meaningless.

Since there is no single uniform dependency perspective among its proponents (i.e., Furtado, 1965; Sunkel, 1993; Cardoso, 1972; Faletto, 1979) Blomstrom and Hettne (1984) have abstracted six dimensions of the dependency syndrome. These include holism vs. particularism, external vs. internal, economic vs. sociopolitical analysis, sectoral/regional contradiction vs. class contradiction, underdevelopment vs. development and voluntarism vs. determinism.

## Sustainable Development and Human Rights Approaches

### Sustainable Development (SD) Theories

Since the 1970s a new and an important dimension and approach has been added to the concept and process of development, sustainable development (SD). The rate and pattern of economic development and the unbridled economic growth pursued by developed and developing nations have led to a sort of rat race to plunder the Earth's limited natural resources, particularly the nonrenewable ones, the mineral and fossil fuels on which the current technologies depend, which result in a severe depletion of natural resources on the one hand and serious ecological imbalances and environmental degradation on the other ranging from soil erosion, desertification, deforestation, floods and droughts, and air pollution, to shrinking of the ozone layer, pollution of the world's oceans and lakes, global warming, climatic changes, and so on. What the planners and policy makers of economic growth failed to realize was that growth is often illusory and the prosperity and welfare that it is expected to generate is transitory since the apparent gain in income means a permanent reduction in the stock of environmental assets. The conventional national accounts as an indicator of long-term sustainable economic growth do not reflect the diminished potential for future production caused by the depletion of nonrenewable resources.

Conceptions of SD are many and varied. The term sustainability is derived from the Latin word sustainere, meaning to hold up/to endure and has been interpreted differently by different scholars. Whereas to the agricultural scientist SD means maintaining the momentum of the green revolution, to the ecologist it means a way of providing sufficient food and other goods without degrading natural resources. To the economist it stands for efficient long-term use of resources, to the sociologist and anthropologist it is that pattern of development that preserves traditional values, including care and concern for preservation of natural resources, and to the political scientist it signifies the broader, environmentally harmonious, enduring development that ensures intergenerational, intragenerational, and intergender equity and justice.

Sustainable Development is a process in which development can be sustained for generations—that form of development that affords to the future generations the same, if not more capacity and resources as to the present generation. The concept of SD thus espouses a pronounced concern for accountability, ethics, morality, cultural mooring and ethos as well as environmental stewardness—the protection and survival of the blue spaceship, the planet Earth with all its complex and diverse living organisms.

In its human development report of 1991, the United Nations Development Program (UNDP) defines SD as "development that improves health care, education and social well-being. "Such human development is now recognized as critical to economic development and to early stabilization of the population. It also states that "men, women and children must be the center of attention with development woven around people and not people around development." In its 1992 report, the UNDP defined SD as "a process in which economic, fiscal, trade, energy, agriculture and industrial policies are all designed to bring about a development that is economically, socially and ecologically sustainable". In its report "Our Common Future," the World Commission on Environment and Development (also known as the Brundtland commission) conceptualizes SD as "development that meets the needs of the present without compromising the ability of the future generations to meet their own needs."

Development and conservation of nature are synergic since development cannot subsist upon a deteriorating environmental resource base and the environment cannot be protected when growth ignores the costs of environmental destruction. These problems are linked in a complex system of cause and effect, and as such cannot be treated separately by fragmented policies. An integrated, holistic, comprehensive approach is at the center stage of SD, as Engel and Engel (1990) state. It is the moral, ethical, legal, and political responsibility of every human being, society, polity, economy, and culture, international organizations, to protect and preserve the living planet Earth for promoting SD everywhere.

## Human Rights Approach

The human rights approach to the conceptualization of development has been covered. In addition, the SD approach also involves the integral and intrinsic dimension of human development, which in our view is the result of human rights' fulfillment and realization. We would like to avoid repeating these facts here.

From the first Human Development Report in 1990, which is prepared under the leadership of Mahbub-ul-Haq, the UNDP criticized the income measurements and presented a more comprehensive concept of human development (UNDP, 1990). The report defines "human development as a process of enlarging people's choices." At first the focus was on three essential areas of choice: the opportunity to lead a long and healthy life, the opportunity to acquire knowledge, and the opportunity to have access to the resources needed for a decent standard of living. To these were later added opportunities for political freedom and human rights, human development for women as well as men, environmental and other aspects of sustainability, and opportunities for citizen participation to effect political decisions in society.

What was originally launched as an alternative goal of development in this way (Martinussen, 1997) gradually became a new framework for research as well as development cooperation- the new paradigm for sustainable human development (Haq, 1995; Banuri et al., 1995).

## CONCLUSION

The time-honored issue of development raised thousands of years ago is still being pondered today. It is one of the great and important concepts in social sciences around which a number of theories have been propounded. The debate and discourse on development is as old as the dawn of human consciousness. There is historical, literary, archaeological, and other evidence to indicate that significant scholarly contribution to the conceptualization of the term development came from ancient societies of India, China, Egypt, Babylonia, and Assyria some 4000 to 5000 years ago and from ancient Greek and Roman civilizations and sources about 2500 years ago. Attempts to define and theorize the term have continued throughout human history The idea of development has had a checkered history. Over the centuries it has changed its meanings and connotations many times. Far from being a static concept, development has evolved into a dynamic one. This is evident from the currency of the concept, starting as "progress" and "evolution" of man and moving on to "civilization," "development," "social change," "Westernization," and "modernization." An in-depth study of the term unfolds the truth that development is a very difficult term to define, that it is a conundrum because it is a value-oriented, protean, multidimension-al, multivariate, multilevel, umbrella concept. Its various dimensions include: norma-tive, empirical, qualitative, quantitative, rural, urban, social, political, administrative, legal, economic, cultural, demographic, physical, intellectual, mental, moral, spiritual, material, personality (psychological), individual, group, local, state and regional, national, international, and global aspects, facets, and features. The multidimensional concept and process of development thus call for an all-embracing, comprehensive, integrated, and holistic perspective and interdisciplinary and multidisciplinary meth-odology; that is, the systems analysis in which there are definitive roles and functions for the state, market, society, household (family), individuals, groups, and civil society organizations to bring about all-around sustainable human development.

The study establishes the fact that the emergence of the concept and process of development has led to the birth of the social science. As far as the idea or issue of development is concerned we no longer speak of various social sciences but the social science, the raison d'être being that all those concerned with development—scholars, planners, and policy makers alike—have no option but to use conceptual frame-works that integrate and synthesize the society, polity, economy, culture, and personality in their approach. Such a framework, which emphasizes the interactions and interrelatedness in all forms of social behavior among these actors and players, is popularly known under the rubric of the systems approach (Lipset, 1972).

In the ultimate analysis, development is SD; that is, environmentally synergic human progress. It is human ascent and development, centering on an increase in the standard of living and the level of welfare and well-being of all people—women, men, and children—in every society, together with conservation of natural resources and ecological balance. Its operational definition is freedom from hunger, poverty, disease, illiteracy, inequality, ignorance, and insecurity, and liberation from all exploitation and discrimination. In short, development is the removal of poverty, unemployment, and inequality from every country, and within each country, between different segments and regions by ensuring that every member enjoys all human rights.

## REFERENCES

Adiseshiah, M. (1966). What Is Development? New York: McGraw Hill.
Adiseshiah, M. (1970). Development as People: The Total Approach. Paris: UNESCO; The Second Development Decade.

Adiseshiah, M. (1977). Planning and development. In: Sharma, S. K., ed. Dynamics of Development: An International Perspective. Vol. II. New Delhi: Concept, pp. 279–286.

Almond, G., Powell, B. (1966). Comparative Politics: A Developmental Approach. Brown, Boston: Little.

Amin, S. (1976). Unequal Development. Sussex: Harvester.

Apter, D. E. (1965). The Politics of Modernization. New York: Harper and Row.

Arora, S. K. (1976). Pre-empted future? Notes on political development. In: Kothari, ed. State and Nation Building. New Delhi: Allied, pp. 23–66.

Banuri, T., Hyden, G., Juma, C., Rivera, M. Sustainable Human Development from Concept to Operation: A Guide for the Practitioner. New York: UNDP.

Baran, P., Sweezy, P. M. (1968). Monopoly Capital: An Essay on American Economic and Social Order. Harmondsworth: Penguin.

Bava, N. (1981). Approaches to development. Indian J polit. sci. 11(2):41–57.

Bava, N. (1984). People's Participation in Development Administration in India. New Delhi: Uppal.

Bava, N. (1992). The Social Science Perspective and Method of Public Administration: Public Policy and Development Administration Approach. New Delhi: Uppal.

Bava, N. (1993). Development and the Social Science Method: An Interdisciplinary and Global Approach. New Delhi: Uppal.

Bava, N. (1997). Towards an integrated theory of people's participation through NGOs in nation-building and development. In: Bava, N.,, ed. Non-Governmental Organizations in Development: Theory and Practice. New Delhi: Kanishka, pp. 3–20.

Bava, N. (2000). Paradigms of development. In: Bava, N., ed. Public Policy and Administration: Normative Concerns. New Delhi: Uppal, pp. 235–256.

Bava, N. (2000). Democracy, development, peace and human rights. In: Bava, N., ed. Human Rights and Criminal Justice Administration in India. New Delhi: Uppal, pp. 1–10.

Beck, L. (1988). Shifts in concept and goals of development. Goals of Development. Belgium: UNESCO, pp. 43–53.

Blomstrom, M., Hettne, B. (1984). Development Theory in Transition: The Dependency Debate and Beyond. London: Zed.

Braibanti, R. (1977). Political development: Contextual non-linear perspective. In: Sharma, S. K., ed. Dynamics of Development. New Delhi: Concept, pp. 178–181.

Buzan, B. (1991). People, State and Fear: An Agenda for International Security Studies in the Post-Cold War Era. London: Harvester Wheat Sheaf.

Cardoso, F. H. (1972). Dependency and Latin America. New Left Rev 74.

Cardoso, F. H., Falletto. (1979). Dependency and Development in Latin America. Berkeley, CA: University of California Press.

Chai-Anan, S. (1991). The three dimensional state. In: Manor, J., ed. Rethinking Third World Politics. London: Longman.

Chien, D. J. (1977). People development: A developmental alternative for Asia. Indian J Pub. Admin. XXIII (3):594–605.

Chodak, S. (1973). Societal Development: Five Approaches with Conclusions from Comparative Analysis. New York: Oxford University Press.

Comte, A. (1898). A General View of Positivism. New York: Dutton.

Deutsch, K. (1961). Social mobilization and political development. Ameri. Pol. Sci. Rev. 493–514.

Engel, J. R., Engel, J. G. (1990). Ethics of Environment and Development: Global Challenge, International Response. London: Belhaven.

Frank, A. G. (1969). Capitalism and Underdevelopment in Latin America. New York: Monthly Review Press.

Furtado, C. (1965). Development and Underdevelopment. Berkeley, CA: University of California Press.

Gant, G. (1979). Development Administration: Concepts, Goals and Methods. Madison, WI: University of Wisconsin Press.

Gore, M. S. (1973). Some Aspects of Social Development. Hong Kong: Dept. of Social Work, University of Hong Kong.

Gore, M. S. (1988). Social development. Bharatiya Samajik Chintan XI:1–4.

Gunnel, J. G. (1970). Development, social change and time. In: Waldo, D., ed. Temporal Dimensions of Development Administration. Durham, NC: Duke University Press, pp. 47–89.

Hagen, E. (1962). On the Theory of Social Change: How Economic Growth Begins. Homewood, IL: Dorsey.

Harris, D. B. (1967). The Concept of Development: An Issue in the Study of Human Behaviour. Minneapolis: University of Minnesota Press.

Haq, M. (1995). Reflections on Human Development. New York: Oxford University Press.

Heady, F. (1979). Public Administration: A Comparative Perspective. New York: Marcel Dekker.

Hirschman, A. O. (1958). The Strategy of Economic Development. New Haven, CT: Yale University Press.

Hozelitz, B. (1960). Sociological Aspects of Economic Growth. Glenco, IL: Free Press.

Huntington, S. P. (1965). Political development and political decay. World Politics XVII (2):386–430.

Inayatullah. (1967). Towards a non-western model of development. In: Lerner Scvana, D., ed. Communication and Change in Developing Countries. Honolulu: East–West Centre. pp. 100–110.

Islam, N., Henault, G. M. (1979). From GNP to basic needs: A critical review of development and development administration. Internat. Rev. Admin. Sci. VL(3):253–267.

Jagannadham, V. (1978). Administration and Social Change. New Delhi: Uppal.

Jauguribe, H. (1973). Political Development: A General Theory and Latin American Study. New York: Harper and Row.

Jose, A. S. M. (1976). Comparative analysis of development and underdevelopment. In: Kothari, R., ed. State and Nation Building. New Delhi: Allied, pp. 99–101.

Kothari, R. (1976). State and nation building in the third world. In: Kothari, R., ed. State and Nation Building. New Delhi: Allied, pp. 3–20.

Kuhn, T. S. (1962). The structure of scientific revolution. In: International Encyclopaedia of United Science. Chicago: University of Chicago Press.

Lehmann, D. (1979). Development Theory: Four Critical Studies. London: Frank Cass.

Lewis, A. (1955). The Theory of Economic Growth. London: Allen & Unwin.

Lin, P. (1976). Development guided by values. In: Kothari, R., ed. State and Nation Building. New Delhi: Allied, pp. 149–192.

Lipset, S. M. (1972). Politics and the Social Sciences. New Delhi: Wiley Eastern Pvt.

Martinussen, I. (1997). Society, State and Market: A Guide to Competing Theories of Development. London: Zed Books.

Meier, G. M. (1989). Leading Issues in Economic Development. New York: Oxford University Press.

Michelena, J. A. (1976). Comparative analysis of development and underdevelopment. In: Kothari, R., ed. State and Nation Building. New Delhi: Allied, pp. 3–113.

Mc Clelland, D. C. (1961). The Achieving Society. Princeton, NJ: Van Nostrand.

Myrdal, G. (1968). Asian Drama: An Inquiry into the Poverty of Nations. Penguin: Harmondsworth.

Nurkse, R. (1953). Problems of Capital Formation in Underdeveloped Countries. Oxford: Blackwell.

Ogburn, W. F. (1922). Social Change. New York: B. W. Huebesch.

Parsons, T., Shils, E. Toward a General Theory of Action. New York: Harper and Row.

Prebisch, R. (1984). Five stages in my thinking on development. In: Meir, G., Seers, D., eds. Pioneers in Development. New York: Oxford University Press.

Preston, P. W. (1985). New Trends in Development Theory. London: Routledge and Kegan Paul.

Pye, L. (1966). Aspects of Political Development. New Delhi: Amerind.

Riggs, F. W. (1964). Administration in Developing Countries: The Theory of Prismatic Societies. Boston: Houghton Mifflin.

Riggs, F. W. (1961). The Ecology of Public Administration. Bombay: Asia Publishing House.

Riggs, F. W. (1966). Administrative development: an elusive concept. In: Montgomery, J., Siffin, W., eds. Approaches to Development: Politics, Administration and Change. New York: Mc Graw Hill, pp. 225–235.

Riggs, F. W. (1976). Further considerations on development. Admin Change 4(1).

Rodan, R. P. (1943). Problems of industrialization of eastern and south-eastern Europe. Econ. J.

Rostow, W. W. (1962). The Stages of Economic Growth: A Non-communist Manifesto. Cambridge; England: Cambridge University Press.

Rustow, D. (1967). A World of Nations: Problems of Political Modernization. Washington, DC: Brookings Institute.

Schumpeter, J. (1947). Capitalism, Socialism, and Democracy. London: George Allen & Unwin.

Seers, D. (1972). What are we trying to measure? J Dev. Stud. April.

Shamuyarira, N. M. (1976). Political development in new African states. In: Kothari, R., ed. State and Nation Building. New Delhi: Allied, pp. 229–268.

Smelser, N. J. (1968). Essays in Sociological Explanation. Prentice Hall, NJ: Englewood Cliffs.

Srinivas, M. N., Seshiah, S., Parthasarathy, V. S. (1976). Dimensions of Social Change in India. Bombay: Allied.

Sunkel, O. (1993). Development from Within: Towards a Neostructuralist Approach for Latin America. Boulder, CO: Lynne Rienner.

United Nations Development Program, Human Development Report. (1990). New York: Oxford University Press.

Waldo, D. (1977). Democracy, Bureaucracy and Hypocrisy. University of California: Institute of Government Studies.

Weber, M. The Protestant Ethic and the Spirit of Capitalism. New York: Scribner's.

Webster, A. (1984). Introduction to the Sociology of Development. London: Macmillan.

Weiner, M. (1966). Modernization: The Dynamics of Growth Forum Lectures.

Weidner, E. (1977). The goals, strategies and environment of development. In: Sharma, S. K., ed. Dynamics of Development: An International Perspective. New Delhi: Concept, pp. 31–39.

Welch, C. E. Jr. (1967). Political Modernization: A Reader in Comparative Political Change. Belmont, CA: Wordsworth.

World Commission on Environment and Development. Our Common Future. Delhi: Oxford University Press.

# 8

From Development Administration to
New Public Management in
Postcolonial Settings
*Internal Problems, External Prescriptions*

**O.P. DWIVEDI**
*University of Guelph, Guelph, Ontario, Canada*

**JORGE NEF**
*University of South Florida, Tampa, Florida, U.S.A.*

## INTRODUCTION

The internationalization of the theory and practice of public administration is a phenomenon closely related to the creation and evolution of the modern world system (Galtung, 1980: 107–178). Its roots are found in the European colonial expansion into the New World and subsequently into Asia and Africa. The overseas empires and administrative systems that evolved there corresponded to particular modalities of accumulation in different historical periods. In the earlier cases of seventeenth century Spain and Portugal, the mold was mercantile, while in the cases of British, French, Dutch, or Belgian expansion in the eighteenth and nineteenth centuries, modern capitalism prevailed.

The disintegration of the imperial order after the Second World War brought about the coexistence of neocolonialism with autonomist attempts under the banners of the United Nations' development decades and the development policies of multilateral and bilateral assistance (Pérez-Salgado, 1997:247). A Western-centered paradigm of government administration emerged in the postcolonial and Cold War context, development administration (DA). This "orthodox" model posited that higher efficiency and effectiveness was a function of the entrenchment of the bureaucratic standards—often referred to as scientific management—present in the most advanced industrial societies (Heady, 1966: 38–40; Karl, 1976: 494–495). The transformation of the public service from a traditional to a modern bureaucratic organization in underdeveloped countries was seen mainly as the result of external inducements, transfer of technology, and training by foreign experts. The ideas of planning and induced material and industrial expansion were central to DA, whose earlier testing grounds in the industrial world were the New Deal and European reconstruction under the Marshall Plan. The early antecedents of current administrative reform efforts can be traced back to such initiatives as President Truman's Point Four program in the late 1940s, the Colombo plan in the late 1950s, the U.N. First Development Decade, and the U.S.-sponsored Alliance for Progress in the early 1960s.

In postcolonial settings, this managerial transformation involved the conversion of a colonial "law and order" form of organization and modus operandi into a "rational productivity bureaucracy" that would provide the institutional conditions for economic "takeoff" (Rostow, 1960). In the context of the Cold War, the trend toward an administrative state was furthered by the need to institutionalize precarious and fragmented political systems and enable them to accomplish nation building and economic growth to stifle insurgencies. The bureaucratic model behind this view of management and organization was based on the dichotomy between politics and administration. It was also based upon other "principles," such as hierarchy, vertical departmentalization, unity of command, political neutrality, relative autonomy, recruitment and promotion based on merit, public service accountability, objectivity, and probity. At the end of the U.N. Second Development Decade (1961–1971), the assumptions of the prevailing paradigm began to crumble. Deep political, economic, social, and cultural-ideological crises spread throughout the West and its periphery, bringing the era of post-World War II economic *dirigisme* to an end.

As the Keynesian "administrative state" fractured under the double pressure of the worldwide fiscal crisis of the late 1970s and an accelerated transnationalization of capital, a "new orthodoxy" emerged. The paradigm to replace the DA model involved a combination of neoliberal economics and "new public management" (NPM). The slogan of a "leaner but meaner state" implied the belief that a small core of public servants everywhere could be simultaneously better trained, more professional, more globally minded, more ethical, more productive, more customer-oriented, and more responsive to the demands of business in general. In the context of a triumphant hegemonic neoliberal and monetarist ideology, the expectation was that a smaller civil service would result in better efficiency and responsiveness, thus eliminating the opportunity as well as the enticement for corruption. Based on this premise, the public sector itself was to retreat, privatize, deregulate, downsize, outsource, and localize. Supposedly the gap created by a shrinking government sphere was to be filled by a concomitant vitalization of civil society and the private sector. The expected outcome in the postsocialist and post-welfare state would be development and prosperity on a national and global scale.

As with the "old" orthodoxy, however, instead of democracy, probity, and prosperity, most developing nations faced growing poverty, civil strife, and a host of insoluble developmental, environmental, and human problems. By and large, a truly effective public management system never materialized. While the West was celebrating the retreat of the state and the collapse of socialism, deprivation expanded at an accelerated rate worldwide, corruption increased, and civil society as well as social capital deteriorated. As with its Keynesian predecessor, the net effect of the structural adjustment policies derived from the new formula was that the practices, styles, and structural arrangements succeeded in reproducing the symbolism but not the sub stance of modern developed administrative systems. Furthermore, the above-mentioned unsolved problems have not been limited to the Third World. The former socialist Second World and ever-growing segments of the population in the West live today under precarious conditions and expanding insecurity. Meanwhile, a privileged minority in all these "worlds" has accumulated wealth and power at an unprecedented scale. Confronted with widespread corruption, an ineffectual civil service, and largely immobile governing institutions, the standard solution has been to call for more of the same administrative reforms that created these problems. A vicious cycle ensues, in which international financial and technical cooperation agencies find themselves deeply entangled.

When looking at metropolitan influences upon the administrative systems of postcolonial countries it is useful to make a distinction between two historical patterns. One is that of the Latin American nations—when formal independence took place in the earlier part of the nineteenth century—which evolving into a neocolonial mold ever since. The other is that present inasmuch larger group of countries in Asia, Africa, the Middle East, the Pacific, and the Caribbean, whose emergence resulted from the disintegration of the British, French, Dutch, and Belgian empires following the Second World War. In the first group, in addition to the Iberian and Romanesque administrative legacy, a string of early twentieth century reforms— some externally induced but others "homegrown"—have shaped their administrative systems. Cases in point are the numerous experiences with the welfare and administrative states, import substitution industrialization (ISI), the modernization of budgetary and accounting practices, the development of public corporations, and the efforts at creating professional administrative cadres. Although the newer "emerging" (non-Latin American) nations inherited more advanced colonial bureaucracies, many of these possessed at a minimum the outward characteristics of modern civil services, yet these features favored a resilience of colonial administrative forms, practices, and personnel, in often at odds with local needs and realities. In some cases, such as in the Indian subcontinent, such colonial administrative innovations as a professional administrative class preceded similar developments in Europe. Moreover, some of the features of the administrative states in this region (including planning practices and the very concept of DA) became exportable benchmarks of administration for development elsewhere. At close scrutiny, DA was a synthesis of pre-existing local doctrines and traditions in the South, enduring colonial modalities, and essentially Western ideas connected to scientific management, the administrative state, and the reconstruction efforts under the Marshall plan. It was also immersed in a view of development that saw it as part of a larger counterinsurgency strategy to prevent Third World revolutions.

This largely interpretative chapter will examine the above-mentioned continuities (as well as discontinuities) in development thinking and administrative paradigms in both DA and NPM. An important task in this regard is to explain why both the "old" and the "new" models have had very limited success, to put it mildly. Concurrently, the very notions of development and administration that underpin these paradigms will be explored from a critical standpoint. The focus of the analysis will be a general discussion of the most salient and common features in the relationships among public administration, public sector reform, and development strategies "down there." We will approach the subject from both a historical and a systemic perspective. First, the crises and continuities leading to the present paradigm shift will be briefly analyzed. Subsequently, attention will be paid to the current administrative practices (namely, NPM) in lesser-developed countries, with special reference to the context, culture, structure, and processes and the broader developmental effects of these practices. To achieve this, a number of broadly comparative and operational questions will be addressed: (1) What changes in administrative structures, culture, and behavior have occurred in the "Third World" as a result of economic and political reforms in the past two decades? (2) To what extent do the administrative systems in these regions increasingly present legal-rational characteristics? (3) Are these systems of public administration becoming more efficient and/or effective in delivering services? (4) Is there a noticeable tendency of government agencies to become more— or less—client- or service-oriented? (5) What is happening to public trust, account-ability, and probity, and more specifically, what is the role of corruption in this process? (6) Finally, the perennial question: what has been the extent of public administration's contribution to national and regional development under these auspices?

## THE HISTORICAL LEGACY

As was mentioned at the outset, colonial administrations were modernized long before independence and the "spirit of Bandung." For instance, the Bourbon reforms emanating from Spain and Portugal in the eighteenth century, or the creation under British rule of the All-India Civil Service in the midnineteenth century were attempts to make colonial extraction more efficient. Likewise, administrative systems in sub-Saharan Africa (with the exception of Ethiopia's traditional monarchy), particularly in such nations as Ghana, Guinea, Mali, Nigeria, Ivory Coast, Sierra Leone, Tanzania, Kenya, Uganda, Malawi, Zambia, Cameroon, and Gabon, had inherited a European-based colonial administrative system, albeit with different nomenclatures among the colonies (Balogun and Mutahaba, 1999: 196). Subsequent external induce-ments to reform came via bilateral and multilateral conditionalities attached to foreign aid, trade, and military assistance. More often than not these efforts linked the interests of Northern with local, *comprador* elites. The aforementioned moderniza-tions have entailed protracted phases of colonial assimilation, decolonization, nation building, early institutionalization, indigenization, bureaucratization, authoritarian rule, and more recently, liberalization and transitions to limited democracy.

### From Development Administration and Bureaucratic Authoritarianism

Development administration and administrative development in the 1960s were clearly part of a conscious strategy relying on modernization as counterinsurgency (Nef and Dwivedi, 1981). Foreign aid, professionalization and development planning were central in a broad effort at refurbishing the civil services of South and Southeast Asia, Africa, the Middle East, and Latin America. Under USAID and European sponsorship, increasing numbers of students and trainees from these regions were exposed to Western—especially American—ways. Financial assistance poured in to carry on domestic programs of technical cooperation in educational, agrarian, and tax reforms, and also for the training and rationalization of the public sector under the principles of scientific management and DA.

Broadly speaking, the DA model presented a number of shared characteristics: (1) the fundamental goals of the state were induced development and nation building, (2) government planning was paramount in the attainment of these goals, (3) rational administration manifested itself in central agencies for program and budget planning, personnel management, standardized procedures, and decision making, (4) the state was to undertake anticyclical, demand-side management to reactivate and direct the economy, (5) regulation and protectionism to attain import-substituting industrialization complemented state ownership and operations, (6) the state provided a social package in health, education, and welfare and managed labor relations, (7) the backbone of induced development was a career, professional civil service, (8) the public service constituted a large administrative apparatus departmentalized by major purpose and having a wide developmental mandate, and (9) to accomplish these tasks in a more effective manner, the administrative machinery included a complex body of autonomous agencies (parastatals) charged with strategic development tasks.

At least equally important in Western eyes were the modernization and retooling of the security apparatus along national security and counterinsurgency lines, as was the case in Iran, South Korea, Pakistan, and throughout Latin America (Barber and Ronning, 1966). In fact, in numerous countries administrative and military reforms went hand in hand, and many saw officers as Nasserite or Kemalist nation builders. While the reforms of the civil service, though extensive, remained narrowly focused, "technical," and piecemeal, the thoroughgoing transformation of the security apparatus had a much deeper, longest term, and often dramatic impact. On the one hand, it generated institutional imbalances between the civilian and military cadres of the state. On the other, as military aid was the main external power leverage by core countries the proclivity to create entangled North–South praetorian linkages in a Cold War environment became entrenched.

## Democratic Transitions and Receiver States

The illusion of officers as disciplined and "altruistic" bearers of national development and nation building—as well as the idea of bureaucratic authoritarianism as a "fourth way" to development—vanished toward the end of the Cold War. Military aid was costly, it was rarely related to developmental outcomes, and more often than not it had failed to constitute a reliable leverage. Bureaucratic authoritarianism was certainly repressive, but also cumbersome and hardly developmental. Worse, the belief that the so-called national security regimes would bring order and stability was exaggerated, as such regimes were on the whole neither secure nor really national. Repression and the militarization of development were often the flip side of intrinsic weakness and illegitimacy on the part of client regimes. Instead, more often than not this paved the way to popular rebellions. Most important, with the deflation of the socialist "Second World," there appeared to be no need for dictatorial regimes to protect Western security and economic concerns. As authoritarian bureaucracies and national security doctrines in the South became ever more associated with gross human rights violations, sheer terror, incompetence, and wholesale corruption, the public service function, both military and civilian, also lost prestige.

With the inauguration of the Carter administration, a new economic and political development paradigm began to take shape, combining a return to a restricted form of democracy with liberal, market-oriented reforms. This perspective, referred to as Trilateralism, offered a common ground for Western and Southern elites (Sklar, 1980). The implicit transnational alliance of central and peripheral capital constituted a seemingly workable form of power sharing capable of reducing the North–South cleavage of previous decades. First World critics had began to perceive such repressive regimes as those of the shah of Iran, Somoza, Pinochet, Marcos, Zia ul Haq, or Suharto as a liability for the long-term survival of their economic and political interests. Carefully orchestrated transitions to limited forms of democracy ensued, superintended by the United States and its allies within the G7. This "transition" had strict limits and conditionalities. On the whole and despite an appeal to human rights, they maintained the socioeconomic and political forces that had benefited decades of Cold War authoritarian rule, while excluding radical and popular sectors in the new democracies. The existing security establishment was to be both the warrantor of the process and the central authoritarian enclave and the insurance policy of the new institutional arrangement. This "low-intensity" democracy (Gil et al., 1993) also preserved the basic pro-business and pro-Western economic policies of the authoritarian era. Chief among the institutional legacies of the authoritarian regimes was a "receiver state," primary goal was to manage fiscal bankruptcy and facilitate IMF-inspired conservative economic reforms (Vilas, 1995). The administrative corollary of the new state was the NPM doctrine. The political formula prescribed a "subsidiary" state whose main functions were similar to those of the predevelopment administration, law-and-order system, except for two features. The first is the truly global nature of the public policy context, inserted in a unipolar international order with limited national sovereignty. The second is the profound transformation and transnationalization of the state, related to the aforementioned "receivership" role.

Latin America became a test-case scenario for the emerging strategy combining liberal economic reforms with constricted democracy. Although market-friendly reforms have been associated with the explicit unfolding of a Friedmanian neoliberal agenda (Friedman, 1962; 1964) in the 1990s, many national security regimes had forcefully attempted "monetarist" structural adjustments and "shock treatments" along similar lines at least a decade earlier. In fact, these efforts involved considerable privatization, denationalization, deregulation, and downsizing while making the national economies more hospitable for foreign investment. The examples of Indonesia, Brazil, the apartheid regime in South Africa, Chile, and to a qualified extent the Asian "tigers," involved the coexistence of monetarist, pro-Western, and pro-business policies side by side with a large public sector and a repressive state. Of all these, only the Chilean and South African experiments effected a transition from import-substitution and protectionism to full-fledged neoliberalism while undergoing a conditional democratization. These "experiments" soon evolved into a model for Asia, Africa, and years later for the "transitional" postcommunist societies of Eastern Europe and Central Asia. In the words of a perceptive observer

> [the] state reform agenda for. . .developing countries is based on the approaches of the World Bank and other multilateral financial organizations. At the beginning, the emphasis of reforms was put on a number of policies to shrink the state and transfer most

intervention activities to the market. These recommendations were called the "Washington Consensus." They arose in the context of fiscal and financial problems resulting from the 1980's [debt] crisis (Vilas, 2000: 25).

The emergence and consolidation of Thatcherism, "Reaganomics," and other right-wing regimes officialized a new hegemonic ideology at a time when the Cold War and international socialism appeared exhausted.

## New Public Management and Neoliberal Reform

The neoliberal paradigm entrenched a "categorical imperative" type of discourse, Margaret Thatcher's now famous "there is no alternative" (TINA) principle. This dictum would soon become acceptable common sense in the development community. During the last two decades of the twentieth century, especially on the heels of the crumbling administrative state, neoliberal economic reforms everywhere replaced DA in redefining the role of the state and its agencies. The prescriptive package contains a series of policy and administrative measures to reduce constraints on the classic "invisible hand," in sharp contrast with the preceding tradition. These measures include: (1) downsizing the public sector, (2) privatizing government services and economic activities, (3) reducing the state's role in direct economic management and social programs, (4) deregulating government controls in the private sector, (5) reducing direct corporate taxes, (6) cutting expenses and balancing the budget, (7) drastically downscaling and even eliminating protectionism, (8) outsourcing services whenever possible, and (9) localizing government functions.

In addition to these tasks, the public sector has also faced a myriad of challenges emerging from a more complex and transnationalized political and economic context, which is encapsulated in the term globalization. Unlike the administrative state, in which the notion of the public or national interest was considered an objective policy parameter defined by a "common good," policy objectives are determined by multiple transnational transactions geared to optimal macroeconomic balances while realizing gains for those who control the market forces.

Initially the neoliberal formula was extremely successful as a political project in the developed world. Although its experimental origins were in the dictatorship of General Pinochet in Chile under the intellectual mentorship of Friedrich von Hayek and Milton Friedman, it subsequently found legitimacy in the conservative electoral victories in the United States, the United Kingdom and Canada, as well as in other Organization for Economic Cooperation and Development (OECD) countries. From there it evolved into an article of faith in such bilateral and pseudo-multilateral agencies as the IMF, the World Bank, and the Inter-American Development Bank. It finally became the hegemonic discourse in most Western intellectual establishments. It was largely through the structural adjustment condition attached to Third World debt relief by lending agencies that neoliberal policies were entrenched (see International Development Research Centre [IDRC], 1992), but despite this early success, less than two decades later the outcome has been more successful for its pervasiveness than for its social effects.

The combination of incomplete and democratic transition, restricted democracy, and the widespread existence of receiver states has had deleterious effects upon the administrative systems in peripheral countries. Privatization, budget cuts, downsizing, deregulation, and denationalization—especially in the developmental, social, energy, agricultural, and industrial areas—have dramatically reduced the scope and functions of the state.

Moreover, the continuity of the institutional and cultural features of repressive practices has stunted further democratization of both state and society in a way similar to the continuity of colonial administrations after independence. As profit and personal gain on the one hand and the national interest on the other become blurred in the new ideological domain privileging private interests and greed, the notion of public service becomes increasingly empty. Furthermore, with the status and income levels of civil servants declining, and with an illegal economy (such as drug and weapons) thriving worldwide, systemic corruption has become rampant, reaching the highest levels of government and the bureaucracy (Lee, 1988). Under these circumstances, externally induced efforts to making public administration more accountable, responsible, universalistic, effective, and client-oriented and less corrupt become as formal and ineffectual as the DA prescriptions of the 1960s.

In a nutshell, this is the crux of the "catch 22"-type dilemma of public administration in developing nations. On the one hand, the existing international "development" practices create conditions incompatible with any administrative reform to make such systems work. On the other hand, the administrative prescriptions couched in technical lingo tend to be more often than not either patchwork or simple rhetoric. Bureaucracy nevertheless continues to be a favored organizational form in East and Southeast Asia, although "its longevity varies considerably between countries, and there are differences in its operations across the region" (Turner and Halligan, 1999: 131).

## A COMPARATIVE PERSPECTIVE

The bulk of the literature on comparative administration evokes a universalistic trend. The circumstances, outcomes, and effects of administrative change, however, tend to be region-and country-specific. Administrative systems are also conditioned by the current modality as well as the legacy of state–society relations; they are not divorced from politics. On the contrary, management and organization are not "technical," but eminently political issues.

From this perspective, administrative changes have to be conceived as driven by political interests and having political implications for the relationship between state and society. The point of convergence between politics and administration is public policy, and this is especially the case with development policy. Outcomes related to growth and distribution result from actions, inactions, and interactions among various internal and external political actors using limited resources and possessing diverse development ideologies that justify their interests (Stallings, 1978: 1–14).

Two aspects in the theory and practice of administration seem to have remained constant throughout. One is that the source of conceptual innovation has continued to be distinctively Western, more specifically serving the interests of a powerful minority in the global core. The other is the reciprocal relationship and identity between administrative theory and the development model, one in which these elites' ideas have remained simultaneously dominant and hegemonic (Cox and Gramsci 1983).

To build an "ideal type" that portrays the public administration system for the entirety of the underdeveloped world with any rigor and precision is a nearly impossible task. Despite the great diversity and complexity among the countries making up the Third World, however, there are sufficient structural commonalities to configure an identifiable set of economic, social, and political traits, especially by contrast to the developed states of the G7 and OECD nations. In this sense it is possible to sketch a general outline of the structural, functional, behavioral, and attitudinal traits present in the complex conglomerate of state agencies in underdeveloped and lesser sovereign regions. These agencies comprise a wide array of public organizations in the central government, functionally decentralized entities, and such territorially decentralized units as state and local governments.

An important premise of the analysis is that in all societies the public and private sectors and their respective cultures tend to intersect, particularly at the level of the power elite (Mills, 1957). The same applies to the distinction between the civilian and military spheres of the state. Complex organizations, whether business or public, civilian or military, are not compartmentalized in complete isolation from each other and the broader political, social, or economic forces, both internal and external; rather, they are inserted in the fabric of societies, their problems, and their culture, including historical memories, myths, and symbols, as well as past and present cleavages. They are also affected by the international and especially by the regional environments in which these administrations operate.

Development administration, as a Western "soft technology" artefact to be applied in the periphery, assumed many entrenched Euro-American managerial values. These included the separation of politics from administration and the belief that First World-style progress was not only inherently good, but essential to stop revolution. "Rational" thinking, for example, presupposed that public sector management would be the realm of professional administrators, the latter ably assisted by "objective" economic plans formulated to achieve national goals.

In this "factual" model there was no place for political considerations, let alone "ideological" preferences in development and its administration. As the post-1974 Vietnamese, post-1979 Iranian, or Nicaraguan experiences proved, however, politics could not be kept separate from economic planning, management of resources, or administration of the public sector. Either the administrative system responded to changing political contexts or the indigenous political leadership simply bypassed the established administrative apparatus and created its own mechanisms to accomplish its objectives. In a way the same was true for radically conservative reforms, as in the Asian Newly Industrializing Countries (NICs) or in Latin America. The separation of politics from administration remained artificially embedded in the parlance of the theories of DA, while political factors dominated the practice of economic, social, and even managerial concerns. This conceptual schizophrenia is yet to be acknowledged by many scholars, practitioners, and international aid personnel.

By their very nature, developmental issues are *political* because they deal with the authoritative allocation of values in the context of limited and sometimes rapidly diminishing resources. In developing countries, therefore, public sector management cannot remain purely within the domain of so-called value-free administration, otherwise irrespective of the amount of international aid, history may repeat itself, as in the failed experiment of America's massive involvements in Iran or Vietnam.

## THE STRUCTURAL CONTEXT OF PUBLIC ADMINISTRATION

The historical continuities and discontinuities discussed above have resulted in the coexistence of numerous and often incongruous traits in the relationship between administration and development in postcolonial societies. These include an uneasy coexistence between foreign and domestic influences, attempted and failed reforms, and persistent crises. The aforementioned legacy manifests itself into three deep and interconnected structural contradictions that set the operational context of administration.

1. The first is the persistent and unresolved tension between expanding social expectations and shrinking economic capabilities. Whether we talk about Asia's or Latin America's emerging markets, the desperate plight of Africa, the peculiarities of Middle Eastern economics, or postcommunist transitions in Eastern Europe and Central Asia, reinsertion in the global economic order has meant extreme vulnerability and hardship, compounded by weak and unstable growth for all regions. After a protracted period of dismal economic performance for Latin America and Africa in the 1980s, the unevenly distributed recovery of the 1990s was once again thwarted by subsequent crises, this time in Asia and in the former Second World. Chronic underdevelopment and unemployment translate into shrinking resources, extremely limited mobility opportunities, systemic frustration, and a severe lack of governance.

2. The second tension is the one between the "haves" and "have-nots." Constricted generation of surplus, worsened by extreme forms of wealth and income inequality, reduces the possibilities for consensual, liberal-democratic forms it conflict management. For example, most populations in the Third World experience the paradox of living in favorably endowed regions in terms of resources while coexisting with some of the worst forms of poverty and inequity. While contemporary social conflict throughout the world does not present the outwardly subversive characteristics of the revolutionary confrontations of the Cold War, social unrest has not subsided. As its underlying causes persist so does its intensity, irrespective of the changing manifestations of mass–elites relations. The conflict today is not so much perceived as a cleavage between social classes but between privileged elites and a somewhat amorphous "rest of society." Either way, the result is a sort of catastrophic equilibrium involving an uneasy mixture of autocracy, oligarchical rule, protracted violence, a growing legitimacy vacuum, messianism, and corruption.

3. This proclivity for disequilibria connects to the third systemic tension: that between the formality of sovereignty and the reality of dependence. Many countries outside the G7 and the OECD are penetrated political systems with ever more precarious control over external actors, events, and policies. Their economic foundations are still built upon a skewed and exogenous mode of development, with boom and bust cycles compounded by massive debt burdens, current conditionalities, and rapid transnationalization.

Growing governmental illegitimacy tends to produce a vicious cycle of substitution of external First World support, for internal support, leading to greater illegitimacy and a greater need for external supports. Often the presence of these regimes leads to ever-expanding cultural resentment, with very little "elbow room" for compromise and accommodation. The combined effect of such contradictions upon the political system manifests itself in a highly conflictual zero-sum—or even "negative-score"—game, in which politics is an unstable mixture of rebellion, repression, and stalemate (Nef, 1982). The implications of this political environment for public policy in general, and public administration in particular, are cardinal; they set the constraints and possibilities for socioeconomic reform in peripheral societies.

It has become fashionable to talk about democratic transition in developing nations, especially by contrast to the "exceptional conditions" existing in many such nations in the 1970s and 1980s. At close scrutiny, however, this characterization is deceiving. The type of restricted democracy to emerge in most countries bears little substantial similarities to Western democracy or evenly, the democratic practices existing in some of these societies prior to the emergence of authoritarian rule.

The alleged democratizing trend is basically a formal and exclusionary arrangement sustained by pacts of elites, including foreign elites, in which the key function of the state is to be a receiver and administrator of structural adjustment packages. Current modalities of administration for development, such as NPM, enhance this exclusionary style. More than the oft-repeated issue of ungovernability, a lack of democratic governance is at the center of the continuous crisis. While facilitating elite control of popular demands, limited democratic participation reduces the scope of legitimacy. The key concept to understanding the current crisis is deinstitutionalizations—the extent to which the liberalization packages have failed to address the question of legitimization.

Illegitimate regimes are unsustainable, irrespective of the social engineering to keep their administrative machineries running. Administrative efficiency without public support is simply ineffectual. Both public disillusionment with government and the increasing meaninglessness of the "new" democracies are ubiquitous. If the state cannot maintain political and economic sovereignty, protect the life and well-being of its citizens, safeguard democratic rights, and assure participation—in a word, provide for human security (Nef, 1999)—its very reason for existence becomes problematic.

Furthermore, as the prevailing neoliberal ideological and policy agendas reduce the state role to that of protecting business interests, there is little the public sector—no matter how efficient, effective, or transparent—could do. In the absence of a strong and legitimate political order and community, the NPM formula, with its corollaries of privatization, downsizing, deregulating, localizing, and outsourcing, has potentially destabilizing effects. Moreover, without a pre-existing cohesive and vigorous civil society, administrative modernization is simply a means to a vacuous end.

## The Impact of NPM

The NPM movement was launched in the 1980s in the West to improve the financial problems that beset their governments. The various versions of the welfare—and the "warfare"—state had become too costly, and the Keynesian principles on which they were based were discredited because politicians had taken to running systematic deficits in order to finance government programs and satisfy special interests. There were also instances of growing militancy on the part of public sector unions, numerous strikes, and the rigidities resulting from the combination of big government with collective bargaining.

Furthermore, the 1980s was a period of revival of conservative ideologies disguised as "tax revolts." The election of Margaret Thatcher in Britain and Ronald Reagan in the United States gave powerful support to a new "managerial" and businesslike approach to public sector management. In reality, this trend had deep historical roots in the Wilsonian Administrative Reform Movement in the late nineteenth and early twentieth century, in its quest for business principles, efficiency, and depolitization (Karl, 1976: 490). The novelty of the approach was that it occurred at a time in which the New Deal had become exhausted and national industrial capitalism had mutated into transnational global finance.

The NPM movement espoused a number of operational "principles," namely: (1) need for budget restraint, (2) reduction of bureaucracy, (3) accent on results, (4) service to the public, (5) decentralization and devolution, (6) contracting out, (7) performance pay, and (8) accountability. These principles translate into an emphasis on results more than processes, in both planning and evaluating programs and people, and in service to the public. Quality is paramount, as the citizen is defined as a "client" or user capable of demanding services. Delegation of authority is instrumental to these objectives, as are other businesslike incentives for motivating employees, such as merit pay, mission statements, "strategic planning," and quality circles (Dwivedi and Gow, 1999:130).

This means bringing decisions as close as possible to the level of action and empowering employees to take the initiative. There is greater attention to cost reduction through comprehensive auditing, contracting out, and introduction of competitive external bids. The NPM has also introduced such notions as corporate management, corporate culture, and bottom-line management, an essentially market-driven rhetoric. This paradigm is based on the premise that by reducing the opportunities for incompetence and corruption through the narrowing down of the scope of government activities, efficient, transparent, effective and accountable governance would appear.

The expectation is that with fewer bureaucratic structures to deal with there would be fewer administrative problems. Once more, the heavy emphasis is placed on objective business criteria of responsibility and accountability, with a blind faith on flimsy culture-bound practices and little concern for subjective and intercultural dimensions. As the 2001 Enron and subsequent business scandals revealed, deeply seated corruption in the higher levels of corporate America had become a fact of life; business ethics could not be seen as a paradigm for transparency or accountability.

Developing nations are being urged to have market-friendly governance and administration. Since the public sector is posited more as a problem than a solution, NPM in the garb of "development management" is recommended as a cure-all. International aid is being made conditional upon accepting this prescription. Shrinking the bureaucracy, eliminating subsidies, tearing down protectionism, accepting currency devaluations, and other changes in monetary and fiscal policy translate in many instances into societies even more exposed to the ravages of Western and local economic elites. In a broader sense, these adjustments mean the end of Keynesianism and the welfare state. Constrained by supply-side monetarist policies designed by economists and business administration experts, the role of public administrators appears to be presiding over their own demise (Dwivedi, 1994).

## The Limits of NPM

There is no doubt that the emphasis on result-based performance is of value. There is, however, a danger of neglecting political, institutional, and cultural dimensions that represent deeply seated values. At the same time, faced with the complexities of day-to-day operations and the conflicting values that the system has thrust upon them, development administrators need some fundamental reference points to implement policies. In this respect a public manager differs essentially from a private executive. While the latter is trained to regard the law as a costly constraint that must be obeyed only if it cannot be circumvented, the public manager must uphold it.

To be sure, public management proponents usually say that they are aware that the state is not a business, but the values of public accountability and respect for the law tend to be eclipsed by bottom-line considerations. In practice, though very few public servants in the developed and underdeveloped worlds actually believe that government should be thought of as a corporation, the marching orders are precisely to do so. The greatest problems with managerialism in the public sphere are its reductionism, its deconstruction of the notion of public good, and its overall ethnocentrism. It tries to reduce a complex phenomenon to a single idealized model drawn from business (Dwivedi and Gow, 1999:178).

A great paradox with NPM is that at close scrutiny it is a powerful ideology posing as an "objective" technique (Manzer, 1984:27). Public management also appears to neglect the importance of law and legality in public administration. By introducing such notions as corporate management, corporate culture, and even that of management itself, it tends to obscure the fact that relations between senior officials and politicians are legal-normative in nature. As John Rohr states, the Constitution must serve as a source of regime values for administrators. At the lower levels of administration, the law is a guarantor of due process: "Government by law is the most bureaucratic of all institutions because to a greater extent than other institutions it feels bound by its own rules" (Rohr, 1988:171).

Perhaps a more appropriate normative image for the public administrator is that of the steward, not the entrepreneur. This leads to another NPM paradox. Astley and Van de Ven have observed that there are two versions of organization theory, one that is basically deterministic and one that is proactive in its outlook (Astley and van de Ven, 1983).

The deterministic school sees management as fine-tuning, adapting organizations to changes occurring in the environment, an objective situation that administrators cannot change. The proactive outlook takes a strategic view; the context and circumstances of administration are challenges to be acted upon. While the language of NPM is full of references to proactive stances in which where strategic planning, innovation, change, and growth are promoted as in an idealized business environment, its basic thrust is profoundly deterministic. Its message is that really there are no choices (beginning with the nature of the economic model and policy) and that structural economic conditions and world trade competition are *natural* forces governments all over the world must adhere to. This obscures the fact that in reality governments in developed countries do things very differently. For instance, continental European countries favor a more corporatist form of national bargaining with business and labor, while Britain, the United States, and Canada prefer a more liberal approach, in which individualism is seen as supreme. The NPM also masks the fact that there are other models of the state and of policies besides the market model (Dwivedi and Gow, 1999).

## THE DYNAMICS OF REFORM: PROCESSES AND EFFECTS

Administrative change in the periphery has been for the most part either externally induced or heavily assisted by external actors. Colonial reforms, the desire of local elites to modernize, the presence of international missions and consultants, development administration, and today's NPM with Structural Adjustment Programmes (SAPs), are all cases in point (Dwivedi, 1994). The instances of indigenous administrative reform have been fewer, piecemeal, heavily localized, and mostly reactive to deep discontinuities. The common denominator of all administrative reforms for development in the Third World, whether internally or externally induced, is—despite technical rhetoric—its distinct political intent, for such initiatives, irrespective of the antiseptic language in which they are wrapped, could strengthen, weaken, consolidate, or challenge existing power relations. Furthermore, they all operationalize in organizational and managerial terms a broader political, social, and economic project.

Administrative modernization in the 1990s has predicated in a very different domestic and international environment—and on very different programmatic objectives—from those of the structural reforms of the 1960s. The policy framework for international cooperation continues to be distinctively neoliberal, not Keynesian. Markets rather than planning and government intervention are central, although this policy switch has been and still is contingent upon strong state enforcement.

Many developing countries came out of the Cold War through a transition to a limited and not very transparent form of democracy brokered by external agents. The countries were also saddled with enormous and unmanageable debt burdens. The international financial community and its international bodies used debt management to impose stringent conditionalities. The latter included a number of measures for attaining macroeconomic equilibrium via debt reduction, open market policies, and institutional reforms.

It is precisely in the context of these structural adjustment policies that the bulk of the prescriptions for the current administrative reform have to be seen. As has already been mentioned, the administrative corollary to the neoliberal package contained in the SAPs is the NPM paradigm, well known in the in the United States through *Reinventing Government*, by Osborne and Gaebler (Osborne and Gaebler, 1992), yet its lineage can be traced back to the conservative administrative reforms in the 1980s in England, New Zealand, Australia, and Canada that materialized what was then called a "neoconservative" agenda. Its administrative correlate has been a profound shift from civil service to the new management.

Downsizing government, making it publicly more accountable and transparent, and turning it into a more efficient mechanism for delivering services on its own (or in partnership with private and/or voluntary organizations) are not purely isolated measures to secure "better" service. They are all manifestations of a broader ideological rationale that includes a number of articulated prescriptions: re-establishing the rule of the market over the "collectivist" idea of the "public good"; reducing taxes and public expenditures; deregulating the private sector; and privatizing the public sector (Nef and Robles, 2000). The role of the state under this model is mainly subsidiary; that is, its main directive is to protect the functioning of the market and private property. The basic "social contract" is post-Fordian in the sense that it reduces and fragments the role of workers in the system of labor relations, enhancing instead the uncontested hegemony of big business, both foreign and domestic. The notion of popular and national sovereignty is replaced by the sovereignty of capital. A new type of state thus displaces the liberal-democratic hybrid: a plutocracy with popular support and massive abstention. This state arrangement manifests itself in labor, taxation, and welfare policy. It also means a "postmodern" return to patrimonialism.

Over the last two decades there has been a redefinition of the role of the state throughout most of the globe along the lines mentioned above. This has manifested itself in a transition between two models: the Keynesian "administrative state," the central mission of which was the attainment of national development, and a "receiver" state, the principal role of which is the management of structural adjustment and the subsidiary role of which is the implementation of palliative development.

Such development refers mostly to targeted programs to address the plight of those who fall off social safety nets as a result of orthodox economic policies by means of microcredit, sustainable livelihoods, capacity building schemes, and the like. This transformation, as mentioned earlier, came at the heels of the bureaucratic authoritarian restructuring of the 1970s and was largely facilitated by it. It has been accomplished by closures, privatization of many activities—especially in public utilities, health, social security, and education—and outsourcing in the private sector. A myriad of private entities have emerged to take on these downloaded public functions with captive clienteles and low elasticity.

The record of privatization has shown mixed results, ranging from greater quality and rationalization of service, to more effective costing and profitability, to situations of exclusion and manifest decline in quality, coverage, and accessibility. In some cases, it has given an impetus for modernization and improved standards, and has generated sources of new investment and even cheaper and better products (as in telecommunications).In many other cases, however (as in power utilities, medicare, education, and social security), it has spearheaded at best speculative appropriations at the public expense, widespread fraud, and large-scale corruption. Downsizing the civil service has led to a proliferation of personnel on limited service contracts and a large quantity of private consultants. It is not uncommon to see parallel structures to the officially downsized agencies made of contractual and external personnel. More often than not this "temporary" structure evolves into a persistent clientele conditioned to the ups and downs of patronage politics.

Fiscal management has moved to the center stage of public administration. By and large, the financial base for public programs has been significantly reduced, while budgetary processes have been streamlined and expedited. Budget cuts have been geared to attaining fiscal balance, improving efficiency in cost, and above all, facilitating the entrenchment of structural adjustment policies. In addition to the macro issues of privatization and fiscal management, the administrative reform under NPM has had some remarkable achievements throughout the Third World, especially when it comes to the "micro-" and efficiency-oriented aspects of administration. Of all the activities implemented, the most clearly successful have been the efforts to rationalize procedures and debureaucratize and computerize services. The quality and time of service rendered to customers has clearly improved in many lesser-developed countries. This applies especially to licenses, certificates, income taxes, and a reduction of red tape. More substantial structural reforms have met with less success, ranging from limited accomplishments (e.g., localization), to mere cosmetic changes, to complete ineffectiveness, or worse. Basic issues, such as corruption, an inability to meet public needs, and systemic breakdown, stand as the most nefarious outcomes of the new orthodoxy.

## CONCLUSIONS

Though tentative, this interpretative exploration has allowed us to construct a basic outline of the relationships among the administrative values, structures, and functions sketched above and the larger social and political order in which development takes place. It has also suggested some conjectures regarding the dynamic relationship between such patterns and attempts of reform. As a general conclusion, nine propositions with prescriptive overtones can be derived from the preceding analysis.

1. The administrative systems of the Third World reflect the distinctiveness and complexity of the various national realities and common regional and global trends. The latter include persistent dependence, the perpetuation of rigid and particularistic social structures, chronic economic vulnerability, weak and unstable growth, social marginalization, low institutionalization, and acute social and political polarization, all of which translate into high levels of ambiguity and uncertainty. Administrative life in these nations is conditioned more by these circumstances than by the declared goals of "technical" reform. Ostensibly, structural transformations have taken place, yet administrative culture and behavior have persisted, producing syncretistic adaptations rather than profound reorganizations. On the whole, the political economy of public administration in postcolonial societies has been conditioned by a bias for the maintenance of the domestic and regional status quo.

2. In general, the administrative systems in most of the Third World have exhibited for quite some time the formal attributes of bureaucracy. Successive reforms have entrenched these traits, yet under the circumstances described here, the presence of "legal-rational" and "managerial" characteristics do not constitute substantive indicators, let alone predictors, of responsiveness, effectiveness, or democratic accountability; rather, the formality of the legal-rational model often hides the reality of a "mock" bureaucracy, in which complex procedures and technical trappings are geared to a dysfunctional mixture of issue nonresolution and nonissue resolution. Public administration in these countries has been distinctively derivative. As a reflection of an entrenched center-periphery regional and global order, it has tended to follow vogues, recipes, and solutions manufactured in the developed societies. In this sense, it has been exogenous in its motivations, problem identification, and prescriptions. The tendency to define problems and questions from the vantage point of rather standard answers and solutions has provided for a rather mechanistic and acritical approach. The scientific and technological institutions in the region have been more interested in reproducing the prevailing modes of social engineering than addressing larger contextual and politically contentious issues. Technical cooperation has not fared any better.

3. One emerging cultural pattern with a deep impact on administration is cultural globalization. This trend toward one homogeneous managerial "monoculture" has its roots in scientific management and DA. The ideas of efficiency, the automaticity of the market, and the myth of achievement are all hallmarks of Western administrative culture.

   As the Soviet-led Marxist–Leninist strain of modernization fell in disrepute in Eastern Europe, its capitalist variety has become the dominant paradigm by default. There seems to be no alternative hegemonic discourse at the present time other than the reassertion of some indigenous model of development—including Islamic revivalism—or the nostalgic critique offered by the postmodernism of Western intellectuals.

4. Even under the guise of internationalization, the above-mentioned global thrust often means technological dependence and continued reliance on the grafting of theories and methodologies of First World administrative modalities. This translates into the transplantation and replication of ideas, institutions, and "know-how" in postcolonial contexts. Under the language of "flexibility," the management style continues to be hierarchical, patrimonial, and centralized.

   Internationalization also requires that Western values and practices prevail everywhere, with standards of performance based on the indicators developed in the core. An imitative and replicative system of public management emerges that favors downsized and streamlined government, the freeing of the business sector from overregulation and controls, and an efficient delivery of public goods and services. It is thus no surprise that Western (or Western-trained) advisors recommend government restructuring, public service reforms, campaigns against corruption, and extensive training and education for public servants, along the lines of the NPM reforms undertaken in the United States, the United Kingdom, France, Germany, Australia, New Zealand, or Canada.

   Third World nations may have no choice but to accept the prevailing prescription, but the result of the therapy is often a hodgepodge of updated colonial or neocolonial administrative practices superimposed on ineffective bureaucracies being pulled in different directions. The world of the twenty-first century may be ready for fast food chains, blue jeans, and soda pop, but certainly not for the Western notion of "one size fits all" in the field of governance and administration. There is no question that the Third World will have to set its house in order by controlling corruption and waste and curbing the dominance of special interests in its own systems of governance. Developing countries have a lot to change, but so do the developed nations.

5. During the last two decades of the twentieth century, there were ostensible improvements in "debureaucratizing," "decluttering," reducing waiting times, and cutting down of red tape. This has been accompanied by deregulation, a reduction of the size of the civil service, and a transfer of many public functions into private agencies. The failure of the democratizations of the 1980s and 1990s, as well as the debt crises and structural adjustments, have altered the content and instrumentalities of public policy (Nef, 1997). Peripheral administrative systems have been directly affected by cur-

rent circumstances and challenges derived from a concerted effort at neo-liberal modernization along the lines of the prescriptions of First World governments and international agencies.This alteration has not resulted into substantively greater efficiency, however let alone effectiveness to "get things done" for the public; nor does it seem to effect a deep transformation of administrative practices and behavior.

6.  The same applies to the question of administrative responsiveness to public demands. In a narrow technical sense, the transformation of the recipient into a "client"—as has been attempted in numerous reforms—does not substantially alter the intrinsic quality of the service. The irony is that while social demands on the public sector to tackle mounting problems and to provide more services are growing, the state apparatus is shrinking. What is happening instead is a revolution of rising frustrations resulting from the inability of the political systems and their bureaucracies to tend to the most basic problems people face in their daily lives.

7.  The inability to control corruption is indicative of the very incongruous logic of the current prescriptions. Such prescriptions are not only flawed but also hypocritical. Administrative systems are immersed in a larger cultural matrix, containing values, practices, and orientations toward the physical environment, economy, social system, polity, and culture itself. This matrix defines the parameters of both "public" and "private" spheres. Corruption in these cases is not only public; it is systemic (Caiden et al., 2001).

A predatory attitude toward the environment and resource extraction (often fueled by a mounting foreign debt), possessive individualism, amoral familism and clientelism, a weak civic consciousness, and a tendency to imitate the "modern" configure a reactionary mind-set with ethical double standards. This also engenders irresponsibility and a lack of capacity and will to anticipate and make strategic policy shifts.

Administrative reforms promoting privatization, a smaller role for the state, deregulation, downsizing, outsourcing, and formal decentralization have not addressed the fundamental issues of inequality, lack of democracy, and abuse that underpin administrative structures and practices. The existence of corruption and inefficiency is continually eating away the public trust in effective governance. Red tape, ambiguous laws, rampant graft, and very slow redress by judicial mechanism have all effectively produced a sense of collective impotence and distress. Cynicisms and apathy prevail, along with frustration and rage. At the same time, ever-growing numbers of people end up accepting corruption and abuse as a normal way of life.

The *mantra* for survival becomes pay or suffer; without the ability to pull strings in the corridors of power, nothing will get done, from erratic electric power and water supply to ill-maintained roads and street lights, illegal encroachments, open drains, and practically useless sewage disposal facilities, to tardy public transport. At the same time, for those who can pay, everything is available. For most of the two-thirds of humanity in the Third World, these challenges appear to be monumental.

Despite widespread corruption, however, there are pockets in the bureaucracy and the body politic devoid of the scourges of dishonesty and inefficiency. The picture is complex. For example, the 1997 *World Bank*

*Report* stated: "[I]n South Asia... in many countries state inefficiency and corruption have co-existed with a relatively competent and efficient civil service, albeit one whose quality has suffered a noticeable decline" (World Bank, 1997:165).

8.  Historically, the administrative experience of the Third World has been molded by numerous failed attempts at modernization and recurrent crises. This results in a protracted condition of institutional underdevelopment. It has also contributed to perpetuating a self-fulfilling prophecy of immobility. Without real political and institutional development, addressing real issues such as poverty, unemployment, or lack of effective citizenship, administrative reforms—even wrapped in the rhetoric of public sector modernization—are merely patchwork. The contribution of the current vogue to real development and democracy remain marginal, as the protection of market forces, not development and democracy, are its prime directives.

    Despite the historical differences among the countries comprising the lesser-developed component of the "Third World," their objective insertion into the international division of labor as export economies configured a postcolonial order based upon commodities and rent. This characterization now also includes the "transitional" societies of the former socialist world that became peripheralized in the 1990s. The dependent nature of such commodity states has continuously affected the basic functions of their administrative systems and the scope of possible reform. This may help to explain why the attempts at modernization via DA strategies in the 1960s and NPM at present just reenforced pre-existing inequities and vulnerability, increasing social unrest and political turmoil.

9.  The fundamental issue is not as much management as governance. Perhaps the United Nations Development Programme (UNDP) offers the most comprehensive definition of such "good governance." To the UNDP it entails among other things government that is "participatory, transparent, and, accountable. It is also effective and equitable. And it promotes the rule of law. Good governance ensures that political, social and economic priorities are based on broad consensus in society and that the voices of the poorest and the vulnerable are heard in decision-making over the allocation of development resources" (UNDP, 1998:3).

    This definition evokes the concept of human security (Nef, 1999). First of all, it involves public participation in decision making. Second, it implies impartial enforcement of the rule of law. Third, it means transparency in and access to the governing process, including institutions and information sources. Fourth, it requires responsiveness of institutions to the needs of all stakeholders. Fifth, it necessitates consensus among different and divergent interests in the society. Sixth, it translates into the assurance of equity for all individuals in the pursuit of their well-being. Seventh, it means effective and efficient responsibility and accountability of institutions, including the statecraft to serve the basic needs of all by using public resources with optimum accountability (Caiden and Dwivedi, 2001: 251–253). Eight, it requires strategic vision on the part of the leaders toward broad-range and long-term perspectives on sustainable human development. Finally, a central requisite is stewardship, whereby governing elites are dedicated to serve to the public interest. Substantively and especially in developing nations, good governance and sustainable human development also demand conscientious attempts at eliminating poverty, sustaining livelihoods, fulfilling basic needs, and offering an honest and open administrative system.

No country seems to be immune to the global ethical breakdown we have witnessed recently. Even the People's Republic of China, hailed as a paragon of public virtue and morality by visitors and observers in the 1970s, has revealed a much different face. In many nations, a widespread sense of moral disarray and decay exists, and neither developed nor developing countries are exempt.

The need for probity is clearly imperative. This is especially so in societies in which traditional organizational and managerial values drawn from indigenous religious and secular sources were displaced by Western-style management, consumerism, and individualism. By casting out these fundamental beliefs and with insufficient time and conditions for the "modern" values to take root, no specific standards were left against which the conduct of public officials (as well as business people) could be measured. Religious and other leaders with moral authority were told to keep out of the state affairs.

The protective layer of public morality was thus left exposed to the onslaught of dishonesty, sleaziness, deception, and possessive individualism. That axiological protective layer in the body politic needs to be reaffirmed, for no nation or society, irrespective of its political, religious, or secular orientation, can sustain itself in a moral vacuum. The presence of "self-evident" articles of faith (drawn from societal values, cultural traditions, and spiritual ideals) governing peoples' lives is in this sense not only an ethical but a practical necessity. Good governance is essentially moral governance (Dwivedi, 1987).

Contrary to the optimistic predictions derived from conventional modernization theory (Keynesian, Marxist, and neoliberal), in hindsight these generalized dismal results for the security and livelihood of most people should have been predictable. So far, the existing wisdom has tended to dismiss these failures as singular anomalies, yet when these cumulative discontinuities became too many to be treated as exception, the validity of existing models and vogues ends up being largely irrelevant. We once used the expression "a fence around an empty lot" to refer to DA in the 1970s. The same is happening now with NPM.

Any profound administrative transformation involves both structural and attitudinal (as well as much more profound value) changes. Efforts at administrative restructuring, "modernization," and the like need to first address, either directly or indirectly, the nature of administrative culture and the issue of democracy (or rather lack of democracy) throughout the globe. Administrative culture is something heterogeneous, and dynamic. Syncretism, continuities, and discontinuities are part and parcel of its fabric and texture. A lack of democracy, or put more directly, the contradiction between liberalism and democracy (Macpherson, 1977), lies at the core of the current governance problem. From the era of bureaucratic authoritarianism to that of the new public managers, "governability," disempowerment, and exclusion have been constants in the conventional political and administrative formula. The "problem" has been identified as "overparticipation." The solution of choice has been to control, domesticate, or punish social demands. Administrative modernizations without real political democratic reform beyond purely electoral and institutional facades are fatally flawed and destined to failure. Paraphrasing what John Start Mill pointed out over a century and a half ago; small tinkering with big problems does not produce small solutions; it produces no solutions at all.

## REFERENCES

Astley, W. G., Van de Ven, A. (1983). Central perspectives and debates in organization theory. Admin. Sci. Q 28:245–273.

Balogun, M. J., Mutahaba, G. (1999). Redynamizing the African Civil Service for the twentyfirst century. In: Henderson, K., Dwivedi, O. P., eds. Bureaucracy and the Alternatives in World Perspective. London: Macmillan, pp. 190–216.

Ban, C. (1995). How Do Public Managers Manage? Bureaucratic Constraints, Organizational Culture and the Potential for Reform. San Francisco: Jossey Bass.

Barber, W., Ronning, N. (1966). Internal Security and Military Power: Counterinsurgency and Civic Action in Latin America. Columbus: Ohio State University Press.

Baumgartner, T., Burns, T., DeVille, P. (1977). Reproduction and transformation of dependency relationships in the international system: A dialectical systems perspective. Proceedings of the Annual North American Meeting of the Society for General Systems Research, pp. 129–136.

Bonifacio, J. A. (1995). Modernizacion del servicio civil en el contexto de la reforma estatal. Revista centroamericana de Admnistracion Publica 28 and 29:5–26.

Braudel, F. (1980). History and the social sciences: The longue durée. In: Braudel, F., ed. On History. Chicago: University of Chicago Press, pp. 25–54.

Caiden, G. E., Dwivedi, O. P. (2001). Official ethics and corruption. In: Caiden, G.E., Dwivedi, O.P., Jabbra, J.G. Where Corruption Lives. Bloomfield, CT: Kumarian.

Caiden, G. E., Dwivedi, O. P., Jabbra, J. G. (2001). Where Corruption Lives. Bloomfield: Kumarian.

CLAD's Scientific Council. (Feb. 1999). A new public management for Latin America. Revista del CLAD, Reforma y Democracia. no. 13.

Cox, R., Gramsci, A. (1983). Hegemony and international relations: An essay on method. Millen J Internat Stud 12(2):163–164.

Crowther, W., Flores, G. (1984). Problemas latinoamericanos en administración pública y dependencia de soluciones desde Estados Unidos. In: Flores, G., Nef, J., eds. Administración Publica: Perspectivas Criticas. San José, Costa Rica: ICAP, pp. 59–89.

David, E. (1957). An approach to the analysis of political systems. World Pol 9(3):384–385.

Dwivedi, O. P. (1987). Moral dimensions of statecraft: A plea for an administrative theology. Can J Polit Sci 20(4):699–709.

Dwivedi, O. P. (1994). Development Administration: From Underdevelopment to Sustainable Development. London: Macmillan.

Dwivedi, O. P., Gow, J. I. (1999). From Bureaucracy to Public Management: The Administrative Culture of the Government of Canada. Peterborough, ON, Canada: Broadview.

Freire, P. (1971). Pedagogy of the Oppressed. New York: Herder and Herder.

Freire, P. (1976). Education, the Practice of Freedom. London: Writers and Readers Publishing Cooperative.

Friedman, M. (1964). Capitalism and Freedom. Chicago: University of Chicago Press.

Friedman, M. (1962). Essays in Positive Economics. Chicago: University of Chicago Press.

Galtung, J. (1980). The True Worlds: A Transnational Perspective. New York: Free Press.

Giddens, A. (1998). The Third Way: The Renewal of Social Democracy. Cambridge, UK: Polity Press.

Gil, B., Rocamora, J., Wilson, R. (1993). Low Intensity Democracy: Political Power in the New World Order. London: Pluto.

Gouldner, A. (1954). Patterns of Industrial Bureaucracy. Glencoe: Free Press.

Graf, W. D. (1988). The Nigerian State: Political Economy, State Class and Political System in the Post-Colonial Era. London: James Currey.

Graf, W. D. (1995). The state in the third world. In: Panitch, L., ed. The Socialist Register. London: Merlin, pp. 140–162.

Graf, W. D. (1996). Democratization for the third world. Can. J. Dev. Stud. 37–56.

Heady, F. (1984). Public Administration: A Comparative Perspective. 3rd ed. New York: Dekker, pp. 338–342, 174–221; also 1st ed., Englewood Cliffs, NJ: Prentice-Hall, 1966, pp. 38–40.

IDRC. (1992). The Global Cash Crunch: An Examination of Debt and Development. Ottawa: IDRC.

Islam, N. (1989). Colonial legacy, administrative reform and politics: Pakistan 1947–1987. Pub Admin Dev 9(3):271–285.

Karl, B.D. (1976). Public administration and American history: A century of professionalism. Pub. Admin. Rev. 36(5):489–503.

Keen, B. (1992). A History of Latin America. Boston: Houghton-Mifflin.

Kliksberg, B. (1984). La reforma de la administración pública en América Latina. Elementos para una evaluación. Alcalá de Henares, Spain: Instituto Nacional de Administración Publica.

Kliksberg, B. (1987). Nuevas fronteras tecnológicas en materia de gerencia en América Latina. Revista de la CEPAL 31:179–199.

Lee, R. W. (1988). Dimensions of the South American cocaine industry. J. Interamer. Stud. 30(3):87–104.

Macpherson, C. B. (1977). The Life and Times of Liberal Democracy. Oxford: Oxford University Press.

Malloy, J. (1977). Authoritarianism and corporatism in Latin America: The modal pattern. In: Malloy, J., ed. Authoritarianism and Corporatism in Latin America. Pittsburgh: Pittsburgh University Press, pp. 3–19.

Manzer, R. (1984). Policy rationality and policy analysis: The problem of the choice of criteria for decision-making. In: Dwivedi, O. P., ed. Policy and Administrative Studies. Guelph: University of Guelph, pp. 27–40.

Marini-Ferreira, C. M. (1999). Crise e reforma do estado: uma questão de cuidadania e valorizaç ão do servidor. Rio de Janeiro: Escola Nacional de Administração Pública, pp. 1–37.

Maturana, H., Varela, F. (1980). Autopoiesis and Cognition: The Realization of the Cognitive. Boston: Reidell.

Mesa-Lago, C. (1999). Desarrollo social, reforma del Estado y de la seguridad social al umbral del Siglo XXI. Revista del CLAD. Reforma y Democracia 15:7–70.

Mills, C. W. (1957). The Power Elite. New York: Oxford University Press.

Moore, B. (1966). Social Origins of Dictatorship and Democracy: Lord and Peasant in the Making of the Modern World. Boston: Beacon.

Morstein-Marx, F. (1963). The higher civil service as an action group in Western political development. In: LaPalombara, J., ed. Bureaucracy and Political Development. Princeton, NJ: Princeton University Press.

MST (Landless Rural Workers Movement). (2000). Fundamental principles for the social and economic transformation of Brazil. J Peasant Stud 28(2):153–161.

Nef, J., Robles, W. (2000). Globalization, neoliberalism and the state of underdevelopment in the new periphery. J Dev Soc XVI, Fascicule 1:27–48.

Nef, J., Bensabat, R. (1992). "Gobernability" and the receiver state in Latin America: Analysis and prospects. In: Ritter, A. Cameron, M. Pollock, D., eds. Latin America to the Year 2000: Reactivating Growth, Improving Equity, Sustaining Democracy. New York: Praeger, pp. 171–175.

Nef, J., Dwivedi, O. P. (1981). Development theory and administration: A fence around an empty lot? Indian J Pub Admin XXVIII(1):42–66.

Nef, J. (1982). Empate político, inmobilismo e inflación: Algunas notas preliminaries. Revista Centroamericana de Administración Pública 3:141–155.

Nef, J. (1997). Estado, poder y políticas sociales: una visión crítica. In: Urzúa, R., ed. Cambios Sociales y Política públicas en América Latina. Santiago: Andros, pp. 233–262.

Nef, J. (1999). Human Security and Mutual Vulnerability: The Political Economy of Development and Underdevelopment. Ottawa: IDRC.

O'Donnell, G. (1977). Corporatism and the question of the state. In: Malloy, J., ed. Authoritarianism and Corporatism in Latin America. Pittsburgh: Pittsburgh University Press, pp. 47–84.

Ormond, D., Löffler, E. (1999). Nueva Gestión Pública ¿Que tomar y que dejar? Revista del CLAD. Reforma y Democracia 11:141–172.

Osborne, D., Gaebler, T. (1992). Reinventing Government: How the Entrepreneurial Spirit Is Transforming the Public Sector. Reading, MA: Addison-Wesley.

Péréz Salgado, I. (1997). El papel de la cooperación técnica internacional en el proceso de modernización del Estado y la gestión en América latina. Revista del CLAD. Reforma y Democracia 8:247–270.

Raphaeli, N. (1967). Readings in Comparative Public Administration. Boston: Alyn and Bacon.

Rifkin, J. (1995). The End of Work: The Decline of the Global Labor Force and the Dawn of the Post-Market Era. New York: Putnam's.

Riggs, F. (1967). The Sala model: An ecological approach to the study of comparative administration. In: Raphaeli, N., ed. Readings in Comparative Public Administration. Boston: Alyn and Bacon, pp. 415–416.

Robles, W. (2000). Beyond the politics of protest: The landless rural workers movement of Brazil. Can J Dev Stud XXI(3):657–691.

Rohr, J.A. (1988). Bureaucratic morality in the United States. Internat Polit Sci Rev 9(3):167–178.

Rostow, W. W. (1960). The Stages of Economic Growth: A Non-Communist Manifesto. Cambridge: Cambridge University Press.

Santana, L., Mario, N. (1996). Reinventing government: Nueva retórica, viejos problemas. Revista del CLAD. Reforma y Democracia 6:147–164.

Sklar, H. (1980). Trilateralism: Managing dependency and democracy—An overview. In: Sklar, H., ed. Trilateralism: Elite Planning for World Management. Montreal: Black Rose Press, pp. 1–55.

Smucker, J. (1988). La culture de l'organisation comme idéólogie de gestion: une analyse critique. In: Symmons, G., ed. La Culture des Organisations. Québec: Institut québécois de recherche sur la culture, pp. 39–68.

Stallings, B. (1978). Class Conflict and Economic Development in Chile 1958–1973. Stanford, CA: Stanford University Press.

Theobald, R. (1995). Globalization and the resurgence of the patrimonial state. Internat Rev Admin Sci 61(3).

Turner, M., Halligan, J. (1999). Bureaucracy and the alternatives in East and Southeast Asia. In: Henderson, K., Dwivedi, O. P., eds. Bureaucracy and the Alternatives in World Perspective. London: Macmillan, pp. 129–159.

UNDP. (1998). Good Governance and Sustainable Human Development. New York: UNDP.

Vilas, C. (1995). Economic restructuring, neoliberal reforms and the working class in Latin America, In: Halebsky, S., Harris, R. eds. Capital, Power and Inequality in Latin America. Boulder, CO: Westview, pp. 137–138.

Vilas, C. (2000). ¿Más allá del Consenso de Washington? Un enfoque desde la política de algunas propuestas del Banco Mundial sobre reforma administrative. Revista del CLAD. Reforma y Democracia 18, 25–76.

World Bank. (1997). World Development Report. Washington, DC: World Bank.

# 9

# Evaluating Indicators for Rural Women's Socioeconomic Development
## *The Case of Thailand*

**ANGELINE L. AMES and TODD T. AMES**

*National University of Singapore, Singapore*

## INTRODUCTION

The debate concerning women's economic development has been a controversial one for several decades. In the world economic system based on the capitalist mode of production, women's integration into waged labor has evolved into a leading topic in development studies. Many aspects of development research throughout the world have focused on women's integration into waged labor as a development tool for women to initiate social change (Taplin, 1989; Boserup, 1970). Integration in the early 1970s meant that women needed to be included in industrial labor (Pearson, 1998:172). Some argued that industrial integration had positive implications for women (Lim, 1990:111 c.f. Pearson, 1998). Research in Ghana suggests that women who worked in the formal sectors of the economy were better off economically than most women, who remained in the informal sector (Ninsin, 1991). Fairly recently, however, development research has highlighted the negative aspects of integration for women in developing countries (Thomson, 1996; Kaosa-ard, 1995; Rosa, 1994; Mies, 1991). Studies of the formal economic sectors in Southeast Asia and Mexico indicate that although many women have been incorporated into the industrialization process, most work as low-paid waged laborers and facilitate the process of capital accumulation (Ahmad, 1998; Bell, 1997; Arizpe and Aranda, 1986). Further research into the informal sectors of the economy in Kenya, Malaysia, and Thailand suggests that women in agriculture and home-based production usually work as paid laborers and independent commodity producers with inadequate social protection (Ariffin, 2000; Suda, 1996; Kaosa-ard, 1993; Lee, 1993). In Thailand, the informal home-based sector is defined as "lacking in structure, with no labor regulations, no clear cut employee/employer relations in work arrangements, and low capitalization" (Lee, 1993:84). The question is then why the majority of women's work in developing countries has resulted in low pay, limited employment, and poverty when certain aspects of the development process resulted in shifts from subsistence economic activity through cash-crop production to waged labor.

This chapter is designed to evaluate rural women's socioeconomic development in Thailand as it relates to their integration into wage labor, to the gross domestic product (GDP),[1] and to changes in state policies toward women's development. Special attention is paid to shifts in GDP and social policies for rural women's economic development in Thailand, as both have had a tremendous impact on rural Thai women's socioeconomic development (McMichael, 1996; Ames and Ames, 2002).

For the purpose of this study, the concept of women's socioeconomic development is taken from the United Nations Fourth World Conference on the Status of Women (United Nations, 1995). The U.N.'s overall concept of socioeconomic development for women stresses basic changes in the social and economic relations of women caused by their integration into waged labor (United Nations, 1995). In this chapter, the focus is on changes in rural Thai women's integration into waged labor with an emphasis on female employment and education. Interviews, literature, and past research (Ames and Ames, 2002; Ariffin, 2000; Rahman and Aziz, 1998; Ahmad, 1998) have identified changes in employment patterns and educational levels as valuable indicators in measuring women's abilities to benefit from waged labor. The chapter evaluates the validity of these two indicators as they relate to rural Thai women's socioeconomic development and examines the role of GDP and state policy in this regard. Finally, it explores how these evaluations can be used to construct comprehensive, multi-indicator measures that can better address rural women's socioeconomic development.

## STATE POLICY, GENDER, AND GROSS DOMESTIC PRODUCT IN THAILAND

In analyzing the roles played by state development plans, GDP, and waged labor in women's socioeconomic development, it is useful to consider the economic processes at work that influence the situation. Until the late 1970s, Thailand had relatively abundant land resources, and agricultural exports provided the primary source of foreign income. The agricultural sector had the single largest demand for labor, both for rural women and men. Between 70–80% of the total female workforce outside the Central Region (Bangkok) was still employed in the agricultural sector in the late 1970s, and nonagricultural employment played a relatively minor role in terms of Northern rural women's labor activities (Kaosa-ard, 1995:5). In the economic restructuring of Thailand, however, state development plans focused on a push to industrialize. The importance of the agricultural sector began to decline and rural women migrated to Bangkok in pursuit of industrial wage-labor opportunities. These women found wages to be extremely low compared to the wage rates in some other Southeast Asian countries.[2]

The decline in the importance of agriculture to the national economy of Thailand was not the only factor that contributed to rural women's integration into waged labor; the level of land ownership had also declined (Ames and Ames, 2002). Many of the smaller landowners in northern Thailand had sold their land and gone to work in Chiang Mai City or to agricultural estates, either private or government-owned. Rural women in Chiang Mai Province became commodity producers, growing fruits and vegetables and selling their products to export processing plants (Interviews, 1998). Limited access to land was an important contributor to rural poverty (UNESCAP, 1998:7). Other causal factors of rural poverty in northern Thailand included low literacy rates, urban/rural dichotomies, and limited access to markets, materials, credit, inputs, and technology (Ames and Ames, 2002). Various politicoeconomic factors that contributed to rural poverty included land reforms' bias toward development in urban infrastructures; the lack of irrigation facility, rural electricity, and rural roads for transport; and the lack of legitimate access to rural credit (UNESCAP, 1998:7–10).

The transitional economic situation in Thailand has created a great need to develop economic opportunities for low-income rural women and opportunities in the form of education or re-education, as well as alternative labor or employment opportunities in small-scale or income-generating activities. State planning in Thailand has been in line with the above—formulating socioeconomic plans for rural areas, while emphasizing the modernization of traditional methods of production and a shift toward waged labor for rural women. Rural development strategies have focused on providing modern farming opportunities, value-added processing of agricultural products, and integration of women into the nonfarm and off-farm labor force. Some of the programs that have been implemented in the rural areas include setting up markets in urban areas; holding skill and training workshops; encouraging cooperatives, village industries, and rural entrepreneurships; establishing microcredit facilities and related supports; and adopting income-generating projects (Ames and Ames, 2002).

As concluded by Thailand's Report on the Status of Women (National Commission Women's Affairs, 1994), positive social effects are seen when women's socioeconomic roles and relations improve. A decline in female poverty is seen when employment and family income increase, female rural–urban migration decreases, and female literacy or educational levels rise (Dulansey and Austin, 1985:83–84). Because increasing rural women's earnings is so important, an improvement in their social and economic relations is central to their socioeconomic development. These undertakings were demonstrated in the national development plans of Thailand and the strategies used to promote women's socioeconomic development. (See Table 1.)

An emphasis within the fourth national development plan of Thailand was on women's employment and educational development. This fourth plan noted the lack of women's educational opportunities and their discrimination with respect to professional advancements. The plan also noted that the male population had greater educational opportunities, which is evident in the female and male illiteracy rates of 25.2%, and 11.1%, respectively. The plan also pointed out the discrimination in terms of professional advancement and salaries (Sookasame, 1989:204; National Commission Womens' Affairs, 1985:20). In this plan, economic development for women was designed and implemented predominantly through training programs. These training programs were to assist rural women in gaining the skills needed to compete in the changing labor market.

**Table 1**   State Policies for Women's Socioeconomic Development (1972–1986)

| Time frame | National economic and social development plans | Women's socioeconomic development strategies |
|---|---|---|
| 1972–1976 | Third National Development Plan | Women's role in family planning issues major focus (reproductive roles). Targeted Thai women as a group for social development. Wage and labor protection. |
| 1977–1981 | Fourth National Development Plan | Education and employment development for women. Employment training programs for rural women. Small-scale industries to develop economic opportunities for women in rural areas. |
| 1982–1986 | Fifth National Development Plan | Poverty alleviation and reduction programs in rural areas. Income generation projects established with national funding provided. Productive roles needed to be developed, female labor opportunities needed to improve in both urban and rural areas, educational levels for women needed to be raised, and political matters that did not equate Thai women to an equal status needed to be addressed. |

*Source*: Interviews, 2001; UNDP, 2000; Sookasame 1989; National Commission on Women's Affairs, 1985.

For the first time in Thai state policy, the fifth plan fully identified Thai women as a specific target group and emphasized poverty alleviation in the poorer north and northeast regions of Thailand. Income generation became a top priority for rural women's economic development, and their vocational and skills training became a major policy for both government and nongovernmental organizations. The emphasis on rural women's productive roles in the fifth plan was a clear indicator of the change in policy focus that took place in the 1980s (Ames and Ames, 2002). Connected to the fifth plan was the long-term women's development plan (1982–2001), which also focused on poverty alleviation for the rural women in Thailand. Despite such state policy to promote poverty alleviation, there is disparity among Southeast Asian countries in terms of the number of rural women in poverty. Although the percentage of Thai rural women in poverty was lower than in Malaysia or Indonesia, over half of Thai rural women still lived in poverty. (See Table 2.)

Both Indonesia and the Philippines recorded higher numbers of rural populations in absolute poverty than did Thailand. In fiscal year 1995, the Thailand Community Development Board's budget for women and children in rural areas was 390 million baht (Thai currency), and in 1996, it increased to 500 million baht. Even with this slight increase, the budget for the development of rural women still accounted for less than 0.07% of the total government budget (Kaosa-ard, 1995:18–20).

**Table 2**  Estimated Number in thousands, and Percentage of Rural Women Living Below the Poverty Line in 1988

| Country | Number of rural women | Rural population in absolute poverty | Percentage of rural women in poverty |
|---|---|---|---|
| Thailand | 9040 | 14,464 | 63 |
| Malaysia | 1572 | 2161 | 73 |
| Indonesia | 23713 | 34,608 | 68 |
| Philippines | 12245 | 22,390 | 55 |

*Source*: Corner, 1997:6.

The sixth, seventh, and eighth national development plans continued to promote strategies for Thai women's socioeconomic development. (See Table 3.) During the eighth plan (1997–2001), a five-year women's development plan was adopted. One main objective of this plan was to provide women with access to the decision-making process (UNDP, 2000:15). While international organizations continued to treat gender as a separate, cross-cutting issue within development and

**Table 3**  State Policies for Women's Socioeconomic Development (1987–2001)

| Time frame | National economic and social development plans | Women's socioeconomic development strategies |
|---|---|---|
| 1987–1991 | Sixth National Development Plan | Included women who were on the margins of Thai society, such as agricultural workers, Buddhist nuns, women officials, state enterprise women workers, imprisoned women, and prostitutes. |
| 1992–1996 | Seventh National Development Plan | Crucial policy framework that emerged during this time was that trafficking and prostitution of Thai women and Thai children had to be addressed. |
| 1997–2001 | Eighth National Development Plan | The Eighth Plan was geared toward fostering and developing Thai women's physical, intellectual, and spiritual well-being, and strived to more fully develop their human potential and ensure full human participation. This included raising the education of labor up to the secondary level. |
| | | Mainstreamed women into policy development and design by setting up the term gender as a focal point within the larger plans. |
| | | Government commitment to the Convention on the Elimination of All Forms of Discrimination Against Women (CEDAW) and the Beijing Platform for Action. |

*Source*: Interviews, 2001; UNDP, 2000; Sookasame, 1989; National Commission on Women's Affairs, 1985.

social welfare, the Thai national policy assumed that the gender issue would automatically be considered at all levels of development (Ames and Ames, 2002).

When considering a rise in GDP as a clear indicator of development, many authors (McMichael, 1996; Webster, 1992; Weeks, 1981) have noted numerous drawbacks in using GDP as a valid measure of development. Some of the more obvious problems include the fact that greater outputs do not necessarily indicate rising standards of living or equitable distribution of wealth and resources.

What has been noted by development agencies such as the United Nations Economic and Social Commission of Asia and the Pacific (UNESCAP), however, is that an increase in wealth and resources, measured in terms of GDP, is necessary to provide the resources for improving the social and economic standards of living for the population of the less-developed countries. For developing countries such as Thailand, an increase in output requires extensive increases in labor inputs. In this sense, economic growth in the form of increasing GDP is useful in that it can be considered a readily available indicator of increased employment and incomes for a greater number of people. This increase in income results in a greater ability to pay for such social services as education (UNESCAP, 1999:113–114). In addition, rising income is related to the supply of resources, the investment climate, and the demand of the private sector to provide higher-quality social services (UNESCAP, 1999:113–114). The question is, however, whether or not rural women, like their male counterparts, are experiencing similar increases in income.

Thailand's case certainly illustrates these points; its per capita GDP rose from $688 in 1980 to $2833 in 1995, and during the same period, government expenditures on education increased eightfold (UNESCAP, 2001:1, 3). One simple indicator of the effects of these policies and resource allocations is the concomitant increase in the adult literacy rate during this period, increasing from 92.3/82.6 (male/female) to 96.4/92.0 (male/female (UNESCAP, 2001:1). The purposeful targeting of education in general and women's education in particular in the national development plans was seen as a way to achieve socioeconomic development. Up until the crisis, the government allocated about 21% of the national budget to education (UNESCAP, 2001:2).

Following the crises of 1997, by 1998 per capita GDP had fallen to $1828, and the rate of growth dropped from 7.9% in 1995 to −10.1% (negative growth) in 1998 (Vimolsiri, 1999:268; UNESCAP, 2001:1). The impact of this decline has been an increase in unemployment, from 1.9% in 1997 to 4.4% in 1998. Overall, 13.4 million people lost their jobs. Women made up 80% of the unskilled labor laid off in the manufacturing sector (UNESCAP, 1999:119).

Loss of family income has been directly attributed to causing 254,000 students in Thailand to end their educations prematurely. The hardest hit was basic education, with 47% dropping out of primary schools (UNESCAP, 1999:126). While the government expenditure for education increased slightly after the economic crisis to 23% in real terms, the amount declined due to the devaluation of the baht (UNESCAP, 2001:2). This resulted in an estimated layoff of 70,000 primary school teachers by 1997, which was largely due to the government's attempt to drastically cut costs in the face of the crisis (UNESCAP, 1999:119).

The government's response was to initiate a program providing comprehensive assistance to the poor in the form of employment generation and training. Against some opposition to the borrowing of outside funds during its financial hardship, the

Thai government decided to accept the "Miyazawa plan," a combination $1.45 billion package from the World Bank, the Japan Exim Bank, and the Organization for Economic Cooperation and Development (OECD) (UNESCAP, 2001:28). The funds from this plan were to create employment for both men and women. One of the main emphases was also to provide funds for community education and training in both marketing and the production of handicrafts. The plan also included a large component of social investment in the form of job creation and vocational training for 10,000 women, youth, and the disabled (UNESCAP, 1999: 129). For policies to be implemented, the political and public will needs to exist. As noted by one Thai government official, a good example of the importance of this issue is the recent adoption by Thailand of job protection regulations for women, which have been largely ignored by most employers (Interview, 2001).

## INTEGRATION OF THAI WOMEN INTO WAGED LABOR

Among the various industrial sectors in Thailand, foreign direct investment had been more involved in manufacturing, accounting for one-third of the total foreign investment inflows during the 1980s. Food, textiles, electronics, chemicals, machinery and transportation equipment, petroleum products, and construction materials were among the major industries with substantial foreign investment. The United States and Japan were the two countries that initially invested the most foreign capital in Thailand. Combined, the United States and Japan accounted for over 60% of total foreign investment between 1970 and 1985 (Tambunlertchai, 1993:134). Newly industrialized nations in Asia, particularly Taiwan, Hong Kong, and Singapore, became the sources of foreign investment from the mid-1980s onward. Japanese and Taiwanese investments had been in industries under the Board of Investment (BOI)[3] and operated in collaboration with the Thai business elites, whereas the United States invested mostly in the energy sector, which is outside the BOI (Tambunlertchai, 1993:135–136). Although in the past Thailand received less foreign investment than most of its fellow Association of South East Asian Nations (ASEAN) members, such investment in export-led industries increased throughout the 1980s. By 1988, foreign investment averaged 38.5% of the total equity capital of all BOI-promoted industries (Tambunlertchai, 1993:136). Foreign investors had control over the multinational firms, as they were the ones supplying capital, expertise, and technology. It was during this time that the integration of rural Thai women into the capitalist labor process intensified throughout the export-oriented and import-substitution industries.

> [A] key to Thailand's international market-oriented success story has been what investors, bankers, planners, and analysts refer to as "the low-wage, docile, and disciplined work force," a very indirect way of designating women. Export-oriented manufacturing of items such as electronics, ready-made clothes, processed food, jewelry, shoes, and leather ware are made mostly by women. They [women] constitute over 70 percent of the workers in each of these industries (National Commission on Women's Affair's, 1994:5).

Wanting to make as much profit as possible, multinational corporations limited Thai women workers "to certain levels of the occupational hierarchy and for them [the workers] there is little hope of learning useful skills" (Charoenloet, 1991:1).

As of 1990, there were three large-scale export-oriented factories and sixteen small-scale factories in Chiang Mai Province (northern Thailand), of which only one was involved in agro-export. Most of the rural women in the large-scale garment factories were paid on the basis of piece rates, estimated at around 2000 baht per month (Gray, 1990:48). For those in small-scale factories, such as broom or umbrella factories, the average pay was 25 to 160 baht per day. One woman we interviewed in 1998 estimated that her daughter made 5000 baht a month by working as a semiskilled assembly worker at a silver/jewelry factory in Lamphun (Ames, 1999).

As women's economic roles continued to change, so did their sources of income. From 1986 to 1992, rural Thai women's major source of income shifted from profits to wages as their economic roles continued to change from commodity production to waged labor (Kaosa-ard, 1995:7). For the whole nation, there was an increase of 26% in wages and salaries between 1976 and 1992, while there was a decrease in profits during the same period. (See Table 4.)

For rural women in northern Thailand, the overall contribution to household cash income increased from 22–43% during this period (Kaosa-ard, 1995:7). As state policy continued to promote industrial development, more and more rural Thai women found themselves involved in the manufacturing and agro-export sectors. The strong push for industrialization was not, however, the only reason Thai women found themselves more and more dependent on an industrial economy. The agricultural sector had been pushed to its limits, creating another change in the occupational structure in Thailand.

> By 1980, it was apparent that Thailand had reached the limits of its agricultural expansion. As the supply of land for cultivation became increasingly scarce, women were the first group of surplus household labourers to leave the agricultural sector. Between 1983 and 1988, there was a net withdrawal of female workers from the agricultural sector, evident even during peak growing seasons. This movement of labour out of the primary sector has enabled the growth of Thailand's export market, which is based on labour-intensive manufacturing. Thus, released from the agricultural sector and readily employed in manufacturing, services, and commerce sectors, rural Thai

**Table 4**   Sources of Income by Year and Gender (1976–1992)

| Sources of income by years | Females (percentage per year) | Males (percentage per year) |
|---|---|---|
| Wages and salaries | | |
| 1976 | 38.5 | 32.4 |
| 1988 | 60.0 | 51.5 |
| 1992 | 64.3 | 48.5 |
| Profits | | |
| 1976 | 47.2 | 61.1 |
| 1988 | 38.3 | 47.0 |
| 1992 | 33.7 | 49.4 |
| Other | | |
| 1976 | 14.3 | 6.5 |
| 1988 | 1.6 | 1.5 |
| 1992 | 2.0 | 2.1 |

*Source*: Kaosa-ard, 1995:30.

women made the shift from home-based (and often unpaid) employment to non-farm, wage-paying employment in the 1980s (Kaosa-ard, 1995:6).

The decline in the agricultural sector also resulted in the expansion of the informal sector, in which many rural Thai women are engaged today (Ames and Ames, 2002). A regular wage is the distinguishing feature between formal and informal sectors; the formal sector is made up of "regular organized occupations with steady pay, and the informal sector of self-employment, irregular employment, and often intermittent or varying remuneration" (Pine, 1982:396). While the informal sector provides an opportunity for some rural Thai women to work outside the home and receive wages, many more rural women generate their income at home on a subcontracting basis with inadequate social protection. The growth in the informal sector has resulted in patterns of "gender segregation" that reinforce the supporting or secondary economic status of Thai women and the preference for rural women to enter the informal labor force as opposed to continuing their education (National Commission on Women's Affairs, 1994; Chang, 1998). In our interview in 1998, many of the women working in the informal sector reported low levels of education, while those working in the formal sector reported higher levels of education. It is interesting to note that the average income of the informal sector workers was for the most part equivalent to that of the women working in the formal sector of the economy (Ames, 1999). Social protection and a regular wage, however, were lacking in the informal sector.

Changes in economic relations are also seen through changes in the occupational structure of rural women in northern Thailand. Although the percentages of rural women working in agriculture and animal husbandry decreased from 82.2% in 1980 to 46.3% in 1998, in all other sectors of the economy such percentages actually increased. (See Table 5.)

While women's participation in clerical jobs, sales, and services has risen significantly, the increase in their participation in professional, administrative,

**Table 5**  Changes in Occupational Structure for Women in Northern Thailand by Percentage of Labor Force

| Occupations | 1980 | 1991 | 1998 |
|---|---|---|---|
| Professional, technical, and related workers | 2.2 | 4.3 | 7.3 |
| Administrative, executive, managerial workers, and government officials | 0.2 | 0.2 | 1.2 |
| Clerical and related workers | 0.6 | 2.3 | 4.9 |
| Sales workers | 6.8 | 15.2 | 20.5 |
| Agricultural, animal husbandry and forest workers, fisherman and hunters, miners and related workers | 82.2 | 59.0 | 46.3 |
| Transport equipment operators, communications and related workers | 0.1 | 0.4 | 0.3 |
| Craftsmen, production workers, and laborers | 5.8 | 13.6 | 16.0 |
| Service workers | 2.1 | 4.7 | 4.4 |
| Total | 100 | 100 | 100 |

*Source*: 1980 Population and Housing Census; 1991; Office of the Prime Minister, 1998.

executive, managerial, and government services remains insignificant. Although these occupational changes have taken place, the majority of rural women in northern Thailand still work in the primary and services sectors. In 1991, on average, women in urban areas made 9000 baht a year more than women in rural areas (Office of the Prime Minister, 1991:216–217). When members of some projects were asked what type of occupation they would like to see their daughters pursue, the overwhelming majority answered a "government official in the urban areas," since such a job paid so well (Ames and Ames, 2002). In fact, the highest-paying position for Thai women is a government job in a municipal area (Office of the Prime Minister, 1991:218–219). The comments of the respondents clearly indicated the importance of high-income employment for rural Thai women.

In 1990 and 1991, 52% of all Thai women participated in the workforce, while at the same time they performed household chores and were responsible for child-care. The data available in 1991 on wage differentials showed that Thai women earned consistently less than Thai men in agriculture, manufacturing, commerce, and services. On average, Thai women earned approximately 5000 baht a year less than their male counterparts in both urban and rural areas (Office of the Prime Minister, 1991:216–217). In 1993, the national statistical office showed that 80.2% of the female labor force was between the ages of 35 to 39 years and that 57.5% worked in agriculture. Although agriculture remains the most important sector for Thai women, by and large they are still unpaid for their work, whereas Thai men work as wage laborers (National Commission on Women's Affairs, 1994:19). We found this to be true in 1998 as well. Although the female members of the projects under study were working as commodity producers, husbands and sons were overwhelmingly working as waged laborers (Ames and Ames, 2002).

Rural Thai women working in agriculture face multiple forms of income disparities: many of them do unpaid work (UNDP, 1999:234), men earn on average more than women, urban women earn on average more than rural women, and women in the urban service sector earn more than women in agricultural activities. While employment is an important indicator of development in Thailand, income thus varies greatly due to gender, rural–urban distinction in work, and the type of waged labor activities one engages in. In the case of rural Thai women, income would indicate that they are not sufficiently integrated into waged labor activities in Thailand. This would also suggest that despite state policy and national development plans the government is not completely in control of the economy.

The government's inability to control the economy was clearly illustrated by the effects of the Asian economic crisis on the Thai population. The crisis resulted in a massive devaluation of the baht, from which many Thai people not only lost their life savings but also were robbed of their right to work. As export-oriented factories moved out of Bangkok literally overnight, the vast majority of their employees, especially women, were left jobless (Interviews, 1998, 2001). These women were not paid before the companies pulled out, and they had no legal means or financial backing to ensure that they would receive the money owed to them by many of these industrial firms (Interviews, 1998). This loss was felt throughout Thailand, as the majority of these women were supporting themselves, their families, and their parents. This is especially true for the rural women in northern Thailand, where their role in the family was primarily economic and their remittances used to be extremely high (Interviews, 1998; Kaosa-ard, 1993). Following the economic crisis, when demand for the products of Food and Agricultural Candy project was falling and its need for subsequent labor inputs was declining, instead of laying off some members of the project, the decision was made to cut back on hours worked while retaining the full employment of all members (Ames and Ames, 2002). Instead of having some members unemployed, all chose underemployment. Similar patterns were seen in Indonesia following the financial crisis of 1997, when the returning wage laborers were absorbed back into family farming activities with no substantial rise in outputs (Ames, 2002). The case of Thai rural women illustrates how falling demands and incomes can still allow for high levels of employment, suggesting again the important interlinkages in developing economies among production, employment, and income.

## EDUCATION, GENDER, AND DEVELOPMENT IN THAILAND

Varying degrees of gender equality exist in Thailand's education system. In 1999, primary and secondary net enrollment rates[4] (percentage of female and male) were 103% and 97%, respectively. Varying degrees of gender equality also exists in the ASEAN region as a whole. (See Table 6.)

Overall, the levels of enrollment in the ASEAN region are impressive, and net enrollment in Thailand is high for females. As is rightfully noted in UNIFEM's (2000) report on targets and indicators, however, the gender-specific measures need to be developed by taking into account the completion rates and types of studies female students pursue. Although the gender gap found at the primary and secondary levels appears minimal in the region, studies have shown that equal years of female and male education do not lead to equal job opportunities and equal pay (UNIFEM, 2000:17).

Kaosa-ard's (1993) research in rural northern Thailand demonstrates how employment opportunities had a significant impact on the secondary enrollment ratios between the male and female populations. When there were industrial job opportunities in a village, the enrollment ratio of female students at *Matayomsuksa* 5 (upper secondary education) was only 27.8%, compared to 42.9% for male students. In advanced agricultural-related villages, however, in which many children provide family labor, the reverse was seen; female students' enrollment ratio was 48%, while male students' enrollment ratio was 40% (Kaosa-ard, 1993:15–16).

**Table 6**   1999 Gender Gap in Education in Selected ASEAN Countries (Percentage Female/Male)

| Country | Adult literacy | Primary net enrollment | Secondary net enrollment |
|---------|----------------|------------------------|--------------------------|
| Thailand | 96 | 103 | 97 |
| Philippines | 99 | 100 | 102 |
| Singapore | 91 | 98 | 98 |
| Malaysia | 90 | 100 | 115 |
| Indonesia | 88 | 99 | 91 |

*Source*: UNDP, 2000:5.

**Table 7**  Occupational Structure for Women in Northern Thailand by Primary and Secondary Educational Attainment (1998)

| Sector | Total[a] | None | Less than Pratom 4 | Pratom 4 | Pratom 7 | Matayomsuksa 3 | Matayomsuksa 5 |
|---|---|---|---|---|---|---|---|
| Agriculture | 1015.9 | 144.6 | 47.0 | 573.8 | 176.7 | 45.2 | 19.2 |
| Manufacturing | 253.7 | 8.4 | 4.4 | 111.2 | 52.4 | 38.3 | 20.4 |
| Services | 274.1 | 10.7 | 4.2 | 74.1 | 27.4 | 26.2 | 18.0 |

*Note*: Nonmunicipal area.
[a] In thousands.
*Source*: Report of Labour Force Survey, 1998:161.

Although enrollment for Thai female students at the primary and secondary levels of education appears to be equivalent to that of male students, this is not the case in universities or vocational schools or in the technical fields. In terms of vocational areas, Thai women are more likely to be enrolled in home economics, hotel and catering, tailoring, and commerce. Informal training for women focuses on their reproductive rather than productive roles, and entrepreneurship courses are more likely to teach domestic skills (UNDP, 2000:2–8). Sex quotas for entrance into such schools as medicine are evident, and indicate a preference for male students (UNDP, 2000:8). In 1995, only 23% of female tertiary students were enrolled in science (UNDP, 1999:230).

Members of the projects studied said that they wanted their daughters to go to college, because this was the only way to obtain a job outside the villages (Ames and Ames 2002). This indicates a change in Thai women's perceived needs for education. In the past, women went to school to gain knowledge in the domestic sphere. Today, women are obtaining education to compete in the ever-changing labor market. (See Tables 7 and 8.)

As Tables 7 and 8 demonstrate, education plays a decisive role in the female occupational structure. On the one hand, over half of the women working in the primary sector of Thailand's economy reported low levels of education (*Pratom* 4 or

**Table 8**  Occupational Structures for Women in Northern Thailand by Tertiary and Other Educational Attainment (1998)

| Sector | Total[a] | University degree | Short course vocational | Technical vocational | Teacher training |
|---|---|---|---|---|---|
| Agriculture | 1015.9 | — | 7.0 | 2.0 | — |
| Manufacturing | 253.7 | 3.3 | 8.9 | 4.6 | 1.3 |
| Services | 274.1 | 40.5 | 13.4 | 14.1 | 45.0 |

*Note*: Nonmunicipal area.
[a] In thousands.
*Source*: Report of Labour Force Survey, 1998:161.

lower, which is equivalent to four years in primary school). On the other hand, women working in the services sectors reported high levels of education (university, vocational, and teacher training). Almost half the women working in the services sector reported tertiary educational attainment. Over half the women working in manufacturing reported their educational attainment to be *Pratom* 7 and under.

What is most interesting about Tables 7 and 8 is that the majority of the women surveyed reported *Pratom* 4 educational attainment. This was found in all three sectors, which demonstrated that women who moved into waged labor in northern Thailand had only four years of primary education. Such a low level of education for these women in northern Thailand was also evident in the projects we studied. Out of 43 respondents, 58.25% (n = 25) had four years of primary school, 11.65% (n = 5) completed *Pratom* 7 (which is equivalent to upper-level elementary school), and 4.66% (n = 2) completed *Matayomsuksa* 3 or lower secondary school. Only 2.33% (n = 1) had a bachelor's degree from a university, and another 2.33% (n = 1) had a diploma from a technical college. It should be highlighted that these two women were in their mid-twenties,[5] and they had gone back to their villages during the economic crisis to work in the projects.

The educational levels of the respondents were significantly different from the educational levels of their daughters. Out of 27 daughters reported, 25.02% (n = 6) ranged from day care to secondary school level, and 12.51% (n = 3) had already completed secondary school and were working. About 25.02% (n = 6) were either in the process of completing or had already obtained a bachelor's degree, and 20.85% (n = 5) had received diplomas from technical colleges. Only one respondent said that her daughter had obtained a master's degree. The remaining 25.02% (n = 6) listed only occupations for their daughters without reporting their educational levels. The reason given for their daughter's higher levels of education was simple. They mentioned that they now had money earned from the projects and that they were using it to keep their daughters in school. Money is important because, as mentioned before, about 47% of Thai students at the primary level had to leave schools by July 1998, because of the lack of family income during the economic crisis (UNESCAP, 1999:126).

The validity of education as an indicator of women's socioeconomic development is a tricky one and is very hard to use on its own. Our research indicates that gender, job opportunities, and adequate sources of income all have an impact on educational levels. Although there is an improvement in the levels of education for women in Thailand, the situation of their economic well-being does not seem to be improving. This is especially true for women in rural areas and poverty-stricken households. It can thus be concluded that education as an indicator used to measure socioeconomic development and women's integration into waged labor tells us the following: educational attainment is changing for rural Thai women, but it is yet to have a significant impact on their attainment of high-paying jobs. While women in all sectors of the rural economy reported similar monthly incomes, in the municipal areas urban women earn an estimated 50% more than women engaged in agriculture (Office of the Prime Minister, 1991:216–217). Women in urban areas need the higher levels of education to obtain better-paying jobs. Despite various limitations faced by rural women, significant changes in their levels of education do tell us that values and norms concerning their educational need are changing, but these changes in educational levels have yet to be used as a tool to promote their socioeconomic development. To adequately use education as a valuable indicator in this regard, one must consider such factors as the levels of educational attainment, kinds of studies pursued, differences in gender, types of occupations available, and availability of funds for schools.

## CONCLUSION

The ways in which Thai women's social and economic relations have changed depends in part on their socioeconomic backgrounds. As they are finding themselves incorporated into waged labor, some are able to pursue professional careers based on their educational levels and their access to the urban labor force. For most of them, however, incomes remain low and waged employment is limited mainly to agriculture. Rural women with limited education and vocational skills work in home-based production and the informal sector of the economy, in which there has been little change in rural women's social and economic relations. Tools needed for economic mobilization and upward mobility, such as autonomy, political participation, and education, are still not available to most of these women. Contemporary jobs and incomes still create an inferior economic standing of women, which is reinforced by state policy. Although Thai women were involved in their rural economic development at the micro level, there is little indication that they were involved in the actual development of macro economic policies that had a direct impact on their access to the economic resources and economic power needed for ensuring equality in pay and educational attainment.

Available national statistics and our research data demonstrate that integration into the formal sectors had not been as high for Thai women as it had been for Thai men. Rural women working in the formal sectors have found themselves concentrated in low-skilled (often unpaid) work in the agricultural sector, semiskilled assembly work in the manufacturing sector, and domestic work in the services sector. There are other factors involved in the economic integration of rural women that have been discussed in this chapter. These factors include selling of land and changes in state policy, which have pushed women out of their traditional farming roles. What need to be further explored in the area of rural women's employment are the types of informal work they do, which includes subcontracting work, piecework, off-farm employment, and small-scale income-generating programs. If employment is an indicator of rural women's socioeconomic development, it must include their work in both the informal and formal sectors to accurately reflect their economic integration and employment.

Increasingly high levels of primary and secondary educational enrollment have benefited Thai women. It was demonstrated that female illiteracy rates dropped over the past two decades. By 1997, female adult literacy had reached 92.8% (UNESCAP, 1999:230). There was no indication of differences between the sexes in net primary enrollment or net secondary enrollment. As Chang (1998) noted, however, rural women tend to stop their education after the secondary level to enter work in the informal sectors, hence the levels of university enrollment would apply more to women who continued their education after secondary school, especially urban women from higher socioeconomic backgrounds (Ng, 1999). Female university enrollment rates therefore may not necessarily indicate higher education for rural women.

As Thailand experienced high GDP growth rates, women were able to obtain more advanced education. This had provided them with the opportunity to pursue high-paying jobs outside agricultural activities, but Thai women still lag behind their male counterparts in terms of the income they earn from such nonagricultural jobs. Much of this can be attributed to male–female differences in educational subjects and length of education, thus although education remains an important contributing factor to determining one's employment and income in Thailand, a more accurate indicator would encompass completion of educational programs, subjects pursued, and attainment of higher degrees.

The situation in Thailand before and after the 1997 crisis suggests the interlinking nature of such indicators as GDP, employment, income, and education, especially when considering the degree of the country's socioeconomic development. While GDP has been faulted in the past when overused as an indicator of economic development, in the case of Thailand it has been an important means to generate the resources necessary for social development. This was evident during the period up to the 1997 crisis and its aftermath, when the collapse of the economy and the fall in GDP led to the erosion of jobs, income, and educational resources in Thailand.

Finally, perhaps the most notable relationship found was between the three primary sectors of the economy (agriculture, industrial, and services) and women's work. Policies to push for economic growth had pulled women out of traditional economic roles and into waged labor. At the same time, state policies to promote women's socioeconomic development were included in the national plans, which aimed at promoting the educational and productive needs of rural women. When income, occupational structure, and education level are used to indicate rural women's development, however, the answer is still the same; rural women have not experienced the development needed to permanently lift themselves out of poverty. Their socioeconomic development is a process of interrelated and interdependent factors. A more comprehensive, multifactor indicator of these women's development would include their employment and income in both the formal and informal sectors as well as their university enrollment, subjects of study, and degrees attained. While we feel it is important to continue to utilize changes in employment patterns and levels of education as indicators of rural women's economic integration in Thailand, we suggest that what is needed at this stage is more disaggregated data on rural women while studying this and other related topics.

## NOTES

1. According to UNDP (1999:254), "Gross domestic product (GDP) The total output of goods and services for final use produced by an economy by both residents and non-residents, regardless of the allocation to domestic and foreign claims. It does not include deductions for depreciations of physical capital or depletion and degradation of natural resources."

2. In 1975, only Indonesia paid its female workers wages as low as Thailand's (McMichael, 1996:97). As has been mentioned, nonagricultural employment played a relatively minor role in terms of northern rural women's labor activities during this time. This is quite unlike Malaysia, in which the majority of industrial female workers came from the rural areas (Ariffin, 1994).

3.  The (BOI) was set up in 1959–1960. This new agency's main task was to guarantee that the Thai government would not make public or compete with firms promoted under the BOI umbrella (Muscat, 1994;104).

4.  The net primary enrollment rate indicates the ratio of enrolled primary-school-age children to all primary-school-age children. This is different from the gross enrollment rate, the most commonly available indicator, whose greatest drawback is that school enrollment is only a proxy for actual school attendance (World Development Report, 2001:18).

5.  Of the 43 women interviewed within the projects, the ages ranged from 20 to 67 years. Of those interviewed, 11.65% (n = 5) were in their twenties, 25.63% (n = 11) in their thirties, 30.29% (n = 13) in their forties, 18.64% (n = 8) in their fifties, and 13.98% (n = 6) in their sixties.

## REFERENCES

Ahmad, A. (1998). Country Briefing Paper: Women in Malaysia. Manila: Asian Development Bank.

Ames, A., (1999). Changes in social and economic relations among rural women in northern Thailand. master's thesis, University of Victoria, Victoria, BC, Canada, and Chiang Mai University, Chiang Mai, Thailand.

Ames, T. (2002). Changes in wage labour and small and medium businesses in Tana Toraja: A rural community's responses to economic and social change. J. Anthro. Indonesia.

Ames, Ames. (2002). Women's poverty, social welfare, and state-economic development policies in northern Thailand. In: Thang, L. L., Wei-Hsin, Y. eds. Women, Work, and Family in Asia. Singapore: Times Academic.

Ariffin, J. (1994). From Kampung to Urban Factories: Findings from the HAWA Study. Kuala Lumpur: University of Malay Press.

Ariffin, R. (2000). Globalization and its impact on women workers in Malaysia. paper presented at Workshop on Globalization and Labour in Malaysia. Bongi, Malaysia: Universiti Kebangsaan.

Arizpe, L., Aranda, J. (1986). Women workers in the strawberry agribusiness in Mexico. In: Leacock, E., Safa, H., eds. Women's Work. MA: Bergin and Garvey, pp. 174–193.

Bell, P. F. (1997). Thailand's economic miracle: Built on the backs of women. In: Somswasdi, V., Theobald, S., eds. Women, Gender Relations, and Development in Thai Society. Chiang, Mai, Thailand: Ming Muang Navarat, pp. 55–82.

Boserup, E. (1970). Women's Role in Economic Development. New York: St. Martin's Press.

Chang, T. P. (1998). Women in the Informal Sector: Household Ethnography. Kuala Lumpur: Faculty of Economics and Administration.

Charoenloet, V. (1991). Factory Management, Skill Formation, and Attitudes of Women Workers in Thailand: A Comparison between an American Owned Electrical Factory and a Japanese Owned Electrical Factory. Thailand: Mahidol University Press.

Corner, L. (1997). Rural Development and Poverty Alleviation in ASEAN: A Gender Perspective. Bangkok, Thailand: UNIFEM.

Dulansey, M., Austin, J. (1985). Small-scale enterprises and women. In: Austin, J., ed. Gender Roles in Development Projects. CT: Kamarian, pp. 79–131.

Gray, J. (1990). The road to the city: Young women and transition in northern Thailand. Ph D dissertation. Macquarie University, Sydney, Australia.

Kaosa-ard, S. (1993). Employment, income, and education of northern women. Thai. Dev. Res. Inst. Q. Rev. 8(3):9–17.

Kaosa-ard, S. (1995). Women in Development: Enhancing the Status of Rural Women in Northern Thailand. Bangkok, Thailand: Thailand Development Research Institute (TDRI).

Lee, R. (1993). Labour issues in the informal sector in Thailand with special emphasis on homebased workers. In: Lazo, L., ed. From the Shadows to the Fore: Practical Actions for the Social Protection of Homeworkers in Thailand. Thailand: International Labour Organization, pp. 82–92.

McMichael, P. (1996). Development and Social Change—A Global Perspective. Thousand Oaks, CA: Pine Forge Press.

Mies, M. (1991). Gender and global capitalism. In: Sklair, L., ed. Capitalism and Development. London: Routledge, pp. 107–122.

Muscat, R. J. (1994). The Fifth Tiger. Helsinki, Finland: United Nations University Press.

National Commission on Women's Affairs (1985). Women's Development in Thailand. Bangkok, Thailand: National Committee for International Cooperation.

Ninsin, K. (1991). The Informal Sector in Ghana's Political Economy. Ghana: Freedom Publications.

Ng, C. (1999). Positioning Women in Malaysia: Class and Gender in an Industrializing State. New York: St. Martin's.

Pearson, R. (1998). Nimble fingers' revisited: Reflections on women and third world industrialization in the late twentieth century. In: Jackson, C., Pearson, R., eds. Feminist Visions of Development, pp. 171–188.

Pine, F. (1982). Family structure and the division of labour: Female roles in urban Ghana. In: Alavi, H., Shanin, T., eds. Introduction to the Sociology of Developing Societies. New York: Monthly Review, pp. 387–405.

Rahman, A., Aziz, A. (1998). Economic reforms and agricultural development in Malaysia. ASEAN Econ. Bull. 15(1):59–76.

Report of the Labour Force Survey. (1991). Bangkok: National Statistical Office, Office of the Prime Minister.

Report of the Labour Force Survey. (1998). Bangkok: National Statistical Office, Office of the Prime Minister.

Rosa, K. (1994). The Conditions and Organizational Activities of Women in Free Trade Zones: Malaysia, Philippines, and Sri Lanka, 1970–1990. In: Rowbotham, S., Mitter, S., eds. Dignity and Daily Bread: New Forms of Economic Organizing Among Poor Women in the Third World and the First. New York: Routledge, pp. 73–99.

Sookasame, K. (1989). Women's Development in Thailand's National Development: Social and Economic Background. Bangkok, Thailand: Thai University Research Association, pp. 197–233.

Suda, C. (1996). The political economy of women's work in Kenya: Chronic constraints and broken barriers. In: Ghorayshi, P., Belanger, C., eds. Women, Work, and Gender Relations in Developing Countries: A Global Perspective. Westport, CT: Greenwood, pp. 75–90.

Tambunlertchai, S. (1993). Manufacturing. In: Warr, P. G., ed. The Thai Economy in Transition. Cambridge: Cambridge University Press, pp. 118–150.

Taplin, R. (1989). Economic Development and the Role of Women: An Interdisciplinary Approach. Aldershot, Hampshire, UK: Gower.

National Commission on Women's Affairs. (1994). Thailand's Report on the Status of Women and Platform for Action. Bangkok: Prime Minister's Office.

Thomson, S. (1996). Gender Issues in Small and Medium Enterprise: Development in Northeast Thailand. Bangkok: Gender and Development Research Institute.

UNDP (1999). Human Development Report. New York: Oxford University Press.

UNDP (2000). Gender and Development. Thailand: United Nations Development Program.

UNESCAP. (1998). Economic Reforms and Rural Poverty Alleviation: An Enquiry into the Asian Experience. New York: United Nations Press.

UNESCAP (1999). Development, Research and Policy Analysis Division (DRPAD). Economic and Social Survey of Asia and the Pacific. Bangkok: United Nations Economic and Social Commission of Asia and the Pacific.

UNESCAP (2001). Development, Research and Policy Analysis Division (DRPAD). Economic and Social Survey of Asia and the Pacific. Bangkok: United Nations Economic and Social Commission of Asia and the Pacific.

UNESCAP. (2001). Thailand Page: Statistical Data. www.unescap.org/stat/statdata/thailand. htm.

UNIFEM. (2000). Targets and Indicators: Selections from Progress of the World's Women. New York: UNIFEM's Biennial Report.

United Nations. (1995). Fourth World Conference on Women: Draft Platform for Action. A/CONF.177/L.1. New York: United Nations Press.

Vimolsiri, P. (1999). Growth with equity: Policy lessons from the experience of Thailand. In: Growth with Equity: Policy Lessons from Experiences of Selected Countries in the ESCAP Region. pp. 267–311; www.unescap.org/drpad/publication/growth.

Webster, A. (1992). Introduction to the Sociology of Development. Hong Kong: Macmillian Education Ltd.

Weeks, J. (1981). Population. NJ: Wadsworth.

World Development Report (2001). Attacking Poverty. New York: Oxford University Press.

# 10

## Fossilization of Chinese Customs Under Colonial Rule in Hong Kong
### Implications for Gender and Development

**SELINA CHING CHAN**

*National University of Singapore, Singapore*

## INTRODUCTION

What was the traditional customary inheritance pattern in colonial Hong Kong? Why did the male and female villagers differ so much in opinion over the reform of the Chinese customary inheritance pattern? What is the meaning of tradition in the modern cosmopolitan city of Hong Kong? What is the impact of the colonial policy on this rapidly developed city? This chapter examines how "tradition" was contested in the colonial era by different parties: namely, women's groups, male villagers, female villagers, the general public, and the colonial government. It studies the way in which different parties were involved in the public discourse of patriarchal tradition and gender inequality. In addition, the changing meanings of tradition in the process of economic development are illustrated within the context of colonial policy.

Anthropologists and sinologists have claimed that the Chinese traditionally tend to practice the patrilineal inheritance pattern (Cohen, 1976:70; Jamieson, 1970:25; McCreery, 1976; Watson, 1984). Past research on inheritance in the New Territories merely focused on the discussion of men's rights (Baker, 1979:9; Freedman, 1966:55; Potter, 1968; Watson, 1975:188; 1985:109).[1] It was widely known that a man's estate should be divided more or less equally among all his sons. Daughters were not entitled to any inheritance, although they might be given some movable property at marriage in the form of dowry.[2] Goody (1990:79) suggests that dowry was a form of premortem inheritance. The value of the dowry was negligible, however, when compared to that of the inheritance obtained by sons, and hence was insignificant in the parents' estate. It was thus argued that dowry would not bear the meaning of premortem inheritance (Chan, 1997:153).

Due to an emphasis on the patrilineal inheritance pattern, existing studies have portrayed villagers as passive followers of tradition (Baker, 1979:9; Freedman, 1966: 55; Potter, 1968; Watson, 1975:188; 1985:109).[3] Daughters' attitudes toward inheritance practices were largely omitted in such studies on inheritance in Chinese society, which concentrated mostly on men's rights,[4] thus this study of a rare organized rebellion of daughters is quite different from previous works examining how different women resisted the patriarchal control of the family within the context of marriage (e.g., Jaschok and Mier, 1994). Indeed, previous studies on women's resistance to patriarchy were mainly conducted in the context of renouncing marriage; having special living arrangements after marriage; getting a "compensating bridedaughter" by paying the husband a certain amount of money to obtain a concubine; and building girls' houses, vegetarian halls, and houses for spinsters (Stockard, 1989; Watson, 1994).[5] This chapter examines women as active agents who openly voiced their grievances on the unequal inheritance tradition. It also argues that both men and women are active agents who engage in the process of interpreting, reinterpreting, and inventing tradition. On such invented tradition, Hobsbawm and Ranger (1983:1–2) write

> It includes both "traditions" actually invented, constructed and formally instituted. . . . "Invented tradition" is taken to mean a set of practices, normally governed by overtly or tacitly accepted rules and of a ritual or symbolic nature, which seek to inculcate certain values and norms of behaviour by repetition, which automatically implies continuity with the past. . .the peculiarity of "invented tradition" is that the continuity with it is largely factitious.

This chapter argues that this tradition was also formed through the continuous process of negotiation between the colonial government and the villagers. It suggests that the over 100 years of colonial rule since 1898 had "respected" the Chinese custom by "fossilizing" the customary inheritance pattern with reference to the legal order in the Qing period (1644–1911). This policy led to the nondevelopment of gender roles and to the invention of tradition. This chapter also suggests that it was the colonial government that fossilized Chinese customary inheritance through the legal order and objectified it as an invented tradition. Such enforcement of this fossilized inheritance law consequently forbade the extension of women's rights of inheritance and the development of gender equality. Ironically, it was also the colonial regime, with its Western ideas, feminist ideology, and increased educational opportunities for women that led to the changing gender dynamics in Hong Kong during the past few decades.

The chapter stresses, however, that the locals were not entirely passive in reacting to the invented tradition. The invented tradition gained new meaning in response to local socioeconomic environment. In fact, the locals have different ways to interpret and handle the invented tradition. It is suggested here that the "traditional" gender ideologies were a political construction that was attached to the particular economic and political process during the colonial regime. It was also an invented tradition with marked inflexibility, which perpetuated gender stereotyping and patriarchal power reproduction. As far as the gender dimension of societal development is concerned, this colonial reproduction of a patriarchal power structure was hardly progressive, and such a legacy still has a considerable bearing upon the gender question within the current developmental framework in Hong Kong society.

The present study is mainly based on anthropological fieldwork conducted in Hong Kong in 1993 and 1994. A wide range of New Territories villagers, who are diverse in terms of class, background, and gender, were interviewed. Subsequent visits to the New Territories villages were also made in 1995 to 1997, 1999, and 2000. These visits were primarily for gaining a better understanding of the impact of the reform adopted in 1994 in response to the female villagers and organizations discussed below.

## MODERNITY VS. CHINESE TRADITION

The reform of the New Territories Ordinance was initiated by the persistent efforts of female villagers and women's organizations and can be traced to several incidents in 1993 and 1994. In August 1993, the Hong Kong government issued the *Green Paper on Equal Opportunity for Women and Men*. This green paper aimed to investigate gender inequality by focusing on the opportunity for participation in the major socioeconomic and political spheres of contemporary Hong Kong. It thus aroused public interest in the issue of gender equality. Quite a number of women's organizations commented that the green paper did not make enough suggestions for improvement in the unequal right of inheritance among the indigenous villagers in the New Territories of Hong Kong. Some 40,000 signatures were collected from the general public by the women's groups to urge the government to revise the New Territories Ordinance.

In October 1993, concerns over the inheritance rights for women were first raised when the housing authority made a public statement declaring that inheritance patterns during the first fourteen phases of the home ownership scheme were bound by the New Territories Ordinance because these homes were built on land within the New Territories.[6] Under the New Territories Ordinance, the inheritance of all kinds of land and housing in the New Territories had to follow Chinese tradition. Women were therefore precluded from inheriting home ownership scheme homes. In November 1993, the government announced the New Territories (Exemption) Bill, which served to exempt all nonrural land from the ordinance. It provided relief to the concerns of the 340,000 owners of nonrural land or property who were largely not in favor of the customary rule of succession. Women thus became able to inherit property on nonagricultural land in the New Territories, just as in the rest of Hong Kong. This amendment went through peacefully and was widely welcomed by the public all over Hong Kong, including the villagers in the New Territories.

These two incidents provoked a general interest in gender equality among the Hong Kong people outside the New Territories. Their attention was drawn to the practice of "unequal" rights of inheritance in the New Territories indigenous villages, a practice supported by the New Territories Ordinance.[7] It was under this particular environment that some village women who felt victimized started to seek help from social workers and external pressure groups—women's groups in the city—in order to fight against this male-biased tradition in the village. They were unlike male villagers, who had direct access to the political center of the lineage through such local political organizations as the Heung Yee Kuk and the village council.[8] It is indeed a common characteristic in many developing socities to have men's access to the power center institutionalized while women are left marginalized. This was also the first time that these village women established contact with any women's organization in Hong Kong. With the help of some women's organizations, the reform of the New Territories Ordinance was put forward with the intention of giving daughters in the New Territories the same right to inherit as sons and daughters living elsewhere in Hong Kong.[9] According to most legislative councilors, the amendment was aimed at ensuring that men and women are entitled to equal inheritance rights. It was generally perceived by the public and the government as a means to remove gender inequality.

Significantly, the controversy over the reform of the New Territories Ordinance revealed the conflict between modernity and tradition, or more specifically, between gender equality and patriarchy. This conflict was crystallized in a showdown on October 13, 1993. Four female villagers protested against the "discriminatory" tradition by wearing a version of the traditional Chinese costume and giving pieces of roasted pork to male councilors entering the building but not to their female counterparts (*South China Morning Post*, 1993). As these village women delivered pork to the men and not to the women outside the legislative council building, they also symbolically portrayed themselves as victims under the oppression of patriarchy. The roasted pork was meant to symbolize inheritance from ancestors. This action was intended to draw the analogy with the unfair practice in the New Territories giving men but not women the right to receive pork from ancestral estates. An image of victimization under the oppression of male kinfolk was consequently constructed for public display. This was a breakthrough, as village women were hardly seen in the public sphere and were not vocal or outspoken.[10] This was indeed the first time that daughters acted collectively as active participants, openly demanding equal inheritance rights while also challenging the legal, institutional, and social forces in public.

This vivid image of the way in which tradition was used against village women was highly publicized.[11] To illustrate this oppression at a personal level, several women recounted their experiences publicly. One of them had seven siblings, all of whom died at a young age. She was thus the only child left in the family. Her father died when she was twelve, leaving behind three houses and four pieces of land. Following the customary way of inheritance, she was not entitled to inheriting her father's property, although she was the sol heir in the family. By custom, the property was subsequently passed on to her father's brother's sons.

The experience of another village woman also portrayed how she as an individual became a victim of tradition. This village woman was not married and was staying in her father's house since her father had died some years earlier. Her brothers, who inherited the house, suddenly decided to sell it. She was thus forced to leave the house and as a result became homeless. In this context, tradition is portrayed not only as depriving a woman of her right to inherit her father's property, but also as causing her to become homeless.

The active effort to inform the general public of their personal stories also reveals that these women felt oppressed by the patriarchal system, and therefore actively challenged it. Such activism challenges past studies that viewed women as conformists to the patriarchal system although they were recognized as participants in the everyday running of the family (Ebrey, 1991; Judd, 1989; Watson, 1991). More recently, women became active, openly challenging the legal, institutional, and social forces in public. This is an important hallmark in Hong Kong's social history, because it represents the first incident in which the actions and voices of New Territories' women were featured by the mass media.[12]

In sum, the protestors argued that Chinese tradition discriminated against women in the New Territories because it forbids them from inheriting land and property. The logic underlying the condemnation of such a tradition was based on the principle that each individual is a single and independent entity and should therefore receive an equal share of the inheritance regardless of sex. In addition, the women's groups also hoped to eradicate discriminatory practices against women in both the public and private spheres by pressing the government to introduce the U.N. Convention on the Elimination of All Forms of Discrimination Against Women.

Indeed, active village participants who fought for the reform of the customary inheritance were daughters.[13] With the help of the Association for the Advancement of Feminism and some female social workers, these daughters eventually formed the Anti-Discrimination Female Indigenous Inhabitants' Committee in November 1993. They staged a series of demonstrations to fight for equal inheritance rights in different public places. Indeed, this was the first time that daughters came together and staged an organized rebellion to fight against the patriarchal system. This contradicts the findings of past studies that described rebellion on an individual basis and mainly on matters related to marriage.

The action of these daughters had not only caught the attention of the indigenous inhabitants, it had also aroused the interest of the general public. This could be observed in the two declarations published in newspapers by the general public. On October 13, 1993, a declaration entitled "Stop Discriminating the New Territories Women, Revise the New Territories Ordinance Immediately," was published by 352 individuals from different backgrounds as well as forty-one organizations, including various women's organizations, political parties, religious organizations, family organizations, social workers, transport organizations, student unions, labor unions, and residential committees (*Ming Pao*, October 13, 1993). On April 7, 1994, another declaration, entitled "Support Gender Equality, Fight for Equal Inheritance Rights," was published by twelve women's organizations in the same newspaper. Gender equality was highlighted as the main reason behind these demands for a reform of the New Territories Ordinance. The general public and the media perceived that it was Chinese tradition that prevented women in the New Territories from inheriting and and property. It was argued that the individual, whether a man or a woman, should be the unit for claiming inheritance.

## DEFENDING THE CHINESE TRADITION: VIEWS OF MALE VILLAGERS AND HEUNG YEE KUK

The proposed amendment of the New Territories Ordinance nevertheless, provoked outrage among the male villagers, who were mainly represented by the Heung Yee Kuk. The Heung Yee Kuk claimed that the peaceful way of life of New Territories villagers was at risk of being destroyed by these external pressures and initiated the *Baoxiangweizu* movement, which literally means the "protect the community and defend the lineage" movement. This movement involved a series of activities, some of them taking place in the villages in the New Territories, and some of them taking place in the city. On April 17, 1994, more than 1000 male villagers joined a demonstration at a secondary school that was located in Sheung Shui of the New Territories.

Shortly afterwards on the same day, a demonstration was held to commemorate what had happened ninety-five years before, when on April 16, 1899, British troops built a temporary camp and hoisted a flag in Tai Po. The villagers were furious then and claimed that the erection of a camp was detrimental to the geomancy there. They burned part of the temporary camp and attacked the British troops, leading to much fighting between the villagers and the troops. One thousand male villagers from different places in the New Territories took part in ancestor worship at some graves in Yuen Long. These graves contain the bodies of those who died fighting against the British in 1899. Significantly enough, this was the first time such elaborate rituals had been performed during ninety-five years of the colonial regime. The act of worship itself was highly symbolic at this particular moment. Its aim was not purely to venerate the ancestors; it was intended on the one hand to commemorate the sacrifice of the ancestors resulting from the intrusion of the British, and on the other hand to inform the ancestors about the repeated intrusions on their tradition—customary inheritance—in the 1990s.

On April 26, 1994, about 2000 villagers participated in a demonstration in Tsuen Wan City Hall in the New Territories. At night, villagers were urged to switch off their lights at home for ten minutes to protest against the impending approval of the amendment to the New Territories Ordinance that would gave equal inheritance rights to all. The resulting span of darkness symbolized the sadness and death of tradition brought about by the reform. On June 20, two days before the third and final reading of the motion to reform the New Territories Ordinance, about 1000 villagers from different villages were mobilized by the Heung Yee Kuk. These villagers were divided into six sections to take shifts in a continuous thirty-six-hour demonstration outside the building of the legislative council. When the bill of amendment to the New Territories Ordinance was finally approved (thirty-six for and two against), some villagers pinned black armbands on their sleeves and some waved black cloths outside the legislative council's building. The act of using black cloth to express disappointment and sadness was significant, since the wearing of black armbands is a practice commonly observed at funerals in mainland China. This represented the dissolution of the family and lineage system that the villagers argued that the reform would cause. The pain and sadness that resulted from the intrusion on tradition were therefore powerfully communicated.

Apparently, the reform was perceived by the Heung Yee Kuk as a threat to village tradition. Tradition was reified as patrilineal inheritance and was interpreted as the will and wish of the ancestors. Being established in the immemorial past, tradition was therefore sacred and not to be changed. The Heung Yee Kuk pointed out that land should be passed on only to members of the patrilineage—only the sons. Daughters' holdings of such land would lead to an "occupation" of lineage land by nonlineage members in future generations through marriages with outsiders. It was argued that the transfer of land to nonmembers of the patrilineage is a violation of tradition. Some informants further explained that if houses in the village were given to daughters, there would be many non-lineage members living in the village in the future. Indeed, the effect of this challenge on the villagers' tradition of was believed to lead to a dissolution of their clan system.

Significantly, the controversy over the reform of the New Territories Ordinance revealed the conflict between modernity and tradition, or more specifically that between gender equality and patriarchy. In this context, tradition had been reified as the customary inheritance practice that was laid down in the Qing dynasty and that had been followed ever since. In the Baoxiangweizu movement, the villagers argued that their tradition should not be abolished, and in particular, that customary inheritance should continue. The reason is clearly pointed out by one of my informants, who said: "The son gets a share from his father because he is a son. The daughter obtains her share from her husband's family.[14] That is very fair. If a daughter is entitled to receive a share from her natal family, then together with the share that she gets from her husband's family, she would have two shares. This is unfair." This viewpoint was widely shared by male villagers. The explanation of the custom as being a fair one revealed the unique cultural ideal that they held. The logic is that the individual is not the smallest property-owning unit in the Chinese kinship system. The perception that a married daughter together with her husband should be treated as a single unit and thus have a single share of inheritance together was derived from the patrilineal descent ideology in the Chinese kinship system.

A fuller understanding of the patrilineal descent ideology may be obtained through an examination of the native concepts of *qi* (chi) as explored by Chun (1990), and *fang* as explored by Chen (1984). Qi means breath or ether, but in the present context it means the shared and transmitted substance that passes from father to son (Chen, 1984). Qi serves as the basis of a symbolically constituted relationship between a father and his son as well as between brothers of a common father (Chen, 1984). The term qi indicates the continuous sharing of substance from father to son in every generation from the infinite past into the infinite future. It also runs through the whole lineage and is a metaphor for the descent ideology. Unlike sons, daughters do not share qi with their fathers. Similarly, fang denotes the descent status that a man holds by virtue of being a son (Chen, 1984). A daughter does not hold independent fang status, as a son does (Chen, 1984). Before marriage, a daughter belongs to her father's fang. After marriage, she belongs to her husband's fang. Following the descent model, only the fang, which is either a son or a son together with his wife, is a proper and independent property-owning unit. Based on this principle, it is therefore fair for those who own fang status to obtain a share of inheritance from their father.

More significantly, the close relationship between the descent status and the right to inherit may be further understood from following statement made by an informant: "Sons are meant to carry on the *xianghuo*.[15] Daughters do not; they are supposed to marry out. Therefore only sons can inherit property." Carrying on the xianghuo means continuing the descent line of the family, which is one of the most important ends in Chinese kinship ideology. Only sons can carry on the descent line and assume the role of offering sacrifices to their fathers and ancestors. Daughters cannot continue the family line and therefore do not have rights of succession.[16] The above description shows how the objectified tradition may remain an obstacle to gender equality, which is considered a basic component of development in all modern societies, including Hong Kong.

## MAINTENANCE OF CHINESE CUSTOM UNDER COLONIAL RULE

While fighting for the maintenance of Chinese customary inheritance, the Heung Yee Kuk and the male villagers apparently attempted to portray the New Territories' inhabitants as having a distinctive tradition. The occupational and educational profile of these villagers had become very similar to the rest of the Hong Kong people, however. These indigenous inhabitants were no longer farmers as their ancestors were in the beginning of the century. In fact, the contrast in lifestyle between the New

Territories and the rest of Hong Kong was clear only at the beginning of the century. The New Territories were purely a rural area then, while the center of colonial and commercial power was in Hong Kong island. The discourse in custom and tradition embodies an understanding of relations between the rural areas and the city, respectively, representing the New Territories and the rest of Hong Kong in the early twentieth century. In the New Territories today, agriculture and fishing have waned considerably. The blurring of distinction between the lifestyles in the village and in the city had in fact started ever since urbanization and town planning began in the 1950s. One would therefore wonder why the Heung Yee Kuk used tradition as a weapon to fight against the reform. The reason was because tradition had a special political significance in the New Territories. This has to be understood in the context of Hong Kong's unique colonial background.

Unlike the rest of Hong Kong, the New Territories were a piece of leased land. The New Territories were leased by China to the United Kingdom in 1898, while Hong Kong was ceded in 1842. It was because the New Territories were a piece of leasehold land that the British colonialists had obligations to respect the tradition and customs there. In fact, the British colonialists guaranteed at the outset of their colonial rule that the inhabitants of the New Territories should be administered with tact, discretion, and sympathy (Chan, 1999). This was specified in the proclamation issued by Sir Henry Blake on February 19, 1900, in which the customs and tradition of these inhabitants were promised to be respected (Haydon, 1962). This preferential treatment of the New Territories is due to the fact that the New Territories were on land leased from China, and thus subject to the special agreements made between the foreign affairs officials of China and Britain. It was announced that customs on houses, land, and graves in these villages were permitted to continue (Wesley-Smith, 1983). It was exactly because the New Territories were a piece of leasehold land that the British, who were merely the "tenant," had no right to interfere with the customs of the New Territories villagers. The New Territories were administered differently from the rest of Hong Kong, which was in contrast a ceded area (Chan, 1999).[17] In particular, the customary inheritance in the New Territories was respected and enforced by the colonialists.

The different treatments of culture in the New Territories and the rest of Hong Kong were revealed from the exclusive enforcement of the New Territories Ordinance in the former. The ordinance granted full power to the Court to "recognize and enforce any Chinese custom or customary right in relation to land" in the New Territories.[18] According to the Chinese customary inheritance under the Qing law, sons were entitled to inherit their fathers' property while daughters were not. This is interesting because men and women living outside the New Territories in Hong Kong have enjoyed equal rights of inheritance since 1971,[19] but in the New Territories, in the absence of a will, daughters were not entitled to inherit from their fathers, unlike daughters in the rest of Hong Kong. This has resulted in a fossilization of custom and tradition, although in practice there is a wide range of acceptable customs with considerable diversity. The tradition of gender inequality based on the fossilized Chinese customs thus continued to be an obstacle to gender equality in the New Territories.

## THE GUARDIANS OF CHINESE TRADITION?

The prominent voices from the Heung Yee Kuk represented mainly the male villagers, which was understandable since the holders of political power in the village and in the

Heung Yee Kuk were men. These men were indeed the beneficiaries under the customary inheritance pattern. While they struggled against the reform to preserve their tradition, they were at the same time attempting to protect their economic interests because land and houses were valuable resources in a land-scarce city such as Hong Kong. Most of the "rural" and that exists now is—through lease or sale—used for residential or commercial purposes. The bulk of the village land has been sold to the private sector and the government for development since the 1950s (Chan, 1997). In fact, the villagers made handsome profits from these land sales and had become very rich over the past two decades.

In addition, there were some contradictions between what the Heung Yee Kuk claimed and what the villagers actually practiced. As mentioned earlier, one of the arguments put forward by the Heung Yee Kuk was that the inheritance of land by daughters would constitute a threat to the clan and lead to the disruption of the "homeland." This argument was based on the assumption that the lineage would be dissolved if nonlineage members were to own lineage land. Land was claimed to be inalienable from the patrilineal members of the lineage; namely, sons, grandsons, great-grandsons, and so forth. In practice, the meaning of land has been transformed in recent decades. The ownership of land is no longer maintained within the lineage. Villagers do not condemn each other for not following the traditional norm of discouraging the sale of land to nonlineage members. In fact, they are more concerned with the search for the highest bid in their land sales. In other words, economic interests are the real motive behind the ownership of land and houses. As was noted in the case of one of the five major lineages in the New Territories, nearly half of the lineage land had been sold to outsiders who were not lineage members. The result of giving land to daughters and of selling it to outsiders is similar in the sense that such land would end up in the hands of nonlineage members.[20] Despite a decline in the quantity of lineage landholdings, the lineage has not dissolved but has actually flourished in new ways (Chan, 2001). The tradition that was actually practiced is quite different from the traditional customs highlighted by the Heung Yee Kuk during the Baoxiangweizu movement. In fact, the village men were protecting their own economic interests when they defended their traditional inheritance rights.

Besides, the reaction of the Heung Yee Kuk to the passage of the amendment to the New Territories Ordinance on June 22, 1994, was interesting. The most significant sequel to this was the Heung Yee Kuk's plan to help villagers draw up wills in order to ensure that the customary practice of patrilineal inheritance would be maintained and that landed property would be passed on only to sons in perpetuity. Needless to say, having a will to arrange for the disposal of one's property after death is not a Chinese custom. As noted by Chen (1984), the traditional Chinese inheritance pattern does not admit individual disposal, since it is the descent ideology as embodied in the concepts of fang and qi that determine the pattern of inheritance. The Chinese father simply performs the role of a trustee and passes the family property from his generation to the next. There is no such concept as an "individual will" in Chinese society.

Interestingly, none of the villagers disagreed with the idea of making wills or considered it a violation of tradition. The irony was that in claiming to defend tradition, the "guardians" of tradition proposed a nontraditional means to achieve it. In other words, the Heung Yee Kuk attempted to preserve tradition through a way that defied tradition itself. In addition, the intent behind this attempt to maintain tradition was to protect economic interests of village men rather than their love for tradition as such. Irrespective of these shifts in means and motives of maintaining the traditional inheritance system, such a system is antidevelopmental to the extent that it is not conducive to gender equality.

## CONCLUSION

Hong Kong was transformed from a fishing village to a cosmopolitan city under the colonial rule. Paradoxically, the colonial government petrified the customary inheritance pattern in accordance with the Qing law without any significant reform. The colonial policy resulted in an invented tradition with marked inflexibility, which perpetuated gender stereotyping and patriarchal power reproduction. In other words, the patriarchal control was maintained and reproduced through the institutionalization of tradition. The case of the New Territories was similar to many other colonies in which the colonial government played an important role in creating or reinforcing patriarchal control. In many African societies, the colonial government also imposed patriarchal values onto the local communities while ignoring the traditional rights of women (Boserup, 1970). Indeed, the British rulers often imposed the traditional Western values of Victorian England on its colonies, which reinforced gender inequality during the colonial period (Charlton, 1997:10).

In the New Territories, the village men granted a new meaning to their traditional inheritance rights. They make use of the traditional gender ideologies to perpetuate their economic interests in the process of building a capitalist economic system. While the prices of property skyrocketed, they managed to maximize their economic interests by selling their ancestors' land or houses at high prices. In contrast, village daughters did not benefit from this economic progress; they were marginalized, because the houses and land went to male villagers, who were the sole beneficiaries of the traditional inheritance system, although they tried to reinterpret such a system in the process of engaging themselves with the outside world.

It is clear from this chapter that the system of unequal gender relations that is rooted in the traditional inheritance pattern based on Chinese customs hardly changed in the New Territories under British colonial rule and that it continued in more recent times under a new pretext. The perpetuation of this gender-biased tradition remains a critical barrier to gender equality, and thus to any gender-sensitive social development. Unlike more conventional forms of gender inequality, this tradition-bound inequality is more difficult to eradicate in most societies because it may require a fundamental change in the traditional male-dominated belief system and demand measures beyond legal institutions. These are critical concerns for ensuring a mode of development that guarantees gender equality.

## NOTES

1.  J. Watson (1975:188n) discussed a son's inheritance right to his father's property in the Man lineage of the New Territories. For cases in which two brothers only manage to have one son between them, the son has to succeed both descent lines and hence inherits from two "fathers." R. Watson (1985:109) also pointed out that in Ha Tsuen, which is another lineage in the New Territories, only sons who are socially accepted as legitimate by lineage members are entitled to inherit.

2. Dowry in the New Territories was mainly composed of furniture (cupboard, chairs, clothes) and jewelry (earrings, rings, bracelets, necklaces)—and sometimes a young servant girl (R. Watson 1985:131–132). Since the 1990s, the dowry is mainly in the form of jewelry, such as gold and sometimes diamonds.

3. A few exceptions are found in recent works. Chan (1997:154) discussed how village men reinterpreted the traditional inheritance pattern. Wolf (1994:253) also doubted that women were passive recipients of a men's culture in her re-examination of the uterine family system.

4. Past studies on women's property in natal families were confined to dowry, the value of which is negligible when compared to that of the inheritance obtained by sons.

5. Existing studies on other unmarried women, such as bondservants, slaves, and prostitutes, were mainly done to examine whether women in these jobs were fairly treated as human beings.

6. This was a housing scheme that sold the homes to the lower middle class at lower prices.

7. The indigenous villages in the New Territories have long been occupied by the indigenous villagers whose ancestors were living in the New Territories villages before the British entered the territory in 1898 (Chan, 1998).

8. In fact, the indigenous inhabitants are led by three levels of political leadership: the Heung Yee Kuk, the rural committees, and the village council. At the lowest level of this hierarchy, village representatives are elected by their respective villages—one representative for each village—to chair the village council, which is an informal political organization at the village level that takes care of the internal affairs within the village. This council usually comprises male villagers. Exceptions may be found, however, in a few villages in which most males villagers had already migrated abroad, leaving women as the majority. All the village representatives would hold seats in the rural committee at the district level. Councilors in each rural committee have to elect from among themselves a chair and a vice-chair to lead the committee. The holders of these two positions in the rural committees automatically and jointly form the Heung Yee Kuk. The Heung Yee Kuk has acted as a leader in protecting the interests, mainly on land, of the indigenous inhabitants in the New Territories throughout the process of modernization. Daughters outside the New Territories have enjoyed the same rights of inheritance as sons since 1971.

9. Daughters outside the New Territories have enjoyed the same rights of inheritance as sons since 1971.

10. In general, women in the New Territories villages were hardly seen in such public place as village halls and ancestral halls. They were not expected to participate in village meetings either. During my fieldwork in the Pang village, I had never seen a woman in the village hall or in a village meeting.

11. This is the first time that village women had access to any women's organization. The village women wanted to fight for their own interests. As for the women's organizations, the objective was to fight for gender equality. In this particular incident, one group, named the Association for the Advancement of Feminism, offered substantial help to the village women. It helped the female villagers to form the Anti-Discrimination Against Indigenous Women Committee. The four female protestors turned out to be active participants in

the committee. In fact the Association for the Advancement of Feminism also tried to broadcast its message to people overseas.

12.  The controversy over the reform of the female inheritance rights had become the talk of the town.

13.  Wives benefit indirectly from their husbands' share while unmarried daughters do not. On the other hand, an unmarried daughter traditionally got to receive maintenance allowance granted from her father's bequest while a married daughter had no such benefit.

14.  The daughter and her husband jointly get a share.

15.  *Xianghuo* literally means the "incense and fire" of the family.

16.  In the case of uxorial marriages, a daughter still cannot continue the descent line of the natal family. It is her son who takes the name of her natal family and who carries on the line of her family.

17.  In theory, tradition in the New Territories was to be accorded with "exceptional kindness" and "particular respect and preservation." In practice, many of the traditional customs, such as the customary ownership of land in the New Territories, were ignored by the colonial government. (For details, see Chan, 1999.)

18.  Before 1961, the land officer had the power to enforce any customary right. After 1961, this power was transferred to the high court.

19.  Indeed, even the People's Republic of China had already abolished the Qing Law of customary succession by the enactment of the marriage laws in 1950. Ironically, Hong Kong, despite being a cosmopolitan city, maintained the traditional Chinese customs of the Qing dynasty in the New Territories while under the colonial regime.

20.  Village houses were rarely sold to outsiders, and thus the lineage continues to control the village hamlets.

## REFERENCES

Baker, H. D. R. (1979). Chinese Family and Kinship. London: Macmillan.

Boserup, E. (1970). Women's Role in Economic Development. New York: St. Martin's.

Chan, S. C. (1997). Negotiating tradition: Customary succession in the New Territories of Hong Kong. In: Evans, G., Tam, M., eds. Hong Kong: The Anthropology of a Chinese Metropolis. HI: Curzon, pp. 151–173.

Chan, S. C. (1998). Politicizing tradition: The identity of indigenous inhabitants in Hong Kong. Ethnology 37(10):39–54.

Chan, S. C. (1999). Colonial policy in a borrowed place and time: Invented tradition in the New Territories of Hong Kong. Eur. Plan. Stud. 7(2):231–242.

Chan, S. C. (2001). Selling the ancestors' land: A Hong Kong lineage adapts. Mod. China 27(2):2–284.

Charlton, S. E. (1997). Development as history and process. In: Visvanathan, N., Duggan, L., Nisonoff, L., Wiegersma, N., eds. The Woman, Gender and Development Reader. London: Zed Books, pp. 7–16.

Chen, C. N. (1984). Fang and Chia-tsu—The Chinese kinship system in rural Taiwan. PhD dissertation, Yale University, New Haven, CT.

Chun, A. (1990). Conceptions of kinship and kingship in classical Chou China. T'oung Pao 76:16–33.

Cohen, M. (1976). House United, House Divided: The Chinese Family in Taiwan. New York: Columbia University Press.

Ebrey, P. (1991). Marriage and inequality. In: Ebrey, P., Watson, R. S., eds. Chinese Society. Berkeley, CA: University of California Press, pp. 1–24.

Freedman, M. (1966). Chinese Lineage and Society: Fukien and Kwangtung. London: Athlone.

Goody, J. (1990). The Oriental, the Ancient and the Primitive. Cambridge: University Press.

Haydon, E. (1962). The choice of Chinese customary law in Hong Kong. Internat. Compar. Law. Q. 11:231–250.

Hobsbawm, E., Ranger, T. (1983). The Invention of Tradition. Cambridge: University Press.

Jaschok, M., Mier, S. (1994). Women and Chinese Patriarchy: Submission, Servitude, and Escape. Hong Kong: University Press.

Jamieson, G. (1970). Chinese Family and Commercial Law. Hong Kong: Vetch and Lee (first published in 1921).

Judd, E. (1989). Niangjia: Chinese women and their natal families. J. Asian Stud. 48:525–544.

McCreery, J. (1976). Women's property rights in China and South Asia. Ethnology 15:74–163.

Ming Pao. Oct. 13, 1993.

Ming Pao. April 7, 1994.

Potter, J. (1968). Capitalism and the Chinese Peasant. Los Angeles: University of California Press.

South China Morning Post. Oct. 14, 1993.

Stockard, J. (1989). Daughters of the Canton Delta: Marriage Patterns and Economic Strategies in South China: 1860–1930. Stanford, CA: University Press.

Watson, J. (1975). Agnates and outsiders: Adoption in a Chinese lineage. Man 10:193–306.

Watson, R. (1984). Women's property in Republican China: Rights and practice. Repub. China 10(1):1–12.

Watson, R. (1985). Inequality Among Brothers. Cambridge: University Press.

Watson, R. (1991). Women, property, and the law in the People's Republic of China. In: Watson, R., Ebrey, P., eds. Marriage and Inequality in Chinese Society. Berkeley, CA: University of California Press, pp. 313–346.

Watson, R. (1994). Girls' houses and working women: Expressive culture in the Pearl River Delta, 1900–41. In: Jaschok, M., Miers, S., eds. Women and Chinese Patriarchy. Hong Kong: Hong Kong University Press, pp. 25–42.

Wesley-Smith, P. (1983). Unequal Treaty 1898–1997. Hong Kong: Oxford University Press.

Wolf, M. (1994). Beyond the patrilineal self: Constructing gender in China. In: Ames, R. T., Dissanayake, W., Kasulis, T. P., eds. Self as Person in Asian Theory and Practice. Albany, NY: State University of New York Press, pp. 251–270.

# 11

## Information and Communication Technologies as Tools for Development
### Between Skepticism and Optimism

**BARBARA FILLIP**

*Consultant, Arlington, Virginia, U.S.A.*

Many people have come to speak of new information and communication technologies (ICTs) as a magic bullet for developing countries to use to advance their social and economic development. ... Is the "leapfrogging" of development through ICTs feasible? The short answer ... is *Maybe*. The slightly longer answer is *We Are Trying to Figure This Out*. And the most insightful answer from the people who devote their lives to these questions is *We Really Hope So* (Kirkman, 1999).

## INTRODUCTION

This chapter provides an overview of information and communication technologies (ICTs) as an emerging component of the development discourse and of development activities around the globe. While information technology is having a global impact, this chapter will focus on the potential of ICTs for developing countries and how ICTs are being viewed and applied as tools for development.

The current development discourse is full of references to the *digital divide*. Whether the glass is half empty (i.e., the digital divide is threatening to increase inequality and further marginalize the "unconnected") or half full (i.e., the digital age is bringing new opportunities for developing countries to leapfrog and catch up with the developed world), it is clear that ICTs provide both challenges and opportunities for developing countries. Information and communication technologies are not a panacea—they are tools. As with any tool, an individual user's ability to access and make effective use of ICTs is more important than direct ownership of ICTs.

It is also clear that the current focus has been perhaps unjustly set on new ICTs, such as the Internet, casting a shadow on a range of other ICTs with important potential, such as radio, television, personal digital assistants (PDAs), smart cards, and cellular phones. While the advantages and disadvantages of various ICTs can be debated, they all have potentially important applications. Such applications will be illustrated throughout this chapter with brief case studies. The case studies are also meant to illustrate the range of sector-specific applications of ICTs for development purposes as well as the range of organizations involved in supporting access and effective use of ICTs in developing countries.

## UNDERSTANDING THE DIGITAL DIVIDE WITHIN THE EVOLVING DEVELOPMENT DISCOURSE

### Optimists and Pessimists Within the Mainstream

Within the current development discourse, two main positions regarding the digital divide are commonly expressed. On the one hand, the optimists argue that ICTs provide new opportunities for developing countries to participate in global markets—to leapfrog and catch up with the rest of the world. The optimists tend to refer to digital opportunities and avoid the term digital divide (Drake, 2000). On the other hand, the pessimists worry that the digital divide will result in increased inequalities as the opportunities made possible by ICTs will remain unavailable to those who do not have access to these new tools. Mohsen Tawfik (1999) of UNESCO's communication, information, and informatics sector provides a detailed account of both these two extreme positions.

Whether optimists or pessimists, these two positions are firmly within the mainstream of the development discourse. In practical terms, the differences tend to be less important at the level of implementation as long as opportunities and challenges are both taken into consideration in the design of programs and projects to address the digital divide or take advantage of digital opportunities. Whether the glass is half full or half empty, it takes the same amount of water to fill it. In addition, since we are primarily dealing with "potential" beneficial or detrimental impacts of the digital divide, the key is in what we are able to do, the approach we take to transform that potential into reality. In the words of a participant in this author's course on ICTs for developing countries

> When I began the first paragraph of the first reading of the course, I sighed a little and hope that this would not be another academic discussion about potential potential potential. I realize that potential is the key word, but it's also one that I get tired of hearing down south. I want to see actualized potential. I want to see real differences in real peoples' lives, preferably those who are really in need of socio-economic upliftment (participant from South Africa in the first online session of "ICTs for Developing Countries," E-mail message of April 20, 2001).

With that in mind, both optimists and pessimists would probably agree that the focus should be on finding appropriate strategies and approaches to ensure that the opportunities brought about by ICTs are made available to all. Their differences refer primarily to differences in emphasis within the same basic paradigm.

## Critics of Mainstream Perspectives

Critics of these mainstream perspectives argue that ICT dissemination is part of the expansion of global capitalism, cultural imperialism, and an instrument of globalization, linking urban centers in developing countries to centers in capitalist economies and further marginalizing rural areas (Verzola, 2002).

While the majority of the emerging literature on ICTs for development (now often shortened as ICT4DEV) sees ICTs as intrinsically beneficial to development, some are concerned that too much is being made of their potential positive impacts and not enough attention is paid to the fact that ICTs are tools. As with any tools, how they are used is what is really important.

> The trouble with ICTs, however, is that although they offer the technical means for establishing channels, networks, and sites, they cannot by themselves ensure either that these are used for deliberation, that they promote participation, or that they provide access to needed information. The actual social uses of ICTs are to a large extent guided by the political-institutional arrangements within which they are embedded. Whether the potential to support social development will be realized depends much more on the institutional environment of the technology than on its technical features *per se*. Therefore analysis of the relation between ICTs and social development has to give ample attention to their policy context (Hamelink, 1998).

Manuel Castells argues, for example, that "uneven development isn't about first world/third world dichotomy so much as between dynamic segments of countries which form the global network society and 'switched off territories' and people on the other hand" (Castells, 1998: vol. III, p. 354). Furthermore, within this framework of the new informational economy, a fourth world is emerging. This fourth world consists of a significant portion of the world population that is shifting from a position of exploitation to a position of irrelevance (Castells, 1998). Unless measures are taken to reform the current development model, Castells warns, this fourth world may become the source of increased criminal activity and violence across the globe. The result is, as noted by Fernando Henrique Cardoso (1993) that "we are no longer talking about the South that was on the periphery of the capitalist core and was tied to it in a classical relationship of dependence…we are dealing…with a crueler phenomenon: either the South (or a portion of it) enters the democratic–technological–scientific race, invests heavily in R&D, and endures the 'information economy' metamorphosis, or it becomes unimportant, unexploited, and unexploitable." Within the mainstream discourse, a link is made among ICTs, knowledge, and development. In short, ICTs are seen as facilitating the transfer of knowledge.

## North–South Knowledge Transfer and the Modernization Paradigm

The promises of the new technologies for developing countries are formulated within a broad discourse of modernization and development that is based on the assumption that a deficiency in knowledge is partly responsible for underdevelopment (Schech, 2002). A simple example of an activity that would fit perfectly within this argument is the digitization of libraries full of knowledge that can be made available to developing countries through the World Wide Web or CD-ROMs. This recipe of development through knowledge delivered via new ICTs falls within a long tradition of Western thought that seeks solutions of the world's ills and ultimate salvation in technological breakthroughs (Wertheim, 1999; Noble, 1997).

Starting from this simple conceptualization of ICTs' role in development, the field, while still young, is rapidly evolving. It is now more widely recognized that: (1) ICTs are not a panacea, (2) programs and projects based on straight North–South transfer of knowledge facilitated by ICTs are bound to fail because they do not recognize that existing power structures tend to direct the benefits of new technologies to the already privileged, and (3) North–South knowledge transfers will not empower the poor.

## ICTs and Horizontal Global Communications

The hope is that ICTs make horizontal global communications possible. Some governments might look at this as a potential danger, however. Whether locally based or global, virtual or not, communities are faced with new opportunities to represent themselves, network, and gather support for their cause. The Zapatista movement is most often cited as an example. Following their brief rebellion in 1994, the Zapatistas pioneered the use of the Internet by a guerrilla group, creating a Web site to encourage international support for their fight for Indian rights and democracy.[1] The hope again is that effective use of ICTs can and will lead to empowerment of marginalized, impoverished communities. The reality may be different.

### Realities of Development Work

Most development practitioners focus on developing strategies for successful ICT projects and programs without looking beyond their immediate goals or questioning the rationale for what they are doing. Working within the mainstream means identifying what works and what doesn't work, lessons learned, best practices within a common framework, and an understanding that ICTs have become essential tools for communities to be part of the global society. Another danger is that within the international development community, those working on ICTs are often working with blindfolds, suddenly forgetting everything they know about sustainable development in general and the socioeconomic contexts within which they are attempting to support ICT applications in particular.

Most of this chapter describes mainstream activities. The main difference between today's discourse surrounding the digital divide and traditional modernization theory is the reduced importance of the state in the knowledge diffusion process.

### Wave of Events

New "issues" emerge on the agenda of the international development community on a regular basis. Whether it is the environment, gender, governance, or some other topic, annual reports of such international organizations as United Nations Development Program (UNDP) and the World Bank illustrate well the changing priorities (fads) of the international development community. While some organizations engaged in activities related to communication for development issues have been pioneering and advocating the use of ICTs for many years (such as Canada's International Development Research Center), the growth of organizations now entirely focused on ICTs for development or having developed new ICTs for development strategies within the past decade has been very impressive (and this is not necessarily a good thing). In addition, most development organizations, big and small, are now adding some ICT projects or programs to their portfolio.

## Global Knowledge Partnership (GKP)

In June 1997, members of the international development community gathered in Canada to address a new issue on the horizon, the role of knowledge in development. Titled Global Knowledge for Development, the conference paid particular attention to the increasing role played by ICTs in the global economy as well as to their potential in developing countries. As a follow-up to this conference, the Global Knowledge Partnership, or GKP was formed. The GKP is a loose alliance of organizations within the international development community, but also comprises members of the private sector. Additional follow-up conferences were held in Kuala Lumpur, Malaysia, in 2000 and Addis Ababa, Ethiopia, in 2002. Beyond the conferences, GKP is a network of networks, focusing its activities on facilitating coordination.

## World Bank Development Report 1998–1999 and Knowledge Initiatives

Other key events occurred in parallel to the GKD conferences. The World Bank's 1998–1999 development report focused on knowledge for development. A centerpiece of the Bank's new knowledge strategy has been the development of the Global Development Gateway. Designed to be a supersite on the Internet where everyone everywhere would be able to access all the available knowledge on development issues, the gateway was highly controversial from the start. The gateway is further discussed later in the chapter.[2]

## The UNDP's Human Development Report of 2001

The UNDP's human development report of 2001 focused on "making technologies work for human development," and offered a highly optimistic vision of how information and genetic technologies offered opportunities for tackling poverty. This was seen as a departure from UNDP's previous stance regarding ICT issues. Whereas UNDP had previously counterbalanced the World Bank's market-oriented approach with more human-centered development, this report was seen as very (perhaps excessively) optimistic about the new opportunities for leapfrogging.[3]

## DOT Force

The focus in the summer of 2000 of the annual meeting of the G-8 countries in Okinawa were the new ICTs. With a large financial commitment from Japan, the summit followed through on its commitment to set up a digital opportunity task force, otherwise known as the Digital Opportunities Task (DOT) force. A highly unusual initiative for the G-8, the DOT force consisted in country task forces comprising government, industry, and civil society members. In addition, representatives from a small number of developing countries as well as international development agencies were invited. Following a series of consultations around the world, the DOT force submitted its report in May 2001, and the report was adopted by the Genoa meeting of the G-8 in the summer. The various parties involved are now working out the implementation details.[4]

## U.N. ICT Task Force

From another front, the United Nations launched its own ICT task force, mandated by U.N. Secretary-General Kofi Annan to find ways to spread the benefits of the digital revolutions to those currently excluded from its opportunities. The members of the task force come from the public and private sectors, civil society, and the scientific community, and provide a mix of leaders from developing and industrialized countries.[5]

## Upcoming World Summit on the Information Society (WSIS)

The most important event in the near future is the World Summit on the Information Society under the auspices of the International Telecommunications Union (ITU). The summit will occur in two phases, first in Geneva in 2003 and then in Tunisia in 2005. The summit is being preceded by a series of regional consultations and virtual processes.

It should be clear from all these activities that coordination of these high-level global activities is taking up a lot of energy and these activities are often seen as quite remote from the concerns of those involved in the implementation of pilot projects on the ground.

## Digital Divide

The term digital divide has been rejected in many quarters, for a range of reasons. As has already been noted, the optimists prefer to talk of digital opportunities. Those who have tried to address information and knowledge issues for many years argue that it is not as much a "digital" divide as an "information" or knowledge divide. The earlier terms "information haves" and "information have-nots" reflected this focus on the message as opposed to the channel. The term digital tends to reflect a focus on new technologies and in particular the Internet.

While twenty years ago the report of the Maitland commission noted that Tokyo had more telephone lines than the entire continent of Africa (and this fact was unfortunately repeated in almost every piece of literature related to the digital divide), it is no longer true. The divide is a changing, moving target. For example, mobile telephone technologies are emerging as the predominant form of communication in many African countries. As a recent ITU report notes, by the end of 2001, more than twenty eight African countries had more mobile than fixed subscribers.[6]

New gaps are emerging, however, in particular with regard to access to the Internet. It is now more commonly recognized that access is not just a question of a person's ability to get a connection to the Internet. Access must now be measured in terms of quality, and therefore bandwidth. While many in Africa now have "access" to the Internet, their access is often limited to E-mail, and at best, very slow, painfully frustrating access to the World Wide Web.

In short, while the telephone gap is shrinking, the Internet gap is widening. Mobile telephones are making it possible for countries to increase their telephone density by a factor of 6 in six years, while it had taken thirtyfive years to increase telephone density by a factor of 3 before the introduction of mobile telephones. As a recent ITU report notes, "The nature of the digital divide is shifting, from quantity to quality... Effective solutions will require a triumvirate pact between governments, development agencies and the private sector" (International Telecommunications Union, 2002).

## Hype or Not?

The digital divide is really an economic divide. Why the hype then? Is there not a similar health divide, education divide, and wealth divide? Why are ICTs different? Information and communication technology are seen as different because they potentially affect all sectors of society. The potential negative impacts of staying on the wrong side of the divide are seen as leading to further marginalization of those countries already at the bottom of the list in terms of "development." The potential positive impacts of leapfrogging are seen as offering opportunities for escaping their "developing" status and graduating to "emerging" economies.

## ADDRESSING THE DIGITAL DIVIDE

As noted above, effective strategies to address the digital divide are likely to be based on close collaboration among governments, international development agencies, and the private sector. Less often mentioned, the potential role of the emerging global civil society should not be ignored.

### Global Strategies

The key initiatives launched in the past few years and already mentioned, have all come up with global strategies emphasizing a very similar set of necessary steps to be taken. We can only hope that the DOT force, U.N. ICT task force, and other global and regional initiatives will fully coordinate their efforts. The other challenge is that of transforming broad statements and strategies into actions that can be implemented at ground level.

### Donor Agencies

A number of multilateral and bilateral agencies have now developed specific policies or strategies to address ICTs. The World Bank started a range of initiatives related to ICTs in the mid-1990s, including the infoDev program, WorldLinks for Development, and Global Development Learning Network (GDLN). From a wide range of scattered initiatives, the Bank has now established an organizationwide strategic vision. The Bank recently developed a framework for supporting client countries in the "knowledge economy." Within this framework, the World Bank developed a sector strategy paper that focuses on information infrastructure development.[7] This paper was developed by the recently formed Global Information and Communication Technology Department.

The Inter-American Development Bank (IDB) spells out on its Web site how the institutional structure has evolved to address the emerging needs in terms of IT (note that the term information technology is used rather than ICT). The IDB is now in the process of designing and implementing a series of ICT projects that follow an integrated approach.[8] Citing the findings of the digital opportunities initiative, an IDB project in Guyana is being planned with a comprehensive and holistic approach that will cover the regulatory area, access through telecenters, and applications to enhance trade.[9]

With limited resources, UNDP has focused its attention on working in partnership with others. In particular, it is now implementing its digital opportunity initiative in partnership with Accenture and the Markle Foundation. The aim of the program is to identify the roles that ICT can play in fostering sustainable economic development and enhancing social equity.[10]

On the bilateral front, the United States Agency for International Development (USAID) had focused a lot of its earlier attention on Africa with the Leland initiative, facilitating the early spread of the Internet over the continent. USAID is now implementing a new global program called DOT-COM (Digital Opportunity through Technology and Communication). DOT-COM emphasizes both policy making and capacity building with regard to ICTs.[11] It is a set of three cooperative and interrelated initiatives to promote information and communication technology for development. DOT-COM activities cross all sectors, including education, economic growth, women in development, agriculture, trade, health, environment, and telecommunications/E-commerce policy. The three DOT-COM cooperative initiatives provide expertise and services in policy, access, and learning systems.[12]

## National Strategies

Even within a market-based development model, governments have an important role to play in terms of developing and implementing the appropriate mix of policies that will encourage private sector investment in telecommunications while taking measure to ensure universal access to telecommunications and enable individual users and enterprises to benefit from such telecommunication infrastructure.

A number of the initiatives supported by donors have paid significant attention to the necessary steps that governments must take in order to take advantage of digital opportunities and ensure that the benefits of the digital revolution are distributed evenly within the population. Some countries have made significant efforts to develop national strategies related to ICTs and the information society. For example, Tanzania developed its own ICT strategy in 2001 with assistance from the Swedish development agency (SIDA).[13]

In many cases the governments have sought partnerships with the private sector in order to address both key telecommunication infrastructure challenges and challenges in the application of technologies in various sectors of the economy. This has been the case most recently with Mexico's E-Mexico initiative and the involvement of Microsoft.

The most common ground-level activity in the field of ICTs for development to date has been the development of telecenters. A telecenter is defined as "a shared site that provides public access to information and communication technologies" (Proenza et al., 2001). The donor literature presents the telecenter as the key solution for community access to ICTs. The range of options in designing and implementing telecenters is almost without limits, however. The growing literature on telecenters has tried to identify the advantages and disadvantages of key approaches, as well as the key lessons learned.[14]

## ICTs FOR WHAT? SECTOR APPLICATIONS OF ICTs FOR DEVELOPMENT PURPOSES

Information technology can be seen both as a sector that has significant potential for creating employment and generating revenues and as a tool for development. One example can illustrate the difference. India has a very important IT sector, focusing on software development, but India still has a long way to go to effectively use ICTs as a tool for social development. While it is important to address the digital divide and provide "access" to ICTs, it is also essential to focus on what this access is truly expected to do from a development perspective. "Access for what?" is the question increasingly asked.

## Entertainment and Social Purposes of ICTs

If access is to have a clear development impact, telecenters must become truly multipurpose, with, for example, rural health workers using some of the available ICTs to communicate with urban counterparts to transfer health data and access information databases, or with agricultural extension workers using the same computers to communicate with research centers and get access to essential information. Ideally, all members of the community within reach of the telecenter would be able to take advantage of distance learning opportunities brought about by the telecenter.

Perhaps more important, the telecenter can become a new tool for community building and community-driven development. The telecenter can become a new place of assembly, community discussion, and so forth. The telecenter will not, however, operate in a vacuum; community leadership and power structures are likely to impact how a telecenter's resources are used.

## ICTs for Better Health

Most health workers in developing countries operate in an environment in which access to information is one of many challenges; for example, shortages of medical equipment sometimes as basic as rubber gloves, inadequate supplies of drugs, sometimes even basic medicines such as aspirin, lack of training, and poor pay, resulting in a brain drain of some of the best doctors to Europe and North America. Access to information is appalling. Training textbooks are often out of date, and access to information on the latest drug developments or preventive treatments are limited. Doctors feel isolated because they cannot get advice on making a diagnostic. How can ICTs help? What roles can ICTs play in addressing these challenges? There are five key ICT applications for better health. Each will be briefly addressed below.

## Handling Surveillance and Epidemiological Information

Information and Communication Technologies can help to collect and transfer surveillance and epidemiological data more effectively and quickly than before. In one project in India, rural health workers were given a PDA to help them collect basic patient information. The use of PDAs has reduced the time health workers spend on record keeping by 40–60%, allowing them to focus more on delivering quality health care. In addition, the use of PDAs increases the accuracy of the records.[15]

## Disseminating Personal and Community Information

In Africa, a partnership between the WorldSpace Foundation, a digital radio pioneer, and Satellife, a pioneer in ICT for health, has resulted in the development of the Public Health Channel, which is being piloted in Zimbabwe, Kenya, Uganda, and Ethiopia, and will target the information needs of hospitals, medical schools, medical libraries, health clinics, health ministries, and medical research institutions.[16] More generally, radio has been used extensively for the diffusion of health messages to the public.

## Managing Health Services

Information and communication technologies can facilitate the management of
health services by increasing efficiency in decision-making processes. Over the entire
continent of Africa, researchers have been mapping malaria risk using geographic
information systems (GIS) to integrate spatial malaria and environmental data sets.
The researchers are able to produce maps of the type and severity of malaria
transmission. Based on those maps, the most appropriate levels and types of
interventions can then be deployed, thereby helping to rationalize the allocation of
scarce resources for malaria control.[17]

## Accessing Knowledge and Medical Literature

Information and communication technologies can facilitate access to a broad range of
health information, including essential medical journals, but they can also facilitate
networking among health professionals. As the medical literature available on the
Internet is not always particularly relevant to addressing the most pressing health
issues facing developing countries, the example highlighted below specifically
addresses the needs of developing countries. Under a project funded by USAID,
Management Sciences for Health (MSH) developed the manager's electronic resource
center (ERC). The ERC is a collection of management information products designed
to meet the needs of health professionals around the world with varying levels of
Internet access. The ERC provides access to both Web and E-mail products.[18]

## Facilitating Clinical Decision Making

Information and communication technologies can also help health practitioners in
clinical decision making. This is most often referred to as telemedicine applications,
whereby interactive audio, visual, and/or data communication is used to provide
medical care.

Fancy telemedicine applications have been implemented around the world, up to
the point in which a doctor in London can operate on someone in New York. These
advanced telemedicine applications are of little relevance to developing countries.
There are cases, however, in which telemedicine can help to address specific challenges.
For example, a project was developed in Ethiopia to link rural clinics and the main
hospital in Addis Ababa through a teleradiology application. Ethiopia suffers from a
severe shortage of health care professionals, especially in remote and rural areas. There
are fewer than ten radiologists in the country for a population of 60 million people.
There are, however, twenty-one radiologist centers with the necessary equipment. As a
result, the radiologists must travel from center to center to examine patients. Two
options were envisaged. The first one was to install equipment in one or two remote
clinics to link them with the urban hospital and facilitate remote consultation. The
second one was to connect a doctor traveling from village to village within the remote
region of Tigray.[19]

## ICTs for Education and Learning

Information and communication technology applications in the education sector
and the ever-expanding lifelong learning area have been key to the deployment of

ICTs in developing countries. Two important applications of ICTs in education have taken off on a wide scale: (1) ICTs in schools and (2) ICTs for enhanced distance learning.

## ICTs in Schools

There are a number of different rationales for using computers in classrooms. For example, students need to become familiar with the tools of the information society, the use of technology in the classroom can enhance existing curriculum, and technology can be used to access remote databases and sources of information, as well as communicate with other schools (Perraton, 2000). What follows are two examples of programs that have brought ICTs into the classroom.

## WorLD—World Links Program for Development

WorLD was created in 1997 as a pilot initiative of the World Bank. Its mission is to open a world of learning with the help of IT. WorLD is building global, educational online communities for secondary school students and teachers around the world in order to expand distance learning opportunities, enhance cultural understanding across nations, build broad support for economic and social development, and train teachers to integrate information technology into the classroom. Forty developing countries from all regions of the world have been initially targeted to participate in the program, with a goal of thirty to fifty schools participating per country.[20]

## Enlaces—Chile

Chile's computers in schools program, Enlaces, started as a pilot project in 1993. The goal was to create a telecommunications and computer network among 100 Chilean primary schools and associated institutions. By the end of 1995, Enlaces had surpassed its original target and had incorporated computers into some 180 schools at both the primary and secondary levels. This still represented a very small percentage of schools. The project was then converted into a national program. As more and more countries are developing policies related to the use of ICTs in education, more and more countries are looking to put computers into classrooms. The most important challenges, however, are in making all the necessary changes to make effective use of the computer rather than the technical challenges of actually setting up computer labs in schools.[21]

## ICTs for Enhanced Distance Learning

Distance education is not new, and the use of ICTs for distance education programs is not new either. Radio broadcasting and television programs have been used for decades to reach a range of target groups in developing countries with educational programs. In some cases, distance education using ICTs has actually provided an alternative to traditional classroom schooling. In isolated region in which there are no schools, ICTs can bring much needed educational programs to children and adults alike.

In other cases, distance education programs are used in conjunction with traditional classroom settings, in which ICTs are used to allow access to high-quality materials and teaching methods and supplement poorly qualified teachers in the classrooms. Finally, with advanced technologies, many universities across the world are experimenting with virtual networks and online learning. Three examples using three different technologies are briefly presented below.

### African Virtual University (AVU)—Satellite Education in Africa

The AVU is an example of a continentwide collaborative initiative among universities to deliver high-quality content via videoconferencing of lectures from key institutions. World-class professors from universities around the globe deliver lectures from a studio classroom. The lecture is transmitted via satellite to participating campuses in Africa. The typical AVU classroom has approximately twenty-five to thirty students sitting at their desks watching the broadcast on large-screen projectors, television monitors, or computers. On-site moderators guide the students, and some real-time interaction with lecturers is possible. The AVU started as a World Bank-funded project and is now struggling to become financially sustainable on its own.[22]

### Telesecundaria—Television-Based Education in Mexico and South America

Telesecundaria is a TV-based program developed in Mexico in 1968 that offers a complete junior secondary curriculum (grades 7 to 9) to rural populations where access to traditional secondary schools is not possible. The program has been so successful that it has continued to expand both within Mexico, where it also now targets grades 10 to 12 and junior high adult education, and within Central America, where it is being used and adapted by a number of other countries. Between 1998 and 2002, the Ministry of Public Education was planning to open 4500 new Telesecundaria schools to address the needs of another 250,000 students. In 2002, a complete high school program should be available on a national scale (Calderoni, 1998). While many schools have requested videoconferencing that would allow interaction between students and the television presenters, the high costs of this technology renders its use unlikely anytime soon.

### Educatodos—Radio for Out-of-School Youth

Educatodos is a program supported by USAID in Honduras that has provided interactive radio instruction (IRI) for out-of-school youth. While primary enrollments are relatively high in Honduras, repetition rates in early grades are very high, resulting in a large number of students dropping out by sixth grade if they have repeated some grades and are "too old" to continue studying in traditional schools. The program started in 1995, addressing education needs in grades 1 through 6. The program is managed by the Ministry of Education and is part of the formal education system, providing equally valid certificates of completion for each grade. The programs, which combine broadcast and audiotaped lessons and text materials, are run at the local level by a total of about 4000 volunteer facilitators, who are members of the communities in which the Educatodos groups meet. Since 1999, Educatodos has implemented a pilot phase for grades 7 through 9 (Corrales, 1995).

## Key Issues Regarding ICT Applications for Health and Education

There are hundreds if not thousands of examples of existing projects of various scale putting ICTs into use for education and health purposes. Across these two "social" sectors, a number of similar issues have emerged. Impact and cost-effectiveness have not always been carefully monitored and measured. While the focus is often on providing access to the technologies, human capacity issues are often ignored or not adequately addressed. Sustainability is emerging as a central issue. Most projects funded by external actors are likely to fall apart when donor funding ceases because they have failed to develop a postdonor model for sustainability. In this context, whatever impact the pilot donor-funded project may have had, long-term impact is likely to be limited. In both health and education, the local production of content and local knowledge as well as local capacity must be better used and strengthened in order to maximize impact and local empowerment.

## E-Commerce

### What Do We Mean by E-Commerce?

Electronic commerce is a generic term to describe the way in high organizations trade electronically. It uses such technologies as the Internet, intranets, electronic data interchange (EDI), and smart cards to communicate with customers or other companies, to carry out research or information gathering, or to conduct business transactions.

### Can E-Commerce Be an Engine of Development?

The most recent studies on E-commerce for developing countries highlight both the opportunities offered by new ICTs and the continuing challenges facing developing countries in transforming potential into reality (UNCTAD, 2001): "the potential of e-commerce to become an engine of development will not be realized if investment in infrastructure, equipment and human resource development does not go hand in hand with profound modifications in the organization and management of companies and (as far as they have an impact on the operation of businesses) government agencies" (UNCTAD, 2001). Often highlighted is the potential of E-commerce in the tourism sector for many developing countries. Tourism is a very information-intensive industry and among the sectors most quickly adopting the Internet for business.[23] Other opportunities often highlighted for E-commerce in developing countries concern business-to-business (B2B) applications. For all this to work, however, the appropriate legal and regulatory frameworks must be in place. This includes finding solutions to address global transactions and dispute resolution mechanisms, privacy and security issues, legal recognition of electronic signatures, and taxation issues. Other key obstacles include managing payments online and actually delivering physical products to their destinations. In the LDCs (least developed countries), entrepreneurs who wish to engage in E-commerce face serious difficulties, including a lack of infrastructure, IT skills, legislation, payment methods, and financial resources. Governments of LDCs have also shown very little interest in E-commerce and have not paid much attention to the need to establish the appropriate legal and regulatory frameworks.

For LDCs, the key to success is often being able to identify niches for E-commerce projects. The most serious problem for LDC enterprises who embark on E-commerce is not technology but the need to change their business culture and practices (UNCTAD, 2001). Some examples of niches for E-commerce in LDCs include offline teleservicing. This includes transcription services, data input, software development, remote access server maintenance, Web development, creation of databases, digitization of old documents, translation, and editing. While a lot of attention is being paid to E-commerce, the broader area of effective use of ICTs by enterprises is receiving less attention (Heeks and Duncombe, 2001).

### PeopLink

The best known example of developmental E-commerce is PEOPLink.[24] PEOPLink is a nonprofit organization helping producers in remote communities all over the world market their products on the Internet. PEOPLink is building a global network of trading partners (TPs) that in turn provide services to several community-based artisan producer groups. The TPs provide the artisan groups with digital cameras and train them to capture images and edit them in a compressed format suitable for transmission via the Internet. PEOPLink then places images of the crafts on the PEOPLink Web page and promotes them to retail and wholesale buyers in the industrialized countries. The Web page also contains educational materials, sent electronically by the TPs, about the work and lives of the artisans. PEOPLink also help the TPs build and maintain their own Web catalogs and provide online training and product development support.

Clearly, there are opportunities for E-commerce in developing countries. With some help in the form of assistance from organizations such as PEOPLink, these opportunities can even benefit poor artisans or isolated rural communities. In the meantime, the success of these small-scale activities should not obscure the need for government action at the level of the legal and regulatory environment to ensure that the proper incentives are in place for enterprises to embrace E-commerce and take their place in global markets.

## E-Governance/E-Government

### What Is the Difference Between E-Governance and E-Government?

E-governance goes beyond E-government. While E-government deals primarily with governments' use of electronic means to provide services to the public, E-governance includes a broader range of activities enabling citizens to take part in government activities. Michiel Backus (2001) provides the following definition of E-governance: "The application of electronic means in: (1) the interaction between government and citizens and government and businesses, as well as in (2) internal government operations." Just as successful E-commerce requires changes in how business is conducted, E-government must be accompanied by changes in how government business is conducted. In short, E-government is not just about setting up a government Web site to disseminate information, although it may start with such a Web site as a first step.

### Recent Literature

The recent report of the Pacific Council on International Policy entitled "Roadmap for E-Government in the Developing World" identified ten key questions that E-government leaders should ask themselves. Along the lines of this chapter, the report notes that E-government is not a shortcut to economic development, budget savings, or clean and efficient government: "E-government is a process... and often a struggle that presents costs and risks, both financial and political" (Pacific Council on International Policy, 2002). Two examples of E-government and E-governance are presented below.

## E-Government in India

The Department of Revenue in Karnataka, India, has computerized 20 million records of land ownership of 6.7 million farmers in the state.[25] Previously, farmers had to seek out the village accountant to get a copy of the record of rights, tenancy, and crops (called an RTC). This is a document needed for many tasks, such as obtaining bank loans. There were delays and harassment, and bribes had to be paid. Today, for a fee of Rs.15, a printed copy of the RTC can be obtained online at computerized land record kiosks. In the next phase, all the databases are to be uploaded to a Web-enabled central database. The RTCs would then be available online at Internet kiosks, which are likely to be set up in rural areas.[26]

## ICTs and Participation in Democratic Processes in Indonesia

In Indonesia, DISCUSS (Democracy Initiative Through Sustainable Community Discussion), a project funded by the US government and managed by the U.S.-based NGO PACT, has helped to combine face-to-face community discussions with systematic dissemination of information through a wide range of media, including radio, press, television, and the Internet. Discussions were facilitated at the community level in collaboration with local NGOs. The results of the discussions were collected and national and provincial databases are compiled balance accessible to decision makers, policy analysts, advocates, media organizations, and ordinary citizens. Providing a platform for community empowerment, the discussions resulted in recommendations to authorities, action plans, dispute resolutions, and so on.

The key point of this example is that face-to-face communications should not be ignored in the age of the Internet and that there are many ICTs (beyond the Internet) that can contribute to information dissemination and participation in democratic processes. E-democracy may be primarily about online voting, but ICTs in a broader sense can have an important role to play in facilitating democratic processes.

## KNOWLEDGE NETWORKING FOR DEVELOPMENT

### ICTs as Tools for Development Work

There is a certain degree of confusion within the development community about ICTs for development and ICTs for development assistance. The focus of this chapter up to this point has been on ICTs for development. This section focuses more on ICTs for development knowledge; that is, using ICTs to disseminate knowledge about development.

### Electronic Networking for Rural Asia–Pacific (ENRAP)

ENRAP is an initiative funded by the International Fund for Agricultural Development (IFAD). The initiative supports Internet use and knowledge sharing among rural development projects in the Asia–Pacific region. ENRAP pursues a participatory approach. All stakeholders are engaged in the process and strategies are devised to ensure future sustainability. The key goal of the initiative is the development of local applications for electronic networking, referring to ICTs that fit the communicational and informational needs of users in response to specific development issues.

Through the use of local applications for electronic networking, it is envisioned that IFAD project staff will be better able to communicate and share relevant information not only with their project co-workers, but also with stakeholders, beneficiaries, and other IFAD project staff members domestically and internationally. ENRAP uses this process of communicating and/or sharing information among community individuals for the purpose of achieving project objectives and ultimately alleviating rural poverty. ENRAP's aim is to introduce ICTs as a means of assisting stakeholders to meet their communication and information needs. The ICTs that are selected by the stakeholders may range from CD-ROMs to E-mail and the World Wide Web. The participatory development process for local applications involves a series of mini-workshops among key stakeholders as a first step (Richardson and McConnell, n.d.).

While this example specifically addresses the knowledge needs of development agencies and donor-funded projects managed by IFAD, the next example more directly addresses the knowledge needs of individuals at the grassroots level.

## Knowledge Network for Augmenting Grassroots Innovations (KnowNet-Grin)

Honey Bee Network brings together those creative and innovative farmers, artisans, mechanics, fishermen and women, and laborers who have solved a problem through their own genius without any outside help, whether from the state, market, or even NGOs. Such self-triggered and a developed innovations—whether technological or institutional—are scouted, supported, sustained, and scaled wherever possible with or without value addition or linkage with formal science and technology. The idea is to generate incentives and benefits for the innovators. The innovations could be developed by individuals or groups. These may have been developed in the recent past or long and sometimes these innovations or creative practices might have become part of traditional knowledge. We thus also look for outstanding examples of traditional knowledge that help in conserving and utilizing natural resources in a sustainable manner. The name Honey Bee signifies a philosophy of discourse that is authentic, accountable, and fair. The honey bee does two important things: it collects pollen without impoverishing the flowers and it connects flower to flower through pollination. The idea is that when the knowledge of people is collected the same people do not become poorer after sharing their insights. Further, innovators are connected with one another through feedback, communication, and networking in the local language.

Initially the Honey Bee Network was text-based. The process of scouting innovations, publishing them in a newsletter, receiving feedback from readers, and enabling innovators to incorporate this feedback in their innovation proved to be very long, given the limitations of a quarterly publication in six languages. The process was not only very long and limited in its usefulness to the innovator, but it was also of limited use to illiterate innovators and potential users of the innovations. The network is now turning into a multimedia and multilingual network providing real-time connectivity among grassroots innovators. This will help to connect grassroots innovators in real time and solve problems much faster, therefore demonstrates the value of the network, which in turn will result in more incentives for innovators to become part of the network.

## CONCLUSIONS

### Key Points

Throughout this chapter, I have tried to make a number of key points that will be summarized here. First, while everyone agrees that ICTs offer important potential for contributing to development, it is not clear that the transformation between potential and reality is automatic or that the process will have a significant beneficial impact on the poverty or inequalities in developing countries.

Second, while it is clear that there are many examples of applications of ICTs for development, most of these have been developed on a pilot basis and with substantial donor funding. Their sustainability is often in doubt, and their impact is limited to the nature of small-scale pilot projects.

Third, while the term ICT is often used to refer to computers and the Internet, there is a much wider range of ICTs (old and new) that may better address the specific needs of developing countries, including increasingly mobile and relatively inexpensive PDAs, digital radios, and smart cards.

Fourth, while the international development community is struggling to learn from its early experiments with ICTs for development, there are growing pressures to come up with sustainable solutions that can be implemented on a large scale to have greater impact than what has been done to date. "Scaling up," as it is referred to, involves more than just doubling budgets and size. To the extent that projects cannot be scaled up, whether because human and/or financial resources are not available or for some other reason, the potential of ICTs will not be realized.

Fifth, even if it is possible to scale up some of these ICT applications for development, as in the case of the Grameen Bank's village phone program, the beneficial impacts are not always clearly measured. The international development community has a long way to go to implement monitoring and evaluation mechanisms that truly reflect impact rather than output-based outcomes.

### Where to Go from Here: Integrating and Mainstreaming

While there is clearly scope for such sector-specific initiatives such as those highlighted in the previous sections on health, education, E-commerce, and E-government, there is also a need for integrated approaches and for mainstreaming ICTs in development activities rather than focusing on stand-alone ICT projects. This is particularly true in the LDCs, which ICTs alone cannot address the needs of communities and risk creating imbalances in the allocation of scarce resources.

As mentioned earlier, the IDB is developing an ICT project in Guyana that is going to take a comprehensive and holistic approach. Citing the final report of the DOI, the project document suggests that "a comprehensive and holistic approach is the most effective way to promote synergies and maximize the impact of ICTs."[27] The result is a project that will cover a range of interrelated initiatives, such as: (1)

improvements in the legal framework, (2) increased use of ICTs in the public sector (E-government), (3) community outreach (community access centers), and (4) promotion of ICT service exports (E-exports). Two additional types of activities will support the four listed above: (5) network connectivity, and (6) human resources development. It could be argued that the issue is not ICTs for development but rather development supported by ICTs (Ballantyne, 2002).

For example, the World Bank's ICT strategy notes that more work needs to be done to effectively integrate ICTs in all Bank activities, including sector strategy papers, poverty reduction strategy papers, and country assistance strategy processes (World Bank, 2002). Just as the expression "mainstreaming gender" in development activities has become commonplace, the expression "mainstreaming ICTs" will (or should) become commonplace.

## Beyond the Hype, Beyond the Internet

While a lot of ongoing activity and interest focuses on the Internet, a broader approach to a range of ICTs would be more appropriate for many developing countries and in ICTs. In many ways, the Internet is *not* necessarily the most powerful tool for information dissemination, communication, or knowledge sharing. In many cases, other ITs are more appropriate (or a combination of ICTs, as in the case of the DISCUSS project previously discussed). It is not a debate about old and new technologies. Some "old" technologies are evolving rapidly and offering new opportunities, such as digital radio. Some of the newest technologies may also provide better opportunities if they are cheaper and more mobile than the currently predominant desktop/laptop paradigm (smart cards, PDAs).

## NOTES

1. A detailed account of the Zapatistas' Netwar can be found in "The Zapatista 'Social Netwar in Mexico,'" 1998; URL: http://www.ezln.org.
2. This author is an advisor to the ICTs for Development section of the Global Development Gateway. The home page is at the following URL: a http://www.developmentgateway.org/node/133831/.
3. For a critique of the UNDP report, see ITDG's formal response at http://www.itdg.org/html/whats_new/docs/ITDGResponseToHDR%20June2.PDF.
4. The Web site of the DOT force is at http://www.dotforce.org.
5. For more information, see the U.N. ICT task force's Web site at http://www.unicttask-force.org.
6. New efforts are also being implemented to better measure the digital divide. For example, IDRC has been developing new maps of the digital divide in Africa that represent the international bandwidth available in bits per capita. See http://www.idrc.ca/acacia/info/info.html.
7. The executive summary of the sector strategy can be found at http://info.worldbank.org/ict/assets/docs/ExecSum.pdf
8. The IDB's IT for development program is at http://www.iadb.org/sds/itdev/.
9. The proposal document for the Guyana project can be found at http://www.iadb.org/EXR/doc98/pro/uGY0066.pdf.
10. A short concept paper can be found at http://sdnhq.undp.org/it4dev/ffICTe.pdf. The Web site for the digital opportunity initiative is at http://www.opt-init.org.
11. The DOT-COM Web site is currently at http://www.usaid.gov/info_technology/dotcom/.

12. Find more information about DOT-COM at http://www.usaid.gov/info_technology/dotcom/.
13. The draft of Tanzania's ICT strategy can be found at http://www.moct.go.tz/ict/zerothorder.pdf. For other examples, see Pakistan http://itcommission.gov.pk/itpolicy.htm); Egypt (http://www.mcit.gov.eg/national_plan.html), and Mexico (http://www.e-mexico.gob.mx/).
14. See Proenza et al. (2001), as well as Jensen and Esterhuysen (2001) and Latchem and Walker.
15. India Health Care Project—"Use of Information Technology for Delivering Quality Health." ongoing project funded by infoDev. at http://www.infodev.org.
16. The URL for WorldSpace: http://www.worldspace.org; URL for Satellife: http://www.satellife.org.
17. The URL for the Mapping Malaria Risk in Africa (MARA) project: http://www.mara.org.za/ about.htm.
18. The URL for the ERC: http://erc.msh.org.
19. The URL for the project description: http://www.ehto.org/midjan/regions_Ethiopia.html.
20. For more information, see http://www.worldbank.org/worldlinks/english/.
21. For more information, see http://www.enlaces.cl.
22. For more information, see http://www.avu.org.
23. For a developmental example, see the Kiskeya project which enables electronic commerce for sustainable tourism, at http://kiskeya-alternative.org/descrip-eng.html.
24. PEOPLink's Web site can be found at http://www.peoplink.org.
25. For additional case studies on E-government, see the World Bank's E-government site at http://www1.worldbank.org/publicsector/egov/sitemap.htm. For a wide range of case studies on E-governance, see the Digital Governance's Web site at http://www.cddc.vt.edu/digitalgov/gov-cases.html.
26. URL: http://www1.worldbank.org/publicsector/egov/bhoomi_cs.htm.
27. URL: http://www.iadb.org/EXR/doc98/pro/uGY0066.pdf.

## REFERENCES

Ballantyne, P. (March 2002). I-connect newsletter.

Backus, M. (2001). E-governance in Developing Countries. IICD research brief no. 1. URL: http://www.ftpiicd.org/files/research/briefs/brief1.doc. accessed Nov. 1, 2002.

Calderoni, J. (1998). Telesecundaria: Using TV to Bring Education to Rural Mexico. Washington, D.C.: World Bank Education and Technology Technical Notes Series. Vol. 3. no. 2.

Cardoso, F. E. (1993). North–South relations in the present context: A new dependency? In: Cornoy, M., Castells, M., Cohen, S., eds. The New Global Economy in the Information Age: Reflections on Our Changing World. University Park, PA: Pennsylvania State University, pp. 149–164.

Castells, M. (1998). The Information Age: Economy, Society and Culture. Vols. 1–3. Oxford: Blackwell.

Castells, M. (1993). The informational economy and the new international division of labor. In: Cornoy, M., Castells, M., Cohen, S., eds. The New Global Economy in the Information Age: Reflections on Our Changing World. University Park, PA: Pennsylvania State University, pp. 15–43.

Corrales, C. (1995). Adult Basic Education in Honduras: Managing Multiple Channels. LearnTech Case Study Series. no. 9.

Drake, W. J. (2000). From the Global Digital Divide to the Global Digital Opportunity: Proposals submitted to the G-8 Kyushu-Okinawa Summit 2000. World Economic Forum

Global Digital Divide Initiative. URL: http://www.weforum.org/pdf/Projects/From-TheGDDivideToTheGDOpportunity.pdf. accessed Nov. 1, 2002.

Government of Egypt. (2002). National Plan for Communications and Information Technology. URL: http://www.mcit.gov.eg/national_plan.html. accessed May 23, 2002.

Government of Pakistan. (2002). IT Policy. URL: http://itcommission.gov.pk/itpolicy.htm. accessed May 23, 2002.

Government of Tanzania. (2002). National ICT Policy of Tanzania—Draft. URL: http://www.moct.go.tz/ict/zerothorder.pdf. accessed May 23, 2002.

Hamelink, C. (1998). ICTs and Social Development: The Global Policy Context. Papers presented at the UNRISD Conference on Information Technologies and Social Development. URL: http://www.unrisd.org/infotech/conferen/icts/icts.htm#TopOfPage. accessed June 4, 2002.

Heeks, R., Duncombe, R. (2001). Information, Technology and Small Enterprise: A Handbook for Enterprise Support Agencies in Developing Countries. IDPM, University of Manchester, UK: URL: http://idpm.man.ac.uk/idpm/esahndbk.html. accessed June 4, 2002.

Inter-American Development Bank (IDB). (2001). Guyana: Information and Communication Technologies, Profile II. URL: http://www.iadb.org/EXR/doc98/pro/uGY0066. pdf. accessed May 23, 2002.

International Telecommunications Union. World Telecommunication Development Report 2002. Geneva: ITU.

Jensen, M., Esterhuysen, A. (2001). The Community Telecenter Cookbook for Africa. Paris: UNESCO, URL: http://unesdoc.unesco.org/images/0012/001230/123004e.pdf. accessed June 4, 2002.

Kirkman, G. (1999). It's More than Just Being Connected: A Discussion of Some Issues of Information Technology and International Development. A working paper presented at the Development E-Commerce Workshop, Aug. 16–17, 1999; Media Laboratory at the Massachusetts Institute of Technology, Cambridge, MA, URL: http://www.cid.harvard.edu/ciditg/papers/itg-beingconnected.pdf. accessed June 4, 2002.

Latchem, C., Walker, D. (2001). Telecenters: Case Studies and Key Issues. Commonwealth of Learning. URL: http://www.col.org/telecentres. Accessed June 4, 2002.

Noble, D. F. (1997). The Religion of Technology: The Divinity of Man and the Spirit of Intervention. New York: Knop.

Pacific Council on International Policy. (2002). Roadmap for E-Government in the Developing World: 10 Questions E-Government Leaders Should Ask Themselves, http://www.pacific-council.org/pdfs/e-gov.paper.f.pdf. accessed June 4, 2002.

Perraton, H. (2000). Information and Communication Technologies for Education in the South. report prepared for the Department for International Development (DFID); URL: http://www.globalisation.gov.uk/BackgroundWord/EducationInTheSouthHilaryPerraton.doc. accessed June 4, 2002.

Proenza, F., Bastidas-Bush, R., Montero, G. (2001). Telecenters for Socioeconomic and Rural Development in Latin America and the Caribbean. Washington, DC: InterAmerican Development Bank, URL: http://www.iadb.org/ict4dev/telecenters/fullrep.pdf. accessed June 4, 2002.

Richardson, D., McConnell, S. (2002). Electronic Networking for Rural Asia-Pacific (ENRAP): A Participatory Approach to Developing Local Applications; URL: http://www.enrap.org/pub_docs/Final_Report.doc, n.d. accessed June 5, 2002.

Schech, S. (2002). Wired for change: The links between ICTs and development discourses. J Internat Dev 14(1):13–23.

Tawfik, M. (1999). Information and Communication Technologies: Hope and Concern for the Future. WebWorld. Point of Views, URL: http://www.unesco.org/webworld/point_of_views/tawfik_2.shtml. accessed Nov. 1, 2002.

UNCTAD. (2001). E-commerce and Development Report 2001: Trends and Executive Summary. United Nations; New York: URL: http://www.unctad.org/ccommerce/docs/ cdr01_en.htm. accessed June 4, 2002.

UNDP. (2002). Driving Information and Communication Technologies for Development: A UNDP Agenda for Action, 2000–2001; URL: http://sdnhq.undp.org/it4dev/ffICTe.pdf. accessed May 23, 2002.

Verzola, R. (2002). The Internet: Toward a deeper critique. April 3, 2002; URL: http://www.by-tesforall.org/news/default.asp?DocID = 4&channelId = 16&Tablename = Document. accessed Nov. 1, 2002.

Wertheim, M. (1999). The Pearly Gates of Cyberspace. London: Routledge.

World Bank. (2002). Information and Communication Technologies: A World Bank Group Strategy, URL: http://info.worldbank.org/ict/assets/docs/ExecSum.pdf. accessed May 23, 2002.

# 12

# Smallholder Response to Population Pressure and Adversity in Rwanda

**CYNTHIA DONOVAN, EDSON MPYISI, and SCOTT LOVERIDGE**

*Michigan State University, East Lansing, Michigan, U.S.A.*

## INTRODUCTION

Africa's agricultural sector is often characterized as stagnant. By many measures, the assessment is justifiable. Food production in Africa is not keeping pace with population growth, and yields for many crops are well below the levels achieved by developing countries in other regions (Binswanger and Townsend, 2000). African policy makers are criticized for low investment in agricultural research and infrastructure development, while World Bank efforts to produce structural (market and macroeconomic) reforms seem to yield disappointing returns (Easterly, 2001). Others point out that agricultural progress in sub-Saharan Africa is hindered by the placement of its ports, the remote location of its high-quality soils, how its latitude affects crops, and the prevalence of disease (Bloom and Sachs, 1998).

The typical farmer in sub-Saharan Africa tills the soil without the benefits of mechanization, improved seed varieties, chemical fertilizer, and pesticides. In short, much of Africa has not participated in the technological revolution that released millions from starvation and subsistence farming in other parts of the world. The situation in Rwanda—the country examined in this chapter—is in many ways representative of the overall status of agriculture in sub-Saharan Africa.

While the pace of technical change and overall output growth are slow, Africa's agricultural sector is dynamic in other ways. This chapter demonstrates that farmers seem to assess their situation and are capable of making fairly rapid transitions in cropping patterns when faced with new constraints or opportunities. Surveys of agricultural households over the last decade reveal tremendous changes in Rwandan agricultural outputs. The traditional Rwandan farmer has apparently responded to changing sociopolitical, agroclimactic, land resource, and economic circumstances by making radical shifts among crops. For some crops, the change in output may primarily be the result of secular shifts in productivity driven by lack of resistance to disease. In other cases, land availability, prevailing prices, lack of labor, lack of land, or food security may be the primary drivers behind substantial crop shifts by small-holders.

The purpose of this chapter is to first document and highlight some of the major shifts in output over the past ten years and then provide some working hypotheses about the reasons behind the changes. We also document troubling trends in overall productivity in the traditional agriculture sector, underscoring the need for more off-farm employment and for improved agricultural input and output systems. Rwanda's status as one of Africa's most densely populated countries makes it a good case study for what policy makers in other countries may soon face as populations grow.

The rest of this chapter is laid out as follows. The second section provides a brief history of Rwanda and some of the basic facts of its geography. The third section presents the data and methodology. The fourth section presents a comparison of the main crops and livestock in 1990 and 2001. The fifth section provides selected information at the provincial level, focusing on areas in which there have been substantial changes. The six section suggests potential explanations for the large shifts in Rwanda's agricultural sector, while the seventh section summarizes what the combined changes mean in terms of overall nutrient availability. The eighth section describes specific implications and recommendations for improving Rwanda's agricultural sector, and the final section relates Rwanda's situation to the rest of Africa and other regions.

## A SUMMARY OF RWANDA'S TURBULENT HISTORY

Rwanda is a small mountainous country situated on the western edge of East Africa.[1] It shares borders with Burundi, Democratic Republic of Congo, Tanzania, and Uganda. Prior to the arrival of European colonizers, Rwanda was a highly organized feudal society, with Tutsi pastoralists forming a ruling class. The majority of the population are members of the Hutu group, who were traditionally agriculturalists. The Twa minority were traditionally hunter-gatherers. Rwanda's feudal ruler, known as the mwami, had better military defenses than many other groups in nearby regions. The military defenses were originally designed to protect Rwanda from incursions by nearby groups and also from the slave trade, but later served to buffer Rwanda from colonial rule. The strong local military defenses and fertile high-altitude volcanic soils translated into a high population density.

Recognizing the costs of subduing such a strong nation, German colonizers elected to negotiate an arrangement that left the mwami in control and did not formally merge Rwanda or neighboring Burundi into its Tanganyika colony. Rwanda is landlocked, with few transportation routes to Europe for high-value exportable natural resources. As such, the German interest in Rwanda was minimal. As part of treaties negotiated at the end of World War I, Germany was stripped of its colonies. Colonial administration of Rwanda, on the border of what was then called the Belgian Congo, was transferred to Belgium.

Belgium exerted a much stronger influence on Rwanda than had Germany, but it continued Germany's practice of working closely with the mwami. This had the effect of directing more resources toward the Tutsi ethnic group. The Tutsi group became much wealthier and better educated than Rwanda's other ethnic groups; the socio-economic gap between Tutsis and Hutus was thus exacerbated during the colonial time.

The long history of differential access to resources translated into bloody conflicts and several instances of mass exodus by members of both major ethnic groups in the postcolonial era. Land abandoned in ethnic conflicts was rapidly occupied by others, making it difficult to repatriate refugees. The largest and most widely publicized of these conflicts was in 1994, when radicals associated with a Hutu-dominated regime organized the mass genocide of Tutsis and also murdered Hutus who did not support the genocide. Roughly 10% of the population died or fled. The genocide generated international support for a new government. The new government made repatriation of refugees a major priority, opening new areas for farming, and dividing the land of families with large farms to make room for the refugees. The repatriation of refugees together with a high birth rate combined to make Rwanda more populated than it was prior to the 1994 genocide.

Today more than 90% of Rwanda's population is rural. Most of the rural population is engaged in some kind of farming, making agriculture the largest sector in the economy. Investment in research and programs to train farmers in new techniques suffered from the political turmoil of the past few decades. Technical advances in Rwanda's agricultural sector have been few. There is almost no mechanization; farmers typically use short-handled hoes to cultivate the land. Few varieties have been introduced recently, and with some exceptions farmers apply very little fertilizer, herbicide, or pesticide. The result is declining land and labor productivity in agriculture. Population increases made Rwanda's average farm size shrink about 30% between 1986 and 2002 (Mpyisi et al., 2002; Ministry of Agriculture, 1992). The typical farm family now grows six crops on land that is roughly 810 square meters in size (Mpyisi et al., 2002).

## DATA AND METHODOLOGY

In what follows, our basic information comes from data collected by the Ministry of Agriculture's statistical unit between 1986 and 2001. We focus our attention on two years. The 1990 data set reflects the situation in the last prewar year during which data could be collected without political disruptions and weather and agricultural outputs were fairly normal; 1990 is thus a good year to represent the prewar status of agricultre. The 2001 data set is the most currently available information, and it is considered a relatively good production year.

In both years, the basic method of data collection is the farm-level household survey; commercial farms and the landless are excluded from our sample. The information here reflects the situation of family farms. The households are selected based on a statistically valid clustered random sample designed with assistance from the U.S. Bureau of the Census. Enumerators visited each household periodically for an entire crop year[2] to collect information about the quantities harvested. The 1990 survey visited each household monthly for information on production, sales, and so on, whereas the 2001 survey data are based on seasonal visits to households, thus with longer recall and possibly lower accuracy. In both years, the harvest information is complemented with measurements of the size of the household's fields and basic data

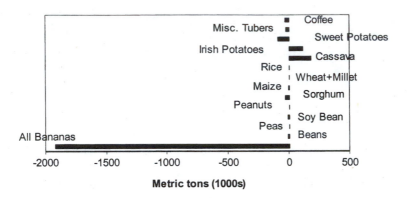

**Figure 1**   Production change (1990–2001). *Source*: FSRP/DSA household surveys.

about the characteristics (gender, age, etc.) of household members and use of inputs. The 1990 sample size was 1284 households versus 1584 households in 2001. These relatively small sample sizes resulted in a high variability of measurement of geographically restricted or rare crops. We therefore focus here on the major crops, which account for the much of food consumption. Readers requiring a more complete description of the survey method are referred to Mpyisi et al. (2002) and the Ministry of Agriculture (1992).

## CHANGES IN NATIONAL CROP OUTPUT AND LIVESTOCK INVENTORIES (1990–2001)

Figures 1 and 2 present the change in output of major smallholder crops between 1990 and 2001. In terms of the percentage of change, the greatest decreases in production were in coffee, soybeans, various tubers, and bananas, while Irish potato and cassava production surged. In terms of quantity, the 1,910,000-ton drop in banana ouput dwarfs all other changes, although there was a substantial reduction in sweet potatoes

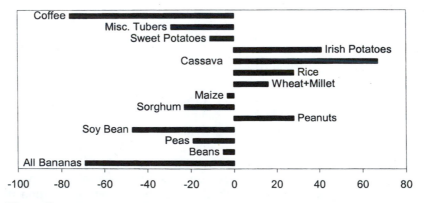

**Figure 2**   Percentage production change (1990–2001). *Source*: FSRP/DSA household surveys.

and large increases in Irish potatoes and cassava production. Overall, livestock inventories, particularly poultry and small livestock, dropped substantially over the same time period, (Donovan et al., 2002).

## SELECTED COMPARISONS AT THE PROVINCIAL LEVEL

This section explores patterns of the changes at the subnational level. Because the borders of Byumba and Kibungo were redrawn in 1996 to create Umutara, direct comparisons of 1990 and 2001 production in these three provinces is only possible by aggregating them into a single "eastern zone" (Figure 3).[3]

Our maps (Figure 4–6) illustrate that the distribution of changes in production patterns is by no means uniform across Rwanda. The estimated tonnages by province are available in Donovan et al. (2002). Kibuye was the only part of the country with increased banana production. The reduction in banana output was most dramatic in the Kigali Rurale province, where output fell 91%. The areas surrounding Kigali Rurale also experienced substantial declines in bananas. Several regions experienced gains of over 100% in Irish potatoes, and Butare and Gikongoro provinces also posted impressive gains. The traditional epicenter of Rwandan Irish potato production, Ruhengeri, lost about 50% of its production. Both Ruhengeri and Kigali Rurale lost almost all their coffee production. Coffee harvests were substantially reduced in the other regions as well. To summarize the findings from these maps, production in some crops expanded in some regions even as national production fell dramatically, while production of Rwanda's main internationally traded crop (coffee) dropped across the

**Figure 3**   Rwandan provinces and the Eastern Zone.

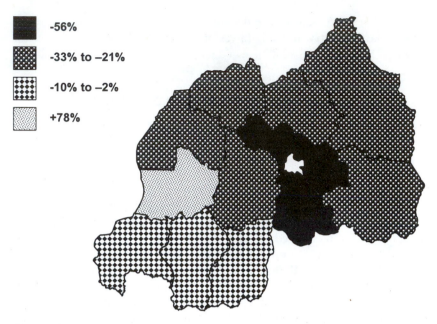

**Figure 4**   Change in Banana production (all varieties) by province (1990–2001). *Source*:
MINAGRI household surveys. Note that Kibungo and Byumba were divided in 1996 to create
Umutara, so all three provinces are treated as a single unit.

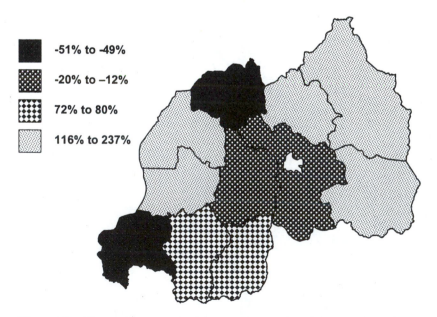

**Figure 5**   Change in tons of Irish potatoes produced by province (1990–2001). *Source*:
MINAGRI household surveys. Note that Kibungo and Byumba were divided in 1996 to create
Umutara, and thus all three provinces are treated as a single unit.

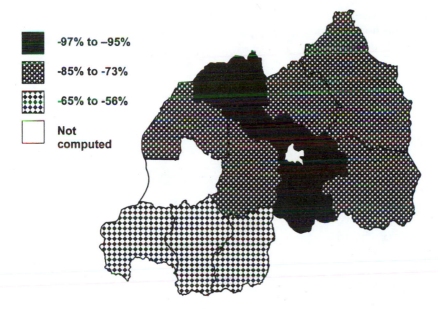

**Figure 6**   Change in tons of coffee produced by province (1990–2001). *Source*: MINAGRI household surveys. Note that Kibungo and Byumba were divided in 1996 to create Umutara, so all three provinces are treated as a single unit. No estimate of 1990 Kibuye coffee production is available.

whole country. With such dramatic regional differences within Rwanda, it is clear that production of locally marketed crops is heavily influenced by local conditions, not just national policy or international prices.

## WHY RWANDAN AGRICULTURE IS CHANGING

We now explore potential reasons why agriculture in Rwanda changed so dramatically over the eleven-year interval. Change can come from differences in yields, area planted per farm, or number of households planting the crop. The production data themselves provide information about the number of households producing each crop. Table 1 presents the change in the percentage of households engaged in cropping each of the major crops. For example, in 1990, 42% of farm households harvested coffee, but by 2001, only 18% of farm households produced the crop. Table 1 therefore reports a change of negative 24% (18% minus 42%) for coffee. A main finding from Table 1 is that fewer or more farmers growing a crop can provide an explanation for changes in overall output for some crops but not others. Coffee, sweet potatoes, and bananas all experienced national declines in output as well as declines in the proportion of households harvesting the crop. The proportion of households producing cassava declined, while total output rose by 67%. There was little change in the proportion of households producing Irish potatoes, while total national output rose by 41%.

Our discussion here is enhanced by interactions with a wide array of people who work in agriculture on a regular basis, including the Ministry of Agriculture, Forestry

**Table 1**  Change in Proportion of
Households Producing a Crop
(1990–2001)

| | |
|---|---:|
| Coffee | −24% |
| Sweet potatoes | −10% |
| Irish potatoes | 1% |
| Cassava | −13% |
| Bananas (all types) | −19% |
| Miscellaneous tubers | −27% |
| Rice | −1% |
| Wheat/millet | −1% |
| Maize | 4% |
| Sorghum | −9% |
| Peanuts | 2% |
| Soy beans | 3% |
| Peas | −14% |
| Beans | 0% |

*Source*: MINAGRI household surveys.

and Livestock Resources (MINAGRI) personnel, the agricultural faculty from
National University of Rwanda, and staff of nongovernmental organizations (NGOs)
active in agriculture. Our data confirmed impressions the agricultural professionals
had about overall crop production trends through their field work. The possible
reasons why they listed the changes in production vary substantially from crop to crop.
Table 2 summarizes the discussion. Munyemana and von Oppen (1999). Loveridge

**Table 2**  Summary of Reasons for Changes in Crop Output

| Increases | Decreases |
|---|---|
| Irish potatoes | Bananas |
|   Increased technical support from NGOs |   Disease, drought, and theft |
|   Increased availability of inputs |   Political turmoil, lack of maintenance |
|   Increased acreage (deforestation) |   Reduced government investment in bananas |
|   Interest in potatoes by larger-scale |   Reduced use of manure as fertilizer |
|     farmers and traders | |
| Cassava | Sweet potatoes |
|   Distribution of cuttings drought years |   Poor rains in 1997, 1998, 2000 |
|   Drought resistance |   Lack of planting material |
|   Flood resistance |   Disease and caterpillars |
|   Increased demand for cassava products |   Fewer households producing |
|   Substituting cassava for sweet potatoes | |
| | Coffee |
| |   Liberalization—farmers now allowed |
| |     to remove trees |
| |   Low international prices |
| |   Low-quality output and poor processing |
| |   Old trees and low yields |

et al. (2002) provide a discussion on the decline and prospect of the coffee production in Rwanda.

## MACRONUTRIENT PRODUCTION FROM OWN CROPS

We now examine what the changes in cropping patterns likely mean in terms of Rwanda's access to basic nutrients. There are three main macronutrients that we will examine here: kilocalories (see Figure 7), lipids, and proteins. The production for each of the main crops is converted into the values of each macronutrient provided and then summed across the crops. Rwanda's recently completed Integrated Living Conditions Survey, (known by its French initials, EICV) (Ministry of Finance and Economic Planning, 2002)[4], shows that over 60% of rural households do not sell their agricultural production.

Earlier research (Loveridge, 1992) found that the fifteen[5] main crops included in the analysis provide 50% of the lipids, 95% of the proteins, and 96% of the calories consumed by rural households. The main question is whether households can get their nutritional needs from their own production. Households differ in their consumption needs, depending upon the household's age and gender composition, so production by household is reported in per adult equivalent (AE) terms instead of per capita terms (Ministry of Finance and Economic Planning, 2002).

In terms of total calorie intakes from these crops, in 1990 Rwandan farm households covered 82% of their daily calorie needs per AE; but in 2001 that coverage fell to 65% (see Figure 8). Looking at the other two major macronutrients, lipids from

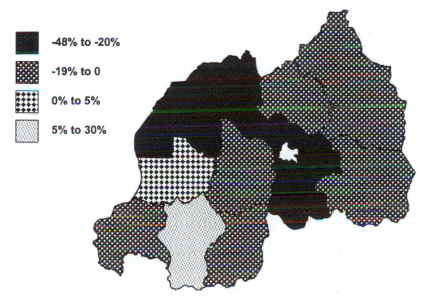

**Figure 7** Change in percentage of kilocalorie needs produced on farm (1990–2001). *Source*: MINAGRI household surveys. Note that Kibungo and Byumba were divided in 1996 to create Umutara, so all three provinces are treated as a single unit. Calculations based on production per adult equivalent, excluding animal products and small horticultural products.

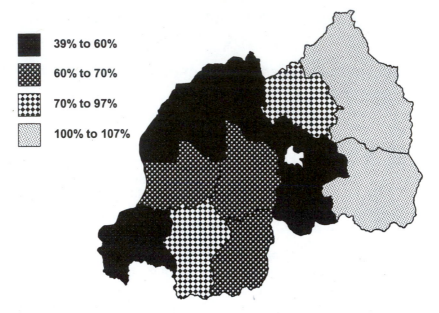

**Figure 8**   Percentage of daily calorie needs produced on farm (2001). *Source*: MINAGRI household surveys. Note that Kibungo, Byumba, and Umutara are treated separately here. Calculations are based on production per adult equivalent, excluding animal products and small horticultural products.

own crop production basically remained stagnant at 17% of needs, although the eastern zone and Butare saw increases due to groundnut production. Own production of proteins fell from 72% to 60% of needs, with declines in sweet potatoes, bananas, and soybeans. Further shifts in production would have localized consequences on nutrient availability. A decline in bean production in Kigali Rurale, for example, resulted in a sharp fall in protein availability. Some of the shifts might be short-term responses to risky weather in previous seasons, particularly in Kigali Rurale and Butare, where rainfall had been unreliable.

## IMPLICATIONS OF CROP CHANGES

Rwanda's agriculture, while relatively stagnant in terms of technology and limited resources, is highly dynamic in one respect. It is capable of adapting quite quickly in response to new opportunities and constraints. Smallholders appear to quickly seize new varieties and inputs, as demonstrated by Irish potatoes and cassava. They also seem to be capable of quickly moving away from crops that are no longer profitable (coffee) or crops with declining yields (bananas and sweet potatoes). Farmers continue to hedge their risk through diversification of their crop portfolio, producing an average of 6.42 crops per household in 2001. Despite these positive aspects of Rwanda's agriculture, our overall data reveal some troubling trends that deserve immediate and sustained attention from policy makers. While Rwanda's situation is unique in some respects, many of the trends identified in our data seem as if they will play out in similar ways in other African countries. Rwanda is a demographic forerunner in that its population density surpasses other countries in sub-Saharan Africa, so other countries may face similar circumstances in the near future. Solving these problems in Rwanda may help find solutions elsewhere. The remainder of this chapter explores the implications of these trends for Rwanda, and proposes steps policy makers can take to improve the situation.

## Potential of Reduced Access to the Cash Economy

In 1990, bananas (including the value-added activity of brewing banana beer) and coffee were by far the two largest sources of cash income for Rwandan agricultural households (Kangasniemi, 1998). The substantial declines in these cash crops may translate into reduced access to market goods, including imported food. Nationally, only 60% of households sell their agricultural outputs (Ministry of Finance and Economic Planning, 2002). The limited access to cash may impact farmers' ability to acquire improved inputs when opportunities arise. Plans for distribution of inputs to improve specific crops need to take this lack of cash into account. Scaling purchased inputs to a very small and therefore more affordable amount or providing credit for input purchase are potential avenues for overcoming this barrier to improved agricultural productivity.

## Effect of Crop Mix on Food Security

Production of beans, peas, and soybeans has declined in overall terms since 1990, thus in per capita terms, production has also has fallen, and the household production of lipids, proteins, and calories has dropped. Moving away from these high-protein crops implies a less healthy diet unless the gap is made up through imports of protein-rich foods. Rural Rwandans have been able to purchase substantial quantities of imported beans in the past (Loveridge, 1989), but with reduced access to cash, this strategy to obtain a nutritionally balanced diet may not be feasible in the future. Chronic food insecurity may worsen, although a shift to more drought-resistant crops (cassava in particular) may be a household strategy to reduce drought-related food shortages. Further exploration of the reasons behind the reduction in these crops might help determine appropriate policy mechanisms (e.g., improved systems for supporting animal agriculture, such as veterinary services, might speed the postwar recovery of livestock inventories.)

## Marketing Infrastructure

Improved systems to process and deliver Rwandan agricultural outputs to the national and international market are needed. As noted in Rwanda's poverty reduction strategy paper (Ministry of Finance and Economic Planning, 2002), commercialization of diversified agricultural products is based upon competitiveness. Rwanda's climate is highly advantageous for exporting certain high-value crops to the northern hemisphere, but these markets cannot be reached without better secondary and tertiary roads, market information systems, and agricultural processing facilities. Improved marketing infrastructure will also help farm families combat nutritional deficiencies through lower-cost food imports and reduce the cost of agricultural inputs while improving incomes from marketed crops.

## Extension Services

In the United States, the cooperative extension service is widely recognized for contributing substantially to the country's movement from a largely agrarian society to one in which 3% of the population can produce more than enough food to feed the whole population (Campbell, 1995; McDowell, 2001). The United States provides annual federal appropriations to designated state universities. The universities then manage a network of extension field offices tied directly to university research. Farmers and others thereby gain easy access to the latest university research. Feedback loops from field extension offices help identify questions for further university investigation. Funds from local and state governments supplement federal base funding, assuring some national consistency of programs and also tailoring of programs to meet local needs.

Most other countries employ extension services that are separate from university research. In some cases, the work of educating farmers is blended with enforcing environmental regulations or collecting production statistics. This alternative model detaches the extension educator from the researcher. When the extension educator must also enforce regulations, a lack of open dialogue between the educator and the farmer can also emerge.

In Rwanda, extension work has been arranged through several models. During the 1980s and early 1990s, several regional government projects supported extension services and the government had many more extension agents, called *monagris*. The monagri system included both data collection and code enforcement, and it was abolished after the genocide. The replacement model of regional government projects seems to be resulting in reduced access to extension services by farmers.

At the same time, farmers indicate that a lack of knowledge is the principal reason for not using fertilizers to enhance productivity (Kelly et al., 2001). Farmers' organizations and NGOs are increasingly responsible for providing extension services, but with short project cycles little institutional capacity may be built for the long term (Bingen and Munyankusi, 2002). The government has recently begun revamping the curriculum at the National University of Rwanda to include more applied research and outreach programs, but these efforts are generally restricted to the region near the university. Still, it is a promising effort if it can be sustained and enlarged.

## Soil Fertility

A decreased area in crops providing good soil protection, such as bananas and mulched coffee, could have rapid, deleterious effects on Rwanda's soil fertility, particularly if these crops are replaced with cassava or cereals (which can exacerbate soil erosion). Among crops common in Rwanda, coffee and bananas provide the greatest protection against erosion (Lewis, 1988), and soil fertility was a major policy concern even before the crop shifts took place (Clay, 1996). The problem is compounded by the lack of fertilizer and the rapid decline in fallow fields documented by Mpyisi et al. 2001. Only 6.9% of households report using purchased inputs (Ministry of Finance and Economic Planning, 2002). Loss of manure due to reduced livestock inventories is another factor putting soil fertility at risk. Rwanda has traditionally been an exporter of animal products (Gabriel, 1974), so the reduced livestock inventories documented here have implications for both income and soil fertility. Research is needed regarding the ways to revitalize animal agriculture, along with studies to help identify other means to sustain or build soil fertility under the prevailing conditions. Again, this require a long-term program with consistent funding. When research is available, policy makers should shift more attention to extension efforts to teach farmers how to improve or maintain soil fertility.

## Other Biophysical Measures to Enhance Land and Labor Productivity

More research is also needed to develop plant varieties in order to increase resistance to disease and improve yields from selected crops. The feasibility of chemical or other treatments to reduce disease should also be explored. Research and U.S.-style extension efforts to develop efficient crop management practices can complement the efforts to improve soil fertility.

## Consistent Investments in Data Gathering

It is impossible to track changes in the agricultural sector or make appropriate decisions for research and extension investments without deep understanding of the market and nonmarket forces at play in setting the stage for agricultural production. Rwanda has several sets of data about rural conditions due to the willingness of policy makers to invest in data gathering. Regular studies of production trends and prices are necessary elements for continued tracking of progress in the agricultural sector and for developing early warning systems to reduce transitory food insecurity.

## RWANDAN POLICY RESPONSE AND CHALLENGES

In summary, Rwanda's farmers are faced with a variety of forces, some favorable and others unfavorable. Rural households are responding to pressures created by the reduced availability of land per capita, rainfall deficits, reduced prices and yields of selected crops, and limited availability of improved inputs and varieties in other crops. They also respond to better marketing opportunities and higher prices. The challenge is to provide the incentives for changes that increase the long-term sustainability of the system while improving farm incomes and generating greater nonfarm linkages. With the severe constraints on land, employment in nonfarm activities or in urban areas is necessary to reduce pressure on agricultural land. It has been observed that such land pressure-and the lack of basic environmental resources (fuel, water, food) that is associated with the land-scarce situation-generates much of the internal conflict present in developing countries (Homer-Dixon, 1999).

Within agriculture, for soil fertility and erosion control, banana cropping can be expanded by improving the productivity and marketing of bananas. For coffee, efforts are focused on accessing the high-priced coffee markets. Lowering fertilizer costs and increasing fertilizer availability are seen as strategies to get more farmers using fertilizers to enhance both land and labor productivity. Farmers demand more information on the use of fertilizers and management practices to lessen weather risks and increase yields, however, If better systems to support agriculture are put into place, the sector will respond with greater productivity.

Rwanda's story provides a cautionary tale for policy makers in other African countries. Land and population pressures coupled with lack of appropriate investments to steer a better path for agricultural productivity create a volatile mix that can lead to both misery and conflict. Some of Rwanda's problems are of its own making. For example, the previous regimes implemented policies that mandated certain crops (coffee) or soil preservation techniques (erosion control ditches) without regard to farmers' incentives. Other problems result from the lack of interest in supporting long-term research investments. The successes enjoyed by the agricultural sector in affluent countries came as a result of consistent investments in research and dissemination of research results among farmers. The system of three-to-five-year projects currently employed by many donor agencies seems unlikely to generate an indigenous knowledge base required for real advances in agricultural productivity.

Other changes are required at the regional or international level if African agricultural productivity is to reach the levels enjoyed in other regions. Reducing formal and informal barriers to trade can enhance the border trade between Rwanda and its neighboring countries. In the past, too much attention was paid to trade linkages with Europe at the expense of a well-developed regional trade policy. Coordinated investments in transportation infrastructure from Rwanda to major cities and ports in nearby countries could enhance the overall trade outlook of the region. Similarly, a mutually supported system of regional price reporting could facilitate the movement of food to areas where it is most needed. Donors could play a role in establishing basic trust and vision for better regional cooperation so that each country fulfills its potential through trade.

The experience of Rwanda offers lessons that can be instructive to policy makers dealing with the problem of Africa's low agricultural productivity. The path for reversing Africa's declining per capita food availability seems clear. Policies must change to embrace long-term locally based research and other investments that help translate the research results into viable economic activities that smallholders can willingly adopt. Failure to make these improvements may lead to further collapse of African socioeconomic systems. The world is no longer a place in which one large region will suffer in isolation while another prospers. Complacency about the status of African agriculture can have consequences for other regions. Making better investments in African agriculture thus is simply the right thing to do.

## NOTES

1. Additional details of Rwanda's political history can be found at: Newafrica.com. Rwanda History, http://www.newafrica.com/history/country.asp?countryid = 40 (accessed March 2002); African Studies Center. Rwanda–History, University of Pennsylvania, http://www.sas.upenn.edu/African_Studies/NEH/rw-hist.html (accessed March 2002).
2. To be consistent with major planting and harvest times, the crop year runs from September through August.
3. The eastern zone integrates Byumba, Kibungo, and Umutara into one region.
4. The EICV was a household survey conducted in rural and urban areas based on a nationally representative sample frame. By design, the majority of households in the FSRP/DSA 2001 sample are included in the EICV sample.

5.  The fifteen crops are beans, peas, peanuts, soybeans, maize, sorghum, wheat, millet, rice, sweet potatoes, cassava, Irish potatoes, taro, yams, and bananas.

## REFERENCES

Bingen, J., Munyankusi, L. (2002). Farmer Associations, Decentralization, and Development in Rwanda: Challenges Ahead. FSRP/DSA publication 4E. Kigali, Rwanda: Food Security Research Project and MINAGRI Division of Agricultural Statistics.

Binswanger, H. P., Townsend, R. F. (2000). The growth performance of agriculture in sub-Saharan Africa. Amer J Agri Econ 82(5):1075–1086.

Bloom, D. E., Sachs, J. D. (1998). Geography, demography, and economic growth in Africa. Brookings Papers Econ Act 2:207–295.

Campbell, J. R. (1995). Reclaiming a Lost Heritage: Land-Grant and Other Higher Education Initiatives for the Twenty-First Century. Ames, IA: Iowa State University Press.

Clay, D. C. (1996). Fighting an Uphill Battle: Population Pressure and Declining Land Productivity in Rwanda. International Development working paper no. 58. East Lansing, MI: Michigan State University.

Donovan, C., Mpyisi, E., Loveridge, S. (2002). Forces Driving Change in Rwandan Agriculture, 1990–2001. FSRP/DSA working paper. Kigali, Rwanda: Food Security Research Project and MINAGRI Division of Agricultural Statistics.

Easterly, W. (2001). The Elusive Quest for Growth: Economists' Adventures and Misadventures in the Tropics. Cambridge, MA: MIT Press.

Gabriel, E. (1974). Les Routes d'Exportation du Betail Rwandais. Bulletin Agricole du Rwanda 7(1):22–29.

Homer-Dixon, T. F. (1999). Environment, Scarcity, and Violence. Princeton, NJ: Princeton University Press.

Kangasniemi J. (1998). People and Bananas on Steep Slopes: Agricultural Intensification and Food Security under Demographic Pressure and Environmental Degradation in Rwanda. PhD dissertation, Michigan State University, East Lansing, MI.

Kelly, V., Mpyisi, E., Shingiro, E., Nyarwaya, J. B. (2001). Agricultural Intensification in Rwanda: An Elusive Goal. Fertilizer Use and Conservation Investments. FSRP/DSA publication no. 3F. Kigali, Rwanda: Food Security Research Project and MINAGRI Division of Agricultural Statistics.

Lewis, L. A. (1988). Measurement and assessment of soil loss in Rwanda. Catena Suppl 12:151–165.

Loveridge, S. (1989). Importance du Haricot et du Sorgho dans le System de Production des Cultures Vivrieres au Rwanda: Disponibilites Actuelles et Projections pour l'Avenir. Kigali, Rwanda: Ministry of Agriculture, Animal Resources, and Forestry (MINAGRI), Division des Statistiques Agricoles.

Loveridge, S. (1992). Les sources de revenu des ménages agricoles Rwandais, les exportations et leur impact sur la disponibilité alimentaire en milieu rural (année agricole 1990). Kigali, Rwanda: Ministry of Agriculture, Animal Resources, and Forestry (MINAGRI), Division des Statistiques Agricoles.

Loveridge, S., Mpyisi, E., Weber, M. (2002). Farm Level Perspectives in Rwanda's Coffee Supply Chain Coordination Challenge. FSRP/DSA Policy Synthesis no. 2E. Kigali, Rwanda: Food Security Research Project and MINAGRI Division of Agricultural Statistics.

McDowell, G. R. (2001). Land-Grant Universities and Extension into the 21st Century: Renegotiating or Abandoning a Social Contract. Ames, IA: Iowa State University Press.

Ministry of Agriculture, Forestry and Livestock Resources (MINAGRI). (1992). Division des Statistiques Agricoles. Enquete Nationale Agricole 1990, Production, Superficie, Rendement, Elevage et Leur Evolution 1984–1990: Publication DSA no. 26. Kigali, Rwanda: MINAGRI Division of Agricultural Statistics.

Ministry of Finance and Economic Planning. (2002). A Profile of Poverty in Rwanda: A Report Based on the Results of the Household Living Standards Survey. English version. Kigali, Rwanda: Ministry of Finance and Economic Planning.

Mpyisi, E., Shingiro, E., Nyarwaya, J. B. (2002). Statistiques Agricoles: Production Agricoles, Elevage, Superficies et Utilisation des Terres, Annee Agricole 2001. Document DSA no. 5F. Kigali, Rwanda: MINAGRI Division of Agricultural Statistics.

Munyemana, A., von Oppen, M. (1999). La Pomme de Terre au Rwanda: Une Analyse d'une Filiere a Hautes Potentialites. Lima, Peru: Centre International de la Pomme de Terre (CIP).

# 13

# Structural Adjustment in Bulgarian Agriculture

**MONICA KOUBRATOVA HRISTOVA**

*Institute of Agrarian Economics, Sofia, Bulgaria*

## INTRODUCTION

Bulgaria is a small country in the southeastern part of Europe with a territory of 110,910 square km and a population of nearly 8 million. The average population density in 2000 was 72 people per square km. Roughly 43.6% of the population lives in the rural areas, which account for 81.4% of the territory. Until 1989, Bulgaria was part of the communist bloc. In November 1989, Bulgaria started a unique process of transition from a centrally planned economy to a market-oriented economy. There is no adequate theory to explain the way this transition took place.

This chapter examines the structural adjustment of Bulgarian agriculture during this transition period. Agriculture has been and is an important sector in the economy of Bulgaria because of its favorable natural conditions and good farming traditions. The second section of this chapter reviews the macroeconomic situation and dynamics during the transition period. In the third and fourth sections present the role of agriculture in the national economy and its development. Section five summarizes the main features and impacts of the land reform, privatization, and irrigation-management transfer. In the sixth section, an analysis of farming structure is made on the basis of the recent farm surveys. Section seven explores the impacts of agricultural policies while the eighth section summarizes some lessons learned from Bulgarian experience in agricultural adjustment. The final section presents some overall conclusions.

## THE MACROECONOMIC SITUATION

The transition period in Bulgaria was characterized by political instability, especially before 1997, when there was a new government almost every year. During this period, the structural reforms took the formed privatization and liquidation of enterprises, although comprehensive structural reforms had not yet begun (Angelov et al., 1999: 249).

The transition period may be divided into two periods—before and after the introduction of the currency board in June 1997. During the first period, the macroeconomic situation was characterized by high instability and uncertainty. The consumer price index was three-digit, and achieved its highest level of 1182.3% in 1997. Interest rates were high and the devaluation of national currency was progressive. The decline in the gross domestic product (GDP) was significant; the GDP in 1997 was 66% of the GDP in 1990. (See Table 1.) To counter the economic decline, the policies of privatization, market liberalization, and demonopolization were launched in order to create a conducive environment for the market economy.

At the beginning of the reforms, the unemployment rate increased and reached 13.7%. The real monthly wage fell to 28% of the wage in 1990, and the real monthly pension reached its lowest point (22%) in comparison with 1990 (Angelov et al., 1999: 264). The share of food, beverages, and tobacco in household expenditures increased to 54.3% in 1997.

In June 1997, a currency board was introduced under the pressure of both the International Monetary Fund (IMF) and foreign creditors after a deep financial crisis (Nenovsky, 2001: 36). The national currency was pegged to the German mark, and later to the euro. Since 1997, the economy has stabilized, and further trade and price liberalization has been achieved. In 2001 the consumer price index came down to 109%, and the GDP growth rate was 4%. There were some negatives features, however. In 2001, the registered unemployment rate rose to 14%. In rural areas unemployment was more than 50% of the active population.

The foreign trade balance was negative as a result of many factors, and the foreign direct investment was only $1944 million until 2000 (*Statistical Yearbook*, 2002: 99). The governmental debt was $8.4 million in the first months of 2002 and the foreign debt/GDP ratio was 59%. Investments are still at a very low level; commercial banks do not adequately function as financial intermediaries (Angelov et al., 1999: 14).

**Table 1**   Main Macroeconomic Indicators in Bulgaria

| Indicators | 1990 | 1993 | 1995 | 1997 | 1999 | 2000 | 2001 |
|---|---|---|---|---|---|---|---|
| GDP growth (%) | −9.1 | −1.5 | 2.9 | −7 | −1.5 | 0 | 4 |
| Private sector share in GDP (%) | 9.1 | 35.4 | 48.0 | 56.5 | 64 | 70 | 74 |
| CPI—average annual (%) | 123.8 | 156.1 | 163.0 | 1182 | 101 | 107 | 109 |
| Nominal interest rate | 4.5 | 48.0 | 50.1 | 176 | 4.8 | 5.5 | 6 |
| Real interest rate | 0.3 | −5.2 | −3.6 | −1024 | 3.8 | −1.5 | −3 |
| Nominal exchange rate (BGL/$) | 2.84 | 27.6 | 67.2 | 1674 | 1.84 | 1.81 | 1.78 |
| Real exchange rate (BGL/$) | 2.84 | 3.7 | 3.2 | 3.6 | 3.3 | 3.1 | 2.8 |
| Trade balance (mln.$) | −552 | −885 | 120 | 380 | −750 | −800 | −900 |
| Current account (mln.$) | −1180 | −1386 | −59 | 427 | −850 | −900 | −1000 |
| Unemployment (%) | 1.5 | 16.4 | 11.1 | 13.7 | 15 | 15 | 14 |

*Source*: Angelov et al., 1999: 264.

In general, the currency board had positive stabilizing effects on the economy, but now a new policy is needed to increase economic growth (Getchev, 2000: 44). It is necessary to continue the reforms and the institutional building of the market economy in order to better use the positive results of the liberalization and privatization effort (Minasian, 2002: 36).

## THE ROLE AND DEVELOPMENT OF AGRICULTURE

### The Role of Agriculture

During the transition period, the share of the agriculture and forestry sector varied betwen 10.6% (in 1993) and 26.6% (in 1997) of the GDP, which is similar to its relative importance during the previous regime of the centrally planned economy. Since 1997, a decrease in income has been observed, in both the agriculture and forestry sectors mainly because of the drought in 2000 and 2001. There are also clear signs of the decreasing economic role of the sector as a whole.

Today the agriculture sector in Bulgaria is largely private. In 2001, the private sector created 99% of the agricultural output, employed 98% of people working in the sector, and cultivated 97% of the arable land. Before 1989, agriculture was an export-oriented sector. Agricultural and food export accounts for 10% of the total value of Bulgarian export (Ministry of Agriculture and Forestry, 2001a: 104). Agriculture is the main economic sector in rural areas that is still active. Its important social role is due to the lack of an appropriate national social policy to mitigate the decline in real income and the high unemployment rate during the current transition period.

The overall impact of agriculture on the environment is positive because of the lower level of fertilizer and chemical use in Bulgaria. In many areas, wetlands have been restored, the number of birds is increasing, and the rich biodiversity is being preserved. In comparison with the agri-environmental measures undertaken in the countries of the European Union (EU) and in some Central and East European countries, however, there is a delay in implementing an appropriate agri-environmental policy in Bulgaria.

### The Development of Agriculture

During the transition period, the agricultural sector has undergone extensive changes. A quicker increase of input prices than output prices has resulted in a decrease in the use of fertilizers, chemicals, irrigation, and machinery. Another reason was the creation of new agricultural producers who lacked working and investment capital. In 2000, the rate of fertilizer use was 35 kg per ha (Ministry of Agriculture and Forestry, 2001a: 70). The usage of agricultural machines has declined for various reasons; in 2001, for example, the number of tractors and combines represented, respectively, 65% and 52% of the numbers used in 1989. Before 1990, Bulgaria had 1.2 million ha of irrigable land, which was about 20% of its total arable land. During the transition period, the irrigable area decreased to 13% of the arable land, partly because of the delay in irrigation management reform. Despite the drought and the significant state subsidies for irrigated water during the period for 1999 to 2001, only 9.7% of the irrigable area was reported as irrigated (Ministry of Agriculture and Forestry, 2001a: 64).

During the transition period, people employed in agriculture represented 17–26% of the working population, but there has been an increasing involvement of older people in agriculture, and thus there is a need for improvement in the qual-

**Table 2**   Main Agricultural Products—Area, Yields, and Output (1998–2000)

| Crops | Average area (in thousands of ha) | Average yields (t/ha) | Output (in thousands of t) |
|---|---|---|---|
| Wheat | 1029 | 2.73 | 2809 |
| Barley | 266 | 2.68 | 712 |
| Maize grain | 466 | 2.67 | 1245 |
| Sunflower | 547 | 0.94 | 516 |
| Tobacco | 27 | 1.19 | 32 |
| Tomatoes | 29 | 14.85 | 424 |
| Red and green peppers | 21 | 9.16 | 196 |
| Potatoes | 52 | 9.24 | 480 |
| Apples | 14 | 4.56 | 636 |
| Wine grapes | 99.8[a] | 3.14 | 314 |
| Table grapes | 14.2[a] | 2.64 | 38 |

[a] Area in 1999.
*Source*: 2000 Agrarian Report, MAF.

ification and the skills of farmers and agricultural employees. During the socialist period there was a clear specialization of agricultural workers. Today the new conditions required new skills and knowledge, especially in relation to the management and marketing of agricultural output.

Bulgarian has 4.9 million ha of arable land. The fallow and uncultivated areas increased during the transition period, which amounts to 16% of the arable land, according to the Ministry of Agriculture and Forestry (MAF) and 30% according the National Statistical Institute (Bansik, 2001:13; National Statistical Institute, 2002: 130).

In terms of composition of gross agricultural output, in 2000 the share of crop production was 41%, livestock 42%, farm services 5%, and nonagricultural secondary activities 12% (MAF, 2001a: 52). Table 2 contains data on crop production for the main crops grown in Bulgaria. The present yields are at the level of the 1970s, because of the fragmentation of land, lack of management knowledge and advice service, use of low-quality seeds, lack of working and investment capital, and low level of application of fertilizers and chemicals. In terms of crop production, during the transition period, there was a shift toward the production of cereals and sunflowers (covering about 50% of the arable land). These crops may be stored for a longer time and are produced with less labor and fewer production costs.

## LAND REFORM AND PRIVATIZATION

### Land Reform

During the socialist period, private land was never nationalized, but a process of gradual collectivization of private land started in 1946, resulting in the creation of the socialist production cooperatives. In 1956, cooperatives already cultivated 65% of the arable land (National Statistical Institute, 1957: 145).

Land reform started in 1991 when the Ownership and Use of Farmland Act (OUFA) was introduced by the general assembly. At the beginning of the transition, the land reform was seen as the main reform in agriculture. It was expected that the private ownership rights on land and other production factors would automatically create a market economy. Land reform was a very complicated process, and lasted for almost nine years.

The main issue of the OUFA is the restoration of land property rights to former owners and their heirs within actual boundaries "where they exist or can be established" (OUFA). When changes in the land occurred during the previous years, the restoration of land property rights was made through land division plans. The second issue of the OUFA is the dissolution of the former cooperatives by the liquidation boards. The liquidation boards had to carry out the valuation of cooperative property, distribute assets among owners of land and workers according to some specific rules, and conduct necessary economic activities.

The land reform was reported as being complete in 1999, but the process of issuing notarized ownership for agricultural land is still going on. Until 1997, only 19% of the owners had received their documents (see Table 3). This slowed down the land market. The completion of land reform was very important for the creation of stable new agricultural producers.

The negative impact of land reform on the future of the agricultural sector is the increase of land fragmentation. The estimation is that after land reform is complete there will be more than 20 million parcels, with an average size of 0.2 ha (Rissina et al., 2001: 5). The restoration of land property rights from the period prior to the socialist one has restored the structure of Bulgarian agriculture of that period characterized by small farms, with 3.9 ha average size comprising ten to fifteen plots (Hristova et al., 1993: 109). The decrease of farmland and the increase in the numbers of heirs are the main reasons for the present farm structure. There is no legal framework to regulate further land fragmentation among the heirs. The rapid fragmentation of land has made the purchase or leasing of land difficult.

Another negative result of land reform was the increased number of absentee landowners who are not direct agricultural producers. About 62% of landowners are now living in the towns, and another 20% are pensioners living in the villages (Rissina et al., 2001:5). During the land reform, land was given for temporary use to producers who could not use it as collateral and followed a short-term strategy. This created a very weak and unstable agricultural sector. In addition, there was waste of resources; for example, animals were distributed among people who could not take care of them. Many agricultural buildings were destroyed or left unused.

Since 1999, the land market has been more active with the accelerated process of issuing notarized deed. About 10,710 transactions for 18,000 ha were registered during

**Table 3**  Progress in the Restoration of Land Property Rights in Bulgaria

| Year | 1992 | 1993 | 1994 | 1995 | 1996 | 1997 | 1998 | 1999 |
|---|---|---|---|---|---|---|---|---|
| Restored property (as percentage of total land) | 6 | 14 | 32 | 48 | 57 | 66 | 74 | 99 |
| Notarized deeds issued (%) | 0 | 0.1 | 0.3 | 3.0 | 6.8 | 19 | 25 | 90 |

*Source*: National Statistical Institute.

1999 and 2000. The number of transactions and the amount of land sold increased by about three times in 2000 and 2001. Average land prices have slowly increased from $685 per ha to $705 per ha (SAPI, 2000: 13). The state does not intervene in the agricultural land market and land is still not subject to a tax. The discussion showed that such a tax would not be desirable. Landowners preferred to keep their land parcels, expecting better prices and more favorable conditions for agricultural business. Landowners are keeping land as insurance against unfavorable economic conditions.

## Privatization of Agricultural Enterprises

The privatization of state-owned enterprises in the Bulgarian economy started in 1992 with the implementation of the Public and Municipal Enterprises Privatization Law. The speed of privatization in agriculture has been very slow. In 2000, the MAF announced that 67% of state-owned assets were privatized. The privatization in other Central and East European countries was completed in 1995.

At present there are 100 state-owned enterprises in the agricultural sector, but 79 of them have undergone insolvency or are in liquidation (MAF, 2001a: 16). The main problems of state-owned enterprises are the high level of loan indebtedness and the lack of competitiveness of their products and amortized facilities, but many of the privatized enterprises have also failed to improve their performance.

State representatives are appointed to defend the state interest and control the state-owned enterprises. In fact, these representatives are active defenders of the interests of these enterprises because they receive an additional salary for their work. On the other hand, any change in the government is usually followed by a change in the management of state-owned enterprises. This has become a source of influence and corruption in the decision making in the Ministry of Agriculture dealing with agricultural development. More specifically, funds from the state-owned enterprises have often been used to support political parties.

## Transfer of Irrigation Management to Water User Associations

During the transition period, the MAF did not undertake any reform to adapt the irrigation management to the private land ownership and new market conditions. Nowadays, irrigation is in crisis, which is evident in the insignificant level of irrigated land and insufficient irrigation facilities.

In 2001, the first serious step was undertaken by creating water user associations (WUAs) to take up the responsibilities of irrigation management. The experience until now has shown that the transfer of irrigation management would be very slow and with doubtful success. The main obstacle is that WUAs didn't receive enough financial incentives for their establishment and activity. There was a privileged treatment of the state-owned irrigation company in comparison with WUAs.

## THE EVOLUTION OF AGRICULTURAL PRODUCTION UNITS

The comparison of the farming structures before and during the transition period shows that they are similar. The farming structure is bimodal, and large production units coexist with small family farms.

During the socialist period, the main agricultural production units were the cooperatives. They operated about 80–90% of the arable land. Small producers with limited land and mechanization facilities cultivated the rest of the land. In 1985, small producers operated 10% of the agricultural land (National Statistical Institute, 1986: 264). An important feature of the small producers' activity was the help they received from the cooperatives.

During the transition period, the bimodal farming structure continued to exist, producing agricultural output in different environments and trying to survive in very difficult and unfavorable conditions with limited state support. The statistical data about agricultural producers are still incomplete and sometimes controversial. It is observed that there is a slow and gradual concentration of production units. The tendency is toward a decline in the number of small farms and land cultivated by them and an increase in the number of large agricultural units.

The agricultural producers may be classified into two main groups on the basis of the marketability of their output. The first group includes the agricultural units producing for the market. An MAF survey showed that in 1999 and 2000 these producers operated more than 85% of the arable land and represented 6% of the total number of production units (Bansik, 2001: 1). The second group includes mainly small farms, the so-called subsistence farms, that do not produce for the market. They operated 15% of the land, grew 75% of the cattle, goats, and sheeps, and represented 94% of the total number of agricultural production units.

## Large Production Units

In 2000, the number of large production units was 13,162, of which 3861 were agricultural production cooperatives, 327 legal entities, and 8843 private individuals. In comparison with 1996 their number has increased respectively by 11%, 69%, and 12%. The statistical register showed that 65% of the farms were in crop production, 16% in livestock production, 6% in crop and livestock production together, and 13% in mechanization services (Bansik, 2001: 12).

Large agricultural production units are specialized in intensive production, mainly in cereal production, profiting the economy of scale. They operated 89% of the area of wheat, 85% of barley, 93% of maize, and 94% of sunflowers in 2000 (MAF, 2001b: 5–6). They were well equipped with agricultural machinery, and 90% of the machines were their private property. The land cultivated by the large-scale production units is leased, and well-qualified specialists are hired for production. The survey of MAF showed that the average size of these production units was 540 ha, with an average number of eleven employees.

Production cooperatives cultivate more than 40% of the arable land and have about 774,000 members. The average size of a cooperative is about 700 ha of land and 240 members, usually pensioners. The existence of the production cooperatives is due to the lack of opportunities for the new landowners and unfavorable conditions for both the establishment of private farms and the development of the agricultural sector.

The majority of the machines in the cooperatives are from the socialist period and are already amortized (Valchev, 1999: 210).

Agriculture was the main activity for 97% of the managers. Ninety-four percent of the cooperatives provided mechanization services as complementary activities, while 30% of the juridical entities were in the trade business and 16% in food processing.

The managers of the large production units have the education necessary for agriculture. The results of the survey of MAF showed that 65 % of its managers had agricultural education, 9% of the cooperative managers were younger than 40, and 29% were older than 60. The managers of the legal entities were younger—16% of them were younger than 40, while 21% of them were older than 60 (Bansik, 2001: 11).

There are not enough data about the performance of the production units. The survey showed that one worker in a large production unit operated 3.8 ha, while one worker in the small farms operated 0.5 ha.

## Family Farms

The majority of the family farms—the smallest ones—are subsistence farms. Their size is too small to provide enough income for their managers. For 36% of them agriculture was their main activity. There are no data about the number of farms that are market-oriented.

The small farms specialize in the production of vegetables and fruits that are labor-intensive crops (Valchev, 1999: 204). The survey of MAF showed that the average size of the small farms was 62 ha. In principle, they used their family labor, and the average number of workers was two.

Usually the managers of small farms are old people with no managerial experience and adequate skills. Forty-seven percent of small farms managers were over 60, and only 12% of them have passed some agricultural training (MAF, 2001b:11).

The preliminary data of the census of population and agricultural farms showed that in March 2001 there were 1.453 million family farms in Bulgaria cultivating 0.93 million ha (Table 4.).

The data show polarization among agricultural farms. Farms up to 1 ha represented 83% of the total number and cultivated 26% of the land, while farms bigger than 10 ha represented only 0.4% of the total number and cultivated 17% of the arable land.

A comparison between the results of the 2001 census with a similar survey made in 1996 shows that there is a 13% decrease in arable land cultivated by family farms and an 18% decrease of their number. The concentration of farms is obvious. Each year some 80,000 small farms (up to 1 ha) go out of production, and some 5000 farms with an average size of 3 ha emerge.

**Table 4**   Size Distribution of Individual Farms in Bulgaria in 2001

| Size of the land (in ha) | Number of farms (in thousands) | Structure (%) | Arable land, (in thousands of ha) | Structure (%) |
|---|---|---|---|---|
| Up to 1 | 1212.7 | 83.4 | 2438.1 | 26 |
| From 1.1 to 2 | 133.3 | 9.2 | 1759.7 | 19 |
| From 2.1 to 5 | 84.5 | 5.8 | 2441.3 | 26 |
| From 5.1 to 10 | 17.6 | 1.2 | 1121.3 | 12 |
| More than 10.1 | 5.2 | 0.4 | 1603.7 | 17 |
| Total | 1453.3 | 100 | 9364.1 | 100 |

*Source*: National Statistical Institute.

**Table 5**   Distribution of Animals in Family Farms (Percentage of the Total Number in 2001)

| Animal | Up to 2 | From 3 to 30 | More than 30 | Total number |
|---|---|---|---|---|
| Cattle | 82.5 | 17.3 | 0.2 | 232364 |
| Cows | 90.8 | 9.1 | 0.1 | 211169 |
| Goats | 70 | 29.88 | 0.12 | 462722 |
| Sheep | 30.2 | 69.5 | 0.3[a] | 316369 |
| Pigs | 87 | 12.99 | 0.01[a] | 175124 |
| Poultry[b] | 68.4 | 31.36 | 0.24 | 803739 |

[a] More than 20.
[b] For poultry—up to 10, from 11 to 50, more than 51.
*Source*: National Statistical Institute.

Farms up to 2 ha decreased their cultivated arable land by 1.2 million ha and their number by 345,000. The changes in the biggest farms were in the opposite direction. Farms with a size from 2.1 to 10 ha increased their number by 20, 000 and their arable area by 607,000 ha.

It was observed that around 80–90% of the farms had one or two different animals (Table 5). In comparison with data from 1996 there was a general decrease in the total number of animals kept in the family farms and a decrease of the number of animals kept by farms with up to two animals.

The data from the census show that 1.45 million family farms owned 35,719 tractors, 25,227 cultivators, 2883 combines, and 19,201 trucks. The data also show that every 42nd farm had a tractor and every 60th farm had a cultivator. These numbers show the very low level of mechanization and the need for investments.

## AGRICULTURAL POLICY

Until 1997, agricultural policies were mainly directed toward the establishment of private property in the sector and less focused on the help and establishment of viable farming structures. Land reform and privatization were the main reforms and started in the first years of the transition. The unstable macroeconomic situation had a negative impact on the development of the agricultural sector as a whole. This coincided with both land reform and the national consumer protection policy. Price and trade liberalization was delayed by five years in comparison with the beginning of the transformation process. Every study about state support for Bulgarian agriculture has demonstrated a significant trend toward consumer protection and agricultural producers' taxation during this period.

Since 1997 agricultural policies have been more focused on the creation of favorable conditions for agricultural producers. Further price and trade liberalization was undertaken, subsidies and investments for agriculture increased, and some tax and social insurance preferences were given to agricultural producers.

During this period MAF started to produce an annual report on agriculture in which the objectives and priorities of future agricultural policy were defined. The objectives of the MAF policy were to develop an efficient and competitive export-oriented agriculture, improve rural incomes, and prepare for admission to the EU.

There has been a discrepancy between these objectives and the concrete measures that have been undertaken by the different governments. Even now similar problems occur each year with different accuteness, and the MAF applies the same obsolete measures without any effect; no preliminary analysis has ever been made of the impact, beneficiaries, or losers of any agricultural policy or measure in Bulgaria.

In general, the agricultural sector may be considered as a free market one because the intervention of the government in the sector is very limited as to budget and efficiency. State support for agriculture accounts for less than 0.15 % of the government's budget.

## Price and Trade Liberalization

Because of the decreased internal market demand, foreign trade restrictions, and price controls on twenty main agricultural and food products, there was a sharp increase in input prices and a lower increase in output prices. The protection of the national consumer was accomplished through taxation of exports, export quotas, a temporary export ban, and licenses for export. At the same time the subsidies for agriculture were restricted and land reform and liquidation of former cooperatives continued. All these conditions resulted in the losses for the majority of the agricultural producers as well as high indebtedness.

Further liberalization of prices of the main agricultural and food products occured in 1997. In 1998 all quota bans and restrictions on imports and exports of agricultural goods were abolished and the customs regime was simplified in accordance with IMF and the World Bank requirements. The average arithmetic tariff rate for agricultural goods was 27.45% in 1998 and 22% for the period from 1999 to 2001 (MAF, 2001a: 103), but until now agricultural importers have profited more from these conditions than agricultural exporters. Customs duties are not used enough to protect national agricultural producers.

The state does not currently intervene in the formation of prices of agricultural and food outputs and inputs except for tobacco and irrigation water. The price of tobacco is decided each year by the Council of Ministers, thus ensuring a stable income for tobacco producers. In 2001 some 53.9 thousand producers cultivated tobacco, 83% of which were located in the semimountainous areas in southern Bulgaria. The support of tobacco has an important social role for people living in these areas.

The state started to subsidize the price of irrigation water in 2000 because of the drought. The state subsidy covered the difference between the actual irrigation water prices set by the state-owned irrigation company and the price level defined by the MAF. The subsidies for irrigation water have limited impact because they affect only the agricultural producers who use irrigation water. This policy encouraged the inefficient use of irrigation water, created expectations that the state would continue the support in future, and discouraged water users to take over the management of the irrigation systems. Currently, there is no other price subsidy for agricultural and food products in Bulgaria and there are no export subsidies for Bulgarian agricultural and food products.

## Subsidies for Agriculture

During the transition there was permanent support to cereal producers via short-term measures to ensure the cereal balance of the country. Short-term credits and subsidies for the purchase of seeds, fuel, spare parts, fertilizers for wheat, maize, barley, sunflowers and potatoes were and continue to be distributed to producers. In the early years of the transformation process, the subsidies for agriculture were distributed by a special regulation issued each year. Now the support is given by State Fund "Agriculture" as it is defined in the Agricultural Producer Support Law. The beneficiaries have to apply and must meet some minimum requirements. Some $87 million was spent for short-term subsidies for the period from 1997 to 2001. The allocation of the short-term budget showed that 70% of the support was spent for northern Bulgaria because the subsidized crops were mainly cultivated there. The short-term credits and subsidies replaced the low level of credits provided by commercial banks to the sector.

## Investment Policy

Investments are very important for the installation and restructuring of the newly established agricultural producers. Since 1997 there have been different investment programs for which agricultural producers may apply and receive preferential credits. Until 2000 the short-term budget was higher than the budget for the investments in agriculture. For the period from 1997 to 2001 the State Fund "Agriculture" spent some $93 million for 1545 investment projects.

Commercial banks are very cautious in providing loans to the agricultural sector because of its low level of profitability, the existing uncertainties, and some restrictions on bank activity. For the period from 1997 to 2000 loans for agriculture were 2.2% of the total amount of credit given to the other economic sectors (Marinova, 2002: 13). Their interest rate varies between 12% and 18%, with collateral of at least 150% of the credit amount.

For the period from 1999 to 2001 the structure of the financed investment projects showed that 39% of the total number were for purchasing agricultural machinery, 28% for purchasing productive animals, and 11% for creating permanent crops. Problems exist because of the considerable paperwork, and controls on how the money is spent are lax.

## Tax and Social Insurance Preferences

The first tax preferences for agricultural producers were introduced in 1991 by the OUFA. Agricultural producers and corporate bodies are not required to pay profit tax for unprocessed crop and livestock production until 2005. This tax concession is valid if any profit is reinvested in the same activities. To use the preferences the producer has to generate a profit. Statistical data show that most agricultural enterprises experience losses.

The income of individual producers from unprocessed crop and livestock production, rent, leases, and other transactions related to a transfer of tenure to agricultural land is also tax-exempt. Some transactions by agricultural cooperatives profit a value-added tax exemption, and dividends of the cooperative members are not taxed. Agricultural land, forests, and farm buildings used for production are exempted from taxes levied on real estate.

Social insurance preferences for individual agricultural producers' (who are physical entities) were introduced in 2000. Juridical entities have to follow the general rules for social insurance payments. The Social Insurance Institute reported that in 2001 only 10,000 agricultural producers paid social allowances. Individual agricultural producers do not make social insurance payments partly because the majority of them are pensioners.

## Other Support Measures

### Support for the Market Infrastructure

The MAF supports the construction of market infrastructure in the country. A project for the construction of wholesale markets for fruits, vegetables, and flowers in eleven big towns in Bulgaria has been financed by a loan of the European Bank of Reconstruction and Development and MAF. Until 2002 investments were made in five wholesale markets. The major problem has been the low level of agricultural production and the inability of the markets to collect enough income to disburse the loans.

The MAF is subsidizing about 80% of the budget of a market information company that regularly provides basis information about input and output prices in agriculture, especially to the central administration.

### Support for Hydromeliorative Infrastructure, Antierosion Works, and Improvement of Agricultural School Facilities

This type of state support is characterized by the application of old practices that haven't changed since their introduction at the beginning of the transition. The distribution of the limited budget is not based on any economic or financial analysis of the projects. There are a significant number of projects, and small amounts are distributed among them each year. There is no monitoring and analysis of investment impact. The lack of transparency and accountability related to the distributed funds creates the appearance that money is wasted and that there is corruption (Koubratova, 2000:11).

### Advice Services

The National Agricultural Advice Service was created in 1995. Until now it has had limited activity. It has twenty-eight regional services and 150 employees. The main problems are the limited budget and the lack of training of the specialists and advisers. The data show that each specialist of the National Agricultural Advice Service advised an average of sixty agricultural producers in 2000. The participation of farmers at the organized seminars was very low—an average of 22 farmers per seminar (MAF, 2001a: 55).

### Institution Building

During recent years a number of new agencies and service institutions were established within the system of the MAF. Some of them are linked to the increased requirements related to the accession of Bulgaria to the EU. The number of people employed in them is about 22,000. There is still a lack of coordination between the activities of these institutions. The same is true for the directories of the MAF. The institutions and directories compete with each other (in order to keep their job positions) instead of coordinating and complementing their activities. The main reason for this is that there is no division of tasks and no common strategy for the development of the agricultural sector.

There are no clear criteria for analyzing the agencies' work and how their budgets are spent. Accountability to society and to agricultural producers is missing. The communication between the MAF and the agricultural producers is very poor. The agricultural policies are defined without the participation of the beneficiaries or their representatives. Nongovernmental organizations of producers have recently been established. In some sectors there is more than one organization defending the interest of a limited number of producers. In other cases, the organizations are not fully represented. They often try to please the MAF rather than defend their members' interests.

## Accession to the European Union

The main economic indicators show that the Bulgarian economy lags behind in comparison with the EU member countries. In 2000, the GDP per person in Bulgaria was only 22% of the corresponding indicator for the EU. The average salary was 18% of the average EU salary, and labor productivity was 27% of EU labor productivity (Angelov et al., 2001: 185).

As stressed in the regular EU report for 2001, the Bulgarian economy is not ready to respond to the pressure of opening its markets to the EU. There is a consensus within the society that Bulgaria has to become member of the EU, however. Despite this consensus, there are several important unsolved problems in the agricultural sector.

One of the main problems will be the adjustment of Bulgarian agricultural policy to the common agricultural policy (CAP). The latter is not only changing, but it implements different intervention mechanisms from the ones used in Bulgarian agriculture. Considerable effort, money, and time will be needed in order to implement them in Bulgarian agriculture. Bulgarian agricultural policy exists with limited state intervention, while in the EU countries agricultural policy is based on substantial and costly intervention. On the other hand, Bulgaria is not rich enough to support the agricultural sector to the same extent.

The adjustment to the CAP will create additional shocks for Bulgarian agriculture and producers, the effects of which are unknown. The official position of the government for the negotiations in the field of agriculture has not been announced and agricultural producers don't know what to expect from future changes. Measures to adapt the sector and mitigate the negative impact are needed, but they are not even being discussed (Simova, 2002: 32).

In recent years the EU countries have been the main trading partners of Bulgaria. Trading with EU member countries is based on mutual granting of trade preferences. Bulgarian agriculture cannot profit from these preferences because of the extensive development of agriculture, low productivity, slow adjustment of the sector, and the presence of nontariff barriers (such as sanitary standards) for Bulgarian products. Bulgarian agricultural products cannot compete with the highly subsidized products of EU countries; cheap agricultural products are imported from neighboring countries that have higher productivity and more subsidies for agricultural production. This creates strong pressure on Bulgarian producers and has generated losses.

## LESSONS LEARNED

The lessons learned from the Bulgarian experience as well as some proposals for further improvements are discussed below. It is worth stressing that the structural adjustment in Bulgarian agriculture is less efficient when compared with the changes in agriculture in most other Eastern and Central European countries in transition.

It is also important to stress that agricultural adjustment in Bulgaria coincided with the radical economic and political changes undertaken in the country. This made the changes slow and painful when agriculture was treated as an ordinary sector of the economy. The economic instability and land reform resulted in a significant drop in agricultural production. Nowadays some of the negative effects of land reform are obvious, but in 1991 land reform was a political imperative. The slow process of the completion of land reform, reduction of subsidies, formation of policies for protecting national consumers, and lack of investments in agriculture created unfavorable conditions for the establishment and successful development of viable agricultural producers.

Since the introduction of the currency board in 1997 the macroeconomic situation has stabilized. At the same time, the restored rights on land reached 66% of the total land, but only 19% of the land has notarized deeds, and agricultural producers continue to suffer losses.

The price and trade liberalization have been undertaken after a delay of five years. The opening of the national market for importers and the corruption among customs officers resulted in an abundance of imported cheap agricultural products, creating additional pressure on agricultural producers. This imposes a better use of trade policy instruments in order to protect national producers in an optimal way.

Because of the lack of sufficient studies and reliable information on Bulgarian bimodal agriculture during the transition period, the statistical data are unreliable and controversial. It is worth spending more money to study and register the agricultural producers.

The Bulgarian experience showed that it is impossible to have a successful support policy for agriculture without knowing its target groups and their main features and needs. For this reason it is very important to identify and support the market-oriented agricultural producers who can ensure the development of the sector. There are some large production units that are performing very well and are exporting goods to European countries without any support or subsidies from the state.

Subsistence farming plays an important role in providing food because the social policy and the budget deficit could not provide enough support for pensioners, unemployed persons, and other groups. The measures related to subsistence farming should be different from the ones for competitive producers. This differentiation can improve the efficiency of the agricultural policy and the use of the budget.

The state showed a willingness to support the agricultural sector, but the applied policies and measures have been incorrectly tailored and have resulted in money being wasted. The only objective of the measures was to show that the state has been distributing money for agriculture. A strategy for the development and restructuring of Bulgarian agriculture is still missing and the support policies in agriculture have been not coordinated as to field and period of application.

## CONCLUSIONS

Agriculture is an important sector of the Bulgarian economy, but its importance as a share of the GDP and employment decreases as the performance of the other sectors increases. Eleven years after the beginning of the transition period, Bulgarian agriculture is based on private ownership of the land. More efforts are nevertheless needed to quickly end the privatization of state-owned enterprises in the sector. Land fragmentation will continue to be of main concern during the future and impede the further restructuring of the sector.

A slow and gradual concentration of agricultural production units has been observed. The rate of their adjustment will depend upon which agricultural policy measures are undertaken. Agricultural units producing for market have to be clearly distinguished from the small subsistence farms, and policy measures have to be undertaken separately for both types of farms.

The restructuring of ownership is an important instrument for increasing competitiveness and economic performance of the agricultural sector, but it has to be accompanied by a complex arrangement of policies and measures, including macro-economic and sectoral ones, that have to create favorable conditions for agricultural producers. These conditions include human resource development and an increase in the efficiency of advice services and vocational training, easier access to investments, and an increase in the efficiency and accountability of the institutions involved in the sector.

It is necessary to elaborate and agree on a strategy for restructuring and developing the agricultural sector as a part of a national strategy. The adjustment of the agriculture sector is impossible without appropriate macroeconomic policies. Agricultural policies have to be changed and adapted to the new challenges of the market economy and the accession to the EU that may create new shocks and the need for further adjustment.

## REFERENCES

Angelov, I., Dimitrov, A., Hubenova-Delisivkova, T., Krayninska, I., Tcharevski, V., Tchanev, V., Beleva, I., Konsulov, V., Koparanova, M. (1999). Economic Outlook of Bulgaria by 2001 and Beyond by 2010. Sofia: Friedrich Ebert Stiftung.

Angelov, I., Hubenova-Delisivkova, T., Krayninska, I., Koparanova, M., Konsulov, V., Tcharevski, V., Tchanev, V., Bankov, G. (2001). Bulgarian Economy and the European Union—Pre-accession Period. Sofia: Friedrich Ebert Stiftung, Economic Institute of the Bulgarian Academy of Science.

Bansik. (2001). Final Results of the Occupation and Use of the Territory of Bulgaria in 2001. Sofia: Ministry of Agriculture and Forestry.

Hristova, M., Popov, T., Keremedchiev, S., Georgieva, M. (1993). Agrarian Reform and Agricultural Organizations. Sofia: NSA.

Getchev, R. (2000). Bulgarian economy—Conditions and alternatives for development. Econ Thought 3:26–44.

Koubratova, M. (2000). The Agrarian reform in Bulgarian agriculture: Purposes and achievements. Proceedings of the Third National Conference of The Union of Bulgarian Agricultural Economists. Sofia: Gorexpress, pp. 128–142.

Marinova, M. (2002). Financial Policy and Tax Preference for Agriculture. Report on AGRA 2002. Plovdiv.

Minasian, G. (2002). Financial Stabilization and Economic Growth. Sofia: Economic Institute of Bulgarian Academy of Science, Academic Publishing House "Prof. Marin Drinov."

Ministry of Agriculture and Forestry. Annual Report. 2000. Sofia: MAF.

Ministry of Agriculture and Forestry. Agro-statistic. Structure of the Agricultural Holdings in Bulgaria During the Period 1999/2000. Sofia: MAF.

Nenovsky, N. (2001). The currency board in Estonia, Lithuania and Bulgaria: Comparative analysis. Econ Thought 3:24–46.

Rissina, M., Yanakieva, Y., Kyosev, G., Mitzev, V., Yovtcheva, P. (2001). Problems of Land Ownership. Sofia: Institute of Agrarian Economics.

SAPI. Conditions and Trends in the Development of the Land Market in Bulgaria. Sofia: AMIS Ltd, Ministry of Agriculture and Forestry.

Simova, A. (2002). About some controversial questions in the agricultral sector associated with Bulgarian join to the European Union. Journal of Agricultural Economics and Management. Sofia: Institute of Agrarian Economics, Bulgarian Association of Agricultural Economists, Center for Scientific Technical Information, pp. 31–34.

National Statistical Insitute. (1957). Statistical Yearbook. Sofia: National Statistical Institute.

National Statistical Institute. (1986). Statistical Yearbook. Sofia: National Statistical Institute.

National Statistical Institute. (2002). Statistical Yearbook. Sofia: National Statistical Institute.

Valchev, N. (1999). Agrarian Structure of Bulgarian Agriculture. Sofia: Gorexpress.

# 14

## Factors Affecting Sustainable Health Care Management Programs in Post-Soviet Transitional Economies

**PATRICIA A. CHOLEWKA**

*Columbia University, New York, New York, U.S.A.*

### INTRODUCTION

Dynamic changes are occurring on a worldwide basis in the organization, financing, and delivery of health care services. This is especially true for the social welfare sector within the transitional economies of the post-Soviet nations. Various factors are driving this sector's transformation, including demands by both practitioners and patients for advanced medical technology and improved health care services and the burgeoning use of economic accountability standards by government and international investors.

In order to restructure their organizations to remain viable within these new constraints, health care system administrators are realizing that they need to utilize more effective management methods. Such management methods as total quality management (TQM), developed and used in the United States and the European Union (EU) have been sought for incorporation into these public administration systems.

This chapter will identify and discuss many enabling and inhibiting environmental factors that health care sector stakeholders should consider so that sustainable TQM programs can be successfully implemented and institutionalized within the health care systems of these transitional economies.

## HISTORICAL BACKGROUND: SOVIET HEALTH CARE SYSTEM ADMINISTRATION

Socioeconomic and organization management studies by the World Health Organization (UNICEF, 1992), the United States Agency for International Development (USAID) (Cleland, 1997), the Commission of the European Communities (CEC, 1997) and the International Bank for Reconstruction and Development (World Bank, 1993; Hirschler, 2001) have shown that under Soviet political administration, standards for hospital management, financial accounting, and clinical practice were either inadequate or inconsistently enforced. Within economic transition efforts there is a need for modernization of administrative and budgetary procedures, as these countries prepare for inclusion into the EU and other global organizations, such as the North American Treaty Organization (NATO).

Under the Soviet system, organization and administrative directives were forcibly imposed by a centralized authority, and operational innovation was seen as counterproductive to the Communist Party influence and control (Leites, 1985; Schubert-Lehnhardt, 1995; Yanowitch, 1979; 1985). Various socioeconomic and managerial reports have shown that under the Soviet system, hospital management, medical practice, and finance and accounting standards for monitoring the use of resources were either ineffective or inadequate according to Western management standards (Cholewka, 1997; Gefenas, 1995; Kaminski, 1995; Lee et al., 1992; Leites, 1985; Yanowitch, 1979).

According to Leites (1985), the regard for quality of life, and hence the quality of patient care and effectiveness of treatment, was never addressed effectively. To question patient care practices or health care management methods by practitioners would have been questioning the authority and management expertise of the central Communist Party. It was more important within the Soviet economy, including the health care system, for Communist Party officials to create jobs to keep people employed than to achieve efficiency, quality, or equality in the services being provided.

In Western terms, the Soviet Union suffered from overemployment, using too many people to deal with too little work (Shapiro and Godson, 1994). Economic plans for crash industrialization gave way to a race for the maximum. Overfulfillment of quotas was the target, and awards went to directors who produced 120% of the quota, although these quotas were often misreported. In order to reach this inflated goal, however, resources had to be obtained at the expense of other industries: "The method, in fact, is not strictly speaking that of a planned economy, it is, rather, that of a competitive expansion without regard to allocation of resources or to the necessity of the goods produced. This system gave rise to enormous dislocations" (Conquest, 1990: 20).

According to Minev et al. (1990), important questions to consider when analyzing the Soviet health care system are why the system of health care failed to abolish or at least sharply reduce inequalities of outcomes in Soviet health care between rural and urban areas and between the Soviet health care system and that of developed countries. These questions become very important because the idea of equal access and treatment lies at the heart of the Soviet health care system.

A major factor to consider thus must be the character of the system. Early Soviet improvements to the health care system were based on widening public access to existing facilities. This idea for improvement was quickly checked, however. Health problems became more complex, and soon demands for more resources, better quality services, better working conditions, and increasing ecological issues quickly surfaced.

Semashko (1935), the founding father of the Soviet public health system, wrote that the duty of every member of the Soviet of Workers' and Peasants' Deputies was to inspect the work of the medical and prophylactic institutions to secure efficiency, help overcome shortcomings, improve economic management, and ensure that proper attention be given to the needs of the workers and peasants. He advocated that existing programs be inserted in keeping with set criteria, and that thus maintaining—not improvement—was the key to keeping the health care system functioning (Semashko, 1935).

Moreover, Lisitin and Alekandrov (1967) wrote that the basic principles upon which the public health system of the Soviet state was established included: (1) the state nature of the system, including planning on a state basis and the fact that it was free of charge, universally accessible, and provided a high standard of medical care, (2) an emphasis on prophylaxis, (3) close links between medical research and practice, and (4) the broad participation of the people themselves in developing the public health system. The Soviet state assumed full responsibility and control for the organization, planning, and provision of services. As outlined in the economic plans for national economic development, the Supreme Soviets of the union republics determined expenditure on public health in the budgets of the republics.

In reality, however, the social welfare system (and the health care sector in particular, since it was considered an unproductive part of the overall economic system) continued to receive low priority after the introduction of central planning. This resulted in making most cash benefits dependent on prior employment, of introducing the principle of earnings-relatedness for those who were entitled, and of excluding substantial occupational and ethnic groups from coverage altogether (Shapiro and Godson, 1994). The much-touted universal access into the Soviet social wefare system thus in actuality was quite limited.

Rowland and Telyukow (1991) stress that post-Soviet reformers are striving to reconstruct a health care system that was plagued by chronic underfunding, antiquated and deteriorating facilities, inadequate supplies and outmoded equipment, poor morale, few incentives for health care workers, and consumer dissatisfaction: "The central planning process embodied in the five-year plans emphasized quantitative rather than qualitative goals and resulted in concern with expanding the absolute number of facilities and providers without regard to quality or competence. New construction [and expansion] rather than renovation was rewarded" (Rowland and Telyukow, 1991: 83).

As a result of these Soviet administrative policies, prereform output was largely overstated and postreform production was undermeasured. Mezentseva and Rimachevskaya (1990) wrote that 7 million people were employed in the Soviet public health care system (i.e., 6% of the total active population), but the lack of proper attention to public health care led to a level of salaries that was among the lowest in the national economy.

According to Minev et al. (1990), the achieved level of Soviet public health care did not meet the population's requirements, and now there is a problem of the economic self-interest of medical employees in raising the efficiency of their work. In the Soviet centrally planned societies, collective goals were set and did not involve the participation or input of those directly involved in carrying out the production process (Leites, 1985; Rowland and Telyukow, 1991; Schubert-Lehnhardt, 1995; Yanowitch, 1979). Policy making at the central level was hampered by a poor flow of information from throughout the system for the tracking and evaluation of health system trends.

Consequently, standards were determined by arbitrary statistical norms, leading to many imbalances. Misinformation caused the resulting problems of poorly targeted investment, inadequate integration between the different parts of the system, excessive specialization, a narrow base for financing, and grossly deficient incentives to efficiency (Preker and Feachem, 1994). A worker or manager was not necessarily matched to a position by experience or educational qualifications; political considerations were important when considering employment applicants. It was not necessary to monitor and evaluate a worker's performance, since it would mean that both the worker and the manager had to be accountable for what good was produced or service provided.

Cantor (1978) defines accountability as the condition of being answerable for one's own action and lack of action. Under Soviet health care system administration, service or quality problems were not discussed because by not acknowledging them they did not "officially" exist. Yanowitch (1979) has found that even a cursory acquaintance with the Soviet literature on labor problems provides abundant evidence of chronic difficulties with excessive labor turnover, poor work discipline, faulty work organization, and disappointing productivity performance.

In order to counteract these factors that affected production capability, Soviet sociological and managerial studies from the mid-1960s through the 1970s had begun to stress greater democratization of work, with worker participation in the management of production. This meant more than just using the official channels of participation; serious efforts were made to pose the issue of changing the distribution of managerial authority and providing opportunities for genuine forms of worker initiative in plant-level decision making. Some more progressive Soviet managers argued that the enrichment of the work process must be seen as significantly dependent on production independence or on-the-job independence of the worker; that is, the degree to which the functions of planning, organization, and control of the work process are directly delegated to the ordinary worker.

These recommendations were never put into practice, however, since loss of control threatened the political ideology of the Soviet system (Yanowitch, 1985). Acknowledging poor performance would mean perhaps a demotion, loss of employment, deportation, or worse (depending on the political regime) for the worker and manager. Accountability was important only when the system failed to produce prescribed quotas imposed by the central governing authority. Leites (1985) writes that the Communist Party used degrees of kontrol; that is, the surveillance and correction of one's performance by others, to ensure work success and the feeling of responsibility to society.

Although in theory the party believed that the worker's conscience was the best controller, in reality, when performance was low the party looked for low kontrol as the cause. Conversely, when kontrol was high, the party believed that its decisions would be carried through, and the party promoted norms favoring cohesion; that is, the principle of collective responsibility for defective performance. Minev et al. (1990) contends that the patient was the last to be considered in the health care scheme. The system was not geared to take into account the significant impact of an individual's lifestyle on health status. Although individual health status was considered partly dependent upon one's own behavior, the health system was depersonalized, collective in focus, and therefore by its core ideology could not influence health status by changing individual behavior.

Moreover, according to Leites (1985), in managing both society and the economy, there was a pervasive distrust by Soviet authority of ordinary human beings, of human nature, and perhaps of what was seen by the Soviet leadership as distinctive attributes of the human material that made up the mass of Soviet society: "Regional planning, far from respecting regional diversity, was a tool to impose uniformity... minority differences were disregarded and ... subjected to pressures to conform" (Barr, 1994: 86).

Within Soviet society, specific education was needed to perform certain tasks, but in most cases educational advancement and technological improvements were not necessary once a system was in place (Schultz, 1989). Direction, which was provided by a central committee far removed from the region or country involved, prevented the realistic means to problem solve and stifled initiative and innovation, and while the party stressed initiative, in theory, acting without orders was frowned upon and punished (Leites, 1985; Yanowitch, 1979; 1985). Analysis of the Soviet socialist experience in the national health system shows "that relying too heavily on a state monopoly in a centrally planned and supply-driven health sector lowers the efficiency and quality of care. This must be quickly corrected if health services in [these independent nations] are to be successfully integrated into the emerging market economies" (Preker and Feachem, 1994: 290).

Total hospital budgets were calculated as the sum of the various per capita service expenditure norms for different patient or hospital categories, including such things as food, medicine, physician visits, and even linen changes. Each category's ruble amount (expenditure norm) was then multiplied by the corresponding expected number of patient days per year to determine the needs of the specialized hospital. Thousands of such norms for each spending category were issued by the Ministry of Finance and the specialized ministries under the old system (Bird et al., 1995).

## POST-SOVIET HEALTH CARE SYSTEM ADMINISTRATION

The newly independent nations of the former Soviet Union include Albania, Armenia, Azerbaijan, Belarus, Bosnia and Herzegovina, Bulgaria, Croatia, Czech Republic, Estonia, Georgia, Hungary, Kazakhstan, Kyrgyz Republic, Latvia, Lithuania, former Yugoslav Republic of Macedonia, Moldova, Poland, Romania, Russian Federation, Slovakia, Slovenia, Tajikistan, Turkey, Turkmenistan, Ukraine, Uzbekistan, and the Federal Republic of Yugoslavia. These countries began their reforms from somewhat different initial conditions and have followed somewhat different reform strategies (i.e., their macroeconomic positions were quite dissimilar when reforms were initiated and there were substantial dissimilarities in the timing of and approach to reforms) (Blejer et al., 1993). Also, although many are showing positive economic growth a decade after the initiation of economic reforms, there are marked variations in economic performance with prospects getting less favorable as one moves across the region from west to east (World Bank Group, 2002). To varying degrees within this economic environment these nations are also faced with managing a health care system that was once operated within a centrally planned, hierarchically structured economy that appropriated and used resources, including facilities, equipment, supplies, and personnel, without consistent accountability standards regarding how, when, for whom, and by whom these resources were used (Cholewka, 1999a).

With independence from the Soviet Union in 1990, the centralized economic funding source in Moscow, Russia, was no longer providing operating capital, supplies, and materials to these nations. Reimbursement for social services and allocation of technologically advanced equipment and materials to health care facil-ities were now controlled by their national ministries of health, and the amount varied according to the policy interpretations by and political influence of health care institutions. With a decrease in operating revenue, national governments were forced to reduce the size and scope of health and other social services, and this affected the operating budgets of regional and local health care entities that provided much of the social welfare services.

At the same time, providers of health care services, including physicians and dentists, were investigating ways to privatize their practices and become fee-for-service, primary care providers. New health care financing models, promulgated by the adoption of new national health insurance systems, dictated that services that were once completely funded were not reimbursed, only partially reimbursed, or paid on a sliding scale according to the financial ability of the patient/consumer. Once this fee-for-service payment concept was introduced into some of these health care systems, the health care providers (hospitals and/or physicians) gradually became aware of the role the consumer had in causing some competition within the system by defining health care quality and choosing the best service provider (Cholewka, 1999b).

Increasingly, the funding and management of hospitals and health-related facil-ities are being transferred from the central level to the local level of government. This transfer raises a concern as to whether national standards will be maintained by local governments (e.g., criteria for hiring credentialed medical and nursing personnel). Requirements concerning these and other practice standards should therefore be a condition of funding. Another concern is how much decentralization is appropriate (e.g., developing other decentralization strategies for reducing the number of facilities, improving those that remain, and appointing district health directors who will be responsible for all public health activities in their districts) (Bird et al., 1995).

The major focus of the World Health Organization (WHO) for this restructuring of post-Soviet health care systems is for sustainable development that directs the reorganization of medical care toward health promotion, prevention, and primary health care. This objective would incorporate community participation and intersectoral cooperation (Towers, 1992:191). Tisch and Wallace (1994) believe that sustainable development should be a participatory process that involves the community in the design and implementation of development activities, and that since donor aid is limited, attempts must be made to ensure that local capability can continue development activities once the donor funding ceases. They stress that in order for development to be sustained the following issues must be addressed: (1) utilizing existing local leadership instead of creating new structures that may not be socially or historically sustainable, (2) stressing intersectoral participation; (3) ensuring that accountability for project implementation is intersectoral and not merely the re-sponsibility of a few people, (4) practicing an open management style that includes project beneficiaries to help ensure a wide base of participation and support, (5) creating new institutions only when the existing institutions prove to be inefficient and ineffective, (6) building the local capacity to provide technical assistance services, and (7) consciously planning and nurturing sustainability (Tisch and Wallace, 1994: 42).

In some cases, sustainability efforts can be eased through government decentralization of the control of the functions of the health care facility to allow greater efficiency of operations. By controlling finance, personnel, and operations locally, facility managers can react faster to environmental changes and make decisions that are advantageous to both the organization and the community. In order to evaluate the outcomes of operational management decisions, it is essential to establish management information systems that will require investment from various sources, including the state, private business, and other investors. Aid agencies have tried to initiate political and economic reforms during the past decade with mixed results. Evaluation of their experience with past programs shows that the trend is for sustainable programs that must be developed on a country-by-country and even an organization-by-organization basis, much as occurs within the U.S. health care system. An approach that uses a universal management model of one system fits all is neither workable nor sustainable (Cholewka, 2001).

This need for new management systems creates a challenge for health care management consultants to develop and present management training programs that are culturally sensitive, adaptable, and sustainable to the organizational and socioeconomic needs of these countries. McLaughlin and Kaluzny (1994) define TQM as a comprehensive approach to improving an organization's economic competitiveness through efficiency, effectiveness, and flexibility by involving each individual at every organizational level in the planning, organization, and understanding of each activity. Total quality management must start at the top of the organization with a continuing demonstration of executive management's commitment to incorporating quality concepts. This commitment ensures the adoption of a strategic overview of quality with a focus on the prevention, not detection, of problems through process management.

The core concept of TQM is the customer–supplier relationship. Holt (1993) defines efficiency as the result of making decisions that lead to doing things right, which helps to achieve the objectives of an enterprise with fewer resources and at lower costs. He defines effectiveness as the result of making decisions that lead to doing the right things, which helps to fulfill the mission of an enterprise.

In the U.S. health care industry, TQM programs gradually evolved into the continuous quality improvement (CQI) approach to managing health care service delivery. This approach adapted concepts from the industrial TQM model and used teams to measure the effectiveness (quality) and efficiency (resource utilization) of practitioners' services to identify and pursue opportunities to improve service outcomes to meet or exceed customers' expectations.

Since these expectations are subjective and can change continuously, improvement would have to be considered continually (McLaughlin and Kaluzny, 1994). The health care management consultant thus plays a pivotal role in guiding health care organizational change strategies. The consultant assists in the stabilization of transitional organizational processes by providing technical assistance and guidelines that can improve the way health care resources are utilized, how they are managed, and how their service outcomes are monitored (Cholewka, 1997).

## Management at the Microeconomic Level

Post-Soviet health systems faced profound challenges during the period of political and economic change. Within the first few years of transition, government spending on the social sectors decreased as economic focus was placed on macroeconomic development and growth. Infectious disease rates related to socioeconomic disadvantage, health-risk behaviors, and the overcrowded penal system rapidly increased, while the capacity to deal with them decreased because of funding cuts, outdated diagnostic techniques and treatments, and the mismanagement of public health system restructuring efforts (World Bank Group, 2002).

In response to economic restructuring, hospital management had to adapt at the microeconomic or organizational level and to develop its own management criteria. Hospital management reduced the scale and scope of its operations by downsizing, eliminating, merging, or privatizing services, and this led to the elimination of health care positions through attrition, retirement, or the creation of part-time positions (Cholewka, 2001; 1999a).

At present, with the assistance of USAID, World Bank (WB), and other EU sources, ministries of health and health care facility managers are redesigning and managing health care delivery systems in a different manner from which they were accustomed. By designing this new system, they are participants in the change effort and are building self-reliance and self-sufficiency (Cholewka, 1997). This concept of independent management is directly in opposition to Soviet political ideology, which stressed following health service provision dictates without questioning centralized authority and directing all efforts to the general good of the state. Independent thought and innovation was discouraged.

Under Soviet administration, there was no legal concept regarding the rights of the individual. Since independence this new organizational planning effort, resulting from economic and budgetary constraints, has forced some hospital managers to initiate policy changes to build consensus and the momentum for change. Perhaps the most important reason for hospitals and other health-related facilities to seek the development of autonomous organization management systems is for the improved ability to collect revenues through insurance payments and user fees and maintain control over these resources. Because the current economic environment has severely affected the ability of facilities to provide adequate levels of patient care, the efficient use of available funds and the collection of adequate operating revenues are of utmost importance to the survival of the organization (Cholewka, 1999a).

## Organization Development and Culture Change

As the ministries of health introduced restructuring and refinancing models and reactive changes were taken by management, few managers and practitioners understood the changes to the organizational culture and the necessary changes in behavior that the different incentives of a new system would require. Old beliefs and standards were being challenged and changed. Mistrust and suspicion of organization management by staff resulted in resistance to change efforts that affected hospital routine. Some personnel wanted more rapid, radical changes, while others were incapable of or had no interest in adjusting to the management needs of a new results-oriented economic system and opted to leave the system through early retirement financial incentive arrangements. Other personnel tried to resist using independent problem-solving or innovative management methods and relied on the tried and true method of waiting for orders from the top.

Some managers were ready to initiate departmental changes but needed guidance in advanced health services and human resources management to increase the efficiency of their departmental operations. Hospital executive management realized that a more managed organizational response was needed to adapt to continuous changes brought on by an unstable external environment. This response recognized that it was essential for personnel to be directed in a team effort and focused on the overall objective of the organization for the hospital to be viable (Cholewka, 1997).

A very important factor that should be addressed regarding the sustainability of management reform programs is the high level of corruption that existed, and still exists, at every level of every organization and government entity in these nations. The aid policies of USAID, WB, and EU agencies for the nations of the former Soviet Union were standardized in format and focused on both establishing civil societies with democratic institutions and jump-starting free markets in places in which these institutions were scarcely understood (Hirschler, 2001).

In the guise of following these policy directives, these countries, using entrenched Soviet-style administrative practices, implemented a maze of economic legislation and regulation without any advanced public consultation, prior analysis, feedback from the citizenry, or performance review of the agencies in charge, and just as in the old Soviet system, the only way that any economic activity could survive in such a large-scale, nontransparent environment was through collusion with and/or the bribing of public and the newly "privatized" sector officials (Thomas, 2001).

With the apparent breakdown in the provision of pharmaceutical products, medical equipment, and supplies to health care providers, the use of a black market supply and distribution network is tacitly endorsed by government authorities. Patients are willing to pay substantial gratuities to physicians for referrals through the health care system and for other medical and surgical services, and to health care staff for bed linen, hospital food, or supplies during their hospital stay. Many health care providers working outside the public sector see unrestrained privatization within an excessively relaxed regulatory framework as the means to use unscrupulous profiteering and pillaging tactics to supply their new "private" practices. Although they do not pay rent or fees for the use of office space within the hospital, they continue to use the public health care facilities as their extended private offices through the use of hospital rooms, equipment, supplies, diagnostic, and other therapeutic services for patient care (Cholewka, 1999a).

Corruption and a lack of the rule of law continue to be ongoing problems of conducting business and implementing free market policies in these transitional economies and have caused international aid organizations to re-evaluate development policies and approaches that were "misguided at best, and downright unhelpful at worst" (Hirschler, 2001: 3). The failure of so many of these countries to adopt economic reforms is because the people who controlled the state assets or enjoyed close ties with the old political elite benefited from such early reforms as liberalization and privatization that tended to be unchecked and unrestrained in "entrepreneurial" deals. These same people still tend to oppose subsequent reforms that erode their gains (World Bank Group, 2002).

In response to unsuccessful program implementation and pending EU membership, efforts are being made by aid organizations to promote anticorruption practices by developing a universal set of norms and principles defining ethical and professional conduct. These supposedly universal standards are clearly derived mainly from idealized Western standards, however, and are meant to supersede local customs, practices, and value systems: "Notwithstanding these efforts, corruption, fraud and economic crime remain widespread in many EU candidate countries, where they contribute to a lack of confidence by the citizens and discredit reforms" (Cirtanautas, 2001: 7–8).

## FACTORS INFLUENCING TQM PROGRAM DEVELOPMENT AND SUSTAINABILITY

### National and Organizational Culture

Historical influences are key to understanding the cultural legacy of the present post-Soviet health care systems. Although each nation is unique, many commonalities exist in the financing, structure, and function of these health care systems. In addition, environmental factors, internal and external to the hospital organization, influence the continued development and sustainability of health care management reform efforts. Countries that have succeeded in their development efforts have all encouraged entrepreneurship and reduced government harassment and obstacles to private enterprise. Each did this in its own way, however (Hirschler, 2001).

Unique organizational concerns specific to cultural differences indicate that specific management reform programs geared to meeting health care organizational needs have to be developed, applied, and tested for effectiveness. This has not been done so far in the apparent rush to change for change's sake. Now there is a growing trend to incorporate results from qualitative research studies with a participant observer component as a counterweight to some grandiose and nonsustainable economic development plans.

World Bank efforts within the health systems of these regions are aimed at making health care delivery more relevant to community needs, improving the cost-effectiveness of practitioner services, and supporting a new system of health insurance administration. World Bank lending for health, nutrition, and population projects in this region grew from 1991 to 2001 to a cumulative total of almost $1.3 billion (World Bank Group, 2002). Currently, with the movement to incorporate into the EU, NATO, UN, and other global organizations, this appears to be an opportune time for these nations to continue to implement organizational change strategies to improve hospital services.

Aligned to this new focus, TQM concepts would be helpful to hospital management to fashion a hospitalwide quality management program specific to planning, monitoring, and evaluating its health care provision and budget issues. Increased participation by providers in this change process could also increase their motivation to work within a system that they can help influence and improve. If the decision is made by these post-Soviet health system managers to adopt and implement a health care quality improvement program, strategies for more intensive training and development programs would have to be determined to address the specific human capital and institutional capacity needs of the health care facility (Cholewka, 1999a).

Before developing a TQM model, a very important issue to consider is the place that health care has within the context of each country's culture. One way to understand this place is to approach health care as a cultural system built out of meanings, values, and behavioral norms of the national culture. Differences in the style, methods, and forms of medical diagnosis and treatment, as well as the manner of system and organizational management, are linked to national socioeconomic ideologies.

Likewise, medical and nursing education, practice, and system management concepts are culturally and ideologically based. For example, Western democratic concepts and beliefs about health care—that is, the financing of (system versus program), responsibility for (individual versus state), and access to [universal (male and female children and adults of all ethnic groups) versus elite groups]—might not be similar in every region of the world, therefore a Western-style management model based on Western-style democratic ideology and developed to address the operational needs of organizations functioning within a market economic culture, might not be easily applied transculturally. The primacy now placed by development agencies for cost-saving measures through participatory planning involving the community and stressing primary care might be seen as a method of eroding the political autonomy and organizational culture of local health care practitioners (nurses and physicians) and managers.

Because the transition to the new socioeconomic capitalistic-based culture requires their cooperation, a management paradigm incorporating TQM concepts requires cultivation and nurturing by development organizations. This is something that has not happened, as evidenced by an unsuccessful rate of implementation in these countries within the decade after their independence.

It is therefore important to keep in mind that these development organizations are attempting the process of building a health care organizational culture within a dynamically evolving national culture. This process requires a period of incorporating new concepts with anticipated behavior changes that are completely foreign to the present ideology. The old communist ideology, forcibly imposed by Soviet authorities with military backup, took between fifty to seventy years to become established. It might take just as long for the new economic paradigm to take root. (See Table 1.)

## Professional and Managerial Education and Training

The health sectors of the nations of the former Soviet Union have a basic physical infrastructure (although deficient) and basically educated and trained health care practitioners (i.e., physicians, nurses, ancillary personnel). Because of past educational practices, human capital and institutional capacity in these nations are low. Under the old system, which had no intention of changing communist administration ideology, there was minimal contact outside the communist world for scientific research and exchange of clinical practice standards and technological information. There was a xenophobic attitude toward the noncommunist world. Learning was carried out in a didactic fashion in an environment that placed the teacher as the information authority dispensing facts that students learned as precisely as possible. Learning facts was more important than learning how to learn. Students in these countries were not expected or encouraged to apply their knowledge in a variety of clinical or research situations since independent thought and questioning established practice was discouraged (Barr, 1994).

**Table 1**  Total Quality Improvement Program Development and Sustainability Factors Specific to Health Care Systems in Post-Soviet Transitional Economies

National factors
  Political and economic stability of national health care system
  Government (Ministry of Health) support; nonconflicting, unambiguous policies consistently enforced
  Government–practitioner partnership to develop practice standards, audit criteria, reachable goals, and corrective action plans
  Intersectoral cooperation and participation
  Financial incentives to organizations to meet quality and cost-containment goals
  Micro- versus macroeconomic approach
  Acknowledgment of consumer role within health care system
  Western management and information technology support
Organizational factors
  Management long-term commitment and support with demonstrable "buy-in"
  Resource support to encourage and reward innovative ideas
  Managerial knowledge and skills to assess, motivate, support, and maintain staff *behavior change* (and *readiness to change*)

*Note*: Anticorruption methods (e.g., fraud and abuse monitoring) must be incorporated into any TQM program.

Excessive specialization led to the absence of a broad education and to the development of skills that are now difficult to adapt to the more complex demands of a market economy. Outdated skills are a widespread problem because of the few incentives to upgrade the skills of the staff. There is no significant focus on training in modern management functions (in addition to qualitative and quantitative analytical training). In the West emphasis is placed on inductive reasoning; that is, developing the life-long skill of independent problem solving by applying knowledge gained from an academic environment, and through experience, to a current situation (Cholewka, 1999a).

## Organizational Management

Under the previous system of Soviet Union health care, administration was a top-down affair, and even after a decade of economic transition training programs, old ways of thinking are still pervasive. There is still a widespread misunderstanding and an entrenched distrust of "the West" and such "Western values" as capitalism, individualism, "rights" of the patient or individual, critical thinking, interdisciplinary team problem solving, decentralized control, orientation to productivity and profit, and accountability to the planning and accomplishment of service outcomes.

It will take time for a societal paradigm shift; that is, to change the passive mentality of reliance on a centralized decision-making authority to an active mentality of self-reliance and independent decision making. Transition to a market economy is placing heavy demands on the skills of administrators to plan new administrative structures and to use new management concepts (i.e., planning, organizing, leading, and controlling functions attributed to management versus administration), which need time to take root (Cholewka, 1997; 1999a).

During this period of socioeconomic transition these nations need human capital capable of competing effectively with the countries of the EU, to which they aspire for incorporation. At present

> the gap in health status between the former socialist economies and highly industrialized, market-oriented economies is wide and growing, especially in the cohorts of working age. This places an economic burden on these nations due to lost investment in human capital (that is, those who die in middle age and have already received publicly funded education and other services; medical expenditures made prior to their deaths; and the more general opportunity cost of lost lives) (Preker and Feachem, 1994: 294–295).

When an organization seeks out new knowledge to effect change, it is already poised for a change transformation, but in order to accept and use new concepts to change the management paradigm of the current health care system, there has to be motivation linked to an incentive to change. One motivation for the health care organizations within these countries to change management style is the economic reality of the scarcity of economic resources with which to continue to operate. A second would be the possibility of making a profit by operating in a more efficient manner, while enforced government directives to do so—with legal and/or monetary sanctions—would be a third (Cholewka, 1997).

## Donor Activity

The political and macroeconomic restructuring of these societies has caused the health care infrastructure to be in a constant state of flux stemming from unclear, inconsistently enforced directives and/or ever-changing government administrators at the ministry of health level. Meanwhile, while addressed by aid organizations, programs stressing system and organization management are not emphasized in this period of transition. In reality, emphasis is placed on crisis intervention at a specific program level. Current programs are developed and managed by economists, physicians, and/or public health professionals, who, while not educated in management concepts per se, apply the medical model of treatment for both program development and administration. The public administration of the health care system should incorporate resource planning, cost analysis, policy implementation, monitoring and evaluation, quality improvement, human resource management, information management, and health insurance/financial management when developing sustainable health care management programs.

Donor activity in the region has been unbalanced, with some countries receiving assistance from a multitude of donors for a variety of institutions, while other countries remain regrettably neglected. Many development programs are focused on the political agenda of the donor agency, however, and leave no room for input by the recipient nation. After a decade of unsuccessful development program outcomes in these nations, the WB acknowledges that a key challenge is building state institutions capable of governing a modern market economy by integrating lessons learned into its operations. The WB sees the need to build strong public support for its programs by holding consultations with a wide range of players in the design and implementation of programs that don't just sound good on paper, but can actually be implemented. There is also a great need for monitoring the impact of reform efforts. The new focus is to assist their clients in successfully carrying through reforms while limiting the inflow of private investments relative to needs (World Bank Group, 2002).

After a decade of economic transition programs, the validity of these transformation efforts is being scrutinized by donor and aid organizations and challenged by recipient nations. What is being evaluated is the persistent problem inherent in these reforming socialist countries that is a combination of plans without controls and markets without incentives. Due in part to financial mismanagement and political corruption, at the macroeconomic level there is an absence of effective program coordination and accountability mechanisms. If democratization and globalization efforts are to continue, there is a need for continued privatization and increasing fiscal revenues, but the greatest long-term challenge is for managing change at the enterprise level, especially within the social sector.

After a decade of independence, health care reform in most post-Soviet nations today is still slow, fragmented, and managed by crisis intervention. Although health care providers are anxious to acquire technological advancement within their individual practices, they are also anxious to see improvement in the total quality of clinical practice, service provision, and overall organizational management. Their ability to monitor and control costs, to develop and implement professional practice standards like those being used in Western countries, and to manage and develop human resources is still rudimentary. Sustainable programs for system improvements are hampered by changes in governance and policy at the ministry of health (national) level and the managerial ability and strength of commitment to change programs by leadership at the organization (local) level (Cholewka, 1999b).

## Corruption

Corruption at every level of post-Soviet society is a major factor to be acknowledged before any real reform outcomes can be realized. Donor aid programs should incorporate accountability methods to measure outcomes—agreed-upon reforms and standards—to prevent corrupt operational and reporting practices that might be used to circumnavigate funding criteria. An anticorruption culture should be developed with accountability standards and penalties that are enforced. Development outcomes should be evaluated for continued funding. It has been shown that for the sake of satisfying Western development organizations, those in power have learned to spout an adapted Western-style business lexicon and phraseology, but they have not demonstrated measurable systemic changes (Hirschler, 2001).

## The Emerging Role of the Health Care Consumer

The emerging sense of product and service quality (value) by the citizenry will eventually have to be effectively addressed by both the public and private economic sectors. Successful economic outcomes within these new market economies, whether for public or private health care enterprises, will be governed by the "survival of the fittest"; that is, the survival of which provider can provide the best quality health care (the most affordable, accessible, appropriate, equitable, safe, and effective health care services) within such external and internal economic constraints as consumer demand, investment criteria, and government regulation. The education of organization personnel in health services management technology using TQM methods, incorporating consumer satisfaction surveys, is therefore the most logical and appropriate way to ensure a competitive edge for economic survival of these health care service providers (Cholewka, 1997).

## SUMMARY AND POLICY CONSIDERATIONS

This chapter presented a brief overview of some issues that face development organizations, management consultants, and national policy makers as they design sustainable health care management programs for implementation into the public administration systems of the post-Soviet nations of Central and Eastern Europe. Daunting challenges still lie ahead.

These nations are moving from a secondary (state responsibility) health care culture to a primary (individual responsibility) health care culture within a decentralizing economic environment that is dynamically moving toward a national insurance-based reimbursement structure. It would therefore be useful to be aware of the differences between the health care systems of these countries, not only in terms of their health care socioeconomic spending, but of where the concept of health is situated within their social traditions, culture, and political systems.

After a decade of economic transition programs, the effectiveness of these transformation efforts is being scrutinized by donor and aid organizations and challenged by recipient nations. Increasingly, recipient nations are questioning the practicality of increasing their national debt by accepting financial loans for institutionalizing expensive, unworkable "development programs." Donor organizations are evaluating the persistent problem in these reforming socialist countries that is a combination of plans without controls and markets without incentives. At the macroeconomic level, there is an absence of effective program coordination and accountability mechanisms, but the greatest long-term challenge is for managing change at the enterprise level, especially within the social sector.

There is an increasing trend to link development with health-related outcomes when designing international assistance programs. At present, development programs seem to stress economic development with income, education, and health as the main components. In reality, however, while acknowledging the importance of health-related issues that affect national socioeconomic growth and development, the management and coordination of the health care sector is mostly ignored or underfunded. Health care system management programs are virtually nonexistent, considering the importance of health to a nation's economic viability (gross national product/GDP) and the education of its citizenry. Keeping this in mind, it can be said that one cannot educate a dead man.

Modern economies involve close coordination of a very large number of complex decisions that require systemic transformation at the microeconomic level. An effective way to start is with the incorporation of TQM programs into system, organization, and community-related health care operations. These programs stress participation by health care practitioners in the planning, monitoring, and evaluation of and accountability for the efficiency and effectiveness of clinical services. Ideally, and at the expense of sounding too simplistic, intersectoral cooperation within a culture of openness and information sharing would need to be developed and maintained to accomplish these goals. According to Dixon et al.

> financing systems are only one among many factors needed to cope effectively with the undoubted inefficiency within the health sector [of these post-Soviet countries.] The multifaceted problems faced in the region demand a well-conceived and long-term health sector reform strategy, with specific programmes, a clear governance framework, skilled and committed health care management and administration and support from health care

professionals and the public for the aims and goals of the reforms. Unfortunately, none or few of these elements have been assembled so far in the region to the extent needed. These are but a few of the challenges that lie ahead for the region in the next 10 years, and perhaps beyond (Dixon et al., 2002: 23).

## REFERENCES

Barr, N. (1994). Labor Markets and Social Policy in Central and Eastern Europe: The Transition and Beyond. Washington, DC: Oxford University Press.

Bird, R. M., Ebel, R. D., Wallich, C. I. (1995). Decentralization of the Socialist State: Intergovernmental Finance in Transition Economies. Washington, DC: the World Bank.

Blejer, M. I., Calvo, G. A., Coricelli, F., Gelb, A. H. (1993). Eastern Europe in transition: From recession to growth? Proceedings of a conference on the macroeconomic aspects of adjustment, co-sponsored by the International Monetary Fund and the World Bank. Washington, DC: the International Bank for Reconstruction and Development/the World Bank.

Cantor, M. M. (1978). Achieving Nursing Care Standards: Internal and External. Wakefield, MA: Nursing Resources.

Cholewka, P. A. (1997). Transferring management technology: Healthcare quality improvement education in Central and Eastern Europe. J Healthcare Qual. 19(4):29–33.

Cholewka, P. A. (1999a). Comparative Analysis of Two Healthcare Organizations in Post-Soviet Lithuania and Ukraine: Implications for Continuous Quality Improvement. Ann Arbor, MI: University Microfilms (UMI).

Cholewka, P. A. (1999b). Reengineering the Lithuanian healthcare system: A hospital quality improvement initiative. J Healthcare Qual. 21(4):26–37.

Cholewka, P. A. (2001). Challenges to institutionalizing sustainable total quality management programs in healthcare systems of post-Soviet countries. Internat. J. Econ. Dev. (E-journal). Penn State University.

Cirtanautas, A. (2001). Anticorruption campaigns: How to get rid of paradoxes and inconsistencies. Trans. Newsl. 12(4):7–10.

Cleland, C. F. (1997). Improving health status: Health care quality in the context of health reform. International ISQua Conference on Quality in Health Care, Chicago.

Conquest, R. (1990). The Great Terror: A Reassessment. New York: Oxford University Press.

Commission of the European Communities. (1997). Agenda 2000. Vols. 1 and 2: The Challenge of Enlargement. Brussels.

Dixon A., Langenbrunner J., Mossialos E. (2002). Facing the challenges of health care financing: A background paper for USAID Conference, Ten Years of Health Systems Transition in Central and Eastern Europe and Eurasia. Washington, DC, pp. 1–25.

Gefenas, E. (1995). Health care in Lithuania: From idealism to reality? In: Seedhouse, D., ed. Reforming Health Care: The Philosophy and Practice of International Health Reform. New York: Wiley, pp. 121–127.

Gulens, V. (1995). Distortions in personality development in individuals emerging from a long-term totalitarian regime. J Balt. Stud. 26:267–284.

Hardt, J. P., Kaufman, R. F. (1995). East-Central European Economies in Transition. Joint Economic Committee, Congress of the United States. New York: Sharpe.

Hershey, P., Blanchard, K. H., Johnson, D. E. (1996). Management of Organization Behavior Utilizing Human Resources. 7th ed. Englewood Cliffs, NJ: Prentice-Hall.

Hirschler, R. (2001). Interview with Nick Stern, senior vice president and chief economist of the World Bank. Transition Newsl. 12(4):1–4.

Holt, D. H. (1993). Management: Principles and Practice. 3rd ed. Englewood Cliffs, NJ: Prentice-Hall.

Kaminski, B. (1995). The legacy of Communism. In: Hardt, J. P., Kaufman, R. F., eds. East-Central european Economies in Transition. New York: Sharpe, pp. 9–23.

Lee, S., Luthans, R., Hodgetts, R. (1992). Total quality management: Implications for Central and Eastern Europe. Org. Dynam. 20(4):42–55.

Leites, N. (1985). Soviet Style in Management. New York: Crane Russak.

Lieven, A. (1994). The Baltic Revolution: Estonia, Latvia, Lithuania and the Path to Independence. 2nd ed. New Haven, CT: Yale University Press.

Lisitin, Y. P., Alexandrov, O. A. (1967). The System of Public Health Services in the USSR. Moscow: Ministry of Health of the USSR.

McLaughlin, C. P., Kaluzny, A. D. (1994). Continuous Quality Improvement in Health Care: Theory, Implementation, and Applications. Gaithersburg, MD: Aspen.

Mezentseva, E., Rimachevskaya, N. (1990). The Soviet country profile: health of the USSR population in the 70s and 80s: an approach to a comprehensive analysis. Soc. Sci. Med. 31(8):867–877.

Minev, D., Dermendjieva, B., Mileva, N. (1990). The Bulgarian country profile: The dynamics of some inequalities in health. Soc. Sci. Med. 31(8):837–846.

Preker, A. S., Feachem, R. G. A. (1994). Health and health care. In: Barr, N., ed. Labor Markets and Social Policy in Central and Eastern Europe. New York: Oxford University Press, pp. 288–321.

Rowland, D., Telyukow, A. V. (1991). Soviet health care from two perspectives. Health Aff. 10(3):71–86.

Schubert-Lehnhardt, V. (1995). Who should be responsible for a nation's health? In: Seedhouse, D., ed. Reforming Health Care: The Philosophy and Practice of International Health Reform. New York: Wiley, pp. 167–170.

Schultz, T. W. (1989). Investing in people: Schooling in low income countries. Ec. Ed. Rev. 8(3):219–223.

Semashko, N. A. (1935). Health Protection in the USSR. New York: Putnam.

Shapiro, L., Godson, J. (1994). The Soviet Worker: From Lenin to Andropov. New York: St. Martin's Press.

Tisch, S., Wallace, M. (1994). Dilemmas of Development Assistance: The What, Why, and Who of Foreign Aid. Boulder, CO: Westview.

Thomas, S. (2001). Petty corruption in the wild, wild east. Trans. Newsl. 12(4):5–6.

Towers, B. (1992). From AIDS to Alzheimer's: policy and politics in setting new health agendas. In: Bailey, J., ed. Social Europe. New York: Longman.

UNICEP/WHO. (1992). The looming crisis in health and the need for international support: Overview of the Reports on the Commonwealth of Independent States and the Baltic countries. Collaborative missions with the participation of UNFPA, WFP, and UNDP.

World Bank. (1993). World Development Report 1993: Investing in Health. New York: Oxford University Press.

World Bank Group. ECA Regional Brief. online. available at: http://www.worldbank.org/eca/, Jan. 18, 2002.

Yanowitch, M. (1979). Soviet Work Attitudes: The Issue of Participation in Management. New York: Sharpe.

Yanowitch, M. (1985). Work in the Soviet Union: Attitudes and Issues. New York: Sharpe.

# 15

# The Impact of HIV/AIDS on Economic Development in Sub-Saharan Africa
## Policy Implications

**ALEX SEKWAT and SANGHO MOON**

*Tennessee State University, Nashville, Tennessee, U.S.A.*

## INTRODUCTION

This chapter reviews both the impact of acquired immunodeficiency syndrome (AIDS) and human immunodeficiency virus (HIV) on economic development in sub-Saharan Africa and the policy measures needed to mitigate its effects. Recent studies suggest that the HIV/AIDS epidemic poses one of the greatest challenges to long-term economic development in sub-Saharan Africa [United Nations Joint Program on HIV/AIDS (UNAIDS) and World Health Organization (WHO), 2001; Kabbaj, 2001; World Bank, 2000]. The epidemic has slowed economic growth in more than half of the countries in the subregion and threatens to reverse decades of gains in human resources development, education, health, and business and undermine the well-being of Africa's future economic growth and development.

HIV/AIDS impacts sectors of social and economic development, ranging from the "capacity of the household to provide for the needs of its members to the capacity of governments to protect the rights of their people to health, education, and income security" [International Labor Organization (ILO), 2000: 21]. It incapacitates and kills farmers, teachers, civil servants, health workers, private sector workers, and professional or skilled and unskilled workers in virtually all sectors of the economy. HIV/AIDS has evolved from a health problem in the 1980s to a serious economic development issue during the past decade. In general, researchers widely agree that HIV/AIDS affects economic growth through two routes. The first is through the illness or the death of productive working adults (Loewenson and Whiteside, 1997: 21). HIV/

AIDS outbreaks mainly occur in two specific age groups; that is, infants and adults aged 20 to 40 years. The high prevalence of the epidemic among the highly productive working-age population (aged 20 to 40) causes significant productivity loss. The second path is through the diversion within an economy (or consumptive allocation) of resources from savings (and eventually investment) to health care. The argument on the impact of HIV/AIDS on savings (and hence investment) is simple: individuals who fall ill will divert their savings (for future consumption) into current consumption in order to maintain themselves and their dependents. They will also liquidate their existing savings and possibly their wealth (or assets) to finance upcoming health care costs associated with HIV/AIDS. Diversion of resources from savings into health care will lead to less investment for future production, and shrinking investment will be directly associated with a decline in the macroeconomic growth rates accompanied by high rates of unemployment.

The linkage between HIV/AIDS and economic development has become an important public policy issue in recent years. Policy makers in the countries hardest hit by the epidemic are under pressure to devise the most effective ways to respond to the deadly disease. This chapter reviews the impact of HIV/AIDS on economic development in sub-Saharan Africa and the policy measures necessary to mitigate its effects. It begins with a review of the epidemiological impact of the epidemic in the subregion, then it reports on the impact of HIV/AIDS on major sectors of economic activity, including households, agriculture, business, health, and education. Next, the chapter reviews the macroeconomic effects of the disease in sub-Saharan Africa. The chapter concludes with a summary of the policy implications of HIV/AIDS on economic development and the measures necessary to reduce its effects.

## EPIDEMIOLOGICAL IMPACT

The HIV/AIDS pandemic is a global problem. It has spread to every region and country in the world since the first cluster of clinical illness caused by the disease was reported in the medical literature in 1982. In late 2001, an estimated 40 million people worldwide were living with HIV/AIDS and a staggering 70% of them were living in sub-Saharan Africa (Dixon et al., 2002). A recent report released by UNAIDS and WHO revealed that 5 million people became infected worldwide in 2001 (UNAIDS and WHO, 2001). Furthermore, data on AIDS-induced mortality indicated that the disease has surpassed malaria as the leading cause of death in sub-Saharan Africa. Since the onset of the pandemic, about 22 million people have succumbed to it, of which 12 million were Africans (Hecht et al., 2002).

Projections by the World Bank (1997) indicate that by the year 2020 HIV will account for 37.1% of deaths among people between the ages of 15 and 59 in developing countries, compared to 8.6% of deaths from infectious disease in 1990. According to Parker (2002), structural inequities in all societies continue to fuel the epidemic, with the greatest concentration occurring in the poorest and marginalized sectors. While mortality rates have leveled off in developed countries, the picture remains bleak in the developing world, especially in sub-Saharan Africa and Southeast Asia. Recent UNAIDS and WHO (2001) projections indicate that sub-Saharan Africa and Southeast Asia have the highest rates of infection. Within sub-Saharan Africa, infection rates vary among countries, with the highest prevalence in southern and eastern African countries. The infection rates range from about 2% of the adult population in some West African countries to more 30% in southern Africa. Prevalence rates in Central and East Africa fall in between (2–30%). In Zimbabwe, Namibia, Swaziland, South Africa, and Botswana, for example, HIV prevalence among 15 to 49 year olds ranges from 20–26%. Among these countries, life expectancy is projected to drop from 60 to 70 years to 30 to 40 years within the next two decades (Shapourand and Rosen, 2001).

The epidemiological impact transcends the number of adult HIV infections and AIDS deaths. Infant, child, and female mortality and tuberculosis cases are on the rise. Women and children are the most vulnerable to HIV infections in Africa. Women account for 55% of HIV-infected adults in sub-Saharan Africa, and children in the subregion account for 75% of the world's infections and 90% of orphans. Moreover, because HIV/AIDS strikes people in their most productive years, the labor force is severely impacted. Labor supply is impacted through increased morbidity and mortality of the working adult population.

## SECTORAL EFFECTS

HIV/AIDS affects all aspects of social and economic development in the world's hardest hit regions, especially in sub-Saharan Africa. The economic effects of HIV/AIDS are first felt at the micro level by individuals, then by households. They are then felt by whole communities and eventually affect the development aspects of society and the macroeconomy (Guinness and Alban, 2000). When individuals fall ill, they cannot work and are forced to depend on their families for care and support. In turn their families are compelled to deplete their savings to pay for medical expenses or other forms of treatment. Moreover, traditional support systems are overstretched and families and communities lose their economic, social, and cultural viability. Eventually the effects of HIV/AIDS spill over to the macroeconomy as infection rates increase in the adult working population. In sum, the AIDS epidemic shrinks household resources and increases levels of poverty at the micro level, resulting in increased health sector expenditures, job absenteeism, loss of skilled workers, reduced productivity, and ultimately reduced national growth and development. Specific sectors affected by the HIV/AIDS epidemic include households, education, health, agriculture, and business.

### Households

The economic effects of HIV/AIDS on individuals and households in sub-Saharan Africa are significant. Households come under increasing economic difficulties because of the lack of income resulting from the prolonged sickness caused by HIV/AIDS. According to a recent study, the immediate effects of the AIDS epidemic include a reduction in household income, increased debt, the early entry of children into the labor market to supplement family income, the continued presence of older household members in the labor market, and the withdrawal of children from school (Gonzalez, 2001). If a working adult—especially the breadwinner—is infected, the long-term welfare of the entire household is jeopardized. First, the food supply at the household level becomes increasingly unsustainable. Typically, the household is compelled to deplete accumulated savings to pay for food, medical care, and funeral expenses. Second, school-aged children are forced to drop out of school because of dwindling resources and/or because their services are needed to care for ailing parents.

Studies on the economic effects of HIV/AIDS on households in sub-Saharan Africa indicate that the effects are severe. In the most affected countries, estimates show that the number of individuals living in poverty increased by 5% as a result of HIV/AIDS (UNAIDS and WHO, 2001). In urban areas of Ivory Coast, the epidemic reduced food consumption per capita by 41% and household spending on education by 50% (UNAIDS and WHO, 2001). In addition, a household with a member afflicted by AIDS spent "twice as much on medical expenses as other households, with 80 percent of expenditures devoted to the person with HIV/AIDS rather than other family members" (USAID, 2001a: 12). In Botswana the per capita income for the poorest 25% of households is estimated to fall by 13% in the next decade because of the effects of the HIV/AIDS epidemic (Greener, 2000; Guinness and Alban, 2000). Studies in Rwanda have revealed that "households with a HIV/AIDS patient spend on average 20 times more on health care annually than households without an AIDS patient" (UNAIDS and WHO, 2002: 3). In Ethiopia, the average cost of HIV/AIDS treatment and funeral expenses exceeded the average household income (USAID, 2001b). In Tanzania a study of adult mortality "found that 8 percent of total household expenditure went to medical care and funerals in households that had an adult death in the preceding 12 months" (Stover and Bollinger, 1999: 4). The loss of household assets and members ultimately jeopardize the household's long-term ability to survive.

## Health Sector

HIV/AIDS impacts the health sector by increasing the demand and cost for health services. Recent studies indicate that the demand for health care by HIV/AIDS patients is overstretching the meager resources of households and the already feeble health systems of sub-Saharan African countries. The cost of providing health services to HIV patients accounts for a large proportion of the total health expenditures for most countries in the subregion. Estimates by UNAIDS indicate that public health spending on HIV/AIDS in 1997 exceeded 2% of gross domestic product (GDP) in seven of sixteen African countries in which total health expenditure from public and private sources on all diseases accounts for 3–5% of GDP. In southern Africa, total health expenditure per capita ranges from $9 in Malawi to $203 in south Africa. These amounts correspond to 0.2% and 4.1% of per capita health spending in the United States, respectively. In Zimbabwe, projections indicate that by 2005 the epidemic will account for more than 60% of the Ministry of Health's budget and more than 50% in Kenya (USAID, 2001a). A study in Ivory Coast revealed that HIV/AIDS-related costs accounted for 11% of the public health budget in 1997 (Guinness and Alban, 2000). In Malawi, AIDS-related expenditures accounted for 20% of the total Ministry of Health's budget in 1996 (Guinness and Alban, 2000; World Bank, 1998).

Studies on HIV/AIDS-related hospital bed occupancy rates show an increasing trend in many sub-Saharan African countries. In Burundi and Kenya HIV-positive patients occupy 50% of the beds in urban hospitals, and in Botswana the hospital bed occupancy by HIV/AIDS patients has reached about 60% (USAID, 2001a). In

Tanzania patients afflicted by HIV/AIDS-related diseases occupy over 60% of hospital beds (Msobi and Msumi, 2000). Projections indicate that the number of hospital beds needed for AIDS patients will exceed the total currently available in Namibia by 2005 (USAID, 2001a).

The health sector labor force is vulnerable to the negative effects of HIV/AIDS in several ways. Many health workers in sub-Saharan Africa are affected by the disease. A recent USAID-funded study identified the following ways in which the epidemic impacts the effectiveness of the health labor force (Drysdale, 2000). First, HIV/AIDS increases the stress level of health care workers, mainly because of the fear of becoming infected or contracting the disease from patients (Drysdale, 2000). Second, the USAID study noted an increase in the rate of infection among health workers. Consequently, morbidity, mortality, and absenteeism rates have risen in countries with high levels of HIV seroprevalence among health workers. A preliminary pilot study in Zambia revealed that "mortality among female nurses rose 13 times from 1980 to 1991 to 2.67 percent and further rose to 4 precent in 1994. Absenteeism among the health workforce rose from 'about 10 percent to about 15%'" (Drysdale, 2000: 2). Third, there is a shortage of experienced health workers, as many succumb to the disease or leave the health profession entirely due to burnout, fear of infection, or other related problems. According to a recent UNAIDS and WHO (2001) report, up to 25% of health care workers are lost as result of HIV/AIDS in some sub-Saharan African countries. The same report noted that illness among health workers in Malawi and Zambia "increased five-to-six fold and death rates have reduced personnel, increased stress levels and workload for the remaining employees" (UNAIDS and WHO, 2001: 8).

## Education Sector

HIV/AIDS profoundly impacts the demand for educational services at the household level and the entire school age population in many countries throughout sub-Saharan Africa (World Bank, 2000). The epidemic impacts the entire education sector in several major ways. First, it reduces the supply of teachers as a result of AIDS-related illnesses and deaths. Increased morbidity and mortality among teachers negatively impacts the supply of educational services through premature deaths, increased absenteeism, and reduced productivity. Recent studies indicate a significant reduction in the number of teachers in the countries hit hardest by the epidemic. In Zambia, for instance, the mortality rate among teachers in 1998 reached thirty-nine per 1000, 70% higher than that of the 15 to 49, age group in the general population (Kelly, 1999). According to the World Bank (2000), the annual rate of deaths of teachers and education officers in Zimbabwe caused by AIDS would reach about 2.1% during the 2000–2010 decade, and the estimates for Zambia, Kenya, and Uganda would be 1.7%, 1.4%, and 0.5%, respectively, over the same period of time. The average professional time lost by each infected teacher and education officer in the four countries studied by the World Bank (Kenya, Uganda, Zambia, and Zimbabwe) amounted to "six months before developing full-blown AIDS and then 12 additional months more after developing the full disease" (World Bank, 2000: 6). In the Central African Republic, AIDS-related deaths accounted for 85% of teachers' mortality between 1996 and 1998. In Zambia, about 1300 teachers died as a result of AIDS in 1998 (World Bank, 2000).

Second, the epidemic reduces school enrollment by forcing school-aged children to care for sick family members, work to generate income for the family, or drop out simply because their families can no longer afford the cost of their education (due to illness or the death of a working parent). Projections by the World Bank (2000: 5) show that "the size of the primary school age population in Zimbabwe would be 2.98 million in 2010 under a no AIDS scenario but 2.27 million under the current AIDS situation, a difference of 24 percent." In Zambia, the primary school-aged population would be 2.71 million in 2010 without AIDS, but 2.16 million with AIDS (World Bank, 2000). In this case, the differential would be more than 20%. In Kenya and Uganda, the differences in the size of the primary school-aged populations in 2010 would be 13.8% and 12.2%, respectively, between the without AIDS and the with AIDS projections (World Bank, 2000: 7).

Third, the human resources at risk also include all individuals who have roles in the delivery of educational services, both in the private and public sectors, including those working in departments of education and those involved in the education and training of teachers (Cohen, 1999). Moreover, staff absenteeism is rising for the same reasons noted above. According to Cohen (1999), high morbidity and mortality rates caused by HIV/AIDS are reducing institutional and human capacities in many sub-Saharan African countries.

Last, the estimated costs of HIV/AIDS to the education sector are staggering. A recent report titled *Education and HIV/AIDS: A Window of Hope* projected the cost of replacing teachers who have died of HIV/AIDS at $25 million between 2000 and 2010 in Zambia, and twice as much in Mozambique (World Bank, 2002). In Swaziland, "the cost of sickness and death benefits for teachers, plus the extra cost of hiring and training new teachers is projected to exceed U.S. $200 million by 2016—more than the 1998/99 government budget for all goods and services" (USAID, 2001a: 16).

## Agricultural Sector

The agricultural sector is the backbone of the economies of most African countries. According to a recent ILO (2000: 7) study, "farming and other rural occupations provide a livelihood for 70 percent of the population in Sub-Saharan Africa." It is the largest employer of labor and the largest contributor to the GDP in many African countries. In Tanzania, agriculture accounts for 52% of the GDP and employs up to 83% of the labor force. Labor remains a vital factor of agricultural production in Africa because of its limited utilization of mechanized farming or new technology. HIV/AIDS induces labor shortages in the agricultural sector since it affects adults in their most productive years. According to a study sponsored by the U.S. Department of Agriculture (USDA), the level of agricultural productivity and per capita food consumption declined in sub-Saharan Africa during the past two decades (Shapour and Rosen, 2001). A study in Zimbabwe reported a decline in production of up to 50% of the normal levels in such crops as maize, cotton, peanuts, and vegetables (UNAIDS and WHO, 2000; ILO, 2000). Similar studies in Tanzania, Burkina Faso, and Ivory Coast reported declines in production [ILO, 2000]. Although the net effect of HIV/AIDS on economies dependent on agriculture is unknown, Shapouri and Rosen (2001) contend that the spread of the epidemic in rural areas will have a direct effect on food production and security in the most severely affected countries.

In Zimbabwe, "the death of a breadwinner from AIDS was found to reduce the marketed output of various crops anywhere from 29 percent to 61 percent" (USAID,

2001a: 14). The reduction in output is induced by losses in labor and increased medical expenses (Kwaramba, 1997; Stover and Bollinger, 1999). A study by the Food and Agricultural Organization (FAO, 1997) in Burkina Faso showed that households affected by AIDS experienced a 25–50% decline in net revenues from agricultural production. AIDS impacts agricultural production by forcing farmers to change cropping patterns by switching to less labor-intensive crops. In many cases this may mean switching from export crops to food crops. In that sense HIV/AIDS could affect the production of cash crops and some food crops. Furthermore, cash crops are often abandoned in favor of less labor-intensive subsistence crops (UNAIDS and WHO, 2000; Topouzis, 1998; Economic Commision for Africa, 2000). Similarly, "livestock production is also affected as animals are sold to generate cash or are sacrificed" (Economic Commision for Africa, 2000).

Overall, the quality and quantity of agricultural production is rapidly declining in the hardest hit countries, causing malnutrition and a reduction in food security. At the macroeconomic level changes in the supply and quality of farm labor as well as changes in the supply and demand for agricultural produce entailed by the epidemic will alter the relative prices of commodities on local and international markets as well as interest rates and wages (Cohen, 1992: 10).

## Business Sector

HIV/AIDS affects business activity by either increasing costs or reducing revenues. The degree of impact of the epidemic depends on the type of business, how labor is utilized, the type of labor employed (skilled or unskilled), and the type of benefits provided (e.g., health insurance, pensions). The major effects of HIV/AIDS on businesses include increased operating costs, reduced productivity, reduced labor supply, increased absenteeism, diminished profitability, low employee morale, poor labor relations, and reduced business competitiveness in the global market (Guinness and Alban, 2000; USAID, 2001a).

The major HIV/AIDS-related factors leading to increased business expenditures stem from both internal and external effects (Simon et al., 2000). The internal effects include increased absenteeism due to AIDS-induced morbidity, a decline in morale and work discipline, higher health care costs, higher medical insurance, burial fees, and increased training and recruitment costs (Simon et al., 2000; Stover and Bollinger, 1999). The external effects relate to changes in the external market environment, such as reduced demand for businesses' products, increasing wages, and the rising costs associated with institutional breakdowns (Simon et al., 2000). Recent studies show that HIV/AIDS-related absenteeism has detrimental effects on labor costs, productivity, and profitability. A study of AIDS-related absenteeism in eastern and southern African businesses revealed that the epidemic accounted for 25–50% of total costs (ILO, 2000). According to a study by the ILO (2000: 14), the high numbers "stem from the disruption of the production cycle, the underutilization of equipment and the costs of temporary staff." A similar study in a Zimbabwean transportation company revealed that HIV/AIDS-related absenteeism accounted for 54% of AIDS costs, followed by absenteeism due to HIV-related symptomatic illness at 35% (Whiteside and O' Grady, 2000).

Studies indicate that HIV/AIDS-related labor costs can reduce business profits and productivity. One study projected a reduction of "profitability by 6 to 8 percent annually and productivity by 8 percent" (USAID, 2001a: 16). In Kenya and South

Africa, recent estimates indicate the substantial impact of HIV/AIDS on profitability (Morris et al., 2001; Roberts et al., 1996). HIV/AIDS impacts labor productivity because a sick person is either unable to work or his or her job performance is lowered by physical and psychological factors.

The effects of HIV/AIDS vary by type of business, the ease or difficulty of replacing workers, and the skill levels utilized. Both labor-intensive businesses and businesses that rely heavily on migrant labor are highly vulnerable to the effects of the epidemic. Recent studies show that infection rates are highest in industries that are labor-intensive or rely heavily on migrant workers, such as commercial farming, mining, and transportation. In labor-intensive businesses, labor productivity is the most important determinant of output and profitability. One study examining the workforce of a sugar mill in South Africa indicated that HIV-infected workers accounted for 26% of all those tested (Morris et al., 2001). A similar study of a commercial Kenyan sugar estate revealed that 25% of the workers were HIV-positive (Roberts et al., 1996). Another study by South Africa's Medical Research Council revealed that at least 25% of miners are infected, and the rate is projected to increase to 30% by 2005 (ILO, 2000).

## MACROECONOMIC EFFECTS

Starting in the early 1990s, studies on the macroeconomic effects of HIV/AIDS increasingly appeared in the economics literature. Cuddington (1993), Cohen (1992), and Over (1992) were among the first group of researchers to examine the macroeconomic impact of HIV/AIDS (Whiteside, 1996: 111). Specifically, Cuddington (1993) attempted to model the macroeconomic impacts of AIDS in Tanzania, and Over (1992) provided an overview of the macroeconomic impacts of HIV/AIDS in sub-Saharan Africa. Cohen (1992) looked at the ways in which AIDS disrupts social and economic systems (Whiteside, 1996). Other early studies included the work of Kambou et al. (1992), Cuddington (1993), and Cuddington et al. (1994).

The early studies demonstrated that the macroeconomic impacts of HIV/AIDS are difficult to estimate. Methodological issues couple with persistent problems in developing countries, including droughts, conflicts, corruption, economic mismanagement, political instability, and changes in oil prices, obscure assessment of the macroeconomic impacts of HIV/AIDS (USAID, 2001a; 2001b: 6). In addition, measurement of HIV/AIDS prevalence and economic growth presents difficulties in the estimation of the economic impact of AIDS, thus the findings of previous studies tend to vary according to the methodologies and assumptions made by researchers and the social and economic conditions of individual countries. For instance, early macroeconomic models examining the relationship between HIV/AIDS and economic growth in sub-Saharan countries suggest that HIV/AIDS is adversely related to the rates of economic growth, and that the epidemic reduces the overall growth rates of the economy (Cuddington, 1993; Cuddington et al., 1994). The implications of the macroeconomic impact within the economic growth models remain unclear, however, because the two sets of projections employed (i.e., the AIDS epidemic trend and economic growth rates) are difficult to combine in a sufficiently simplified economic model and are vulnerable to uncertainty and measurement errors in estimation (Loewenson and Whiteside, 1997: 7). The macroeconomic factors susceptible to

HIV/AIDS broadly range from economic growth rates, the level and/or distribution of national wealth, and the allocation of resources between savings and health care, to employment rates as a summary measure of macroeconomic outcomes. Overall, from the perspective of mainstream economists who believe in the macroeconomic growth model (Cuddington, 1993; Cuddington et al., 1994), the prevalence of the AIDS epidemic slows down economic growth and has the potential to reverse the development gains of the last forty years.

Other empirical evidence suggests that the economic impact of HIV/AIDS worldwide is not significant and that the epidemic may have little effect at the macroeconomic and sectoral level. Loewenson and Whiteside (1997) analyzed preliminary data based on fifty-one countries, and reported only a small, statistically insignificant negative impact of HIV/AIDS on macroeconomic indicators. Other studies in Tanzania (Cuddington, 1991) and Zambia (Forgy and Mwanza, 1994) reported similar findings. Furthermore in a cross-country analysis, Bloom and Mahal (1995) found little evidence supporting claims that the AIDS epidemic slows the growth rate in per capita income. They noted that "we find no evidence that the economies of the countries where the (HIV/AIDS) epidemic is already advanced grew at a significantly slower pace between 1980 and the early 1990s than those of other counties in which changes in the cumulative prevalence of AIDS was lower" (Bloom and Mahal, 1995: 21).

Recent studies on the macroeconomic effects of HIV/AIDS, particularly in sub-Saharan Africa, however, revealed significant effects on growth rates. A study by Bonnel (2000) found the effects of HIV/AIDS on GDP to be severe. He found that for a typical sub-Saharan country with "AIDS prevalence rate of 20 percent, the growth rate of GDP would be some 2.6 percentage points less each year and at the end of a 20 year period GDP would be 67 percent less than otherwise" (Bonnel, 2000: 846). Bonnel (2000) called this a "vicious downward spiral." Arndt and Lewis (2000) agree with Bonnel's (2000) conclusions. By employing a computable general equilibrium model for South Africa containing fourteen productive sectors and generating simulation results, Arndt and Lewis (2000: 856) found the GDP to be "17 percent lower in the AIDS scenario as opposed to the non-AIDS scenario" in South Africa. Moreover, they noted that nearly half the deterioration in growth performance is attributable to the shift in government spending toward health expenditure (Arndt and Lewis, 2000). Finally, Arndt and Lewis (2000) suggested that the slow and gradual nature of the impact of the epidemic over a long period points to a drag in the rate of capital accumulation (through a savings to current expenditure), and that these effects become amplified over time.

Another recent study found that the annual per capita growth in half of the countries of sub-Saharan Africa fell from 0.5–1.2% as a direct result of AIDS. According to Guinness and Alban (2000), per capita GDP by 2010 in some of the hardest hit countries may drop by 8%, and per capita consumption may fall even further. In some countries estimates indicate that the number of people living in poverty has already increased by 5% as a result of the pandemic. Moreover, countries with an adult population infection of less than 5% are estimated to experience a modest HIV/AIDS impact on GDP growth rate—about a 0.6% decline per annum. According to the UNAIDS and WHO (2000), GDP growth may decline by 2% annually as the HIV prevalence rate rises to 20% or more. In South Africa, where the rate of prevalence of the epidemic has reached 20% of the population, HIV/AIDS is projected to reduce the economic growth rate by 0.3–0.4% annually, resulting by the year 2010 in a GDP 17% lower than it would have been without AIDS and wiping out. $22 billion from the country's economy (UNAIDS and WHO, 2000). In Botswana, where infections have reached 36% of the population, AIDS is estimated to reduce the government's budget by 20% and the income of the poorest households by 13% (USAID and WHO, 2001). Botswana's GDP is also estimated to decline by 1.5% annually, thus shrinking the economy by nearly one-third by 2025 (Guinness and Alban, 2000).

In sum, recent studies focusing on the macroeconomic impacts of HIV/AIDS in sub-Saharan Africa suggest that a rising HIV/AIDS epidemic will lead to negative growth, a fall in the level of GDP, and a substantial decline in domestic savings.


## POLICY IMPLICATIONS

HIV/AIDS presents major challenges to policy makers in sub-Saharan Africa. The disease is only one of numerous problems that plague social and economic development in the subregion. Countries in Africa are mired in such problems as high debt, endemic poverty, political instability, and civil conflicts. These problems require fiscal resources, which are in short supply in Africa. One major challenge faced by policy makers is how to prioritize programs and make prudent budget allocations in light of limited fiscal resources. Within the health sector, there is competition for scarce resources by the other critical diseases that—along with HIV/AIDS—kill most Africans annually, including malaria, diarrhea, and respiratory infections. To ensure adequate allocation of budgetary resources toward combating HIV/AIDS, policy makers must elevate the epidemic to the top of their respective national development agendas. As noted by the United Nations Development Program (UNDP), "national development plans and poverty reduction strategies must take full account of the challenge of both slowing the spread of the epidemic and coping with its impact" (UNDP, 2001: 2).

Loewenson and Whiteside (1997: 2) contend that any efforts to mitigate the impact of AIDS must be based on a sound analysis of the scale and nature of that impact. According to them, it is crucial for policy makers to support further research and analysis of the effects of the epidemic. In addition, one of the important challenges is to identify how best to ensure that existing research is effectively translated into action. Bonnel (2000: 846) suggests that reversing the "vicious downward spiral" caused by the spread of the HIV/AIDS epidemic and mitigating its impact requires three sets of measures: "First, sound macro-economic policies to achieve growth which will enable governments to engage with the epidemic and its impacts; second, sound structural reform aimed at addressing some of the factors accounting for the spread of HIV in the first place, in particular social, gender, income, and ethnic inequality; and third, modification of the incentives for people to change their behaviors."

Researchers and policy makers at the 2000 AIDS and Economics Symposium in Durban, South Africa, contend that no country in Africa has developed concrete programs to control the disease, even though the problems caused by the adverse effects of the AIDS epidemic on both the micro and the macro levels of the economy have existed in the region for nearly two decades. The final statement from the AIDS and Economics Symposium (2000) recommends that individual African countries raise awareness among policy makers and communities about social and economic losses due to HIV/AIDS, design cost-effective programs at the community and national levels to control the disease, stimulate research into finding a vaccine against HIV/AIDS, and better manage national health services and delivery systems (Mwabu, 2000). Moreover, the process of policy development must include the active participation of HIV-infected individuals. These individuals can provide a more effective perspective and clearer understanding of the disease, how it is transmitted, how it can be prevented, and how to live with it.

The UNDP contends that any response to HIV/AIDS must be directed at reducing the number of new infections and reversing the spread of the epidemic, expanding access to care and treatment for HIV/AIDS patients, and mitigating the impact of the epidemic on social and economic development by intensifying national poverty reduction efforts and providing support for individuals affected by the epidemic (UNDP, 2001). Overall, policy makers must undertake or support the following strategic measures to mitigate the effects of the epidemic.

First, they policymakers must identify ways and means to reduce the number of HIV infections in their respective countries. While 'technical solutions,' such as safe blood transfusions, treatment of sexually transmitted diseases and condom utilization are important in the fight against HIV/AIDS, prevention is the most effective means to reduce the rate of infection. Ways to prevent new infections include funding programs that promote information dissemination, education, and communication, establishing program of voluntary testing for HIV/AIDS, and prohibiting discrimination against HIV/AIDS patients. To implement this strategy, leaders at all levels of government including those at the community level, must initiate a dialogue with civil society groups and leaders in all economic sectors on measures to reduce the spread of the disease. The dialogue should focus on modes of HIV transmission, reduction of the stigma of the disease, and prevention of infection. Through open dialogue with civil society, national and community leaders in Uganda, Tanzania, and Senegal have executed such a prevention strategy, which according to current research findings has made significant advances in reducing HIV infection rates (UNDP, 2001). The success in these countries is the outcome of visionary leadership and commitment at the highest political levels. The same measures can be replicated in other African countries.

Second, governments need to adopt a multisectoral approach to mitigate the effects of the epidemic. National and local leaders must mobilize households, local communities, the business sector, the education sector, the health sector, and government ministries to effectively fight HIV/AIDS. As noted by Stover and Bollinger (1999: 12), "by stimulating and supporting a broad multi-sectoral approach that includes all segments of society, governments can create the conditions in which prevention, care and mitigation programs can succeed and protect a particular country's future development prospects." At the household level, the effects of HIV/AIDS can be reduced if adequate resources are available to fund programs that support families with infected adults, such as home care for ill individuals, foster care for AIDS orphans, and support for the educational expenses of children orphaned by AIDS (Stover and Bollinger, 1999). Furthermore, policy makers can mitigate the impact of HIV/AIDS at the household level "by working through existing indigenous traditional community mechanisms instead of displacing them" (UNAIDS, 1999: 11).

The education sector plays a key role in the identification of opportunities for remedial action and containment of HIV/AIDS. The policy implications for decision makers in the education sector include the need for more flexibility to accommodate children or orphans who must work to support themselves or their families, the need to pay for the educational expenses of children whose parents have died or are ill as a result of AIDS, and the need to replace teachers who succumb to AIDS. The business community should formulate a set of practical guidelines to assist individual firms in developing or expanding prevention programs in the workplace, such as providing HIV/AIDS education, along with condoms and health services. Such programs are critical in those business sectors with a higher incidence of HIV infection, such as commercial farming, transportation, and mining. Businesses should work in partnership with nongovernmental organizations (NGOs) and governmental agencies to create an environment that fosters HIV/AIDS prevention. The health sector should play the most important role in the sectoral response to combat the AIDS epidemic. It must therefore be adequately funded to provide comprehensive care and support for HIV-positive individuals. Comprehensive care must encompass the provision of both lifesaving drugs and psychological support to HIV-positive individuals, along with their families and their communities, to cope with the economic and social consequences of sickness and death due to AIDS. In addition, there must be training for health care workers. The support of international community is crucial to implement a comprehensive care program since African health systems lack the technical knowhow, AIDS-related drugs, diagnostic equipment, and necessary infrastructure to fight HIV/AIDS.

Finally, a strong commitment by the top leadership in each country is crucial in the fight against HIV/AIDS. According to Stover and Bollinger (1999), policy makers must elevate AIDS to the top of the national policy agenda. Akukwe (2000) contends that the ultimate responsibility for managing and ultimately controlling the spread of the HIV/AIDS pandemic lies with Africans and their leaders. Without sustained progress in improving governance (e.g., adequate political representation of various shades of opinion at the highest decision-making apparatus of government, implementation of transparent macroeconomic policies that promote private enterprise, and engagement of community-based entities and NGOs in the design and provision of grassroots health programs), no amount of international donor assistance will resolve the current HIV/AIDS crisis (Akukwe, 2000). A UNDP (2001) study identified several ways of effective governance in response to HIV/AIDS, centering on elevating key policy makers, including executive leaders, prominent politicians, business leaders, and traditional or community leaders, to the top of the anti-HIV/AIDS campaign. In other words, effective response to the epidemic requires political will, clear vision, and the commitment of leaders at the highest level of government. Experience in countries with successful HIV/AIDS campaign programs indicates that success (in the reduction of infection rates) is an outcome of committed and visionary leaders who managed to allocate adequate resources to the health sector and mobilize communities, the private sector, government entities, and civil society to fight HIV/AIDS. Furthermore, it takes responsible leaders to develop a "large-scale strategic response to HIV/AIDS which involves multi-sectoral planning providing the necessary framework for a coordinated response of diverse range of partners" (UNDP, 2001: 1). Effective governance of the HIV/AIDS response is also contingent upon the ability of governments "to decentralize and empower local authorities and provide adequate resources and work hand in hand with communities that are at the front lines of prevention and care" (UNDP, 2001: 2). Finally, the HIV/AIDS governance challenge must encompass the development of national capacities for effective management and implementation of programs in which special efforts are needed to "establish strong accountability frameworks, budgeting systems, managerial capacities and monitoring and evaluation systems that will facilitate the rapid disbursement of funds and effective implementation at scale" (UNDP, 2001: 2).

In sum, African leaders need to take the lead against mitigating the effects of HIV/AIDS. They must mobilize civil society, donors, the private sector, and the general public, and place the epidemic at the center of their development agendas. Success ultimately depends on full mobilization of all sectors and levels of government and civil society (UNDP, 2001).

## REFERENCES

Akukwe, C. (2000). HIV/Aids in Africa: Rethinking Current Strategies. http://allafrica.com/stories/200204010527.html.

Arndt, C., Lewis, J. D. (2000). The macro implications of HIV/AIDS in South Africa: A preliminary assessment. *J South Afr Econ* 68(5):856–857.

Bloom, D. E., Mahal, A. S. (1995). Does the AIDS Epidemic Really Threaten Economic Growth? *NBER Working Paper*. New York: National Bureau of Economic Research Publication.

Bonnel, R. (2000). HIV/AIDS and economic growth: A global perspective. *J South Afri Econ* 68(5):820–855.

Cohen, D. (1999). The HIV Epidemic and the Education Sector in sub-Saharan Africa. UNDP Issues Paper no. 32. New York: UNDP. Available at http://www.undp.org/hiv/issues.english/issue32e.htm.

Cohen, D. (1992). The Economic Impact of the HIV Epidemic. UNDP Issues Paper no. 2

Cuddington, J. (1993). Modelling the macro-economic effect of AIDS with an application to Tanzania. *World Bank Econ Rev* 7(2):173–189.

Cuddington, J., Hancock, T., Roberts, A. (1994). A dynamic aggregative model of the AIDS epidemic with possible policy intervention. *J Policy Model* 16(5):473–496.

Dixon, S., McDonald, S., Roberts, J. (Jan. 26, 2002). The impact of HIV and AIDs on Africa's economic development. *Brit Med J* 324:232–235.

Drysdale, S. (2000). *Health Sector*. Durban, South Africa: AIDS Brief for Sectoral Planners and Managers.

Economic Commission for Africa. (2000). HIV/AIDS and Economic Development in Sub-Saharan Africa. Addis Ababa, Ethiopia.

FAO (1997). *The Rural People of Africa Confronted with AIDS: A Challenge to Development*. Rome: FAO.

Forgy, L., Mwanza, A. (1994). *The Economic Impact of AIDS in Zambia*. Lusaka, Zambia: Report for the Ministry of Health/USAID.

Gonzalez, M. (2001). The Development Context: What Is the Impact of HIV/AIDS? available at: http://www.caa.org.au/world/health/hiv/study/index.html#development.

Guinness, L., Alban, A. (2000). The economic impact of AIDS in Africa: A review of the litreature. UNAIDS Background Paper for African Development Forum 2000, AIDS: The Greatest Leadership Challenge, Addis Ababa, Ethiopia, available at: http:\\www. unaids. org.

Hecht, R., Adeyi, O., Semini, I. (2002). Making AIDS part of the global development agenda. *Finan Dev* 39(1):36–39.

ILO (2000). *HIV/AIDS in Africa: The Impact on the World of Work*. Addis Ababa, Ethiopia: International Labor Office Publication Bureau.

Kabbaj, O. (2001). The African Development Bank Calls for Partnership in Order to Face the HIV/AIDS Pandemic in Africa. available at: http://www.afdb.org/knowledge/speeches2001/pdt-aid-pandemic-in-africa-2001e.htm.

Kambou, G., Devarajan, S., Over, M. (1992). The economic impact of AIDS in an African country: Simulation with a general equilibrium model of Cameroon. *J Afr Econ* 1(1):103–130.

Kelly, M. J. (1999). The impact of HIV/AIDS on schooling in Zambia, XIth International Conference on AIDS and STDs in Africa, Lusaka.

Kwaramba, P. (1997). The Socio-Economic Impact of HIV/AIDS on Communal Agricultural Systems in Zimbabwe. Zimbabwe Farmers Union, Friedrich Ebert Stiftung Economic Advisory Project. working paper 19. Harare, Zimbabwe.

Loewenson, R., Whiteside, A. (1997). Social and Economic Issues of HIV/AIDS in Southern Africa. SAFAIDS, Harare, Zimbabwe: http://www.iaen.org/impact/sfaids1.pdf.

Morris, C., Burdge, D. R., Cheevers, E. J. (2001). *Economic Impact of HIV Infection on a Cohort of Male Sugar Mill Workers in South Africa from the Perspective of Industry.* Vancouver, BC, Canada: University of British Columbia.

Msobi, N. Msumi, Z. (2000). HIV/AIDS and other chronic conditions: Home based care study, Bagamoyo District, Tanzania. AIDS and Economics Symposium, Durban, South Africa.

Mwabu, G. (2000). Summary and closing remarks. AIDS and Economics Symposium, Durban, South Africa, http://www.iaen.org/conferences/durbansym/papers/mwabuclose.pdf.

Over, M. (1992). The Macro-Economic Impact of AIDS in sub-Saharan Africa. technical working paper no. 3. Washington, DC: World Bank.

Parker, R. (2002). The global HIV/AIDS pandemic, structural inequities, and the politics of international health. *Amer J Pub Health* 92:343–346.

Roberts, M., Rau, B., Emery, A. (1996). *Private Sector AIDS Policy: Business Managing HIV/AIDS.* Arlington, VA: Family Health International/AIDSCAP.

Ruger, J. P., Jamison, D. T., Bloom, D. E. (2001). Health and the economy. In: Merson, M. H., Black, R. E., Mills, A. J., eds. *International Public Health.* Gaithersburg, MD: Aspen, pp. 617–666.

Shapouri, S., Rosen, S. (2001). Toll on agriculture from HIV/AIDS in sub-Saharan Africa. In: Issues in Food Security. Washington, D.C.: USDA, Economic Research Service. Agriculture Information Service bulletin number 765-9.

Simon, J. L., Rosen, S., Whiteside, A., Vincent, J. R., Thea, D. M. (2000). The response of African businesses to HIV/AIDS. *HIV/AIDS in the Commonwealth 2000/01.* London: Kensington.

Stover, J., Bollinger, L. (1999). *The Economic Impact of AIDS.* The Futures Group International in collaboration with Research Triangle Institute (RTI) and the Center for Development and Population Activities (CEDPA), Washington, D.C.

Topouzis, D. (1998). The Implications of HIV/AIDS for Rural Development Policy and Programming: Focus on Sub-Saharan Africa. New York: UNDP study paper no. 6.

UNAIDS (2002). *Report on the Global HIV/AIDS Epidemic 2002.* Geneva, Switzerland: UNAIDS.

UNAIDS (2002). *A Review of Household and Community Responses to the HIV/AIDS Epidemic in the Rural Areas of sub-Saharan Africa.* Geneva, Switzerland: UNAIDS.

UNAIDS and WHO. (2001). AIDS Epidemic Update: December 2001. Geneva: WHO.

UNAIDS and WHO. (2000). AIDS Epidemic Update: December 2000. Geneva: WHO.

UNDP. (2001). HIV/AIDS, Governance Challenge. Bureau for Development Policy (BDP), Special Initiative on HIV/AIDS, UNDP, New York. Available at: http://www. undp.org/hiv/HIVgovern.pdf.

USAID (2001a). *Leading the Way: USAID Responds to HIV/AIDS.* Washington, DC: United State Agency for International Development.

USAID (2001b). *The HIV/AIDS Crisis: How Does HIV/AIDS Affect African Businesses?* Washington, DC: United State Agency for International Development.

Whiteside, A. (1996). *The HIV/AIDS epidemic: Background, implications and concepts.* Paper prepared for the workshop, Including HIV/AIDS in Development Aid. Durban, South Africa.

Whiteside, A., O'Grady, M. (2000). The Economic Impact of HIV and AIDS in Southern Africa. available at http://www.idsnet.ch/modules.php?name = NewsletterArticle&-sid = 160.

World Bank. (1997). *Confronting AIDS: Public Priorities in a Global Epidemic.* New York: Oxford University Press.

World Bank. (1998). *Malawi AIDS Assessment Study.* Washington DC: World Bank.

World Bank. (2000). *Exploring the Implications of the HIV/AIDS Epidemic for Educational Planning in Selected African Countries: The Demographic Question.* Washington DC: World Bank.

World Bank. (2002). Education and HIV/AIDS: A Window of Hope. Washington, DC: World Bank.

# 16

## Industrial Development Policies and Strategies
### The African Case

**DESTA MEBRATU***

*UNIDO Consultant, Addis Ababa, Ethiopia*

## INTRODUCTION

In the 1950s and 1960s, Africa held great promise for its people. Two world wars left Africa largely unscathed, destructive civil wars had been uncommon, and independence brought a wave of optimism that anything could be achieved. Since the 1960s, there have been a plethora of development strategies that have been prescribed for promoting development in Africa. Africa's economic performance during the following two decades was nevertheless conspicuously disappointing compared to its past achievements and relative to its potential and rich endowment. Although some African countries showed a positive growth trend in the 1990s, the region as a whole is still faced with various problems that are associated with underdevelopment.

The objective of this chapter is to review the different categories of development strategies promoted in the region over the last decades, evaluate their development impact, analyze their limitations, and identify the core development challenges that need to be addressed in policy making. Accordingly, the first section presents the major categories of development strategies in Africa. This will be followed by the performance of the national economies in general and the industrial sector in particular. The

*Current affiliation: Program Officer, Regional Office for Africa, United Nations Environment Program, Nairobi, Kenya

third section analyzes the source of limitations of the development strategies. Finally, the core development challenges that need to be addressed in the region and the corresponding strategic elements are presented in the fourth section.

## MAJOR CATEGORIES OF DEVELOPMENT STRATEGIES

Since the 1960s, a number of development strategies have been prescribed for promoting development in Africa. An overview of development efforts in Africa shows that there are three major groups of development strategies that have influenced national development strategies: (1) the United Nations (U.N.) development initiatives, (2) the regional development initiatives, and (3) the Bretton Woods institutions initiatives. The following subsections present the main features of these three major categories of development strategies.

### United Nations Development Initiatives

The core element of these initiatives is designing development decades in different sectors. The concept of development decades evolved as the United Nations sought to promote active programs of development for the third world that would halt the widening gap between developed and developing countries. The United Nations Third Development Decade, which began in 1981, was based on the assumption that reforming the international economic system was essential for the health of both developed and developing countries. Since then, there have been numerous development initiatives adopted specifically for Africa by the U.N. General Assembly. Some of the major industry-related development initiatives adopted by the United Nations include (Mebratu, 2000a): (1) the U.N. Industrial Development Decade for Africa (UN-IDDA) in 1980, (2) the U.N. Transport and Communications Decade in Africa (UNTACDA) in 1980, (3) the U.N. Program for Action for African Economic Recovery and Development (UNPAAERD) from 1986 to 1990, and (4) the U.N. System-Wide Special Initiative for Africa in 1995.

The development decades of the United Nations have been limited to the broad recognition of the need for promoting social development in Africa. The UN-IDDA was based on the much wider concept of designing and constructing internal engines of growth in Africa to replace the long and accelerating weakening of an external engine of growth resting on trade and economic relations with the developed economies of Western Europe and the United States. The focus of the program was the production, supply, and use of factor inputs for designated core industries and the use of the outputs of core industries for promoting the growth of strategic sectors (UNECA and UNIDO, 1989).

### Regional Development Initiatives

In parallel with the U.N. development initiatives, there have been numerous regional initiatives promoted by the United Nations Economic Commission for Africa (UNECA) and the Organization of African Unity (OAU). The regional development initiatives were guided by the principles of the Lagos Plan of Action (LPA), which was adopted by the Summit of African Heads of States in 1980. Some of the major development initiatives that belong to this group are (Mebratu, 2000a): (1) Africa's Priority Program for Economic Recovery (APPER) from 1986 to 1990, (2) the African Alternative Framework for Structural Adjustment Programs (AAF-SAP) in 1989, (3) the treaty for the African Economic Community in 1991, and (4) the Cairo Agenda for Action in 1995.

A thorough assessment of African socioeconomic development toward the end of the 1970s prompted the member states of the OAU to adopt the LPA and the Final Act of Lagos for the collective industrialization of Africa. The adoption of LPA was based on the two principles of self-sustained and self-reliant industrialization. The principles of self-reliance involve the use of indigenous raw materials, indigenous labor and management, domestic and regional markets, and so on (UNECA, 1980). Self-sustainment relies on internal as opposed to external requirements and stimuli. The LPA not only emphasizes industrial growth, but more specifically, self-sustained industrialization designed to meet domestic needs. A number of strategic measures were proposed, such as (UNECA, 1980): (1) the building up of an industrial production structure capable of meeting changing domestic needs through the preparation and implementation of an integrated industrial development program, (2) the establishment of a core of production, marketing, research, and development activities that provide the impetus for economywide growth processes, (3) the selection of products appropriate to the satisfaction of the basic needs of the mass of the population and to the promotion of self-sustaining development, (4) the expansion and restructuring of domestic markets by integrating the rural economy with the modern sector through the construction of the necessary infrastructure, (5) subregional economic integration aimed at developing basic and capital goods industries in integrated subregional markets, and (6) the generation and use of information and data as required by governments in their economic planning and decision making.

The core element of the Final Act of Lagos was the promotion of regional integration as the principal instrument for Africa's self-sustainment. As was pointed out by UNECA (1998:21), however

> the African experience in economic integration has so far produced very limited results. Progress is scanty in the areas of production, infrastructure and other elements that could sustain development efforts. The institutional framework for integration is faced with several difficulties that are far from being resolved. In addition to the lack of funds for their implementation, integration programs and schemes are so discordant from one subregion to another that they give rise to hopeless situations. All actors are not allowed to participate in the integration process, which is seen so far as an affair of governments.

## Bretton Woods Institutions (BWI) Initiatives

The other group of initiatives that has affected the course of events since the 1980s has been the interventions made by the World Bank and the International Monetary Fund (IMF) in economic policy making of most African countries. The African economic crises were exacerbated in the beginning of the 1980s by the collapse of their balance-of-payments situation, their growing indebtedness, and their urgent need for resources and foreign currency for developmental purposes. This has left African countries with no option but to approach the World Bank and IMF for "bail-out" support (UNECA and UNIDO, 1989). In response to these crises, the Bretton Woods Institutions (BWIs) came up with a package of assistance that contained key policy and institutional reforms as conditions of participation. These included (Mebratu, 2000a): (1) a structural adjustment program (SAP) since 1982, (2) an enhanced structural adjustment facility (ESAF) since 1988, and (3) a highly indebted poor countries (HIPC) initiative since 1996.

Starting in 1980, the Bretton Woods initiatives—led by neoliberalism and the regional initiatives led by the LPA—competed for dominance in influencing Africa's development policies and strategies. A closer look at the philosophical and episte-mological foundation of these groups of strategies shows that the initiatives promoted by UNECA and the Bretton Woods initiatives were fundamentally different. The regional strategic initiatives spearheaded by UNECA were based on the achievement of self-reliance and self-sustainment through active state intervention (UNECA and UNIDO, 1989). In contrast, the initiatives promoted by the BWIs were based on the promotion of a laissez-faire approach governed by the market.

Until the early 1980s, the national development strategies of most African countries promoted active state intervention in development planning and implementation. The financial crises of the 1980s forced most African countries to accept the policy reform requirements of the BWIs. As a result, an increasing number of African countries participated in one form or another of SAP. By 1993, a total of thirty-five sub-Saharan African countries had implemented SAPs (Stein, 1998). According to the World Bank (1989), however, the lack of full-fledged political commitment to the reform process at the national level did not lead to the desired results in most of the countries in which SAP was implemented.

## THE PERFORMANCE OF THE AFRICAN ECONOMY

Despite the numerous international and regional initiatives and interventions that have been made, Africa as a region continued to show negative economic growth over the past two decades. It is true that the recent economic recovery in Africa that began in 1994 has given grounds for renewed optimism both within and outside the region. The recovery, however, is fragile, and its sustainability is in question, not only because it has not been underpinned by a strong investment performance, but also because it has been highly vulnerable to external shocks, including weather and the terms of trade. This section presents the major features of African countries' economic performance. The first subsection discusses the overall national economic performance, while the second subsection covers the development and performance of the industrial sector.

### National Economic Performance

In general, the economy of Africa declined from the 1970s through the mid-1990s. Tables 1 and 2 show how the African economy declined in terms of gross domestic product (GDP) and per capita GDP after an impressive start at independence. As can be seen from Table 1, Africa had an annual average real GDP growth of 4.7% between 1966 and 1973. This declined to 1.5% between 1990 and 1995. In 1996, for the first time in the last two decades, the average growth in GDP reached 4.4%. This was due to a number of favorable conditions, including a good harvest and a price increase in the primary commodities exported from Africa.

Similarly, Africa registered 2.0% average per capita growth between 1966 and 1973. This figure declined to −1.1% for the period between 1991 and 1995. The figures

**Table 1** Growth in GDP in Africa

| 1966–1973 | 1974–1980 | 1981–1990 | 1990–1995 | 1996 | 1997 |
| --- | --- | --- | --- | --- | --- |
| 4.7 | 2.8 | 1.9 | 1.5 | 4.4 | 3.0 |

*Note*: annual percentage change in real GDP.
*Source*: Extracted from World Bank, 1997.

showed some improvement in 1996 and 1997 as a result of the improvement in GDP during those years.

In contrast to (or as a result of) its dismal state of economic growth, Africa's debt has grown geometrically during the last three decades. In 1960, Africa's external debt amounted to less than $3 billion, and the average debt service ratio was only 2% of exports. During the 1970s and 1980s indebtedness advanced rapidly, from $84,049 million in 1980 to $223, $298 million in 1995. In 1996, the total debt increased by about 5%, to $235.4 billion. The region's aggregate ratio of debt to exports was estimated at 239.9% in 1996. Table 3 shows the extent of Africa's debt as measured by its GDP and export earnings.

Africa has also missed out on the large expansion of international trade. Africa's share of global trade has fallen from around 3% in the 1950s to around 1% in 1995. Its contribution to global manufacturing was a mere 0.3% in 1995. The problem is not only in relative terms to the rest of the world, but also in absolute terms. According to the African Development Bank (ADB, 1997), in 1995, total African exports in nominal dollar terms were actually 10% below the level of 1980. Unlike much of the rest of the world, exports relative to GDP ratio have actually declined, from 31% in 1980 to 28% in 1995 (World Bank, 1997). What is particularly interesting is the structure of exports. In 1970, 92% of African exports were in primary commodities (e.g., fuels, minerals, and metal). In 1991, the figure was exactly the same (World Bank, 1993).

The terms of trade for Africa have increasingly declined in the past fifteen years. The average annual declines were −6.2, −2.5, and −3.2, respectively, for the periods 1980–1985, 1986–1990, and 1991–1995 (ADB, 1997). The relative decline in the terms of trade in Africa is also directly related to the shifting nature of global production. The emphasis on raw material and primary product export is very problematic in an era in which knowledge becomes a larger proportion of the value added to commodities (Stein, 1998). The poor performance on the export side of manufacturing is also reflected in the production side. Between 1980 and 1993 manufacturing in sub-Saharan Africa increased by only 0.9% per annum compared to the preadjustment decade when it increased by a reasonable 4.3% per year (World Bank, 1995). Relative to GDP, industry in sub-Saharan Africa fell between 1980 and 1995. One

**Table 2** Africa's Gross Domestic Product Growth per Capita

| 1966–1973 | 1974–1990 | 1991–1995 | 1996 | 1997 |
| --- | --- | --- | --- | --- |
| 2.0 | −0.7 | −1.1 | 0.8 | 1.8 |

*Note*: annual percentage change.
*Source*: Compiled from World Bank, 1997.

**Table 3**  External Debt and Related Statistics for the Whole of Africa

| Indicator | 1996 | 1997 | 1998 |
|---|---|---|---|
| Total debt (in billions of dollars) | 340.6 | 344.1 | 350.1 |
| As a percentage of GDP | 67.8 | 64.7 | 65.5 |
| As a percentage of exports of goods and services | 293.4 | 283.9 | 302.8 |
| Debt service (in billions of dollars) | 31.0 | 33.0 | 35.7 |
| As a percentage of exports of goods and services | 29.3 | 21.3 | 30.9 |

*Source*: Compiled from UNECA, 1999c.

indicator of the lack of progress in this area is the percentage of the laborforce in industry, which was 9% in 1994. In 1960, the figure was 7% (UNDP, 1997).

In general, the preceding discussion indicates that by all major economic indicators Africa is in a worse position than it was in the 1970s. The economic malaise facing Africa today is serious. About three-fourths of the countries in the region are classified as low-income. Of all the developing regions in the world, Africa is the most overburdened by foreign debt, the most dependent on foreign financial and technical assistance, and the most dependent on food aid and imported food. On the social front, the social development efforts undertaken by African national governments, bilateral development agencies, and international organizations have led to some positive but limited results.

For instance, between 1960 and 1994, life expectancy increased from forty years to fifty-two years, while since the mid-1980s the proportion of the population with access to safe water has almost doubled, from 25–43% of the total (Stein, 1998). During the past two decades adult literacy advanced from 27–55%. Between 1960 and 1991 female school enrollment at the secondary level quadrupled, from 8–32%. Over the past three decades, the infant mortality rate fell from 167 live births per 1000 to 92 per 1000. Even if there are some improvements in the sphere of social development, Africa still has the worst record on social indicators.

## The Performance of the Industrial Sector

One of the major reasons for the failure of African economic growth is the poor performance of the manufacturing sector (UNECA, 1999a). The performance of Africa's industrial sector over the past two decades has showed neither meaningful progress in industrial growth nor significant structural change. The average regional annual growth has been only 0.6% since 1990 (while the population growth rate for the same period has averaged 3%), and the share of manufacturing in GDP averaged only about 11% in the 1990s (UNECA, 1996). The industrial sector is also characterized by both a low level of capacity utilization (30–50% on average) and extreme dependence on foreign inputs, expertise, and exchange.

In general, the industrial sector in the region is very weak, contributing only about 1% to the world's industrial output. Even that small contribution comes mainly from twelve of the fifty-three African countries, which more or less possess a relatively diversified industrial base. The remaining forty-one countries contributed only 28% of the region's manufacturing value added (UNECA, 1996).

The average figures of the different economic groupings are shown in Table 4. Africa registered 2.0% of total MVA (Manufacturing Value Added) growth rate and

**Table 4**  Total MVA Growth Rate and per Capita MVA Growth Rate

| Economic groupings/regions | Total MVA growth rate (%) | | Per capita MVA growth rate (%) | |
|---|---|---|---|---|
| | 1980–1990 | 1990–1998 | 1980–1990 | 1990–1998 |
| Low income | 6.7 | 6.5 | 4.2 | 4.4 |
| Middle income | 6.8 | 5.7 | 4.3 | 3.4 |
| High income | 2.6 | 3.1 | 0.4 | 1.5 |
| Africa | 4.3 | 2.0 | 1.3 | −0.6 |

*Source*: Compiled from UNIDO, 2001a.

−0.6% of per capita growth rates between the years 1990 and 1998. The corresponding growth rate for low-income countries is 6.5% for total MVA and 4.4% per capita.

Africa's percentage share of the world's MVA remained almost constant from 1990 to 1999, having the same 1% share in both years. As can be seen in Table 5, Africa's percentage share of MVA from developing countries declined from 5.8% in 1990 to 4.3% in 1998. On the other hand, its share of population from the developing world increased from 14.7% in 1990 to 15.7% in 1998.

As can be seen in Table 6, the average share of MVA in the GDP of African countries declined from 13.4% in 1985 to 12.9% in 1998. If we look at the trend of the low-income groups, the average share of MVA in GDP grew from 16.4% in 1985 to 20.3% in 1998. Similarly, the share of MVA in GDP grew from 20.2% in 1985 to 22.9% in 1998 for middle-income countries. In the case of the high-income countries, however, the share of MVA in GDP decreased from 22.5% in 1985 to 21.2% in 1998. This could be explained by the shift in the industrial structure from manufacturing to services at the later stage of the industrialization process.

According to UNIDO's country performance survey (2001a), out of forty-five African countries covered in the survey, thirty-two had better performance, both in terms of total MVA growth rate and per capita MVA growth rate, between 1980 and 1990 than between 1990 and 1998. Again out of the forty-five countries, thirty registered a negative per capita MVA growth rate for the period from 1990 to 1998. Algeria, Burundi, Cameroon, and Democratic Republic of the Congo have shown the largest decline, both in terms of total MVA and per capita MVA growth rate.

**Table 5**  Africa's Share of MVA and Population from the World and Developing Countries

| | 1990 | 1995 | 1996 | 1997 | 1998[a] | 1999[b] |
|---|---|---|---|---|---|---|
| Percentage share in world's total MVA | 1.0 | 0.9 | 0.9 | 0.9 | 1.0 | 1.0 |
| Percentage share from developing countries' MVA | 5.8 | 4.4 | 4.3 | 4.2 | 4.3 | |
| Population share from developing countries | 14.7 | 15.3 | | | 15.7 | |

[a] Provisional.
[b] Estimate.
*Note*: at constant 1990 prices.
*Source*: Compiled from UNIDO, 2001a.

**Table 6**   Average Share of MVA in GDP of Economic Groupings and Regions

| Developing countries/region | 1985 | 1990 | 1995 | 1996 | 1997 | 1998[a] |
|---|---|---|---|---|---|---|
| Low income | 16.4 | 18.6 | 20.4 | 20.7 | 20.7 | 20.3 |
| Middle income | 20.2 | 22.1 | 22.8 | 23.0 | 23.5 | 22.9 |
| High income | 22.5 | 21.8 | 21.0 | 21.1 | 21.2 | 21.2 |
| Africa | 13.4 | 13.4 | 12.7 | 12.5 | 12.8 | 12.9 |

[a] Provisional.
*Source*: Compiled from UNIDO, 2001a.

Thirteen of the countries have managed to maintain a positive growth rate both in total and per capita MVA. It is only Uganda, however, that has managed to register a significant growth rate both in terms of total MVA (4.4–14.2%) and per capita growth (2.1–11.0%).

If the sectoral structure of the manufacturing industry in Africa is considered, it can be seen that the African manufacturing industry is dominated by production for domestic demand and the processing of raw materials for export. As can be seen from Table 7, agroindustries are the most dominant industries in the manufacturing sector, followed by the mining industry. The chemical and engineering industries

**Table 7**   Distribution of Value Added (Percentage) of Selected Branches (1990 and 1997)

| Industrial classifications | 1990 | 1997 |
|---|---|---|
| Food products | 9.8 | 8.7 |
| Beverages | 12.9 | 12.4 |
| Tobacco | 8.6 | 6.5 |
| Textiles | 8.5 | 7.1 |
| Wearing apparel | 6.1 | 7.1 |
| Leather and fur products | 6.0 | 6.8 |
| Footwear | 8.0 | 8.0 |
| Wood and cork products | 12.2 | 9.6 |
| Paper | 4.8 | 3.6 |
| Industrial chemicals | 4.1 | 3.1 |
| Other chemicals | 5.0 | 4.8 |
| Petroleum refineries | 8.7 | 7.2 |
| Products of petroleum and coal | 2.4 | 2.2 |
| Rubber products | 4.2 | 3.7 |
| Pottery, china, earthenware | 9.4 | 7.7 |
| Glass | 3.8 | 3.6 |
| Other nonmetallic mineral products | 10.9 | 9.2 |
| Iron and steel | 4.1 | 3.2 |
| Nonferrous metals | 4.4 | 3.6 |
| Metal products | 7.1 | 5.3 |
| Nonelectrical machinery | 2.4 | 1.8 |
| Electrical machinery | 2.7 | 1.4 |
| Transport equipment | 3.1 | 1.6 |

*Source*: Compiled from UNIDO, 2001a.

**Table 8** Number of Enterprises and Employees (1995–1998)

| Country | Number of enterprises | | | | Number of employees | | | |
|---|---|---|---|---|---|---|---|---|
| | 1995 | 1996 | 1997 | 1998 | 1995 | 1996 | 1997 | 1998 |
| Algeria | 23,902 | 23,230 | | | 373,826 | 326,669 | | |
| Burkina Faso | 235 | 263 | 285 | 304 | | | | 12,065 |
| Cameroon | 212 | 194 | 206 | 198 | 50,863 | 53,606 | 53,754 | 53,092 |
| Egypt | | | 9511 | | | | 1,099,400 | |
| Eritrea | 138 | 157 | 205 | 223 | 13,872 | 13,354 | 14,921 | 15,103 |
| Ethiopia | 501 | 642 | 741 | 762 | 90,213 | 90,039 | 92,365 | 93,216 |
| Kenya | 3685 | 3843 | 3524 | 4355 | 204,793 | 210,423 | 214,490 | 216,889 |
| Malawi | 102 | 102 | 102 | 102 | 35,630 | 38,834 | 36,892 | 40,160 |
| Mauritius | 927 | 896 | 882 | 927 | 110,439 | 107,354 | | |
| Morocco | 6259 | 6282 | 6396 | 6578 | 453,575 | 463,237 | 475,267 | 489,854 |
| Mozambique | 391 | 390 | 318 | 166 | 42,745 | 36,260 | | |
| Niger | 47 | 49 | | | | | | |
| Senegal | 231 | 245 | 248 | | 31,885 | 38,850 | 35,348 | |
| South Africa | | 25,839 | | | 1,440,100 | 1,456,400 | 1,395,600 | 1,333,800 |
| Tunisia | 10,985 | 12,667 | 11,372 | 11,847 | 273,588 | 287,397 | 288,262 | 292,078 |

*Source*: Compiled from UNIDO, 2001a.

make only a modest contribution to the African manufacturing. Beverages, wood products, and nonmetallic minerals made the highest contribution. With the exception of apparel and leather products, the contribution of all subsectors declined from 1990 to 1997.

In terms of the number of enterprises, the overall trend has shown an increase. With the exception of Cameroon and Mozambique, in which there was a decline, and Malawi and Mauritius, in which the number remained the same, the other countries showed an increase from 1995 to 1998. Even if most countries showed an increase in the number of enterprises, the corresponding increase in the number of employees is minimal. For instance, in the case of Ethiopia, the number of enterprises increased by almost 50% from 1995 to 1998. (See Table 8.) The corresponding increase in the number of employees is less than 4%, however. Similarly, the number of enterprises in Eritrea grew by almost 65% from 1995 to 1998, but the corresponding growth in the number of employees was about 9%. In the case of Ethiopia, this can be explained by two factors. Primarily, most of the new industries are micro and small-scale industries that generate few jobs per industrial unit. Second, the marginal employment gain from the increased number of enterprises was partially lost because of the layoffs resulting from the restructuring and/or privatizing of the already existing medium- and large-scale enterprises that used to be owned by the government. As a whole it can be said that the contribution of the African manufacturing sector in terms of employment generation is still very low.

In general it can be concluded that the contribution of the manufacturing sector to sustainable development in Africa has been minimal. In fact, especially during the second half of the 1980s and the first half of the 1990s, the significant slowdown in industrial growth that is associated with slightly declining rates of growth in GDP reflects a changed structural relationship in the form of deindustrialization (UNIDO, 1999a). Manufacturing, which has been the lead sector in the fast-growth developing countries in Asia and Latin America, has been a lagging sector in Africa since the 1980s. In view of the central role of the manufacturing industry in fulfilling the sustainable development objectives of African countries, African governments and their international partners should put more effort into expanding the manufacturing sector of the region on a sustainable basis.

## ANALYSIS OF DEVELOPMENT POLICY FAILURES IN AFRICA

There is very little disagreement regarding the severity of the economic crises facing most African countries. However, there are divergent views regarding the causes of such poor economic performance. This section presents the divergent views regarding the reasons why the various development strategies failed in Africa and analyzes the basic reasons for their failure.

### The Divergent Views

The World Bank and IMF relate the failure of development strategies in Africa to the macropolicy distortions that are induced by African governments. According to this group, the situation is aggravated by such endogenous factors as inappropriate economic development policies and market distortion, a lack of political will to make the necessary economic reform, lack of skilled manpower for public sector management and entrepreneurial development, and high population growth, which exceeds 3% per annum for many African countries. There are others who blame forces beyond the control of economic policy makers in the region for the poor performance. According to this group, the following are some of the exogenous factors that are most commonly cited as reasons for Africa's economic failure (Mebratu, 2000a): (1) an inequitable global trading system, which led to the continuous decline of the prices of primary commodities, (2) the increasing debt burden, for which debt servicing will require up to 85% of export earnings, (3) the lack of foreign direct investment in African economies, (4) the continuous decline of overseas development assistance, and (5) natural calamities, such as drought.

When one looks at the better performance of Africa in earlier periods in which there were similar external shocks, and the faster growth of low-income countries in other regions that have faced similar external conditions as Africa, the contribution of disoriented domestic policies to economic problems seems to weigh more heavily. As pointed out by Hyden (1983), changes in the international environment may accelerate or impede social and economic processes within a given country but these factors are not determining elements. Even if the exogenous factors exacerbated the situation, what makes the economies of Africa particularly vulnerable to exogenous shocks and natural disasters are the peculiar domestic conditions prevailing in Africa. Factors such as the rudimentary nature of its infrastructure, its limited technological base, and the structural disarticulation of its economies, with domestic production almost totally dependent on imported capital and intermediate goods, contribute to under-development.

Others argue that the reason is more than policy failures on the African govern-ment side, even if they have been contributing factors. Howard Stein argues that the reason is largely theoretical. According to Stein (1998:12), "adjustment theories have their roots in neo-classical economic theory which is badly flawed as a guide to under-standing how to build economies capable of structural transformation and sustainable development." In other words, it is not an implementation problem but a conceptual problem. Also according to Stein (1998), the thinking behind the model is rational-deductive and axiomatic. It is rational-deductive in the sense that the behavior of agents is predetermined by a set of rational rules that are deductively posited.

This rationally predictable behavior arises from a set of market signals. It is axiomatic in the sense that consumers and private producers are assumed to be utility and profit maximizers that rationally respond in an efficient manner if the market signals are correct: "The obvious problem with the approach is that the need for adjustment is a product of the model of adjustment. The model of adjustment is a product of a series of theoretical premises of abstraction. Thus any divergence of the real cause from the premised cause will lead to serious errors in the realm of policy formulation and implementation" (Stein, 1998:13).

Similarly, UNECA (1989) argues that the conventional SAPs promoted by the World Bank and IMF are inadequate in addressing the real causes of African crises, which are structural in nature. According to UNECA (1991:23), "the analysis of the evaluation carried out by the World Bank in 1988 indicated that sub-Saharan African countries implementing structural adjustment programs, experienced, after adoption of SAPs: GDP growth declines from 2.7 percent to 1.8 percent; a decline in the investment/GDP ratio from 20.6 percent to 17.1 percent; a rise in the budget deficit from −6.5 percent to −7.5 percent of GDP; and a rise in debt service/export earning ratio from 17.5 percent to 23.4 percent. The figure also shows that there has been only a minor improvement in the current account/GDP ratio from −9.4 percent to −6.5 percent."

UNECA (1989) concluded that both on theoretical and empirical grounds the conventional SAPs are inadequate in addressing the real causes of economic, financial, and social problems facing African countries, which are structural in nature. UNECA further proposed an alternative framework for a structural adjustment program that advocates the need for adjustment programs to emphasize structural transformation in the case of Africa and take into consideration the structure of production and consumption and the people. The failure of structural adjustment programs in Africa has compelled even the major financing institutions to recognize the positive role the state can play in the process of development beyond acting as night watchman.

## Factors of Limitations

Many authors have tried to analyze the limitations of the development strategies promoted in Africa from different perspectives. Most of these analyses do not go beyond finding an explanation as to why a specific development strategy failed due to factors that fall outside the process of developing the strategy in the first place. It is true that both endogenous factors and exogenous factors have significant influence on the effectiveness of a given policy framework. Nevertheless, it is important to critically evaluate the basic premises of the policy formulation process in order to overcome the limitations of the development policy framework in Africa. The following are some of the major factors that affected policy development and implementation in Africa.

1. *Preanalytic vision*: Self-reliance and self-sustainment as described in the LPA have been the key elements of the preanalytic vision for most strategies developed at the regional level. While self-reliance and self-sustenance that take the internal and external environments into account are very much desirable, the interpretation given to them in the African context seems to be very much influenced by the desire to be free of any colonial vestige. Furthermore, their implementation has had limited success because of the lack of the necessary prerequisites for implementation at the national level. On the other hand, neoclassical economics has been the dominant school of thought providing the preanalytic basis for most of the strategies that have been developed by the BWIs. The success of the neoclassical economic model is dependent on the fulfilment of the basic assumption of a perfectly competitive market and rationally deductive behavior of consumers who exist in a very different context in Africa (if they do at all). The incompatible preanalytic visions adopted for Africa have been one of the major sources of flaws in African policy development.

2. *"One-size-fits-all" model*: Most of the development efforts that have been undertaken so far are based on imposing a development model that has been thought to be successful somewhere else with the general assumption that it should work for promoting development in Africa. The effort of imposing the dominant model in Africa has failed because of the absence of the basic prerequisite for the success of the neoclassical model. An SAP

is characterized by its package of reform measures that are developed based on the theoretical assumptions of the neoclassical economic model, which includes the presence of a uniformly functioning market. In the face of local realities significantly varying from the theoretical assumptions, this one-size-fits-all model fails. Degefe (1998:14) noted that "while this modality may be correct for those economies where markets are very well developed and are at the full employment level, this 'one-fits-all' model approach is wrong for those countries suffering the consequences of high unemployment of natural and human resources and the market is in the process of development."

3. *Local responsiveness*: Both the regional initiatives and the strategies promoted by the BWIs suffer from a lack of understanding of how the local socioeconomic dynamics function. Africa's primordial and patrimonial relationship, which has been referred to as the "economy of affection" by Hyden (1983), has never been given due consideration in either economic analyses or strategy development. It is the lack of consideration of this important aspect of the African socioeconomic fabric that has led to failure after failure of development strategies promoted by the various national and international organizations. This disregard of the local dynamics of the African socioeconomic structure has stymied the effectiveness of the proposed development policies as instruments of a meaningful transformational process.*

4. *Sectoral synergy*: One of the shortcomings of development policy analysis in the African context is the limited attention given to understanding and strengthening sectoral synergies and complementarities that are critical to the promotion of development. As a result, most of the policies and strategies have the tendency to promote favoritism in one sector or emphasize one sector's development at the expense of another. This has negatively affected the dynamic nexus that needs to be developed between such major sectors as the public and the private sectors, the agriculture and industrial sectors, and the formal and informal sectors.

5. *Factor variation*: From a systems dynamics perspective, it is crucial to make distinctions between the fundamental and facilitating factors of the development process and understand the interaction within and between these factors (Mebratu, 2000b). Even if there are numerous factors that may influence the development process, all of these factors can be categorized into fundamental and facilitating factors, depending on their level of influence in the whole process. The level of distinction made between and the treatment given to fundamental and facilitating factors of the development process is a critical element in determining the effectiveness of a development strategy. The dominant strategies that have been promoted so far in Africa do not make any distinction between the fundamental factors that determine the nature and direction of the development process and the facilitating factors that determine the pace of the development process. The enormous

---

* Even if Hyden presented the "economy of affection" as a threat to modern economic development, it may have some positive elements that could be useful to promote development in an African context.

effort that has been put into creating the facilitating factors thus has had limited success in the absence of having the fundamental factors in place.

6. *Socioecological consideration*: The predominant notion of socioecological considerations in the policy arena is to address them in the context of developing addon environmental policies. The add-on approach has a limited success both as a policy and as a technical intervention (Mebratu, 2000b). In the policy domain, sustainable development requires main-streaming socioecological and socioeconomic principles in development policies and strategies. Studies conducted in different countries have, however, indicated that all macroeconomic policies have different forms of socioecological impacts. In order to avoid adverse socioecological impacts, it is advisable to give early consideration to socioecological factors in the process of generating development strategies. Virtually no consideration is given to socioecological issues in most development strategies. Even those that give minor recognition to socioecological factors have not gone beyond a brief statement about the importance of giving them due consideration.

7. *Adaptive mechanisms*: The failure of the principal development strategies prescribed for Africa has been evident since the early years of their imple-mentation. There have been some attempts to learn from the lessons, but they were not aimed at reviewing and reorienting the whole process of the strategy development process. The process of strategy development involves a sequence of interacting stages that determine the whole effectiveness of the strategy. This process includes the preanalytic vision, procedures, model, detailed strategies, implementation, and indicator parameters for evalua-tion. Most of the review processes in Africa were limited to the manipulation of the indicator parameters, implementation factors, and some of the strat-egy elements; they have never gone to the level of reviewing the whole process of strategy development. Considering the chronic nature of strategic failure in Africa, a review process that is limited to the lower end of the strategy development process cannot lead to any improvement.

8. *Socially efficient privatization*: Experience from other parts of the world shows that the development of the domestic private sector is a crucial ele-ment for developing national capacity and promoting industrial develop-ment. In this context, privatization in Africa should have been used as a strategy for the transfer of state assets to strategically selected domestic private capital or as an instrument of creating a broad national entrepreneurial base. Empirical evidence shows that privatization in Africa has not been premised on that objective. According to Mkandawire (1998), privatization in Africa has been largely driven by the fiscal concerns of the state, the pronouncements on the inefficacy of public enterprises and ide-ological aversion to state ownership, and the unfounded belief that state investment always "crowds out" private investment or is inherently inferior in performance to private investment.

9. *Informal and small-scale sectors*: A study of the recent economic history of many African countries that have gone through periods of internal tur-moil shows that it is the informal and small entrepreneurs that have kept the economies going. As it stands today, the bulk of their activity is in the nature of trading, but in the process, business skills and cost-effective

management of men, materials, and money have been developed. What is needed is to transfer this skill to an industrial culture that becomes part of the formal economic structure. In recent years most of the national programs have recognized this potential and proposed measures for strengthening and developing the small and medium-sized industries. What is contemplated is a progressive process of graduation to larger scales of industrial activity.

## Lessons to Be Drawn

At independence in the 1950s and 1960s, newly elected sub-Saharan administrations saw industrialization as the logical, preferred road to self-sufficiency and self-sustained growth. It was intended that the shift of labor and other resources from low-productivity agriculture to high-productivity manufacturing, and the development of linkages among enclave mining, energy, or plantation agriculture and an emergent, modernizing manufacturing industrial sector, would create millions of new jobs, simultaneously raising living standards (UNIDO, 1999a). Since then, national industrial development policies and strategies have gone through different stages, which are listed in Table 9.

Although these initiatives have had limited success in terms of promoting industrial development, they provided a basis for understanding what kind of policy interventions do not work within the region. The following are some of the major lessons that could be drawn from the initiatives in Table 9:

Limitation of supply-driven initiatives: The development and promotion of "supply-driven" and "top-heavy" regional initiatives in the absence of the appropriate mechanisms, infrastructural foundations, and sense of ownership at the national level has limited possibility of success, hence the development of national industrial development strategies that are responsive to local and global socioeconomic dynamics should be given priority.

**Table 9**  The Evolution of Industrial Policy (1960–2000)

| 1960–1979 | 1980–1995 | 1995–2000 |
|---|---|---|
| Intervention and regulation | Market-orientation and deregulation | Industrial governance |
| Self-sufficiency and indigenization | Foreign direct investment (FDI) | Privatization and FDI |
| Public ownership | Privatization | Public–private sector cooperation |
| Import controls and tariff protection | Trade and investment liberalization | Promotion of clusters |
| Inward-driven industrialization | Outward orientation | Supply-side support from SMEs |
| Industrialization to achieve structural transformation | Promoting efficient industries | Global competitiveness |

*Source*: Adapted from UNIDO, 1999b.

Transformational rather than transplanting process: Attempting to bring about industrial development through the promotion of economic reform packages under one-size-fits-all models has had limited success. The promotion of sustainable industrial development will require a transformational process that provides the context for the development of flexible and responsive strategies that evolve with changing circumstances.

Complementary roles of market and governments: Markets and governments have complementary roles in industrialization. Examples of successful industrialization in other regions over the last few decades indicate that government intervention should be supportive of market trends and competitive forces and should facilitate change. It should be targeted in such a way as to address specific market failures or externalities directly, but there do remain cases in which selective and temporary support by government is warranted.

Industrial competitiveness as the key factor: Success in economic development depends on a country's ability to break into the virtuous cycle of investment-economic growth-competitiveness-investment. Competitiveness at the national level depends increasingly on productivity as the offspring of technological advancement. In an era of an increasingly globalized and competitive economy, African countries should continuously improve their competitiveness even in the traditional sectors in which they are believed to have a comparative advantage.

Infrastructural prerequisites for regional integration: In the context of regional integration efforts, member states should focus on creating the necessary infrastructural prerequisites for widening industrial cooperation and inter-Africa trade. In this context, the countries with well-performing industrial sectors in each subregion should take the initiative to promote industrial cooperation within their respective subregion.

Strengthening the entrepreneurial base: For any kind of industrial transformation, entrepreneurial capacity is synonymous with human capital. In this context, Africa must urgently deal with the transformation of the informal sector and the strengthening of small-scale industries. There is evidence to suggest that at this level of operation the indigenous base can be developed to put in place a sustainable industrial culture.

Capacity for a knowledge-based-economy: The traditional labor-intensive and resource-based industries are losing market share to the fast-growing skills-, information-, and knowledge-intensive industries. While Africa does not enjoy a comparative advantage in these industries, the region risks being locked into a slow growth path of traditional industries if technology is not upgraded. Even traditional industries lose competitive advantage if they fail to upgrade technology and skills. In this context, African countries need to enhance their capacity for being active participants in the evolving knowledge economy.

In general, most of the regional initiatives developed as collective expressions of the political will of the governments that have emerged from the struggle for political independence have limited responsiveness to both local and global factors of dynamics. In this context, it is hoped that the recent development initiatives promoted by regional and international organizations can accommodate some of the lessons discussed above. This includes the New Partnership for Africa's Economic Development (NEPAD), which is expected to be implemented by the newly established African Union (AU),* and the Comprehensive Development Framework (CDF) promoted by the World Bank.

## THE WAY FORWARD

### Development Models

During the twentieth century human endeavor was directed largely at creating economic growth through the use of natural resources and sustaining expansion by subordinating nature to satisfy human needs. Practiced in both the industrialized world and the developing countries, this endeavor has not only strained the physical resources that sustain human organizations, it has also created many social tensions that threaten mankind today.

Consequently, a number of new problems appeared at the turn of the twenty-first century. These problems have manifested themselves in social and ecological limits to realizing and maintaining widespread public welfare. This situation calls for finding ways of achieving organizational stability and social equity and adapting society to live as a part of the global ecosystem (Meadows, et al., 1992).

From a policy perspective, the distinction to be made between growth and development has held a prominent place in the debate. In this context, it will be important to understand the distinctions and relationships among economic growth, social development, and sustainable development. In the context of this chapter, such distinctions and relationships can be depicted by the scheme given in Figure 1. Productive engagement constitutes the basis for this scheme (Mebratu, 2000a), without which neither growth nor development will be conceivable. Productive engagement thus constitutes the common denominator for economic growth, social development, and sustainable development.

Neoclassical economics, which has been the theoretical underpinning of economic growth, assumes that the issue of wealth distribution and equity can be met through the "trickle-down" effect of wealth accumulation while ecological factors can be addressed through resource substitutability and the "internalization of externalities" through market instruments. While both the trickle-down effect and the internalization of externalities may make some positive contributions, recent trends and the current state of the world clearly show that these instruments are far from being sufficient in addressing the problem.

The recognition of the limitation of exclusively "growth-centered" policies in terms of addressing the issue of wealth distribution has led to a second form of policy, which is "development-centered" (Mebratu, 2000a). The evolution of other schools of economic thought has played a significant role in the promotion of development-centered policies that combine competition-based economic growth with social welfare. In these kinds of policy systems, an improved environmental quality

---

* African leaders decided in 2001 to transform the OAU to the AU, with the mandate of promoting economic development and cooperation in the region.

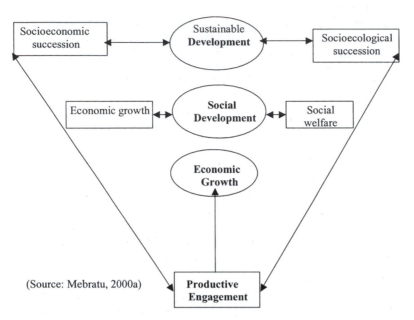

(Source: Mebratu, 2000a)

**Figure 1**  Distinction and relationship among economic growth, social development, and sustainable development.

for living is addressed as one of the elements of social well-being. As a result, countries that have adopted development-centered policies have a better record in environmental quality and management in addition to having improved social equity when compared to countries that promote growth-centered policies.

The increasing evidence showing different aspects of global ecological imbalance and the growing global economic disparity, however has necessitated the evolution of a third generation of policies—those that are "sustainability-centered" (Mebratu, 2000a). These kinds of policies will focus on promoting a productive engagement that ensures the socioeconomic and socioecological success of societies. This does not in any way exclude competition-based economic growth, but promotes a qualitatively different kind of economic growth that is responsive to socioecological and socioeconomic requirements.

## The Policy Challenges

Understanding the nature of the socioecological signals within the African socioeconomic context is important in effectively responding to these signals and promoting sustainability within the region. The major sociological signals related to the source- and sink-function indicate that the region is faced with major challenges that can only be overcome through a fundamental socioeconomic transformation process that is responsive to the emerging global socioeconomic reality. The transformation of the socioeconomic structure of the region through sustainable industrialization constitutes the core element of this socioeconomic transformation. The following are identified as the principal policy challenges that have significant influence on the promotion of sustainable development in Africa.

## Carrying Capacity and Population Mismatch

At the turn of the twentieth century, the total population of Africa was only 118 million, 7.4% of the world's population (UNEP, 2000). In the next fifty years the population grew slowly. There has been a dramatic population increase since the 1950s because of the sharp decline in mortality rates. By 1997, the population was estimated at 778.5 million, more than 13% of the world's population (UNFPA, 1996). It is projected that by the year 2025, the population in Africa will almost double to 1453 million, representing about 18% of the world's population (UNFPA, 1996). Despite such rapid population growth, Africa remains underpopulated. Its population density of 249 per 1000 hectares* is low, compared to the world average of 442 per 1130 found in Asia (WRI, UNEP, UNDP, and WB, 1998).

The population pressure becomes significant when it is seen within the context of the carrying capacity of the African natural resource base. Land is the critical resource and the basis for survival for most people in Africa. Agriculture contributes about 40% of regional GDP and employs more than 60% of the labor force (World Bank, 1998), yet this continent, perhaps more than others, has real physical constraints on the productivity of its land. Climatically, Africa can be distinguished as one of the driest continents. About 50% of the continental surface has a rainfall deficit season of sufficient magnitude to restrict agriculture and make the area arid or semiarid (Lewis and Berry, 1988). This situation manifests itself in a significant mismatch between the population and the carrying capacity of the resource base.

*Policy Response.* Addressing the mismatch between the carrying capacity of African natural resources and the increasing population pressure would require transformation at the following two levels: demographic transformation and economic transformation. The demographic transformation should be aimed at containing the momentum of population pressure to a sustainable level within the limit of the carrying capacity of the natural system. The economic transformation should be aimed at reducing the environmental load from socioeconomic activities so that it would be within the limit of the assimilative and regenerative capacities of the natural environment. There is a strong complementarity and interdependence between the demographic and economic transformation, one having either a positive or negative influence on the other.

One of the key elements in the promotion of these transformations is the issue of land tenure. Throughout history, patterns of land ownership have shaped the relationship between nature and society and the patterns of human relations in nearly all societies. They have also helped to determine the possibility and pace of structural transformation and economic change (Mebratu, 2000a). Some tenure patterns have manifested and solidified social inequality, while others have promoted social mobility—or even equity in some cases. Some tenure patterns have blocked technological progress, while others have encouraged it. In essence, changing the relationship of people to the land has meant changing the relationship of people to one another (Eckholm, 1979). Despite the issue of land reform being at the core of political reforms

---

* There is a wide variation in population density within the region. Mauritius has the highest population density in Africa, at 5562 per 1000 hectares, while Namibia's 19 people per 1000 hectares is the lowest (WRI, UNEP, UNDP, and WB, 1998).

in the last three decades, most African countries are still lacking an appropriate property rights framework that promotes sustainable development (Mebratu, 2000a).

From a sustainable development perspective, it would be unrealistic to think of a single property rights model that could be applicable for all African countries. As pointed out by Hanna and Munasinghe (1995), sustaining environmental resources is not dependent on a particular structure of property regime, but on a well-specified property rights regime and a congruency of that regime with its ecological and social context. In this context, African countries need to address the policy challenge of developing a property rights regime that would promote economic efficiency, social equity, and effective environmental resource management.

*Strategies.* The following are some of the major strategic measures that need to be taken in order to address the issue of carrying capacity and resource mismatch:

> *Efficient land tenure*: Promote the establishment an effective land tenure system as part of all environmental resource management (protection) programs by developing a combination of private, communal, and state ownership structures and adopting dynamic and transparent mechanisms for the definition and effective protection of property rights.
>
> *National industrial development strategies*: Develop comprehensive national industrial development strategies that take into account the resource potential of the country within the context of the regional and global economy and promote the structural transformation of the national economies on a sustainable basis.
>
> *Community-based family planning*: Family planning programs have been around for decades in most African countries, but their effectiveness has been limited. For family planning to be effective, it needs to be community-based, -developed, and -implemented within the specific socioeconomic context. In this regard, African countries need to develop national population control strategies that are mainly structured around community-based family planning.

### Poverty and Environmental Degradation

For the last few decades, the top political imperative and policy challenge throughout the continent has been (and remains) the poverty of the majority of the people. According to recent projections, Africa is the only continent in which poverty is expected to rise during the coming decades if things are not changed. The human and income poverty indicator produced by UNDP (2001) shows that fifteen of the twenty-two countries that have more than 40% of their population below the national poverty line are in Africa. The nation with the highest percentage of poor people (86% below the national poverty line) is an African country. According to UNECA (1999b), about 44% of Africa's population was living below a poverty line of $39 per person per month in the early 1990s. Poverty and environmental degradation are linked in a vicious circle in which people cannot afford to take proper care of the environment. Almost 40% of people in sub-Saharan Africa live below the poverty line, and both income poverty and human poverty are increasing (UNDP, 1997).

Industrial development contributes to alleviating poverty by raising productivity, reducing risk exposure, and increasing the physical income-generating assets of the poor. The growth of nonfarm employment is an important means of income stabilization for the poor, and job creation is undoubtedly central to poverty alleviation. There is a growing consensus that a main concern of industrial policies and strategies in African countries should be poverty alleviation through industrial development. Sustainable poverty reduction through industry requires (UNIDO, 2001b): (1) development of a coherent systemwide industrial strategy, (2) improvement of industrial governance processes and development of a supportive institutional infrastructure, (3) strengthening of micro, small, and medium-sized enterprises and creation of sustainable employment, (4) an upgrade of technological capacities and skills and an increase in the access of countries to knowledge and modern technology, and (5) effective integration of the least developed countries into global production networks.

*Strategies.* The following are identified as the major strategies that would require global and regional cooperation to reduce and eradicate poverty within the region through sustainable industrial production: (1) *structural transformation of the economy*—take the structural transformation of the economy as the highest policy priority in terms of alleviating poverty and protecting the natural environment, (2) *business incubator programs*—develop and implement small business incubator programs that facilitate the transformation of the informal sector to formal sector production, and (3) *agroindustrial support*—provide targeted technical and financial support programs that promote the development of micro and small enterprises, with special focus on agroindustries.

## Financial Resource Depletion

Financial resources are one of the major resources that have been seriously depleted in Africa over the last decades. Between 1982 and 1991, capital flight from the severely indebted, low-income countries in sub-Saharan Africa was about $22 billion (Ajayi, 1997). This was equivalent to about half the external resources required for development, as estimated by Amoako and Ali (1998). It should also be noted that as Africa struggles to cope with debt, the average capital flight/debt ratio was over 40% for about eighteen African countries. For some countries it is even higher.

For instance, this figure was 94.5% for Nigeria, 94.3% for Rwanda, and 74.4% for Kenya (UNECA, 1999c). Relative to other regions, Africa invests less of its own capital at home than other developing areas. Ajayi (1992) indicated that despite a lower level of wealth per worker than any other region, Africa's wealth owners have relocated 37% of their wealth outside the continent. This compares to a ratio of 17% in Latin America and only 3% in East Asia.

*Strategies.* The following are identified as the major strategies that would require global and regional cooperation to contain and reverse the flow of capital from African countries and thereby enhance their domestic investment capacity for sustainable development.

> *Fighting corruption*: Corruption raises transaction costs and its unpredictability makes returns on investment uncertain, discouraging private investment. African countries has need to develop efficient anticorruption systems that include the introduction of clearly defined policy regimes and the facilitation of transparent decisionmaking at all levels of government.

*Promotion of capital market*: Capital markets spread risks among investors and can create investment opportunities for the nonprofessional and typically small investor. In this context, African countries need to take the necessary steps to encourage the establishment and strengthening of an efficient and transparent capital market.

*Confidence-building measures*: The problem with African capitalists is not a lack of thriftiness but a lack of faith in their own countries as investment sites and the consequent propensity to expatriate capital abroad. In this connection, African countries need to take the necessary confidence-building measures to develop faith among domestic investors.

## Human Resource Depletion

Human capital plays a decisive role in the process of economic development, and investment in this field constitutes a prerequisite for sustained economic growth. Most African countries suffer from a low level of investment in human capital. This has been further aggravated by a massive outflow of the few skilled workers they have trained using scarce domestic resources. In a 1995 World Bank study, it was noted that some 23,000 qualified academic professionals emigrate from Africa each year in search of better work conditions. As a result, African countries have lost as much as one-third of their highly skilled personnel in recent decades, having already lost an estimated 60,000 middle- and high-level managers between 1985 and 1990 (Aredo and Zelalem, 1998).

Another major development challenge that has been faced by Africa from a human resource perspective is the alarming spread of the AIDS (acquired immuno-deficiency syndrome) epidemic in the region. In 1982 there was only one country in sub-Saharan Africa (SSA) that had the prevalence rate of above 2%. By 1998, twenty-one countries in SSA had a prevalence rate that is above 6% (Mebratu, 2000a). It is not only the sheer size of the population affected by AIDS (Acquired Immunodeficiency Syndrome) that is a grave concern for SSA, but its attack on the most productive segment of the society—those persons between 18 to 45–makes it detrimental to the overall development efforts in SSA. The number of people living with AIDS in sub-Sahara African countries in 1999 has been estimated to be 8.7% of the total population (UNDP, 2001). This is the highest among regions when compared to 0.3% for high-income countries, 1.0% for middle-income countries, 1.3% for low-income countries, and 1.1% for the world average.

*Policy Response.*   The policy responses that have been promoted to contain and/or reverse the brain drain can be broadly categorized into the following two groups on the basis of the approaches they employed. The first approach considers the brain drain as a loss and devises the following policy measures to counteract this loss (Brown, 2000): (1) *restrictive policies* that are designed to make migration more difficult through different mandatory requirements, including compulsory national service, (2) *incentive policies* that are designed to make emigration less attractive, for instance by offering highly skilled workers incentives to remain in their home countries, and (3) *compensatory policies* whereby either the receiving country or the individual migrant gets taxed in order to compensate the sending country for the loss of its human capital.

The limited effectiveness of the above policy measures has led to a new form of thinking around the brain drain issue that recognizes the potential that a country's highly skilled expatriate presents to its development process. This approach has led to the development of the following two options (Brown, 2000):

The *Return option* was first implemented in the 1970s through the 1980s and 1990s when a few countries encouraged their highly skilled expatriates to return home. A few countries, such as India, South Korea, and Taiwan, have been able to implement this strategy effectively.

The *Diaspora option* is based on the recognition of brain drain as a potential gain to the sending country. The diaspora option promotes the creation of networks of highly skilled expatriates that are referred as expatriate knowledge networks. The idea is to set up connections and linkages between highly skilled expatriates and their counterparts in their country of origin.

While the long-term effectiveness of the restrictive policy option could be questionable, each of the other options may make its own contribution in terms of enabling African countries to utilize the skills of their citizens for their development effort. African countries should thus give the highest policy priority to develop a coherent policy and strategy based on the combination of the above options.

More important, however, African countries need to review their human resource management strategies. The human resource management strategies of most African countries are mainly based on a tactical approach that emphasizes administrative rules, procedures, authorities, power dynamics, heavy reliance on past experience, and short-term decisions. Since it rejects new developments and seeks to perpetuate the status quo, it has limited tolerance and attraction to a highly skilled group. In this context, African countries need to adopt the "strategic management approach" that focuses upon communication, participation, teamwork, appraisal, training, and organizational development strategies (Mebratu, 2000a). The shift from the tactical to strategic human resource management approach and the reversal of the brain drain should be taken as a major challenge for the promotion of sustainable development in the region.

*Strategies.* The following are identified as the major strategies that would require global and regional cooperation to contain or reduce the impact of the brain drain on African countries' development effort.

*Conducive environment*: Most of the push and pull factors that drive the brain drain process are related to the economic and institutional conditions of the working environment. In this context, African countries need to strive to create a conducive working environment with merit-based incentive systems that are manageable within their own means.

*Expatriate knowledge networking*: The development of networks that facilitate the exchange of information and cooperation among highly trained and skilled expatriates spread all over the world should be promoted by African countries. In this context, countries can get an insight from African knowledge networks such as the South African Network of Skills Abroad (SANSA).

*Reorientation of technical cooperation*: Technical cooperation aimed at capacity building for development constitutes the major part of development cooperation over the last few decades. If technical cooperation is to become more effective, it needs to be reoriented in such a way that it will promote endogenous capacity utilization and serve as a vehicle for reversing the brain drain.

*Community-based education*: The major factor that aggravated the spread of AIDS within Africa is the lack of awareness about the disease and the low level of attitudinal change. The experience of some African countries has shown that consistent community-based education complemented with prevention support measures is the most effective strategy to contain the spread of AIDS.

## Mainstreaming Sustainability

One of the key challenges of African countries in the context of sustainable development is the challenge of meeting the development aspirations of their people within the limits of the regenerative capacity of the source function and the assimilative capacity of the sink function of the natural ecosystem. The major limitation that emerges from policy analysis with respect to environmental issues is the limitation of considering environmental issues as an add-on element in development policies and strategies (Mebratu, 2000b).

Most of the intervention measures so far have not seriously considered altering economywide policies to achieve broad environmental objectives on a sustainable basis, but instead have chosen to rely on specific complementary measures to mitigate environmental harm (Munasinghe, 1996). Even if the role of add-on environmental laws and regulations is significant in terms of reducing the impact of existing environmental problems, the promotion of sustainable development will require a systematic integration of environmental considerations in national development policies and strategies. In this context, examining the environmental implications of macroeconomic and sectoral policies of an economywide nature and facilitating the mainstreaming of environmental issues in national policy regimes become vital.

Panayotou and Hupe (1996) concluded that using environmental and social policies as add-ons or as supplementary and compensatory parallel policies to mitigate or cushion the environmental and social impacts of macroeconomic policies is second best to the full integration of these policies with the economic policies in the context of a sustainable development strategy. In this context, African countries would have an added benefit by mainstreaming environmental considerations in their industrial development strategies, as most of them are in the process of developing such strategies.

*Strategies.* The following are identified as the major strategic measures that would require regional and global cooperation in terms of achieving the mainstreaming of sustainability:

*Training of policy makers on SID*: Provide training for middle- and high-level policy makers on the basic principles and tools of sustainable industrial development to facilitate the mainstreaming of sustainability in industrial policies and strategies.

*Reorient tertiary-level education*: Develop selected course modules on sustainable industrial development that could be provided to tertiary-level education in selected fields, such as engineering, management, and economics.

*Ecoindustrial parks*: The development of new industrial zones and/or estates is one of the core elements of the industrial development strategies of most African countries. The development of these industrial zones or estates as ecoindustrial parks that are based on ecoefficient industrial arrangement can provide the basis for mainstreaming sustainability in the industrial development effort of the region.

## Globalization and Marginalization

Globalization has been less favorable to Africa than to other developing regions and has created a divergence in living standards in relation to those of developed countries and the fast-growing industrializing countries of East and Southeast Asia. Africa's failure to penetrate international markets for manufactured goods highlights the region's vulnerability to globalization (UNIDO, 1999b). To make things worse, existing manufacturing industries are increasingly going out of business (even from the national market) because of their inability to compete with imported industrial products from other countries through the liberalized trade regimes.

International trade is an important source of industrial growth. In this context, African industry will need to diversify away from its traditional trade patterns, which are marked by excessive dependence on exports of raw materials and semiprocessed goods and on traditional comparative advantages of raw materials and unskilled labor, which are becoming increasingly less important for world competitiveness. Development of domestic manufacturing is particularly important because globalization fosters industrial agglomeration, especially within increasing returns of scale for industry. Manufacturing firms concentrate in locations with easy access to dense networks of input suppliers. The wage differential effect, which is expected to counter this agglomeration tendency, is becoming weaker over time as the share of labor costs in total costs falls in a widening range of manufacturing activities (UNCTAD, 1999).

*Policy Response.* The African experience shows that without enhancing domestic manufacturing capacity globalization in the form of trade and investment liberalization leads to marginalization. The region's "speed of integration index" was negative between 1961 and 1990. In the 1990s it averaged 0.9 annually, compared with 6.0 for low- and middle-income regions as a whole. The main challenge facing African decisionmakers is to reverse the region's marginalization in the world economy and enhance the competitiveness of domestic industries. This requires strong industrial growth in line with economic transformation experienced by other developing regions. Deindustrialization, as reflected in a declining share of MVA in GDP, must be halted in all countries. At the same time, the share of Africa in world manufacturing value added, which has hardly changed over the last two decades, will need to increase significantly (UNIDO, 1999b).

Very low and in some cases declining levels of factor productivity is the fundamental problem that has undermined the ability of industrial enterprises in Africa to withstand heightened import competition and break into export markets (Bennell,

1994). In this context, African countries need to take the improvement of productivity and competitiveness of their industries as one of their priorities in order to reduce their marginalization from an increasingly globalized economy. As was pointed by the African Roundtable of Eminent Persons (2001), to be part of the globalized economy Africa has to move from being primarily a producer of agricultural products and other commodities to a manufacturing, value-added economy.

*Strategies.* The following are identified as the major strategic measures that would require regional and global cooperation in terms of avoiding the increasing marginalization of Africa from the globalized economy:

> *Industrial productivity and competitiveness*: For African industries to be competitive in the global market, they need to improve their productivity significantly. In this context, African countries and their partners need to develop support programs aimed at improving industrial productivity, which leads to improved competitiveness and reduced environmental impacts.
>
> *Regional cooperation and integration*: Regional trading blocks are emerging as the major vehicles for maintaining and/or gaining the maximum benefit from the increasingly globalized economy. This is particularly important for most African countries, which have significant resource and market limitations when facing the challenge of globalization. In this context, African countries need to develop the necessary physical and institutional infrastructure in order to strengthen their regional cooperation and integration efforts.
>
> *Industrial technological capability*: The development of industrial skills and technological capability is the basic prerequisite for African countries to expand their manufacturing base and effectively participate in the global economy. The slow development of such skills and capability could be a binding constraint on any country's sustainable industrialization effort.

## Trade, Environment, and Development

One of the major conclusions reached during the Earth Summit of 1992 was that "the major cause of the continued deterioration of the global environment is the unsustainable pattern of consumption and production, particularly in industrialized countries" (UN, 1992). The Earth Summit underlined the deep divide in consumption and pollution between developed and developing countries, whereby 20% of the world's population in the rich North accounts for 50–90% of consumption and pollution (IIED, 1997). To remedy this, Agenda 21 called on industrialized countries to take the lead in making the shift toward sustainable consumption and production. Agenda 21 also called for the promotion of a balance among international trade flows, development needs, and environmental sustainability and for making them mutually reinforcing.

The issue of sustainable production and consumption has been expressed in a surge of measures as policy makers, businesses, and citizens try to interpret and implement the sustainable consumption and production agenda. European governments have set health standards for such products as food and clothing that affect the human ecology of production across the globe. Consumer demand for organic products is opening up new trade opportunities for producers in the South. Corporations are integrating environmental specifications into their supplier policies, and some are demanding independent verification of environmental performance (Robins et al., 2000). Many of these actions have implications for international trade, and these implications are expected to increase in the following years as more and more measures are taken to promote sustainable consumption and production.

*Policy Response.* It is generally believed that the shift toward sustainable consumption and production will lead to multiple socioeconomic and socioecological benefits; nevertheless, the atmosphere surrounding international discussion on trade and the environment has been to a large extent polarized between two conflicting fears of "environmental protectionism" and "environmental dumping" (IIED, 1997).

Most developing countries, including African countries, express concern that green consumer preferences and rising standards in the industrialized world could constrain markets for their exports, particularly when they are imposed unilaterally and in ways that discriminate against the production process. This leads to environmental protectionism.

On the other hand, concerns have also been raised, mostly in the industrialized world, about the negative environmental impacts of trade liberalization. This group believes that trade liberalization heightens both the risk of encouraging overexploitation of natural resources for short-term gain and a downward pressure on global standards, leading to environmental dumping.

Less has been said about the positive impacts (environmental opportunities) that changes in consumption and production patterns in developed countries could have for exports in developing countries of environmentally and socially preferable goods and services. Products from developing countries that currently have environmental advantages in the markets of industrialized nations include organically grown food, reusable and recyclable materials, biomass fuels, natural fibers, and sustainably harvested forest products, but it is believed that the broad-based nature of sustainable consumption and production provides a potentially wide range of opportunity sectors, including advanced manufacturing goods and services. The success of the effort to promote sustainable production and consumption will be significantly influenced by the level of success of replacing the environmental protectionism mind-set with the environmental opportunity mind-set. This would require addressing issues of constrain, including the following:

Primarily, the measures taken by industrialized countries in terms of influencing consumers' choice and market decisions should be matched by a concerted effort to enhance the national capabilities of developing countries to benefit from the environmental opportunities of promoting sustainable consumption and production.

Second, as much as they advocate broad-spectrum trade liberalization for developing countries, industrialized countries should commit themselves to look at most of the subsidy regimes that have significant impacts on the export earnings of African countries, which are to a large extent based on primary commodities.

Third, in view of the dominant role that has been played by transnational companies on global trade and environment forums, it would be important to provide the necessary institutional and technical support to ensure the active and informed involvement of African countries in such forums.

In a nutshell, the challenge of instituting a transparent process and the challenge of enhancing the capacity of African countries to take an active part in the global negotiation process are two of the major challenges that have to be faced by the international community in terms of creating a global trading regime that would promote sustainable development. For Africa to benefit from this global transition, it needs to come out of the "protectionist" mind-set and explore the opportunities that would provide additional benefit to the region.

*Strategies.* The following are the strategic measures that may require regional and global cooperation in order to positively manage the links among trade, the environment, and development:

> *Export promotion through ecoefficient production*: African countries need to refocus their attention on identifying the environmental advantages or opportunities they have from the promotion of sustainable consumption and production in industrialized countries and find ways of exploiting these opportunities. In this context, African countries need to develop "export-promotion strategies through ecoefficient production." This would require establishing and strengthening the activities of centers such as national cleaner production centers.
>
> *Multiple level of liberalization*: Although trade liberalization has the potential to promote efficiency and economic benefits, the liberalization process has to be commensurate with the production and institutional capacity of the countries. Considering the varying levels of countries' development it is important to enable African countries to develop and implement multiple levels of trade liberalization that reconcile their national economic capacities with the challenges of globalization and environmental requirements.

## The Knowledge Economy and the Digital Divide

The increasing influence of the advances made in the field of information and communication technology over the last decade, the various potential opportunities and challenges posed by the advances that have been made in the field of biotechnology, and the evolution of nanotechnology from scientific breakthroughs in the field of engineering and science at the molecular level constitute the three major building blocks of the knowledge economy in the twenty-first century. Application in information and communication technology is further ahead of those in biotechnology and nanotechnology. Besides being pervasive input to almost all human activities, the advance of information and communication technology (ICT) breaks down barriers to human development in at least three ways not possible before (UNDP, 2001).

> *Breaking down barriers to economic opportunity*: The expansion of ICT offers the potential for developing countries to expand exports, create good jobs, and diversify their economies.
>
> *Breaking down barriers to knowledge*: Access to information is as central as education to building human capabilities. While education develops cognitive skills, information gives content to knowledge. The Internet and the World Wide Web can deliver information to the poor and the rich alike.
>
> *Breaking down barriers to participation*: Poor people and communities are often isolated and lack means to take collective action. Global Internet commu-

nications have empowered many global civil society movements in recent years to express themselves in an effective way. The world over, citizens are increasingly able to use the Internet to hold governments more accountable.

While the evolving knowledge economy is expected to open new opportunities for developing countries, it is feared that the existing level of information and communication infrastructure in most African countries will act as a major constraint to exploiting these opportunities. This has led to the concern that African countries could be faced with a digital divide unless they take the necessary measures.

*Policy Response.* The view that the knowledge-driven economy is not relevant to manufacturers or only to high-technology manufactures is entirely wrong (UNIDO, 1999b). All manufacturers, whether large or small and whether from a traditional or a high-technology sector, must see themselves as part of the knowledge-driven globalizing economy. New competition in global markets of such products as garments, gloves, shoes, and processed fruit is driven by quality, production flexibility, and networking. The supply chain management and technological innovation by leading firms is also changing rapidly (UNIDO, 1999b).

During the last few years, the African telecommunications sector has shown a more liberal policy in attracting foreign investment and improving its infrastructure and services. By the start of 1998 (UNECA, 1999c), (1) a total of twenty countries had established independent regulatory agencies compared to two in 1990, and some countries are in the process of following suit, (2) a total of seventeen African telecom operators had allowed some degree of privatization and/or foreign ownership, and (3) the African mobile cellular market had shown steady growth.

African countries need to do much more in terms of developing their institutional and physical infrastructure for improved access of ICT to their people, however. Moreover, as was pointed out by UNDP (2001), African countries need to realize that the most limiting factors for utilizing the potential for the knowledge economy in general and ICT in particular are human imagination and political will. In this context, African countries need to put the necessary mechanisms in place to explore and exploit the maximum benefit from the knowledge economy.

*Strategies.* The following strategic measures are proposed to ensure that African countries will avoid the adverse impact of the digital divide and secure the maximum benefit from the evolving knowledge economy:

*Developing ICT infrastructure*: The development of ICT has provided new ways of partially overcoming the limitation caused by the lack of physical infrastructure, but there are still some basic infrastructural requirements to which African countries should give priority.

*Liberalizing the ICT sector*: The active involvement of the private sector in the ICT business is vital to gain the maximum benefit from the knowledge economy. In this context, African countries need to take the necessary steps to liberalize the ICT sector.

*Support to knowledge-based activities*: Most African countries have the potential to be active contributors to the global knowledge economy. In this context, African countries need to explore the possibilities and provide active support to firms that can participate in knowledge-intensive economic activities.

## CONCLUSION

Africa is the least developed region in the world, and is locked in a vicious circle of underdevelopment, poverty, and environmental degradation. The region that came out of the colonial era with the greatest sense of hope and aspirations has now become synonymous with the numerous vices of underdevelopment. Despite the various forms of policy interventions made over the decades, the economic perform-ance of most African countries still leaves much to be desired.

Manufacturing, which was the lead sector in the newly industrializing countries, has been a lagging sector in Africa since the 1990s. The contribution of the manufac-turing sector for sustainable development in Africa over the last decades has been minimal. In fact, the significant slowdown in industrial growth in Africa associated with slightly declining rates of growth in GDP, especially since the second half of the 1980s, reflects a changed structural relationship in the form of deindustrialization.

The priority issues in the context of promoting sustainable industrial devel-opment in Africa are addressing the mismatch between carrying capacity and pop-ulation, deindustrialization, the marginalization impact of globalization, poverty reduction through sustainable industrialization, capacity building for mainstreaming sustainability and policy coordination, building the necessary physical and institu-tional infrastructure for regional cooperation and integration, and redefining the linkages among trade, the environment, and development. In view of the central role of the manufacturing industry in contributing to the sustainable development ob-jectives of African countries, African governments and their global partners should put much more effort into expanding the manufacturing sector of the region on a sustainable basis.

Despite the overwhelming challenges that Africa is facing, the region has con-siderable potential to pursue sustainable development in ways that would benefit its people and the whole world. This can be a reality, provided that African governments stand up to the leadership challenges of creating an enabling environment and global partners are able to provide the necessary technical and financial support for the integration of Africa into the global economy. The key step in this regard is the development of a dynamic development policy framework that is primarily respon-sive to the national development settings and aims at enhancing the development management capacity of the individual countries in the region.

## APPENDIX: ACRONYMS

| | |
|---|---|
| AAF-SAP | African Alternative Framework for Structural Adjustment Programs |
| ADB | African Development Bank |
| AIDS | Acquired immunodeficiency syndrome |
| APPER | Africa's Priority Program for Economic Recovery |
| ARB | African Research Bulletin |
| AU | African Union |
| BWIs | Bretton Woods Institutions |
| CDF | Comprehensive development framework |
| ESAF | Enhance structural adjustment facility |
| GDP | Gross domestic product |

| HIPC | Highly indebted poor countries |
| ICT | Information and communication technology |
| IDDA | Industrial Development Decade for Africa |
| IIED | International Institute for Environment and Development |
| IMF | International Monetary Fund |
| LPA | Lagos Plan of Action |
| MVA | Manufacturing value added |
| NEPAD | New Partnership for Africa's Development |
| OAU | Organization of African Unity |
| OECD | Organization for Economic Cooperation and Development |
| SANSA | South African Network of Skills Abroad |
| SAP | Structural Adjustment Program |
| SID | Sustainable industrial development |
| SSA | Sub-Saharan Africa |
| UN | United Nations |
| UNDP | United Nations Development Program |
| UNEP | United Nations Environment Program |
| UNECA | United Nations Economic Commission for Africa |
| UNIDO | United Nations Industrial Development Organization |
| UNPAARED | United Nations Program of Action for African Economic Recovery and Development |
| UNTACDA | United Nations Trade and Communication Decade in Africa |

## REFERENCES

ADB (1997). African Development Report. Oxford: Oxford University Press.

African Roundtable of Eminent Persons. (2001). Statement of the Roundtable). http://www.johannesburgsummit.org/web_pages/africa_roundatble_report.htm>.

Ajayi, S. (1992). An Economic Analysis of Capital Flight from Nigeria. World Bank Working Paper Series. no. 993. Washington, DC: World Bank.

Ajayi, S. (1997). An Analysis of External Debt and Capital Flight in the Severely Indebted low-Income Countries in Sub-Saharan Africa. IMF Working Paper no. WP/97/68. Washington, DC: IMF.

Amoako, K. Y., Ali, A. A. G. (1998). Financing development in Africa: some exploratory results. paper presented at the Plenary Session of the African Economic Research Consortium (AERC) Workshop, Nairobi.

Aredo, D., Zelalem, Y. (1998). Skilled labor migration from developing countries: an assessment of brain-drain from Ethiopia. Proceedings of the Seventh Annual Conference of the Ethiopian Economy. Addis Ababa: Ethiopian Economic Association.

Bennell, P. (1994). British Manufacturing Investment in Sub-Saharan Africa: Corporate Response During Structural Adjustment. Institute of Development Studies, Working Paper no. 13.

Brown, M. (2000). Using the intellectual diaspora to reverse the brain drain: some useful examples. presented at a regional conference on brain drain, Addis Ababa.

Degefe, B. (1998). Relevance of structural adjustment policies in a subsistence economy. Economic Focus. Vol. 1:3. Addis Ababa: Ethiopian Economic Association.

Eckholm, E. (1979). The Dispossessed of the Earth: Land Reform and Sustainable Development. Washington, DC: World Watch Institute.

Hanna, S., Munasinghe, M. (1995). An introduction to property rights and the environment.

In: Hanna, S., Munasinghe, M., eds. Property Rights and the Environment. Washington, DC: Beiger International Institute of Ecological Economics and the World Bank.

Hyden, G. (1983). No Shortcuts to Progress: African Development Management in Perspective. London: Heineman.

IIED. (1997). Unlocking Trade Opportunities: Case Studies of Export Success from Developing Countries. New York: United Nations.

Lewis, L. A., Berry, L. (1988). African Environments and Resources. Boston: Unwin Hyman.

Meadows, D., Meadows, D., Randers, J. (1992). Beyond the Limits. London: Earthscan, pp. 313.

Mebratu, D. (2000a). Strategy framework for sustainable industrial development in sub-Saharan Africa. Ph.D. dissertation, Lund: Lund University.

Mebratu, D. (2000b). Transdisciplinarity and the developing world. Proceedings of the International Transdisciplinarity 2000 Conference. Zurich: Swiss Federal Institute of Technology, pp. 289–294.

Mkandawire, T. (1998). Thinking about development states in Africa. International Conference on African Development in the 21st Century. Tokyo: United Nations University.

Munasinghe, M. (1996). An Overview of the Environmental Impacts of Macroeconomic and Sectoral Policies. In: Munasinghe, M., ed. *Environmental Impacts of Macroeconomic and Sectoral Policies*. Washington D.C.: International Society for Ecological Economics, The World Bank and UNEP.

Panayotou, T., Hupe, K. (1996). Environmental impacts of structural adjustment programmes: synthesis and recommendations. In: Munasinghe, M., ed. Environmental Impacts of Macroeconomic and Sectoral Policies. Washington, DC: ISEE, WB, and UNEP, pp. 55–100.

Robins, N., Roberts, S., Abbot, J. (2000). Sustainable Trade: Who Benefits? London: IIED.

Stein, H. (1998). Globalization, Adjustment and the Structural Transformation of African Economies. Paper presented to a Regional Conference on Globalization. Addis Ababa: UNECA.

UN (1992). Agenda 21. New York: United Nations.

UNCTAD. (1999). Trade, Sustainable Development and Gender. Geneva: UNCTAD.

UNDP. (1997). Human Development Report 1997. New York: Oxford University Press.

UNDP. (2001). Human Development Report 2001. New York: Oxford University Press.

UNECA. (1980). Lagos Plan of Action. Addis Ababa: UNECA.

UNECA. (1989). African Alternative Framework for Structural Adjustment Program (AAF-SAP). Addis Ababa: UNECA.

UNECA and UNIDO. (1989). Mid-term Evaluation of IDDA-I and the Proclamation of IDDA-II. Addis Ababa: UNECA.

UNECA. (1996). Focus on African Industry: Africa in the 21st Century. Addis Ababa: UNECA.

UNECA. (1998). Emerging Trends in the Negotiations under WTO: Pertinent Issues of Concern to African Countries. Addis Ababa: UNECA.

UNECA. (1999a). Growth Strategies for Africa: Lessons and Proposals. Working Paper of Economic and Social Policy Division. Addis Ababa: UNECA.

UNECA. (1999b). Economic Report on Africa 1999: The Challenge of Poverty Reduction and Sustainability. Addis Ababa: UNECA.

UNECA. (1999c). The challenges of financing development in Africa. Seventh Session of the Conference of African Ministers of Finance. Addis Ababa: UNECA.

UNEP. (2000). African Perspectives: Extract from GEO 2000. Nairobi: UNEP.

UNFPA. (1996). Annual Populations 1950–2050 (the 1996 revision). New York: United Nations.

UNIDO. (1999a). UNIDO Annual Report 1998. Vienna: UNIDO.

UNIDO. (1999b). African Industry 2000: The Challenge of Going Global. Vienna: UNIDO.

UNIDO. (2001a). International Yearbook of Industrial Statistics. Vienna: UNIDO.

UNIDO. (2001b). Building Productive Capacity for Poverty Alleviation in Least Developed Countries: The Role of Industry. Vienna: UNIDO.

WRI, UNEP, UNDP, WB. (1998). World Resources 1998–99: A Guide to the Global Environment. New York: Oxford University.

World Bank. (1989). Sub-Saharan Africa: From Crisis to Growth. Washington, DC: World Bank.

World Bank. (1993). World Development Report. London: Oxford University Press.

World Bank. (1995). World Development Report. London: Oxford University Press.

World Bank. (1997). World Development Report. London: Oxford University Press.

# 17

## Science and Technology Policies for Development
### The Case of Singapore

**HABIBUL HAQUE KHONDKER**

*National University of Singapore, Singapore*

## INTRODUCTION

The last quarter of the twentieth century saw the emergence of various terms to re-define the current age, such as the "postindustrial society," the "information society," the "knowledge society," and the "third wave." A common feature of all these redefinitions is the centrality of knowledge (especially scientific knowledge) in modern society. Today, for survival and competition, no nation can ignore the use of scientific knowledge in its production, consumption, and betterment of the human condition. In almost all countries, the application of scientific knowledge is at the forefront of policy agenda adopted to reduce poverty, control endemic diseases, overcome environmental degradation, and enhance the quality of life.

This is not to endorse a technocratic, futuristic worldview that regards science as the panacea, however. What to make of science and how to integrate it within a broader social and ethical framework is a question that puzzles policy makers and deserves serious consideration. A number of writers (Moravcsik, 1975; Morgan, 1984; Shahidullah, 1991; Mowery, 1994, among others) have emphasized the importance of scientific knowledge in the sustainability of socioeconomic development and quality of life for people around the world. Andre Danzin, a noted French science planner, suggests that in view of the fact that a considerable fund of scientific and technical knowledge has been accumulated over the past hundred years, it ought to be used to satisfy the fundamental needs of the people (Danzin, 1979:206).

In the development field, the interaction among science, technology, and development has been a matter of great interest. Science can play a role in economic transformation and improvement in the infrastructure of production. Since the United Nations Conference on the Application of Science and Technology in Underdeveloped Areas in 1963, a great deal of attention has been focused on the need for the promotion of science and technology in the Third World. One writer suggests that by adopting science policies and investing in science, many poor countries can achieve economic growth (Cooney, 1983:280). Apart from a large number of international conferences sponsored by the United Nations, the political leaders as well as intellectuals of the Third World have emphasized the importance of science in the modernization process. For example, Jawaharlal Nehru, the first prime minister of India, was a champion of science, and recognized the power of scientific and technological knowledge in modernizing India. He once commented: "What is planning if not the application of science to our problems?" (cited in Gandhi, 1969:10). Nehru emphasized the development of a scientific outlook that he called the "scientific temper." He once observed that: "Who indeed can afford to ignore science today?...The future belongs to science and those who make friends with science" (Nehru, quoted in Morehouse and Gupte, 1987:193).

Syed Hussein Alatas (1976) argued that science and modernization are inseparable. For him, modernization is a process of the expansion of scientific knowledge in all domains of human life. In East Asia in general and Japan in particular, the culture is considered favorable to the inculcation of science and technology. According to Bartholomew, Japan's dominant Confucian intellectual tradition was loosely structured and relatively tolerant of new ideas and perspectives. Controversial theories in Western science, including heliocentrism or the origin of species, aroused little opposition and were readily accepted; Japanese scientists did not have to slay the dragons of traditional religion to accommodate new scientific ideas (Bartholomew, 1989:3). In Japan, governmental leadership since the Meiji restoration of 1868 has been crucial in the development of science and technology. The accumulation of technical skills and a strong commitment to education played an important part in Japanese industrialization, in which governmental steps strengthened rather than displaced private incentives (Rosenberg, 1990:152). In the case of South Korea, it can be observed that the development of scientific and technological capacity captured the attention of the government from as early as in the 1960s. The Korea Institute of Science and Technology was founded in 1966 and the Ministry of Science and Technology (MOST) was established in 1967 (Khondker, 1988:135).

Despite the growing significance of science and technology, no country should take its scientific and technological edges for granted. In the global competition in research and development (R&D), there are losers and winners, with profound implications for overall socioeconomic development. For countries that are yet to participate in this global race, the future is simply bleak. Countries that choose to neglect the importance of science and technology are not going to just stagnate, they will be in a reverse developmental direction, while other countries with a rational worldview will continue to progress. This chapter discusses the role of the state with regard to science and technology in the development of Singapore. The chapter also alludes to the possibility of drawing certain lessons from the Singapore case in building scientific capacity as an aid to economic development for the developing countries.

## DEFINING SCIENCE POLICY AND DEVELOPMENT

The first major concept requiring clarification in this chapter is science policy, but the definition of science policy is not free from problems. Under such policy, one can include: (1) those mechanisms by which science and technology can contribute to the mitigation of certain socioeconomic problems, and (2) those mechanisms that strengthen the major components of science and technology, such as a pool of trained scientists and engineers and the educational system utilizing available scientific knowledge (Fusfeld, 1979). According to UNESCO, an appropriate national science policy must enhance the advancement of science for its own sake and facilitate the application of science to technology for the production of goods and services (UNESCO, 1970: 104).

In recent years the discussion of the development of science policy and building scientific capacity has emphasized the interaction among government, industry, and universities (Etzkowitz and Leydesdorff, 1997). Others have emphasized the role of the research universities in the globalization of scientific knowledge (Skolnikoff, 1993), yet the involvement of government remains a catalytic factor. With regard to the relationship between government and science, the Enlightenment philosopher Condorect wrote: "In every century Princes have been found to love the sciences and even to cultivate them, to attract Savants to their palaces and to reward by their favours and their amity men who afforded them a sure and constant refuge from world-weariness, a sort of disease to which supreme powers seems particularly prone" (quoted in Salomon, 1973:1). With the advent of modern sciences and with the state taking a role in the process of modernization, the relationship between science and public authority became more formal and institutional.

Just as the state's favorable guidance can be a blessing, if the state turns against science and higher education on ideological reasons the consequences can be equally disastrous. The case of China (PRC) illustrates this problem quite well. During the Cultural Revolution, major centers of higher education and such institutes as the Chinese Academy of Sciences were devastated on the ideological ground that theory, including scientific theory, must emerge through practice. Later, Deng Xiaoping took a pro-science position in light of its role in technological and economic development. The debate over science policy was resolved through the resolution of ideological debates. Science and technology are seen by China's current leadership as key to its modernization program. Along with agriculture, industry, and national defense, science and technology constitute one of the major components of the "four modernizations." Deng Xiaoping himself was concerned that the lack of theoretical research was holding back China's economic progress (Saich, 1989:9).

The absence of a systematic science policy is not the monopoly of the developing world. Even in the advanced industrialized countries, a systematic and organized process of formulating science policy has a short history. In the United States, for example, the federal government had no organized policies about science until World War ll. The growth of science in universities during the nineteenth and early twentieth centuries was slow and incremental: "Academic concerns were primarily practical and local, not theoretical and national" (Nichols, 1993:199). It is only after World War II that systematic policies emerged toward achieving competence in science by international standards. This was fuelled in part by postwar confidence in science. Funding increased dramatically; total academic R&D spending rose from a few hundred million dollars per year in the 1950s to more than $19 billion by 1992. Federal funds accounted for 60–70% of the total (Nichols, 1993:200).

For the developing countries, it is not too late to devise an appropriate science policy. We thus emphasize such concerns as the building of institutions and capacities for the generation, inculcation, and utilization of scientific knowledge. All these must be guided by a utilitarian aspect of science—that it helps improve the quality of life. Again quoting the report of UNESCO: "The progress of a country depends on its capacity to identify, resolve and decide upon the scientific and technical problems which confront it at the successive stages of economic and social development. This is particularly relevant to the change-over from the traditional industries to the new forms of production, and to the integration of modern techniques into the national production system" (UNESCO, 1970:103).

It must be readily acknowledged here that we are dealing with a narrow definition of science in examining its policy and leaving out a number of sociologically meaningful issues. Issues such as the relationship between society and science, the emergence of scientific thinking and rationalization, and the autonomy of science are subjects of perennial interest to students of the sociology of science, but given the focus of this chapter, we limit the discussion only to matters covering policy issues.

The second major concept used in this chapter is development, which is broadly defined as improvement in the quality of life. What constitutes quality of life, however (assuming it has a common definition), and how to attain this objective are issues that divide social scientists. Focusing on the qualitative dimension, Dudley Seers and Amartya Sen suggest that development can be attained through enhancing the capabilities or potential of the people in a society. A number of economists define development in terms of economic growth combined with equitable income distribution, with long-term sustainability in economic, political, cultural, and ecological terms. In this regard, the idea of "sustainable development" evoked wide interest among policy makers and development experts. The Brundtland report defines sustainable development as "development that meets the needs of the present without compromising the ability of the future generations to meet their own needs" (WCED, 1987:42). As for the Asian Development Bank (ADB), sustainable development "is a process of change in which the exploitation of resources, the direction of investments, the orientation of technological development and institutional change are all in harmony and enhance both current and future potential to meet the human needs and aspirations" (ADB, 1992:211).

The policy makers in Singapore have not ignored the goal of sustainable development as revealed in both the orientation of technological development and the outcome of reasonably equitable growth. Although no one can deny the positive role of the Ministry of Environment, a governmental arm, in keeping Singapore green and clean, there are instances in which priorities in economic goals override the objectives of conservation of nature. In so far as the development of science and technology is concerned, the government has remained steadfast. It has been recognized that in order to maintain competitiveness, "Singapore needs to move to an innovation phase of our development and promote activities with more innovative and design content. This means mastering science and technology. Singapore must increase her capacity to undertake research and development of international standard" (NSTB, 1991:i). The next section deals with Singapore's science policy and its role in the development of this country.

## THE CONTEXT OF SINGAPORE

A number of countries in East Asia and Southeast Asia have enjoyed a high rate of economic growth for the past two decades. In the 1980s, East and Southeast Asian newly industrializing countries (NICs) maintained high growth rates, with the exception of a temporary slowdown in Singapore and Hong Kong during the period for 1985 to 1986. Despite the "Asian crisis" of 1998–1999, by the 1990s Singapore successfully graduated from a Third World to a First World country in three decades. In 2001, Singapore's per capita gross national product (GNP) stood at US$24,740 (World Bank, 2002). The story of Singapore's rapid economic development has now become an exemplar for development experts. The World Economic Forum ranked Singapore fourth in global competitiveness in 2001. In fact, Singapore was ranked first in three consecutive years (from 1997 to 1999) (the Straits Times, Oct. 19, 2001). From a very early stage of development in this city-state, its leaders have shown a favorable view and deep appreciation of the role of science and technology. The modernizing attitudes of these leaders have been a catalyst for development in Singapore. Systematic policies were not developed until the late 1970s, however.

By any standards, Singapore's economic performance during the last three decades deserves proper appreciation. It has achieved rapid economic growth that benefits the great majority of the populace. This achievement is particularly impressive in view of the fact that the country has hardly any natural resources; the only gift of nature is its location at the maritime crossroads. One important point in Singapore's economic performance is that it has an open but not a lasissez-faire economy (Castells, 1988:3). By this, Castells alludes to the strong development policies guided by the state that led Singapore to compete successfully in the world economic system. In his words, Singapore is "the quintessential developmental state" (Castells, 1988:4). It is important to note that the concept of the developmental state was first applied to Japan by Chalmers Johnson in the early 1980s.[1] It would be somewhat simplistic, however, to divide the development options into two: state-led versus market-led. In addition to the state-led or plan-rational and the market-led or market-rational models, there are the plan-ideological and market-ideological models (Applebaum et al. 1992:18–20). Wade's (1990) distinction between "governed market" and "free market" is a useful distinction that provides the basis for the above ideal-typical classification.

The recent history of the growth of science and technology has shown that the ideology of the free market can have negative implications, while excessive state control can stifle such growth. The models for socioeconomic development in general are applicable to the developments in science and technology as well. In this regard, the role of the developmental state in the promotion of science and technology deserves special attention. As far as Singapore is concerned, its pragmatic leaders have always been in the forefront of planned development, which began to change in the mid-1980s as policy makers began to realize that one cannot be too careful and meticulous in planning. A flurry of forward plans and documents on the visions of Singapore's future in both technological and economic terms were perhaps an inadvertent outcome of this rethinking. It is important to understand the spurts in the science and technology policies in light of this overall shift in policy orientation. Although the leadership in Singapore has been quite sensitive to the needs of science and technology development from the very outset, there was room for improvement. The policy shift in the 1980s reflected such a realization on the part of the leadership in Singapore.

From the early years of Singapore's independence in 1965, it was realized that in order to attract foreign investment Singapore must have a good supply of technical and scientific manpower. The emphasis on high-quality education and especially technical education paved the way for development in science and technology. Singapore is also attuned to the need of constantly upgrading its technological capabilities and building a strong scientific infrastructure. In the 1981 budget statement, Goh Chok Tong (the then minister of trade and industry) unveiled the economic plan for the 1980s, the main objective of that plan was to transform Singapore into a modern industrial economy based on science, technology, skills, and knowledge (Lim et al., 1988:67).

## SCIENCE POLICY AND DEVELOPMENT IN SINGAPORE

The formulation of a coherent science policy and its implementation played a major role in the socioeconomic development of Singapore. The role of science and technological development in Singapore's economic development is especially important because of the very limited endowment of natural resources. From the very beginning, the Singapore government recognized the need for technological improvement. Policy initiatives were undertaken to expand R&D activities for productivity and quality enhancement (Lim et al., 1988:447–448). In Singapore, as in Korea, the development of science and technology was viewed as an integral part of overall economic development (Choi, 1983:125). The priority of science and technology has been accepted by leaders in Singapore. It is recognized that in order to enhance its national competitiveness in the industrial and service sectors, Singapore has to be developed into a center of excellence in selected fields of science and technology (NSTB, 1991:1). What is noteworthy here is that emphasis has been placed on the promotion of science and technology in "selected fields" in which the country can expect to have comparative advantages. This pragmatic approach has been quite rewarding and is consistent with the trends in other NICs. Major strides have been made in Singapore toward excellence in science and technology, particularly in such export industries as consumer electronics, pharmaceuticals, and industrial chemicals.

Among Asian countries, according to a National Science Foundation (NSF) report, China, India, Japan, Singapore, South Korea, and Taiwan emphasized scientific and technological education for their brightest young people and increased their R&D expenditures. The total R&D expenditures of these six countries reached US$91 billion in 1987, which was 25% below the U.S. sum for that year. The NSF report also added that more than 90% of the students sent to America by Taiwan and India are enrolled in science and engineering (International Herald Tribune, Aug. 27, 1993:6).

In attaining the specific development goals appropriate policies were carefully devised and successfully implemented. One of the policy areas that played an important role in the development of Singapore is an appropriate science policy. It is recognized that "[T]he emergence of South Korea, Singapore and Taiwan into the community of industrialized nations is, in large part, due to their ability to master industrial technology quickly and to use it to attain competitiveness in quality and price in rapidly expanding world markets" (Weiss, 1990:17). In 1978, Lee Kuan Yew, the founding leader of Singapore, mentioned in a speech that "What made Singapore different in the 1960s from most other countries of Southeast Asia was that she had no xenophobic hangover from colonialism." He continued: "Mankind's progress has been what it is because one man's discovery, whether it is the first spark of fire, or the first atomic explosion, does not have to be painfully and painstakingly rediscovered by all those who seek the benefits of the original discovery" (Lee, 1978).

To embark on and sustain progress in science and technology, education and training are crucial. The foundation of Singapore's economic growth has been education and training. Although the subject of science policy is often discussed separately, it may be useful to see it in conjunction with policy issues in higher education, manpower training, and human resources development. In Singapore, total full-time university enrollment grew from about 5700 in 1968 to about 10,000 in 1981. Polytechnical-level enrollment grew from 1900 in 1968 to 5700 in 1981 (Mattar, 1981). In recent years Singapore has seen a steady growth in the area of tertiary education, in which the focus has been more on quality than quantity. Although investment in R&D in Singapore was only 0.23% of GDP in 1978 (lower than the 0.50% recommended by the United Nation for developing countries), as its economy went through structural transformation in the late 1970s, new priorities in science and technology policies emerged. Emphasis was placed on high value-added, technology-intensive industries and services. The promotion of science-based and research-oriented industries was actively pursued. With the move toward industrial upgrading in 1979, the Singapore government began to formulate a long-term R&D plan. The importance of science and technology as an instrument for restructuring the economy was reflected in these policy shifts ("Singapore: Science and Technology," 1986:3).

In Singapore, R&D expenditure grew from 0.2% of GDP in 1978 to 1% in 1990. The number of research scientists and engineers grew from 818 to 4276. In terms of the number of research scientists and engineers per 10,000 people in the labor force, the increase was 8 in 1978 to 28 in 1990. This is a remarkable development in its own right, although compared to other NICs, the performance may not be significant.[2] It may be mentioned here that the United States, France, and the United Kingdom devote a significant proportion of their R&D budgets to military programs. If only civilian R&D is considered, the five countries that exceed 2% of GDP are Switzerland, Japan, Germany, Sweden, and the Netherlands (OECD, 1987:9). Of the $638 million or 1% of GDP spent on R&D in Singapore, the private sector accounted for 59%. Of the remaining 41%, 22% was spent by the governmental sector and 32% by the higher education sector (NSTB, 1991:9). In 2001, the overall investment in R&D reached 3.2 billion Singapore dollars, or 2.1% of GDP (ASTR, 2002).

## INSTITUTIONAL CAPACITY FOR DEVELOPING SCIENCE IN SINGAPORE

Barely a year after the independence of Singapore in 1965, its leaders started to pay due attention to the issue of science. In February 1966, the Singapore government launched a dual project to mobilize scientific and technical talent so that they can be utilized to further the economic and other development interests of Singapore society. Over time there emerged a series of state-sponsored institutions to enhance the development of science in Singapore. Some of these major institutions are briefly discussed in this section.

## The Science Council of Singapore

The Science Council of Singapore was established in 1967 through an act of the parliament. The primary role of this council was to assist the government in promoting the development of the nation's scientific and technological capabilities. It advised the government on scientific and technological matters related to the training and utilization of manpower, R&D, and the relationship with other scientific organizations. It also undertook such promotional activities as seminars and industrial and scientific exhibitions, televised competitions, project and policy studies, and educational publications. The main aims of the Singapore Science Council were to: (1) foster encouragement and expand scientific education in schools and universities in the state, (2) encourage the maintenance of scientific standards, (3) oversee a study of scientific manpower to assess the needs and to suggest ways and means of utilizing the manpower, (4) assess research projects of various individuals in the state and make recommendations to government, (5) encourage research projects in the private sector, (6) advise the government on capital expenditure with regard to scientific matters, and (7) undertake the study of projects that will be of economic interest to the state (the Straits Times, Feb. 9, 1966).

## Singapore National Academy of Sciences

The Singapore National Academy of Sciences was inaugurated on July 31, 1967, with the following broad objectives: (1) to promote the advancement of science and technology in the Republic of Singapore, (2) to discuss scientific, technological, and socioeconomic problems, in particular those of national interest, and (3) to represent the scientific opinion of the members and fellows of the academy (Journal of the Singapore Academy of Science, 1969).

The president of the academy, Professor T. H. Elliot urged that Singapore should produce its own scientists, whose permanent affiliations would be with the country. To achieve this aim, he suggested that future scientists should receive most of their scientific education at home, take science as a career, and build a scientific community of their own (the Straits Times, Oct. 25, 1967). The main aim of the academy was to bring science and technology to the people so that they could understand and appreciate the government's "tremendous industrialization programme" (Kiang Ai Kim, quoted in Khondker, 1994). In his opening address at the First Congress of the National Academy of Science, Dr. Toh Chin Chye, the then minister for science and technology, highlighted the importance of national scientific bodies in advising the government in formulating scientific policies in developing countries.

In 1990 the National Science Council was relinquished and gave way to the establishment of the National Science and Technology Board. The two major achievements of the National Science Council were the Research and Development Assistance Scheme (RDAS) and the Science Park. One of the major responsibilities of the Science Council was to promote and encourage medium- and long-term research activities through RDAS. Between 1984 and 1990, ninety-eight projects worth $63 million were funded under the RDAS (Science Council, 1990:5). On the other hand, the Science Park became the cornerstone for what has become known as Singapore's technology corridor. Its role in creating a high-tech culture is comparable to that of Silicon Valley in the United States and Tsukuba City in Japan.

## The National Science and Technology Board

In January 1991, the National Science and Technology Board (NSTB) was formed "to develop Singapore into a centre of excellence in selected fields of Science and Technology" in order to enhance its competitiveness in various sectors (Window of Opportunities, 1991). In the report of the NSTB, it was stated that the average growth of R&D in Singapore from 1978 to 1990 was 26% per year. The main mission of the NSTB was to promote R&D to boost national competitiveness. The major strategies undertaken in this regard include the promotion of R&D through financial and fiscal incentives and the funding of R&D manpower development through scholarships and other schemes. To achieve its mission, the NSTB sought to identify all the resources necessary to enable the profit-driven private sector to undertake R&D.

The NSTB facilitated various initiatives to develop a favorable environment for knowledge creation and the enterprising use of science and technology. In the meantime, Singapore's economy also moved toward an information economy, thanks to the ability of the policy makers to identify the major trends in the global economy. By joining the information revolution, which generated a new frontier in global economic relations, Singapore was able to reap the benefit through such institutions as the NSTB. Early in 2002, the NSTB changed its name to the Agency for Science Technology and Research, with Philip Yeo as its new chairman. With changing circumstances, the focus has been shifted from information technology (IT) to "life sciences."

## Other Research Institutions and Centers

In Singapore, there are other research institutes and centers providing an enabling environment for the development of human resources, skills, technology, knowledge, and products in the private sector. Since the late 1980s, the following institutions have continued to play the role of prime R&D centers in Singapore:

1. The Institute of Molecular and Cell Biology (IMCB), a basic research institute established in 1987 within the National University of Singapore, established a coherent and viable base of strategic research in health care and cell regulation. It is the first organization in the world to commercialize transgenic rat technology.

2. The Information Technology Institute was formed in 1986 as the applied R&D arm of the National Computer Board. Its research activities are market-driven and focused on creating useful innovations using emerging IT.

3. The GINTIC Institute of Manufacturing Technology was set up in 1985 by Nanyang Technological University with the assistance and expertise of Grumman International, a U.S.-based company.

4. The Institute of System Science was formed in 1981, primarily as a teaching institute. Its R&D program began in 1986.

5. The Singapore Institute of Standards and Industrial Research its an institution in which more than 30% of the 452 existing staff members was directly involved in R&D work in the late 1980s. More than half of the staff members hold postgraduate degrees (NSTB, 1991:50–52). Singapore was successful in creating a science and technology infrastructure in the first two decades of its independence.

## CONCLUSION

Even in its purest form, science is not completely isolated from technology (Sarlemijn and Kroes, 1990:5). Many developing countries had the popular notion that they should not worry about basic scientific research and should instead concentrate on technology development. Even with regard to technology, a distinction is made between original innovation and improvement in application, but this distinction is not that clear-cut. Without a foundation in science, the selection of technology, let alone its improvement, becomes difficult. As new technology is highly science-based, there is no scope for neglecting science, even if the orientations are very pragmatic. Singapore's experience shows that although initially its focus was more on technology development than science, over time it began to develop both.

The situation of Singapore, as in other NICs, is different from both the developing and developed countries. In developing countries, there is more emphasis on the use of science and technology for survival, modernization, and coping with the challenges posed by adverse socioeconomic conditions. The application of appropriate agricultural technology to improve food production and the use of scientific knowledge and technology for birth control are two common areas. In developed capitalist countries, scientific innovation and technology development are often proactive. In the case of NICs, it can be said that the development of science and technology is often imitative, and thus appropriate science policy remains a prerequisite. There is no justification for downplaying the importance of imitation in the areas of science and technology, however. As the Japanese experience shows, the transition from imitation to innovation is a clear possibility. The role of basic scientific research is invaluable even in terms of maintaining the status quo or upgrading technology. It would be unwise to neglect basic research (unless it is too capital-intensive) in promoting science and technology.

In reaping the benefits of investments in science, it would be unrealistic to expect immediate returns. Many policy makers tend to take a short-term approach, while growth in science and technology is a long-term affair. This gap in perception has consequences for budgetary allocations for R&D. According to Fusfeld, "'Productivity' is a word that must be carefully used in connection with R&D." While in manufacturing productivity means more results, in science, new understanding, new concepts, and new frontiers are important (Fusfeld, 1979:17). In Singapore political leaders are not afraid to take a long-term view with regard to science and technology, even though from the point of political expediency it may not always be ideal. Despite the rhetoric of "Asian values" and so on, the Singapore leadership never lost its emphasis on modernization, science, and technology in fuelling economic growth and management. As one writer commented, "we must admire the Singapore minister's constant search for a vision and belief in their policies... at the same time [there is] a willingness to re-examine and re-evaluate policies, and readjust them and reset goals if needed" (Cheng, 2001).

The focus on science and technology in the early years was compatible with the needs for export-oriented industrialization. Following the economic recession of 1986, the leadership reoriented its focus on IT and biotechnology. As IT gained prominence in the advanced industrialized countries, Singapore was quick to change its priorities. The pro-IT and pro-globalization policies have eventually paid off. The economic slowdown was seen neither as permanent nor as a devastating feature in Singapore.

The government was on course following its new emphasis on biotechnological research and embarked on new projects in the life sciences in the midst of the economic slowdown in the late 1990s. It followed the strategy of promoting science and technology under the active guidance of the state with collaboration from the private sector and increasingly from tertiary educational institutions. As the experience of Singapore's economic success shows, it took place not simply due to unregulated market forces; the role of the government has always been central. Similarly, in the realm of developing science and technology, a carefully calibrated and informed state policy contributed to—and did not displaced—private initiatives.

The strength of Singapore's science and technology policy lies in its ability to adapt to changing global circumstances. In recent years the following changes are noticeable:

1. A rapid expansion of tertiary education.
2. A shift in the focus of education from rote learning to creative education. Here a glaring weakness has been detected and remedied. Although Singapore's education in the early phase was suitable for human resource development in an export-led economy, it was lacking in innovative thinking and scientific creativity.
3. A major initiative was taken by the government in the 1990s to attract researchers and scientists from overseas by providing them with incentives that included immigration opportunities. The program commonly known as recruitment of "foreign talents" generated some local resentment, yet the government stood by the policy and tried its best to convince the citizenry of the economic benefits of this initiative.

The coordination of policies toward higher education, infrastructure development for science and technology through the creation of science parks and technology corridors, and a drive to attract foreign talents is indicative of a thinking government in tune with the "paradigm shifts" of the global environment. The most important lesson that Singapore can offer to the policy makers of the developing countries is the will to learn and to change.

## NOTES

1. The developmental state is characterized by: (1) state capacity, often enhanced by a highly capable bureaucracy; (2) a monolithic, corporatist political system that grants the bureaucracy a great deal of autonomy and keeps the other claimants to political power such as the working class under control; (3) an ability to forge a close relationship between corporations and the government, fine-tuning policies to the advantage of the corporations; and (4) a commitment to granting welfare provisions for the people, such as housing, public education, and health care, that have direct and indirect economic benefits. In light of the above characteristics, Singapore state is clearly a developmentalist state.
2. In 1989 Korea spent 1.8% of its GDP on R&D, with a target of raising expenditures to 5% by the year 2000. Taiwan also planned to raise such speading from 1.3% (in 1988) to 2% by the end of the 1990. The comparable figures for Japan, Germany, and the United Kingdom in 1988 was 2.9% (NSTB, 1991:16).

## REFERENCES

ADB (Asian Development Bank). (1992). Asian Development Outlook. Manila: Asian Development Bank.

Alatas, S. H. (1976). Erring modernization: The dilemma of developing societies. In: Atal, Y., Piers, R., eds. Asian Rethinking on Development. New Delhi: Abhinav.

Applebaum, R. P., Henderson, J. (1992). States and Development in the Asian Pacific Rim. Newbury Park, CA: Sage.

ASTR (Agency for Science Technology and Research, Singapore). (2002). R&D Survey of 2001. Singapore: Government of the Republic of Singapore.

Bartholomew, J. R. (1989). The Formation of Science in Japan. New Haven, CT: Yale University Press.

Castells, M. (1988). The Developmental City-State in an Open World Economy: The Singapore Experience. Berkeley, CA: University of California. (BRIE paper no. 31).

Cheng, C. (Nov. 22, 2001). Learning lessons from a focused Singapore. South China Morning Post.

Choi, H. S. (1983). Bases for Science and Technology Promotion in Developing Countries. Tokyo: Asian Productivity Organization.

Cooney, S. (1983). Progress through technology: An innovative model. Impact. Sci. Soc. 134/135.

Danzin, A. (1979). Are science and technology leading to a new pattern of development? Impact Sci. Soc. 29:3.

Etzkowitz, H., Leydesdorff, L. (1997). Universities in the Global Knowledge Economy: A Triple Helix of Academy-Industry-Government Relations. London: Cassell.

Fusfeld, H. I. (1979). Science and Technology Policy: Perspectives for the 1980s. New York: New York Academy of Sciences.

Gandhi, I. (1969). Moving Asia Forward. Impact Sci. Soc. 21:7.

International Herald Tribune, Aug. 27, 1993, pp. 6.

J. Singapore Acad. Sci. 1969.

Khondker, H. (1988). Science and development: Some lessons from India and South Korea. Asian Profile 16:2.

Khondker, H. (1994). Science Policy in Singapore. research report. Singapore: Department of Sociology, National University of Singapore.

Lee, K. Y. (Oct. 5, 1978). Extrapolating from the Singapore experience. special lecture at the 26th World Congress of the International Chamber of Commerce, Orlando, FL.

Lim, C. Y., et al. (1988). Policy Options. Singapore: McGraw-Hill.

Mattar, A. (1981). Science as an instrument for economic development. Speeches Monthly Coll. Minis. Speeches 5:1.

Moravcsik, J. (1975). Science Development: The Building of Science in Less Developed Countries. Bloomington, IN: PASITAM.

Morehouse, W., Gupte, B. (1987). India: Success and failure. In: Segal, A., ed. Learning by Doing: Science and Technology in the Developing World. Boulder, CO: Westview Press.

Morgan, R. P. (1984). Science and Technology for International Development. Boulder, CO: Westview Press.

Mowery, D. C. (1994). Science and Technology Policy in Interdependent Economies. Boston: Kluwer Academic.

Nichols, R. W. (1993). Federal science policy and universities: Consequences of success. Daedalus 122:4.

NSTB (National Science and Technology Board). (1991). National Technology Plan: Science and Technology: Window of Opportunity. Singapore: Government of the Republic of Singapore.

OECD. (1987). Science and Technology Indicators Report. Paris: Organization for Economic Cooperation and Development.

Rosenberg, N. (1990). Science and technology policy for the Asian NICs: Lessons from economic history. In: Evenson, R., Ranis, G., eds. Science and Technology: Lessons for Development Policy. Boulder, CO: Westview Press.

Saich, T. (1989). China's Science Policy in the 1980s. Manchester: Manchester University Press.

Salomon, J. J. (1973). Science and Politics. London: Macmillan.

Sarlemijn, A., Kroes, P. (1990). Between Science and Technology. Amsterdam: North-Holland.

Science Council (Singapore). (1990). Annual Report. Singapore: Science Council.

Singapore: Science and technology. (1986). Sci. Am. 254:6.

Shahidullah, S. M. (1991). Capacity Building in Science and Technology in the Third World: Problems, Issues, and Strategies. Boulder, CO: Westview Press.

Skolnikoff, E. B. (1993). Knowledge without borders? Internationalization of the research universities. Daedalus 122:4.

Straits Times Feb. 9, 1966.

Straits Times Oct. 25, 1967.

Straits Times Oct. 19, 2001.

UNESCO. (1970). Science and Technology in Asian Development. Paris: Unesco.

Wade, R. (1990). Governing the Market. Princeton, NJ: Princeton University Press.

WCED (World Commission on Environment and Development). (1987). Our Common Future. New York: Oxford University Press.

Weiss, C. Jr. (1990). Scientific and technological constraints to economic growth and equity. In: Evenson, R., Ranis, G., eds. Science and Technology: Lessons for Development Policy. Boulder, CO: Westview Press.

World Bank. (2002). World Development Report. Washington, DC: The World Bank.

# 18

## Organizations, Agencies, and Other Entities That Impact the Developing World
### Internet Sources

**THOMAS S. CHAPMAN**

*The Ohio State University, Columbus, Ohio, U.S.A.*

## INTRODUCTION

Delving into issues concerning developing countries can be a daunting task. Polysyllabic terms and long agency names are often reduced to a confusing set of acronyms. The complex interactions among government agencies, nongovernmental organizations, and other institutions may overwhelm those not familiar with global affairs. This chapter explores the actors involved in international development issues. The focus is on familiarizing the reader with the actors in the global development arena, with an emphasis on data sources that can be utilized to explore policies related to economic progress, population pressures, health, food security, civil rights, social concerns, and environmental degradation.

This chapter examines many different types of organizations: U.S. governmental departments and bureaus that have an international focus, foreign government

Information about the goals and activities of organizations in this chapter has been compiled directly from the Web pages listed. Websites are constantly being developed and changed. If any of the pages listed in this chapter has changed, you may consider using a search engine such as Yahoo! or Excite to search for the new Web address. I would like to mention that Professors Douglas Graham, Fredrick Hitzhusen, Douglas Southgate, and Luther Tweenten of the Department of Agricultural, Environmental, and Development Economics at The Ohio State University made helpful suggestions as this chapter was being developed.

agencies that are also concerned with international development, international organizations to which individual nations belong and provide financial support, non-governmental organizations (NGOs) that seek to influence government policies and/ or impact the lives of people in the developing word, and other organizations (e.g., businesses, the press, universities, religious institutions) that significantly impact international development. Rather than attempting to be all-encompassing, this chapter should be seen as a gateway to the entities that are concerned with development policy. The list of organizations included here is not exhaustive. In addition to discussing what these organizations are, this chapter notes the types of data they provide, with a special emphasis on data sources available through the Internet.

## THE U.S. GOVERNMENT

The U.S. government has three branches, fourteen executive departments, and many bureaus, agencies, and other entities. Several different organizations within the federal government are concerned with the problems and policies of the developing world. A good place to start looking for government information is First Gov (firstgov.com), a government Website that provides access to online U.S. federal government resources. Fed Stats (www.fedstats.gov) and Fed World (www.fedworld.gov) are additional government Websites that may be useful for finding government research and data.

### The State Department

The State Department (www.state.gov) is the lead U.S. foreign affairs agency, and the secretary of state is the president's principal foreign policy adviser. The State Department maintains embassies in about 180 foreign countries (usembassy.state. gov). Embassies are usually located in a host country's capital. The United States also has consulates in other large commercial centers. Six geographic bureaus and one office coordinate the conduct of U.S. relations overseas. These are the Bureau of African Affairs, the Bureau of East Asian and Pacific Affairs, the Bureau of European Affairs, the Bureau of Near Eastern Affairs, the Bureau of South Asian Affairs, the Bureau of Western Hemisphere Affairs, and the Office of the Special Advisor for the New Independent States. The Bureau of International Organization Affairs develops and implements the policies of the U.S. government within the United Nations and its affiliated agencies, as well as within certain other international organizations. The Bureau of Democracy, Human Rights, and Labor ensures that human rights and labor conditions in foreign countries are taken into account in the U.S. policy-making process. The Bureau for International Narcotics and Law Enforcement Affairs works with foreign governments to reduce illicit drug crop cultivation and trafficking through crop control, enforcement, and alternative development programs. The Bureau of Oceans and International Environmental and Scientific Affairs deals with such global issues as biodiversity, global climate change, and environmental pollution. The Bureau of Population, Refugees, and Migration coordinates policy on global population, refugees, and migration issues and manages migration and refugee assistance appropriations. Travel advisories and *consular information sheets* (www.travel.state. gov/travel_warnings.html) issued by the State Department contain information about crime and safety concerns, political situations, and health issues for every country in the world. The State Department also maintains a Web page devoted to important international topics and issues (www.state.gov/interntl/index.htm) and prepares *background notes* on many foreign countries (www.state.gov/r/pa/ei/bgn). The Office of International Information Programs (usinfo.state.gov) develops and implements a variety of information initiatives and strategic communications programs aimed at the foreign affairs community.

## The U.S. Agency for International Development

The Agency for International Development (USAID—www.usaid.gov) is an independent federal government agency that receives overall foreign policy guidance from the secretary of state. USAID provides humanitarian aid and foreign assistance to the developing world. The agency works in six principal areas crucial to achieving both sustainable development and advancing U.S. foreign policy objectives: economic growth and agricultural development; population, health, and nutrition; environment; democracy and governance; education and training; and humanitarian assistance. USAID provides assistance in four regions of the world: sub-Saharan Africa, Asia and the Near East, Latin America and the Caribbean, and Europe and Eurasia. Among the types of assistance provided by USAID are immunization programs, agricultural research, family planning programs, and loans to small entrepreneurs.

## The Central Intelligence Agency

The Central Intelligence Agency (CIA—www.cia.gov) is an independent agency responsible to the president and accountable to the intelligence oversight committees of the U.S. Congress. The mission of the CIA is to provide foreign intelligence on national security topics and conduct counterintelligence activities, special activities, and other functions related to foreign intelligence and national security as directed by the president. The CIA produces *The World Factbook* (www.cia.gov/cia/publications/factbook), an excellent source of information on foreign countries. Originally a classified source of basic intelligence, *The World Factbook* has been available to the public since 1975 and is frequently cited by researchers working in developing countries.

## The Department of Commerce

Many trade and other economic issues are the province of the Department of Commerce (www.doc.gov). The International Trade Administration (ITA—www.ita.doc.gov) is the lead unit for trade in the Department of Commerce. It promotes U.S. exports of manufactured goods, nonagricultural commodities, and services. The ITA participates in formulating and implementing U.S. foreign trade and economic policies and monitors market access and compliance of U.S. international trade agreements. Although not concerned with international development issues, the Economic Development Administration (EDA—www.osec.doc.gov/eda) does focus on economic development in economically distressed areas of the United States. Within the Commerce Department is the Census Bureau (www.census.gov), which not only conducts the population census every ten years, but also keeps statistics on imports and exports and collects demographic information on 200 countries. Population pyramids and summary demographic information are available from the International Data Base of the Census Bureau (www.census.gov/ipc/www/idbnew.html). The

Census Bureau also maintains the HIV/AIDS Surveillance Data Base (www.census. gov/ipc/www/hivaidsd.html).

## Agencies Within the Office of the President

Within the Office of the President are two key components of the U.S. foreign policy team. The U.S. trade representative (www.ustr.gov) is America's chief trade negotiator and the principal trade policy advisor to the president. The trade representative has a Web page devoted to trade and development (www.ustr.gov/gsp). The National Security Council provides the president with a national security and foreign policy staff within the White House. The National Security Council, which is chaired by the president, includes the vice president, the secretaries of state and defense, the chairman of the Joint Chiefs of Staff, and the director of central intelligence. The secretary of the Treasury, the U.S. representative to the United Nations, the assistant to the president for national security affairs, the assistant to the president for economic policy, and the chief of staff to the president are invited to all meetings of the council. The attorney general and the director of the Office of National Drug Control Policy attend meetings pertaining to their jurisdictions, and other officials may be invited when appropriate. The newly created Office of Homeland Security (www.whitehouse.gov/homeland) is also within the Office of the President.

## The Department of Agriculture

The Department of Agriculture (www.usda.gov) helps ensure open markets for U.S. agricultural products and provides food aid to needy people overseas. The Foreign Agricultural Service (FAS—www.fas.usda.gov) monitors and assesses global food aid needs, maintains an international field structure that includes agricultural counselors and agricultural trade offices, and administers a variety of export promotion, technical, and food assistance programs. The FAS publishes reports and statistics on foreign countries. Many of these reports may be accessed online (www.fas.usda.gov/country.html).

## Centers for Disease Control and Prevention

The Centers for Disease Control and Prevention (www.cdc.gov), an agency within the Department of Health and Human Services, has increasingly taken a global perspective, since pathogens and health problems ignore international borders. The CDC works with the Joint United Nations Programme on HIV/AIDS and other organizations to monitor and combat the spread of HIV infections. The National Center for Infectious Diseases maintains a traveler's health Web page that contains information about diseases and outbreaks throughout the world (www.cdc.gov/travel).

## The Military

The U.S. military, with an annual budget in the hundreds of billions of dollars and a global presence, cannot be ignored when discussing the problems and policies of the developing world. The United States maintains bases in such places as Turkey and Panama. The closing of a military installation, such as Subic Bay in the Philippines, may have a major impact on the local economy of a developing country. Military aid may provide security to a government, and the choices of where to send troops, advisors, and military equipment impact the balance of power in the developing world.

The Library of Congress maintains a database on country studies prepared for the Department of the Army (lcweb2.loc.gov/frd/cs). The Department of Defense may be a useful source of additional information (www.defenselink.mil).

## Other Federal Agencies

The Peace Corps (www.peacecorps.gov) was formed in the 1960s to promote world peace and friendship. The Peace Corps, which currently has volunteers serving in seventy-six countries, has been involved in projects in 134 nations. Peace Corps programs aim to bring clean water to communities, educate children, help start new small businesses, and stop the spread of AIDS. The Smithsonian Institution (www.si.edu) is composed of sixteen museums and galleries, the National Zoo, and research facilities in the United States and abroad.

Other government agencies may have special departments devoted to food, population, and environment concerns, and agencies may work together on particular issues. The USAID, FAS, NASA, and other agencies maintain the Famine Early Warning System (www.fews.net). The Department of Justice has a center devoted the global challenge of crime (www.ojp.usdoj.gov/nij/international). NASA has a Web site called Visible Earth (visibleearth.nasa.gov), which provides satellite and other images and includes visualizations of the human impact on the earth. The Small Business Administration and other agencies are developing the U.S. Export Advisor (www. tradenet.gov). The Export-Import Bank (www.exim.gov) and the Trade and Development Agency (www.tda.gov) also have trade information. Refugee information may be gained from the Department of Health and Human Services' Office of Refugee Resettlement (www.acf.dhhs.gov/programs/orr) or the State Department (www.usinfo. state.gov/topical/global/refugees). The United States Environmental Protection Agency's has a Website called Enviro$en$e (es.epa.gov/cooperative/international/), which contains information on international pollution control programs. The EPA also has an office of international activities (www.epa.gov/oia). One objective of the Federal Reserve, the central bank of the United States (www.federalreserve.gov), is to provide financial services to the U.S. government, the public, financial institutions, and various foreign institutions. Economic data and research produced by the Federal Reserve Banks (www.federalreserve.gov/rnd.htm) may be found online.

## FOREIGN GOVERNMENT AGENCIES

Foreign countries may be useful sources of information in two ways. Developed countries may have agencies that focus on international development, similar to USAID. Developing countries also provide information on themselves. As English is the common language in international affairs, many foreign organizations have English versions of their Web pages.

The United States is not the only country that provides foreign aid and assistance. As a percentage of GDP, many countries provide more foreign aid than the United States. The government of Germany has an agency called the GTZ (www. gtz.de/english/index.asp), which has the goal of improving the living conditions in developing and transition countries while conserving natural resources. The Canadian International Development Agency(www.acdi-cida.gc.ca/INDEX-E.HTM) seeks to improve basic human needs, infrastructure, the private sector, and the environment while promoting gender equality and good governance. The Japan International

Cooperation Agency (www.jica.go.jp/english) is a major source of development aid. In the United Kingdom, the Department for International Development (www.dfid.gov. uk) is responsible for promoting development and the reduction of poverty. When looking for information about international aid to a particular country, it is often the nations with which the countries share a colonial legacy that are the largest donors.

Foreign governments maintain relations with the United States through their embassies. The embassies of developing countries may provide useful information about their home countries. Embassy.org provides a list of foreign embassies in Washington, D.C. (www.embassy.org/embassies), including their addresses, phone numbers, and Web pages. Foreign government agencies may make information directly available, and several sites provide links to foreign governments. Some Websites focus on governments and political parties (www.politicalresources.net and dir.yahoo.com/Government/Countries), while others focus on constitutions and laws (www.psr.keele.ac.uk/const.htm). The Bank for International Settlements (www.bis.org/cbanks.htm) compiles links to central banks' Web pages, as does a private individual (adams.patriot. net/~bernkopf) who also has links to ministries of finance and economy. The International Foundation for Election Systems and the Cable News Network (CNN) manage a Website on elections throughout the world (www.cnn.com/WORLD/election.watch).

## INTERNATIONAL ORGANIZATIONS

Countries may band together to meet certain objectives. They sign agreements, treaties, and conventions, and they establish agencies and forums to work toward their common goals. Some organizations are based on geography or particular issues, while others are truly global.

### The United Nations

One hundred eighty-nine countries (Switzerland being a notable exception) belong to the United Nations (UN—www.un.org/english). The four purposes of the United Nations are to maintain international peace and security, to develop friendly relations among nations, to cooperate in solving international problems and in promoting respect for human rights, and to be a center for harmonizing the actions of nations. The organizational structure of the United Nations is complex, but it publishes a useful chart (www.un.org/aboutun/chart.html) that contains embedded links. The United Nations has six principal organs. The General Assembly functions as a parliament for all member nations. The Security Council, which has five permanent members (the United States, China, France, the Russian Federation, and the United Kingdom) and ten elected members, attempts to maintain international peace and security. The Economic and Social Council, with fifty-four elected members, oversees the economic and social programs of the United Nations and its related organizations. The Trusteeship Council was established to provide international supervision for territories (such as Pulau) seeking self-government or independence. The International Court of Justice, which consists of fifteen judges elected by the General Assembly and the Security Council, settles disputes between member countries. The Secretariat, led by the Secretary-General, carries out the substantive and administrative work of the United Nations.

Within the United Nations are several programs and funds. The United Nations Children's Fund (UNICEF—www.unicef.org) serves as an advocate for the protection of children's rights and works to improve the basic needs and opportunities of children. UNICEF provides statistical data relating to mothers and children by country (www.unicef.org/statis). The World Food Programme (WFP—www.wfp.org) is the food aid organization of the United Nations. The United Nations Population Fund (www.unfpa.org) works with developing countries to find solutions for their population problems and is the largest international source of population assistance. The United Nations Environment Programme (www.unep.org) promotes sustainable resource use and environmental conservation. The Office of the United Nations High Commissioner for Refugees (UNHCR—www.unhcr.ch) coordinates international action for the worldwide protection of refugees and the resolution of refugee problems. The United Nations Human Settlement Programme or UN-HABITAT (www.unhabitat.org) works for sustainable human settlements and adequate shelter for all. The United Nations Development Programme (UNDP—www.undp.org) works to reduce poverty and supports technical cooperation among developing countries. Within the UNDP are the United Nations Development Fund for Women (UNIFEM—www.unifem.undp.org), which works for gender equality, and the United Nations Population Information Network (www.undp.org/popin), which facilitates and enhances the availability of population information. The United Nations Drug Control Programme (UNDCP—www.undcp.org) fights illicit drug use and international crime. The Office of the United Nations High Commissioner for Human Rights (OHCHR—www.unhchr.ch) promotes universal respect for and observance of human rights and fundamental freedoms. The Universal Declaration of Human Rights was passed by the U.N. General Assembly in 1948 (www.unhchr.ch/udhr/lang/eng.htm). The United Nations Conference on Trade and Development (UNCTAD—www.unctad.org) helps to integrate developing countries into the world economy and publishes reports on international trade and investment. The United Nations University (UNU—www.unu.edu), headquartered in Tokyo, has thirteen research and training centers and programs around the world.

## Organizations Associated with the United Nations

Several autonomous organizations are joined to the United Nations through special agreements. The International Labour Organization (ILO—www.ilo.org) formulates international labor standards. The Food and Agriculture Organization of the United Nations (FAO—www.fao.org) strives to raise levels of nutrition and standards of living, to improve agricultural productivity, and to better the condition of rural populations. The FAO maintains several statistical databases related to food production and consumption (apps.fao.org). The United Nations Educational, Scientific and Cultural Organization (UNECO—www.unesco.org) promotes education for all, cultural development, protection of the world's natural and cultural heritage, and international cooperation in science. The World Health Organization (WHO—www.who.int) aims to solve health problems and attain for all people the highest possible level of health.

The World Bank group (www.worldbank.org) provides loans and technical assistance to developing countries to reduce poverty and advance sustainable economic growth. The World Bank consists of the International Bank for Reconstruction and Development (IBRD), the International Development Association (IDA), the International Finance Corporation (IFC), the Multilateral Investment Guarantee Agency (MIGA), and the International Centre for Settlement of Investment Disputes (ICSID). A wealth of individual country data (www.worldbank.org/data/countrydata/countrydata.html) is available from the World Bank. The International Monetary Fund (IMF—www.imf.org) promotes international monetary cooperation and exchange stability. While the World Bank is concerned with technical programs to promote development, the IMF is focused on currency exchange and balance of payment issues. Information for individual countries is available through the IMF Web page (www.imf.org/external/country/index.htm), but some publications are only available for purchase. The World Trade Organization (WTO—www.wto.org) focuses on the rules of trade between nations. The WTO has produced *Trade Policy Reviews* for several countries (www.wto.org/english/tratop_e/tpr_e/tpr_e.htm).

The International Fund for Agricultural Development (IFAD—www.ifad.org) was formed to combat hunger and rural poverty in developing countries. The United Nations Industrial Development Organization (UNIDO—www.unido.org) promotes the industrial advancement of developing countries through technical assistance, advisory services, and training. UNIDO has industrial data for select countries (www.unido.org/Regions.cfm). Other autonomous international organizations associated with the United Nations include the International Civil Aviation Organization, the Universal Postal Union, the International Telecommunication Union, the World Meteorological Organization, the International Maritime Organization, the World Intellectual Property Organization, and the International Atomic Energy Agency.

## Other International Organizations

The International Food Policy Research Institute (IFPRI—www.ifpri.org) identifies and analyzes policies for sustainably meeting the food needs of the developing world. The research divisions of IFPRI concentrate on environment and production technology, markets and structural studies, food consumption and nutrition, and trade and macroeconomics. Country-level research published by IFPRI (www.ifpri.org/country/country.htm) is available for many developing countries. The Consultative Group on International Agricultural Research (CGIAR—www.cgiar.org) supports a network of international agricultural research centers that focus on increasing agricultural productivity, protecting the environment, saving biodiversity, improving public policy, and strengthening research at the national level. CGIAR holds in trust a large collection of germplasm samples.

Not all international organizations have a global perspective. The African Development Bank (www.afdb.org), Asian Development Bank (www.adb.org), Caribbean Development Bank (www.caribank.org), and Inter-American Development Bank (www.iadb.org) are international organizations that work to reduce poverty in their respective regions. The European Investment Bank (eib.eu.int) has projects in the transition countries in Central and Eastern Europe. The Organization of American States (www.oas.org), Organization of African Unity (www.africanunion.org), and Association of Southeast Asian Nations (www.aseansec.org) have geographically based foci. The Organization of Petroleum Exporting Countries (www.opec.org), is made up of developing countries (including Venezuela, Nigeria, and Indonesia) that are heavily reliant on oil exports as a source of income. As trade has become more important, regional free-trade associations have been formed, such as the North

American Free Trade Agreement (NAFTA—www.nafta-sec-alena.org/english/index.htm), the European Union (europa.eu.int/index_en.htm), and Mercosur (www.mercosur.org) in South America. The West Africa Monetary Union includes eight nations that share a common currency (www.bceao.int). The Asia–Pacific Economic Cooperation (www.apecsec.org.sg) promotes open trade and economic cooperation among the countries of the Pacific Rim.

The Organisation for Economic Co-operation and Development (OECD—www.oecd.org) is an association of countries with a commitment to market economics and pluralistic democracy. Organizations such as G-7, G-8 (www.g8.utoronto.ca), and G-20 (www.g20.org/indexe.html) are forums in which finance ministers and central bank governors can discuss important international economic issues. The North Atlantic Treaty Organization (www.nato.int) is an alliance that seeks to safeguard the freedom and security of its nineteen member countries. The Organization for Security and Co-operation in Europe (OSCE—www.osce.org) is a security organization made up of fifty-five countries from Europe, Central Asia, and North America. The Commonwealth (www.thecommonwealth.org) is an association of fifty-four countries that were once part of the British Empire.

## NONGOVERNMENTAL ORGANIZATIONS

Filling a gap between the public and private sectors are thousands of NGOs, which play a critical role in issues of food, population, and the environment in the developing world. Some are very localized, while others have achieved global prominence. Many are useful sources of information, but remember to be wary when using data from an NGO publication if you are unfamiliar with the NGO.

The World Resources Institute (WRI—www.wri.org) works to reverse the degradation of ecosystems, halt climate changes caused by human activity, reduce the use of materials and generation of wastes, and guarantee access to information regarding natural resources. The WRI publishes the biennial *World Resources* texts. EarthTrends (earthtrends.wri.org) is a WRI Website dedicated to environmental and sustainable development information and contains country profiles with key environmental facts. The World Wildlife Fund (WWF—www.panda.org) and Green Peace (www.greenpeace.org) are two highly visible organizations that combat environmental degradation. Resources for the Future (RFF—www.rff.org) is a think tank devoted to social science research into environmental and natural resource issues. The Nature Conservancy (nature.org) and Conservation International (www.conservation.org) are concerned with environmental conservation.

Care International (www.care.org) is a large organization that delivers relief assistance to people in need and seeks long-term solutions to global poverty. CARE originally stood for Cooperation for American Relief Everywhere, but it is now truly a global organization. Oxfam (www.oxfam.org) attempts to address the structural causes of poverty and related injustice. Some of the largest relief organizations, such as Catholic Relief Services (www.catholicrelief.org) and World Vision (www.worldvision.org), have religious affiliations. Médecins Sans Frontières, also known as Doctors Without Borders, (www.msf.org), provides medical aid wherever it is needed. The International Federation of Red Cross and Red Crescent Societies (www.ifrc.org) is the world's largest humanitarian organization.

Transparency International—TI (www.transparency.org) is dedicated to curbing corruption at both the international and national levels, and has developed the

Corruption Perceptions Index (http://www.transparency.org/cpi/index.html), which ranks ninety nations in terms of the degree to which corruption is perceived to exist among public officials and politicians. It also produces country and issue papers. Human Rights Watch (www.hrw.org) is dedicated to protecting the human rights of people around the world. Amnesty International (www.amnesty.org) campaigns to free all prisoners of conscience, ensure fair and prompt trials for political prisoners, abolish the death penalty, torture, and other cruel treatment of prisoners, end political killings and disappearances, and oppose human rights abuses by opposition groups. Freedom House (www.freedomhouse.com) ranks all countries in the world in terms of civil and political liberties. The Heritage Foundation (www.heritage.org) published the *2002 Index of Economic Freedom*, which ranks almost 150 countries in terms of economic opportunities and regulation. An interactive online version (www.heritage. org/index) is available. The Economic Freedom Network (www.freetheworld.com) also rates countries on economic freedom.

The Population Reference Bureau (PRB—www.prb.org) provides information on U.S. and international population trends and their implications. The PRB and USAID have developed a very useful Website (www.popnet.org) with population data and links. The International Planned Parenthood Federation (www.ippf.org) campaigns to increase support for reproductive health and family planning worldwide. Planned Parenthood and the United Nations Population Information Network have developed country profiles of sexual and reproductive health (www.ippf.org/regions/countries/index.htm).

The World Economic Forum (www.weforum.org) brings together government, business, and other leaders. The annual meeting in Davos, Switzerland, has a major impact on international issues. The International Chamber of Commerce (www.iccwbo.org) is a business organization with companies and associations in over 130 countries.

Many more NGOs exist. Action Without Borders (www.idealist.org) has many links. The Union of International Associations (www.uia.org) claims to have information on thousands of international nonprofit organizations.

## MEDIA, ACADEMIA, AND OTHER ENTITIES

The news media are an excellent source of information on countries. The Cable News Network (CNN—www.cnn.com/WORLD), the British Broadcasting Company (BBC—www.bbc.co.uk), the Associated Press (AP), and Reuters have bureaus throughout the world. Yahoo! (news.yahoo.com) picks up wire stories from AP and Reuters and other sources. The National Technical Information Service of the Department of Commerce compiles news from foreign sources (wnc.fedworld.gov). The *Christian Science Monitor* (www.csmonitor.com) has more of a global outlook than other daily newspapers. The *Financial Times* (www.ft.com) and *Wall Street Journal* (www.wsj.com) may also be helpful, especially with economic and business news. The *Economist* (www.economist.com) carries international news and frequently runs special profiles of countries and regions. A sister group of The *Economist*, the Economist Intelligence Unit (www.eiu.com), publishes a *Country Report* and a *Country Profile* for most countries. News magazines with regional themes, such as the *Far Eastern Economic Review* (www.feer.com), are invaluable for certain parts of the world. *National Geographic* (www.nationalgeographic.com) has maps and articles on environmental conditions in various countries.

Academic sources are also helpful. Journals such as *Foreign Affairs* (www.foreignaffairs.org) and *Current History* (www.currenthistory.com) have articles on countries that may delve more deeply into issues than the popular press. Databases are maintained by academic sources. The University of California, San Diego, has a catalog of social science data (odwin.ucsd.edu/idata). The University of Texas at Austin has an online collection of maps (www.lib.utexas.edu/Libs/PCL/Map_collection/Map_collection.html). The Penn World Tables (pwt.econ.upenn.edu) contain macroeconomic data for most countries. Resources for Economists (rfe.wustl.edu/Data/World/index.html) has links to other international data sources. The Internet has yet to completely replace libraries, and many university libraries have large collections of books and other media with information about developing countries and development issues.

Individual countries may have other actors that play important roles in development policies. Religion may be influential, especially when it is state-sponsored or the cause for political division. The relationship between local business interests and multinational corporations that seek natural resources, relatively cheap labor, new markets, and lax regulatory standards is key to economic and social development. *Fortune* magazine publishes an annual list of the 500 largest corporations (www.fortune.com/lists/G500/index.html) in the world, as ranked by annual revenues. These corporations have a truly global reach (e.g., McDonald's has restaurants in 121 countries throughout the world). Countries that have experienced a large amount of emigration find that their diaspora are often an important source of foreign currency and investment. Sports may have a major impact on a country. The International Olympic Committee (www.olympics.org) consists of 199 national Olympic committees.

## CONCLUSION

This chapter is meant to be a guide to agencies that play a role in the problems and policies of international development. It is certainly not comprehensive, nor is it supposed to be. Internet and library searches should lead you to new organizations, data sources, and issues that you will want to explore, but always maintain a certain level of skepticism when doing research. It can be very simple and inexpensive to start an organization and put out publications through the Internet. It is becoming increasingly common for charlatans to start charities with official-sounding names to defraud well-meaning individuals. Similarly, a group with an extreme political agenda can easily form an organization with an innocuous-sounding name to misinform the public. Well-established organizations work hard to protect their reputations, and their information is usually trustworthy. It is important, however, to investigate the objectives, funding sources, and membership of any organization before you cite its research. This includes government sources, especially in the developing world. Government agencies often have their own agendas, and the data they report are sometimes inaccurate or purposely misleading. It is often wise to seek out multiple sources to confirm what you find on the Internet.

Additionally, this chapter mainly profiles organizations related to economic and political development; literature, art, and music are ignored. Cultural factors have enormous influence in the developing world. To gain a true insight into many issues in the developing world, both local and external cultures must be studied.

# 19

# The Role of Nongovernmental Organizations in Rural Development

**GEDEON M. MUDACUMURA**

*Pennsylvania Treasury Department, and Pennsylvania State University, Harrisburg, Pennsylvania, U.S.A.*

## INTRODUCTION

Brown and Korten (1991) recognized that the decade of the 1980s saw a rapid increase of interest in nongovernmental and nonprofit organizations within the international development community. The Bretton Wood Institutions, the world's biggest financial institutions, have selected nongovernmental organizations (NGOs) for the implementation of their development projects in developing countries (Beckmann, 1991). The expanding role of NGOs has also been recognized by international agencies, including the Club of Rome and the Development Assistance Committee of the Organization for Economic Cooperation and Development (OECD) (OECD, 1988). In fact, the number of NGOs registered within the OECD countries grew from 1600 in 1980 to 2970 in 1993 (Smillie and Helmick, 1993).

The rationale behind this increasing interest in NGOs is probably their presumed success in reaching the poor and addressing their socioeconomic problems more adequately than government agencies. A second justification for the rise and growth of NGOs is supposedly related to the increasing availability of funding under the New Policy Agenda. The latter is driven by two basic sets of beliefs organized around two poles: neoliberal economics (free markets and privatization) and liberal democratic theory (democratization and strengthening civil society) (Edwards and Hulme, 1996).

During the United Nations Conference on Environment and Development (UNCED) in Rio de Janeiro (1992), world leaders demonstrated that no one group of nations could continue progressing while the majority of its people remained hungry and poor (Dwivedi, 1994). The preamble of Agenda 21:1.1 of the Rio Declaration began on an optimistic note.

> Humanity stands at a defining moment in its history. We are confronted with a perpetuation of disparities between and within nations, a worsening of poverty, hunger, ill health and illiteracy, and the continuing deterioration of the ecosystems on which we depend for our well-being. However, integration of environment and development concerns, and a greater attention to them will lead to the fulfillment of basic needs, improved living standards for all, better protected and managed ecosystems and a safer, more prosperous future. No nation can achieve this on its own; but together we can—in a global partnership for sustainable development.

The income disparity between the "haves" and the "have-nots" was demonstrated clearly from the United Nations Development Programme's (UNDP) statistics on the global distribution of income. The statistics showed that the richest 20% of the world's population received 82.7% of the world's total income, while the poorest 20% got only 1.4% (UNDP, 1992).

According to the World Development Report (2000/2001), the world has deep poverty amid plenty. Of the world's 6 billion people, 2.8 billion—almost half—live on less than $2 a day, and 1.2 billion—a fifth—survive on less than $1 a day. The average income in the twenty richest countries is thirty-seven times the average income in the poorest twenty—a gap that has doubled in the past forty years. Ultimately, these statistics reveal that global economic growth had hardly filtered down, and that the optimism that so-called modern development would have floated people on a rising tide of wealth and prosperity was misplaced (Pezzoli, 1998).

A close examination of the depressing statistics on the increasing levels of poverty may lead to the conclusion that poor countries' development policies have failed to properly address the crucial needs of the majority of the population. It is an indisputable fact that the official development policies have not reached the majority of the people living in rural areas. As a result, the incidence of debilitating, dehumanizing poverty persists at unacceptable levels in most developing countries.

Brown and Korten (1991) argued that the advances achieved through economic modernization have left large segments of the population poorer than what they were before the introduction of modern technologies in many countries. To critics, the primary causes of extreme poverty are immaterial, lying in certain deficiencies in education, organization, and discipline. Without these, all resources remain latent, untapped potential (Schumacher, 1973). To what extent do NGOs fulfill the challenging tasks of educating and organizing the masses of poor people in the design and implementation of adequate development policies?

The economic literature mentions two opposing perspectives on poverty reduction—the technocratic and the institutional. Economists prefer to rely on the technocratic approach, when emphasizes designing development policies that target the poor as effectively as possible. Others, including NGOs, are more comfortable with the institutional approach, which fosters the development of institutions and the improvement of government policies of alleviating poverty (Besley, 1996).

This chapter aims at ascertaining the role of NGOs in building local capacity, a sine qua non for sustaining rural development. Focusing on the institutional approach, the first section briefly reviews the emergence of NGOs in the development arena while highlighting their critical mission of building the organizational capacities necessary to mobilize the energies and creativity of the poor to solve their own problems. The second section explores the interplay between local and international NGOs in fulfilling their challenging mission. Considering the complex development issues, the author recommends networking all NGOs in the third section, and concludes the chapter with a call for development scholars and practitioners to conduct empirical research geared toward assessing the effectiveness of NGOs in reaching the poor and furthering rural development.

## NONGOVERNMENTAL ORGANIZATIONS—A CRITICAL MISSION

Historically, government agencies have been the dominant actors in the planning and implementation of development policies. The wide range of development theories initiated in the 1950s and 1960s emphasized the role of the central government, and little thought was given to self-direct capacity for organization among rural constituencies. For instance, early development theorists stressed the need for transferring Western technologies and management approaches to the illiterate and backward people of the developing nations, whose production techniques were hopelessly behind the times.

As Esman (1980) remarked, the elements of the prevailing development paradigm were that all societies could modernize and grow economically in a sequence of historically verified stages that had occurred in Western nations over the previous two centuries and that this modernization and growth could be accelerated in developing countries through the transfer of resources and technologies from industrialized nations. The state would be the principal instrument of development.

The appropriate development approach was thus to replace backward production techniques with advanced methods that rural people would be taught to adopt. Modernization theorists argued that modern cultures must replace traditional cultures for progress to occur. Indigenous local organizations were bound to be traditional and thus obstructive to the kind of change considered necessary by the agents of modernization (Apter, 1965).

Emerging economic development theories of the 1970s identified the development needs that were to be filled by transfering technology and resources from richer to poorer nations. Such transfers led to an organization gap between central government agencies and the rural communities they were supposed to help, a gap that is believed to be the major limiting factor to effective development (Uphoff and Esman, 1974).

Owens and Shaw (1972) were among the first development scholars to highlight the relevance of bridging the organization gap separating central government agencies and local development communities. Building on Owens and Shaw's insights, other scholars posited that like the economic factors of land, labor and capital, organization, technology, and resource transfers are complementary elements of larger processes (Uphoff and Esman, 1974).

The underlying assumption behind the importance of organization was that if the poor could become organized, they could both acquire more resources to enhance their productivity and well-being and deploy those resources more effectively. International development donors and national governments turned to NGOs as potential instruments for organizing the poor and implementing official development projects. Public and private development funds were thus channeled through NGOs.

## INTERPLAY—LOCAL AND INTERNATIONAL NGOs

Brown (1992) conceived NGOs as typical private, nonprofit groups organized around shared values and visions for a better world. Similarly, the World Bank considered NGOs as private organizations pursuing activities to relieve suffering, promote the interests of the poor, protect the environment, or undertake community development (World Bank, 1988). The terms nonprofit, nongovernmental, and private voluntary organizations are often used interchangeably to denote any organization engaged in international and national relief and development work.

Many NGOs perform their traditional and operational relief and welfare roles by providing goods, services, and logistical support, while others are considered solely as development catalysts that concentrate on stimulating and developing institutional capacities to produce long-term change. As mentioned earlier, the focus of this chapter is on NGOs that develop institutional capacities by building grassroots organizations for self-help and self-reliance and serving as facilitators of development issues that governments have either chosen to ignore or ineffectively addressed.

NGOs are not a novel social formation of the 1970s or 1980s. Cernea (1988) argued that such organizations have existed for longer than most governments. Focusing on the recent explosive emergence of NGOs, he pointed out three characteristics related to NGOs engaged in development.

First, many NGOs have started in both developed and developing countries in most areas of public endeavor and are active on behalf of either local or national interests. Second, old NGOs have taken up functions that are new for them, adding development-oriented and production-support activities (e.g., agricultural development work) to their traditional concern for relief and welfare. Third, NGOs, particularly the those organizations for the poor, have become internally sophisticated, better organized, and more aware of their power, and thus have increased their militancy and mobilization capabilities.

To complement each other, networks of NGOs are being created and NGO councils and federations have been established at national and international levels. Have, however, these experienced international NGOs been successful in organizing the poor of the developing nations, helping them to become actively involved in the formulation of policies that affect their daily lives?

Korten (1986) and Van Sant (1986) further contended that the international nongovernment organizations (INGOs) act as intermediary facilitators, helping local NGOs to become more effective agents of rural development. A closer look at the type of collaboration that exists between INGOs and local NGOs reveals that traditional "top-down" assistance has failed to provide sustainable improvements in the lives of the poor. Jones (1993) remarked that developing countries' right and ability to control their own development is forcing INGOs to change their role. Along the same line, the international donor community is recognizing poor countries' growing leadership capacity to the point of bypassing INGOs and directly funding local NGOs.

The World Commission on Environment and Development (WCED, 1987) broadly suggested the type and nature of collaboration that should exist among local and international NGOs as follows:

> The vast majority of the [NGO] bodies are national or local in nature, and a successful transition to sustainable development will require substantial strengthening of their capacities. To an increasing extent, national NGOs draw strength from association with

their counterparts in other countries and from participation in international programmes and consultations. NGOs in developing countries are particularly in need of international support—professional and moral as well as financial—to carry out their roles effectively...Governments should establish or strengthen procedures for official consultation and more meaningful participation by NGOs in all relevant intergovernmental organizations.

While INGOs provide the necessary financial support and technical training to local NGOs, such collaboration should focus primarily on the genuine empowerment of NGOs, getting them ready to take over sustainable and innovative development work. Empowerment is here conceived as the enabling process that allows the intended beneficiaries of development programs and projects to exert a more positive influence on activities that will influence the direction of their lives. From that perspective, development scholars and practitioners have been debating the extent to which NGOs strive to empower people at the grassroots level.

For instance, the World Bank provided the opportunity for NGOs to participate in the elaboration of the poverty reduction strategy paper (PRSP) process, ensuring that the government draws the development strategy together with a broad range of national stakeholders. From a theoretical standpoint, such opportunity maximizes the involvement of NGOs in the policy process, while institutionalizing such involvement so that it becomes the norm in all future policy debates.

Along the same line, the United States Agency for International Development (USAID) clarified the aim of all its programs; that is, to enhance participation and to encourage accountability, transparency, decentralization, and empowerment of communities and individuals (Sholes and Covey, 1996). International NGOs should thus concentrate their efforts on organizing and empowering local communities, the best strategic approach leading to successful formulation and implementation of development policies (Drabek, 1987; Paul and Israel, 1991).

Emphasizing the importance of the participation of the poor in rural development, Nindi (1993) viewed cost reductions, greater efficiency, greater profits, job enrichment, happiness, solidarity, and community development as the main objectives of participation. Participation is here defined as the process through which development stakeholders influence and share control over priority setting, policy making, resource allocations, and access to public goods and services (World Bank, 2001).

Along the line of building local capacity, Schumacher (1973) viewed the aims of international development aid as providing the people of the developing nations with the material opportunity for using their talents and for of living a full and happy life, highlighting that the best aid to give to developing countries is intellectual aid, a gift of useful knowledge that is infinitely preferable to a gift of material things. As Schumacher (1973) summed it up, the gift of material goods makes people dependent, but the gift of knowledge makes people free.

Ultimately, NGOs may have not been very successful in building local knowledge. In fact, critics argue that both the people and governments of Africa rely increasingly on NGOs to provide services that would ordinarily be filled by the state http://www.nytimes.com/2002/03/22/international/africa/22NGO.html).

Moreover, a close examination of the negative impacts of the current foreign debt on poor nations may lead one to question the extent to which INGOs collaborate with their counterparts in developing nations to train individuals, freeing them from the burden of unbearable foreign debts. A huge part of the economies of poor countries is devoted to producing goods for export, with the resultant income sent back out of the economy and not available for domestic use, even for such important domestic needs as health care, education, and infrastructure.

Along the same lines, an analysis of foreign debts also pushes one to seriously think about the effectiveness of the international financial institutions that supposedly play the role of bridging research and practice. In that respect, Wolfenson (1996) noted that the World Bank serves as a global clearinghouse that identifies and seeks out the best ideas, develops their practical applications, and gets them to end users in time to apply them to the real problems people face.

Looking at the current socioeconomic indicators that highlight the continual rise of poverty in developing countries, one would question the efficacy of the best ideas promoted by the leading international development agency. Brown (1992) reported that NGOs' participation in World Bank projects increased sevenfold, from an average of fourteen new projects a year between 1973 and 1988 to an average of ninety-six new projects a year between 1989 and 1990. While involving more NGOs in the implementation of development policies, the World Bank's statistics revealed that the number of individuals living in poverty failed to decrease (2.718 billion living on less than $2 a day) (World Bank, 2000).

Based on these statistics, to what extent have NGOs sponsored by the leading international financial institution successfully conveyed the best ideas and best practices to improve the living standards of the poor while helping them to get out from under their unbearable foreign debt? Are these NGOs acting as pressure groups mobilizing citizens to devise specific development policies geared toward improving societal welfare?

## Strengthening Grassroots Organizations

The emerging capacity-building perspective regards beneficiaries as active creators of change rather than as victims of a disaster or consumers of services, leading to the speculation that active creators are potentially self-reliant participants and partners rather than passive recipients of development aid (Brown, 1992). This perspective explains the underlying raison d'être of development NGOs, which is to mobilize people into organized structures of voluntary group action for self-reliance and self-development (Cernea, 1988).

Once people are organized, the ultimate goal is to make better use of their own local productive resources, to create new resources and services, to promote equity and alleviate poverty, to influence government actions toward these same objectives, and to establish new institutional frameworks that will sustain people-centered or actor-centered development (Cernea, 1988). By prioritizing people's organization, NGOs recognize the centrality of people in development policies, as opposed to conventional approaches, which focused on technology alone or on financial resources alone, considering people as an afterthought. Considering that development is about transforming societies, improving the lives of the poor, and enabling everyone to have access to health care and education (Stiglitz, 2002), it is not surprising that official development policies devised along the lines of conventional practices failed to improve the lives of the beneficiaries.

Emphasizing the importance of putting people first, Schumacher (1973) warned that the results of the second development decade would be no better than those of the first unless there was a conscious and determined shift of emphasis from goods to people. Without such a shift, the results of development aid would become increasingly destructive. Three decades later, most development scholars and practitioners are realizing that there is no other way to sustain development without paying special attention to the social dimension. Have NGOs been real development catalysts, engaging positively in the transformation of poor nations' societies and enabling the majority of the poor to improve the quality of their lives?

## Serving as Development Catalysts

Before exploring the role of NGOs as development catalysts, it is important to remember that there is no agreed-upon definition of the concept of development. From an institutional perspective, Brown and Korten (1991) conceived of development as a process by which the members of a society develop themselves and their institutions in ways that enhance their ability to mobilize and manage resources to produce sustainable and justly distributed improvements in their quality of life consistent with their own aspirations.

NGOs engaged in development as defined above should be driven by shared values. Such shared values can be powerful guides offering community members a sense of efficacy in molding the world to fit a collectively desired vision. Assuming that the superordinate goal of the community is to improve the living standards of its residents, NGOs sharing that vision would work toward achieving it.

Moreover, it is argued that development catalyst organizations use temporary interventions to promote the creation of sustainable locally accountable institutions that improve humans' quality of life. Their role should be temporary, since their actions are directed to induce changes that produce self-directing, self-financing local institutional arrangements that could survive after the departure of the NGOs (Brown and Korten, 1991).

Development catalyst NGOs should thus build self-reliant, sustainable institutions accountable to the people. Such NGOs should identify themselves with the interests of the poor while constantly interacting with them, enabling them to analyze their problems, to understand their problems better, and to articulate their felt needs (Nindi, 1993). Such interactions should be structured around the main objective of strengthening the management and analytical skills of individuals comprising grassroots organizations.

## Empowering Local People

Many scholars push the task of catalyst NGOs a further step, suggesting that local beneficiaries working with catalyst NGOs should feel more comfortable in discussing their development concerns. To reach that point requires NGOs to properly distribute the gift of useful knowledge. One would agree with Schumacher that such appropriation of the gifts of knowledge to thousands of beneficiaries would undoubtedly open up a new and much more hopeful era in the history of development.

Knowledgeable beneficiaries, interested in self-reliance, driven by mutual benefit sharing, and committed to building democratic structure, would be more effective only when they opt to pull together their efforts, creating their own organizations, often called "peoples' organizations" (POs) or "grassroots organizations." The fundamental importance of the latter is to maintain the dynamism of a society. Peoples' organizations give voice to those who have been historically marginalized and provide them with a crucial vehicle for exercising their rights while holding their governments accountable (Miller, 1994).

Development catalyst NGOs should have a central task to empower the people through the formation of grassroots organizations, helping them to assume key economic and political roles in improving their own situations, including exerting influence over the decisions of other agencies that affect them. Once initiated, POs should work seriously toward making their activities self-supporting and locally sustainable. Esman and Uphoff (1984) and other development scholars provided evidence supporting the strong relationships between the presence of local organizations and economic and social improvements.

Peoples' organizations can be critical actors in local development success and sustainability. For instance, the postevaluations of the World Bank projects revealed how local organizations that were involved in the formulation and implementation of development projects took over a project and sustained its activities (Cernea, 1987).

A successful takeover step implies that people's organizations recognize early the relevance of relying on their own financial and technical means, realizing that excessive outside financial assistance may create dependence and work to the detriment of the organizations over the long run (Brown and Korten, 1991). Effective development catalyst organizations should explore the possibilities of linking with others to share experience and successful technologies and exchange information. One may question how development catalyst NGOs have been effective in helping grassroots organizations devise suitable intermediate technologies.

## Focusing on Intermediate Technology

As discussed earlier, economic development theorists of the 1950s and early 1960s viewed the process of development as a series of successive stages of economic growth. The economic theory of development primarily focused on the notion that the right quantity and mixture of savings, investment, and foreign financial and technical assistance were all that was necessary to enable poor countries to get developed. During the decades following the 1950s, unsuccessful efforts were deployed in transferring Western technologies to developing countries.

Some of the main reasons for such failures had to do with the belief in the universal application of Western technologies—more concretely, the erroneous conception that what has worked in the developed countries should work in the developing nations.

The underestimation of local cultures was another big factor responsible for the failure of development policies. As Soedjatmoko and Murase (1985) put it, in their preoccupation with growth and its stages and with the provisions of capital and skills, development theorists paid insufficient attention to institutional and structural problems and the power of historical, cultural, and religious forces in the development process.

The report of the Commission on Global Governance (1995) refers to NGOs as key organizations that can test innovative ideas and devise appropriate technologies because of their direct knowledge of local needs. Are current NGOs concerned with the development of intermediate technologies with a human face, technologies that reintegrate the human being with his skillful hands and creative brain into the productive process?

Wellard and Copestake (1993) claimed that the slow growth of food production and the persistence of unacceptable levels of poverty in sub-Saharan Africa were explained by the inadequate supply of productivity-enhancing technology appropriate to the needs of poor farmers. Lappe and Collins (1977) further recognized the existence of local technology, suggesting that the role of NGOs or other development agencies should be to help local people share their knowledge and experience while combining the best elements in the elaboration of suitable technologies.

Such an approach would allow people to be part of a dynamic unfolding of events rather than be on the receiving end of a technical exercise (Lappe and Collins, 1977). Also, Farrington and Biggs (1990) revealed that NGOs that apply the approach of participatory research play an important role in devising new technologies and methods.

Developing countries need more intermediate technologies designed for the purpose of effectively using the available labor in rural areas. NGOs should concentrate on the identification and diffusion of these intermediate technologies that are appropriate for labor-surplus societies. The diffusion will be more effective when local NGOs make a firm commitment to work together, sharing their experience through networks.

## NETWORKING DEVELOPMENT NGOs

Considering a network as a noncentralized system of autonomous segments with multiple leaders that is sustained by shared values and interests, networking makes it possible to link together like-minded organizations for sharing information, planning joint activities, and making a united response to political pressures from governments and the demands of international development agencies. From this perspective, networking development NGOs could strengthen their collective advocacy efforts since they are all concerned about the sustainability of local development initiatives. Such a functional multiorganizational network requires maintaining a vision, promoting changes in attitudes and perceptions, and ensuring continuous communication exchanges among network members (Chisholm, 1996).

Networking is one appropriate approach that would enable NGOs to ensure that their local development initiatives are materialized and sustained while sharing individual resources in mutually supportive ways. Building such network associations would further serve as important channels for the diffusion of ideas and technologies for development policies.

Moreover, Carroll and Montgomery (1987) considered networking as a means of sharing experiences and methodologies and conducting joint projects, as well as a useful course of action in negotiating with international donors. With the current trend toward globalization, networking NGOs at the local, national, regional, and global levels could strengthen local capacity while maintaining the flow of development approaches and other useful development techniques that local NGOs might apply to achieve their developmental goals.

By focusing on the development and dissemination of the intermediate technologies with a human face through local, national, regional, or global networks, development NGOs could succeed at making local development more people-centered. Proponents of "people-centered development" emphasize human development, equitable distribution of resources, and long-term ecological sustainability as central concerns of development strategy.

It is worth recalling that before the 1970s, development was always seen as an economic phenomenon in which rapid gains in overall and per capita Gross National Product (GNP) growth would "trickle down" to the masses (Todaro, 1996). During that period, economists treated development as if it were nothing more than an exercise in applied economics, unrelated to political ideas, forms of government, and the role of people in society. Owens (1987) suggested considering not just ways in which societies can become more productive but the quality of these societies that are supposed to become more productive—the development of people rather than the development of things.

In fact, the World Bank, which championed economic growth as the goal of development, readjusted its views based on clear indications that economic growth was not necessarily accompanied by improvements in the distribution of output, leaving the bulk of the people poor and deprived (Maku, 1994). The Bank asserted that the challenge of development was to improve the quality of life, claiming that a better quality of life not only involves higher incomes, but also encompasses as ends in themselves better education, the highest standards of health and nutrition, less poverty, a cleaner environment, more equality of opportunity, greater individual freedom, and a richer cultural life (World Bank, 1991).

In the early 1970s, Goulet (1971) suggested sustenance, self-esteem, and freedom as the core values representing common development goals sought by all individuals and societies. Concretely, sustenance refers to the ability to meet basic human needs, including food, shelter, health, and protection. Self-esteem is a sense of worth and self-respect, of not being used as a tool by others for their own ends. Freedom relates to a sense of emancipation from alienating material conditions of life and from social servitude to nature, ignorance, other people, misery, institutions, and dogmatic beliefs. These values, which are related to the fundamental human needs expressed in almost all societies and cultures, would be given appropriate consideration if NGOs involved in rural development were brought together through local, regional, and global networks.

It is worth remembering that the institutional approach relies on social institutions to improve the human needs of the less fortunate and considers NGOs as major players in building local capacity and lobbying governments to change development policies (Besley, 1996). One would thus expect that NGOs committed to having an impact on the lives of their constituencies would effectively gear their efforts toward empowering the poor, helping them to achieve a remarkable level of knowledge and decent living standards.

Unfortunately, there are some indications that NGOs are not as effective as many people think. Indeed, one may question the efficiency of NGOs during the period for 1980 to 1991, when sub-Saharan Africa experienced an erosion of the substantial improvements in life expectancy, literacy, and access to education and health services made in the early days of independence (Fowler, 1991). Several critics argue that NGOs do not perform as effectively as had been assumed in terms of poverty reach, cost-effectiveness, sustainability, popular participation, and innovation (Tendler, 1981; Fowler, 1993; Carroll, 1992; Riddell and Robinson, 1992; Wellard and Copestake, 1993).

## CONCLUSIONS

The decade of the 1980s saw a rapid increase of interest in NGOs within the international development community. The rationale behind such an increase is probably the NGOs' presumed success in reaching the poor and addressing their socioeconomic problems more adequately than government agencies.

From a theoretical standpoint, development NGOs' primary emphasis is on organizing people with the ultimate goals of helping them to make better use of their own local productive resources, to create new resources and services, to promote equity, to influence government, and to establish new institutional frameworks that will sustain people-centered development. NGOs as development catalysts should concentrate on stimulating and developing institutional capacities to produce long-term change, building grassroots capacities for self-help and self-reliance and serving as facilitators of development issues that governments may have overlooked or ineffectively addressed.

Throughout the chapter, the author questioned the extent to which development NGOs succeed in building organizational capacities necessary to mobilize the energies and creativity of the poor to solve their own problems. The strategic goal of building local capacity is to provide an ongoing stream of development benefits, and one may wonder if NGOs are fulfilling such a challenging task.

The international development community has opted to work with NGOs despite some evidence that NGOs do not perform as effectively as had been assumed in terms of poverty reach, cost-effectiveness, sustainability, popular participation, and innovation. Considering the lack of empirical studies highlighting the effectiveness of NGOs, it behooves development scholars and practitioners to explore the extent to which NGOs reach the poor and help them achieve the self-awareness that leads to recognition of their inherent collective strength.

Concretely, development researchers should investigate how NGOs operating in poor countries effectively build the institutional capacity that facilitates and promotes the process of human development. Such empirical research should shed light on the main factors that determine NGOs' effectiveness in furthering rural development in poor nations.

## REFERENCES

Apter, D. (1965). The Politics of Modernization. Chicago: University of Chicago Press.

Beckmann, D. (1991). Recent experience and emerging trends. In: Paul, S., Israel, A., eds. Nongovernmental Organizations and the World: Cooperation for Development. Washington, DC: World Bank.

Besley, T. (1996). Political economy of alleviating poverty: theory and institutions. In: Bruno, M., Pleskovic, B., eds. Annual World Bank Conference on Development Economics. Washington, DC: World Bank.

Borgin, K., Corbert, K. (1982). The Destruction of a Continent: Africa and International Aid. San Diego: Harcourt Brace Jovanich.

Brown, D. L. (1992). Nongovernmental Organizations as Development Catalysts. Boston: Institute for Development Research.

Brown, D. L., Korten, D. C. (1991). The Role of Voluntary Organizations in Development. Institute for Development Research.

Carroll, T. F., Montgomery, J. D. (1987). Supporting Grassroots Organizations. Cambridge: Lincoln Institute of Land Policy.

Carroll, T. (1992). Intermediary NGOs: The Supporting Link in Grassroots Development. West Hartford, CT: Kumarian.

Cernea, M. (1988). Nongovernmental Organizations and Local Development. World Bank discussion papers. Washington, DC: World Bank.

Cernea, M. (1987). Farmer organizations and institution building for sustainable agricultural development. Reg. Dev. Dialogue 8(2):1–24.

Chisholm, R. F. (1996). On the meaning of networks. Group Org. Mgt. 21(2):216–235.

Drabek, A. G. (1987). Development alternatives: The challenge for NGOs. World Dev. 15(suppl):9–15.

Dwivedi, O. P. (1994). Development Administration, from Underdevelopment to Sustainable Development. New York: St. Martin's.

Edwards, M., Hulme, D. (1995). Non-Governmental Organizations—Performance and Accountability: Beyond the Magic Bullet. London: Earthscan.

Edwards, M., Hulme, D. (1996). Beyond the Magic Bullet: NGO Performance and Accountability in the Post-Cold War. Ithaca, NY: Kumarian.

Esman, M. J. (1980). Paraprofessionals in Rural Development. Ithaca, NY: Cornell University.

Esman, M. J., Uphoff, N. T. (1984). Local Organizations: Intermediaries in Rural Development. Ithaca, NY: Cornell University Press.

Farrington, J., Biggs, S. D. (1990). NGOs, agricultural technology and the rural poor. Food Pol. 15:479–492.

Fowler, A. (1991). The role of NGOs in changing state–society relations: perspectives from Eastern and Southern Africa. Dev. Pol. Rev. J. Overseas Dev. Inst. 9(1):54–84.

Fowler, A. (1993). NGOs as agents of democratization: An African perspective. J. Internat. Dev. 5(3):325–339.

Goulet, D. (1971). The Cruel Choice: A New Concept in the Theory of Development. New York: Athenaeum.

Korten, D. C. (Aug. 1986). Micro-policy reform: the role of private voluntary agencies. NASPAA Work Paper 12.

Lappe, F. M., Collins, J. (1977). Food First, Beyond the Myth of Scarcity. New York: Ballantine.

Maku, M. J. (1994). Africa after more than thirty years of independence: still poor and deprived. J. Third World Stud. 11(2):13–58.

Miller, V. (1994). NGOs and Grassroots Policy Influence: What Is Success? Boston: Institute for Development Research.

Nindi, B. C. (1993). Dilemmas of development in rural institutions in sub-Saharan Africa. J. East Afr. R. & D. 23:140–150.

Norman, H., Streeten, P. (1979). Indicators of development: the search for a basic needs yardstick. World Dev. 7:567–580.

Organization for Economic Cooperation and Development (OECD). (1988). Voluntary Aid for Development: The Role of Nongovernmental Organizations. Paris: OECD.

Owens, E., Shaw, R. (1972). Development Reconsidered: Bridging the Gap between Government and People. Lexington, MA: Lexington Books.

Owens, E. (1987). The Future of Freedom in the Developing World: Economic Development as Political Reform. New York: Pergamon.

Paul, S., Israel, A. (1991). Nongovernmental Organizations and the World Bank. Washington; DC: World Bank.

Pezzoli, K. (1998). Human Settlements and Planning for Ecological Sustainability: The Case of Mexico City. Cambridge: MIT Press.

Riddell, R., Robinson, M. (1993). The Impact of NGO Poverty-Alleviation projects: Results of the Case Study Evaluations. ODI working paper 68. London: Overseas Developmental Institute.

Schumacher, E. F. (1973). Small Is Beautiful: Economics as if People Mattered. New York: Harper Perennial.

Sholes, R., Covey, J. (1996). Partners for Development: USAID and PVO/NGO Relationships. Boston: Institute for Development Research.

Smillie, I., Helmich, H. (1993). Non-Governmental Organizations and Governments: Stakeholders for Development. Paris: OECD.

Soedjatmoko, A., Murase, A. (1985). The Primacy of Freedom in Development. Lanham, MD: University Press of America.

Stiglitz, J. E. (2002). Globalization and Its Discontents. New York: Norton.

Tendler, J. (1982). Turning Private Voluntary Organizations into Development Agencies: Questions for Evaluation. Evaluation Discussion Paper no. 10. Washington, DC: U.S. Agency for International Development.

Report of the Commission on Global Governance. (1995). Our Global Neighbourhood. New York: Oxford University Press.

Todaro, M. P. (1996). Economic Development. Reading, PA: Addison-Wesley.

Uphoff, N., Esman, M. J. (1974). Local Organization for Rural Development: Analysis of Asian Experience. Ithaca, NY: Cornell University.

UNDP. (1992). Human Development Report. New York: Oxford University Press.

Van Sant, J. (1986). The Role of International and Host Countries NGOs as Intermediaries in Rural Development. Washington, DC: Development Alternatives, Inc.

Wellard, K., Copestake, J. (1993). Non-Governmental Organizations and the State in Africa. London: Routledge.

World Bank. (Aug. 1988). Operational Manual Statement: Collaboration with Nongovernmental Organizations. 5(30):1. Washington, DC.

World Bank. (1991). World Development Report. New York: Oxford University Press.

World Bank. (2001). World Development Report: Attacking Poverty. Washington, DC: World Bank.

World Bank. (2000). Global Economic Prospects and the Developing Countries. Washington, DC: World Bank.

World Development Report. (2000/2001). http://www.worldbank.org/poverty/wdrpoverty/.

World Commission on Environment and Development. (1987). Our Common Future (the Bruntland commission's report). New York: Oxford University Press.

# 20

## Transforming a Large-Scale Microfinance Institution
### Strategies and Challenges in Bangladesh

**EDWARD T. JACKSON**

*Carleton University, Ottawa, Ontario, Canada*

**P. DAL BRODHEAD**

*New Economy Development Group, Ottawa, Ontario, Canada*

## INTRODUCTION

Development projects are —rather, *should be*—policy experiments. From experimentation and piloting through replication and dissemination, projects can serve as tools to explore, test, refine, and monitor the implementation of policies (Brinkerhoff and Crosby, 2002; Chambers, 1997; Rondinelli, 1993). There is a tendency in current development thinking, however, to overlook projects as being too micro level to achieve significant results. This is a misconception, because it is precisely the ability of projects to generate interactions and synergies among all levels of intervention—macro (policy), meso (institution), and micro (community, enterprise, household, and individual)—that defines their potential to serve as effective policy experiments (Jackson, 2000).

In this regard, this chapter examines the strategies and challenges of a decade-long experimental process to transform a government microfinance program into an independent nonprofit foundation—the Palli Daridro Bimochon Foundation (PDBF) or Rural Poverty Alleviation Foundation—in Bangladesh. In launching the PDBF on July 9, 2000, the former prime minister of Bangladesh, Sheikh Hasina, said that "We have to increase the purchasing capacity of the rural population." Established by an act of Parliament and supported financially by the Canadian

International Development Agency (CIDA), the PDBF was designed as an auton-omous, self-supporting microcredit institution in order to alleviate rural poverty or enhance the socioeconomic advancement of the rural poor in Bangladesh (Bangla-desh Observer, 2000).

Why was there a need to create such an institution in Bangladesh, which already has the world's largest microfinance programs, such as the Grameen Bank (Rural Bank), the Bangladesh Rural Advancement Committee (BRAC), and Proshika—three major nongovernmental organizations (NGOs)? The fact is that at best the combined reach of all NGO microfinance programs in Bangladesh has been capable of serving the credit needs of no more than 10–20% of the nearly 50 million rural Bangladeshis living in extreme deprivation (Asian Development Bank, 1999). The government therefore had to play a role by creating an institution such as PDBF, which is the largest government-sponsored microcredit program, serving one-third of the districts of Bangladesh. In examining this case, this chapter may provide useful insights to scholars and practitioners regarding the government's role in poverty reduction, microfinance institution effectiveness and sustainability, and institutional change and capacity building.

## THE SIGNIFICANCE OF THE MODEL

The PDBF has much in common with other microfinance institutions (MFIs) in Bangladesh. Its lead product is very small loans to rural, landless citizens, using solidarity or peer groups to promote high repayment rates. The PDBF aims to expand the size of its loan portfolio in order to cover an increasingly larger proportion of its credit operations through interest-related revenue. The PDBF also mobilizes the savings of the poor to lever even more lending to its clients. At the same time, PDBF provides income generation, leadership, and social development training to its beneficiaries, most of whom are women. These services are subsidized by external grants. In these and other respects, the PDBF thus resembles many other MFIs.

Where the foundation departs from most MFIs is in the role it has configured for the government. To a considerable degree, this model draws on the Canadian experience with many incorporated "crown" corporations, arm's-length research foundations, and quasi-NGOs. In these cases, the government plays a sponsoring role, but does not become directly involved in program management and service delivery. Government is kept at arm's length, but it is nonetheless actively engaged.

In essence, the PDBF model strikes a "middle way" for government to play a role in poverty reduction generally and microfinance in particular. Situated between the polarities of direct government delivery of services on the one hand and pure regulation on the other, this model offers a different kind of role for the state. In terms of governance, the government of Bangladesh is represented on PDBF's board of governors, which also includes representation from the private and NGO sectors as well as from the borrowing clients served by the institution. In terms of operations, the PDBF's credit strategies, together with its personnel policies, are geared toward achieving maximum staff productivity, rapid portfolio growth, high loan repayment rate, and ultimately, financial sustainability. Overall, the PDBF operates at arm's length from government, but engages government as an active stakeholder with other social actors. In this model, the state is neither dominant nor marginalized.

Within the framework of the United Nations' Millenium Development Goals, the international development community is aiming between 1990 and 2015 to halve the proportion of people whose income is less than $1 a day between 1990 and 2015, and also to halve the proportion of people who suffer from hunger (UNDP, 2001a). Effective and efficient strategies are required to attain these objectives. In this regard, current development discourse offers two different visions of what governments can do. In one approach, government is urged to play a direct, "hands-on" role in implementing program-level approaches, such as poverty reduction strategy papers (PRSPs) and sectorwide approaches (SWAps) (CIDA, 2001; OECD, 2000). In much microfinance discourse, however, NGOs are viewed as the most desirable implementing agencies, while government is urged to play a purely regulatory role (e.g., Ledgerwood, 1999). In contrast, the PDBF model suggests that there is a "third-way," a "blended" model whereby government works actively with other stakeholders but is not responsible for day-to-day operations.

## THE COUNTRY CONTEXT AND ORIGIN OF PDBF

### Country Context

Through the 1990s, Bangladesh struggled to reduce the worst effects of the widespread poverty among its people. The decade saw the population of the country increase from about 120 million in 1992 to 135 million in 1999, but gross domestic product (GDP) per capita rose only modestly during the same period, from about $1120 to nearly $1500. Consequently, the country remained very low on the list of low-human development countries, ranking 146 out of 173 countries on the human development index in 1992 and 132 out of 162 countries in 1999, thus roughly maintaining the same position relative to the rest of the world (UNDP, 1994; 2001b).

To be sure, some indicators improved markedly. The average life expectancy in the country continued its upward trend begun in the 1980s, rising from 52 in 1992 to 58 in 1999, and infant mortality per 1000 live births was almost cut in half, from 109 to 58, during the same period. Furthermore, the adult literacy level increased significantly (37–59%) in the 1990s. Nonetheless, by 1999, the government reported that fully 30% of the population (some 40 million people) lived on less than $1 per day, and about 36% (about 48 million), was living below nationally defined poverty line (UNDP, 1994; 2001b; ADB, 2000).

Of course, socioeconomic data tell only part of the story. The 1990s in Bangladesh were also characterized by growing political instability and reduced governability. Partisan political strikes, election violence, and scandal-heated political discourse, together with deep-seated corruption and patronage systems, all contributed to legislative gridlock as well as policy uncertainty for donors and business. While governing politicians and bureaucrats sought to effect public-sector reforms for greater effectiveness and transparency, they were rarely able to deliver on their commitments.

One bright spot in this otherwise sobering picture, however, was the impressive work of Bangladesh's MFIs (Sharif and Wood, 1997). Mostly comprising NGOs, these MFIs provided between 5 and 9 million assetless individuals—the majority of whom have been women—with access to very small loans for off-farm and on-farm income-generating activities (ADB, 1999). In fact, in the 1990s, Bangladeshi MFIs lent more to the rural poor than the entire formal financial sector (ADB, 1999). Led by the Grameen Bank and the BRAC—with 2 million and 1 million members, respectively— these programs generally employed peer-group lending methods, often (but not always) supported by ancillary training, to compensate for the borrowers' lack of collateral and to maintain high repayment rates. Among Bangladeshi MFIs, the Rural Development Project 12 (RD-12) of the parastatal Bangladesh Rural Development Board (BRDB) was the largest government-run microcredit program (see Hye, 1996; Khandker, 1999). RD-12 was later to become the PDBF.

## The Origins of the PDBF

The origins of the PDBF can actually be traced back nearly forty years. In the 1960s, the Bangladesh Academy for Rural Development designed what came to be known as the Comilla model of two-tiered rural cooperatives. The model called for the organization of village-level (or primary) cooperative societies to enable farmers to mobilize and distribute inputs (seeds, fertilizers, pesticides, credit). In turn, clusters of village societies were federated into thana- (subdistrict) level cooperative societies in order to gain economies-of-scale efficiencies. In 1971, the government of newly independent Bangladesh adopted the Comilla model as its national development strategy, which was implemented through the Integrated Rural Development Program. The model was soon criticized for not targeting the landless, however. Efforts to incorporate the poor into existing societies were unsatisfying and slow. Consequently, in 1978, a separate program—Rural Development-1—was started, expressly to organize new societies exclusively for the landless; this program was completed in 1983 (Hye, 1996; Khandker, 1999).

In 1982, a new government parastatal, the BRDB, was created to manage a wide range of donor-financed, credit-oriented projects focused on rural men and women who owned less than an acre of land. Operating under the Ministry of Local Government, Rural Development and Cooperatives (MLGRDC), BRDB worked through the two-tiered cooperative system, but provided credit rather than other agricultural inputs as its main service (Hye, 1996; Khandker, 1999).

Services for the cooperatives of the landless came to be known as the Rural Poor Program, which was funded by CIDA. From 1984 to 1988, CIDA supported a follow-on phase of this project known as RD-12, which promoted the organizing of separate cooperatives for landless men and women. RD-2 established 5600 *bittaheen* cooperative societies, as they were known, more than one-third of which were expressly for landless women (RD 12,1991).

In 1988, a larger and more ambitious collaboration began between CIDA and BRDB. The RD-12 was an eight-year initiative that aimed "to assist assetless rural men and women by providing them with skills, training and credit necessary for income generation, and to strengthen the capacity of BRDB to plan, implement and sustain development among the rural poor" (RD-12,1991:2). Hiring a Canadian executing agency (CEA) to provide technical assistance to BRDB, CIDA committed C\$15 million to the project, which worked in 139 thanas (or upazillas) in six greater districts, covering one-third of the country. RD-12 emphasized the mobilization of solidarity groups for lending, more flexible and rapid credit arrangements, and more focused training for beneficiaries and project staff (RD-12,1991).

Chronology of the PDB Foundation Project

1984
Rural Development Project 2 (RD-2) implemented by BRDB, supported by the
International Development Association, United Nations Development Program,
Overseas Development Administration, and CIDA.
Canadian-funded resource team advises BRDB.
1988
Rural Development Project 12 (RD-12) approved by government of Bangladesh
(GOB) and supported by CIDA.
1991
Canadian executing agency (CEA) begins work as advisor to BRDB.
Gender and social development strategy prepared for RD-12.
1992
Internal evaluation of training component carried out by Y. Kassam and M. Kamal.
1996
RD-12 closes.
1997
With support from CIDA, the Rural Bittaheen Institution Project (RBIP) starts to
transform RD-12 assets to an autonomous, self-financing institution.
1999
PDBF Act passed by Parliament of Bangladesh.
RBIP project closes.
2000
PDBF officially launched by prime minister of Bangladesh.
Assets transferred from
RD-12/BRDB to PDBF.
2001
First full year of operations of PDBF.
Senior management team in place.
New employee service rules and compensation scale introduced.
2002
Evaluation of PDBF performance.

## RD-12 ACHIEVEMENTS AND LIMITATIONS

### Major Achievements

1. *Coverage*: At the village level, by late 1996 the project had organized some
   12,000 bittaheen women's societies and 4600 bittaheen men's societies, whose
   combined membership was approximately 450,000. Of these members, about
   330,000 received loans. Eighty percent of all RD-12 borrowers were landless
   women. Moreover, by late 1996, the project had mobilized over Taka 200
   million in savings deposits from society members, enabling the lending of
   much more credit than what could be financed solely by the CIDA grant
   (E.T. Jackson and Associates, 1997).
2. *Training*: RD-12 invested heavily in training at all levels. Between 1988 and
   1992, for example, some 60,000 beneficiaries (49% of whom were women)
   received over 570,000 person days of training in leadership, income gen-

eration, and social development. Nearly 2000 field functionaries (41% of whom were female) participated in 45,000 person days of training. The unit cost of training per person was C$48 for beneficiaries and about C$190 for field staff (Kassam and Kamal, 1992; Kassam, 1998).

3. *Gender equality*: As indicated by the data on training access, the RD-12 project took a decisive shift toward women's participation in its latter years. For example, of about 44,000 assetless members receiving skills training for income generation between 1992 and 1994, some 32,000, or fully 80%, were women (Lily 1994a), but that indicator was only one of many demonstrating that RD-12's gender-equality efforts were making gains. By 1994, 44% of all field officers and about 40% of thana-level officers were women (Lily, 1994b), percentages that compare favorably with other MFIs in Bangladesh.

## Limits of the Model

While these and other indicators of achievement were indeed impressive, the limits of the model of a government-owned and -operated microfinance program were reached by the end of RD-12.

1. *Underperforming thanas*: At the thana level or district, RD-12 loan re-payment rates were suffering in underperforming thanas. The legal rigidities of cooperative regulations and inadequate management capacity, together with local corruption and patronage, combined to bring down the performance of a subset of thana societies.

2. *Overdue loans*: Throughout the 1990s, RD-12 worked hard to monitor and improve loan repayment rates, making frequent field visits by head office staff, backstopping field staff collection activities, and publishing district- and thana-level comparative data on loan repayment performance. In the early 1990s, the repayment rate ranged in aggregate from 88–91%, but it was a constant struggle to maintain these levels (Matienzo, 1991; Sardar, 1993; Deb Roy, 1995).

3. *Interest rate*: For most of the duration of RD-12, the project's interest rate charged to borrowers remained significantly below that of its major counter-parts. RD-12's rate stood at 16% (declining balance), while Grameen and BRAC's were both set at 20% (flat rate) (Khandker, 1999). Each time CIDA and other stakeholders pressed for BRDB to raise the interest rate, in the interest of financial sustainability, the board delayed and deferred; its ability to resist political pressure simply proved to be too weak.

4. *Human resources*: In the Bangladeshi tradition, the board also found it difficult to fire underperforming or corrupt staff, especially senior-level ones. In a number of cases, when the Canadians pushed for this to happen and were told it had been done, it later became evident that underper-forming personnel had merely been transferred elsewhere.

5. *Sustainability*: Taken together, all of these factors—underperforming thanas, underperformance in loan repayments, a low interest rate, and rigid and counterproductive human resources practices—meant that there was no way that institutional sustainability could be achieved under the BRDB model. CIDA, the CEA, and some GOB officials believed that what was needed was a *new* model that involved a performance-driven, auto-

nomous institution operating at arm's length from government. The new institution needed to be business-oriented and guided by the disciplines inherent in financial sustainability.

## Performance of RD-12 vs. Other MFIs

In the mid-1990s, the World Bank carried out a landmark comparative study of the performance of Bangladesh's three largest microcredit programs: RD-12, the Grameen Bank, and BRAC. Published widely (Rahman and Khandker, 2000; Khandker, 1998; 1999), this research confirmed that RD-12 was performing as a world-class MFI in terms of scale, reach, and poverty impacts, but the study also illuminated certain areas of underperformance that were limiting RD-12's ability to move faster toward institutional sustainability.

1. *Socioeconomic impacts*: Drawing on survey data for about 1800 households across Bangladesh, the World Bank study found that in terms of targeting, 58% of RD-12 participants owned no more than half an acre of land, compared to 55% for Grameen and 65% for BRAC. It was also found that every Taka 100 increase in credit to women participants produced increases in the nonland assets of women borrowers by Taka 29 in RD-12, compared with Taka 15 in BRAC and Taka 27 in Grameen. Household production of program participants increased by 48% for RD-12, 56% for Grameen, and 57% for BRAC. Notably, in RD-12, the research showed that 6% of households rose above the poverty line each year, compared to 5% and 3%, respectively, for Grameen and BRAC; "Poverty reduction was thus highest for RD-12," concluded the study (Khandker, 1999: 56). Also, at the village level moderate poverty was reduced by 14% in RD-12 villages, 12% in Grameen villages, and 10% in BRAC villages (Khandker, 1999). In general, then, RD-12 performed at a similar, and sometimes higher, level than these two better-known MFIs, on participant-, household-, and village-level indicators of effectiveness.

2. *Institutional sustainability*: At the same time, however, the Bank's findings also pointed to some important weaknesses in RD-12's performance, especially in relation to institutional sustainability. On the positive side, all three MFIs were able to double their membership in the early 1990s, almost entirely among women, and on average, increased their annual loan disbursement by a factor of five. Both RD-12 and BRAC doubled their staff size to accommodate this growth, although in contrast, Grameen's staff complement remained the same.

RD-12 was found to underperform on two indicators that are crucial to institutional sustainability, however. First, in RD-12, member savings constituted about three-quarters of the value of loans outstanding, whereas the ratio for the other two MFIs ranged between one-quarter and one-third. In other words, comparatively speaking, RD-12 was not leveraging borrower savings to the maximum extent. Second and perhaps most tellingly, in 1994 RD-12 reported annual loan disbursements per staffperson of Taka 277, compared with Taka 1418 for Grameen and Taka 638 for BRAC. Further, 1994 member savings per staffperson were Taka 83 for RD-12, Taka 259 for Grameen, and Taka 136 for BRAC (Khandker, 1999).

Viewed alongside an interest rate that continued to be considerably lower than that of its counterpart MFIs and the organizational rigidities and patronage systems associated with the public sector in Bangladesh, these findings underscored the limits of the government-run model.

## TRANSITION TO A NEW MODEL: THE RURAL BITTAHEEN INSTITUTION PROJECT

In 1997, CIDA and the GOB started a new joint initiative: the Rural Bittaheen Institution Project (RBIP). A direct response to the limitations faced in the previous project, RBIP had three ambitious objectives: (1) to transform RD-12 into an autonomous, self-financing institution, (2) to establish the foundation for financial self-reliance, and (3) to strengthen and modify current RD-12 (RBIP) operations and services in 139 thanas. The project was divided into two parts: a three-year (1997–1999) transition phase, and a two-year (2000–2002) start-up phase for the new institution (see RBIP Quarterly Reports, 1996–2000).

1. *Business plan*: After much work and several revisions, a business plan for RBIP covering the period 1996 through 1999 was approved by the governments of Bangladesh and Canada. The goal of the plan was "to create a new autonomous (self-governing) institution which will conduct a sustainable program for poverty alleviation" in order to "enhance the economic and social well-being of the Bittaheen (rural assetless poor)." The two primary management roles of the three-year project were first, to strengthen project operations and build the basis for financial self-reliance, and second, "to perform the tasks necessary to ensure transformation of the project to a new institution" (GOB/GOC, 1997: i–ii).

   The business plan detailed measures to create the governance structure of the new entity, draft enabling legislation, transfer all RD-12 assets (revolving loan fund, loan portfolio, personnel, equipment) to the new institution, delink employee terms of service from government regulations, streamline operations, promote a culture of efficiency and customer service, design new credit products, strengthen internal audit and accountability procedures, organize informal primary groups rather than registered cooperatives, and enhance the supervision of thana-level societies.

   By early 1999, a new business plan had been prepared for the soon-to-be launched PDBF. Underpinned by the same principles and strategies as the 1997 business plan, the new plan based its projections on RD-12's final balance sheet and detailed list of assets, as well as a number of operational innovations, especially in credit and finance, instituted during the transition phase (E.T. Jackson and Associates, 1999). The plan also provided new projections for a six-to-eight-year period for the new foundation to achieve operational sustainability.

2. *Legislation*: After extensive research and consultation, stakeholders chose a foundation model as the legal structure for the new institution. Draft articles and bylaws for the new foundation, prepared by a consultant viewed as credible by the GOB, were approved in principle by the prime

minister's office and the cabinet in late 1998, but it was not until a full year later—after intensive lobbying by Canada and Bangladeshi advocates—that the cabinet and Parliament officially approved the foundation's enabling legislation. This approval was finally achieved largely because of CIDA's threat to withdraw its support of the project altogether unless the PDBF Act was passed, and the eventual willingness of the GOB to assume the operating costs of the project.

3. *Governance*: The RBIP project also saw the design and implementation of a structure of governance for the new foundation. Transiting from the Project Steering Committee of the RD-12 Project, a new steering committee was formed, which later became the first board of governors of the foundation. While the foundation is autonomous, its board is chaired by the secretary of MLGRDC, with the director-general of BRDB as vice-chair: A senior official of the Ministry of Finance is the third government representative. At the same time, the board also includes three representatives of the private sector and four representatives from the foundation's client group, Bittaheen women and men.

4. *Internal audit*: During the RBIP project, the Canadian technical-assistance team placed emphasis on building substantial internal audit capacity that was later to be transferred to the new institution. (RD-12 had not incorporated an internal audit function.) The CEA designed, staffed, and supervised a unit of six junior auditors that was transferred to the new institution at start-up. The unit began conducting field audits in late 1997 and continued to do so until the new foundation was launched.

5. *Accounting and financial systems*: Another outcome of the RBIP was a totally renovated accounting and financial system characterized in 1999 by a shift to a standardized double-entry accrual system, a centralized review and control system for a consolidated balance sheet and profit and loss statement for thana cooperatives, centralized budgetary control procedures, a continually improving project balance sheet, and conversion to computerized record keeping and reporting at the central and thana levels.

6. *Protection of the revolving loan fund*: Through a range of innovative and activist measures, the CEA worked with field staff to protect the revolving loan fund in the face of many challenges. (See below.) Consequently, the RBIP project was able to transfer to the foundation a loan portfolio valued, after loan-loss provisions, at approximately C$13 million, as well as C$9.4 million in cash, and client savings of about C$12 million (PDBF and CRT, 2002).

7. *Gender policy*: Like earlier projects, women's participation was strong in RBIP at the micro level, where 72% of members and 82% of borrowers were women, and at the meso level, where 40% of field staff were women (E.T. Jackson and Associates, 1999). This phase, however, also saw a concerted effort to establish a gender *policy* for the new institution, at every level and in all of its activities. The goal of the policy, developed in 1997, was: "Poverty reduction through equal participation of women and men in all spheres of activities of the institution and thereby move towards equal partnership" (RBIP, 1997:3). To be reviewed by senior management semiannually; the policy called for specific actions in every area of the new institution, including

management, human resources, social development, group mobilization, financial management, credit and savings, and monitoring and evaluation. RBIP was the first government-sponsored project to have developed such a policy, and as such, was seen a best-practice innovation. It was also recognized, however, that the policy "provides only leverage: in itself, it does not transform the institution, but it at least sets out the rules of the game" (Rowe, 1997:7). By 1999, some 250 senior staff of RBIP had received orientation training on the gender policy.

8. *Social outcomes*: As in RD-12, RBIP continued to engage local society members in an array of social-development training and awareness activities—often linking with other agencies that would actually deliver these services—on a range of issues, including adult literacy, family planning, public health, and primary education for girls and boys. A 1998 study of more than 200 beneficiaries in six regions confirmed what earlier internal analyses of RD-12 had indicated: that the program was contributing to significant social outcomes as well as economic ones. For example, the RBIP research found that two-thirds of the beneficiaries practiced family planning (as compared to the national average of just under 50%), two-thirds of RBIP families used sanitary latrines (versus the national average of 45%), and two-thirds of participants reported that the school-attendance rate of their children was between 90–100%. Overall, one-quarter of respondents said that they highly valued the increased dignity and status, as well as increased mobility and social interaction, that participating in RBIP conferred upon them. The study concluded that the social and economic development of landless citizens, especially women, represent an interactive and mutually reinforcing process (Sultan, 1998).

## CHALLENGES TO RBIP

1. *Floods*: In 1998, widespread flooding brought suffering to more than 30 million people across Bangladesh. An estimated 135,000 RBIP members were affected, either directly or indirectly. Like other MFIs in Bangladesh, RBIP devised a short-term relief plan for affected members, though one that sought to reinforce rather than erode credit discipline. The effects of the flooding tended to increase arrears for the next 18 months. By late 1999, however, the demand for new loans had returned to preflood levels.

2. *Loan arrears and delinquency*: While the loan portfolio of RBIP grew in the late 1990s, reaching about Taka 670 million in 1999, so did the volume of loans in arrears, which stood at Taka 132 million in early 1999, representing about 20% of the overall portfolio. One of the factors associated with this trend was the uncertainty surrounding the future of the project. Legislation for the new institution had been delayed, and former RD-12 personnel were operating with little or no job security. In the absence of BRDB leadership, the CEA team played a very active role in visiting field staff to encourage increased supervision of borrowers. An incentive-driven collection system for field staff was also instituted. All of these measures kept the arrears portfolio from getting worse, but were not sufficient to reduce it significantly.

3. *Senior management:* The RBIP period was also characterized by an almost complete lack of senior-management presence or commitment on the part of BRDB. After all, the board was about to lose responsibility for a program it had built up to an impressive scale. In fact, some middle and senior BRDB managers actively *opposed* the transfer of the project to the new institution, delaying the foundation's start-up. This vacuum in day-to-day senior management was filled by the technical assistance team, primarily to protect the revolving loan fund that had been financed by CIDA, GOB, and member savings. The CEA and CIDA also were obliged to lobby the GOB heavily to counter internal opposition to the transition.

4. *Field staff:* The morale of some 2000 field staff members of RD-12 suffered the most from the uncertainty over the project's future during the RBIP period. The CEA team worked hard to communicate to the field positive messages about the transition. Also at issue for some field personnel was the proposed delinking from government terms of service by the new institution. Further, the new performance-oriented staff assessment procedures to be used by the new institution threatened nonperforming field staff. More pointedly, by 1999, the CEA had identified 400 underperforming RD-12 field staff who, it proposed, should be released. Alhough preliminary and supposedly confidential, informal news of this proposal strengthened the resolve of the opponents of the transition.

5. *Managing change:* One of the "metalessons" of the RBIP period was that stakeholder politics are just as important—or perhaps more important—in large-scale institutional transformations than the technical work needed to renovate policies and systems. Change agents must manage both the political and technical dimensions at the same time, and they must manage ongoing relations with both proponents and opponents, up and down (and across) the project structure. All of this takes people and money—and staying power. In order to achieve enduring change, change, it turns out, must be endured.

6. *Gender policy:* While RBIP's new gender equality (GE) policy was indeed an important achievement, it also became evident during this phase that inertia and resistance were limiting progress in implementing this policy. Among the factors contributing to these limitations were lack of leadership by both Canadian and Bangladeshi stakeholders in advancing gender issues at the broader strategic level, steady internal criticism directed at project advocates of gender equality, and the subordination of GE to other—primarily financial—priorities in the overall organizational transformation process. Consequently, the GE policy remained largely unimplemented at the completion of RBIP and through start-up of the foundation.

7. *Gender dynamics:* An internal RBIP study sought to understand the gender dynamics of loan ownership and utilization, issues that are receiving increased attention in microfinance worldwide. While only 7% of women (and only 2% of men) reported that they felt their spouse controlled the loan, two-thirds of women said that the use of the loan was a joint decision made with their spouse. In assessing the *utilization* of credit provided to women, the study found that in practice less than 40% of women actually controlled the use of their loans. In one-third of loans to women, the husband or son controlled their utilization. Notwithstanding this, it was also found that 54%

of both women and men felt that their spousal relationship had improved during their participation in the program (Sultan, 1998). These complex findings parallel the experience of other Bangladeshi MFIs and deserve further study and action.

## THE NEW FOUNDATION (PDBF): GAINS, LIMITS, AND RESULTS

### Initial Gains of PDBF

While the start-up process for the PDB foundation brought many challenges, by early 2002, the new institution was also able to point to a number of important gains in key areas

1.  *Loan disbursement*: In both 2001 and 2002 (through April 2002), the foundation lent more than Taka 1 billion to borrowing members. This quantum of lending was considerably larger than annual loan disbursement levels during the RBIP period, thus even in its start-up phase and in spite of other countervailing factors, the foundation succeeded in growing the loan portfolio (see Brodhead, 2001).
2.  *Client savings*: At the same time, the foundation was able to slightly increase the size and proportion of client savings in the revolving loan fund. Savings deposited by foundation clients reached the C\$12 million mark by 2002. Again, given other negative factors internal and external to the project, this achievement was a notable one.
3.  *Staff training*: In addition, the foundation was very active in training at all levels during its first two years of operation. In 2000 and 2001, the foundation provided more than 1100 days of management and operations training for operational staff and partners. The next year, more than 2700 training days for foundation staff were provided.
4.  *Client training*: As with previous projects, the foundation invested heavily in client training. During its first two years of operation, the new institution organized 2000 person days for training more than 400 paratechnicians, some 31,000 training days in branch-level income-generating activities (IGAs) for society members, and more than 45,000 training days for members in society-level IGAs. In the areas of gender and social development, over the same period the foundation provided 42,000 person days of leadership training for solidarity group members, and more than 330,000 days of adult literacy training.

### Confronting Problems

Notwithstanding the important gains made during the initial start-up phase of the foundation, there were the following problems to be confronted:

1.  *Labor disruptions*: A combination of insecure field staff, disgruntled nonperforming managers, and opportunistic union organizers led to the periodic occupation in late 2001 and early 2002 of a number of foundation offices and the intimidation of many staff members. While most project stakeholders on both the Canadian and Bangladeshi sides were not opposed to collective

bargaining and unions in general, partisan, corrupt, and nonperforming staff members had captured the union organizing drive and sought to turn back the clock to terms of service that, to say the least, would not be performance-oriented. It is worth noting that most MFIs in Bangladesh, including Grameen and BRAC, are *not* unionized, for some of the same reasons. Consequently, the foundation and its proponents fought the occupations and the union, a battle that continues.

2. *Governance*: Furthermore, some GOB representatives on the board of governors of the foundation also sought to roll back the clock, trying to reassert the government's control over the program. The rest of the board, CIDA, and Canadian consultants resolutely resisted this "rollback" effort. This battle, too, continues, although it is dissipating as time goes on.

3. *Interest rate*: Up until mid-2002, the foundation maintained the same low interest rate—16% on a declining balance basis—that had held back the financial sustainability of the program in earlier phases. An external evaluation commissioned by CIDA was critical of this rate. In mid-2002, however, the board of the foundation voted to raise the interest rate to a level approaching that of the other major MFIs. As of this writing, the interest rate is 24% (declining), only slightly below the average current MFI rates in Bangladesh.

4. *Product mix*: The CIDA evaluation was even more critical of the foundation's failure to diversify its product mix. While the average loan size continued to rise compared to previous projects, the basic financial product offered to clients was the same in 2002 as it had been a decade earlier. The experience of MFIs in Bangladesh and elsewhere, however, indicates that product (and client) diversification is a prerequisite for the financial sustainability of microcredit programs. Much work remains to be done on this issue by the foundation.

## The Aggregate Results

It is useful to view the results of the foundation and its precursor projects from a long-term perspective. When the results of the RD-12, RBIP, and PDBF projects are aggregated, it becomes evident that the stakeholders achieved some remarkable things together, as follows:

1. Almost C$230 million was lent cumulatively to landless Bangladeshi citizens, mostly women, from 1988 through early 2002. (See Table 1.)

2. During the same period, more than C$12 million in client savings was mobilized for use, several times over, in the program's revolving loan fund (RLF).

3. Between 1988 and 2002, the GOB contributed a total of nearly C$19 million (about C$14 million toward operating costs, and nearly C$5 million to the RLF).

4. For its part, CIDA provided C$41 million toward operating costs and nearly C$15 million to the RLF over the life of the three projects.

5. Table 2 shows that the three projects' clients provided about 38% of the cost of the RLF, with CIDA contributing about 47% and the GOB 15%. Note, though, that the *combined value of both Bangladeshi stakeholders/groups—*

**Table 1**  Cumulative Loan Disbursements (1988–2002)

| Fiscal year | During the year (Tk.) | Cumulative (Tk.) | Cumulative (CDN$) | Exchange rate (CDN$/Tk.) |
|---|---|---|---|---|
| RD-12 | | | | |
| 1988–1989 | 19,778,490 | 19,778,490 | 659,283 | 1:30 |
| 1990–1990 | 44,663,490 | 64,441,980 | 2,148,066 | |
| 1990–1991 | 87,485,250 | 151,927,230 | 5,064,241 | |
| 1991–1992 | 221,492,950 | 373,420,180 | 12,447,339 | |
| 1992–1993 | 476,942,310 | 850,362,490 | 28,345,416 | |
| 1993–1994 | 702,660,930 | 1,553,023,420 | 51,767,447 | |
| 1994–1995 | 722,776,810 | 2,275,800,230 | 75,860,008 | |
| 1995–1996 | 653,477,140 | 2,929,277,370 | 97,642,579 | |
| RBIP | | | | |
| 1996–1997 | 643,040,620 | 3,572,317,990 | 111,634,937 | 1:31 |
| 1997–1998 | 797,424,010 | 4,369,742,000 | 136,554,438 | |
| 1998–1999 | 912,567,160 | 5,282,309,160 | 165,072,161 | |
| 1999–2000 | 804,513,310 | 6,086,822,470 | 190,213,202 | |
| Foundation | | | | |
| 2000–2001 | 1,016,727,190 | 7,103,549,660 | 200,099,990 | 1:35.5 |
| 2001–2002 (up to April 2002) | 1,011,593,500 | 8,115,143,160 | 228,595,582 | |

*Source*: PDB and CRT, 2002.

*the government and the clients—represented 53%, slightly more than half of all RLF funding.*

6. As Table 3 indicates, from 1988 to 2002 the three projects provided more than 5.5 million person days of training to both project beneficiaries (over 5.4 million days) and project staff (more than 100,000 days);

7. Two-thirds of project trainees were women, representing a major long-term investment in the human-resource capacity of landless women in particular.

Of course, development interventions are much more than statistics. These numbers are testimony not only to the breadth, however, but also to the depth of the results generated by the three projects over some fourteen years. The data also underscore the fact that, especially in terms of shared financial contributions, these

**Table 2**  Stakeholders' Contributions, 1988–2002 (C$ millions)

| Stakeholders | Operating costs | Revolving loan fund | Total |
|---|---|---|---|
| CIDA | 41.34 | 14.68 | 56.02 |
| GOB | 13.91 | 4.95 | 18.86 |
| Clients | – | 12.29 | 12.29 |
| Total | 55.25 | 31.92 | 87.17 |

*Source*: PDB and CRT, 2002.

**Table 3**  Person Days of Training (1988–2002)

| Categories | Person days of training | Women trainees (%) |
|---|---|---|
| Beneficiaries | 5,409,177 | 67 |
| Staff | 105,500 | 43 |
| Total | 5,514,677 | 66 |

*Source*: PDB and CRT, 2002.

interventions were driven by a practical, productive three-way partnership involving CIDA, the GOB, and landless Bangladeshi citizens.

## TRANSFORMATION STRATEGIES AND POLICY IMPLICATIONS

### Strategies for Transformation

It was no accident that such impressive results were generated. A number of strategies were intentionally employed in support of the transformation process toward a more efficient, autonomous, and sustainable MFI, yet at the same time—almost dialectically—countervailing challenges to the change process played themselves through the evolution of the various projects, especially over the past five years, when the process directly confronted entrenched interests, both nationally and locally.

1.  *Strategies*: Five major strategies were employed in this transformation effort. First, a significant investment was made at all levels of the program in training all key project players, from borrowers who received training on income-generating techniques to field officers on group mobilization, to headquarters staff on management information systems and human resources policies. Second, a sustained effort was made to integrate a gender equality perspective into all aspects of the program through policies, credit targeting, training, and tools. Third, new management methods were introduced to senior staff, with an emphasis on performance-based personnel policies, From a Bangladeshi perspective, this was perhaps the most countercultural and threatening of all the strategies used. Fourth, a significant push was made by the consulting team to strengthen the banking and credit capacity of the program, particularly with respect to arrears monitoring and the internal audit function. Finally, in order to create and sustain the momentum and legitimacy required for these changes, much effort was put into the education of, and relationship-building with, key government officials in order to ensure senior-level support.

2.  *Challenges*: At the same time, an array of internal and external challenges constrained the transformation process. One challenge was Bangladesh's volatile natural environment, in which episodic floods and hurricanes too often decimated the modest socioeconomic gains made by villagers through credit and income activities. In parallel, an equally volatile political environment produced a steady flow of political strikes (known as *hartals*), standoffs, and violence that frequently slowed the machinery of both the state and the development agencies to a crawl. Inside the network of project stakeholders, there also were marked challenges. Efforts to fire corrupt and

ineffective staff too often met with resistance from their allies and the patronage networks they fed, as well as from Bangladeshi organizational traditions more generally. Furthermore, threatened by the performance-based focus of the new foundation, some disaffected and nonperforming personnel organized demonstrations that intimidated staff and slowed the start-up of the new institution. Finally, the efforts of certain senior-level government opponents of the change process intensified on many fronts, including through the government's role on board of governors of the foundation, where these opponents worked hard to actually return the program to full government control and management practices.

3.  *Reflections on practice*: In applying these strategies and meeting these challenges, the consulting team (comprising two Canadians and seven Bangladeshi professionals) in particular learned (and relearned) key lessons about the organizational transformation process.

    a.  *Resources*: Large amounts of time and money were required to implement the change process. A mix of advanced skills on the consulting team—especially in stakeholder management and credit and banking, but also in other areas—proved crucial.

    b.  *Roles*: The consulting team found it had to play a variety of roles, from internal monitoring of program operations (its main role), to managing stakeholder politics (especially in RBIP and foundation start-up), to (briefly, only in RBIP) actual program management— depending on the needs of the particular phase in the change process. In managing both stakeholder and formal politics, the team learned that both foreign (for distance, and association with the donor) and local (for proximity, and textured understanding) players are necessary. In a broader sense, because of their longer tenure and more extensive knowledge of the project (compared to other, more transitory players) the consultants also became the stewards and the "corporate memory" of the longer-term change process.

    c.  *Rotation*: The institutional practices of both CIDA and the GOB resulted in a continuous rotation in and out of the project by representatives for each of these stakeholder groups. The consulting team devoted time to building relationships and briefing, educating, and supporting each of these representatives, as well as enabling them to interact with each other as required.

    d.  *Resolve*: On both the GOB and CIDA sides, the consulting team also found that it needed at critical moments to strengthen the resolve of key players to press for maximum change; this was part of the consultants' strategic change role.

    e.  *Reduced focus*: Organizational transformation is fundamentally a continuous, multitasking process. Many policies, systems, programs, and people must be changed at the same time. This was a very large-scale intervention, however. Early on, the team found that within a given year or even project phase, only a few areas could be caused to undergo real thoroughgoing change—and even that was difficult. The consultants thus worked with other stakeholders to focus on only a few strategic priorities for major change at a time. In the latter stages of the change process, for better or worse the consultants, CIDA and the GOB chose to emphasize banking, credit, and governance change and gave less priority to gender policy and social development change.

Overall, the consulting team experienced the organizational transformation process as demanding, time-consuming, complex, unpredictable, at once political and technical, partial, contradictory, and uneven—as did other stakeholders. There were both proponents and opponents of change inside and outside the project structures, and for every gain or success, there was an equal or greater number of losses or failures. This kind of large-scale organizational transformation is, to put it mildly, very hard work.

## Development Policy Implications

The case study examined here helps to shed light on a number of development policy issues that are currently the subject of debate and experimentation among scholars, donor officials, policy makers, NGO personnel and consultants, as follows:

1. *Appropriate role for the state in the microfinance sector*: Governments still operate in large swathes of the microlending market in developing countries. There are some notable examples of high-performing public-sector MFIs, such as Bank Rakyat Indonesia and Badan Kredit Kecamatan (also in Indonesia) (Ashe and Wilson, 1996), which have restructured their operations from supply-driven credit systems to demand-oriented, profit-sensitive, full-service banking operations. Apart from these individual cases, however, the bulk of international experience suggests that governments are ill-suited to directly manage efficient, high-growth, and sustainable microfinance programs. In particular, states are vulnerable to the negative influences of corruption, patronage, and bureaucratic rigidities and delays. In the field of microfinance at large, dominated as it is by NGOs, there is a strong prejudice against any active role for government other than a regulatory one (Ledgerwood, 1999). The case examined here, however, offers evidence of a "third way" between the polarities of active state management and pure regulation. The PDBF—with senior government officials playing a central role on its board of directors and utilizing converted government assets (capital, personnel, equipment)—offers a "blended" model.

2. *Appropriate role for microfinance in the "new architecture" of aid*: Current development discourse promotes multistakeholder policy- and program-level interventions, such as poverty reduction strategy papers (PRSPs) and sector-wide approaches (SWAps), that call for pooled (rather than individual) investments by donors in country-driven plans (CIDA, 2001; OECD, 2000; World Bank, 2001). The case of the PDB Foundation draws attention to the possibility that governments can play an arm's-length role in promoting scaled-up and effective microfinance within the broader framework of national poverty reduction efforts (Kassam, 2002). Further, there is a role for external technical assistance to ensure that this role is played effectively *and* that government is not permitted to reassert full ownership and control over the microfinance intervention. In PRSPs or SWAps, governments can thus choose to play the role of policy formulator and reg-

ulatory enforcer in microfinance, but in addition, they may also choose to play an arm's-length partnership role in order to gain a "window" on policy implementation in this important field of poverty reduction.

3. *Methods for achieving the sustainability of microfinance institutions*: Perhaps more than any other sector, the microfinance sector globally has been pre-occupied by—and has generated a host of innovations for—achieving institutional sustainability. This usually involves some combination of raising interest rates, increasing lending volume, improving system efficiencies, and diversifying across other products (adding mortgages, insurance, credit cards) and clientelle (including the nonpoor) (Fernando, 2000; Hulme, 2000; Ledgerwood, 1999). The PDBF case demonstrates the power of mobilizing group-member savings as a means of levering external capital to boost lending volume and operational scale. The foundation's predecessor projects, however, suffered both from an unwillingness to raise interest rates and from low staff productivity, as measured by loan-disbursement per field employee. The foundation has so far also failed to diversity its product line and clientelle. Furthermore, like other MFIs, the foundation also intentionally continued to "carry" a major training component that required significant subsidy, affirming that this was part of its blended model.

4. *Strategies for effecting large-scale institutional transformation and capacity development*: Institutional change and capacity development are central concepts in today's development discourse, as they should be. The PDBF case shows that capacity-development must involve all levels of intervention, from individual borrowers and lending groups, to the national institution, to the level of law and policy. In the PDBF case, most work focused on the micro and meso levels for a full decade before serious efforts were made to draft and lobby for enabling legislation for the foundation model. Ultimately, this change process was also a matter of staying power—of sheer endurance. Large amounts of money and time were required to transform what began as a government rural development project to a nonprofit, business-oriented MFI. This continuity enabled the proponents of change to counter opposition to it and to strengthen the resolve of stakeholders in moments of conflict or indecision.

5. *Strategies for promoting gender equality in poverty reduction*: In development cooperation, there remains a strong Northern and significant Southern constituency for promoting GE in poverty reduction. In the case of PDBF, there were sustained efforts to promote GE at the micro and meso levels for more than a decade. At the macro level, the act bringing the foundation into existence makes special reference to giving preference to women as borrowers. The lack of implementation of the new institution's gender policy, however, demonstrated the inertia and resistance by project leadership, both Bangladeshi and Canadian, to more thoroughgoing changes than hiring a larger percentage of women field staff and lending to a larger percentage of women borrowers. In one of the intervention's most serious failures, gender policy implementation was in effect subordinated to banking and credit issues. Finally, the effect of lending on intrahousehold gender and income dynamics remains fairly opaque, as it does for other MFIs (see Rahman, 1999; Mayoux, 1998), and needs much more work.

## CONCLUSION

In development practice, there are no perfect projects. As with this case study, there are only dialectical dualities: achievements and challenges, victories and failures, solidarity and conflict. In the end, the most important *permanent* task is to learn— and to improve.

In fact, the experience of the PDB Foundation could accurately be viewed as a series of successive approximations in trying to get government-sponsored micro-finance "right." After more than a decade, the PDBF model is elaborated and in place, and some of its components have been tested on a large scale. Still more remains to be done, however. The model has not yet been *fully* tested, nor have its opponents been fully appeased. The Foundation *has* become a reality, however, and the longer it perseveres, the greater the chance it will have of achieving its goal of sustainability— both institutionally, and for the households it serves. The project—and the policy experiment—continues.

## ACKNOWLEDGMENTS

The authors would like to thank the following individuals for their advice and assistance over the years on the project analyzed here. Mike Adair, Brodie Anderson, Nick Adams-Aston, Jeff Ashe, Ferdousi Begum, Arabinda Deb Roy, H.I. Haleem, Jim Halliday, Kazi Reazul Hoque, Mufazzel Hossam, Hasnat Hye, Yusuf Kassam, Rokeya Khatun, Huguette Labrosse, Joanna Ledgerwood, Evelyn Lee, Rudi Ma-tienzo, Ralph McKim, Abdul Momin, John Moore, Kamal Mustafa, Dale Posgate, Ayub Quadri, Daudur Rahman, Brian Rowe, S.A. Salik, A.Q. Siddique, Kevin Smith, David Spring, Bob Woodhouse, Doris Wong. We wish to pay special tri-bute to two project leaders whose efforts were essential to the success of the project: Shahid Talukder and Russell Pepe, who changed others, changed themselves, and endured.

## REFERENCES

ADB. (2000). Facts and figures. 32(1):23.

ADB. (1999). The Role of Central Banks in Microfinance in Asia and the Pacific. Manila.

Ashe, J., Wilson, K. (1996). The transformation of three public microfinance institutions and the role governance played. Ottawa, Ontario, Canada: Report prepared for the RD-12 Project, through E.T. Jackson and Associates Ltd.

Bangladesh Obs. (July 10, 2000). PDBF launched: Make each family self-reliant. Dhaka.

Brinkerhoff, D. W., Crosby, B. (2002). Managing Policy Reform. Bloomfield, CT: Kumarian.

Brodhead, D. (2001). Quarterly financial review for the period ended December 31, 2000. Dhaka/Ottawa: Palli Daridro Bimochon Foundation.

CIDA (Canadian International Development Agency). (2001). Strengthening Aid Effective-ness. Hull.

Chambers, R. (1997). Whose Reality Counts? Putting the First Last. London: Intermediate Technology Publications.

Deb Roy, A. (1995). Productivity of field functionaries and impact of loan delinquency. Ideas Act. 5(2):1–2.

E.T. Jackson Associates Ltd. (Feb. 28, 1997). RD-12 Quarterly progress and financial report (July 1–Dec. 31, 1996). Ottawa, Ontario, Canada.

E.T. Jackson and Associates Ltd. (1999). Foundation for the Elimination of Rural Poverty: Business Plan. Dhaka/Ottawa, Ontario, Canada.

Fernando, N. A. (2000). Financial innovation: Key to microfinance development. ADB Fin. Poor 1(2):4–6.

Government of Bangladesh and Government of Canada. (1997). Memorandum of Understanding: Rural Bittaheen Institution Program. Dhaka/Hull.

Hulme, D. (2000). Impact assessment methodologies for microfinance. World Dev. 28(4):79–98.

Hye, H. A. (1996). Below the Line: Rural Poverty in Bangladesh. Dhaka: University Press Limited.

Ideas Act. (1991). RD-12: A project that builds on and promotes changes in BRDB.

Kassam, Y. (1998). Combining participatory and survey methodologies in evaluation: The case of a rural development project in Bangladesh. In: Jackson, E. T., Kassam, Y., eds. Knowledge Shared: Participatory Evaluation in Development Cooperation. West Hartford/Ottawa: Kumarian/International Development Research Centre, pp. 50–63.

Kassam, Y. (2002). SWAps and the microfinance sector: Issues and possibilities. report prepared for the PDBF Project, through E.T. Jackson and Associates Ltd. Ottawa, Ontario, Canada.

Kassam, Y., Kamal, M. (1992). Final report of the evaluation study of the training component of RD-12. for the RD-12 Project through E.T. Jackson and Associates Ltd. Ottawa, Ontario, Canada.

Khandker, S. R. (1999). Fighting Poverty with Microcredit: Experience in Bangladesh. New York/Washington, DC: Oxford/World Bank.

Khandker, S. R. (1998). Microcredit programme evaluation: A critical review. IDS Bull. 29(4):11–20.

Jackson, E. T. (2000). The front-end costs and downstream benefits of participatory evaluation. In: Feinstein, O., Picciotto, R., eds. Evaluation and Poverty Reduction. Washington, DC: World Bank, pp. 115–126.

Ledgerwood, J. (1999). Microfinance Handbook: An Institutional and Financial Perspective. Washington, DC: World Bank.

Lily, J. (1994a). RD-12: A model for training. Gender Persp. 2(4):9.

Lily, J. (1994b). RD-12 ensures a voice for women. Ideas Act. 4(6):1–3.

Matienzo, R. (1991). RD-12 repayment credit rates moving into a very critical phase. Ideas Act. 1(2):6–7.

Mayoux, L. (1998). Participatory learning for women's empowerment in microfinance programmes. IDS Bull. 29(4):39–50.

OECD (Organization for Economic Cooperation and Development). (2000). Dev. Coop. DAC J. 1(1).

PDBF and CRT (Palli Daridro Bimochon Foundation and Canadian Resource Team). (2002). Project data. Dhaka.

Rahman, A. (1999). Women and Microcredit in Rural Bangladesh. Boulder; CO: Westview Press.

Rahman, R. I., Khandker, S. R. (2000). Editors' introduction. the Bangladesh Development Studies. 2/3 (special issue on microfinance and development):i–x.

Rondinelli, D. A. (1993). Development Projects as Policy Experiments. 2nd ed. London: Routledge.

Rowe, B. (1997). Social development and the RBIP:Status Report. E.T. Jackson and Associates Ltd. Ottawa, Ontario, Canada.

Rural Bittaheen Institution Program. (1997). Gender Policy, Dhaka.

Rural Bittaheen Institution Program. (1996–2000). Quarterly Progress and Financial Reports. E.T. Jackson and Associates Ltd. Ottawa, Ontario, Canada.

Sardar, N. I. (1993). RD-12 management action to improve overdue loan situation. Ideas Act. 3(2):1, 3.

Sharif, I., Wood, G. D. (1997). Conclusion. In: Wood, G. D., Sharif, I., eds. Who Needs Credit? Poverty and Finance in Bangladesh. London: Zed, pp. 371–379.

Sultan, M. (1998). Report on Organizational Development and Social Development. Dhaka: Rural Bittaheen Institution Program.

UNDP (United Nations Development Program). (1994). Human Development Report. New York: Oxford.

UNDP (United Nations Development Program). (2001a). Millennium Development Goals. New York (www.undp.org).

UNDP (United Nations Development Program). (2001b). Human Development Report. New York: Oxford.

World Bank. (2000). Overview of Poverty Reduction Strategies. Washington, D.C. (www.worldbank.org/poverty/strategies).

# 21

# Decentralization and Local Protectionism in China

**YONGSHUN CAI**

*National University of Singapore, Singapore*

## INTRODUCTION

For a state with multiple-level governments, the process of decentralization, which is the transfer of authority or responsibility to local-level governments, is often seen as an important condition for economic development (Rondinelli and Nellis, 1986). It is emphasized that as the local government has access to more relevant information than the central government about local conditions, it is likely to make better decisions (Hayek, 1945). Decentralization also promotes efficiency by introducing competition among local jurisdictions, which has significant implications for overall economic development (Tiebout, 1956; Brewley, 1981). As Wallace Oates suggests, "The tailoring of outputs to local circumstances will, in general produce higher levels of well-being than a centralized decision to provide some uniform level of output across all jurisdictions" (Oates, 1994). In addition, say Montinola et al., "Competition among jurisdictions provides incentives to replace poorly chosen strategies with variants of strategies that appear to succeed elsewhere" (Montinola et al., 1995: 59).

In line with the above findings, the importance of decentralization has been highlighted repeatedly in studies of China's economic reform and development. Susan Shirk (1993), for example, suggests that playing to the provincial governments was an effective strategy employed by Deng Xiaoping to promote economic reform in China. Those measures, including the fiscal decentralization and an active participatory role assigned to provincial leaders, provided a strong incentive for local cadres to carry out reforms. Montinola et al. (1995) point out that decentralization has been a significant factor for China's economic development, working as both an incentive and a guarantee for such development. The Chinese style of decentralization is based on federalism, and not only encourages local governments to speed up economic development but also prevents the central government from overextracting resources from local authorities or curtailing the reform process. Jean Oi (1999) explores the effect of fiscal decentralization on the governments at the county and township levels, and finds that the reform measure also served as a strong incentive for local cadres to develop township and village enterprises.

It is beyond dispute that decentralization is an important precondition for the economic development of China, yet inherent in this delegation of power to local governments is the problem of the lack of guarantee that local authorities will use their power to benefit the localities or the country as a whole. From the perspective of a principal-agent relationship, interest divergence between the central government and lower-level governments is inevitable (Moe, 1984). Because of such interest divergence, a possible consequence of decentralization is that the pursuit of local interests by local governments may create a "collective bad" for the country. To some extent, this is the situation today in China. In this regard, a serious problem faced by both the central and local governments is so-called local protectionism—local governments imposing restrictions on external business entities in order to protect their local interests. Local protectionism not only poses a significant hurdle to the creation of a common market in the country, it also hinders national economic development in that it discourages local enterprises from improving their performance and becoming competitive in domestic and international markets.

Fully aware of the problems arising from local protectionism, the Chinese central government has made a number of attempts to address the issue, but with only little progress and thereby limited success. This chapter addresses the rationale behind local protectionism in China and why the central government is not in a position to stop the practice. It suggests that driven by the pressure of the creation of employment and the generation of revenue, local governments see local protection as a necessary option. While the central government is determined to stop such activities, the existing political system undermines its efforts because of the difficulties in imposing credible punishment on local officials. The issue of local protectionism suggests that a strong and determined central state is necessary to create a common market and promote long-term economic development in China.

The remainder of the chapter covers the following. First, the chapter discusses the system of local protectionism in China by using the beer manufacturing industry as an example. Second, it explores the rationale of local governments for engaging in such activities by highlighting the pressure they themselves face in revenue generation and the creation of job opportunities. Third, the chapter demonstrates the negative effects of such local protectionism on the development of the national economy in China. It also addresses the measures adopted by the central government, and explains why such measures have only limited effectiveness. Finally, it concludes by emphasizing the importance of the state's capacity in economic transition and development.

## THE SYSTEM OF LOCAL PROTECTIONISM IN CHINA

In China, local protectionism means that based on its administrative power, the local government provides protection for local firms that engage in legal or even illegal businesses. In so doing, local governments employ various means to resist, sabotage, or even ignore state policies and laws in order to set up trade barriers. This is true for local governments at the provincial, city, and county levels. The spread of local protectionism has hurt the Chinese economy in many ways. First, it segregates the markets and increases transaction costs. The lack of a common market will have a lasting negative effect on China's economic development. Second, as local protectionism often violates laws, it damages the reputation of legal institutions—the foundation of a market economy—and leads to chaos in the market in China. Third, it prevents the emergence of competitive companies at the national level, severely hindering industrial development in China.

In resorting to local protectionism, most policies or measures adopted by local governments are aimed at providing monopolized power to local firms. There are numerous protected industries or businesses, including the car industry, the beer manufacturing industry, and the cigarette manufacturing industry, and the purchase or sale of such production materials and consumer goods as TV sets. The list has expanded further in recent years to include cement, chemical fertilizers, steel, cotton, wool, cocoon, coal, and other sectors, and "trade wars" have emerged between regions over these sectors (Xin, 2001). These trade wars happen either because the local government does not allow external business entities to buy raw materials produced locally or because it prohibits external enterprises from selling their products in its local market.

The scope of protective measures of local governments is quite broad. One simple practice is to impose additional charges on nonlocal companies. In 2001, for example, a competitive TV manufacturer from Guangdong province was charged a 16-million-yuan (Chinese currency) fine in Nanjing, Jiangsu province, under the pretext that the company did not follow local regulations (Wang, 2001). Each local government may also make up specific regulations regarding the purchase of various products needed for the production or utilization purposes of local public agencies. In a county in Henan province, for example, the local government stresses that "to protect the manufacturing of chemical fertilizers in our county, any work unit or individuals must not purchase the product externally. For those who violate this regulation, the government will not only confiscate their business income but will also impose severe punishment. The major leaders involved will assume both administrative and economic responsibilities" (Xin, 2001). Similarly, to protect the local cigarette industry in a city in Jiangsu province, the local government has the provision that the work units are prohibited from using public funds to buy nonlocally manufactured cigarettes, which implies that they can only purchase local products (Yan, 2000a). With regard to various forms of local protectionism, the state council presents the following major types in its 2001 directive:

1. Using various means to designate particular work units or individuals as the only qualified party for certain businesses
2. Setting up checkpoints along the road, railway, bus station, port, or airport to prevent the import of nonlocal goods or the export of local goods
3. Practice discrimination of both taxes imposed on nonlocal products and regulations regarding prices or standards
4. Imposing different technological requirements and standards on nonlocal products to limit their entry
5. Adopting different licensing or approval procedures to restrict the import of nonlocal products

6.  Restricting or excluding nonlocal enterprises from participating in local biddings
7.  Restricting or excluding nonlocal enterprises from establishing their agencies and imposing discriminating regulations to encroach on their legal interests (Liu, 2002)

A good example to demonstrate the degree and methods of local protectionism in China is the beer industry. By 1999, China was the second largest country in the world in terms of its beer production and consumption after the United States, but the unique characteristic of China's beer industry is that it is populated by small enterprises. The number of beer-manufacturing factories in China totaled 650 by the end of the 1990s, which is about one factory in every three to four counties on average. Only two of these factories have an annual output of 1 million tons, accounting for 10% of the total output in China. In other words, the Chinese beer industry does not reap the benefits of the economy of scale. In contrast, the output of only two beer companies in the United States—Anheuser-Busch and Miller Brewing—equal the amount of beer manufactured by all the beer factories in China. In 1999, Anheuser-Busch's share of the U.S. market was 47.5%, and that of Miller Brewing was 21.4% (Guo, 2000).

The existence of such a large number of small manufacturers in China cannot simply be attributed to the different tastes of locals or the lack of competition among manufacturers. As a matter of fact, the competition in the beer industry is intense, and the coexistence of these numerous beer factories is largely due to local protectionism. As beer has a high tax rate, the industry often contributes significantly to the fiscal revenue of local governments. Local governments thus have the incentive to exclude external beer manufacturers from entering the local market. For this purpose, local governments have employed administrative means to increase the operation costs of external manufacturers or to prevent local consumers from buying nonlocal beers in the name of "developing the local economy by drinking local beer." The major mode of protection is to impose exorbitant taxes on imported beer or simply to prevent its sale. Some local governments even confiscate nonlocal beers. For example, a city of Heilongjiang province confiscated about 5000 boxes of beer from a nonlocal manufacturer in the name of getting rid of fake goods (Guo, 1998). Some local governments impose extra taxes or fees on external beers or impose heavy fines on those who sell nonlocal beer. Others adopt specific regulations discriminating against external beers. Protection may also take a less direct form. For example, some local governments reduce the cost of production of the local factories by granting them a delay in the payment of taxes.

In a city in Hubei province, the government imposed administrative restrictions on the sale of nonlocal beers. In 1996, the city government established a beer market management office, which is funded and headed by the local beer manufacturer. The office is also located in the local beer factory. In March 2001, as another organizational effort to boost the production of local food and beverage industries, the local government formed a food and beverage business inspection group, mostly consisting of important government organs—the local cigarette and alcohol bureau, the quality and technology inspection bureau, the industrial and commercial bureau, the tax bureau, the hygiene inspection station, and the public security bureau.

In the meantime, the city government also employed other protectionist measures. First, it provided policy support to local beer producers. In 2001, the city alcohol management bureau issued a notice stating that "Without approval, non-local beers cannot be sold in local stores, restaurants, and hotels," but it was very difficult to obtain such approvals. In contrast, shops that sell the local beer do not need such approval. Second, in the guise of market management, local government organs carried out inspections and imposed fines on those who sold nonlocal beer. In the first half of 2001, the inspection groups confiscated 6000 boxes of a nonlocal beer. Because of such protectionist policies, sellers of nonlocal beers were often threatened, stalked, molested, and even beaten up (Leng, 2001).

The above situation in this city in Hubei province is not an isolated case; similar ones have occurred elsewhere. For example, the government in a city in Liaoning province requires retailers to sign an agreement with local beer producers to sell only their products. Those who violate the agreement may have their licenses revoked and will be fined up to 20,000 yuan. The departments concerned are required to carry out inspections around the clock and confiscate nonlocal beers (Yan, 2000). In 1999, the local government in a city in Jiangsu province stated that nonlocal beers must be checked by the local technology supervision bureau before they could be sold in local markets. This became an effective check to prevent nonlocal beer from entering the local market, as the technical requirements were often difficult to meet (Yan, 2000). Similarly, in 2000 the Quality and Technology Inspection Bureau of Jiangxi province issued a directive stating that the local beer was a provincial product that should be protected. Only this bureau has the right to check the quality of the beer. If there are problems with the quality of the local beer, they should be reported to the bureau. Action can be taken only after the approval of this bureau (Hu and Liu, 2000).

These above protectionist measures represent a fundamental reason for the coexistence of numerous small-scaled beer manufacturers in China. This case indicates the severity of local protectionism and points to the fact that there are many such cases of protectionism at the local level in China. As this issue has significantly affected economic activities across China, it is thus necessary to examine the rationale of the local government in adopting local protection.

## LOCAL GOVERNMENT'S RATIONALE FOR PROTECTIONISM

Local protectionism was not a problem in China before the economic reform, when local governments faced a different incentive structure. In a planned economy, competition among jurisdictions was not necessary, because the production and consumption of products were planned and allocated by the state. Local governments were thus not under pressure to generate fiscal revenue and create jobs for the local population. The current reform measures of decentralization have not only granted them power, however, but have also transferred to them many responsibilities. Fiscal decentralization has provided an incentive for local governments to speed up economic development. On the other hand, however, most local governments have to be financially self-dependent. As more revenue has been channeled to higher-level governments at the provincial and central levels after the 1994 fiscal reform, a large number of lower-level governments have failed to generate the required revenue. Among more than 2300 counties in China, at least 25% are in deficit. The failure to pay their employees has become a national phenomenon in China since the 1990s (Zhou, 2001a).

Local officials in China are often evaluated on the basis of their ability to develop the local economy and maintain social stability. In this regard, a daunting challenge for the governments at both the central and local levels is the increasing rate of unemployment caused by the reform of state-owned enterprises. Thus far tens of millions of workers have been streamlined in the reform process. Laid-off workers and other unemployed people have become a serious concern for the Chinese government, as they may threaten social and political stability (Cai, 2002; State Economic Planning Commission, 2000). In this context, the central government requires local governments to provide subsistence subsidies to these people and create jobs for them. Whether local governments can fulfill the two tasks largely depends on the performance of local business entities. Because of the pressure, few local governments are willing to see their local firms wiped out by market competition. On the contrary, it is their primary goal to sustain the operation of their firms. Local protectionism thus has a political and economic rationale.

This tendency of local governments to protect local businesses is reflected in their attitudes toward sham-goods production. China has been severely plagued by these sham goods—which are unqualified or illegal products or illegal duplications of well-known products—since the 1990s. In 1998, for example, it was estimated that the sham goods sold on the market were worth about 133 billion yuan. Those enterprises whose products were illegally duplicated suffered significant losses. The widespread prevalence of sham goods has not only prevented the development of a market economy in China, it has also increased difficulties for Chinese enterprises to export their products. Chinese Premier Zhu Rongji also acknowledged the severity of this problem. The list of these goods ranges from cotton to motor vehicles. As Table 1 suggests, the number of sham-goods manufacturers is significant in China.

These products not only disrupt the market order, they have also affected the public's health and safety. For example, some peasants bought fake seeds and reaped nothing after working hard on the land for several months. Others were disabled or even lost their lives when they used uncertified products. The alcohol manufacturing industry is a good example. By the late 1990s, in addition to those small-scaled and unregistered factories, the number of alcohol manufacturers in China was 46,000, but a significant number of them were producing sham alcohol. It is estimated that about 80% of the well-known brands of alcohol and beer in China are used illegally

**Table 1**   The Crackdown of Sham-Goods Manufacturers in 2000

| Categories | Number of cases | Number of sham-goods manufacturers |
|---|---|---|
| Food | — | 20,420 |
| Medicine and medical instruments | 38,700 | 1534 |
| Agricultural production materials | 29,400 | 5117 |
| Cotton products | 2005 | 981 |
| Cars | 3478 | 1338 |

*Source*: The Website of the State Economic and Trade Commission (available at http://www. setc.gov.cn/mysc2001).

by other factories. As the manufacturers of sham alcohol often fail to meet the technical requirements, tragic incidents have occurred to consumers across the country. By late 1998, the number of cases in which consumers were poisoned reached 700, and the total number of people affected was about 6000. About 200 of them died, and more than sixty lost their eyesight (see also Table 2).

While the reasons for the spread and persistence of sham-goods production are complex, local protectionism is one of the most critical factors. Theoretically, sham goods should not be a problem as long as the market operates according to the rules. As time passes, sham goods will lose their share of the market, but this is premised on the assumption that the market has mechanisms to identify and punish the fraudulent cases. The lack of such mechanisms allows the persistent supply of such goods. For example, during the period 1991 to 2001, the amount of detected sham goods was very limited, worth only about 30 billion yuan (Website of the State Economic and Trade Commission, 2000). This does not mean that local governments in China encourage their enterprises to make life-threatening products, but their half-hearted efforts to prevent this practice is a crucial reason for the continuity of sham-goods production. As the production of these goods is a source of revenue, some local governments lack the determination to eradicate them. This can be reflected in their perfunctory implementation or ignorance of the central government's regulations.

In a county in Zhejiang province, for example, the provincial law-enforcement group intended to investigate sham products and informed the local leaders in the hope of obtaining their support, but when the investigation group arrived in the locality, the local leaders did not even meet the group, giving the excuse that they had more important things to do. Similarly, in a county in Guizhou province, the provincial sham-goods investigation office found out that a factory manufacturing cigarettes was using the brand name of another factory. The local government was required to help solve the problem, but when the investigation office took action, none of the local leaders joined in (Zhang, 2000).

Some local governments even provide direct help to enterprises engaged in the production of sham goods. For example, in a county in Jiangsu province, the local quality and technology inspection bureau investigated a factory that was producing

**Table 2**  Examples of Poisoned Alcohol Drinkers

| Year | Locality | Persons disabled/wounded | Number of deaths |
|------|----------|--------------------------|------------------|
| 1992 | Heilongjiang | 6 | 7 |
| 1993 | Sichuan | 7 | 4 |
| 1993 | Henan | 25 | 4 |
| 1994 | Hubei | | 3 |
| 1994 | Sichuan | 1 | 8 |
| 1994 | Guangxi | 2 | 5 |
| 1995 | Guizhou | | 5 |
| 1996 | Yunnan | 6 | 35 |
| 1998 | Shanxi | | 37 |

*Source*: Jialin Wang, "Jiude yongtan" ("The Story of Wine") *Dadi* (*Land*), 4: 1998. 2–5.

sham goods, but the county government accused the bureau of violating the local regulation in this investigation. It emphasized that "Any law-enforcement inspection within the county must submit the information on the time, location, reasons, modes, and contents to the county government for approval before taking action." When carrying out the inspection, a stamped approval of the county government must be presented, otherwise the inspected organizations have the right to reject it. Those who carry out inspections without approval are also subject to punishment.

The State Quality and Technology Inspection Bureau admits that sham goods are difficult to eliminate because some local leaders see the production of such goods as an engine of local economic development. The head of the National Industrial and Commercial Bureau also points out that the production and sale of sham goods are more or less related to local protectionism. Such goods will not be eliminated without the removal of this source (Huang, 2000), therefore if local governments close an eye to the manufacture of illegal or unqualified products, it is unrealistic to expect that they would stop to protect local business activities in their localities. What are the implications of this local protectionism for economic development? The next section deals with this question.

## THE IMPLICATIONS OF LOCAL PROTECTIONISM FOR ECONOMIC DEVELOPMENT

Local protectionism may benefit a locality in the short term, but the aggregate outcome is anything but desirable, because it poses a serious challenge in a county to the development of a market economy. A mature market economy is based on laws, and firms compete with each other in line with the rules regulating their business activities. The competition pushes firms to continually improve their performance and profits in order to survive, leading to a more optimal use of resources, but this does not mean that government intervention is absent in the market economy. In fact, government intervention in the economy is common, and the question is more likely to be how much and what kind (Evans, 1995). Existing studies suggest that a fundamental aspect of government intervention is the formation of a reciprocal relationship between the government and businesses (Amsden, 1989). In other words, firms that receive help from the government should improve their performance and become self-dependent or competitive after receiving protection for a certain period, hence government protection can be seen as being less effective or failing if the protected firms remain uncompetitive after a significantly long period of protection.

Local protectionism in China has not been effective or productive because it fails to push local firms to improve their technology and performance. Over the years, many Chinese state-owned enterprises (SOEs) enjoyed a monopoly status, partly because of the local protectionism that prohibited competition from nonstate sectors and external companies. Such lack of competition undermined the SOEs' incentive to improve their products or to focus on research and development because they faced fewer problems of survival. Consequently, many Chinese industries, including vehicle manufacturing, telecommunications, and the computer industry, lack international competitiveness. As the chief executive officer (CEO) of a Chinese SOE admits, "Chinese state-owned enterprises can be the champion of the Olympic Games in the business field. But they are the champion of the Olympic Games for the disabled"

(Wang and Duan, 2002). In other words, Chinese SOEs can survive, but mostly in the domestic (or more accurately, the local) market with government support. This problem has been fully reflected in the car industry, as detailed below.

The Chinese government has planned to develop the car industry as one of the most important industries in China, but very limited progress has been made. The fundamental problem is that most car manufacturers in China are very weak in technological development. It is almost universally agreed that this weakness may undermine their competitiveness after China's entry into the World Trade Organization (WTO). For example, a survey of about 400 consumers in Beijing in 2002 found that almost 71% reported that the competitiveness of the cars made by Chinese firms would undoubtedly decline after China's accession into WTO. Although the Chinese government has obtained a five-year period of protection for the Chinese car industry, these consumers believe that this measure is far from sufficient to save the industry (CICN, 2002). While the reasons for the technological backwardness are complex, a most important reason is local protectionism, which fails to provide incentives for car manufacturers to improve the quality of their cars. This is because despite their lack of technological development, their market shares are guaranteed in their localities.

About two-thirds of the provinces in China have decided that they would develop car manufacturing as a major industry, but the industry is considered to be "dispersed, disordered, and small-scaled." China had over 120 car manufacturers and about 500 assembly factories by the early 2000s. The annual number of cars manufactured is about 1 million. In contrast, the United States has eight car manufacturers, but its output is 10 million (Yan, 2000). A unique phenomenon is that despite the small scale of production, many car manufacturers in China have been able to make profits. This is because car prices are much higher in China than in some developed countries such as the United States or Japan, in both absolute and relative (to individual incomes) terms.

The reason why the car industry can survive despite its small scale of production is the protection offered by the government. At the international level, the central government imposes strict restrictions on the import of foreign cars. Domestically, local governments prevent the competition of nonlocally manufactured cars. A typical practice is to impose extra fees or much stricter technical requirements on nonlocally manufactured cars. A number of local governments have imposed various fees on externally produced cars. For example, in 1997 the Hubei provincial government issued a notice that required local public agencies to buy the locally manufactured car (i.e., the only important car made in the province), otherwise they would not receive their fund allocation or purchase permission. Also, the public security department would not issue the registration. Other work units or individuals who buy the locally made car would be exempt from some local taxes and fees. Similarly, in 1999 the government of Jilin province adopted a regulation that "Those who buy local vehicles will be exempted from local fees and charges. They will also be given the priority of going through the procedures of registration" (Zhang, 2000a).

Against this background, it is not surprising that the practice of local protectionism may lead to trade wars. For example, in the late 1990s the Shanghai government pronounced that the users of locally manufactured cars needed to pay 20,000 yuan for the license, whereas those who used nonlocally manufactured cars would have to pay 98,000 yuan. In retaliation, the government of Hubei province regulated that local users who bought the car made in Shanghai (i.e., the one protected by the

Shanghai government) must pay an extra 70,000 yuan, which was over 41% of the price of the car. The extra fees were collected to support the "particularly unstable enterprises" in the province. For example, in this province a work unit bought a car made in Shanghai at a price of 170,200 yuan, but it had to pay about 150,000 yuan in fees in order to get the licenses. The Hubei government claimed that it imposed fees not to prevent the Shanghai-made car from entering the market in Hubei but to force the Shanghai government to allow the Hubei-made car into its market. As a matter of fact, by early 2001 about thirty cities had put restrictions on the purchase of cars (Zhou, 2001,), hence the unique trend that taxies in each city are locally made (if the locality manufactures cars), a direct outcome of local protectionism (Chen and Li, 2000).

A fundamental goal of decentralization is to introduce competition across jurisdictions, but local protectionism prevents it. Because of such intervention, car manufacturers are less worried about the market for and the improvement of their products. Technological innovation and research are thus extremely inadequate among Chinese car manufacturers. As a result, "After 50 years of development, the car manufacturing industry in China is still unable to develop its products, adopt new modes of production, or manage sales. The ability to compete with others is poor" (Zhang, 2002). This is also the major reason why this industry lags behind other neighbors, such as South Korea (not to mention Japan). As a CEO of a car manufacturer in Shanghai also admits, "It is better for us to stop the internal war. We should change the segregation of the market and strengthen the cooperation in order to face international competition" (Zeng and Li, 2000). With China's entry into the WTO, the car manufacturing industry in China is already facing tremendous pressure from external competition. Because the lack of technology, the most practical strategy of all major car manufacturers in China is to form joint ventures with foreign companies in order to use their technology to upgrade domestic products.

The car manufacturing industry in China indicates the negative impact of local protectionism on the promotion of competitiveness of some Chinese firms or the formation of a reciprocal relationship between the government and the firms. It also points to another unique phenomenon in China—no matter how intense the competition among enterprises across jurisdictions becomes, it seldom leads to mergers. This is because the local government simply believes that it will lose control of its enterprise if a merger occurs and that local revenue and employment will be negatively affected. This is particularly true in the sector of TV manufacturing in China. Local protectionism makes it possible for less profitable TV manufacturers to survive. In 2001, the sector as a whole made little profit. Among the more than seventy TV manufacturers in China, about 28.6% manufacture 80% of the total number of TV sets. In other words, the remaining 71.4% of the manufacturers only make 20% of the total number of TV sets. One result is the waste of resources, as most of these manufacturers only utilize half of their production capacity. The CEO of one of the largest electronics companies in China, TCL, points out the reason:

> The TV industry has not established a mechanism of exit. TV manufactures in many places are the protected firms as they are important tax payers. They are crucial to the local revenue and employment. Because of local protection, although they make little profit or even make losses, they do not exit. As a result, over the years, this industry only stresses the expansion of scale but ignores the development of technology. The competition can only be based on prices. But in price competition, technology is indeed very important as suggested by the practice of foreign companies. Last year [2000], Tony and

Toshiba made new TV sets and sold them in China. The price was over 10,000 yuan per set. A few months later, when our domestic companies manufactured the same products, the price fell to 5,000 yuan to 6,000 yuan (Wu, 2001).

The cases of the car industry and TV manufacturing indicate the significant negative impact of local protectionism on the enhancement of the competitiveness of Chinese firms. The central government has fully realized the problems with local protectionism or the "feudal economy" and has adopted some measures to address this problem, but because of the political arrangements discussed below, the elimination of local protectionism still has a long way to go. It remains a formidable obstacle to the market-driven strategy of economic development currently pursued by the Chinese government.

## THE CENTRAL GOVERNMENT AND THE CURBING OF LOCAL PROTECTIONISM IN CHINA

Local protectionism has become a "collective bad" in China, as it has increased transaction costs and weakened the competitiveness of local enterprises. Theoretically, this problem can be addressed in two ways. The first way is that the local government realizes that ceasing this practice works to the advantage of their localities in the long run. This is because the withdrawal of local protectionism can be propitious for the desirable business environment needed to attract investors. Moreover, it would also increase the competitiveness of their enterprises in the future. For many local officials who are reshuffled every few years, however, the long-term interests of locality may not be sufficient to give up such immediate concerns as employment and revenue. Instead, local officials may believe in Keynes's oft-quoted saying, "In the long run, we are all dead."

Given the lack of incentives on the part of local governments, the other solution is the maintenance of a powerful central state to assume the responsibility of building a common market (Montinola et al., 1995). As mentioned earlier, a unified domestic market is crucial in China, both for its long-term economic development and for its image as a responsible member of the WTO. Since the 1990s, the central government has tried to reduce local protectionism or the so-called feudal economy. In 2001, the state council issued *The Decision on the Prohibition of the Use of Local Protectionism in Market Activities*, which stipulated the consequences local governments would have to bear if they were engaged in such a practice. In particular, any local government that sets up trade barriers is to be penalized by its higher-level counterparts. Cadres that are directly responsible for local protectionism, depending on the severity of the offense, will be demoted, removed, or have legal punishment imposed. As usual, however, the problem is not whether there are laws to abide by but whether violations are punished. As discussed above, since the divergence of interests between local and central governments may not disappear, it poses a significant obstacle to the central government's efforts. It becomes even more difficult because of the limited access to the central government.

In China, a level-by-level monitoring system has been most frequently used to discipline lower-level governments. This system has two significant limitations. On the one hand, the central government must have an effective information-gathering system. On the other hand, the punishment imposed by the central government must be effective and credible in order to serve as a warning. As a matter of fact, information collection and monitoring have always been a problem for China's central government because of the very large number of lower-level governments (Cai, 2000). For this reason, the central government has to rely on higher-level local governments to monitor lower-level local governments. Under this system a lower-level government is often held directly accountable to its immediate high-level counterpart. For example, it is often the city government that disciplines county government officials. It is also true that the higher-level government may directly handle high-profile cases when lower-level governments violate laws or regulations.

There are two significant implications of this system for policy implementation in China. First, a patron–client relationship can develop between governments of different levels, which undermines the credibility of punishment. This is all the more true if cadres of different levels have good personal relations. Second, as lower-level cadres are assigned with multiple tasks, punishment for violations is less credible because some of the tasks inherently conflict with each other. This being the case, the local government may be in a position to choose its priority: "The power to choose is the power to manipulate, holdup, and exact" (McCubbins et al., 1989: 439–440). An important aspect of the Chinese political norm is collective-interest exemption, which means that as long as local officials work for the benefits of their localities (i.e., collective interests) rather than themselves, their wrongdoings (such as the violation of state laws or regulations) are not taken seriously, because they had good "intentions" or "motivations." The exception is when such a case catches the attention of the high-level government using the case to demonstrate its determination to adhere to the bidding of the central government, but even then, few cadres receive legal punishment.

In the case of antilocal protectionism, the central government faces the same problem. In its directive issued in 2001, the state council pronounced that "For those local governments or their organs that engage in, tolerate, or prevent the investigation of cases of local protectionism, the provincial (or municipality) government will mete out punishment accordingly. As for provincial-level governments that engage in such activities, the central government will determine the course of action" (Liu, 2002). Because of the reasons discussed above, despite the severity of this issue in China few cadres that adopt local protectionism have ever been punished, hence as in the case of the beer manufacturing industry, regardless of government regulations, local governments continue to require local citizens to buy locally produced beer. It is also partly for this reason that sham goods are far from being wiped out. The persistence of local protectionism itself suggests that the provision of punishment failed as a deterrent. This issue also implies that if local officials in China are still evaluated on the basis of local economic development and revenue generation, local protectionism may persist because the incentive structure will remain unchanged. Within the existing political system, the cooperation of high-level government, especially at the provincial level, would be crucial for the central government to address this issue.

## CONCLUSION

Decentralization is believed to be important in promoting economic and social development because it provides incentives to lower-level governments by granting them the power of decision making and by rewarding their efforts. China's development initiatives also point to the importance of decentralization. Over the past twenty years, the phenomenal economic growth has largely been the result of both the openness and the reform policies that provided a strong incentive to local governments to develop local economies. This Chinese-style federalism is thus crucial to the understanding of China's development.

Decentralization has also created some problems in China, however, especially the system of local protectionism discussed in this chapter. Local governments have often abused their administrative power by adopting discriminatory regulations regarding economic activities in their localities. As local governments are responsible for local revenue generation and employment, they are thus strongly motivated to sustain the operation of local firms. For this purpose, some of them set trade barriers to prevent external businesses from entering the markets. While local protectionism may help some firms survive, it creates a "collective bad" for economic development in China. It hinders the development of a common market and increases the costs of transactions. It also reduces competition across jurisdictions, and thereby undermines the incentive of SOEs to improve their performance. Thus far, very few value-added Chinese industries are competitive internationally. A significant reason is that the protection offered by the local government undermines their incentive to make investments in long-term research and development. This is why most exports from China are not technologically advanced products and can be easily replaced by outside manufacturers.

The Chinese central government is fully aware of the problems arising from local protectionism and has taken a number of measures to address the issue, but this crusade still has a long way to go. Theoretically, local protectionism may cease if the local government realizes that this practice will hurt local interests in the long run, but as mentioned above, not many local officials are concerned about future benefits because they are reshuffled every few years. Another solution is the existence of a powerful central government. As local protectionism is often seen as a violation of government policies rather than state laws, local governments engaged in such a violation often face administrative rather than legal punishment. Because of the huge number of local governments, however, especially at the county and city levels, the central government is not in a position to monitor them.

Moreover, the central government's use of high-level local governments to discipline the lower-level ones is less effective, because of their common local interests and patron–client relations. The situation is likely to improve, however, as the Chinese government is under increasing international pressure to address the issue after its entry into the WTO. To keep its promise, the government will have to put more effort and resources toward tackling this problem and thus speed up the process of creating a common market in China. If seriously pursued, this government initiative will also have favorable implications for future economic development in China, especially in terms of greater local competition and innovation and higher international competitiveness.

## REFERENCES

Amsden, A. (1989). Asia's Next Giant—South Korea and Late Industrialization. New York: Oxford University Press.

Brewley, T. (1981). A critique of Tiebout's theory of local public expenditures. Econometica 49:713–739.

Cai, Y. (2002). The resistance of Chinese laid-off workers in the reform period. China Q 170:45–62.

Cai, Y. (2000). Between state and peasant: Local cadres and statistical reporting in rural China. China Q 163:783–805.

Chen, G., Li, F. (2000). No one can benefit from local protectionism. Renminluntan (People's Forum) 9:2–5.

CICN. (Jul. 22, 2002). Zhongguo gongshang shibao (China's Industrial and Commercial News).

Evans, P. (1995). Embedded Autonomy: States and Industrial Transformation. Princeton, NJ: Princeton University Press.

Guo, Q. (Jan. 22, 1998). A factory director was frustrated to tears by local protectionism in Heilongjiang province. Gongren ribao (Workers' Daily).

Guo, H. (2000). Who is going to take over the beer market? Dadi (Land) 16:12–16.

Hayek, F.A. (1945). The use of knowledge in society. Amer. Ec. Rev. 35:519–530.

Hu, X., Liu, J. (Oct. 27, 2000). Why is only local beer available here? Zhonghua xinwen bao (China News).

Huang, C. (Nov. 29, 2000). Breaking local protectionism is a precondition for eliminating sham goods. Jingji ribao (Economic Daily).

Leng, X. (2001). Hoping to have a unified big market. Nanfengchuang (Window for the South Wind) 11:2–8.

Liu, H. (Jan. 21, 2002). Local protectionism: Small actions and large damages. Hebeishangbao (Hebei Business News).

McCubbins, M., Noll, R., Weingast, B. (1989). Structure and process, politics and policy: Administrative arrangements and the political control of agencies. V. Law. Rev. 75:439–440.

Moe, T. (1984). The new economics of organization. Amer. J. Polit. Sci. 28:739–777.

Montinola, G., Qian, Y., Weingast, B. (1995). Federalism, Chinese style: The political basis for economic success in China. World Pol. 48:50–81.

Oates, W. (1994). Federalism and government finance. In: Quigley, J.M., Smolensky, E., eds. Modern Public Finance. Cambridge: Harvard University Press, pp. 126–164.

Oi, J. (1999). Rural China Takes off. Berkeley, CA: University of California Press.

Rondinelli, D., Nellis, J. (1986). Assessing decentralization policies in developing countries: The case for cautious optimism. Dev. Pol. Rev. 4:3–23.

Shirk, S. (1993). The Political Logic of Economic Reform in China. Berkeley, CA: University of California Press.

The State Economic Planning Commission. (2000). China's social situation at the turn of the new century. Jinji gongzuozhe xuexi ziliao (Study Materials for Economic Workers) 23:2–11.

Tiebout, C. (1956). A theory of local expenditures. J. Pol. Econ. 64:416–424.

Wang, J. (1998). The story of wine. Dadi (Land) 4:2–5.

Wang, K. (Jan. 16, 2001). Why was Kangjia fine in Nanjing? Caijin shibao (Financial Times).

Wang, N., Duan, Y. (April 26, 2002). Why can China not have companies as large as General Motors? Zhongguo jingji shibao (China Economic Times).

Wu, B. (Jan. 15, 2001). Who will be the ultimate winner of the competition of TV manufacture? Beijing chenbao (Beijing Morning News).

Xin, W. (Dec. 12, 2001). Local protectionism should be stopped. Ershiyi shijie jingji baodao (21st Century Economic Report).

Yan, Y. (April 22, 2000). Can the directives of the Cultural Revolution Committee manage the market economy well? Fazhiribao (Legal News Daily).

Yan, Y. (2000a). Removing the local protectionism. Dadi (Land) 5:3–7.

Zeng, G., Li, F. (2000). No one benefits from local protection. Renmin Luntan (People's Forum) 9:11–12.

Zhang, G. (Dec. 28, 2000). The roots of effective fighting against sham goods—Local protectionism. Shichangbao (Market News).

Zhang, Y. (2000a). A critical test of the Chinese car industry. Nanfengchuang (Window for the South Wind) 4:12–15.

Zhang, X. (April 1, 2002). International problems plaguing China's car industry. Nanfangdushibao (Southern City News).

Zhou, D. (2001a). Why was teachers' salary payment delayed to the new century? Liaowang (Perspective) 9:50–51.

Zhou, F. (April 1, 2001). What is the end of administrative monopoly? Fazhiribao (Legal News Daily).

# 22

## Panchayati Raj
### The Indian Model of Grassroots Democracy and Decentralized Rural Development

**NOORJAHAN BAVA***

*University of Delhi, Delhi, India*

### INTRODUCTION

The Republic of India is considered the largest of the world's democracies, and it represents one of the "functioning democracies" among developing nations (Kohli, 2001). India also has one of the oldest traditions of local self-government, popularly known as panchayati raj (PR). This village administration functioned through indigenous political institutions called panchayats. Traditionally every village (gram) had a panchayat consisting of five selected representatives (panches). History of India is replete with evidence that its ancient landscape was dotted with hundreds of panchayats or "village republics," through which the rural communities were governed even though throughout the Indian subcontinent the prevailing form of central government was monarchy (Majumdar et al., 1978). Despite their checkered history, there exists a remarkable continuity in the traditional and contemporary types of panchayats.

### THE PHILOSOPHY OF PANCHAYATI RAJ

#### Participatory Governance

Panchayati raj, the name given to the contemporary Indian model of local self-government in rural areas, rests on the foundation of a democratic ethos, as well as

*Dr. Bava is retired.

many democratic principles and institutions. The underlying philosophy of the contemporary PR signifies the realization of *village democracy (gram swaraj), the empowerment of rural people, participation of all citizens in the process of self-government, and decentralized rural development*. Village (grassroots) democracy had to operate through direct and indirect institutions, namely the village assembly (gram sabha) and elected representative bodies called panchayats constituted at various levels. The lofty goal of empowering the rural populace calls for devolution of powers, functions, finance, authority, and responsibility to local government units by their respective state governments. It implies the doctrine of popular sovereignty and the principle of decentralized governance. Above all, the panchayats serve as the institutional mechanism for channeling the *participation* of all citizens, not only in the process of governance, but also in multilevel planning and decentralized rural development.

Panchayati raj is based on the vision of gram swaraj of Mahatma Gandhi, who emphasized decentralized governance by stating that democracy could not be achieved by some men sitting on the top but had to be achieved from below by the people of every village. To Jayaprakash Narain, a close follower of Gandhi and a strong advocate of partyless direct democracy, the gram sabha signified village democracy, and he desired that at least one level of government should be a direct democracy. The relationship between the panchayat and gram sabha should be that of cabinet and assembly.

## Decentralized Planning

Panchayati raj represents the triangular relationship that exists among democracy, decentralization, and development (Maddick, 1963, 1970). In a democratic polity such as India, democracy has to be both an end in itself as well as a means to an end. Democracy is a development goal as well as the strategy for achieving other goals, such as eradicating poverty, unemployment, inequality, ill health, malnutrition, illiteracy, and ignorance. Panchayati raj operationalizes the concept of decentralized, multilevel planning and enables rural citizens to participate in the decision making for development. Panchayats at the village, intermediate, and district levels are the units for development plans and programs at their respective levels.

## Citizens' Participation

Panchayat raj institutions (PRIs) serve as the channel for mobilization, participation, and involvement of the rural citizens in decentralized governance and socioeconomic development at the grassroots level. Noorjahan Bava (1984, 1997) argues that citizens' participation in the various interfaces of the developmental decision-making process is the essence of democracy. It is crucial for development administration and the sine qua non of success, equity, effectiveness, and stability of development programs. Citizen participation is both a means to an end as well as an end in itself. For community development, participation is a "means," and for political development and participatory democracy, it is an "end" in itself.

If citizen participation is the vital means of achieving development goals, *decentralization* (political, economic, functional, and financial) is the instrument for eliciting and invoking citizen participation for democratic governance and socioeconomic development. In other words, decentralization is at the center stage of both democratic governance and planned development (Cheema and Rondinelli, 1983). Achievement in development, social change, and economic growth requires the spreading of efforts so that local communities and individuals can participate and bring under ideal grassroots conditions local energy, enthusiasm, initiatives, and resources for development activities. It is also true that only when people have control over both decisions and their execution can government and administration become transparent, accountable, free of corruption, and responsive to citizens' felt needs.

## The Empowerment of the People

One of the objectives of PR is the empowerment of rural people in general and of the weak, poor, and downtrodden (and of women in particular). Political empowerment takes place through citizens' political participation as members of panchayats, state assemblies, and parliament. These include various forms of participation: (1) contesting and getting elected to the panchayats, (2) taking part in the deliberations and decision making in PRIs to bring about change in rural society and improve the living conditions and standard of the people, (3) resolving local problems, (4) fulfilling the felt needs of the people, (5) mobilizing and managing local community resources in a sustainable manner, and (6) delivering such public services as health care, education, housing, roads, and essential commodities in an efficient and speedy manner.

The above duties related to performance of the role of members of panchayats as political leaders are indeed spectacular acts of exercising de jure sovereignty that enables local people to gain control over their lives. As the *Human Development Report* (1993) puts it, "Any proposal to increase people's participation must pass the empowerment test—does it increase or decrease people's power to control their lives. This test applies to all institutions that organize or affect human lives."

Conceptually, panchayats are the elected institutions of the rural people for their empowerment, socioeconomic transformation, and self-governance rather than agents of the state government. There is no doubt that with the three-tier panchayats, political empowerment of rural people, especially that of women and those belonging to scheduled castes and tribes, can become a living reality, with mandatory reservation of 33.3% in the seats and chairpersonships of all panchayats for these weaker sections of society.

Further, it is possible for a full-blown direct democracy to flourish in rural India when the constitutionally mandated gram sabha—the village assembly—functions as the bedrock of the PR system. It has enormous powers of direction, supervision, and control over elected members of the panchayats, local members of the Legislative Assembly (MLAs), and area members of Parliament (MPs). It also has control of the panchayat budget, approval of development plans and projects, and power of social audit, which paves the way for good governance.

## PANCHAYATI RAJ (PR): THE FIRST EXPERIMENT AND ITS DECLINE

Having included the subject of local government in the state list, the constitution of India provides in Article 40 that the "state shall take steps to organize village panchayats and endow them with such powers and authority as to enable them to function as units of local self-government." Many interpreted this provision as a token of respect shown by the founding fathers for Mahatma Gandhi's concept of gram swaraj, while social scientists such as Maddick (1963) saw a threefold objective behind the constitutional provision, including: (1) fostering the involvement of individuals throughout the nation in the process of democratic governance, (2) gaining villagers' participation in national development from the village level upwards, and (3) lessening the burden of the state administration through decentralization.

## Origin and Structure of PR

The failure of the Community Development Program (launched in 1952 to bring about integrated rural development in India on the initiative of the central government) was attributed by the Balwant Rai Mehta committee to the absence of an institutional mechanism in the countryside to channel villagers into participating in the development program. As a solution, in 1957 the committee recommended the introduction of a scheme of "democratic decentralization," popularly known as panchayati raj, that would establish a model of three-tiered panchayats—the gram panchayat, panchayat samiti, and zila parishad—at the village, block/intermediate, and district levels respectively. (The exact number of tiers was left to the discretion of the state governments.) Panchayati raj sought to achieve three objectives: (1) to ensure maximum participation of the people in socioeconomic development, (2) to decentralize the administrative apparatus down to the village level, and (3) to carry the democratic process and local self-government institutions to rural areas (Singh and Mishra, 1993).

All state legislatures enacted panchayat legislations and established panchayats—three tiers in most states, two tiers in a few, and only one tier in Kerala and Jammu and Kashmir. In their process of growth, the first-generation panchayats witnessed three phases: the golden period (1957–1964), stagnation (1965–1969), and decline (1970–1977), as pointed out by the Ashok Mehta committee (1978). The first experiment of PR failed to take off.

## Causes for the Decay of Panchayati Raj

The continuing decay of the PR till 1992 was brought about by a number of factors. One of the most important was the determination and effort by political leaders at the central and state levels to end the threat to their leadership from the panchayat leaders at the grassroots level by undermining PRIs in every possible way. After the death of Prime Minister Nehru, central- and state-level politicians began to wreck the PR. The center, for its part, established its own project offices, and the District Rural Development Agency, equipped with its own staff, funds, and guidelines, implemented such centrally sponsored schemes as the Integrated Rural Development Program (IRDP) and the National Rural Employment Program without involving the panchayats at all.

For their own part, the state governments strangled the PRIs by maintaining the Department of Rural Development independently from the Department of Local Administration and Panchayat Development without any coordination between the staff or the programs between the two departments. They also failed to grant adequate funds and power to the panchayats. No elections were held to the panchayats for many years—as long as twenty to twenty-two years in some cases.

Instead, officers on special duty were appointed to manage local government affairs. All these factors created conditions that were conducive for collusion between rural development bureaucracy, which was largely made up of state government officials on deputation to district administration downwards, and panchayat leaders, consisting of dominant caste/class leaders, landlords, and money lenders. Further, there was rampant corruption, factionalism, and politicization, resulting in the near collapse of the system (Sharma, 1994). The monumental failure of the denial of devolution of power, funds, and functions to the PRIs reduced them to the status of mere agents of their respective state governments. Criminal negligence and arbitrary action by state governments contributed to the emasculation of PRIs in many states over the years (Khanna, 1994).

## The Revival of PR

Many steps were taken by the central government to arrest the decay of PR. These included the appointment of the G. V. K. committee (1985) and the L. M. Shingivi committee (1986) by then Prime Minister Rajiv Gandhi, and conferences and work-shops on PR attended by district collectors, and nongovernmental organizations (NGOs). Also included was the introduction of the 64th Amendment Bill (1989) and success of getting it passed by a two-thirds majority in the lower house (Lok Sabha). It was, however, struck down by the upper house (Rajya Sabha) by just two votes. The next government, headed by V. P. Singh, also made an effort, but failed to provide constitutional status to PRIs. The Congress Party renewed its commitment to the philosophy of "power to people," successfully fought the general elections with this plank, formed the government headed by P. V. Narsimha Rao and introduced the Seventy-Third Constitutional Amendment Bill in December 1991 in the Parliament. The bill was passed by both houses and became an act on April 24, 1993.

## THE SEVENTY-THIRD CONSTITUTIONAL AMENDMENT AND THE NEW PANCHAYATI RAJ

### Salient Features

The 73rd and 74th Amendments have indeed revived, rejuvenated, and revolutionized the PRIs and urban local bodies, respectively. They are landmark developments in the evolution of democratic decentralization and local self-government in the country in the sense that they mandate the "third tier" of government in the federal democratic polity of India (Bava, 2000; Mathew, 1994).

The Amendment Act has not only bestowed upon the PRIs their much-needed "constitutional status." It also provided for a mandatory reservation of seats for scheduled castes and tribes in proportion to their number in the total population in the panchayat area, as well as a 33.3% reservation for women in all seats and chairperson positions for all levels of the panchayats. Although the act did not create a "local list" of power, it did add the Eleventh Schedule, consisting of twenty-nine items, to the Constitution. Article 243G envisaged the panchayats as institutions of local self-government so that they would enjoy functional, financial, and administrative autonomy. In the spirit of Article 40 (Joshi, 1998), the act left it to the state legislatures to devolve adequate power, authority, and resources to the panchayats through enactment of conformity legislations.

The act mandated the establishment of the gram sabha (village assembly)—an institution of direct democracy—in each village as the foundation of PR. It also provided for representative bodies consisting of a uniform structure of three-tiered panchayats at the village, block, and district levels in each state, except Jammu and Kashmir, Nagaland, Mizoram, Meghalya, and scheduled and tribal areas.

In keeping with the centrality of elections in a democracy, all members of all panchayats are to be directly elected by the rural citizens. While the chairpersons of block and district panchayats are to be elected indirectly, the president (sarpanch) of a village panchayat is to be elected directly or indirectly, as the state government dictates. The term of every panchayat being five years unless it is dissolved earlier under relevant law, elections to a panchayat must be held before the expiration of its term or by at least six months from the date of its dissolution. Every state should appoint: a state election commission for superintendence, direction, and control of the preparation of the electoral rolls and to conduct panchayat and municipal elections; a finance commission to distribute financial resources between the state and panchayats and to provide for audit of the panchayat accounts; and a district planning committee for integrated development of both rural and urban areas by planning and implementing for economic development and social justice.

## The Working of the New PR

Various states and Union Territories enacted their conformity legislation before April 24, 1994, and held elections to the panchayat bodies. According to Kuhn (1998), thanks to the 73rd Amendment Act, the number of rural self-government institutions with elected representatives rose to around 500 bodies at the district level, 5000 at the block level, and 2,25,000 at the village level. According to the study conducted by the Institute of Social Sciences (1998) in the country as a whole, 7,68,582 women (31.37%) members have been elected to the gram panchayats, 38,582 (20.7%) to the panchayat samitis, and 4030 (31.8%) to the zilla parishads.

In a patriarchal society such as India, in which women have been subjected to centuries-old gender discrimination, deprivation and inequality, PR has indeed opened the door to emancipation, participation, and political empowerment. In order to enable women members to achieve results in their political role, a number of interventions are necessary. They need continuous orientation training, sensitization, capacity building, information, and counseling in both governmental and nongovernmental organizations. When they respond to sociopolitical challenges in society, they are to be supported by civil society organizations such as NGOs that are working for empowerment of women. Above all they need the backup of their families, relatives, friends, and neighborhoods (Palanithurai, 2001).

Panchayati raj has been a great liberating force as far as the poor, weak, downtrodden, dalit (socially and economically backward classes), and scheduled caste (SC) and scheduled tribes (ST) are concerned. A 1998 study conducted by the Institute of Social Sciences revealed that as of May 31, 1998, there were 3,43,792 SC members in the gram panchayats, 18,867 SC members in the panchayat samitis, and 1904 in the zilla parishads—an average of 16.73% SC representatives in the country as a whole.

The same study also shows that 2,40,178 ST members had been elected to gram panchayats, 8442 at the block level and 1247 at the district level—an average of 7.95% as of May 31, 1998. These empirical findings established the fact that the constitutional provision for mandatory reservation for the SC and ST population in the PRIs has been an important step toward empowering one of the most economically and socially deprived sections of society. In a caste-ridden society, a mere increase in the numerical representation of SC and ST cannot by itself empower these weaker sections without land reforms leading to land ownership. The spectacular achievement of West Bengal and Kerala in PR is the direct function of the successful land reforms and political will in these states.

## Successful Case Studies in PR

The state of West Bengal is a typical example of what political will, commitment, ideology, political stability, and economic (land) reforms can play to ensure the spectacular success of PR. It is the first and only Indian state that has seen timely and regular panchayat elections on a party basis every five years since 1978, a year after the Left Front government was elected to power. It goes to the credit of the Left Front government that unlike other states it has never postponed or rescheduled panchayat elections, even when political compulsions dictated otherwise (Mathew, 2001). The Left—headed by the Communist Party of India-Marxist (CPI-M)—came to power on two planks of its election manifesto; namely, vigorous agrarian and political reforms. Its agrarian reform program involved both the forceful implementation of existing tenancy laws that gave security of tenure and a legally determined right to maximum crop sharing to tenants, and the distribution of surplus land above the land ceiling limit to small, marginal farmers and landless agricultural laborers.

In terms of its achievement on both these counts, it is by far the leading state in the country (Gazdar and Sengupta, 1997). Its political reform program consisted of empowering the three-tiered panchayat system with a gram panchayat (village council) for a cluster of villages at the lowest level, a panchayat samiti for a block, and a zilla parishad for a district (Ghatak and Ghatak, 2000). Although the Congress government passed laws on land reforms and strengthening of panchayats, they were not seriously implemented. It was left to the Communist government to combine political will and ideological commitment to egalitarian reforms to ensure serious and effective implementation of reforms by the administration.

During Congress rule (from 1967 to 1970), a million acres of good agricultural land were taken over by the government. This considerably weakened the hold of the big landlords, who had been the traditional rulers of rural society. When the first panchayat elections took place in 1978 the power structure in the rural areas thus had already changed. As a result, instead of empowering the already powerful landlords, panchayat elections placed power in the hands of newcomers, who could be relied upon to implement land reforms faithfully. In this way land reforms and the panchayats supported each other (Gazdar and Sengupta, 1997).

Without land reforms panchayat elections would undoubtedly have continued the rule of the landed gentry in rural areas of the state. This is a marked difference between West Bengal and other states (except Kerala). Because there is no land reform in other states, landlords and elites easily get elected to the PRIs, and they corner the benefits of rural development programs for themselves and perpetuate inequalities in society.

The newly elected members of the West Bengal panchayats in turn played an active role in the enforcement of the agrarian reform program of the Left government. This involved identifying the beneficiaries, supporting them against possible threats from landlords, and helping revenue bureaucrats (thehsildars) register the leases of sharecroppers so that the benefits of tenancy laws would go to them. Many people from the lower and middle strata of the rural society—poor peasants, sharecroppers, agricultural laborers, and school teachers—could thus for the first time hold the seats of power and resources distribution. In the 1978 panchayat elections 75% of the elected representatives of the village councils came from households owning less than two acres of land.

The hallmark of a direct democracy is the direct participation of citizens in the administration and management of public affairs. The 73rd Amendment provided for a statutory body called the gram sabha (village assembly), a collective political body of all persons registered in the electoral rolls of a village located in the area of panchayat, precisely for this purpose. West Bengal has taken a step forward by providing for gram sansad (GS) constituency meetings in every gram panchayat area to enable rural citizens to take part directly and intensively in the process of governance and development. It is required to guide and advise the gram panchayat (GP) regarding schemes of economic development and social justice for the area.

Statutorily, the GS may identify or lay down principles for identifying schemes for economic development of the village; select beneficiaries for poverty alleviation programs; constitute one or more beneficiary committees that are not members of the GP; mobilize mass participation for community welfare, adult education, and family and child welfare; promote solidarity and harmony among all sections of the people, irrespective of religion, faith, caste, and creed; and record its objection to any action of the pradhan or members of the GP for failure to implement any development scheme properly or without the active participation of the people of the area (Datta and Sen, 2000). It meets twice a year (May and December), and if the pradhan/uppradhan does not convene the sansad, the state government is empowered to remove the member from office. Further, the GP has to consider every resolution adopted at the village constituency meetings, and decisions and actions taken on them will have to be reported at the next meeting. If this does not happen or if the GP fails to place the draft budget and statement of accounts and audit reports, it would be considered a serious lapse and the auditor could declare all expenditures of the GP as illegal in his report. The gram sansad has thus emerged as an innovative institution contributing to the realization of the ideal of participatory governance (Ghatak and Ghatak, 2000).

Despite its success in some aspects of PR, however, West Bengal lags behind Kerala, Madhya Pradesh (M.P.), and Karnataka on such indicators as the power to prepare local plans, the power to transfer funds, and the power to transfer or control the local staff. In particular, the extent of the devolution of the state government's power, finances, and functions to the panchayats and the extent of the participation of the people in the planning process is less in West Bengal than in Kerala.

Kerala, the southernmost state of the Indian Union, is another oft-cited example of a successful experiment in PR and decentralized/participatory rural development. The state had only one tier—the village panchayat—from 1957 to 1990, and the second tier—the district council—was only established in 1991. For the first time the three tiers of PR were established under the Kerala Panchayati Raj Act of 1994, which provided for the village, block, and district panchayats.

In accordance with Article 243A of the Constitution, the Kerala Panchayat Act also provides for gram sabha, the institution of direct democracy and the cornerstone of the PR system. What is unique to Kerala is that it provides for a gram sabha for every ward in the panchayat because of the large population (10,000 to 75,000 people) in village panchayats. By the 1999 amendment to its panchayat act, Kerala has also paved the way for greater and more intensive participation of the rural citizens in self-governance by giving legal recognition to even smaller units called ayalkutams, or neighborhood groups of around sixty households each.

Immediately after assuming power in 1996, the Left Democratic Front (LDF) government in Kerala launched what has come to be called the peoples' campaign for local bodies-oriented participatory planning for rural–urban development through operationalization of the concept of microlevel planning. The LDF decided to prepare and implement the Ninth Five-Year Plan by involving the PRIs and municipal bodies in a big way in the process of "planning from below." The experiment brought to the fore the lack of experience in grassroots planning; the absence of necessary laws, rules, and regulations; and the lack of adequate government personnel and experts.

The government decided to overcome the hurdles by launching a five-month-long peoples' campaign on August 17. It was hailed as the first instance of planning from below, with citizens' participation in the real sense (Namboodripad, 1996a). It involved conducting seminars and workshops at both the gram sabha and ward levels, as well as at various panchayat and municipal levels. Training was given in both the preparation of village, block, and district plans and how to integrate the village plans with block plans—the latter with the district plan prepared by the district planning committee. In all 400 persons were trained at the state level, 15,000 at the district level, and one lakh at the panchayat and municipal levels.

Such a massive campaign for training personnel for planning from below had never been attempted in this state (Namboodripad, 1996b). The most important step was the decision of the state government to devolve 40% of the state plan outlay of Rs.15,000 crore to local bodies to kick start participatory decentralized planning. Dreze and Sen (1993), Kurien (1995), and George (1997) think that the much lauded Kerala model resulted in remarkable achievements in such key areas of human development as health, education, and economic equity, which were achieved through the combination of government redistribution policies and mass mobilization. Kerala's experience shows that the conditions of the people can be improved even at a low level of economic growth, provided there is growth in mass awareness and collective action to utilize available facilities.

Oommen and Annamalai (1994), however, hold that the Kerala model of development resulted in a virtual stagnation and even decline in the sphere of employment and material production. In their view, the highly polarized politics in the state, such as that between the United Democratic Front (UDF) and LDF, which alternately form the government with slender majorities, often compelled them to pursue highly populist policies to please the voters, focusing on welfare and social service sectors and neglecting agricultural and industrial sectors. One can even conjecture that the people's campaign for the Ninth Plan was a strategy to overcome the political stalemate and economic stagnation. The thrust of LDF government's policy now is to involve people in production-oriented planning.

## ISSUES IN PANCHAYATI RAJ

### The Emerging Local Political Leadership in PR

Empirical research in some states—Haryana, Rajasthan, West Bengal, and so on (Nandini, 2000; Thakur, 2001)—on the socioeconomic profiles of elected members of panchayats at various levels reveals that the rural political leaders of PR institutions are predominantly agriculturists (marginal and small farmers), most of whom own land up to one to five acres. The traditional landed gentry consisting of landlords and big farmers (with ten to fifteen acres and more) have also been elected to the panchayats, but their numerical strength has decreased, compared to their position in the first-generation panchayats.

Successful land reforms in such states as West Bengal and Kerala have opened up many avenues for poor farmers, including getting elected to the panchayats. In other words the emerging panchayat leadership represents more socially and economically backward castes and classes than its counterparts in the 1960s to 1980s. Mandatory reservation for SC, ST, OBCs, and women has also led to their empowerment and participation in local governance. Gender discrimination against women is slowly but surely being done away with, although women panchayat members face many hurdles and problems in their efforts to become joint rulers and equal partners in the grassroots democratic institutions.

Once a male bastion, panchayats still continue to be so to some extent in the patriarchal rural society of India, even after the 73rd Amendment, although some progress has been made in the male monopoly of political power at the local level. As representative bodies today's PRIs are more broad-based and represent wider segments of society than before. Studies also indicate that the new panchayat leadership is more literate (ranging from primary to higher secondary level), youthful, and energetic, as they broadly belong to the age group of thirty to fifty years as compared with the gerentocracy of the first-generation panchayat leaders.

In Rajasthan and Haryana, most (80%) of the new panchayat leaders and their family members are found to be politically conscious; they have been members of one political party or other, and 35% of them have had political experience as members of GPs. It is hoped that the presence of such leadership qualities in PR members as dynamism, enthusiasm, enlightenment, public-spiritedness, a keen awareness of individuals' problems, and the skill and capacity for decision making will transform PR into a vibrant democracy at the grassroots level.

It is true that less than 10% of the contemporary leaders of the panchayats are power/status seekers, but the vast majority have been elected to the PRIs for the avowed purpose of working for the betterment and well-being of their fellow citizens. In the words of J. S. Mill, there are more "other-regarding" than "self-regarding" members in the new PR, which is a sign of a healthy democracy.

## Participatory Democracy and Good Governance

No doubt direct voter participation in the gram sabha, ward sabha, and gram sansad augurs well for good governance at the local level. Also, in conformity with the provisions of the 73rd Amendment, all state panchayat acts have created the gram sabhas and designated them as institutions of direct democracy and instruments, of social audit, accountability, and transparency. In reality, however, their functioning leaves much to be desired. For one thing, the Constitution has left it to the state legislatures to specify the powers and functions of the gram sabha, with the result that they have been reduced to mere "advisory" bodies instead of a "controlling" authority over the panchayats (Datta and Sen, 2000).

In Kerala it is obligatory on the part of the president or the vice president to explain to the GS as to why a particular decision taken by it could not be implemented.

Except in Kerala and Madhya pradesh, the advice and suggestions of the GS are not even binding on the GP (Participatory Research in Asia, 1997).

In most states, the functional domain of GS is limited to the discussion of the annual statement of accounts and administration reports and the selection of beneficiaries of the antipoverty programs (Oommen, 1996). In Andhra Pradesh, Bihar, Gujarat, Karnataka, Madhya Pradesh, Rajasthan, and Andaman and Nicobar Islands, the GS reviews programs of work for the current year and new programs for the next year. It mobilizes voluntary labor and contribution in kind or in cash for community welfare, adult education, and family welfare in Bihar, Karnataka, Kerala, Punjab, Rajasthan, Sikkim, Uttar Pradesh (U.P.), and West Bengal, and in addition to the above, GS promotes unity and harmony among all sections of society in West Bengal and Tamil Nadu (Jain, 1999b).

While in Haryana and Kerala the GS considers and scrutinizes existing schemes, all completed works, and all kinds of activities of panchayats, as well as maintains a complete register for all development works undertaken by the GP or government department, the GS in Gujarat, Haryana, Karnataka, and M.P. considers budgets prepared by GP and future development programs and plans for the sabha area (Jain, 1999a). Andhra Pradesh, Goa, and Orissa have given the GS the important fiscal power to identify and recommend areas for additional taxation and revenue generation.

The 1999 amendment of M.P. goes beyond any state panchayat legislation in empowering nontribal GS in the state with wide-ranging powers of the kind envisaged in the central act—provisions of panchayats (extension to scheduled v. areas) 1996 for the GS in unscheduled areas. These included the power to: (1) exercise control over the institutions and functionaries in the social sector transferred or appointed by the GP (such as primary school teachers and health care workers); (2) manage natural resources, including land, water, forests, and minerals within the areas of the village in accordance with the provisions of the Constitution and other relevant laws in force for the time being; (3) advise GPs in the regulation and use of minor bodies of water and award minor mineral leases; (4) impose prohibition; and (5) be consulted before land acquisition, along with the right to recall elected members of the village panchayat after they have completed half their term.

The actual implementation of the above provisions by the administrative officials, however, is not in accord with the spirit of the statute. For instance, the power of control over forests translates into instructions that revenues from nontimber forest produce (NTFP) may not be retained by the state government except for 20%, which would meet administrative costs. The 80% collected by the state government is to be returned to the actual collectors of NTFP (30%) and to the cooperative of NTFP collectors (50%), which would almost overlap with the GS, for financing development works. The spirit of the law, however, actually suggested a transition from joint to community forest management, in which the GS is empowered to take all decisions regarding protection and sustainable use, but this has not yet been acceded to.

## Decentralized Rural Development through PR

Although most state governments have empowered the GSs to plan for development works at the village level, in the sphere of development planning rarely has this power meant beyond the approval of beneficiaries. As Mander (1999) says, "Procedural lacunae and absence of political and administrative will have ensured that even these instructions are frequently breached."

The only exception to this nationwide phenomenon is Kerala, in which the government took the historic decision to earmark 35–40% of the state plan outlay as untied funds for projects planned by local bodies. Of this as much as 70% was devolved to village panchayats. The first step in decentralized planning is the identification of the felt needs of the local people. This was done by convening and conducting gram/ward sabha meetings (on holidays so that all members can attend).

Prior to these meetings, public consciousness and awareness was heightened by mass organizations, NGOs, and active peoples' campaigns. It was estimated that 3 million persons participated in these meetings, of which 27% were women. The felt needs of the local people were gauged through their realistic and meaningful participation in discussions at GS meetings in groups of twenty-five to fifty members— one for each development sector, one for the SC and ST, and one for women and child development.

Such meetings were facilitated by resource persons who were locally identified and trained for the purpose. The GS prepared village development plans based on the felt needs on the one hand, and the technical standards and norms of the district planning board on the other. These plans gave priority to public health, including health care, drinking water, and nutritional care of preschool children. The public health sector received 12.34% of the funds allocated to the peoples' plan in the state.

The decentralized, peoples' participation-oriented development model of Kerala succeeded because of the interplay of political, administrative, social, economic, and financial factors. Of these, a proactive political and administrative leadership at various levels—the center, state, and local levels—is essential. There must be ample demonstration of political will and commitment to decentralized development. The state legislators and government must provide for the adequate devolution of powers, funds, functions, and responsibility upon the PRIs and municipal bodies.

In other words, political, administrative, financial, and personnel devolution to the panchayats at the village, block, and district levels should be statutorily provided and wholeheartedly implemented. Panchayat raj institutions must have the authority to raise their own cadre of staff. Last but not least, people who are the objects and subjects of the development programs have to be as literate, educated, enlightened, and aware of their rights as the people of Kerala.

## Bureaucratic Control over PRIs

A serious hurdle to the effective functioning of PR in all states is the bureaucratic control and stranglehold over the panchayats at various levels. The District Rural Development Agency (DRDA) serves as the conduit for the center's unwarranted, undesired interference with rural development administration through the district collector and the project officer. The survival of DRDA even after the 73rd Amendment is an anachronism, and violates the letter and spirit of the amendment, which provides a constitutional status to the PRIs as units of local self-government. Even today, all centrally sponsored schemes, such as IRDP and Jawahar Rozgar Yojana, are implemented in the states through the DRDA and not directly by the panchayats. The recent announcement by the central government that the president of the district panchayat would be chairman of the DRDA and the district collector (DC), its chief executive officer is a calculated move to continue to maintain the grip of the center over the local bodies and smacks of the ambivalent attitude of the central leadership toward PR.

The Bharatiya Janta Party (BJP) ruled Gujarat government, which postponed the GP elections twice in the recent past because of drought, has now come out with the undemocratic, fascist strategy to do away with elections by offering a special incentive of Rs 1 lakh to those GPs that avoid contests in panchayat elections and select all the members and the sarpanch and upsarpanch unanimously under the samras gram (harmonious village) scheme. The move cuts at the very roots of local democracy, and as the 2001 Institute of Social Sciences study says, it leads to perpetuation of the hegemony of the resourceful upper-caste few at the grassroots level.

There are reasons to believe that this reward-induced mechanism for *guided democracy* may be extended to other levels, and in the process the voice of the weak—dalits, tribals, backward classes, women, and minorities—will be suppressed in the name of harmony. By a notification dated November 23, 2000, the Gujarat government unconstitutionally denied reservation to tribals in the seats and chairpersonships in the Fifth Scheduled Area panchayats in the state, in which the population of the ST is less than 25% of the total population of a GP. This notification is a blatant violation of Article 244, which stipulates that no regulation amending the application of any act—central or state—to a Fifth Schedule Area will have effect unless it has been made after consulting the state's tribal advisory council and has received the consent of the president. In another arbitrary exercise of power, just two days prior to the election notification, the government reorganized thirty-four GPs and delimited or created eighty-one GPs out of them.

In Rajasthan the government's control over PRIs starts from the beginning and is sustained till the end (Thakur, 2001). For instance, the block development officer (BDO) is not placed fully under the control of the chairperson of the panchayat samiti. The latter can exercise supervision and control over the BDO only for securing implementation of the resolutions or decisions of the panchayat samiti or its standing committee, provided these are consistent with the provisions of the act. The government may order the removal of any member or chairperson or vice-chairperson of any panchayat from his office.

The panchayat act empowers the state government to act as the chief superintending and controlling authority in all matters relating to the administration of PRIs. It can cancel any resolution or order of any panchayat, and in an emergency the collector can suspend a resolution passed by a panchayat on grounds of health, security, peace, and so on. The government can fix the standard for performance of a panchayat if, in its opinion, it has failed to perform its duties. It can dissolve a PRI at any time for incompetence or default or absence of power. Devolution of power, functions, or funds is not adequate to enable the PRIs to function as units of self-government.

In M.P., the district panchayat presidents have complained that they have been given limited financial and administrative powers, impeding the effective functioning of the panchayats, and they are not able to use even these limited powers because of the obstructive mindset of the bureaucracy. They have suggested there should be greater coordination between the district panchayat president and the chief executive officer (CEO).

In Haryana, Gram Vikas Samitis (GVS)—a nominated body running parallel to the elected GPs has come into being, and the deputy commissioner of Sonepat district has asked sarpanches and panches to extend their full cooperation to GVS. This is an attempt on the part of the government and bureaucracy to browbeat the elected panchayats. In violation of the constitutional provisions, many states have postponed panchayat elections with impunity. Mahipal (1999) says the powers of the gram sabhas in schedule V areas have also been eroded in many states. The center has a constitutional responsibility to ensure that the states are governed in accordance with the constitutional machinery (Articles 355 and 356). The rule of law, the heart of democracy, must prevail at all levels of government—central, state, and local.

## THE RELEVANCE OF THE PANCHAYATI RAJ FOR OTHER DEVELOPING NATIONS

In the previous section, we looked critically at the actual working of the new PR system of grassroots democracy and decentralized development in rural India as it unfolds in various states of the federal polity of the country. In the following pages, an attempt is made to answer a key academic and a central policy question. What relevance does PR—the Indian model of rural/grassroots democracy and decentralized development—have for realizing these lofty goals in other developing countries? In other words, what lessons can other developing countries learn from the Indian experience of rural local self-government and decentralized development through PR?

Most developing countries have been confronted with the following common problems in the wake of their political independence from colonial rule at the end of the Second World War: (1) predominantly agrarian economies with low productivity, antiquated agricultural technology, single cropping pattern, dependence on monsoon rain for irrigation, unemployment and underemployment, low growth rate, and low gross national product; (2) population explosion with attendant poverty, malnutrition, ill health, and illiteracy, resulting in low productivity and production; (3) gender discrimination, inequalities, crime, and violence against women, girl children, and the socially and economically weaker sections of society; (4) the lack of citizen participation in governing and development processes; (5) the subordination of the common people to the elite and the absence of empowerment of large segments of society from the centers of power and influence; and (6) at the international level, the subjection of these weak and poor nations to unequal exchanges, inequalities, trade discriminations, heavy dependence on the rich industrial nations for capital, modern technology, and huge borrowing at exorbitant interest rates from the World Bank and International Monetary Fund (IMF), resulting in mounting public debt.

The type of political system and the governance pattern chosen by the political leaderships of these developing nations to resolve those problems, however, varies widely, ranging from constitutional monarchy, authoritarian, totalitarian regimes, communist party dictatorships or military dictatorships, guided democracies, and basic democracies to full-blown constitutional democracies. In short, there were more dictatorships and authoritarian regimes than genuine democracies in the political landscape of the African–Asian region.

### India and China: A Comparative Analysis

India and the People's Republic of China, the seats of ancient civilizations in southern Asia, became politically independent in 1947 and 1949, respectively. They chose two diametrically opposed political systems and development models. Indian political leadership under the influence of Prime Minister Nehru, a staunch democrat and a strong believer in socialism, voted in favor of the liberal democratic model of governance within the framework of a federal polity with a parliamentary form of government through the Constitution of India, which was promulgated in 1950.

The Republic of India, in keeping with her great and unique legacy of a non-violent, peaceful struggle for freedom, consciously and deliberately chose the paradigm of development through democracy. For India and her more than 1 billion people, democracy is an article of great faith. That democracy is both a desirable polity and a great development goal for India is not only writ large in her constitution, but is also proven by the fifty-five-year postindependence history of the country. Panchayati raj represents the culmination of the democratization of the Indian polity by creating the third tier of government at the village, block, and district levels. It encourages the state governments to devolve adequate and sufficient local autonomy, power, functions, duties, responsibilities, resources, and funds to the PRIs through a statute under the 73 Constitutional Amendment Act of 1993.

Furthermore, the PR philosophy stands for such democratic values and strategies of development as greater participatory/democratic governance; decentralized planning and development; full participation of the local populace, resources, energies, and initiatives in the management of local government affairs and rural development; and the empowerment of the people. With this philosophy as the guiding star thousands of panchayats in the country have been working resolutely since 1993 to achieve the twin purposes of the new PR.

On the other hand, China rode to political independence through a bloody revolution, coming under the inspiration and influence of Marxism–Leninism and Maoism to build the dictatorship of the proletariat under the vanguard of the Communist Party of the country. In the beginning China consciously and deliberately adopted the revolutionary model of development of the Soviet Union, but abandoned it in favor of the Maoist doctrine of a highly centralized central government. It acted under the supreme command and control of the Politburo of the Central Committee of the Communist Party of China.

Although the constitution of China provided a chapter on citizens' fundamental rights and described China as a "democratic peoples' republic," it was a single party dictatorship without the right of the people to contest elections to the National People's Congress or the provincial peoples congresses under a multiparty system, or the right to oppose or criticize the government or the Communist Party. Mao Zedong introduced the Cultural Revolution to curtail the growing powers of the bureaucracy in the name of democracy, but it soon degenerated into violence and the abuse of power at the hands of the party cadres. Rural China, which was governed through the communes, was forced to sell the produce of the collective farms at arbitrary prices fixed by central government officials. Throughout the Maoist regime of 1949 to 1975 there was no democracy in China.

A new chapter in the history of China began with the rise of Deng Zio Ping after the death of Mao. Under his leadership, China took the road of capitalist development. His four modernization programs—of agriculture, industry, science and technology, and the army—became the foundation for China's policy shift toward economic liberalism, entailing privatization, marketization, and globalization. Neither Deng nor the Communist Party demonstrated any political will to introduce democracy in China, however.

China remains a highly centralized unitary state since its beginning as a developing country in 1949. For purposes of administration, China is divided into a number of provincial governments. After the collapse of the communes in the late

1980s the central government provided for village elections in the Organic Law in 1987. It did not begin until 1990, however. Village self-governance (VSG) operates through three political institutions—the village assembly, the village representative assembly, and village committees.

> Village assembly (VA)—China's 900 million rural people live in 100 million villages. The village assembly consists of all adult villagers of a village or one representative from each household. Although under the law the VA is the highest decision-making body on all major matters of the village, it has fallen into disuse. It is rarely convened, because the large size of a Chinese village—usually consisting of 1000 to 3000 persons—make it impossible to call all villagers for meeting and decision making.

> Village representative assembly (VRA)—Since 1993, the Ministry of Civil Affairs has promoted VRAs. By 1994, half of all villages in China had VRAs. A VRA consists of heads or deputy heads of small village groups reminiscent of production teams of the commune days, village committee members, and delegates of local women's federations, youth leagues, the militia, and representatives of the elderly.

> A VRA offers a check against the power of the party branch and village chief, gives voice to the villagers in making decisions most directly affecting them, and fosters greater transparency. Village representative assemblies also have more power and greater moral authority than the village committees. They have the right to decide important village affairs, participate in their management, oversee and vote on major expenditures, supervise village heads, and veto decisions of village committees. They are deeply embedded in village life and have the good of the villagers in their hearts.

> Village committee (VC)—The VC is the only organization required by law to be democratically elected. The Ministry of Civil Affairs has set forth four fundamental principles essential to democracy: that the chairman and members of the VCs should be directly elected by the villagers themselves, that the number of candidates exceeds the number of positions, that voting should be by secret ballot, and that the winning candidate receive more than half the votes.

> The role of the VC is dual and sometimes contradictory. On the one hand, it has to implement the decisions made by the VRA. On the other hand, it is responsible for publicizing government policies and persuading villagers to follow those policies even when the government policies are not entirely popular. Under the law, the VC is responsible for mediating in civil disputes, helping to maintain social order, and reporting popular opinions and proposals to the government. Beyond this, specific functions of VCs vary from place to place.

## India and Thailand

Thailand, a developing country in Southeast Asia, is another example of a highly centralized unitary state with a long-standing tradition of local government under provincial and central governments. It has never had local self-government, despite having changed its constitution sixteen times. Even the present constitution, the sixteenth in the series, does not provide for local self-government. On the contrary, the foundation of the country's structure of administration into three levels—central, provincial, and local—established under the Public Administration Act of 1993 remains intact even today.

It is important to note that the scope of local government function is very limited in Thailand. There are no data available on what role the local bodies play in rural development or the involvement of the local populace in governance and development processes. It is found that the overlapping of authority between local and provincial administrations has limited the role and functions of the local authorities.

For instance, many functions at the local level are performed by the central government departments of revenue, public works, public health, and country and town planning (UNESCAP, 1997). This leaves no room for the growth and development of local government at all, let alone local self-government.

Citizens' participation is found to be minimal, because of the absence of any legal provision in local government legislation, thus in case of conflicts between citizens and local government, they go to the street or to the media. Disputes between central and local governments or among local governments go to the Department of Local Administration. The culprit for this entire negative scenario is the overdose of centralization in Thai administration.

The Constitution of 1997 contains some remedial steps. Article 282 stipulates that the central government must allow autonomy to local governments. Article 283 mandates that the supervision of a local government by the central government should be as required by law and if it is in the best interest of the local people. It also stipulates that local governments must have the authority to formulate their own policies, both in government and in general, personnel, and financial management, and to determine their authority vis-à-vis the central government or other local governments (UNES-CAP, 1997).

It further states that in order to bring about true decentralization, appropriate legislation specifying the plans for and the implementation process of decentralization must be passed and reviewed not longer than five years. The year 2002 reminded the Thai government that the time for such review was in the offing.

In our perception, although the constitution of Thailand has paved the way for decentralized government at the local level, much needs to be done to introduce and work out true self-government in the rural and urban areas of the country. At this critical juncture of its journey toward local democracy the Thai government may turn toward the Indian model of PR for inspiration.

## India and Australia

There are many similarities between India and Australia. Both countries were former colonies of the British Empire and are presently members of the Commonwealth of Nations. Both are federal polities with a parliamentary system of government and a good deal of decentralization—political, administrative, economic, and financial—effected between the central and the state governments by their constitutions.

Both are developing nations with a deep faith in democracy and decentralized development. The government and the political leadership in both countries have shown the will and commitment to find democratic solutions to the problems and challenges of development. There is a genuine attempt to strengthen the institutions of local democracy. We have seen how India is trying to succeed in its efforts to work out local self-government and people-participative, decentralized development in rural areas through PR.

A real political will and remarkable commitment for grassroots democracy is found in Australia, and this is evident from the fact that the country adopted the Declaration on the Role of Australian Local Government (ALG) in 1997. The ALG states that the role of local government (LG) is a standard to which all Australian governments should aspire in their efforts to achieve a more effective democratic process and secure the environmental, social, and economic well-being of their constituents.

Quoting the fundamental principles of LG, "ALG must be a partner in the Federal system; will be responsible and accountable to the local community and will provide good Local Governance, must exercise Local Autonomy, will provide Leadership and Advocacy, will provide Active Citizenship at Local Level; will foster Local Identity and Civic Pride; will secure Community Cohesion; will ensure Local Service Delivery; will facilitate Community Development; will foster Regional Cooperation and will adapt to Change" (http://www.loc-gov-focus.aus.net/1997/december/declare.htm).

Like Australia, India and other countries should adopt and sign the World Declaration on Local Self-Government and translate it into reality, for local government is the place in which local democracy is born.


## GLOSSARY

Readers are advised to go through the English meaning of the following terms, which are frequently referred to in contemporary discourse, discussions, and writings on local self-government in India, popularly known as panchayati raj (PR). These terms are written in Hindi, the roots of which are in Sanskrit, one of the oldest languages in the world. The Hindi term, its abbreviation, and then the meanings are given below.

| Hindi word | Meaning |
| --- | --- |
| Gram (G) | A village. |
| Sabha (S) | An assembly. |
| Gram sabha (GS) | A village assembly/general body of all adult members of a particular village meeting at a common place, usually under a tree. According to the 73 Constitutional Amendment Act of 1993 the GS is a mandatory statutory body of all those citizens who are registered in the electoral rolls of a village within the area of jurisdiction of a panchayat. |
| Gram swaraj | Village self-rule, democracy. |
| Panch | Number 5 in Hindi—a member of a panchayat. |
| Panches | Members of a panchayat. |
| Panchayat (P) | A statutory body of five to nine members elected or chosen by all the adult members of a village. It manages the general affairs of the village. |

| | |
|---|---|
| Nyaya panchayat (N P) | Panchayat in charge of the administration of justice. |
| Raj | Rule or governance. |
| Panchayati raj (PR) | Rule or government by panchayat. It is the name given to rural local self-government in India, thus PR signifies grassroots democracy. |

Tiers of panchayati raj
First tier

| | |
|---|---|
| Gram panchayat (GP) | Village panchayat (VP). It is at the lowest level, the basic unit of PR system. |

Second tier

| | |
|---|---|
| Panchayat samiti (PS) | That is the Block or middle-level panchayat. In some states it is also known as taluka (a revenue division ) panchayat. |

Third tier

| | |
|---|---|
| Zilla parishad (ZP) | The panchayat at the district or apex level. A district is the most important unit of field administration for revenue, law and order, and development administration below the state level. It has a number of blocks within its jurisdiction. The district collector/district magistrate/deputy commissioner is not only the kingpin of the district administration but also the chief executive officer of ZP. |
| Sarpanch (SP) | President of village panchayat. |
| Upsarpanch (UP) | Vice-president of village panchayat. |
| Pramuk or pradhan | President of panchayat samiti. |
| Uppramuk or Uppradhan | Vice-president of panchayat samiti. |
| Vikas samiti. | Development committee. |
| Sansad | Parliament. |
| Gram sansad | Village parliament or constituency meeting. |
| Ward sansad | Ward meeting. |
| Lok sabha (LS) | House of the People, the lower house of the Indian Parliament. |
| Rajya sabha (RS) | Council of States, the upper house of the Indian Parliament. |

# REFERENCES

Bava, N. (1984). People's Participation in Development Administration in India: An Empirical Study of Tamil Nadu. New Delhi: Uppal.

Bava, N., ed. (1997). Non-governmental Organizations in Development: Theory & Practice. New Delhi: Kanishka.

Bava, N. (2000). Democracy, decentralization and development in India. In: Bava, N., ed., Development Policies and Administration in India. New Delhi: Uppal Publishing House, pp. 3–27.

Cheema, S., Rondinelli, D. (1983). Decentralization and Development. Beverlly Hills, CA: Sage.

Datta, P., Sen, P. B. (2000). Participatory rural governance in India. Indian J Pub Admin XLVI(NOI):38–49.

Dreze, I., Sen, A. (1993). Hunger and Public Action. Delhi: Oxford University Press.

Gazdar, H., Sengupta, S. (1997). Agrarian politico and rural development in W. Bengal. In: Dreeze, J., Sen, A., eds. Indian Development: Selected Regional Perspectives. New Delhi: Oxford University Press, pp. 137.

George, J. (1997). Panchayats and participatory planning in Kerala. Indian J Pub Admin XLIII(NOI):79–92.

Ghatak, M., Ghatak, M. (Jan. 2000). Recent reforms in the panchayat system in West Bengal: Towards greater participatory governance? Econ Polit Wkly 5:45–58.

Government of India. (1957). Report of the Team for the Study of Community Development Projects and National Extension Service. New Delhi.

Government of India. (1978). Report of the Committee on Panchayati Raj. New Delhi: Ministry of Agriculture and Irrigation.

Institute of Social Sciences. (1998). Panchayati Raj Update. VIII (11).

Jain, S. P. (1999a). Devolution of Power, Function and Authority to Panchayats in Different States. Hyderabad: National Institute of Rural Development.

Jain, S. P. (1999b). Gram Sabha. Proceedings of the National Conference on Gram Sabha, Hyderabad, National Institute of Rural Development.

Joshi, R. P. (1998). Constitutionalisation of Panchayati Raj. Jaipur: Rawat.

Khanna, B. S. (1994). Panchayati Raj in India: Rural Local Self-government. New Delhi: Deep and Deep.

Kuhn, B. (1998). Participatory Development in Rural India. Delhi: Rawat.

Kohli, A., ed. (2001). The Success of India's Democracy. Princeton, NJ: Princeton University Press.

Kurien, J. (1995). The Kerala model: Its central tendency and the outlier. Social Sci 23(1–3):70–90.

Maddick, H. (1963). Democracy, Decentralization and Development. Bombay: Asia.

Maddick, H. (1970). Towards direct democracy. Kurukshetra 48(1):2–13.

Mahipal (1999). Gram sabhas in fifth scheduled areas. Kurukshetra 48(1):46–72.

Majumdar, R. C., Ray Chaudhuri, H. C., Datta, K. (1978). An Advanced History of India. 4th ed. Delhi: Macmillan Company of India.

Mathew, G. (Dec. 9, 1994). 73rd and 74th Amendments: A revolutionary step. Hindustan Times. Delhi ed.

Mathew, G. (Jan. 20, 2001). Panchayat elections: Dismal records. Econ Polit Wkly.

Namboodripad, E. M. S. (Sept. 5, 1996a). From land reforms to people's planning. People's Dem.

Namboodripad, E. M. S. (Oct. 18, 1996b). A Kerala experiment: Planning from below and above. Frontline.

Nandini, D. (2000). Relationship between political leadership and bureaucracy at the grassroots level: An empirical study of selected districts in Haryana. PhD dissertation, University of Delhi, Delhi.

Oommen, J., Annamalai, V. (1994). Emerging structure of panchayati raj in India: A comprehensive analysis of new acts of states. Indian J Pub Admin 40(4):590–605.

Oommen, M. A. (1996). Panchayati Raj Development Report. New Delhi: Institute of Social Science.

Palanithurai, G. (2001). The genre of women leaders in local bodies: Experience from tamilnadu. Indian J Pub Admin XLVII(1):38–50.

Participatory Research in Asia. (1997). Proceedings of the seminar on strengthening panchayati raj institutions in India. New Delhi: India International Center.

Sharma, K. L. (Sept. 25,1994). Panchayati raj: An experiment in the empowerment of the rural people. Kurukshetra.

Singh, S. S., Mishra, S. (1993). Legislative Framework of Panchayati Raj in India. New Delhi: Intellectual Publishing House.

Thakur, B. P. (2001). Emerging pattern of rural leadership: A study of new panchayati raj in sawaimadhopur district of Rajasthan. PhD dissertation, Delhi University, Delhi.

UNDP. (1993). Human Development Report. Delhi: Oxford University Press.

UNESCAP. (1997). Local Government in Asia and the Pacific: A Comparative Study. Country Paper: Thailand, http://www.loc-gov-focus.aus.net/1997/december/declare.htm.

# 23

## Good Governance in Africa
### Decentralized Planning and Means of Participation in Development in Botswana

**KESHAV C. SHARMA**

*University of Botswana, Gaborone, Botswana*

## INTRODUCTION

In general, governance is a broader notion than "government," which is composed of such elements as the constitution, the legislature, the executive, and the judiciary. Governance involves interaction between these formally defined institutions and those of civil society. Existing cultural values, social norms, and traditions or structures have important influences on this institutional interaction (Corkery, 1999: 14–15). Due to the lack of a precise definition of governance, there are different explanations of the concept. The United Nations Development Program (UNDP, 1997) defines governance as "the exercise of political, economic, and administrative authority to manage a nation's affairs." The World Bank (1997) defines it as "the manner in which power is exercised in the management of a country's economic and social resources for development." According to a working group of the International Institute of Administrative Sciences (1997), "Governance refers to a process by which diverse elements in a society wield power and authority and thereby influence and enact policies and decisions concerning public life, and economic and social development. These involve the relationship of individual men and women to the state, the organization of organs of state, the generation and management of resources for current and future generations, and the relation between states."

Like other countries all over the world, African countries have shown an increasing interest in identifying and promoting the major characteristics of good governance, such as democracy, decentralization, public participation, and accountability. Summarizing its characteristics, Hope (1997: 126–137) observes that good governance exists where there is political accountability, bureaucratic transparency, the exercise of legitimate power, freedom of association and participation, freedom of information and expression, sound fiscal management and public financial accountability, respect for the rule of law, a predictable legal framework encompassing an independent and credible justice system, respect for human rights, an active legislature, enhanced opportunities for the development of pluralistic forces, including civil society, and capacity building. For the World Bank, good governance is epitomized by "a predictable, open, and enlightened policy making (that is, transparent processes); a bureaucracy imbued with professional ethos; an executive arm that is accountable for its actions; and a strong civil society participating in public affairs." Sound management of economy is another significant dimension of good governance. This includes prudent public policies, creation of an enabling environment for investment, the provision of sound infrastructure, an incentive system, the equitable distribution of resources, and effective public participation in development planning and management.

## PUBLIC PARTICIPATION IN DEVELOPMENT MANAGEMENT: AN ESSENTIAL COMPONENT OF GOOD GOVERNANCE

Popular participation in development management, an essential ingredient of good governance, is generally viewed as the active involvement of people at the grassroots level in the choice, execution, and evaluation of programs designed to improve their livelihood. Local participation encompasses the establishment of a new power base at the community level. Oyugi (2000) observes that the success of popular participation depends on a positive orientation on the part of the political leadership and the political system, the existence of formal and institutionalized provisions for it, and the willingness and ability of the people themselves to participate. According to Nyong'o (quoted in Oyugi, 2000), individuals' participation involves and encompasses their own politicization and political action. It involves citizens' participation in governance and development at the local level through democratic, free, and fair elections, the democratic exercise of power by the center, and the devolution of power to the localities. It also calls for the respect of ethnic and regional diversity and communal rights, including the right to participate in cultural activities and to give expression to identities. The UNDP views participation as a means of raising social awareness and encouraging local initiatives. Local decision-making structures facilitate the genuine involvement of people in issues of direct concern to their needs. Grassroots democracy is also considered the best means of ensuring the equitable distribution of resources. It can therefore be argued that popular participation is the cornerstone of good governance. Popular participation enables stakeholders to express their voice in the decision-making process. It also guarantees the impartial application of the rule of law.

Development is now increasingly being conceived of as a state of human well-being rather than the state of national economy. "People-centered" development is conceived and measured not only in economic terms but also in terms of social well-being, political structures, and the quality of the physical environment. This concept of development is characterized by relatively less concern about the quality of production or output and more concern about general quality of human life. This is reflected in dissatisfaction with the use of such indicators or measures of development as per capita income or the rate of growth of national income and the corresponding search for alternative or additional indicators, such as life expectancy, standard of health or literacy, access to various social or public services, freedom of speech, and the degree of popular participation in government (Conyers and Hills, 1984).

Popular participation is an essential ingredient of good governance and a prerequisite of development that is in keeping with the felt needs, problems, aspirations, and priorities of the people. Popular participation in development and good governance can be considered significant for a number of reasons. First, it is a means of obtaining information about local conditions, needs, and attitudes, without which development programs and projects could fail. Second, people are more likely to be committed to a development project or program if they are involved in its planning and preparation. It is necessary to have such a commitment in order to ensure that a project will be accepted or adopted. It is also important for getting local assistance in the construction or maintenance of the project. Local contributions in cash or in kind may be easier to get for "self-help" projects if people see these as something they have helped to initiate. Third, the involvement of people in their own development is considered to be in line with the concept of people-centered development, in which development is for the benefit of the individual rather than the individual being merely an agent of development (Conyers and Hills, 1984).

Popular participation is both a means and an end. As an instrument of development, it provides the driving force for the collective commitment for the determination of people-based development processes and the willingness by the people to undertake sacrifices and expend their social energies for its execution. As an end in itself, popular participation is the fundamental right of the people to fully and effectively participate in the determination of the decisions that affect their lives at all levels and at all times. The African political context has been characterized in many cases by overcentralization of power, with impediments to effective participation of the people in social, political, and economic development. As a result, a large number of people have not been able to contribute to the development process, and their creativity has been undervalued and underutilized.

## THE AFRICAN SCENARIO: A DISAPPOINTING TRACK RECORD OF GOVERNANCE

With the exception of a few African countries, the record of accomplishment in governance has been quite disappointing. African countries are faced with poverty, inequality, a heavy debt burden, weak currencies, capital flight, brain drain, poor infrastructure, unemployment, and crime. In addition, many countries are torn by political and civil strife, ethnic conflict, civil wars, and natural disasters. Governments in these countries are characterized by dictatorship, one-party rule, military coups, political intolerance, a lack of discipline, and arrogance in leadership. Failure or ineffectiveness of governance has not only made the task of development more difficult, it has also resulted in the denial of justice, nepotism, corruption, and a lack of accountability. Poor governance has been a major factor in the deterioration of economic crisis in African countries. The denial of democracy, misguided public policies, the mismanagement and misuse of scarce resources, inequitable distribution, the lack of an enabling environment for development, and limited domestic and foreign investment have been manifestations of poor governance. A conference of social scientists of southern African universities held at Lusaka in 1999 (Frimpong and

Jacques, 1999: 275–278) expressed concern about the poor record of democratic rule and governance on the African continent, military intervention in civilian governments, the lack of ethical behavior and accountability among leaders, and rampant corruption and its disastrous economic and social consequences. Undemocratic governments, based on a one-party system, military dictatorship, and a lack of popular participation, have brought untold suffering to the peoples of Africa. The lack of democratic governance in Africa seriously undermines the legitimacy of government and state institutions.

African countries have a disappointing record in the two essential ingredients of good governance: decentralized government and popular participation in development administration. The experience of many countries in Africa demonstrates that there are more cases of failure than success associated with decentralization efforts, whether political or administrative. Oyugi (2000) observes that decentralization efforts in Africa have "failed to act as a spur to democratic development management and efficient and effective delivery of services." He attributes these failures to "poor design of decentralization programmes, imitative nature of decentralization programmes which fail to take into serious consideration their feasibility, the prevailing political environment, notably interference in the governance process caused by untested ideologies and militarization of political life and, even more importantly, the lingering culture of central hegemony over the localities, whether political or administrative" (Oyugi, 2000: 20). Balogun (2000: 170) also observes that "the cause of decentralization has not been well served by the centre's monopoly of power and resources. Rather than encourage popular participation in local governance and development, the centrally engineered measures (deconcentration, delinking, and devolution) have kept substantive power in the hands of the central government elite and their local allies." Further, "where the communities are ethnically mixed, opportunistic leaders may hijack the governance and development process to serve their own personal interests."

## THE CASE OF BOTSWANA: AN OASIS OF POSITIVE GOVERNANCE IN AFRICA

While many countries on the African continent are characterized by poor governance as outlined above—which has led to economic crisis, political instability, regional–ethnic tensions, mismanagement of resources, a lack of integrity in the civil service, and authoritarian leadership—Botswana has experienced political stability and sustained economic growth, and has been relatively free of regional and ethnic tensions. A World Bank study therefore concluded some years ago that Botswana had built an enviable reputation as having one of the most effective public sector management systems in Africa (Raphaeli et al., 1984). Botswana has also been pointed to as a model of success (Picard, 1987). Based on its performance record, Botswana was ranked seventy-first out of 178 countries by the UNDP in its development report of 1996 (using the human development index for 1993) (Government of Botswana, 1997).

When Botswana became independent in 1966, its GDP per capita was one of the lowest in the world, and the country was among the least developed. At that time, an overwhelming rural population depended mainly on agriculture for livelihood. Beef production was the mainstay of the economy in terms of output and export earnings. Over 30% of Botswana's men between the ages of 20 and 40 were working in South Africa. Communications and infrastructure were barely developed. Prospects for rapid development of the economy seemed bleak, and the government was dependent on foreign aid not only for all its investment projects, but also to finance its recurrent expenditures (Government of Botswana, 1997).

During the last decades, there has been remarkable economic development in the country, resulting in increasing access to water, roads, health, and education. The growth in GDP has averaged around 6% per annum over the entire postindependence period. The structure of the economy is dominated by the emergence of the mineral sector, which has continued to expand, stimulating infrastructure development and financing the expansion of government services.

## Nature and Characteristics of Development Planning

Development planning in Botswana is undertaken within the framework of a mixed economy, in which the private sector plays a significant role. The government welcomes foreign investment and has offered many incentives to attract it. The government has always been against nationalization and has lately been pursuing the policy of privatization. The government is committed to the principle of a free market economy and endeavors to create a conducive or enabling environment for the private sector to operate effectively as an engine of growth. The government provides infrastructure and ensures that prices and other economic incentives stimulate producers to use the resources at their command effectively. The government concentrates its efforts on setting the legal, fiscal, and monetary framework for private sector development. The government's overall economic strategy has been to achieve rapid and large returns from intensive capital investment in mining, particularly the country's large diamond resources, and to reinvest those returns to improve the living standards of those who do not benefit directly from the mining sector's expansion. Further, government policies have emphasized the complementary themes of employment creation and rural development, including improvements in infrastructure, education, and health facilities.

Botswana has formulated eight development plans since independence in 1966. Local authorities (LAs) have concurrently produced their fifth plans, the timing of which now covers the period of the national plan. This will facilitate greater coordination between LA plans and national plans. Urban authorities have also produced plans for the first time so that they too can have a medium-term horizon of development within a coherent framework that can allow interested stakeholders to objectively evaluate their policies, plans, and programs (Government of Botswana, 1997).

## The Central Planning Machinery

Administrative machinery for development planning in Botswana consists of a number of organizations, including political executive, ministries, interministerial committees, public enterprises, private firms, local government, district-level organizations, nongovernment organizations (NGOs), and community-based organizations (CBOs). Planning in Botswana is an outcome of communication and coordinated effort among a number of organizations operating vertically and horizontally throughout the central government as well as the periphery.

The cabinet and the parliament have the highest authority for public policy making and development planning. Below this level, the Ministry of Finance and

Development Planning (MFDP) plays a central role. Staff members from this ministry are second to its ministerial planning units, which are responsible for project preparation and evaluation in addition to plan preparation and policy advice at the ministerial level. The MFDP staff is responsible for project appraisal, advice on sectoral policies, and the monitoring of project implementation. There is also active participation by the Directorate of Public Service Management, the Department of Statistics, the Bank of Botswana, and the planning units of various ministries and district-level organizations. A significant organization for major policy decisions and development strategy is the Economic Committee of the Cabinet, which consists of all the ministers and permanent secretaries, the attorney general, the head of the police, the commander of the defense force, and the governor of the Bank of Botswana.

The government has established several institutions to assist with coordination in designated fields. In view of the increasing importance attached to private sector development, the government established a high-level consultative committee (HLCC) in 1995 that brings together members of the cabinet, senior civil servants, chief executives of major parastatals and executives from the private sector. The HLCC is chaired by the president, and serves as a major consultation forum between the private and public sectors (Government of Botswana, 1997). There are committees at the ministerial level that report to the HLCC, which are called HLCC sectoral committees.

The Rural Development Council (RDC) is charged with coordinating rural development activities, a task that cuts across the activities of virtually all ministries. Chaired by the minister of finance and development planning, the RDC reviews all plans for rural development, monitors implementation, and receives regular progress reports. The membership of this body includes most permanent secretaries and representatives of district councils, brigades, the private sector, and trade unions. On the other hand, the National Employment Manpower and Incomes Council (NEMIC) includes representatives of government, parastatals, and employee organizations, and serves as a consultative body to advise on the formulation and implementation of manpower, employment, and income policies.

## The Process of Planning

The national development plans (NDPs) involve the following process of plan formulation in Botswana. The preparation of the NDPs begins with the keynote policy paper of the MFDP, which identifies the theme of the next plan as well as indicates the preliminary resources position and major issues for discussion and resolution. This is followed by the preparation of sectoral keynote policy papers (SKIPs) by ministries, LAs, and other interested parties. At this time the LAs are engaged in consultations with their various constituencies and ministries on projects to consider for the next plan. A meeting of local and central planners is called to discuss how national projects are to be distributed across various LA boundaries.

A meeting of the National District Development Conference, which includes representatives of LAs, ministries, and NGOs, is called to debate the issues raised by the various SKIPs. The resolutions of the conference and comments by various ministries and organizations are consolidated into a major issue paper by MFDP for presentation and discussion by the economic committee of the cabinet, which determines the final resolution of such issues.

Following a detailed macroeconomic forecast by the MFDP, a draft macroeconomic outline is prepared and circulated for comments from ministries, parastatals, LAs, and other interested organizations. The macroeconomic outline both presents the underlying economic environment for the next planning period and sets out the expenditure and manpower ceilings, on which ministries can base their sectoral chapters. The document also provides a preliminary version of the macroeconomic chapters of the next plan document.

A meeting of the economic committee of the cabinet is reconvened to make a final resolution about resource allocation among various ministries and organizations and to settle any outstanding policy issues before ministries and LAs prepare their sectoral chapters. During the budget formulation of the first year of the plan, a draft NDP document is normally circulated for consideration by the economic committee of the cabinet and then by the cabinet before it is presented to Parliament.

## Decentralized Local Development Planning

The district development plan (DDP) is the collective effort of a number of district-level organizations. The district administration (district commissioner's office), district council, land board, tribal administration, and district development committee (DDC) are the main organizations involved in the district-level planning. In addition, such forums as village development committees, NGOs, and CBOs also make contributions to local-level planning. In the urban areas, the town and city councils play a role in planning the development of areas under their jurisdictions. The district commissioner's office plays a central role in the formulation, implementation, and monitoring of DDPs. As chairman of DDC, he or she is responsible for coordinating rural development activities. He displays leadership, builds teamwork, and gets the cooperation of the district council, land board, tribal administration, government ministries, and public.

The district council consists of elected representatives of the people at the district level and performs certain statutory functions related to primary education, primary health, village water supply, rural roads, community development, and social welfare. All these are vital areas for rural development and planning. The role of district councils in district planning therefore becomes obvious. As representatives of the people, the councellors are expected to articulate their felt needs, problems, and priorities. The district council gives the final formal approval of the district plan after it is finalized by the DDC. As land boards have the authority to allocate tribal land for residential, arable, commercial, agricultural, or development purposes, they assume a significant role in DDP. Land boards are represented in DDCs.

Traditional leaders (chiefs, headmen) also contribute to the process of planning and development in their own areas. They serve as a two-way channel of communication between the government and the people. They provide leadership in retaining the best customs and traditions of the local community. *Kgotla* (the traditional village assembly) has traditionally been a forum for communication and consultation with the community and continues to play that role in the formulation of DDPs (Sharma, 1999a).

The DDC is one of the most significant organizations at the district level for the formulation, coordination, and monitoring of DDP implementation. The DDC is a forum for communication among all the district-level organizations involved in rural development. All the significant organizations operating at the district level, such as the district administration, district council, land board, tribal administration, and the district-level officers of ministries, are represented in this body, which is chaired by the district commissioner.

## Features and Process of Decentralized District and Urban Development Planning

The Botswana government has declared its commitment to decentralized planning. According to the district planning handbook of the government of Botswana

> [O]ne of the primary aims of district planning process is to ensure that people are involved in rural development, so it must address the problems, opportunities and priorities as identified by the communities this development is intended to benefit. If this aim is to be achieved then a dialogue must be established between the community and development authorities. If sustained development is to be realized then the concept of participation must be pursued. Development is not a process whereby planners prescribe what is 'best' for others and then simply provide resources, which, it is hoped, will accomplish the prescribed development. True participation demands that beneficiaries are brought into the decision making process in a real way (Government of Botswana, 1999).

The process of district-level planning initiated in the 1970s has continued to improve. In previous plan periods, DDPs were prepared every three years, as compared to the six-year period covered by national plans. This method was premised on the notion that one DDP would be based on the existing NDP's sectoral plans and financial ceilings, while the second DDP would provide some basis for determining the priorities of the next NDP. After 1989 this approach was abandoned in favor of preparing DDPs to cover six years, beginning two years before a new national period. For example, DDP-4 covered 1989 to 1995. The period of DDP-5s was synchronized with that of NDP-8 to run from 1997 to 2003. The interim period from 1995 to 1997 had to be bridged by district annual plans, which were more in the form of implementation schedules (Mandlebe and Raphaka, 11–24). Apart from following the same time frame in preparation and implementation, the two sets of plans (NDP and DDP) also use a series of matrices to coordinate the precise details of ministry–LA project plans and activities, budgeting, and annual phasing (Government of Botswana, 1997).

The DDP-5s were drafted simultaneously with NDP-8. According to NDP-8, districtwide community consultations were held in 1995 for more than six months before the drafting of the plans could begin: "The Local Authorities Key Issues Papers (LAKIPs) reflected the major concerns of their communities, plus the input of the political and administrative authorities in each district. The Ministerial Sectoral Key Issues Papers (SKIPS) and Macro-Economic outline for this plan took into account the policy issues, facts and figures outlined in the LAKIPPs" (Government of Botswana, 1997: 466). The urban areas prepared an urban development plan (UDP-1) for the first time, covering the NDP period. Some capacity constraints are experienced in the urban areas, in which the central government's cadre of economic and land-use planners does not exist (Government of Botswana, 1997: 466).

## MAJOR STRENGTHS AND LIMITATIONS OF DECENTRALIZED DEVELOPMENT PLANNING

A number of attributes of the Botswana experience can be identified (Sharma and Mhlauli, 1996: 101–112). The country has established development planning machinery at the district level, and so far five DDPs have been formulated, as compared to eight NDPs. Procedures for the formulation, implementation, and monitoring of DDPs have been put in place and are constantly being improved. (Sharma, 2000a; 2000b). The vertical linkages between the center and the districts have improved. The principle of bottom-up planning has been accepted by central and district planning organizations, public servants, and the people in the districts. Generally, the system uses the existing administrative organization instead of creating a large number of additional structures. Such traditional authorities as village chiefs have been integrated into the modern setup of public administration, and the traditional forums, such as kgotla, are used for communication between the government and the people and for consultation on local development plans. Foreign aid and indigenous resources are utilized prudently. The image of the country's administrative machinery has not been tarnished by widespread corruption. Above all, the administrative capacity of local-level organizations has improved steadily. In spite of these positive attributes, however, district-level planning in Botswana is faced with some limitations and challenges.

*First,* decentralized development planning has faced a number of constraints and challenges. The constraints related to formulation, implementation, monitoring, guidance, and vertical and horizontal two-way communication create a gap between the intention and the reality of bottom-up planning. The country is constantly learning from experience, however, and improvements are being made. This can be discerned from the weaknesses pointed out by the Ellison (consultancy) report in 1990. The improvements were noted by the Phaleng and Peer consultancy report in 1997.

*Second,* translating the intention of "bottom-up planning" into a desired outcome remains a serious challenge. The nature of the planning process in Botswana is not fully decentralized. Development plans in the past were formulated at the center, where policies were determined with regard to the allocation of resources. The contribution of district-level organisations has increased steadily, however, which can be discerned from the observation of the Phaleng and Peer consultancy report on the preparation of DDP-5 and UDP-1 in 1997 that "the institutional structure in Botswana for development planning at local level is quite good" (Ellison, 1990: 27).

*Third,* in the past the DDPs were prepared after the NDP had already been finalized. This procedure for plan formulation made integration of DDPs into an NDP difficult. The situation in this regard has improved, as NDP and DDPs now follow the same calendar. The integration of the two components, however, needs further improvement. The effective coordination of DDPs and NDP depends to a considerable extent on the cordial relationship between the center and the districts and on satisfactory two-way communication. In order for NDPs and rural development policies to be in line with the felt needs and priorities of the people, the center has to more effectively utilize the mechanisms of communication with the public and their organizations.

The district-level organizations also have to remain adequately informed about the nationally determined strategy, resource position, national priorities, and constraints so that they can organize their own efforts accordingly and make worthwhile inputs into the formulation and implementation of rural development programs. The mechanisms for formulating DDPs and UDP, and processes for their integration in to the NDPs are being improved constantly. In the process of preparing DDP-5 and the UDP-1 and coordinating with the NDP-8, there was considerable improvement over the past years' experience. The consultancy report of 1997 on the preparation of DDPs and UDPs documented these procedures. At that time, a drafting team was set up at each LA under the joint auspices of the district commissioner and the council secretary. Various drafts of each LA's plans had to be approved first by the local DDC or urban development committee, and then by the relevant council, which bore the ultimate responsibility for the plans. There were two high-level government bodies—the District Plans Committee and the NDP-8 reference group— supervising the processes of preparing the LA plans and the NDP-8. Writing the DDP-5 and UDP-1 was the responsibility of the LAs themselves, but editing each draft was undertaken by the Ministry of Local Government, Lands and Housing (MLGLH).

*Fourth,* the process of preparing DDP-5 and UDP-1 during the preparation of NDP-8 showed considerable improvement. The previous consultancy report submitted in 1990 by Kenneth Ellison identified a number of organizational and implementation constraints in the district planning process. He observed that project implementation was adversely affected by infrequent consultation with district staff and was delayed by inflexible bureaucratic structures. Project implementation was not properly coordinated because of the exceedingly autonomous operations of sectoral ministries at the district level. There were delays in implementation because districts had limited control over financial resources. Significant advances were made in land-use planning in many districts, but implementation of these plans was constrained by the lack of integrated development planning and project design capacity (Ellison, 1990: 28).

*Fifth,* just as organizational deficiencies and unsatisfactory vertical linkages create problems in district-level planning, ineffective horizontal linkages and coordination also pose a serious challenge. As district-level planning machinery consists of a number of organizations (particularly district administration, district council, land board, and tribal administration) and their inputs have to be effectively coordinated, a harmonious and coordinated relationship among them is essential. These issues were identified in NDP-8. In 2001 the government convened a presidential commission to address these issues.

*Sixth,* the DDC has served as a worthwhile organization for coordinating DDPs; however, many problems and weaknesses have continued to hamper its operation. The DDC's membership continues to be quite large and unwieldy. Its membership needs to be reviewed to reduce it to a smaller and more manageable size. As chairman of DDC, the district commissioner finds it difficult to get the cooperation of all of the members. The commissioner has to depend on persuasion, human relations, and leadership qualities for developing team spirit among his colleagues who are members of DDC.

*Seventh,* in terms of the effectiveness of community participation, if "planning from below" has to be realized, citizen participation in the formulation and implementation of plans is essential. This participation has to be real rather than ceremonial. A decentralized planning system has been organized in Botswana at the district level with this objective, although ensuring effective participation in the formulation and implementation of development plans remains a challenge.

For increasing the involvement of people and enhancing their participation, the planning process has to be decentralized not only up to the district level; it has to be decentralized further down to the village level. The district-level organizations have to do more to promote such decentralization, which could strengthen such bodies as the village development committees (VDCs) or other NGOs. In the future, decentralization will be incomplete if it stops at the district level (Sharma, 1992: 96–115). Village-level organizations will have to receive greater attention and authority for participation in district-level planning.

In Botswana's experience, the performance of VDCs, which were created in 1968 to encourage self-help in village communities, has varied. Some have been quite active, but others have contributed very little. Communication between district councils, government ministries, and VDCs needs to be strengthened. The VDCs need to be integrated into the stream of decision-making activities regarding development planning. They generally continue to operate on their own. Councellors, members of parliament, traditional authorities, and community development workers need to better assist the VDCs.

Civil society organizations have been growing in both number and strength in Botswana. The government is recognizing the role that the NGOs and CBOs can play in the process of governance and service delivery. There are now many societies, community groups, church-based agencies, and NGOs representing a wide range of interests and concerns, including gender, youth, culture, human rights, the disabled, entrepreneurs, agriculture, and the environment. In 1995, NGOs set up the Botswana Council of Non-Governmental Organisations (BOCONGO) to help create an enabling environment for the operation of NGOs. The participation of NGOs and civil society is gradually growing. In order to facilitate this, an NGO policy is being developed. On the other hand, although the government has identified the private sector as an engine of growth and has renewed its emphasis on policies of privatization and public–private partnership, governance at the local level continues to remain confined to the work of government organizations. In addition, although the media are not seriously constrained in their freedom of expression, they do not yet reach the majority of poor, uneducated, deprived, and underprivileged people, although the state-run radio network is now reaching a large number of people, even in the remote rural areas.

## RECOMMENDATIONS FOR DECENTRALIZED DEVELOPMENT THOUGH POPULAR PARTICIPATION

### Strengthening the Resources of Local Authorities

There is widespread concern about the continuing shortages of qualified staff in district- and local-level organizations. The government has assumed the responsibility for human resource development in the country, and various efforts have been made to strengthen different kinds of educational and training programs. There has been an expansion of education at the primary, secondary, and tertiary levels, and preservice and in-service training programs have been introduced or expanded. More concerted efforts, however, are needed for human resource development for district- and local-level organizations (Sharma, 1999b:73–90).

Besides the need for strengthening education and training, the personnel involved in governance at the local level have to be part of a sound personnel management system that can attract, retain, and motivate staff of good caliber and keep their morale high by giving them attractive service conditions. The LAs have continued to lose some well-qualified staff. Innovative measures can help retain deserving staff and keep them committed. The Local Government Service Management, which is responsible for re-cruitment, placement, transfers, training, and discipline of all LA employees in the country, has made significant improvements in the service conditions. It needs to be improved further, however. Personnel management of LAs needs greater autonomy from central controls and more decentralized personnel management and training functions.

The financial strength of local governments in Botswana has been limited, as these "are almost wholly dependent upon Central Government for their revenue. In 1995/96 for instance, the Revenue Support Grant from the Central Government represented 64%, 92%, and 91% of the recurrent income of Urban Councils, District Councils and Land Boards, respectively. In addition, councils receive 100% of their development funds in the form of grants from Central Government" (Government of Botswana, 1997:467) Given their limited financial resources and such dependence on grants, decentralization remains quite handicapped (Sharma, 1997: 61–77). In this regard, the NDP-8 states the following:

> [T]he financial dependence of Local Authorities upon the centre places a considerable constraint on decentralisation. It breeds an unhealthy reliance upon Central Govern-ment, forcing Local Authorities to look to the Central Government for advice and direction on even the smallest matters. It reverses the desirable direction of accountability, making Local Authorities less responsive to the needs of their constituents. Decreasing the financial dependence of Local Authorities upon the Central Government, and thereby increasing their autonomy and accountability to their own constituents, is a primary policy goal of MLGLH during NDP8 (Government of Botswana, 1997:467).

The government of Botswana has initiated a number of measures in this area. A new formula of revenue support grants was approved in 1994 and was first implemented during the financial year 1996–1997. The formula provides a specific level of support from the central government to LAs, which can be calculated well in advance by LAs themselves. The intention of the new system, according to NDP-8, "is to change the financial incentives that Local Authorities face, forcing them to finance incremental expenditure from increased revenue from their own sources or else from cost savings" (Government of Botswana, 1997:467).

The financial strength of LAs will depend not only on the availability of finances, but to a large extent on their sound management. Sound management of local government finance will require qualified personnel with high standards of profes-sionalism and integrity. The recruitment, promotion, placement, and general conduct of staff dealing with financial management will have to emphasize the principles of merit and objectivity. The autonomy of LAs will have to be backed by a well-established system of public accountability. Independent auditing machinery may have a vital role in enforcing accountability. The mandate of such organizations as the

Directorate on Corruption and Economic Crime and the office of Ombudsman will ensure that the central and local government bureaucracies operate in accordance with the established rules and procedures and in a transparent manner. Management of finance will not only have to be in accordance with the established authority, rules, and regulations; considerations of prudence, economy, and productivity should also be borne in mind. Political and bureaucratic leadership in the local and central government should have a strong commitment to establishing high standards of ethics in the management of finances.

Local government is entrusted with public money, which has to be used in accordance with the laws, prescribed authority, instructions, and directions. The government bureaucracy has to exercise reasonable precautions to safeguard the collection and disbursement of public funds. Before 1994, the LAs were audited by the Department of Local Government Audit, which was part of the MLGLH. After 1994, the local government audit was made a part of the office of the auditor general. It now enjoys greater independence compared to the past. Local government audit is seriously handicapped, however, because of unsatisfactory recordkeeping and bookkeeping in the LAs. The effectiveness of the audit machinery in Botswana is limited not because of lack of freedom or authority but because of the continuing shortage of qualified staff. As government departments do not have sufficient accountants, the standards of accounting also remain unsatisfactory. The local government audit reports reveal the nature of inadequate and unsatisfactory bookkeeping, recordkeeping, and general financial management in some LAs. Efforts for strengthening the local government audit and the operation of the recently established Local Authorities Public Accounts Committee are expected to improve financial management in LAs, however.

Corruption, which is a worldwide problem, has also affected Botswana. One of the concrete measures undertaken by the government of Botswana to check the growth of corruption includes the Directorate on Corruption and Economic Crime established by the Corruption and Economic Crime Act (1994). This directorate is headed by a director who is authorized to receive and investigate any complaints involving alleged corruption in any public body. He has the authority to require any person to produce records, reports, data, and documents relating to functions of any public or private body. He may require any person to provide information or to answer any questions considered necessary in connection with the investigation.

Another measure undertaken for uncovering maladministration and enhancing the accountability of government bureaucracy is the establishment of the office of ombudsman by the Ombudsman Act (1995). The ombudsman is authorized to investigate any administrative action of any government organization from which a member of the public may have experienced injustice. The impact of the ombudsman office will only be felt over time. At present, the very awareness of public officials that their actions, inactions, or maladministration could be subjected to investigation by an independent authority such as this is likely to contribute to their increased alertness and more responsible behavior (Ayeni and Sharma, 2000: 60–63).

Besides its concern for checking corruption and making public bureaucracy more responsive, the government is concerned with enhancing the productivity of the central and local government. As part of its efforts to increase productivity, the government has established the Botswana National Productivity Centre, which organizes productivity improvement and management programs, conferences, and workshops for public servants as well as private sector employees. The government has also created work improvement teams (WITs), which consist of public servants of different ranks from the same work unit. The WITs are expected to meet regularly to identify, analyze, and solve problems relating to their work unit and to propose and implement improvements. The WITs are expected to enhance team spirit, improve human relations, develop positive attitudes toward work, facilitate communication between managers and employees, provide quality services, and ensure job satisfaction.

## Vertical and Horizontal Coordination

Local governance and poverty reduction measures require well-coordinated efforts of a large number of governmental organization and NGOs at the central and local levels. The input of these organizations has to be harmonized in the formulation and implementation of development plans. Effective two-way communication is required to build a healthy partnership among the center, the districts, and the urban centers. The grassroots organizations below the district level also have to be taken into consideration. In order to ensure that the NDPs are in line with the needs, problems, and priorities of the people, the central planning machinery has to establish mechanisms of communication with the district-level organizations and urban centers. The district and urban planning units, on the other hand, have to remain informed of the nationally determined strategy, resource situation, and national priorities so that they can organize their own plans accordingly and provide necessary inputs into the national planning process.

Although Botswana has developed mechanisms and procedures to promote vertical and horizontal coordination, there are weaknesses that need to be remedied (Sharma, 2000a: 85–105). In the past the NDPs and DDPs were formulated following such different time schedules that the inputs of districts into the national plan remained nominal. Now that the two planning processes follow the same timetable and cover the same six-year period, their harmonization is more likely. Urban councils have also improved their planning mechanisms. It should be realized, however, that satisfactory integration of district and urban plans into the national plan can only be accomplished over time. Structural and procedural reforms have to continue to improve the existing situation. Greater sensitivity on the part of the central government about the problems and expectations of the lower levels is required for good governance at the local level.

## Accountable, Responsible, and Responsive Bureaucracy

Good governance requires a responsible, responsive, sensitive, caring, and accountable public bureaucracy. Responsible behavior by the public bureaucracy implies an adequate understanding by public servants of their roles, functions, and authority. The public expects, demands, and deserves satisfactory services from the government. Public servants need to have the proper appreciation of the problems faced by the public they are expected to serve. Public officials at the district level and below need those qualities to effectively plan and implement rural development programs. The public bureaucracy in Botswana has undergone considerable reorientation in its attitude toward the public. It has to be more sensitive to the needs and aspirations of poor and underprivileged people in the rural areas.

## Committed Political and Bureaucratic Leadership

For strengthening local governance, the strong commitment of political and bureaucratic leadership at the highest level of government is an essential prerequisite. Without it, the effectiveness of local governance may merely remain rhetorical. In order to translate the declared intention and objectives into reality, top-level political executives and public servants have to adopt concrete measures to promote effective decentralization of authority and resources for strengthening local governance.

The commitment of local-level political leaders and their harmonious relationship with public servants are also essential. As the local-level organizations in Botswana are still not adavanced, it may be unrealistic to expect the same high standards that are found in well-established institutions in developed countries. It is hoped that with the passage of time, the caliber, experience, and leadership roles of these organizations will improve. Their elected politicians and public servants also need to work as a team, with a proper appreciation of each other's role and responsibility. Public servants have to operate as politically neutral advisers to politicians and execute the policies made collectively by them. Politicians should operate as representatives of the people and articulate their felt needs. Public servants need to inform and advise the elected officials on the procedures, regulations, and implications of different policies or decisions. This desired process should be understood by both sides.

## CONCLUSION

As outlined above, Botswana has displayed a number of characteristics of good local governance, as evident from its decentralized development planning and its mechanisms for public participation in development management. Administrative structures for popular participation in local-level development have continued to grow. There has been a steady growth of civil society, NGOs, and CBOs. The government continues to pursue its efforts for promoting decentralization in development planning and management. The government has also been able to promote successful integration of traditional and modern administrative institutions. Public education and awareness of participation in political and economic activities have grown as well.

In spite of these strengths, the country has faced various constraints that have inhibited the effectiveness of such decentralized development planning and popular participation. The realization of the ideals of decentralized, bottom-up planning thus remains a challenge. The integration of DDPs into the NDPs also continues to face several constraints. Vertical and horizontal coordination in development planning and management is not entirely satisfactory. The administrative capacity of local government remains limited because of the scarcity of the human and financial resources needed for decentralization. Such grassroots organizations as VDCs are effective only in some areas.

The strengthening of decentralized development planning and the mechanisms of popular participation in development management require the following conditions: (1) the strong commitment of political leaders and public servants to further decentralization, (2) continued improvements in the organizations and procedures to integrate DDPs into NDPs, (3) more vertical and horizontal coordination among relevant organizations, (4) the enhanced capacity of LAs and greater decentralization of their financial and human resources, (5) greater strength of such grassroots organizations as VDCs, and (6) further involvement of such traditional authorities as village chiefs and such traditional institutions as kgotla in the process of local-level planning and development management.

## REFERENCES

Ayeni, V., Sharma, K. C. (2000). Ombudsman in Botswana. London: Commonwealth Secretariat.

Balogun, M. J. (2000). The scope for popular participation in decentralization, community governance and development: towards a new paradigm of centre-periphery relations. Reg. Dev. Dia. 21:1.

Corkery, J. (1999). Governance: Concepts and Applications. Brussels: International Institute of Administrative Sciences.

Conyers, D., Hills, P. (1984). An Introduction to Development Planning in the Third World. New York: Wiley.

Ellison, K. H. (1990). Report and Recommendations of the District Development Plan 4 Consultancy. Gaborone: Government of Botswana, Ministry of Finance and Development Planning and MLGLH.

Frimpong, K., Jacques, G. (1999). Corruption, Democracy and Good Governance in Africa: Essays on Accountability and Ethical Behaviour. Gaborone: Light Books.

Government of Botswana. (1997). National Development Plan 8: 1997/98-2002/03. Gaborone: Government Printer.

Government of Botswana. (1999). District Planning Handbook. Gaborone: Ministry of Local Government, Lands, and Housing.

Hope, K. R., Sr. (1997). The political economy of policy reform and change in Africa: the transition from the statism to liberalization. Reg. Dev. Dia. 8:1.

International Institute of Administrative Sciences. (1997). New Challenges for Public Administration in the 21st Century: Efficient Civil Service and Decentralized Public Administration. Proceedings of the Third International Conference of Administrative Sciences, Brussels.

Mandlebe, W., Raphaka, T. Y. (1994). Integrating district and national planning. In: Report of the Proceedings of the 16th CPO/Do(D) Annual Seminar on the Theme: Focus on District Development Planning with Special Emphasis on Implementation of Development Programs. MLGLF Gaborone, Government Printer.

Oyugi, W. O. (2000). Decentralization for good governance and development: concepts and issues. Reg. Dev. Dia. 21:1.

Picard, L. A. (1987). The Politics of Development in Botswana: A Model for Success. London: Lynne Reinner.

Raphaeli, N., et al. (1984). Public Sector Management in Botswana: Lessons in Pragmatism. Washington, DC: World Bank.

Sharma, K. C. (1992). Bureaucracy and co-ordination of rural development policies at the district level in Botswana. In: Asmerom, H. K., Hoppe, R., Jam, R. B., eds. Bureaucracy and Development Policies in the Third World. Amsterdam: Free University Press.

Sharma, K. C. (1997). The capacity, autonomy, and accountability of local government in local level governance. Reg. Dev. Dia. 18:2.

Sharma, K. C. (1999a). Traditional leadership and contemporary public administration: The case of Botswana. In: Valsan, E. H., ed. Democracy, Decentralization and Development. Brussels: IASIA.

Sharma, K. C. (1999b). Botswana: Decentralization for democratization and strengthening of local government. In: Reddy, P. S., ed. Local Government, Democratization and Decentralization: A Review of Southern African Experience. Cape Town: Juta.

Sharma, K. C. (2000a). Decentralized district development planning and management in Botswana. In: Olila, P. O., Kosura, W. O., eds. Regional Development Policy and Practices in Africa and Asia: A Comparative Study. Nairobi: UNCRD.

Sharma, K. C. (2000b). Popular participation for good governance and development at local level in Botswana. Reg. Dev. Dia. 21:1.

Sharma, K. C., Mhlauli, E. G. M. (1996). Botswana: confronting the realities of capacity building. In: Picard, L. A., Garrity, M., eds. Policy Reforms for Sustainable Development in Africa: The Institutional Imperative. London: Lynne Rienner.

UNDP (United Nations Development Programme). (1997). Governance for Sustainable Human Development. New York: UNDP.

World Bank. (1997). Partnership for Capacity Building in Africa. Washington, DC: World Bank.

# 24

# The Political and Institutional Dilemmas of Sustainable Development

**ROBERTO P. GUIMARÃES**

*U.N. Economic Commission for Latin America and the Caribbean (ECLAC), Santiago, Chile*

## INTRODUCTION

The environmental crisis that underlies repeated calls for a new, sustainable style of development draws attention to the fact that we are running out of resources and out of places to store or dispose of wastes. It also reveals that we are living in an age in which existing institutions are inadequate for facing the realities of this truly "ecological transition"—from simpler, quasi-natural systems to more complex patterns of interactions between humans and nature.

The emergence of this ecological dimension in social life poses hitherto unforeseen challenges to the social sciences, as well as to the everyday concerns of citizens, government, and private enterprises. In effect, how a collectivity deals with nature discloses as much about its internal social relations as the other way around. It therefore seems pertinent to explore the political and institutional dimensions of the current discourse on sustainable development, as well as its implications for development policies, particularly in view of the realities of developing countries.

The analysis that follows thus departs from clearly characterizing the political nature of the environmental crisis underneath the so-called crisis of sustainability, exploring the implications of nature being incorporated into human culture. Next a brief description of how public perceptions about sustainable development emerged. In this section the institutional evolution of sustainable development policies, particularly in terms of integrating intersectoral policies and promoting public participation, are analyzed against the backdrop of the current process of globalization.

The analysis then turns to the challenges that still prevail on the long road toward sustainable development, with special emphasis being placed on the evolution that led to the World Summit on Sustainable Development, which took place in Johannesburg from August 26, to September 4, 2002. In the concluding portion of the chapter, the specific threats faced by the new international agenda for sustainable development are scrutinized, particularly the asymmetrical results of the globalization process so far, and the new realities of international terrorism after the September 11 attacks on the United States.

## THE POLITICAL NATURE OF THE CRISIS OF SUSTAINABILITY

> The struggle to enlarge the world of beauty, of nonviolence, of peacefulness, is a political struggle. The reassurance of these values, in restoring the Earth as a human environment, is not just a romantic and poetic idea, which concerns only the privileged. It is today a matter of survival (Herbert Marcuse cited in Mansholt et al., 1972: 77).

In 1970, 300,000 persons died in Bangladesh when a cyclone drove a huge wave over the Ganges delta, in what has been described as the greatest natural disaster in history. In 1984 the world was struck by the image of millions of Ethiopians dying of starvation. Some 700,000 persons lost their lives between 1991 and 2000 as a result of natural disasters, and over 90% of the victims lived in developing countries. According to recent studies carried out by the International Federation of Red Cross and Red Crescent Societies (IFRC, 2001), in Latin America, more than 20,000 persons lost their lives to climate-related disasters between 1990 and 1999, and the total number of persons affected came to nearly 4.5 million. The tragic effects of hurricane Mitch on Central America in 1998 were mainly responsible for the difference between the two decades. How many North Americans will perish when the San Andreas Fault—an intricate fault network that is 800 miles long and at least ten miles deep along the California coast—moves once again sometime in this century? All of these situations can be predicted well in advance. The Ganges delta is a flat lowland known for its climatic instability, whereas the nature of Latin America's physical environment means that there is a particularly serious risk of the occurrence of climate-related phenomena capable of producing a disaster. Africa, which was essentially self-sufficient in food, began to show increasing signs of declining per capita grain production at the beginning of the 1970s. Finally, in 1906 San Francisco was literally destroyed by a major earthquake, and surveying through the San Andreas Fault, shows a drift at the rate of as much as two inches per year.

Even though most of these examples refer to so-called natural disasters, they all show a dramatic failure to cope with the laws of nature. Even in the case of San Francisco, Bangladesh, and portions of Central America, one may argue that in allowing human concentration in such highly unstable environments we actually help those natural occurrences to become disasters. There are undoubtedly social and political variables that may explain this "failure," but the truth is that there has been a persistent disregard, by social scientists and decision makers alike, of the rules that regulate the world surrounding us.

This *ecopolitical* approach assumes, as John Passmore (1974) points out, that an ecological problem cannot be confused with "a problem in ecology." The latter is essentially a scientific challenge, of understanding some particular ecological phenomena, whereas an ecological problem is fundamentally *social* in nature, a predicament that we believe society would be better off without in the first place. In fact, an adequate understanding of the current crisis must acknowledge that the ecological outcomes of the way people use the Earth's resources are ultimately related to the modes of relationships among people themselves. Unless we devise new ways to integrate the wisdom of the natural and social sciences, we may end up spending considerable effort to add less knowledge about more obscure or irrelevant phenomena. Never before have we been so close—not to disaster in the way many zealous environmentalists believe—to experiencing on a planetary basis the limitations of our fragile life-support systems. Activists and intellectuals alike tell us that nothing short of a system of planetary ethics must arise if we are to survive as a species. Anything short of ecopolitical knowledge is bound to render the work of social scientists and policy makers substantially meaningless in their attempts to both understand society and formulate better policies for improving the quality of life of its members.

## The Incorporation of Nature into Human Culture

If there was a book of life on planet Earth, it would probably contain the following entry:

> Once upon a time—in fact, some nine thousand years ago—there was a man and his name was Gentile. Gentile had a small family: himself, his wife and two children (a boy and a girl), four altogether. His wife wanted to have more children but Gentile was very conscious of the need to maintain a harmonious relationship with nature, so he had decided not to overpopulate his surroundings. All in all, he seemed to have a good and peaceful life. Suddenly, Gentile realized that he was getting tired of being a hunter. Not that he disliked hunting. Of course, his heart wept a bit every time he had to kill another *eco-creature*. But he was also very much aware of the need to maintain a balance among *eco-species*, so in a way Gentile felt proud of performing his *eco-duties*. No, it was not dislike of hunting. Yet, somehow, he felt he could be a little happier. ... His family! That was it, that was it! What was really bothering him was that he had to spend so much time away from home, from his wife, from his children, from his fellow *eco-neighbors*, and could not share his happiness with them as much as he would like to. If there were only a way of feeding his family and staying close! ...
>
> Then, one day he woke up with a strange feeling that he could keep some animals around his house, thus he would not need to run after them anymore. Without quite understanding why, he also had the idea that he could clear part of a plot nearby, assigning different spots for vegetables, herbs, fruits, and so forth. How come? He just could not believe it. Somehow, he still felt that he could keep animals around, and also that in one spot he could grow potatoes—only potatoes, imagine!—in another corn, and in another, beans, and in another, and another, and another. ... For the first time in his entire life Gentile used the word garden (from *garth* and also *yard*—enclosure). That night Gentile did not sleep well. Despite his wonderful discoveries, he went to bed overwhelmed by his power. He knew there was much to be gained, and he felt happy for that. But he also knew that he was losing something. He did not know exactly what, but he felt sorry for it (Guimarães, 1986: 21–22).

From then on, the fate of human society was determined. Gentile's decision would inexorably lead to the ultimate ecological disruption: the advent of agriculture. It is indeed ironic—Is it not?—that thanks to that disruption civilization became possible. Considering this long-standing patter of occupation of the planet, it seems to have been indeed a step toward the contemporary concept of *sustainable* development. The "modern" notion of sustainability has its origin in the international debate that began in 1972 in Stockholm and that was consolidated twenty years later in Rio de Janeiro. Notwithstanding the variety of interpretations found in the literature and in political discourse, most of these dwell on the definition suggested by the World Commission on Environment and Development, presided by the then prime minister of Norway (Brundtland, 1987): Sustainable development is that which meets the needs of the present generation without compromising the possibilities of future generations to satisfy their own needs.

## The Ecopolitics of Sustainable Development

*Ecopolitics* is thus a short word for the *ecological politics* of sustainable development (Guimarães, 1991). It emerges from the recognition that to overcome the current ecological crisis of sustainability—poverty and social destitution coupled with scarcity of natural resources and environmental services—political decisions will have to be made. In this process some interests will be favored over others, both within and between nations. To recognize the ecological roots of most of our current political problems is not only a matter of survival, as proposed by Marcuse's quote mentioned above (cited in Mansholt et al., 1972: 77), but also a logical conclusion. Its urgency stems from the fact that time, the scarcest resource of all, is running out fast, or at least it is running out faster than the ability of our social and political institutions to face reality. The emergence of this new, sustainability-related dimension in our lives poses hitherto unforeseen challenges to both the social sciences and the everyday concerns of citizens and governments. This of course has both theoretical and practical implications.

For one thing, as our brief fable about Gentile was intended to suggest that the roots of the ecological crisis trace back to the introduction of agricultural and pastoral activities. Until recently, however, human beings have been able to remain largely unaware of this. Now that human beings count themselves not in the thousands but in the billions, they cannot avoid recognizing their dependence on the exchanges between economic activities and natural systems. It is realistic to conclude that as a result of the same forces that allowed us to built complex and advanced societies, "many parts of nature are becoming more fragile in our hands—and our lives may become more fragile with them" (Deutsch, 1977: 4). This fragility has become more fully apparent only recently, and many still do not appreciate it.

The development of civilization was—and in many respects still is—based on the naive and optimistic view that natural resources are practically inexhaustible. Despite that, the "environmental crisis" underneath the unsustainability of extant development styles underscores the fact that we are running out of resources and out of places to dispose of our wastes. These problems are not exclusive to rich or poor countries; absolute and relative scarcity—actual lack of resources and lack of access to resources—equally affect central and peripheral nations. We are also living in an era in which adequate institutions are scarce, and which there is a scarcity of political will as well. The vast majority of our social and political institutions were not designed for the basic dilemma of ecological scarcity; they can barely operate within its parameters, and they are ill-suited to solve it. Consequently, to understand the implications of sustainable development, one must attempt to grasp the social process behind it, since the ecological outcomes of the way people use the Earth's resources are ultimately related to the modes of relationships among people. The possible solutions to the crisis of sustainability must be found within the social system itself.

## Competing Political Forces and the Institutional Dimension of Sustainable Development Policies

Any discussion of sustainable development policies requires a political treatment instead of a technical one (Guimarães, 1991). At stake in these ecopolicies is much more than the simple arrangement of public actions in one area; it is the concept of development itself that is being called into question. As with most policies, some interests will be favored over others. Whereas most policies allow for a somewhat clear identification of *winners* or *losers*, however environmental policies are much more difficult to treat in this respect. Furthermore, the outcomes of sustainable development policies are not open to direct measure or individualization. One can measure the results of, say, industrial or agricultural policies, and identify which groups benefit most from decisions in these areas, but which particular groups stand to gain from drinking water free of pollutants or from preventing the depletion of the ozone layer? Finally, perhaps one of the most important dimensions of sustainable development, the ultimate beneficiaries of these decisions are not yet participants in today's struggle for survival. Current decisions must take into consideration the needs and the conceivable aspirations of generations to come, whereas we educate, feed, shelter, and do justice to a population that is already alive.

The holistic and, at the same time, the specific nature of ecological problems also underscores the political foundations of ecopolicies. Because we cannot deal with all problems at once, we are forced to choose particular areas or problems for concentrated governmental efforts. By singling out any given area, however, we are bound to provoke jurisdictional disputes within and between bureaucratic and societal institutions. This is in addition, of course, to the problems derived from an application of what Herbert Simon (1957) calls "bounded rationality"—the limited capacity of the human mind compared to the scope of the problems it needs to address—to complex ecological relationships. As a result, what are often considered "technical" criteria (standards, regulations, norms) will have to be bargained for; that is, politically negotiated.

These three notions—that ecopolicies question development processes, that they generate jurisdictional disputes, and that they are hardly quantifiable and individualized—all lead to one crucial feature of the policy context in which they emerge. Within the cultural framework of modern civilization, in which human beings are not part of but rather apart from nature, sustainable development policies are clearly unsympathetic, bothersome, and stand out from other public policies by being the "spoiler." We thus arrive at the core of the dilemmas faced by policy makers formulating and struggling to implement such policies today. On the one hand, their stand must be adversarial, almost by definition. On the other hand, decision makers are compelled to exercise persuasion and inducement in a continuous learning process. Not surprisingly, it requires much more political will to break the inertia of sustainable development policies than it does in other areas of public action. For the same reasons, it takes much less political clout on the other side to reach a situation of virtual stalemate, to immobilize sustainability-oriented programs and activities.

The crucial question, then, turns out to be whether conflict is being well administered or not. There are plenty of indications that these intrinsic tensions have not been well administered so far. (See, e.g., Guimarães, 1991.) First of all, the negotiation that allows any conflict to be addressed presupposes the existence of actors that share more or less equivalent control over political resources. Nothing could be further from the truth than the politics surrounding sustainable development. On one side is a strong group of businesspeople, developers, and multinational corporations, all of whom benefit greatly from accelerated economic growth. On the other side is a loosely related group of conservationists, community-based organizations, experts, and persons directly affected either by poverty or by pollution and the depletion of natural resources, (or more often than not, by both). In the middle—in some sense over both groups—stand the governmental bureaucracies and private, transnational conglomerates.

## THE EVOLUTION OF GLOBAL PERCEPTIONS CONCERNING SUSTAINABLE DEVELOPMENT

> He will manage the cure best who foresees what is to happen from the present condition of the patient (Hippocrates: 460–337 B.C.).

The 1990s began with significant changes in the international debate on environmental problems. The highest level of attention to the impending environmental crisis was the Summit of the Earth which took place in Rio de Janeiro in 1992. Rio-92 laid the foundations for a new world vision about the environment, turning the global agenda into one of sustainable development. The conventions on biological diversity and climate change represented paramount steps in this direction. In short, the Earth summit heightened public awareness about the interconnections among the environmental, social, cultural, and economic dimensions of development. Gradually, sustainable development began to penetrate the economic and political discourse.

### Institutional Ups and Downs Since the Earth Summit of 1992

The opening of new international decision-making forums to include emerging issues brought up by renewed signs of environmental stress worldwide has been closely related to the evolution of the actual situation as well as of the agenda in many regions of the world. This process has deepened in the decade since Rio-92 as a direct result of globalization, as indicated by the United Nations Economic Commission for Latin America and the Caribbean (ECLAC, 2002a). Among many aspects, globalization reinforced in real trends the concept in vogue at the end of the 1980s relative to the exhaustion of specific models of economic and social organization, while revealing at the same time the insufficiencies of the prevailing styles of development to respond to the new challenges. Styles of development in which the traditional problems of poverty and inequality have now been aggravated by the ecological limits and environmental requirements to achieve sustainable development in the twenty-first century (Guimarães, 2001a).

This became quite clear in the text of Resolution 44/228 of the U.N. General Assembly, which was adopted without a vote on December 22, 1989, and which convened the Rio conference three years later. As stated in the resolution, governments were "gravely concerned that the major cause of the continuing deterioration of the global environment is the unsustainable pattern of production and consumption, particularly in industrialized countries." In effect, if the need to increase national wealth to satisfy the basic needs of a growing population can represent severe pressures upon the endowment of natural resources, the increment of extractive and industrial activities may entail an even sharper deterioration in the carrying capacity of the ecosystems that provide essential environmental services for sustained economic output.

Since Rio, the evolution in perceptions about current challenges, along with the concrete actions that have resulted from the new global agenda, allow for an overall positive assessment of the international context for sustainable development. New concepts have been enshrined in multilateral treaties and conventions, such as the principle of "shared yet differentiated responsibilities," the "polluter pays" principle, and the "precautionary" principle. New, nonstate and civil society actors have also been incorporated, with unforeseen and unprecedented weight, among these, environmental nongovernmental organizations (NGOs) in general and the scientific community in the specific instance of climate change. (See, e.g., Born, 1998.) It should be stressed, however, that the emergence of new actors does not necessarily mean the abolition or a weakened role of the state. Quite the contrary—it has been increasingly recognized in recent years that despite the ideological sways of the last decade the state still holds key responsibilities both in regulatory matters and in articulating the diverse productive, community, and social sectors, especially in education, public safety, and the environment (Guimarães, 1990; 1996a). This recognition assumes ever more importance when it is acknowledged that governance—referred to until very recently as the transition of authoritarian to democratic regimes, or in relation to the need to tame hyperinflation and economic instability—is founded today on the possibilities of overcoming poverty and inequality.

As stated in the 1994 edition of the United Nations Development Program (UNDP) human development report, nobody should be condemned to a brief or miserable life only because he or she was born in the wrong class, in the wrong country, or with the wrong gender. The new foundations of civilized life that will provide governance to political systems worldwide therefore require the emergence of a new *development paradigm*. In this context, the state still provides a contribution to development that is *unique, necessary,* and *indispensable* (Guimarães, 1996a): *unique* because its logic transcends the logic of market forces, particularly in such dimensions as equity and social justice, which are foreign to market mechanisms and institutions, and also incorporates so-called diffuse rights intrinsic to citizenship; *necessary* because the very logic of capital accumulation requires the production of "public goods" that cannot be produced by competitive actors in the marketplace, particularly in such imperfect markets as the ones of developing countries; and *indispensable* because it addresses climate change, biodiversity depletion, and many other issues not amenable to the microeconomic calculus of discount rates and rates of return, especially when future generations (who by definition cannot participate in today's market) are brought to the forefront of environmental regimes.

In addition, one must remember that the challenges posed by social inequality or environmental decay cannot be defined as *individual* problems, embodying instead social, *collective* problems. It is definitely not the case of guaranteeing access via the marketplace to education, housing, health, or an environment free of pollution; instead, these entail the recovery of collective (solidarity) practices of fulfilling the material and spiritual needs of human well-being.

From a less positive standpoint, the evolution of the global agenda concerning environmental regimes and sustainable development has also entailed new threats. One must keep in mind the warnings made in the mid-1990s that concerns for the environment allow for the introduction of new "conditionalities" in international development aid. Countries should also resist the tendency to replace development aid for trade, what was summarized in Rio in the "trade, not aid" proposal. To many public and private sectors, the principles of environmental protection and of sustainable development are still considered a restriction to economic growth. This has severely limited the public capacity to halt and reverse the increasing environmental deterioration of critical ecosystems and to control pollution.

## Expansion of an International Environmental Regime

In terms of its actual decisions, the Rio conference was a landmark event because it produced agreements that afforded more a comprehensive treatment of global environmental issues by focusing on the goal of sustainable development. The five Rio agreements represented the most universal and coordinated political step taken in the early 1990s toward establishing an international system of cooperation for mainstreaming the environmental dimension into development. These instruments explicitly incorporate the concept of "common but differentiated responsibilities" first formulated in Stockholm and fully acknowledged in principle 7 of the Rio Declaration.

The accelerated pace of globalization has also given rise to greater ecological and economic interdependence (MacNeill et al., 1991). Thanks to the worldwide awareness of countries' interdependence in the face of global environmental problems, the legally binding instruments formulated in Rio de Janeiro were adopted and ratified more quickly than in previous decades and by practically all member states of the United Nations. The essential change of this new generation of multilateral agreements has been the acknowledgment of an explicit correlation among environment, health, and production and consumption patterns on the one hand, and economic, commercial, and social policies on the other. This has been particularly evident in the Kyoto and Cartagena protocols and the Rotterdam and Stockholm agreements. Other advances post-Rio have also been evidenced in multilateral agreements emphasizing emergent environmental issues brought up by the advance in scientific knowledge. This has been the case, for example, with the Global Program of Action for the Protection of the Marine Environment from Land-based Activities (1995), the Rotterdam Convention on the Prior Informed Consent Procedure for Certain Hazardous Chemicals and Pesticides in International Trade (1998), and the Stockholm Agreement on Persistent Organic Pollutants (2001).

The increase in multilateral environmental treaties, the proliferation of forums and secretariats for these treaties, and the growing number of intergovernmental organizations created to follow up on them have underscored the need to streamline the international management structure for sustainable development, however. The existence of more than 500 legal instruments—which in many cases have no practical connections between one another—has thus given rise to a multilateral environmental treaty "traffic jam." Accordingly, a matter of particular concern has been the almost complete absence of synergies among these accords, even though when they are viewed from a territorial perspective some major areas of common ground can be found.

Additionally, attempts to reconcile commercial goals and environmental issues have often failed, mainly due to limited economic approaches that deem it necessary to assign "correct prices" to environmental services and natural resources. These efforts have been hindered by uncertainties about the source, scope, and magnitude of the harm done to health and the natural habitat by pollution, which makes it difficult to accurately calculate the costs of past and present damage, and of the economic benefits of abating pollution or conserving natural resources. In contrast to the multilateral trading system, the management of international environmental affairs is marked by a scattered, structure that is far from coherent.

Against this backdrop and using biodiversity as an example, establishing the links between environmental and trade agreements is clearly a pending assignment. Developing countries are also under growing pressure to incorporate environmental components into trade agreements (ECLAC, 2002a). The main objectives for this have been to prevent the emergence of competitive advantages deriving from lax environmental standards ("environmental dumping") and to ensure that legislation is not used for protectionist purposes. It has thus been correctly argued that the pressure to sustain competitiveness to which countries are subjected by globalization may prevent governments from taking steps to internalize environmental costs and improve their ecoperformance if this entails higher costs for domestic producers (Zarsky, 1997).

In short, it is correct to suggest that almost ten years after Rio, the world has hardly begun the path toward sustainable development. It is true that most countries assumed with enthusiasm the commitments of the summit of 1992, and have attempted to bring to fruition the many Rio conventions, the Rio Declaration, and Agenda 21, but the achievements so far have been clearly insufficient. This process has not been carried out only by national governments; many civil and private organizations, universities, and research centers, as well as countless local governments, have become more and more involved in the implementation of the Rio "spirit" and actual decisions, yet much is still to be done to confront the many and varied challenges ahead, some of which did not exist at the time governments met in Rio ten years ago.

## Improvements in the Integration of Public Policies and in Citizen Participation

The process of integrating environmental policies into other sectoral policies has also had its ups and downs (ECLAC and UNEP/ROLAC, 2001). In most countries, the concept of sustainable resource use and environmental conservation is only just beginning to be incorporated into the different economic sectors. Traditionally, macroeconomic policy and sectoral policies in the fields of health, education, agriculture, mining, and so forth have taken very little account of the environmental dimension. Numerous "market failures," which are identified as one of the main underlying causes of environmental deterioration, reflect this situation. This is also the case in those sectors that make direct or indirect use of biodiversity, such as the agricultural, forestry, fishery, and water resources sectors.

Consequently, with regard to economic and social policies, the balance sheet of what was achieved in the 1990s is clearly mixed. In the economic field, there has been considerable progress in correcting fiscal imbalances, reducing inflation, promoting exports, reviving regional integration processes or starting new ones, attracting new flows of foreign direct investment, and restoring economic growth. Significant progress has also been made in the development of strong macroeconomic institutions and, although with some delay, new institutional challenges have been tackled in other fields, such as the regulation of financial services, the promotion of competition, and the regulation of public services.

On the negative side, the achievements in terms of economic growth and increasing productivity over the same period have been frustrating. The ups and downs of the economy and the frequency of financial crises indicate that not all the causes of instability have been eliminated, and some of them may actually have gotten worse. In this context, the scope for orienting public policies toward sustainable development becomes more uncertain, since priority tends to be given to sectoral-type policies rather than integrative policies, such as those for sustainable development. The institutions regulating environmental and social matters face the growing challenge of designing management instruments that can be both effective and economically efficient in the pursuit of environmental and social objectives, especially in view of the perception that traditional regulatory schemes have not been successful in dealing with the processes of inequality and environmental deterioration. Furthermore, due the fiscal restrictions faced by most countries, authorities have less scope for strengthening their capabilities through higher budget allocations and must therefore explore other means for self-financing management.

A novel component of the concept of sustainable development since the Earth summit has been the promotion of the participation of civil society and the productive sectors in the decision-making process (Bárcena, 1999). The possibility of developing sustainable societies requires the provision of the necessary information to civil society so that its members can take part in the adoption of decisions affecting them and play a constructive leading role. This approach resulted in the institutionalization of citizen advisory bodies of varied and representative composition, and this process sped up from Rio-92 onward, when many national sustainable development councils or commissions were set up. Their function is to ensure that national plans comply with the objectives of Agenda 21, to promote participation in the process of generating public policies, and to open up spaces for the discussion of medium-and long-term strategies. Various factors militate against the consolidation of these spaces at the national level. The fact that their functions are not clearly defined, the conflicts that hinder them from ensuring multisectoral composition, and the difficulty of exerting real influence on other sectors are all obstacles that limit the influence of this organ at the national level.

These difficulties are somewhat lessened when local actors undertake these actions, and decentralization processes have made a contribution in this respect, furthering democracy and bringing government closer to its citizens. Although concrete results are not yet sufficiently widespread, there is a very proactive tendency among local authorities to use long-term local development strategies adopted on the basis of participatory planning processes, which many actually refer to as Local Agenda 21. Among the many actions taken within this framework are sustainable land use, the fight against unemployment and social disintegration, the application of appropriate population and spatial distribution policies, the rational use of energy, the establishment of sustainable systems of transport and communications, the conservation and rehabilitation of historical and cultural heritage landmarks, and the improvement of rural settlements.

Another avenue for public participation has been expanding by the more active role of the legislature. Most countries have provided in their legislation for various forms of specialized participation in environmental matters, including mechanisms that give citizens access to information at different levels, representation of citizens' organizations on various collective bodies (councils on protected areas or river valley areas, national commissions on climate change or biodiversity, etc.), and public hearings about granting environmental licenses for large-scale or infrastructure projects. In sum, there has been a growing movement toward changes in terms of civil society's organizations that increasingly demand greater room for participation: in issues concerning gender, youth, and indigenous groups, business and trade associations, and consumers' groups. This tendency has been strengthened in recent years by the explosive growth of information and communications technologies and networks, thereby enabling these organizations to obtain information very rapidly and to work quickly in close coordination.

## OLD AND NEW CHALLENGES ON THE ROAD TO JOHANNESBURG

Three decades after the Stockholm Conference of 1972, there should not remain any doubt, as we stated just a few months after Rio-92 (Guimarães, 1992), that from the times of *Only One World* (Stockholm-72), through *Environment and Development* (Rio-92), to *Sustainable Development* (Johannesburg-2002), the world's perception about the environmental crisis has irrevocably changed. The international debate, which began in Stockholm and consolidated after Rio, should have definitely overcome the exclusively technocratic perspective, the naïve illusion caressed in Stockholm that the advances of scientific knowledge would be enough in themselves to allow for the emergence of a sustainable style of development. Likewise, it does not make any sense to still confront the environment and development, since the former is simply the result of the failings of the latter. The problems of the environment are those of development, of an unequal development for human societies, and of a harmful one for natural systems. These do not constitute a technical problem, but a social and political challenge, as became unmistakably plain ten years ago in Rio de Janeiro.

## A New Paradigm for the Formulation of Development Policies

The transition to sustainability implies a profound change in the prevailing archetype of civilization, particularly in what is referred to as its cultural pattern of articulating humans and nature. An adequate understanding about this transition imposes the recognition that humankind is facing the exhaustion of a style of development that is *ecologically wasteful* (depletes the natural resource base), *socially perverse* (generates poverty and inequality), *politically unjust* (freezes absolute and relative scarcity of access to resources), *ethically objectionable* (disrespects human and nonhuman life forms), and *culturally alienated* (estranges and subjugates nature).

The often-repeated statement that human beings must constitute the center and the raison dêtre of development thus calls for a new development style that must be (Guimarães, 2001b): (1) *environmentally* sustainable in the access and use of natural resources and in the preservation of biodiversity, (2) *socially* sustainable in the reduction of poverty and inequality and in promoting social justice, (3) *culturally* sustainable in the conservation of the system of values, practices, and symbols of identity that in spite of their permanent evolution determine national integration through time, (4) *politically* sustainable by deepening democracy and guaranteeing access and participation of all sectors in public decision making, and (5) able to be guided by a new development *ethics*, one in which the economic objectives of growth are subordinated both to the laws governing the operation of natural systems and to the criteria of respect for human dignity and improvement in the quality of life for current and futures generations; in short, a development paradigm that respects the integrity of the life-support systems of the planet.

Needless to say, recalling the U.N. General Assembly Resolution 44/228 of 1989 that the developed world bears a greater and differentiated responsibility in the search of solutions for the most urgent planetary problems, the contribution of our ecological disorder to global ecological disorder is still quite limited. None can escape from the reality that it will only be possible to attain a style of development that is environmentally and socially sustainable if all countries are willing to change their current patterns of growth and of incorporation of the natural endowment in economic activities.

In order to undertake the transition to a sustainable future, all countries need to introduce far-reaching economic and social changes, starting by restructuring production in a way that meets the threefold objective of increasing competitiveness, reducing social asymmetries, and reversing the environmental deterioration associated with current patterns of productive specialization. On the legal and institutional front, the world is faced with the task of adapting current planning systems to make it easier for management instruments to operate at the different levels of government. The territorial specificity of sustainable development means there is a need to establish solid operational links with local authorities by means of strategies that tie the whole range of administrative structures to the ecological characteristics of each subnational region (Guimarães, 2001c).

If it is true that the post-Rio decade has witnessed intensive economic changes with most developing regions now more integrated into the world system, it is also appropriate to note that these countries are more than ever subject to tensions that generate new and heightened uncertainty and instability. At the same time, the benefits of recent global processes have not yet reached the vast majority of people, and progress toward the goals of equity has stagnated everywhere.

As a result, the world is no more socially or economically sustainable than it was ten years ago. Recent data put out by the United Nations Environment Programme (UNEP, 2000) clearly indicate that the environmental situation is not showing any clear signs of progress toward sustainability, either. The last decade witnessed a marked degree of vulnerability to a series of more intense and frequent natural phenomena that are continuing to impact on increasingly fragile ecological and social systems. This has resulted in greater human, environmental, and economic insecurity, further undermining sustainability and generating heightened uncertainty and political strain upon institutions.

## Sustainable Development in an Era of Globalization

Again one must acknowledge that developing countries will not be able to confront all the challenges of the transition toward sustainability alone. In short, the viability of global, regional, and domestic agendas will be largely determined by the progress made in the international agenda. Globally, it is indispensable to reform the world financial system in light of sustainable development imperatives. The Johannesburg summit could be a good opportunity for progress in this debate on the basis of the results that came out of the United Nations Conference on Financing for Development, including the industrialized world's pledge to commit new financial aid for sustainable development (ECLAC, 2002b). The search of adequate answers to the sustainability challenges will require new forms of articulation and coordination among developing countries, since the developed countries have demonstrated the lengths to which they will go to defend their interests. This has been demonstrated through recently declassified confidential documents that reveal that even before Stockholm, the so-called Brussels's group—Belgium, France, Germany, The Netherlands, the United Kingdom, and the United States—plotted to resist the creation of UNEP and to undermine environmental regulations. Indeed, according to a note of one of the group's first meetings written by a civil servant in the British Foreign and Commonwealth Office, the behind-the-scenes maneuvers of this "unofficial policy-making body to concert the views of the principal governments concerned will have to remain informal and confidential." This meeting took place in July 1971, nearly a year before Stockholm. Written by an official in what was then the British Department of the Environment, this note underscores that Britain wanted to restrict the scope of the Stockholm conference and reduce the number of proposals for action. In an indirect reference to what would later become UNEP, the paper says that "a new and expensive international organisation must be avoided, but a small effective central coordinating mechanism. . .would not be welcome but is probably inevitable" (Hamer, 2002).

To further complicate matters, most scenarios discussed today about the new millennium emphasize the process of *globalization*, often defined exclusively in economic, financial, or commercial aspects. Many—including myself—consider it more revealing to unveil globalization from a *sustainable* development perspective. This brings into question, for instance, the economic rationality of globalization in its many dimensions vis-à-vis the logic and the pace of natural processes. In other words, capital (flows) may have become "globalized," yet the same process has not taken place with respect to labor or natural resources. Indeed, the prospects of a process of globalization founded upon an upward, unlimited, and unchecked economic growth model are also seriously disputed, particularly in view of the reality of exhaustion of many natural resources (e.g., fauna, flora, nonrenewable sources of energy) as well as of deterioration of natural processes that are crucial for the ecosystem viability of life on the planet (ozone layer, climate, etc.). As Kenneth Boulding, a leading pioneer of sustainability, suggested, "anyone who believe that exponential growth can go on forever in a finite world is either a madman. . .or an economist." Finally, those subscribing to these and other serious reservations also point to the growing consensus about the social unsustainability of the current styles of development, a reality of globalization in the midst of increasing social inequality and exclusion, a reality that certainly preceded but has been exacerbated by the very process of globalization. (See, e.g., Sen, 1989.)

One may deepen this *socioenvironmental* standpoint by asserting that the character of globalization, or at least of the neoconservative corporate ideology underlying and legitimating the hegemonic modernity of today's world, appears to leave only two alternatives to emerging countries. Either these integrate themselves fully—albeit subordinated and dependent—in the globalization bandwagon of the world market, or it will not remain anything more to those countries than the reality of backwardness masked behind the illusion of autonomous development.

At the heart of today's challenges lies not inevitable insertion into an increasingly global world, however, but what mode of insertion is convenient to emerging economies, whether or not the prevailing patterns of insertion allow these countries to retain national control of growth and what sorts of alternatives allow these societies to maintain and foster social cohesion, cultural identity, and environmental integrity. As suggested in a brilliant book debunking neoliberalism (Calcagno and Calcagno, 1995: 265)

> We are told that we must all board the modernity train (as if there was only one), even though we do not know where it will take us, we do not know whether we will be allowed to board it as full-fare passengers or service personnel who are sent back to their origin once the journey is over, or whether we will become immigrant labor at the final destination. In short, we are being counseled, as sovereign countries, to adopt a behavior that no liberal (as a matter of fact, not even a sane person) would embrace at a railroad station.

## CONCLUDING REMARKS: HAVE THE PROSPECTS FOR SUSTAINABLE DEVELOPMENT WORSENED?

> The environmental crisis is an outward manifestation of a crisis of mind and spirit. There could be no greater misconception of its meaning than to believe it to be concerned only with endangered wildlife, human-made ugliness, and pollution. These are part of it, but more importantly, the crisis is concerned with the kind of creatures we are and what we must become in order to survive. (Lynton Caldwell, 1973: 18).

Humankind has given the impression, especially in the past decade, that it is acquiring a clear understanding of the challenges that modern civilization will have to overcome in order to survive, yet the issues that seem to permeate the political debate within and between nation-states bear little resemblance to ecopolitics. Certainly there is much talk about starvation in Africa, the moral obligation to improve the distribution of resources on a global scale, and the need to reverse the degradation of tropical rain forests, which harbor most species. "Defense"-related subjects nonetheless dominate the public agenda. Governments all over the developed world recognize that starvation, pollution, and the squandering of resources are all part of the same ecopolitical equation. At the same time, their actions entirely elude the nature of the environmental crisis. The naiveté of many world leaders today recalls the example offered by Alvin Toffler (1974) about the simpleminded-ness of the elders of an Indian tribe that for centuries lived off the produce of a river at its doorstep. Its culture and economy are based upon fishing, boat building, and cultivating the land fertilized by the river, so that the future of this community merely repeats its past. What happens, however, when this tribe pursues its tra-ditional style of development unaware that a dam is being built upstream? Its image of the future is misleading—dangerously misleading—for the river will soon dry up or become a trickle.

In short, the single most important challenge facing the world in the new millennium is in fact the *quality* of growth (i.e., the increase in the levels of well-being and the reduction of socioeconomic inequalities) much more than its *quantity* (i.e., the simple increment of material output). In his prologue to a book of the University of the United Nations on the implications of the process of globalization, U.N. secretary general Kofi Annan, stated that "millions of people around the world experience it not as an agent of progress but as a disruptive and even destructive force, while many more millions are completely exluded from its benefits" (Grunberg and Khan, 2000, p.v.). One of the editors of this book goes on, indicating that "globalization was seen as inevitable. It is driven by technology and market. But it is not a force of nature, rather it is the result of man-made processes. It must be shaped to serve humanity. To that end, it needs to be carefully managed by countries nationally and through international cooperation" (Grunberg, 2000, p.18).

One must also pay close attention to the implications of globalization for gov-ernance at all levels—planetary, regional, national, and subnational, because, among many reasons, as the authors of the book introduced by the secretary general poignantly remark, world affairs are less and less the combined interdependencies among individual countries. Many global dynamics simply ignore national bound-aries. The erosion of nation-states brings with it powerless governments and may lead to the end of governance. In their words, "many applaud this erosion of governance—indeed, many see it as the main attraction of globalization. *These are the true anarchists, perhaps more so than the masked youth that smashed windows at the WTO meeting of Seattle in 1999*" (Grunberg and Khan, 2000:3, emphasis added).

Last but not least is the cause for alarm regarding the new geopolitical reality of security brought about by the events of September 11, 2001. Indeed, one of the most positive traits of the previous international atmosphere was the relative openness of the avenues for international negotiation, until the mid-1980s obstructed by the strategic security interests dominating the Cold War. This evolution had allowed humankind to put the environmental crisis at the forefront of the global agenda, not as a collateral effect of growth but as an intrinsic characteristic of the prevailing styles of development. It was for this reason that we left Stockholm after a narrowly devised conference, designed to analyze the deterioration of the *human environment,* arrived in Rio aware of the bonds between *environment and develop-ment,* and were expected to land in Johannesburg to finally adopt decisions for *sustainable development.*

The brutal attack inflicted on the United States skyrocketed insecurity in the main world power to levels comparable only to the Berlin blockade or to the Soviet Missile Crisis in Cuba. The initial and still predominantly military response resurrects the specter of a new cold war, a most unfortunate setback in international relations. Indeed, it would be unfortunate for the efforts of paving the transition to sustainable development if the world were to subordinate the social, environmental, and institutional challenges of sustainability to exclusively geopolitical considerations—that is to say, according to the limits and always problematic interpretations about what constitutes terrorist actions and movements or nationalist actions of protest or legitimate resistance to foreign encroachment in national affairs. History is full of examples of the perverse results of extreme fundamentalism.

The previous millennium started with the globalization that has influenced civilization ever since—the Christian Crusades against the Islamic world. The specter of this easy "globalism" once again in Western and Eastern societies' opposing and capricious economic and religious fundamentalism. One should not forget that the religious fundamentalism of some countries today dates back precisely to resistance movements during the Crusades—the premodern version of the hegemonic, corporate-driven "economic wisdom" of today. Many of those same highly organized movements that one could classify nowadays as being terrorist have their historical roots in this very same resistance to the Western heavy-handed worldview.

If it had seemed correct to suggest that the historical shift of the international agenda from an exclusively environmental one to one of sustainable development could be mostly explained by its ethical character, much in the same vein as the evolution experienced by its predecessors, the gender and the human and civil rights agenda (Guimarães, 1996b), many have been warning about the threats posed to these not yet attained civil liberties by the measures being suggested to confront the new threats of international terrorism. Equally unfortunate would be the subordination of the collective interests of well-being and material and spiritual growth to the fundamentalist interests of many market forces. It would definitely represent a step backward to allow the advances achieved in Western civilization, to a certain degree deepened by the new wave of globalization, to now be threatened by the struggle against global terrorism.

No less disturbing has been the tendency of granting priority to the individual, economic, and strategic interests of hegemonic countries, downgrading the fight against poverty and the reduction of inequities in wealth distribution, and maintaining the carrying capacity of life-support ecosystems at the lower levels of international priorities. As Stiglitz, the 2001 Nobel Prize winner in economics, recognized one month after the fall of the Twin Towers, "there is the growing feeling that maybe we have made a mistake by putting too much emphasis in the selfish material interests, and too little in shared ones" (Stiglitz, 2001). The risk of making backwards steps on the path to sustainability is thus real. As Stiglitz suggests, the understanding will hopefully prevail that "with globalization, comes interdependence, and with interdependence comes the need to adopt collective decisions in all areas that affect us collectively."

In other words, the sad reality today is that thirty years after Stockholm, the warnings voiced by Margaret Mead (1970) still have not been echoed by world leaders. In her wise words, "we can recognize that the ways of our forebears are ways to which we can never return, but that the more we can recapture of this earlier wisdom, in a form we can understand, the better we can understand what is happening today, when a generation almost innocent of a sense of history has to learn how to cope with an unknown future, one for which they were not reared." (Mead, 1970: 70). Three decades later, and in light of the sustainable development agenda and its actual accomplishments, Lourdes de Santiago is also right when she reminds us of the saying of a Mexican peasant that summarizes the present predicament with profound wisdom: "we were better off when we were worse off" (De Santiago, 2002:16). One cannot deny either that the world has become extremely more complex in recent decades, and that the generalized feeling these days, despite the technocratic naiveté of the Stockholm pioneers about sustainability, is that those certainly were happy times, although we did not know it.

## REFERENCES

Bárcena, A. (1999). Bases para Una Ciudadanía Ambiental. Mexico City: UNEP/ROLAC.

Born, R. H. (1998). Os Regimes Internacionais da Rio-92: A Participação de Atores Não Governamentais. PhD dissertation, University of São Paulo, São Paulo.

Brundtland, G. H. (1987). Our Common Future: From One Earth to One World. New York: Oxford University Press.

Calcagno, A. E., Calcagno, A. F. (1995). El Universo Neoliberal: Recuento de sus Lugares Comunes. Buenos Aires: Alianza Editorial.

Caldwell, L. K. (1973). Environmental policy in a hypertrophic society. In: Utton, A. E., Henning, D. H., eds. Environmental Policy: Concepts and Applications. New York: Praeger.

De Santiago, L. G. (2002). La Gobernabilidad en América Latina en el Siglo de la Globalización. MA dissertation, Alberto Hurtado University, Santiago de Chile.

Deutsch, K. W. (1977). Eco-social Systems and Eco-Politics: A Reader on Human and Social Implications of Environmental Managamente in Developing Countries. Paris: UNESCO.

ECLAC (United Nations Economic Commission for Latin America and the Caribbean). (2002a). Globalización y Desarrollo. Santiago de Chile: ECLAC, LC/G.215(SES.29/3), April 9.

ECLAC (United Nations Economic Commission for Latin America and the Caribbean). (2002b). Growth with Stability: Financing for Development in the New International Context. Santiago de Chile: ECLAC Books Series no 67 (LC/G.2171-P), International Conference on the Financing of Development, Monterrey, March.

ECLAC and UNEP/ROLAC-Regional Office for Latin America and the Caribbean of the U.N. Environment Programme. (2001). The Sustainability of Development in Latin America and the Caribbean: Challenges and Opportunities. Santiago de Chile: ECLAC, doc. LC/G.2145(CONF.90/3), Oct. 5.

Guimarães, R. P. (1986). Ecopolitics in The Third World: An Institutional Analysis of Environmental Management in Brazil. PhD dissertation, University of Connecticut, Storrs.

Guimarães, R. P. (1990). El Leviatán Acorralado: Continuidad y Cambio en el Papel del Estado en América Latina. Estudios Internacionales 63: April–May 45–81.

Guimarães, R. P. (1991). The Ecopolitics of Development in the Third World: Politics and Environment in Brazil. Boulder, CO: Lynne Rienner.

Guimarães, R. P. (1992). El Discreto Encanto de la Cumbre de la Tierra: Una Evaluación Impresionista de la Conferencia de Rio. Nueva Sociedad 122: Nov.–Dec. 86–103.

Guimarães, R. P. (1996a). ¿El Leviatán en Extinción? Notas sobre la Reforma del Estado en América Latina. Pretextos Nov. 9:115–143.

Guimarães, R. P. (1996b). Nuevas Temáticas en las Políticas Públicas. In: Guzmán, V., Hola, E., eds. El Conocimiento como un Hecho Político. Santiago de Chile: Centro de Estudios de la Mujer, pp. 135–146.

Guimarães, R. P. (2001a). Tierra de Sombras: Desafios de la Sustentabilidad y del Desarrollo Territorial y Local ante la Globalización. Simposio Internacional Integración Regional, Globalización y Desarrollo, Santiago de Chile, July.

Guimarães, R. P. (2001b). The politics and ethics of "sustainability" as a new paradigm for public policy formation and development planning. Internat J Econ Dev 3, 3.

Guimarães, R. P. (2001c). Fundamentos Territoriales y Bioregionales de la Planificación. Santiago de Chile: ECLAC Environment and Development Series. no. 39 (LC/L.152-P), July.

Grunberg, I. (2000). Globalization, Governance and the Role of the United Nations in Economic Affairs. In: Grunberg, I. and Khan, S., eds. Globalization: The United Nations Development Dialogue: Finance, Trade, Poverty, Peace-Building. New York: United Nations University Press.

Grunberg, I., Khan, S. (2000). Globalization: The United Nations Development Dialogue: Finance, Trade, Poverty, Peace-Building. New York: United Nations University Press.

Hamer, M. (Jan. 2002). Plot to undermine global pollution controls is revealed. New Sci 2 (electronic version http://www.newscientist.com/hottopics/pollution/pollution.jsp?id = ns99991734).

IFRC (International Federation of Red Cross and Red Crescent Societies). (2001). 2001 IFRC World Disaster Report. Geneva.

MacNeill, J., et al. (1991). Beyond Interdependence. New York: Oxford University Press.

Mansholt, S., et al. (1972). Ecología y Revolución. Santiago de Chile: Editorial Nueva Universitaria.

Mead, M. (1970). Culture and Commitment. New York: Doubleday.

Passmore, J. (1974). Man's Responsibility for Nature: Ecological Problems and Western Traditions. New York: Scribner's.

Simon, H. (1957). Models of Man. New York: Wiley.

Stiglitz, J. (2001). Cambiar la Prioridades. El País, 11, Oct. electronic version www.jubilee2000uk.org/analysis/articles/Cambiar_las_prioridades.htm.

Toffler, A. (1974). The psychology of the future. Learning for Tomorrow: The Role of the Future in Education. New York: Random House.

UNDP (United Nations Development Program). (1994). Human Development Report, Mexico City: Fondo de Cultura Económica.

UNEP (United Nations Environment Programme). (2000). GEO: América Latina y el Caribe. Perspectivas del Medio Ambiente. San José de Costa Rica: UNEP.

Zarsky, L. (1997). Stuck in the Mud? Nation-States, Globalization and the Environment. electronic version http: //www.nautilus.org/papers/enviro/zarsky_mud.html.

# 25

## Security, Defense, and Development in the Current Age

**HO-WON JEONG and ELEFTHERIOS MICHAEL**

*George Mason University, Fairfax, Virginia, U.S.A.*

### INTRODUCTION

Our history is full of major wars and other manifest conflicts as well as the divide between rich and poor (1). Although the threat of nuclear weapons has become less visible following the end of the bipolar system of the Cold War era, new weapons of mass destruction are still being developed, deployed, and tested. At the same time, millions of people are suffering from malnutrition, starvation, poverty, and economic exploitation. Protracted intrastate (mainly ethnic and/or civil war) conflicts, similar to the Rwandan and Yugoslavia situations, are not likely to cease in the near future as various groups seek autonomy that cannot be fulfilled within an existing nation-state framework.

In understanding the quest for peace in the twenty-first century, we thus, need to consider not only the prevention and management of violence (Cahill, 1996; Wallensteen, 1998; Lund, 1996), but also changes that will eliminate oppressive social and economic structures. In particular, a response to the threats of international terrorism requires dealing with the sources of social instability in Afghanistan, Somalia, Sudan, Yemen, and other conflict-ridden countries. Holistic approaches to security, development, and defense have been advocated by many educators, philosophers, historians, artists, grassroots activists, and politicians.

While this chapter reviews the traditional security paradigms based on military power that have dominated interstate relations for centuries, it stresses the need for a more holistic approach to peace building, which can help strengthen resilience to future violence (2). After briefly looking at military security and defense strategies, the chapter delves into a discussion about the necessity for nontraditional means of security, such as civilian-based defense, disarmament, economic conversion and development, nonviolence, and conflict resolution. An expanded notion of security and defense can be considered in terms of the control of military violence, the peaceful settlement of conflict, cooperation for economic and social development, ecological balance, a respect for human rights, self-determination, and nonviolent structural change (3).

## SECURITY AND DEFENSE BASED ON MILITARY POWER

### Balance of Power

The traditional way of maintaining peace is considered in the context of a military alliance system and political arrangements between states (Waltz, 1979). The balance of power has often been referred to as the most classic alliance security system designed to maintain peace by historians and political strategists. The nineteenth century European multiple state system is given as a successful example of maintaining stability by means of a balance of power. The balance of power was considered successful to the extent that while frequent wars were inevitable, they were kept local. Relations among states were managed by means of making, breaking, and shifting alliance ties. A balance of power "is ill-suited to deal with conflicts that, although internal, threaten international peace and security," however, (Goodby, 1996). The success of balance of power as a policy tool to prevent war is ascribed to a diffused power structure in an international system, diplomatic skills, the absence of ideological impediment in coalition building, little influence of public opinion on diplomacy, and the existence of a state qualified for a balancing role between different power blocs.

These classic assumptions, however, have not been applied since the end of World War II. The Cold War period is characterized by the concentration of overwhelming power in the hands of the two superpowers, an ideological split and political confrontation, and difficulty in shifting an alliance relationship. From the 1990s, we have seen hegemonic power exercised by a single superpower. Overall, a balance-of-power system is severely constrained by a changing international environment. An equilibrium managed by skillful politicians cannot be easily achieved in the contemporary world, in which a power situation changes very rapidly with the development of new technologies as well as the fluctuation of an economy that influences the military budget. As we observed in the Iran–Iraq War, the strength of military power can be easily misjudged, and thus it leads to a gamble for war. The greatest defect is that the efforts to maintain a balance of power often produce an arms race even in periods of peace.

### Collective Security

Contrary to the balance of power system, which does not have any supranational agency responsible for coordinating power relations, a collective security system has a centralized mechanism to eliminate the pattern of competitive alignments. The preponderance of power achieved through cooperation within a community of nation-states is assumed to provide security for all and discourages a potential aggressor from taking the risk of attacking another state. For strategic reasons, during the Cold War a collective security system was defined in terms of collective defense systems, such as North Atlantic Treaty Organization (NATO) and World Trade Organization (WTO) (where presumptive aggressors were clearly defined), and was limited to member states.

The core principle of collective security "is the respect for the moral and legal obligation to consider an attack by any nation upon any member of the alliance as an attack upon all members of the alliance" (Morgenthau, 1953, cited by Goodby, 1996). The successful operation of a collective security system therefore requires such conditions as a consensus on the identification of aggressive parties and compliance with the obligations of states to take actions against attacks on another member state. The serious limitation of collective security is that it does not work in a situation in which major powers are involved, either directly or indirectly, in the aggressive action. The failure of a collective security system under the United Nations is mainly caused by the absence of institutionalized procedures specifying the rules and parameters of an operation and the lack of an agreement among major member states to form multinational coalitions to enforce a particular course of action in response to aggression and/or the aggressor.

In practical terms, a collective security system was not able to operate under the bipolar international system of the Cold War period. The present global power configuration marked by the supremacy of a U.S.–dominated Western alliance system may offer a better chance to punish aggressors—as is being tested in Serbia, which is engaged in ethnic cleansing and genocide. Uneasy feelings about the use of power against aggressors, however, illustrates that policy makers are not naive about power but unrealistic about what can be achieved by collective security.

The use and manipulation of power can be used as a peace approach—merely concerned with the absence of war—but this can be irrelevant to the solution of basic problems. The maintenance of the status quo can become an obstacle to the changes needed to improve the conditions for satisfying human needs. In that sense, efforts to maintain the traditional power-oriented social and international order may lead to future dilemmas of insecurity. As John Burton argued, "power politics has failed domestically and internationally, but no alternative has been articulated and applied as policy. This is the bankrupt state of civilization at the end of the twentieth century (4)." Basically, peace built on military power increases the necessity for armament and justifies war for peace. It results in the heavy dependence on a small number of military and political elites for the security of ordinary people. The rapid development of military technology makes the traditional security system more vulnerable.

## Peacekeeping

In controlling violence, peacekeeping has emerged in reaction to the failure of the collective security system under the United Nations to prevent violent intrastate conflicts from expanding into enormous dimensions (5). Peacekeeping operations are designed to prevent the escalation of conflicting situations and the involvement of outside forces in support of belligerent parties (Naidu, 1996). The role of peacekeeping forces, which mostly consist of soldiers from neutral countries, are thus restricted to acting as a buffer force, maintaining order along borderlines or providing conditions for implementing a cease-fire. In accordance with U.N. resolutions, they are thus not asked to defeat any aggressor (Boutros-Ghali, 1992; 1995). The neutral forces are allowed to stay in the conflicted area by the invitation of a host country. The United Nations Force in Cyprus (UNFICYP) is generally viewed as a classic example of U.N. peacekeeping operations. Training and financial arrangements for U.N. peacekeeping operations require cooperation among member states under the leadership of the secretary general. Peacekeeping forces cannot be automatically used in any kind of dispute, especially those involving big powers; their effective operation has to rely on the intensive coordination among the states contributing their soldiers to the operations, the states involved in the conflict situations, and the coordinating authority.

Although it prevents regional conflict from spreading, peacekeeping efforts do not entail a problem-solving process. In fact, the existence of peacekeeping discourages further efforts to resolve deeper problems and only freezes the conflict situation into conditions characterized by a cease-fire agreement, or the "absence of war." In response to this limitation, the "third generation" peacekeeping operation is engaged in providing assistance in restorating basic services, food distribution, and transportation of refugees beyond patrolling demilitarized zones (Roberts, 1996; Druckman et al., 1999). Its overall goal, however, is restrained to the preservation of the status quo and much less for the implementation of long-term structural peace-building policies, or what has been referred to as structural, long-term conflict prevention policies (Smith, 1999; Wallensteen, 1998) (6).

## ARRANGEMENTS FOR HUMAN SECURITY

Building coalitions for peace from the bottom up is concerned with disarmament, demilitarization, the peaceful use of resources (natural and human), and the ultimate change in military institutions (Jeong, 2000; Barash, 1991). The significance of grassroots movements lies in citizen involvement in and demand for participation in the areas in which only government elites have traditionally exercised control and in which the nation-state has been unsuccessful in meeting basic human needs. Protection of human life and well-being rather then preservation of territorial borders with destructive weapons has begun to draw new attention.

### Civilian-Based Defense

Civilian-based defense relies on a noninstitutionalized structure to wage an effective struggle against foreign invasion. The nonmilitary defense strategy widely adopted by Scandinavian and small European countries needs a trained civilian population to defeat military aggression. Resistance is used by the civilian population as a whole on the assumption that massive, nonviolent resistance and noncooperation makes it impossible for the enemy to occupy and maintain political control. It is also assumed that highly visible preparation and the effective communication of the will to resist convinces the potential aggressor to believe that invasion could not succeed or at best not be beneficial.

Although nonmilitary civil resistance is sometimes criticized for the reason that it lacks sufficient deterrent capabilities, it may become a valuable means by which people can build up a self-sufficient, autonomous defense system on the basis of a nonmilitarized society. Despite the fact that the civil nonmilitary defense system may not function at 100% all of the time, civilian defense by social, political, and psychological means is a credible alternative security system (Moeller, 1996). With nonmilitary means, people would safeguard themselves better than the uncertain security given by military organizations—citizens' security can be made even more vulnerable to the weapons systems of adversarial countries.

## Disarmament

Disarmament can be considered along with nonmilitary defense methods and conversion of military production for civilian use. Global disarmament will be meaningful only when it deals with armaments around the world, both conventional weapons and nuclear weapons. Equally important, disarmament will be effective when it is associated with the creation of a mechanism that allows the promotion of peaceful change and renders the use of arms ineffective in determining world affairs.

In reaction to the problems that arise from the use of power for achieving peace, disarmament aims at the prohibition of research, tests, production, possession, and use of weapons. The establishment of a monitoring system is needed to implement an agreement on disarmament (Rogers, 1996). The difficulty in achieving disarmament stems from such political obstacles as the rejection of international verification by sovereign states. They would not want to give up exclusive control over an armament process because of a lack of mutual trust and good will in an existing international system. Some other technical problems include inaccuracy in comparing one weapon system with another and the uneasy distinction between defensive weapons and offensive ones.

## Economic Conversion

Conversion efforts are directed toward changing militarized society and industry by transforming the capabilities and facilities for producing armaments. The idea of conversion emphasizes the fact that the continuation of the arms race poses not only a great danger to world peace but a threat to human welfare as well. The precondition for the conversion of resources from military use to civilian use is not general and complete disarmament; a conversion is also possible by partial disarmament or merely a reduction in expenditures on armaments.

On the other hand, a successful conversion process at factories and laboratories may encourage disarmament. As is suggested by the slow conversion process in the post-Cold War era, however, the lack of cooperation from businesses and governments can be an obstacle to the transformation of the armament industry for commercial purposes. For successful conversion, political will is required, as well as the effective operation of the converted industries.

## Nonviolent Movements for Peace

In challenging dominant political and military institutions, nonviolent struggles can be based on organized campaigns of direct resistance against a hegemonic system, social oppression, or economic exploitation. Demonstrations, economic boycotts, nonlethal sabotage, and other types of nonviolent techniques have been popularly employed by organizers of peace movements (Jeong, 2000). Peace movements believe that alternative security can be promoted by abolishing military institutions.

Despite their fragmented and discontinuous character, peace movements illustrate that ordinary people can be engaged in opposition to mobilization for war. Campaigns against militarism on a sustained basis can be successful when they have a strong communal base of organizations and their commitments are supported by an ideology or religion that transcends national boundaries. It can be argued that peace movements were credited to some degree with ending the Cold War through their successful challenges to state power and security policies. The recent opposition to war against Iraq shows that the issues of peace have become transnationalized and globalized. In spite of their promises, however, peace movements can be hindered by a gap between the leadership and the grassroots base and an armorphous coalition character.

Various feminist movements link women's increased role in society to peace. They suggest that oppression of women reflects the special nature of the global dominance system; militarization is analyzed by the sociopolitical aspects of sexism and the underlying psychological factors. In feminist perspectives of peace and security, militarization thus results from social norms and relations and a culture that encourages masculine modes, values, and priorities. Human security can be enhanced by the equity of women in all cultural, social, and ideological contexts. In that context, feminism can become a significant tool for a demilitarization process through the particular role of women and the effort to equalize society.

## CONFLICT RESOLUTION: A PROBLEM-SOLVING APPROACH

If conflict can be resolved peacefully, there is no need to go to war. Peaceful settlement, better known in recent practice as conflict resolution, institutionalizes arbitration, mediation, conciliation, negotiation, and other methods in exploring suitable terms of agreement without using violence. Despite its promising assumption that war can be avoided by political arrangements, the traditional method of bargaining tends to produce only temporary solutions to the problem in favor of the stronger party and leaves the real source of conflict unsettled. Negotiation and bargaining among politicians and diplomats often disregards the desires and needs of the people directly involved in conflicts.

Traditional methods of dispute settlement based on the bargaining of narrowly defined self-interests have not seriously considered broad social and economic conditions as a source of adversarial relationships. Compared with state-centric models of dispute settlement, problem-solving approaches to conflict resolution shift their focus from a state to an identity group and from power to a social relationship on the assumption that only finding the hidden needs of people can lead to the real solution of problems. Collaborative problem solving is designed to discuss the underlying issues that do not come to the surface in power bargaining (Beckett, 1997). As Burton (1997) argues

> relationships are affected by the total social environment, including the family, education, health, housing, conditions of employment and almost every social condition experience by members of the society. If there is power domination in one part of the system, this will affect others. If there is to be a legitimization of authorities in societies, then it must be at all authorities. In short, a shift from power to problem solving can be practical only if it takes throughout the whole system, from personal and family relationships, through work relationships, to relations with authorities (7).

While the traditional settlement process is merely concerned with the maintenance of existing institutions and the preservation of the status quo, basic needs approaches to conflict resolution aim at structural changes. When vital values and needs are at stake, adversaries need to reach an agreement through understanding of each other's perceptions and values. The dissatisfaction of needs for identity, recognition, security, autonomy, and participation directly constitutes the source of international conflict. The unit of conflict and the locus of power thus have to reside in identity groups (characterized by ethnicity, religion, culture, and economic and social status) that are not represented by states. This approach may be effectively applied in places in which power negotiations within the framework of existing structures are unlikely to solve conflicts, such as Palestine, Northern Ireland, the former Yugoslavia, and Sri Lanka. As demonstrated in South Africa, the resolution of manifest conflict cannot be achieved without distributive justice (van der Merwe, 1998).

## SELF-DETERMINATION AND HUMAN RIGHTS

Self-fulfillment of individual human beings can be promised by a harmonious communal society that exists in decentralized political structures. Large-scale impersonal institutions rely upon force and intimidation rather than voluntary patterns of cooperation. Radical reform at all levels of social, economic, and political organizations is essential for self-realization, and justice can be achieved only through the decentralization of power. Self-autonomy and justice in communal life is the main goal of peace for minority group members in multiethnic societies.

Self-determination is a basic principle not only for realizing freedom to control one's own life but also for achieving a positive human condition. The quest for self-determination thus reflects the aspiration of an individual human being rather than aspiration of a nation. A human being's loyalty does not necessarily reside in the state system, and individuals can be reincorporated into a new sociopolitical framework.

Self-determination as a basic norm for the construction of a peaceful world provides such notions: the basic need of an individual human being should be a more primary concern than the goal of the state; personal freedom can be interpreted in the context of an individual human being's control over his or her own life; and self-determination includes the liberation from oppression and deprivation as its goals. Individual human beings endlessly look for various group identities to satisfy their aspirations; the state system is not a good unit for fulfilling a functional need for human welfare.

The demand for human rights is based upon the aspiration for the betterment of social and political conditions and liberation from injustice, poverty, and other human suffering (Naidu, 1996). Human rights have multifaceted aspects: political, civil freedom, socioeconomic well-being, and nondiscrimination. Scientific and technological developments in economic and social conditions affect the way in which human needs are perceived, and this makes the demand and achievement of human rights more universal and transnational. Protecting the rights of an individual or a group of people from state power imposes some limitations on state sovereignty, and states are obliged to meet certain standards in how they treat their citizens.

Since social order founded on injustice and violation of human rights leads inevitably to violence, the satisfaction of human rights is the precondition for peace. Human rights are inseparable from the achievement of social justice. In this sense, human rights can become an essential means to achieving the goal of peace. Human rights and self-determination seek the liberation of individual human beings from injustice and oppression in their endeavor to seek self-realization. Peaceless situations do not simply arise from the absence of manifest violence but from the condition or structure that leads to the unjust distribution of resources and power, a lack of freedom, and human deprivation. Human rights and self-determination promote the conditions for attaining positive peace.

## ECONOMIC SECURITY

### Development and Modernization

Many political institutions collapse when they are not fulfilling basic human needs or when satisfactory alternative social structures are not available, (Burton, 1979). During the Cold War, capitalism and socialism competed for adherence throughout the world. Neither of these social-political and economic systems was ever pure, and they can be labeled as mixed economies since most of the macroeconomic policies were managed by national governments. In the current international system of the post-Cold War era, the emphasis is on the prospect of rapid growth based on free trade, open market systems, and the free flow of foreign investments. This may offer efficiency in production that advances industrialized or developed countries. The classic model for development, replacing European colonialism, was based on the idea that the gap between rich and poor and developed and less developed countries "could be diminished if the rich countries provided development aid to the poor countries so that they could 'take off' and become developed" (Alger, 1999).

Similarly, modernization theories assumed that less developed countries should be patterned after the industrialized or developed countries, such as those in Western Europe and North America. In cultural terms, this linear process distorts centuries-long local traditional values and sees tradition as a burden for long-term economic and social progress. Modern social values are based on pseudo-universal industrial standards rather than ethnic and family ties. As a result, modernization theory, born within this context, gives more priority for building infrastructure and less priority for food and agriculture. Although some would argue that both bilateral and multilateral economic aid programs have often contributed to maintaining peace, they have not completely eliminated poverty, malnutrition, and the constantly increasing rate of people affected by AIDS and other diseases in many countries around the world (United Nations, 2001).

Modernization theorists distinguish between traditional economies, in which "patterns of behavior tend to remain constant from generation to generation," and modernization, which can be described as "a process of rapid changes in human affairs" (Black, 1966) (8). In a modern society, the individual is part of a "revolution of rising expectations," and citizens have less control over their environment than in traditional societies. Modern society thus alienates and deprives its members from the traditional community and can be traced directly to social disintegration. This gives rise to the "micro-war-zones" in the poor areas of the inner cities, in which the standard of living is low and poverty is widespread (Garbarino, 1999).

The discourse of modernization has been controlled by the dominant logic of power and justice (Foucault, 1977). Those who oppose the existing social order in an "industrialized revolutionary" society have been deprived of opportunities for developing their human potential. The gaps between nations at different stages of development and with different economic and military capabilities have further been expanded.

## Economic Well-Being and Equity

Economic well-being can be attained by equitable socioeconomic and political conditions. Structural changes are needed to create a society in which individuals' control over their lives can be maximized. In order to eliminate poverty, alienation, and political oppression, development should be based on human needs, self-reliance, and ecological balance. The conventional modernization paradigm, which serves the interests of modern political and economic elites, is often a threat to social stability in many Third World countries. In contrast to growth-oriented approaches, basic need development creates nonhierarchical economic structures at various levels, from the village to the global society. Given its grassroots orientation and reliance on indigenous values, technologies, and practices, an alternative development model can deal with the causes of structural violence related to the conventional modernization process, including the vulnerability of modern industrialism, bureaucratic control, urbanization, and the imbalance between society and the ecological system.

Indigenous development strategies are not compatible with an exploitative international economic system. The frustration that arises from a center-periphery relationship produces tensions between the North and the South. The elimination of an exploitative relationship results from the division of labor between poor and rich countries (Jeong, 1998). To weaken the infrastructure of dominance, developing countries need to depend on collective self-reliance and the effective use of their local resources. In promoting self-reliance and autonomy, priorities can be given to citizens' needs.

## ENVIRONMENTAL SECURITY

In a modern Darwinian world, our collective history indicates that as a species we have generated wars against other humans. At the same time we are held responsible for the extinction of other species. A genesis of violence can be explained in part as a struggle for hegemonic power over scarce resources. The Gulf War in 1990 is an example of this. The great ecological dangers that the inhabitants of the Earth face include total nuclear wars, industrial pollution, overpopulation, and the exhaustion of resources, to mention a few. Ecological threats are far more destructive than any war ever fought on Earth. Unless its inhabitants begin to view Mother Nature as a single unit made up of highly interdependent groups, humans are likely to perish arithmetically from pollution and related diseases, from malnutrition, or by nuclear war or accidents. In this regard, environmentalists developed the term ecocide to explain the capacity of humans to make the Earth an unfit place to live.

The threat to the future survival of humanity comes from the destruction of the global environment as well as catastrophic wars. Unsustainable economic growth diminishes the Earth's capacity to support life. Rapid industrial development, as well as the growing population, makes the management of the global environment more difficult (Zebich-Knos, 1998). Reversing global climate changes, acid rain, air pollution, and other problems requires international coordination.

Those who affect the conditions of the global environment should be responsible for their actions, and there should be certain norms applied to all. Conflict over the distribution of resources in the global commons, such as the oceans and outer space, also raises questions about exclusive national jurisdictions. Reaching international agreements on the management of our shared human heritage is essential for preventing future conflict.

## POLITICAL INSTITUTIONS AND GOVERNANCE

A world government has never been seriously considered by politicians as a means to overcome the problems associated with the anarchistic state of a multistate system. Some legal scholars, however, argue that the establishment of a central authority with real power can help maintain order through law and coercion. Skeptical of individual states as a reliable means, its proponents suggest that a world government is needed to eliminate the capacity of states to fight against each other, but an overemphasis on the role of concentrated, coercive power instead of political adjustment and accommodation does not guarantee peace, and a central authority may face an internal split and resistance.

Based on the assumption that people will easily recognize the necessity for change of the existing state structure and the establishment of a world system, international federalists emphasize an education and propaganda campaign to put pressure on political elites to accept the need for a supranational government and create a new constitution. This approach depends too much on the political elite for the creation of new global institutions. Moreover, it can be easily argued that the federalist government is not a good unit for political harmony and economic welfare, because a global-level political system cannot easily maintain internal coherence and keep balance between centrifugal forces and centripetal forces.

Overall, integrating and organizing various aspects of life is not necessary for human welfare. The experience of creating a federalist government at a national level (to which federalists often refer) may not be easily transferred to the creation of a global-level authority. It would be an unrealistic dream to maintain peace through a vertical integration process. Attempts to accomplish a universal, complete armament will face stiff resistance from nation-states.

Some believe that global organization would naturally be created by the necessities of humankind. An appeal to common sense in looking for practical solutions to problems faced by humanity can lead to building a scheme for the comprehensive reform of international political arrangements (Glossop, 1994). On the other hand, state elites would attempt to reverse the process of transferring political power to supranational organizations.

On the basis of the experiences of the European Union and its predecessor, the European Common Market, neofunctionalists try to establish supranational institutions through the fusion of economic interests. The "spillover effect" is the main strategy for the creation of a new political union. A neofunctionalist approach requires certain conditions for its success, including economic equality and a symmetrical relationship between member states, the existence of pluralist interest groups, the capacity of political elites and bureaucrats to adopt and respond to change, and the sharing of similar views among elites.

Differences in culture and economic and political systems limit the general applicability of a neofunctionalist approach to the creation of a supranational organization on a global scale. Moreover, the achievement of regional cooperation may hamper the effort for global cooperation and decrease the need for functional cooperation with other regions of the world. While international businesses and bureaucrats are likely to shape the process of global integration, ordinary citizens would play a less important role in a more integrated international political structure.

Given the strong sentiment of nationalism even in industrialized countries, exemplified by Quebec in Canada and Scotland in the United Kingdom, close economic relationships would not necessarily lead to maintenance of political integration. Beyond a high level of coordination of environmental, economic, and social policies, political integration may not benefit ordinary citizens.

The concentration of power at the center, whether it is for a world government or a new political union, is based on the assumption that a multistate system cannot serve for the common goal of humanity, peace, and welfare, and should be integrated in a more centralized power structure. Centralized power is assumed to operate better than small units, yet conflict cannot be solved by the mere integration of different societies based on various cultures, social traditions, and value systems. A more broadly and generally integrated society would not satisfy the diverse range of demands and the needs of various groups.

## CONCLUSION

Traditional approaches of security to maintaining peace are mostly concerned with the manipulation of military alliance systems and political arrangements. Conventional paradigms based upon elite diplomacy within a state-centric framework cannot answer very important questions when we define peace not only in terms of the absence of war but also in terms of certain social and economic conditions. Ignorance about unacceptable social conditions leads us to fail to see both manifest and latent causes of intra- and intersociety conflict and violence (Jeong, 1999).

If peace research should realistically assess the political feasibility of preventing violence and beyond that achieving social justice, more attention needs to be paid to transforming social systems as well as the processes of solving such imminent problems as the protection of refugees and humanitarian intervention. The quest for peace should be concerned with the elimination of structural violence that is not committed by individual actions but is built into the social system that is responsible for uneven chances in life.

Security and development should promote economic and social conditions that help individual human beings fulfill their capacity and value expectations. Revealing social forms of dominance allows us to find the conditions needed for structural transformation. The search for peace requires the examination of a structural environment that creates social harmony. The sources of contention in different types of conflicts are related to uneven decision-making power over the distribution of social and economic resources. In a more transdisciplinary and transacademic peace research tradition (9), peace values can guide both theory and practice.

## NOTES

1. Also see Sandole (1998). According to the author, "it is based on the assumption that 'mapping' any particular conflict in terms of various categories–e.g., (i) conflict; (ii) conflict causes and conditions; and (iii) conflict intervention perspectives and processes–constitutes a preliminary step to designing and implementing an effective intervention into it."
2. Cousens et al. (2001; "Introduction"). The authors argue that "although the idea of post-conflict peace-building appeared to hold great promise after the end of the Cold War, within a very few years the opportunities for peace-building seemed to pale beside the obstacles to it. This volume examines the successes and failures of large-scale interventions to build peace in El Salvador, Haiti, Somalia, and Bosnia-Herzegovina."
3. This chapter has significantly benefited from Chadwick F. Alger's pioneering work (Alger, 1999). He suggests a twenty-two-piece peace builder's tool chest that has chronologically evolved from the nineteenth century. The purpose of this chapter is more related to the assessment of various types of peace policies that are relevant to building peace in the twenty-first century.
4. See Sandole and van Der Merve, (1993: 57).
5. See Boutros-Ghali (1992; 1995).
6. Wallensteen (1998) differentiates between structural and direct conflict prevention policies. The former has a long-term perspective, "aiming at constructive future relations among contending groups." The latter has a short-term perspective and focuses on "managing the immediate conflict process."
7. Burton (1997) states that symmetry versus asymmetry may also apply at the international level. Power domination in the international and global level affects the relationships between the actors'-nation-states. (pp. 67–68).
8. See Black (1966: 9).
9. For an excellent review of the development of peace studies programs in North America and Western Europe, refer to Harris (1998).

## REFERENCES

Alger, C. (1999). The expanding tool chest for peacebuilders. In: Jeong, H., ed. The New Agenda for Peace Research. Aldershot, U.K.: Ashgate, pp. 13–44.

Barash, D. (1991). Introduction to Peace Studies. Belmont: Wadsworth.

Beckett, G. (1997). Social theory and the theory and practice of conflict resolution. In: Broadhead, L., ed. Issues in Peace Research, pp. 59–86.

Black, C. (1966). The Dynamics of Modernization. Princeton, NJ: Princeton University.

Boutros-Ghali, B. (1992). An agenda for peace, preventive diplomacy, peacemaking and peacekeeping. Report of the secretary-general pursuant to the statement adopted by the summit meeting of the Security Council on Jan. 31, 1992. New York: United Nations.

Boutros-Ghali, B. (1995). An Agenda for Peace. New York: United Nations.

Burton, J. (1997). Violence Explained: Political Analysis. Manchester University Press.

Burton, J. (1979). Deviance Terrorism and War. New York: St. Martin's.

Cahill, K. (1996). Preventive Diplomacy: Stopping Wars Before They Start. New York: Basic Books and the Center for International Health and Cooperation.

Cousens, E., Kumar, C., Wermester, K. (2001). Peace-building as Politics: Cultivating Peace in Fragile Societies. CO: Lynne Rienner.

Druckman, D., Wall, J., Diehl, P. (1999). Conflict resolution roles in international peace-keeping missions. In: Jeong, H., ed. The New Agenda for Peace Research. Aldershot, U.K.: Ashgate, pp. 105–134.

Foucault, M. (1977). Discipline and Punish: The Birth of the Prison. New York: Vintage Books.

Garbarino, J. (1999). Lost Boys: Why Our Sons Turn Violent and How We Can Save Them. New York: Anchor Books.

Glossop, RJ. (1994). Confronting War. London: McFarland.

Goodby, J. (1996). Can collective security work?—Reflections on the European case. In: Crocker, C., Hampson, F.O., eds. Managing Global Chaos: Sources of and Responses to International Conflict. Washington, DC: USIP, pp. 237–253.

Harris, I. (1998). A portrait of university peace studies in North America and Western Europe at the end of the millennium. Internat J Peace Stud 3(1):91–112.

Jeong, H. (2002). Peace building design. In: Jeong, H., ed. Approaches to Peace Building. Houndmills, U.K.: Palgrave.

Jeong, H. (2000). Peace and Conflict Studies: An Introduction. Aldershot: Ashgate.

Jeong, H. (1999). Research on conflict resolution. In: Jeong, H., ed. Conflict Resolution: Dynamics, Process and Structure. Aldershot: Ashgate.

Jeong, H. (1998). The struggle in the UN system for wider participation in forming global economic policies. In: Alger, C., ed. The Future of the United Nations System. Tokyo: United Nations University Press, pp. 221–247.

Lund, M. (1996). Preventing Violent Conflict: A Strategy for Preventive Diplomacy. Washington, DC: USIP.

Moeller, B. (1996). UN military demands and non-offensive defense security. *Peace Confl Stud* 3(2):1–20.

Morgenthau, H. (1953). Politics Among Nations. New York: Knopf.

Naidu, MV. (1996). Dimensions of Peace, Multi-Disciplinary Investigative and Teaching Association. Canada: Brandon.

Roberts, A. (1996). The Crisis in U.N. Peacekeeping. In: Crocker, C., Hampson, FO., eds. Managing Global Chaos: Sources of and Responses to International Conflict. Washington, DC: USIP, pp. 297–320.

Rogers, P. (1996). Nuclear weapons—Disarmament, control or transition? In: Broadhead, L., ed. Issues in Peace Research, 1995–1996. Department of Peace Studies. Bradford, U.K.: University of Bradford, pp. 59–78.

Sandole, D. (1998). A comprehensive mapping of conflict and conflict resolution: A three pillar approach. Peace Conflict Stud 5(2):2–29.

Sandole, D., Van der Merwe, H. (1993). Conflict Resolution Theory and Practice: Integration and Application. Manchester, U.K.: Manchester University Press.

Smith, D. (1999). Preventing Conflict Escalation: Uncertainty and Knowledge. In: Jeong, H., ed. The New Agenda For Peace Research. Altershot, U.K.: Ashgate, pp. 161–178.

United Nations (2001). Human development report. UN Development Program, http://www.undp.org/hdr2001/.

van der Merwe, H. (1998). Facilitation and mediation in South Africa: Three case studies. Peace Conflict Stud 5(1):56–76.

Wallensteen, P. (1998). Preventing violent conflicts: Past record and future challenges. Department of Peace and Conflict Research. Uppsala, Sweden: Uppsala University Report no. 48.

Waltz, K. (1979). Theory of International Politics. New York: Random House.

Waltz, K. (1959). Man, the State, and War: A Theoretical Analysis. New York: Columbia University Press.

Zebich-Knos, M. (1998). Global environmental conflict in the post-cold war era: Linkage to an extended security paradigm. Peace Conflict Stud 5(1):26–40.

# 26

## Democratization, Demilitarization, and Development in Africa:
### *Theory and Experience*

**LLOYD J. DUMAS**

*University of Texas, Dallas, Texas, U.S.A.*

## INTRODUCTION

During the Cold War, Africa was seen by much of the world as just another "playground" for the global geopolitical struggle between capitalism and communism. Most of the attention paid to Africa and the aid given by the superpowers and their allies was intended to do little more than secure the political and economic allegiance of African leaders. A great deal of the aid took the form of military assistance, but even when the aid took more benign forms, very little of it had anything to do with real concern about the political or economic condition of the African people themselves. It is therefore no surprise that when the Cold War ended, so did much of the attention and aid.

The truth is that for a very long time Africa has been viewed by the politically and economically dominant European and European-based societies (such as the United States) as a source of raw materials, and shamefully, for centuries, even as a source of raw labor. The intellect, creativity, and culture of the African people, especially the people of sub-Saharan Africa, have been considered something of a curiosity—when they have been considered at all. This attitude continues, despite the fact that, for example, two of the most influential and popular movements of twentieth century culture clearly had their roots in Africa—modern art (especially cubism) and rock music—and it persists even though it is by now generally understood that the entire human enterprise itself began in Africa. In a very real sense, all of us owe our intellectual, social, and cultural achievements—our very existence—to events that transpired on this continent millions of years ago.

To judge from much more recent events, Africans have not thought that well of themselves either. When colonialism in Africa finally gave way to self-determination movements, in all too many places oppressive colonial governments were replaced by authoritarian African governments. These governments often depended for support on Cold War military rivals and other outsiders intent on maintaining some species of neocolonial control. Despite rhetoric to the contrary, foreign supporters may well have preferred governments that ruled with an iron hand because they could deliver political and economic concessions without the messy, time-consuming, and uncertain business of democratic debate. Such authoritarianism would not have been possible, however, without the willingness of some Africans to dominate and exploit other Africans, to enrich themselves even at the cost of undermining any real chance their people had for development. The nations of Africa have yet to reach the point at which the great mass of the African people experience the tide of economic uplift that many expected or at least hoped for when the formal bonds of colonialism were first broken.

The end of the Cold War and the growing "globalization" of the world economy has done little for Africa: ethnic rivalries continue to flare around the continent, taken even to the extremes of genocide, as in Rwanda and Burundi; wars continue to erupt; and HIV/AIDS continues to ravage the continent. The images of Africa that Europeans and Americans see are images of starvation, sickness, and slaughter, reinforcing their basic prejudices. This has gone on far too long. It cannot be allowed to continue.

Economies built on extraction and exploitation and political systems built on militarism and authoritarianism offer no hope for a better life; they are recipes for more of the same. It is long past time for Africans to take control of their own future, not by isolating themselves from the rest of the world, but by moving in directions that can create the kind of political and economic environment in which the inherent creativity and intellectual capability of the African people can flourish. It is important to hold to the vision of a prosperous, democratic, and free Africa, but if that vision is to be more than a mirage, we must also find practical ways to build a road that can take us there.

Real economic development, not merely economic growth, is the key to a sustainable, long-term rise in the material standard of living of the vast majority of the African people. Real democracy, not merely formal elections (even honestly conducted contested elections), is the key to planting and nourishing the institutions and attitudes of freedom and democracy deep in the core of African society, and demilitarization is critical to both democracy and development.

## DEMILITARIZATION AND DEMOCRACY

People do not ordinarily relish the idea of killing other people, or look forward to putting themselves in the position of being killed or seriously injured, yet stripped of the pomp and ceremony and of the uniforms and rituals that is exactly what militaries are all about. Soldiers must be ready to offer themselves up to kill or be killed or militaries cannot do what they have been designed to do.

Accordingly, military training must be designed not merely to teach people to use weapons, but to take away their individuality and train them to unthinkingly do what they are told to do when they are told to do it. There is no room for questioning authority, no place for free and open debate; in the midst of military action, votes cannot be taken on which tactics to use. Military organizations are simply not effective without authoritarian command structures, and they cannot be built around democratic principles. It is therefore very difficult for truly democratic political systems to develop and prosper in militarized societies.

The simple fact that a society builds and maintains a military force does not by itself mean that society is militarized. Nearly all of the democratic nations in the world today have military forces. Some, such as Britain, France, and the United States, have very large, well-funded militaries. In all these nations, however, military forces are subordinated to and can only be activated by democratically elected civilian officials. Furthermore, there are strict and effective rules that limit the use of military force inside the borders of the nations themselves. There are also laws, or at least well-established social norms, in all of these countries that inhibit the formation and sharply limit the impact of armed paramilitary forces. They do not always work perfectly—witness the long history of the Irish Republican Army and the Ulster Defense Forces in Northern Ireland and the alarming growth of the so-called militia movement in the United States in the 1990s—but even in the United Kingdom and United States, both the level of violence and the general influence of these paramilitary groups on life in the wider societies have actually been quite limited.

The mere existence of national military forces may not be incompatible with democracy, but in order for democracy to reach its full potential there must be a major reduction in the size, power, and influence of national and subnational armed forces. Even where democratic institutions are firmly established, there is no question that a large, well-funded military establishment, together with its economic allies, exerts a corrupting influence on the political life of the nation. On leaving the U.S. presidency more than forty years ago, one of the most successful military commanders of the twentieth century, General Dwight David Eisenhower, chose to focus his farewell address to the nation on a warning: "In the councils of government, we must guard against the acquisition of unwarranted influence·by the military-industrial complex. The potential for the disastrous rise of misplaced power exists and will persist....We must never let the weight of this combination endanger our liberties or democratic processes (1)."

The full flowering of democracy not only requires that governments be elected by popular vote, but also that they are structured to reflect the hopes and desires of all of a nation's people. In that respect, even the well-established democracies still have some distance to go. Electing governments by popular vote is not enough. The qualified electorate and the range of political contestants must be broad enough to express the opinions and interests of all the nation's people. There must be a sufficiently free flow of information in the society that those who want to go to the polls can be well enough informed about the issues to cast a considered vote. People of widely differing political viewpoints must not only be free to speak out, but must also have access to whatever it takes to seek political office and make themselves heard by the electorate.

It is not particularly easy to establish these conditions. They are not fully established even in the advanced democracies of Western Europe, Japan, and North America. In the United States, for example, questions persist as to whether the votes of even all the qualified voters who went to the polls in the 2000 presidential election were actually counted. Likewise, the continuing problem of the corrupting influence of money on politics has once again emerged as a big public issue. Despite the many difficulties, however, it is important to keep trying to move political systems in that direction.

It is important to pay attention to the structure of the formal institutions of democratic government. James Madison, the principle drafter of the U.S. Constitution, strongly believed that people pursued their self-interest even when it ran counter to the "aggregate interests of the community," and so could not be trusted when it came to political power (2). This led him to argue for the establishment of an elaborate system of checks and balances, enshrined within the basic structure and organization of government, to protect against the undue exertion of power by any one faction (3). With specific powers vested in different parts of the government and no one part possessing the power to override the authority of the others, the tendency of those that people any branch of government to try to enhance their own power would be held in check by the same tendency on the part of those that make up the other branches. An underlying respect for and belief in the rule of law was also a vital component supporting this carefully constructed constitutional edifice.

Some argued that these precautions were unnecessary in a democracy, because the "people" do not need to be protected against their own will, but Madison understood that power corrupts and that since human beings are corruptible, the mere existence of democracy is not enough to assure honest and even-handed government. Without an elaborate constitutional system of checks and balances and a respect for the rule of law, it is all too easy for representative democracy to deteriorate into a "tyranny of the majority (4)." It is the combination of representative democracy, constitutional checks and balances, and commitment to the rule of law—the combination that has come to be known as "liberal democracy"—that is the best guarantor of government driven by the will of the majority but protective of the rights of the minority. With the benefit of two centuries of hindsight, it is even clearer today than in Madison's time that his depressing conclusions about the nature of human political corruptibility were essentially correct and that his strategy for dealing with this problem was basically sound.

The full flowering of democracy is not restricted to the establishment of the formal institutions of democratic government; it is also important to build the underlying infrastructure of civil society from which democracy draws its strength and durability. Civil society is neither government nor business, but both the set of formal institutions and the informal relationships and traditions that promote trust, a sense of wider community, and a shared obligation for building a better common future (5).

In strongly centralized states, such as those of Europe, civil society occupies the political space created when the power of the state is restricted by the process of democratization. Making use of the freedom to speak and organize for direct action or to influence the policies of the state, the institutions of civil society become critical to assuring that the public has enough ongoing political leverage to nourish and support the continuation and expansion of democracy. In Africa, in which much of the population lives not so much under the authority of a strong central state as under the authority of strong chiefs who combine judicial, legislative, and executive authority and rule by unwritten "customary law," the development of civil society might serve as a buffer against this authority as well, providing the wedge necessary to enhance freedom and democracy by facilitating the development of alternative sources of power and influence (6).

The formal institutions of civil society are nongovernmental, nonprofit organizations created by the people of a country. They are established for a wide variety of reasons: to help those who need help; to raise public awareness of social inequities and political injustices; and to further a social or political cause in which their members believe by providing information and encouraging peaceful civil action. A truly democratic society not only permits such organizations to exist and operate independently of control by business or government, it encourages and facilitates their formation.

The informal relationships and traditions of civil society are also of great importance. Democracy requires open civil discourse with tolerance of, if not respect for, the expression of opinions that may not only be critical of the government, but with which many of the people of the nation may disagree. Shutting out those who express contrary opinions—a phenomenon that, I'm sad to say, has increasingly narrowed political discourse in the United States in recent decades—has no place in civil society, but it is not so much precluded by government or formal civil institutions as it is inhibited by the culture and traditions of open civil discourse. Simplistic slogans, satire, and ridicule, on the other hand, do have their place in free political debate, although they too tend to close the mind to alternative points of view, and as the saying goes, "Minds, like parachutes, work best when they are open."

The formal institutions and informal traditions of civil society have little room to operate within the authoritarian structure of military organizations. Freestanding, independent organizations of soldiers that might serve as alternative centers of power and influence cannot be permitted. Debate about policies, strategies, and tactics is severely circumscribed. While militaries do encourage cooperation and joint effort in the service of an objective, their culture of obedience and discipline, their formal hierarchical command structure, and their tradition of rank and privilege are not conducive to either the open discourse or the freedom of action that are essential to civil democracy.

## DEMILITARIZATION AND DEVELOPMENT

Economic development is much more than growth in the money economy as measured by gross domestic product (GDP), because economic activity is much more than carrying out money-valued transactions. Economic activity includes the production and distribution of all goods and services that add to the material well-being of the population, whether or not they are bought for money. By that definition, economic activity does not include the production of goods and services that do not add to material well-being, even if money is paid for them.

Military-related activity belongs to this latter class. Whatever else can be said for it, military-oriented activity does not grow food, produce clothing, build housing, or keep people amused. It also does not create the kind of machinery and equipment that can be used to grow food, produce clothing, build housing, and so on. The military is simply not an economic institution; its activities are intended to serve other noneconomic purposes. The purposes the military does serve may be important, but they have nothing to do with the objectives of the economy. Military-oriented activities have no *economic* value because they do not directly contribute to material well-being, to the material standard of living (7).

While they have no economic value, however, they do have considerable economic cost. Military expenditures divert labor, machinery, equipment, and other economically productive resources that could otherwise be directed to projects capable of raising the standard of living. Their true cost is what economists call "opportunity cost," the material well-being that has been sacrificed as a result of this resource diversion. To this must also be added the economic cost of the loss of human life, the destruction of property, and the economic activity foregone because of the chaos and disruption that warfare causes. In the more developed countries, this cost has been high. In Africa and much of the developing world, the cost has been nearly incalculable.

Economic development cannot succeed without a great deal of economic investment. Education to raise the skill of the labor and improved infrastructure are the two most important investments for generating strong, sustained development. In fact, it is difficult even to imagine how economies can mature beyond pure dependence on the export of extracted raw minerals and inefficiently produced specialized crops without major investments in education and infrastructure.

There is no force for development more powerful than growth in the skills and capabilities of the labor force. People are at once both the object of and the most important means for economic development. As important as it is, however, education is not magic. It must be paralleled by and coordinated with investments in infrastructure and other necessary capital that create not only jobs, but the opportunity for productive, sustained, and decently paid work. Raising education levels will only serve to frustrate people unless there is also the opportunity for them to use and be properly compensated for their newly acquired skills.

Large-scale investments in education and infrastructure are critical, but they are also expensive. Countries of limited means cannot make the required investments and still maintain large, well-funded militaries. It is as simple as that.

In 1948, reacting to this simple fact, the government of Costa Rica decided to eliminate its national military forces entirely and channel what resources were available to more productive pursuits. During the past half century, Costa Rica has remained independent and been the most stable, democratic, and prosperous nation in Central America, while the rest of Central America has suffered serious economic troubles and terrible spasms of violence.

If the nations of Africa are to succeed in substantially raising the living standards of their people and replacing the bonds of economic dependence on the rest of the world with more balanced, mutually beneficial trade relations, they must accelerate their rate of economic development. Oversized, overfed, overly influential militaries are incompatible with broad-based economic development. Unilateral disarmament is certainly not required, but a substantial degree of demilitarization is a prerequisite for success.

## GETTING THERE: THE PROCESS OF DEMOBILIZATION

In the United States, the former Soviet Union, and many of the more developed countries of the world, the end of the Cold War raised the challenge of converting unneeded military bases and military industrial capacity to civilian use. Though it has been very poorly implemented in all too many places, this type of economic conversion has been well studied and is rather well understood. It has been one of the major themes of my professional work, in papers and books spanning more than thirty years (8). Demobilization has been given much less attention, however, largely because it has not been that much of a problem in countries with well-developed economies that can absorb soldiers returning to civilian life.

In Africa, in which few nations have a significant military industry, demobilization is a first-order problem. In Ethiopia, for example, after the end of the war in which Eritrea gained its independence, many soldiers were simply released from their military duties and told to go home. No special attempt was made to integrate them into civilian life. Many of them had been in the military so long that they knew little—if anything—else, so when they were sent home, they took their guns with them. Used to a military life and without any real civilian skills, they turned into roving bandits who preyed on people in the countryside and further disrupted economic life. A great deal of damage was done before the government finally decided to undertake a variety of programs specifically aimed at retraining and otherwise reintegrating former soldiers into civilian life. These programs have apparently met with considerable success. It was a painful but important lesson to learn.

Both retraining and reorientation are key components of successful demobilization of military and paramilitary forces, as well as to their thoroughgoing reintegration into civilian society. Many troops within official military and unofficial paramilitary forces in less developed countries have relatively little skill relevant to civilian economic activity. This is especially true where armed conflicts have been protracted and where many have entered the military or paramilitary as children, as has become increasingly common in Africa and elsewhere.

It is necessary to help those who are being demobilized to acquire skills that will make them more suitable for employment in already existing or newly emerging economic opportunities within their country. It is just as important to help them adopt ways of thinking that are more compatible with the civilian world and to help them unlearn some of the mental orientation they developed as soldiers. The demobilized soldier must learn to abandon the mindset of unquestioned obedience and the use of extreme violence to achieve objectives in favor of a way of thinking that is oriented to creation, initiative, and peaceful cooperation as the means to success. It is not safe to assume that such an alteration in ways of thinking will happen automatically, especially if the demobilizing soldiers began their military careers as children.

There have been a number of attempts at demobilization in Africa since the early 1980s, some successful, some unsuccessful. They include, for example, reductions in the size of military security forces in Chad, Eritrea, Ethiopia, Mozambique, Namibia, Uganda, and Zimbabwe. Typically, the ex-combatants being demobilized are at best only partially illiterate. They are generally low skilled and have little or no personal property, housing, or land. At the same time, they may have many dependents. In addition, at least some have suffered significant physical and/or mental trauma as a result of their combat experiences, as is true of many, if not all, combat veterans. Such individuals cannot simply be mustered out of the armed forces and told to go home.

Nicole Ball has suggested an analytically useful division of demobilization into four main phases: assembly, discharge, short-term reinsertion, and long-term reintegration (9). Assembly brings soldiers to a specific geographic area so they can be counted, registered, and disarmed. Because they must be supplied with shelter, food, clothing, sanitary facilities, and medical care while in these special assembly enclaves, there are strong financial pressures to discharge them quickly. When demobilization is the result of negotiation rather than the defeat of one side by the other, a maximum time span for discharge is often written into the agreement.

For various reasons, including the importance of having sufficient time and resources to retrain and reorient the demobilizing soldiers properly, several years of assembly and encampment might be required. This is particularly true when large numbers of former combatants are being demobilized. Gathering them in one place may reduce the cost of retraining and reorientation as well. The assembly period is also used to provide information and tangible packages of cash and/or in-kind assistance, such as civilian clothing, household utensils, building material, seeds, or tools.

During the discharge phase, it is a good idea to transport the ex-soldiers (and their dependents) to the areas in which they intend to settle rather than leaving them to find their own way. This is not only helpful to them, it helps assure that the ex-combatants do not all congregate in the same place and create problems in the future.

Once transported to their settlement areas, the short-term reinsertion phase begins. Reorientation sessions in their new surroundings can help them readjust to the civilian roles they are now expected to play. People from the local community should probably be involved in these reorientation sessions as well. Other short-term reinsertion assistance, such as providing some food, household goods, and temporary shelter, may also be useful, but it is important not to go too far lest demobilizing soldiers get the idea they will be permanently on the dole. Too much assistance may also generate resentment on the part of their neighbors that can interfere with their ability to successfully reintegrate into civilian society in the long term.

Even if the other stages of demobilization succeed, long-term reintegration of ex-combatants can still be difficult. Reintegration does not just involve economic success; former soldiers and their families must also become an accepted part of the communities in which they now live. If they are veterans of a popular war or successful liberation struggle, they may be seen as heroes, in which case social acceptance will not be a problem, but if they have been part of a government or guerrilla force that killed many of their own people, destroyed a great deal of property, and made the lives of people in the community miserable, long-term reintegration will be much harder to achieve. It must therefore unavoidably be part of a long, painful, and complex process of reconciliation.

There are too many people with too many guns in too many places in Africa. Even when they are not killing people, destroying property, and disrupting life, they are draining the economy and holding back political progress toward democracy. Demilitarization is vital, but it cannot succeed without effective programs of demobilization, programs that can ease the transition of soldiers to economically productive civilians.

## WHAT ABOUT SECURITY?

It may be true that overlarge, overly influential armed forces burden the economy and interfere with the full development of democracy. Still, internal and external security are important to both political stability and successful economic development. Neither democracy nor development can flourish in the midst of chaos. Militaries and police forces under the control of democratic governments have a role to play, but the inherent tension between democracy and development on the one hand and armed forces on the other makes it wise to put the greatest emphasis on alternative security mechanisms.

Interestingly enough, there is evidence that both democracy and economic development may themselves be powerful sources of security. Although it is not without controversy, a substantial theoretical and empirical literature exists in political science in support of what has become known as the "democratic peace" proposition—the idea that clearly democratic states rarely fight wars with each other (10). Furthermore, truly free and democratic societies can be more internally secure. Since there are many mechanisms for expressing dissent and redressing grievances, those who feel ill treated are not as likely to resort to violence to make themselves heard. This is strengthened when the formal institutions of democracy are supplemented by a well-developed and vigorous civil society.

No one needs to tell Africans how destructive and violent exploitative economic relationships can be, but successful economic development facilitates building *mutually beneficial* trade among African nations and between Africa and the wider world. Balanced economic relationships are much easier to establish and maintain among countries at higher levels of development; they have more to offer each other. Also balanced relationships that benefit all parties not only increase economic well-being all around, they reduce the threat of violence and war among the trading nations (11). More prosperous people are also less likely to arm themselves and fight when conflicts arise within the nation.

That balanced economic relations can provide security and help keep the peace is not merely a nice thought or a theoretical speculation; the European Union (EU) is a clear demonstration that it can and does work. The nations that belong to the common market of the EU have not only fought with and dominated the people of other nations, they have fought countless wars with each other. Some of the same nations that now are members of the EU also played key roles in two of the most deadly conflagrations of the twentieth century, World War I and World War II. Yet today, if you were to go to any of the nations that are part of the EU, stop people on the street, and ask them what they thought the odds were that their country would go to war with any other EU country in the next fifty years, they would laugh at you; it would not even be considered a serious question.

There are many conflicts among the EU member nations, some of them quite serious, but these nations are part of a web of balanced economic relations that is so valuable to all of them that they no longer think in terms of going to war with each other. They argue, they debate, they shout—but they no longer mount organized military campaigns against each other or against each other's interests.

In the past, Africans have experimented with common market arrangements, such as the Economic Organization of West African States (ECOWAS), with limited success, but such arrangements will have a much higher probability of fulfilling their economic and political promise when African nations are able to raise living standards enough to expand both their market potential and the range of goods and services they can offer each other.

## CONCLUSIONS

The military model is inherently rigid, authoritarian, and hierarchical; it is not a model from which free, open, and democratic political systems can be readily derived. If democracy is to grow in Africa, the power and influence of military and paramilitary organizations will have to be reduced and subordinated to the control of governments put into office in free and fair popular elections. The institutions, culture, and traditions of civil society must be allowed to flourish and weave themselves into the political and social fabric, becoming an inseparable part of the way things are.

Demilitarization is also key to the acceleration and sustainability of economic development in Africa. Africa is a continent of rich natural resources, but the only resource that can really make development happen is the people. Major investment in their skills and education, coordinated with investment in the capital with which they must work, is critical. These are very expensive investments; it is difficult enough for nations with limited means to afford them. In the face of the resources required to support extensive armed forces, it is impossible.

Militaries can only succeed in winning a conflict if they are able to defeat their enemy. The only way to gain by military activity is to take what you want and need from the vanquished. It is at best a zero sum game. Economic activity is a very different game. Not only is it possible for all participants to gain, in the long run it is likely that each will gain more when all the participants share in the winnings.

The dream of a more democratic, peaceful, and prosperous Africa is a workable, practical vision. It is not going to be easy to achieve. It will not be simple, it will not happen quickly, and it will not be cheap, but if Africans can throw off the militarized, hierarchical colonial model they have inherited and the authoritarian, exploitative way of thinking that goes with it, if they can reclaim and redirect the resources now being siphoned into economically unproductive military activity, there is no doubt that they can turn that vision into reality. The Africa of tomorrow will indeed be a much more peaceful, democratic, and prosperous place than the Africa of today.

## NOTES

1. This famous warning was delivered at the end of Dwight Eisenhower's second term as president of the United States. Eisenhower, Dwight D. "Farewell Radio and Television Address to the American People," delivered from the president's office, 8:30 p.m. Jan. 17, 1961, Section IV.
2. Madison, James. *Federalist Paper #10*. See, for example, F. Quinn, ed. *The Federalist Papers Reader*. Washington, D.C.: Seven Locks Press, 1993, pp. 70–77.
3. Madison, James. *Federalist Paper #51*. In, F. Quinn, ed. *The Federalist Papers Reader*. Washington, D.C.: Seven Locks Press, 1993, pp. 131–136.
4. It was the concern of James Madison and his colleagues Alexander Hamilton and John Jay about such possibilities, that led to their belief that representative democracy was superior to direct democracy. Attacked by their critics as elitist, they believed that representative democracy, with checks and balances, would provide "filters" that would refine the will of the people to the general benefit of society. See *The Federalist Papers*.
5. See, for example, the Institute for Civil Society, One Bridge Street, Suite 101, Newton, MA 02158.
6. It is worth noting that this kind of multisided authority of chiefs may have been largely an artifact of the colonial era, established by colonial rulers for their own convenience or to enhance their own control. Prior to that time, chiefs may have

ruled by customary law, but their authority tended to be more restricted. (I am indebted to Mahmoud Mamdani for his insights along these lines.)

7.  For a much more complete version of this analysis, see Dumas, Lloyd J. *The Overburdened Economy: Uncovering the Causes of Chronic Unemployment, Inflation and National Decline*. Berkeley, CA: University of California Press, 1986. A shorter and simpler exposition can also be found in Dumas, Lloyd J. *The Socio-Economics of Conversion: From War to Peace*. Armonk, NY: Sharpe, 1995, Chap. 1.

8.  See, for example, Dumas, Lloyd J. *The Socio-Economics of Conversion: From War to Peace*. London and Armonk, NY; Sharpe, 1995; also *Making Peace Possible: The Political Economy of Arms Reduction*. Oxford: Pergamon, 1989, and *Reversing Economic Decay: The Political Economy of Arms Reduction*. Boulder, CO: American Association for the Advancement of Science and Westview Press, 1982.

9.  This framework is embedded in a very interesting discussion of the requirements for successful demobilization and reintegration, derived from an analysis of a sample of successful and unsuccessful attempts in Africa. See Ball, Nicole. "Demobilizing and Reintegrating Soldiers: Lessons from Africa." In: *Rebuilding Societies After Civil War*. Kumar, K., ed. Boulder, CO: Lynne Rienner, 1997, pp. 85–105.

10. The empirical literature supporting this observation includes, for example; Bremer, Stuart. "Dangerous Dyads: Conditions Affecting the Likelihood of Interstate War, 1816–1965." *Journal of Conflict Resolution*, 36: 309–331, 1992; Maoz, Zeev and Bruce Russett. "Normative and Structural Causes of Democratic Peace: 1946–86." *American Political Science Review*, 87 (Sept.); 1993; 624–648, Thompson, William and Richard Tucker. "A Tale of Two Democratic Peace Critiques." *Journal of Conflict Resolution*, 41(3): 428–454, 1997; Henderson, Errol. "Through a Glass Darkly: Afrocentrism, War and World Politics." *New Political Science*, 23(2): 203–223, 2001; Russett, Bruce and John O'Neal. *Triangulating Peace*. New York: Norton, 2001. For an exploration of the argument as to why democracies rarely go to war with each other (even though they have often gone to war with undemocratic nations), see Russett, Bruce. "Politics and Alternative Security: Toward a More Democratic, Therefore More Peaceful World." In: Burns, Weston, ed., *Alternative Security: Living Without Nuclear Deterrence*. Boulder, CO: Westview Press, 1990. For an interesting critique of both the empirical and theoretical literature supporting the democratic peace proposition, see Henderson, Errol A. *Democracy and War: The End of an Illusion?* Boulder, CO: Lynne Rienner, 2002.

11. On the proposition that trade between pairs of nations is a powerful force toward keeping the peace, see Polachek, Solomon. "Conflict and Trade." *Journal of Conflict Resolution*, 24 (March): 55–78, 1980. In later work, Polachek argues that trade, more than democracy as such, is the reason why war between democratic nations has become so rare. See, for example, Polachek, Solomon. "Why Democracies Cooperate More and Fight Less: The Relationship Between International Trade and Cooperation." *Review of International Economics*, 5(3); 205–309, 1997. For a broad exposition on the importance of balance and other characteristics of economic structure and relationships in maintaining the peace, see Dumas, Lloyd J. "Economics and Alternative Secu-

rity: Toward a Peacekeeping International Economy." In: Weston, Burns, ed. *Alternative Security: Living Without Nuclear Deterrence.* Boulder, CO: Westview Press, 1990.

## BIBLIOGRAPHY

Ball, N. (1997). Demobilizing and reintegrating soldiers: Lessons from Africa. In: Kumar, K., ed. Rebuilding Societies After Civil War. Boulder, CO: Lynne Rienner, pp. 85–105.

Bonn International Center for Conversion. Conversion Survey 1999: Global Disarmament, Demilitarization and Demobilization. Baden-Baden, Germany: Nomos Verlagsgesellschaft.

Bremer, S. (1992). Dangerous dyads: Conditions affecting the likelihood of interstate war, 1816–1965. J Confl Res 36:309–331.

Dumas, L. J. (1982). The Political Economy of Arms Reduction. Boulder, CO: Westview Press.

Dumas, L. J. (1986). The Overburdened Economy: Uncovering the Causes of Chronic Unemployment, Inflation and National Decline. Berkeley, CA: University of California Press.

Dumas, L. J. (1989). Making Peace Possible: The Political Economy of Arms Reduction. Oxford: Pergamon.

Dumas, L. J. (1990). Economics and alternative security: Toward a peacekeeping international economy. In: Burns, W., ed. Alternative Security: Living Without Nuclear Deterrence. Boulder, CO: Westview Press.

Dumas, L. J. (1995). The Socio-Economics of Conversion from War to Peace. Armonk, NY: Sharpe.

Henderson, E. (2001). Through a glass darkly: Afrocentrism, war and world politics. New Poli Sci 23(2):203–223.

Henderson, E. (2002). Democracy and War: The End of an Illusion? Boulder, CO: Lynne Rienner.

Kingma, K. (1997). Demobilization of combatants after civil wars in Africa and their reintegration into civilian life. Policy Sci 30:151–165.

Maoz, Z., Russett, B. (1993). Normative and structural causes of democratic peace: 1946–86. Amer Poli Sci Rev 87:624–648.

Polachek, S. (1980). Conflict and trade. J Confl Res 24:55–78.

Polachek, S. (1997). Why democracies cooperate more and fight less: The relationship between international trade and cooperation. Rev Internat Ec 5(3):205–309.

Russett, B. (1990). Politics and alternative security: Toward a more democratic, therefore more peaceful world. In: Weston, B., ed. Alternative Security: Living Without Nuclear Deterrence. Boulder, CO: Westview Press.

Russett, B., O'Neal, J. (2001). Triangulating Peace. New York: Norton.

Spencer, D. (1997). Demobilization and Reintegration in Central America. BICC paper 8, Bonn International Center for Conversion, Bonn, Germany.

Thompson, W., Tucker, R. (1997). A tale of two democratic peace critiques. J Confl Res 41(3):428–454.

Tulchin, J. S., Brown, A. (2002). Democratic Governance and Social Inequality. Boulder, CO: Lynne Rienner.

# 27

## Transnational Labor Migration, Gender, and Development in Southeast Asia

**BRENDA S. A. YEOH, THERESA WONG, and ELAINE HO**

*National University of Singapore, Singapore*

## INTRODUCTION

In the last few decades, considerable literature has been produced on transnational labor migration, mainly attempting to "measure its extent, to define dominant characteristics, and particularly to evaluate its contribution to socio-economic development" (Goss and Lindquist, 1995:317). Castles and Miller (1998) outlined three main types of migratory flows: student mobility, refugee movement, and labor migration. Of these, transnational labor migration is the most significant in terms of its magnitude and subsequent sociocultural, economic, and political repercussions on both the host and sending countries.

Up to the early 1980s, labor migration not only took the form of unskilled labor, it also included a "small component of skilled personnel who were part of the 'brain-drain'—typically from less developed economies to more developed economies" (Iredale, 1997:1). In recent decades, however, under the forces of globalization labor migration flows have been quickened and their nature changed. Instead of a "singular great journey from one sedentary space to another," "multiple, circular and return migrations...occur across transnational spaces" and people "follow multifarious trajectories and sustain diverse networks" (Lie, 1995:304). New streams of migration have evolved, rapidly transforming the lives of millions of individuals and their families while inextricably linking the fates of states and societies together for better or worse. In this chapter, we examine the impact of transnational labor migration on the social development of Southeast Asian countries, paying particular attention to the identity negotiations and (dis)empowerment of women, gender relations, and notions of the "family," as well as policy issues pertaining to gender, migration, and development.

## TRANSNATIONAL FLOWS OF SOUTHEAST ASIAN LABOR MIGRANTS

The unprecedented pace and scale of economic, political, social, and demographic change in Asia in recent decades has brought about a parametric increase in the level of human mobility, the complexity of their spatial pattern, and the diversity of their group affiliations (Hugo, 1996). Southeast Asian countries represent an important scene for the emergence of what Castles and Miller (1998:141) call "new migrations," and function as both the "source" and "destination" of such migrations. Table 1 illustrates the stock of registered migrants *to* selected Association of Southeast Asian Nations (ASEAN) countries, while Table 2 depicts the stock of registered migrants *from* the same countries.

Migration flows originating from Southeast Asia to destinations beyond the region began in the 1960s, when discriminatory legislation against Asian immigrants was repealed in the United States, Australia, and Canada. Migration rapidly expanded in the 1970s and 1980s, when increased investment and trade networks between Southeast Asian nations and these Western countries, as well as large-scale refugee flows stemming from the Vietnam War, created the impetus and stimulated corresponding population movement. The American military presence in East and Southeast Asia further forged transnational linkages facilitating migration to the United States, particularly in the form of foreign brides (Castles and Miller, 1998:142–146).

Since the oil price rise of 1973, especially during the 1980s, the Middle East has also become an important destination for migrants from the Philippines, Indonesia, and Thailand. Although 450,000 Asians were repatriated during the Gulf War crisis, demand for foreign labor surged again after the war, partly because of reconstruction needs in Kuwait, and also the political sensitivities involved in employing both Palestinians in Kuwait and Israel and Yemenis in Saudi Arabia. While most migrants to the Middle East in the 1970s were males employed in construction, there was an increase in demand for domestic servants during the 1980s, leading to the feminization of contract labor. Asian contract labor migration to the Middle East operates within rigid frameworks; the migrants not only have to endure difficult working and living conditions, but also face a different cultural atmosphere, especially with regard to the status of women in society. The migrants, particularly women, are susceptible to abuse and exploitation, despite attempts of their home governments to guarantee their

**Table 1**   Stock of Registered Migrants to Selected Southeast Asian Countries

| Destination | Year | Stock | Source |
|---|---|---|---|
| Singapore | 2000 | 612,000 | Yap, 2002:282 |
| Malaysia | 2000 | 900,000 | Kassim, 2002:243 |
| Thailand | 1999 | 40,934 | Chalamwong, 2002:292 |
| Philippines | 1999 | 5956 | Go, 2002:278 |
| Indonesia | 1998 | 33,295 | Nazara, 2001:228 |

**Table 2**  Stock of Registered Migrants from Selected Southeast Asian Countries

| Origin | Year | Stock | Source |
|--------|------|-------|--------|
| Malaysia[a] | NA | NA | NA |
| Thailand | 1999 | 202,416 | Chalamwong, 2002:304 |
| Philippines | 2000 | 841,628 | Go, 2002:276 |
| Indonesia | 1998 | 380,173 | Nazara, 2001:225 |
| Vietnam | 2000 | 30,000 | Cu, 2002:319 |

[a] Official records for emigration from Malaysia were unavailable.

protection and ensure safe transfer of remittances through official channels (Castles and Miller, 1998:147–149).

In the 1970s, with the ascent of the first-tier newly industrializing economies (NIEs) in East and Southeast Asia—Hong Kong, Taiwan, South Korea, and Singapore—demand for low-skilled Filipino, Indonesian, and Thai workers grew rapidly. This emergence of NIEs and their concomitant economic progress created educational and occupational opportunities for their citizens, leaving other sectors in need of workers willing to take up jobs in the "3D" (dirty, dangerous, and difficult) category (Go, 1998:30). East Asia is the primary destination for Thai migrants (Chalamwong, 2002:293), and demand for Indonesian workers in the region has increased. While the deployment of Filipinos in East Asia (and the Middle East) declined in 2000, more Filipinos were migrating to European countries, especially Italy. Compared to a 16.2% increase in the number of Europe-bound Filipino migrants in 1999, the numbers increased by 28% in 2000 (Go, 2002:262). Nonetheless, Japan and Hong Kong are still important destinations for female Filipinos working as entertainers and domestic workers respectively. In addition, a relatively newcomer to the scene is Vietnam, with South Korea forming the largest market for Vietnamese emigrants (Cu, 2002).

Compounding these migratory flows are developments in the 1990s that point to a noteworthy shift toward intra-Southeast Asian migration, indicating that the region's less developed economies with surplus labor supply migrants to first- and second-tier NIEs (Malaysia and Thailand are in the latter category) with labor shortages. Migration is intrinsically linked to economic status, as gaps in living standards and disparities in capital and labor among Southeast Asian nations create the conditions for intraregional migration. Southeast Asia represents an eclectic mix of countries of destination, countries of origin, and countries that both send and receive migrants (ESCAP, 2002:10), thus intra-Southeast Asian migration is emerging as a significant dimension of transnational labor migration. In Thailand, Malaysia, and Singapore alone—three major Southeast Asian destination countries—there were an estimated 1.3 million foreign workers by the end of 1998. (See Table 3.)

The primary labor-importing countries in Southeast Asia are Singapore and Brunei Darussalam. Both Brunei and Singapore attract mostly regular migrants (professionals and less-skilled) from other Southeast Asian countries, such as Malaysia, the Philippines, Indonesia, and Thailand (ESCAP, 2002:1; 11). There were more than 612,000 foreigners in Singapore in 2000, comprising 29% of its labor

**Table 3**  Composition of Regular Migrants in Thailand, Malaysia, and Singapore

|  | Indonesia | Philippines | Thailand | China | Bangladesh | Burma | Others | Total |
|---|---|---|---|---|---|---|---|---|
| Thailand | — | — | — | — | — | 75,091 | 15,381 | 90,472 |
| Malaysia | 490,550 | 14,828 | 7,222 | — | 224,609 | — | 37,501 | 774,710 |
| Singapore | 100,000 | 60,000 | 60,000 | 46,000 | — | — | 184,000 | 450,000 |

*Source*: ESCAP (2002:1).

force. Foreign workers were concentrated in the low-skilled jobs, with 75% working as production-related workers, cleaners, and laborers, and 12% as administrators/ managers and professionals (Yap, 2002:282). While the numbers of foreign workers by nationality are not available, piecemeal reports suggest that the presence of Southeast Asian migrants in Singapore's labor force is not small. For example, skilled Malaysian expatriates constitute one of the largest groups of employment pass holders in Singapore; about 200,000 Malaysians migrate to Singapore to work, of which 30,000 are daily commuters (Kassim, 2002:9; ESCAP, 2002:13). On the other hand, Thai workers constitute around a third of the total number of workers in the construction sector, and it has been reported that in addition to the 50,000 to 60,000 legally employed Thai workers, there are similar numbers of illegal Thai workers in the country (Wong and Chong, 2000). It should be noted that even in this primarily labor-importing country, the inflow of foreign workers is matched by an outflow of Singaporeans to other countries, mainly as skilled economic migrants. To support and sustain the growth and expansion of the Singaporean economy, the government is encouraging Singaporean-based businesses and Singaporean professionals to venture beyond the territorial limits of the city-state. This regionalization process, which is also becoming increasingly internationalized, has been referred to as Singapore's "external wing" (Yeoh and Willis, 1999).

Thailand and Malaysia, the second-tier NIEs in Southeast Asia, are labor-importing-cum-sending countries. Economic growth in the 1990s had halted labor emigration in Thailand, but high unemployment rates during the 1997 Asian economic crisis prompted the government to encourage it again. Male contract labor constituted more than 81% of the 202,416 regular Thai emigrants in 1999 (Chalamwong, 2002:293), and there has been an increasing proportion of Thai females who work as domestic workers and entertainers, many of whom enter their destination countries as illegals (Chantavanich and Risser, 2000:16–17). The lack of job opportunities and fall in incomes in their own countries and the appeal of higher wages in the countries of destination are important stimuli for Thais to migrate to East Asia, Southeast Asia, the Middle East, and Africa (Chalamwong, 2002:293). Likewise, many skilled, semiskilled, and unskilled workers in Malaysia find employment in Europe, Australia, Canada, the United States, Japan, and Taiwan for similar reasons (Kassim, 2002:235).

In the case of Malaysia, the 900,000 foreign workers registered in 2000 were mostly engaged in manufacturing, plantations, agriculture, domestic services, and construction. The majority of these workers were from Indonesia (70.2%) and Bangladesh (23.1%), with others coming from India, Cambodia, Pakistan, Myanmar, Nepal, the Philippines, Thailand, and Sri Lanka (Kassim, 2002:243). Although female migrants have diversified to manufacturing and other services (Kassim, 2001a: 115), domestic and general services still tend to be female domains, while migrant women employed in the manufacturing sector, such as in the industrial zone of Seberang Jaya in Penang, are perceived by locals as a source of social problems (Kassim, 2001b:267).

The labor-supplying countries in Southeast Asia are the Philippines, Indonesia, Myanmar, Cambodia, Laos, and Vietnam. The Philippines supply the largest number of workers of varying skill levels, who migrate to more destinations of the world than migrants of other nationalities (ESCAP, 2002:12). The occupational profile of Filipino workers has undergone several shifts over the years in response to changes in international demand. Although the bulk of emigrants in the 1970s were professionals (38.1%) and service workers (22%), these two categories showed a sharp decline in the early 1980s. Instead, there was greater demand for construction workers in the Middle East, which expanded its contributing proportion of total worker outflow from 20.8% in 1975 to 64.4% in 1980. Demand for construction workers fell thereafter, however, because of the fall in oil prices, a decline in the number of construction projects, and the increasing budgetary deficit in Saudi Arabia. In contrast, the share of service workers and professionals (particularly medical workers, such as nurses) rose sharply, from 34.7% in 1985 to 52.4% in 1987. In the mid-1990s, the demand for construction workers surged again (from 33.2% in 1987 to 38.2% in 1995) because of the economic boom in the NIEs. At the same time, the proportion of service workers, particularly domestic helpers and performing artists or entertainers, has continued to rise (Go, 1998:13–15).

Indonesian migrants are mostly unskilled and directed toward Malaysia and Singapore because of their geographical proximity and cultural similarity to Indonesia. Approximately 96% of all Indonesians deployed in the ASEAN region headed for these two countries in 1998. Female workers mainly work in domestic service or as nurses, although they can also be found in the finance, insurance, building, and land-leasing sectors, while male migrants are concentrated in transportation, communication, storage (Saudi Arabia, Korea, United States, and Singapore), and construction (Malaysia and Brunei) (Nazara, 2001:216–217,226).

Like Indonesia, Vietnam exports mostly unskilled workers who are employed in the construction or garment industries. Previously, emigration was concentrated in Laos and Cambodia, but the destination countries for Vietnamese migrants have recently diversified. Vietnamese migration to Asian countries increased in the last few years, with South Korea representing the major share, followed by Laos and Japan. Beside that, Vietnamese migrants also go to countries such as Liberia and Kuwait. In 2000, Vietnamese emigrants numbered 30,000, compared to only 12,000 in 1995 (Cu, 2002:319). In such cases as Myanmar, Laos, and Cambodia, transnational migration consists mostly of unauthorized cross-border flows into Thailand involving seasonal agricultural workers, construction workers, and garment workers, as well as commercial sex workers (Chantavanich and Risser, 2000:17; Piper, 2002:9–10).

In 1997, the Asian economic crisis set back the magnitude and patterns of migration temporarily, especially for the most crisis-stricken countries in East and Southeast Asia (Simpson, 2001; Iguchi, 2001). Foreign workers were particularly vulnerable to displacement, because the manufacturing and construction sectors that they were employed in underwent disproportionately greater sectoral contractions. The labor-receiving countries—Singapore, Thailand, and Malaysia—sought to limit and combat illegal immigration. As for documented immigration, Malaysia actively reduced the number of documented foreign workers, while Singapore continued to stress the necessity of foreign labor for the sustenance of its economy. Meanwhile, labor-sending countries in Southeast Asia faced high unemployment rates and undertook proactive roles in encouraging their citizens to seek overseas employment: the Philippine government identified key market niches in which Filipino workers could have a competitive edge, Thailand provided low-interest loans for emigrants, and the Malaysian government withdrew the ruling that its citizens apprehended abroad for overstaying should have their visas impounded by the immigration authority upon their return (Simpson, 2001:12–13).

Given such sweeping changes in the trajectories and constitution of migration flows among Southeast Asian countries in the past decades, an important trend noted from the 1980s is that women were taking an increasingly prominent part in the contract labor system (Wille and Passl, 2001; Truong, 1996). The "feminization of migration" is largely due to increasing demand for labor in the service and entertainment industries in the Middle East as well as Asia. Women now comprise the majority of legally deployed migrant workers from the Philippines and Indonesia, most of whom are employed as domestic workers and entertainers (in the case of the Philippines) (ESCAP, 2002:12). In 1998, for example, 308,280 Indonesian females were deployed abroad, compared to only 71,893 males migrants (Nazara, 2001:224). Similarly, in the Philippines, the number of new hires of female workers increased by more than 16% in 1999, whereas that of men increased by only 0.1%. Female workers accounted for almost two-thirds of the total outflow in 1999 (Simpson, 2001:15).

## GENDERED MIGRATION AND DEVELOPMENT

It has been argued that gender-differentiated movements such as those we have sketched are especially significant in societies facing developmental change, since such population movements mirror the way "sexual divisions of labour are incorporated into spatially uneven processes of development," which become "a template for subsequent social and economic evolution in developing societies" (Chant and Radcliffe, 1992:1). The developmental impacts of gender-differentiated transnational labor migration can be felt at two main levels.

First, gendered labor migration is altering the way households and communities function, with consequences for familial relations, the gender division of labor, and the traditional (read "patriarchal") balance of power in Southeast Asian societies. Second, at the policy level, labor in-migration is viewed as a solution to local labor shortages, while labor out-migration is seen as a means of shedding excess labor or earning foreign exchange. Both constitute strategies for national development for various Southeast Asian states. At the same time, international labor migration is also increasingly regarded as a growing phenomenon that must be better understood and regulated at the policy level, especially with respect to the increasingly gender-differentiated streams that are giving rise to a large number of "vulnerable" female migrants on foreign soil.

## Gendered Migration and Impacts on the "Family" or "Household"

The "family" or "household"* is gaining recognition as a vital unit of analysis in studies of the developmental impacts of migration (Zlotnik, 1995). It is at the family or household level at which migration dynamics are most keenly felt and individual actors constantly rework their roles and responsibilities within the framework of changing circumstances in their family situations. In fact, Castles (1998:221) valorizes the family over the state in migration decision making in Asian countries, attributing labor migration flows to the "micro-level rationality of family survival strategy." The increasing participation of Southeast Asian women in migration has highlighted the need for a "family perspective" in migration studies (Yeoh et al., 2002a), primarily because women are still considered the lynchpin of the typical "Asian" family and accepted as "a traditional institution, reflecting a time-tested Asian way of living that is so valuable that it should not and cannot be questioned" (PuruShotam, 1998:12). The ideology of familism (Stivens, 1998)—with women positioned as the upholders of Asian family values and tradition—continues to remain entrenched in the modernizing of Asia and often features as a defining characteristic to distinguish what is Asian from what is non-Asian. The increasing participation of women in various labor migration streams—leading to women's absences, sometimes for long periods, from home—thus now raises the level of anxiety about the well-being of the family considerably more than when only men migrated without their families. With increased mobilities of the female workforce within and across national borders, there has been increasing interest in the question of what will become of the "Asian family" in the midst of Southeast Asian development.

Current research indicates the detrimental nature of the social and emotional consequences for the "left-behind" families, particularly for dependent members. In the case of the left-behind households of Filipino navy stewards, le Espritu argues that the prolonged absence of husbands often saddled their wives with a disproportionate share of household tasks (see Yeoh and Willis, 1999), while many navy children were "latchkey kids" at a young age, or had to "mother" younger siblings during their parents' absence. Hugo (2002) catalogues a number of effects from the strain of family separation, including a higher incidence of mental disorders among women and children, lower levels of school performance and impeded social and psychological development among children, and the abandonment of the elderly as a result of the dwindling of the "carer generation." He also provides evidence from fieldwork in East Flores, Indonesia, to support the view that the extended absence of the migrant can lead to marital instability and the consequent breakup of the family unit, which is evident from a higher incidence of divorce among migrant households

---

* The terms family and household mean different things. The "household" is concerned with such activities as production, consumption, and reproduction directed toward the satisfaction of human needs, while "family" is seen as inhering symbols, values, and meanings. As Croll (2000: 107, quoting Rapp) argues, however, it is important not to miss the "essential connections" between them, for "it is through their commitment to the concept of the family that people are recruited to the material relations of the household."

and abandoned families left to fend for themselves. Polygamous unions also represent one way in which fractured families are reconstituted, with male migrants taking second wives in the destination countries. The formation of liaisons based on unequal power relations between male migrants from developed economies and the local women has also been noted. In this regard, Yeoh and Willis (forthcoming) provide examples of Singaporean males who have migrated to China as professional, managerial, or entrepreneurial workers.

It should be noted, however, that the adverse social and emotional effects on familial relations is not predetermined. Hugo (2002) notes that of key importance is the presence of support networks for left-behind families of low-skilled migrants in maintaining resilient family lives in the absence of one parent. Migrants themselves who are physically absent from "home" may still contribute to the durability of the family. Asis (2002), for example, shows that while some Filipino women migrants she interviewed spoke of troubled marital relations and wayward children, the majority actively worked at maintaining "a sense of connection" with their children through phone calls, letters, and other means of long-distance communication. Hondagneu-Sotelo and Avila (1997: 550) present it as transnational "circuits of affection, caring and financial support" that succeed in keeping the families physically and emotionally intact during the period of their absence. Whatever may be the costs and benefits, it is clear that establishing and maintaining the family itself is a challenge in these circumstances.

Economic considerations often provide a major impetus for the migration of one or more members of the family. Economic disparities between sending and receiving nations evidently come into play, and opportunities to attain a better life for families at home have been the driving force for the large flows of low-skilled labor migrants from the Philippines and Indonesia to receiving countries, such as Singapore and Malaysia. In many developing countries in Asia, migration constitutes one of the strategies for the survival of the family or household, especially when it is faced with little or no surplus income (Asis, 2000). Flows going in the opposite direction are also economically driven, such as that of Singaporean men heading to China for investment opportunities (Yeoh and Willis, 1999). In this context, migration is undertaken not to alleviate poverty, but to create even greater surpluses, either for their families or for themselves. For both groups, the act of sending remittances back home is an integral part rather than a "random product" of the strategy behind migration (Sofranko and Idris, 1999: 468).

As migration facilitates the distribution of family members across space, remittance flows often feature as an important link between family members located in both "source" and "destination" countries. A study by Menjivar et al. (1998) comparing remittance patterns between Salvadoran and Filipino migrants, show that ties to family networks have a strong influence on the remittance behavior of both groups of migrants. Focusing on short-term circulations of the Indonesian transmigration program, Leinbach and Watkins (1998) find that remittance behavior is spatially controlled and temporally variable. The increasing feminization of migration in Asia has also led to the growing importance of remittances by female migrants working as domestic labor (Menjivar et al., 1998; Sofranko and Idris, 1999).

Analyses of the use of remittances by left-behind families show that although there is a general consensus that remittances constitute a valuable economic contribution to the family, their long-term effects are contentious. Among the uses of remittances are the fulfillment of basic necessities, investment, and the purchase of luxury goods. While a large proportion of remittances are used to sustain basic necessities, the distribution of remittances to other expenses, mitigated by kin obligations, help determine the long-term economic benefits to the family. Sofranko and Idris (1999) argue that rather than being an antimodern construct, the extended family helps to utilize migrant remittances for business investment purposes through the provision of information, thereby facilitating wealth creation for left-behind kin. Some households, however, remain trapped in the vicious cycle of poverty, even upon the receipt of remittances from migration. It should also be noted that not all members of the left-behind family benefit equally from the receipt of remittances. In many parts of Southeast Asia, the privileging of male over female offspring often means that the income and remittances sent back by young women migrants are channeled to their brothers' education or to facilitate their migration, while the women themselves are not accorded similar opportunities for self-improvement (Asis, 2000).

Remittances have been found to constitute an obligation on the part of migrants, especially if their migration had been financed by the immediate or extended family. Remittance activity is said to be set within a context of exchanges between the home family and the migrant, with the home family providing essential services, such as child care. The migrant's ties to the family sometimes rob him or her of control over his or her wages earned abroad, however. In her study of Filipino female migrants and their agency, Barber (2000:402) found this to be true, especially for the Filipino women working in Canada. These women carry with them ingrained expectations to be mindful of the wellbeing of their families back in the Philippines. Barber argues that this is an expectation of both the family and the Philippine state, rooted in the idea of the woman's duty to the home. In a similar vein, Woelz-Stirling et al. (2000) find that Filipina women continue to feel the obligation to remit money even as they begin new lives in Australia, often leading to conflict between themselves and their Australian husbands, which stem from different cultural practices toward money and family ties.

Beyond the fact that both the sending and receipt of remittances tend to be inflected in different ways by questions of gender, the act of migration itself impacts the reconfiguration of gender relations in complex ways. This has two main aspects. First, studies have shown that migration is a means of female empowerment, whether as a conscious strategy or an unintended by-product of the migration experience. Theoretically, migration may improve women's social position if it leads to increased participation in wage employment, more control over earnings, and greater participation in family decision making (Pessar, 1984). While migration may potentially open up space for resistance, disruption, and emancipation (Lavie and Swedenburg, 1996), and in so doing reconfigure gender hierarchies so as to improve immigrant women's positions of power and status relative to men's in the country of settlement, it may also leave gender asymmetries largely unchanged or even further deepen some aspects of women's subordination (Yeoh and Huang, 2000). For example, while it has been noted that through their work in foreign countries women migrants learn skills that they can then bring back to their own countries and households, the apparent benefits of migration for individuals do not apply to all who have migrated abroad for work. Indeed, deskilling often occurs in female migration streams that originate from developing countries and that flow to developed economies. One well-documented example is the employment of thousands of university-educated Filipino women in domestic work in such countries as Malaysia, Singapore, and the oil-rich states in the Middle East (Zlotnik, 1995). It has also been noted that generalizations about the positive economic impacts of migration on the family unit as a whole may not hold true for individual members, particularly women. In a study of the occupational mobility of migrants in Malaysia, Chattopadhyay (1997) found that while men managed to derive socioeconomic advantages out of family migration, the women who accompanied their husbands in migration did not obtain any economic gains, and even suffered economic losses if they happened to be unemployed. Evidently, either migration decision making only takes into account the economic benefits accruing to men, or sex discrimination in the labor market has been responsible for these male–female differentials. In sum, the existing literature on migration and changing gender relations suggests "contradictory outcomes whereby the position of immigrant women is improved in some domains even as it is eroded in others" (le Espiritu, 2002: 48).

Second, gender-differentiated migration may also lead to altered gendered divisions of labor within the left-behind household, the configurations of which depend on the existing divisions of power, negotiated along the lines of age, gender, and the relationships among members of the household (Chant, 1998). While the migration of the male heads of households may lead to women and children performing tasks traditionally done by men, including agricultural work (Hugo, 2002), the migration of women does not necessarily see men taking on the roles previously assumed by women (Asis, 2000; Lam et al., 2002; le Espiritu, 2002). As women—traditionally linked with care giving and the upkeep of the household (Zlotnik, 1995)—respond to the economic pull of new feminized migrant labor streams, they leave gaps in household work that are often picked up by other female members of the household, such as grandmothers, sisters, and aunts (Yeoh and Huang, 2000). Whether or not this empowers women is a question that does not lend itself to easy generalizations. Women who are left behind in the source area from which menfolk migrate may also find themselves taking on a wider range of roles and responsibilities, becoming more autonomous and involved in decision making within the family and community. In contrast, le Espiritu (2002) argues that while being left behind may give Filipino women more authority over family governance, it also increases their domestic burdens and overall workloads.

It should also be noted that while migration may lead to the redefinition of women's roles of being a "good mother" beyond that of "nurturer" to include that of "provider" (Asis, 2002: 92), the personas of migrant women (in the case of foreign domestic workers in Singapore) "as daughters, sisters, mothers or wives are not suspended while they are away from home; instead they continue these roles transnationally" (Yeoh and Huang, 2000: 428). None of the women interviewed in Yeoh and Huang's (2000) study saw themselves as "replacing any (living) male member of their families economically or otherwise, or talked of their status [vis-à-vis men's] as being enhanced by their sojourn overseas." Clearly, then, while the question as to whether or not migration is a strategy of empowerment for Southeast Asian women yields rather mixed conclusions, depending on the perspective taken, it is unlikely, at least in the short term, that there would be significant changes in women's identity as lynchpins of the family, even with the enlarged sphere of autonomy opened up to women as a consequence of migration.

## Gendered Migration and Policy Challenges

Increased mobilities in a spatially fluid Southeast Asian world and the feminization of migration present a range of challenges to the national policies of both migrant-sending and-receiving countries. Despite some differing opinions as to whether current policies are gender-blind (Piper, 2002) or overregulated with respect to gender (Abella, 1995), it is clear that there is increasing awareness that the experiences of male and female labor migrants are different. As such, policies can no longer take the experiences of male migrants as the norm or passively assume that the effects of policy are somehow gender-neutral. It is largely agreed that female labor migrants in Southeast Asia are more vulnerable to exploitation and abuse than men, with women largely being channeled into stereotypically "women's jobs," which are low-skilled and low-paying. Where the combination of these factors already leaves large numbers of foreign women workers vulnerable to abuse and exploitation, the fact that most of these women are in domestic work adds another level of vulnerability as women become dispersed among and subsequently sequestered in individual households. Not only are they subject to the vagaries of their employers' control within the privacy of the domestic sphere, they are denied access to collective bargaining power and are often beyond the reach of public surveillance. Moreover, governments tend not to police the private sphere, as this is not equated with the workplace (Piper, 2002:1, 7, 12). Governments, however, are beginning to recognize the need to regulate female migration, sometimes going to the extent of attempting to tightly control the flow of women in ways that worsen the problem of female vulnerability (Abella, 1995); for example, limiting women to typically "female" jobs, such as domestic helpers and entertainers.

## Policy Initiatives at the International Level

The challenges faced by transnational migrants have long been recognized in the international arena. To date, three international instruments have been developed to protect migrant workers and their families. The first two, adopted by the International Labour Office (ILO), are the Migration of Employment Convention of 1949 (ILO Convention no. 97) and the Migrant Workers (supplementary provisions) Convention of 1975 (ILO Convention no. 143). While these conventions are motivated by socioeconomic changes in Europe—particularly the desire to regulate the movement of surplus labor in Europe and to control illegal migration—these treaties also reinforce the Universal Declaration of Human Rights. A third instrument—the United Nations International Convention on the Protection of the Rights of All Migrant Workers and the Members of their Families (MWC)—extends basic human rights to all migrant workers, whether documented or undocumented, with additional provisions for documented migrant workers and their families.[*]

In practice, however, these instruments currently have few teeth. The MWC, for example, has been ratified by nineteen member states, but requires twenty

---

[*] Hune (1991: 812) feels that the convention does not go far enough to address the special situation in which migrant women find themselves, arguing that it does not address the fact that women's work and men's work are generally not the same, that there is no protection from the inequity of men's wages and women's wages, and that there is a lack of specific attention to the sexual exploitation and victimization of women migrant workers.

signatures before it comes into force, which still has not happened twelve years after its adoption.* Most of the states that have ratified the convention are migrant-sending rather than migrant-receiving countries. Of these states only two are in Southeast Asia—including the Philippines which sent 800,000 female labor migrants abroad in 1999 and is the largest exporter of labor migrants in the region.

## Policy Initiatives at the National Level and Bilateral Agreements

The ratification status of international policy instruments on migrant protection points to a divergence between migrant-sending and migrant-receiving countries on the issue; while sending states are under pressure to protect their citizens abroad, receiving states are hard-pressed to police the large numbers of migrants arriving in their territory. The specific policies of sending and receiving states reflect varying responses to gender-differentiated migration.

The major migrant-sending states in the region include the Philippines, Indonesia, and Thailand. Female labor migration is perceived as beneficial by these states in terms of the remittances sent back by migrants, as well as a means by which to alleviate unemployment. As Truong (1996: 43) argues, "balance of payment and debt politics [in labor-exporting countries] have instumentalized female migrant workers as a source of remittance and hence foreign exchange." The Indonesian government actively promotes international contract labor, focusing its efforts on certain parts of the country and offering to pay the expenses and insurance of initial migrants. The Thai government increased its efforts to promote contract labor, especially during the financial crisis in 1997, and the Filipino government has in place institutions to regulate the deployment of Filipinos overseas, as well as pre-departure training (Wille and Passl, 2001). The promotion of contract labor can result in the channeling of women into a small range of occupations that leave them vulnerable to exploitation, however (Piper, 2002:6). Even more pervasive is the promotion of certain occupations deemed to be typically "male" or "female." Tyner (1996:408), for example, shows the extent to which policies in the Philippines deliberately promote the socially constructed sexual division of labor as "natural"—Filipino men serving as navy stewards, for example, while Filipino women are typecast as nurses and domestic workers. In short, the transnational labor market is "not only segmented but also gendered" (ESCAP, 2002: 25).

Oishi (2001) argues that emigration policies for women tend to be "value-driven," while those for men are "economically driven." Stories of abuse and exploitation of local women in foreign countries often draw emotional responses from the public, appealing to the idea of women as the weaker sex. She believes that this has prompted countries to place controls on women where such regulations do not exist for men. These include the Indonesian government's stipulation that women must be at least twenty-two years old to migrate, and as domestic workers, that are restricted to certain destination countries. The Indonesian government also attempts to regulate recruitment firms that deal with overseas labor (Wille and Passl, 2001). The Thai government has in place a ban on the recruitment of women except in the

---

* In December 2002, the MWC came into force with its ratification by East Timor, the 20th signatory. However it remains to be seen what impact the MWC will have on migrant workers' rights.

case of selected destination countries, and in Myanmar the recruitment of female workers is banned, except for professional women.

In the Philippines, women who wish to work as overseas contract workers (OCWs) must be at least twenty-one years old; nurses must possess a degree in nursing and have had at least one year's work experience in the Philippines. Value-driven policies for female migrants have an additional resonance here. It was the execution of a domestic worker (Flor Contemplacion) for murder in Singapore in 1995 that led to a tremendous public outcry over the plight of overseas workers and catalyzed the policy process. The Migrant Workers and Overseas Filipino Act—the "Magna Carta" for OCWs—was passed in the same year, mandating all government efforts to protect the rights and welfare of overseas Filipinos. While the Philippines has taken the lead among Southeast Asian countries in formally recognizing the contribution of OCWs to the national economy, and with the 1995 act, put "in black and white what the government should do to better manage both the functional and dysfunctional dimensions of the diaspora" (Gonzales, 1998: 130, quoting Battistella, 1995), few of the other labor-exporting countries in the region place an accountable system of protection of the rights of migrant workers (Truong, 1996: 43).

Even in the case of the Philippines, negotiating formal bilateral labor agreements for the protection and welfare of their OCWs is ridden with difficulties. Gonzalez (1998: 133) notes that the two most common arguments raised by receiving countries that balk at such negotiations are that "(1) OCWs are subject to the same laws and regulations as nationals and therefore need no special attention and (2) terms of employment are negotiated between OCWs and private employers or agencies, which is a procedure that [the host government] would not like to get involved in." In Singapore, where about 80,000 Filipinas work as domestics, one stumbling block to achieving a mutually agreeable bilateral agreement lies in the fact that eight out of ten Filipinas who come to Singapore for jobs arrive as tourists, thereby bypassing the processing and orientation programs conducted by Philippine state agencies. While the Singapore government is prepared to grant these tourists-turned-workers pre-approved work permits collected on arrival, the Philippine government deems this "illegal" overseas employment. This "discrepancy" makes it harder for Philippine state agencies to track and protect their own nationals working abroad.

As Battistella (quoted in Gonzales, 1998: 137) notes, "while citizens abroad are covered by a whole range of standards (international law, humanitarian law, bilateral and multilateral agreements), the actual implementation of the law is limited by the standards and practices of the host country." The "limits" of the law and associated policies in host countries often stem largely from the notion that labor migrants of the unskilled or less skilled categories should constitute a transient workforce (Yeoh et al., 2002b), and therefore must be discouraged from putting down roots in the host society. Such policies include contracts allowing migrant workers to stay in the receiving country for only a limited period of time (usually two years) (Wille and Passl, 2001), and limiting their mobility by requiring them to stick to assigned sectors or specific employers (ESCAP, 2002: 40). Family reunification in the host country is proscribed, and in Singapore, not only is marriage between foreign domestic workers and Singaporean men prohibited, migrant women working as domestics are screened twice yearly for pregnancy, HIV/AIDS, and sexually transmitted diseases (STDs) on pain of repatriation. In short, unskilled and low-skilled labor migrants "are only allowed to take part in the economic life of their host countries and are excluded from the social, cultural and political realms [as well as] deprive[d] of the right to have a family life" (ESCAP, 2002: 40).

It has been argued that the experiences of female migrant workers are different from men's because they endure "triple oppression" or are "doubly disadvantaged," as they are "more susceptible to exploitation, including sexual abuses, as foreigners, workers and females in the intersection of nationality/race/ethnicity, class and gender" (Hune, 1991: 807). It is important to recognize that migrant women who become domestic workers are subject to an added dimension of vulnerability because they undertake reproductive work that is not only undervalued but located at a site—the employer's home—that is marked out as a private sphere deemed out of the jurisdiction of the authorities. In Singapore, for example, the wages and other conditions of service of foreign domestic workers are left to market forces, a situation the state has consistently maintained is preferred because of the "nature of domestic work" (Yeoh et al., 2002b).

On a more positive note, there is growing awareness among receiving states that foreign female labor is becoming increasingly significant to their socioeconomic ambitions. Foreign domestic workers, for example, take over the duties of housework and child care, allowing local women to play an active role in the economy. Without significant changes in the organization of reproductive work in the host country—work usually assumed by women—importing female migrants to fill this niche is a strategy that takes advantage of the cheaper cost and flexibility of migrant labor (Truong, 1996). In Singapore, for example, one out of every seven households employs a foreign maid (*The Straits Times*, Jan. 13, 2002), a clear indication of the nation-state's dependence on female migrant workers to help sustain family life amid the major economic restructuring wrought by the demands of globalization. Countries such as Singapore therefore may not be able to put off calls for policies providing greater protection to vulnerable populations of female migrant workers. Countries that supply domestic workers from time to time have responded to cases of abuse and mistreatment of their women workers abroad by means of bans, and while these are neither effective nor practical in stopping the migrant flow, they have provided the impetus for the negotiation of labor agreements between sending and receiving countries. The realization that foreign domestic workers constitute a necessary part of the economy of globalizing cities as well as their isolation from society, the Singapore government has recently amended its penal code to increase penalties for maid abuse and to bar abusive employers from hiring foreign domestic workers, even though it has not been receptive to changing its immigration and labor laws to accord more rights to migrant workers (Yeoh et al., 2002b).

## CONCLUSION

As Hugo (1999: 31) notes in the context of Asia, "it is apparent that the gap between male and female mobility has closed and in many international and internal flows females now outnumber males." Truong (1996: 42) further observes that "international migratory processes in the last two decades have shown a clearly articulated gender dimension to which structures of states (*e.g.*, juridical-legislative, policy-making-making and bureaucratic execution), political institutions (*e.g.*, trade unions and political parties), and other organizations in civil society (*e.g.*, church groups, women's groups) cannot adequately respond." There have been strong calls for the range of organizations involved to work together "to devise rules and mechanisms to lessen the vulnerability of migrants and promote a more equitable sharing of benefits and responsibilities brought about by migration" (ESCAP, 2002: 41). In particular, the need for "a better protection regime and more efficient safety nets...to assist vulnerable female migrants" (Wille and Passl, 2001: 265) has been noted with increasing urgency.

As a starting point, Hugo (1999: 31) argues that migration policy in Asia needs to be better informed by stronger research efforts to clarify and valorize the developmental impacts of female migration. In particular he notes that "there has been an underestimation of the scale and significance of the impact both in terms of the economic contribution of women both through their involvement in work at the destination and their sending of remittances to their origins" (Hugo, 1999: 31).

Beyond focusing attention on more research in this area, it is clear that the negative aspects of female transmigration can only be ameliorated by the concerted efforts of a range of institutions and actors. At the very top, "decision-makers (both politicians and bureaucrats) must show strong political will to carry out much-needed reforms" to ensure that the issues are featured prominently on both national and international agendas (Gonzales, 1998: 150). Regional dialogue and bilateral (if not multilateral) agreements between sending and receiving countries that look beyond economic benefits to the overall welfare of the migrants and their families as well as their communities of origin and destination are crucial to create an effective "culture of co-responsibility" (Truong, 1996: 43).

Beyond the roles of sending and receiving states, it is also important to ensure that "civil society support and vigilance (e.g. NGOs, media, academe, women's groups, labour organizations, think-tanks, churches, and so on)" is strong and vibrant in sustaining policy implementation, especially the delivery of protective and preventive services (Gonzales, 1998: 150). A wide range of nongovernmental organizations (NGOs), for example, is involved in all phases of the overseas contract work cycle and should be treated by governments as partners that supplement and complement the activities of state agencies in responding to the needs of female migrant workers (Gonzales, 1998: 140). Involving NGOs also brings to bear different perspectives and helps widen our understanding of the issues involved. For example, in the case of the trafficking of women and girls, while governments tend to treat trafficking as a border security issue, many NGOs attach a human rights perspective, emphasizing the sexual exploitation and abuse of women (Piper, 2002). NGOs and other civil society organizations also provide avenues to encourage active networking among female migrant workers, thus allowing them to participate as active agents in welfare-oriented or advocacy work. As Law (2002) illustrates, this has the potential to take on transnational dimensions as female contract workers form cross-national alliances to negotiate for rights and better working conditions.

Finally, it is crucial to remember that a number of issues embedded in Southeast Asian women's migration go beyond the reach of migration policy. For example, one of the consequence of gendered cross-border flows is the spread of diseases such as HIV/AIDS. (See Bain, 1998.) Mobile populations are found to be vulnerable to HIV infection "due to the greater likelihood of being engaged in risk behaviour when outside their normal social environments" (National Committee for Control of AIDS, 2000:5). In Laos, these mobile populations include groups that are highly differentiated along the lines of gender; for example, male truck drivers and construction workers and female sex workers. Such issues cannot be dealt with simply within the ambit of migration policy, but must be addressed by social developmental policies (Piper, 2002: 15). To take a different example, Truong (1996: 44) argues that protecting the rights of female migrants who become domestic workers goes beyond migration policy and requires attention to family law (including the recognition of domestic violence as a reality) and labor legislation and enforcement "to minimize the instrumentalization of their labor, and the treatment of their personhood as an expendable commodity." At the heart of the dilemmas that beset socioeconomic development on the one hand and women's mobility and vulnerability on the other, is the need to valorize women's reproductive work, to respect their personhood, to eschew gender stereotypes, and to work toward greater equality in gender relations in largely patriarchal countries in Southeast Asia.

## REFERENCES

Abella, M. I. (1995). Sex selectivity of migration regulations governing international migration in Southern and South-eastern Asia. In: United Nations, ed. International Migration Policies and the Status of Female Migrants. New York: United Nations, pp. 241–252.

Asis, M. M. B. (2000). Imagining the future of migration and families in Asia. Asian Pac. Migr. J. 9(3):255–272.

Asis, M. M. B. (2002). From the life stories of Filipino women: Personal and family agendas in migration. Asian Pac. Migr. J. 11(1):67–94.

Bain, I. (1998). Southeast Asia. Internat. Migr. 36(4):553–585.

Barber, P. G. (2000). Agency in Philippine women's labour migration and provisional diaspora. Women Stud. Internat. Forum 23(4):399–411.

Battistella, G. (1995). Phillipine Overseas Labour: From Export to Management. ASEAN Economic Bulletin 12(2).

Castles, S. (1998). New migrations in the Asia-Pacific region: A force for social and political change. Internat. Soc. Sci. J. 50(2):215–227.

Castles, S., Miller, M. (1998). The Age of Migration: International Population Movements in the Modern World. Basingstoke, Hampshire, U.K.: Macmillan.

Chalamwong, Y. (2002). Thailand. Organisation for Economic Cooperation and Development. Migration and the Labour Market in Asia: Recent Trends and Policies. Paris: OECD, pp. 289–308.

Chant, S. (1998). Households, gender and rural-urban migration: Reflections on linkages and considerations for policy. Environ. Urban. 10(1):5–21.

Chant, S., Radcliffe, S. A. (1992). Migration and development: The importance of gender. In: Chant, S., ed. Gender and Migration in Developing Countries. London: Belhaven, pp. 1–29.

Chantavanich, S., Risser, G. (2000). Intra-regional migration in Southeast and East Asia: Theoretical overview, trends of migratory flows, labour linkages and implications for Thailand and Thai migrant workers. In: Chantavanich, S., et al., eds. Thai Migrant Workers in East and Southeast Asia: 1996–1997. Thailand: Asian Research Centre for Migration, pp. 10–27.

Chattopadhyay, A., 1997. Gender differences in the effect of family migration on occupational mobility in Malaysia. PhD dissertation, Department of Sociology, Brown University, Providence, Rhode Island.

Croll, E. (2000). Endangered Daughters: Discrimination and Development in Asia. London: Routledge.

Cu, C. L. (2002). Vietnam. Organisation for Economic Cooperation and Development. Migration and the Labour Market in Asia: Recent Trends and Policies. Paris: OECD, pp. 309–336.

Economic and Social Commission for Asia and the Pacific (ESCAP). (2002). International Migration: An Emerging Opportunity for the Socio-economic Development of the ESCAP Region. New York: United Nations.

Go, S. P. (1998). Towards the 21st century: Whither Philippine labour migration? In: Cariño, B. V., ed. Filipino Workers on the Move: Trends, Dilemmas and Policy Options. Philippines: Philippine Migration Research Network, pp. 9–44.

Go, S. P. (2002). The Philippines. Organisation for Economic Cooperation and Development. Migration and the Labour Market in Asia. Paris: OECD, pp. 257–280.

Gonzales, J. L. (1998). Philippine Labour Migration: Critical Dimensions of Public Policy. Singapore: Institute of Southeast Asian Studies.

Goss, J. D., Lindquist, B. (1995). Conceptualising international labour migration: A structuration perspective. Internat. Migr. Rev. 29(2):317–351.

Hondagneu-Sotelo, P., Avila, E. (1997). I'm here, but I'm there: The meaning of Latina transnational motherhood. Gender Soc. 11(5):548–571.

Hugo, G. (1996). Asia on the move: Research challenges for population geography. Internat. J. Pop. Geo. 2:95–118.

Hugo, G. (1999). Gender and Migrations in Asian Countries. Liège, Belgium: International Union for the Scientific Study of Populations.

Hugo, G. (2002). Effects of migration on the family in Indonesia. Asian Pac. Migr. J. 11(1):13–46.

Hune, S. (1991). Migrant women in the context of the International Convention on the Protection of the Rights of All Migrant Workers and Members of their Families. Internat. Migr. Rev. 25(4):800–817.

Iguchi, Y. (2001). Migration policies in East and South-east Asia in the 21st century. Organisation for Economic Cooperation and Development. International Migration in Asia: Trends and Policies. Paris: OECD, pp. 21–34.

Iredale, R. (1997). Skills Transfer: International Accreditation Issues. Wollongong, Australia: University of Wollongong Press.

Kassim, A. (2001). Integration of foreign workers and illegal employment in Malaysia. Organisation for Economic Cooperation and Development. International Migration in Asia: Trends and Policies. Paris: OECD, pp. 113–134.

Kassim, A. (2001). Recent trends in migration movements and policies in Malaysia. Organisation for Economic Cooperation and Development, International Migration in Asia: Trends and Policies. Paris: OECD, pp. 261–284.

Kassim, A. (2002). Malaysia. In: Organisation for Economic Cooperation and Development, ed. Migration and the Labour Market in Asia. Paris: OECD, pp. 231–255.

Lam, T., Yeoh, B. S. A., Law, L. (2002). Sustaining families transnationally: Chinese-Malaysians in Singapore. Asian Pac. Migr. J. 11(1):117–144.

Lavie, S., Swedenburg, T. (1996). Introduction: Displacement, disapora and geographies of identity. In: Lavie, S., Swedenburg, T., eds. Displacement, Disapora and Geographies of Identity. Durham, NC: Duke University Press, pp. 1–26.

Law, L. (2002). Sites of transnational activism: Filipino non-government organizations in Hong Kong. In: Yeoh, B. S. A., Teo, P., Huang, S., eds. Gender Politics in the Asia-Pacific Region. London: Routledge, pp. 205–222.

le Espiritu, Y. (2002). Filipino navy stewards and Filipina health care professionals: Immigration, work, and family relations. Asian Pac. Migr. J. 11(1):48–66.

Leinbach, T. R., Watkins, J. F. (1998). Remittances and circulation behaviour in the livelihood process: transmigrant families in South Sumatra, Indonesia. Ec. Geo. 74(1): 45–63.

Lie, J. (1995). From international migration to transnational diaspora. Contemp. Soc. 24(4): 303–306.

Menjivar, C., DaVanzo, J., Greenwell, L., Valdez, R. B. (1998). Remittance behaviour among Salvadoran and Filipino immigrants in Los Angeles. Internat. Migr. Rev. 32(1):97–126.

National Committee for Control of AIDS. (2000). HIV/AIDS Country Profile—Lao PDR 2000. Joint United Nations Programme on HIV/AIDS (UNAIDS), Lao PDR, Vientiane.

Nazara, S. (2001). Recent trends in labour migration movements and policies in Indonesia. In: Organisation for Economic Cooperation and Development, ed. International Migration in Asia: Trends and Policies. Paris: OECD, pp. 211–229.

Oishi N. (2002). Women in Motion: Globalization, State Policies, and Labor Migration in Asia. PhD dissertation. Department of Sociology, Harvard University, Cambridge, MA.

Pessar, P. (1984). The linkages between the household and workplace in the experience of Dominican immigrant women in the United States. Internat. Migr. Rev. 18(4):1188–1211.

Piper, N. (June 2002). Gender and migration policies in Southeast Asia—Preliminary observations from the Mekong region. IUSSP Regional Population Conference on Southeast Asia's Population in a Changing Asian Context, Bangkok, pp. 10–12.

PuruShotam, N. (1998). Between compliance and resistance: Women and the middle-class way of life in Singapore. In: Sen, K., Stivens, M., eds. Gender and Power in Affluent Asia. London: Routledge, pp. 127–166.

Simpson, J. (2001). Introduction. In: Organisation for Economic Cooperation and Development, ed. International Migration in Asia: Trends and Policies. Paris: OECD, pp. 7–17.

Sofranko, A. J., Idris, K. (1999). Use of overseas migrants' remittances to the extended family for business investment: A research note. Rur. Soc. 64(3):464–481.

Stivens, M. (1998). Sex, gender and the making of the new Malay middle classes. In: Sen, K., Stivens, M., eds. Gender and Power in Affluent Asia. London: Routledge, pp. 87–126.

The Straits Times. (Jan. 13, 2002).

Truong, T. D. (1996). Gender, international migration and social reproduction: Implications for theory, policy, research and networking. Asian Pac. Migr. J. 5(1):27–52.

Tyner, J. A. (1996). The gendering of Phillipine international labor migration. Prof. Geogr. 48(4):405–416.

Wille, C., Passl, B. (2001). Female Labour Migration in South-East Asia: Change and Continuity. Bangkok: Asian Research Centre for Migration, Institute of Asian Studies, Chulalongkorn University and the Asia-Pacific Migration Research Network.

Wong, D., Chong, C. L. (2000). Men who built Singapore: Thai workers in the construction industry. In: Chantavanich, S., et al. eds. Thai Migrant Workers in East and Southeast Asia 1996–1997. Bangkok: Asian Research Center for Migration, Institute of Asian Studies, Chulalongkorn University and the Asia-Pacific Migration Research Network, pp. 58–107.

Yap, M. T. (2002). Singapore. Organisation for Economic Cooperation and Development, Migration and the Labour Market in Asia. . Paris: OECD, pp. 281–288.

Yeoh, B. S. A., Willis, K. (1999). "Heart" and "wing," nation and diaspora: Gendered discourses in Singapore's regionalisation process. Gender Place Cult. 6(4):355–372.

Yeoh B. S. A., Willis K. (Forthcoming). Constructing masculinities in transnational space: Singapore men on the "regional beat." In: Jackson, P., ed. Transnational Spaces. London: Routledge.

Yeoh, B. S. A., Huang, S. (2000). "Home" and "away": Foreign domestic workers and negotiations of diasporic identity in Singapore. Women Stud. Internat. Forum 23(4):413–429.

Yeoh, B. S. A., Graham, E., Boyle, P. J. (2002a). Migrations and family relations in the Asia-Pacific region. Asia Pac. Migr. J. 11(1):1–11.

Yeoh B. S. A., Huang S., Devasahayam T. W. (2002). Diasporic subjects in the nation: Foreign domestic workers, the reach of law and civil society in Singapore. Symposium on the Reach of Law in the Pacific Rim, 28–29, May 2002, University of British Columbia, Vancouver, BC, Canada,

Woelz-Stirling, N., Manderson, L., Kelaher, M., Gordon, S. (2000). Marital conflict and finances among Filipinas in Australia. Internat. J. Intercult. Relat. 24(6):791–805.

Zlotnik, H. (1995). Migration and the family: The female perspective. Asian Pac. Migr. J. 4(2–3): 253–271.

# 28

# Transforming the Developmental State in Korea Under Globalization
## The Case of the IT Industry

**SEUNGJOO LEE**

*Yonsei University, Wonju-si, Kangwon-do, South Korea*

## INTRODUCTION

Is the developmental state destined to fade away in the age of globalization? Since the outbreak of the Asian crisis in 1997, critics of the developmental state have argued that it would no longer be able to provide strategic guidance for the national economy (Kim, 1999). In their view, as its institutional foundations have eroded in the face of the forces of globalization and the exponentially increasing complexity of the world economy, the developmental state would converge toward the Anglo-American model. Given the recent track record of liberalization measures undertaken by East Asian developmental states, the empirical basis of these arguments seems credible.

The examination of the liberalization process of the South Korean information technology (IT) industry demonstrates, however, that the developmental state has a great deal of adaptive capability in dealing with new challenges (Weiss, 2000; Vogel, 2001). In the early 1990s, the Korean state embarked on "strategic liberalization" in the IT industry, which aimed at introducing competition among domestic companies before opening up the market to foreign firms. Ironically, liberalization was implemented not through the retreat of the state but by active state intervention.

In this chapter, I first present a brief survey of existing explanations on liberalization. Second, I discuss the liberalization processes in the Korean IT industry. Third, I provide a schematic theoretical framework explaining why Korea ended up with a unique pattern of liberalization. Finally, based on the case of the IT industry, I draw broader theoretical implications about the limitations and efficacy of the developmental state in the era of globalization.

There are several explanations on the determinants of liberalization. For example, it is argued that liberalization occurs as internationalists led by competitive export-oriented sectors gain political strength vis-à-vis nationalists (Frieden, 1991; Frieden and Rogowski, 1996; Milner, 1988), but this formulation has difficulty in demonstrating how to overcome collective action problems. When the benefits of liberalization are dispersed and the costs concentrated, the potential beneficiaries of liberalization are not willing to bear the costs; that is, interests and preferences often do not correspond. In this case, only the government—if insulated from societal pressure—may proceed with liberalization. Moreover, in the case of Korea, its unique industrial structure makes it difficult to identify sectoral interests. Because big conglomerates in Korea, known as *chaebol*, are highly diversified and involved in both export-oriented and import-competing industries, there is no evidence that export-oriented sectors favored liberalization.

Moreover, the formulation falls short of capturing key features of liberalization in Korea, such as the mode and timing of liberalization. What made the Korean state decide to introduce liberalization in the first place? Why did liberalization in the Korean IT sector proceed through the active involvement of the state and not by the retreat of the state? To answer these questions, I argue that an ideological shift within the political leadership and an institutional transformation in the IT sector combined to determine the outcome. First, in terms of managing the economy, the political leadership made a fundamental change toward liberalization, departing from the past legacies of developmentalism. Second, the Korean state undertook a major restructuring of the government in order to build highly integrated *sectoral institutions* in the IT industry. Largely reflecting the emerging technological change, the reformulation of institutions minimized the functional mismatch between ministries' jurisdictonal authority and new business realities, thereby making it possible for the Korean state to make decisions in a coherent and timely manner. The Korean government also managed to maintain a close relationship with the private sector, thereby making information sharing between them possible. Moreover, since the late 1980s, Korea was under rampant bilateral (by the United States and European Union) and multilateral (by the World Trade Organization) pressures for market opening in the IT sector. While sufferng from it, the Korean state strategically utilized the pressure to enhance its capability vis-à-vis domestic interest groups and successfully pre-empted their potential opposition.

## THE LIBERALIZATION PROCESS IN KOREA

Together with the finance sector, the IT sector has been one of few areas within which full-scale liberalization and regulatory reforms were introduced in the 1990s. One of the most distinctive characteristics of the liberalization process of the IT sector is that it was a government-led *discretionary* liberalization. It was the Korean government itself that made major decisions, such as how many entrants to allow and how strong these entrants had to become to effectively compete with the vertically integrated dominant incumbent carrier. A brief overview of the liberalization process of the Korean IT industry is in order.

In 1989, the United States and Korea ran into trade conflicts with each other over the IT industry when the U.S. government first designated Korea as a priority foreign country. The U.S. government cited such problems as discriminatory government procurement practices, a lack of transparency, and trade protection (Hyun and Lent, 1999: 393). Through a series of negotiations, the two governments agreed on two points: (1) the Korean government agreed to lift investment restrictions on U.S. value-added network businesses from 1994, and (2) the Korean government would open government procurement bidding corresponding to the level suggested by the General Agreement on Tariffs and Trade (GATT) (1).

At the same time, the agreement provided a strong impetus for the 1990 reform plan, which brought competition into the Korean telecommunications services market for the first time. Despite strong pressure from domestic firms to delay the market opening and an early liberalization of the domestic market, the Korean government was firm in its stance to introduce competition. As a consequence, in 1991 duopoly competition (KT and DACOM) in the international long-distance market was first introduced. In addition, permission was granted for complete competition in the value-added service market. (See Table 1.)

In 1994 and 1995, the Korean government unveiled two more government-led liberalization programs. This time, the multilateral negotiations by the WTO's nego-

**Table 1**   Major Liberalization Measures in the Korean IT Industry

|  | Changes in services | Competition in markets |
|---|---|---|
| 1990 | Specify basic telecom services: general (voice telephony) and special (mobile) | Competition for value-added network services introduced |
|  |  | Second international call carrier (1991) |
|  | Accept the concept of value-added services | Wireless pager (1992) |
|  |  | Mobile service provider (1994) |
| 1994 | Drop the distinction between general and special services | Domestic long-distance call market |
|  |  | Relieved the ownership limits of service providers on equipment manufacturers |
|  | The concept of new value-added service providers enlarged | Allowed KT to enter special service markets |
| 1996 |  | Decided to provide new services, including PCS, TRS, and CT-2 |
| 1997 |  | Twenty-seven new service providers licensed |
|  |  | Korea Electric Co. allowed to enter telecom market |
|  |  | Nine new service providers licensed in the following areas: local telephone services (1), TRS (4), leased line services (2), radio paging (1), and long distance (1) |
|  |  | Revision of classification of telecommunication services, introducing new category of "special telecommunication service providers" (voice resale and Internet telephone) |

*Source*: MIC.

tiating group on basic telecommunications (NGBT) provided a new impetus for liberalization in the Korean IT industry. The policy goal was to improve the competitive environment in all segments of the IT industry. First, in 1995 DACOM entered the domestic long-distance market. Second, the government-owned Korea Electric Power Corporation (KEPC) was permitted to enter the IT market. In addition, many chaebol were given entry into the IT service market, either by forming a consortium with other small and medium-size firms or through strategic alliances with foreign telecom companies (*Joongang Ilbo*, Dec. 15, 1995). For example, the top three chaebol—Samsung, Hyundai, and Daewoo—participated in the Hanaro Telecom consortium. As a result, by June 1996, twenty-seven companies acquired, the rights to start various IT services businesses, such as personal communication service (PCS), trunked radio system (TRS), cordless telephone second generation (CT-2), wireless data communication, international call services, communication network leasing, and paging (2). It is noteworthy that this liberalization drive was carried out three years ahead of a full-scale market opening as stipulated under the new world order of the WTO. This fact indicates that rather than merely reacting to external pressure, the Korean government made a strategic move to create a competitive domestic environment (*Korea Times*, July 5, 1995).

In 1996 and 1997, the second bilateral negotiations with the U.S. government (3) and the 1997 Basic Telecom Agreement accelerated the liberalization process in Korea. Moreover, the 1997 Asian financial crisis provided further bureaucratic justification for the government's commitment to an early full-scale liberalization of the IT industry. By the late 1990s, therefore, Korea had introduced competition—albeit managed competition—to all segments of the IT market. As of April 2000, there were fifty-two facility-based service providers (FSPs) and 229 special service providers (SSPs), whereas the number of value-added service providers had increased to 3279. With mounting pressure and an urgent need for restructuring the IT industry, the Korean government also removed price regulation and introduced full-scale price competition in all segments of the market except for local service (OECD, 2000:89–98).

With this backdrop, the impact of liberalization on the IT industry began to materialize, as vindicated in the exponential growth and enhanced competitiveness in many segments of the Korean IT industry. In terms of mobile phone users, as of 2001 Korea boasted one the highest penetration rates in the world in this area—50.6%, far above the 27.6% in the United States and 42.1% in Japan and. As Table 2 demon-

**Table 2**  Selected Index of the IT Industry in Korea (2001)

|       | Number of Internet users (1,000)[a] | Internet penetration (%; per 100 capita)[b] | Number of DSL subscribers (unit 1000)[c] | Number of CATV Internet subscribers (1000)[d] |
|-------|-------------------------------------|---------------------------------------------|------------------------------------------|-----------------------------------------------|
| Korea | 20,093                              | 43.9                                        | 3,784                                    | 2,156[e]                                       |

[a] March 2001,
[b] March 2001,
[c] September 2001,
[d] June 2001,
[e] August 2001.
*Source*: http://kidbs.itfind.or.kr/KIDBS/statistics_info.html.

strates, the robust growth of the IT industry in Korea is also evidenced by other indicators, such as the number of Internet users, Internet penetration rates, the number of DSP subscribers, and the number of cable television (CATV) Internet subscribers (4).

## MAIN FEATURES OF LIBERALIZATION IN THE KOREAN IT INDUSTRY

As illustrated in Table 1, in the course of the liberalization process, Korea has largely replicated the past practices of state intervention in economic affairs, as it was essentially state-led. Although the Korean government, particularly the Ministry of Information and Communication (MIC), did not initiate liberalization, it carefully designed the liberalization process and significantly influenced the final outcome of liberalization. In addition, the Korean government found a new activist role for itself at a time on which other rival ministries, such as the Ministry of Industry, Trade and Energy (MOITE), had begun to reduce state intervention in the economy. This is in stark contrast to the cases of the United States and the United Kingdom, in which political leaders and bureaucrats created new regulatory bodies and delegated their regulatory responsibilities to them. Even compared with the experiences of other East Asian countries, the Korean case is unique. For example, unlike Japan, in which the Ministry of Posts and Telecommunications (MPT) deliberately pursued liberalization as a means to augment its power (Vogel, 1996), the Korean MIC—as a unified body of promoters and regulators of the IT industry—did not explicitly seek to design liberalization so as to increase its power at the expense of other government ministries and the private sector; that is, the primary goal of the MIC was to foster a competitive market in the IT industry.

A close examination of the liberalization processes in the Korean IT industry reveals that it was a response to domestic pressure for liberalization as well that reflected the political calculus of Korea's top leadership. This determined the nature of liberalization programs in the Korean IT industry in terms of policy goals, the pace and intensity of liberalization, and the pattern of political intervention.

First, in terms of policy goals, the Korean government aimed to enhance competition in the IT industry. Second, in terms of the pace and intensity of liberalization, Korea experienced a relatively condensed process; liberalization took about one-half the time it took in Japan. While Japan was one of the first movers that had embarked on liberalization as early as 1985, it took Japan about fourteen years to complete the process. In contrast, in the face of intense U.S. pressure, Korea accomplished a similar degree of liberalization over a seven-year period beginning 1990.

Third, in terms of the degree of political intervention, the liberalization process in Korea was relatively depoliticized. Although some major decisions were subject to mediation by top leadership, intervention by politicians and various interest groups with keen interests in the IT industry remained minimal. This provided an institutional capacity for the MIC to take an initiative in the liberalization process. This does not, however, imply that liberalization in Korea was free from political intervention. As demonstrated in the decision to designate SK as a second mobile service provider and LG's takeover of DACOM, the liberalization process in Korea was politicized in the various stages of liberalization; rather, even when the liberalization process was subject to politicization, the final outcomes still did not deviate from those envisioned by the MIC. In most cases, the MIC was able to impose its policy preferences on the courses of liberalization.

## THE KOREAN DEVELOPMENTAL STATE AND THE POLITICS OF LIBERALIZATION

As discussed in the previous section, the liberalization process in Korea reveals many interesting features. Where do such features originate (5)? I argue that two factors were fundamental in determining the nature of liberalization in Korea: top leadership's political orientation and the transformative capability of the Korean government, particularly in the IT sector.

### The Political Leadership's Orientation

There are divergent paths to liberalization. The path a country chooses is hinged on the way key actors involved in the industry perceive the impact of liberalization and the subsequent restructuring of the industry. At the same time, this choice largely reflects the policy orientation of the political leadership in each country. Given that political leadership in each country has a different policy agenda—a product of its relationship with the society—liberalization is essentially a political choice. This is why it was politicians rather than bureaucrats who initially took the lead in the liberalization process. In short, the political calculus of top leadership led government ministries to seek a specific path to liberalization (6). In the course of liberalization, lead ministries get engaged in the strategic behavior by juxtaposing two seemingly conflicting goals: (1) to create competitive market environments and (2) to maintain or increase their governments' regulatory powers. While both goals are important, in each country the specific combination of the two inherently reflects the political calculus of the top leadership. In the case of Korean liberalization, the primary goal was to create a more competitive environment among domestic firms before opening up the market to foreign firms, thus giving secondary emphasis to reinforcing the MIC's regulatory power.

The initial liberalization drive in Korea dates back to the Chun Doo Hwan government's penchant for realigning the state's role in the economy (Moon, 1988). In the early 1980s, quagmired in a serious economic crisis stemming from political upheavals following the assassination of president Park Chung Hee, the Chun government launched a major economic restructuring program. At the same time, the Chun government attempted to break away from the state-guided model by implementing liberalization in order to shore up its political legitimacy. Although it was primarily financial liberalization that was undertaken, there was an overall relaxation of the state's control of the private sector. Ultimately it signified that a fundamental shift in policy orientation was being made within Korea's top leadership.

This ideological shift within the government continued into the mid-1990s. As President Kim Young Sam came to power, the Korean government launched the political campaign of *segyehwa* (globalization). In this segyehwa drive, the implementation of liberalization was considered crucial in upgrading the Korean economy. This was symbolized in the Korean government's penchant for joining the Organization for Economic Cooperation and Development (OECD). In order to enter into the OECD, the Kim Young Sam government found it necessary to undertake further liberalization measures. It was against this backdrop that the liberalization of the IT industry was implemented in the 1990s. In other words, the liberalization of the IT industry largely reflected the political leadership's ideological shift toward a drastic relaxation of state control over the national economy.

This shift was gradually implanted into the bureaucracy, as reflected in the changes in the recruitment pattern of government officials. In the 1980s, the top bureaucrats, who had been educated during the Japanese colonial period and hence were ingrained with developmental ideology, began to be replaced by U.S.-trained bureaucrats. By the early 1990s, these new bureaucrats took key positions within the government and emerged as champions of liberalization.

The IT industry was not an exception to this overall trend. Liberal-minded bureaucrats within the MIC actively launched liberalization programs. Compared to other government ministries, this ideological shift was even more conspicuous in the MIC. Rather than being limited to the MIC's top positions, the shift spread deep into the middle rank of the ministry, which ultimately influenced the ministry's policy making. It was vividly evidenced in the recruitment pattern in Korea Information Strategy Development Institute (KISDI), a government think tank under the MIC. Most researchers at KISDI had American Ph.D.'s and were indoctrinated in liberal ideology. They played a pivotal role in promoting liberalization in the IT sector, as the MIC actively embraced their policy recommendations. This signified that a fundamental reorientation was being made in every corner of the MIC. The newly empowered neoliberal bureaucrats endeavored to distance leaving from the past practices of developmentalism.

Because of this, policy makers in Korea recognized that the early opening up of the IT sector would not seriously impair the overall competitiveness of domestic firms (7); rather, in the Korean government's view it would nurture domestic, competitiveness before intensified competition between domestic and foreign companies unfolded. Although new regulations were instituted, they inherently aimed at establishing a competitive market environment. The logic of asymmetric competition was prevalent in policy makers' thoughts. Specifically, this served as a powerful constraint on the incumbent, Korea Telecom (KT). While carrying out diverse liberalization measures, the Korean government therefore made conscious efforts to limit KT from expanding into new areas and launched many preferential policies for new entrants. For example, KT was not allowed to enter the field at mobile phone service until 1997. Ultimately these efforts brought a "leveling-the-playing-field" effect in this segment of the Korean IT industry as well as other tangible effects, such as lowering prices, improving service quality, introducing new services, and promoting the invention of new technologies.

## The Transformative Capability of the Korean Government

Although the ideological shift spearheaded by top leadership and ingrained in the bureaucracy had a significant bearing on the pattern of liberalization, it does not fully explain the specific path to liberalization that the Korean government took—state-led liberalization; that is, while the shift signaled an abrupt departure from the developmentalism of the past decades, it did not lead to a fundamental breakup of the Korean developmental state into the Anglo-American-style regulatory state. The Korean liberalization process was completed not by the retreat of the state, but by the Korean state's new activist role. What made such a unique path to liberalization possible in Korea? The answer to this question lies in whether or not a given country has the institutional foundations to undertake a specific form of liberalization. I argue that the transformative capability of the Korean state made state-led liberalization possible. Spefifically, three factors were crucial: the ability to maintain institutional integrity in a given sector, the ability to maintain a close relationship with the private sector, and the ability to strategically utilize foreign pressure.

First, the Korean state maintained a highly unified institutional structure in the IT industry in that jurisdictional authority was centralized within a single ministry. First of all, the ministry in charge of the IT industry—the MIC—was a promoter as well as a regulator. In addition, the MIC in Korea was relatively free from challenges from the incumbent KT as well as bureaucratic wrangling with other ministries, which ultimately allowed the MIC to implement drastic liberalization. By the early 1990s, it was obvious that in the Korean IT industry, old regulatory schemes such as a state-run monopoly carrier in the basic telecommunication market and a high level of state intervention in the value-added service and equipment industries had become serious obstacles to the rapid growth of the newly emerging IT industry. Moreover, over-lapping jurisdictional authority over the IT industry caused a policy gridlock, as various government ministries competed with one another.

Recognizing this deadlock, various efforts were made to create a unified policy-making structure in the IT industry under the Kim Young Sam government. In December 1994, these efforts materialized in the form of a government reorganiza-tion plan (Hahm and Kim, 1999; Moon and Ingraham, 1998). In this plan, the MPT, which was renamed the Ministry of Information and Communications (MIC), became the only ministry in charge of the telecommunications industry. The MIC absorbed the industrial policy function of the IT industry, which had previously been under the jurisdiction of MOITE (8). Jurisdiction over the software industry was also transferred from the Ministry of Science and Technology (MOST) to the MIC. The MIC's dominance in the IT industry was completed in June 1996 when the planning office of the Information Society was placed directly under the authority of the MIC.

Although the organizational reform did not completely remove competition among ministries and bureaucratic wranglers, the MIC clearly gained power over MOITE and other ministries, thereby pre-empting the possibility of bureaucratic conflicts over the rapidly proliferating IT industry. The organizational shake-up removed one of the chronic problems in Korea's high-tech policy making since democratization in 1987: the lack of policy coordination (Moon and Mo, 1998). The relative absence of bureaucratic turf wars in the IT industry provided the MIC with the institutional foundations to take the lead in the liberalization process.

In short, being relatively free from bureaucratic rivalry, the MIC had fewer incentives for reregulation to consolidate and expand its jurisdictional boundaries and enhance its status within the Korean government. Furthermore, the MIC was in a good position to impose its policy preferences on the key issues related to liberalization in the private sector. Because of this, rather than taking an incrementalist and gradualist approach to liberalization, the MIC was able to speed up the liberalization process to improve the competitive environment in the IT industry (interview with an MIC official, Dec. 2001) (9). More specifically, the Korean government was able to manage the competition in the IT services industry primarily through the control of competitors' entries in each market segment.

Second, while being insulated from societal interests, the MIC managed to maintain a close relationship with the private sector, which in turn helped the MIC establish a channel that could facilitate the information flow between the government and the private sector. The MIC's efforts originated from its quest for transforming itself into a policy ministry. Until the mid-1980s, the MIC was merely a policy implementation ministry. Its weak link with the private sector was a serious obstacle to the MIC's rise as a policy ministry, because the MIC lacked policy expertise, even on issues within its jurisdiction. In order to cope with this, the MIC regarded cooperative relationships with the private sector as essential, because these would facilitate the flow of information about technology changes and market dynamics.

This was done in various ways. At the tope level, the MIC was in a good position to capture future technological and market trends in the IT sector. Since the 1980s, MIC ministers had been recruited from the private sector. Many of them were the top managers of IT-related companies, such as Daewoo Electronics and Samsung Electronics. A flow of information from the government to the private sector was also made possible in the 1990s as many more midlevel bureaucrats more actively sought their second career in the private sector than in the past. As the IT industry emerged as a booming sector in the 1990s, many bureaucrats emigrated into private firms. These bureaucrats served as liaisons between the MIC and the private sector. In the IT sector, therefore, two-way information sharing was relatively well maintained, while not impeding the autonomy of the state. As a result, the MIC successfully emerged as a policy ministry in the mid-1990s (10). The MIC's status as a policy ministry was further solidified when the Institute for Communications Research (ICR) was created under it in 1985 (11).

This institutional characteristic ultimately influenced the pattern of liberalization in Korea; that is, the MIC's interest in becoming a policy ministry, combined with its close relationship with the private sector that it cultivated, prevented the MIC from engaging in reregulation during the liberalization process.

Third, foreign pressure for liberalization also contributed to enhancing the Korean state's transformative capability. In the Korean IT industry, the initial impetus for liberalization came from external sources. On the one hand, liberalization in Korea was in part a response to a neoconservative deregulation movement begun in the United States and the United Kingdom in the 1970s. On the other hand and more important, Korea had faced bilateral and multilateral pressure for liberalization of the IT industry since the late 1980s. At the bilateral level, Korea, together with the EU, Japan, and Mexico, was designated by the U.S. government as a priority negotiation country (PFC), as stipulated by Section 1377 of the Omnibus Trade and Competitiveness Act of 1988 bilateral negotiations. At the multilateral level, Korea was subject to WTO basic telecommunications negotiations that subsequently wielded an enormous impact on the Korean IT industry (12). These pressures served as a catalyst in expediting the liberalization of the IT industries in Korea. Evidence of this lies in the fact that major liberalization programs to enhance the competitive environment in Korea were carried out immediately after Korea completed either bilateral negotiations with the United States or multilateral negotiations in the Uruguay Round.

Rather than resisting foreign pressure, the Korean government took advantage of it to speed up the liberalization process. As the lift of protection on domestic firms became imminent, other actors in the IT industry were worried that too rapid a liberalization process would drive domestic firms from even their own captive home market. By locking itself in liberalization programs as demanded by foreign countries and multilateral institutions, however, the Korean government assured those in the IT industry that liberalization was both inevitable and irreversible. As a result, the Korean government was able to lead an orderly structural reform of the IT industry. In this process, KT was forced to give up some of its existing privileges (13). If the institution's structure had been dispersed, it would have been more difficult for the Korean government to strategically utilize foreign pressure, because some actors within the Korean government would have attempted to collaborate with other domestic forces opposing liberalization to block it, thus making an orderly implementation of liberalization difficult.

This does not imply that the Korean government was always able to utilize foreign pressure in its favor, however. Foreign pressure brought an unintended consequence to the liberalization process as well; the liberalization drive under foreign pressure opened the way for chaebol—previously prohibited for entering the IT industry—to participate in various IT services as a major stockholder. As demonstrated in LG's successful bid to take over DACOM, chaebol adroitly exploited the overall relaxation of restrictions on ownership to start businesses in this sector.

As chaebol's influence increased, the concern about limiting chaebol from unduly expanding its power in the IT industry also increased. This concern was firmly shared by both small and medium-size firms, as well as the general public. In their view, uncoordinated liberalization would simply exacerbate the problem, making the establishment of a competitive market difficult. This provided the Korean government with the political justification for embarking on government-led liberalization. In the case of the IT industry, the Korean government endeavored to check the rampant power of chaebol by allowing foreign companies' early entry into in the industry and by introducing various competition-enhancing measures such as a transparent accounting system and corporate restructuring.

## CONCLUSION

This chapter attempted to explore the unique pattern of liberalization in the Korean IT industry by focusing on the political leadership's orientation and the transformative capability of the developmental state. Liberalization in Korea was government-led, and the Korean government was active in speeding up the liberalization process. The primary momentum for such drastic liberalization was essentially derived from the ideological orientation of the Korean political leadership, which attempted to distance itself from previous regimes. Institutional foundations were also favorable for the government to take the lead in the liberalization process. Through a major government reorganization plan, the MIC was effectively able to claim sole jurisdiction over the IT industry, which prevented it from seeking reregulation. The close relationship between the MIC and the private sector facilitated information sharing between them. Foreign pressure further strengthened the Korean government's institutional capacities, as it strategically employed foreign pressure to impose its policy positions on the private sector and to pre-empt potential opposition to liberalization.

The examination of the liberalization of the Korean IT industry leads us to reconsider the efficacy of the developmental state model in the age of globalization. Many scholars contend that as the pace of technological change quickens and market dynamics get complicated, government–business relations have shifted in favor of the latter (Moon and Prasad, 1994; Kim, 1997). Moreover, various forces of globalization seem to make the East Asian developmental state model less tenable. Citing the 1997

Asian financial crisis as the manifestation of these accumulated structural problems, they go on to argue that developmental states in East Asia can no longer play a role of policy innovator and ultimate coordinator of conflicting interests.

Does this imply that the developmental state is destined to fade away? Although government-led liberalization does not warrant success, the liberalization process in the Korean IT industry suggests that the developmental state may still be effective if the state has the ability to maintain institutional integrity or to transform itself in the face of a changing environment. Korea plunged into the Asian financial crisis, and even after the crisis, it suffered from serious policy gridlocks because it failed to recreate institutional foundations in coordinating diverse interests in financial liberalization (Thurbon, 2001). It is noteworthy that financial liberalization in Korea involved the abrupt relinquishment of the state's governing capability, as was symbolized by the elimination of the Economic Planning Board (EPB) under the Kim Young Sam government (Weiss, 2000; Lee, 2000). On the contrary, Korea implemented liberalization in the IT industry without serious disruption as the government played the role of ultimate coordinator. The Korean case therefore requires us to focus on the sources of sectoral variations before discarding the developmental state model. The case of the Korean IT industry also suggests that even in the age of globalization government intervention can be beneficial if top leadership's political orientation is effectively embedded in institutional structure in a given sector.

Another theoretical implication of this study pertains to the impact of globalization on domestic policy making—whether globalization will wipe out national diversities or whether nations will still take divergent paths toward development. Proponents of the globalization thesis argue that nations will ultimately converge and flatten out differences among themselves—between the West and the East as well as between advanced and developing countries (Ohmae, 1995). In this view, the convergence will not be limited to advanced countries, but will expand to developing countries because the regulatory reforms undertaken by advanced countries powerfully shape a future path that developing countries will follow. Given this sturdy impact of globalization, Korea is expected to ultimately converge toward one model of development to invite more competition and reduce state intervention in the managing of the economy.

Although I do not deny that the forces of globalization powerfully constrain a range of choices available to states, I contend that nations will still take divergent paths toward development, as demonstrated in the Korean case. This is because each country has different ideas of how to respond to the challenges presented by globalization, and there are variations in the way the forces of globalization are channeled through and mediated by domestic institutions. These ideas and institutions are inherently created, developed, and maintained within the political, historical, and cultural contexts of each country, and the path toward liberalization will be a path-dependent rather than a universal one (Carlile and Tilton, 1998).

## NOTES

1.   The agreement had an immediate effect on the Korean procurement market. For example, in terms of government procurement in 1992, 8.8 billion out of a total 21.6 billion won was

subject to open bidding. In the case of KT's procurement, 39.7 billion out of 49.7 billion won was open to U.S. companies.

2. The Korean government's efforts to bring in competition were soon expanded to other segments of the market. In 1997, in the local call service market Hanaro was selected as a second service provider. In the long-distance service market, Onse Telecom, an international phone service provider, became the third long-distance service company.

3. In 1996, the U.S. government, with very specific demands on its agenda, resumed the second bilateral negotiations. The U.S. government asked to eradicate such problems as government intervention in equipment purchases of private companies and limitations on foreign investment in the Korean market (Joongang Ilbo, Dec. 20, 1996).

4. In terms of its overall capacity to take advantage of IT, however, Korea's performance is less impressive. This does not necessarily mean that the impact of liberalization on the IT industry has been modest in Korea, given that this capacity also reflects the overall national regulatory environment and not just the competitiveness of the IT industry. In a recent survey conducted by the Center for International Development (CID) at Harvard University, Korea ranked twentieth in a seventy-five-country list (*Korea Times*, March 1, 2002). This was based on the networked readiness index (NRI), which assesses countries' capacities to explore the opportunities offered by information and telecommunications technologies. In another survey, conducted in May 2001 by the Economist Intelligence Unit, Korea ranked twenty-first in the world in terms of an E-commerce environment (The Economist Intelligence Unit/Pyramid Research E-readiness Rankings, 2001).

5. One may argue that the sense of urgency for liberalization was great in Korea, particularly as Korea headed into the financial crisis of 1997. According to this view, in order to escape the impasse caused by the crisis, Korea had no choice but to speed up liberalization. Although this argument seems plausible, it does not aptly capture reality in the sense that liberalization in the IT industry should be understood in tandem with the liberalization processes in other parts of the economy. The initial stage of the liberalization drive in Korea dates back to the early 1980s under the Chun Doo Hwan government. In the early 1990s, the Kim Young Sam government further expedited the process.

6. There is a wide spectrum in the patterns of liberalization. At one extreme, one could find drastic liberalization, primarily aimed at enhancing consumers' interests. The assumption underpinning this is that national competitiveness will ultimately be enhanced by intensifying competition and weeding out underperforming companies. To invite foreign companies into the domestic market will further facilitate this development, which in turn will significantly alter the landscape of the industry. At the other extreme is "predatory reregulation," in which in the liberalization process, government ministries seek to reinsert new regulatory measures to enhance their power. This practice is often implemented at the expense of both producers and consumers. This schematic typology should be understood as a continuum within a broad spectrum, however, rather than as two discrete alternatives, because most countries lie between these two categories.

7. In this period, Korean policy makers had two industry policy goals in mind: (1) to localize basic telecommunications equipment, and (2) to satisfy basic telecommunications service needs. As Korea successfully developed a switching system, TDX, they believed that TDX would fend off foreign penetration into the Korean procurement market. For this point, see Hyun and Lent (1999: 393).

8. In addition to its traditional jurisdictional authority over telecommunications services, radio waves, and national post offices, the MIC took charge of the national information infrastructure. In contrast, MOITE was reduced in size and renamed the Ministry of International Trade and Industry (MITI). MITI had to abolish the Bureau of Electrics and Electronics.

9.  The MIC's decisions were essentially market-conforming, however, in that by maintaining a close relationship with the private sector, the MIC could acquire its views on key issues.
10. The rise of the MIC began as early as the late 1980s, as reflected in its recruitment pattern. In the late 1980s, for example, Oh Myung became the first minister to come from the ranks of the MPT (MIC).
11. In 1988, ICR was renamed the Korean Information Society Development Institute (KISDI).
12. The successful conclusion of the Group on Basic Telecommunications (GBT) signified that beginning in January 1998, over 90% of the world's basic telecommunications market would be liberalized according to the schedules submitted by individual countries.
13. This is well represented in the remarks of MIC Minister Kang Bong Kyun: "[we have to] introduce a competitive system *among domestic companies prior to opening the market to foreigners*" (Han, 1998: 107).

## REFERENCES

Carlile, L. E., Tilton, M. C. (1998). Is Japan Really Changing Its Ways? Regulatory Reform and the Japanese Economy. Washington, DC: Brookings Institution.

Frieden, J. A. (1991). Invested interests: The politics of national economic policies in a world of global finance. Internat. Org. 45.

Frieden, J. A., Rogowski, R. (1996). The impact of the International Economy on National Policies: An Analytical Overview. In: Keohane, R. O., Milner, H. V., eds. Internationalization and Domestic Politics. New York: Cambridge University Press, pp. 25–47.

Hahm, S. D., Kim, K. W. (1999). Institutional reforms and democratization in Korea: The case of the Kim Young Sam administration, 1993–1998. Governance Internati. J. Policy Admin. 12, 479–494.

Han, S. U. (1998). Inmaek euro bon jeongbo jeonchaek ilgochal Jeongbo Sahwoe Yeongu [Information Society Research], 10:101–125.

Hyun, D., Lent, J. A. (1999). Korean telecom policy in global competition: Implications for developing countries. Telecom. Policy 23:389–401.

Kim, E. M. (1997). Big Business, Strong State: Collusion and Conflict in South Korean Development, 1960–1990. New York: State University of New York Press.

Kim, E. M. (1999). Crisis of the developmental state in South Korea. Asian Persp. 23:35–55.

Korea Times. (March 1, 2002).

Lee, S. (July 20, 2000). U.S. pressure may give Japan IT industry boost. Daily Yomiuri.

Lee, Y. (2000). The failure of the weak state in economic liberalization: Liberalization, democratization and the financial crisis in South Korea. Pac. Rev. 13:115–131.

Milner, H. (1988). Resisting Protectionism: Global Industries and the Politics of International Trade. Princeton: Princeton University Press.

Moon, C., Mo, J. (1998). Epilogue: Democracy and the origins of the 1997 Korean economic crisis. In: Moon, C., Mo, J., eds. Democracy and the Korean Economy. Stanford: Hoover Institution Press, pp. 171–198.

Moon, C. (1988). The demise of the developmentalist state: The politics of stabilization and structural adjustment. J. Dev. Soc. 4:67–84.

Moon, C., Prasad, R. (1994). Beyond the developmental state: Networks, politics, and institutions. Governance Internat J Policy Admin 7:360–386.

Moon, M. J., Ingraham, P. (1998). Shaping administrative reform and governance: An examination of the political nexus triads in three Asian countries. Governance Internat. J. Policy Admin. 11:77–100.

OECD. Regulatory Reform in Korea: OECD Review of Regulatory Reform. Paris: OECD.

Ohmae, K (1995). The End of the Nation State: The Rise of Regional Economies. London: Harper Collins.

The Economist Intelligence Unit/Pyramid Research E-readiness Rankings. (2001); <http://www.ebusinessforum.com/index.asp?layout = rich_story&doc_id = 367>.

Thurbon, E. (2001). Two paths to financial liberalization: South Korea and Taiwan. Pac. Rev. 14:241–267.

Vogel, S. K. (1996). Freer Markets, More Rules: Regulatory Reform in the Advanced Industrial Countries. Ithaca, NY: Cornell University Press.

Vogel, S. K. (2001). The crisis of German and Japanese capitalism: Stalled on the road to the liberal market model? Compar. Polit. Stud. 34:1103–1133.

Weiss, L. (2000). Developmental state in transition: Adapting, dismantling, innovating, not normalizing. Pac. Rev. 13:21–55.

# 29

## Understanding the Postsocialist Transition

**NADIA LISOVSKAYA**

*University of Manchester, Manchester, United Kingdom*

> No one, I think, in studying the question of the economic system in Russia has denied its transitionary character... But what does the word "transition" mean? Does it not mean, as applied to an economy, that the present system contains elements, particles, fragments of both capitalism and socialism? Everyone will admit that it does. But not all who admit thus take the trouble to consider what elements actually constitute the various socio-economic structures that exist in Russia at the present time. And this is the crux of the question.
>
> V. I. Lenin (1918)

### INTRODUCTION

Regardless of the fact that over a decade has passed since the collapse of the USSR, the political economy of transitional countries remains largely misunderstood. This group of countries is often confused with developing or developed ones. This chapter aims to identify the institutional and structural specificity of postsocialist transitional economies. Institutions are defined in this context as rational frameworks for politicoeconomic behavior, the basic institution being ownership. Structures are understood here as economic categories linked to the notion of "value": costs of production, price, utility, and scarcity.

## DEFINING THE PHENOMENON AND SETTING THE FRAMEWORK

The analysis presented in this chapter is grounded on a basic assumption: that the genesis of the East European transition toward market economies lies in the central planning that preceded it. What this assumption implies is that in order to understand transitional countries one must first understand the specific economic anatomy of central planning—its institutions and structures. The main economic features that distinguished centrally planned countries from the rest of the world were the institutions of state ownership and planned exchange. This specific institutional arrangement affected the structural composition of centrally planned countries and how those structures could subsequently evolve. Thus in order to disclose the mechanism of postcentral planning transition, (1) the economic essence of centrally planned institutions must be defined and their influence on domestic structures grasped, and, (2) the logic of dynamic institutional and structural transformation from central planning to a market economy must be perceived.

There is probably no single theoretical school in contemporary politicoeconomic discourse that does not endeavor to explain the postsocialist transition. Here the neoclassical, Keynesian, evolutionary, and institutional approaches are among the best known. Given this multiplicity of approaches, the need arises to evaluate them.

When evaluating the appropriateness of these various theoretical approaches, two views can be distinguished. According to the first one, the positivistic nature of economic science endows its schools of thought with an ontological commonality that significantly narrows their capacity to explain the phenomenon of postsocialist transition; namely, all of these theories, which emerged from the Western academic environment and theorized according to what they observed, take private ownership and competitive exchange for granted, whereas these are fundamentally incompatible with, and in diametric opposition to, the nonprivate ownership and the noncompetitive exchange of central planning. The second view, mainly held by the mainstream economic theory, assumes the possibility of the application of abstract theoretical models on various case studies regardless of the historical or social context.

Of the aforementioned approaches, neoclassical economic theory is the least equipped for explaining postsocialist transition. As a result of its abstractness from institutional dynamics, it increasingly operates with static models. The structural dynamics are connected with the shift in the institutional layout, because the extraction of profit from a commodity is preceded by the transformation of the commodity in question from public or state to private property. Transitional countries represent a case of dramatic institutional change, which caused unique structural regularities.

In contrast, the institutional school possesses the greatest potential to disclose the postcentral planning transition, since it operates with institutions and their dynamics, but it too has limitations. In the definition of institution, there is a dominance of behavioral elements. Consider the following definition of institution given by Veblen (1994:190):

> Institutions are, in substance, prevalent habits of thought with respect to particular relations and particular functions of the individual and of the community; and the scheme of life, which is made up of the aggregate of institutions in force at a given time or at a given point in the development of any society, may, on the psychological side, be broadly characterised as a prevalent spiritual attitude or a prevalent theory of life. As regards its genetic feature, this spiritual attitude or theory of life is in the last analysis reducible to terms of prevalent type of character.

In contradistinction, our claim is that the institutions of central planning and transition are to be analyzed primarily from a rational angle, in terms of the consequences that necessarily unfold from the logic of a given economic system, and without this emphasis on social and psychological aspects. The reason for this is that state ownership and planned exchange were established in countries with diverse cultural and religious backgrounds, and hence these factors could not have played a decisive role in the characteristics and transformation of centrally planned institutions and structures; otherwise central planning would be a phenomenon tethered to a certain combination of social and psychological circumstances. As a result of their ontological and methodological limitations, the theories mentioned above often record but cannot explain the anomalies of economic transformation in Eastern Europe.

Aside from the aforementioned established theoretical frameworks, three approaches hold much promise for understanding postcentral planning transformation. A first approach is found in those authors who specifically aimed at conceptualizing central planning. The problem here is that the majority of publications do not go further than administrative (e.g., central planning boards and ministries) or purely political studies. As a result, the economic essence of central planning institutions and structures has remained considerably unexplored until now. The best publications include those of such Soviet theorists as Preobrazhenski, and Bukharin, as well as von Mises, von Hayek, Nove, and Lavigne.

A second approach may derive from those schools that aim to construct the theory of dynamics. Here, Keynesian and Schumpeterian contributions are of particular importance. The Keynesian approach is convenient, as it provides a framework for the understanding of transition. It is assumed that the possibility of additional factor employment in some transitional countries over the last few years was secured by a very low capacity utilization of production in the early mid-1990s, reaching sometimes only 50% of the 1980s level. This understanding of growth is very similar to the Keynesian "full employment." Schumpeter's understating of development as a process linked to innovations is crucial for the conceptualization of the lack of structural development in central planning, as the latter was unable to absorb innovations and remained static. Both Keynes and Schumpeter use the notion of static, nonexchange, and nonmonetary economy as an antipode to a dynamic economy. This concept, used by both authors as an abstract analytical tool helping to clarify the theory of dynamics (growth and development), is extremely close to the economic essence of central planning.

A third and final approach may be derived from those writings that emerged at the dawn of political economy as a science, which can be observed in the pioneering works of Smith, Ricardo, Marx, and the marginalists. This was the time when the most simple and basic notions of the discipline—including the categories of ownership, exchange, value, and commodity—were objects of doubt and discussion. Private ownership and competitive exchange, which together constitute the ontological commonality that bars various contemporary schools from grasping the nature of centrally planned economies, were at this point not yet taken for granted. Conclusions were drawn that were rarely revisited later, and instead of being subject to critical inquiry, served as the foundations of the present theoretical frameworks within economic science. It was early in the history of economic science, before these tentative positions acquired their foundational status, that efforts were made to comprehend nonprivate ownership and nonexchange (i.e., the theoretical possibilities that were later actualized in centrally planned economies). Taking the most basic elements of these classic politicoeconomic discussions—the functions of money and the principle of value exchange—as our basic assumptions and a starting point, the third approach becomes none other than a simple historicological approach. By not demanding any peculiar empirical or theoretical conditions, this method proves to be readily adjustable to the central planning and transitional environment.

Given these diverse approaches, the following sections offer an approach to understanding the institutional and structural specificity of central planning and transitional countries. Since many of the scholars from the various approaches mentioned above touch on elements discussed in our analysis, appropriate reference will be made in order to place the proposed framework within the broader context of existing economic schools.

## INSTITUTIONS AND STRUCTURES: CENTRAL PLANNING

Planned exchange takes place when the state determines both the prices and the volumes of goods to be bought and sold. It is commonly understood that apart from state ownership, socialist economies were also characterized by this particular exchange system. Indeed, there are many studies describing the organization of planned exchange in centrally planned economies (Kornai, 1992; Jeffries, 1990; Lavigne, 1995; Nove, 1983). These are not discussed here in detail. What is neglected in the literature that merits attention, however, is the following question—Was planned exchange (central planning) inevitable in state ownership of the means of production? Although planned exchange was instituted in various socialist countries, it was not clearly elaborated by Marx and Engels, who did not explicitly discuss planned exchange as it was carried out in the USSR. Implicit references to planning, however—though with regard to community not the state—can be found in the classic texts. (See Brus, 1972.) The notion of a plan becomes a central part of policy making and academic language only after the Revolution. For instance, in 1922 Bukharin and Preobrazhenki mentioned the necessity of planning (1969:114).

We may begin answering this issue by examining the attempts of Soviet theorists to define labor. Remuneration was said to be determined on the basis of "the main economic law" and "the law of distribution according to labor,"[2] neither of which contains concrete economic mechanisms for the evaluation of labor. To compensate for this inadequacy, the state, in the context of state ownership by which it both owns the means of production and is an employer), must define the value of labor administratively. Applying Marx's principle that labor is the principal source of the value of commodities, this case yields the following conclusion: under conditions in which the state owns the means of production, the state fixes prices. This is one of the two features of planned exchange.

The fixation of prices, however, does not automatically entail the other feature of planned exchange—that the physical volumes of goods to be exchanged are determined by the state. It is possible for an enterprise to sell more if it has produced more (escaping such determination) in two ways: if a new demand appears or if prices fall. The first scenario, under conditions of state ownership, is problematic because enterprise demands cannot arise spontaneously, as they would in a market economy. A certain investment decision must be made in order to increase the domestic demand

(3) and this demand then allows for a change in the physical volumes of goods to be exchanged. This investment decision is made by the state, however, controlling the demand and thereby controlling the physical volumes of goods to be exchanged. In consequence, this first possibility only amounts to a circuitous fixation of the physical volumes of goods to be exchanged. The second possibility, that prices fall, is to be disregarded in contexts in which the state owns the means of production, for it was argued above that state ownership implies the fixation of prices, excluding this possibility.

Our starting point was that the planned exchange of goods means the fixation of both prices and physical volumes; that is, there is a fixation of value in central planning, and money serves as a measurement of fixed values. What does it mean for the remaining functions of money—means of payment, means of exchange, and store of value?

In market countries competition minimizes prices. The aim of enterprises is therefore to produce a new product, which will either have the same qualities as those of its competitors but a lower price, or offer a product with the same price but a wider range of qualities. Both types of competition can be reduced to the minimization of costs of production. Since there was no competition in central planning, there was no pressure on price or costs, as these were fixed. These costs, realized in price, were countervailed by a fixed amount of the monetary mass in circulation.

Since the centrally planned system does not recognize the scarcity of resources, it does not seek means for economizing these resources, which is what innovations attempt to do. This understanding of innovations is rooted in the classic political economy approach; namely, that of Ricardo's and Marx's. As Marx observed, "Every new invention that enables the production in one hour that which hitherto been produced in two hours depreciates all similar products on the market. Competition forces the producer to sell the product of two hours as cheaply as the product of one hour" (Marx, 1956:72). In other words, the minimum necessary labor time for production is established through competition. Competition demands decrease this time, and invention provides the producer with such a possibility. This is one of the most laconic of formulae codifying the essence of intellectual products. It should be noted that it is principally rooted in a Ricardian elaboration of costs, which equals labor multiplied by time (cost $=$ labor $*$ time). The emphasis on time provided in the Ricardian and Marxist approaches is acceptable if we stick to the labor theory of value. As this discussion goes beyond the scope of the current work, we will take a more conservative stance; the capacity of economizing material costs as well as time is considered here as the most important feature of innovations.

The system does not demand innovations and as a result cannot develop structurally. Technological backwardness became an endemic feature of central planning. In the years from 1981 to 1985, the average terms for the use of equipment was forty-five years in the USSR versus seventeen in the United States (Schmelev and Popov, 1992: 67). This structurally frozen system was extensive by nature; it grew but did not develop; it was static in time. Of all those who touched on the issue of invention in central planning, von Mises provides one of the most scientific explanations. He lists dynamics forces: changes in external nature, quality and quantity of the population, quality and quantity of capital goods, technique of production, organization of labor, and change in demand (von Mises, 1936:196). Further, von Mises argues that socialism cannot cope with these dynamics factors, since it is essentially a static system. Von Mises points out that due to the lack of incentive for labor to increase productivity, the increase of productivity of labor must inevitably decline. Innovations, according to von Mises, are elements of a dynamic system.

Alongside the impossibility to absorb innovations, another phenomenon became prominent in the centrally planned economies. Even if central planners made a decision to create an innovation, the resources for this new combination have to be taken from the current or circular flow. In market countries, as was shown by Schumpeter (1961), this is realized by the creation of ad hoc money and its exchange for real goods and services from the current circulation; that is, there is an exchange occuring in time— future goods, yet to be invented, are exchanged for those in the current circulation.

In central planning this does not happen, since all values of the goods are fixed in the plan. Their extraction will lead to the distortion of the chain of production plans they are related to. This in turn will lead to the distortion of the equilibrium between the values of goods and money.

What follows is that monetary units in central planning were means of only instantaneous payment and exchange. They performed these functions only in a current, circular flow, and these functions cannot be realized in time. Exchange and payment took place only in the fixed by plan volumes and values of money and goods. The storage of monetary units for future purchasing power was senseless and impossible in central planning, since these monetary units were used only with instantaneous exchange. In other words, the function of money as a means of storage—a function that clearly points to money as a means of connection between past, present, and future—was nonexistent in central planning.

A difference should be made between the intermediary or industrial and final consumption sectors. In the sector of industrial consumption the values of goods were fixed in the plan. It appeared that everything that was offered had to be bought and therefore money completely lost its function as a store of value. In the sector of final consumption values also were fixed; workers' wages, which constituted incomes to be spent on goods, on the one side, and the prices of goods, on the other, were determined by the plan. The demand side could not be fixed easily by the plan, however, because it was impossible to plan individuals' preferences. Here people could postpone their consumption, accumulate a particular amount, and buy an expensive good, or each time consumers went to shop, they could choose a new combination of goods and services. It looks as though money was more real in this sector since it could serve as a means of exchange and payment and the store of value.

Now we need to define the value of money in a centrally planned economy in general. It was concluded that there was an "instant" or current (or circular, using Schumpeter's term) value created in the industrial sector. Part of this value referred to the means of production and another part to goods of final consumption. Let us look in closer detail at the value of the means of production. If innovations are the sources of new value, then it follows that no new value was created in central planning. The value of the means of production, which was fixed in an economy at the point of the establishment of central planning, therefore was not added with new value in the course of the existence of central planning. Does this mean that this magnitude of value remained fixed? No, for the means of production partially transform their value by those goods that are produced by them. The means and instruments of production experience physical and moral aging, as a result of which their value gradually decreases. Even if some equipment was able to work for many decades (e.g., for thirty or more years, as it was in central planning), its real value was very little because of moral aging. We therefore conclude that no new value could be created in the industrial sector, and moreover that the value fixed at the point of the establishment of the centrally planned system has gradually decreased.

Now let us look at the sphere of final consumption. Since consumers had more choice to buy or not to buy, they generated a pressure on prices. This pressure, however, did not make much sense, since the price of a good for final consumption was part of a larger plan that fixed this as well as other prices. This means that it was practically impossible for producers to respond to consumers' preferences and minimize prices and therefore sell their goods. It appears that some goods were sold and some could never even be purchased. Most probably, this last category of goods went to waste. Let us note that not all goods that do not meet consumer preferences have to be wasted; these goods can be exported. In central planning, however, exports and imports were also included in the plan. Besides, it was quite senseless. If, for instance, an enterprise exported its goods and gained currency, the latter could not be used for any industrial purchase in the country, as all internal goods flows were fixed in the plan. We conclude that the value of some goods was not realized; some value was bound to be wasted.

The scenario could be worse, however. The factor that made it better was that in centrally planned countries as well as in any other country, there is a source that creates value "from nothing." This has to do with natural resource endowment, such as land, water, and mineral resources. These resources are a country's idle resources. Before discovery or even extraction, they were not used as input factors in any production process. Their use in the economy therefore is not overshadowed by the creation of a gap in the present circulation, as it is in the case with innovations, which combine resources already in use.

A centrally planned state owning these resources does not need to create an ad hoc monetary mass in order to employ these newly excavated natural resources. Therefore, with the employment of natural resources, a new value is being added into the circular flow. Incidentally, since circular flow has a fixed amount of monetary mass, the addition of new value without the change of money supply may explain the decrease of prices, which was characteristic to centrally planned economies at the early stages.

We thus saw that the value created in central planning was constituted from (1) goods of industrial usage; that is, means of production, the value of which was steadily decreasing; (2) final consumption goods, among which a certain waste inevitably took place; and (3) the excavation of natural resources. If the first two value sources had a declining tendency, the third was a source of an increase in value. If we define development in a broad sense—that is, new value creation—then the third source did lead to development, but this development originated not from a more effective use of known and already employed resources, but from the addition of new ones. This was therefore an extensive type of development. It was the employment of these idle resources, which cost nothing but created value, that was the source of the enigmatic growth of centrally planned economies. This growth had to take place in the early decades of the centrally planned system, when the value of industrial goods was diminishing but had not yet reach the point at which it could not be covered by value created by natural resources. It was thus mainly this source that kept the centrally planned economies extensively developing for some time.

What does this amount of value mean for money? According to Schumpeter, capital and money are the same. Capital is that amount of ad hoc created monetary resources that have a purchasing power and that can be used for buying goods and services from the circular flow. This ad hoc money is not different in any way from money in the circular flow; it is not bound to any particular good or service. It follows that the monetary units of central planning could be denoted as money in a very limited sense. The instant purchasing value of these monetary units can be estimated as a sum of value of (1) the means of production, whose value by the end of central planning was probably zero because of physical and moral aging, (2) final consumption goods, whose value was also insignificant because of waste, and (3) the value of employed natural resources. Therefore, such monetary units in central planning were limited.

This picture of values had some inevitable consequences on the sphere of distribution. Budget is a manifestation of a state regardless of its politicoeconomic character; the origin of the budget has nothing to do with the form of ownership or the planned/market mode of resource allocation, since it is an economic manifestation of the state. State ownership and the plan as the main method of allocation of resources nevertheless caused a modification of the functions and composition of the budget in centrally planned economies. The fact that profit, taxes, and current and capital expenditures were transformed through the state budget meant that the division between state and enterprise financial resources was arbitrary and nominal. These resources, including the profit of an enterprise, represented the resources of the state. The fact that practically all economic resources in the country had a state origin and hence enterprises did not have any incentive for profit implies that the conventional budget tools—subsidies and taxes—did not have the same economic meaning in central planning as in a market economy.

## INSTITUTIONAL AND STRUCTURAL DYNAMICS: POSTCENTRAL PLANNING TRANSFORMATION

The transformation of state ownership into private ownership happens in two ways: first through transferring the existing capital assets to new owners and second through creating conditions for the emergence of new nonstate capital assets. In both cases, the formal transformation of ownership destroys the basis of planned exchange: state ownership of capital assets.

The transformation of planned exchange to competitive exchange involves the loss of its distinguishing elements, because neither the prices nor the volumes of goods bought and sold remain fixed. Here a problem arises. In central planning the function of exchange was performed by planning and money as an economic category became obsolete. The problem is that the abolition of planning is not automatically accompanied by the creation of money. The space that was once occupied by the plan is not immediately occupied by money, for the latter has yet to exist. This phenomenon, which may be suitably referred to as a *monetary vacuum*, is the essence of the specificity of the postcentral planning transition. It is precisely monetary and not simply an investment vacuum, since it refers to the lack of all categories of money: M1, M2, and M3.

The implication of a monetary vacuum for the institutions of ownership should be that they become characterized by slowness, a nonlinear privatization process, and a gap between formal and actual ownership rights. Indeed, the formal transference of assets from state to private hands should not occur as soon as monetary inflows to enterprises fail to appear. Of course, the first characteristic implies certain political commitments, and the erratic privatization process in Belarus, and Uzbekistan well illustrates the point. The degree of democracy does resolve the issue of the speed of privatization, however, as the recent claims for renationalization in a more democratic Czech Republic confirm. The other characteristic of ownership, the gap between formal and actual ownership rights, means that a problem endemic to transition is ownership rights' enforcement, particularly the enforcement of intellectual ownership rights (4).

The consequences of a monetary vacuum for another institutional element, the sphere of exchange, should imply mutual indebtedness between enterprises; maintenance of various forms of price regulations; preservation or creation of mechanisms of nonmonetary exchange, such as barter or compensatory agreements; creation of hybrid distribution arrangements; and the exercise of methods of administrative control on private enterprises. These arrangements are nonexistent in both centrally planned and market economies, and evolve as a result of the monetary vacuum phenomenon. *Kontserns*, for instance, particularly popular in the former Soviet Union countries, represent a voluntary unification of enterprises and occupy a middle position between ministry and enterprise (5). The major function of such kontserns is to resolve the sale and supply problem. In a way these kontserns can resemble Indian "canalizing agencies," with the major difference being that concerns are created to resolve a transformational problem—the monetary vacuum. Financial-industrial groups (FIGs), mostly popular in Russia (6), were created as a result of the sharp demand for financial resources in industry, which clashed with the logic of financial institutions, which due to high inflation, tend to concentrate their activity in short-term trade and speculative deals, and not in large and long-term industrial projects. The objective of the FIGs therefore is seen as the unification of financial and industrial capital, thus providing working and investment capital for enterprises. Other measures of state-enterprise interaction contain various intergovernmental agreements on the barter supply of goods and declarations on the facilitation of industrial cooperation between industrial enterprises of Commonwealth of Independent States (CIS) countries (7). On the other hand, transitional countries lack forms of monetary arrangements practiced in the West: statutory marketing boards, export marketing boards, regulatory marketing boards, fiscal monopolies, and canalizing agencies. Such enterprises do not exist in Estonia (8). Mongolia, Bulgaria, Georgia, Albania, Romania, Hungary, Czech Republic, and Slovenia. Poland and Latvia maintain marketing boards, and Kyrgyzstan has a fiscal import monopoly. It is noticeable, however, that these structures cover a very limited range of products and are not effective (9).

Budgeting will also possess specific transformational features preconditioned by a monetary vacuum. We can recall that the budget played a minor role in central planning. This budget now has to perform the role of the main state mechanism of resource distribution. Such a role, however, which covering areas that had earlier been regulated by the nonmonetary plan, cannot correspond to the capacity of the small postcentral planning budget. A suddenly arising massive budget deficit should be a structural inevitability in transitional countries. In order to reduce the gap between expenditures and revenues, transitional countries therefore have to activate the fiscal function; extremely high taxes should be a chronic feature in postsocialist countries. It should be emphasized that earlier we noted that "subsidies" and "taxes"—meaning in principle 100% provision and confiscation of resources by the state in respect to industrial units—implied that these two economic categories were senseless in central planning. This was additionally aggravated by the distorted value system resulting in the disappearance of money as an economic category. That is why the transformation from plan to market implies not the decrease of these 100% taxes and 100% subsidies up to a reasonable level, say 30% of taxes on enterprises and a corresponding share of the budget, for subsidizing various items. Instead, the described peculiarities of subsidies, taxes, the value system, and money create a situation in which there are neither taxes nor subsidies (nor money in the economy). Transitional states therefore have to impose extremely high taxes in order to pay for minimum public programs. Those programs in turn are bound to be very limited, since money is lacking not only in the public purse, but also in enterprises' and households' spheres.

## CONCLUSION

The specificity of transitional countries is rooted in the lack of normal commodity exchange in central planning. It was argued that money did not exist as an economic category under central planning. The functions of money were performed by the plan. The abolition of the plan does not create money in itself, but the creation of the market mechanism necessitates the existence of money in the economy. The space occupied by the plan under central planning and by money in market economies is empty, leaving a vacuum where money should be. This monetary vacuum is the principal feature of transitional countries, making them not an odd variety of developed, developing, and newly industrialized countries, but a group of countries in which every seemingly chaotic and irrational irregularity is underpinned by a peculiar and highly logical order.

On the methodological front, the assertion according to which the positivist limitations of social sciences restrict the capacity of applying a particular theory in different contextual conditions was questioned. It was shown that Joseph Schumpeter, who died in 1950 when the socialist countries had not even officially entered their stage of "advanced socialism" (1970s) and when the transition to a market economy was far off, nevertheless offered a theory that is able to explain the important issues in both centrally planned and transitional economies. In the framework of the present analysis, the problem with theory is therefore reduced not to the positivist limitations of social science theories, but to the quality of theories. The answer can already be found, in fact, in the works of XIX economists. In other words, we can arrive at a conclusion regarding the institutional and structural specificity of transitional countries by pure logical thinking and primary data analysis if we can recall some of the principal politicoeconomic assumptions, especially those relating to value exchange and the functions of money, developed by Smith, Ricardo, and Marx. These observations bring us to the consideration that at least in the case of the politicoeconomic explanations of transition, the possibility of many alternative explanations is doubtful. A more acceptable conclusion is that for the concrete characteristics of a phenomenon with a coherent logic the principal answers should not be much different.

## NOTES

1.  The author is indebted to Professor Terence Rajivan Edward and Professor Hakan Samur for their invaluable help and encouragement.

2. The first law claimed "the achievement of full welfare and free and rich development of all members of the society in socialised order on the basis of constantly progressing labour productivity." The second law declared the remuneration according to the amount of work done.

3. We consider only the relations between enterprises. The demand in question thus relates to enterprises, not final consumers.

4. This is supported by legal studies. In 2001, a special edition, "Enforcement of Industrial Property Rights in Eastern Europe," was issued by the journal *International Review of Industrial Property and Copyright Law*. The results of detailed studies in the region were presented. The important conclusion is that it is not formal codification of intellectual property rights, but their enforcement that constitutes the real problem in transitional countries.

5. Like ministries, concerns have certain functions of state supervision and administrative, nonfinancial assistance. Unlike ministries, however, these concerns are financed by deductions from the net profit of enterprises.

6. There were seven of them in 1993–1994, twenty one in 1995, seventy in 1998, and about 100 in 1999 (Voitenko, 2000; 2001; Vinslav et al 2000).

7. Intergovernmental Agreement of April 15, 1994, "On the Facilitation in the Creation and Development of Industrial, Commercial, Credit-Financial, Insurance and Mixed Transnational Organisations." On April 15, 1994, all the CIS countries signed an agreement on the facilitation of the creation and development of industrial, commercial, credit-financial, insurance, and mixed transnational companies. In the course of the realization of the agreement six bilateral agreements on major principles of the creation of financial-industrial groups (with Belarus, Kazakhstan, Ukraine, Uzbekistan, Tadjikistan, and Kyrgyzstan). In the agreement on the creation of a monetary union among CIS countries, signed on October 21, 1994, the sides have taken obligations to create preferential credit banding and currency-financial conditions for the creation and development of transnational structures. On March 29, 1996, in the agreement among Russian, Belarus, Kazakhstan, and Kyrgyzstan on the deepening of integration in economic and humanitarian branches, the countries have been obliged to elaborate and realize a system of measures of state support for the development of industrial cooperation and the creation of transnational structures.

8. There are two state-trading enterprises in Estonia, mainly resulting from the remaining state ownership on the bodies in question, but the Estonian government has committed itself to eliminating them.

9. In Latvia, for instance, the government has not been supplying its market boards with financial resources, and its activities therefore were negligible.

## REFERENCES

Brus, W. (1972). The Market in a Socialist Economy. London: Routledge and Kegan Paul.

Bukharin, N., Preobrazhenski, E. (1969). The ABC of Commuinism. London: Penguin.

Hayek von, F. (1988). The Fatal Conceit: The Errors of Socialism. London: Routledge.

Keynes, J. (1960). The General Theory of Employment, Interest and Money. London: Macmillan.

Kornai, J. (1992). The Political Economy of Communism. Oxford: Clarendon.

Lavigne, M. (1995). The Economics of Transition: From Socialist Economy to Market Economy. Basingstoke: Macmillan.

Lenin, V. ([1918] 1965). Left-wing childishness and the petty bourgeois mentality. In: Lenin V., ed., Collected Works. 4th English ed. Moscow: Progress Publishers pp. 323–354.

Marx, K. (1956). The Poverty of Philosophy. London: Lawrence & Wishart.

Nove, A. (1983). The Economics of Feasible Socialism. London: Allen & Unwin.

Shmelev, N., Popov, V. (1989). Na perelome: ekonomicheskaya perestroika v SSSR (At the

Turning Point: Economic Perestroika in the USSR). Moscow: Izdatelstvo agenstva pechati novosti.

Schumpeter, J. (1961). The Theory of Economic Development. An Inquiry into Profits, Capital, Credit. London: Oxford University Press.

Veblen, T. (1994). The Theory of the Leisure Class. London: Routledge/Thoemmes Press.

Vinslav, U., Voitenko, A., Germanova, I., Voroshchuk, A. (2000). Razvitiye postsovetskih TNK: ekonomicheskiye, pravovye i politicheskie problemy. Rossiiskiy ekonomicheskiy zhurnal  423–34.

Voitenko, A. (2000). Sostoyaniye I perspektivy ofitsial'nyh finansovo- promyshlennyh grupp v Rossii. Rossijskij Ekonomicheskii Zhurnal 1:22–28.

Voitenko, A. (2001). Sostoyanie I perspektivy ofitsial'nyh finansovo-promyshlennyh grupp v Rossii. Rossiiskiy ekonomicheskiy zhurnal 2:22–29.

von Mises, L. (1936). Socialism: An Economic and Sociological Analysis. London: Jonathan Cape.

# 30

# The Growing Challenges of Globalization to Self-Reliant Development in Developing Nations

**M. SHAMSUL HAQUE**

*National University of Singapore, Singapore*

## INTRODUCTION

In recent decades, one of the most significant human phenomena affecting all societies and nations has been the process of "globalization," encompassing economic production and consumption, political ideology and state formation, cultural norm and identity, and intellectual orientation and information exchange. Although various modes or forms of globalization occurred in the past—which can be traced back to the advent of capitalism in the early sixteenth century (Frank, 1998) and found in such historical events as the conquest and colonization of new territories, cross-national migration of people, diffusion of ideas and technologies, and expansion of transport and communication networks—the contemporary phase of globalization surpasses all the early epochs in terms of its scope, pace, intensity, complexity, and impacts. The current phase encompasses all social domains, represents unprecendented speed and intensity, shapes national and international concerns, and affects almost all layers of human existence, including the realm of private space and individual choice.

Due to the practical significance of globalization, it has become one of the most widely debated academic issues in various disciplines or fields of study, including political science, international relations, economics, sociology, geography, history, and philosophy. These multidisciplinary interpretations make the understanding of globalization complex and controversial, which is reinforced further by the diverse viewpoints expressed by the multiple actors and interests involved in the globalization process. The major actors or forces of globalization include the dominant states (especially the United States), transnational corporations, and international agencies, such as the World Bank, International Monetary Fund (IMF), World Trade Organization (WTO), and International Finance Corporation (IFC) (Martin, 1993; Ramonet, 2000). In facilitating globalization, there are also major regional economic and trade blocs, such as the Organization for Economic Co-operation and Development (OECD), Asia-Pacific Economic Cooperation (APEC), European Union (EU), North American Free Trade Area (NAFTA), Association of Southeast Asian Nations (ASEAN), Organization of American States (OAS), and Organization of African Unity (OAU) (ILO, 1999).

These diverse actors and interests have led to the emergence of various ideological perspectives on globalization, including the conservative, progressive, nationalist, and radical outlooks. In general, however, globalization is defined as a process of growing interdependence among people across nations, as a shift from distinct national economies to an internationalized economy, and as a worldwide network of finance, production, and information based on the international mobility of capital, people, and goods and services (CIDA, 1996; ILO, 1999; OECD, 1998). This interpretation does not address the noneconomic dimensions of globalization and its unequal structure. In this chapter, globalization is thus largely understood as *a process of integrating regions, nations, societies, and peoples in the domains of economics, politics, culture, and knowledge through means such as capital, technology, production, exchange, and information owned and controlled unequally by various states, organizations, classes, and individuals.*

With this brief overview of the significance and meaning of globalization, the main objective of this chapter is to explore its implications. Although the current literature covers enormous studies on the consequences of globalization for a variety of issues, such as national sovereignty, unemployment, economic inequality, gender issues, and cultural identity (Kochler, 1999), this chapter specifically focuses on its impact on self-reliant development. In most development studies, the realization of self-reliance (as opposed to dependence) has been a common concern (Bjonnes, 2002). It is observed by some scholars that the process of globalization—by expanding the forces of the free market, reinforcing a unipolar global structure, imposing international agreements and economic policies on governments, eroding state autonomy and capacity, and exercising a "new phase of colonization"—tends to undermine national self-reliance (Haque, 2002; OECD, 1998; Köchler, 1999). In fact, globalization often represents an antithesis of a self-reliant mode of development, especially for developing nations. This chapter explores the impacts of globalization on three major domains of self-reliance, including the economic-financial, politicoideological, and cultural-intellectual spheres, which represent the dimensions of a comprehensive view of development.

## GLOBALIZATION AND ECONOMIC–FINANCIAL SELF-RELIANCE

### The Extent of Globalization

The economic and financial factors constitute one of the most basic dimensions of self-reliant development. In this sphere, the process of globalization has been intensified through the current policies of deregulation, privatization, and liberalization adopted by countries worldwide (Khor, 2000; Haque, 2002), which have diminished state intervention and protectionism and unleashed the power of global market forces to take over national assets and public enterprises, maximize cross-border capital mobility, ensure free trade, and facilitate foreign investment. Beyond the advanced market economies in Western Europe and North America, during the recent decades these globalization-friendly policies have been embraced by most developing countries in Asia, Africa, and Latin America, as well as by the former socialist states in Eastern Europe. For instance, since the mid-1980s, East and Southeast Asian countries liberalized and deregulated trade and finance in order to attract more foreign direct investment (FDI) and expand the volume of export (Montes, 1997). South Asian countries have also undertaken such policies to reduce trade barriers, withdraw capital controls, permit foreign ownership, encourage foreign investment, and so on (Haque, 2001).

Facilitated by these conducive policies in favor of global market forces, the value of world exports increased from $315 billion in 1970 to $3.4 trillion in 1990 (Khor, 2000:4). By 1996, while the value of world exports reached $6.3 trillion, the value of world imports rose to $6.4 trillion (ILO, 1999). Similarly, the amount of cross-border capital flows (excluding FDI) increased from $536 billion in 1991 to nearly $1.3 trillion in 1995, and the total stock of the world's liquid financial assets rose from $10.7 trillion in 1980 to $41.5 trillion in 1994 (Fraser and Oppenheim, 1997). According to the ILO (1999), in the 1990s the list of the fastest-growing countries in exports and imports included China, Indonesia, Malaysia, the Philippines, Singapore, Thailand, Argentina, and Poland.

Another indicator of economic–financial globalization is the worldwide expansion of FDI. With the growing integration of the world market, by 1996 the total inflow of FDI reached $349 billion and outflow $347 billion, and the inward FDI stock rose to $3.2 trillion and outward stock to $2.8 trillion (ILO, 1999; World Bank, 1996). While the main investors have been the United States, the United Kingdom, Japan, France, and Germany, an increasing number of developing countries became the major recipients of FDI in the 1990s. The average annual share of total FDI flows to developing countries increased from 17% in 1981–1990 to 32% in 1991–1995 (Khor, 2000:4). There are considerable variations among the developing regions and countries in receiving FDI, however. For instance, in 1996 over 80% of all FDI flows to the developing world went to Latin America and the Caribbean (30%) and to East Asia and the Pacific (50%) (ILO, 1999). Within the East Asia-Pacific region itself, the main recipients of FDI have been China, Malaysia, Indonesia, the Philippines, Singapore, Taiwan, and Thailand (ILO, 1999; Kyloh, 1998).

In addition to FDI, there has been an unprecedented proliferation of foreign portfolio investments. For instance, for major industrial nations, the value of cross-border transactions in bonds and equities increased from 10% of gross domestic product (GDP) in 1980 to 150–250% of GDP in 1995, while for developing countries portfolio investments constituted 38% of all private investment flows (bonds 19% and equity 18.8%) in 1996 (ILO, 1999). The U.S. investment flows into foreign securities increased from $74 billion in 1982 to $1.27 trillion in 1996 (ILO, 1999). In addition to such liberalization of investment, this economic–financial globalization has been facilitated by institutional and strategic arrangements, such as the creation of the aforementioned regional trade blocs and the worldwide expansion of free trade zones and export-processing zones.

## The Impacts on Self-Reliance

*First*, the new set of policies (liberalization, deregulation, privatization) under which the current phase of intensive globalization is being realized has diminished the self-reliance of national economies, especially in developing countries. Increasingly, these countries have become the major markets for exports and investments from advanced capitalist nations. It was observed in 1994 that about 42–47% of total exports from the United States, Japan, and Western European nations went to developing countries and the former socialist states ("Global Economy," 1994:10). Such massive exports to developing countries have been detrimental to the self-reliant development of indigenous industries and markets in these countries. In fact, the end of protectionism and the expansion of free trade have not been favorable for developing countries with regard to the terms of trade for their own products. It has been observed that for these countries, the terms of trade for nonfuel commodities fell by 52% between 1980 and 1992 (Khor, 2000:10). The situation became worse in the 1990s; between 1996 and 1999 the prices of oil and nonoil primary commodities produced by developing countries fell by 16.4% and 33.8% respectively (Khor, 2000:11). According to Khor (2000:10–11), the current liberalized trading system has favored the manufactured goods exported by advanced capitalist nations, disadvantaged the raw materials and primary commodities exported by the least developed countries, and eroded the self-reliance of their national economies.

*Second*, the loss of economic self-reliance caused by globalized markets, finance, and trade is also indicated by the growing worldwide dominance of transnational corporations (TNCs) emerging from developed nations. Between 1970 and 1995, the number of TNCs increased from 7000 to 40,000, and while 90% of these TNCs are based in advanced industrialized nations (mostly in France, Germany, Japan, the Netherlands, Switzerland, Sweden, Canada, the United Kingdom, and the United States), they have 250,000 foreign affiliates operating in countries all over the world (Karliner, 1997). Today these TNCs shape the world economy in terms of trade, finance, investment, technology, and so on (Pha, 2002). It has been observed that the revenues earned by only two American TNCs (General Motors and Ford) surpass the combined GDP of all sub-Saharan African countries; the sales of six Japanese trading companies (Mitsubishi, Mitsui, Sumitomo, etc.) are equal to the combined GDP of all South American countries; 70% of world trade and 90% of world technology and product patents are held by TNCs; and about 51% of the 100 largest world economies are represented by corporations rather than national economies (Karliner, 1997). Such colossal economic powers of large corporations based in advanced capitalist nations, which represent the major forces of globalization, have worsened the vulnerability and external dependence of developing countries, and thus adversely affected their self-reliant development.

*Third*, in the process of globalization, the liberalization of foreign investment and foreign ownership has considerably expanded the extent of foreign ownership in many countries. According to the ILO (1999), the new opportunity for FDI has been one of the most effective avenues for entering foreign markets and acquiring foreign assets since the mid-1980s. The above-mentioned TNCs have thus expanded worldwide ownership, especially by purchasing privatized assets in all major sectors, including oil, airline, power supply, telecommunication, automobile, electronics, and food processing (Haque, 1999b; Karliner, 1997). In the developing world, the primary targets of foreign investment and ownership have been countries in Southeast Asia (e.g.,

Indonesia and the Philippines) and Latin America (e.g., Argentina, Brazil, Mexico, and Venezuela) (ILO, 1999). This increasing foreign ownership in developing countries has diminished their control over their own national economic activities and perpetuated their external dependence.

Fourth, the external dependence of developing countries has also been reinforced by their increasing external debts; they borrowed heavily to pursue market-led policies and export-led production in order to compete in the global market. Between 1990 and 1998, the total external debt rose from $55.3 billion to $154.6 billion in China, $83.7 billion to $98.2 billion in India, $69.9 billion to $150.9 billion in Indonesia, $35.0 billion to $139.1 billion in South Korea, $28.1 billion to $86.1 billion in Thailand, $119.9 billion to $232.0 billion in Brazil, and $104.4 billion to $160.0 billion in Mexico (World Bank, 2001; 314–315). In addition to foreign debt, the worsening global inequality also represents a challenge to the economic self-reliance of poorer developing countries as they become increasingly powerless in unequal international markets and dependent on few affluent nations dominating the global economic and financial structures. In line with the growing economic polarization among countries caused by the forces and processes of globalization, by 1993 developed nations (20% of the world's population) shared more than 78% of the $23 trillion global GDP, while developing countries (80% of the world's population) accounted for less than 22% of such global GDP (UNDP, 1996). Due to the deeper integration of all national economies into the world capitalist system, this worsening inequality among countries certainly weakens the economic autonomy and self-reliance of poorer countries in relation to affluent capitalist nations.

## GLOBALIZATION AND POLITICO-IDEOLOGICAL SELF-RELIANCE

### The Extent of Globalization

Beyond the economic–financial arena, politico-ideological autonomy is crucial for a self-reliant mode of development, which has been significantly affected by the current phase of globalization encompassing all nation-states. While the postwar period saw the emergence of welfare capitalism in Western Europe and North America, socialism in Eastern Europe and other regions, and nationalist developmentalism in most Asian, African, and Latin American countries, since the early 1980s all these state-led ideological frameworks began to weaken under the increasing pressure created by the above-mentioned forces of globalization, and these earlier ideological traditions were eventually replaced with a neoliberal ideology that favors global market forces (Hildyard, 1997; Haque, 1999b). As McChesney (1999b) mentions, neoliberalism is the "defining paradigm" of the current age, which has dominated the global politico-ideological trend in recent decades.

This neoliberal ideology—which is endorsed by the advocates of neoclassical theory, public choice school, monetarist policy, and free trade (especially the multilateral agencies, advanced capitalist states, transnational commercial banks, and neoconservative think tanks)—prescribes fiscal discipline, privatization, deregulation, trade liberalization, foreign investment, subsidy cuts, and market-based exchange and interest rates (Pereira, 1993:19). The underlying assumptions and rationales of neoliberalism are that market competition serves the public interest based on individual choices, maximizes individual prosperity by efficient allocation of resources, encourages private enterprise and initiatives, eradicates waste and incompetence, ensures the determination of prices based on supply and demand, and so on (Hildyard, 1997; McChesney, 1999b).

During the last two decades, this neoliberal ideology has been globalized often by influence and pressure exerted on various developing countries in Asia, Africa, and Latin America. In Africa, the application of neoliberal ideology has been realized by implementing such structural adjustment policies as divestment, subsidy withdrawal, price deregulation, and trade liberalization (Corkery, 1997). In Latin America, since the early 1980s Chile and Mexico have embraced neoliberal reforms, such as a reduction in public spending, the elimination of trade barriers and foreign investment regulations, and the privatization of public assets (Pereira, 1993:28–40). Bolivia and Venezuela introduced similar neoliberal reforms based on the adjustment programs prescribed by the IMF and the World Bank. Even the populist regimes, such as those of Alberto Fujimori in Peru and Carlos Menem in Argentina, also adopted neoliberal reforms, despite the serious limitations and adverse consequences of such reforms (Pereira, 1993:44–46). In Asia, the neoliberal approach has been followed by such countries as India, Pakistan, Bangladesh, Malaysia, the Philippines, Thailand, and South Korea (Haque, 2003).

On the other hand, the globalization of neoliberal ideology has led to fundamental changes in the political system, especially in the formation of the state. In this ideological context, the earlier formations of the welfare state, socialist state, and developmental state dominated by the public sector, have been replaced with a market-friendly state structure, which is variously termed as the privatized state, the minimalist state, the contract state, the hollow state, the managerial state, or the skeleton state (Clarke and Newman, 1997). The main features of this new state formation include its minimal intervention and regulation, its supportive rather than leading role in producing and delivering services, its initiatives to downsize the public sector and expand market forces, its policy to liberalize trade and investment, and its withdrawal of subsidies and use of market principles (Carlos and Pereira, 1998; Hildyard, 1997; Haque, 2002).

In various degrees, these features of new state formation have become global as most developing countries and postsocialist nations have moved toward downsizing public bureaucracy, deregulating market controls, privatizing public enterprises, and eliminating trade and investment barriers. In Asia, the restructuring of the state and its role has been pursued in many countries (e.g., Bangladesh, India, Malaysia, Nepal, Pakistan, Singapore, Sri Lanka, and Thailand), although there are variations in the extent and pace of such changes in the direction of a minimalist state (Schmidt, 1998; Haque, 1998; 2001). Similar antipublic sector and market-friendly trends in state formation can be observed in Africa and Latin America, such as in Argentina, Chile, Mexico, Uganda, and Zimbabwe (Kaul, 1996; Oszlak, 1997). The examples of Arab countries following the minimalist state model include Algeria, Jordan, Morocco, and Yemen (World Bank, 1996).

## The Impacts on Self-Reliance

The globalization of neoliberal ideology and the minimalist state model has serious implications for political self-reliance, especially in developing countries. *First*, the autonomy and self-reliance of the state itself may have come under challenge. While the state had relative autonomy to pursue its national policies in various sectors, in the

current neoliberal global context dominated by international agencies and corporations, states in the developing world have lost their self-reliant policy preferences
(Khor, 2000). It has been pointed out that due to the integration of these states into the
neoliberal ideological framework, their policy decisions are often dictated externally
by the dominant capitalist states (Khor, 2000; Hildyard, 1997). In fact, the range of
promarket policies associated with structural adjustment and stabilization programs is
not necessarily chosen by states in developing countries; such policies have usually
been imposed on them by the World Bank, the IMF, and the WTO (Jiyad, 1995; Khor,
2000). The state often had no choice but to adopt market-led policies as a precondition
for obtaining foreign loans from international agencies. As Khor (2000:6) mentions,
today "domestic economic policies of developing countries are thus being made in the
WTO negotiations, rather than in parliament, bureaucracy or cabinet at the national
level."

In the case of Latin America, the autonomous policy choices of the state, especially in countries with huge external debt and dependence, have been constrained
by covert and overt pressure created by the U.S. government, the IMF, and the World
Bank (Haque, 2002; Pereira, 1993). Similarly, in South and Southeast Asia, the
traditional developmental policies were compromised and the externally prescribed
policy reforms had to be introduced, often because of pressure from international
agencies and foreign donors. It has also been observed in the case of North Africa and
the Middle East that policy reforms in favor of global free trade and market forces
were imposed as loan conditionalities by international agencies, especially the World
Bank. (See World Bank, 1996.)

*Second*, the diminishing political self-reliance in developing countries is also
evident in the decline of their state capacity in the context of globalization. In the
absence of an advanced market system in these countries, the state used to play a
crucial role to ensure some degree of national self-reliance by undertaking massive
developmental initiatives and protecting national interests. Today, however under the
current global context of neoliberal market ideology, the emerging minimalist states in
these countries have lost a certain capacity to maintain their self-reliance; it is
mentioned by the World Bank (1997) itself that most countries in sub-Saharan Africa
are facing the crisis of state capacity. More specifically, the capacity of minimalist
states has diminished because of the externally imposed privatization of its profit-
making enterprises, reduction in its tax revenues and overall budget, and its obligation
to pay debt services (Ferge, 1999).

Beyond this growing financial incapacity, the state is also likely to face the
problem of human resources because of the prescribed policy of streamlining or
downsizing its public sector by retrenching employees, reducing job security, and
cutting wages (Meyer-Stamer, 1997). In addition, the policy of deregulation has
weakened the state's capacity to exercise effective control over national economic
management; the globalization of deregulated market forces is now eroding the state's
capacity to manage and monitor the activities of TNCs, the cross-border flow of goods
and services, external trade, the international monetary exchange, and so on (CGG,
1995). Due to this weakening capacity of the state—caused by its growing financial
difficulties, human resource constraints, and loss of effective regulatory controls under
the neoliberal policy agenda—it is less capable today to pursue a self-reliant mode of
development based on domestic resources and local needs rather than foreign loans,
investments, and demands.

*Third*, at the micro-grassroots level, the self-reliance of workers and citizen has come under challenge due to the adoption of neoliberal policies and the new role of minimalist states to meet the demands of international agencies and global market forces. More specifically, due to the diminishing policy autonomy of states mentioned above, they have autocratically introduced the unpopular structural adjustment policies without public consultation or consent. Such policies may satisfy global demands, but they adversely affect citizens' interests (Pereira et al., 1993; Hildyard, 1997). For example, the globalization-led neoliberal policies have diminished the rights of workers and trade unions in terms of their job security, labor relations, safety and health, and bargaining power (Schmidt, 1998; WCL, 1997). Under market-driven neoliberal policies favoring the global economic powers during the 1990s, the rights of workers and their unions deteriorated in many countries in Asia, Africa, Latin America, and Eastern Europe (WCL, 1997). These trends imply a decline in workers' power, security, and self-reliance.

Similarly, under global pressure, the adoption of neoliberal structural adjustment by the minimalist state (e.g., the reduction in subsidies and withdrawal of social programs) has led to the erosion of citizens' entitlement to such basic services as education, health, and housing, and affected their overall well-being and self-reliance. In certain years during the 1980s and 1990s in Asia and Africa, government spending on education dropped in such cases as Malaysia, Indonesia, Myanmar, Tanzania, Uganda, Zaire, and Zimbabwe (UNDP, 2001; World Bank, 2000; Tevera, 1995). Between 1980 and 1996, there was similar decline in education expenditure in Chile, Costa Rica, Ecuador, El Salvador, Panama, and Peru (World Bank, 2000). There was also a drop in government expenditure on health, especially in such African countries as Ghana, Egypt, Kenya, Nigeria, Somalia, and Uganda (UNDP, 1995). Under market-led policy reforms, while public expenditures on basic services have not improved, the conditions of unemployment and inflation have worsened in many countries in Asia, Africa, Latin America, and Eastern Europe (Pereira et al., 1993; WCL, 1997). The global proliferation of neoliberal ideology, minimalist state, and market-driven policies has thus led to the erosion of citizens' entitlement and access to basic services, and diminished their self-reliance and well-being.

## GLOBALIZATION AND INFORMATIONAL-CULTURAL SELF-RELIANCE

### The Extent of Globalization

In the current age, cultural and informational self-reliance has become increasingly critical for human development. In this regard, the most outstanding feature of contemporary globalization is the worldwide expansion of information technologies and communication networks integrating all societies and peoples in terms of information, knowledge, and culture through varieties of electronic and print media. While the domain of media, information, and culture was largely under state regulation prior to the 1980s, today—under pressure from international agencies and market forces—the media and information networks have been privatized, deregulated, and globalized under the dominance of a few media giants (McChesney, 1997). The deregulation and privatization of media ownership under the neoliberal framework allowed foreign ownership of various media networks and created lucrative markets worldwide (McChesney, 1999). The process of such globalization has been facilitated by new satellite and digital technologies that allow for instant communication and information access, and for television signals to be broadcast to any part of the world (Rothkop, 1997).

Behind this intensive process of informational and cultural globalization however, are certain transnational media corporations, the number of which had shrunk from fifty in 1984, to 23 in 1990, to only ten in 1996 (Bagdikian, 1997). Today there are eight such media giant of which the five largest ones (in terms of sales) include Time Warner ($24 billion), Disney ($22 billion), Bertelsmann ($15 billion), Viacom ($13 billion), and Rupert Murdoch's News Corporation ($11 billion) (McChesney, 1997). The examples of other first-tier media giants are General Electric, AT&T Liberty Media, and Sony. There are also various second-tier media corporations, including Dow Jones, Gannett, Knight-Rider, Mediaset, Pearson, and Reuters (McChesney, 1999a). Most of these global media corporations are engaged in multiple media industries, including television channels and networks, film production, cable and satellite systems, music production, book publishing, retail stores, magazines, and newspapers (McChesney, 1997).

Since the early 1980s, facilitated by the above-mentioned policies of deregulating and privatizing the media and communication systems in most countries, these giant media corporations have expanded their outlets worldwide and globalized their informational and cultural products (Covington, 1994). More specifically, Time Warner has more than 200 subsidiaries worldwide and 1000 movie screens outside the United States; Viacom's Nickelodeon offers programs in various languages and broadcasts children's programs through 90 million TV sets in seventy countries; and Viacom's MTV is a global music channel available to 280 million homes worldwide. Disney has already expanded its channels to countries in North America, Western Europe, and East Asia, and ESPN International broadcasts televised sports in 165 countries in twenty-one languages (Akande, 2002; McChesney, 1997).

In the arena of news and information, only four Western news agencies— Reuters (United Kingdom), AFP (France), AP (United States), and UPI (United States)—provide 55–75% of international news published in the Asian, African, and Latin American dailies (Roach, 1990; Haque, 1999a). CNN has become one of the most globalized television news channel with 90 million subscribers worldwide, and AP has 300 news bureaus in more than seventy countries (Olson, 1993; McChesney, 1997). The most recent addition to the globalization of information and communication networks is the proliferation of the Internet. It is estimated that the number of Internet hosts increased from 100,000 in 1988 to 36 million in 1998. The number of Internet users expanded from 26 million in 1995 to 250 million in 2000, and these users are from more than 150 countries (Haque, 2002; Norris, 2000; Kim, 1998). The Internet has revolutionized the nature of global communication by enhancing interpersonal exchange or correspondence and providing instant access to news, articles, reports, and information on virtually everything imaginable or conceivable (CGG, 1995; Kim, 1998).

## The Impacts on Self-Reliance

The current phase of intensive globalization in the realm of information, knowledge, and culture examined above is considered a serious threat to national identities or traditions. Such a concern has been expressed by policy makers, academics, indig-

enous people, and antiglobalization groups. For instance, in 1998 the culture ministers from twenty countries met in Ottawa to discuss the possibility of setting some
"ground rules" to protect their cultural traditions from the global culture industry
dominated by the United States (McChesney, 1999a, b). There are certain valid
reasons for this concern about the erosion of informational and cultural self-reliance
and the perpetuation of external dependence in this domain.

*First*, as discussed above, the ownership and control of the information networks
is dominated by transnational media corporations located predominantly in the
United States. In addition, the United States is the leading cyberpower, dominating
the computer industry and information highway; representing the major computer
giants, such as Microsoft, Intel, and IBM; and managing the Internet systems and
Internet hosts (Ramonet, 2000). It has been mentioned that only 1% of the films
watched in America are foreign productions, whereas American films, television series,
and news media flood the world every day (Ramonet, 2000). By 1990, about 750
million TV sets were broadcasting such imported programs to 2.5 billion people in
more than 160 countries (Kellner, 1990:1). This extreme inequality in the flow of media
products and information represents a dependency relationship based on the dominance of the core nations (especially the United States) and the vulnerability of
peripheral countries in the developing world (Kim, 1998).

*Second*, based on the severe inequality in the ownership and control of global
media networks, the cultural self-reliance of developing countries has come under
challenge, because through such media, the indigenous cultural beliefs and artifacts of
these countries are being marginalized every day by foreign images, values, and
symbols (Akande, 2002). The commoditized and packaged cultural products imported
from advanced industrial nations (especially the United States)—including films,
music, cartoons, comics, videos, clothes, and sports—tend to render indigenous
cultural symbols obsolete (Akande, 2002). The global dominance of American movies,
television programs, and software is so immense that even Western countries, such as
France and Canada, have passed laws to stop the satellite dissemination of them
(Rothkop, 1997). For the relatively powerless developing countries, it is more difficult
to maintain their cultural self-reliance under pressure created by cultural globalization
or McDonaldization (Akande, 2002).

*Third*, there is growing consumerism in developing countries (especially in terms
of a fetish for foreign goods) reinforced by the advertising industry, which also
threatens cultural self-reliance. Through the above-mentioned global media, commercial advertising has significantly multiplied in these countries (UNDP, 1998). Today
the "global elites" across nations have developed preferences for imported goods, and
they tend to identify with Western brands, songs, idols, and gadgets that are publicized
or advertised worldwide through the media (UNDP, 1998; Ramonet, 2000). These
global elites in developing countries are very similar to those in developed nations in
terms of their lifestyle; they speak English, dress in business suits, carry cellular
phones, travel abroad frequently, drive luxurious cars, consume imported goods,
prefer Western film and music, and avoid local products (Schmidt, 1998; Rothkop,
1997). It is thus not only external cultural influence created by media, it is also the
foreign lifestyle and consumption behavior of local elites that may pose a threat to the
national cultural self-reliance of developing countries.

*Finally*, cultural self-reliance has also come under challenge because of the
growing threat of hegemonic global media to local languages (which sustain indig-

enous cultures) in different parts of the world. Unfortunately, in addition to the various forms of global media (e.g., radio, television, films, newspapers, magazines, books, journals) dominated by English, the current worldwide dissemination of information, knowledge, and cultural products through the Internet is mostly in English. It is observed that English represents about 90% of global traffic on the Internet; the Internet is anchored in the United States, most software for navigating the Internet is in English, and it is considered an effective means for Western "cultural imperialism" (Kim, 1998). In the current age, English has become the language of global business and politics, the language of computers and the Internet (The Triumph of English, 2001). Because of such dominance of English over the media, information, business, and communication, globally it is now the first language for 380 million people and the second language for 250 million. One billion more are trying to learn it, and about half of the world's population may be able to speak the language by 2050 (The Triumph of English, 2001).

In the above context of the global hegemony of English, thousands of local languages in the developing world are under threat. It is found that more than 5000 languages (6800, according to some estimate) are characterized as endangered (Tuhus-Dubrow, 2002; Cheruiyot, 2003). According to Akande (2002), even optimistic estimates predict that about 90% of the languages spoken worldwide will disappear by the next century, and with them, some basic components of various cultures will also die. In short, due to the overwhelming dominance of English in the globalization process, many indigenous languages and traditions are dying in developing societies, and their cultural self-reliance as a part of authentic development is being diminished every day.

## CONCLUDING REMARKS

It has been explained in this chapter that unlike the previous epochs, the current phase of globalization has been most unprecedented in terms of its scope, speed, and intensity. It encompasses almost all domains, societies, institutions, and individuals. This phase of all-pervasive globalization, however, has been most unequal and hegemonic in terms of its main actors and beneficiaries. Although the process of such globalization has impacts on every national and international concern or issue, the main agenda of this chapter has been to explore its implications for a self-reliant (as opposed to dependent) mode of human development, especially in developing countries. From various empirical sources and descriptive studies, it has been explained that the contemporary phase of globalization has adversely affected all major domains of self-reliant development, including the economic, political, ideological, intellectual, and cultural spheres.

Despite these adverse implications of globalization, especially for the self-reliance of developing societies, it continues to expand and deepen worldwide due to its major beneficiaries and vested interests, such as the business elites, transnational corporations, capitalist states, and international agencies advocating and facilitating globalization and controlling or managing its major factors and processes. Under the globalization-led policy context dominated by privatization, deregulation, liberalization, foreign investment, and foreign ownership, while these vested interests gained considerably by expanding their worldwide empires in technology, finance, utilities, transport, information, media, and the culture industry, the self-reliance of developing countries declined in each of these sectors, and the poorer sections of the population lost their basic rights or entitlements. The forces of globalization are so influential and powerful—because of their alliance with dominant states, access to policy-making circles, influence over international bodies, and control over capital, technology, and information—that no single poor country can oppose or avoid them. In such circumstances, there is a need for exploring effective alternatives to escape from the grasp of the globalization forces in order to realize self-reliant development.

*First*, it is necessary to deconstruct or demystify globalization by assessing its adverse impacts on economic self-reliance, financial autonomy, ideological choices, political rights, cultural identities, and social justice. (Some of these have been discussed in this chapter.) For instance, despite the advocacy of structural adjustment programs by the World Bank and the IMF as the panacea for economic development, in actuality these programs have mainly subordinated the developing economies to the global capitalist system, eroded their economic self-reliance, and worsened their external dependence. These detrimental outcomes, according to Chossudovsky (1994), largely represent a form of "market colonialism" and "economic genocide." Similarly, while the global television and information networks dominated by the U.S. media giants are presented as objective and neutral, in reality they often present biased information, images, and interpretations; manufacture events and issues based on distortion and fabrication; and shape the world's opinion about critical human concerns by using various forms of manipulation and sensationalism (Ramonet, 2000; Kellner, 1990; Whitney, 1994). These are just a few examples showing why there is a need for the critical assessment of all domains (economic, political, ideological, and informational) of globalization.

*Second*, in order to counter the hegemonic forces of globalization, the powerless developing nations need to reinforce their solidarity at the regional and cross-regional levels based on geographic proximity, economic interdependence, cultural similarities, and so on. In this regard, the earlier South–South cooperation reflected in the formation of the Group of 77, Non-Aligned Movement (NAM), New International Economic Order (NIEO), and New World Information and Communication Order (NWICO), which emerged in the 1970s, became virtually nonexistent during the past two decades. Even the existing regional associations in Asia, Africa, and Latin America have become subservient to various international bodies, such as the WTO and the IMF. On the other hand, there are organizations such as NAFTA, OAS, and APEC that are complicated by allowing both the powerful developed nations and the powerless developing countries to be their members. Since the process of globalization expanded the power of the dominant capitalist states (OECD, 1998), what remains essential today is to enhance unity among the peripheral developing nations by reviving some of the existing options (NAM, NIEO, NWICO) and creating more effective organizations and forums. These poorer countries need to overcome their historical differences, build mutual trust and cooperation, and adopt collective initiatives and organizational alternatives in order to counter global powers, bargain for greater participation in international bodies, and maintain their economic, political, and cultural self-reliance (Haque, 1999a; Khor, 2000).

*Finally*, it is necessary to rethink the role of the state in developing countries, which has lost considerable autonomy and capacity under the current context of globalization, requiring the government to adopt market-driven neoliberal policies. In the absence of an advanced market economy and the predatory intervention of global economic powers in these countries, the state has a critical role to play to counter global forces, protect national economy, build local capital and entrepreneurship, satisfy citizens' basic needs, ensure equity and distributive justice, preserve indigenous culture and knowledge, and thus realize a self-reliant form of development (Polidano, 1998; Theobald, 1997). The state itself needs to be restructured, however, in terms of overcoming its past bureaucratic elitism, eliminating its administrative inefficiency and corruption, enhancing its transparency and accountability, and ensuring its people-oriented policies and programs.

The above observations basically represent some generic policy recommendations; more detailed policy options have to be worked out by the policy makers in developing countries while addressing the adverse implications of globalization for their self-reliant development. These policy makers themselves need to be careful, however, in deciphering the causes, actors, beneficiaries, and outcomes of globalization explained by its advocates worldwide. Even the United Nations is not neutral; its Human Development Report 1999 endorsed the globalization of markets despite its urge to make "globalization works for people" (CGG, 1999). Similarly, U.N. Secretary General Kofi Annan appeared to be too simplistic when he asked the people in North Africa and Central Asia to embrace globalization in order to enhance human development ("Embrace Globalization,"2002). Today there are thousands of such studies, reports, and opinions on globalization, which are often the main source of confusion. If the policy makers in developing countries are genuinely interested in self-reliant development, they should thus take a cautious and critical approach to assess diverse interpretations and viewpoints about the impacts of globalization on their economic, political, and cultural self-reliance.

## REFERENCES

Akande, W. (2002). The drawbacks of cultural globalization. Yellow Times Nov. 10, http://www.globalpolicy.org/globaliz/cultural/2002/1110cult.htm.

Bagdikian, B. H. (1997). The Media Monopoly. 5th ed. Boston: Beacon.

Bjonnes, R. (2002). Strategies to eradicate poverty: An integral approach to development. In: UNESCO, ed. The Encyclopedia of Lifesupport Systems. Paris: UNESCO.

Carlos, L., Pereira, B. (1998). Managerial public administration: Strategy and structure for a new state. J Post Keynesian Ec. 20(1):7–24.

CGG (Commission on Global Governance). (1995). Our Global Neighborhood: The Report of the Commission on Governance. Oxford, UK: Oxford University Press.

CGG (Commission on Global Governance). The Millennium Year and the Reform Process. London: Commission on Global Governance.

Cheruiyot, K. (2003). Our languages are dying. One World Feb. 24, http://www.globalpolicy.org/globaliz/cultural/2003/0224language.htm.

Chossudovsky, M. (1994). Global impoverishment and the IMF-World Bank economic medicine. Frontline. Aug. 12.

CIDA (Canadian International Development Agency). (1996). Globalisation and Gender Development Perspectives and Interventions. Quebec, Canada: Women in Development and Gender Equity Division, Policy Branch, CIDA.

Clarke, J., Newman, J. (1997). The Managerial State: Power, Politics and Ideology in Remaking of Social Welfare. London: Sage.

Corkery, J. (1997). International Experience with Institutional Development and Administrative Reform: Some Pointers for Success. ECDPM working paper no. 15. Maastricht: ECDPM, March.

Covington, R. (1994). American TV invades the world. Internat. Herald Trib. 11–18. Oct. 19.

Embrace globalization, Annan tells Muslim states. (2002). Arab News Oct. 29, http://www.globalpolicy.org/globaliz/cultural/2002/1029annan.htm.

Ferge, Z. (1999). The need for social policy reforms: The global scene. In: Nelson, J. M., Tilly, C., Walker, L., eds. Transforming Post-Communist Political Economies. Washington, DC: National Academy Press, pp. 299–321.

Frank, A. G. (1998). ReOrient: Global Economy in the Asian Age. Berkeley, CA: University of California Press.

Fraser, J., Oppenheim, J. (1997). What's new about globalization? McKinsey Q 2:168–179.

Global economy: War of the worlds. (1994). Economist.

Haque, M. S. (1998). New directions in bureaucratic change in Southeast Asia: Selected experiences. J. Polit. Mil. Sociol. 26(1):96–114.

Haque, M. S. (1999a). Restructuring Development Theories and Policies: A Critical Study. Albany, NY: State University of New York Press.

Haque, M. S. (1999b). Globalization of market ideology and its impact on Third World development. In: Kouzmin, A., Hayne, A., eds. Essays in Economic Globalization, Transnational Policies and Vulnerability. Amsterdam: IOS Press. pp. 75–100.

Haque, M. S. (2001). Recent transition in governance in South Asia: Contexts, dimensions, and implications. Internat. J. Pub. Admin. 24(12).

Haque, M. S. (2002). Globalization, new political economy, and governance: A Third World viewpoint. Admin. Theory Praxis. 24(1):103–124.

Haque, M. S. (2003). Reinventing governance for performance in South Asia; Impacts on citizenship rights. Internat. J. Pub. Admin. 26(8–9):1–23.

Hildyard, N. (1997). The World Bank and the State: A Recipe for Change? London: Bretton Woods Project.

ILO (International Labour Office). (1999). Globalization and Workers' Rights. Geneva: International Labour Office.

Jiyad, A. M. (1995). The social balance sheet of privatization in the Arab countries. Third Nordic Conference on Middle Eastern Studies: Ethnic Encounter and Culture Change, Joensuu, Finland, June 19–22.

Karliner, J. (1997). The Corporate Planet: Ecology and Politics in the Age of Globalization. San Francisco: Sierra Club Books.

Kaul, M. (1996). Civil service reforms: Learning from commonwealth experiences. Pub. Admin. Dev. 16(2):131–150.

Kellner, D. (1990). Television and the Crisis of Democracy. Boulder, CO: Westview.

Khor, M. (2000). Globalization and the South: Some Critical Issues. discussion paper no. 147. Geneva: United Nations Conference on Trade and Development.April.

Kim, S. (1998). Cultural imperialism on the Internet. Edge E-J. Intercult. Rel. 1(4).

Kochler, H. (1999). Philosophical aspects of globalization. International Roundtable on the Challenges of Globalization, 18–19, March University of Munich, Germany.

Kyloh, R. (1998). Governance of globalisation: ILO's contribution. working paper. Jan. Geneva: International Labour Organization, http://www.ilo.org/public/english/dialogue/actrav/publ/global.htm.

Martin, B. (1993). In the Public Interest: Privatization and Public Sector Reform. London: Zed Books.

McChesney, R. W. (1997). The global media giants: The nine firms that dominate the world. FAIR Nov./Dec. http://www.fair.org/extra/9711/gmg.html.

McChesney, R. W. (1999a). Rich Media, Poor Democracy: Communication Politics in Dubious Times. Urbana: University of Illinois Press.

McChesney, R. W. (1996b).Noam Chomsky and the struggle against neoliberalism. Monthly Rev. April 1.

Meyer-Stamer, J. (1997). New patterns of governance for industrial change: Perspectives for Brazil. J. Dev. Stud. 33(3):364–391.

Montes, M. F. (1997). The economic miracle in a haze. In: Montes, M. F., Quigley, K. F. F., Weatherbee, D. E., eds. Growing Pains: ASEAN's Economic and Political Challenges. New York: Asia Society.

Norris, P. (2000). The worldwide digital divide: Information poverty, the Internet and development. Annual Meeting of the Political Studies Association of the UK, London School of Economics and Political Science, April 10–13.

OECD (Organisation for Economic Co-operation and Development). (1998). OECD Economic Outlook. Paris: OECD.

Olson, G. E. (1993). America's Cable News Network. Amer. Stud. News. 30:38–42.

Oszlak, O. (1997). The Argentine civil service: An unfinished search for identity. Conference on Civil Service Systems in Comparative Perspective, Indiana University, Bloomington, Indiana, April 5–8.

Pereira, L. C. B. (1993). Economic reforms and economic growth: Efficiency and politics in Latin America. In: Pereira, L. C. B., Maravall, J. M., Przeworski, A., eds. Economic Reforms in New Democracies: A Social Democratic Approach New York: Cambridge University Press, pp. 15–76.

Pereira, L. C. B., Maravall, J. M., Przeworski, A. (1993). Economic Reforms in New Democracies: A Social Democratic Approach. New York: Cambridge University Press.

Pha, A. (2002). TNCs stride the world. Guardian (Australia). http://www.thirdworldtraveler. com/Controlling_Corporations/TNCs_Stride_World.html.

Polidano, C. (1998). Don't Discard State Autonomy: Revisiting the East Asian Experience of Development. Public Policy and Management Working Paper no. 9. Manchester, UK: Institute for Development Policy and Management, University of Manchester, Sept.

Ramonet, I. (2000). United States goes global: The control of pleasure. (transl. H. Forster). Le Monde Diplomatique, May.

Roach, C. (1990). The movement for a new world information and communication order: A second wave? Media. Cult. Soc. 12(3):283–307.

Rothkop, D. (1997). In praise of cultural imperialism? Effects of globalization on culture. Foreign Pol. June 22.

Schmidt, J. D. (1998). Southeast Asia Between Global Neoliberal Discipline and Local Quests for Welfare. working paper no. 84. Perth, Australia: Asia Research Centre, Murdoch University. Feb.

Tevera, D. (1995). The medicine that might kill the patient: Structural adjustment and urban poverty in Zimbabwe. In: Simon, D., et al., ed. Structurally Adjusted Africa: Poverty, Debt and Basic Needs. London: Pluto Press.

(2001). The triumph of English: A world empire by other means. Economist, Dec. 20.

Theobald, R. (Sept 1, 1997). Enhancing public service ethics: More culture, less bureaucracy? Admin. Soc. 490.

Tuhus-Dubrow, R. (2002). World's languages are fast disappearing. Independent April 25, http://www.globalpolicy.org/globaliz/cultural/2002/0425fast.htm.

UNDP (United Nations Development Programme). (1995). Human Development Report 1995. New York: Oxford University Press.

UNDP (United Nations Development Programme). (1996). Human Development Report 1996. New York: Oxford University Press.

UNDP (United Nations Development Programme). (1998). Human Development Report 1998. New York: Oxford University Press.

UNDP (United Nations Development Programme). (2001). Human Development Report 2001. New York: Oxford University Press.

WCL (World Confederation of Labour). (1997). Report on Trade Union Rights Worldwide–1996–1997: Impact of Globalization on the International Labor Standards. Brussels: World Confederation of Labour, http://www.cmt-wcl.org/en/pubs/report96-97.html.

Whitney, C. R. ( 1994). Cold war radios feel pinch: Free Europe and liberty reel from big cuts. Internat. Herald. Trib. Aug. 22.

World Bank. (1996). World Bank Annual Report 1996. Washington, DC: International Bank for Reconstruction and Development.

World Bank. (1997). World Development Report 1997: The State in a Changing World. New York: Oxford University Press.

World Bank. (2000). World Development Report 1999/2000. New York: Oxford University Press.

World Bank. (2001). World Development Report 2000/2001. New York: Oxford University Press.

# 31

# The Impact of Globalization on the Developmental Role of Local Government in South Africa

**HEATHER NEL**

*University of Port Elizabeth, Port Elizabeth, South Africa*

## INTRODUCTION

In South African legislation there is a strong focus on progressively building local government into an effective, frontline development agency capable of bringing about the social and economic uplift of local communities. Local authorities are no longer mere providers of such services as water and electricity; rather, the emphasis has shifted to developmental local government in which it is the central responsibility of local authorities to work together with local communities to find sustainable ways to meet their needs and improve the quality of their lives.

Linked to this is the fact that the concepts of reconstruction and participation in South Africa call for a special kind of development planning. The most fundamental feature of these concepts of development is a people-centered orientation that stresses not only economic growth, but also social well-being and the sustained quality of the physical environment, in line with what the United Nations terms "sustainable human livelihoods." The argument is that unless people are at the center of development, no significant development will take place. To enhance people-centered development in South Africa, there is a need for a strong civil society that is guided by the principle of every community member being dynamically involved in the process of reconstruction and development within the local government sphere.

Added to the above are the challenges posed by globalization with respect to diminishing the role of the state in all spheres of government, including local government. Increasing emphasis is placed on enhancing the role of the private sector, and this is translated into legislation pertaining to local government whereby public–private partnerships and alternative service delivery mechanisms are encouraged. It is in this respect that civil society organizations need to play a vigilant role to ensure that the imperatives of globalization do not compromise the role of local government as an agent of people-centered development.

This chapter will therefore aim to explore the impact of globalization on the developmental role of local government in South Africa. Specific aspects to receive attention include the South African policy framework for developmental local government, global imperatives impacting upon the developmental role of local government in South Africa, alternative service delivery mechanisms in terms of local government service delivery, and the role of civil society organizations (CSOs) and their relationship to developmental local government in South Africa. Particular emphasis will be placed on the concept of local government "partnering" with CSOs in fulfilling its development mandate. It is first necessary, however, to provide an overview of South African legislation with respect to developmental local government.

## DEVELOPMENTAL LOCAL GOVERNMENT: THE SOUTH AFRICAN POLICY CONTEXT

The *Constitution of the Republic of South Africa* of 1996 (Act 108) (Republic of South Africa, 1996) indicates the objectives of local government in Section 152: to provide democratic and accountable government for local communities, to ensure the provision of services to communities in a sustainable manner, to promote social and economic development, to promote a safe and healthy environment, and to encourage the involvement of communities and community organizations in the matters of local government.

The South African Constitution furthermore stipulates the developmental duties of municipalities in Section 153. In this regard, it is stated that a municipality must structure and manage its administration, budgeting, and planning processes to give priority to the basic needs of the community, to promote the social and economic development of the community, and to participate in national and provincial development programs.

It is therefore apparent that the South African Constitution upholds and entrenches the right of the existence of local government, especially with respect to implementing development programs. This developmental orientation of local government is supported by the *White Paper on Reconstruction and Development* (Republic of South Africa, 1994), in that local government is assigned a vital role in implementing the Reconstruction and Development Programme (RDP). It is acknowledged that local authorities are the key institutions for delivering basic services, extending local control, managing local economic development, and redistributing local resources. Wallis (1996) asserts that the priorities of local government in terms of the RDP are twofold and need to be approached in tandem. First, the delivery of services needs to be improved or extended to new localities, and second, institutional capacity needs to be developed in ways that create conditions conducive to the implementation of the RDP.

Liebenberg and De Kock (1995) reinforce local government as the pivotal focus of the RDP and recommend that the developmental tasks of the three spheres of government be as follows:

National government should fulfill a coordinating role and focus its attention on the attainment of economic growth and the delivery of services in line with the RDP.

Provincial/regional government should oversee regional infrastructural developments and could assist local governments by creating an atmosphere in the region conducive to community empowerment and development.

Local government should directly identify needs, provide services, and cooperate with community organizations in implementing development projects.

Emphasizing the developmental role of local government, the RDP lists integrating areas that were once divided under apartheid, providing and maintaining affordable infrastructure services, strengthening the capacity of local government to provide services, ensuring a more equitable role for women, and ensuring meaningful participation by residents and stakeholders. The *White Paper on Local Government* of 1998 (Notice 423) (Republic of South Africa, 1998) is another policy document that has significant implications for local government in South Africa. The white paper puts forward a vision of "developmental local government" that centers on working with local communities to find sustainable ways to meet their needs and improve the quality of their lives. It establishes the following characteristics of developmental local government: (1) exercising municipal powers and functions in a manner that maximizes their impact on social development and economic growth, (2) playing an integrating and coordinating role to ensure alignment between public and private investment within the municipal area, (3) democratizing development, and (4) building social capital through providing community leadership and vision and seeking to empower marginalized and excluded groups within the community.

The white paper provides approaches to assist municipalities in becoming more developmental, such as integrated development planning and budgeting, performance management, and working together with local citizens and partners. It is thus apparent that under the postapartheid South African Constitution, local government has a new, expanded role to play. In addition to providing many of the traditional municipal services—such as ensuring water provision and refuse collection—local authorities must now lead, manage, and plan for development. Their task—together with national and provincial government—is to eradicate poverty, boost local economic development and create jobs, and carry forward the process of reconstruction and development.

Local authorities are expected to provide clear and accountable leadership, management, budgeting, and direction in such areas as participation of the community in its own government; communication and cooperation between community and government; integrated development and management of the municipal areas; provision of infrastructure, household, and community services; land-use regulation and planning; housing and township establishment; development planning and local economic development; environment and health care; and local safety and security.

Local authorities will be expected by their constituents to address this "package" of responsibilities to the greatest extent possible within the constraints of available resources and abilities. Furthermore, planning and management for development must also combine and integrate all important aspects of development: social, economic, environmental, ethical, infrastructural, and spatial. To achieve all of this, local authorities must mobilize the participation, commitment, and energies of residents and stakeholders by establishing participatory processes that are constructive and effective. Competing claims on the limited available resources might lead to conflict, and local authorities will have to provide direction and leadership, ensure fairness, and build agreement and consensus around common shared goals (www.local. gov.za).

This is elaborated upon in Section 25 of the *Municipal Systems Act* of 2000 (Act 32) (Republic of South Africa, 2000a) in that it describes an "integrated development plan" as a single inclusive and strategic plan for the development of a municipality that links, integrates, and coordinates plans and takes into account proposals for the development of the municipality, aligns the resources and capacity of the municipality with the implementation of the plan, and constitutes the policy framework and general basis on which annual budgets must be based.

Added to the above, municipalities are encouraged to facilitate "local economic development" (LED). It is acknowledged that local government can play an important role with respect to promoting job creation and boosting the local economy. This can be achieved by providing cost-effective services and establishing a sound infrastructure, reviewing existing policies and procedures (e.g., procurement procedures) to ensure that they promote LED, and providing special economic services, such as investment support and small business support and targeting assistance to particular sectors in the local economy with the potential to expand (Republic of South Africa, 1998).

Local economic development needs to take place within the context of increasing global competition between cities for limited investments. Local governments are thus under tremendous pressure to exploit their natural resources and other competitive advantages to attract both domestic and foreign investors. Local economic development plans should be formulated within the parameters of national and provincial policies, however, and could include infrastructure investment objectives, job creation through community public works programs, a framework for public–private partnerships, and spatial planning to integrate various communities.

A further piece of legislation impacting upon the developmental role of local government in South Africa is the *Development Facilitation Act* (DFA) of 1995 (Act 67) (Republic of South Africa, 1995). Chapter 1 of the DFA sets out principles that affect decisions taken by local authorities with respect to the development of land. These principles include provisions that all laws, policies, and administrative practices affecting land development should inter alia facilitate the development of both formal and informal existing and new settlements, promote sustainable development, and provide guidance and information to stakeholders involved in or affected by land development rather than simply attempting to control the process and the people. Authorities in each sphere of government must coordinate the various sectors involved in or affected by land development to minimize conflict over scarce resources.

In addition to the above, the DFA requires that local authorities submit land development objectives (LDOs) to the provincial government for approval. The LDOs focus on four main areas, namely, objectives relating to the sorts of services a local authority will provide: the standard of the services and the level at which they will be provided, urban and rural growth and form, including a range of issues traditionally recognized as part of town and regional planning, the development strategies a local authority will utilize to manage the proposed development, and the targets set by the local authority against which its performance in meeting development objectives can be measured.

It is essential to point out that LDOs are not something separate from or supplementary to the integrated development plan (IDP) of a local authority; rather, the requirements of LDOs need to be utilized as a broader framework within which local authorities determine their development goals, detailed strategies, action plans, and budgets. In turn, the IDP of a local authority serves as the basis for the conception of various development projects.

From the above it is apparent that local government in South Africa is expected to fulfill a vital role in development at the grassroots level. In terms of the legislation, South African local authorities are regarded as the frontline agencies of national and provincial government institutions in implementing development programs to the benefit of the masses that have been historically disadvantaged as a result of the separate development policies of the pre-1994 government. Pragmatically, the national development policy framework in South Africa requires local authorities to actively initiate and implement development programs and projects in collaboration with local stakeholders, including local communities, nongovernmental organizations (NGOs), and the private sector. Local government is thus no longer viewed in terms of legislation as the sole agent of service delivery, but as an enabler or facilitator of development at the grassroots level.

To this end, local authorities in South Africa need not only take cognizance of the requirements of national legislation with respect to their developmental role; in addition, it is imperative that local government politicians and officials have a sound understanding of the impact of global forces on their roles and responsibilities with respect to local development. For this reason, the following section will focus on the impact of globalization on local government in South Africa.

## THE IMPACT OF GLOBALIZATION ON THE DEVELOPMENTAL ROLE OF LOCAL GOVERNMENT IN SOUTH AFRICA

In analyzing the impact of globalization on local government in a developing nation such as South Africa, it is first necessary to clarify the meaning of the concept.

### Conceptualizing Globalization

Globalization is defined by Ronnie (www.cosatu.org.za, Aug. 20, 2001) as the social, political, economic, and cultural trends that characterize the ever-increasing integration of the world economy. It permeates all spheres of the capitalist economy, such as production, trade, and labor relations, and has been greatly aided by the enormous technological strides made in recent times. Kristoff (www.globalpolicy. org, Aug. 19, 2001) notes that globalization is "a new and powerful force that is erasing national borders and linking the world in an unprecedented web of trade and investments."

Held (1992) states that globalization implies a distinctively new international order involving: the emergence of a global economic system that stretches beyond the control of a single state, the expansion of networks of transnational linkages and communications over which particular states have little influence; a growth in international organizations that can limit the scope of action of the most powerful states, and the development of a global military order that can reduce the range of policies available to governments and their citizens.

The essential elements of globalization are integration and the lesser significance of the nation-state. This is aptly illustrated by Kaigee (1999) when he points out that: of the 100 largest companies in the world today, fifty-one are individual transnational enterprises; only forty-nine of the world's biggest economies are nation-states; Ford's economy is bigger than either Saudi Arabia's or South Africa's; and five transnational corporations alone control 50% of the global market in seven industries, namely, consumer durable, automotive, airlines, aerospace, electronic components, electrical goods, and steel.

The trend toward globalization affects the management of the public sector in that the spread of ideas and the impact of technology occur so rapidly that national barriers are becoming increasingly blurred. Furthermore, in a world of economic competition, the role of governments and the public sector can be important determinants in creating competitive advantage.

## The Impact of Globalization on the Public Sector

### National Competitiveness and Capacity Development

There is a close link between the quality of public service delivery and national economic performance, particularly in the areas of health, education and training, taxation, and the encouragement of small and medium-size enterprise development. Given the role of the public sector in boosting national competitiveness, it is not surprising that there is a concomitant emphasis on building the capacity and competence of public officials.

In this regard, it is interesting to note that the United Nations Development Program (UNDP) supports a "governance approach" to capacity development. This approach maintains that capacity development designs and processes need to incorporate key characteristics of good governance in order to ensure sustainability and ownership. These characteristics include transparency, effectiveness and efficiency, equity, stakeholder participation in decision making, and responsiveness to the needs of the community being served (http://magnet.undp.org).

### Paradigm Shift Toward Managerialism

Hughes (1998) points out that since the mid-1980s there has been a transformation in the management of the public sectors of advanced countries whereby the rigid, hierarchical, and bureaucratic form of public administration is changing to a flexible, market-based form of public management. This is not merely a matter of reform, but a fundamental paradigmatic shift that poses a direct challenge to several of what had previously been regarded as fundamental and almost eternal principles of public administration. These principles include (1) that the classic Weberian bureaucracy is the single best way of operating a public institution, (2) that public institutions should be regarded as the direct providers of services, (3) that politics and administration can be separated, and (4) that public administration requires professionals who are employed for life to serve any political "master" equally.

In contrast, the "new public management" paradigm focuses on a managerialist and minimalist state. Within this paradigm, the role of the public sector is reduced, and there is a focus on management in terms of both producing results and outcomes and enhancing efficiency. Furthermore, there is an emphasis on the public sector, not as a sole service provider but as a catalyst for other sectors—private, voluntary, community—to act in the interests of meeting community needs.

In this respect, Denhardt and Denhardt (2000) note that public management has undergone a revolution in recent times in that public administrators are responding to admonishments to "steer rather than row" and to be the entrepreneurs of a new, leaner, and increasingly privatized government. These authors point out, however, that in giving public administrators more power through encouraging them to "steer" public service delivery, essentially what transpires is that they forget who owns the "boat." It must be kept in mind that the government belongs to the citizens and public administrators should accordingly focus on their responsibility to serve and empower citizens as they manage public institutions and implement public policy. In other words, it is argued that with the citizens at the forefront, the emphasis should not be placed on either steering or rowing the governmental boat, but on building public institutions characterized by integrity and responsiveness.

The minimalist approach to the state is a key component of neoliberalism, which views the state as fundamentally inefficient with respect to service delivery and state spending as a disincentive to private sector investment. The implications of this approach for the public sector include a vision whereby public institutions are redefined into "core" administrative units that focus on strategy and serve to regulate service delivery rather than directly provide services; enter into a series of contracts, partnerships, and network arrangements with a range of service providers both internal and external to the public sector; and are urged to become "internationally competitive." A further global trend impacting on the role of the public sector is that of commercialism.

## Commercialism

The above conception of the public sector emphasizes delivering those services that users can afford rather than those services that users need. As a result, service delivery is commercialized through turning citizens into consumers who have a commercial relationship with the service provider; expecting users to pay the full costs of services with very limited cross-subsidization or other forms of subsidization; and such that public institutions only continue to provide services that are financially viable (http://www.cosatu.org.za/samwu/sandra1.htm).

From the above, it is clear that the boundaries between the public and private sectors are increasingly blurring. For example, the *White Paper on Municipal Service Partnerships* (Notice 1689) (Republic of South Africa, 2000b) in South Africa describes a "municipal service partnership" (MSP) as an arrangement whereby a municipality partners with the private sector, NGOs, or other public institutions in providing municipal services. This white paper argues that if they are well structured and properly implemented, MSP arrangements can lead to significant improvements in the efficiency of municipal service delivery. Greater efficiency means that significantly more services can be delivered while still remaining within the municipal council's overall budget limits.

This white paper further argues that contracting a specialist service provider can have several advantages. In addition to providing specialist knowledge and expertise, such a service provider can often gain efficiency from economies of scale that may not be available to a municipal council.

Municipal service partnerships also permit municipal councils to reduce their expenses for equipment rental, lease costs, initial purchase costs, and technology licensing arrangements. Over time, municipalities can save on the capital costs of infrastructure expansion and technology upgrades. By linking the provision of municipal services to a definitive contractual arrangement, municipal councils are also able to know their costs in advance and therefore are in a better position to prepare their budgets and plans. In addition, by requiring a number of potential service providers to bid for the provision of municipal services, municipal councils can gain from the benefits of competition. Despite the apparent advantages of several of these trends related to globalization, it is important to note the impact thereof on poverty eradication and sustainable development.

## The Impact of Globalization on Poverty Eradication and Sustainable Development

Woodward (1998) asserts that it is difficult to envisage the "frontiers of globalization being rolled back in the near future—and still more difficult to imagine this being done in such a way as to benefit the poor in developing countries." He adds that the effects of globalization are mediated by the nature of the international system in terms of the institutional framework and the development strategies it promotes.

These have five fundamental shortcomings, namely: (1) the nature of the production of and trade in advanced manufactured goods and primary commodities is such as to confer strong economic advantages on producers of the former (primarily developed countries), while disadvantaging the latter (most developing countries); (2) the international "rules of the game" are skewed heavily toward the developed countries and against developing countries, partly because of the weak institutional position of the latter in the bodies that formulate them; (3) partly as a result of this, international markets for goods, services, and factors of production function in such a way as to widen the gap between developed and developing countries rather than to close it; (4) the development strategies being promoted by the international financial institutions exacerbate this problem by actively enforcing a competitive rather than a cooperative approach to development; and (5) despite claims by developed country governments and international financial institutions that poverty reduction is an important priority of their policies toward developing countries, in practice it is no more than a hoped-for by-product of the development process that they promote.

If the process of globalization is to be harnessed for effective and sustainable development and poverty reduction, it is essential that these problems be resolved. This will require a fundamental review, both of the international institutional framework and the currently dominant neoliberal view of development. The fundamental question that needs to be posed is: Given the increased pace of globalization, to whatparadigm should development be geared? The UNDP proposes the concept of sustainable human development as an alternative to neoliberal paradigms of development.

## Sustainable Human Development as an Alternative to Neoliberalism

There are both common points and important contrasts when one compares human development and neoliberalism as development paradigms. The common ground is most notably the fact that both are rooted in liberal individual philosophy, emphasizing freedom of choice exercised within a democratic framework. Human development goes beyond the neoliberal framework in many respects, however, in that it also emphasizes the need to strengthen human capabilities if choices are to be exercised purposefully and creatively. It also recognizes economic and social rights and the need for a stronger state to ensure that such rights are available to all.

Also as a paradigm human development contrasts with liberalism. Human development focuses on people, not markets, is multidisciplinary, not just economic, and emphasizes ends, not means. Changes are needed, both nationally and internationally, if human development is to receive more serious attention in policy analysis, formulation, and implementation. Some of this has been taking place as countries, universities, and NGO groups show more interest in the human development approach. Much of this is self-generated interest, but in poorer countries international support has helped. In these countries, more support could be useful. Internationally, two important challenges relate to growing inequality and environmental pressures. Both will require much more serious international action, backed up by stronger national support, especially from the industrial and better-off developing countries (Jolly, www.globalpolicy.org, Aug. 20, 2001).

Through its annual human development report (HDR), UNDP has advocated the concept of sustainable human development (SHD), or the process of enlarging individuals' choices. The most critical choices are: (1) to lead a healthy life, (2) to be educated, (3) to enjoy a decent standard of living, and (4) to enjoy freedom, self-respect, and the respect of others. If SHD is about enlarging individuals' choices, then poverty means that those choices are denied. Poverty therefore is much more than a lack of income, but rather a form of *deprivation* that can be better described as *human poverty*.

Human poverty is multidimensional in that it severely constrains human choices and results in vulnerability and a perpetuation of inequalities. These inequalities manifest themselves between women and men, rural and urban, developed and underdeveloped regions, and different ethnic groups. Seldom are these inequalities isolated; instead they are interrelated and overlapping. Given these various dimensions, it is also apparent that poverty eradication cannot be achieved through sector-specific interventions (e.g., public works, training of health workers). Human poverty is both a condition and a process. It does not imply that poor men and women are passive victims of their plight, but that they are constantly coping and adapting to, and more importantly fighting, impoverishment processes.

In this context, traditional development concepts, policies, and policy instruments and activities may not be entirely adequate to meet emerging challenges. New concepts, tools, methodologies, and approaches are needed to address the various dimensions of human poverty and to examine the relationship between human poverty and the environment, health, and education (http://www.undp.org/sl/ Documents/Global_prog/SLGLOPROFIN.doc).

Ultimately, a more holistic approach is needed if poverty eradication and SHD are to become a reality. The concept of sustainable livelihoods (SL) is one way to approach the twin issues of combating human poverty and promoting SHD.

## Sustainable Livelihoods

The UNDP has defined *livelihoods* as the assets, activities, and entitlements that people utilize in order to make a living. In this particular context, assets are defined as not only natural/biological (e.g., land, water, common-property resources, flora, and fauna), but also social (e.g., community, family, and social networks), political (e.g., participation and empowerment), human (e.g., education, labor, health, and nutrition), physical (e.g., roads, clinics, markets, schools, and bridges), and economic (e.g., jobs, savings, and credit).

The sustainability of livelihoods becomes a function of *how* men and women utilize asset portfolios on both a short- and long-term basis. *Sustainable livelihoods* are those that are able to cope with and recover from such shocks and stresses as drought, civil war, policy failure through adaptive and coping strategies; that are economically efficient, or able to use minimal inputs to generate a given amount of outputs; that are ecologically sound, ensuring that livelihood activities do not irreversibly degrade natural resources within a given ecosystem; and that are socially equitable, which suggests that promotion of livelihood opportunities for one group should not foreclose options for other groups, either now or in the future.

The added value of the SL concept and methodology is that it approaches poverty reduction in a sustainable manner. First, it attempts to bridge the gap between macro policies and micro realities (and vice versa), an effort that neither poverty reduction programs nor participatory development initiatives have been able to accomplish successfully. Antipoverty endeavors have usually been conceived and implemented from the national level, using per capita income or consumption measures and manipulation of sectoral policies as points of departure. Little if any attention is paid to the manner in which (or where) people live, the resources (assets) used for pursuing livelihoods, or the human, environmental, and financial costs associated with the implementation of national program through a centralized bureaucracy. On the other hand, participatory development on the whole has managed to understand how men and women prioritize needs, exploit resources, and offer solutions to their pressing problems. The missing link, however, is examining how macro and sectoral policies affect the livelihood options available to a particular community or individual.

Participatory development initiatives thus remain isolated from broader economic processes, while traditional antipoverty programs may overlook local disparities and power relations. By using both participatory and policy (cross-sectoral) tools, the SL approach highlights the interlinkages between livelihood systems at the micro level and the macro policies that affect these livelihoods. Understanding such processes allows the policy-making process and the implementation of these policies to be better informed and reoriented to serve the interests, needs, and capacities of marginalized groups. Policy implementation is mediated through mesolevel institutional linkages, such as local government, NGOs, and community-based organizations (CBOs) (http://www.undp.org/sl/Documents/Global_prog/SLGLOPROFIN.doc).

For example, through formulating their IDP, local authorities in South Africa are compelled to embark on community participation initiatives to obtain the views of their local communities regarding which development programs and projects to prioritize. Local communities, particularly those in poverty-stricken areas, are thus given an opportunity to shape the budget and projects of the local authority in a manner that takes cognizance of their needs and development priorities. The IDP thus serves as a policy instrument within the local government sphere in that it guides local development initiatives, yet it is formulated in close collaboration with the local community and other stakeholders to ensure that their needs are met through the programs and projects undertaken. In turn, IDPs also serve as the linkage between local activities and the macro policy context in that they act as a mechanism to ensure that the guidelines and imperatives set out in national development policies are implemented at a micro level. In this regard, it is important to further analyze the role of local government in an SL context.

## LOCAL GOVERNANCE IN THE SUSTAINABLE LIVELIHOODS CONTEXT

Governance can be regarded as the exercise of economic, political, and administrative authority to manage a country's affairs at all levels. In this perspective, governance comprises the mechanisms, processes, and institutions through which citizens and groups articulate their interests, exercise their legal rights, meet their obligations, and mediate their differences. In an SL context, governance is said to have three legs: economic, political, and administrative. Economic governance includes decision making processes that affect a country's economic activities and its relationships with other economies. Political governance is the process of decision making to formulate policy, while administrative governance is the system of policy implementation.

As suggested above, SL is a radical departure from previous perspectives on development and poverty eradication. By implying the need to start with the constraints and opportunities facing individuals, households, and communities, there is a rationale for a coherent and concise definition of governance that suits this objective. There are two aspects of the governance concept that need rethinking in relation to SL. The first is that governance is associated with regime rather than the state or civil society. This means that the concept refers to the constitution or reconstitution of normative rules that guide public or political action. Governance is just one aspect of politics; it focuses on the basic—or constitutional—rules that determine behavioral conduct and action. The second is that governance is different from policy making, public administration, or project management. As is suggested in Table 1, governance takes place at an analytical meta level, meaning that the other activities listed above are circumscribed by the rules established at the regime or governance level.

Governance here means that it is possible to distinguish between two sides of politics. One is the distributive side, which addresses the perennial question of

**Table 1**  Governance and Its Relation to Other Concepts
and Activities

| Level | Activity | Concept |
| --- | --- | --- |
| Meta | Politics | Governance |
| Macro | Policy | Policy making |
| Meso | Program | Public administration |
| Micro | Project | Management |

who gets what, when, and how. This side of politics is usually referred to as political economy because it focuses on how public resources are allocated in society. The other side is the constitutive side, which addresses the question of who sets what rules, when, and how. This is what we here call governance, because it focuses on the rules of the political game. This distinction is particularly important in relation to SL. The conventional needs approach relies more on the distributive side and does not ask for changes in the rules of the game to achieve its objectives. On the other hand, SL, which focuses on empowerment and enhanced access to resources, calls for a change in the rules, and by implication, a shift in power relations. As an approach to poverty eradication, SL therefore requires attention to the constitutive side of politics, (i.e., governance) (http://www.undp.org/sl/Documents/Strategy_papers/Governance_and_SL.htm).

In this respect, local government in South Africa has an important role to play at the micro level in ensuring that disadvantaged communities are empowered and uplifted through the implementation of development projects that make up a broader IDP. The impact of globalization is experienced even at this level of governance, however, in that increasing pressure is placed on local authorities to privatize and thereby adopt a minimalist approach to service delivery and development. This is heavily contested by CSOs in South Africa, particularly trade unions, in that it is viewed as a process that will lead to job losses and the further alienation of poverty-stricken communities that cannot afford to pay for services provided by the private sector.

It is in this respect that CSOs have an important role to fulfill in ensuring that local government retains its significance as a facilitator and agent of sustainable development. In ensuring that local government is truly developmental in the sense of positively contributing to poverty alleviation and sustainable livelihoods, it is vital that civil society organizations fulfill a watchdog and advocacy role.

## THE ROLE OF CIVIL SOCIETY ORGANIZATIONS IN ENHANCING THE ROLE OF LOCAL GOVERNMENT AS AN AGENT OF DEVELOPMENT IN SOUTH AFRICA

The suggestion that local governments do not have to deliver services themselves has serious implications that need to be considered. First, local governments may use this to derogate on their responsibility to deliver services by handing them over to the private sector and NGOs. Essentially what results is a self-fulfilling prophesy on the inherent inefficiency of the public sector in terms of service delivery. Second, it is implied that government should only take on "core" functions that no one else can do. The "noncore" functions are then privatized or outsourced thereby creating a "contracting state" in which the government as far as possible outsources rather than uses its own capacity. This strategy typically empowers public managers in terms of defining core functions (often with the assistance of consultants) to the extent that even when resources remain in state hands, they are under the control of autonomous managers. In addition, to compensate for budget cuts and limited resources, local governments attempt to bring in private capital by entering into partnerships with companies, and this enhances the influence of capital over government (http://www.cosatu.org.za/docs/lgdp.htm, Aug. 20, 2001).

With respect to the above, it is imperative that CSOs in South Africa assume an advocacy function in the sense of actively promoting and protecting the plight of the poor, who are the most adversely affected by these trends in local governance. It is interesting to note that Congress of South African Trade Unions (COSATU) argues in this regard for: a national service delivery framework that addresses the need to extend municipal services to historically neglected areas; the need to retain service delivery within the domain of the public sector; the right of the public not to have it service delivery undermined by the inability to pay; human resources development to capacitate public officials to render services effectively and efficiently; a financial framework with a strong redistributive element; and the promotion of citizen participation, particularly in the budgetary process (http://www.cosatu.org.za/docs/lgdp.htm, Aug. 20, 2001).

The RDP acknowledged the role of local government as the "hands and feet" of meaningful development in society, and this sentiment needs to remain on the agenda of national government, especially in light of the findings of the UNDP poverty report of 2000. According to this report almost three-fourths of South Africa's poor live in underdeveloped rural areas, many people lack adequate housing and access to basic social services, and it is estimated that one in every four citizens will be infected with HIV/AIDS by 2010 (http://www.undp.org/povertyreport, Aug. 19, 2001).

Contrast this with the fact that since 1997 both the public and private sectors have shed more than half a million jobs. Added to this, nearly 70% of unemployed people in South Africa have never worked and those most affected by unemployment are women and the young (http://www.polity.org.za/govdocs/reports/poverty.html). Despite the high unemployment rate in South Africa, however, various municipalities are embarking on the process of privatization using various methods, including public–private partnerships.

The national government clearly supports such restructuring initiatives in that it set aside 500 million Rands in the 2000–2001 budget for this purpose. From this it is clear that the tenets of the macroeconomic policy GEAR (growth, employment, and redistribution strategy) have not only failed to eradicate poverty in South Africa, but have also to a large extent contributed to creating poverty and deepening inequalities. In essence, it is a strategy that redistributes wealth from the poor to the rich.

The challenge confronting CSOs in a context of globalization is to ensure that the poor and the vulnerable are placed at the center of development. In this regard, CSOs can adopt various strategies of influence; namely, forming coalitions with other like-minded groups in an effort to strengthen their cause and mandate, engaging in the discourse and debate concerning the implications of globalization for the poor and informing government of viable policy alternatives to promote sustainable livelihoods, particularly at a grassroots level, embarking on political protests and campaigns to raise the awareness of government as well as the general public of the adverse effects of globalization, serving as the guardians of public accountability by acting as watchdogs over state expenditure on social services and poverty eradication, and where appropriate and local government lacks capacity, acting as a channel for alternative service delivery by managing projects to benefit the poor.

Civil society organizations thus can and should fulfill an important role in rolling back the onslaught of neoliberalism within the local government sphere in South Africa. To do so, however, they need to critically evaluate their strategies and ensure that they build their internal capacity. This will enhance their ability to effectively advance socioeconomic transformation in a manner that elevates the majority of the South African population out of abject poverty to a level of which they can enjoy the benefits of SL. In this respect, it is important to analyze the role of CSOs as mechanisms for alternative service delivery within the local government sphere (http://www.sangoco.org.za).

Too often the concept of minimizing the role of the state is equated with an attempt to actively promote the private sector as the only viable alternative in terms of service delivery. Civil society organizations, however, have been playing an increasing role in recent years in the provision of social services in response to fiscal stress, state weakness or inefficiency, and an ideological environment favoring non-state action. In positive terms, CSOs are perceived to have certain inherent characteristics capable of providing better quality and more equitable service. It is argued that CSOs are more participatory and less bureaucratic and more flexible and cost-effective, with a particular ability to reach the poor and marginalized in society.

It is worth noting that interaction with CSOs with respect to municipal service delivery could prove to be instrumental both in facilitating empowerment in that these organizations fulfill a vital role in capacity building or ensuring the acquisition of skills and competence within disadvantaged communities and thereby reducing a culture of dependency, and in enabling or generating the ability among members of disadvantaged communities to participate effectively in the process of development planning (Davies, 1993).

Davies (1993) supports this and adds that CSOs require a facilitating environment in which to operate. In particular, these organs of civil society need support from local government institutions, at least to the extent that their role in development is acknowledged and understood. In encouraging such a mutually supportive relationship, local government managers can be instrumental in providing opportunities (e.g., through training) for local CSOs to strengthen their capacity in servicing development needs within the communities being served; expanding information sharing and networking activities with local CSOs with respect to development initiatives; and encouraging national government and multilateral agencies to channel more aid to CSOs with a recognized ability to undertake development projects effectively and efficiently.

The Report on Municipal Community Partnerships (MCPs) suggests that the following sectors should be prioritized as the lead components of an MCP strategy within the local government sphere in South Africa: (1) basic services, such as water and sanitation, refuse collection, roads, and environmental maintenance, (2) social housing in metropolitan areas, cities, and towns, (3) local economic development strategies, and (4) revenue management, including billings and revenue collection (www.local.gov.za).

Fredericksen and London (2000) elaborate by stating that partnerships between the government and CSOs have proven to be central to long-term neighborhood revitalization in many settings in the United States. It is argued, however, that in their haste to contract with community partners, local governments may not be considering the serious possibility that such organizations do not have the capacity to deliver services or effectively manage projects over time. It is recommended that particular attention be devoted to the elements of the organizational capacity of CSOs when engaging in empowerment strategies: (1) leadership and vision, (2) management and planning, and (3) operational support, including skilled staff and adequate infrastructure.

It is thus apparent that in a context of globalization, local governments in developing nations such as South Africa have a crucial role to play with respect to the development of their local communities. Contrary to this, global forces have been influencing governments to minimize their role and increasingly contract out service delivery to the private sector. It was pointed out above, however, that in the interests of local empowerment, local governments have the option of partnering with CSOs in municipal service delivery. To ensure the success of such municipal–community partnerships, it is imperative that local government in South Africa create an enabling environment within which CSOs can develop their capacity to assist local authorities with service delivery in their particular communities. It was furthermore emphasized above that CSOs need to be vigilant in ensuring that poor and marginalized communities in South Africa are not further disadvantaged by the forces of globalization with respect to municipal service delivery.

## CONCLUSION

This chapter clearly indicates that local government has been assigned an important developmental role in South Africa. Municipalities are expected to actively participate in the implementation of national and provincial development programs and thereby promote the social and economic development of their communities. It was pointed out, however, that the neoliberal trends associated with globalization have impacted on the role of local government in South Africa in that the emphasis of national government has shifted to reducing the role of the state and cutting back on expenditures on service delivery.

As a result, public institutions in all spheres of government are being encouraged to restructure themselves in such a way as to contract out certain noncore functions through alternative service delivery mechanisms, including public–private partnerships. This enhances the influence of private capital on government and leads to a managerial state whereby the intervention of political leadership in public service delivery is undermined. Added to this, such restructuring initiatives are contributing to enhancing rather than eradicating poverty in that they invariably lead to job losses in a country in which unemployment is already at an unacceptably high level.

The overarching contention of this chapter is that realizing the goal of SL requires an emphasis on local government as an agent of development and societal empowerment. Developmental local government has the potential of meeting basic social and economic needs, alleviating poverty, and reducing inequalities. The concept has been turned into an approach that emphasizes competition and the profit motive as the only way to develop the economy, however.

To realize its true potential, developmental local government needs to focus on addressing the needs of the poor in a manner that enables poverty-stricken communities not only to rely on the government to alleviate their plight, but to become actively engaged in development initiatives and projects aimed at poverty eradication. To this end, local authorities in South Africa need to recognize that they need not be victims of the forces of globalization by mindlessly privatizing or contracting out their services and functions; rather, local government can embark upon alternative service delivery mechanisms, such as municipal–community partnerships, whereby local communities partner with their local authorities in implementing development projects that will meet their needs and build their capacity. This supports the notion of SL in that such development initiatives focus on how to enhance the quality of life of communities at a micro level while simultaneously drawing on and capitalizing on the assets local communities have to offer.

Such an approach is contrary to national and international pressures for minimal state intervention in terms of service delivery and increasing privatization, however. It thus needs to be actively endorsed and promoted by CSOs through various strategies of influence as a means of addressing the plight of the poor in South Africa.

## Web Sites

http://magnet.undp.org
http://www.anc.org.za
http://www.cosatu.org.za/docs/lgdp.htm
http://www.globalpolicy.org/globaliz
http://www.local.gov
http://www.polity.org.za/govdocs/reports/poverty.html
http://www.sangoco.org.za
http://www.undp.org/povertyreport/countryprofiles/safrica1.html
http://www.undp.org/sl/Documents/Strategy_papers/Governance_and_SL.htm
http://www.undp.org/Documents/Global_prog/SLGLOPROFIN.doc

## REFERENCES

Davies, B. (1993). Empowering the poor: Capacity-building in the Eastern Cape. Indic. South Africa 11;1.

Denhardt, R. B., Denhardt, J. V. (2000). The new public service: Serving rather than steering. Pub. Admin. Rev. 60;6.

Fredericksen, P., London, R. (2000). Disconnect in the hollow state: The pivotal role of organizational capacity in community-based development organizations. Pub. Admin. Rev. 60;3.

Hughes, O. E. (1998). Public Management and Administration: An Introduction. 2nd ed. Basingtoke, UK: Macmillan.

Kaigee, H. (1999). The challenges of globalisation for the 21st century: Lessons for a development approach. Umrabulo 7(3).

Liebenberg, I., De Kock, P. (1995). Some conjectures and perspectives on the RDP white paper. Politeia 14;1.

Republic of South Africa. (1994). White paper on reconstruction and development: discussion document. Pretoria: Government Printer.

Republic of South Africa. (1995). Development Facilitation Act (Act 67 of 1995). Pretoria: Government Printer.

Republic of South Africa. (1996). Constitution of the Republic of South Africa (Act 108 of 1996). Pretoria: Government Printer.

Republic of South Africa. (1998). White Paper on Local Government (Notice 423 of 1998). Pretoria: Government Printer.

Republic of South Africa. (2000a). Local Government: Municipal Systems Act (Act 32 of 2000). Pretoria: Government Printer.

Republic of South Africa. (2000b). White Paper on Municipal Service Partnerships (Notice 1689 of 2000). Pretoria: Government Printer.

Woodward, D. (1998). Globalization, Uneven Development and Poverty: Recent Trends and Policy Implications United Nations Development Programme, working paper 4.

# 32

# Raising Voices
## *Satellites, the Internet, and Distributive Discourse*

**MARGARET GRIECO**

*Napier University, Edinburgh, United Kingdom*

## INTRODUCTION: THE CASE FOR CONNECTIVITY

Recently, there has been a growing emphasis in the development field on the need to pay attention to the "voices of the poor" (World Bank, "Voices of the Poor"). With the help of the World Bank, "voicing" has unambiguously arrived as a development methodology (Ardener, 1993; Gilligan, 1982; Hanak, 1997). International institutions have finally come to appreciate that the experts on poverty are the poor themselves and that the condition of poverty is the outcome of power relations.

> At the turn of the new millennium, the World Bank collected the voices of more than 60,000 poor women and men from 60 countries, in an unprecedented effort to understand poverty from the perspective of the poor themselves. Voices of the Poor, as this participatory research initiative is called, chronicles the struggles and aspirations of poor people for a life of dignity. Poor people are the true poverty experts. Poor men and women reveal, in particular, that poverty is multidimensional and complex—raising new challenges to local, national and global decision-makers. Poverty is voicelessness. It's powerlessness. It's insecurity and humiliation, say the poor across five continents (World Bank, 2000).

This new methodological thrust is linked with the recognition that projects, programs, and policies must involve the end users in the design and decision-making processes; the poor are no longer to be regarded as clients or customers in the development equation, but as participants and managers in the positive alteration of their circumstances (Chambers, 1995). The focus is on participant or participatory management of development projects.

As it has developed in the recent policy practice and policy literature, voicing currently has two components: (1) the "capture" of "voices" through the collection of perspectives and biographies and the presentation of these by other agencies on a global stage through the use of new information communication technologies, such as the World Wide Web (i.e., the World Bank Voices of the Poor Initiative funded by DFID), and (2) the involvement of the disadvantaged in local project design and operation—the participation of all voices in opposition to past practices of project design in whom only "experts" and "leaders" were consulted and involved.

Both these perspectives on voicing have their clear limitations, however. The perspective adopted in the World Bank Voices of the Poor initiative is indeed one of the capture of voices rather than one of "direct voicing": the voices captured have no control over how their voices are to be used and they are not enabled by the project to initiate future discussion or to come together in discussion independently of the agency that has captured their voices. Voicing has been reduced to interviewing the poor and archiving their responses. While such a development has its benefits in amplifying the concerns expressed by the poor as presented by an interlocutor and does indeed possess an authenticity that is superior to the past practice of neglecting the voices of the poor, it does not represent a direct, autonomous voice of the poor.

In the direct voicing of the poor on the contemporary global policy stage, connectivity (access to information communication technology) is critical. Connectivity permits the disadvantaged to have a "view" into other arrangements and better-resourced worlds, and enables the sharing of experience among those who are geographically separated but experience similar constraints. Most important, connectivity enables the disadvantaged to directly communicate their views on their circumstances, needs, and desires to relevant policy agencies, governments, and other potential partners in development. To be authentic, voice must be able to initiate conversations and not simply operate as a response to be summoned by another. As of yet, the issue of ensuring the connectivity of the poor has not received systematic development community attention; this must necessarily be viewed as a weakness in the current "voicing methodologies."

Within the World Bank Voices of the Poor initiative, the "collection" of voices was viewed as a mechanism for sensitizing project selection and improving project design to meet the needs of the poor. It was a step on a path to shifting activity away from large public sector programs into decentralized community-driven initiatives. These community-driven initiatives and the policy space for the representation of the voices of the poor within them are highly localized; the involvement of the poor in small local projects not only brings participation but also brings operating responsibilities without necessarily delivering commensurate additional resources to effect such projects or without ensuring the connection of the poor to the forums that control the macro resources.

In this way, the focus on community-driven initiatives typically—in the absence of connectivity—draws an artificial boundary around the speech communities involved in development policy and suspends the metadiscussion of entitlement to share in regional, national, or global wealth. As the development form of preference moves toward decentralized, community-driven initiatives and away from the large public sector projects of the past, connectivity for those involved in such community-driven initiatives is critical.

Connectivity enables networking between and among community-driven initiatives and enlarges the stage on which voices converse. It allows communities to reflect on their experiences and exchange information with others similarly placed. Most important, it allows challenge to be articulated on resource allocation, governance practices, and the direction of development. There are agencies such as IDRC that have begun to attend to this need to ensure that community-driven initiatives do not remain localized but obtain the communications resources necessary to their networking at every level of the global hierarchy. A model is to be found in the IDRC-supported village information technology project in Pondicherry, India (http://www.mssrf.org/informationvillage/assessment.htm).

New information communications technology enables those from remote locations to directly voice their needs interests, and preferences through a range of modes and mediums—videoconferencing, Web pages, E-mail, online forums, electronic commerce—and most important the new technology offers options that do not necessarily depend on literacy. Video clips on Web pages or the use of icons can and have been used to communicate in contexts in which literacy is low and the immediacy of the message is paramount. In the new information age our ability to rapidly transmit and receive the visual image and to track the spatial location of that image opens up checks on authenticity and abilities to audit beyond imagination a decade ago.

The ability to combine the immediate transmission of a visual image with aural or audio enhancement from any location no matter the state of its existing infrastructure opens up the prospect of new policy processes and protocols. In the past, the grassroots did not have the capability of transmitting its view or perspective on the world directly and immediately onto the global stage. The recognition that connectivity offers new ways of enabling the illiterate to directly participate and that the ability to participate over distance is dramatically transformed by the new information technologies places pressure upon the development community to intervene in the development of technology applications and ensure that these are designed to better meet the needs of the world's poor and harness the potential of "oculacy" that the new technology provides. New information communication technologies are not constrained by traditional infrastructural requirements, such as the presence of electrification; satellite-linked, handheld, solar-powered communication technologies are not subject to many of the maintenance constraints past technologies have experienced in remote locations.

To summarize, communities from remote locations historically had no effective technologies available to them that respected the intactness of their authority to speak in the presentation of their views. The views of client groups were largely articulated through professional brokers, such as the staff of international organizations. The Internet enables member-based organizations to communicate directly and to take a direct seat in the halls of discourse and to further distribute that discourse (Holmes et al., 2002). The ability to do this virtually increases the real resources available to member-based institutions in their bargaining for improvements in their conditions and status. Voicing as it has now emerged in the development discourse is the correction of historic practices of "silencing," "muting," and "exclusion," but to be effective in contemporary times, such policy must not only address traditional assymetries in localized discourse but must also now pay attention to the communication assymetries of the present globalization of governance, and at the heart of this redress is connectivity. There is a potential benign policy fit between voicing and ensuring access to the new communications information technology; equally, a failure to address the issue of universal connectivity represents a violation of voicing and an increasing power distance (Hofstede, 1980) between the poor and the communications-rich.

## LITERACY BARRIERS AND DIGITAL DIVIDES: A LAGGING POLICY FRAMEWORK

Universal education is a generally accepted policy goal, while universal connectivity is frequently viewed as a form of luxury or an unreachable social goal. Universal connectivity can be viewed, however, as a contemporary counterpart of universal education. Literacy or formal education are social forms tied to the historical primacy of print as a communication technology; speech and visual or oculate forms can readily share with print within the framework of new information communication technologies, and the virtual transference of such forms can greatly reduce the transport and transaction costs of obtaining relevant information.

Connectivity has a role to play as both a complement to and a substitute for traditional educational systems. New technologies enable voicing to take place and be communicated outside the traditional pedagogic boundaries of literacy. Therapeutic drama can be undertaken with street children in Africa. The immediacy of such expression can be captured through video and relayed across the Internet. Similarly, street children in one African location can gain a view of the circumstances of street children in another African location or of children in more privileged locations. Such technical capabilities and potential open up prospects for new processes of consultation for more directly involve the end users of the development process.

At present, Web sites carrying the voices of African street children do so in a primarily literate, reported frame (http://www.childhopeuk.org/voices.htm; http://www.geocities.com/african_alternatives/streetchildren/), and there is little evidence that African street children have been provided with "open access" to Internet facilities. There is no good reason why this should continue to be the case, however. In Latin American, "Internet for street children" projects have been set up as a consequence of IDRC support (Eberlee, 2000). They provide street children with a period of open Internet access (Street Children's Project, Ecuador/Colombia—http://www.chasquinet.org/ninosdelacalle/e-result_ta1.html#2) in recognition of the fact that the access of such children to formal education is severely limited. In the interaction with the technology, literacy skills are developed, along with such technical skills as scanning, editing, and CD making; street children interact with children in other countries through chat rooms and E-mails with significant consequences for self-esteem.

The Latin American use of Internet technology to enable street children to gain control over their environments contrasts with the use of the same technology in the Philippines as a technology for tracking and administering the management of street children (http://www.fit-ed.org/program.html).

> Another program will assist DSWD (Department of Social Welfare and Development) in pooling all their information and databases on street children. This will enable the

department to document and track the progress of street children more effectively, assist in placing them in the proper rehabilitation centers and educational institutions, or return them to their families, and possibly lessen the number of children who go back to the streets. The street children database program will also allow the department and its NGO partners to coordinate more effectively in the many programs geared towards aiding the street children. FIT-ED continues to support DSWD in their social development goals by helping them attain their IT objectives, especially in assisting them fulfill their computer hardware and networking requirements.

While international institutions have been slow to see the potential of connectivity—most particularly rural connectivity—for communication, development, and participation, and lagged behind in the development of an appropriate policy framework, within the India subcontinent and in many parts of Asia this potential has been recognized.

The development of rural information technology infrastructure services in India (Pondicherry online project report: http://www.mssrf.org/informationvillage/assessment.htm) provides a useful example of current Asian policy trends. In a group of six villages in Pondicherry in South India.

> [a] project has established a hub-and-spoke model of data-cum-voice communication. The village centers can communicate with each other as well as to the Internet. A hybrid of technologies is used—wired with wireless for communication and solar with mains for power supply. The hub provides connectivity to the Internet through dial-up telephone lines, and the staff there creates locally useful content. The village centers receive queries from the local residents and transmit information, collected from the hub, back to them. An important feature of this project is the strong sense of ownership that the village communities have developed towards the village centers. The other key feature is the active participation of rural women in the management of the village center as well as in using it. A system of close consultation between the project staff and the rural users has been evolved, so that information needs are realistically assessed (online project report).

The online project report records the role of project staff in transforming external materials into information that is useful to this village information network.

> The project staff have designed and developed many locally useful databases. Many of them are frequently updated and some are updated even twice daily. A considerable part of information is accessed from the local sources, on the web or otherwise. A critical portion comes from the web, from national and international sources. All of them are transformed into locally useful material, in format (voice/digital audio, in some cases) and in language (Tamil, spoken by 98% of the population).

This particular project has major gender benefits.

> It is significant to note that assetless, ultra-poor families are among the major users. About 18% of the users are women, which is much higher than the proportion of women users in village public reading rooms (less than 3%). This combined figure also conceals the fact that the proportion of women users in older centers is much higher. These two results are indicators of the success of the project approach emphasizing the participation of women and the assetless families. The pattern of usage...indicates that educational purposes (such as use of CD-ROMs) and accessing government sector data are the two most important uses of this system (online report).

The range of uses to which information is put within this village information communication technology network is indicative of the role that connectivity occupies in linking citizens to government services.

Availing farm labour insurance by landless Women; 157 women obtained this insurance

School examination results and marksheets downloaded from the web; over the last 2 years about 2100 students in all the centers have used this option and saved waiting time by at least one week per person.

Ease of contacting medical practitioners and veterinarians: the local databases have been found specific and useful.

Price information related to grain sales: this is the most important benefit according every farmer (121 interviewed in June 2000) as it helps him/her with better negotiating position in dealing with price-fixing middlemen.

Fishing hamlet receives information on wave heights downloaded twice daily from the US Naval Oceanographic laboratory. This is viewed by the craft-vessel fishermen as life-saving.

Largest number of users find govt. sector data most useful; at least 147 individuals reported deriving benefits from housing schemes.

In addition to provision of data and information, each of these centers has become a routine, operational contact point between government agencies and local families. Government departments such as agriculture, rural development, fisheries, and the State Electoral Office frequently and regularly use the village centers to dissemination information to the village families. This development has been rated well by the local families.

Perhaps the best known example of a connectivity program that services rural women is that of the Grameen Bank field phone in Bangladesh (http://www.apnic.-net/mailing-lists/s-asia-it/archive/2000/03/msg00033.html). The Grameen Bank challenged many of the conventional assumptions of banking when it embarked upon its major program of microfinance in Bangladesh. Its movement into rural communication infrastructure services has once again challenged many orthodox assumptions about the prospects for rural women's connectivity. Don Richardson's summary of the Grameen experience provides a succinct account of these key developments (http://www.apnic.net/mailing-lists/s-asia-it/archive/2000/03/msg00033.html).

Grameen Telecom's Village Phone pilot project currently involves 950 Village Phones providing telephone access to more than 65,000 people. Village women access micro-credit to acquire digital GSM cellular phones and subsequently re-sell phone calls and phone services within their villages. Grameen Telecom staff have announced that when its programme is complete, 40,000 Village Phone operators will be employed for a combined net income of $24 million USD per annum.

The Grameen Telecom experience points to a potential solution for telecom operators facing the significant challenge of managing the last mile of rural telecom operations: link existing and successful micro-credit organizations with telecom operators (fixed line and/or wireless) to expand public call office (PCO) coverage in rural areas. Small loans to rural entrepreneurs (perhaps targeted to women and youth) can enable entrepreneurs to establish PCOs and provide a range of services including telephone, fax, email and even web, photocopying and computer word-processing services. A franchise programme of this sort would also establish consistency of service across a region that would, in turn, support local social and economic development.

The Grameen model does not yet seem to have captured or developed the local database characteristics of the Pondicherry model, but the potential for such a development is clearly present and its scale is substantially larger than the Pondicherry coverage. Once again the IDRC has been involved in financing the evaluation of the Grameen project.

Both the Pondicherry and the Grameen projects have brought information communication technologies to contexts in which there is a high level of female illiteracy, and the link between voicing and illiteracy is often repeated in the literature and in the policy field. Yet another interesting project is found in the south of India and has as its label and motto voicing silence (http://www.mssrf.org.sg/9-pa403.html). This project in Tamil Nadu, developed by the same foundation that developed the Pondicherry project, is focused on the voicing and empowering of girls through drama. An account of the program is provided on a Web site, but the Web site does not yet contain video clips, and it has not been used to place girls in contact with girls in other locations and cultures.

> Continuing its efforts to refine perception and articulation through theatre as part of the process of empowerment, workshops were organised for adolescent girls. Working for 100 hours over a span of 3 months in three schools in Chennai, "Voicing Silence" attempted to concentrate on self-exploration through creative movement with IX and XI grade girls. These workshops involved 17 resource persons from the city, working separately or together, with a shared approach. Giving them a free hand to choose the area they wished to address and the mode of expression, such as dance, improvisation, games or puppetry, the workshop concentrated only on the process and not the product.

The projects evidenced here are given as examples of the potential of new information communication technologies in contexts in which issues of social vulnerability, gender, and illiteracy may have been presumed to militate against the use of these new digital, electronic, and cellular forms. Furthermore, it has been indicated that new information communication technologies can be combined with a range of alternative pedagogic forms to complement or substitute for traditional educational arrangements. Despite its potential, widespread policy attention on the role of connectivity in participation has lagged behind both the speed of development of the new technologies and the successful pilot or model projects already found within the development field. Such policy attention is critical if the interventions necessary to the interests of raising the voices of the poor are to take place in the development of the technology.

## VOICE AND TECHNOLOGY: MODELS IN PRACTICE

The Cybertracker is a palm-top computer that can be connected to a geographical positioning system (GPS) that was explicitly developed to benefit the Bushmen of the

Kalahari Desert in South Africa (http://www.cybertracker.co.za/), enabling them to participate in modern environmental management in which their traditional skill of animal tracking plays an essential part. The designer of the Cybertracker provides a set of social reasons as part of the objective or motivation for the design of the technology: (1) creating employment opportunities in local communities, thereby providing social benefits and giving conservation an economic value, (2) using the Cybertracker to provide prestige to the work of field rangers, enhancing their motivation and self-esteem, (3) giving traditional knowledge a value in a modern context while revitalizing aspects of traditional culture for the future, and (4) using the Cybertracker to develop tracking into a modern science that may have far-reaching implications for conservation.

The Cybertracker technology can be viewed as having been developed to preserve the voice of the Bushmen of the Kalahari. The technology makes use of icons and has an Etch-a-Sketch function; it is a technology that depends on oculacy and that is quintessentially portable and thus fits the needs of a nomadic lifestyle. It also has considerable utility as a field recording tool. Its Web page description carries the following caption: "The most efficient way to gather large quantities of data for field observations, even by non-literate users, at a level of detail not possible before."

This model technology development preserves both the voice and skill of a vulnerable community and integrates these aspects of community in a cutting-edge data collection technology with major scientific benefits. The Cybertracker that has been developed for environmental management and to amplify and accentuate the tracking skills of the Bushmen of the Kalahari could also with small adaptations be used to summon emergency vehicles or medical help in the event of crises of disease and sickness or to collect data on a range of social, health, or participation issues.

The Cybertracker was also developed as Greenware; that is, it was designed to have environmental benefits, and has been utilized worldwide.

> CyberTracker projects have now been implemented, or are in the process of being implemented, in more than 30 countries worldwide: Africa—South Africa, Namibia, Botswana, Mozambique, Zimbabwe, Congo-Brazzaville, Cameroon, Chad, Central African Republic, Equatorial Guinea, Gabon, Ghana, Burkina Faso, Benin, Niger, Senegal, Kenya, Tanzania, Uganda and Egypt. South America—Suriname, Guyana, Brazil. Asia & Pacific—India, Borneo, Australia. Europe—UK, Germany, France, Italy, Spain. USA and Canada. Arctic and Antarctic

The designer of the Cybertracker also hosts discussion from users of Cyber-tracker technology on his Web site. The Cybertracker projects thus enable the raising of voices at many levels.

Yet another model of development embracing the disadvantaged is to be found in the *favelas* of Brazil. Rodrigo Baggio, a computer expert with social work experience in Brazil's favelas, or slums, has set up over 300 computing schools (http://members.tripod.com/vstevens/papyrus/2001/pn010802a.htm) for the youth of the favelas. His inspiration came in a dream (http://www.iadb.org/idbamerica/archive/stories/2000/eng/JAN00E/e200p.htm).

> One night he had a dream in which he saw poor children using computers "to discuss their own reality." The dream set off a chain reaction that culminated the following year, when Baggio formed the Committee for Computer Science Democratization (known as CDI in Brazil). His goal was to teach "computing and citizenship" to young

people in favelas so that they could improve their chances of finding a job while discussing ways to tackle their communities' problems. The idea was dismissed as crazy "by 99 percent of the people I shared it with," recalls Baggio. Eventually, through sheer persistence, Baggio found a Catholic Church in the Santa Marta favela that agreed to give him space to start the school. A large clothing store donated five state-of-the-art computers, and a nongovernmental organization agreed to coordinate everything.

Baggio's favela computing project is remarkable both for its scale and its sustainability:

> Since 1994, CDI has helped open a total of 107* computing schools in poor neighborhoods in 13 Brazilian states. Some 32,000 youths have already taken the courses. Though the schools continue to depend on donated computers and facilities, they are financially self-sufficient, thanks to a modest tuition fee, averaging $3 per month, that provides a decent wage for instructors—all of whom must live in the community where the school is located.

The scale of the favela computing schools suggests that connectivity projects aimed at the vulnerable have considerable policy potential both as a mechanism for participation and for education. Initially, only a few of the computing schools had online connections, but as of June 23, 2002, 102 computing schools were online (http://www.cdi.com.br/). The vision of individuals is clear in the development of the best practice models of connectivity and voicing; the policy vision of the large institutions still lags.

Warschauer (2001) summarized the key characteristics of the favela computing schools as follows: (1) visionary leadership, (2) emphasis on human and social possibilities that can be enhanced by the use of computers, (3) promoting of power among the most marginalized sectors of society, whether due to poverty or additional types of social inclusion, (4) development of meaningful partnerships, both with the grassroots organizations and the private sector businesses that can help provide funding, and (5) a well-elaborated curriculum integrating both social content and IT that is flexible enough to be adapted in appropriate ways according to local circumstances. These characteristics connote an outstanding model for social empowerment through technology (http://members.tripod.com/vstevens/papyrus/2001/pn010802a.htm).

The embeddedness of the computing schools in wider social action appears to be a very important dimension of their success; membership of the computing schools helps communities better organize a range of social, political, and economic activities. It increases the bargaining capabilities of the communities in which the computing schools are located.

## TRACKING AND TRANSPARENCY: THE PARADOX OF POWER IN AN INFORMATION AGE

The advent of the new IT, with its increased data processing capacity and the ability to immediately relay or exhibit processed information globally through the wide-

---

* Since this date the number of schools has expanded to over 300.

spread distribution of this communication technology, has resulted in a tightening of the tracking and transparency of the powerful. For example, the advent of the widespread use of the Web and the development of a World Bank anticorruption site (http://www1.worldbank.org/publicsector/anticorrupt/) occurred at roughly the same time. The World Bank makes a global invital upon its site to world citizens to report relevant corruption. The site markets the position of the Bank on corruption through the very technology that enables individual reports of corruption to reach it effectively and until recently relatively autonomously. The "war on terror" is producing substantial scrutiny of E-mail and of "virtual journeys," such as visits to Web pages or chat rooms. This scrutiny may have impact on the use of electronic forms to alert the international institutions to problems of corruption. Despite this caveat, the electronic form results in the ability of the citizenry to better track the behavior and resource accumulation of the powerful.

The larger the institution, the more likely that material can be accumulated on its performance and cross-checked with other sources of data. The distributed character of technology means that many "eyes" can be used to observe the powerful; it is the paradox of power in the information age.

Once again, India figures strongly in the connectivity/raising voices equation. CUTS is an Indian organization that focuses on grassroots monitoring and perceptions of corruption (http://www.internationalbudget.org/cdrom/papers/systems/transparency/grassrootsperception.htm). The use of new information communication technology in tracing and tracking corruption is widespread. Similarly, new IT have been widely used by communities to map their own poverty and disadvantage and to identify the geography of hazards where these have conventionally been concealed by government from the public at large.

The distributed character of the new information communication technology enables large numbers of people to enter individual units of information into cumulative frames of information at low individual transaction costs. Communities can develop databases and archives of information that previously were solely the province of large administrative agencies. In the northeast of the United Kingdom such a database was developed on transport difficulties experienced by low-income communities that were dependent on public transport (http://www.goneat.org.uk). This community monitoring project received over 6000 visits on its Web site in the week in which it ran a trial monitoring the used various forms of new information communication technology.

The evidence is that both democracy and an effective media raise the social bargaining power of low-income communities. In such a frame, it seems clear that connectivity is likely to have the same consequence, and indeed this question has become the issue of economic research conducted by Professor Tim Besley of the London School of Economics.

## CONCLUSION: MANAGING MANY CONVERSATIONS—THE NEED FOR STRATEGIES

It is clear from this short account of developments in the connectivity and voicing of the disadvantaged that many conversations are possible between those having connectivity and seeking to exercise their voice. Such conversations need to be well managed by their owners. Identifying channels of influence and effectiveness outside the voiced group or community is as important as achieving equity in voice within a community.

Similarly, identifying those sharing predicaments and negative circumstances is important in developing solidarity networks that can be used for effectively challenging traditional power arrangements, which disempower the many and generate social descriptions of marginality. With connectivity, networks and alliances can be built at substantially lower transaction costs than those experienced in a period in which contact between those having similar interests or circumstances could only be achieved by physical travel. Out-of-locality networking provides information on a greater range of solutions than can be found in any one location. It provides an opportunity to learn about technical as well as social, political, and economic solutions. Pondicherry developed solar backup systems to deal with power outages or breakdown, which are so common in India. Solar backups are likely to be of relevance to connectivity projects in many developing countries.

The scale of information available through connectivity will require local thought about the screens to be applied in information search and the priorities that need to be respected in the construction of locally relevant databases. Context is key, and a register of best practices that helped provide key contextual indicators would be a very useful tool. The advent of community metadata—a process that is rapidly progressing in the United States but that on the last report neither the World Bank nor IMF were signed up to—will increasingly enable communities and groups to identify the data and information they require more rapidly and through simpler search protocols. The need for the international agencies to sign up to major metadata protocols becomes imperative if they are to be of use to communities in developing countries.

Raising voices requires connectivity, but it also requires well-organized and easily accessed and transparent information. Perhaps a policy vision that begins to tackle metadata issues will convert into a voicing vision that no longer sees the voice of the poor as being confined to localized participant management initiatives but enables it to take its place as a powerful global lobby in a world of increasing global governance.

## REFERENCES

Ardener, S. (1993). Introduction. In: Ardener, S., ed., *Defining Females: The Nature of Women in Society*. 2d ed. Providence, RI: Berg.

Barr, D. *Integrated Rural Development Through Telecommunications*. http://www.fao.org/sd/CDdirect/CDre0029.htm.

Chambers, R. (1995). Paradigm shifts in the practice of participatory research and development. In: Nelson, N.Wright, S., eds., *Power and Participatory Development: Theory and Practice*. London: Intermediate Technology Publications.

Eberlee, J. (2000). *Using the Internet to Help Street Children in Latin America*. Canada: IDRC (http://www.idrc.ca/reports/read_news.cfm?article_num=725).

Gilligan, C (1982). *In a Different Voice: Psychological Theory and Women's Development*. Harvard University Press.

Hanak, I. (1997). Speech strategies and gender exclusion in a rural development project. *Austrian J. Dev. Stud.* 3:257–281 (http://www.univie.ac.at/ecco/doc/hanak-031997-speech.pdf).

Hofstede, G (1980). *Culture's Consequences: International Differences in Work-Related Values.* Beverly Hills, CA: Sage.

Holmes, L., Hosking, D., Grieco, M. (2002). *Organising in the Information Age: Distributed Technology, Distributed Leadership, Distributed Identity, Distributed Discourse.* Aldershot: Ashgate.

World Bank. Voices of the Poor; http://www.worldbank.org/poverty/voices/overview.htm.

World Bank. Gender Issues in Participation; http://www.worldbank.org/wbi/sourcebook/sba209.htm.

# 33

# Sustainable Development Through Good Governance in India
## Challenges and Strategies

**R. B. JAIN**

*University of Delhi, Delhi, India*

## INTRODUCTION

More than a generation has passed since the process of decolonization has changed the contours of the world map and set the emergence of the so-called Third World countries. While the patterns of political change have differed among these societies, in most of them there has been a persistence of a juridical state, even if some of these have often lacked effectiveness and internal legitimacy. The image of the state in these societies has, however, varied from one of a strong society molding into new shapes and forms to one of a weak state virtually helpless in the swirl of dizzying social changes.

In all these societies, however, despite the fragmentation of social control, states have grown and have expanded their jurisdiction and resources considerably. Scholars advocating the concept of "strong corporate" or "bureaucratic authoritarian" states comment upon the control of state agencies over nearly every aspect of social life. In some societies, the demands on the state by both the unorganized and organized groups have grown to such an extent that the state is said to have become "incapable of governing," despite all the resources and tools that it may be able to command. This incapacity of Third World states to respond to the demands of their societies has been the one single factor responsible for a deviation from the Weberian rational pattern of bureaucratic behavior.

On the other hand, a common feature that has dominated the countries in the Third World has been the "ideology of development," incorporating the social and economic progress that determines the boundaries of political and social action. Bureaucracy as an instrument of state action seems to have become the principal vehicle for the accomplishment of developmental goals in all Third World countries, however. Concerns have been expressed about the prospective role of bureaucracies and the possibility that they may stray from their instrumental role to become the primary powerholders in societies. The political role of bureaucracy has been one of the principal issues of discussion in Third World countries. Many of the characteristics of the colonial governments have permeated the successor states. In addition, because of the growing intervention of the state in most human collective activities and resultant public enterprises, the state in the Third World has found itself deficient in skilled and technically competent manpower, resulting in low administrative capacity (Jain, 1989).

## CONCEPT OF GOOD GOVERNANCE

The two terms that are very often talked about these days are governance and corruption, but these not only remain largely undefined, but even the relationship between the two is either not properly understood or well defined. While corruption is commonly defined as the abuse of public office for private gains, governance is a broader concept, defined as the exercise of authority through formal and informal traditions and institutions for the common good. Governance encompasses the process of selecting, monitoring, and replacing governments. It includes the capacity to formulate and implement sound policies, and it assumes a respect for citizens. From this framework, governance can be construed as consisting of six different elements. These are: (1) voice and accountability, which includes civil liberties and freedom of the press, (2) political stability, (3) government effectiveness, which includes the quality of policy making and public service delivery, (4) quality of regulations, (5) rule of law, which includes protection of property rights and an independent judiciary, and (6) control of corruption. In the situation that many countries face at the start of the twenty-first century, especially in the developing world, controlling corruption emerges as just one of the most closely intertwined elements of governance. Combating corruption leads to improving the quality of governance. The key question therefore is what strategies lower corruption and strengthen the quality of governance.

Improving the quality of governance requires a system of checks and balances in society that restrain arbitrary action and harassment by politicians and bureaucrats, promote voices and participation by the population, reduce incentives for the corporate elite to engage in state capture, and foster the rule of law. A meritocratic and service-oriented public administration is a salient feature of such a strategy. Synthesizing the strategy of key reforms for improving governance and combating corruption is a particularly daunting challenge, however, as is the task of detailing and adapting a strategy to each country-specific reality. Governance is more than fighting corruption. Improving governance should be seen as a process integrating three vital components: (1) knowledge, with rigorous data and empirical analysis, including in-country diagnostics and dissemination and utilizing the latest information technology tools, (2) leadership in the political, civil society, and international arenas, and (3) collective action, via systematic participatory and consensus-building approaches with key stakeholders in society (which the technology revolution is also assisting). No two countries arrive at the same strategy, but to maximize the prospects of success, any country serious about improving governance for sustainable development must involve all key stakeholders, guarantee a flow of information to them, and lock in the commitment of the leadership (Kaufman, 2001).

## CHALLENGES IN THE TWENTY-FIRST CENTURY

### Challenges to Governance

The threshold of the twenty-first century heralds the advent of the corporate millennium. The politicoadministrative system in India now has to face a growing number of challenges. In the coming years, there is likely to be a growing commitment to a free market and global economy, and therefore corporate governance is going to be a crucial factor in efforts to restructure governing institutions. With the end of the Cold War in the 1980s, the victory of capitalism, the emergence of new industrialized countries around the world, and the development of the new technological revolution, along with political, economic, and social phenomena, have in many respects bypassed the border of the state and acquired a global dimension.

Under globalization, citizen demands are more diversified and sophisticated. They want choice, improved responsiveness, and improved quality of services. With the diminished role of the state, a market-oriented economy supported by a democratic government with an efficient and quality-oriented public administration is conceived as the formula for both economic development and the well-being of the people. Privatization, deregulation, debureaucratization, and decentralization are the current political issues. Performance-oriented governance and management strategies are advocated to improve responsiveness and accountability. No wonder the concept of *development management,* which has gradually expanded to encompass bureaucratic reorientation and restructuring, the integration of politics and culture into management improvement, participatory and performance-based service delivery and program management, community and nongovernmental organizations (NGO) capacity-building, and policy reform and implementation, is increasingly gaining ground, especially in the context of developing countries (Brinkerhoff and Coston, 1999).

Development management specialists now need to hone in on the critical managerial features of the problems that are preoccupying decision makers and demonstrate how the discipline is relevant and useful. It is these decision makers who must be convinced of the fit between development management and current global issues. Development management has made a difference in the lives of the citizens in the developing world, but continuing to contribute means remaining "in good currency." This is as much a challenge to the subfield as renewing and advancing development management's practical and applied research agendas (Brinkerhoff and Coston, 1999). The policy makers in India today face a formidable challenge in striking this balance as a strategy for good governance. Given the present politico-social scenario of the country, the ability of the system to respond to these new challenges is a big question for concerned citizens in India today.

The triumph of corporate millennium and world capitalism has led to a veritable tidal wave of economic and financial reforms in developing and transitional economies in the form of structural adjustment programs. Coupled with the increased financial power of transnational corporations, the pace of technological innovation has led to an increased search for new products, new production methods, and new markets. The revolution in information technology (IT) has not only made the world smaller, but has also led to profound changes in the reorganization of production and industrial establishments. Both businesses and governments are under intense pressure and scrutiny because people share instant information through a worldwide telecommunication network. There has been an expansion of world trade on a more competitive basis. The system of American-dominated multinational enterprises is being replaced by a system of multinational alliances in airlines, telecommunications, banking, insurance, and so on. At the same time the resurgence of massive international migration flows caused by the global economic structuring and information and technological revolutions have caused worldwide demographic changes.

Along with global transformation, the role of the state has also been changing. The trend is to shift from a system for which the state is the center of the world to a system for which the territorial principle has to come into balance with the interdependency principle. The political power of the states has been weakened by supranations, subnations, economic forces, and macroregions, In many countries, traditional bureaucratic public management is under severe criticism and is being gradually replaced by a new performance, result-oriented management, along with efforts toward downsizing government bureaucracy, empowering the local community, and encouraging private incentives. The tendency both at the national and local levels is to evolve a common concept of governance implying a leaner, fairer, and more representative government that allows for both more individual freedom and active participation in civil society. Citizens are increasingly coming together and organizing to represent their interests, express their views, and undertake actions to assist themselves, either independent of or in partnership with the government. In the globalizing world of the twenty-first century, civil society takes on an increasingly powerful role in development and in influencing policies.

This rearrangement of roles among the market, the state, and the people gives more space for civil society to organize itself to effectively voice the interests of both the people and the common good. It also gives more responsibility to civil society to take up the interests of the people whose voices would otherwise be overwhelmed and drowned and by the business interests of the politically powerful (Parr, 1997).

## Challenges to Sustainable Development

Ever since the Brundtland report of 1987, which defined the concept of sustainable development (SD) as "development that meets the needs of the present without compromising the ability of future generations to meet their own needs....A process of change in which exploitation of resources, the direction of investments, the orientation of technology development, and institutional change are all in harmony and enhance both current and future potential to meet human needs and aspirations," the central rationale for SD has been to increase the standard of living (broadly defined), and in particular, the well-being of the least advantaged people in societies, avoiding uncompensated future costs. Sustainable development highlights the importance of the sustainability of ecological and social systems rather than economic sustainability alone. It is also defined as development that improves health care, education, and social well-being. Such human development is now recognized as critical to economic development and human prosperity, which in the context of developing countries is intertwined with poverty-removal strategies. It is a fact that despite the apparent economic growth and development in many developing countries the poor are still poor (and have even increased in absolute numbers). Their critical basic needs in education, health, welfare, and infrastructure, along with the need for clean drinking water, still remain unmet.

In the same vein, the concept of SD also raises the issue of the need for institutional and technological devices in order to secure a semblance of clean and healthy living for the proliferating masses, especially in developing countries. The national concerns about the environment are such that the policy to think globally and act locally is most appropriate. Many of the environmental problems are the outcomes of international factors beyond the boundaries of a nation-state, and are coupled with extreme poverty and illiteracy, uncontrolled population growth, and development challenges. The mere construction of a legal and administrative framework for environmental management thus, does not solve the problems of environmental degradation or provide an ecological balance for SD. A strong political will to enforce environmental policies, the ability of administrative institutions to work in the most objective, efficient, and effective manner based on technoeconomic and social considerations, and a bold approach for reconciling the goals of development with those of preserving of environmental equities among the various diversified and deprived section of the population are essential conditions for the success of any strategies for managing the environment for SD.

In a recent article, Hyden (2001) linked the concept of SD to the substantive goal of poverty reduction, a practical policy concern currently shared by most members of the international development community, and believes that it is a complex policy issue because conditions for its realization vary from place to place. Furthermore, SD is multisectoral, bringing together a range of socioecological concerns, and involves a nexus between conservation and development. It is in this context that governance becomes important, because it points to the need for changing institutional relations and rules. Although Hyden argues that no consensus on what the concept really means has emerged so far, governance provides an opportunity for rethinking macro–micro relations in ways that not only enable, but also reassure local actors—individuals and communities—that the efforts to improve their livelihoods are worthwhile. The governance dimension of SD is thus vital to the realization of its objectives. Being able to put in place a system of rules that (1) allow actors in society to realize that politics is a positive-sum game, and (2) provides guarantees that the rights of the poor cannot be trampled upon with impunity is the highest priority in order to make SD a reality. The SD approach has the advantage of being comprehensive, and thus views the condition of the poor in both socioeconomic and civil-political terms (Hyden, 2001).

It also follows that the goals of SD can only be achieved by making changes in the present political, economic, and technological system at the global level and by making major changes in the management of planet Earth. There is a need to evolve a new global psychology, a fresh way of thinking about both political and economic change and society's relationship with nature. International cooperation must develop and continue so that there could be effective global environmental management.

Themes of "international governance" (the way the global environmental policy for development is governed and administered) and its improvement primarily in the North/South context are the starting point of an increasing number of international commissions and working groups of independent experts or decision makers. Their published reports all suggest a reform of the given mechanisms of international governance, called the consultative group (CG) mechanism framework, which will bring donors together who have a long-term interest in supporting particular developing countries. Consultative group meetings are chaired by the World Bank. The International Monetary Fund is closely associated with the World Bank in this international framework of aid coordination. On the national level, the United Nations Development Programme (UNDP) is supposed to take the institutional lead in aid coordination on the basis of its round table (RT) mechanism.

The main challenge for international development cooperation toward SD in the new century will thus be to bridge the economic political divide. This will require integrating the democracy and governance agendas into a single strategy addressing the intricate links between economic and political reforms *simultaneously*. The recent initiative by the World Bank on the "comprehensive development framework" (CDF) constitutes such an attempt. The CDF process stresses the necessity of devising comprehensive and coherent aid strategies based on an integrated conception of development linking economic and political challenges (Santiso, 2001).

## INDIA'S EXPERIENCES IN GOVERNANCE AND ADMINISTRATIVE DEVELOPMENT

The threshold of the new millennium has furnished us with a good occasion to reflect upon and evaluate India's experiences in administrative development toward its pursuit of good governance and ponder over the likely emerging trends and the lessons learned for the future. Reflecting on the realities of the public administration system in India over the last half century is not a simple exercise, for India is a complex society composed of diverse languages, social systems, ethnic, tribal, and caste groups, religions, regions, and cultural patterns, along with unlimited environmental factors that shape the behavioral patterns of the masses and public functionaries at all levels. All those factors affect the idea of rationalism in administrative behavior; it is very difficult to objectively evaluate their impact on governance. Since Independence in 1947, the government of India has taken a number of steps to revamp the system of administration at different stages of its evolution with a view to secure objectivity, transparency, efficiency, and responsiveness in the administrative process—the basic ingredients of good governance in a democratic system based on the concepts of the rule of law and the public welfare.

As it appears, the search for the elusive goal of good governance in India has been concurrent with the evolution of a constitutional democratic government, a government that is limited, stable, and truly representative of the majority of the people, maintains its territorial integrity and national sovereignty, accelerates economic growth and development, upholds the rule of law and renders justice without fear or favor and without delay, and ensures the welfare of all sections of the people. These objectives were sought through the adoption of the Republican Constitution in 1950. Despite the lofty ideals and the values of good governance enshrined in the Constitution, however, we find ourselves today in a state in which the system has not been able to provide either a stable government or stable policies.

What has gone wrong in our constitutional and administrative system during the last fifty years has been a subject of endless debate and discussion, and a number of prognoses have been made by constitutional and administrative experts, political leaders and policy makers, and various commissions and committees to reform and restructure the system to be able to achieve the objectives of good governance. "Has the system of government failed in India or we have failed the system?" is a question being raised again and again without any satisfactory answer.

As Jain (2001) emphatically suggested, it is wrong to always blame the structural aspects of the governmental system for our failures. Given the normal wear and tear in the edifice of the governmental and administrative system over a period of over fifty years, the system as a whole has not only survived, but also admirably borne the brunt of the times, in comparison to the scores of examples of other countries in the developing world in which such structures have crumbled completely.

At the same time, however, a number of serious distortions have crept into the system over the years, giving validity to the dictum of Woodrow Wilson that "it is easier to make a constitution than to run it." The foremost and most fundamental reason for all these aberrations has first been the existence of a dual system of values on the part of the political and administrative elites in India, who have the basic responsibility of implementing the system. In their public pronouncements and external behavior, they are highly idealistic and show deep concern for integrity, equity, and justice—the prime values of good governance. In practice, however, when it comes to actual decision making and its implementation, the same political and administrative elites are vulnerable to all kinds of narrow prejudices, biases, and pressures of caste, community, or religion—political compromises—in order to continue to remain in power by all possible means—fair or dubious. This has been a marked trend in India's political and administrative development, especially since the 1960s. The public postures of political and administrative leaders hardly match their actual behavior in the positions they hold and the values they espouse.

Second, there has been a growing sense of zealousness among the people from all walks of life in India about their constitutional rights and administrative privileges without paying due attention to the corresponding duties that go with them. The level of tolerance among the people in India, which was the hallmark of their social, cultural, and political behavior in the first two decades of the republic, seems to have been lost somewhere in the labyrinth of the struggle for power. People will go to any length of aggressive, unfair, immoral, and unjudicial conduct to achieve their selfish goals.

This general decline in standards of behavior and conduct of mutual relations has been more prominent in the floors of our legislatures, once considered the temples of democracy. The honorable members of these august bodies increasingly seek to settle their individual and political scores by blocking proceedings, creating pandemonium, showing fists, hurling shoes, chairs, and microphones, and breaking the heads and teeth of political opponents. All these occurrences have had some disastrous consequences for the social and political system as a whole. People in all professions and occupations will go to any extent and resort to any form of agitation in demanding their rights, but would not care for the obligations that such rights carry. Whether it is student bodies, academics, labor organizations, or business or industrial groups, there are agitations galore for all kinds of demands on the state and against any move of the government to bring about any reform or semblance of discipline in the system, holding the citizens at large to ransom, and throwing the daily lives of the people out of gear and at the same time putting strains and pressures on the performance of the system.

Third, at the same time, the total lack of a notion of accountability and responsiveness on the part of both our legislators and administrators has eroded the very essence of a responsible government. There are political rhetoric and polemics, but no substantial accomplishment in respect of the citizens' needs and aspirations. There are innumerable grandiose policies, plans, programs, and projects (four P's) that we are very apt to formulate, but no plans or will to implement them. The result is either stagnation or a very slow growth in the realm of progress and development.

On top of everything else, the bureaucracy in India is cold, slow, and somewhat inhuman in dealing with the complaints of its citizens. Worse, it carries an image of being the most corrupt among the world bureaucracies. Instances of administrative excesses, police brutality, and the nexus among politicians, bureaucrats, and criminals for securing political and personal ends appear in the media practically every day. Billions of rupees are being spent every day on the security, privileges, and "welfare" of politicians, legislators, ministers, and other political and administrative functionaries, but without any proportionate return on the welfare of the masses. There is open exploitation of money power, muscle power, and mafia power all around for securing personal and material gains without the slightest qualms about one's own responsibility for efficient and effective governance.

Fourth, in India the poor are still poor and have even increased in absolute numbers. Economic gains have been wiped out by population growth. Although India has an economically powerful middle class, a vibrant software industry, and nuclear capability, a huge number of India's citizens continue to eke out a living under conditions of extreme poverty and deprivation. The government's capacity to perform is still weak, and the resources available for public investment and development are still scarce. Local jurisdictions are particularly starved. The critical basic needs in education, health, welfare, infrastructure, and clean drinking water for the masses still go unmet. Many of the poor are in fact worse off now than they were a decade or so ago. It is no wonder that India ranks very low in the human development report prepared each year by the UNDP. Human development is the strand that holds together concerns on political institutions and governance, social institutions and culture, and science and technology. Ultimately what really matters is how the interaction between globalization and these different institutions redounds to higher levels of human development.

As one of the observers of the Indian political scene has rightly put it

> poverty is the biggest political constituency in India. Not only do our politicians feed off it like vultures but supposedly pro-poor activists and NGOs also rush around condemning economic reforms on the grounds that the poor will not benefit. . .. A favorite whipping boy of the "pro-poor" activists is globalisation. This they tell us is definitely anti-poor but again they do not ask if globalisation is an option anymore or a reality we have to face. There are not many countries left in the world so over regulated as we are. . .there is much we can gain by learning from other kinds of systems of governance where we went wrong (Singh, 2000).

What particular social and economic model can be devised at this juncture of the evolution of the Indian polity, with vociferous disruptive tendencies and without any coherent ideological stance, remains the biggest challenge for the policy makers in India at the beginning of the millennium.

## TOWARD A STRATEGY OF GOOD GOVERNANCE FOR SUSTAINABLE DEVELOPMENT

In light of these developments around the world, the fundamental question that arises is to devise strategies that would be conducive to nations for striving toward SD. Besides the institutional and structural innovations that make for a system of good governance, corruption-free SD requires a "moral determination" (Dwivedi, 1987; 2001). Recognition of such moral determination in governance marks the direction in which those who govern must channel their efforts if they are to justly serve society. That direction calls for individual moral responsibility and accountability, sacrifice, compassion, justice, and an honest effort to achieve the common good. Ultimately, it is moral determination that provides the foundation for governance toward corruption-free SD.

### Adopting a Normative Model of Governance

The need at present thus seems to be to adopt a normative model of a *good management approach* incorporating both the politico-administrative as well as the moral dimensions of good governance. This should include (1) a more strategic or results-oriented (efficiency, effectiveness, and service quality) orientation to decision making, (2) the replacement of highly centralized organizational structures with a decentralized management environment that integrates the new rural, urban, and municipal Institutions in which decisions on resource allocation and service delivery are made close to the point of delivery, (3) the flexibility to explore alternatives to direct public provision that might provide more cost-effective policy outcomes, (4) a focus on matching authority and responsibility as key to improving performance, including the mechanism of explicit performance contracting, (5) the creation of competitive environments within and between public service organizations, (6) the strengthening of strategic capacities at the center to steer government to respond to external changes and diverse interests quickly, flexibly, and at the least cost, (7) greater accountability and transparency through requirements to report on results and their full costs, (8) servicewide budgeting and management systems to support and encourage these changes, (9) the most important task—to break the growing nexus of bureaucrats, politicians, and criminals, leading not only to a breakdown of the total system but also to a sense of cynicism among the citizenry, (10) adapting of innovations and evolving suitable mechanisms to eliminate corruption at both the political and administrative levels and to strengthen citizens' grievance system, (11) improvement of the system of delivery at the cutting edge of administration by replacing the existing archaic bureaucratic procedures by absorbing some appropriate precepts inherent in the philosophy of new public management, and (12) improvements in the working atmosphere of the government institutions and offices to reflect a new work culture and a changed administrative behavior incorporating the principles of transparency, responsiveness, accountability, participation, and citizen-friendly management.

## The Public–Private Sector Synergy

There is no doubt that the process of globalization and the simultaneous rapid economic and technological changes have greatly affected the pattern of governance in modern times. Scholars have argued that the actual pattern of governance in internationalized environments can be related to the respective governance capacities of public and private actors, which hinge in turn on the strategic constellation underlying the provision of public goods. The specific strategic constellations vary along three dimensions; namely, the congruence between the scope of the underlying problem and the organizational structures of the related actors, the type of goods problem, and the institutional context.

For their part, each of these combines a number of factors (Knill and Lehmkuhl, 2002). On the basis of this concept, four ideal types of governance have been identified, enabled by their differing configurations of public and private capacities to formally or factually influence in various ways the social, economic, and political processes employed in the provision of certain goods. Assessing the implications of economic and political internationalization on the governance capacities of public and private actors, internationalization has been described as a process in which the patterns of governance are transformed along three paths: from interventionist regulation to regulated self-regulation, from interventionist regulation to private self-regulation, and from interventionist regulation to interfering regulation. An analysis of the consequences of internationalization for the patterns of governance further suggests that the expectation of the weakening of the state, or a mutual driving out of governance activities of public and private actors, can hardly be confirmed.

The relationship between public and private actors is not free from conflict; neither is it paralyzed by conflict. In essence there is a dynamic, synergetic relationship, with public and private contributions reinforcing each other over time. Such mutual dependencies between public and private actors, however, and their concepts of coping with specific problems, are apparent only in the implementation of certain regulatory arrangements and do not take into account the problems related to accountability and the democratic legitimacy of regulatory structures. A crucial question thus becomes important: How is it possible to ensure that private governance activities are kept responsive to wider societal interests? The question of accountability therefore becomes a key factor and an issue of good governance.

## Accountability as a Basic Requisite for Governance

If the concept of accountability refers to the degree to which public servants and others in nongovernmental sectors providing public programs are responsive to those they serve, then there is a need for multidimensional methods to measure how different institutional arrangements are advantageous to different forms of responsiveness. The traditional measures of accountability that rely on line or top-down measures do not necessarily provide a good guide to the accountability culture as a whole. As service delivery systems move to more complex forms of agency, accountability at other levels must be expected to undergo a dynamic process of evolution, adaptation, and in some cases crisis. It is clearly not enough to bemoan the decline of a parliament or the weakness of the consumer.

Institutional development must fit each case. Vertical strength can be improved with stronger roles for parliamentary committees, ombudsmen, and so on. Tools for greater horizontal accountability will need to be different for competitive systems and for those using more collaborative methods. In both cases, a focus upon the role of reflexive feedback or improvisation offers a means to reopen the organizational process box without the perils of reregulation. This new domain of accountability will take some time to develop its own regime of measures, standards, and rules. Perhaps the most important step needed is the recognition that multidimensionality of accountability means both multiple measure and new mandates (Considine, 2002).

## Adoption of Information Technology and the Concept of E-Governance

The revolution in IT has brought into focus its adoption for good governance. There is a talk of E-governance all over the world. E-governance implies a smoother interface between government and citizen. While it cannot entirely replace manual governance, even its limited applications are good enough to affect day-to-day living. It can fulfill, roughly speaking, the four purposes for which citizens generally interact with the government: (1) paying bills, taxes, user fees, and so on, (2) complying with registration formalities, whether of a child's birth, a house purchase, or a driver's license, (3) seeking information, and (4) lodging complaints. E-governance can reduce distances to nothing, linking remote villages to government offices in the cities, and can reduce staff, cut costs, check leaks in the governing system, and make the citizen-government interaction smooth, without lines and the tyranny of clerks. It must be remembered, however, that E-governance is only a tool for good governance. It can't succeed independent of responsive officers, and it has to be owned by the political leadership; otherwise, it will only be a bureaucrat's game (*India Today*, 2000). How to rebuild the system of governance on these new premises without the majority of population even being literate is a real challenge for all concerned with new innovations in the performance of the government in India.

## The Citizen-Oriented Paradigm of Governance

The corporate millennium has brought into focus a new concept of governance based on the interests of the shareholders (i.e., the citizens), which has signaled the role of transparency, accountability, and merit-based management and a sense of morality and ethics that rests on the principle of "concern for others." An ethical organization—more so a government—not only stands for people with a set of values, but for a positive attitude that generates a culture within the organization in which every member feels a sense of loyalty and belonging and the leaders are responsible for initiating dialogues across a wide range of levels and functions so as to operationalize values in practical policies.

Modernization of government and public administration involves a redefinition of government responsibilities. The state system of the twenty-first century will have to see a redistribution of duties and responsibilities among government, business, and society. The guiding principle is the idea of the "empowering state" that leaves more space for society and individual commitment. The internal structures of government administration should also become part of this developmental process. This would require the introduction of modern management techniques with quality control, budgeting, and cost-benefit analyses. In the future, public authorities are meant to be results-oriented in providing public services. Modern management and E-government are two central means of achieving fundamental changes in public administration. The goal is an administration that does more and costs less. E-government projects are not only modernizing public agencies and authorities, but are also making administrative procedures more transparent for ordinary citizens, which in turn also makes new demands on personnel to be more accountable.

Managers must respond flexibly to the changing demands and expectations of the public and the ever-changing nature of public problems, yet they must do so in a manner that provides accountability to both the public and political overseers. A dichotomous approach to the study of leadership as management action and the governance structures within which managers operate has inhibited the search for a public management theory that reconciles the dilemma. Managers must attend to demands for both flexible leadership action and structures that promise account-ability. The capacity to perceive this relationship offers managers a means to keep flexibility and accountability in a dynamic tension. It has been suggested that public management scholars can elevate this understanding from an implicit "theory in use" to an explicit "espoused theory." This approach could be a productive one for public management scholarship and. ultimately for its practice (Feldman and Khademian, 2001).

## Combating Corruption in Governance

From the foregoing discussion, it is more than evident that the concept of quality governance is premised on a corruption-free administrative system. Combating corruption for SD calls for (1) reducing opportunities and incentives for corrupt behavior and increasing the sense of accountability on the part of public officials, (2) effective implementation of anticorruption measures, which would imply that measures should be logically consistent with regard to the phasing of a timetable for speedy investigation and conviction, (3) a strong political commitment to implement the strategies and enforce anticorruption measures, and (4) the active participation from below in the enforcement of administrative, legal, and judicial measures, thus mobilizing the public against corruption in public life.

Apart from the above fundamental conditions, it must be emphasized that fighting corruption requires: (1) the formation of a national coordinating body responsible for devising and following up on a strategy against corruption, along with a citizens' oversight board, (2) the existence of a high-powered independent prosecuting body to investigate and prosecute all such known cases of corruption, (3) the setting up of special courts for trying such cases so that the cases come to their legitimate conclusion without any delay, (4) a thorough overhaul and reform of the system of electoral laws and economic regulations, minimizing the temptation to indulge in corruption, (5) enact appropriate legislation to limit the number of ministries and departments both at the center and the states so that the temptation of expanding ministries only for political gains could be minimized, and (6) by providing specialized technical assistance to anticorruption agencies, the organiza-tion of high-level anticorruption workshops or strategic consulting or hiring inter-national investigations to track down ill-gotten deposits overseas.

At the same time, it is also important that international institutions take steps to encourage participatory approaches in developing countries in order to build consensus for anticorruption drives and associated reforms. Civil society is likely to be a major ally in resisting corruption. Moreover, it is this ally that seeks concrete support from more developed Western countries and international agencies in actively combating corruption (Kaufman, 1997). International cooperation can help national leaders develop political resolve, and international action can convey the useful truth that we are all involved in the problem of corruption and that we must find solutions together.

## CONCLUDING OBSERVATIONS

In conclusion, it should be remembered that for achieving good governance, no amount of planning and thinking in the above areas would be useful unless the governments at all levels of the polity are capable enough to make hard and unpleasant decisions and have the will and capacity to implement and continuously monitor and evaluate their impacts. At the same time, the political leadership has to demonstrate its strong determination to undertake reforms by first cleaning its own stable from corrupt and criminal influences and setting ethical standards of quality governance both at the political and administrative levels.

In the perspectives of the worldwide developments at the threshold of the twenty-first century, this chapter discussed some of the emerging challenges to quality governance on which the strategies for growth and SD outlined above can be built and operationalized. It is heartening that people in almost all countries have recognized their importance, and it is likely that the growing concerns about achieving SD, fighting corruption, and devising innovations for "quality governance" may turn out to be a concerted international movement, not merely confined to the realm of academic discussions or writings in specific contexts, but constructive actions for positive results transcending the jurisdictions of national boundaries. This is the only hope for achieving universally good and corruption-free good governance—for the very survival of humanity—toward which we must all strive.

## REFERENCES

Brinkerhoff, D. W., Coston, J. M. (1999). International development management in a globalized world. Pub. Admin. Rev. 59(4):346–361.

Considine, M. (2002). The end of the line? Accountable governance in the age of networks, partnerships, and joined-up services. Gov. Internat. J. Policy. Admin. Inst. 15(1):21–40.

Dwivedi, O. P. (1987). Moral dimensions of statecraft. Can J. Polit. Sci. 20(4):609–709.

Dwivedi, O. P. (2001). The challenge of cultural diversity for good governance. U.N. Meeting on Managing Diversity in the Civil Service, organized by the U.N. Division of Public Economics and Public Administration (DPEPA), U.N. Department of Economic and Social Affairs, New York May 3–4, 2001.

Feldman, M. S., Khademian, A. M. (2001). Principles for public management practice: from dichotomies to interdependence. Gov. Internat. J. Policy. Admin. 14(3):339–361.

Hyden, G. (2001). Operationalizing governance from sustainable development. J. Dev. Soc. 11:13–31.

India Today, (Dec. 11, 2000). pp. 70–76.

Jain, R. B. (1989). Bureaucratic Politics in the Third World. New Delhi: Gitanjali.

Jain, R. B. (2001). Public Administration in India: 21st Century Challenges to Good Governance. New Delhi: Deep & Deep.

Kaufman, D. (summer 1997). Corruption: the facts. For Policy 130.

Kaufman, D. (Jan. 30–31, 2001). New empirical frontiers in fighting corruption and improving governance—Selected issues. OSCE Economic Forum. Brussels, pp. 1–3.

Knill, C., Lehmkuhl, D. (2002). Private actors and the state: internationalization and changing patterns of governance. Gov. Internat. J. Policy. Admin. Inst. 15(1):41–63.

Parr, S. F. (1997). Sustainable Human Development in a Globalizing World. New York: Human Development Report Office, pp. 1–2.

Santiso, C. (2001). Development cooperation and the promotion of democratic governance: promises and dilemmas. Internationale Politik und Gessellschaft (International Politics and Society) 4:386–397.

Singh, T. (Dec. 11, 2000). Poverty politics. India Today 26.

# 34

## Citizen Participation and Development Policy Studies
### *The Limits of Concept Transfer*

**HINDY LAUER SCHACHTER**

*New Jersey Institute of Technology, Newark,*
*New Jersey, U.S.A.*

## INTRODUCTION

This chapter examines some aspects of the diffusion of new public management's customer model of citizenship to developing and newly industrialized countries. New public management, or reinventing government, is a public-sector innovation that appeared almost simultaneously in many countries during the first half of the 1990s. The essence of its approach is the application of business practice to the public sector (Denhardt, 1993: 8–9). Its maxims include injecting competition into service delivery, orienting government to results, driving organizations through missions rather than rules, decentralizing polities, and centering administration on customers (Osborne and Gaebler, 1992). As an apolitical theory of management, it presents itself as a suitable candidate for adoption by any jurisdiction (Osborne and Plastrik, 1997:47). In this regard it is similar to the "principles" literature of the first half of the twentieth-century, which insisted that identical maxims applied to managing public and private organizations around the world (e.g., Urwick, 1944).

Like individuals, polities depend on peers for cues to behavior (Elkins, 2001). Seeing another jurisdiction use a concept or slogan shows that a set of ideas exists that a polity can integrate into its own political life. Some change-related uncertainty evaporates when policy makers see a concept receive support in another domain. Such external support may even make the idea more politically palatable among the citizenry, hence political and administrative fads often sweep across nations.

Countries with varied political and social histories adopt similar public-sector reforms (Schwartz, 1998).

Our era is particularly suited for the diffusion of concepts because of the relative ease of communication. Before they can borrow a concept, policy makers must first know it exists. In a global society, information moves quickly across national boundaries. Policy makers have many ways of becoming aware of innovative strategies, including professional organizations and policy communities, along with their various conferences and publications (Dolowitz and Marsh, 2000). Ease of travel allows policy makers, experts, and consultants to interact personally with peers across the globe (Mossberger and Wolman, 2001).

Sometimes this ease of communication facilitates the transfer of concepts that are advantageous to the recipients. At other times it exacerbates the probability that leaders will make one of two mistakes. They may transfer a concept that works well in the originating polity but that is inappropriate for them because of political, economic, or cultural differences. Welch and Wong (1998) argue that when developing or newly industrialized nations apply to themselves a concept designed for the West, they find that it rarely fits well.

Leaders also may transfer a concept whose defects in the originating polity are still unpublicized at the time of transfer. This second problem is particularly likely to occur if adoption takes place almost simultaneously in several countries. The new speed of diffusion allows problematic concepts to travel widely before their weaknesses are revealed. At some later period, originators and borrowers will then both have to grapple with the same infelicities.

In this vein, one criticism of importing new public management to East Asia lies in cultural incompatibility. A concept designed for one context is taken into another that is vastly different. Au et al. (2001) consider it alien to Chinese culture to have civil servants view the public as paying customers. Similarly, reinvention threatens traditional Korean values that stress communal harmony rather than individual aggrandizement.

Any analysis of the customer model in East Asia also has to deal with the metaphor's similar trajectory in the West and the East, however. The problem is not simply that East Asian jurisdictions borrowed a model unsuited for their cultures, but also that they were too quick to borrow a metaphor that was conceptually problematic in any democracy. Reinvention and traditional administrative values clash in the West as well as in Asia. New public management trumpets its distance from the older administrative model wherever it goes.

This chapter examines the diffusion of the customer model to East Asia not to emphasize cultural differences between Anglo-Saxons and Asians but rather to suggest how the search for ready-made solutions led Asian policy communities to accept an innovation without thinking through its rationale or consequences—in ways that would become clear to both the originators and the receivers after the innovation was in place. If problems attendant on Asian reinvention emanate exclusively from cultural incompatibility, we would expect that Asian critics of new public management would raise issues ignored by critics in the West. If, however, reinvention engendered convergent difficulties in the West and the East, then we would expect scholars in the originating and borrowing polities to offer similar critiques. This analysis shows that the latter scenario actually occurred.

The chapter opens by describing the essence of the customer model in America as seen through the National Performance Review (NPR). It then describes the implementation of this model in Hong Kong, Malaysia, South Korea, and Taiwan, four capitalism-oriented East Asian polities. In the early 1990s all four were newly industrialized jurisdictions. Each fit Lee's (1998) category of the "developmental" state, which she defines as a state whose legitimacy principle includes promoting and sustaining development. Each was taking steps to promote democracy. Hong Kong's colonial governor wanted some semblance of citizen participation before the territory's handover to China. Malaysia, South Korea, and Taiwan had recently increased the democratic nature of their governments after periods of authoritarianism.

In all five states, similarities are evident in new public management's implementation. In all these countries, change had top executive backing. Governments stressed the citizen-as-customer metaphor, meaning that citizens were seen as customers warranting high service-delivery standards rather than potential decision makers involved in determining public policies. Governments also introduced new electronic communication techniques.

This chapter describes key aspects of reinvention in these states. It then proceeds to offer representative critiques from American and Asian commentators and show their similarities. The author does not maintain that reinvention is widely discredited in any of the countries. Many officials in both the East and the West still say that gains in economy or customer satisfaction engendered by the new system are worth abstract concerns about democratic accountability (Haque, 2002). The chapter simply shows that among reinvention's critics similar analyses emanate from scholars in America and Asia. This convergence supports the contention that new public management results in similar conceptual difficulties in the East and the West.

## NEW PUBLIC MANAGEMENT IN AMERICA AND FOUR ASIAN COUNTRIES

### United States of America

The NPR, a six-month study of the American government chaired by then vice president Al Gore, opens with the brief that "it is time for a new customer service contract with the American people, a new guarantee of effective, efficient, and responsive government" (Executive Office of the President, National Performance Review, 1993:i). For the NPR, the problem is "not *what* government does, but *how* it works," and the solution is to treat taxpayers as business treats customers (Executive Office of the President, National Performance Review, 1993:2). Effective governments insist on customer satisfaction. They use surveys and focus groups to discover what customers want and then they restructure operations to provide it.

The NPR assumed that improved customer relations required performance standards. To prepare such standards, American agencies created reinvention teams. In September 1994 the government published a compendium of over 1500 standards that it saw as emblematic of quality service (Executive Office of the President, National Performance Review, 1994). Most deal with service delivery or courtesy. The Internal Revenue Service developed standards to mail refunds within forty days and to resolve account inquiries in an average of twenty-one days. The Social Security Administration developed a standard to be polite to customers, and another to inform people of the social security benefits for which they qualify.

In keeping with the focus on how government works, the NPR supported rapid development of electronic government, including systems to distribute public benefits electronically and to use information technology in agency work. The NPR criticized government agencies for not responding as readily as the business sector to the needs of innovative computer use.

## Hong Kong

As part of the 1992 public-sector reform, the colonial governor, Chris Patten, tried to foster a culture in which civil servants viewed the public as paying customers (Au et al., 2001). The government created an efficiency unit, whose motto "serving the community," meant developing a culture of customer satisfaction. Reporting to the chief secretary, one of the governor's chief advisors, the efficiency unit strove to implement "A culture that recognises the public as the paying customer and treats him or her accordingly" (Howlett, 1997:22).

To enhance customer satisfaction, agencies developed performance standards. They set standards on maximum waiting times for care at public hospitals, police officer response to calls, replies from tax authorities, and receipt of licenses. Other reform proposals included the use of customer surveys, customer liaison groups, and designated customer service officers. The land registry hired a customer service manager and held customer liaison meetings. The health department appointed a patient relations officer, put telephones and drinking facilities in clinics, and required staff members to wear name tags. It also opened additional clinics to serve more customers (Lam, 1997).

This was a turbulent period for Hong Kong, as it was slated to become a special administrative unit of China in 1997, but the strong colonial-era executive propelled thorough implementation of the new customer-oriented changes. By mid-1993, eleven departments had performance standards (Burns, 1994). In 1995, all forty-seven departments directly serving the public had set standards (Huque, 2002). The efficiency unit and the performance standards remained in place after Hong Kong's transfer to China.

## Malaysia

Beginning in 1993, Malaysia's Client Charter embraced a customer perspective on citizen–government relations. The chief secretary of the Malaysian government declared "the customer is king" (Ali, 2001:281). The government pledged to use total quality management to give each citizen "high quality services that are built around their own needs" (Ali, 2001:281). The aim was "total customer satisfaction" (Chiu, 1997:177).

Agencies translated quality pledges into standards. At Sultanah Aminah Hospital, quality pledges included providing an internal shuttle service, a choice of menus for patients in the first-class wards, and faster ambulance service (Rahman, 1996). Other departments enacted standards on providing facilities so that customers could wait in comfort and on placing signs for efficient customer travel in government buildings (Hamid, 1995).

Public organizations displayed client's charters that told citizens which services were available at a given location. They gave delivery times and often included information on costs, accessibility, and courtesy standards. Office counters held customer questionnaires. People could fill them out and report whether or not agency personnel actually met standards (Chiu, 1997).

Information technology changes accompanied the customer service paradigm. To ensure "convenience and comfort," the government embarked on an E-public program to allow citizens to have electronic access to services at any time and from any place (Ali, 2001:281). Functions encompassed in the original E-service pilot were driver and vehicle registration, licensing, utility bill payments, and online health ministry information.

## South Korea

In 1993, the Korean president pushed reinventing government with its customer focus as a world trend that his nation should follow (Moon and Ingraham, 1998). His inauguration slogan was "reinventing a new Korea" (Kim, 1997a: 107). In 1993 the Administrative Innovation Commission (AIC) began to make changes "to improve citizens' convenience in service delivery" (Kim, 1999:171) and "to provide service to customers in a timely, polite, efficient, and cost-effective. . .manner" (Kim, 1999:172). One scholar describes the ensuing shift as a movement away from following rules and procedures to maximizing customer value (Kim, 1998).

The AIC solicited suggestions from individuals as well as administrative agencies for proposals on deregulating, decentralizing, and abolishing red tape. In the first year and a half, it received over 13,000 proposals, with about 68% coming from individual citizens (Kim, 1997a). Unnecessary paperwork was simplified. To notify the government of a change of address became a one-step procedure rather than a six-step one.

Many agencies adopted citizens' charters similar to those used in Britain (Kim, 2000). These charters are supposed to set out in clear language service-quality information pertinent to customers. The AIC also acted as a complaint hot line. In 1998, the Office of Government Reform was created to oversee reinvention efforts.

## Taiwan

Taiwan began its administrative reform program and government reinvention in 1993 (Chu and Wang, 2001). Seeking a client orientation, the executive Yuan, the highest administrative agency in the central government, focused on satisfying customers. It pledged to raise service quality and implement "one-window service" (Kuo, 2001). Administrators were asked to have a customer-service mentality (Chen et al., 2003). Taipei, the capital city, opened an integrated service center as a one-stop location that people could visit to file complaints.

As in the other polities, Taiwan pushed electronic government as a particularly important goal (Kuo, 2001). In 1995, Taipei's mayor launched an electronic mailbox for individual complaints. Government viewed this channel as a low-cost, convenient medium by which people could voice their day-to-day problems (Chen et al., 2003).

## A CRITIQUE OF NEW PUBLIC MANAGEMENT

By the mid-1990s new public management and the customer metaphor came in for criticism in America. This criticism focused on the model's blind spot for the difference between the public and private sectors' goals. It questioned whether or not customer satisfaction should be a government's overarching aim, and whether or not such an aim did not diminish democratic citizenship.

Traditional theories of citizenship link the public to administration through elected representatives (Frederickson, 1991). People vote for legislators and a chief executive, who in turn exert control over bureaucracies. For some theorists this link provides sufficient popular control. Proponents of strong democracy, on the other hand, argue that this connection is necessary but insufficient; people need additional participation forums, including neighborhood assemblies in which they can gather to discuss issues (e.g., Barber, 1984). Scholars were debating the feasibility of representative versus strong democracy just as the customer model reared its head. (For an Asian summary of this debate, see Chen et al., 2003.)

Suddenly both representation and active citizenship models were in peril. New public management's critics saw the customer model as eroding both representation and active citizenship. One strand of their criticism explores how NPR diminishes democratic accountability. Another strand questions if "customer" is an appropriate metaphor to use for citizens in a democratic polity. These critiques become clear if we examine some American and East Asian analyses. We will see similar lines of argument from both perspectives with critiques centering on new public management's relationship to democratic accountability, defects in understanding the customer role, and the problems of expecting better client service at a time of downsizing.

### The Customer Model and Democratic Accountability

An early critique by Ronald Moe (1994) of America's Congressional Research Office questions the new public management emphasis on entrepreneurial government at the expense of democratic accountability. Traditional administrative paradigms construct America as a country with a government of laws passed by an elected legislature; the president and the administrators have a duty to implement the laws passed by Congress. The Gore report, however, envisions agencies as entrepreneurial entities. Congress becomes a nuisance whose micromanaging stifles administrator initiative. For Moe (1994:114), this is an "extraordinary misunderstanding about the role of public law in the designing and management of agencies." His analysis stresses the dissimilarities between managing government and private firms. Public agency missions have to come from elected representatives rather than administrators. He concludes that implementing the NPR yields a government that is less accountable to citizens.

Yong Duck Jung's (2000) critique of South Korea's reinvention uses concepts similar to Moe's analysis of NPR. He scores Korea's new public management because it does not stress the rule of law and democratic control. After thirty years of authoritarian rule, Korea finally has achieved free elections. As important as these contests are, however, citizens cannot use them to control public policy. Jung suggests that Korea needs a good-governance model of administration rather than reinvention. In such a model, the government would foster additional forums for people to evaluate policies and thus give the public input into decision making. For Jung, the alternative could mean great policy failures and the loss of public-sector creditability.

## What Kind of Customer Model?

Several American critics of new public management blame the customer metaphor for portraying citizenship as an essentially passive role. With this metaphor, administrators set the policy agenda. Citizens as customers simply react to the service choices that are available to them. Richard Box (1998) describes such citizens as free riders; these individuals pay scant attention to policy matters and let other people help make decisions without their input. Schachter (1997) urges people to use an owner metaphor rather than a customer metaphor for citizenship.

Myungsuk Lee (2001) decries the customer metaphor in the Asian context. He believes that government cannot work properly without active citizen participation, a concept better represented by an owner metaphor. Like Schachter (1997) he argues that active citizenship will increase when governments provide better information to the public. He sees such increased activity as essential for a democratic polity. Similarly, Won-Yong Kwon (2002:v) says that in Korea, "citizens do not want to remain just consumers of government services. Citizens demand that governments treat them as owners." Such treatment entails giving the public information on how governments provide services.

Not all American criticism of NPR opposes the customer metaphor. Some authors question whether or not reinvention works on its own terms as a strategy to foster customer satisfaction. Schachter (1997) notes that new public management actually trivializes what governments can do to delight customers. The emphasis is on a small part of the customer role—improving delivery rather than the services on offer. The assumption seems to be that a bank's customers only care about the length of its lines, not the nature of its interest rates. In keeping with this assumption, social security standards include one on courtesy but none on substance. The Gore report ignores substantive policy change even as a way to please clients.

South Korea's Pan Suk Kim believes that satisfying customers is a legitimate government objective, nevertheless he enlarges on the notion that reinvention's focus is narrow even within a customer framework. Kim differentiates between the quality of service delivery and the quality of service outcomes (1998). Reinvention brings quality in a delivery context, or what Kim (1997a:113) calls "administrative reform for convenience of daily life." The focus is on improving delivery of existing services rather than increasing the range of services offered. When reinvention proponents talk about customer impact, they mean immediate impact at the service delivery point rather than consequences over a period of years. They want to alleviate anger at waiting five minutes rather than slow wasting from receiving an inadequate pension. Other Korean critics echo the concern that reinvention concentrates on small problems, on "symbolic rather than substantive reforms" (Hahm and Kim, 1999:490). They label the AIC reforms as "microscopic...and not fundamental" (Kim, 1997b: 248).

Lee (2002) finds a similar problem in Hong Kong. She argues that its current performance standards often do not reflect what the public perceives as good service. Hong Kong agencies put great efforts into meeting their standards, but these goals may not reflect a client's real needs. How useful are they? Often they merely state current practice at the time in which they are written (Burns, 1994).

Some evidence exists from the Asian context that citizens have different service priorities than those fostered by new public management. The director general of Malaysia's complaints bureau once evinced surprise that so few citizens completed the customer questionnaires placed in government offices, and opined that "This suggests a need to change the mindset of customers" (Chiu, 1997:178). He proposed to accomplish this shift by giving people small presents for completing the questionnaires. What the lack of interest may suggest, however, is that citizens do not see delivery as central to service quality. They do not believe that completing questionnaires will actually bring substantive improvement. These citizens may not see a choice of meals on first-class wards in public facilities as fundamental improvement. They might prefer spending a greater percentage of GNP on health care or abolishing the distinction between first- and other-class wards in public hospitals; even customers have broader agendas than reinvention imagines.

## Downsizing and the Customer Model

Wherever it goes, new public management aims to produce a significant shift in agency culture. It wants to move administrators away from a bureaucratic model and toward customer service. Phil Nufrio (2001) suggests that this shift has not occurred in America because of the downsizing attendant on reinvention; administrators who fear losing their jobs are not the best specimens to delight customers.

In similar fashion, Sung Deuk Hahm and Kwang Woong Kim (1999) relate Korean agency downsizing to the lack of culture change in that polity. The 1993 reforms in South Korea eliminated over 1000 administrative positions, and employee morale rapidly diminished. As their positions disappeared, administrators were not in the proper frame of mind to improve customer service. M. Shamsul Haque (1998; 2000) discusses downsizing in Southeast Asian nations, such as Malaysia. Position elimination hurt the morale of even the remaining workers; they lost the intrinsic motivation attendant on being a member of an authentic public institution dedicated to promoting the whole community. They felt neither proud of nor comfortable with a customer-service image. Under such conditions, how could they concentrate on helping customers? A clash developed between new public management's low-cost and customer-service imperatives.

## ANALYSIS AND CONCLUSION

Considerable literature suggests that the problem in transplanting new public management results from the cultural differences between East and West. United Nations documents warn Asian nations against cookie-cutter borrowing without regard to their own cultural traditions and needs (e.g., United Nations Development Program, 1999). If cultural incompatibility were the prime mover behind the critique of reinvention in Asia, however, we would expect to see conceptually variant arguments from Anglo-Saxon and Asian experts. Asian scholars, for example, might base their approaches on the Confucian or Buddhist traditions. In actuality, however, many themes used by American scholars to critique the NPR reappear in Asian scholars' analyses.

In the early 1990s the public administration literature in America and Western Europe included many paeans to aspects of new public management (e.g., Wagenheim and Reurink, 1991). At start-up time a number of newly industrialized countries in East Asia borrowed parts of the model, including the customer focus. Later in the decade scholars in America analyzed defects of this orientation. As this chapter shows, Asian analyses of these defects appeared simultaneously and concurred with

Western critiques. A basic aspect of both sets of critiques is the distance between customer and good-governance models of citizenship—the need for a broader approach to participation that includes a place for citizens in decision making (e.g., Smith, 1996; Bowornwathana, 2000).

The transfer problem is not as much cultural incompatibility as an inability to foresee problems that would later become apparent in any polity accepting the new concept. Borrowing an innovation requires information and processing skills. Each policy community brings to this task the biases and assumptions that make up its managerial logic (Afuah, 1998:97). Although in theory a borrowing jurisdiction can correct any mistakes the pioneering polity may have made, it will fail to do so if the jurisdiction's managerial logic restricts its scan for information that would indicate either a compromised rationale or unforeseen consequences. In this case, the four Asian states' managerial logic propelled them to see advantages rather than disadvantages to innovations emanating from Anglo-Saxon countries.

Elite groups in each state shared an interest in assimilating policy information from the Anglo-Saxon world. For much of this period, Hong Kong was a British colony with a colonial governor well placed to borrow goals, instruments, content, and ideas from his homeland. As relative newcomers to developed status, the other three countries had leaders who were eager to learn about innovations from nations with longer histories of developed status. Malaysia's policy experts were influenced by English and American models of governance (Common, 1999). Its ministers tended to use English in their speeches at official functions (Rajamoorthy, 1999). South Korea's public administration scholars used American textbooks. Their articles cited American sources more often than Korean works (Chung, 1998). One observer has described Taiwan's intellectual community as outstandingly Western-ized, with a majority of government ministers holding doctorates from American universities (Whitehead, 1999). It is easy to see why American and other English-language ideas seemed unproblematic to this audience. In the early 1990s, neither their government officials nor their policy scholars extensively questioned the suitability of the citizen-as-customer concept to participative democracy. Their managerial logic led to them to overgeneralize from a few poorly documented success stories in the West.

A transfer process by which borrowing polities understand all of a paradigm's potential flaws is impossible for two reasons. First, policy officials satisfice; they tend to look for innovations that are good enough for a specific short-term purpose. Second, some problems manifest themselves on a case level. They do not occur in the originating polity; they only appear in the borrowing state.

Contemporary transfer speed can make the process more dysfunctional as well as more easy, however. Increased speed means that policy experts are often assessing a new concept before it has any chance of showing strengths or weaknesses in the originating state. Diffusion in a hurry increases the likelihood that polities will not discover problems until after implementation. The probability is particularly high if the borrowing polity sees the originating jurisdiction as a model or exemplar in any significant way.

The public administration literature already notes the advantages of speedy diffusion of information across the globe (e.g., Cleveland, 1985). Such advantages are real, but policy makers must also understand the negative dynamic of swiftly diffusive and transportable information. Learning from the mistakes of others may become an outdated concept if as in the diffusion of the citizen-as-customer metaphor, polities all over the world adopt a trend before anyone can analyze its insufficiencies.

# REFERENCES

Afuah, A. (1998). Innovation Management. New York: Oxford University Press.

Ali, T. S. (2001). Serving in the knowledge age: Public service for knowledge advantage. Internat. Rev. Admin. Sci. 67(2):273–285.

Au, K., Vertinsky, I., Wang, D. (2001). New public management in Hong Kong: The long march toward reform. Jones, L., Guthrie, J., Steane, P, eds. Learning from International Public Management Reform. Amsterdam: JAI, pp. 311–335.

Barber, B. (1984). Strong Democracy. Berkeley, CA: University of California Press.

Bowornwathana, B. (2000). Governance reform in Thailand: Questionable assumptions, uncertain outcomes. Governance 13(3):393–408.

Burns, J. (1994). Administrative reform in a changing political environment: The case of Hong Kong. Pub. Admin. Dev. 14(3):241–252.

Box, R. (1998). Citizen Governance: Leading American Communities into the 21st Century. Thousand Oaks, CA: Sage.

Chen, D. Y., Huang, T. Y., Hsaio, N. (2003). The management of citizen participation in Taiwan: A case study of Taipei city government's citizen complaints system. Internat J Pub Admin. 26(5):525–540.

Chiu, N. K. (1997). Service targets and methods of redress: The impact of accountability in Malaysia. Pub Admin Dev 17(1):175–180.

Chu, P. Y., Wang, H. J. (2001). Benefits, critical process factors, and optimum strategies of successful ISO 9000 implementation in the public sector. Pub. Perf. M. Rev. 25(1):105–121.

Chung, S. H. (1998). From imitation to creation: Public organization research in Korea, 1967–1996. Internat. J. Org. Theory. Behav. 1(3):321–362.

Cleveland, H. (1985). The twilight of hierarchy: Speculations on the global information society. Pub. Admin. Rev. 45(1):185–195.

Common, R. (1999). Accounting for administrative change in three Asia-Pacific states: The utility of policy transfer analysis. Pub. M. 1(3):429–438.

Denhardt, R. (1993). The Pursuit of Significance: Strategies for Managerial Success. Belmont, CA: Wadsworth.

Dolowitz, D., Marsh, D. (2000). Learning from abroad: The role of policy transfer in contemporary policy-making. Governance 13(1):5–24.

Elkins, Z. (2001). Designed by diffusion: International networks of influence in constitutional reform. Annual Meeting of the American Political Science Association, San Francisco.

Executive Office of the President, National Performance Review. (1993). From Red Tape to Results: Creating a Government That Works Better and Costs Less. Washington, DC: U.S. Government Printing Office.

Executive Office of the President, National Performance Review. (1994). Putting Customers First: Standards for Serving the American People. Washington, DC: U.S. Government Printing Office.

Frederickson, H. G. (1991). Towards a theory of the public for public administration. Admin. Soc. 22(4):395–417.

Hahm, S. D., Kim, K. W. (1999). Institutional reforms and democratization in Korea: The case of the Kim Young Sam administration, 1993–1998. Governance 12(4):479–494.

Hamid, T. (1995). Government in transition: Building a culture of success—the Malaysian experience. Pub. Admin. Dev. 15(3):267–269.

Haque, M. S. (1998). Impacts of globalization on the role of the state and bureaucracy in Asia. Admin. Theory Praxis 20(4):439–451.

Haque, M. S. (2000). The new crisis in administrative ethics in developing nations: Trends and implications. International Political Science Association meeting, Quebec City, Canada.

Haque, M. S. (2002). Globalization, new political economy and governance: A third world viewpoint. Admin. Theory Praxis 24(1):103–124.

Howlett, B. (1997). Hong Kong, 1997. Hong Kong: Information Services Department.

Huque, A. S. (2002). Administrative reform in Hong Kong: Rationale, strategies and results. In: Farazmand, A., ed. Administrative Reform in Developing Nations. Westport, CT: Praeger, pp. 89–103.

Jung, Y. D. (2000). Great policy failures, public administration credibility, and good governance in Korea. Internat. Rev. Pub. Admin. 5(1):125–129.

Kim, P. S. (1997a). Public management reform in Korea. In: Kim, B., Kim, P., eds. Korean Public Administration. Elizabeth, NJ: Hollym, pp. 97–124.

Kim, B. W. (1997b). Revitalizing the local public service in South Korea: New challenges, barriers, and strategies. In: Kim, B., Kim, P., eds. Korean Public Administration. Elizabeth, NJ: Hollym, pp. 238–258.

Kim, P. S. (1998). Revolution in public service delivery. Internat. J. Org. Theory Behav. 1(2): 129–162.

Kim, P. S. (1999). Government reform in Korea. In: Wong, H., Chan, H., eds. Handbook of Comparative Public Administration in the Asia-Pacific Basin. New York: Marcel Dekker, pp. 163–178.

Kim, P. S. (2000). Administrative reform in the Korean central government: A case study of the Dae Jung Kim administration. Pub. Perf. M. Rev. 24(2):145–160.

Kuo, Y. Y. (2001). New public management in Taiwan: Government reinvention. In: Jones, L., Guthrie, J., Steane, P., eds. Learning from International Public Management Reform. Amsterdam: JAI, pp. 337–351.

Kwon, W. Y. (2002). Preface. In: Holzer, M., Kim, B.J., eds. Building Good Governance: Reforms in Seoul. Seoul, Korea: National Center for Public Productivity and Seoul Development Institute, pp. v–vi.

Lam, J. (1997). Transformation from public administration to management: Success and challenges of public sector reform in Hong Kong. Pub. Produc. Mgt. Rev. 20(4):405–418.

Lee, E. (1998). The political economy of public sector reform in Hong Kong: The case of a colonial-developmental state. Internat. Rev. Admin. Sci. 64(4):625–641.

Lee, E. (2002). The changing relationship between the state and the voluntary sector in Hong Kong. American Society for Public Administration meeting, Phoenix, Arizona.

Lee, M. (2001). New public management, new governance and administrative reform in Korea. American Society for Public Administration meeting, Newark, NJ.

Moe, R. (1994). The "reinventing government" exercise: Misinterpreting the problem, misjudging the consequences. Pub. Admin. Rev. 54(2):111–122.

Moon, J. M., Ingraham, P. (1998). Shaping administrative reform and governance: An examination of the political nexus triads in three Asian countries. Governance 11(1):77–100.

Mossberger, K., Wolman, H. (2001). Policy transfer as a form of prospective policy evaluation. Annual Meeting of the American Political Science Association, San Francisco.

Nufrio, P. (2001). Changing Organizational Culture: A Study of the National Government. Lanham, MD: Rowman and Littlefield.

Osborne, D., Gaebler, T. (1992). Reinventing Government: How the Entrepreneurial Spirit Is Transforming the Public Sector from Schoolhouse to State House, City Hall to Pentagon. Reading, MA: Addison-Wesley.

Osborne, D., Plastrik, P. (1997). Banishing Bureaucracy: The Five Strategies for Reinventing Government. New York: Addison-Wesley.

Rahman, A. A. (1996). Public service innovations in Malaysia. In: Salleh, S. ed. Public Sector

Innovations—the ASEAN Way. Kuala Lumpur: Asian and Pacific Development Center, pp. 63–112.

Rajamoorthy, T. (1999). Globalization and citizenship in Malaysia. In: Davidson, A., Weekley, K., eds. Globalization and Citizenship in the Asia-Pacific. New York: St. Martin's, pp. 87–103.

Schachter, H. L. (1997). Reinventing Government or Reinventing Ourselves: The Role of Citizen Owners in Making a Better Government. Albany, NY: State University of New York Press.

Schwartz, H. (1998). Reinvention and retrenchment: Lessons from the application of the New Zealand model to Alberta, Canada. J. Policy. Anal. Mgt. 16(3):405–422.

Smith, B. (1996). Sustainable local democracy. Pub. Admin. Dev. 16(2):163–178.

United Nations Development Program, Regional Bureau for Asia and the Pacific. Public Sector Management Reform in Asia and the Pacific: Selected Experiences from Seven Countries. (retrieved from http://undp.un.org.pk/rgp/).

Urwick, L. (1944). The Elements of Administration. New York: Harper and Brothers.

Wagenheim, G., Reurink, J. (1991). Customer service in public administration. Pub Admin Rev 51(3):263–270.

Welch, E., Wong, W. (1998). Public administration in a global context: Bridging the gaps of theory and practice between Western and non-Western nations. Pub. Admin. Rev. 58(1):40–50.

Whitehead, L. (1999). The democratization of Taiwan: A comparative perspective. Tsang, S., Tien, H., eds. Democratization in Taiwan. New York: St. Martin's, pp. 168–185.

# 35

## Decentralization, Democratic Centralism, and Citizens' Exclusion
### A Case Study of Nebbi District in Uganda

**ALFRED LAKWO**[*]

*Catholic University of Nijmegen, Nijmegen, The Netherlands*

## INTRODUCTION

The increasing challenge to development policies and practices is evident from the widening socioeconomic and political gaps between rich and poor nations and continually generate new prescriptions suggested by donor countries concerned with the current *development impasse*. Decentralization policy is one such new prescription. This chapter focuses on the practical problems associated with the implementation of decentralization policy and explores the discourse on the issue. The chapter draws empirical evidence from Nebbi district, which is considered one of the best-performing districts in Uganda, and shows the irony of the ideal construct of development policy processes, which still seems to be a taken for granted and is endorsed by both the national elites and the elected representatives of local governments. It is posited that while decentralization is being popularized as a new approach to development, it is characterized by the usual top-down structure and the negative policy externalities that hamper the effectiveness of decentralization.

The chapter starts by exploring one of the growing trends in promoting decentralization in the Ugandan context. It also presents an overview of decentral-

* The author is a Ph.D. student at the Center for International Development Issues, Nijmegen, (CIDIN), Catholic University of Nijmegen, The Netherlands, and Uganda Martyrs University, Nkozi, Uganda. I appreciate the comments on this piece from Aldelbert Kamanzi, Hebe Verrest, Wilfred Cwinyaai, and Frans J. Schuurman.

ization and explores the policy-making process within the decentralized structure of local government, emphasizing popular participation. The chapter then focuses on the crucial challenges to decentralization with regard to legal, institutional, funding, participatory, and communication limitations. It recommends a genuine people-centered government committed to citizenship building, a managerial reorientation, and a devolution of power to the people as invaluable ingredients of local-level development.

## DECENTRALIZATION: THE NEW DEVELOPMENT PATH

Changes in the global political climate and a shifting view of the role of government have led to the "rolling back of the state," with the concomitant increase in the role of nonstate actors in development (1). This ideological reversal has been evolving since the 1970s, and the focus has been on people first, development through learning, decentralization, diversity, local knowledge, transparency and accountability, good governance, small groups, community action, participation, and partnership. Decentralization is considered a possibility that can salvage the situation of underdevelopment in the Third World (2).

The popularization of decentralization in the 1970s and 1980s in developing countries (Rondenelli, 1981: 133–134) was an attempt to undertake the development paradigm that could integrate the structural approach with neoliberalism (3). The premise is that decentralization opens up government systems—which used to be solely for the elites—for citizen participating in local governance. It provides for capacity building for local managers and organizations in grappling with their development issues, and it transforms the development process from an inside-out approach that draws on the social capital of the people.

The supply-oriented premises upon which decentralization is supposed to succeed require the creation and/or strengthening—financially or legally—of subnational governmental units, the activities of which are substantially outside the direct control of the central government, and the creation of synergy in local–central government relations to the advantage of local governments (Dunleavy, 1980: 116) (4). In short, the supply side should meet the demand side by ensuring that while power is returned to the people who need government services, most decisions should be made by them, depending on the issues at stake (Standish, 1983: 224; Crosby and Orsini, 1996). Failure is tantamount to what the other development approaches (both in their processes and end products) yielded, which according to Verhagen (1987: 8) reduced the status of the poor to that of "beneficiaries" of development projects, "adopters" of new technologies, and consumers of ill-coordinated public welfare services, all which imply a high degree of dependence on the benevolence, entrepreneurial capacities, and economic means of others. Two critical issues still remain pertinent, however; that is, (1) the state still wields the monopoly power to provide development, and (2) democratic institutions need to be established to build a synergy between state-led development and the citizen, probably within the civil society (a third sector) or by appending both the civil society and the citizens to the state's control (Thompson, 1995).

At the practical level, however, participatory development embedded in decentralization is increasingly linked to democracy and human rights—strong civil societies are seen as providing a force that countervails the powers of government, thus making development responsive to the needs of the people; sectorwide programs generated through dialogue are increasingly preferred to the isolated projects popularized by nongovernmental organizations (NGOs) in the 1980–1990s; responsibilities for program identification and implementation are being delegated to the lowest level of government possible; and financial as well as management responsibilities are being devolved to democratically elected lower authorities.

As a policy goal and a policy instrument, decentralization aims at shifting the responsibilities for development to local authorities; that is, bringing at the decision-making process closer to the people so that they become the agents of their own change (Stocker 1988: 244; SNV, 1999: 27; Ofei-Aboagye, 2000) through improved local democracy, accountability, and sustainability of quality and cost-effective "locally" chosen service delivery. Although it is evident that the decentralization policy in Uganda undertook a centralized and political process with a pragmatic (preserving the monopoly of governance) and reformist agenda (opening governance to the populace), this requires that the pillars of community-based strategic and participatory policy process are upheld (SNV and District Planning Unit, 1997).

## THE DECENTRALIZATION PROCESS IN UGANDA

Factional politics controlled by the elites is characteristic of Ugandan politics. The inability of the elites to commit academic suicide explains why the constitution in 1962 results from independence was abrogated in 1967, leading to a new constitution that centralized the hitherto decentralized local governance. Between 1986 and 1992, however, when the National Resistance Movement (NRM) came to power, local governments tended to decentralize through the local councils. While at the initial stage there was more political decentralization (as in the ten point Programs, through the resistance/local council structures running from village to district), by 1992 the decentralization process started in a geographically phased manner (phase 1, thirteen districts, phase 2, fourteen districts, and phase 3, twelve districts). This was accompanied by legislative, financial, and personnel decentralization. The 1995 constitution and the 1997 Local Governments Act which firmly committed to decentralization in Uganda.

Now in power for sixteen years, the government of Uganda, is committed to the decentralization policy as an engine for stimulating local development. This explains the transfer of responsibility for planning, management, and the raising and allocation of resources from the central government to local governments. This requires, however, that all stakeholders—the leaders and the followers and the public, private, and civil society institutions—share as partners and not be co-opted during implementation in decision making (Mosse, 1994; Fowler, 1998; Guijt and Shah, 1998; Cornwall, 1999; Kothari, 2001). This demands a mutual interlinkage, partnership, and joint actions with due consideration of the community—the end users of services. This has not been the case, however; instead a top-loaded hijacked placement has been in operation that decides for the community, speaks on its behalf, takes what actions it thinks are best for the community, and finally earns credit for itself—leaving the community in the perpetual limbo of poverty.

Nsibambi (1998) pointed out that the objectives of decentralization in Uganda are in line with statutes no. 15 of 1993, and include: (1) transferring real power to the local governments and thus reducing the workload on remote and underresourced central officials; (2) bringing under control (political, managerial, and administrative) the delivery of services to local people to improve effectiveness and accountability and to promote a sense of citizen's ownership of local government programs and projects; (3) freeing managers in local government from the constraints of central authorities to allow them to develop organizational structures that are tailored to local conditions; (4) improving financial accountability and responsible use of resources by establishing a clear link between the payment of taxes and the provision of the services they finance; and (5) improving the capacity of local governments to plan, finance, and manage the delivery of services to their constituents.

The above objectives may be summarized as the creation of functioning local bureaucracies under the direction of accountable and democratically elected leaders (councils) that take responsibility for the development and good governance of the people in the geographical areas under their jurisdiction. The objectives also indicate that decentralization should put people first, respect local knowledge and skills, empower local communities, provide for local autonomy, and prioritize locally engineered activities. In the development debate, as Bossuyt and Gould (1999: 1–17) argued, decentralization remains a political process with vested interest in power and access to resources aimed at reducing poverty through empowerment, resource mobilization strategy, and effective basic social services delivery. Are these ideals the same as what is being practiced? In answering this question, I will argue that decentralization has promoted democratic centralism within the local government circles and excluded other would-be nonstate actors.

Practically, as stipulated in the Local Governments Act (LGA) of 1997, local governments are expected to: (1) provide vertical and horizontal information and insights to all stakeholders; (2) coordinate the mapping and mobilization of local capacities and resources, especially the informal private sector, with the expectation that this will promote local economic growth, employment, and the production of surplus that the local government can in turn tax; (3) provide a domestic framework to promote the participatory formulation, conceptualization, and operationalization of local development plans; (4) ensure the fair and equitable targeting of poverty reduction programs at the local level; (5) facilitate the development of socioeconomic and physical infrastructure; and (6) generate greater trust and accountability between the state and its citizens by involving local leaders, entrepreneurs, and civic organizations in both democratic dialogue and the workings of government.

Local governments are thus supposed to catalyze the processes of development, acting as facilitators rather than as controllers of the processes. It is in these new roles and expectations that a major challenge to "responsive action" is embedded. The basis of this challenge lies in participatory public policy formulation, which requires openness since it involves a multitude of processes and actors, as opposed to the traditional policy process, which is the preserve of the elites in government.

## DECENTRALIZATION AND THE POLICY-MAKING PROCESS

Public policy under decentralization comes to the forefront because the role of the nation-state in the provision of common goods and services is questionable in view of the increasing demand for accountability, transparency, democracy, and legitimate leadership; that is, good governance (5). This demands that the policy-making process become gateless, with actors mutually transparent and accountable for their actions.

The dynamics in the policy-making chain require many strategic approaches with objectivity and inclusiveness, as well as logically conscious and participatory actions, because although it appears cyclical, a policy-making process is actually messy (Hogwood and Gunn, 1984: 24; Clay and Schaffer, 1984; Van Horn et al., 1989: 59–158; Dresang and Gosling, 1989: 146–172; Juma and Clarke, 1995). This should accommodate political, organizational, personal, policy, and ideological values, and needs, equity, quality, professionalism, and politics, as well as the basic rationality (political, technological, public, ethical, etc.) involved (Anderson, 1984: 11–13, 23–43; Edwards, 1980: 53–87; Nakamura and Smallwood, 1980: 46–66; Levine et al., 1990: 81–99; Cusworth and Franks, 1993: 85–175).

From the above, a "new tyrant"—popular participation—in development emerges (White, 1996; Pietersen, 1998; Cooke and Kothari, 2001). A number of reasons are cited for popular participation in the policy-making process; namely, an increased likelihood of successful policy implementation and share of manager's dilemmas (Cernea, 1991); the empowerment of the beneficiary (Frischtak, 1994; Clark, 1991; Carroll, 1992; Bratton, 1990); improved service delivery (Picciotto, 1995); cost sharing through the beneficiaries' contributions and more efficient use of resources (Alesina, 1994); inclusiveness and transparency effects against policy opposition (Hyden, 1992); and strategic needs targeting or policy responsiveness (Sharpe, 1998).

The need for popular participation calls for participation beyond the informative and consultative level to shared, collaborative mechanisms in local governments (see Chambers, 1993; Burkey, 1993; Pretty, 1994; Eade, 1996; Blackburn and Holland, 1998), what Rahman termed "people's self-development" (Rahman, 1993: 178) because it creates policies and development that are: "'needs-oriented, geared to meeting both material and nonmaterial human needs. It is 'endogenous' stemming from the heart of each society; it is 'self-reliant' implying that each society relies primarily on its own strengthen and resources; it is 'ecologically sound' rationally utilizing the resources of the biosphere; and based on 'structural transformation' as an integrated whole." (See also Hoogvelt, 1982: 15–20; Burkey, 1993: 30–32; Booth, 1995: 17–18.)

What gives real meaning to popular participation, however, is the collective effort of the people concerned to pool their efforts and other resources to attain objectives they set for themselves (Slater and Watson, 1989: 153; Higgins, 1996: 447). According to Rondenelli, this is necessary to increase the scope of decision and thus create an incentive to local participants, structures, focus, and stability (Rondenelli, 1983: 113; compare Samoff, 1979: 33), but is it an actual practice or rhetoric of the elites to perpetuate their position of power?

Keely and Scoones (2000) caution on the leading role that politics play in shaping policies, and Rebecca Sutton (1999) reaffirms that policy process should be owned by the people and involve organizations outside the government as well. (See Cockery et al., 1997; Komba, 2000.) Timmer (1998) thus concludes that one of the reasons for the failure of policies is simply the efforts to implement policies that are unrealistic; that is, not based on careful analysis of the constraints that policy managers and implementers are likely to face (budget, bureaucratic capacity, physical infrastructure, supply and demand parameters, and politics).

Policy makers are therefore obliged to supply according to the demand of their clients—the community. It is doubtful, however, that this can fit within the bureaucratic culture of governance (Cockery et al., 1995: 12). With the growing concern in political–citizen relations, however, popular participation is not only the democratization of decision making but also the sharing of decision-making dilemmas between all actors and holding government accountable to the public for its action. This need not use public opinion for the legitimization of a pluralistic interest. It should be based on deliberation and not information and/or debating (Klein, 1994: 1003–1012; Saltman and Figueras, 1997: 112; Ling, 1999: 107–119). It also demands that the elite's control of the decision-making process be reduced (Gulhati, 1990: 15).

## Planning as a Policy Management Tool

Decentralization policy implementation in Uganda aims at bringing governance closer to the grassroots level to improve public service delivery, to foster democratization, and to strengthen national unity, thereby making government more effective, efficient, and flexible, as well as cheaper and more accountable and responsive to the needs of the common person (6). A question that is always sidelined is "What is the appropriate forum for building synergy between the led and leaders?" The best opportunity is in the local government development planning process, which comprises the operational values and interests among different stakeholders at various levels. The planning process provides a fertile opportunity for a critical analysis of who gets what, what is offered, why it is offered, where it is offered, and how it is delivered effectively, honestly, and without a hidden agenda.

The Constitution of 1995 [articles 97, 98, 176(2), 190 and the sixth schedule], as enshrined in the Local Governments Act of 1997 (sections 7, 31, 36–38, 75, and the second and fourth schedules), stipulates the roles and functions of local councils in regard to planning—which Hilliges and Rademaker (2000) point to as accountability—a critical role in public policy management. As the body corporate, local governments are expected to: (1) establish a functional district planning unit charged with planning facilitation, coordination, and negotiation roles at the district level; (2) have a functional technical planning committee composed of technical personnel within the local government (i.e., both government and NGOs) and headed by the chief administrative officer (CAO) at the district level and the subcounty chief at the subcounty level; and (3) develop a comprehensive and integrated three-year development plan incorporating the plans of the lower-level councils. It is noteworthy that both horizontal and vertical planning approaches exist, irrespective of the approach balance. The local council plans both for its council and for the various sectors. At the district level, however, much emphasis is placed on sector plans that cut across all the administrative units, while at the subcounty local council level (LCIII) effort is put on administrative unit plans. This should recognize, however, the national priorities that are set relative to the national target.

## THE EXPERIENCE IN NEBBI DISTRICT

Nebbi district was one of the fourteen districts that were decentralized in the second phase of the 1994/1995 decentralization process. The district is located in northwestern Uganda over 400 km from the capital, and has three counties (Jonam, Padyere, and Okoro) comprising sixteen subcounties and three town councils (Pakwach, Nebbi, and Paidha). These are further subdivided into eighty-four parishes with 1221 villages (LC1). A mutual political and administrative structure exists at all these levels save for LCI to ensure the coherence of and complementarity in policy formulation and implementation.

In essence, under decentralization the district planning process should begin at the village level, ascending to the parish level and the subcounty level with a preliminary plan conference. During the conference, at the village and parish levels, the parish development committees (PDCs)—established with support of UNICEF in only two parishes of the four pilot subcounties—lead the planning process. This process involves debriefing the community on the budget framework paper, the annual and medium-term budget, and the annual and medium-term plan.

It also involves: the review of past performance—budget, projects, and linkages established; soliciting of proposals for implementation in the coming year; and prioritizing of the activities identified. Note that this process does not take place in areas without PDCs because the lead agencies—subcounty councillors and technical staff—are subcounty-based; information from collaborating NGOs are not available at that level; and national priority program areas are unheard of.

Ideally, the above process is to be replicated at the parish level with feedback to the village on what priority areas have been identified and listed for submission to the subcounty level. At the subcounty level, a similar process should be completed, and an annual plan should be submitted to the district level for the formulation of a district comprehensive plan. Implicitly, then, the levels of a comprehensive plan start at the parish level, ascending to the district level, with each plan at these levels clearly indicating both the priority areas of its lower-level units and all actors. (See Figure 1).

When properly followed, the processes in Figure 1 should open up the local government system, just as nonstate actors have been accommodated at the central government level because of donor pressure (i.e., civil society participation), result-

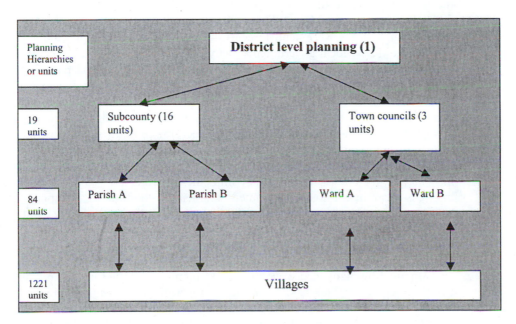

**Figure 1**   Schematic layout of planning process; Nebbi district setting. Note: Wards in towns are the equivalents of parishes in a subcounty administration.

ing in the transparent participation of all actors. What, however, does democratic centralism have in practice? This is the focus of the next section, which looks at the failure to achieve a participatory planning process.

## CHALLENGES TO THE PARTICIPATORY PLANNING PROCESS

The ideal planning processes noted above have had minimal impact on the formulation and implementation of the Nebbi district development plan. The current rolling three-year plan (1999–2002) was not formulated with the participation of the village communities, and its implementation does not refer to their needs. This is because of a number of pitfalls, which are discussed below.

### Legal Framework Limitations

The planning process under decentralization is undertaken within stipulated legal requirements that ideally ensure coherence and complementarity between the various levels of local government institutions.

The Constitution of 1995 and the LGA of 1997 provide for the establishment of a "national planning authority." This is to provide regulatory, supervisory, and advisory roles to the district and national planning functions to ensure conformity and quality. In the absence of this institution, the districts especially are shadowed by the Ministry of Planning, Finance and Economic Development, which to date has shown limited interest in the local government planning process except for technical specifications to meet donor requirements. In the end, even at the district level, there is little conformity in the annual plans of the various departments. Different departments use different formats, according to their funders' preference. Attempts by the Ministry of Local Government, Decentralisation Secretariat, in providing a working guide for local governments has yielded limited adoption impact.

The law also provides for the establishment of a district technical planning committee (DTPC). In Nebbi district, while this committee took over from the defunct District Development Committee (DDC), it is inactive. The sub-county technical planning committees are not functional at all. The frequency of DTPC meetings compared to that of sectoral committee, and district council meetings shows a great disparity. This has led to the hijacking of the DTPC roles by the sectoral committees and district council, and hence a mismatch in the compliance of policy implementation.

While it is clear in the local government financial regulation what happens before a budget is approved (e.g., the 20% expenditure limit), the law is silent on the direction local councils are to take in the wake of failure by either a department or a local council to prepare a plan to accompany the annual budget. The assumption is that all local government budgets should be accompanied by plans, hence the "implied" plans as reflected in the annual budget documents. This has led the local government councils to prepare annual budgets without annual plans. Much emphasis is put on the preparation of annual budgets, indicating the local council's overreliance on revenue control and not mobilization and guided utilization.

The autonomy of local councils (LCs) has not met expectations, especially at the subcounty level (LCIII), where they were meant to provide a link between the lower councils and the district council. Apart from the finance and general administration interface, this position has reduced the pace at which district development plans can be prepared. An explicit example is a contribution by one of the LCIII representatives during a meeting to review the district development plan: "We are given the discretion of planning and managing our finance. Our priority as of now is not a development plan but safe water and environmental sanitation." While this remark indicates the limited knowledge and appreciation of planning it also shows the inability of the district to prepare an integrated development plan (i.e., a bottom-top plan), since it has no mandate to dictate the timing within which the subcounty council can prepare its plan.

One of the essential elements of decentralization was to reduce the overcentralized workload at the ministerial level. This has been accomplished by limiting the role of the ministry to policy formulation and quality assurance. The effectiveness and efficiency of local governments, however, rest on the level of support supervision they receive both from the center for district levels and from the district to field-based staff. A number of ministries have shied away from this role. A case in point is the statistics departments of the Ministry of Finance and Economic Planning (MoFEP), which up to now has focused on national-level data generation without the capacity-building component of district-based staff. Besides being aware of the difficulty of downloading nationally and/or regionally conducted survey data into useable district planning data/information (because of the sample sizes normally used), districts are left on their own to fund the costly, needed planning data collection initiatives. This is replicated within local government. The subcounties don't receive technical advice from the district except for the marginally funded programs.

## Institutional Limitations

The established institutions within the local governments are the focal points for enhancing planning functions. These have not been effective, however, apart from the aspects seen above, because of

Management by crisis. While the major departments are used to a top-bottom planning approach coupled with the limited capacity-building initiative from the center, the district has loop sided to the utilization of its available resources within a "utilization schedule." Even the annual budgets that lack the accompanying plans suffer from gross budgetary indiscipline; funds are not allocated per the budget target but as per political needs, consequently the would-be linkage among policy, plan, and budget that is the foundation for planning is lost.

A manpower gap between approved and filled vacancies. Although the public service ban on recruitment affected staffing, more important were the high costs, which consume about 70% of the district's total budget. Compounded by the low operational funds and momentum for planning, there is person–job gap that can in part be bridged by adequate funding, continuous training, and tooling. It was not surprising that in 2002 the local government development fund remittance (and approval) was delayed.

Inadequate linkage, coordination, and networking between departments, sectors, development actors, and line ministries in the district council. As a result, for instance, there is a low level of integration of NGOs and community-based organisations (CBOs) into the development policy process. Policies are therefore not binding to all, and if they are enforced at all it is to the detriment of the district.

Political interference as opposed to political intervention. Because of the blurred boundary of the political–policy line against policy management and implementation, the politicians more often hijack the roles of technical staff. A notable illustration was the imposition of teachers' transfer as well as the stripping of the role of personnel teachers' duties by the secretary for social services.

## Funding Limitations

The realization of a plan is dependent on the adequacy of the funding available for the implementation of the planned activities. This is lacking, however. Although the budget value has increased in real terms from Ushs 3.2 billion in 1995/1996 to 11.1 billion in 2000/2001, Nebbi district is heavily dependent on a remittance from both the central government and donors to run its cash budget. This is evident from the drastic decline in the local district's actual revenue, from 13% in 1995/1996 to 2% in 2000/2001. (see Table 1).

The financial situation of the district is in part due to the effect of household poverty on local tax revenue. Even then, the g-tax performance is aggravated by poor registration, enumeration, assessment, and collection methods coupled with the inadequate support and supervision of revenue collectors.

As a result, the collection performance of local revenue has been generally low and the capacity of the councils to implement the activities budgeted for is greatly affected. The council now suffers from a big backlog of activity rollover and out-

**Table 1**  Income Budget Performance by Source, Nebbi District (1995–2001)

|  | 1995/1996 | 1996/1997 | 1997/1998 | 1998/1999 | 1999/2000 | 2000/2001 |
|---|---|---|---|---|---|---|
| Local revenue |  |  |  |  |  |  |
|   Budget | 33% | 25% | 13% | 14% | 7% | 4% |
|   Actual | 13% | 7% | 5% | 11% | 5% | 2% |
| Donor funds |  |  |  |  |  |  |
|   Budget | 16% | 14% | 8% | 8% | 3% | 19% |
|   Actual | 4% | 13% | 7% | 5% | 9% | 18% |
| Central government funds |  |  |  |  |  |  |
|   Budget | 51% | 61% | 79% | 78% | 90% | 77% |
|   Actual | 83% | 79% | 88% | 84% | 86% | 81% |
| Total budget | 100% | 100% | 100% | 100% | 100% | 100% |
| Total actual | 100% | 100% | 100% | 100% | 100% | 100% |

*Source*: Office of chief finance officer (audited accounts for FY 1995/6–2000/01).

standing debts (in terms of salaries and wages, tenderers' arrears, etc.). Box and Kruiter (1998:1) caution that the sustainability of the development policy is linked to the ability of local institutions to generate adequate resources as opposed to aids an addiction and dependency syndrome. The district is operating on a purely cash budget, and coupled with a resource allocation based on political needs and not the plan, the zeal of departmental heads has been lost.

## Weak Community Participation

Community participation has been upheld in the promotion of local development because of its contribution toward ownership and sustainability for self-sustained growth. Seen this way, community participation is a means; injection input and an end product of development (Oakley and Marsden, 1984). This is because popular participation ensures the collective effort of the people concerned to pool their efforts and resources to attain objectives they set for themselves. In this regard, participation is viewed as an active process in which the people take initiatives and actions stimulated by their own thinking and deliberation and over which they can exert effective control.

Weak community participation is in part attributed to centralized planning functions within the district departments, in which planning is still viewed purely as the role of the head of the department. The involvement of departmental staff is minimal. As a result, departmental plans are not comprehensive. Besides, because of inadequate professionalism in participatory planning methodologies as well as institutional "biases" (Chambers, 1983) the people are not involved. At the same time, "representative politics" has continued to limit community participation; perceived plans are exclusively the views of the politicians and their sectoral staff. No consultation is made by the politicians, and the views and/or opinions of the community in regard to their needs are not sought. This is tantamount to abuse of office, wastage of resources, lack of community mobilization, a weak coordination mechanism, and corruption. In such a situation, the established local council structures end up oppressing the community, hence the inability to know "which needs and whose needs will be met through the distribution of the scarce resources."

Furthermore, there is a lack of visible results of from the community planning processes. Some community members complain that despite the repeated prioritization of problems and solutions in their plans, local governments ignore their priorities. The community members therefore see no reason for being involved in continuous politically motivated and domineered assessments that do not yield any positive result for them—what they term "being present for the government officials to justify their expenditures."

## Communication Limitations

Many of the planning problems have an element of poor communication to them. The subcounties are not informed of district investments. The local government budget framework paper (in which many of the conditional grants are negotiated) is agreed upon before the subcounty priorities are sent to the district. There is little or no feedback from the district on subcounty plans and budgets. (Sometimes there is even no acknowledgment that they have been received.) National policies remain unknown at the lower parish and village levels.

Added to the above, the neglect of a reporting culture at both the subcounty and district levels has hampered monitoring of local government performance. First, subcounty staffs look at the district level for channeling their reports. Apart from loosening their support ties, this trend of events thrives on hindering performance-related monitoring (i.e., output-oriented accountability).

During the two training session I participated in (United Nations Children's Fund and European Union, funded in late 2001 and early 2002) the development committees at both the subcounty and parish levels pointed to information central-ization at the district level. They were not even aware of either their own budget estimates or key policies, such as on sanitation, immunization, and agricultural modernization. How can an uninformed actor demand effectively and/or supply as expected?

## What Happens Next?

Planning functions is to accelerate the pace and spread the benefit of growth with efficient allocative geographic dimension (where to place investments); social dimen-sion (who should benefit from the investments); and institutional dimension (what agency or who should be in charge of it) (Prud'homme, 1995) basing on resource envelops (Sai, 1993: 11–12). In the absence of these, Nebbi district is experiencing a development process whereby political decisions are guided by the perceptions of the politicians who are policy makers. A notable example is the School Grant Facility, where political controversy emerged as to the location of the project. Services are not provided by demand but by political weight; other actors become co-opted as implementers; the private sector stampedes for contracts by winning political favors; ethnic citizenship is promoted at the expense of the district's population; the ability of the people to own their destiny is lost; and corruption has become rampant (Rothchild, 1994; Bates and Krueger, 1993) (7).

## CONCLUDING REMARKS

Power in the local government system is vested in the hands of the ruling elites and elected politicians. The decentralization of power from the central government to local government has met with a recentralization of power at the local government level. The participation of nonstate stakeholders is marginal, if any. They are not allies but are seen as beneficiaries of political actions. As a result, service delivery concentrates on (1) the late 1950s and 1960s ideology of development by modernization through infra-structures, (8) and (2) a strong but faulty belief that improving only the capacity of local governments will improve the situation—sidelining the civil society, especially the weak social movements embedded in community-based organizations (CBOs). Politics has become cheaper than salt—an end to power acquisition and domination. Its destiny in guiding the future of the population is becoming increasingly questionable (Hirschman, 1975). This perpetuates the "I don't care" attitude in the population and thus the continued nonparticipation by citizens in local government policy process (Rothchild, 1994, Frischtak, 1994; Hirschmann, 1993).

I argue that the "political gatedness" rather than the claimed ignorance of channels of access and the lack of capacity to take part and contribute to policies (see Bratton, 1989) builds lack of interest and resistance alongside the standing history of "government delivers all" to perpetuate a noninclusive policy process and thus decentralized centralism. (See Bates and Krueger, 1993; Putnam et al., 1993.) The better way out includes strengthening the capacity of both the state institutions (and all its bureaucracies—the power source that government thrives on) and the nonstate actors (the cogs of the development wheel) to ensure genuine partnership. This will create a demand and supply interplay. A democratic citizenship needs to be built, however, to ensure that government officials are held more accountable and transparent (Nerfin, 1987).

Citizenship building should not, however, lean on the current ethnic or indigenization approach whereby the national government seems to propagate the autonomy of local governments as a leeway for its maneuvers—think local, act local—what Mamdani (1996) calls retribalization. (See Marcussen, 1996; Mohan and Stokke, 2000; Mohan, 2001.) At best neopatrimonalism should be avoided (Medard, 1991; 1996).

Unless redirected, the development of the masses cannot be envisaged. This is in line with the observation of Schuurman (1997: 152), who pointed out that

> Decentralization itself in no way guarantees that things will improve for the poor. Where national political interest is focused on neo-liberalism and on an export oriented development disembbeded from the welfarists state policy, then decentralization is powerless to prevent spatial inequalities from persisting or even increasing. Political participation at local government level will only reflect the fragmentation of civil society and neo-feudal attitude of political parties vis-a-vis social movements.

The lessons that the Ugandan story depict for the rest of the developing world, in which decentralization is (un)consciously being popularized, are: (1) establishing a decentralization policy and its effective implementation requires legal instruments and its coherence to practical situations, particularly in the local-central government nexus; (2) a sound institution (with adequate logistics, motivated visionary personnel, and people-centered culture) is a must and the opportunity costs of hurried establishment with the aim of gradual improvements is tantamount to an unacceptable debt-based investment error; (3) a reliable self-funding base is necessary to avoid donor dependence and manipulation by externally engineered (and nationally predetermined) priorities not cognizant of local peculiarities and particularities; (4) the community is the driving force for participation, thus its capacity and capability to demand as well as that of government and civil society institutions to supply need a juxtaposition within the policy process; and (5) the adequacy, relevance, timeliness, and effectiveness of communication among all actors is paramount in bridging under- and overflow of information and its associated drawbacks, such as "corruption gossips."

In the same vein, there is a need for rethinking the national development vision—outside the World Bank and IMF prescription—in view of "alternative development," which requires, in Chambers's words, "handing over the stick." The national government's strength in changing from a traditional development engine status to a facilitator with the acuity to "read development" will provide for building synergy between all actors, allowing for "just" opportunity costs in interest and value considerations. The current umbrella concept of good governance, democracy, transparency, and accountability will only become a reality when the people to whom they should apply take the lead in spearheading them (in context, content, and principles).

## NOTES

1. Decentralization is defined as the transfer of responsibility for planning, management, and the raising and allocation of resources from the central government ministries and agencies to field units of central government ministries or agencies (deconcentration); subordinate units or levels of government (devolution); semiautonomous public authorities (delegation); or nongovernmental private or voluntary organizations (privatization)(Rondenelli and Nellis, 1986: 8). These constitute the basis upon which Litvack and Seddon identify three main types of decentralization: (1) political decentralization, which basically aims at a pluralistic politics and representative government whereby citizens or their elected representatives have more power in public decision making (i.e., the formulation and implementation of policies); (2) administrative and fiscal decentralization, which seeks to redistribute authority, responsibility, and financial resources for providing public services among different levels of government by the transfer of responsibility for the planning, financing, and management of certain public functions; and (3) economic or market decentralization, in which there is shift in responsibility for functions from the public to the private sector.

2. de Haan (2000: 7–12) discusses the "shrinking of the Third World," beginning from the assumed meaning of Third World—poor, hardly developed, oppressed, and exploited. With the asymmetrical relationship with the countries at the center (dependency theory) being broken, the rising of the standards of living of the newly industrializing countries, different poor countries with highly developed areas, and the falling of the "Second World," characterized by the fall of the Berlin Wall in 1989, he argues geographically that the Third World does not exist. The term is used here consciously, however, only to suit the mental map contextualization and not as a geographically applicable term.

3. This approach was based on experience from the Far East where local development increased with the increasing role of the state as an animator providing a strategic and dynamic role and synergy in ensuring a conducive "invisible hand," of the market partly by harnessing domestic and international forces. (See Onis, 1991: 109–121.) Structuralism is the antithesis of neoliberalism. It approaches the process of eliminating poverty, ignorance, and disease through central planning and social engineering based on the tendency of resource exploitation from potentially productive sectors and siphoning them through public monopolies, economic regulators, and law enforcers. It also opposes capitalism that seems immature in developing countries, since perfect competition is impeded by inequalities in access to and control over resources, information, and technologies. Neoliberal ideology and politics entrust the preservation of the market economy and free competition in conjunction with the minimal necessary regulatory role of the state. It views development from a capital-intensive aspect of industrialization, heavy infrastructure investment, and the transformation of the traditional values. (See Gilpin 1987; Weigle, 1996: 437; Marshall, 1996: 427–430.)

4. Ofei-Aboagye (2000: 1) defines local governance as the active involvement of the local population within the territorial boundaries of a local government in ensuring improved quality of services and leadership at the local level. It includes greater participation by civil society in the decision-making process and involves consensus building and civic awareness.

5. For details, see Heidenheirmer et al., (1990). They point out that public policy is a process of how, why, and to what effect different government pursues particular courses of actions or inactions. Compare this with Hogwood and Gunn, (1984: 12–24), who look at policy as a label for a field activity; as an expression of general purpose; as a specific proposal; as

decisions of government; as formal authorization; as a program; as an output; as an outcome; as a theory/model; and as a process.

6.  It should be noted that the legal requirement of all local governments to plan is based on the fact that the development plan

    Acts as a management tool in guiding operational directions placing the local government mission first. The various development actors are therefore guided by the plan to pull all resources (manpower, finance, time, and logistics) in one direction, thus reducing the popular tendency of management by crisis.

    Is a resource mobilization guide. Given the fact that local government resource envelop is limited, there is a great need to balance local choices and needs against the available resource capacity. A plan provides a shopping guide for additional resource mobilization from outside the local government coffers, intended to facilitate the realization of the local government's goal and to bridge the funding gap.

    Is a monitoring and evaluation tool kit. While local government autonomy is guaranteed, its integrity is dependent on the level of service delivery, transparency, and public accountability. A plan therefore provides an avenue for measuring the delivery status of local governments in relation to the community-set target.

    Is a means of accounting between the actors. Gunther Hilliges and Jan Rademaker (2000) argue that accountability is a multitier concept that requires reciprocity and equality between actors. It is a transparent process of identifying, analyzing, planning, implementing, monitoring, and evaluating activities. It is not only money-focused; it involves a horizontal and vertical and mutual bridge for involving, maintaining, and ensuring joint action partnership at all levels. Accountability therefore entails open and transparent practices through

    The way in which criteria for project selection and priority setting are established
    How evaluation criteria and measures of success are established and measured
    How project/program information is used and presented
    The way in which any funds raised or provided will be used and what share will go to activities and administration
    The way in which issues will be presented in any fund raising and information campaign, for example, appeals on solidarity and compassion, and its long-term benefits or joint responsibilities

7.  See a survey of community perception of government institutions and services as depicted from the draft national integrity survey report (Lakwo, 1998), which pointed out within 30 days prior to the survey of 16,139 households covered, only 35% had access to government services (and local government services accounted for only 7%), of which 50% were satisfied with the speed of services and the behavior of government staff, 43% made extra payment to service workers to access services, 54% were asked for extra payment, 18% and 64% of service workers perceived the magnitude of corruption as "very much and somewhat," respectively, compared to 39% and 41% of household and donor (and NGO) project were considered least corrupt, respectively.

8.  Note that the term development itself is contestable. Its evangelization was based on world blocking (Oruka, 1997), and it hinged on western technology, technical assistance, and finance, making the "so-called developing countries," the "other" of "the west" (Sachs, 1992; Nduhukire-Owa-Mataze, 2000). The universalization of development led to the failure to liquidate "underdevelopment" (Chambua, 1994). Critics of this theory include Köhler, et al. (1996), Albow (2000), and Stiglitz, (2001), whose focus includes the need for respecting local diversity, indigenous knowledge, the consideration of truth as a negotiable variable, the recognition of power relations, and the localization of action (de Haan and Blaikie, 1998).

## REFERENCES

Albow, M. (2000). Globalisation after modernization: A new paradigm for development studies. In: Schuurman, F. J. , ed. Globalisation and Development Studies: Challenges for the 21st Century. Amsterdam: Thela Thesis.

Alesina, A. (1994). Political models of macroeconomic policy and fiscal reforms. In: Haggard, S., Webb, S. B., eds. Voting for Reform: Democracy, Political Liberalization and Economic Adjustment. New York: Oxford University Press.

Amanor, K., Annan, J. (1999). Linkages between Decentralisation and Decentralised cooperation in Ghana. ECDPM discussion paper No. 9.

Anderson, C. H. (1976). The Sociology of Survival: Social Problems of Growth. IL: Dorsey.

Anderson, J. E. (1984). Public Policy-Making. 3rd ed. New York: CBS College Publishing.

Baeck, L. (Jan. 1998). Thematisation and Canon Building in Post War Development Studies. In: Discussion Paper Series DPS 98.01. Katholieke Universitet Leuven, Centre for Economic Studies.

Bates, R. H., Krueger, A. (1993). Political and Economic Interactions in Economic Policy Reform: Evidence from Eight Countries. Oxford: Basil Blackwell.

Blackburn, J., Holland, J. (1998). Who Changes: Institutionalising Participation in Development. London: Intermediate Technology Publications.

Booth, D. (1995). Marxism and development sociology: Interpreting the impasse. In: Corbridge, S., ed. Development Studies: A Reader. London: Edward Arnold.

Bossuyt, J., Gould, J. (1999). Synthesis: Elaborating the linkage. In: de Jong, K., Loquai, C., Soiri, I., eds. Decentralisation and Poverty Reduction: Exploring the Linkages IDS, University of Helsinki and ECDPM, Maastricht, The Netherlands, policy paper 1/1999, pp. 1–17.

Box, L., Kruiter, A. (April 1998). Sustainable Finance for Development Activities: A Matter of Creativity and Skills. Maastricht, The Netherlands, ECDPM Policy Management Brief no. 10.

Bratton, M. (1989). The politics of government-NGO relations in Africa. World Dev 17(5):569–589.

Bratton, M. (1990). Non-governmental organizations in Africa: Can they influence public policy? Dev. Change 21:87–118.

Bujo, B. (1998). African Christian Morality at the Age of Inculturation. Makuyu, Kenya: Pauline Publications Africa.

Burkey, S. (1993). People First: A Guide to Self-Reliant, Participatory Rural Development. London: Zed.

Carroll, T. F. (1992). Intermediary NGOs: The Supporting Link in Grassroots Development. West Hartford, CT: Kumarian.

Cernea, M. (1991). Putting People First: Sociological Variables in Rural Development. 2nd ed. New York: Oxford University Press for the World Bank.

Chambers, R. (1983). Rural Development: Putting the Last First. London: Intermediate Technology Publications.

Chambers, R. (1987). Sustainable Livelihoods, Environment and Development: Putting Poor Rural People First. Sussex, UK: IIED.

Chambers, R. (1993). Challenging the Professions: Frontiers for Rural Development. London: Intermediate Technology Publications.

Chambers, R. (1994). Participatory rural appraisal (PRA): Analysis of experience. World Dev 22(9):1253–1268.

Chambua, E. S. (1994). The development debates and the crisis of development theories: The case of Tanzania with special emphasis on peasants, state and capital. In: Himmelstrand, U., Kinyanjui, K., Mburugu, E., eds. African Perspectives on Development. Nairobi: EAEP.

Clark, J. (1991). Democratizing Development: The Role of Voluntary Organizations. West Hartford, CT: Kumarian.

Clay, E., Schaffer, B., eds. Room for Manoeuvre. London: Heineman.

Cockery, J., Land, A., Osborne, D. (1997). Governance and Policy Formulation. Maastricht, The Netherlands: ECDPM.

Cockery, J., Lands, A., Bossuyt, J. (Dec. 1995). The policy formulation: Institutional path or institutional maze? A study based on the introduction of cost-sharing for education in three African countries. Maastricht, The Netherlands: Policy Management Report no. 3. ECPDM and AAPAM.

Conyers, D., Hill, P. (1984). An Introduction to Development Planning in the Third World. Wiley.

Cooke, B., Kothari, U. (2001). Participation: The New Tyranny? London: Zed.

Cornwall, A. (1999). Making a difference? Gender and participatory development. IDS Discussion Paper 378.

Crosby, B. L., Orsini, D. M.(1996). Developing lobbying capacity for policy reform. Washington, DC: U.S. Agency for International Development, Implementing Policy Change Project. Technical note no. 7.

Cusworth, J. W., Franks, T. R. (1993). Managing Projects in Developing Countries. England: Longman.

De Haan, L., Blaikie, P. (1998). Reading maps in the dark: Route planning for development geography in post-ist world. In: de Haan, L. J., Blaikie, P., eds. Looking at Maps in the Dark: Direction for Geographical Research in Land Management and Sustainable Development in Rural and Urban Environments of the Third WorldUtrecht/Amsterdam: Royal Dutch Geographical Society, pp. 148–164.

de Haan, L. J. (2000). Livelihood, Locality and Globalisation. Nijmegen, The Netherlands: Nijmegen University Press.

Decentralisation Secretariat. (1994). Handbook for Facilitators of Decentralisation System Seminar. Kampala.

Decentralisation Secretariat. (1995). Decentralisation in Uganda: Policy and Implication. Vol. 2. Kampala.

Decentralisation Secretariat. (1996). Data and Analysis Needed for Decentralized Planning and Coordination in Uganda (draft). Kampala.

Decentralisation Secretariat. Decentralisation Implementation Review Workshop Report. Feb. 12–14, 1996. Kampala: ICC.

Decentralisation Secretariat. (1996). *The Local Government Budgeting Cycle*. Kampala.

Dresang, D. L., Gosling, J. J. (1989). Politics, Policy and Management in the American States. New York: Longman.

Dunleavy, P. (1980). Social political theory and the issue in central–local relations. In: Jones, G. W., ed. New Approaches to the Study of Central-Local Government Relationships. Gower.

Eade, D. (1996). Capacity Building: An Approach to People-Centred Development. Oxford: Oxfam.

Eade, D., Williams, S. (1995). The Oxfam Handbook of Development and Relief. Vol. 1 and 2. Oxford: Oxfam.

Edwards, GC III (1980). Implementing Public Policy. Washington, DC: Congressional Quarterly Press.

Fowler, A. (1998). Authentic NGDO partnerships in the new policy agenda for international aid: Dead end or light ahead? Dev. Change 29 (1):137–159.

Fox, J. (1996). Decentralization and Rural Development in Mexico: Community Participation in Oaxaca's Municipal Funds Program. La Jolla, CA: Center for U.S.–Mexican Studies, University of California.

Frischtak, L. (1993). Comparative Research on Governance and Adjustment: Project Description. Washington, DC: Private Sector Development Department, World Bank.

Frischtak, L. (1994). Governance Capacity and Economic Reform in Developing Countries. Washington, DC: World Bank, technical paper no. 254.

Gaventa, J. (1998). The scaling up and institutionalisation of PRA: Lessons and challenges. In: Blackburn, J., Holland, J., eds. Who Changes: Institutionalising Participation in Development. London: Intermediate Technology Publications.

Gilpin, R. (1987). The Political Economy of International Relations. Princeton, NJ: Princeton University Press.

Government of Uganda. (1999). Vision 2025: A Strategic Framework for National Development. Kampala: Ministry of Finance Planning and Economic Development.

Griffin, K. (1990). Alternative Strategies for Economic Development. London: Antony Rowe.

Grindle, M. (1990). The new political economy: Positive economics and negative politics. In: Meier, G. M., ed. Politics and Policy Making in Developing Countries: Perspectives on the New Political EconomySan Francisco: ICSICS, pp. 41–42.

Grindle, M., Thomas, J. (1990). After the decision: Implementing policy reforms in developing countries. World Dev. 18(8):1163–1181.

Grindle, M., Thomas, J. W. (1991). Public Choices and Policy Change: The Political Economy of Reform in Developing Countries. Baltimore: Johns Hopkins University Press.

Guijt, I., Shah, M. K. (1998). General introduction: Waking up to power, process and conflict. In: Guijt, I. Shah, M. K., eds. The Myth of Community: Gender Issues in Participatory Development. London: ITP, pp. 1–23.

Gulhati, R. (1990). The Making of Economic Policy in Africa. Washington, DC: World Bank–EDI Seminar Series.

Heidenheirmer, A. J., Hedo, H., Adams, C. T. (1990). Comparative Public Policy: The Politics of Social Choice in America, Europe and Japan. 3rd ed. New York: St. Martin's.

Higgins, B. (1968). Economic Development: Principles, Problems and Policies. New York: W.W. Norton and Co., Inc.

Hilliges, G., Rademaker, J. (April 2000). A new understanding of accountability in towns and development.In Advancing the Policy and Practice of Capacity Building in International Development Cooperation. Maastricht, The Netherlands, Capacity Org. Iss. 5: ECPM.

Hirschman, A. O. (1975). Policymaking and policy analysis in Latin America: A return journey. Policy Sci. 6.

Hirschmann, D. (1993). Institutional development in the era of economic policy reform: Concerns, contradictions, and illustrations from Malawi. Pub. Admin. Dev. 13(2):11–28.

Hogwood, B. W., Gunn, L. A. (1984). Policy Analysis for the Real World. New York: Oxford University Press.

Hoogvelt, A. M. M. (1982). The Third World in Global Development. London: Macmillan.

Hyden, G. (1992). Governance and the study of politics. In: Ilyden, G., Bratton, M., eds. Governance and Politics in Africa. Boulder; CO: Lynne Rienner, pp. 1–27.

Hydén, G. (1994). Changing ideological and theoretical perspectives on development. In: Himmelstrand, U., Kinyanjui, K., Mburugu, E., eds. African Perspectives on Development. Nairobi: EAEP.

Juma, C., Clark, N. (1995). Policy research in sub-Saharan Africa. Publ Admin Dev 15:121–137.

Kanyandago, P. (1998). The role of culture in poverty eradication. In: Carabine, D. O'Reilly, M., eds. The Challenge of Eradicating Poverty in the World: An African Response. Nkozi, Uganda: UMU.

Keely, J., Scoones, I. (2000). Environmental Policy-Making in Zimbabwe: Discourses, Science and Politics. IDS working paper. Brighton, UK: University of Sussex.

Klein, R. (1994). Can we restrict the health care menu? Health Policy 27:1003–1012.

Köhler, G., Gore, C., Reich, T., Ziesemer, T., eds. (1996). Questioning Development: Essays on the Theory, Policies and Practice of Development Interventions. Mauburg: Metropolis-Vertag.

Komba, A. A. (2000). The Teaching and Researching in Public Policy in Contemporary African Universities and Implications for Democratic Governance. Dar-es-salaam: University of Dar-es-salaam.

Kothari, U. (2001). Power, knowledge and social control in participatory development. In: Cooke, Kothari, eds. Participation: The New Tyranny? London: Zed, pp. 139–152.

Lakwo, A (March, 1998) National Integrity Survey (NIS). District Draft Report. Nebbi.

Lamb, G. (1987). Managing Economic Policy Change: Institutional Dimensions. Washington, DC: World Bank. Discussion paper no. 14.

Levine, C. A., Guy Peters, B., Thompson, F. J. (1990). Public Administration: Challenges, Choices, Consequences. IL: Scott Foresman.

Ling, T. (1999). Reforming Health Care by Consent: Involving Those Who Matter. Oxford: Radcliffe Medical Press.

Litvack, J., Seddon, J. Decentralisation Briefing Notes. World Bank Institute. Working Paper in collaboration with PREM Network. Washington, D.C.: The World Bank.

Magesa, L. (1998). African Religion: The Moral Tradition of Abundant Life. Nairobi: Pauline.

Mamdani, M. (1996). Citizen and Subject: Contemporary Africa and the Legacy of Late Colonialism. London: James Currey.

Manor, J. (1995). Democratic decentralization in Africa and Asia. IDS Bull 26(2).

Marcussen, H. S. (1996). NGOs, the state and civil society. Rev. Afr. Pol. Ec. 69: 405–423.

Markus, S. (Nov 2000). Monitoring and Evaluation Support to Decentralisation: Challenges and Dilemas. Maastricht, The Netherlands, ECDPM. Discussion Paper no. 19.

Marshall, D. D. (1996). From the triangular trade to (N)AFTA: A neo-structuralist insight into raised Caribbean opportunities. Third World Q17(3):427–453.

Medard, J. F. (1991). The historical trajectories of the Ivorian and Kenyan states. In: Manor, J., ed. Rethinking Third World Politics. London: Longman, pp. 185–212.

Medard, J. M. (1996). Patrimonialism, neo-patrimonialism, and the study of the postcolonial state in sub-Saharan Africa. In: Marcussen, H. S., ed. Improved Natural Resource Management—The Role of Formal Organisations and Informal Networks and Institutions. Roskilde: occasional paper no. 17. International Development Studies, Roskilde University, pp. 76–97.

Ministry of Finance, Planning and Economic Development. (May 2000). National Program for Good Governance in the Context of the Poverty Eradication Action Plan (PEAP) Uganda Governance Capacity Assessment Project. Kampala.

Ministry of Finance, Planning and Economic Development. (2000). Uganda's Poverty Eradication Plan: Summary and Main Objectives, Kampala.

Ministry of Finance, Planning and Economic Development. (2001). Uganda Poverty Status Report 2001: Milestones in the Quest for Poverty Eradication. Kampala.

Mohan, G. (2001). Beyond participation: Strategies for deeper empowerment. In: Cooke, B., Kothari, U., eds. Participation: The New Tyranny? London: Zed, pp. 153–167.

Mohan, G., Stokke, K. (2000). Participatory development and empowerment. Third World Q 21(2):266–280.

Mosse, D. (1994). Authority, gender and knowledge: Theoretical reflections on the practice of PRA. Dev. Change. 25(4):497–526.

Mutajwaha, S. (1992). Some Recent Insights in the Philosophy of the Other. Rome: Urbaniana University Press.

Nakamura, R. T., Smallwood, F. (1980). The Politics of Policy Implementation. New York: St. Martin's.

Nduhukire-Owa-Mataze (2000). Critical Reflections on Development Theory and Uganda's Past Growth, Corruption and Politics. Nkozi, Uganda: UMU Press.

Nebbi District Local Government. (1998). Nebbi District Local Government Development Plan, 1999–2002. Department of Planning, Nebbi District Local Government, Nebbi, Uganda.

Nellis, J. R. (1983). Decentralisation in North Africa. In: Chema, G. S., Rondenelli, D. A., eds. Decentralisation and Development. Sage.

Nelson, J. (1994). Linkages between politics and economics. J Dem 5(4):49–62.

Nerfin, M. (1987). Neither prince nor merchant–citizen: An introduction to the third system. Dev. Dialogue 1:170–195.

Nsibambi, A. (1998). Decentralisation and Civil Society in Uganda: The Quest for Good Governance. Kampala: Fountain.

Oakley, P. (1995). People's Participation in Development Projects. London: INTRAC.

Oakley, P., Marsden, D. (1984). Approaches to Participation in Rural Development. Geneva: ILO.

Ofei-Aboagye, E.(Oct 2000).Promoting the Participation of Women in Local Governance and Development: The Case of Ghana. Maastricht, The Netherlands, ECDPM discussion paper no. 18.

Oitamong, D. (1996). Decentralisation in Nebbi District: A Story of A Frontline Team. Nebbi District Administration, Uganda.

Onis, Z. (1991). The logic of development state. Compar. Politics 24(1):109–121.

Oruka, O.H. (1997). Practical Philosophy: In Search of an Ethical Minimum. Nairobi: East African Educational Publisher.

Picciotto, R. (1995). Putting Institutional Economics to Work: From Participation to Governance. World Bank Discussion Paper no. 304. Washington, D.C.: The World Bank.

Pieterse, J. N. (1998). My paradigm or yours? Alternative development, post-development, reflexive development. Dev. Change 29:343–373.

Pretty, J. N. (1994). Alternative systems of enquiry of sustainable agriculture. IDS Bull 25(2).

Prud'homme, R. (1995). The dangers of decentralisation. World Bank Res Obs 10(2).

Putnam, R., Leonardi, R., Nanetti, R. (1993). Making Democracy Work: Civic Traditions in Modern Italy. Princeton, NJ: Princeton University Press.

Rahman, M. D. A. (1993). People's Self Development: Perspective on Participatory Action Research-A Journey Through Experience. London: Zed.

Rondenelli, D. A. (1981). Government decentralisation in comparative perspective: Theory and practice in developing countries. Internat Rev Admin Sci XLVII, 2.

Rondenelli, D. A. (1983). Implementing decentralisation policies: An introduction. In: Chema, G. S., Rondenelli, D. A., eds. Decentralisation and Development. London: Sage.

Rondenelli, D. A., Chema, G. S. (1984). Decentralisation in Developing Countries: A Review of Recent Experience.World Bank working paper no. 581. Washington, D.C.: The World Bank.

Rondenelli, D. A., Nellis, J. R. (1986). Assessing decentralisation policies in developing countries: The case for cautious optimism. Dev. Policy Rev. 4.

Rothchild, D. (1994). Structuring state–society relations in Africa: Toward an enabling political environment. In: Widner, J. A., ed. Economic Change and Political Liberalization in Sub-Saharan Africa. Baltimore: Johns Hopkins University Press, pp. 201–229.

Rothchild, D., Chazan, N. (1988). The Precarious Balance: State and Society in Africa. Boulder, CO: Westview Press.

Sachs, W. (1992). Participation. In: Sachs, W., ed. The Development Dictionary. London: Zed.

Sai, E. (1993). Priorities for action. DPMN Bull. 1(2).

Saltman, B., Figueras, J. (1997). European Health Care Reform: Analysis of Current Strategies. Copenhagen: WHO.

Samoff, J. (1979). The bureaucracy and the bourgeoisie: Decentralisation and the class structure in Tanzania. Soci. Hist. 21.

Schuurman, F. J. (1997). The decentralisation discourse: Post-Fordist paradigm or neo-liberal cul-de-sac? Eur. J. Dev. Res. 9(1):150–164.

Sharpe, B. (1998). First the forest: Conservation, community and participation in southwest Cameroon. Africa 68(1):25–45.

Serageldin, I. (1996). Sustainability as opportunity and the problem of social capital. Brown J. World Aff. 3(2):187–203.

Slater, D. (1992). Theories of development and politics of the modern: Exploring a border zone. Dev. Change 23(3):283–319.

Slater, R., Watson, J. (1989). Democratic decentralisation or political consolidation: The case for local government reform in Karnataka. Pub Admin Dev 9(2).

Smith, B. G. (1985). Decentralisation: The Territorial Dimension of the State. London: George Allen and Unwin.

SNV (Uganda) and District Planning Unit-Nebbi. (1997). Nebbi Capacity Building Programme: Project Proposal. Dec. 1996; and 1998–2001 Programme Proposal. July.

SNV. (1999). Decentralisation and Empowerment: From Rehabilitation to Growth in West Nile Region, Uganda. Report of the External Review Commission, Kampala.

Standish, B. (1983). Power to the people? Decentralisation in Papua New Guinea. Pub Admin Dev. 3.

Stiglitz, J. E. An agenda for new development economics. Draft paper prepared for the discussion at the UNRISD meeting, the Need to Rethink Development Economics, 7-8 Sept. 2001, Cape Town, South Africa.

Stocker, G. (1988). Politics of Local Governments. London: Macmillan.

Sutton, R. (1999). The Policy Process: An Overview. London: Overseas Development Institute.

Thomas, J. W., Grindle, M. S. (1990). After the decision: Implementing policy reforms in developing countries. World Dev. 18(8):1163–1181.

Thompson, J. (1995). Approaches in government bureaucracies: Facilitating the process of institutional change. World Dev. 23(9):1521–1554.

Timmer, C. P. (1998). Adding Value Through Policy-Oriented Research: Reflections of a Scholar-Practitioner. Washington, DC: International Food Policy Research Institute.

Todaro, M. P. (1992). Economics for a Developing World: An Introduction to Principles, Problems and Policies for Development. New York: Longman.

Uganda Participatory Poverty Assessment. (2000). Participatory Planning for Poverty Reduction: Capacity Needs Assessment Synthesized, National Report. Kampala,

Uganda. Republic of The Constitution. (1995). Entebbe.

Uganda. Republic of (1997). The Local Governments Act. Entebbe.

Van Horn, C. E., Bauman, D. C., Gormley, W. T., Jr. (1989). Politics and Public Policy. Washington, DC: Congressional Quarterly Press.

Verhagen, K. (1987). Self Help Promotion: A Challenge to NGO Participation to NGO Community. Amsterdam: Royal Tropical Institute.

Weigle, M. M. (1996). Political liberalism in post communist Russia. Rev. Politics 58(3).

White, S. (1996). Depoliticising development: The uses and abuses of participation. Dev. Prac. 6(1):6–15.

Whitely, P. F. (1995). Rational choice and political participation: Evaluating the debate. Polit. Res. Q. 48(1):211–233.

# 36

## Participatory Development Policy Design
### Integrating Instrumental and Democratic Rationality

**GEDEON M. MUDACUMURA**

*Pennsylvania Treasury Department, and Pennsylvania State University, Harrisburg, Pennsylvania, U.S.A.*

## INTRODUCTION

Policy analysts have paid little attention to the creative process of designing solutions to public policy issues. The current knowledge about which policy strategies work best under which conditions is at best rudimentary (Linder and Peters, 1985). Without such knowledge, society must rely upon trial and error for developing the solutions to its policy problems. The tasks confronting development policy scholars become more challenging when one thinks about both the multidimensionality, uncertainty, and complexity surrounding the concept of development and the increasing demand for democratic participation.

While the first tradition of policy scholars considered policy analysis as a management science characterized by an ambition to take a relatively broad look at problems of political feasibility and at the range of available alternatives (Quade, 1970), the second tradition assigned policy analysis a more grandiose role as a new supradiscipline that is more concerned with the contributions of systematic knowledge, structured rationality, and organized creativity to better policy making (Dror, 1971).

Commenting on the role of policy analysis as problem-oriented scholarship, Laswell (1971) stressed that this problem orientation demanded a focus on the basic conflicts in our civilizations—the fundamental problems of man in society—rather than upon the topical issues of the moment. He further underscored that the analysis was open to the contribution of a diversity of methods and that it was based on a contextual understanding of the larger social setting of the events studied as well as of their evolution over time (Laswell, 1951).

Building on Laswell's line of thought, if policy scientists must take the contextuality and problem-orientation requirements seriously, connecting the studies of the policy processes to political and societal macroanalyses is not an option, and such connection may require the policy-oriented scholar to cultivate the practice of thinking of the past and the future as parts of one context (Wittrock and deLeon, 1986).

For years, policy scholars have focused their attention on methods, emphasizing the assessment of preordained and well-defined alternatives. The claim that attention to designing solution strategies may improve policy performance has recently been embraced by a number of policy researchers, including but not limited to Dryzek (1983), deLeon (1988–1989), Weimer (1993), Linder and Peters (1991), Ingraham (1987), Schneider and Ingram (1997), and Hoppe et al. (1987), whose primary goal was to shift the core of policy analysis toward policy design. As Linder and Peters (1988) noted, an emphasis on design in policy research forces the analyst to focus more attention on different stages in the policy process than does the more conventional emphasis on either ex-post analysis of policy decisions or the analysis of specific alternative strategies through methodologies such as cost-benefit analysis.

This chapter explores the underlying theoretical framework of policy design, highlighting the key conceptual definitions most referred to in the policy design literature. The diversity of policy stakeholders, and the multidimensional, evolutionary, and complex development problems constitute a great challenge to development policy scholars, whose uncoordinated efforts will hardly lead to an agreed-upon theoretical framework for policy design. These theoretical constraints reinforced by the current split between positivists and postpositivists make it difficult to build a strong body of policy design knowledge.

Before the concluding remarks, the chapter alludes to a participatory policy design approach that integrates the best of both instrumental and democratic rationality, an attempt to bridge the gap between positivists and postpositivists. Such integration requires bringing together a multidisciplinary team of development policy scholars, practitioners, and various development stakeholders for the purpose of designing relevant development policies. Understanding the intricacies of devising sound policy is timely, particularly when financial assistance is tied to well-designed development policies. In fact, President Bush announced recently that the United States will increase its core assistance to developing countries. The increased assistance will come as a reward to sound policy decisions that support economic growth and reduce poverty.

Before delving into the underlying premises of policy design, a brief overview of policy-making's theoretical framework is provided.

## THE THEORETICAL FRAMEWORK OF POLICY MAKING

Attempts to devise public policies geared toward solving large-scale socioeconomic problems have been the business of governments since the dawn of history. As a field, public policy focuses on what Dewey (1927) expressed as the public and its problems, and a public policy is here conceived as an intentional course of action followed by a government institution or official for resolving an issue of public concern (Cochran et al., 1990).

Hisschemoller and Hoppe (1995) defined a policy problem as a gap between the existing and normatively valued situation that is to be bridged by a government action. Policy scholars have struggled to come up with a suitable definition. Most definitions include the notion of purposive action, directed toward problems or goals; action taken by government agents or collectivities that can be defined as agents of government; rules that specify who is to do what, when, why, and how; tools that provide incentives and motivations for individuals to undertake the policy-preferred behavior; and causal theories that link the actions of agents to the behavior of targets and the behavior of targets to outcomes (Schneider and Ingram, 1990).

Two types of problems have been discussed extensively in the policy literature: "well-defined or structured problems" and "ill-defined or unstructured problems." A structured problem is one presenting a high degree of consensus and certainty, while an unstructured problem presents neither consensus nor certainty, but a widespread discomfort with the status quo. Solving the problems of the former type requires the application of standardized quantitative techniques and procedures. Technical methods appear inadequate to provide solutions to unstructured problems, which are too controversial and ambiguous. In addition to the inadequacy of the technical methods, the complexity and uncertainty surrounding policy choice are frequently sufficient to render ineffective any attempt to solve social problems through public policy (Dryzek, 1983).

Roe (1990) further noted that "problem structuring" involves the confrontation, evaluation, and integration of as much contradictory information as possible. Considering the crucial role of participants who see each other not as self-interest maximizers but as persons presenting information on the issue at stake, problem structuring requires a shared sense of social and political responsibility. The sense of social responsibility implies social rationality, which enables people to get to know and respect each other as persons, while political rationality centers on the communication process, which establishes and certifies the production, dissemination, and use of knowledge for solving the policy problems (Diesing, 1962).

While Dery (1984) viewed policy problems as opportunities for improvement, Dunn (1988) warned against classifying problems according to the required method for solving them, arguing that the appropriateness of a particular type of method is a function of its congruence with the type of problem under investigation. Building upon Dunn's principle of methodological congruence and recalling the multidimensionality of development problems, one may appreciate the challenging task for devising appropriate methods to development problems. Failure to devise an appropriate method for each problem may imply limited chances to come up with the right solution.

For instance, in his discussions of problems related to pollution, Majone (1976) concluded that no single policy solution could uniformly achieve environmental effectiveness, economic efficiency, political and administrative feasibility, flexibility, and compatibility within the institutional framework of a market economy. Considering the tendency to capitalize on the sole criterion of economic efficiency, Majone (1976) suggested that a joint optimization of economic incentives and regulatory approaches could be superior to either approach single.

The concept of joint optimization makes sense when one considers the tendency to separate social science theory from the design of practical policy, which inhibits the application of insights from research to the design of concrete solutions (Linder and Peters, 1985). Similarly, Weimer (1993) viewed the generality and level of abstraction of the steadily growing stream of policy design literature as the main impediment obscuring its immediate usefulness to practicing policy researchers. Through joint optimization, development policy analysts may bring together the best elements from purely theoretical constructs and commonsense prescriptions grounded in real-life practical observations. The following section highlights various scholars' views on current policy design issues.

## POLICY DESIGN: CONCEPTUAL DEFINITIONS AND THEORY

In the context of development policy issues, design involves both a systematic process for generating basic strategies and a framework for comparing them. Ingraham (1987) argued that putting more emphasis on policy design raised new questions directed toward a new set of concerns: the match between problem and solution, the consideration of possible policy options, and the extent to which more rigorous consideration of the components of design can be incorporated into existing policy processes.

In a nutshell, development policy scholars and practitioners are likely to perpetuate recurring cycles of policy failures unless they have a clear understanding of the problem to be solved and have tested the techniques that will be utilized to solve it. Considering that development problems are multidimensional, evolutionary, and interrelated, one would question the extent to which development scholars understand them. Failing to understand the problem properly minimizes the likelihood of finding a relevant, reliable solution.

Considering policy problems as moving targets, Wittrock and deLeon (1986) add another level of difficulty when alluding to the changing contextuality in which the problems exist. The intricacies of development problems have thus forced policy researchers to retrench intellectually and scrutinize the underlying assumptions of their approaches to policy problems. Moreover, policy scholars grounded in positivism view problems from a closed system perspective, considering them to be static. Treating development problems as static and policy processes as stable is one of the simplifying assumptions that has been an implicit part of development policy research.

Despite the central feature of the design approach to policy inquiry, which is inherently concerned with issues that transcend the analysis of policies themselves, policy design proponents still claim that less attention has been paid to the contextual and value components of policy design, a serious flaw in any policy formulation exercise. As such, Bobrow and Dryzek (1987) viewed policy design as involving the pursuit of valued outcomes through activities sensitive to the context of time and place.

For instance, a policy design perspective that assumes that formal development policies are important because they reflect the culture and values of society itself cannot be effective unless such a design joint-optimizes the political, social, cultural, and economic circumstances of the policy beneficiaries. In other words, assuming that the political system is a given should not lead policy designers into thinking that political feasibility is the sole and main design criteria. In fact, critics contend that the current tendency to adopt policies that street-level bureaucrats can easily enact has led to antidemocratic policy making.

In addition to political feasibility, Linder and Peters (1987) noted economic and ethical criteria that must be considered along with feasibility when designing public policies. More concretely, a conscious design underscores the importance of structuring design as a systematic activity composed of a series of choices: "The design problem is how best to change behaviors, regardless of whether we are motivated by social cost, the public interests, or concern for vulnerable populations" (Linder and Peters, 1991:130).

While some scholars consider behavioral change as a key element in policy design, another stream of scholars focuses attention on crafting and invention. Linder and Peters (1987) refer to policy design as the intentional crafting and manipulation of elements in an effort to produce some agreed-upon results. Policy design is also viewed as the process of inventing, developing, and fine-tuning a course of action with the amelioration of some problem or the achievement of some target in mind. As Simon (1969) put it, everyone designs who devises courses of action aimed at changing existing situations into preferred ones. Policy design thus represents a creative resolution of a problem or at least the outcome of a creative process. It implies careful consideration of problem definitions to ensure that the proper problem, as opposed to the conventional problem, is the one being solved (Linder and Peters, 1987).

Along the same lines, Schneider and Ingram (1990) remarked that a focus on policy design should concentrate on aspects of policy that have been seriously neglected both in terms of theory and analytical methodologies, but as noted earlier, the complexity and uncertainty surrounding policy choice constitute the greatest challenge to designing effective policies. Complexity may be defined in terms of the number and variety of elements and interactions in the environment of a decision system that has difficulty in achieving more than a highly imperfect grasp of that environment.

Taking into account the way in which social scientists oversimplified complex issues, LaPorte (1975) wondered whether or not social scientists could afford to utilize constructs of simplicity in the face of increasing complexity. To the degree that social scientific concepts based mainly upon the assumption of simplicity are used as the basis for action in complex situations, unwanted and unsettling surprises are an inevitable consequence (LaPorte, 1975).

Furthermore, policy scientists confronted with increasing complexity and uncertainty should consider in-depth reflection as the best strategy. In fact, Meizrow (1991) viewed reflection as the central dynamic involved in problem solving, problem posing, and transformation of meaning schemes and meaning perspectives. Cogitation becomes relevant when development policy designers have to grapple with substantive details of particular programs while devising generic strategies for solving problems. The latter are very complex, and one way to handle them is to decompose them into subproblems that can be tackled serially or in parallel.

Although some scholars suggest decomposition as one way to build the overall policy design, it becomes increasingly hard to justify as complexity increases. Failure to decompose may lead one to thinking holistically, but narrow definitions in holistic analysis can be problematic when one recalls the interconnectedness of socioeconomic problems (Brewer and deLeon, 1983).

Moreover, as Weimer (1992) asked that if existing policies could be usefully analyzed by decomposing them into generic instruments, could policies not be designed by combining generic instruments? To a certain extent, Dryzek (1983) agrees with Weimer, suggesting that decomposition can be accepted as the central principle for design under conditions of moderate, static complexity, but since there is no such thing as static complexity in development policy, as complexity increases decomposition becomes less warranted.

In brief, such turbulent and complex development problems challenge development scholars interested in the theory of design to consider the characteristics of the problems, goals, and instruments. Schneider and Ingram (1990) developed a theoretical framework that identifies the agents, target populations, outcomes, and the linkages among these. Consistent with the dynamic nature of policy problems, the process of design is undertaken at multiple levels, by multiple persons, and at multiple points in time. As Schneider and Ingram (1990:83) argued, a theory of design must predict or explain how differences in the design elements produce differences in outcomes. Among other design elements are the choice of target populations, the behavior of direct and indirect targets, the agencies included in the chain, the actions of agencies, the tools and rules, and the implementation pattern itself.

Policies derived from such a theory may increase understanding, reduce the discrepancies in values, and provide for greater consensus instead of perpetuating or exacerbating the conflicts (Schneider and Ingram, 1990). Increasing such understanding may require identifying both the target populations and the policy tools, key concepts explored in the next section.

## Policy Tools and Target Populations

Schneider and Ingram (1990) viewed tools as means imbedded in the policy to increase the probability of agents and targets taking actions in concert with policy objectives. The policy design literature makes reference to five broad categories of tools: authority, incentives, capacity-building, symbolic and hortatory, and learning.

Capacity building and learning are the most discussed policy tools in the development literature. With capacity-building tools, it is assumed that individuals may lack information, resources, and skills, and may rely on shortcuts or rules of thumb. The assumptions under the learning tools are that agents and targets do not know what needs to be done or what is possible to do. Consequently, policy tools are used to promote learning and consensus building while laying the foundation for improved policy.

The bilateral and multilateral development agencies have tried to emphasize capacity tools that provide information, training, education, and resources to enable individuals, groups, or agencies to make decisions or carry out activities. The underlying assumptions of these tools are barriers steming from a lack of information, skills, or other resources needed to make decisions or take actions that will contribute to development policy goals. Being objective and factual, capacity tools may also be used to influence agency practices and to encourage adoption of innovative programs.

Some political economists referred to the proliferation of tools or instruments as the greatest political revolution of our times (Lindblom, 1990), yet the main question confronting policy scholars is the extent to which these tools enable decision or policy makers to solve socioeconomic problems. Moreover, designing an instrument to have a precise effect of a given magnitude is practically impossible (Linder and Peters, 1985). Considering that many of the available instruments work in an antagonistic fashion, Linder and Peters (1985) warn against using one instrument to reach a selected policy target. Because public policy almost always works through people to achieve results, policies are not likely to have the desired effects unless target groups make decisions and take actions consistent with the production of policy purposes (Ingram and Schneider, 1991).

From that perspective, target populations are the most important aspects of policy design. The concept of a target population directs attention to the fact that policy is purposeful and attempts to achieve goals by changing human behavior. Behavioral change is sought by enabling or coercing people to do things they would not have done otherwise (Schneider and Ingram, 1993); "Target populations may be characterized in terms of technical, political, administrative, and normative dimensions" (Schneider and Ingram, 1990:84). Moreover, it may be advisable to pay attention to target groups that are in a position to contribute most directly to the achievement of policy goals, which are among the least well-understood components of policy making.

An approach to development policy design workable within the context of democratic policy-making systems requires some attention to both goal setting and goal clarification through the political process (Linder and Peters, 1985). Considering that policy makers (elected officials), policy implementers (public administrators), and even policy beneficiaries (targets) have agendas other than transforming desired policy goals into concrete achievements, it would be naive to think that policies are designed solely or even primarily to achieve substantive policy goals or to solve social problems (Ingram and Schneider, 1991).

Policy designers thus have a choice among several target groups, any one of which can be more or less credibly linked to the solution of policy problems. For instance, target populations may be beneficiaries, losers, or only instrumental in the achievement of subsequent policy effects, and may be very critical in determining the level of support or opposition that a policy engenders (Ingram and Schneider, 1991). Similarly, Ingram and Mann (1980) remarked that policy success is most likely assured when the policy identifies the target groups connected to the desired ends, who can be motivated to engage in policy participation, and whose choice does not introduce offsetting behavior elsewhere that will counteract policy effects.

From Elmore's (1982) perspective, policy designers should choose policy instruments based on the incentive structure of target groups. While attempting to combine top-down and bottom-up perspectives, Elmore developed the techniques of forward and backward mapping. He defined forward mapping as a process that consists of stating precise policy objectives, elaborating detailed means-ends schemes, and specifying explicit outcome criteria by which to judge a policy at each stage. Similarly, the technique of backward mapping implies stating precisely the behavior to be changed at the lowest level, describing a set of operations that can ensure the change, and repeating the procedure upwards by steps until the central level is reached. Elmore (1979–1980) summarized the backward mapping as follows:

> begin with a concrete statement of the behavior that creates the occasion for a policy intervention, describe a set of organizational operations that can be expected to affect that behavior, describe the expected effect of those operations, and then describe for each level of the implementation process what effect one would expect that level to have on the target behavior and what resources are required for that effect to occur.

By applying the principle of backward mapping, policy designers may find more appropriate tools than those initially chosen (Elmore, 1985), mainly because backward mapping may take into consideration the policy implementers' and policy beneficiaries' interpretations of the policy problem and possible solutions. To that extent, Matland (1995) views backward mapping as a relevant technique allowing policy designers to take into account not only key policy players' views but also those of microimplementers and target groups. In a nutshell, backward mapping so completely blends design with problem definition that it should be considered a technique of policy design (Weimer, 1993).

Moreover, the effective design of development policies may imply involving the full network of multidisciplinary development policy specialists as well as the target groups and all development stakeholders who may influence future development policy actions, thus broadening the spectrum of development policy stakeholders having the ability to scrutinize the initial stage of policy design may reduce the probabilities of including policy aspects that may negatively impact the target populations. Such a broad-based policy-making strategy implies limiting instrumental rationality to make room for discursive and democratic rationality, key concepts that will be discussed under the participatory policy design before the concluding remarks.

It is worth highlighting that the participation envisioned within the design can involve either voluntary utilization of opportunities or compliance with directives. Regardless of the level of participation by a wide variety of development policy stakeholders, one must keep in mind the policy designers' world, one of unbridled social complexity characterized by a turbulent environment, and the uncertainty surrounding policy problems.

## Complexity and Uncertainty in Policy Design

Recognizing the complex world and the uncertainty surrounding policy problems, deLeon (1988–1989) and others emphasize that policy designers are confronted with the challenging tasks of taking into full account the confusion and complexity of the political and social environments, not only those that exist at the moment but those that could occur in the future. Designing policy thus becomes an exercise requiring in-depth thinking when one must recognize that activities taking place during the policy design stage may have a significant influence on the subsequent stages of the policy process. Moreover, coordinating policy design with subsequent stages in the policy process underscores that policy designers have little confidence in predicting what effects various programs will have in future contexts.

From that perspective, uncertainty is one of the major constraints that policy analysts have to contend with when designing policies for the future. While discussing the concepts of complexity and uncertainty, LaPorte (1975:333) questioned the extent to which the various constructs of reality used as a basis for understanding and action are capable of comprehending a social world characterized by an increasing number of quite differentiated elements whose mutual dependencies are continually growing.

In fact, most social science disciplines offer a highly simplified view of complex reality, with some economists offering their discipline as the one that can yield the correct view of policy problem (Amacher et al., 1976). Applying the concepts based on the simplification to systems that are highly complex may very well be disastrous, LaPorte (1975) argued.

To cope with uncertainty, policy designers must put in place feedback mechanisms that will allow a continual flow of the information needed to readjust the designed policies. Rapid feedback enables one to test a large number of alternatives and modifications to them, producing iterative convergence on a desirable set of alternatives. Convergence will occur if policies refined on the basis of the lessons of successive interventions as the sole guide (Dryzek, 1983) and the policy beneficiaries are key elements in providing such critical information for feedback and refinement.

Such refinement underscores the need for policy scientists to explore the relevancy of participatory action research techniques in compiling information for feedback. As alluded to earlier, getting feedback from policy beneficiaries implies broadening the scope of policy stakeholders, a process consistent with participatory policy design that blends instrumental rationality and democratic rationality.

Furthermore, participatory policy design is another indication refuting the old politics/administration dichotomy born of a vision of public administrators as value-neutral implementers of public policy that is determined elsewhere. Such consideration has been found to be a false description of public policy design since public administrators interact with elected officials and citizens as they sense what is good for the public while searching for adequate strategies to solve problems and deliver services (Svara, 1999).

The following section provides a brief theoretical background of participatory policy design. The section further alludes to the tenets of instrumental and democratic rationality.

## PARTICIPATORY POLICY DESIGN

Laswell (1951) launched the policy sciences with the ambitious goal of uniting the social sciences and part of the natural sciences in a policy science of democracy focused on studying how complex societal problems could be tackled and how large processes and big structures could be influenced through public and democratic policy-making processes (Hisschemoller and Hope, 1995). The underlying objective was to foster human dignity, political democracy, and prudent judgment of every participant in the democratic policy-making process.

Despite Laswell's original ideals of a "policy science of democracy," most university departments, government agencies, and policy-analytic consultants are currently engaged in a "policy analysis of technocracy" (Hisschemoller and Hope, 1995). To move away from intractable policy controversies, "policy technocrats" prefer structuring the problems even at the cost of losing touch with the true complexity and normative volatility of the problems. Such structuring is made possible by policy elites through their power to limit the number of participants in a policy arena or by limiting the range of politically acceptable options for policy choice (Hisschemoller and Hope, 1995). Moreover, policy technocrats prefer sticking to scientific rigor, striving to win success by sacrificing the initial ideals of the policy science of democracy.

The search for scientific truth has led policy scientists to assume that the objective scientific quality of their analyses would be more influential in the policy process, but Heineman et al. (1990) remarked that such objectivity rests on a superficial view of the scientific enterprise and a faulty conception of the policy process. One may question the extent to which policy designers abiding by the rules of policy science of technocracy devise policies that promote responsiveness and accountability. Could they subscribe to the rational logic, procedures, and assumptions of the traditional positivist paradigm and still design policies that better suit the needs of the larger constituency? How would policy designers reconcile instrumental rationality with the emerging concepts of democratic rationality? Exploring these questions may require one to review the underlying themes behind instrumental and democratic rationality while keeping in mind the world of policy analysts characterized by the environment of complexity and uncertainty.

## Instrumental Rationality

It is worth remembering that the systems analysts and operation researchers that carried out most of the early policy research were obsessed by instrumental rationality. Premised on the positivists' belief in pursuing a clearly defined objective, instrumental rationality is viewed as the capacity to devise, select, and effect good means to clarified ends. Dryzek (1990) claims that such rationality destroys the spontaneous and egalitarian aspects of human association, fosters an antidemocratic ethos, represses individuals, bungles complex social problems, renders effective and appropriate policy analysis impossible, and informs inappropriate and unfruitful social science instruments and methods.

Concretely, the main argument against instrumental rationality is that the insights of the policy beneficiaries are overlooked. Using the example of policy analysts with an economics background, deLeon (1988–1989) notes how such background reinforced the separation between expert and client by predicating their policy recommendations on objective economic relationships pursued by rational actors, which requires little knowledge of the policy recipient's particular needs and the complex work environment of public policy makers. Some scholars characterize the current instrumental orientation of the field of policy sciences as an impediment to democracy (Bennett, 1986; Fisher, 1990).

Along similar lines, the policy technocrats' pursuit of scientific rigor may lead to numerological forecasts premised on the assumption that the future is related to the past by means of stable numerical relationships. In such forecasts, pure novelty, discontinuity, and the emergence of the qualitatively different are ruled out. Hayes (1974) summarized the numerological forecasters' steps as follows:

> The first step is to measure whatever can be measured. This is okay as far as it goes. The second step is to disregard that which cannot be measured or give it an arbitrary

quantitative value. This is artificial and misleading. The third step is to presume that which cannot be measured easily is not very important. This is blindness. The fourth step is to say what cannot be measured really does not exist. This is suicide.

It is a fact that predicting is limited by a generalized uncertainty principle. Those attempting to predict the future may more likely miss what the future is holding for them. Some scholars rightly argue that predicting is also subjected to an impossibility theorem. The latter states that future events are partly determined by the content of future knowledge. Actually, the mind cannot predict today what it will know tomorrow (or else it would already know it today); therefore future events cannot be predicted (Popper, 1991).

Should policy designers adhere to instrumental rationality centered on positivist methodologies despite the fact that their intellectual foundations were undermined at least a decade ago (Amy, 1984)? Positivism survives because it limits the kinds of questions that analysis can investigate. The increasing demand for societal-provided services implies a heightened demand for delivering goods and services effectively and efficiently. Unfortunately, in the face of this demand the policy research community is confronted with the disturbing realization that in spite of its positivistic promises, it has not been able to deliver a product of value (deLeon, 1988–1989).

## Democratic Rationality

While Lindblom (1990) claimed that social scientists have failed to design the right policies to social problems, Lindblom and Cohen (1979) urged policy scientists to generate more usable knowledge. A critical group of "policy philosophers" demonstrated that the standard policy-analytic methodology, based on such positivistic dogmas as the fact-value dichotomy and value-neutral analysis, was simply unfit to address the underlying value dimensions of most policy issues (Fischer, 1980; MacRae, 1976; Dryzek, 1990; Hawkesworth, 1988).

Along the same lines, Yankelovich (1991) refuted the fact–value dichotomy, contending that knowledge conceived as a body of facts and truths existing apart from human purpose is a myth. Moreover, trying to reduce the policy world to probabilistic projections is almost impossible because of the dynamic nature of the policy sciences phenomenon rooted in an internal tension between knowledge and politics. In fact, through the interplay of knowledge and politics, different aspects of the phenomenon become salient at different moments, and the phenomenon has the potential to develop and change its form (Torgerson, 1986).

Denhardt (1981) warned policy scientists of the potential risks of focusing on value-free techniques, arguing that by limiting ourselves to measurable facts of public policies, policy analysts implicitly endorse the social conditions that have created those facts and behaviors. Swepson (1998) further noted the danger of falling into the idealist trap that occurs when policy scholars overemphasize some of the ideals of research without integrating them into a methodology that can deal with the contingencies of real life.

In light of these warnings, the proponents of democratic rationality call for a recommitment to the policy sciences of democracy that focus on the deeper political and epistemological implications of a participatory methodology (Fischer, 1992). More concretely, democratic rationality is premised on a discursive type of democracy that fosters active citizenship and meaningful public dialogue aimed at transforming our present society into one that is just, rational, humane, and reconciled (Jensen, 1997).

Reforming the most widely practiced kind of policy analysis that aspires to an instrumental rationality may be a challenging task, but a policy science of participatory democracy oriented to the public sphere could reconcile the twin demands of effective social problem solving and democratic principle while avoiding the risks of erecting barriers in the way of important ends of participatory democracy (Jenkins-Smith, 1988).

Specifically, democratic rationality is conceived as a property of intersubjective discourse in which the reflective understanding of competent actors generates normative judgments and actions principles rather than just the selection of means to ends (Dryzek, 1990). The underlying assumption of democratic rationality is that all actors are equally and fully capable of making and questioning arguments and that community members interact in an environment free from domination, an environment in which the force of good argument backed up with reason is the only authority (Dryzek, 1990).

Moreover, citizens' input is often critical in designing policies and programs that work (Brinkerhoff, 1996), and Fischer (1993) recognizes that collaborative citizen-expert inquiry may well hold the key to solving a specific category of contemporary policy problems. A policy design premised on democratic rationality could thus make for much more effective policy because it would be operating under the policy beneficiaries' values.

Furthermore, rebuilding citizen capacity for self-governance through discourse and active participation in policy debates is timely (Becket and Kings, 2002; Hutchinson, 2002; Tat-Kei Ho and Coates, 2002; Ashman, 2001; Eberly, 1994). Ultimately the goal is to get policy beneficiaries involved in the design of policies that affect their lives, moving beyond the typical model of citizen participation in which administrators use citizen involvement processes for "informing, consultation, and placation" (Timney, 1998:97).

## Participatory Policy Design

In light of the above intricacies that complicate the design of policies, paying attention to ideals of either instrumental rationality or democratic rationality cannot provide a strong theoretical framework for policy design. Without abandoning the ideals because they are important guides for actions even though they can never be achieved in the material world, consciously integrating the best of both types of rationality is the underlying rationale for participatory policy design. Such policy design underscores the existence of a multidisciplinary network of policy scholars and practitioners who combine the positivist's penchant for prediction with the post-positivist's preference for understanding while involving policy beneficiaries in the design process.

For instance, the Structural Adjustment Participatory Review Initiative (SAPRI), a tripartite initiative aimed at deliberating on World Bank and International Monetary Fund (IMF) structural adjustment issues, involved civil society organizations (CSOs), World Bank experts, and government officials. Deliberation among stakeholders is considered essential for participatory policy design, representing a democratic process for clarifying the particular as well as the collective goals, values, and potential impacts of alternative strategies (Pelletier et al., 1999; McWilliam, 1997).

From a research perspective, integrating the positivist and postpositivist research traditions may allow policy researchers to gather and test new insights (Lin, 1998), a process that could be achieved through participatory action research, an action-oriented paradigm that gives central importance to policy beneficiaries' beliefs, values, and intentions. Scholars committed to action recognized this method as one powerful research approach to involve community members in solving multifaceted social problems while building social science theories.

Relying on participatory action research may allow policy beneficiaries to be active participants in the policy design, from data collection to data analysis and policy writing. This participatory research method underscores the relevance of involving the end users in design and decision-making processes while considering policy beneficiaries not as clients or customers in the development equation but as active participants and managers in the positive alteration of circumstances affecting their lives (Chambers, 1995).

## CONCLUSIONS

This chapter has offered a brief overview of the underlying rationales of policy making and highlighted the dynamic and complex nature of public policy problems, particularly the challenging tasks of policy design, considered the cornerstone of policy making. Recognizing the complex world of policy analysts characterized by an environment of uncertainty and fierce political competition, the author underscored how policy design becomes a challenge when one acknowledges that activities taking place during the policy design stage will have a significant influence on the subsequent stages of the policy process.

Unfortunately, the current knowledge about which policy strategies work best under which conditions is at best rudimentary. Without such knowledge, society must rely upon trial and error for developing solutions to its policy problems. The reviewed literature makes no reference to a middle-range theory for guiding the design of policy in general. Without even a rudimentary theory, there is no way of assigning a policy instrument to a problem with any confidence of the outcome.

The chapter further addressed the issue of creativity in designing alternative solutions to public problems, describing the development of an alternative as an art that involves solving a puzzle for which the solution specifies a desirable relationship between manipulable means and obtainable objectives (Wildavsky, 1979). Considering the transient and turbulent nature of development policy issues, crafting policy strategies must thus be an ongoing process, a requirement that is not fully emphasized in the policy design literature.

If policy analysis is to contribute to overcoming the political knots of intractable controversies, policy scholars should focus their attention on a participatory policy design approach that integrates both instrumental and democratic rationality. Such integration requires bringing to the same table multidisciplinary teams of scholars, practitioners, various policy stakeholders, and representatives of policy beneficiaries to design adequate policies. By applying participatory action research methods, policy designers may be right on target in integrating realistic information indispensable for generating useful knowledge while contributing to theory building.

## REFERENCES

Amacher, R. C., Tollison, R. D., Willet, T. D. (1976). The Economic Approach to Public Policy. Ithaca, NY: Cornell University Press.

Amy, D. J. (1984). Toward a post-positivist policy analysis. Policy Stud. J. 13:210–211.

Ashman, D. (2001). Civil society collaboration with business: bringing empowerment back in. World Dev. 29(7):1097–1113.

Becket, J., King, C. S. (2002). The challenge to improve citizen participation in public budgeting: a discussion. J. Pub. Budg. Acct. Financ. Mgt. 14(3):463–485.

Bennett, D. (1986). Democracy and public policy analysis. In: Nagel, S., ed. Research in Public Policy Analysis and Management. Greenwich, CT: JAI.

Bobrow, D. B., Dryzek, J. S. (1987). Policy Analysis by Design. Pittsburgh, PA: University of Pittsburgh Press.

Brewer, G., deLeon, P. (1983). Foundations of Policy Analysis. Homewood: Dorsey.

Brinkerhoff, D. W. (1996). Process perspective on policy change: Highlighting implementation. World Dev. 24(9):1393–1401.

Chambers, R. (1995). Paradigm shifts in the practice of participatory research and development. In: Nelson, N., Wright, S., eds. Power and Participatory Development: Theory and Practice. London: Intermediate Technology Publications.

Cochran, C. E., Mayer, L. C., Carr, T. R., Cayer, N. J. (1990). American Public Policy: An Introduction. New York: St. Martin's.

deLeon, P. (1988–1989). The contextual burdens of policy design. Policy Stud. J. 17(2):297–309.

Denhardt, R. B. (1981). Towards a critical theory of public organization. Pub. Admin. Rev. 41(6):628–635.

Dery, D. (1984). Problem Definition in Policy Analysis. Lawrence, KS: Kansas University Press.

Dewey, J. (1927). The Public and Its Problems. New York: Holt.

Diesing, P. (1962). Reason in Society: Five Types of Decisions and their Social Conditions. Urbana: University of Illinois Press.

Dror, Y. (1971). Design for Policy Sciences. New York: American Elsevier.

Dryzek, J. S. (1983). Don't toss coins in garbage cans: a prologue to policy design. J. Pub. Policy 3(4):345–368.

Dryzek, J. S. (1990). Discursive Democracy: Politics, Policy Science, and Political Science. Cambridge: Cambridge University Press.

Dunn, W. N. (1988). Methods of the second type: coping with the wilderness of conventional policy analysis. Policy Stud. Rev. 7:720–737.

Eberly, D. E. (1994). Restoring the Good Society: A New Vision for Politics and Culture. Grand Rapids, MI: Hourglass.

Elmore, R. F. (1982). Backward mapping: implementation research and policy decisions. In: Williams, W. L., ed. Studying implementation: Methodological and Administrative Issues. Chatham, NJ: Chatham.

Elmore, R. F. (1979–1980). Backward mapping: implementation research and policy design. Polit. Sci. Q. 94:601–616.

Elmore, R. F. (1985). Forward and backward mapping. In: Hanf, K., Toonen, T., eds. Policy Implementation in Federal and Unitary Systems. Boston: Martinus Nijhoff.

Fischer, F. (1992). Restructuring policy analysis: a postpositivist perspective. Policy Sci. 25(3):333–339.

Fischer, E. (1980). Politics, Values, and Public Policy: The Problem of Methodology. Boulder, CO: Westview.

Fischer, F. (1993). Citizen participation and the democratization of policy expertise: from theoretical inquiry to practical cases. Policy Sci. 26:165–187.

Fischer, F. (1990). Technocracy and the Politics of Expertise. Newbury Park, CA: Sage.

Hawkesworth, M. E. (1988). Theoretical Issues in Policy Analysis. Albany: State University of New York Press.

Hayes, D. (1974). Energy forecasting. Committee on Mineral Resources and Environment. Albany: National Academy of Science, Washington, D.C.

Heineman, R. A., Bluhm, W. T., Peterson, S. A., Kearny, E. N. (1990). The World of the Policy Analyst: Rationality, Values, & Politics. Chatham, NJ: Chatham House.

Hisschemoller, M., Hoppe, R. (1995). Coping with intractable controversies: The case for problem structuring in policy design and analysis. Knowl. Policy 8(4):40.

Hoppe, R., van de Graaf, H., Van Dijk, A. (1987). Implementation research and policy design: problem tractability, policy theory, and feasibility testing. Internat Rev. Admin. Sci. 53:581–604.

Hutchinson, J. (2002). Citizen participation. J. Amer. Plan. Assoc. 68(2):226–227.

Ingraham, P. W. (1987). Toward more systematic consideration of policy design. Policy Stud. J. 15(4):611–628.

Ingram, H., Mann, D. (1980). Why Policies Succeed or Fail. Beverly Hills, CA: Sage.

Ingram, H., Schneider, A. (1991). The choice of target populations. Admin. Soc. 23(3):333–356.

Jensen, W. (1997). The application of the critical theory: defining the critical theory. GeoCities http://www.geocities.com/athens/acropolis/8548/.

Jenkins-Smith, H. C. (1988). Analytic debates and policy learning: analysis and change in the federal bureaucracy. Policy Sci. 22:169–212.

LaPorte, T. R. (1975). Organized Social Complexity: Challenge to Politics and Policy. Princeton, NJ: Princeton University Press.

Laswell, H. D. (1971). A Preview of Policy Sciences. New York: American Elsevier.

Laswell, H. D. (1951). The policy orientation. In: Lerner, D., Laswell, H. D., eds. The Policy Sciences. Stanford, CA: Stanford University Press.

Lin, A. C. (1998). Bridging positivist and interpretivist approaches to qualitative methods. Policy Stud. J. 26(1):162–180.

Lindblom, C. E. (1990). Inquiry and Change. New Haven, CT: Yale University Press.

Lindblom, C. E., Cohen, D. K. (1979). Usable Knowledge: Social Science and Social Problem Solving. New Haven, CT: Yale University Press.

Linder, S. H., Peters, G. B. (1991). The logic of public policy design: linking policy actors and plausible instruments. Knowl. Policy 4(1/2):125–152.

Linder, S. H., Peters, G. B. (1985). From social theory to policy design. J. Publ. Policy 4(3):237–259.

Linder, S. H., Peters, G. B. (1988). The analysis of design or the design of analysis. Policy Stud. Rev. 7(4):738–750.

Linder, S. H., Peters, G. B. (1987). A design perspective on policy implementation: the fallacies of misplaced prescriptions. Policy Stud. Rev. 6:459–476.

MacRae, D. (1976). The Social Function of Social Science. New Haven, CT: Yale University Press.

Majone, G. (1976). Choice among policy instruments for pollution control. Policy Anal. 2:589–613.

Matland, R. E. (1995). Synthesizing the implementation literature: the ambiguity-conflict model of policy implementation. J. Pub. Admin. Res. Theory 5(2):145–174.

McWilliam, C. L. (1997). Using a participatory research process to make a difference in policy on aging. Can. Pub. Policy (spring supplement):70–89.

Meizrow, J. (1991). Making meaning through reflection. In: Transformative Dimensions of Adult Learning. San Francisco: Jossey Bass.

Pelletier, D., et al. The shaping of collective values through deliberative democracy: an empirical study from New York's North Country. Policy Sci. 32(2).

Popper, K. quoted in Daly H. E. (1991). Steady-State Economics. Washington, DC: Island Press.

Quade, E. S. (1970). Why policy sciences? Policy Sci. 1(1):1–2.

Roe, E. (1990). Narrative Policy Analysis: Theory and Procedure. Durham, NC: Duke University Press.

Schneider, A. L., Ingram, H. (1997). Policy Design for Democracy. Lawrence: University Press of Kansas.

Schneider, A. L., Ingram, H. (1990). Policy design: elements, premises, and strategies. In: Nagel, S., ed. Policy Theory and Policy Evaluation. New York: Glenwood Press.

Schneider, A., Ingram, H. (1993). Social construction of target populations: implications for politics and policy. Amer. Polit. Sci. Rev. 87(2):334–347.

Simon, H. A. (1969). The Sciences of the Artificial. Cambridge: MIT Press.

Svara, J. H. (1999). Complementarity of politics and administration as a legitimate alternative to the dichotomy model. Admin. Soc. 30(6):676–705.

Swepson, P. (1998). Separating the ideals of research from the methodology of research: either action research or science, can lead to better research. Act Res Internat, (http://www.scu.edu.au/schools/sawd/ari/ari-swepson.html).

Tat-Kei Ho, A., Coates, P. (2002). Citizen participation: legitimizing performance measurement as a decision tool. Gov. Finan. Rev. 18(2):8–10.

Timney, M. M. (1998). Overcoming administrative barriers to citizen participation: citizens as partners, not adversaries. In: King, C., Simrell, C., Stivers, C., eds. Government Is Us: Public Administration in an Anti-Government Era. Thousand Oaks, CA: Sage, pp. 88–101.

Torgerson, D. (1986). Between knowledge and politics: three faces of policy analysis. Policy Sci. 19(1):33–60.

Weimer, D. L. (1993). The current state of design craft: borrowing, tinkering, and problem solving. Pub. Admin. Rev. 53(2):110–120.

Weimer, D. L. (1992). The craft of policy design: can it be more than art? Policy Stud. Rev. 11(3/4):370–388.

Wildavsky, A. (1979). Speaking Truth to Power: The Art and Craft of Policy Analysis. Boston: Little, Brown.

Wittrock, B., deLeon, P. (1986). Policy as a moving target: a call for conceptual realism. Policy Stud. Rev. 6(1):44–60.

Yankelovich, D. (1991). Coming to Public Judgment: Making Democracy Work in a Complex World. New York: Syracuse University Press.

# 37

## Decentralized Governance and Participatory Development
### The Asian Experience

**HABIB ZAFARULLAH**

*University of New England, New South Wales, Australia*

## INTRODUCTION

In the current epoch of crafting democratic governance in the newly democratizing polities (NDPs) in Asia under the impetus of both domestic demands and external intervention, decentralization and participation have gained critical significance as instruments of holistic development. The development paradigms of yesteryear became discredited because of their tilt, if by default, toward creating conditions that harbored bureaucratic domination, bred injustice, caused social and economic disparity, destroyed cultural values, produced public sector corruption and inefficiency, and damaged the environment (Goulet, 1992).

The direction of development in today's globalized world cannot be divorced from the worldwide trend to create democratic opportunities for the people (Sen, 1999). Authoritarian regimes are making way for democratic governments, which are expected to establish institutions and processes to facilitate synergy between the state and citizens on the one hand, and between state institutions and civil society on the other. The time-honored hiatus between the state and people, a corollary of overcentralization in an authoritarian–bureaucratic framework, is challenged in the contemporary social-political makeover for democratic governance. The great divide between the powerful and the weak, created under clientelist relationships, asymmetrical political–administrative structures, and lopsided development outcomes, had powerful incentives in weakening state–society relations in Asia. (See Migdal, 1988; Randall and Theobold, 1985.) Economic progress may have been achieved within such political–administrative arrangements in some countries, including some in Asia (Chowdhury and Islam, 1993), but it occurred at the cost of democracy, freedom, and human rights (Sen, 1999). Such an arrangement can at best be ephemeral and is bound to collapse in the long run under a gradually crystallizing democratic ethos.

Important to democratic governance, therefore, is the reconstruction of patterns of relationships among the state, the political structures, the administrative apparatus, and the people. In this course of action, civil society can play a causative role in fostering the nexus to enable people-centered development to happen (Hyden, 1997; Uggla, 1996; Peter, 1996; Eade, 2000). A development strategy that strikes a balance between the forces of globalization and local conditions, including a society's perception and the degree of acceptance of and keenness for democratic values, will for all practical purposes have a greater prospect of sustainable success than one entirely (or almost entirely) based on imported ideas and practices. Each society has its peculiar social, political, and economic values and sets of specific demands that may be important in outlining the pattern of democratic and development governance, therefore any attempt at imposing unfamiliar practices or introducing unusual techniques generates the possibility of being opposed under the prevailing political–bureaucratic culture.

Over the past decade or so, several countries of Asia have attempted wide-ranging reforms to bring their governments in line with the current thinking in democratic, decentralized governance. Many of these reforms have resulted from either local pressures or the dictates of the international donor community (IDC)—or both. In some countries, new decentralization laws have been enacted with new systems, devolving more power to subnational governments gradually put in place. In these new systems, citizens' participation in the management of local affairs and in development planning and implementation has been stressed, and mechanisms has been created to facilitate the practice. Due to structural flaws, procedural intricacies, political and social factors, and bureaucratic resistance, however, participatory development within formal governmental structures has in many situations remained elusive even though the rhetorical stance of the political leadership has been strong and the persistence of civil society intense.

In the absence of genuine formal participatory structures within the machinery of government or because of the protracted nature of decentralization reform implementation, nongovernmental organizations (NGOs) are highly proactive in offering alternative conduits for the people to be both participants in and the beneficiaries of development initiatives, especially poverty alleviation programs, watershed management, social forestry, health services, education, and the like. In essence, barring a few isolated cases in which the state actors have taken the initiative, participatory development in Asia has largely become the domain of NGOs.

This chapter examines the scope and substance of decentralization reforms in several countries of South and Southeast Asia, their implications for citizens' participation in local governance and development, and the role of NGOs in facilitating participation in social development. The focus is on the reforms in selected South and Southeast Asian nations. To provide a conceptual perspective to the Asian experience, we make some general observations on the notions of decentralization and participatory development.

## MANAGING PEOPLE-ORIENTED DEVELOPMENT

Managing people-driven development in Asia—or for that matter in any developing society—is a complex phenomenon. A range of social and economic factors, some apparently conflicting, is always at play. The modalities of operationalizing and managing effective development systems conducive to local needs are therefore continuously being worked out. The political leadership, development policy planners, civil society institutions, and international aid community are all involved in charting the most appropriate course of action for improved governance aimed at providing continuous benefits to the people. Past experiences, however, indicate dissatisfaction with central planning and administration of development programs in Asia, as economic and social benefits were unevenly distributed among the disadvantaged people, thereby failing to alleviate poverty (Rondinelli et al., 1983). The postcolonial centralized state, with its plethora of controls and levers and weak accountability mechanisms, generated a bureaucratic attitude generally opposed to popular participation in development. The interests of dominant elites were prioritized over those of the overwhelming poor. Imperfect systems of allocation and discriminatory access mechanisms stemmed from the bureaucratization of local government (Wood, 1977). Development programs and projects at the local level and the delivery of state services to the people were entirely managed by the local agents of the central administration, and the patterns of relationships between the local bureaucracy and the common people were influence by a network of clientelism.

Early attempts at rectifying these problems by way of decentralizing and debureaucratizing the machinery of government in the newly independent countries miscarried because of political ill will and bureaucratic resistance. At the same time, a new pattern of recentralization and rebureaucratization occurred in some places (Wood, 1984), further widening the gap between the state and the people. The resurgence of interest in governmental reform (which was a common phenomenon in the late 1950s and 1960s), however, and especially the wave of democratization in the developing world since the 1970s, led to the construction of new paradigms and strategies to efficiently and effectively manage governance at the periphery.

The reformulation of the role and structure of the state has accompanied a redefinition of development itself and the process it entails (Haque, 1999: Ch. 9). The technocratic "top-down" approach was gradually replaced by techniques that favored wider association of the people in the planning and implementation of development programs (Johnston and Clark, 1982). The purpose of development was no longer economic progress alone, but embraced a much broader scope with the more formal inclusion of the notion of "human development," which has virtually been at center stage since it was "conceptualized" in 1990. Streeten (1997: 22) rephrases it "as the enlargement of choices, the presentation of options," and equates it with the "development of the people, for the people and by the people." It has to do with jobs and income, social services, and above all, participation of the people in the development process.

### Participation as a Development Variable

Democracy bolsters development both in an ideological and structural sense, and because participation is symbiotically related to democracy, it is hard to think of its existence in an authoritarian, centralized governmental framework. Democracy can provide the institutions and practices to facilitate citizen engagements in governance (Bhagawati, 1995: 54–55). Such engagements can produce useful outcomes for the people, such as wider opportunities to ventilate grievances, formally project local demands, and obtain greater equality of access to services. Without equality of access to participatory structures, social exclusion for certain segments of the population, especially the disadvantaged—women and the poor, for instance—would result. The vitality of poverty alleviation programs—reducing inequality, raising living standards, and creating equitable access relationships—depends in large measure on popular participation (Ingham and Kalam, 1992). The rights-based approach to development, an extended version of the basic needs approach, has now emerged as the preferred paradigm in development. Indeed, citizens' participation as an "overall development strategy" in governance is adjudged a fundamental human right and a variable in social and economic development (DFID, 2000; Commonwealth Foundation, 1999; ILO, 1978: 2; UNDP, 1993) Participation creates opportunities "to increase control over resources and regulate institutions in given social situations on the part of groups. . . hitherto excluded from such control" Stiefel and Wolfe (1994:5). (See also World Bank, 1994a; Love, 1991.) It encourages interactions between individuals or their representative groups and state actors in the policy process.

Furthermore, participation empowers and dignifies the common people, which can shield them from arbitrary state authority (Chambers, 1983). This can influence a change in the patterns of relationships between citizens and the state apparatus. Participation may also create conditions for collaboration and partnership between stakeholders in development. Citizens' capacity to comprehend problems and think constructively is enhanced in a participatory culture, and people are equipped with the appropriate skills to negotiate with other state and societal actors and to manage development activities with conviction and dedication (Love, 1991; Clayton et al., 1997). Common wisdom generated by exchanging information and resources facilitates social transformation (Tandon, 1982). These can be effective learning tools in the practice of democracy at the ground level and create the possibility of "raising the quality of democracy and strengthening civic capacity" (OECD, 2001: 11).

## Participatory Development

The emerging ethos of participatory development subsumes a broader circumference for citizens' participation blended with other dimensions of governance. It goes beyond the community-level project planning and implementation and is strategically placed within the overall national development paradigm and linked to the forces of a market-driven economy (UNDP, 1993: 2). While there are critics of neoliberal economic principles and skeptics of market-driven development (1), fuller participation of the people by way of affording them control over the development process in its totality—initiatives, decisions, and resources (Cornwall, 2000: 35)—is widely supported as a basis for creating a democratic developmental culture in a society. Participatory development implies planned quest and deference for "local views and indigenous knowledge," and acknowledges the role of the common people as "actors" rather than "beneficiaries." (See UNDP, 1998; OECD, 2001: 11.) As a "local-level reflection of good governance," participatory development can effectively uphold transparency, accountability, due process, and the right of the local people to be heard (World Bank, 1994b: 42–43). The World Bank's Comprehensive Development Framework (see Wolfensohn, 1999) is patterned to make participation at the local level "a guiding principle in development, strengthening general capacity for participatory activities, and creating a culture that welcomes the use of participatory approaches" (World Bank, 2001a). Development will have wider resonance if both the primary (the people, especially the poor) and the secondary stakeholders (civil society organizations) are associated with the development of the decision-making process and share control over the use of resources in development. An interactive development network linking the state, people, and civil society will enhance social capital by creating "norms and social trust that facilitate coordination and cooperation for mutual benefit" (Putnam, 1995: 67).

The IDC—the other stakeholders—have different perceptions about participatory development (2). Their views may provide some useful guidance in understanding the options available to the political leadership in different countries to design participatory structures within the governmental framework, but they cannot be taken as absolute aphorisms, nor can they be adopted without relevance to a society's cultural norms or political attitudes. To realize their agreed-upon ends and enable continuity, participatory development has to be processed in concert with the priorities and values of primary and secondary stakeholders and public administrators.

## DECENTRALIZED GOVERNANCE

Decentralization provides an institutional base for participation. If, among other things, the purpose of decentralization is to take the state to the door step of the people, then enlarging the scope of participation becomes critical (UNDP, 2002: 74). The two are symbiotically entwined. Decentralization is ineffectual without participation, and the latter is difficult to operationalize within a centralized structure. A decentralized system can serve as a medium for popular support toward planning, implementing, and managing development initiatives. A sense of local "ownership" of these initiatives can maximize citizens' commitment to and espousal of development activities and make them vigorous and enduring (United Nations, 1962).

In the NDPs, decentralization can be resourcefully used to support community organizations and services, strengthen policy networks, and widen the scope for probing into and evaluating developmental goals (World Bank, 2000a). More important, participation has the potential to enforce bureaucratic accountability, induce greater governmental responsiveness to local needs, and reduce the scope for administrative intransigence, malfeasance, and corruption (World Bank, 1996). Unlike the national bureaucracy, which is remote from the people, a local official "has his master at his door-step" (Maddick, 1963: 58). An effective decentralized governmental system is predisposed to enhance the capacity and character of the array of public service providers.

The degree to which citizens' participation is fostered in development correlates with different forms of decentralization and to the degree of decentralization within each form. Asian countries have been experimenting with some of these forms since the early 1960s with varying results. Some of these served the purposes of authoritarian regimes quite favorably, even if only to meet quick-fix goals of efficiency and economy, while others more attuned to supporting a democratic process have provided effective results, some potentially enduring.

Decentralization may be political, administrative, fiscal, or economical or a combination of these. There may be variants and subvariants of each form based on the mix of principles from each, relevant to particular settings and demands (Tommasi and Weischelbaum, 1999). These forms may range from the narrow to the more extensive, depending on the extent to which national governments are willing to relinquish or share power with nonpublic or subnational entities (Rondinelli, 1983; Ranis and Stewart, 1994). Whatever form of decentralization is put in place, however, has to be accompanied by public and institutional accountability to match outputs to popular priorities (Crook and Manor, 1998: 7).

In fact, in the current worldwide trend toward democratization and economic liberalization all four types are extant in different measures and can effectively contribute to broaden public participation in development. The extent and intensity of each type is conditioned by political, social, and economic factors, the willingness of the political leadership to undertake extensive reforms in governance, and the spontaneity with which the people and civil society endorse and accept the structures created for participation.

In the Asian NDPs, the emphasis today is on political decentralization, which is basically the relocation of power, authority, and decision-making roles to independently elected subnational governments. The increased proximity of decision making to the community directly affected enhances political accountability, ensures center-periphery checks and balances, enlarges possibilities for local participation in development, and promotes efficiency within local governments (Crook and Manor, 1998: 7–14). Political decentralization can encourage healthy competition among subnational jurisdictions that may lead to more innovative and appropriate policies for development (Weingast, 1995).

While administrative decentralization has been common in nondemocratic polities in the past and often with success, it cannot bring about the same results as it would within a democratic framework. The reasons are obvious. Even with comprehensive administrative decentralization leaning toward greater devolution of administrative authority, the chances of securing popular participation will be restrained in the absence of political power at the local level. In essence, administrative decentralization cannot effectively debureaucratize the administrative system, as centrally appointed civil servants continue to play the dominant role in development management.

Three subtypes of administrative decentralization—deconcentration, delegation, and devolution—are common and have been widely referred to in the theoretical literature (Rondinelli et al., 1983; Rondinelli, 1999: 17). In structures pursuing deconcentration the central–local relationship is basically imbalanced, with local affairs dominated from above, and there is no local political base for public participation; the representative element may also be either absent or limited (Turner and Hulme, 1997: 160–161). Authoritarian regimes have often used deconcentration as a clever tool to promote their rhetoric of sharing power with subnational governments (Semboja and Therkildsen, 1994).

Delegation may be a more extensive form of decentralization, but the degree to which it fosters public participation in development depends on each organization's inclination to open up its space and create the structures for the spontaneous involvement of individuals and groups in planning, implementing, and evaluating its programs. Devolution is closer to political decentralization and serves as its basis for greater freedom from central control. From the standpoint of administrative decentralization, however, devolution is nothing more than the transfer of authority to subnational units to undertake a range of economic, social, and administrative functions. Even if they are "representative" of the people, local "political" units cannot go beyond their defined jurisdiction and take extraordinary initiatives to respond to their peculiar problems (Self, 1985: 157). If devolution is practiced within a fundamentally centralized bureaucratic system without sufficient space for pluralist politics to function and limited public or civil society participation in local affairs, it will essentially be politically ineffective behind a façade of local "democracy." On the other hand, if genuine devolution of power is vested on local representative bodies with the bureaucratic apparatus performing under the baton of the elected leadership and independent of central control, the chances are that development management will be more participatory.

Within any form of decentralization, be it political or administrative, the responsibility for managing fiscal affairs in the local development arena is situated in subnational political units. Fiscal decentralization entrusts subnational governments both with the power and authority to generate their own funds for development and welfare purposes through taxation, rates, fees, levies, and so on and with overall control over their efficient and equitable management. Fiscal decentralization becomes necessary, because without sufficient fiscal leverage, and despite their political and representative strength, local units cannot bring government to the doorstep of the common people if they cannot generate the resources themselves and utilize them to meet local needs. The prospect for improved macroeconomic governance is greater in decentralized fiscal systems (Huther and Shah, 1998).

From an economic and market standpoint, privatization of either local public service delivery or development project implementation is a fairly recent phenomenon in Asia, and is gradually gaining ground, with NGOs playing a more robust role in providing some of the basic services at the local level, either alone or in some form of partnership with the government. Deregulation complements privatization. By shifting central control over economic activities at the local level, by removing legal constraints on NGO or private sector involvement in both service delivery and development initiatives, or by encouraging public–private partnership, different dimensions of participation can be ushered in. Indeed, deregulation has knocked down the barriers that previously existed between the state and other stakeholders in development. A deregulated framework supports close synergy between key interests in development.

Nongovernmental organizations have a comparative edge over governmental institutions. They are strategically placed to create a more intimate relationship with development program beneficiaries at the grassroots level on the tenets of voluntarism and therefore can easily apply participatory approaches devoid of the customary bureaucratic inhibitions that typify governmental organizations (Turner and Hulme, 1997: 207–208; Thomas, 1992; Fowler, 1988; Korten, 1980). The strength of NGOs lies in their "task-oriented" approach and their participatory praxis that provides them with a marked degree of functional advantage over government agencies. Furthermore, governments alone cannot cater to the large rural populations in most of Asia;

reliance on or partnership with the "third sector" therefore becomes desirable, both to alleviate poverty and to deliver social development programs.

## DECENTRALIZATION INITIATIVES IN ASIA

The thrust for comprehensive decentralization in Asia came in the wake of the democratization that began sweeping most of the Third World in the 1980s. Over the past two decades, authoritarian or neoliberal regimes, such as those in the Philippines, Indonesia, Thailand, Pakistan, Bangladesh, and Nepal, as well as moderately democratic ones, such as those in India and Sri Lanka, have embarked on organized attempts to restructure their political–administrative systems in line with the current thinking on good governance. In some of these countries the pace of change has been uneven and often sluggish, with little significant impact on human welfare; in others positive advancements have been attained.

Both India and the Philippines achieved remarkable progress in decentralizing power to local institutions in the early 1990s. India has been a continuing democracy since independence, whereas the Philippines experienced years of authoritarian rule before embracing democratic rule. In India, the decentralization initiative came as a normal course of consolidating a democratic structure, whereas in the Philippines the clamor for reforming the local government system became rife after the restoration of democracy in 1986, and a sound and effective decentralized system was considered a "bulwark against the re-imposition of authoritarianism" (Rood, 2000).

The Local Government Code (LGC) of 1991 is a milestone in the political history of the Philippines. It brought about far-reaching changes to the existing system of local governance, which had featured a local political culture antagonistic to democratic practice and a bureaucratic culture that tampered with local management structures and functions. (See Timberman, 1991: 38, 226–227; Hollnsteiner, 1963.) The code is explicit about "genuine and meaningful local autonomy" that would make local government units (LGUs) "self-reliant" and "effective partners in the attainment of national goals." Responsiveness, accountability, efficiency, organizational dynamism, prioritization of community service needs, and local taxing power were designated as key elements of the new decentralization policy. Supervisory and accountability devices were built into the new decentralization system. An intergovernmental supervisory system was designed to restrain local government bodies "from transgressing against regulations and norms," with provinces playing a significant role, thereby relieving the center of some control over local affairs (Ferrazzi, 2001: 5–6; Government of the Philippines, 1991: Ch. 1, Sec. 2).

Structurally, there was little change in the existing hierarchical system, from the governor down to the *barangays* (villages), but the powers and functions of local units were enlarged and the scope of citizen engagement in local development substantially broadened. Central government agencies in the Philippines were to periodically consult with LGUs, NGOs, citizen organizations, and community groups on development project implementation, and the participation of the private sector in the delivery of basic services was judged essential "as an alternative strategy for sustainable development." Recall, initiative, and referendum were incorporated as special mechanisms to ensure accountability. In addition to the normal procedures the LGC highlighted the continuing use of legislative enabling acts and administrative and organizational reforms to enhance local autonomy (Government of the Philippines, 1991: Ch. 1, Secs. 2, 3).

Constitutional changes in India in 1992 provided the statutory basis for the creation and operation of elected *panchayat raj institutions (PRIs)* at the village, intermediate, and district levels, each endowed with the power and authority to function as institutions of self-government and to formulate and implement plans for economic development and social justice. The PRIs now have the opportunity to provide critical inputs to the policy process and effectively contribute toward poverty alleviation and welfare and development programs at subnational levels by generating their own revenue through local taxation or by levying fees and charges. A state government is required to share its revenue with the panchayats and provide them periodic grants-in-aid to undertake development activities. Local-level financial systems are regulated and audited by finance commissions set up in each federating state (Government of India, 1992).

The bureaucracy in India—which had long been at the center of managing development and welfare programs at the subnational level—has been stripped, even if in a formal sense, of many of the powers it had enjoyed in the past. With democratically elected local bodies in place a new pattern of governance has emerged at the subnational level. The new political leadership, basically unfamiliar with the rules of the game, is not expected to have an effortless spell, at least initially. So far, the "transition of power from bureaucratic structures to peoples [sic] elected structures has. . .been somewhat slow and painful on the part of the bureaucracy, and bewildering. . . (for) the newly elected *panchayat* representatives" (Das, 1999: 4). While cohabitation between PRIs and bureaucratic institutions is essential, in practice the bureaucracy continues to operate with the same stance and approach it did in the past—ingeniously dominating the decision-making process and keeping PRI leadership at bay by creating "cumbersome administrative procedures that make life difficult for them" (World Bank, 2000b: x).

The decentralization reforms in the Philippines were not implemented at an incremental pace, as would have been appropriate given the extensive changes that were in order; rather, hasty implementation caused confusion, resentment, and skepticism among stakeholders and independent observers. Problems in transferring functions, appropriating resources to local government units, and framing guiding regulations for routine administration of local affairs were initially handled and partially resolved by a congressional oversight committee, but later it by and large became dormant (Brillantes, 1999:9; Mistal, 1996). The Philippine government also displayed a lack of enthusiasm in building the capacity of local government units, which were "practically left to fend for themselves" (Sosema, cited in Ferrazi, 2001: 8). Consequently, going by the LGC, the LGUs formed bonds among themselves and consolidated and coordinated their efforts and services for common purposes (Government of the Philippines, 1991: Ch. 1, Art. 3f ). To further promote their collective interests LGUs have formed associations at the provincial levels, which in turn have federated at the national plane "to more effectively channel their concerns to the government" (Ferrazzi, 2001:8).

The decentralized structure in India has been in place for only a few years, and while it would be naïve to make any informed and judicious assessment of its performance, indications do point to some inherent problems. One study argues that the scheme "does not go far enough" in addressing "some fundamental issues in a decentralized decision-making system," and a lack of clear prioritization of functions at the village level has produced inequities in fund allocation and utilization (Gaiha, 1995). Even an official report highlights some glaring deficiencies in the Indian decentralization scheme relating to fiscal matters as well as the improper modes for operationalizing the rules: the absence of financial autonomy, inconsistencies in applying taxation principles, a lack of relevant guidelines on PRIs' powers to raise revenue statutorily assigned to them, and inappropriate use or underutilization of grants-in-aid money because of state interference. It has been argued that "PRIs have been given vast functions with few sources of revenue. The functional autonomy of the PRIs cannot be operationalized unless the finances of the PRIs are set on sound footings, with clearly defined sources of revenues" (Government of India, 2001: 20–23).

Pakistan and Bangladesh have had a chequered history in local governance. Regimes of various political shades have experimented with different varieties of local government systems, but in the main, the pattern of central–local relations remained intact since the "basic democracy" model was introduced by the military government in the early 1960s. In both countries, military regimes took a greater interest in initiating reforms than democratically elected governments. The four military regimes in these countries since the mid-1970s can be "credited" for introducing new forms of local governance that had variants of decentralization ensconced in them, although hidden behind the military generals' rhetoric of dispersing power to the people might have been self-seeking intentions. As was the case elsewhere, the military governments in Pakistan and Bangladesh, in reality used the logic of decentralization to establish their legitimacy to govern "without requiring them to surrender real power" (Islam, 2002: 2) and to widen their political support base for the eventual civilianization of their regimes.

For their part, the "democratic" regimes failed to consolidate and extend the reforms undertaken by military rulers, although before being installed in power their leaders were not above making promises to democratize the local government system (Rahman, 2000; Zafarullah, 1997). During the period of civilian rule in Pakistan, however, from 1988 to 1999 and from 1991 to the present, LGUs were further stripped of the already limited fiscal authority they had been enjoying, local government elections became irregular or were manipulated by the ruling party, and local units were curbed from playing their constitutional role and denied the resources they needed for development (Jafri, 1999; Zafarullah, 1997). In fact, the Pakistani polity was capriciously ruled by an ill-motivated political elite through a highly centralized administrative network that both stifled economic growth and human development (World Bank, 2002: 9) and permitted very little scope for citizen participation.

Before the third military takeover in Pakistan, the local government system was under the control of the provinces. The system was highly bureaucratized, with appointed administrators responsible for coordinating public services within their jurisdiction. With the absence of effective public accountability mechanisms, corruption raged at the local level. Political interference was not aimed at improving the character of local governance but at achieving parochial gains (World Bank, 1998a: 95–96). Without any concrete legal form, local administrators performed their functions that were deconcentrated from the provincial governments. In effect, the deputy commissioners became the guardians in the local arena and served either their own interests or those of the local elites with whom they developed a close rapport. In this devious process, "the local government system became obsolete, and service delivery ... suffered" (cited in Islam, 2002: 3).

The current military regime in Pakistan has displayed high degree of earnestness to "reverse decades of overcentralization in the public sector and bring about accountable, empowered local governments, leading to better service delivery" by putting a new local government system in place in 2001 (World Bank, 2001c). Its principal aim is to achieve what the regime advances as the five *D*'s: *devolution* of political power, *decentralization* of administrative authority, *deconcentration* of management functions, *diffusion* of the power–authority nexus, and *distribution* of resources to the districts (Islam, 2002: 5) This has been a bold initiative by the military government in the existing elite-dominated and bureaucratized system. The government is nonetheless highly optimistic about the benefits the proposed decentralization scheme is expected to bring forth at the local level: encouraging competition in the public sector and begetting benefits to the people, spurring the initiatives of individuals entrusted with the responsibility of managing development and welfare programs, decreasing the cost of local services as local institutions respond to "value for money" demand, and creating support institutions at the subnational levels to monitor and evaluate development programs (Government of Pakistan, 2001: 32–33). The World Bank believes the decentralization initiatives have "the potential to deliver better services while opening up political participation to a much wider number of citizens" (World Bank, 2002: 10).

There is definitely an element of altruism in the military government's decentralization plan, as it aims at empowering the common people so that they are at the center of development, enabling a "broader and more equitable sharing of power and authority" among the central, provincial, and local governments, and diffusing the control of powerful elites in local affairs, thereby bridging the persisting gap between the state and the citizens (Government of Pakistan, 2001: 33). The plan envisages a more democratic local government system in which LGUs would have authority, capacity, resources, administrative and financial setups, and accountability mechanisms to serve the people, especially the poor, by delivering public services to them (World Bank, 2001c). Without "extensive support and buy-ins from stakeholders," however, it will be an overwhelmingly challenging to establish effective fiscal decentralization in Pakistan (World Bank, 2002: 10).

In the late 1970s and early 1980s, Bangladesh witnessed two dramatic changes in local government, both initiated by military regimes. The first of these redesigned the system by granting LGUs corporate status and assigning them corrective, financial, developmental, adjudicatory, and welfare functions. Political representation in the lowest tier was enlarged, and gender-based participation was ensured. The higher local government layers were not given any representative character, and they remained in the hands of the bureaucracy, which also continued to influence the administration of local affairs at the lowest tiered LGUs. To widen its power base and strengthen its hold in the rural areas, the regime created another level at the grassroots level—*gram sarkers* (village governments), which would oversee all local-level functions transferred to them through a participatory framework (Khan and Zafarullah, 1981). Intended to operate without direct governmental interference, in reality the degree of influence and control of the ruling party and bureaucracy quashed any commitment to citizen's participation in development activities (Zafarullah, 1997: 40). With limited revenue-raising powers, ill-defined as they were, these bodies were virtually dependent on the central government for financial resources, but recurrent funding was not guaranteed. After two years the floundering system was abandoned (Huque, 1986). The second military regime made some major structural changes to the system of development administration by dismantling the age-old colonial framework of government. It retained the basic goals of development and participation envisaged in the model created by its predecessor. Decentralization became the cornerstone of the new model, and the subdistrict (*upazila*) was made the "prime mover in local-level social and economic transformation, a role which it to play under tremendous political and bureaucratic pressure" (Zafarullah, 1997: 41). While the local government models of both regimes were innovative and had some altruistic purposes in the functional and developmental sense, they were ingeniously used to legitimize military rule. Participation of the poor was limited to casting votes in local elections, which were grossly manipulated by the ruling party, or to provide their labor to local projects for which they were paid a pittance. Nonetheless, the upazila scheme had the makings of an effective local-level planning and implementation mechanism, but was not allowed to function because of self-seeking rural elites, political opportunists, and intransigent bureaucrats (Zafarullah, 1996; McCarthy, 1993). Domination over local development and participation was governed by multiple networks of clientelism in which the political element was significant (Wood, 1992). Within the structures of the "decentralized" scheme, the people remained mere bystanders.

Since the overthrow of authoritarian rule in 1990 and the emergence of democratic politics in Bangladesh, local government has been moved to the sidelines by successive governments. Both parties in power since 1991 have been long on rhetoric but short on action about genuine decentralization reforms. Under the two-tier local government system introduced in 1993, the decentralization reforms of the military regime were reversed and a highly bureaucratized subdistrict administration was created (Westergaard, 2000). Before this scheme could be fully operationalized, the succeeding government sought to replace it by a four-tier system. It was not implemented, however. Representative local government has remained in virtual limbo since the mid-1990s, and development management at the local level has been the domain of the bureaucracy. In the meantime, the government that had introduced the two-tier structure has regained power and is proposing another set of reforms. While the never-ending tussle between the two major parties continues in Bangladesh, decentralized local governance remains a delusion.

The decentralization of Sri Lanka's governmental system was initiated in 1987, mainly to counter the separatist movement in the conflict-ridden parts of the country rather than to demonstrate a determined commitment to take government closer to the people. The scheme was purely ad hoc and was not designed to provide long-term solutions to the country's overwhelming centralized economic management system, which incorporated the process of intergovernmental transfers of funds trapped in bureaucratic complexities and the lack of economic incentives for subnational units. Complete decentralization was never attempted, leaving the local government system highly complex and fragmented, although deficiencies in fiscal decentralization were partially leveled out by capital spending via the provincial setups (Government of Sri Lanka, 2002). The "decentralization" initiatives implemented to date have in effect endured the status quo, as the government in Colombo has been disinclined to withdraw from controlling and overseeing administrative and fiscal functions at the subnational levels. The reliance on central functionaries at the local level to manage local development and welfare programs and the tight fiscal controls of both the central and provincial governments have left local bodies resource-starved and incapacitated in fulfilling their roles in widening the scope for citizen involvement in development activities (World Bank, 2000c: 25).

The United National Party (UNP) government attempted devolution via the 13th amendment to the Constitution, but there were several shortcomings in the plan. Eight provincial councils, which are elected by the people for five-year terms, are basically under the control of governors appointed by the country's president. At the local level there are three types of local authorities that are also elected by the people for four-year terms—municipal councils (in cities and large towns), urban councils (in "less urbanized" areas), and *pradeshiya sabhas* (in rural areas). Local authorities are created or reconstituted by committees whenever the necessity arises, and in this process the central minister responsible for local government takes the initiative. Sectoral committees to assist LGUs have largely remained passive and inadequately represented.

In the meantime, a trend toward delocalization has taken place in Sri Lanka, with many local functions hitherto undertaken by LGUs transferred to governmental, quasi-governmental, or statutory agencies. Being directly linked to the central government, these are mainly controlled either by the political executive at the national level or by legislators rather than by elected LGUs. (See UNESCAP, 2002.) Ambiguity shrouds the entire framework of Sri Lankan decentralization, and both civil servants and the people are confused about the arrangements. Local government is beset with organizational and procedural problems that have eroded the functional viability and efficiency of local governance (DAC, 1997: 63). New proposals to amend the Constitution devolve some power to the regions, which will be responsible for local governance under their jurisdiction, but there are hardly any provisions to construct an effective decentralized system in the country (Government of Sri Lanka, 2000).

The Indonesian Constitution, enacted over half a century ago, still provides the basic framework of local government and decentralization in the country. The principles of decentralization and deconcentration enshrined in the Constitution were elaborated in the statute concerning governance at the regional level. The two principles are juxtaposed in the act. Decentralization affords autonomy to the regions— "right, authority and responsibility of subnational entities to regulate and manage their own affairs"—while according to the deconcentration principle, responsibilities are to be delegated by the central governments, provincial governors and headquarters of line ministries to *their* officers at the subnational levels (Government of Indonesia, 1974: Art. 18). Coadministration has meant merely delegating the implementation of major policy decisions made at the higher levels or administering functions (GTZ Advisory Team, 1997).

The so-called autonomous localities thus work under the tutelage of higher-level governments or their functionaries in the capital cities, and there is considerable overlap among their jurisdiction regarding local government functions as well as variations in the way the several tiers are organized and authorized to oversee local business. For instance, the governor wears two hats, and his roles can be open to conflict, for he represents the central government as the head of the administrative region while as a provincial governor he is expected to serve the interests of his province. Similar roles are performed by county commissioners and mayors at their own levels.

As a matter of fact, the local government system in "New order" Indonesia has featured a unique blending of decentralization, deconcentration, and "coadministration" principles that often worked at cross-purposes and inhibited the development of local democracy. The people have been denied the opportunity to directly elect the heads of their respective local bodies, as the lower house of the legislature holds the right to do so. An LGU has been almost entirely controlled by the appointed commissioner and the local members of parliament (who invariably toe their party line), and together they make the local laws, rules, and regulations and prepare the budget for local administration and development. Local-level planning has basically been a bureaucratized function, with the people or community organizations having little influence in plan formulation. Development plans are prepared and coordinated by the planning agency, which mainly consists of local officials of the ministries. For all practical purposes, until the new decentralization laws were hastily adopted by the parliament in 1999, Indonesia was an "overly centralized" state creating "tenuous links between local demands and decisions on local public services, weak mechanisms for local accountability, and ad hoc allocation of fiscal resources across regions" (Ma and Hofman, 2000: 1).

The new Regional Governance Law is apparently designed to enhance both political and administrative decentralization and lay the foundations for a more democratic local government structure with multiparty elections, sound accountability mechanisms, and efficient service delivery instruments. Except for a few key areas in governance (3), most public service functions have been transferred to the subnational governments, especially districts and cities, with provincial administrations operating as a coordinating layer. The existing hierarchical relationship between subnational governments has been abolished, with district governments (*kotalkabupaten*) gaining "complete" autonomy, and *walikotabupati* (heads of district governments) made responsible to locally elected assembly. The deconcentrated activities of central ministries in the districts are to come under the control of the LGUs. The Law on Fiscal Balance is aimed at transforming intergovernmental fiscal relations in the country. A general allocation fund has been created. Access by LGUs will be governed by "a lock-in share and a transparent allocation formula," while other proposed changes will "yield an *expenditure ratio* for subnational governments...mak[ing] Indonesia one of the most decentralized countries in the world" (Bahl, 2001:3). It has also been suggested that the fiscal initiatives will "establish a social safety net for income redistribution" (Tambunan, 2000).

The "big bang" approach by the Indonesian government in implementing the decentralization reforms has faltered because of the ambiguity in the two plans and the risks the process carries (Hull, 1999; Djalal, 2002): the political and administrative dimensions of the scheme are too broadly defined, creating confusion among the stakeholders, and the lack of clarity in the way subnational responsibilities have been delineated has the risk of intensifying macroeconomic imbalances (Ahmad and Hofman, 2000: 6, 16). The fiscal decentralization scheme restrains the revenue-building capacity of local government and therefore is unable to take in additional spending to meet local needs, thereby compromising local accountability. It has also been argued that the "coincidence of administrative and fiscal decentralization renders nearly impossible the design of an objective equalization scheme" (Ma and Hofman, 2000: 2) With deficient administrative capacity, LGUs will encounter difficulty in speedily and wholly absorbing their mandated responsibilities. The risk of public funds being mis-used or misappropriated is always imminent in the absence of transparency and sound managerial supervision (Ahmad and Hofman, 2000: 3,16).

The development of local government in Thailand has been painstakingly slow because of the uniqueness of the country's political structure, which has undergone several changes, from its shift from absolute monarchy to "democracy," and with intermittent periods of military rule. The first organized local government system came in 1933, with the adoption of the Administrative Law. The central government how-ever, and to some extent the provincial governments, continued to dominate local affairs. In the 1950s, the local government system was enlarged with the creation of specialized rural bodies and partly elected councils at the *tambons* to manage de-velopment at the local level and "to promote and prepare local communities for a self-governing system" (Sopchokchai, 2001). A genuine attempt at decentralizing ad-ministrative power and creating participatory structures came in 1994 with the enact-ment of the Tambon Council and Administration Act.

In Thailand, the 1997 constitution provided for the decentralization of power to local areas "for the purpose of independence and self-determination of local affairs, [to] develop local economics, public utilities and facilities systems and information infrastructure in the locality thoroughly and equally throughout the country," as well as to promote and encourage public participation in sustainable development (Gov-ernment of Thailand, 1997: Secs. 78, 79). In reality, however, decentralization has occurred only theoretically, as administrative power is still concentrated in the central government. The centralized Department of Local Administration oversees and provides direction to both provincial and local administrative apparatuses. In effect, the agents of the central government work in tandem to substantially curb the power and authority of local government units. The Constitution itself does not go far enough in making decentralization of certain sectors (namely, education) mandatory. Indeed, there are conflicts between laws and this seemingly has adverse consequences for true devolution of power to subnational governments. Political controversies, misgivings, and politicization also cloud the decentralization process (Nelson, 2001: 7–8, 13–14).

In rural Thailand, apart from the provincial administrative organization (PAO), two forms of local authorities provide services to the people. These are the tambon (subdistrict) administrative organizations (TAOs) and *sukhapiban* (sanitary) commit-tees. A subdistrict officer, appointed by the provincial governor, heads a TAO, which is a partly appointed and partly elected body representing each village within its juris-diction. Sukhapibans are mainly single-purpose local units created for the purpose of supervising and maintaining sanitation services in both urban and rural areas. They combine both appointive and elective membership. There is considerable functional overlap between PAOs and TAOs because of their direct administrative links from the provincial to the subdistrict levels.

Thai local government has a rather narrow tax base, and its fiscal authority is also limited. While there is a variety of locally raised taxes, very few are generated and utilized at the behest of the LGUs themselves; they merely serve as tax-collecting agents for the central government's coffers. Consequently, LGUs have few funds at their disposal to plan and undertake development work within their jurisdictions and have to rely on the benevolence of the central government for resources to initiate and administer development and welfare programs. By and large, Thai LGUs are resource-starved and lack the capacity to provide basic services to the people.

## PARTICIPATION IN PRACTICE: SOME ASIAN ILLUSTRATIONS

The decentralization initiatives in Asia have no doubt embedded the significance of citizen participation in local governance, especially in such areas as poverty allevia-tion, environmental protection, water resources management, and health delivery systems. Constitutional and statutory provisions have provided the platform for introducing participatory planning and implementation mechanisms in local admin-istration and development. The extent of participation envisaged in these legal instruments differs from one country to another, however, as does the degree of their outcome in practice.

The Indian constitution affords special privileges to disadvantaged segments of the community, not only to ensure the broader participation of the population but also to dismantle prevailing social and economic stratification and power centers at the local level. Positive discrimination allows for greater representation of women and "scheduled" castes and tribal people on PRIs, both as members and in executive leadership positions, thus enabling them to manage their own affairs (Government of India, 1996a: Art. 243D 4). Community empowerment has been supported by creating in each village *panchayat* the *gram sabha* (village council) with all franchised people. This body is particularly significant in the regions mainly inhabited by tribal people, as it is empowered by law to inter alia conserve and protect social customs and traditions, exercise control over institutions and functions in all social sectors, manage natural and community resources, resolve disputes through traditional methods, and retain ownership of minor forest produce. Furthermore, to enable people's participation, the gram sabhas are to be consulted by the state government before making land acquisitions for development projects (Government of India, 1996b: Art. 4). The constitutional move toward decentralization and community empowerment meant a radical departure from the bureaucratic approach to managing local affairs and development activities.

Theoretically, the gram sabha provides a potent ground for citizen participation in local affairs. Participation in the local election process has been high. With the old social configurations and strong elite-based power structures still camouflaged by outward shows of egalitarianism and empowerment, however, the gram sabhas often fail to support the poor and the disadvantaged. According to one study (Alsop et al., 2000: 63) on two Indian states, "villagers are at present more concerned with con-solidating existing economic and social relations rather than using the democratic process to change inequitable rural societies." Gram sabha meetings are manipulated and the decisions are influenced by overbearing PRI members. Rarely are the voices of disadvantaged members heard or heeded in gram sabha meetings (Government of India, 2001: 30–31, 45). The PRIs at the village level appear to be preoccupied with power politics rather than with development issues (Alsop et al., 2000: 63). At the village level, "the resolution of competing village demands is made through less than perfect, sometimes opaque decision processes" (World Bank, 2000c: ix).

On the other hand, unlike most other Indian states, Kerala has been in the fore-front in making the most of the PRI system. The people's campaign for decentralized development there is geared to secure wide participation by the local inhabitants in grassroots planning, thus creating pressure on the government for greater devolution of power and articulating concerns for more resources for development (Krishnakumar, 2000). The planning system has institutionalized both accountability and transparency, while capacity building has been implanted into it by way of mass training programs. The state of Karnataka has also surged ahead in advancing citizen voices and client focus in service delivery by establishing "Panchayat Waves," a radio program aimed at creating awareness about local issues and the role of PRIs among villagers. Although not entirely participatory in nature, the project aims at realizing the "information for empowerment" motto, especially for women (Ananthpur and Prasad, 2000).

While there may be inherent complexities within the PRI system in enforcing participatory routines, in other ways state governments have undertaken sectoral programs that provide opportunities for public participation at the local level. The water sector reform project in Andhra Pradesh in India is a case in point. It has encouraged extensive public participation by transferring irrigation management to farmers, the ultimate beneficiaries. Water users have been mobilized by the state government to form associations and manage water sources on their own (World Bank, undated-a).

In Pakistan the proposed citizen community boards (CCBs) are envisioned as important cogs in the social service delivery process, with a big chunk of the development funds at their disposal. Relying on "voluntary, proactive and self-help initiatives," they are to design development and social welfare projects, implement and manage them, and monitor their performance. They are also expected to realize the empowerment of the people by creating opportunities for them to become "active" participants in the development process (Pakistan NBR, 2002a: 4). On paper, the CCBs may have the capacity to "play a very crucial role in effective democratic local self-governance" (Islam, 2002: 16). The fear that CCBs might be captured by powerful local elites with the connivance of unscrupulous bureaucrats is not unfounded, however, given Pakistan's history of similar conjunction between the two antagonists of citizen participation. Designed to be constituted by unelected groups with the opportunity to raise funds through voluntary contributions, control over these boards could be gained by wealthy local interests (World Bank, 2002: 10).

During the short spell of the *upazila* scheme in Bangladesh (1982–1990), participatory development was a sham, for there was little scope for the primary stakeholders to provide any real input in the local-level planning process. The poor were left out of the process and the mechanisms meant to represent them were abandoned, largely because of the machinations of local politicians, wealthy elite groups, and locally based civil servants. (For details see Zafarullah, 1996.) For them, the best alternative came from a few isolated government-sponsored sectoral projects at the local level and the large array of NGO-organized poverty alleviation and social development initiatives.

In Sri Lanka the principal purpose of establishing *pradeshiya sabhas* was to increase the participation of communities in decision making and development at the local level. The committee system introduced by legislation, however, has failed to serve meaningful purposes in development management at the local level. A USAID (United States Agency for International Development)-sponsored citizen participation project designed to increase citizen participation in local administration and NGO and private sector involvement in local development programs failed to take off because of financial problems. On the other hand, the capacity-building initiatives of the Local Government Ministry that were also intended to enhance citizen participation and reduce citizen–LGU gaps have provided some positive results, although more has to be done to ensure that participation is not subdued by "social differences, politicisation and narrow gauging of functions" (UNESCAP, 2002).

Positive signs of accomplishment in local autonomy were evident within a few years of the adoption of the decentralization scheme in the Philippines as local councils began "asserting their priorities in the delivery of basic services, finding new ways to deliver these services, and forging partnership with the private sector" (Rood, 2000) Citizen participation in development has been fostered by a robust civil society within which NGOs have operated with a sense of collective purpose. They serve as the driving force for the common people in being active participants in the process of development. The people–NGO–LGU nexus has created opportunities for citizen participation. For instance, the three entities have worked together in initiating citizen empowerment structures facilitating community decision making, undertaking communications projects, managing sustainable development programs, facilitating the delivery of health services, establishing "comprehensive" cooperative development programs, promoting advocacy for better governmental performance, conducting systematic monitoring and evaluation of local government activities, and so on (Gonzales, 2000; Rood, 2000; Brillantes, 1999: 11–13).

In the Philippines, the decentralized system appears to be "working and. . .local autonomy has brought about creativity, imagination and innovation at the local level" (Brillantes, 1999: 10). Fewer controls and greater stimuli help in realizing the potential of the people to manage their own destinies. Small fishing communities are thus now entitled to manage their fishery resources, while participatory resource management has aided in the conservation of forest resources (Panayotou, 1994). The Nationwide Coalition of Fisherfolk for Aquatic Reform has employed a participatory process to enable fishing communities to articulate their interests to higher levels of government (Pye-Smith and Feyerabend, 1994).

The Philippine Local Government Code provides opportunities for citizens' organizations to partake in local administration. For instance, the Batman project facilitates participatory development planning and budgeting within *barangays*—the lowest unit of governance in the Philippines—by organizing training programs for officials at the grassroots level. The project has the potential to "strengthen local communities and increase their capability to negotiate their economic and political relations with the larger society" (Rocamora, 2000). This is a unique case of people–government reciprocity, with mutual support of each other's interests. Through the new local government structures people can further their interests and hold local-level public officials accountable for their decisions and actions (Racelis, 1994).

The movement for democracy and subsequent governmental changes in Indonesia have opened up the political space for the people to articulate their demands in a more fulfilling way. Their influence on local governance has been significant, with more openness and greater intensity among regional governments to positively respond to these demands and serve the interests of the people even though the new decentralization laws may not be explicit about citizen participation in development or creating the structures to aid in the local decision-making process. There are indications of some LGUs adopting more "customer-oriented" approaches in responding to demands for services and being open to public discussions about their performance. The provision for choosing the head of an LGU by a locally elected council and allowing local approval of budgets is a step forward in local self-governance and its off shoot—accountability (Alm and Bahl, 1999:15). For their part, regional councils have discovered greater benefits in "cooperating and sharing information with one another and with provincial governments to solve a variety of shared problems" (Asia Foundation, 2002).

The Indonesian government's Integrated Swamp Development Program adopts a participatory approach in the design and implementation of an on-farming water management system (van den Eelaart, 2002). In a similar vein, the strategy of the government to provide low-cost housing to low-income people involves the active participation of the community being served. It has resulted in the formation of people-based organizations in several villages working for community development, beyond managing low-cost housing schemes (UN-Habitat, 1999).

To what extent participation will be achievable under the new decentralization scheme in Indonesia nonetheless remains a big question, for the notion is too narrowly defined and there is a latent irrational bureaucratic fear and skepticism about involving the people in the task of development (GTZ Advisory Team, 1997).

Citizen participation in local affairs or development activities in rural Thailand was virtually an unknown element in the past. Now there is more appreciation of making the people, their organizations, and NGO stakeholders in the process of managing development. The functions of environmental management have been delegated to provincial and local authorities, and the government promotes the idea of NGO–public interaction in environmental matters (Government of Thailand, 1992). The country's constitution also mentions involving the people both in creating sustainable development initiatives and in monitoring, controlling, and overseeing the performance of local bodies (Sopchokchai, 2001), but in practice the existing structures for participation are too complex and the procedures too inflexible for people to meaningfully contribute to local administration, let alone provide essential inputs to development planning and implementation.

As is the case in many other Asian countries, citizen participation in Thailand is confined to voting in periodic elections, resorting to street protests, and signing petitions against adverse governmental action. The Constitution may be explicit in providing to the people the opportunity to lodge formal complaints against local government failures, initiate impeachment procedures against local officials, and propose new sets of community regulations, but these involve a very cumbersome and protracted process that is beyond the time, patience, and resources of ordinary people. They may, however, put collective pressure on their respective LGUs, in collaboration with their counterparts, to take their cause to the higher levels of government. At the local level the people interact with the bureaucracy, which provides the basic services channeled by line ministries, rather than with their elected representatives, who have very little authority to make decisions and approve development plans (Daniel, 2001: 25–32).

## THE NGO CONNECTION IN PARTICIPATORY DEVELOPMENT

In Asia, NGOs have been involved in a range of development activities, such as poverty alleviation, small-scale community development projects, empowerment and capacity building, technical innovation, education and health delivery systems, and disaster relief. Many of the large NGOs began as charitable or relief organizations, but with time they transformed themselves into development organizations (Holloway, 1989: 219). The NGOs have entered the development arena to fill in the void created by nonperforming public institutions in meeting citizens' needs and "to contribute to the democratization of the economy, society and polity" (Uphoff, 1993: 618). The failure of governments in the past to advance the interests of the most disadvantaged people in rural Asia (Narayan et al., 2000) have contributed to the burgeoning of NGOs, which are relied upon by the people and the international donor community, as alternatives to public development agencies or as surrogates for governmental welfare providers.

Not surprisingly, participatory development has been advanced by NGOs, many of which work with the financial support of the IDC, either under contract or in partnership with them. The participatory methods they use are often IDC creations, which are tested in real-life situations by NGOs, occasionally with some form of institutional partnership with public organizations or interactions with occupational groups, such as farmers' associations. A large number of participatory development projects have been in operation in Asia.

The primary purpose of rural NGOs is to accelerate the process of alleviating poverty and empowering the poor. Their projects affect a significant number of the population, especially the disadvantaged and the marginalized living in abject poverty and deplorable social conditions. They seek to achieve this goal through their interventions in a host of activities in such areas as microfinancing, institution building, social mobilization, agriculture, poultry and livestock, fisheries, social forestry, cottage industries, small-scale irrigation, health, and education. Projects are by and large participatory in nature, especially in terms of their long-term sustainability and their promotion of self-reliance among beneficiaries by enabling them to manage their own programs. Empowerment of the poor is activated by creating in them the awareness to identify the social and economic problems that challenge them; NGOs create the appropriate mechanisms to resolve them by helping the people form their own self-help groups.

In social forestry, participation has provided useful results. Forest protection committees in India have shown an exceptional ability in devising innovative ways of protecting their forests from degradation. Group solidarity has enabled villagers to learn the skills to negotiate their demands with the government forest department (World Bank, 1996: 53–59). The power of solidarity has also been proved in other places, such as the Philippines, Nepal, and Bangladesh, in which community-managed irrigation schemes have increased agricultural yields vis-à-vis schemes entirely managed by public agencies (de los Reyes and Jopillo, 1988; Ostrom, 1994; Nathan and Kumar, 2001). The communal irrigation projects in the Philippines also demonstrated the keenness of primary stakeholders in providing inputs and in running their own small-scale irrigations systems (World Bank, 1996: 109–115). Evidence from Indonesia suggests that user preferences in water resource management can be matched only if users are directly associated in the design and selection of water service delivery projects (Isham and Kahkonen, 1999).

There are indications, however, that a state–NGO–people nexus in forestry management schemes can often tilt toward the interests of the rural elites, as is evident in India (Kumar, 2002). Often ostensible participatory development can make a mockery of participation by excluding women (Agarwal, 2001). The state apparatus may also capriciously control such schemes and obviate citizens' interests in social forestry (Pattnaik and Dutta, 1997). In the case of Nepal, common property institutions in social forestry have served their purposes in protecting forests in spite of the ambiguity of such commonality in poverty alleviation (Chakraborty, 2001). Failing motivation among forest users to be involved in forest management may have to be offset by state institutions by meeting certain conditions of participation, as evidenced in India (Lise, 2000). Similarly, indications from watershed projects in India hint that systematic efforts must be made to match the technical skills of development agents with indigenous skills if the desired results are to be achieved (Datta and Virgo, 1998). An ambiguous legal framework and an undue emphasis on economic variables rather than on managerial and capacity problems have often caused obstacles to creating a conducive participative environment in Indonesian fisheries projects (Novaczek et al., 2001).

The government–NGO partnership is increasingly becoming an element in governance in Asia and has replaced the old antagonism that existed between the two. Both entities now realize the gains genuine collaboration can bring in development. Again in social forestry, there are many examples of state–NGO collaboration. Forest user groups, created with the help of government departments, manage forest resources and participate in consultations with public administrators in the "needs and opportunities for management of local forest resources" (World Bank, 1998b: 2). Popular consultation through round tables to formulate and monitor holistic development indicators has been the primary aim of the Sustainable Penang Inititaive (SPI) in Malaysia. The project was conceived by citizens and supported by the state government. The SPI is an excellent example of embedding the notion of popular participation in development planning by incorporating a mechanism that created opportunities for participants to prioritize important local issues (SERI, 1999). The Kerala (India) model of development exhibits the potential benefits that can be gained from the close collaboration among the state, local government, and civil society represented by NGOs (Veron, 2001).

The Palli Karma Sahayak Foundation (PKSF) in Bangladesh provides another example of effective government–NGO collaboration. Designed to support poverty alleviation, PKSF provides interest-free loans to "partner organizations" (the NGOs) to generate income and employment opportunities for the poor. It also provides institutional development services to smaller NGOs. A PKSF is basically an autonomous, community-driven development program operating with political, administrative, and financial flexibility, and with a fair degree of transparency (World Bank, undated-b). This has helped construct an effective synergy among the organization, the government, and the partner NGOs, with positive implications for participatory development.

The NGOs in the Philippines provided significant input in the framing of the Local Government Code and later contributed to its implementation by partaking in pre- and postreform dialogues with policy makers in government and implementing agencies. They have also forged an effective relationship with LGU associations by their active presence in local development councils and health and school boards. Enunciated in the LGC, NGO participation has been a boon for local governance and made the most of by local councils not only in connecting the broad masses of the people with development initiatives and in administering community affairs, but also in consolidating the decentralization reforms and in capacity building at the grassroots level (Tapales et al., 1996; Brillantes, 1998).

## CONCLUDING COMMENTS

In the newly democratizing polities in Asia, decentralized governance is still embryonic and feeling its way into societal, economic, and political structures. Both domestic demands and external compulsions have influenced governments to transform their centralized governmental machinery into more responsive, accountable, efficient, and effective systems by creating mechanisms to inculcate citizen participation either directly or through people's association and NGOs. New local government structures have been either installed, providing for representative bodies to manage local administration and development, or are in the process of being introduced. In general, the legitimacy of these changes derives from constitutional and legislative backing and the integration of the local government framework within the national development system as well as the support stemming from the general public, civil society, and the international development community.

The Asian countries have produced a mixed bag of decentralization measures. India and the Philippines provide two excellent examples of political decentralization in recent times, while in most other Asian NDPs, it has been applied only partially. During military or pseudo-democratic rule in Pakistan, Bangladesh, Indonesia, Thailand, and the Philippines, the general trend was to keep the local government system within the fold of a centralized governmental structure by deconcentrating functions rather than having local affairs managed by representative bodies with significant political powers. Delegation of administrative authority within line ministries has not been uncommon in the Asian NDPs. Some degree of bureaucratic discretion has been permitted to deal with specific problems in the field, but again such an application has been largely restrained by rigid regulations. Recent decentralization reforms in Asia has been primarily concerned with devolution, and constitutional and other legal changes that have been introduced in recent times essentially address this issue. In some countries the intensity of devolution has been high, while in others a more circumspect posture has been adopted. Even where political decentralization has not taken place to the extent desired by advocates of democracy, measures have been instituted to augment the decision-making capacity of local government units (LGUs) to manage local funds they themselves raise or receive from the central government.

Privatization in local administration is still suspect in most of Asia, although much has happened in the national sphere. Contracting out is perhaps the only instrument used by LGUs to deliver some of the services to the community. Self-management, however, has been popular in social forestry, fisheries, and watershed management, and has been partially applied in poverty alleviation schemes. Deregulation—or rather the moderation of rules—has facilitated the burgeoning of NGO activities in rural Asia, however. Government failure to deliver efficient services in certain sectors has pushed NGOs to take over or to enter into effective partnership with public agencies. Indeed, in Asia, NGOs rather than public institutions have been the pivot around which participatory development initiatives have been organized.

The evidence from Asia on the effect of decentralization is too sketchy to enable us to make a reasoned evaluation. It is also too early to evaluate the performance of the several schemes covered in this study, yet the local government systems currently at work have all the essential attributes to improve the delivery of public service at the ground level, efficiently manage public resources, and increase popular participation. The efficacy of the decentralization measures, however, impinges upon the sorts of intergovernmental relations that have crystallized or are emerging. This is especially critical in unitary political systems in which there is no intermediate governmental layer to filter the powerful influences of the central government. In nonfederal systems, therefore, center–local relations require precise and definite delineation of jurisdictions in political, administrative, and fiscal terms to obviate the central government's intrusion into local affairs. Where the local government system is multitiered, the nature of the formal relationship among LGUs both vertically and horizontally calls for defined regulations; otherwise functional and program duplication, overlap, or even conflicts might result. Similarly, lateral interaction between LGUs and NGOs must be permitted under a regulatory regime that is flexible but not oblivious to the salience of public needs. Overall, concrete instruments to keep local government bodies under constant public scrutiny are essential to uphold the tenets of democratic governance.

In the past under undemocratic rule in most of Asia, opportunities for citizen participation in government and development were few. The distance between state and society was too large to permit the common people to have any input in the decision-making process that had ramifications for their well-being. Now, if decentralization is given a fair chance to work, participation will occur and enhance the quality of development. It would develop a deep commitment among primary and secondary stakeholders realized through a sense of belonging. Ownership of development projects causes people to alter their mind-sets and further stimulates them to spontaneously take on greater responsibilities in improving their lots. Genuine participation brings change in social relations and the pattern of interaction among stakeholders in development. Local development through unbound participation, however, runs the risk of being manipulated by powerful social elites, a situation that is not uncommon in Asian societies, or in squandering resources on a plethora of small projects. Caution should thus be applied in keeping local development within manageable proportions so as to make the best use of resources—human, financial, infrastructure, and ideational.

Decentralization is not a cure-all for generating and dispensing the fruits of development to the people, nor is it the remedy for the enduring state–society, rich–poor, or elite–citizen hiatus. The success of decentralization in Asia would depend on a sense of common purpose for the public good, genuine political commitment and administrative backing, an effective public–private collaboration, state–civil society interaction, and reconciliation of conflicting forces, such as globalization vs. localization and marketization vs. state intervention. In all these, ordinary people must be liberated from poverty, discrimination, and social and economic inequality; they must be empowered and given a voice to emerge the ultimate winner.

## NOTES

1. See Haque (1999) for an excellent discussion of various critiques of development theories.
2. The United States Agency for International Development (USAID) provides a "customer" focus, while the World Bank views the participatory process as involving "stakeholders"; namely, elected and appointed officials, specific target groups, and NGOs, as well as its own

officials, who influence and share control (Cornwall 2000: 35). Like the World Bank, the British Department for International Development (DFID), talks of stakeholders, but suggests different participatory roles for each in the decision-making process, mainly in activities pertaining to aid the organization provides (ODA, 1995). The Organisation for Economic Cooperation and Development (OECD) considers participation as "a relation based on partnership with government" (OECD, 2001: 12), while the Swedish International Development Agency (SIDA) takes a much broader view of participation and links it to democracy, social equality, and environmental protection (Rudqvist, cited in Cornwall, 2000: 38–39).

3.  These include *zilla parishads* at the district level (ZP), *panchayat samities* at the block or intermediate level (PS), and gram *panchayat* at the village level (GP).

4.  These areas are: defense, foreign affairs, monetary and fiscal management, and justice administration. (See Articles 7, 9 and 11 of Law 22/99.)

## REFERENCES

Adams, J., Rietbergen-McCracken, J. (1994). Participatory development: Getting the key players involved. Fin. Dev. 31(3):36–37.

Agarwal, B. (2001). Participatory exclusions, community forestry, and gender: An analysis for South Asia and a conceptual framework. World Dev. 29(10):1623–1648.

Ahmad, E., Hofman, B. (2000). Indonesia; Decentralization Opportunities and Risks. Jakarta: IMF and World Bank.

Alm, J., Bahl, R. (1999). Decentralization in Indonesia: Prospects and problems. unpublished paper. Atlanta: Department of Economics, Georgia State University.

Alsop, R. J., Anirudh, K., Sjoblom, D. (2000). Are Gram Panchayats Inclusive? Report of a Study Conducted in Rajasthan and Madhya Pradesh. Washington, DC: World Bank.

Ananthpur, K., Prasad, G. (2000). Governance and Media: Use of Radio in Disseminating Information on Participatory Governance in Mysore District. Brighton, India: Institute of Development Studies.

Asia Foundation. (2002). 1st Indonesia Rapid Decentralization Appraisal (IRDA). Jakarta: Decentralization and Local Governance Program, Asia Foundation.

Bahl, R. (2001). An Overview of decentralization in Indonesia. IRIS/USINDO paper, http://www.inform.umd.edu/IRIS/IRIS/.

Bandyopadhyay, D. (1997). People's participation in planning: Kerala experiment. Ec. Polit. Wkly. 32(39):2450–2454.

Bhagawati, J. (1995). The new thinking on development. J. Dem. 6(4):50–64.

Brillantes, A. B. Jr. (1998). Five-Year Assessment of the Implementation of Devolution in the Local Government Code. Manila: Local Government Academy, Department of the Interior and Local Government.

Brillantes, A. B. Jr. (1999). Decentralization, devolution and development in the Philippines. UMP-Asia occasional paper 44. New York: United Nations, Urban Management Programme.

Chakraborty, R. N. (2001). Stability and outcomes of common property institutions in forestry: Evidence from the Terai region of Nepal. Ecol. Ec. 36(2):341–353.

Chambers, R. (1983). Rural Development—Putting the Last First. New York: Addison-Wesley.

Chowdhury, A., Islam, I. (1993). The Newly Industrialising Economies of East Asia. London: Routledge.

Clayton, A., Oakley, P., Pratt, B. (1997). Empowering People: A Guide to Participation. Oxford: INTRAC.

Commonwealth Foundation. (1999). Citizens and Governance: Civil Society in the New Millennium. London: Commonwealth Foundation.

Cornwall, A. (2000). Beneficiary, customer, citizen: Perspectives on participation for poverty reduction. SIDA Stud 2.

Crook, R. C., Manor, J. (1998). Democracy and Decentralization in South Asia and West Africa: Participation, Accountability and Performance. London: Cambridge University Press.

DAC (Expert Group on Aid Evaluation). (1997). Evaluation of Programs Promoting Participatory Development and Good Governance: Synthesis Report. Paris: OECD.

Daniel, A., (2001). Democracy, Development and Decentralization in Provincial Thailand. Surrey, UK: Curzon.

Das, A. (1999). Experience with Panchayat Law: The 73rd Constitutional Amendment Act and rights of women. Paper presented to a conference organized by the Center for Development Research, Bonn, Tufts University, Boston, and the University of Hohenheim, Stuttgart, Germany, Aug. 26–27.

Datta, S. K., Virgo, K. J. (1998). Towards sustainable watershed development through peoples participation: Lessons from the lesser Himalaya, Uttar Pradesh, India. Mountain Res. Dev. 18(3):213–233.

de los Reyes, R., Jopillo, S. (1988). The impact of participation: An evaluation of the NIA's Communal Irrigation Programme. In: Korten, F., Siy, R. Jr., eds. Transforming a Bureaucracy—The Experience of the Philippine National Irrigation Administration. Bloomfield, CT: Kumarian.

DFID. (2000). Human Rights for Poor People. London: Department for International Development.

Djalal, D. (Dec. 2002). Indonesia: A law unto themsleves. Far East. Ec. Rev. 6.

Eade, D. (2000). Development, NGOs & Civil Society. London: Oxfam.

Ferrazzi, G. (2001). Learning from Decentralization's Implementation: The Philippine Experience and Lessons for Indonesia. Jakarta: German Technical Cooperation.

Fowler, A. (1988). NGOs in Africa: Comparative advantage in relief and micro-development. IDS discussion paper 249. Brighton: Institute of Development Studies.

Gaiha, R. (1995). Poverty, development, and participation in India: A progress report. Asian Surv. 35(9):867–878.

Gonzales, E. M. (2000). Decentralization and political participation in the Philippines: Experiences and issues in societal transformation. Work in Progress Paper. Manila: Institute for Popular Democracy.

Goulet, D. (1992). Development: Creator and destroyer of values. World Dev. 20(3):467–475.

Government of India. (2001). Report of the Working Group on Decentralised Planning & Panchayati Raj Institutions. New Delhi: Ministry of Rural Development.

Government of Indonesia. (1974). Governance at Regional Level. Act 5 of 1974. Jakarta.

Government of Pakistan. (2001). Pakistan: Interim Poverty Reduction Strategy Paper. Islamabad, Pakistan: Finance Division and Planning Commission.

Government of the Philippines. (1991). The Republic Act No 7160. Manila.

Government of the Republic of India. (1992). 73rd Amendment to the Indian Constitution. New Delhi.

Government of the Republic of India. (1996a). The Constitution of the Republic of India. New Delhi.

Government of the Republic of India. (1996b). The Provisions of the Panchayats (Extension to the Scheduled Areas) Act, 1996. New Delhi.

Government of Sri Lanka. (2000). An Act to Repeal and Replace the Constitution of the Socialist Republic of Sri Lanka. Colombo; http://www.lacnet.org/srilanka/politics/.

Government of Sri Lanka. (2002). Connecting to Growth: Sri Lanka's Poverty Reduction Strategy. Colombo: Development Forum.

Government of Thailand. (1992). The Environment Act of 1992. Bangkok.

Government of Thailand. (1997). The Constitution of Thailand. Bangkok.

GTZ Advisory Team. (1997). Support for Decentralization Measures: Discussion Paper on Key Issues in Decentralization and Regional Autonomy in Indonesia. Bonn: German Federal Ministry of Economic Cooperation and Development.

Haque, M. S. (1999). Restructuring Development Theories and Policies: A Critical Study. Albany, NY: State University of New York Press.

Hollnsteiner, M. R. (1963). The Dynamics of Power in a Philippine Municipality. Quezon City: University of the Philippines.

Holloway, R. (1989). Afterward where to next? Governments, NGO and rural development practitioners. In: Holloway, R, ed., Government, NGOs and the Rural Poor in Asia Doing Development. London: Earthscan.

Hull, T. H. (1999). Striking a most striking balance: The implications of Otonomi Daerah for the planning and implementation of development cooperation projects. final report. Canberra: Demography Program, RSSS, ANU.

Huque, A. S. (1986). The illusions of decentralization: Local administration in Bangladesh. Internat. Rev. Admin. Sci. 52(10):79–95.

Hyden, G. (1997). Civil society, social capital and development: Dissection of a complex discourse. Stud. Compar. Internat. Dev. 32(7):3–30.

ILO. (1978). Structure and Functions of Rural Workers' Organization: Participation of the Rural Poor in Development. Geneva: International Labour Organisation.

Ingham, B., Kalam, A. K. M. (1992). Decentralization and development: Theory and evidence from Bangladesh. Pub. Admin. Dev. 12:373–385.

Isham, J., Kahkonen, S. (1999). What determines the effectiveness of community-based water projects? Evidence from Central Java, Indonesia on Demand responsiveness, service rules, and social capital, mimeo. College Park: University of Maryland.

Islam, N. (2002). Local level governance: Devolution and democracy in Pakistan. Workshop on Democratization, April 18–20, University of British Columbia, Vancouver.

Jafri, A. B. S. (Dec. 20, 1999). Towards grassroots democracy. Dawn (Internet ed.).

Johnston, B. F., Clark, W. C. (1982). Redesigning Rural Development: A Strategic Perspective. Baltimore: John Hopkins University Press.

Khan, M. M., Zafarullah, H. (1981). Innovations in village government in Bangladesh. Asian Prof. 9:447–453.

Korten, D. C. (1980). Community organization and rural development: A learning process approach. Pub. Admin. Rev. 40(5):480–511.

Krishnakumar, R. (2000). Democratic decentralisation: A people's movement. Frontline 17(2) (Internet ed).

Kumar, S. (2002). Does "participation" in common pool resource management help the poor? A social cost-benefit analysis of joint forest management in Jharkhand, India. World Dev. 30(5):763–782.

Lise, W. (2000). Factors influencing people's participation in forest management in India. Ecol. Ec. 34(3):379–392.

Love, A. R. (1991). Participatory development and democracy. OECD Obs. 173:4–6.

Ma, J., Hofman, B. (2000). Indonesia's decentralization after the crisis. Prem Notes 43. Washington, DC: World Bank.

Maddick, H. (1963). Democracy, Decentralization and Development. New Delhi: Asia Publishing House.

McCarthy, F. (1993). Deentralization and regime politics in Bangladesh during the Ershad regime. J. Soc. Stud. 61:102–130.

Migdal, J. (1988). Strong Societies and Weak States: State–Society Relations and State Capabilities in the Third World. Princeton, NJ: Princeton University Press.

Mistal, T. (1996). Decentralization: The Philippine experience. In: Logodef, ed. Reform of Centralized Administration Structures in Southeast Asia. Manila: Local Government Centre and Konrad Adenauer Foundation.

Narayan, D., Chambers, R., Shah, M. K., Petesch, P. (2000). Voices of the Poor: Crying Out for Change. Washington, DC: World Bank.

Nathan, D., Kumar, D. (2001). Community fisheries for poverty alleviation. In: Kumar, D., ed. Proceedings of the Network of Aquaculture Centres in Asia-Pacific (NACA) Workshop. Rome: FAO.

Nelson, M. H. (2001). Thailand: Problems with decentralization. International Conference on Building Institutional Capacity in Asia. Jakarta, 12, March.

Novaczek, I., Sopacua, J., Harkes, I. (2001). Fisheries management in Central Maluku, Indonesia, 1997–98. Mar. Policy 25(3):239–249.

Oates, W. (1972). Fiscal Federalism. New York: Harcourt Brace Jovanovich.

ODA. (1995). Note on Enhancing Stakeholder Participation in Aid Activities. London: Overseas Development Agency.

OECD. (2001). Citizens as Partners: Information, Consultation and Public Participation in Policy-Making. Paris: Organization for Economic Cooperation and Development.

Ostrom, E. (1994). Neither Market nor State: Governance of Common Pool Resources in the Twenty-First Century. lecture series no. 2. Washington, DC: International Food Policy Research Institute.

Pakistan, N. B. R. (2002a). Guidelines for Community Boards. Islamabad: National Reconstruction Bureau.

Pakistan, N. B. R. (2002b). Guidelines for Monotoring Committees. Islamabad: National Reconstruction Bureau.

Panayotou, T. (1994). Economic Instruments for Environmental Management and Sustainable Development. Environmental Economics Paper Vol. 16. Geneva: UNEP.

Pattnaik, B. K., Dutta, S. (1997). JFM in South-West Bengal—A study in participatory development. Ec. Polit. Wkly. 32(50):3225–3232.

Peter, E. (1996). Government action, social capital and development: Reviewing the evidence on synergy. World Dev. 24(6):1119–1132.

Putman, R. (1995). Bowling alone: America's declining social capital. J. Dem. 6(1):65–78.

Pye-Smith, C., Feyerabend, G. B. (1994). The Wealth of Communities: Stories of Success in Environmental Management. London: Earthscan.

Racelis, M. (April–May 1994). POs, NGOs and civil society: From the fringes to the maintream. Intersect.

Rahman, H. (Feb. 16, 2000). Revolution through devolution. Dawn (Internet ed.).

Ranis, G., Stewart, F. (1994). Decentralization in Indonesia. Bull. Indonesian Ec.Stud. 30(3): 41–72.

Randall, V., Theobold, R. (1985). Political Change and Underdevelopment: A Critical Introduction to Third World Politics. Durham, NC: Duke University Press.

Rocamora, J. (2000). The left in the Philippines: Learning from the people, learning from each other. speech given in Colombo, Sri Lanka, March 25, www.tni.org/archives/rocamora/colombo.htm.

Rondinelli, D. (1983). Implementing decentralization programmes in Asia: A comparative analysis. Pub. Admin. Dev. 3:181–207.

Rondinelli, D. (1999). Market-supporting governance in an era of economic globalization: Challenges for governments in developing countries. Politics Admin. Change 31:1–27.

Rondinelli, D. A., Nellis, J. R., Cheema, G. S. (1983). Decentralization in developing countries: A review of recent experience. World Bank Staff Working Papers. Vol. 581. Washington, DC: World Bank.

Rood, S. (2000). Decentralization, democracy, and development. In: Timberman, D. G., ed. The Philippines: New Directions in Domestic Policy and Foreign Relations. New York: Asia Society.

Self, P. (1985). Political Theories of Modern Government: Its Role and Reform. Sydney: Allen & Unwin.

Sen, A. (1999). Development as Freedom. New York: Oxford University Press.

SERI. (1999). Penang People's Report. Penang, Malaysia: Socio-Economic & Environmental Research Institute.

Sopchokchai, O. (2001). Good Local Governance and Anti-Corruption through People's Participation: A Case of Thailand. Bangkok: Civil Service Commission.

Sosema, G. C. Jr. (2001). Ten years of local government code. Miscellany 2(1):8–16.

Stiefel, M., Wolfe, M. (1994). A Voice for the Excluded: Popular Participation in Development: Utopia or Necessity? London: Zed.

Streeten, P. P. (1997). Thinking about Development. Cambridge: Cambridge University Press.

Tambunan, M. (2000). Indonesia's new challenges and opportunities: Blueprint for reform after the economic crisis. East Asia Internat. Q. 18:2.

Tandon, R. (1982). A critic of monopolistic research. In: Hall, B. et al., eds. Creating Knowledge: A Monopoly? Participatory Research in Development. New Delhi: PRIA, pp. 79–84.

Tapales, P., Perfecto, P. L., Joaquin Ma, E. T. (1996). Modern Management in Philippine Local Government. Manila: Local Government Center and German Foundation for International Development.

Thomas, A. (1992). Non-governmental organizations and the limits to empowerment. In: Wuyts, M., et al., ed. Development Policy and Public Action. Oxford: Oxford University Press, pp. 117–146.

Timberman, D. (1991). A Changeless Land: Continuity and Change in Philippine Politics. Armonk, NY: Sharpe.

Tommasi, M., Weischelbaum, F. (1999). A Principal-Agent Building Block for the Study of Decentralization and Integration. Cambridge, MA: Harvard University.

Turner, M., Hulme, D. (1997). Governance, Administration and Development: Making the State Work. London: Macmillan.

Uggla, H. A. F. (1996). Making civil society work, promoting democratic development: What can states and donors do? World Dev. 24(10):1621–1639.

UNDP. (1993). Human Development Report 1993. New York: United Nations Development Program.

UNDP. (1996). Human Development Report 1996. New York: United Nations Development Program.

UNDP. (1998). Empowering People: A Guidebook to Participation. New York: CSOPP.

UNDP. (2002). Human Development Report, 2002. New York: United Nations Development Program.

UNESCAP. (2002). Sri Lanka country paper. Local Government in Asia and the Pacific: A Comparative Study. E:\Decent Cases Asia\Local Government in Asia and the Pacific - Sri Lanka.htm.

UN-Habitat. (1999). Submission to the Best Practices Initiative of the Habitat II Conference. Nairobi: United Nations Settlements Programme.

United Nations. (1962). Decentralisation for National and Local Development. New York: United Nations.

Uphoff, N. (1993). Grassroots organizations and NGOs in rural development: opportunities with diminishing states and expanding markets. World Dev. 21(4):607–622.

van den Eelaart, A. (2002). Swamp development in Indonesia. www.eelaart.com.

Veron, R. (2001). The "new" Kerala model: Lessons for sustainable development. World Dev. 29(4):601–617.

Weingast, B. (1995). The economic role of political institutions: Federalism, markets and economic development. J. Law Ec. Org. 11:1–31.

Westergaard, K. (2000). Decentralization in Bangladesh: Local government and NGOs. Colloquium on Decentralization and Development. New Haven: Yale University.

Wolfensohn, J. D. (1999). A proposal for a comprehensive development framework. Washington, DC: World Bank, http://www.worldbank.org/cdf/cdf-text.htm.

Wood, G. (1977). Rural development and the post-colonial state. Dev. Change 8(3):307–323.

Wood, G. (1984). State intervention and bureaucratic reproduction: Comparative thoughts. Dev. Change 15(1):23–41.

Wood, G. (1992). Introduction. In: Kramsjo, B., Woods, G., eds. Breaking the Chains: Collective Action for Social Justice among the Rural Poor in Bangladesh. Dhaka: UPL.

World Bank. (1994a). The World Bank and Participation. Washington, DC: World Bank.

World Bank. (1994b). Governance: The World Bank's Experience. Washington, DC: World Bank.

World Bank. (1996). World Development Report 1996. Washington, DC: World Bank.

World Bank. (1998a). Pakistan: A Framework for Civil Service Reform in Pakistan. report no. 18386-Pak. Washington, D.C.: World Bank.

World Bank. (1998b). Saving Nepal's Forests: The Promise of Community Management. Washington, DC: World Bank.

World Bank. (2000a). World Development Report 2000. Washington, DC: World Bank.

World Bank. (2000b). Overview of Rural Decentralization in India. Vol. 1. New Delhi: World Bank.

World Bank. (2000c). Sri Lanka: Recapturing Missed Opportunities. report no. 20430-CE. Washington, DC: World Bank.

World Bank. (2001a). Participation in Development Assistance. OED Precis 209.

World Bank. (2001b). Decentralization and governance: Does decentralization improve public service delivery? Prem Notes 55.

World Bank. (2001c). Pakistan's Reform Program: Progress and Prospects Report. Washington, DC: World Bank.

World Bank. (2002). Pakistan: Development Policy Review, A New Dawn? report no. 23916-Pak. Washington, DC: World Bank.

World Bank. (undated-a); India: Water sector reform in Andhra Pradesh. www.worldbank.org/participation/web/webfiles/indiawater.htm.

World Bank. (undated-b); Anchoring programs with autonomous funds and existing government agencies. issue paper. www1.worldbank.org/.

Zafarullah, H. (1996). Dilemmas of local level planning. Contemp. So. Asia 5(1):47–65.

Zafarullah, H. (1997). Local government reform and accountability in Bangladesh:The continuing search for legitimacy and performance. Reg. Dev. Dialogue 18(2):37–56.

# 38

## Equity and Efficiency in International Environmental Agreements
### A Case Study of the Kyoto Protocol

**KRISTEN SHEERAN**

*St. Mary's College of Maryland, St. Mary's City, Maryland, U.S.A.*

## INTRODUCTION

Averting climate change is—and will remain—a priority for the global community throughout the twenty-first century. Like the many global public goods that have revived interest in the nature of international cooperation in recent years—the control of infectious disease, international financial stability, biodiversity, and knowledge, just to name a few—mitigating climate change will yield far-reaching consequences for developed and developing countries alike. It can be argued that the concessions made to developing countries under the current climate control framework, the Kyoto Protocol, sacrifice efficiency in the pursuit of equity. Consequently the Kyoto Protocol fails to elicit the level of international cooperation necessary to stabilize greenhouse gas emissions at levels sufficient for preventing catastrophic climate change.

Whether or not the Kyoto framework can be modified or a whole new approach to climate control is warranted remains to be seen. It is evident, though, that successful mitigation of climate change will require rethinking the relationship between equity and efficiency in mitigating climate change. The conclusions that can be drawn from the case of climate change can better inform international negotiations over the provision of other global public goods, particularly when equity for developing countries is a priority.

This chapter develops a framework for understanding why the participation of developing countries in climate control efforts is necessary for efficiency. Al-

675

ternative approaches to climate control that can achieve both efficiency and fairness for developing countries are then explored, including paying developing countries for the climate control benefits provided by their forests. Because the issues surrounding climate change offer a complex backdrop for an analysis of equity and efficiency, an introduction to climate change and the Kyoto Protocol is first provided.

## CLIMATE CHANGE

Climate change refers to a change in the Earth's climate, in excess of natural climate variability, that is attributed directly or indirectly to human-induced changes to the atmosphere's composition (1). Atmospheric concentrations of carbon dioxide and other greenhouse gases warm the Earth's surface by trapping a portion of the sun's outgoing energy reflected by the Earth. Global warming is the result of the intensification of this "greenhouse effect." Scientists predict that climate change could result in a rise in sea levels and flooding, increased incidences of disease, drought, and other weather-related catastrophes, changes in agricultural productivity, and the further impairment of critical ecosystem functions.

Evidence that a warming trend has already begun surrounds us. In its most recent report, the Intergovernmental Panel on Climate Change (IPCC) reports that global surface temperatures have been rising for the past 150 years (2). During the twentieth century alone, the average global surface temperature increased by .6 Celsius degrees, a significantly higher increase than had previously been predicted. In the Northern Hemisphere, warming during the twentieth century was more extensive than during any previous century. The 1990s was the warmest decade and 1998 the warmest year since scientists began tracking temperatures in 1861. The projected rate of warming is also cause for alarm, as it is without precedent during the last 10,000 years. Between 1990 and 2100, the global average surface temperature is predicted to increase by 1.4 to 5.8 Celsius degrees (IPCC, 2001).

According to the IPCC, strong evidence now suggests that most of the observed warming over the past fifty years is anthropogenic in origin (IPCC, 2001). The atmospheric concentration of carbon dioxide has increased by 31% since 1750, the start of the modern industrial age. Roughly 75% of the anthropogenic emissions of carbon dioxide (hereafter referred to as carbon emissions) during the last twenty years is due to burning of fossil fuels for energy. The remaining 25% is a result of land use change, especially deforestation. Functioning as carbon sinks, forests play a critical role in the global carbon cycle. Forests sequester carbon emissions from the atmosphere and store carbon long-term in vegetation and soils.

When forest land is converted to alternative use, however, much if not all of the stored carbon is rereleased into the atmosphere. Moreover, depending upon what use is made of the forest land (e.g., whether it is paved over, reforested, or converted to agricultural use), additional carbon uptake may cease or decline. Despite the very high rates of deforestation that prevailed throughout the 1990s, particularly in the tropics, it is very likely that worldwide carbon sequestration exceeded carbon release from deforestation. If current rates of deforestation worldwide continue, however, forests will no longer be able to function as net carbon sinks (IPCC, 2001).

## THE KYOTO PROTOCOL

Attempts to forge international cooperation on mitigating climate change began in
·1992 with the United Nation's Framework Convention on Climate Change
(UNFCC) in Rio de Janeiro, Brazil. At that time, the participating industrialized
countries agreed to voluntarily reduce their greenhouse gas emissions. The need to
strengthen the UNFCC soon became evident, however, as most of the industrialized
countries failed to meet their voluntary targets and emissions in some countries
actually increased (3). In 1997, more than 150 countries convened in Kyoto, Japan, to
negotiate binding emissions quotas. The product of those negotiations, the Kyoto
Protocol, remains the prevailing international agreement on combating climate
change to date.

The Kyoto Protocol establishes binding emissions limits for industrialized
countries and a range of mechanisms to promote cost-effective compliance. Following
the framework of the UNFCC, the Kyoto Protocol differentiates between two groups
of countries worldwide—Annex I countries, which are subject to emissions limits, and
non-Annex I countries, which have no binding commitments. The list of Annex I
countries includes thirty-nine industrialized countries and countries with economies in
transition.

Although individual country commitments vary, emissions targets for Annex I
countries average 5.2% below 1990 levels during the commitment period (2008–
2012). For example, targets for the European Union, United States, Japan, and the
Russian Federation are 8%, 7.5%, 6%, and 0%, respectively (4).

Policy makers confronted three challenges in designing the Kyoto Protocol.
First, in keeping with the original UNFCC mandate, they were to establish
emissions targets compatible with stabilizing greenhouse gas concentrations in the
atmosphere at levels consistent with preventing catastrophic human-induced climate
change. Second, to improve efficiency and increase the willingness of countries to
participate, policy makers needed to design mechanisms to minimize the costs of
meeting those targets. Finally, to address the historical imbalance in greenhouse gas
production and differences in countries' abilities to pay for abatement, policy
makers had to distribute the costs of preventing climate change equitably across
countries.

The Kyoto Protocol provides countries with three mechanisms for minimizing
the costs of meeting their emissions targets. First, the Kyoto Protocol allows for
international emissions trading between Annex I countries. Emissions trading is key
to an efficient climate treaty because it allows reductions to take place where
abatement costs are lowest rather than requiring each country to meet its target
through domestic measures alone. The commodities to be exchanged through
emissions trading are "emissions credits." A country produces emissions credits
for sale by reducing emissions beyond their required target. A country that buys
emissions credits will apply those credits toward its own commitment, thereby
economizing on abatement at home.

Although emissions trading can decrease the total cost of reducing emissions
worldwide, it may benefit some countries more than others. To a great extent a
country's emissions cap will determine whether it becomes a net buyer or seller of
emissions credits. In turn, this affects income redistribution between countries
under the treaty. For example, the emissions cap for the Russian Federation is

0% below 1990 levels. An unanticipated decline in industrial emissions in Russia throughout the 1990s, however, may generate a surplus of emissions credits to sell in the international market. Prior to withdrawing from the Kyoto Protocol, the United States had indicated its intent to meet most of its emission targets by purchasing emissions credits abroad. The extent of U.S. demand for emissions credits could have driven up the price of emissions credits, precluding many smaller countries from the market. Furthermore, by lowering its own abatement costs, the United States would have had less of an incentive to invest in more energy-efficient technologies to begin the long-term transition away from fossil fuels. For precisely these reasons, many countries mounted objections to full-scale emission trading under the Kyoto Protocol. However, lowering abatement costs allows for an increase in global abatement (Figure 1). Critics should have argued instead for an increase in emissions limits corresponding to the decrease in marginal abatement costs facilitated by emissions trading. In any case, as it now stands there are no quantitative limits on the use of emissions trading between Annex I countries under the Kyoto Protocol (5).

Joint implementation (JI) is the second cost-saving mechanism allowed under the Kyoto Protocol. Under JI, Annex I countries receive credit toward their own emissions targets for implementing projects aimed at reducing emissions in another Annex I country. Again, because abatement costs differ across countries, the aim of JI is to lower total abatement costs by concentrating reductions in the Annex I countries, where they cost least. Finally, the Kyoto Protocol's third cost-saving mechanism, the clean development mechanism (CDM), allows Annex I countries to receive emissions credit for financing projects that reduce emissions in developing countries. Clean development mechanism projects can be unilateral, meaning that developing countries can undertake CDM projects in their own countries without an explicit Annex I partner and market the resulting emissions credits themselves. As with emis-

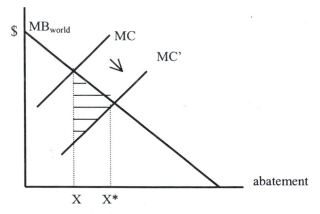

**Figure 1**   Decreasing marginal abatement costs. Initially, optimal abatement occurs at X. If marginal abatement costs decrease from MC to MC', optimal abatement increases from X to X* and generates an efficiency gain equal to the shaded area.

sions trading at this point, no quantitative limits on the use of either JI or CDM credits is specified under the Kyoto Protocol.

A major source of contention in negotiations over the Kyoto Protocol involves the extent to which carbon sequestration by forests and other sinks can be applied toward a country's reduction commitment. The Kyoto Protocol requires Annex I countries to account for "net changes in greenhouse gas emissions by sources and removals by sinks resulting from direct human-induced land-use change and forestry activities, limited to afforestation, reforestation and deforestation since 1990" (Kyoto Protocol, 1997) (6). Only recently have countries reached an agreement as to exactly what sink activities can apply toward emissions targets. Conservation, afforestation, and reforestation within Annex I countries will be eligible for sink credits under the Kyoto Protocol, provided such activities have taken place since 1990. While there is no overall cap on the use of most sinks, limits on sink credits generated from forest conservation have now been established for Annex I countries (7).

A similar controversy surrounds crediting sink activities in developing countries under the CDM. Sink activities under the CDM will be limited to only afforestation and reforestation. Moreover, credits obtained from such projects cannot account for more than 1% of a country's base year emissions. The decision to exclude conservation-based projects from the CDM is in part due to concerns for the *additionality* of emissions reductions. Since forests naturally function as carbon sinks, conservation will have a mitigating impact on global climate change only if it generates carbon sequestration in addition to what would have otherwise have occurred or if it prevents the release of carbon emissions into the atmosphere from forest areas that would have been destroyed. Preserving forest areas that would never have been deforested (i.e., the carbon stored in the forest biomass would never have been released and carbon sequestration would have continued) has no impact on the concentration of carbon dioxide in the atmosphere, in which case substituting conservation for emissions reductions from other sources will not lower atmospheric carbon dioxide concentration.

The Kyoto Protocol is particularly susceptible to the additionality problems posed by forest conservation because absent binding emissions limits for developing countries, there is no independent accounting of net changes in carbon storage and emissions from sink activities in these countries. As Schlamadinger and Marland (2000) explain, under emissions trading or JI, emissions credits created in one Annex I country are subtracted from the assigned amount of another Annex I country in such a way that the total reductions from all countries is unchanged. Under the CDM, when emissions credits created in a developing country are added to the assigned amount of an Annex I country, there is no subsequent subtraction from the assigned amount of developing countries, therefore the total amount of emissions credits allowable worldwide increases. If the credits are granted for activities that fail to generate an additional emissions reduction beyond the status quo or baseline scenario, total emissions worldwide will actually increase (Schlamadinger and Marland, 2000). Under the current Kyoto framework, emissions from deforestation in Annex I countries are counted against their emissions targets. By directly penalizing deforestation, the Kyoto Protocol provides indirect incentives to preserve forests in Annex I countries. Conservation-based CDM projects would have provided the only real incentives for preventing deforestation in developing countries under the Kyoto Protocol.

## EQUITY AND EFFICIENCY IN MITIGATING CLIMATE CHANGE

Concerns for equity motivated a climate control framework in which countries were assigned differentiated responsibilities in recognition of their respective abilities to pay for emissions abatement and their current and historic contributions to the problem of global warming. To minimize the costs of achieving those targets, the Kyoto Protocol included three mechanisms—emissions trading, JI, and the CDM—the purpose of which was to allow emissions reductions to take place in the areas of the world in which they cost the least. Because developing countries were excluded from emissions limits, however, the use of conservation as an option for mitigating climate change in these countries is prohibited. To the extent that conservation offers a cost-effective approach to climate control, excluding conservation options in developing countries may run counter to the Kyoto Protocol's own goal of minimizing abatement costs.

One criticism of the Kyoto Protocol is that it is not likely reduce emissions enough to prevent catastrophic climate change. Emissions are expected to increase at alarming rates in the developing world over the next few decades, particularly in such populous countries as India and China (8). Ratification of the Kyoto Protocol by at least fifty-five countries representing at least 55% of the emissions produced by industrialized countries is required before the treaty can enter into force, therefore if all Annex I countries signed the treaty, at best emissions in industrialized countries would be reduced by an average of 5.2% below 1990 levels. The recent withdrawal of the United States, however, the world's most significant greenhouse gas producer—jeopardizes even this best-case scenario. At worst the Kyoto Protocol will succeed in reducing only 55% of the industrialized world's emissions by 5.2%.

There are thus strong arguments for imposing emissions limits on developing countries for efficiency reasons. The issue remains, *Can imposing emissions limits on developing countries for efficiency reasons be reconciled with equity?* Including developing countries in a climate control treaty would produce an efficiency gain. Depending upon how it was distributed, this could potentially make every country better off, in which case fairness for developing countries could be achieved explicitly rather than implicitly through exclusion from emissions quotas.

There is an efficiency gain generated by including developing countries in a climate control treaty because climate control is a global public good. Carbon emissions are transboundary pollutants that adversely affect all countries (albeit to different extents) via their impact on global climate. Reducing carbon emissions in any one country benefits all countries simultaneously, thus climate control is a classic example of a global public good. Absent an international climate control treaty, countries will fail to provide the optimal levels of global abatement. To understand why, consider that the characteristics of a public good are that it is nonexcludable and nonrivaled in its consumption. Once a public good is provided, it is either impossible or too costly to exclude others from its benefits. Moreover, one's consumption of the public good does not preclude another's.

Public goods give rise to the "free rider" problem; there is no individual incentive to provide public goods if doing so requires paying for the entire cost of its provision while others "ride for free" on the expense. An individual who provides a public good captures only a fraction of the total benefit it generates for others. A rational individual will supply a public good only if the extra benefit *to the individual* from providing another unit of the public good outweighs the extra cost. Since the public good generates external benefits to others in society, the demand for the public good exceeds the willingness of any one individual to pay to provide it.

In the case of climate control, if each country considers only the costs and benefits from its own abatement, it will abate less than is efficient from the perspective of global efficiency. This is why a climate control treaty is necessary to implement the optimal level of global abatement. According to the efficiency criterion, the optimal or efficient level of global abatement maximizes the net social benefit to all countries combined. At the efficient level of global abatement, the marginal cost of abatement in each country therefore must equal the sum of the marginal benefits to all affected countries. Moreover, at the efficient level of global abatement, the marginal cost of abatement must be the same for all countries; otherwise shifting abatement from one country to another could decrease total abatement costs.

## A TWO-COUNTRY MODEL OF EMISSIONS ABATEMENT

A simple two-country model can be used to illustrate why an international climate control agreement is necessary to elicit the optimal level of global abatement. In this model, there are two countries, denoted $C_1$ and $C_2$, that generate carbon emissions. Reducing carbon emissions in either country provides a global public good, abatement. Each country's benefits from total global abatement are a function of the damages that country suffers from carbon emissions. The abatement costs in each country are a function of the opportunity costs of reducing carbon emissions in that country. Each country's benefits are thus a function of total world abatement, while each country's costs are a function of only its own abatement. For simplicity, assume that both countries are identical and have the same abatement benefit and cost functions (9).

Consistent with the principle of diminishing marginal utility, each country's marginal benefits decline as the level of abatement rises. Let each country have a linear marginal benefit function given by $MB_1 = MB_2 = A - X$ where X represents total abatement measured in units of emissions abatement and $A > 0$ is a parameter that reflects the magnitude of each country's abatement benefits. The larger A is, the greater the marginal benefit of abatement will be for any and all levels of abatement. Because abatement is a global public good, if any country reduces emissions it provides a positive external benefit to all other countries. The marginal benefit of abatement worldwide therefore exceeds the marginal benefit to any one country. The marginal benefit function for the world is the horizontal summation of each country's marginal benefit schedule, and is given by $MB_w = MB_1 + MB_2 = 2A - 2X$.

As is typically assumed, each country's marginal abatement costs rise with its level of abatement (10). Let each country have a linear marginal cost function given by $MC_1 = x_1$ and $MC_2 = x_2$ where $x_1$ and $x_2$ represent the abatement levels of each country, respectively, and $x_1 + x_2 = X$. Given equal and rising marginal cost functions, an efficient treaty will assign one-half of the abatement to each country. The marginal cost function for the world therefore is the horizontal summation of each country's marginal cost schedule and is given by $MC_w = X/2$.

At the efficient or optimal level of global abatement, the marginal cost of abatement in each country is equal to the sum of the marginal benefits to all affected countries. Alternatively, optimal global abatement occurs at X* (Figure 2), where

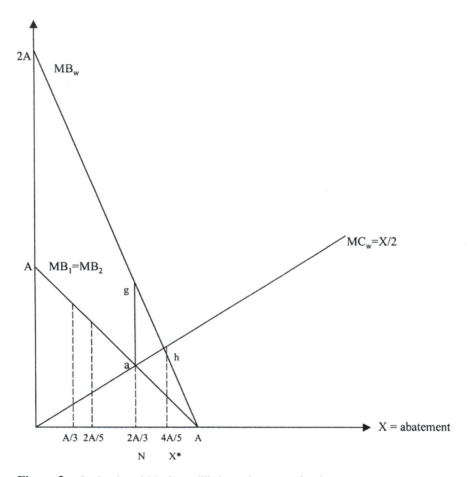

**Figure 2**   Optimal and Nash equilibrium abatement levels.

the marginal benefit to the world from the last unit of abatement is equal to the world marginal cost. Equating $MC_w = MB_w$ and solving for $X^*$ yields $X^* = 4A/5$. In this case, $X^*$ represents the cooperative outcome. As long as each country enjoys a greater net benefit from global abatement at $X^*$ than it would otherwise, each country will voluntarily cooperate and participate in the global climate control treaty.

It is traditionally assumed in theoretical analyses that absent such an international environmental agreement each country will abate at its Nash equilibrium. In a Nash equilibrium, each country takes the abatement level of the other country as given and chooses a level of abatement accordingly to maximize its own net benefit. Each country therefore chooses a level of abatement such that the marginal benefit it derives from its own abatement and the abatement of the other country equals its own marginal abatement cost; that is, in a Nash equilibrium, the following conditions hold for countries 1 and 2 respectively: $MC_1(x_1) = MB_1(x_1 + x_2)$ and $MC_2(x_2) = MB_2(x_1 + x_2)$. Solving these equations finds that each country abates $A/3$, for a total global abatement of $2A/3$ in the Nash equilibrium (11). The Nash equilibrium N in this case represents the noncooperative outcome. Note that N < X* (Figure 2).

Clearly, when each country considers only its own benefits and costs, it abates less than is optimal from the perspective of global efficiency, but neither country has an incentive to abate more than its Nash equilibrium level of abatement unless the other country commits to doing the same. This demonstrates why a credible and enforceable climate control treaty is necessary to overcome the free rider problem and achieve optimal global abatement. Increasing total global abatement from N to X* produces a net global efficiency gain equal to the area of the triangle AGH in Figure 2 (12). In this case, because the two countries have identical costs and benefits, the efficiency gain is split equally between them. Since welfare in both countries improves relative to the Nash outcome, the model predicts that both countries will cooperate and participate in the global climate control treaty.

This simple model with identical countries overlooks a key factor hindering the negotiations over implementation of the Kyoto Protocol, however. Real or perceived differences in costs and benefits across countries influence the incentives of individual countries to cooperate. Studies indicate that abatement costs and damages from climate change may vary widely across countries (13). This suggests that for at least some countries the net benefits from the climate control treaty may be less than the net benefits from the Nash outcome. To be clear, the climate control treaty will always produce a global efficiency gain relative to the Nash outcome. Even though a climate control treaty could potentially make all countries better off, however, whether or not it makes every country better off will depend upon the distribution of costs and benefits.

When abatement benefits and costs differ across countries, side payments may be necessary to induce the participation of some countries in the global climate control treaty. Abatement costs may vary widely across countries because of differences in technology, emissions levels, and income. Capital constraints may prevent many poorer countries from adopting abatement technologies. Moreover, lower levels of abatement in poor as compared to rich countries may reflect a higher marginal valuation on income and consumption in poor countries. In turn, lower abatement levels in developing countries imply lower marginal abatement costs.

An efficient climate control treaty will minimize total abatement costs by allocating abatement across countries until the marginal abatement cost for each country is the same. This means that countries with low abatement costs will abate relatively more under an efficient climate control treaty. As Sheeran (2002) demonstrates, whenever the cost of abatement between countries differs substantially, the country with the lower abatement costs will require side payments to cooperate with an efficient climate control treaty. Similarly, when abatement benefits differ across countries, an efficient treaty that requires all countries to abate may produce more abatement than some countries are willing to pay for. According to Sheeran (2002), whenever abatement benefits differ substantially between countries, the country that benefits less will require side payments to cooperate with the climate control treaty.

Without a careful redistribution of the costs and benefits of abatement, some countries may refuse to participate in a climate control treaty, thereby precluding optimal global abatement. Depending upon the direction of the side payments the treaty requires, an efficient climate control treaty may improve equity in mitigating climate change. This would be the case if the developing countries indeed benefit less and/or can abate at lower cost than the industrialized countries, as is commonly assumed. The industrialized countries would have to pay the developing countries for their cooperation, in which case efficient mitigation of climate change would be compatible with fairness (14).

## AN ALTERNATIVE APPROACH TO CLIMATE CONTROL

While involving developing countries in a climate control treaty that limits their emissions could be justified for efficiency reasons, objections could most certainly be raised on the grounds of equity. However, the issue of where emissions reduction takes place is separable from the issue of who pays for it. It is possible to limit developing country emissions while distributing the cost to the industrialized countries. Because reducing emissions in developing countries generates an efficiency gain, all countries stand to benefit.

Since it is unlikely that the industrialized countries will ever agree to pay developing countries directly for their participation in a climate control treaty, income redistribution will have to be achieved alternatively. For example, in keeping with the current Kyoto approach that relies on emissions quotas, developing countries could be awarded emissions quotas in excess of their current emissions levels (15). Assuming full international emissions trading was allowed, developing countries would have an incentive to reduce their emissions. Similarly, redistributive transfers could also be achieved through the distribution of emissions permits under an international tradable emissions permit system. In this case, developing countries would be awarded emissions permits in excess of their emissions levels. Because developing countries forgo the sale of emissions credits or permits by continuing to emit, both approaches impose a shadow price for emissions equivalent to the global willingness to pay for emissions reduction.

In essence, awarding developing countries emissions permits or emissions quotas in excess of their current emissions levels creates property rights for developing countries over their own emissions abatement. Granting the property right to developing countries amounts to a lump-sum redistributive transfer or potential windfall gain to these countries. To be efficient, however, this approach must require sufficient reductions in industrialized countries to generate emissions prices that are high enough to warrant emissions mitigation in developing countries (16). Moreover, to ensure that developing countries are in fact better off under such an approach, the price they receive for their emissions abatement must exceed their own opportunity costs of abatement. Admittedly, getting the industrialized countries to agree to lower emissions limits may prove to be a difficult political obstacle until damages from climate change become even more striking than they are at present.

Finally, these approaches may circumvent some but not all of the problems involving the additionality of emissions reductions from forest conservation in developing countries. If limits were placed on developing country emissions, developing countries would presumably have to submit inventories of their net emissions, accounting for all emissions by sources and removals by sinks, much like the Annex I countries are required to do under the current Kyoto framework. This means that all emissions from deforestation would be penalized, and thus the appropriate incentives for conservation would be provided. The issue still arises, however, as to how much credit countries should be awarded for sequestration activity within their borders. The Kyoto Protocol currently allows countries to earn credit for carbon sequestration resulting from reforestation and afforestation since 1990. In these limited cases, carbon uptake would be in addition to what would otherwise have occurred, therefore it can substitute for emissions reductions from other sources. This approach does not grant credit for carbon sequestration on existing forest land, however. Many countries, particularly those with abundant forest land, such as the United States have argued that credit should be given for existing forest areas under the Kyoto Protocol. Indeed, concessions were eventually made for these countries. Negotiators made concessions in a way that decreased the total level of emissions abatement under the Kyoto Protocol, however, taking us farther away from the optimal level of global reductions.

Since the net atmospheric concentration of carbon dioxide is the critical variable driving climate change, the same incentives offered for preventing emissions should be offered for sink activities that remove emissions from the atmosphere. It would therefore be inefficient to allow the external benefit of sequestration activity on existing forest land to remain unrewarded. One solution perhaps would have been to award credit to countries for all sequestration activity, but to recalculate each country's emissions quota so that the same target level of emissions abatement was achieved. An alternative tax-subsidy approach to emissions mitigation offers a more straightforward solution, however. According to this approach, countries would be taxed for all emissions from all sources. Moreover, countries would be subsidized for all emissions removals by sinks. The benefit of this approach is that it avoids the additionality problem entirely.

Moreover, the tax-subsidy approach allows for a more immediate solution to the problem of equity. First, it penalizes countries that generate public bads (emissions), while rewarding countries that generate public goods (sequestration). Carbon subsidies could become a significant revenue source for tropical developing countries with abundant forest land or reforestation potential. To correct for historic inequities in the production of greenhouse gases or differences in countries' willingness and ability to pay for emissions reduction, the revenues collected from emissions taxes worldwide could be redistributed to developing countries—a kind of revenue-neutral tax. Tax revenues could be refunded directly or indirectly through capital investments in abatement technologies whose primary beneficiaries would be the developing countries.

Both emissions taxes and such quantity-based approaches as emissions quotas or permits can yield the same (optimal) level of emissions reduction at the same (minimal) total cost. The distribution of income is not necessarily the same under all approaches, however. For example, a government collects tax revenues from polluters, but can distribute permits for free to polluters through a grandfathering system (17). If the government sold permits instead, the distributional effects would be the same, as in the case of a tax. Moreover, if the government were to redistribute pollution taxes back to polluters (i.e., a revenue-neutral pollution tax), the distributional impacts would be the same as in the case of a permit system, in which permits were freely distributed. Many continue to reject emissions taxes on the grounds that the distributional impacts are politically untenable, but as Nordhaus (2002) points out, redistributive transfers under quantity-based approaches such as the Kyoto

Protocol, though certainly more disguised, are likely to be no less objectionable. As Nordhaus states

> The Kyoto Protocol has an arbitrary allocation of transfers. Because it generally used 1990 emissions as a base year when setting targets in 1997, those countries who had high emissions in 1990 (such as the former Soviet Union) will be advantaged while those who have grown rapidly will be disadvantaged....So while the quantity plan looks advantageous because it hides the transfers, when the time comes actually to purchase substantial emissions reductions from Russia, the political glue is likely to come undone (Nordhaus, 2002: 10).

It is possible to use either emissions taxes or permits to compensate developing countries for their participation in a global climate control treaty. A tax-subsidy approach is preferable, if only because it avoids additionality concerns. In turn, this should negate the current objections to including forestry conservation as an option for mitigating climate change. This should lower the total abatement costs, thus increasing the optimal level of global abatement. Moreover, including forestry options in a climate control treaty will help promote sustainable development. Subsidizing carbon sequestration and storage could provide much needed incentives for sustainable land use change and conservation worldwide. Moreover, carbon subsidies could become a significant revenue source for countries with abundant forest resources. Many developing countries, particularly those in tropical regions, may profit from this approach to mitigating climate change.

During the past twenty years, emissions from land use change, especially deforestation, accounted for 25%, or 33 billion tons, of total carbon emissions (IPCC, 2001). The shadow price of carbon emissions can be estimated as the marginal cost of emissions reduction. Estimates of the marginal costs of emissions reduction range from $20 to $220 per ton (18). Assuming a price for carbon emissions within this range, the value of the carbon lost through deforestation over the past twenty years is estimated to be between $660 billion to $7.3 trillion.

Unless countries are paid for the climate stabilization services they provide for the global community, forest areas will continue to decline. This is especially true for developing countries in the tropics, where deforestation rates are the highest. Table 1 details the actual and projected average annual deforestation rates by decade and subsequent carbon loss in Africa, Latin America, and Asia between 1995 and 2045. Throughout the 1990s, an average of 15.6 million hectares of tropical forest were lost each year, 7.8 million hectares in Latin America alone. Assuming emission prices of $20 to $220 per ton, the resulting loss in carbon storage was equivalent to $35 to $389 billion dollars annually.

Deforestation not only releases carbon emissions, however, it decreases carbon sequestration. On average, old-growth forest can sequester 1.5 tons of carbon per hectare per year (19). Table 2 details the average annual value of carbon sequestration and storage for the 1990s for Asia, Africa, and Latin America. Tropical forests provided climate stabilization services, both carbon sequestration and storage, equal to $36 to $395 billion dollars per year (Table 2).

Unless tropical countries can capture the full value of their forests' carbon sequestration and storage services, there is little incentive to protect rather than clear-cut forests for fuel, timber, or agricultural use. Because these services benefit the global community, relying on developing countries to shoulder the entire cost of their

**Table 1**  Average Annual Deforestation and Carbon Loss by Region

|               | 1995  | 2005  | 2015  | 2025 | 2035 | 2045 | Total |
|---------------|-------|-------|-------|------|------|------|-------|
| **Africa**    |       |       |       |      |      |      |       |
| Carbon loss   | 461   | 390   | 334   | 307  | 282  | 283  | 2057  |
| Deforestation | 4575  | 3860  | 3260  | 2900 | 2535 | 2485 | 19615 |
| **Latin America** |   |       |       |      |      |      |       |
| Carbon loss   | 873   | 689   | 598   | 501  | 454  | 453  | 3568  |
| Deforestation | 7757  | 6275  | 5135  | 4160 | 3570 | 3550 | 30447 |
| **Asia**      |       |       |       |      |      |      |       |
| Carbon loss   | 436   | 406   | 363   | 314  | 268  | 254  | 2041  |
| Deforestation | 3283  | 3035  | 2665  | 2170 | 1850 | 1760 | 14763 |
| **All tropics** |     |       |       |      |      |      |       |
| Carbon Loss   | 1770  | 1485  | 1295  | 1122 | 1004 | 990  | 7666  |
| Deforestation | 15615 | 13170 | 11060 | 9230 | 7955 | 7795 | 64825 |

*Note*: Average annual deforestation by decade (1000 ha) and carbon emissions (millions of tons).
*Source*: Trexler and Haugen (1995).

provision means that conservation and sequestration will be suboptimally supplied. Subsidizing developing countries for the value of these benefits will provide real incentives to engage in climate-stabilizing land use change and conservation.

This approach to mitigating global warming could transfer substantial income to the developing world, however. Payments of $20 to $220 per ton of carbon stored or sequestered could transfer $36 to $395 billion to tropical countries per year at the average deforestation and sequestration rates that prevailed in the 1990s (Table 2).

**Table 2**  Annual Value of Climate Stabilization Services

|                   | Annual value of carbon storage | Annual value of carbon sequestration | Total annual value of services |
|-------------------|--------------------------------|--------------------------------------|--------------------------------|
| **All tropics**   |                                |                                      |                                |
| High[a]           | $389                           | $5.2                                 | $395                           |
| Low[b]            | $35                            | $0.5                                 | $36                            |
| **Africa**        |                                |                                      |                                |
| High              | $101                           | $1.6                                 | $103                           |
| Low               | $9                             | $0.1                                 | $9.1                           |
| **Asia**          |                                |                                      |                                |
| High              | $96                            | $1.1                                 | $97                            |
| Low               | $8.7                           | $0.1                                 | $8.8                           |
| **Latin America** |                                |                                      |                                |
| High              | $192                           | $2.6                                 | $195                           |
| Low               | $18                            | $0.2                                 | $18.2                          |

[a] Estimated at $220/ton carbon.
[b] Estimated at $20/ton carbon.
*Note*: Value in billions (1996 U.S. $)
*Source*: Author's calculations.

In contrast, private capital flows to the developing world in 1997 were $90 billion (Heal, 2000). On a per capita annual basis, the subsidies would cost $6 to $66 per person worldwide, or $144 to $1580 per person in the United States alone. Considering the ancillary benefits of protecting tropical forests, such as biodiversity and watershed protection, it may prove a relatively small price to pay for services rendered.

## CONCLUSION

The Kyoto Protocol should be applauded as a critical first step toward mitigating climate change. It is neither the most efficient nor the only equitable means of reducing global emissions, however. To be efficient, a climate control treaty must provide incentives to all countries, including developing countries, to reduce emissions. The costs of reducing emissions can be distributed so that developing countries are no worse off for their participation in the treaty. In fact, because including the developing countries in the treaty lowers global abatement costs and increases the total level of global abatement, all countries worldwide can be made better off under such a treaty, in which case this approach may be no more politically problematic than the Kyoto Protocol.

## NOTES

1.  This definition of climate change is used by the United Nation's Framework Convention on Climate Change.
2.  The Intergovernmental Panel on Climate Change (IPCC) was jointly established by the World Meteorological Organization and the United Nation's Environment Program (UNEP) to assess the science, impacts, and economics of climate change. The most recent IPCC third assessment report incorporates results from the past five years of research. More than 2000 scientists worldwide contributed to this report, which is widely viewed as the authoritative source of climate change information.
3.  Under the UNFCC, countries were to reduce their emissions to 1990 levels by 2000. Since 1990, emissions in the United States have actually increased by 15%.
4.  The protocol allows some countries an increase over 1990 levels. Australia, for example, can increase emissions by 8% above its 1990 levels.
5.  As of the seventh session of the Conference of the Parties to the UNFCC (COP-7) in November 2001.
6.  Afforestation involves planting trees in areas never previously forested. Reforestation converts previously forested land to back to forests. Conservation would prevent the conversion of forest land to alternative uses.
7.  This includes sink credits from forest management generated under JI.
8.  In India, the world's fifth largest fossil-fuel-emitting country, emissions increased 57% between 1990 and 1998. In China, the world's second largest fossil-fuel-emitting country, emissions have increased by 39% between 1990 and 1996 (Marland et al., 2000).
9.  See Sheeran (2002) for more extensive treatment of this model and for extensions of the model that allow benefits and costs to vary across countries.
10. It is assumed that a country exhausts its least-cost options for reducing emissions first; therefore marginal costs rise as the level of abatement increases.

11. $MC_1(x_1) = MB_1(x_1 + x_2) = A - (x_1 + x_2) = x_1$; therefore $x_1 = A/3$. Since the two countries are identical in this model, $x_1 = x_2 = A/3$.
12. The efficiency gain is the increase in net benefits from the climate control treaty as compared to the Nash outcome.
13. See Cline (1992) and Nordhaus and Boyer (2000) for a discussion.
14. See Sheeran (2002) for further discussion.
15. This approach is not without precedence in the Kyoto Protocol. For example, the emissions quota for Australia, an Annex I country, is 8% *above* 1990 levels.
16. Theoretically emissions prices should reflect the marginal damage of emissions.
17. In most cases, pollution permits are distributed to firms in proportion to their pollution levels. For example, a firm that produced 25% of the pollution would receive 25% of the permits. Firms can then trade permits among themselves.
18. Range of estimates as reported by a special issue of The Energy Journal, entitled "The Costs of the Kyoto Protocol: A Multi-model Evaluation," (Weyent, 1999). It is the most comprehensive source of marginal abatement cost estimates to date.
19. Rates of carbon sequestration vary according to region, climate, soil, forest type, and age. The rate of carbon uptake by old-growth forests is lowest, but on average even old-growth forests can sequester 1.5 tons of carbon per hectare per year (Villarin et al., 1999).

## REFERENCES

Brown, P., Cabarle, B., Livernash, R. (1997). Carbon Counts: Estimating Climate Change Mitigation in Forestry Projects. Washington, DC: World Resources Institute.

Chichilnisky, G., Heal, G. (1994). Who should abate carbon emissions? An international viewpoint. Econ Letters 44:443–449.

Chilchilnisky, G., Heal, G. (2000). Environmental Markets: Equity and Efficiency. New York: Columbia University Press.

Cline, W. (1992). The Economics of Global Warming. Washington, DC: Institute for International Economics.

Faeth, P., Cort, C., Livernash, R. (1994). Evaluating the Carbon Sequestration Benefits of Forestry Projects in Developing Countries. Washington, DC: World Resources Institute.

Heal, G. (2000). Nature and the Marketplace: Capturing the Value of Ecosystem Services. Washington, DC: Island Press.

Heil, M. T. (1997). Carbon Emissions and Income: The Effects of Growth and Distribution. PhD dissertation, American University, Washington, DC.

Intergovernmental Panel on Climate Change. IPCC Second Assessment: Climate Change 1995. A Report of the Intergovernmental Panel on Climate Change. New York: Cambridge University Press.

Intergovernmental Panel on Climate Change. Climate Change 2001: Synthesis Report. Summary for Policy Makers (http://www.ipcc.ch/).

Kopp, R., Morgenstern, R., Pizer, W. (Sept. 29, 1997). Something for everyone: A climate policy that both environmentalists and industry can live with. Weathervane. Washington, DC: Resources for the Future.

Marland, G., Boden, T. A., Andres, R. J. (2000). Global, regional, and national $CO_2$ emissions. Trends: A Compendium of Data on Global Change. Carbon Dioxide Information Analysis Center. Oak Ridge, TN: Oak Ridge National Laboratory, U.S. Department of Energy.

McKibben, W. J., Wilcoxen, P. (June 1997). A Better Way to Slow Global Climate Change. Brookings policy brief 17. Washington, DC: Brookings Institution Press.

McKibben, W. J., Wilcoxen, P. (2002). Climate Change Policy After Kyoto: A Blueprint for a Realistic Approach. Washington, DC: Brookings Institution Press.

Nordhaus, W. D. (1994). Managing the Global Commons: The Economics of Climate Change. Cambridge: MIT Press.

Nordhaus, W. D. (2002). After Kyoto: Alternative mechanisms to control global warming. Joint Session of the American Economic Association and the Association of Environmental and Resource Economists, Jan. 4, Atlanta.

Nordhaus, W. D., Boyer, J. (2000). Warming the World: Economic Models of Global Warming. Cambridge: Harvard University Press.

Schlamadinger, B., Marland, G. (2000). Land Use and Global Climate Change: Forests, Land Management, and the Kyoto Protocol. Washington, DC: Pew Center on Global Climate Change.

Sheeran, K.A. (2002). Equity and efficiency in mitigating climate change. PhD dissertation, American University, Washington, DC.

Trexler, M., Haugen, C. (1995). Keeping It Green: Tropical Forestry Opportunities for Mitigating Climate Change. Washington, DC: World Resources Institute.

Victor, D. (2001). The Collapse of the Kyoto Protocol and the Struggle to Slow Global Warming. Princeton, NJ: Princeton University Press.

Villarin, J. T., Narisma, G. T., Reyes, M. S., Macatangay, S. M., Ang, M. T. (1999). Land use change and forestry reference manual. Villarin, J. T., et al. , eds., Tracking Greenhouse Gases: A Guide for Country Inventories. Manila: Manila Observatory.

Weyent, J. P. (1999). The costs of the Kyoto protocol: A multi-model evaluation. Energy J.

# 39

## Policy Implementation in Poor Countries

**JAN-ERIK LANE**

*University of Geneva, Geneva, Switzerland*

**SVANTE ERSSON**

*Umea University, Umea, Sweden*

## INTRODUCTION

In the countries of the Third World, the basic economic and political conditions are intertwined, connected with the problems to implementing public policy. Governments conducting public policies in order to improve the quality of life find that they are restricted by the weak extractive capacity of the state in relation to the economy, as well as by the dissipation of resources through corruption. The basic equation that regulates what governments can do to improve the human predicament thus includes the negative impact from a low gross domestic product (GDP) as well as from political instability.

There are a few bright spots, however, in an otherwise gloomy picture, in which many Third World countries are overwhelmed by poverty and such attendant social problems as the AIDS epidemic. Public policy can also make a difference in a poor country by increasing the quality of life, as for instance when policies in relation to infrastructure, education, and health care work. Whether a top-down or a bottom-up approach to policy implementation is the optimal route to ameliorating the poverty of Third World countries is an open question; the answer depends upon the policy in question and the contingencies. As long as the country has not embarked on a sustained economic growth path, a top-down approach may be the only realistic way. The improvement in reducing poverty depends not only on the economy but also on political stability. Economic development is a necessary condition for policy

**691**

implementation, yet human development or the improvement of the quality of life can only occur when there is political stability.

This chapter presents the argument that policy implementation can improve the quality of life when there is both economic development and political stability, meaning that corruption can be restrained. This optimistic argument consist of two parts, one economic and one political. First, there is a real opportunity for a rapid amelioration of the situation of poor countries provided that they can embark upon sustained economic development. If world poverty were to be reduced, a larger GDP would have to provide the resources that political elites could employ for improving the predicament of their populations. Second, political stability is a necessary condition for turning the possibility of economic improvement of a specific country into reality, otherwise corruption will dissipate the economic opportunity to raise the quality of life. In order to substantiate this argument, which focusses on the negative impact of corruption on Third World development, we make an empirical inquiry based on the findings stated in Appendix 1.

## POVERTY AND POOR COUNTRIES

Despite all the pessimism that surrounds the question of poverty in the world, the possibility of a better world must be emphasized. The widely accepted so-called gap theory claims that the differences between the rich and poor countries keep increasing, but this hypothesis is questionable. Third World countries need both economic development and political development. One may actually wonder whether or not there is cause for more optimism about the first part of the argument—that a sustained process of economic growth would result in significant improvement rather soon—than about the second part. There is more cause for scepticism about the commitment of many Third World political elites to implement policies that really improve the situation of the population.

In the debate abut world poverty the distinction between *economic feasibility* and *political commitment* is blurred. On the one hand there is the deterministic argument that nothing can be done about poverty. Poverty is essentially structural in the sense that the international economy, which based on the distinction between core capitalist countries and the periphery or underdeveloped hinterland, must lead to huge differences between rich and poor countries. This is the position in Marxist theories, including the dependency school and world systems analysis. The spokesmen of governments that have either failed or not even attempted to improve the predicament of their poor populations also frequently employ it, yet one must distinguish between economic possibility and political will.

On the other hand, there is the nondeterministic argument that world poverty can be at least diminished if not eradicated by the choice of the correct public policies. Development comes in two versions. First, there is the top-down perspective, which assigns a crucial role to government planning or so-called development administration. Second, there is the bottom-up perspective, which outlines an alternative public policy approach to the improvement of poverty based on such participatory mechanisms as nongovernmental organizations (NGOs). Without resources, however, self-initiative and grassroots participation will not suffice. Planning too has failed as a development strategy.

We wish to argue that there are economic possibilities to reduce poverty. The political commitment to do so, however, must be 100%. We especially, underline the crucial importance of handling the risk of massive corruption.

Poverty is a word used to describe different human predicaments (Chenery, 1986; Chenery and Srinivasan, 1989; Behrman et al., 1995). The widely held theory that poverty cannot be removed from the social systems of mankind emanates from the concept of relative poverty or focuses on such misery as famine. Relative poverty cannot be counteracted because there will always be differences between the rich and poor in whatever social systems one may conceive. Poverty in this sense applies even to the welfare states in the Organization for Economic Cooperation and Development (OECD) set of countries, as well as to the superrich oil states.

Similarly, the occurrence of famine, although not related to relative poverty, cannot be undone. The argument assumes that the world population is at present increasing in such a manner that in combination with unpredictable food production famines will occur now and then. Famines can only be mitigated by the ad hoc intervention of rich states when they occur.

Here we are looking at absolute poverty as a country feature. This kind of poverty is measured in the form of aggregate statistics about how many people live under a certain acceptable standard of living. The poverty line approach entails the same perspective; this kind of poverty can be counteracted by public policy. Not every poor state faces famine, and what is problematic about poor states is not the occurrence of relative poverty in that country. By tying the concept of poverty to the country, one emphasizes that government has a responsibility for the overall standard of living in a country.

Political stability is a necessary condition if and when the political elites of the Third World are committed to reducing poverty. At the same time, public policy directed against poverty can only be effective if the economy of the country is such that governments can draw upon its physical and human resources. This argument suggests that corruption is *one key* to the probability that public policies will work in Third World countries.

A poor country does not necessarily have to stay poor. Let us first show that it is possible to close the gap between the poor and rich states on the Earth today. Then we will show that even small increments in human development matter crucially for reducing the negative impact of poverty. This requires, however, a certain level of economic development in terms of GDP growth and the containment of political instability in the form of corruption.

## THE "GAP"

It has often been claimed that the distance between rich and poor countries is increasing. It is predicted that the uncontrollable population explosion cannot help but result in a declining quality of life for poor states. Is there no ground for optimism?

When one looks at overall differences among various states, the distance between, for example, the United States and Switzerland on the one hand and India and China on the other is no doubt tremendous. Are there any opportunities for states to take actions that decrease this phenomenal distance? The average country's differences in affluence are truly great, as for example, in the GDP figures for Europe and Africa, yet sustained economic growth has taken place outside the rich world.

The widespread belief that the poverty differences between the First World and the Third World simply increase over time is actually a major stumbling block when searching for policies against poverty. Country developments with regard to overall affluence cannot be subsumed under any such generalization.

Although the affluence per capita is generally higher among the OECD countries, the distance to the Communist and Latin American countries is not dramatic. It is almost ten times higher than in Africa and about six times higher than in Asia. After thirty-five years of unprecedented growth in the world economy the overall picture is somewhat different.

It is obvious that the distance between the OECD countries and the sets of Communist and Latin American countries increased between 1950 and 1985. The stagnation of the Spanish-speaking world is pronounced, but the distance in relation to the African continent has widened even more. The gap theory is questioned and even negated, however, by the sharply shrinking gulf between the OECD countries and the Asian countries. The distance can now be measured by onl a factor of three, and some Asian countries among the newly industrializing countries (NICs) and the newly exporting countries (NECs) are closing in rapidly. It has become less and less accurate to speak about the First World versus the Third World (Lane and Ersson, 2001).

The developments in the early 1990s contradict the gap theory. Not only has Southeast Asia in general, including Mainland China, become a large growth area,

**Table 1**   Human Development Index (HDI) in 1980 and 2000

| Country | HDI (1980) | Country | HDI (1999) |
|---|---|---|---|
| Top | | Top | |
| Argentina | 0.798 | Singapore | 0.876 |
| Uruguay | 0.775 | Republic of Korea | 0.875 |
| Costa Rica | 0.769 | Argentina | 0.842 |
| Singapore | 0.753 | Uruguay | 0.828 |
| Trinidad and Tobago | 0.752 | Chile | 0.825 |
| Chile | 0.735 | Costa Rica | 0.821 |
| Mexico | 0.732 | Kuwait | 0.818 |
| Panama | 0.73 | United Arab Emirates | 0.809 |
| Venezuela, RB | 0.73 | Trinidad and Tobago | 0.798 |
| Korea, Rep. | 0.729 | Mexico | 0.79 |
| Bottom | | Bottom | |
| Malawi | 0.343 | Rwanda | 0.395 |
| Nepal | 0.329 | Mali | 0.378 |
| Senegal | 0.329 | Central African Republic | 0.372 |
| Benin | 0.323 | Chad | 0.359 |
| Burundi | 0.308 | Mozambique | 0.323 |
| Mozambique | 0.303 | Ethiopia | 0.321 |
| Mali | 0.277 | Burkina Faso | 0.32 |
| Burkina Faso | 0.263 | Burundi | 0.309 |
| Chad | 0.255 | Niger | 0.274 |
| Niger | 0.253 | Sierra Leone | 0.258 |

*Source*: UNDP (2001).

but the prospects for increased, affluence in Latin America are much brighter. Chile is a case in point, but Argentina of course fell far behind in 2002. The levels of affluence in the so-called Baby Tigers—South Korea, Taiwan, Singapore, and Hong Kong—are comparable to levels in OECD countries (Lane and Ersson, 2001), the last two city-states outperforming several OECD countries. It is thus possible for Third World countries to close the gap. We emphasize, however, that it requires political stability.

Table 1 lists the Third World countries that were at the top and bottom, respectively, in terms of the index of human development in 1980 and 1999. The Human Development Index, used by the United Nations, reveals not only the immense difference between the First World and Third World countries, but also that several Third World countries have succeeded in improving their quality of life.

## THE LDCs AND THE HIPCs

In 1971, the international community identified a category of countries in profound poverty and with great weakness in institutions. Currently, forty-nine countries with a combined population of 610.5 million—equivalent to 10.5% of the world's population (1997 estimates)—belong to the set of least developed countries (LDCs). These countries face immense difficulties in developing their domestic economies to ensure an adequate standard of living for their populations. These economies are very vulnerable to external shocks or natural disasters. The set of LDCs constitutes the weakest segment of the international community, and the development of these countries represents a major challenge to globalization and its governance. The United Nations has taken actions to help the LDCs that were to be complemented by international support measures.

In various documents, the international community has committed itself to urgent and effective action, based on the principle of shared responsibility and strengthened partnership, to arrest and reverse the deterioration in the socioeconomic situation in the LDCs and to revitalize their growth and development. Declarations at international conferences do not suffice, however. What the LDCs have realized is that they have to lobby for a change in the rules of international trade opening up for unlimited exports to the rich countries.

The heavily indebted poor countries (HIPC) initiative is an example of what global governance can do for reducing poverty. This International Monetary Fund (IMF) initiative is a comprehensive approach to debt reduction for poor countries that requires the participation of creditors, ensuring that no poor country faces a debt burden it cannot handle. The HIPC policy mixes economic feasibility with political commitment; just as important is the country's continued effort toward macroeconomic adjustment and structural and social policy reforms. In addition, this policy tries to come up with financing for social sector programs, primarily basic health and education. Several modifications were approved in September 1999 to provide faster, deeper, and broader debt relief and strengthen the links among debt relief, poverty reduction, and social policies. Even if all of the external debts of these countries were forgiven, however, most would still depend on significant levels of concessional external assistance; their receipts of such assistance have been much larger than their debt-service payments for many years. New initiatives in global governance are important for reducing poverty, but we still maintain that internal factors cannot be bypassed.

Actually, as the new classifications of LDCs and HIPCs show, the variation among Third World countries is now such that it is no longer meaningful to talk about a definitive and unbridgeable gap between rich and poor countries. What is more important for a Third World country than to position itself in relation to a First World country is to see to that it does not fall into the poverty trap. Let us explain.

## THE "TRAP"

Although adherents to the pessimistic theory may admit that there are a few exceptional cases in the form of countries that have managed to make it from poverty to affluence they would probably still maintain that the overall predicament for poor nations is hopeless. The pessimistic theory claims that the distance between the few rich and the many poor is so overwhelming that little can be done, except counteracting sudden famines. Looking at the gap, one certainly notes the sharp difference between the levels of affluence in the OECD countries and those of countries in Latin America, Asia, and especially Africa.

It is true that the step between the rich and the poor in terms of country-level affluence is immense, if it is possible to trust the very complicated calculations that are needed in order to make the measuring rod—an international U.S. dollar—a true quantitative indicator. Poverty, however, is not a strict function of purchasing power. What matters for the policy of eradicating global poverty is not a specific measure of GDP per capita but the quality of life in the country. What the pessimistic theory of world poverty on a country-by-country basis overlooks is the fact that the quality of life is not a strict proportional function of the economic indicator on affluence.

Most important, there is a sharp curve linearity in the connection between economic affluence and general quality of life. (See Figure 1.) Very low levels of country affluence result in truly miserable social conditions, but as the GDP scores ascend toward higher levels, the quality of life indicator at first rises proportionately, but then the curve evens out. Given the relationship between GDP per capita and the quality of life predicament, one must be aware that rapid processes of economic growth will most likely be beneficial quickly for the broad masses in the country's population. The most significant steps out of poverty are taken in the early stages of economic development.

The policy implication is that growth considerations matter more than distributional deliberations. If the national income of many Third World countries could reach a level above 2000 international U.S. dollars, the removal of the most dismal features of poverty in those countries would be helped tremendously.

Positive economic development is thus a necessary condition for improving life in the poor countries of the world. Small increments in GDP per capita would give large increases in the quality of life for the average citizen. Economic resources are not sufficient for eradicating world poverty, however, there must be political stability in the country that attempts to implement policies that ameliorate poverty.

Public policy in a poor country should target those policies that help the country move out of the poverty trap (located on the left side of Figure 1), where a low

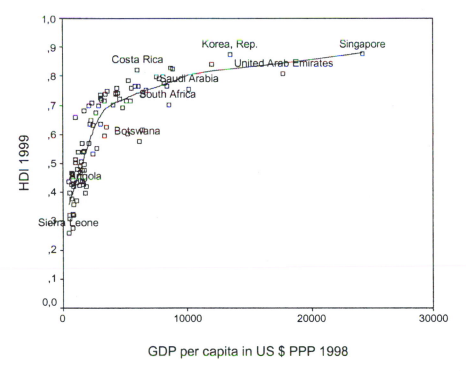

**Figure 1** GDP and Human Development Index (1999). *Source*: World Bank (2000); UNDP (2001).

level of GDP implies a dismal human condition. Public policy can help a Third World country embark on a sustained level of economic development that brings it out of the trap. Small improvements in GDP mean huge increases in quality of life on the left side of Figure 1. Here policies improving infrastructure, education, and health care may pay off handsomely in terms of sustained economic growth, yet there must be political stability in order for a Third World country to leave the poverty trap.

## POLITICAL STABILITY

Policy implementation in a poor country requires state stability. Political elites in the Third World often confess a willingness to conduct policies that would improve the living conditions of their populations. The policy ambition becomes dissipated, however, because of the profound political instability that prevails in many Third World countries. Political instability takes many expressions, but the most damaging one is the massive occurrence of corruption, because it is common, daily, and encompassing.

First, the recurrence of civil wars in Third World countries effectively stops any attempt to improve the predicament of the population. Second, there must be political stability in a more general sense of the enforcement of one political regime over time. State stability measured by looking at the average duration of regimes since 1945 shows the immense political instability of the poor continents.

The average duration of a political regime is sharply lower in Africa, America, and Asia than in Oceania and Europe, in spite of the fact that the extensive regime transformations in Eastern Europe are included in the figures. Typical of the Third World state is the transition from one regime to another. The waning of the Cold War stimulated several countries to install a democratic regime following the rule of law. This applies to both right-wing and left-wing authoritarian regimes from the Cold War period. Whether or not democracy can also be consolidated is more uncertain, however, especially given the risk of massive corruption destroying the rule of law.

One way to tap regime longevity is to look at when the present constitution of a state was introduced. Both indices employed here (the Hudson and Taylor index, referring to the situation from about 1968 to about 1970 versus the Encyclopedia Britannica index, which deals with the situation in 1990) display the great variation in constitutional longevity. The current constitution of a state is much newer than the state itself, meaning that regime changes tend to take place frequently. Some old European states have had numerous constitutional changes, but the most frequent and recent regime changes have occurred in Africa, America, and Asia.

The constitutions of the world are of rather short duration, meaning that they change frequently. Political life is hazardous in many countries, to say the least. The average constitution among the states of the world has been adopted or changed since 1945. This applies particularly to Africa and Asia, where colonial rule received its final blow after the Second World War. Third World countries are characterized by many major constitutional changes.

Regime stability is related to the transitions between the two major types of regimes; that is, democracy versus dictatorship. Although the number of stable democracies does not count for more than one-sixth of the total number of states, the variation over time in the stability of democratic and nondemocratic regimes may be mapped.

Low regime-change scores would be found in the set of states that are either stable democracies or stable dictatorships, mainly the democracies among the OECD set of countries, as well as a few stable authoritarian regimes, mainly right-wing ones. A measurement of regime fluctuations can be based on the standard indices of democracy. High values indicate change over time between democracy and dictatorship, the standard deviation expressing fluctuation between high and low democracy scores.

Regime reshuffling has occurred since the end of World War II on all the continents with the exception of the very stable Oceania. It is particularly pronounced in Latin America and Africa, but has also occurred in several Asian states. Regime instability is pronounced in Latin America and Africa. The movement back and forth between democracy and dictatorship has been strongest first and foremost in Latin America. In Africa there is also general regime instability, but it refers more to the competition between more or less authoritarian civil rule on the one hand and military government on the other. Part but certainly not all of the regime instability in Asia is the result of the difficulties in introducing stable democracy, whereas the late regime transition to democray makes Europe score very high, around 1990. The various measures of political instability—constitutional revisions, coups d'etat, deaths from domestic violence, political strikes—tend to correlate with each other to a considerable degree.

Strictly speaking, regime survival is not a sufficient condition for making and implementing policies that reduce poverty, as an authoritarian regime may intentionally neglect the predicament of the poor. It could remain stable, however, for a long period of time, but only by employing massive resources for repression. In the short run political instability certainly exacerbates poverty.

Governments in the Third World may engage in a variety of social policies that alleviate the harshness of the human condition in these countries. One thinks first and foremost of education and health care policies, but other policies, such as law and order and infrastructure, also benefit the masses. Political instability makes any policy consistency or coherence virtually impossible.

We single out corruption as especially damaging to policy implementation in Third World countries, as it dissipates the few resources availabe and creates cynicism in the political elite. Figure 2 shows the macro relation between the quality of life and corruption, excluding the First World (twenty-four OECD countries).

Figure 2 shows the positive interaction between human development and political stability in the form of a lack of corruption. Here we have circular causation,

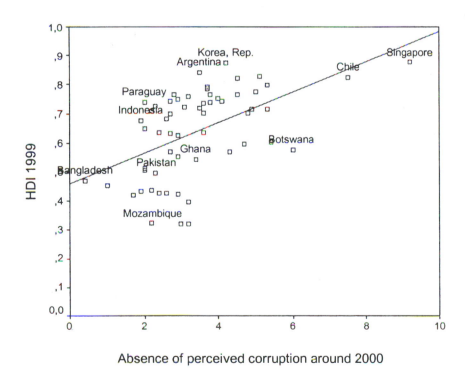

Absence of perceived corruption around 2000

**Figure 2** Corruption and human development (Third World). *Source*: Transparency International (2001); UNDP (2001).

meaning that corruption defeats human development which in turn increases corruption—the vicious circle that prevents public policy and policy implementation to be effective in poor countries.

## CONCLUSION

The implementation of policies for improving poverty in Third World countries requires both economic and political preconditions (i.e., a degree of positive economic development and political stability). Economic growth is only possible through new investments in capital (Jones, 1998) besides the depreciation of already existing capital. How could there be hope, however, for countries in which there is civil war or major regime upheavals, such as military coups, resulting in capital destruction? The poor countries of the world need not only economic development through investment, but also, as we underscore, political stability. The crux of the matter is that political stability and affluence are closely interrelated. In this chapter we have focused on the risk for dissipation of economic benefits through economic growth by corruption in government.

The correlation between a lack of corruption and affluence (GDP) is as high as .75. A low level of affluence leads to political instability, and political instability worsens poverty. If world poverty is to be counteracted, more attention has to be focused on basic political matters, in particular regime stability. It is mainly with regard to the prospects for the political elites in the Third World to arrive at an agreement about basic constitutional questions that one has reason to be sceptical about world poverty. As long as there is fundamental uncertainty about the basic rules of the state, policies cannot be initiated to reduce poverty, and, one may add, the lower the average level of affluence, the more precarious is political stability.

Corruption is a general illness of the state that crushes the hope for economic improvement. It dissipates the economic gains from sustained economic development, and the rumor of massive corruption in a country acts as a warning signal dissuading foreign direct investments. The level of corruption in several Latin American, African, and Asian countries is a major cause of their underdevelopment. Policies against poverty are extremely vulnerable in a general climate of corruption.

**Appendix 1**   Correlations Among Variables

|         |       | HDI vs. corruption | HDI vs. GDP | GDP vs. corruption |
|---------|-------|--------------------|-------------|--------------------|
| Total   | R =   | .715               | .783        | .895               |
|         | Sig = | .000               | .000        | .000               |
|         | N =   | 104                | 135         | 104                |
| Third World | R = | .520             | .717        | .750               |
|         | Sig = | .000               | .000        | .000               |
|         | N =   | 59                 | 90          | 59                 |

*Source*: GDP from World Bank (2000); HDI from UNDP (2001); corruption from Transparency International (2001); corruption perceptions indices available at http://www.transparency.org/cpi/index.html.

## REFERENCES

Behrman, J., Srinivasan, T. N., Chenery, H. (1995). Handbook of Development Eonomics. Vols 3A and 3B. Amsterdam: North-Holland.

Chenery, H. (1986). Industrialization and Growth: A Comparative Study. Washington, DC: World Bank.

Chenery, H., Srinivasan, T. N. (1989). Handbook of Development Economics. Vols. I and II. Amsterdam: North-Holland.

Jones, C. I. (1998). Introduction to Economic Growth. New York: Norton.

Lane, J. E., Ersson, S. (2001). Government and the Economy: A Global Perspective. London: Continuum.

Transparency International. (2001). Corruption Perceptions Indices. available at http://www.transparency.org/cpi/index.html.

UNDP. Human Development Report. New York: Oxford University Press.

World Bank. World Development Indicators CD-ROM. Washington, DC: World Bank.

# 40

## Poverty Reduction
### *The Measurement Question*

**KARIN SCHELZIG**

*Development Alternatives, Inc., Bethesda, Maryland, U.S.A.*

## INTRODUCTION

Poverty reduction has become the core objective of international development efforts in the twenty-first century. The poverty measurement question is therefore of central importance. Small variations in a poverty measurement methodology can make significant differences in the population identified to be poor. This has implications for the design and targeting of poverty reduction or livelihood improvement policies and programs.

This chapter first examines the origins of the "new" poverty focus. It further sketches out some examples of variations in poverty measures. The next section lays out how poverty is measured, with a look at the steps involved in constructing a headcount index (the most widely used poverty statistic)(1). The section after that examines some of the pitfalls of poverty headcounts, with a case study of the Philippines. The chapter concludes by making a case for multidimensional poverty measurement. While more complex, this can correct for errors in such purely monetary indicators as the headcount, and can provide much richer information for better-designed and -targeted poverty reduction strategies.

## POVERTY REDUCTION AS THE GOAL OF DEVELOPMENT

Placed on the back burner for some time while the world focused on structural adjustment and other macro-level interventions, poverty issues began to make their way back to the forefront of the development policy agenda in the early 1990s after the release of two seminal publications: the World Bank's *World Development Report*

(1990) and the first United Nations Development Program (UNDP) *Human Development Report* (1990). The former called for a renewed emphasis on poverty and described poverty reduction as the World Bank's overarching goal, while the latter stressed the importance of focusing on people and expanding their capabilities and choices. During the course of the 1990s, this new trend was confirmed when most donor agencies officially adopted poverty reduction as their main principle. The World Bank motto, for example, became *Our dream is a world free of poverty*. The Asian Development Bank is *fighting poverty in Asia and the Pacific*, while the UNDP builds *partnerships to fight poverty*.

In 1996, the Development Assistance Committee (DAC) of the Organization for Economic Cooperation and Development (OECD) adopted eight international development goals (IDGs), including, at the top of the list, the eradication of extreme poverty and hunger.* By 1999 even the International Monetary Fund had broadened the objectives of its concessional lending to include a specific focus on poverty reduction, and a new poverty reduction and growth facility (PRGF) replaced the enhanced structural adjustment facility (ESAF).

This global emphasis on poverty reduction means that the analysis of poverty plays a key role. To reduce poverty, we have to know who the poor are. Different concepts of poverty will lead to very different measurement outcomes. This was shown early on by Scott (1981), Hagenaars and de Vos (1988), and Glewwe and van der Gaag (1990), among many others. Scott looked at various sets of country data to conclude that "with quite reasonable variations in definition and measurement, the amount of poverty in one country can be made to vary from 26 to 85 percent for the same year. Poverty can also be shown according to the researcher's intent, and without undue violation of the truth, to be declining or increasing over time" (1981:1–2). The Hagenaars and de Vos study applied eight different definitions of poverty to survey data gathered in Holland. The resulting headcounts of the poor population spanned a broad range, from less than one in fifteen to more than one-third of the Dutch population (1988:217).

Why should we revisit the poverty measurement question? Statements about how much poverty there is have wide-ranging political and practical implications and are used for a multitude of purposes. The data are used to justify and rationalize the creation or cutting back of government programs. They are quoted to support the formulation of social policy and to determine funding levels for projects. Social protection and safety net programs use poverty levels for targeting purposes. Poverty is measured to monitor the human impact of donor-funded activities and global economic trends. The increase or decrease of poverty levels is used to underpin political platforms. There is no lack of contradiction; poverty is used to justify increased global trade (trade reduces poverty) *and* to protest globalization (trade harms the poor). Poverty is measured to monitor the achievement of stated global development goals, such as the first MDG to halve the proportion of people whose income is less than $1 a day between 1990 and 2015.

An enormous body of literature spanning multiple disciplines is testament to complex debates over how best to define and measure poverty, but no consensus has

---

* The IDGs later became the Millennium Development Goals (MDGs).

been reached and multiple methodologies are in use today. Furthermore, when academics, development practitioners, and politicians speak about the problem of poverty, chances are that what they actually mean by poverty will vary greatly. At the theoretical level, contradictory poverty statistics can stem from the fact that measures of poverty, while seemingly objective, embody values that reflect the historical, political, social, and ethical forces prevalent at the time of their formation. At a more practical level, variance in poverty statistics can stem from slight adjustments to the parameters in a measurement methodology or a misunderstanding of what exactly the numbers represent.

To explain changes in poverty over time, poverty analysts will turn to such factors as household or country characteristics, safety net interventions and other poverty reduction changes, governance issues, structural features, external shocks, or public spending on such social sectors as health and education. Often overlooked is perhaps the most important factor of all: how the poverty levels are calculated. With the increased enthusiasm among global actors for poverty issues and poverty reduction must come on increased awareness of the simple message that statistics must always be read and quoted with caution.

## HOW POVERTY IS MEASURED: QUANTITATIVE APPROACHES

The main division in the world of poverty measurement falls between conventional income and consumption poverty measures and the rest (i.e., those based on more qualitative or multidimensional definitions) (see Maxwell, 1999). At the outset of the twenty-first century it is generally understood that poverty is more than a simple lack of income and that multidimensional approaches are preferable in theory. Multidimensional approaches to poverty recognize that while income is certainly an important determinant of well-being, it is not the only one. Alternative interpretations that were developed over past decades—largely by social planners and anthropologists working with rural communities in developing countries—allowed for local variation in the meaning of poverty and expanded the definition to include perceptions of nonmaterial deprivation and social differentiation.

These alternative interpretations have evolved and have slowly moved to the forefront of poverty thinking. Robert Chambers's early work informed the multidimensional approach to a great extent when he, putting the last first, developed the notion of integrated rural poverty as consisting of five interconnected dimensions that together make up the deprivation trap: asset poverty, physical weakness, isolation, vulnerability, and powerlessness (1983). The OECD poverty reduction guidelines (2001) lay out five dimensions of poverty: economic, human, sociocultural, political, and protective.

There are some composite indices that take into consideration a number of elements from these dimensions (e.g., the human development index or the human poverty index). There are trade-offs, however, between the breadth and complexity of poverty definition and the ease, precision, and comparability of poverty measurements. Less tangible dimensions of poverty—for example, in the sociocultural or political realms—are more difficult to quantify. How should vulnerability be assessed, for example? Good attempts have been made (see, e.g., Pritchett et al., 2000, Moser, 1998), but standardization is not only elusive but perhaps even undesirable. In standardizing one risks losing the context-specific local community-level applicability that is so valuable for detailed policy planning and monitoring.

In practice, therefore, one-dimensional poverty measurement is applied most frequently. Income and consumption are the narrow focus of conventional poverty measurement, based on the money metric, a theoretical construct based on the assumption that the living standard of a household depends both on its composition and on the commodities it consumes. (See Pyatt, 1996.) These consumed commodities are measured using income (or expenditure) as a proxy (2).

The headcount index is the most commonly used if not the most comprehensive indicator of poverty. The headcount is simply a measure of the proportion of the population living below a given poverty line. Its common usage does not imply that the poverty headcount is the best measure of poverty; problems have been amply discussed in the development literature. (See, e.g., Deaton, 1998; McKinley, 1997.) Briefly, the headcount is a money-metric measure of income poverty that, as discussed above, does not take any wider dimensions of deprivation into account. The figure, expressed as a percentage, furthermore tells the user nothing of the depth or severity of income poverty (as does the poverty gap measure). A person could be close to but just below the poverty line or very far below the poverty line and it would make no difference to the headcount index. Furthermore, the headcount does not change when the overall number of people under the poverty line remains the same but when all or some of those people become much better off or much worse off (as do the Sen or the Foster-Greer-Thorbecke indices). Despite these shortcomings, the headcount remains widely used as a generic indicator of a population's welfare (and changes therein).

Despite its being one of the most "simple" measures of poverty, there are many variables in the establishment of a poverty headcount (see Bidani et al., 2001). The amount of potential variation in methodology is so great that it makes the comparison of data from different assessments very difficult indeed. For poverty numbers to be comparable, the basic building blocks of the measurement methodology must be identical. There are three very general steps. First, a poverty line must be established. Second, a measure of the resources of the population must be conducted. Third, the income or expenditure data must be assessed against this poverty line. Each of these steps involves a number of choices.

## Establishing a Poverty Line

The poverty line is an amount of money without which it is impossible to either (1) survive, or (2) experience a socially acceptable standard of living. The difference between the two is the fundamental difference between an absolute and a relative definition of poverty. The problems with poverty lines are perhaps best summarized by Desai's observation that in creating poverty thresholds, "lines have to be drawn where none may be visible" (1986:1).

On the absolute side, poverty lines are linked to a specific welfare level. They are determined by calculating the value of either food only or a combination of food and nonfood necessities deemed necessary for basic human survival. The establishment of a minimum-needs food basket is difficult, and can seem somewhat arbitrary (not to mention very boring to actually eat) (3). Pricing this minimum-needs food basket results in a food poverty line. Minimum needs *non*food baskets are even more problematic to determine, so the value of the food basket is usually scaled up by a particular multiplier to represent nonfood needs. This avoids having to choose specific nonfood items that should be included. The multiplier by which the value of the food basket is scaled up can be determined in a number of ways. Commonly the spending behavior is observed in families whose total food expenditures just equal the food poverty line. The average total expenditure of these families becomes the poverty line. Sometimes poverty researchers look at the nonfood expenditures of families whose total expenditure just equals the value of the food basket. This results in a very low overall poverty threshold.

The concept of relative poverty was pioneered in the United Kingdom in the 1960s, where, according to Peter Townsend, people were poor if they could not obtain the conditions of life that allow them to play roles, participate in relationships, and follow customary behavior that is expected of them as a result of their membership in a particular society. (See Townsend, 1993.) In other words, the relative formulation of poverty recognizes that different people need different things, in different places, according to different circumstances. Townsend went on to construct complex relative poverty thresholds with respect to commodities and services. Hagenaars and de Vos (1988) constructed an index for Holland using four durable goods (cars, color televisions, refrigerators, and washing machines). As with some other poverty measures, a major problem with the measure of relative deprivation with respect to various commodities is the arbitrary nature of what to include in the list. Furthermore, it does not take into account human's consumption preferences. (Some people choose not to have a television at all, e.g.)

A more simple and attractive relative method is to establish a poverty line in reference to income distribution in society as a whole. The general rationale behind this type of measure is that those falling more than a certain distance below the average or normal income (or expenditure) level in society are unlikely to be able to participate fully in the life of the community. In addition, a relative poverty line rises with overall income or expenditure, hence richer regions logically have higher poverty lines. The European Union (EU) defines poverty in this manner, setting the threshold at 50% of any member country's average income. In Ukraine, a relative poverty line is set at 75% of the median income (4).

## Measuring Resources: The Household Survey

A household survey must be conducted in order to obtain data against which the poverty line is held. Sampling must be very precise; oversampling from well-off or deprived areas will skew results. The units of measurement are significant as well. Should data be collected and poverty analyzed for families or for individuals? Families might be the preferred unit of measurement as a result of economies of scale (five can live almost as cheaply as four, e.g.), but this masks intrahousehold inequalities and distributional issues. It further makes the use of adult equivalents necessary, introducing yet another variable into the mix. Very simply, adult equivalents count the needs of male and female household members of various ages as a fraction of those of the average moderately active adult male. Effective household size is the sum of these fractions and is measured not in the number of persons but in the numbers of adult equivalents. Of course there are choices to be made in the construction of such scales as well. Szckcly et al. (2000) used data from seventeen Latin American countries to test the sensitivity of poverty indexes to the choice of adult equivalent scales and assumptions about economies of scale in consumption. They found that by varying the parameters within reasonable boundaries the proportion of poor could be said to be between 12.7–65.8% of the total population.

## Income or Expenditure?

After setting a poverty line and conducting a household survey, the two must be compared. The income versus expenditure decision will have implications for the results. Income is generally thought to be easier to assess more accurately, but individuals' incomes tend to be highly variable over time. Coping strategies for poor families involve saving in abundant times and drawing on past savings or borrowing in lean ones. Furthermore, income can remain unreported where economic activity takes place in the informal sector. A given year's income thus may not match the level of welfare indicated by expenditure. In Ukraine, for example, the difference between reported income and reported expenditure is considerable, with expenditure averaging 37% more than income (World Bank, 2001). Objections to the measurement of expenditure relate to both the difficulty of obtaining precise consumption data and the fact that consumption choices may be based on taste rather than on the availability of resources. Consumption is nevertheless preferable to income.

Upon implementation of these three steps, then, it is possible to calculate the headcount and arrive at a poverty incidence of, for example, 25% of the population. Without giving the methodological details of this poverty headcount to the end users, it is impossible to know whether the 25% is a measure of the proportion of families *or* individuals that have an income *or* an expenditure that is too low to survive *or* too low to enjoy a socially acceptable standard of living. It cannot be overemphasized how important it is to know what exactly is being presented, as the numbers can differ widely. This is well illustrated with a case study of poverty measurement in the Philippines.

## PROBLEMS WITH POVERTY HEADCOUNTS: A CASE STUDY

There is a wealth of high-quality data available in the Philippines. Official poverty statistics in the Philippines are based on the Family Income and Expenditure Survey (FIES) carried out every three years by the National Statistics Office (NSO). The National Statistical Coordination Board (NSCB) develops the poverty line methodology. The most recent round of the FIES was in 2000 (5).

Unfortunately, despite the availability of such high-quality longitudinal data, looking up the poverty headcount index is not as straightforward as one might think. There are many conflicting figures that can be misused if care is not taken. The problems fall into four categories: subsistence incidence vs. poverty incidence, preliminary vs. revised figures, old methodology, vs. new methodology, and FIES sampling methodology.

### Subsistence Incidence vs. Poverty Incidence

A common cause of confusion is the fact that two different poverty incidences in two different categories are commonly reported in the Philippines. These are the poverty incidence of families, the poverty incidence of the population, the subsistence incidence of families, and the subsistence incidence of the population.

The "subsistence incidence" is a headcount calculated using a basic food poverty line only. It reflects an extreme state of deprivation whereby minimum food needs cannot be met. The "poverty incidence" is a headcount calculated using a poverty line that allows for basic food and nonfood needs. In the Philippine case the food poverty line is scaled up by the nonfood consumption patterns of those families with total incomes at the food threshold. As discussed above, this is an austere method of setting poverty lines.

Confusion arises when studies either do not specify or simply mistake which of the four alternatives they are reporting. The differences in the figures can be quite significant. For 1994, for example, they range from 18.1%, the national subsistence incidence of families, to 40.6%, the national poverty incidence of the population (NSCB, 1996).

An example of mistaken identity of Philippine poverty statistics can be found in a 1993 World Bank discussion paper on the "impressive reductions in poverty" in East Asia. The study is concerned with the numbers of absolute poor, defined by the author as those at or below an income that allows for subsistence levels of food *plus* nonfood necessities (Johansen, 1993:1). The figure quoted for absolute poverty in the Philippines in fact turns out to be the official Philippine subsistence incidence. The report does not specify that this figure is based on a poverty line that allows only for food needs. Conclusions drawn in the study are based on comparing what are in essence noncomparable figures.

## Preliminary vs. Revised Figures

Another source of headcount variation stems from the fact that preliminary figures are released as soon as possible following FIES enumeration. The timely release of data is of course commendable, but the figures are normally revised the following year. Interestingly, the trend among all revised headcounts (both poverty and subsistence, for families and population) is that they are always lower than the preliminary ones.

For example, the 1997 preliminary poverty headcount for the Philippines was reported as 32.1% of families. The revised figure, published later, is 31.8%. Similarly, the 1997 preliminary headcount for Metro Manila was 7.1% of families. The revised figure is 6.4% of families.

## Old Methodology vs. New Methodology

A third issue that creates difficulties in the reporting of Philippine poverty statistics is that there was a major methodology revision in the early 1990s. Prerevision figures sometimes erroneously crop up in current reports.

The approach in place is often referred to as the new methodology, since it has only been used since late 1992 and was first applied to the results of the 1991 FIES. International organizations had suggested that the Philippines model its methodology on that of Indonesia, which according to the World Bank had registered a spectacular reduction in poverty in the past. Fundamental changes, described below, had major effects on Philippine poverty lines and thus on poverty levels.

In the old approach, the nonfood component of the poverty line was determined by the actual expenditure on nonfood items as determined by the FIES results. The food poverty line was scaled up by a coefficient that represented the average ratio of food expenditure to total expenditure for all FIES families.

Under the new approach, the nonfood items are not determined by the actual spending patterns of the population, but are instead set by the NSCB according to how the poor ought to spend their money. The nonfood expenditure is now meant only to include "basic" items, disallowing expenditures on alcohol and tobacco, recreation, durable furniture and equipment, "other" expenditures, and "miscellaneous" expenditures (6). Furthermore, as mentioned above, the food poverty line is now scaled up according to the ratio of food expenditure to total basic expenditure of only the poorest; namely, those whose total household income is within a 10% band around the food poverty line.

A closer look at the new NSCB methodology reveals that it encourages the underestimation of poverty. Surprisingly, even the government's own Presidential Commission to Fight Poverty (PCFP) recognized this. The analysis in *A National Strategy to Fight Poverty* proves that the poorer people become, the fewer poor are counted (NSCB, 1996:7). In using the consumption patterns of those barely able to meet their food needs, the proportion of expenditure going toward nonfood items is bound to be very low. Importantly, it will decline if incomes decline. A declining proportion of expenditure on nonfood items makes the nonfood component lower and results in a lower overall poverty threshold. A lower poverty threshold results in a lower poverty incidence. In essence, the poorer people become, the lower the poverty incidence.

All poverty statistics now reported by the NSCB are "new methodology" statistics; the historical statistics from 1985 and 1988 were retroactively recalculated using the new methodology. The poverty incidence of families for the Philippines in 1988 is now shown to be 40.2%. Under the old methodology it was a great deal higher, at 55% (PCFP,1996:7).

Here again is one of the causes of statistical confusion. Depending on the publication date of the report consulted, historical poverty figures will look very different. Two World Bank reports show two very different numbers for the 1985 poverty headcount: 52% and 44% of families. These figures come from *The Philippines: The Challenge of Poverty* (1988:2) and *The Philippines: A Strategy to Fight Poverty* (1996:3), respectively. If end users of the data do not know that there was a major methodological change between 1988 and 1991, they might erroneously assume that the Philippine government was astoundingly successful at poverty reduction efforts in that time period.

### FIES Samples

So far we have seen that there are many potential ways to err when looking for a poverty headcount in the Philippines; four different types of headcounts, two sets of figures released at different times, and two methodologies mean that sixteen different numbers could be reported (7).

The last issue of the FIES sample is not one of conflicting headcounts, but rather of what exactly the official poverty headcount is measuring in the Philippine case. The FIES does not include families without official and permanent residences in its sample. This is a particularly important point to consider when measuring poverty in urban areas; for example, in Metropolitan Manila. A prominent Filipino economist has found that "estimates of poverty in Manila and other urban centers may be underestimated owing to the omission of families without official and permanent residence.

The poor families in slums and squatter colonies are known to move a lot and are thus likely underrepresented in the survey" (Balisacan, 1994:42).

Informal settlements are by definition unofficial. As this is most likely where the poorest are to be found, they are clearly grossly underrepresented in official statistics. This goes a long way toward explaining the origins of the extraordinarily low poverty headcount for Metro Manila, 6.4% of families in 1997; the poorest families are left out of the sample. It is very difficult to gauge the number of families living in informal settlements in Manila. Figures vary and many are pure estimates, but it is safe to say that the proportion is high (8).

## Poverty Reduced or Poverty Remeasured?

The central lesson from the Philippine case is that where poverty headcounts are concerned, it is expedient that data users know where the numbers come from and what the numbers mean.* Poverty levels and trends can vary enormously if great care is not taken.

It might be argued that the precise levels of poverty do not matter as much as the trends over time; namely, whether poverty is increasing or decreasing, and whether this change is slow or rapid. Even this is impossible to determine with any certainty in the Philippines. According to Stewart, the national poverty incidence increased by 2% between 1988 and 1991 (1995:206). The government, however, reports a decrease of 0.3% for the same time period (NSCB, 1996). There are even conflicting levels and trends reported by the same source. Tables in the *World Development Report 1998/99* show an increase in national poverty rates from 52% in 1985 to 54% in 1991 (World Bank, 1998:197). The World Bank report *Philippines: A Strategy to Fight Poverty* has poverty dropping from 44–37% for this same time period (World Bank, 1996: 3).

Two different researchers using different World Bank and Philippine government reports might easily come up with very different interpretations of what happened to poverty over the same time period. The lesson therefore is that it is essential to investigate where the numbers originate and on what assumptions the measurement is based. A closer look, for example, reveals that the 1998/99 *World Development Report* mistakenly reported old methodology figures (9), whereas the 1999/2000 *World Development Report* reported the preliminary results of the new methodology figures. What might look like impressive poverty reduction thus might not be the result of the increased welfare of a population at all, but rather the result of comparing two different measurement methodologies.

## CONCLUSION: POVERTY IS MULTIDIMENSIONAL

With poverty reduction at the center of development activities, it is essential to take a critical look at poverty measurement; poverty statistics inform development policy choices, programmatic decisions, project assessments, political arguments, and so on.

This chapter has profiled very broadly a number of poverty assessment methods. There are always going to be trade-offs between the breadth and complexity of the

---

* For a more detailed case study of poverty measurement issues in the Philippines, see Schelzig (1999).

definition and the ease and precision (and comparability) of the resulting measure-ment. Conventional income or expenditure poverty is "neater" to measure than poverty defined in a broader, more multidimensional fashion. These conventional poverty measures are therefore most often discussed. Many studies begin with an acceptance of the multidimensional nature of poverty but then revert to income poverty for the sake of simplicity.

Although neater, there are still many choices to make in developing a simple headcount measure, the focus of this chapter. The example of the Philippines shows that changes in poverty headcounts can be a result of a change in the way in which the headcount was constructed. There are many variables in the way in which headcounts are estimated, and small differences in method can lead to significant variance in the resulting poverty measure. In the Philippines, a proliferation of official headcounts (poverty and subsistence, old and new, preliminary and revised) has confused many analysts. This points to the need for being upfront and unambiguous about the principal choices and definitions behind poverty statistics.

The potential for variation in headcounts also presents a strong argument for supplementing them with more multidisciplinary approaches to poverty assessment. Of course income and expenditure should continue to be assessed; money-metric analysis forms a vital part of multidimensional poverty analysis. Multidimensional approaches, however, go well beyond economic interpretation to recognize that the state of poverty arises from many interconnected dimensions that include but are not limited to a lack of income.* Rather than being conceived in merely income terms, poverty should be seen as encompassing such factors as social and human capital, access to common property, political rights, and vulnerability. Furthermore, multidi-mensional approaches to poverty recognize the importance of individuals' own perceptions of poverty, and acknowledge that poverty is highly location- and context-specific.

Multidimensional approaches to poverty assessment can provide much richer information on the state of deprivation and the complex dynamics of poverty reduction than a headcount, allowing for more accurate and results-oriented policy formulation. Nonmonetary indicators can correct for more egregious errors in the headcount index. Assessing poverty levels based only on headcounts incurs a high risk of misinterpretation, which is not ideal, given the current and future centrality of poverty reduction in development policy.

## NOTES

1. The analysis here is focused on national poverty headcounts. For a discussion of interna-tional poverty comparisons and the World Bank's international poverty line of $1/day, see Reddy and Pogge (2002).
2. See White (1999) for the case against the adequacy of income as a proxy for other dimensions of poverty since the correlation is imperfect and the causal mechanisms are far from clear.

---

* See Carvalho and White (1997) on combining quantitative and qualitative approaches to poverty measurement and analysis.

3. It could be, for example, entirely possible to satisfy 90% of daily required calories from rice alone.

4. Importantly, this method is not the same as defining the poor population as a certain percentage from the bottom of the income distribution, (e.g., the lowest 30%). This method means that technically there will always be poverty, even if the lowest 30% of the population are millionaires. In essence, poverty cannot decline under this type of relative poverty measurement without some change in income distribution as a whole.

5. Poverty and other statistics are generally reported from 1985. This is a result of the general unreliability of data during the Marcos dictatorship (pre-1985), a time during which unfavorable statistical series were altered or simply discontinued.

6. Such normative approaches to setting poverty lines are quite common, ignoring the fact that poor individuals' consumption patterns are usually very different.

7. These are the official figures. There are many alternative headcounts as well. Academics, nongovernmental organizations, research institutes, and other government agencies have all contributed their own versions. According to the group Social Weather Stations (SWS), for example, poverty in Manila stood at 50% of families in 1994. The SWS methodology is subjective; families are asked to rate themselves as either poor or not poor.

8. A 1996 NEDA publication states that 36% of Manila's population are squatters, living in 276 major slum areas (NEDA, 1996:17). A technical paper produced for the World Bank that same year reported that 30% of Manila's population live in 591 squatter colonies (Blunt and Moser, 1996:4).

9. This is vaguely ironic, as the theme of the 1998/1999 World Development Report is knowledge for development.

## REFERENCES

Balisacan, A. (1994). Poverty, Urbanization, and Development Policy: A Philippine Perspective. Manila: University of the Philippines Press.

Bidani, B., Datt, G., Lanjouw, J. O., Lanjouw, P. (2001). Specifying poverty lines: How and why. paper presented at the Asia and Pacific Forum on Poverty, Feb. 5–9, 2001. Manila: Asian Development Bank, p. 706.

Blunt, A., Moser, C. (1996). Urban poverty and housing policy in the Philippines. Technical working paper produced for the World Bank Poverty Strategy Report for the Philippines. Washington, DC: World Bank.

Carvalho, S., White, H. (1997). Combining the Quantitative and Qualitative Appproaches to Poverty Measurement and Analysis. World Bank technical paper no. 366. Washington, DC: World Bank, p. 712.

Chambers, R. (1983). Rural Development: Putting the Last First. Harlow, Essex, UK: Longman Scientific and Technical.

Deaton, A. (1998). The Analysis of Household Surveys: A Microeconometric Approach to Development Policy. Baltimore: Johns Hopkins University Press.

Desai, M. (1986). Drawing the line: On defining the poverty threshold. In: Golding, P., ed., Excluding the Poor. London: Child Poverty Action Group, pp. 1–20.

Glewwe, P., van der Gaag, J. (1990). Identifying the poor in developing countries: Do different definitions matter? World Dev. 18(6):803–814.

Hagenaars, A., de Vos, K. (1988). The definition and measurement of poverty. J. Human Res. 23(2):211–221.

Johansen, F. (1993). Poverty Reduction in Asia: The Silent Revolution. Washington, DC: World Bank.

Maxwell, S. (1999). The Meaning and Measurement of Poverty. ODI poverty briefing no. 3. London: Overseas Development Institute, p. 705.

McKinley, T. (1997). Beyond the Line: Implementing Complementary Methods of Poverty Measurement. UNDP technical support document. poverty reduction module 3: Poverty Measurement, Behind and Beyond the Poverty Line. New York: UNDP.

Moser, C. (1998). The asset vulnerability framework: Reassessing urban poverty reduction strategies. World Dev. 26(1):1–19.

NEDA. (1996). Toward a humane world-class metropolis. Philipp. Dev. XXIII(5):14–22.

NSCB. (1996). What Do You Know About Poverty Statistics? Manila: National Statistical Coordination Board.

OECD. (2001). The DAC Guidelines on Poverty Reduction. Paris: Organization for Economic Cooperation and Development.

PCFP. (1996). A National Strategy to Fight Poverty. Manila: Presidential Commission to Fight Poverty.

Pritchett, L., Suryahadi, A., Sumatro, S., (2000). Quantifying Vulnerability to Poverty: A Proposed Measure Applied to Indonesia. World Bank Policy Research working paper no. 2437. Washington, DC: World Bank.

Pyatt, G. Poverty versus the poor. Dies Natalis address on Oct. 10, 1996. The Hague: Institute of Social Studies.

Reddy, S., Pogge, T. (2002). How not to count the poor. Columbia University Institute for Social Analysis, www.socialanalysis.org.

Schelzig, K. (1999). Poverty in Manila: Concepts, measurements, and experiences. PhD dissertation. London: London School of Economics, Development Studies Institute.

Scott, W. (1981). Concepts and Measurement of Poverty. Geneva: UNRISD.

Stewart, F. (1995). Adjustment and Poverty: Options and Choices. London: Routledge.

Szekely, M., Lustig, N., Cumpa, M., Mjia, J. (2000). Do We Know How Much Poverty There Is? Washington, DC: Interamerican Development Bank.

Townsend, P. (1993). The International Analysis of Poverty. London: Harvester Wheatsheaf.

UNDP. (1990). Human Development Report 1990. New York: Oxford University Press.

White, H. (1999). Global poverty reduction: Are we heading in the right direction? IDS Pov Res Prog. Pov. Newsl 3(Spring):5.

World Bank. (1988). The Philippines: The Challenge of Poverty. Washington, D.C.: World Bank.

World Bank. (1990). World Development Report 1990. Oxford: Oxford University Press.

World Bank. (1996). The Philippines: A Strategy to Fight Poverty. Washington, DC: The World Bank.

World Bank. (1998). World Development Report 1998/99. Oxford: Oxford University Press.

World Bank. (2001). Ukraine: Social Safety Nets and Poverty. Report no. 22677 UA. Washington, DC: The World Bank.

# 41

## Conclusion
### Development Agenda for the Twenty-First Century

**GEDEON M. MUDACUMURA**

*Pennsylvania Treasury Department, and Pennsylvania State University, Harrisburg, Pennsylvania, U.S.A.*

## INTRODUCTION

The increasing disparity between the "well-to-do" and the "less-fortunate" was one of the agenda items that world leaders debated during the United Nations Conference on Environment and Development (UNCED) in Rio de Janeiro. The heads of states resolved that no one group of nations could continue progressing while the majority of its people remained hungry and poor. Agenda 21, one of the three landmark documents adopted during the twelve-day conference, spelled out over 120 initiatives to be put into action between 1992 and the year 2000. The preamble of Agenda 21:1.1 of the Rio Declaration began on a foreboding, but optimistic note.

> Humanity stands at a defining moment in its history. We are confronted with a perpetuation of disparities between and within nations, a worsening of poverty, hunger, ill health and illiteracy, and the continuing deterioration of the ecosystems on which we depend for our well-being. However, integration of environment and development concerns, and a greater attention to them will lead to the fulfillment of basic needs, improved living standards for all, better protected and managed ecosystems and a safer, more prosperous future. No nation can achieve this on its own; but together we can—in a global partnership for sustainable development.

The reports of the United Nations Development Programme (UNDP) on the global distribution of income clearly demonstrated this income disparity between rich and poor. The statistics showed that the richest 20% of the world's population

**715**

received 82.7% of the world's total income, while the poorest 20% got only 1.4% (UNDP, 1992).

The 2000/2001 *World Development Report* highlighted that the world has deep poverty amid plenty. Of the world's 6 billion people, 2.8 billion—almost half—live on less than $2 a day, and 1.2 billion—a fifth—survive on less than $1 a day. The average income in the twenty richest countries is thirty-seven times the average income in the poorest twenty—a gap that has doubled in the past forty years. Ultimately, these statistics revealed that global economic growth had hardly filtered down and that the optimism that so-called modern development would benefit all people was largely misplaced (Pezzoli, 1997).

In light of the above situation, none would disagree that development policies geared toward alleviating the conditions of the poor have not been a great success. With some exceptions, international development experts working with governments in poor countries have hardly made much of an impact, thus despite the multitude of research institutions specializing in development issues, researchers have not yet ascertained the underlying causes of this limited impact. Could it be that development policy studies during the last half of the twentieth century failed to address the real issues of development? If the impact has been very limited in the last five decades, how can one presume that the current millennium development goals (MDGs) may set clearer targets to reduce poverty, hunger, disease, illiteracy, environmental degradation, and gender discrimination by 2015?

Recently, the U.N. secretary general and the administrator of the UNDP launched the Millennium Project, which recommends strategies for achieving the MDGs. Over a period of three years, the Millennium Project will work to devise a recommended plan of implementation, allowing all developing countries to meet the MDGs and thereby substantially improving the conditions of their citizens by 2015.

The ten task forces that will perform the bulk of the research comprise academic institutions, the public and private sectors, civil society organizations, and U.N. agencies, with the majority of participants coming from outside the U.N. system. As an advisory body to the United Nations, the Millennium Project will report its findings

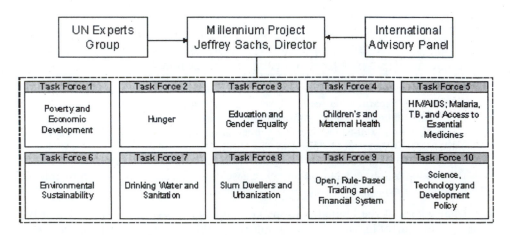

**Figure 1**  Structure of the Millennium Project.

directly to the U.N. secretary general and the administrator of the UNDP. It is structured as shown in Figure 1.

Will the international advisory panel that brings together globally recognized experts in the relevant fields provide relevant and pragmatic insights to solve complex developmental issues? What role will the policy beneficiaries play in the design and implementation of the MDGs strategies? While waiting for the design of the MDG strategies, will the global lending agencies such as the International Monetary Fund and the World Bank, the governments of affluent nations, and international consultants stop urging poor nations to embrace economic belt-tightening policies in exchange for financial aid? The list of such questions can be never-ending. Setting the agenda for future development policy research implies first reviewing what went wrong with the existing development efforts.

This concluding chapter highlights some critical issues that development scholars and experts should consider as the main agenda for the twenty-first century. Such an agenda must underscore the need for a greater understanding of the structure and dynamics of the institutional choices and management systems that enable development policy makers to go beyond a mere description of the multifaceted development issues and pursue a deeper exploration of the interrelationships among development dimensions and the impacts of development policies on individuals' lives and the society at large.

After five decades of development studies, scholars should have a clear understanding of the key development issues that should be taken into consideration while devising and analyzing effective strategies intended to promote societal welfare. Striving for such understanding falls within the framework of overcoming inefficiencies, reducing corruption, and helping people in a changing and competitive world so that the persistence of extreme poverty is not compatible with development efforts. It requires as the cornerstone of development improving the lives of the poor and enabling them to have access to basic services, such as health care and education.

To what extent have development-related disciplines been effective in integrating their research findings for the advancement of humankind? In an effort to break the ground for a plausible integration of such findings, Mudacumura (2002) devised a "general theory of sustainability," which bridges six key development dimensions—economic, social, cultural, political, ecological, and spiritual. In the next section, these dimensions are briefly discussed.

## THE KEY DIMENSIONS OF DEVELOPMENT

### The Economic Dimension

The economic dimension is defined as a dynamic structural change process that preserves cultural values and human dignity while exploring the interconnected relationships geared toward improving citizens' economic welfare at the local, national, and global levels (Mudacumura, 2002). From this definition, improving economic welfare for all the people implies the recognition of interconnected relationships and the realization that economics is only one component of the process needed to achieve development.

This dimension also points to the need for "global equity" based on determined efforts to ensure a just distribution of global resources. In addition, emphasizing intricate development issues leads to a further exploration of how the realization of economic sustainability fits with improving citizens' participation in policy making, preserving cultural practices, and promoting societal welfare—the key issues related to the social dimension.

## The Social Dimension

For Mudacumura (2002), the social dimension implies a participatory decision-making system through which empowered people can devise strategies aimed at fostering global equity and preserving cultural practices while recognizing the complex challenges of securing current and future generations' welfare. Specifically, the social dimension capitalizes on people as a key asset in any development effort. When empowered, people unleash their thinking processes and become active participants in the identification of a community's complex development issues. Empowered individuals at the grassroots level can design suitable development policies that not only foster global equity but also preserve local cultural practices. They can produce effects and can exert their will against adverse forces (Arendt, 1986).

Such empowerment hinges on the existence of an environment that promotes open and undistorted communication; that is, an environment in which local citizens participate as equals in the deliberation of issues affecting their lives. As Sen (1999) asserted, people directly involved must have the opportunity to participate in deciding the appropriate development options that might foster global equity. In this context, participatory decision making is thus acknowledged as the cornerstone of the social dimension.

Moreover, active participation in decision making underscores the relevance of building local capacity, a process of training citizens and equipping them with necessary analytical skills. So armed, local citizens can make valid contributions in development debates. In fact, experience has demonstrated that participation in decision making improves the quality, effectiveness, and sustainability of development policies (UNDP, 1997). Enabling grassroots citizens to play major roles in development decision-making processes is therefore a critical element of the social dimension.

Additionally, the social dimension emphasizes the preservation of local cultural practices. Acknowledging the values of local cultures and ensuring that cultural practices are not overlooked constitute one strategic approach to sustaining development (Chambers, 1997). Historically, development programs that ignored the relevance of local cultural practices failed (Cernea, 1991).

Finally, empowered people working with institutions engaged in sustaining local development pay attention to local cultural practices because culture is intrinsically part of development. Consequently, cultural preservation cannot materialize without a decentralized system of governance and an effective intersectoral collaboration, two of the key components of the political dimension disccused below.

## The Political Dimension

The political dimension can be understood as a decentralized system of governance in which the interlinked, embedded, and symbiotic relationships between public and private development stakeholders' concerns are taken into account while devising development policies. This definition underscores the crucial importance of effective political systems of governance that enable the private and public sectors to collaborate while carrying forward development functions for governance, here conceived as the manner in which power is exercised in the management of a country's economic and social resources for the sole purpose of improving societal welfare.

The above definition emphasizes the effective system of governance to highlight the increasing attention to good governance, a sine qua non for promoting strategies geared toward the betterment of the population at large. Good governance thus implies improving the quality of services and leadership at the local level with decision making decentralized at the grassroots levels.

Concretely, decentralization shifts the responsibilities for development to grassroots organizations and local authorities, thus bringing decision-making processes closer to the people who become the agents in their own change. As such, decentralizing decision making may allow people to be active change agents, a process that might lead to the sustainability of local development.

Decentralization further draws attention to the importance of accountability and participation within a democratic political framework in enhancing public capacity (Doyal and Gough, 1991). Such enhancement includes channels for the public to voice their needs, to influence policy making, and to ensure that those charged with implementing policy remain accountable to those whose livelihoods and futures they will affect (Currie, 1992).

In addition, effective systems of governance imply intersectoral collaboration between public and private development stakeholders who are responsive and accountable to the global population, and pay particular attention to development strategies focused on meaningfully increasing the well-being of all the people. Since neither public nor private development stakeholders have access to the necessary skills, resources, knowledge, and contacts to further development on their own, the collaboration between both sectors is a prerequisite for achieving sustainable development goals. Intersectoral collaboration is thus critical for fostering global solidarity, cultural awareness, and human dignity—the key determinants of the cultural dimension.

## The Cultural Dimension

The cultural dimension is defined as the way in which a community of people acknowledges their complex shared values, beliefs, customs, and skills, and preserves the cultural practices that underpin the community members' synergetic relationships for the sake of maintaining human dignity while promoting global solidarity (Mudacumura, 2002). This definition points to a community's way of acknowledging the key elements that comprise individuals' cultural practices, underscoring that a people's commitment to preserving cultural practices may go beyond local boundaries. Such commitment to preserve a local culture also may enable individuals to recognize the relevance of human dignity.

Specifically, recognizing human dignity entails acknowledging the main beliefs and values to which individuals pay the most attention. Such recognition may further individual self-respect and resistance to exploitation and domination, thus offering real meaning to other values that make individuals' lives more productive in their communities.

Moreover, cultural practices point to the existence of a general set of rules that control the behavior of individuals through recourse to shared values (Gross and

Rayner, 1985). Shared values may thus create a cultural awareness that in turn may explain how individuals with the same core values can initiate building global solidarity, here conceived as a way of preventing any forces that would destroy the global population's cherished values and beliefs.

Furthermore, commitment to global solidarity can help recognize cultural differences while minimizing the risks of divorcing the concrete experiences of a people from their local context. Similarly, community members who are open and receptive to new development insights that do not conflict with their cultural practices may discover that this cultural awareness can be a dynamic source to sustain local development.

Along the same train of thought, the definition of the cultural dimension alluded to the concept of interconnectedness to underscore the extent to which creative expression, traditional knowledge, and other cultural practices are integral parts of individuals' lives in diverse societies. As stated earlier, since it can be argued that culture permeates all aspects of life, any development process must be embedded in local culture for development to be sustainable.

The discussions have so far addressed economic, social, political, and cultural dimensions, providing a definition for each dimension and explaining the extent to which the dimensions are interrelated. It is worth remembering that social, political, economic, and cultural dimensions come into play in a number of ways when addressing ecological and spiritual dimensions.

## The Ecological Dimension

The ecological dimension underscores a holistic decision-making approach that strives to make sense of the interlinked and symbiotic natural and cultural resources that must be preserved while addressing current and future generations' societal welfare (Mudacumura, 2002). The definition emphasizes the interlinked relationships existing in the natural world. Such interrelationships point to the fact that efforts geared toward improving societal welfare are intrinsically dependent on human interactions with the natural world.

Concretely, we may argue that the interlinkages between people and the natural world justify the relevance of paying attention to human culture, particularly when to some tribal groups ecological and cultural well-being are indistinguishable. The interconnectedness of people and nature thus explains the indispensability of searching for adequate means of creating a sustainable society without destroying natural life-support systems.

Furthermore, the impacts of uncontrolled human interactions with natural subsystems may jeopardize these symbiotic relationships, thus leading to genuine ecological crises. Such ecological crises may imply the necessity to emphasize the importance of bringing human development into harmony with the natural environment without jeopardizing the welfare of current and future generations.

Additionally, it is worth recalling that saving the planet and its people from impending ecological crises constitutes the underlying theme of the ecological dimension. Such a theme further underscores the importance of recognizing the welfare interdependence between generations, since each generation has an obligation to protect the productive, ecological, and physical processes that are needed to support future human welfare (Norton, 1996).

Along the same line, the ecological dimension's definition underscores the holistic thinking approach, which recognizes that the whole system is greater than the sum of its subsystems (Kast and Rosenzweig, 1972). Such a holistic approach may explain the interrelated ecological issues transcending life experiences and capabilities of individuals and communities. The holistic thinking approach thus enables development stakeholders to make sense of interconnectedness, empowerment, and the productive, good life, which are basic components of the spiritual dimension of development.

## The Spiritual Dimension

The spiritual dimension is defined as a transcendental value system that connects the self with other interrelated subsystems and functions synergically with the rest of our human faculties through inner-transformational changes leading to productive, good lives (Mudacumura, 2002). This definition points to a transcendental value system that fosters symbiotic interrelationships in which the individual exists and functions as a central part of the integrated overall system. Specifically, the individual is part of a global community consisting of intricately balanced, interdependent parts and processes.

Moreover, as active agents in shaping the global environment, individuals may strive to balance the interdependent parts and processes, a balance without which the survival of mankind can be compromised. Similarly, looking at spirituality as transcending all human subsystems and containing revitalizing power may explain the extent to which individuals' selfish or careless motives may be changed.

It further sheds light on how changed individuals may live productive, good lives in the global community. In this context, a productive, good life means living a complete life, not dying prematurely, having good health, being nourished adequately, and possessing adequate shelter (Nussbaum, 1990). Again, such dynamic, transformational changes leading to a productive, good life underscore the necessity of paying attention to the harmonious relationships that should exist between individuals and the natural environment.

Furthermore, we may argue that the inner-transformational changes suggested by the definition of the spiritual dimension are premised on an understanding of the relations of parts to the whole and of the past to the present and the future (Engel, 1998). Such an understanding might explain why spiritually led citizens work together on faith-based issues, trying to regain their self-worth while living productive, good lives.

Productive, good lives also involve reaching "spiritual fulfillment," a balance between individuals and their surrounding environment. Without a desire for spiritual fulfillment, one might question whether people can lead productive, good lives characterized by peacefulness, joy, happiness, enlightenment, and creative expression, all of which may provide the mental pathways leading individuals away from material consumption and wealth accumulation to a higher level of satisfaction and purpose (Daly, 1991).

Along the same line of thought, the spiritual dimension might explain the need to go beyond accumulating material wealth without considering the effects of that accumulation on the quality of the human condition (Gondwe, 1992), for the underlying rationale behind the spiritual dimension is a focus on individuals' redemptive, inner-transformational changes that may produce renewed individuals who are socially accountable to both current and future generations. This rationale fits with Tawney's (1920) argument that a healthy society comprises people who are trustees in the discharge of a social purpose.

The spiritual dimension further highlights the importance of empowerment, a process whose purpose is to expand human capabilities. Such an expansion involves an enlargement of choices and an increase in freedom (UNDP, 1996). In fact, empowerment underscores that a learning/organizing process exists that allows people to define their development objectives, assess the implications of the development options available to them, and assume responsibility for actions to achieve their agreed-upon objectives.

Finally, the spiritual dimension emphasizes that we should think holistically. It is worth remembering that holism is concerned with interconnections, interrelationships, and long-term underlying systemic patterns (Wheatley, 1992). Relying on holistic thinking may thus explain how an individual may connect with other interrelated subsystems while operating in a symbiotic, global environment.

To recap, a close examination of the underlying premises of the six dimensions (economic, political, social, cultural, ecological, and spiritual) points to the relevance of giving equal consideration to each dimension. The interconnectedness of the discussed dimensions is graphically displayed in Figure 2.

Moreover, the call to bridge the multiple dimensions of development shifts the theoretical focus from reductionism to holism. Concretely, expanding the current

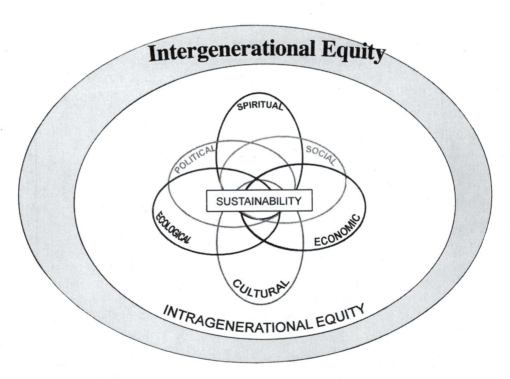

**Figure 2**   General theory of sustainability.

economic development thinking to highlight and include other crucial dimensions for sustaining development may challenge development policy scholars to shift their theoretical underpinnings from reductionism to holism.

One of the propositions of the positivist era was the belief by a dominant group that only their way was worthwhile in tackling problems and setting policy (DeLeon, 1988–1989). On the other hand, considering the interconnectedness of development problems, postpositivists argue that no single approach can claim to have all the answers and that many alternative approaches should be brought to bear on an issue in whatever mix is both appropriate and likely to provide answers.

In light of the multiple dimensions of development, it is necessary to re-emphasize the need for a more broadly based public demand for development policies that "joint-optimize" economic, social, political, cultural, ecological, and spiritual dimensions while being cognizant of the complexity involved. Such complexity also entails considering the imperative to factor in geographical (local, national, regional, and global levels) and temporal (current and future generations) constraints.

Moreover, through the identification of the interlinked development dimensions, one may reiterate the view that the policy-making process is irreducibly complex. For instance, considering simultaneously the six dimensions while devising development policies challenges policy makers to think about the equitable redistribution of global resources, a necessary condition for reducing socioeconomic–political injustices on a global scale. In reality, when financial resources are not distributed evenly, a few cosmopolitan elites accumulate wealth while the urban and rural underemployed lag far behind in poverty (World Bank, 1994).

So far the discussions in this chapter have focused on the six dimensions that interested development policy scholars and practitioners should consider and further explore. Specifically, since there is no comprehensive policy framework that describes various levels of development objectives, the means by which they will be pursued, and the verifiable indicators of their success, this general theory of sustainability may serve as a theoretical umbrella under which development policy scholars could broaden their paradigmatic perspectives while devising development models and policies to address complex development problems. The next section outlines some recommendations for future development research.

## FUTURE RESEARCH RECOMMENDATIONS

The multidimensional and global nature of development problems necessitate appropriate solutions that should derive from a partnership among social scientists from a broad range of development-related disciplines. Leopold (1949:204) alluded to this partnership when he stated that

> one of the anomalies of modern ecological thought is that it is the creation of two groups, each of which seems barely aware of the existence of the other. The one studies the human community, almost as if it were a separate entity, and calls its finding sociology, economics, and history. The other studies the plant and animal community and comfortably relegates the hodgepodge of politics to "the liberal arts". The inevitable fusion of these two lines of thought will, perhaps, constitute the outstanding advance of the present century.

Could the fusion of the social and natural sciences enable researchers to devise easy solutions to multidimensional development problems? Twenty-first century development researchers have the challenge of addressing such problems, which requires a sustained multidisciplinary, multi-institutional approach to generate a range of plausible solutions.

The realization of this multidisciplinary collaboration will require the proponents of various disciplines to shift from closed-system thinking to open-system thinking, basically changing from mechanistic thinking to holistic thinking. Along the same line of thought, Karlqvist (1999) noted that as science moves closer to applications, decision making, and policy making, the identified problems should not be the province of narrow disciplines. The challenges of multifaceted development issues thus cannot be left to ecologists or economists alone, but must involve collaboration among diverse, development-related disciplines.

Development researchers should therefore venture into multidisciplinary research geared toward closing the knowledge gap within and between the disciplines, with the ultimate goal of developing knowledge that is indispensable for multidimensional development issues. Such cooperation would imply an ongoing multidisciplinary dialogue to improve our understanding of both conceptual and pragmatic issues related to social, economic, cultural, ecological, spiritual, and political policy options.

In particular, the multidisciplinary dialogue should address the potential risks of subscribing to narrow perceptions of reality that have been inadequate for dealing with complex development problems. Specifically, the dialogue should rely on the holistic thinking approach to ascertain a deeper understanding and appreciation of how development problems are identified, defined, and solved. This multidisciplinary dialogue should further explore the contending issues among scholars from different disciplines, each working within his or her own methodological traditions and using often incompatible analytical tools and techniques.

Sanchez, the head of the U.N. MDGs hunger task force, used the metaphor of African tribes to illustrate the lack of collaboration among social science disciplines: "Our disciplines are very similar to tribes. We talk our own dialects. We have our own rituals. We publish in our own sources. We distrust the work of others and so on. Typical tribalism. So agricultural economists and anthropologists and so on are just different tribes" (http://www.developmentgateway.org./). Building the multidisciplinary bridge requires finding a common goal that involves specialists from various disciplines.

Ultimately, multidisciplinary collaboration would utilize scientific research methods based on separation of the parts (narrow perceptions of reality), which is believed to be one of the real problems underlying current failures of development policies. As Mudacumura (2002) emphasizes, development problems are closely interconnected and interdependent, so they cannot be understood by using the reductionist/mechanistic method of current academic disciplines and government and nongovernment development agencies: "Such an approach will never resolve any of our difficulties but will merely shift them around in the complex web of social and ecological relations" (Capra, 1982:26).

Additionally, multidisciplinary collaboration should consider academic disciplines' increasing fragmentation of knowledge, which has created an artificial tendency toward area studies in which the researchers often lose the sense of the whole (Wilson, 1998). Recognizing and considering the economic, political, cultural, spiritual, ecological, and social dimensions, however, can help development researchers appreciate the challenges of looking at the multidimensional development issues from a holistic perspective.

## CONCLUDING REMARKS

Complexity in problem solving has been a recurring constraint faced by all societies. Considering the multidimensionality of development issues, the author likes to emphasize the need for development policy scholars to think about the dangers of knowledge fragmentation and the significance of building multidisciplinary approaches while exploring complex development issues.

Such multidisciplinary research collaboration will materialize once the global development community realizes the urgency of turning its primary attention to the poor while making a commitment to replace empty words with effective actions. This requires a change in the mind-set and a commitment to further development. All individuals must show a willingness to collectively set the local, national, and global development agenda and jointly assume responsibility to achieve the agreed-upon outcomes.

The international development research institutions cannot afford to continue their emphasis on fragmented actions that often result in increased human misery. Taking advantage of the current information and communication technologies, the global development research community has an opportunity to network the research institutions at the local and national levels and to ensure a constant information exchange between them. Such research networks might promote a multidisciplinary collaboration and an open forum for constructive debates, which could eventually lead to development policies that are consistent with the needs of local, national, and global communities.

## REFERENCES

Adobor, H. (2003). Managing social change in complex environments: A chaos approach to environmental impacts. In: Mudacumura, G. M., Haque, M. S., eds. Handbook of Development Policy Studies. New York: Marcel Dekker.

Arendt, H. W. (1986). Communicative power. In: Lukes, S., ed. Power. Oxford: Blackwell.

Capra, F. (1982). The Turning Point: Science, Society and the Rising Culture. New York: Simon and Schuster.

Cernea, M. M. (1991). Putting People First: Sociological Variables in Rural Development. Oxford: Oxford University Press.

Chambers, R. (1997). Whose Reality Counts? Putting the First Last. Bath: Bath Press.

Currie, B. (1992). Food crisis and prevention: An analysis in the Indian context. Contemp. So. Asia 1(1):93–111.

Daly, H. E. (1991). From empty-world economics to full-world economics: Recognizing an historical turning point in economic development. In: Goodland, R., Daly, H. E., Serafy, S. E., von Droste, B., eds. Environmentally Sustainable Economic Development: Building on Brundtland. Paris: UNESCO.

DeLeon, P. (1992). The democratization of the policy sciences. Pub. Admin. Rev. 52(2):125–129.

deLeon, P. (1988–1989). The contextual burdens of policy design. Policy Stud. J. 17(2):297–309.

Doyal, L., Gough, I. (1991). A Theory of Human Need. Basingstoke: Macmillan.

Dryzek, J. S. (1990). Discursive Democracy: Politics, Policy Science, and Political Science. Cambridge: Cambridge University Press.

Engel, J. R. (1998). The faith of democratic ecological citizenship. Hastings Ctr. Rep. 28(6): 31–41.

Gondwe, D. K. (1992). Political Economy, Ideology, and the Impact of Economics on the Third World. New York: Praeger.

Gross, J., Rayner, S. (1985). Measuring Culture. New York: Columbia University Press.

Haque, M. S. (1999). Restructuring Development Theories and Policies: A Critical Study. Albany: State University of New York Press.

Hoffman, A. J. (2000). Integrating environmental and social issues into corporate practice. Environment 42(5):22–33.

Kast, F. E., Rosenzweig, J. E. (Dec. 1972). General systems theory: Applications for organization and management. Acad. Mgt. J. 447–465.

Leopold, A. (1949). A Sand County Almanac. New York: Oxford University Press.

Lindblom, C. E. (1990). Inquiry and Change: The Troubled Attempt to Understand and Shape Society. New Haven, CT: Yale University Press.

Mudacumura, G. M. (2002). Towards a General Theory of Sustainability: Bridging Key Development Dimensions Through a Multi-Paradigm Perspective. PhD dissertation. Pennsylvania State University, Harrisburg.

Norgaard, R. B. (1994). Development Betrayed: The End of Progress and a Coevolutionary Revisioning of the Future. New York: Routledge.

Norton, B. G., Toman, M. A. (1997). Sustainability: Ecological and economic perspectives. Land Ec. 73(4):553–568.

Nussbaum, M. (1990). Aristotelian social democracy. In: Douglass, R., Mara, G., Richardson, H., eds. Liberalism and the Good. New York: Routledge.

Pezzoli, K. (1997). Sustainable development: A trans-disciplinary overview of the literature. J. Environ. Plan. Mgt. 40(5):549–574.

Rist, G. (1997). The History of Development: From Western Origins to Global Faith. London: Zed Books.

Sen, A. (1999). Development a Freedom. Oxford: Oxford University Press.

Stiglitz, J. (1998). Towards a New Paradigm for Development: Strategies, Policies, and Processes. Geneva: UNCTAD.

Tainter, J. A. (1996). Getting Down to Earth: Practical Applications of Ecological Economics. New York: Island Press.

Tainter, J. A. (1995). Sustainability of complex societies. Futures 27:397–407.

Tawney, R. H. (1920). The Acquisitive Society. New York: Harcourt Brace & World.

Thompson, F. (1997). The state of public management. J. Policy Anal. Mgt. 16(3):484–507.

United Nations. (1993). Report of the United Nations Conference on Environment and Development. New York.

UNDP. (1992). Human Development Report. New York: Oxford University Press.

UNDP. (1997) Who Are the Questions-makers? A Participatory Evaluation Handbook. New York: Office of Evaluation and Strategic Planning.

Wheatley, M. (1992). Leadership and the New Science. San Francisco: Berrett-Koehler.

Wilson, E. O. (1998). Consilience: The Unity of Knowledge. New York: Knopf.

Wolfensohn, J. D. (1996). The World Bank as a global information clearinghouse: Opening remarks. In: Bruno, M., Pleskovic, B., eds. Annual World Bank Conference on Development Economics. Washington, DC: World Bank.

World Bank. (1994). Governance: The World Bank's Experience. Washington, DC: World Bank.

World Commission on Environment and Development (WCED). (1987). Our Common Future. Oxford: Oxford University Press.

# Index